Modern Chess Openings

MODERN CHESS OPENINGS

Twelfth Edition

Walter Korn

David McKay Company, Inc.
New York

MODERN CHESS OPENINGS

Twelfth Edition, 1982

First printing, 1982

Library of Congress Cataloging in Publication Data

Korn, Walter.
  Modern chess openings.

  First–7th eds. by R.C. Griffith and J.H. White;
8th–9th, 11th by W. Korn; 10th by L. Evans.
  Bibliography: p.
  Includes index.
  1. Chess—Openings.   I. Griffith, R.C.
(Richard Clewin), 1872– . Modern chess
openings.   II. Evans, Larry. Modern chess openings.
III. Title.
GV1450.K67 1980   794.1′22   81–47289
ISBN 0–679–13500–6   AACR2

MANUFACTURED IN THE UNITED STATES OF AMERICA
10 9 8 7 6 5

PREFACE TO THE TWELFTH EDITION

Modern Chess Openings is a compact handbook conveying the basic structures of almost all important openings systems and their strategies. This book is designed to give a comprehensive overview of the game's historic range right through its latest development. The material is presented in columnar tabulation, with supplementing footnotes of the main sub-variations, and with each chapter preceded by an explanatory introduction—all characteristic of *MCO* since its inception.

Looking back over the past forty years of my responsibility for what has become known as "The Chess Player's Bible," I am indeed intrigued how solidly the infrastructure of the game has stood the test of time—embracing both the orthodox and the very modern treatments. Thus, no radical revamping of the established framework was required for *MCO 12*. However, eight years after the appearance of *MCO 11* in 1972, a new enlarged and revised edition became essential because of the immense proliferation of global chess activity, with its resulting benefits such as: new strategic themes; tactical enrichments with refined finesses; and more incisive systems—as will be noticed upon closer inspection by the peruser who wants to keep competitively abreast of the times and the opponents.

MCO strives to achieve an optimum of completeness and clarity while avoiding the unwieldy complexities of too heavy an encyclopedia. Minutely detailed analyses with the latest nuances of the day—subject to fashion after trial and error—are now mostly taken care of by special monographs; by volumes on individual openings with their updating re-editions; or by bulletins and loose-leaf issues—all of them covering specific topics very thoroughly but also exclusively. Each in its own field, and none replacing another, these numerous publications form a useful corollary to the main stream of *Modern Chess Openings*. Our section on Bibliography and the footnoted references within the body of the book, catalogue much of this supplemental literature which the specializing reader may thus acquire separately. (To locate such supplementary sources, *Bowker's Publishers' List of Books in Print* (USA) or Whitaker's *British Books in Print* (UK), available in public libraries and larger book stores can be consulted. Regional chess federations may also be of help.)

While former editions of *Modern Chess Openings* confined themselves with few exceptions to presenting openings variations only and stopping short of the middle game, I have, for the first time, taken the opportunity of expanding some of the given lines into full game scores—more than a hundred of them and many of World Championship caliber. The games are not fully annotated and merely contain some indicative pointers: but they illustrate the underlying technique and the total conception of the game.

As in previous editions, many lines that have become obsolete, have been eliminated, making room for more recent discoveries, refutations and innovations. Some of them have been comfortably incorporated within the existing layout by appending further postscripts to the last footnote of the respective column. Quite a few pages have been fully rewritten and the introductions to the individual chapters have been amplified where warranted. Therefore, the reader is advised to study all inter-related introductions, columns and footnotes in close conjunction, and then evaluate for himself which type of opening and approach he might feel most comfortable with. "Book Theory" is in constant flux, often forged by the master's predilections in the heat of the battle, or by an analyst's abstract reasoning. The ultimate choice is up to the reader.

Chronologically, the present changes again reflect the ever-ongoing progress in the "ultra" elastic and suspenseful handling of both attack and defense not only in some particular old or new debuts, but over the whole spectrum of openings. Distrust of set patterns; sudden departures from conventional lines, producing more flexible maneuvering; or revival of ancient stratagems by means of subtle surprises, etc.; all this has become the order of the day in a contemporary field where psychology complements and/or competes with dogma. Many of the game scores quoted herein illustrate the dynamics which transform a seemingly well-trodden overture into a decisive miniature.

As ever, heed must be paid to potential transpositions, to recognition of similar patterns recurring in different variations or openings but in differing sequences, and what distinguishes them in regard to gaining an advantage or a decisive tempo. I have tried to interlock this element in the footnotes as often as feasible.

The method of transliteration of Russian names and Cyrillic characters into English has remained as spelt out in the eleventh edition. While some codes of transcription may have changed, they are not yet relevant enough to justify resetting.

A delicate dilemma was posed by the controversial alternative of switching to the algebraic notation as used in computer chess and as sponsored by the World Chess Federation or of maintaining the popular descriptive notation as is still used by the majority of publishers and columnists (and also in the Spanish-speaking areas). I concluded that the versatile student of the game really was quite at home in any language of chess, including our native lingo; and that a vast segment of the domestic chess scene was still in favor of the traditional "four-dimensional" (King and Queen winged, Black and White sided) view of the board and description of moves—and ill at ease with the unilateral algebraic view, especially when Black.

I owe gratitude to the many readers and colleagues who kept coming forward with valuable suggestions; who pointed out misprints or mistakes—for which I take the blame; or supplied analytical material when requested. I also thank the numerous friends who assisted in putting together the format of this volume, and the members of Pitman House, London, of David McKay Company, New York and of A&C Black Publishers, London for effectively moving *MCO* along its way to publication. In behalf of McKay, Mr. David Daniels competently carried out the painstaking task of reading and copy-editing the final product, and I am indebted to him for corrections and many valuable pointers. I hope that the many *MCO* adherents, old and new, will derive joyful hours of useful profit from the contents of this latest edition.

WALTER KORN

Contents

SCHEMATIC TABLE OF OPENINGS AND DEFENCES
(For alphabetical listing see "Index," page 451)

I. King's Pawn Openings

CONTENTS

Bibliography

Listed below are some of the important compendia or highly specialized works from which useful references have been quoted in earlier (7th–11th) editions. The compilations still remain valid and, if rare or out of print, they can be obtained from larger (public) library circuits or chess-book dealers. These data enable the reader to search for and critically consult the more extensively detailed treatises on particular opening systems. An asterisk* preceding an author or title denotes source material published after 1973 and added to this, the twelfth, edition.

*J. ADAMS: *The Veresov Opening*.
W.W. ADAMS: *Simple Chess* and *Absolute Chess*.
*L. ALFÖLDY:: *Gambit Eröffnungen* (German).
L. BARDEN, W. HARTSTON and R. KEENE: *The King's Indian Defence*.
A. BECKER: *Die Sizilianische Partie* (German).
*P. BENKÖ: *The Benkö Gambit*.
J. BERGLUND and H. ÅKVIST: *Volga-Gambit* (Swedish).
F. BILGUER: *Handbuch des Schachspiels* and H. KMOCH's *Nachtrag* (German, both referred to as *Bilguer*).
*L.S. BLACKSTOCK: *Ruy Lopez: Breyer System* (algebraic notation).
L.S. BLACKSTOCK, P.J. BOOTH and R.G. WADE: *The Closed Ruy Lopez*.
I. BOLESLAVSKI, P. KERES, A. SUETIN, M. TAIMANOV *et al.*: *Moderne Theorie der Schacheröffnungen*, 8 vols. (Russian and German).
*G.S. BOTTERILL and T. HARDING: *The Scotch*.
*G.S. BOTTERILL and R.D. KEENE: *The Pirć Defence*.
CHESS INFORMANT: Semi-annual Yugoslav publication (Multilingual, referred to as *Informator*), Nos. 1–28.
L. COLLIJN: *Lärobok* (Swedish).
G. DEPPE: *Froms Gambit* (German).
*ENCYCLOPEDIA of CHESS OPENINGS (Yugoslav publication, Multilingual, Vols. A–E — also referred to as *ECO*).
*J. ESTRIN: *The Two-Knights' Defence*.
M. EUWE: *Theorie der Schacheröffnungen*, Vols. I–XII ((German translation).
L. EVANS: *What's The Best Move?* (1970–   ).
R. FINE: *Practical Chess Openings* (also referred to as *PCO*).
R.J. FISCHER: *My 60 Memorable Games*.
T. FLORIAN: *The Schliemann Variation*.

G. Fridshtein: *The Pirć Defence* (Russian and English).

*Y. Geller, S. Gligorić, L. Kavalek and B. Spassky: *The Najdorf Variation* (of the) *Sicilian Defence.*

S. Gligorić: *Selected Chess Masterpieces.*

*S. Gligorić et al.; *The French Defence.*

H. Grob: *Grob's Angriff –g4.* (German)

E. Gufeld and E. Lazarev: *Sitsilianskaya Zashchita* — I (Russian).

G. Gunderam: *Neue Eröffnungswege*, Vols. 1 and 2 (German).

*T.D. Harding: *Irregular Openings.*

*T.D. Harding: *The Leningrad Dutch.*

*T.D. Harding: *Ponziani's Opening.*

*T.D. Harding and G.S. Botterill: *The Italian Game.*

W. Hartston: *The Benoni* and *The Grünfeld Defence.*

A. Hildebrand: *Blumenfeld-gambiten* (Swedish).

*D. Hooper and B. Cafferty: *Petroff's Defence* (2nd edit.)

I.A. Horowitz: *Chess Openings: Theory and Practice.*

S. Jonasson: *Albin's Motgambit* (Swedish).

R.D. Keene: *Flank Openings.*

*R.D. Keene and G.S. Botterill: *The Modern Defence.*

P. Keres: *Teoria shatmatnykh Debyutov*, Vols. 1–4 (Russian).

*G. Koltanowski: *The Colle System.* 10th edition.

*V. Korchnoi and V. Zak: The King's Gambit (referred to as *K/Z*).

W. Korn: *Modern Chess Openings (MCO)*, editor 7th–12th editions; *Moderne Schach Eröffnungen (MSE)* (German); and this author's varied essays and analyses (all referred to as *Comments*; e.g. in *The British Chess Magazine* — "Comments on Current Openings"; *Chess Review* — "Spotlight on the Openings"; etc.).

Yu. Kutyanin and Ya. Estrin: *Zashchita Grynfelda* (Russian).

G. Levenfish: *Sovremenni Debyut* (Russian, referred to as *Debyut*).

*D.N. Levy: *The Sicilian Dragon* and *The Benko Counter-Gambit.*

*J. Marfia and B. Dudley: The *Double Fianchetto Openings.*

A. Matsukevich: *Sitsilianskaya Zashchita* — II (Russian).

O.L. Moiseyev: *Sitsilianskaya Zashchita* — III (Russian).

*J. Moles: *The French Defence Main Line Winawer.*

*H. Myers: *The Nimzovich Defence* and *Reversed King Pawns.*

O. Neikirkh and A. Tsvetkov: *Shakhmatni Debyuti* (Bulgarian).

Ya. I. Neishadt: *Otkazanny Ferzovy Gambit* and *Katalanskoye Nachalo* (Russian).

A.S. Nikitin: *Sitsilianskaya Zashchita* — IV (Russian).

A.O'Kelly: *The Sicilian Flank Game.*

L. Pachman: *Modern Chess Theory*, Vols. I–IV.

V. Panov and Ya. Estrin: *Kurs Debyutov* (Russian, referred to as *P/E*).

R.E. Robinson: *1 P – KB4 (Bird's Opening).*

A.E. Santasiere: *The Futuristic Chess Opening (Santasiere's Folly).*

SCHACH-ARCHIV: Continuous monthly bulletins (German, referred to as *Archives*).

L. SCHIFFLER: *Die Orang-Utan Eröffnung 1 b2 – b4* (German).

R. SCHWARZ: *Handbuch der Schacheröffnungen*, 14 Vols. (German).

B. SHATSKES: *Angliskoye Nachalo*.

A.P. SOKOLSKI: *Lehrbuch der Schacheröffnungen* and *Die Eröffnung 1 b2 – b4* (Russian and German).

*A. SOLTIS: *The Bird Opening* and *Larsen's Opening 1 P – QN3*.

*J. STAKER, A. GLASSCOE and G. STAYART: *The Budapest Defense*.

*A. SUETIN: *Lehrbuch der Schachtheorie* (German translation from Russian).

*SURVEY OF CURRENT CHESS OPENINGS (*RHM*—continuous looseleaf bulletins on specific sections; 1978: *King's Indian Defence*, Part I; 1979–   ; referred to as *Survey*). In algebraic notation.

M. TAIMANOV: *Die Nimzowitsch-Indische Verteidigung* (German).

S.G. TARTAKOWER: (*alias* Xavier Tartakover): *Die Hypermoderne Schachpartie* and subsequent works (German).

P. TRIFUNOVIĆ, B.G. GRUBER and A. BOŽIĆ: *Grünfeldova Indiska Odbrana* (Serbo-Croat).

*E. VARNUSZ: *Die Spanische Partie* (German).

F.A. VASCONCELLOS: *Gambito Budapeste* (Portuguese).

V. VORONKOV: *Novoindiskaya Zaschchita* (Russian).

*N. WEINSTEIN: *The Reti* (booklet).

*N. WEINSTEIN: *Alekhine Defense*.

*R.F. WILLIAMS: *The Real American Wilkes-Barre*.

Other references, often individually acknowledged in the context, have been extracted from annotations of a general nature in the world's leading chess magazines, tournament books and bulletins, such as, to mention a few: *Shakhmatni Byulleten'* (Russian, referred to as *Byulleten*), *Teoriski Bilten* (Yugoslav, referred to as *Bilten*), *Shakhmatna Mis'l* (Bulgarian, referred to as *Misl*), *Échecs Europe* (French), *Fernschach* and *Schach-Echo* (German), *Chess Life & Review* (now *Chess Life*), *The Chess Correspondent*, *Chess Digest Magazine* (all USA), *Chessman Quarterly*, *The New Chess Player*, the *British Chess Magazine*, *Chess*, *Correspondence Chess* (all British), etc.

Explanatory Notes

The variations are evaluated by means of generally known symbols as follows—

+ + after White's (or Black's) move: White (Black) has a clear winning advantage.

+ after White's (Black's) move: White (Black) has a distinct superiority, although there is no immediate forced win.

± White has slightly better chances.

∓ Black has slightly better chances.

= The position offers even chances.

! Good move—or *best choice among several alternatives.*

!? Good move—but open to further research.

? Weak move.

?! Speculative attempt to complicate.

∞ Unclear position, with judgement reserved, or *open to further experimentation.*

† *check*, replacing the symbol "ch" used in former editions of *MCO*.

e.p. pawn capture *en passant.*

Comments—quotations carried over from previous editions or the editor's current present evaluations.

The above symbols are used as guideposts based on contemporary opinion; they may well change in the light of later developments. In no case would we advise readers to forgo their own judgement, as players of different temperaments, or removed from the psychological considerations that govern the choice of a particular variation in tournament or match play, might come to opposite conclusions.

A player should ascertain for himself the why and wherefore of certain moves, as the habit of playing a series of book moves by heart might lead to disaster when the opponent deviates from the "book." To the player who wishes to acquaint himself with the leading variations, we would recommend a study also of all related lines, footnotes, and last-minute postscripts, to familiarize himself with the idea underlying the various alternatives.

As a practical suggestion, two chessboards and men (or pocket sets) may be used when playing through *MCO* columns, making identical moves on both until reaching an important note. The note may be examined on one board, leaving the main position at the other board intact. Subsequently, restore the main position on the other board and again use both boards simultaneously until the next note is reached.

Comparative Chart of Chess Notations

For the benefit of those not familiar with the English (descriptive) notation, we give a diagram of the board with a comparison of the English and algebraic definition of the squares, and a table of international equivalents for the English symbols for the chessmen.

In the English notation, the symbol before the hyphen indicates which piece is being moved, the symbol following the hyphen the square to which it is moved. On the board below, the notation in brackets indicates Black's moves, with the board seen from Black's point of view.

	a	b	c	d	e	f	g	h	
8	(QR1) QR8	(QN1) QN8	(QB1) QB8	(Q1) Q8	(K1) K8	(KB1) KB8	(KN1) KN8	(KR1) KR8	**8**
7	(QR2) QR7	(QN2) QN7	(QB2) QB7	(Q2) Q7	(K2) K7	(KB2) KB7	(KN2) KN7	(KR2) KR7	**7**
6	(QR3) QR6	(QN3) QN6	(QB3) QB6	(Q3) Q6	(K3) K6	(KB3) KB6	(KN3) KN6	(KR3) KR6	**6**
5	(QR4) QR5	(QN4) QN5	(QB4) QB5	(Q4) Q5	(K4) K5	(KB4) KB5	(KN4) KN5	(KR4) KR5	**5**
4	(QR5) QR4	(QN5) QN4	(QB5) QB4	(Q5) Q4	(K5) K4	(KB5) KB4	(KN5) KN4	(KR5) KR4	**4**
3	(QR6) QR3	(QN6) QN3	(QB6) QB3	(Q6) Q3	(K6) K3	(KB6) KB3	(KN6) KN3	(KR6) KR3	**3**
2	(QR7) QR2	(QN7) QN2	(QB7) QB2	(Q7) Q2	(K7) K2	(KB7) KB2	(KN7) KN2	(KR7) KR2	**2**
1	(QR8) QR1	(QN8) QN1	(QB8) QB1	(Q8) Q1	(K8) K1	(KB8) KB1	(KN8) KN1	(KR8) KR1	**1**
	a	b	c	d	e	f	g	h	

Fig.	Eng.	Czech	Dut.	Fr.	Ger.[1]	Hung.	It.[2]	Pol.	Roum.	Russ.	FIDE
♔	K	K	K	R	K	K	R	K	R	K$_p$	K
♕	Q	D	D	D	D	V	D	H	D	ф	D
♖	R	V	T	T	T	B	T	W	T	π	T
♗	B	S	L	F	L	F	A	G	N	C	S
♘	N[3]	J	P	C	S	H	C	S	C	x	N
♙	P	(P)	(P)	(P)	(B)	(g)	(P)	(P)	(—)	(π)	—

[1] These are also used in the Scandanavian and Yugoslav notations.

[2] These are also used in the Portuguese and Spanish notations.

[3] N for Knight in modern usage, replacing the archaic symbol Kt.

Modern Chess Openings

King's Pawn Openings

King's Gambit

(1 P–K4, P–K4; 2 P–KB4)

The King's Gambit, the darling of the romantics, is a swashbuckling opening synonymous with attack, sacrifice, and an exciting open game. *The Chessplayers' Manual* by Gossip and Lipschütz (1874) devotes 237 pages to the gambit without arriving at a conclusion! With the coming of regular clock tournaments its popularity began to wane. The Baden 1914 and Abbazia 1919 gambit tournaments, which proved that Black could maintain a positional edge by returning the pawn at an appropriate moment, all but caused its eclipse in serious chess. Despite Black's ruthlessly precise defences, there have been sporadic attempts to revive the gambit by "chess pirates" like Bronstein, R. Byrne, Pomar, Fischer, and Spasski. Today it is played with a view to obtaining a positional advantage, even if it means an early exchange of queens, and the question whether this is an opening of the future or of the past still remains.

With 2 P–KB4 White stakes a pawn for a dominating centre, better development, and a rapid attack on KB7 which utilizes the open king's bishop's file. Black must decide whether first to accept and shortly return the pawn for equality (with . . . P–Q4), or to hang on to it as long as is practical. The course of the game hinges on this decision. The gambit declined is safer but, as is to be expected, less promising.

In THE KING'S GAMBIT ACCEPTED, against any continuation which after 2 . . . P×P omits 3 N–KB3 (cols. 1–5) Black can achieve at least equality by . . . P–Q4.

Against THE KING'S KNIGHT'S GAMBIT 3 N–KB3, Black has at least five good replies: 3 . . . P–Q4, N–KB3, B–K2, P–Q3, and P–KN4 (cols. 6–20).

THE KING'S GAMBIT DECLINED with 2 . . . B–B4 (cols. 21–5) leads to equality. Unless Black is thoroughly steeped in its intricacies, however, he is advised to try something else. 4 B–B4 is probably White's most solid answer (col. 24, note (*i*)).

1

THE FALKBEER COUNTER GAMBIT with 2 . . . P–Q4 (cols. 25–30) rips the position wide open and leads to early simplifications which are drawish in nature. It is a thoroughly practical defence which operates on the principle that the best way to refute a gambit is to offer still another.

1 P–K4, P–K4; 2 P–KB4, P × P

	Bishop's Gambit 1	Lesser Bishop's Gambit 2	Breyer Gambit 3	Keres Gambit 4	5
3	B–B4	B–K2	Q–B3	N–QB3	
	N–KB3 (a)	P–Q4 (e)	N–QB3 (f)	Q–R5†	
4	N–QB3	P × P	P–B3 (g)	K–K2	
	P–B3 (b)	N–KB3	N–B3	P–Q4	
5	Q–B3 (c)	P–B4	P–Q4	N × P	
	P–Q4	P–B3	P–Q4	B–Q3	B–N5†
6	P × P	P–Q4	P–K5	N–KB3	N–B3
	B–Q3	B–N5†	N–K5	B–KN5	N–QB3
7	P–Q3	B–Q2!	B × P	P–Q4	N × P†
	B–KN5	B × B†	P–B3	N–QB3 (h)	K–Q1
8	Q–B2	Q × B	P × P!	P–K5	N × R
	O–O	P × P	N × KBP	O–O–O	N–K4 (j)
9	B × P	N–KB3	B–Q3 =	B × P	P–KR3 (k)
	R–K1† (d)	N–B3 =		KN–K2 (i)	B–R4 (l)

(a) (A) 3 . . . P–Q4; 4 B × P (4 P × P, Q–R5†; 5 K–B1, B–Q3; 6 N–KB3, Q–R4; 7 N–B3, N–K2; 8 P–Q4, O–O; 9 N–K4, N × P; 10 N × B, P × N =), N–KB3; 5 N–QB3, B–QN5; 6 KN–K2, B × N; 7 NP × B, N × B; 8 P × N, Q–R5†; 9 K–B1, B–N5; 10 Q–K1, Q × Q†; 11 K × Q, P–B6. *Lärobok.* (B) 3 . . . N–QB3; 4 N–KB3, P–KN4; 5 O–O, B–N2; 6 P–Q4, P–Q3; etc., see col. 14. (C) 3 . . . P–KB4?! Lopez Counter Gambit; 4 Q–K2, Q–R5†; 5 K–Q1, P × P; 6 Q × P†, B–K2; 7 P–Q4, N–KB3; 8 Q × BP, Q × Q; 9 B × Q, P–Q4; 10 B–Q3, B–N5† = . (D) 3 . . . Q–R5†; 4 K–B1, P–Q3; 5 N–QB3, B–K3; 6 Q–K2, P–QB3; 7 N–B3, Q–K2; 8 P–Q4, B × B; 9 Q × B, P–KN4; 10 P–K5 (Fischer–Evans, US Chp. 1963–4), P × P; 11 P × P, N–Q2; 12 N–K4, N × P; 13 N × N, Q × N; 14 B–Q2, Q–Q4 = . Fischer.

(b) Tartakover recommends 4 . . . N–B3; 5 N–B3, B–N5; 6 N–Q5, O–O; 7 O–O, N × N; 8 P × N, N–K2; 9 P–Q4, N–N3; 10 N–K5, B–Q3.

(c) (A) Sokolski analyses 5 Q–K2, P–Q4! 6 P × P†, B–K2; 7 P × P, N × P = . (B) 5 P–Q4, B–N5; 6 P–K5 N–K5 (. . . P–Q4; 7 P × N, P × B; 8 P × P, R–N1; 9 N–B3, R × P; 10 O–O ±); 7 Q–B3, P–Q4! 8 P × P *e.p.*, O–O; 9 N–K2, Q–R5†; 10 P–N3, P × P; 11 P × P, Q–N5; 12 Q × Q, B × Q; 13 B–Q3, R–K1 ∓ .

(d) 10 K–B1, B × B = . Euwe.

(e) 3 . . . P–KB4?! 4 P × P, Q–R5†; 5 K–B1, N–QB3; 6 P–Q4, N–B3 = . Alekhin.

(f) (A) 3 . . . Q–R5†; 4 P–N3, P × P; 5 P × P, Q–B3; 6 N–B3, Q × Q; 7 N × Q, B–K2; 8 N–Q5, B–Q1; 9 P–N3, N–K2; 10 B–QN2, O–O ∓ . Korchnoi. (B) 3 . . . P–Q4! 4 P × P, B–Q3 is also promising.

(g) Other recently revived lines are (A) 4 Q × P, P–Q4; 5 P–K5 (5 P × P, N–N5 or 5 N–QB3, B–Q3! or 5 N–KB3, P × P ∓), B–QB4; 6 P–B3 (6 N–KB3, KN–K2!), B × N = . (B) 4 N–K2, N–B3; 5 P–Q4, P–Q4; 6 P–K5, N–K5; 7 QN–B3, B–QN5; 8 B × P, B × N†; 9 P × B, O–O; 10 N–N3, P–B3 ∞ . Tarjan–Pritchett, Internatl. Students Team Tourn. 1969. The column is *Comments.*

(h) Good prospects offer (A) 7 . . . N–K2; 8 N × N, Q × N; 9 P–K5, P–KB3; 11 B × P, P × P; 11 P × P, N–B3; 12 K–B2, B × P; 13 B × B, N × B; and (B) 7 . . . N–KB3; 8 N × N†, P × N; 9 K–Q3, Q–R4; 10 B–K2, N–B3; 11 P–KR3, B × N ∓ . *K/Z.*

(i) 10 P–B4, Spasski–Furman, USSR Chp. 1959, B–N5! ∞ . 4 . . . Q–K2 is interesting.

(j) 8 . . . N–Q5†; 9 K–Q3, Q–B3; 10 P–B3, Q–QR3†; 11 P–B4, B–QB4; 12 P–QN4! N–KB3; 13 P × B, N × P! 14 Q–K1, R–K1 affords Black strong chances. *P/E.*

(k) (A) 9 Q–K1, N×N; 10 Q×Q, N×Q†; 11 K–K1, P–B6+. (B) 9 P–Q4, N×N; 10 P×N, B×P†; 11 K×B, Q–R4†; 12 K–B2, Q×Q+.

(l) 10 P–Q4 (10 R–KN1, Q–N6!), N×N; 11 P×N, B×P†; 12 K×B, Q–R4†; 13 K–N2, Q×Q; 14 B–Q3, Q–R4; 15 B×P ∞. Panov. Instead of 9 . . . B–R4; Black has 9 . . . B×N†; 10 P×B, Q–N6; 11 P–Q4 Q×P†; 12 K–K1, Q–N6†; 13 K–K2, Q–B6†; drawn.

1 P–K4, P–K4; 2 P–KB4, P × P; 3 N–KB3

	6	7	8	9	10
	P–Q4			N–KB3	
4	P × P			P–K5	
	N–KB3 (a)			N–R4	
5	N–B3	B–N5† (e)		P–Q4	
	N × P (b)	B–Q2	P–B3	P–Q4	P–Q3
6	N × N	Q–K2† (f)	P × P	N–B3 (j)	B–B4 (k)
	Q × N	B–K2	P × P (h)	P–KN4	N–QB3
7	P–Q4	P–Q6	B–B4	B–K2	N–B3 (l)
	B–K2 (c)	P × P	B–Q3 (i)	P–N5	P × P
8	P–B4	P–Q4	Q–K2†	O–O	Q–K2! (m)
	Q–K5†	O–O	K–B1	P × N	B–KN5
9	K–B2	N–B3	P–Q4	B × P	P–Q5
	B–KB4	R–K1	B–N5	N–N2	B × N
10	P–B5	O–O	N–B3	N × P	Q × B
	N–B3! (d)	B–KB1 (g)	Q–B2 ∞	N–Q2 =	Q–R5† (n)

(a) 4 . . . B–Q3?! 5 N–B3, N–K2; 6 P–Q4, O–O; 7 B–Q3, N–Q2; 8 O–O, P–KR3? (better is 8 . . . N–B3; 9 N–K4, N–N3; 10 N × B, Q × N; 11 P–B4, B–N5†; or 9 N–K5, N/2 × P; 10 N × N, N × N; 11 B × P, N × B; 12 R × N, Q–N4 =); 9 N–K4, N × P; 10 P–B4, N–K6; 11 B × N, P × B; 12 P–B5, B–K2; 13 B–B2, R–K1; 14 Q–Q3, P–K7; 15 N–Q6! N–B1? (15 . . . B × N!) 16 N × BP, P × R(Q)†; 17 R × Q, B–B4; 18 Q × B, Q–Q2; 19 Q–B4, B–B3; 20 N/3–K5, Q–K2; 21 B–N3, B × N; 22 N × N†, K–R2; 23 Q–K4†, resigns, Spasski–Bronstein, USSR Chp. 1960.

(b) (A) 5 . . . B–QN5; 6 B–B4, O–O; 7 O–O, QN–Q2; 8 P–Q4, N–N3; 9 B–N3, B–N5. Comments. (B) 5 . . . B–Q3; 6 B–B4, O–O; 7 O–O, QN–Q2; 8 P–Q4! N–N3; 9 B–N3, B–KN5; 10 Q–Q3 ± . K/Z.

(c) No weaker is 7 . . . N–B3; 8 B–K2, B–N5; 9 B × P, O–O–O; 10 P–B3, Q–K5; 11 Q–Q2, B × N; 12 P × B, Q–Q4; 13 R–KN1, P–KN3; 14 P–N3, B–N2 ∓ . Pomar–Filip, Stockholm 1962.

(d) 11 B–N5, Q–Q4; 12 R–K1, B–K5; 13 Q–K2, P–B4; 14 B × P, O–O–O; 15 QR–Q1! B–B3! 16 B × N, Q × B; 17 B–K5, KR–K1; 18 B × B, P × B = . Comments. 9 B–K2 is better.

(e) 5 P–B4, P–B3; 6 P–Q4. (A) 6 . . . P × P; 7 P–B5, N–B3; 8 B × P, B–K2; 9 N–B3, O–O; 10 B–QN5, N–K5; 11 O–O, B–N5 = . Tolush–Averbakh, USSR 1959. (B) 6 . . . B–N5†; 7 N–B3, P × P; 8 B × P, O–O; 9 B–Q3, R–K1†; 10 B–K5, N–B3; 11 O–O, N × B; 12 N × N, P × P; 13 B × P, B–K3 = . P/E.

(f) 6 B–B4, Q–K2†! 7 Q–K2, Q × Q†; 8 K × Q, B–Q3; 9 P–Q4, O–O = .

(g) 11 Q–Q3, N–B3 = . Muchnik–Panov, Moscow Chp. 1962. 7B–B4!

(h) 6 . . . N × P!? 7 P–Q4, B–Q3! 8 O–O (8 Q–K2†, B–K3; 9 N–K5 –9 N–N5? O–O! – O–O; 10 B × N, P × B; 11 B × P, N–Q4 ∓), O–O; 9 QN–Q2, B–KN5; 10 N–B4, B–B2; 11 P–B3, N–Q4; 12 Q–Q3 ± . K/Z.

(i). Upon 7 . . . N–Q4 White gains the upper hand after (A) 8 N–B3! B–K2; 9 O–O, O–O; 10 P–Q4, N–N3; 11 B–Q3. Muchnik–Lilienthal, USSR 1967. And (B) 8 O–O, B–Q3; 9 N–B3, B–K3; 10 N–K4 (Spasski–Sakharov, USSR Chp. 1960), B–B2; 11 B–N3, O–O; 12 P–Q4, N–Q2; 13 P–B4, N–K6 = .

(j) 6 P–B4, P–QB3! 7 B–K2, P–KN4; 8 N–B3, B–K3; 9 O–O, R–N1 ∓ .

(k) 6 N–B3, P × P; 7 Q–K2, B–KN5; 8 Q × P†, B–K2; 9 N–Q5, N–QB3; 10 B–N5 O–O = .

(l) 7 O–O, P × P; 8 Q–K2, B–KN5; 9 N–B3, B × N; 10 R × B, Q × P†; 11 B–K3 Q–Q2! = .

(m) (A) 8 P–Q5, N–Q5! (B) 8 O–O, B–KN5 = .

(n) 11 P–N3, N–Q5; 12 Q–K4, Q–K2 = .

1 P–K4, P–K4; 2 P–KB4, P × P; 3 N–KB3

	11	12	13	14	15
	(N–KB3)	.... B–K2		P–Q3 (g)	
4	(P–K5)	B–B4 (c)		B–B4	P–Q4
	(N–R4)	N–KB3 (d)		P–KR3	P–KN4
5	Q–K2	N–B3	P–K5	P–Q4	P–KR4
	B–K2	N × P	N–N5	P–KN4	P–N5
6	P–Q4	N–K5	N–B3	O–O	N–N1
	O–O	N–N4	P–Q3	B–N2	B–R3 (k)
7	P–KN4	P–Q4	P–Q4 (e)	P–KN3 (h)	N–QB3
	P × P† e.p.	P–Q3	B–R5†	N–QB3	P–QB3 (l)
8	Q–N2 (a)	N–Q3	K–B1	P–B3	B–Q3 (m)
	P–Q3	P–B6	N–K6†	P–N5 (i)	Q–B3
9	RP × P	P × P	B × N	N–R4	P–K5
	B–N5	N–R6	P × B	P–B6	P × P
10	N–R2	B–K3	Q–Q3	Q–N3	N–K4
	N × P (b)	O–O ±	B–N5 (f)	Q–Q2 (j)	Q–K2 (n)

(a) 8 P × P, N × P; 9 Q–R2, N × R; 10 B–Q3, P–KB4 = .

(b) 11 R–N1, B–B4; 12 N–KB3, N–R4; 13 R–R1, B–N3; 14 N–B3, N–QB3; 15 B–K3 with pressure.

(c) 4 N–B3, (A) 4 . . . B–R5†! 5 K–K2, P–Q3; 6 P–Q4, B–N5! = . (B) 4 . . . N–KB3; 5 P–K5, N–N5; 6 P–Q4, N–K6; 7 B × N, P × B; 8 B–B4, P–Q3; 9 O–O, O–O; 10 Q–Q3 N–B3; 11 P × P, B × P = . The column is the Cunningham Gambit.

(d) The Wild Cunningham Gambit goes 4 . . . B–R4†; (A) 5 K–B1, P–Q4; 6 B × P, N–KB3; 7 N–B3, O–O; 8 P–Q3 ± , (B) 5 P–KN3, P × P; 6 O–O, P × P†; 7 K–R1, P–Q4 = .

(e) 7 P × P, B × P (7 . . . Q × P; 8 P–Q4, N–K6; 9 B × N, P × B; 10 O–O ±); 8 Q–K2†, Q–K2; 9 Q × Q†, K × Q; 10 P–Q4, R–K1 = .

(f) 11 P × P, P × P; 12 Q × P† ∞ . If 10 . . . P × P; 11 Q × KP, O–O; 12 P × P, B–K2; 13 R–Q1 + .

(g) Fischer's one-time favourite. Tenable but flat is Becker's 3 . . . P–KR3; 4 P–Q4, P–KN4; 5 P–KR4, B–N2; 6 P × P (6 P–KN3, P–Q4! =); P × P; 7 R × R, B × R; 8 P–KN3, P–Q4 = . The text, in conjunction with 4 . . . P–KR3, is the Berlin Defence Deferred.

(h) 7 N–B3, N–K2; 8 P–KN3, QN–B3; 9 P × P, P–N5! ∓ , or 7 . . . B–K3!; 8 B × B, P × B; 9 P–K5, N–QB3 ∓ .

(i) 8 . . . B–R6; 9 P × P, B × R; 10 Q × B, P × P; 11 B × P, Q–B3; 12 B–KN3, O–O–O; 13 QN–Q2, KN–K2; 14 Q–R3†, K–N1; 15 R–KB1, Q–N3; 16 N–R4, Q–N4; 17 KN–B3, Q–N3 = .

(j) 11 N–Q2, N–R4; 12 Q–B2, N × B; 13 N × N, N–K2; 14 N–K3, Q–B3 ∓ . Kaplan-Karpov, Stockholm 1969. The column is the Hanstein Gambit.

(k) 6 . . . N–KB3; 7 B × P, N × P; 8 N–Q2, Q–K2; 9 Q–K2, N × N; 10 K × N, Q × Q†; 11 N × Q = becomes a Kieseritzky Gambit. Hays.

(l) 7 . . . N–QB3; 8 KN–K2, P–B6; 9 N–B4, P–B7†; 10 K × P, P–N6† = , Planinć-Gligorić, Ljubljana 1977.

(m) Or 8 KN–K2, Q–B3; 9 P–KN3, P–B6; 10 N–B4 = .

(n) 11 P × P, Q × KP; 12 Q–K2!

1 P–K4, P–K4; 2 P–KB4, P × P; 3 N–KB3, P–KN4

	16	17	18	19	20
4	P–KR4			B–B4	
	P–N5			P–N5	B–N2
5	N–K5	N–N5		O–O	P–KR4 (*l*)
	N–KB3 (*a*)	P–KR3 (*d*)		P × N	P–KR3
6	P–Q4 (*b*)	N × P		Q × P	P–Q4
	P–Q3	K × N		Q–B3 (*i*)	P–Q3
7	N–Q3	P–Q4	B–B4† (*f*)	P–K5	P–B3 (*m*)
	N × P	P–B6!	P–Q4	Q × P	N–QB3
8	B × P	B–B4†	B × P†	P–Q3 (*j*)	Q–N3
	B–N2	P–Q4	K–K1 (*g*)	B–R3	Q–K2
9	P–B3 (*c*)	B × P†	P–Q4	N–B3	O–O
	Q–K2	K–N2	N–KB3	N–K2	N–B3 (*n*)
10	Q–K2	P × P	N–B3	B–Q2	P × P
	B–B4	N–KB3 (*e*)	B–N5 (*h*)	QN–B3 (*k*)	P × P (*o*)

(*a*) (A) About equality results from 5 . . . B–N2; 6 P–Q4, P–Q3; 7 N × NP, B × N; 8 Q × B, B × P; 9 P–B3, B–K4; 10 B × P, N–KB3; 11 Q–B3, QN–Q2; 12 P–KN3, Q–K2; 13 N–Q2. (B) Unsatisfactory proved 5 . . . P–KR4; 6 B–B4, R–R2; 7 P–Q4, B–R3 (7 . . . P–Q3; 8 N–Q3, P–B6; 9 P × P, B–K2; 10 B–K3 ±); 8 N–QB3, P–Q3; 9 N–Q3, P–B6; 10 P × P ±. Hearst-Evans, USA Jr. Chp. 1947. (C) Experimental is the immediate 5 . . . P–Q3; 6 N × NP, N–KB3; 7 N–B2, R–N1?! 8 P–Q4, B–R3; 9 N–B3, Q–K2; 10 B–B4 (10 N–Q3?– Planinć-Korchnoi, Moscow 1975), R × P; 11 B × P, B × B; 12 Q–B3, R × N; 13 Q × R, B–R3; 14 O–O! +. Korchnoi. Because of these intangibles of the Kieseritzky, Fischer preferred 3 . . . P–Q3 which inhibits N–K5.

(*b*) 6 B–B4, P–Q4; 7 P × P, (A) 7 . . . B–N2! 8 P–Q4, N–R4; 9 O–O, Q × RP; 10 Q–K1, Q × Q; 11 R × Q, O–O ∓. (B) 7 . . . B–Q3 is answered by (1) 8 P–Q4! N–R4; 9 O–O, Q × RP; 10 Q–K1, Q × Q; 11 R × Q, O–O; 12 B–Q3, R–K1; 13 B–Q2, P–B3 ∞. Or (2) 8 O–O, (the Rice Gambit) which is outdated, e.g. 8 . . . B × N; 9 R–K1, Q–K2; 10 P–B3, N–R4; 11 P–Q4, N–Q2; 12 P × B, N × P; 13 P–QN3, O–O; 14 B–R3, N–B6†; 15 P × N, Q × RP; 16 R–K5, B–B4; 17 N–Q2, Q–N6†; 18 K–B1, Q–R7; 19 B × R, P–N6; 20 B–B5, P–N7†; 21 K–K1, Q–R5†; 22 K–K2, N–N6†; 23 K–B2, N–K5 dis †; 24 K × P, N–Q6†; 25 K–R1, Q–R6†; 26 K–N1, K–R1; 27 N × N!∞ Evans.

(*c*) 9 N–B3, N × N; 10 P × N, O–O! = but not 10 . . . P–QB4; 11 B–K2, P × P; 12 O–O, N–B3 ∓. Spasski-Fischer, Mar del Plata, 1960. The column is Fischer's analysis of the Kieseritzky Gambit.

(*d*) Better than 5 . . . N–KB3; 6 P–K5, Q–K2; 7 Q–K2! N–R4; 8 N–QB3, N–N6; 9 Q–B4, N × R; 10 N–Q5, O × P†; 11 B–K2, N–N6; 12 N × P†, K–K2; 13 N–Q5†, etc.

(*e*) (A) 11 B–N3!? (Keres) with two pawns and an attack for the piece. (B) 11 N–B3, B–N5; 12 B–QB4, P × P (or 12 . . . P–B4; 13 P–Q5, QN–Q2); 13 R–N1†, N–N5; 14 Q × P, Q × P†; 15 R–N3, R–B1; 16 B–B4, B–K2 ∓. The column is the Allgaier Gambit.

(*f*) The Urusov Attack. Yet unexplored is 7 N–B3, P–B6; 8 P × P, B–K2 ∞ .

(*g*) For 8 . . . K–N2; 9 P–Q4, P–B6 see col. 17.

(*h*) 11 B × BP, N × B; 12 P × N, Q × P; 13 O–O, B × N; 14 P × B, N–B3; 15 P–B4, Q × P; 16 P–Q5, N–K2; 17 P–Q6, P × P; 18 Q × QP, with a strong attack. Keres.

(*i*) 6 . . . Q–K2; 7 P–Q3! and 8 N–B3 ±. The column is the Muzio Gambit.

(*j*) 8 N–B3, Q–Q5†; 9 K–R1, Q × B; 10 P–Q3, Q–B3; 11 Q × BP, P–B3 =.

(*k*) 11 QR–K1, Q–B4; 12 N–Q5, K–Q1; 13 Q–K2!, Q–K3; 14 Q–B3, Q–B4, draw.

(*l*) The Greco-Philidor Gambit. For 5 O–O, P–Q3; 6 P–Q4, P–KR3 see cols. 14–15.

(*m*) If 7 Q–Q3, N–QB3; 8 P × P, P × P; 9 R × R, B × R; 10 P–K5, B–N2; 11 Q–R7 K–B1; 12 Q–R5, N–R3! 13 N × P, B–KN5; 14 Q–R4, N × P =.

(n) 11 N × P, N × KP; with two practical plans (A) 12 N × P, R–B1; 13 R × P, N–N6; 14 N–R3, P–Q4; 15 B × P, N–K7†; 16 K–B1, N × R; 17 B × N, R × N; 18 B × R†, Q × B; 19 Q × Q†, K × Q; 20 B × P, with 3 pawns for the piece. (B) 12 N × N, Q × N(12 . . . N × P; 13 Q–Q1! P–B6! 14 B–KN5, Q–K4; 15 P × N ±); 13 B × P†, K–Q1; 14 B × P, N × P, 15 B–N5†, K–Q2; 16 Q–Q5! N–K7†; 17 K–B2, Q–N5 ∞ .

1 P–K4, P–K4; 2 P–KB4, B–B4 (*a*); 3 N–KB3 (*b*), P–Q3

	21	22	23	24	25
4	N–B3			P–B3	
	N–KB3			B–KN5	N–KB3 (*j*)
5	B–B4			P × P	P × P
	N–B3			P × P	P × P
6	P–Q3			Q–R4†	N × P (*k*)
	B–KN5	P–QR3 (*g*)	B–Q2	Q–K2
7	P–KR3	N–QR4!	P–B5	Q–B2	P–Q4
	B × N	N–Q5 (*e*)	P–R3	N–QB3!	B–Q3
8	Q × B	N × B	Q–K2	P–QN4	N–B3
	N–Q5 (*c*)	P × N	B–Q2	B–Q3	N × P
9	Q–N3	P–B3!	B–K3	B–B4	B–K2
	P × P!	N × N†	N–Q5	N–B3	O–O
10	Q × NP	P × N (*f*)	B × N	P–Q3 (*i*)	O–O
	R–KB1 (*d*)		P × B (*h*)		P–QB4 (*l*)

(*a*) (A) 2 . . . P–Q3; 3 N–KB3, P × P! see cols. 14–15. (B) 2 . . . N–KB3; 3 P × P, N × P; 4 N–KB3, N–N4; (1) 5 P–B3, P–Q3; 6 P–Q4, N × N†; 7 Q × N, Q–R5†; 8 P–N3, Q–N5! Ravinski; or (2) 5 P–Q4, N × N†; 6 Q × N, Q–R5†; 7 Q–B2, Q × Q†; 8 K × Q, N–B3 (or 8 . . . P–Q3); 9 P–B3, P–Q3; 10 P × P, B × P = . Fischer-Wade Vinkovci 1968.

(*b*) 3 Q–B3, P–Q3; 4 P × P, P × P; 5 Q–KN3, N–KB3! 6 Q × P†, B–K2; 7 N–QB3, O–O; 8 N–B3, N–B3, with excellent development for Black.

(*c*) 8 . . . P × P! 9 B–N5, O–O; 10 B × N, P × B; 11 B × P, with equality. Rubinstein.

(*d*) 11 K–Q1, Q–K2; 12 B × P, R–KN1; 13 Q–R6, R × P; 14 R–KB1! N–K3! 15 B × N! Q × B; 16 B–N5, N–N1; 17 Q–R4, P–KR3, with pressure. Rabinovich.

(*e*) Worth practical try out is 7 . . . B × N?! 8 Q × B, N–Q5; 9 Q–N3! P × P! 10 B × P, N–R4; 11 Q–N4, N × B; 12 Q × N, Q–K2 ∞ .

(*f*) (A) 10 . . . N × KP? 11 O–O! (B) 10 . . . B–R4! 11 Q–K2, Q–Q3; 12 P × P! Q × KP; 13 P–B4, Q–K2; 14 Q–N2 ± .

(*g*) These alternatives seem preferable to cols. 21–2. Black has also (A) 6 . . . B–K3; 7 B–N5! P–QR3; 8 B × N†, P × B; 9 P–B5?! B–B1; 10 B–N5, B–N2; 11 N–K2, Q–K2; 12 Q–Q2, P–Q4 = . Goldstein. (B) 6 . . . N–KN5? 7 N–QR4! N–Q5; 8 N × B, P × N; 9 P–B3, N × N†; 10 P × N, N–B3; 11 Q–K2, Q–Q3; 12 P × P, Q × P; 13 P–B4, Q–K2; 14 Q–N2 ± .

(*h*) 11 N–Q1, O–O; 12 O–O, Tolush-Furman, Leningrad 1947, R–K1 = .

(*i*) White retains an edge after both (A) 10 . . . N–K2; 11 O–O, N–N3; 12 P–QR4 ± and (B) 10 . . . Q–K2; 11 O–O, O–O–O; 12 P–QR4, P–QR4; 13 P–N5, N–QN1; 14 QN–Q2, B–KN5; 15 N–N3, P–QN3; 16 B–K3, N/1–Q2; 17 QR–K1, B–K3; 18 B × B, Q × B; 19 K–R1, Q–K2; 20 QN–Q2, N–N5; 21 B–N1, P–R4; 22 N–B4; P–N4; 23 N × B†, P × N; 24 N–Q2, P–B3; 25 N–B4, K–N2; 26 B × P, N × B; 27 N × RP†, K–B2; 28 N–N6, Q–K1; 29 P–R5, N–Q2; 30 P–N6†, K–N2; 31 P–R6†, K × NP; 32 R–QN1†, resigns. Bronstein-Panov, Moscow Chp. 1947. White's 6th move is Marshall's. In the column, other solid continuations are 4 B–B4, N–QB3; 5 P–B3, N–B3; (A) 6 P × P, P × P; 7 P–Q3, O–O; 8 Q–K2, P–QR4; 9 P–QR4 and (B) 6 P–Q3, B–KN5; 7 P–QN4, B–N3; 8 P–KR3, B × N; 9 P–Q3, B–KN5; 7 P–QN4, B–N3; 8 P–KR3, B × N; 9 Q × B, O–O; 10 P–QR4.

(*j*) (A) 4 . . . P–B4; 5 P × KP! QP × P; 6 P–Q4, KP × P; 7 B–QB4! (B) 4 . . . N–QB3; 5 P–Q4, P × QP; 6 P × P, B–N3; 7 B–N5, B–Q2; 8 N–B3, KN–K2 = . Santasiere-Reshevsky, US Chp. 1946.

(*k*) 6 P–Q4, P × P; 7 P × P, B–N3; 8 P–K5, N–Q4; 9 B–QB4, B–K3; 10 Q–N3, O–O; 11 N–B3, P–QB3; 12 O–O, N–N2; 13 B–K3, N–Q2 = . *Comments.*

(*l*) 11 QN–Q2, N × N; 12 B × N, P × P! 13 P × P! N–B3 = .

1 P-K4, P-K4; 2 P-KB4, P-Q4; 3 KP × P (a), P-K5 (b); 4 P-Q3 (c), N-KB3 (d)

	26	27	28	29	30
5	P × P		Q-K2	N-Q2 (i)	
	N × KP		B-N5 (g)	B-KB4	P × P
6	N-KB3!	B-K3	N-KB3!	P × P	B × P
	B-QB4 (e)	Q-R5†	Q × P (h)	N × KP	Q × P (k)
7	Q-K2	P-N3	QN-Q2	KN-B3	KN-B3
	B-B4	N × P	N-B3	B-B4	B-KN5
8	N-B3	N-KB3 (f)	P × P	B-Q3	O-O
	Q-K2	Q-K2	Q-KR4	N × N	B-B4†
9	B-K3	P × N	Q-N5	B × B	K-R1
	B × B	Q × B†	O-O-O	N × N†	O-O
10	Q × B	Q-K2	Q × Q	Q × N	Q-K1
	N × N	Q × Q†	N × Q	O-O	N-B3
11	Q × Q† ±	B × Q	N-B4	B-Q2	P-QR3
		B-KN5 =	N-N5 =	R-K1† (j)	KR-K1 =

(a) (A) 3 N-QB3, N-KB3, see Vienna Game. (B) 3 N-KB3, P × KP; 4 N × P, N-Q2; 5 P-Q4, P × P e.p. and (1) 6 B × P, N × N; 7 P × N, Q-R5†; 8 P-N3, Q-N5; 9 Q × Q, B × Q; 10 B-K3, N-K2; 11 N-B3, N-B3; 12 B-QN5, B-Q2, drawn. Konstantinopolski-Botvinnik, Sverdlovsk 1943; or (2) 6 N × QP, KN-B3; 7 N-B3, N-N3! 8 B-K2, B-Q3; 9 O-O, O-O; 10 B-B3, P-B3 = . Lutikov-Nikitin, USSR Chp. 1959.

(b) (A) 3 . . . P × P; 4 N-KB3, N-KB3, see col. 6. (B) 3 . . . P × P; 4 Q-B3!, N-KB3; 5 N-B3, B-KN5; 6 Q × P, B-Q3; 7 Q-K3†, B-K2; 8 B-B4, O-O; 9 N-B3, B × N; 10 Q × B, B-B4; 11 N-K2, QN-Q2; 12 P-Q4 ± . Planinć-Gligorić, Yugoslav Chp. 1968.

(c) (A) 4 N-QB3, N-KB3; 5 Q-K2, B-K2; 6 P-QN3, N × P =. (B) 4 B-B4, N-KB3; 5 N-QB3, B-QB4! 6 P-Q4, P × P e.p.; 7 Q × P, O-O; 8 KN-K2, P-B3; 9 P × P, Q-N3 ∓.

(d) (A) 4 . . . Q × P; 5 Q-K2, N-KB3; 6 N-QB3, see note (g-B). (B) 4 . . . P × P; 5 Q × P, N-KB3! 6 N-QB3, B-QB4; 7 B-Q2, O-O; 8 O-O-O, QN-Q2; 9 P-KN3 + .

(e) Weaker are (A) 6 . . . B-KB4; 7 B-K3, P-QB3; 8 B-B4, P-QN4; 9 B-N3 + or (B) 6 . . . B-KN5; 7 B-Q3, P-KB4; 8 Q-K2, Q × P; 9 QN-Q2! ± . Claparède.

(f) 8 P × N, Q × R; 9 Q-K2, B-N5†! 10 P-B3, B-Q3 ∓.

(g) (A) 5 . . . B-KB4; 6 P × P, N × KP; 7 N-QB3, Q-K2; 8 B-Q2, N × N; 9 Q × Q† B × Q!? 10 B × N, B × P; 11 N-KB3 ± . (B) 5 . . . Q × P; 6 N-QB3 (6 N-Q2, B-KB4; 7 P × P, B × P; 8 P-KN4!? N-B3! =), B-QN5; 7 B-Q2, B × N; 8 B × B, B-N5; 9 P × P, B × Q; 10 P × Q, B × B; 11 K × B, N × P; 12 B × P, R-N1; 13 R-K1†, K-Q2; 14 R-Q1, K-B3; 15 B-Q4, N × P; 16 P-KN3, N-K3; 17 B-K3 ± . Bronstein-Szabó, Moscow 1949.

(h) 6 . . . B-N5†; 7 P-B3, O-O; 8 P × P, R-K1; 9 P-K5! B-QR4; 10 N-R3, N × P; 11 B-Q2 ± . Filchev-Shishov, Moscow 1958. The column is *Comments*.

(i) A long buried line now revived is 5 N-QB3, B-QN5; 6 B-Q2, P-K6; 7 B × P, O-O; 8 B-Q2, B × N; 9 P × B, R-K1†; 10 B-K2, B-N5; 11 K-B2! (11 P-B4? P-B3; 12 P × P, N × P; 13 K-B1, R × B! ∓ . Schulten-Morphy, New York, 1857), B × B; 12 N × B, Q × P ∞ . Glazkov in *Byulleten*.

(j) 12 K-Q1 ± .

(k) Equally strong is 6 . . . N × P e.g. (A) 7 Q-B3, N-N5; 8 B-K4, P-KB4; 9 P-QR3, P × B; 10 Q × P†, Q-K2; 11 P × N, Q × Q† = ; or (B) 7 Q-K2†, B-K2; 8 N-K4, N-N5; 9 B-B4, B-KN5; 10 Q × B, N × P†; 11 K-K2, P-KN3 = . The column is *Comments*.

Latvian (or Greco Counter) Gambit

(1 P–K4, P–K4; 2 N–KB3, P–KB4)

This reverse form of the King's Gambit was given a new lease of life by Latvian analysts, notably K. Behting, who restored its theoretical soundness. Recent analysis by Gunderam and a group of Latvian-American masters, in their—now defunct—magazine *The Latvian Gambit*, has come up with several suggestions for Black but they are of a somewhat precarious nature, with unresolved problems pointed up by Hans Müller—and grandmasters rarely employ this defence. Nevertheless, the gambit has been enlarged to five columns (compared to one in the 9th edition) for the simple reason that such wealth of research has been lavished on it, and one never knows when an improvement will revitalize a defence which has already outlasted nine lives.

3 B–B4 (col. 1) is the sharpest "refutation." Keres has subjected it to searching analysis. The result is fireworks!

3 P–Q4 (col. 2) was played in the game Stockholm-Riga, corr. 1936. It opens too many lines and permits Black to resolve all his problems.

3 N×P (cols. 3–4) is stronger than it looks; but Black may be able to thread his way to equality as shown in recent games.

3 P×P (col. 5 is as old as *Bilguer*) is interesting because White strives for a good variation of the King's Gambit Accepted with colours reversed. Here Black must come up with some sound and stubborn planning to counter White's solid treatment; otherwise the Latvian Gambit will remain in the realm of off-beat speculation, despite some enterprising variations of Black's as quoted.

11

1 P–K4, P–K4; 2 N–KB3, P–KB4

	1	2	3	4	5
3	B–B4	P–Q4	N × P		P × P
	P × P (*a*)	BP × P	Q–B3 (*h*)		P–K5 (*p*)
4	N × P	N × P	N–B4	P–Q4	N–K5!
	Q–N4 (*b*)	N–KB3	P × P	P–Q3	N–KB3
5	P–Q4!	B–QB4 (*g*)	N–B3	N–B4	B–K2
	Q × P	P–Q4	Q–KN3 (*i*)	P × P	P–Q3
6	Q–R5†	B–N3	P–Q3	N–B3 (*k*)	B–R5†
	P–N3	B–K3	B–N5	Q–KN3	K–K2
7	B–B7†	B–N5	B–Q2	P–B3 (*l*)	N–B7
	K–Q1	B–K2	B × N	P × P (*m*)	Q–K1
8	B × P (*c*)	O–O	B × B	Q × P	N × R
	Q × R† (*d*)	O–O	P–Q4	N–QB3	Q × B
9	K–K2	N–Q2	N–K5	B–Q3	Q × Q
	P–B3! (*e*)	N–B3	Q–B4	Q–N5	N × Q
10	N–QB3 (*f*)	N × N	P × P	Q–B2 (*n*)	P–KN4
		P × N =	Q × KP† (*j*)	Q × QP (*o*)	N–KB3 (*q*)

(*a*) (A) 3 . . . N–KB3; 4 N × P, Q–K2; 5 P–Q4, N–B3; 6 N–QB3! N × N; 7 P × N Q × P; 8 P–B4, Q–B4 ∞ . Gunderam. (B) 3 . . . P–Q3? 4 P–Q4, see Philidor's Defence, note (*n*).

(*b*) 4 . . . P–Q4; 5 Q–R5†, P–N3; 6 N × P, P × N; 7 Q × P†, K–Q2; 8 B × P, N–KB3; 9 N–B3, Q–K2; 10 P–QN3! R–R3; 11 Q–B7! Q × Q = .

(*c*) If choosing 3 B–B4, safest here is 8 Q–N5†, Q × Q; 9 B × Q†, B–K2; 10 B–Q5, B × B; 11 N–B7†, K–K2; 12 N × B, N–KB3 = . Behting.

(*d*) (A) 8 . . . N–KB3; 9 N–B7†, K–K1; 10 N × R†, P × B; 11 Q × P†, Q × Q; 12 N × Q, wins. Keres. (B) 8 . . . P × B; 9 B–N5†, B–K2; 10 Q × R ± .

(*e*) 9 . . . Q × B; 10 N–B7†, K–K1; 11 N × R†, P × B; 12 Q × P†, K–Q1; 13 N–Q2! ± ; or 13 N–B7†, K–K2; 14 N–B3!. Keres.

(*f*) (A) 10 . . . P–K6; 11 N–B7†, K–B2; 12 B × KP, Q × R; 13 Q–KN5, P–N4; 14 N × P†, P × N; 15 B–B4†, K–N3 ∞ . Lundin-Pupols, Washington 1966. (B) 10 . . . K–B2; 11 B–B4, Q × R; 12 N–B7†, P–Q3; 13 N × P ± . Gunderam. (C) 10 . . . N–B3; 11 Q–N5!, R–N1; 12 Q × N†, B–K2; 13 Q–B7!, R × B (13 . . . P × B; 14 B–N5! Q × R; 15 B × B†, K–B2; 16 Q × R, P–QN4; 17 Q–Q8†, K–N2; 18 N × KP + +); 14 B–N5! Q–B6†; 15 N × Q, P × N†; 16 K × P, B × B; 17 N–K4, B–K2; 18 Q × P, R–K3; 19 R–KN1, P–N4; 20 R–N8†, K–B2; 21 R–K8, resigns. Pupols-Dreibergs, USA 1956.

(*g*) 5 B–KN5, P–Q3; 6 N–B4, B–K2; 7 B–K2, O–O; 8 O–O, P–B3 = . Wolf-Apscheneek, Hamburg 1930.

(*h*) Likewise 3 . . . N–QB3; 4 N × N, QP × N; 5 N–B3, N–B3; 6 P × P, B × P; 7 P–Q4, B–QN5; 8 B–Q3, B–N5; 9 P–B3, B–KR4 = .

(*i*) (A) An unsuccessful attempt is 5 . . . Q–K3; 6 P–Q3, B–N5; (6 . . . P × P†; 7 B–K3, P × P; 8 Q × P allows White an enormous lead in development); 7 P × P, Q × P†; 8 B–K2, B × N†; 9 P × B, P–Q4; 10 O–O! P × N? 11 R–K1 + . (B) 5 . . . P–B3; 6 N × P, Q–K3; 7 Q–R5†! K–Q1; 8 Q–K5, P–Q4; 9 N–N5, Q–K2; 10 Q × Q†, B × Q; 11 N–K5, B × N; 12 N–B7†, K–K2; 13 N × B ± ; (C) 5 . . . Q–B2! 6 N–K3, P–B3! 7 N × P, P–Q4; (1) 8 N–N3, P–KR4! 9 P–KR4, B–Q3 (or 9 . . . P–KN3); 10 Q–B3, N–B3; 11 N/K3–B5, B–B2 = . (2) 8 N–N5, Q–B3; 9 N–B3, B–Q3 (or 9 . . . P–Q5); 10 P–Q4, B–K3; 11 B–Q3, N–Q2; 12 P–KR3, P–KR4; 13 P–KR4, O–O–O; 14 N–N5, R–K1 ∞ .

(*j*) 11 B–K2, N–KB3; 12 O–O, O–O; 13 B–B3, Q–B4; 14 B × P†, N × B; 15 Q × N†, Q–K3 ∞ . *Comments*.

(*k*) More conservative is 6 B–K2! N–B3; 7 P–Q5, N–K4; 8 O–O, N × N; 9 B × N, Q–N3; 10 B–N5†, with better chances. Bronstein-Mikenas, Rostov 1941.

(*l*) 7 Q-K2, N-KB3! 8 P-B3, N-B3; 9 B-K3, B-K2; 10 O-O-O, O-O; 11 P-Q5, N-QN5; 12 P-QR3, P-QR4 = . Muratov-Spasski, USSR 1966.

(*m*) "Chickening out" is 7 . . . N-KB3?! 8 B-K3, B-K2; 9 B-K2!? O-O = .

(*n*) The older line is 10 Q-K3†, B-K2; 11 O-O, N-B3; 12 P-Q5, N-N5; 13 R-B4, Q-Q2; 14 N-N6, RP×N; 15 R×QN, O-O = . Nimzowitsch.

(*o*) 11 B-K3, Q-B3; 12 Q-K2, B-K3; 13 N-K4, Q-K2　　．

(*p*) (A) 3 . . . P-Q3; 4 P-Q4, P-K5; 5 N-N5, B×P; 6 P-KN4! *P/E.* (B) 3 . . . Q-K2?! 4 B-B4, P-Q3; 5 O-O, B×P; 6 R-K1, N-Q2; 7 P-Q4, O-O-O ∞ . Gunderam. (c) 3 . . . N-QB3; 4 B-N5, B-B4; 5 B×N, QP×B; 6 N×P, B×P; 7 Q-R5†, P-N3; 8 N×NP, P×N; 9 Q×R, Q-K2†; 10 K-Q1, B×P! 11 Q×Nt, K-Q2; 12 Q-B4, R-K1 + + . Schiffers-Chigorin, 1878.

(*q*) 11 R-N1, N-B3; 12 R-N3, N-Q5; 13 K-Q1 + . Keres.

Philidor's Defence

(1 P–K4, P–K4; 2 N–KB3, P–Q3)

Philidor promoted this defence in his "L'analyse" (1749), Larsen favoured it in the 1960–70s, but nowadays this defence is adopted only to avoid the better-known variations of other openings, and it has given way in popularity to its counterpart, Pirć's Defence (1 P–K4, P–Q3). By locking in his king's bishop, Black can only hope for equality. He must be constantly on the alert for combinations aimed at his weak king's bishop's pawn. With mechanical moves White can achieve a lasting advantage in space and mobility. Black's game, while sometimes solid, is always cramped, with few chances for any tactical upset.

After 3 P–Q4, N–KB3 was for a long time considered Black's best, developing a piece and attacking the rival king's pawn (col. 1). Possibly White does best to maintain the tension with 4 N–B3, though 4 P × P might lead to a sharp, open game more to the taste of an attacking player.

3 P–Q4, N–Q2—the Hanham Variation—(cols. 2–3) has proved too passive compared to 3 . . . P × P (col. 4) which has undergone a revival.

3 . . . P–KB4?! (col. 5) was played in the good old days, but it is just too risky in this scientific age, although it is exactly this aspect which often tempts Black to spring it as a surprise.

1 P–K4, P–K4; 2 N–KB3, P–Q3; 3 P–Q4

	1	2	3	4	5
	N–KB3......	N–Q2 (The Hanham		P×P	P–KB4
		Variation)			
4	N–B3 (a)	B–QB4		N×P (i)	QP×P (p)
	QN–Q2	P–QB3		N–KB3 (j)	BP×P
5	B–QB4 (b)	O–O........	P–QR4 (h)	N–QB3	N–N5
	B–K2	B–K2	B–K2	B–K2 (k)	P–Q4
6	O–O (c)	P×P	N–B3	B–KB4 (l)	P–K6
	O–O	P×P	KN–B3	O–O	N–KR3
7	Q–K2	N–N5	O–O	Q–Q2	N–QB3
	P–B3	B×N!	P–KR3	P–QR3 (m)	P–B3
8	P–QR4	Q–R5	P–QN3	O–O–O	KN×P!
	P–QR4 (d)	Q–B3 (f)	Q–B2	P–Q4	N–B4
9	P–R3	B×B	B–N2	N×P (n)	N–KN5
	P×P (e)	Q–N3	O–O	N×N	Q–B3
10	N×P	Q–R4	Q–Q2 ±	P×N	B–Q3
	N–B4	N–N3		Q×P	P–KR3
11	R–Q1	B–K2		N–N3	Q–B3
	Q–B2	N–B3		Q–B3	P–KN3
12	B–B4 ±	N–Q2		B–K2	P–KN4 +
		P–KR3 (g)		Q–R5 (o)	

(a) White's pressure seems to evaporate after 4 P×P, N×P; 5 QN–Q2 (5 Q–Q5, N–B4; 6 B–N5, Q–Q2 = ; or 6 N–N5, Q–K2), N×N; 6 B×N, B–K2 (or 6 . . . N–B3 =); 7 B–QB4, O–O = , but the line contains some unexplored possibilities.

(b) A finesse à la King's Indian is 5 P–KN3, B–K2; 6 B–N2, O–O; 7 O–O, P–B3; 8 P–QR4, R–K1; 9 R–K1, B–B1; 10 P–N3 ± . Korchnoi-Guimard, Buenos Aires 1960.

(c) (A) For 6 P–QR4 see col. 3. If (B) 6 P×P?! P×P; 7 B×P†, K×B; 8 N–N5†, K–N1 (if 8 . . . K–N3; 9 P–B₄—not 9 P–KR4, P–KR4; 10 P–B4, P×P; 11 N–K2!, B–Q3; 12 P–K5, N×P! 13 N×P†, K–R3 ∓ –9 . . . P×P; 10 N–K6, Q–N1; 11 N×BP, R–N1; 12 B×P ±) 9 N–K6, Q–K1; 10 N×BP, Q–N3; 11 N×R, Q×P; 12 R–B1, N–B4; 13 Q–K2, B–R6; 14 B–K3, Q×R†; 15 Q×Q, B×Q; 16 K×B, K–B2; 17 N–B7, KN×P! = Vuković. 6 B×P†, K×B; 7 N–N5†, K–N1; 8 N–K6, Q–K1; 9 N×BP ∞ .

(d) (A) 8 . . . P×P; 9 N×P, R–K1 is Larsen's suggestion, but the course of line (B) (2) makes it suspect. In any case, 9 P–QR4 is safer. Comments. (B) 8 . . . Q–B2; 9 P–R3, (1) 9 . . . P–QN3! 10 R–Q1, P–QR3 = . Any impatience of Black's was punished after (2) 9 . . . P×P; 10 N×P, R–K1; 11 B–B4, N–K4; 12 B–QN3, KN–Q2; 13 QR–Q1, B–B1; 14 B–B1, N–B4; 15 B–R2, P–Q4; 16 P–B4! (16 P×P? N–N5!), N/K4–Q2; 17 P–K5, N–N3; 18 P–R5, N/3–Q2; 19 Q–R5, N–K3; 20 N–B5, Q×RP; 21 R–B3, N–N3; 22 R–N3, P–N3; 23 Q–R4, N–R5; 24 R×P, Q–N3†; 25 B–K3, Q–N5; 26 R–QN5, N×N; 27 R×Q, N–K7†; 28 K–R2, N×R; 29 Q×N, B×R; 30 N–R6†, K–R1; 31 P–B5, N–Q1; 32 P×P, BP×P; 33 Q–B4, B–B1; 34 N–B7†, N×N; 35 Q×N, B–K3; 36 B×B, B–N2; 37 B–Q4, QR–Q1; 38 B–B3, P–QN4; 39 B–Q7, R–KB1; 40 Q–K7, resigns. Grefe-Najdorf, Lone Pine 1976.

(e) 9 . . . Q–K1 might maintain some useful tension (Pickett).

(f) 8 . . . P–KN3! 9 Q×B might result in a better endgame for White.

(g) 13 B–K3, B–K3; 14 P–KB4 ± . Khasin-Pines, Moscow 1958.

(h) (A) Dangerous complications where Black may just survive, arise from 5 N–N5, N–R3; 6 O–O (6 P–QR4! Q–B3! 7 P–QB3, B–K2 =) N–N3! 7 B–N3! B–K2; 8 Q–R5, O–O; 9 P×P, P×P; 10 P–KB4, P–B4; 11 P–B3, P×P; 12 B×P, B–N5; 13 Q–R4, Q–Q2; 14 Q–N3, K–R1; 15 N–Q2, B×N; 16 B×B, N–N1 = . PCO. (B) Forthright is 5 N–B3, B–K2; 6 P×P, P×P; 7

N–KN5, B × N; 8 Q–R5, P–KN3; 9 Q × B, Q × Q; 10 B × Q ± . Barden-Klein, British Chp. 1950.

(*i*) No worse is 4 Q × P, N–QB3; 5 B–QN5, B–Q2; 6 B × N, P × B (if 6 . . . B × B; 7 B–N5 ±); and now (A) 7 P–B4, P–B3; with a restrictive defence; or (B) 7 N–B3! N–B3; 8 B–N5, B–K2; 9 O–O–O, O–O; 10 KR–K1 ± . Pachman.

(*j*) An intriguing novelty is 4 . . . P–KN3; 5 N–QB3, B–N2; 6 B–KB4, N–KB3; 7 Q–Q2, O–O; 8 O–O–O, R–K1; 9 P–B3, N–B3! 10 N × N, P × N; 11 P–K5, N–Q4; 12 N × N, P × N; 13 B–KN5, Q–Q2 ∞. Tal-Larsen, match 1969. Here: 6 B–K3! seems best.

(*k*) 5 . . . QN–Q2, see col. 1.

(*l*) One of the more "recent" vogues, as against (A) 6 B–K2, O–O; 7 O–O (7 P–B4, P–B4; 8 N–N3, B–Q2; 9 B–B3, B–B3; 10 O–O, R–K1; 11 B–K3, Q–B2; 12 Q–K2, B–B1 = : Zinn-Diaz, Havana 1968), P–QR3!; 8 R–K1, R–K1; 9 P–QR4, B–B1; 10 B–QB4, QN–Q2; 11 B–KN5, P–R3; 12 B–R4, N–K4; 13 B–N3, P–B3, Drimer-Suetin, Havana 1968; 14 P–KR3 and 15 P–B4 ± . (B) 6 B–N5†, P–B3; 7 B–Q3, O–O; 8 O–O, P–Q4!?∞ . (C) 6 P–KN3, P–Q4; 7 P–K5, N–N5; 8 P–K6, N–KB3 ∞. (D) 6 B–QB4, O–O; 7 O–O, P–QR3! = .

(*m*) (A) A deviation from the classical 7 . . . R–K1; 8 O–O–O, B–B1; 9 P–B3, QN–Q2; 10 P–KN4, N–K4; 11 B–K2, P–QR3; 12 P–KR4, P–QN4; 13 P–R5 ± . Kashdan-Koltanowski, London 1932. (B) Quite important is also 7 . . . P–Q4; 8 P × P, N × P; 9 N × N, Q × N; 10 N–N5, Q–K5†.

(*n*) 9 P–K5, N–R4 (also 9 . . . N–K1); 10 B–K3, P–KN3 = .

(*o*) 13 B × P, N–B3; 14 B–Q6, B × B; 15 Q × B, Q × P; 16 Q–R3, Q × Q = . Kholmov-S. Garcia, Havana 1968.

(*p*) Against this "Philidor's Counter Attack" of Black's, White has a variety of good replies which have refuted the risky 3 . . . P–KB4; e.g. (A) 4 B–QB4, BP × P; 5 N × P, P–Q4; 6 Q–R5†, P–N3; 7 N × P, N–KB3; 8 Q–K5†, B–K2; 9 Q × B†, Q × Q; 10 N × Q, K × N; 11 B–K2 + . (B) 4 N–B3 (1) 4 . . . N–KB3; 5 P × KP, N × P; 6 N × N, P × N; 7 N–N5, P–Q4; 8 P–K6, B–B4; 9 N × KP! + . Analysis by Sozin, Sokolski, and traditional sources. (2) 4 . . . P × QP; 5 Q × P, N–KB3; 6 P–K5! (but not 6 B–KN5, B–K2 =). (C) 4 KP × P, P–K5; 5 N–N5, B × P; 6 N–QB3, P–Q4; 7 P–B3 ± .

Petrov's Defence

(1 P–K4, P–K4; 2 N–KB3, N–KB3)

The Petrov (or the "Petroff" according to the West European spelling adopted before World War I) bears the name of the Russian who practiced it in the nineteenth century, although it was first worked out in some detail by his countryman Jänisch (or Janisch) in 1842. Down through the years the Americans Pillsbury, Marshall, Kashdan and Bisguier have been its outstanding advocates. The defence is theoretically sound but rather limited in strategic conception. The defence was thoroughly re-analysed by the Lithuanian Mikenas and by D. Hooper of Britain.

Black's second move institutes an immediate counter-attack against White's king's pawn and, in this aggressive reaction, is strikingly modern. It can provoke lively counterplay, but lacks fluidity and tension if Black is playing for a win. The forcing character of this defence averts the pitfalls of the Giuoco Piano, Ruy Lopez, and other enterprising systems for White.

3 N × P, P–Q3 (3 . . . N × P?; 4 Q–K2, P–Q4; 5 P–Q3, Q–K2; 6 P × N, Q × N; 7 P × P +); 4 N–KB3, N × P (cols. 1–5) seems to be a somewhat stale method, giving White no more than a minimal edge against 5 P–Q4, P–Q4; 6 B–Q3, B–K2 (cols. 2–3), provided Black rejects the tricky mimicry of 6 . . . B–Q3 (col. 1). However, while this established course has been alive for over a century, the subtle transpositions introduced in the new games added to the vital columns 2–3 prove that there is something new to ring in much of the time even in apparently staid analysis. Black's 6th moves (col. 2) are under a cloud and note *(b)* is the only tenable resource left. Lasker's simplifying 5 Q–K2 (col. 5) is a bid for a favourable end-game which practically leads to a forced draw after the queens are exchanged. Thus, if Black is staking everything on an all-out win, the Petrov is unsuitable, except as a psychological means to differ if the opponent finds it opportune.

17

Moreover, new blood has been infused by lovers of the unexplored, with the revival of Steinitz's 3 P–Q4 (cols. 6–9). The line had, for no real reason, suffered a bad reputation, but is surely White's most dynamic chance. As a rule this early break is undesirable; but here the tempo gained with P–K5 is effective. Col. 8 is an old line, rehabilitated by Fischer, which aims at outright refutation. It is still crucial. Black developed a riposte with 3 . . . P–Q4 (col. 9) which led to further exhaustive experimentation. The Three Knights' Defence (col 10 note *n*) has not gained independent importance. Black can always side-step into the drawish Four Knights' Game, and only 3 B–B4 is still valid ground for further tries.

1 P–K4, P–K4; 2 N–KB3, N–KB3; 3 N × P, P–Q3; 4 N–KB3 (a), N × P

	1	2	3	4	5
5	P–Q4			P–B4	Q–K2
	P–Q4 (b)			B–K2 (n)	Q–K2
6	B–Q3			N–B3 (o)	P–Q3 (s)
	B–Q3?	B–K2 (f)		B–KB4! (p)	N–KB3
7	O–O (c)	O–O		N–Q5 (q)	B–N5
	O–O	O–O	N–QB3	O–O	Q × Q† (t)
8	P–B4 (d)	R–K1 (g)	P–B4 (k)	P–Q3	B × Q
	B–KN5	B–KB4? (h)	N–N5 (l)	N–KB3	B–K2
9	P × P	P–B4	P × P	N × B†	N–B3
	P–KB4	P–QB3	N × B	Q × N†	P–KR3
10	N–B3	N–B3! (i)	Q × N	B–K2	B–R4
	N–Q2	N × N	Q × P	Q–K1	B–Q2
11	P–KR3	P × N	R–K1	P–KR3	O–O–O
	B–R4	B × B	B–KB4	P–Q4	N–B3
12	N × N	Q × B	N–B3	P–R3	P–Q4
	P × N (e)	P × P (j)	N × N (m)	P–B4 (r)	O–O–O =

(a) 4 N–B4, N × P; 5 N–B3, N × N; 6 NP × N, P–KN3; 7 B–K2, B–N2; 8 O–O, O–O; 9 P–Q4, N–Q2 = . Matanović-Alexander, Staunton Memorial 1951.

(b) Tamer but safe is 5 . . . B–K2; 6 B–Q3, N–KB3; (A) 7 O–O, O–O; 8 B–KN5, B–N5; 9 QN–Q2, N–B3; 10 P–B3, P–KR3; 11 B–R4, N–KR4; 12 B × B, N × B; 13 P–KN3, N–KB3; 14 R–K1, Q–Q2; 15 Q–N3, P–B3 = . Keres-Bronstein, USSR Chp. 1961. (B) 7 P–KR3, O–O; 8 O–O, P–B3; 9 R–K1, QN–Q2; 10 B–KB4, R–K1; 11 P–B4, N–B1; 12 N–B3, P–QR3; 13 Q–N3, N–K3; 14 B–R2, B–B1; 15 R–K2, P–QN4; 16 Q–B2, B–N2; 17 QR–K1, P–N3; 18 P–QN4, P × P; 19 B × BP, N–B2 = . Fischer-Petrosian, 5th match game, 1971.

(c) 7 P–B4, B–N5†; 8 QN–Q2, B × N†; 9 B × B, O–O; 10 O–O, B–N5; 11 B–R4, N–QB3; 12 R–K1, N × QP; 13 B × N, P × B; 14 Q × N, P × N = . Tarrasch-Marshall, St. Petersburg 1914.

(d) 8 N–B3, N × N; 9 P × N, P–QB4; 10 P–B4, P × BP; 11 B × P, P × P; 12 Q × P, N–B3 = . Kmoch.

(e) 13 B × P, N–B3; 14 B–B5, K–R1; 15 P–KN4! N × QP; 16 B–K6, B–B2; 17 N–N5! ± . Alexander-Mallison, Brighton 1938.

(f) (A) 6 . . . N–QB3, is a faint possibility. (B) Weak is 6 . . . B–N5; 7 O–O, P–KB4; 8 P–B4, N–QB3; 9 N–B3, B × N; 10 P × B, N × QP; 11 P × N, QP × KP; 12 B × P! Sir G. Thomas—A. R. B. Thomas, Hastings 1937–38.

(g) 8 P–B4, N–KB3; 9 P × P, N × P; 10 N–B3, N–QB3; 11 Q–N3, B–K3! Keres.

(h) In the light of this column, the author's recommendation in MC011 of 8 . . . N–Q3! remains valid.

(i) An improvement which helps clarify White's strategy as is called for; namely, of pressure to bear on Black's backward pawns by forcing exchanges and opening up lines.

(j) 13 Q × P, N–Q2; 14 Q–N3! N–N3; 15 P–B4, Q–Q2; 16 R–N1, P–QB4; 17 B–R3, QR–B1; 18 QR–Q1, Q–B2; 19 R–K5, KR–Q1; 20 B × P, B–B3; 21 R–B5, Q–B3; 22 P–KR3, N–R5; 23 R–K1, R–B2; 24 B–N4, P–KR3; 25 P–Q5, Q–R3; 26 P–Q6, resigns. Kavalek-Pfleger, Montilla 1973.

(k) 8 R–K1, B–KN5; 9 P–B3, P–B4; 10 Q–N3, O–O; 11 QN–Q2, K–R1 (forced); 12 P–KR3, B–R4; 13 Q × NP, R–B3; 14 Q–N3, R–N3; 15 B–K2, B–R5; 16 R–B1, B × N; 17 N × B, B × P†; 18 R × B, N × R; 19 K × N, Q–Q3; 20 N–N5, R–KB1; 21 Q–R3, Q–Q1; 22 B–KB4, P–KR3; 23 N–B3, R–K1; 24 B–Q3, R–K5; 25 P–KN3, R–B3; 26 Q–B5, P–N4; 27 N × P, P × N; 28 B × NP, R/5–K3; 29 R–K1, Q–KN1; 30 P–KR4, R–N3; 31 R × R, resigns. Karpov-Korchnoi, 6th match game, 1974.

(*l*) 8 . . . N-B3; 9 P×P, N×P; 10 N-B3, O-O; 11 Q-N3, B-K3 transposes into note *g*. Black's QNP is poisoned.

(*m*) 13 Q×N, P-QB3; 14 B-R6!! (14 B-Q2 got White nowhere in Yates-Kashdan, Hastings 1931), R-KN1 (14 . . . P×B; 15 R-K5, Q-Q2; 16 QR-K1, B-K3; 17 P-Q5!); 15 R-K5, Q-Q2; 16 QR-K1, B-K3; 17 N-N5! O-O-O; 18 N×BP, B×N; 19 R×B, Q×P; 20 R×B, Q×Q; 21 P×Q, P×B; 22 R-N1, R-N4; 23 P-KR4, R-N4; 24 R×R, P×R; 25 R×RP, R-Q8†; 26 K-R2, R-Q7; 27 R×RP, R×RP; 28 P-R5, R×P; 29 R-R8†, K-B2; 30 P-R6, K-N3; 31 K-R3, P-R4; 32 P-N4, P-N5; 33 P×P, P×P; 34 R-K8, R-B8; 35 K-N2, R-B2; 36 P-N5, R-B4; 37 P-R7, R×P†; 38 K-B3, R-KR4; 39 P-R8/Q, R×Q; 40 R×R, resigns. Browne-Bisguier, US Chp. 1974.

(*n*) 5 . . . P-Q4; 6 N-QB3, B-KB4! 7 N×N, B×N; 8 P-Q4, B-K2 = . Mikenas.

(*o*) 6 P-Q4, P-Q4! 7 B-Q3, B-N5† = .

(*p*) 6 . . . N×N; 7 QP×N, N-B3; 8 B-Q3, B-KN5; 9 B-K4, O-O; 10 O-O ± . Keres-Mikenas, Pärnu 1960.

(*q*) 7 N×N, B×N; 8 P-Q4, P-Q4; 9 Q-N3, N-B3!

(*r*) 13 B-K3, P-Q5; 14 B-B4, N-B3 = .

(*s*) 6 N-B3, N×N; 7 QP×N, B-N5; 8 B-K3 ∞ . Korn-Lommer, London 1949.

(*t*) (A) 7 . . . B-K3; 8 N-B3, P-KR3; 9 B-R4, QN-Q2; 10 O-O-O, O-O-O; 11 P-Q4, P-Q4 = . Comments. (B) 7 . . . QN-Q2; 8 N-B3, Q×Q†; 9 B×Q, P-KR3, 10 B-R4, P-KN3! 11 O-O-O, B-N2; 12 N-QN5, K-Q1; 13 KR-K1, R-K1; 14 KN-Q4, N-B1; 15 P-KB4, B-Q2; 16 N-QB3, K-B1; 17 B-B3, P-B3 = . Kholmov-Bronstein USSR Chp. 1961. The column is Yukhtman-Antoshin, Moscow Chp. 1958.

1 P–K4, P–K4; 2 N–KB3, N–KB3

	6	7	8	9	10
3	P–Q4!. . . . . B–B4 (n)				
	P × P . . . . P–Q4!? (k)			N × P	
4	P–K5 (a)			P × QP	N–B3
	N–K5			P × P	N × N
5	Q × P (b) Q–K2		B–N5†	QP × N
	P–Q4		N–B4 (h)	P–B3	P–KB3
6	P × P e.p.		N × P	P × P	O–O
	N × QP		N–B3	Q–R4† (l)	N–B3
7	N–B3 . . . . B–Q3 (e)	B–K3 (i)	N–B3	N–R4
	N–B3	N–B3!	N × N	P × P	P–KN3
8	Q–KB4	Q–KB4	B × N	Q–K2†	P–B4
	P–KN3 (c)	P–KN3!	Q–R5!	B–K3	P–B4
9	B–Q2	N–B3 (f)	B–K3	N × P	P–N3 (o)
	B–N2 (d)	B–N2 (g)	Q–N5† (j)	P × B (m)	B–B4† (p)

(a) 4 B–QB4, N × P; 5 Q × P, N–KB3, see Bishop's Opening, col. 1.

(b) 5 B–QN5, N–QB3, with Ruy Lopez features safe for Black.

(c) (A) 8 . . . B–K3; (1) 9 B–N5? N × B; 10 N × N, B–Q3; 11 Q–K4, Q–Q2; 12 B–B4, B × B; 13 Q × B, O–O–O ∓. Boleslavski-Maslov, Moscow 1963. (2) 9 B–Q3, P–KN3; 10 N–Q4! B–N2; 11 N × N, P × N; 12 B–K3 ±. (3) 9 B–K3, N–B4! 10 N–QN5, B–N5†; 11 B–Q2, B × B†; 12 N × B, O–O; 13 O–O–O, R–B1; 14 N–KB3, Q–K2; 15 B–Q3, P–QR3 =. Fuderer-Bronstein, Candidates Tournament 1959. (B) 8 . . . B–B4; 9 B–N5! Q–K2†; (1) 10 B–K3, N × B; 11 N × N, Q–N5†; 12 Q × Q, B × Q†; 13 P–B3, B–Q3! 14 N × B†, P × N; 15 O–O–O, B–K3; 16 R × P, B × P; 17 N–Q4, N × N =. (2) 10 K–B1, B–K5; 11 B–Q2, N × B; 12 N × N, O–O–O; 13 R–K1, P–B4; 14 N–B3, Q–B4; 15 N × B, P × N; 16 Q × P, Q–N4†; 17 K–N1, Q × P =. Analysis by Kuypers, and in *Byulleten* 1970.

(d) 10 O–O–O, B–K3 (10 . . . O–O; 11 P–KR4!); 11 B–Q3! O–O; 12 P–KR4, Q–B3; 13 Q–R2, N–K4!

(e) 7 B–N5, N–B3; 8 Q–B3, P–B3; 9 B–KB4, Q–K2†; 10 B–K2, B–K3; 11 QN–Q2, O–O–O; 12 O–O, Q–B2 =. Bogolyubov *et al. v.* Romanovski *et al.*, Leningrad 1924.

(f) (A) 9 O–O, B–N2; 10 B–Q2?! (10 N–B3, B–K3; 11 B–K3, Q–B3 =), O–O (10 . . . B × P; 11 B–B3, B × R; 12 B × B, or 11 . . . B × B 12 N × B with a strong attack); 11 B–B3, B–B4 ∞.

(g) 10 B–K3, B–K3! 11 O–O–O (11 O–O, Q–B3!), Q–B3; (11 . . . O–O; 12 B–QB5), with a tenable but precarious position for Black.

(h) 5 . . . B–N5†; (A) 6 QN–Q2, N × N; 7 B × N, B × B†; 8 Q × B, P–Q3; 9 Q × P, N–B3; 10 B–N5, B–Q2; 11 B × N, B × B; 12 O–O–O ±. *P/E.* (B) 6 K–Q1? P–Q4; 7 P × P e.p., P–KB4; 8 P × P, Q × P; 9 N × P, N–B3 ∓. Kuypers.

(i) 7 N × N, QP × N; 8 N–B3, B–B4; 9 B–K3, P–KR4! =. Klavints-Vistanetskis, Tbilisi 1962.

(j) 10 P–B3, Q–K5; 11 P–KB4, P–Q4; 12 N–Q2, Q–N3; 13 N–B3, P–QB3; 14 O–O–O, B–K2; 15 R–N1, P–KR4; 16 Q–KB2, N–K5; 17 Q–B2, P–N4 ∞, with complications. Tal-Kholmov, Alma Ata 1969.

(k) Also 3 . . . N × P; 4 B–Q3 (4 P × P, P–Q4! 5 QN–Q2, B–KB4; or 5 . . . N–B4; 6 N–N3, N × N; 7 RP × N, B–K2 =), P–Q4; 5 N × P, N–Q2! or 5 . . . B–Q3; 6 O–O, O–O; 7 P–QB4, B × N; 8 P × B, N–QB3; 9 P × P, Q × P; 10 Q–B2, N–N5; 11 B × N, N × Q; 12 B × Q, B–B4; 13 P–KN4, B–N3; 14 P–B4, B–Q6; 15 R–Q1, B–R3 ∞. Browne-Acers, match 1970.

(l) 6 . . . P × P; 7 B–K2, B–QB4; 8 P–B3, P × P; 9 Q × Q†, K × Q; 10 N × P, K–K2; 11 O–O, R–Q1 (Stein-Bronstein, Tbilisi 1967); 12 N–QR4, B–N3; 13 P–N3 ±.

(*m*) 10 N × B, P × N; 11 Q × P†, B–K2 ∓. Prüss-Butler, corr. 1960–61.

(*n*) 3 N–B3, is the Petrov Three Knights' Defence. (A) 3 . . . N–B3, transposes into the Four Knights' Defence. (B) 3 . . . B–N5; 4 B–B4, O–O; 5 O–O, N–B3; 6 P–Q3, B × N, and other lines are flat. The column is the Boden-Kieseritzky Gambit (5 . . . P–KB3!). It can arise from the Bishop's Opening.

(*o*) 9 N–B3, P–K5; 10 N–N5, B–B4†; 11 K–R1, Q–K2; with a yet unexplored configuration.

(*p*) 10 K–N2, P–Q3; 11 P–QN4, B–N3 = . Marchisotti-Rompotti, corr. 1963–4.

Ponziani's Opening

(1 P–K4, P–K4; 2 N–KB3, N–QB3;
3 P–B3)

The ancient Ponziani was strongly advocated by Howard Staunton. Nowadays it is almost extinct, although occasionally an enterprising master like Bisguier will employ it for surprise value. White strives for the better centre, intending to build up with P–Q4 so that he may recapture with a pawn. The lack of a direct threat on his third move permits Black to equalize in a number of ways, but the ensuing game is up to the players!

3 . . . P–Q4 provokes an immediate crisis and puts a finger on the hesitancy in White's strategy but in the long run it might be deceiving. 4 Q–R4, N–B3 (Leonhardt's Defence in col. 1) involves a pawn sacrifice, but Black obtains a quick lead in development and a lasting initiative. 4 Q–R4, B–Q2 (Caro's Defence in col. 2) also involves a pawn sacrifice. Underrated is 4 . . . P–B3 (note (e)) which is Steinitz's solid continuation. 4 B–N5 (col. 3) has hardly been explored. It involves tricky play, particularly in note (i).

The Ponziani Counter-Attack 3 . . . P–B4 (col. 4) is playable with the reinforcement in note (l). Because White has delayed his development with 3 P–B3, Black can afford to gamble for one move.

3 . . . N–B3 (col. 5) is the modern treatment—a solid continuation which gives Black no more or less than easy equality. It has the merit of avoiding the ultra-sharp play in the first four columns.

1 P–K4, P–K4; 2 N–KB3, N–QB3; 3 P–B3

	1	2	3	4	5
	P–Q4			P–B4	N–B3 (o)
4	Q–R4		B–N5	P–Q4	P–Q4 (p)
	N–B3	B–Q2 (e)	P×P	P–Q3 (l)	N×KP (q)
5	N×P	P×P	N×P	KP×P	P–Q5
	B–Q3	N–Q5	Q–Q4 (i)	B×P (m)	N–N1
6	N×N	Q–Q1	Q–R4	B–QN5	B–Q3
	P×N	N×N†	N–K2	P×P	N–B4
7	P–Q3 (a)	Q×N	P–KB4	N×P	N×P
	O–O	N–B3 (f)	B–Q2	B–Q2	N×B†
8	B–N5 (b)	B–B4	N×B	B×N	N×N
	P–KR3	P–B3	K×N	P×B	B–K2
9	B×N	Q–K2 (g)	O–O (j)	O–O	O–O
	Q×B	P×P	N–B4!	N–B3	P–Q3
10	N–Q2 (c)	Q×P†	P–QN4?	R–K1†	Q–B3
	B–Q2 (d)	B–K2 (h)	P–QR4! (k)	B–K2 (n)	O–O = (r)

(a) 7 P–Q4, P×P; 8 B–QR6, B–Q2; 9 B–N7, P–B4; 10 B–B6, O–O = . *Debyut.*

(b) 8 B–K2, R–K1 (8 . . . N–N5? 9 B×N, B×B; 10 P–K5 wins. Swinnerton-Dyer-Barrett, Cambridge 1949); 9 B–N5, P–KR3; 10 B×N, Q×B; 11 N–Q2 ± .

(c) 10 B–K2 could transpose into note (b). If 10 Q×P, R–N1 + .

(d) 11 Q–B2, Q–N3; 12 O–O–O (if 12 P–KN3, P–KB4!), QR–N1; 13 P–KN3, R–N3; with initiative. Mosipan-Romanovski, Kharkov 1959.

(e) Caro's defence. Alternatives are: (A) Steinitz's 4 . . . P–B3! 5 B–N5, N–K2; 6 P×P, Q×P; 7 P–Q4, B–N5; 8 P–B4, Q–K5†; 9 B–K3, B×N; 10 N–Q2, Q–N3; 11 P×B, P×P; 12 B×P, P–QR3; 13 O–O–O, O–O–O; 14 N–N3 ± . (B) 4 . . . P×P; 5 N×P, Q–Q4; 6 N×N, P×N; 7 B–B4, Q–Q2; 8 O–O, B–Q3; 9 R–K1, N–B3; 10 P–Q3 ± .

(f) Stronger than 7 . . . P–KB4; 8 B–B4, B–Q3; 9 P–Q3 + .

(g) 9 P×P, B×P; 10 Q–N3 (Keres gives 10 Q–K2), P–K5; 11 O–O, Q–Q2; 12 P–Q4, O–O–O = .

(h) 11 B×P, O–O; 12 O–O, N×B; 13 Q×N, Q–B2; 14 P–Q4, B–Q3; 15 Q–KR5, QR–K1; 16 B–Q2, R–K3; 17 P–KR3, R–N3; 18 P–QN3, Q–B1; 19 K–R1, B–N1; 20 N–R3, Q–B3; 21 P–Q5, Q–Q3 + + . Zubarev-Tolush, Kiev 1944.

(i) If 5 . . . Q–N4; 6 Q–R4 (or 6 P–Q4, Q×P; 7 R–B1, P–QR3 =), Q×P; 7 R–B1 ± . Keres.

(j) *Lärobok* suggests 9 B–B4, Q–KB4; 10 Q–N3 ± .

(k) Black wins (Schiffers). The threat is 11 . . . P×P; 12 Q×R, B–B4†. Correct was 10 P–Q4, and if P×P e.p. 11 R–Q1, B–B4†; 12 K–B1 (12 K–R1? N–N6†; 13 P×N, Q–R4 mate).

(l) The only way this line is playable is 4 . . . BP×P; 5 N×P, N–B3! = .

(m) (A) 5 . . . P×P; 6 N×P, N×N; 7 Q–R5†! + . (B) 5 . . . P–K5; 6 P–Q5!

(n) 11 Q–K2 + . *Lärobok.* Similar to the Siesta Variation in the Ruy Lopez.

(o) 3 . . . KN–K2; 4 B–B4, N–N3; 5 P–Q4! Rellstab.

(p) 4 P–Q3, P–Q4; 5 QN–Q2, B–QB4 leads to a Philidor Defence in reverse where White has a move in hand.

(q) (A) 4 . . . P–Q4; 5 P×QP, Q×P; 6 B–K2, P×P; 7 P×P transposes into the Danish Gambit, col. 1. (B) Modern, closed, features of the Pirc Defence arise from 4 . . . P–Q3; e.g. (1) 5 B–Q3! B–K2; 6 P–KR3, P×P; 7 P×P, P–Q4; 8 P–K5, N–K5; or (2) 5 P–Q5, N–QN1; 6 B–Q3, P–KN3 ∞ . (C) 4 N–K5 . . . P×P; 5 P–K5, N–K5.

(r) 11 N–Q2, N–Q2; 12 R–K1, N–B3. Keres.

Scotch Game

(1 P–K4, P–K4; 2 N–KB3, N–QB3;
3 P–Q4)

The Scotch Game, known since Ercole del Rio in 1750, got its name from a correspondence match in 1824 between Edinburgh and London. Once a favourite with Blackburne and Chigorin, it was rarely seen in modern tournaments despite attempts at rehabilitation by the Israeli master, Czerniak, but has again been revived by some Russian masters. It is similar to the Centre Game in that White plays the natural P–Q4 early, and it suffers from the same drawback—Black's game is freed too soon. The opening is a classic illustration that a premature centre break, without massive preparation, tends to dissipate rather than generate White's initiative. This assessment holds good mainly for 4 . . . B–B4 in cols. 1–4 which covers the oldest, well-trodden paths, whereas 4 . . . N–B3 (cols. 6–10) has been more actively perused. Noteworthy attempts to strengthen White's play should be studied in cols. 9–10 of the Four Knights' Variation (cols. 8–10), and in conjunction with the Scotch Four Knights' Variation of the Four Knights' Game (see there) from which this system differs in its earlier queen's pawn push. Black might easily equalize in almost every opening variation of these Four Knights' systems but he can hardly hope for more.

The adventurous offsprings of this opening are the *Scotch* and *Göring Gambits* (cols. 11–14) which are rare exceptions inasmuch as they have not been convincingly disproved yet. Both are not necessarily winning propositions, but Black's defences are barely adequate, and he can just hang on to the pawn. Positions similar to the Danish Gambit (see there) arise in these lines and the student should study both openings in close conjunction. The *"Semi"-Danish* was previously found under the Danish Gambit but has since the 11th edition been transferred here as col. 15.

Altogether, considering the vastness of the next openings complex, the Ruy Lopez, which requires thorough professional memorizing of its exhaustive intricacies, the Scotch Game offers the student a chance of a limited, yet comprehensive, acquisition of another conception—as long as Black answers . . . P–K4.

1 P–K4, P–K4; 2 N–KB3, N–QB3; 3 P –Q4, P × P; 4 N × P, B–B4 (*a*); 5 B–K3 (*b*), Q–B3 (*c*)

	1	2	3	4	5
6	N–N5	P–QB3			
	B × B	KN–K2			
7	P × B	N–B2 (*g*)	. . . . B–K2	N–Q2	B–QB4
	Q–R5† (*d*)	P–Q3	P–Q4	O–O (*i*)	N–K4
8	P–N3	B × B	O–O	N × N	B–K2
	Q × KP (*e*)	P × B	B × N	Q × N	Q–KN3
9	N × P†	N–K3	P × B	B × B	O–O
	K–Q1	O–O	P × P	Q × B	P–Q4
10	N × R	B–K2	P–Q5	B–K2	P × P
	N–B3	B–K3	N–K4	P–B4	B–KR6
11	Q–Q6	O–O	Q–R4†	O–O	B–B3
	Q × R	QR–Q1	P–B3	P × P	O–O–O ∓ (*j*)
12	N–Q2	Q–B2	N–B3	N × P	
	N–K1	N–N3	O–O	Q–K4	
13	Q–B4	P–KN3	N × P	Q–Q4 =	
	Q–Q4 (*f*)	B–R6	Q–N3 = (*h*)		

(*a*) After Steinitz's favourite 4 . . . Q–R5, Black wins a pawn but is often exposed to an attack. (A) 5 N–KB3, Q × KP†; 6 B–K2, Q–K2! 7 N–B3, N–B3; 8 B–KN5, Q–Q1! 9 N–Q5, B–K2 = . (B) 5 N–N5, Q × KP†; 6 B–K2, B–N5†; 7 QN–B3, B × N†; 8 P × B, K–Q1; 9 O–O, KN–K2 = . (C) 5 N–QB3, B–N5; 6 N–N5, Q × KP†; 7 B–K2, B × N†; 8 N × B, Q–Q5; 9 B–Q3, N–N5; 10 N–N5†, N × B; 11 Q × N, Q × Q; 12 P × Q, K–Q1; 13 B–B4, P–Q3; 14 R–QB1, B–Q2; 15 N × BP, R–B1 16 B × P, B–B3! = . Chaplinski.

(*b*) 5 N–N3, B–N3; 6 P–QR4, P–QR3; 7 N–B3, (A) 7 . . . Q–B3; 8 Q–K2, QN–K2; 9 N–Q5, N × N; 10 P × N†, N–K2; 11 P–R5! B–R2; 12 P–R4, P–R3; (1) 13 P–N4!? Q–Q3; 14 B–Q2, Q × P; 15 KR–R3, Q–K3; 16 B–K3, P–Q3; 17 O–O–O, O–O; 18 Q–Q2, B × B; 19 R × B, Q–B3; 20 P–N5, P × P; 21 P × P, Q × NP; 22 B–Q3, N–N3; 23 R–R1, B–Q2; 24 K–N1, B–B3! 25 R/3–R3! P–B3! 26 Q × Q, P × Q; 27 B × N, B × R; 28 R × B, R × P, agreed drawn. Padevski-Reshevsky, Tel Aviv 1964. (2) 13 R–R4, O–O; 14 P–N4, P–Q3; 15 P–N5, Q–B4; 16 B–N2, N × P; 17 N–Q4, Q–K4; 18 Q × Q, P × Q; 19 B × N, P × N (Botterill and Harding). (B) 7 . . . P–Q3; 8 Q–K2, B–K3; 9 B–K3, B × B; 10 Q × B, B × N = . Botterill.

(*c*) 5 . . . B–N3; 6 N–QB3, P–Q3; 7 B–K2, N–B3; 8 Q–Q2, N–KN5; 9 B × N, B × B; 10 P–KR3, B–Q2; 11 N–Q5, O–O; 12 O–O–O, B–K3 = . Spielmann-Tarrasch, Breslau 1912.

(*d*) 7 . . . Q–K4; 8 Q–Q5, K–Q1; 9 Q × P, KN–K2∞. Bronstein.

(*e*) 8 . . . Q–Q1; 9 Q–N4, K–B1; 10 Q–B4, P–Q3; 11 N–Q4, N–B3. Euwe.

(*f*) 14 B–B4, Q–Q3; 15 O–O–O, P–B3 + . Bardeleben. 14 O–O–O is better, and so is 8 . . . Q–Q1 in the column, as in note (*e*).

(*g*) (A) 7 P–KB4, B × N! 8 P × B, P–Q4! (Rovner-Borisenko, Minsk 1953); 9 N–B3 O–O = . (B) 7 Q–Q2, P–Q4! 8 N–N5, B × B; 9 P × B! O–O; 10 N × BP, P × P; 11 N × R, R–Q1 = .

(*h*) Alekhin and Reilly-Stoltz and Monosson, Nice 1931.

(*i*) 7 . . . N × N! 8 P–K5! N–B7†! 9 Q × N, Q × P; 10 N–B4, Q–K3; 11 O–O–O, B × B†; 12 N × B, O–O ∓. The column is Mieses-Spielmann 1920.

(*j*) The column is *Bilguer*.

1 P–K4, P–K4; 2 N–KB3, N–QB3; 3 P–Q4, P × P; 4 N × P, N–B3

	6	7	8	9	10
5	N × N		N–QB3 (Four Knights' Variation)		
	NP × N		B–N5		N × P!?
6	P–K5 (a)		N × N		N × KN (k)
	Q–K2	N–Q4	NP × N		Q–K2
7	Q–K2	P–QB4 (d)	B–Q3		P–KB3 (l)
	N–Q4	N–N3	P–Q4		P–Q4
8	P–QB4	B–Q3	P × P		B–QN5
	N–N3	B–R3	P × P		B–Q2
9	N–Q2	O–O	O–O		O–O
	Q–K3 (b)	B × P	O–O		P × N
10	P–QN3	B × B	B–KN5		B × N
	B–K2	N × B	P–B3	B–K3	P × B
11	B–N2	Q–N4	Q–B3	N–K2 (i)	R–K1 (m)
	O–O	N–N3	B–K2 (f)	P–KR3	O–O–O (n)
12	Q–K4	N–B3	QR–K1	B–R4	R × P
	P–Q4	N–Q4	R–N1 (g)	B–Q3	Q–B3
13	P × P e.p.	N × N	N–Q1	P–KB4	Q–K2
	P × P (c)	P × N (e)	R–K1 (h)	B–B4† (j)	P–B4 (o)

(a) 6 B–Q3, P–Q4; (A) 7 P–K5, N–N5; 8 O–O, B–QB4. (1) 9 B–KB4, P–B3; 10 P × P, O–O! = . (2) 9 P–KR3? N × KP! 10 R–K1, Q–B3; 11 Q–K2, O–O! (3) 9 Q–K2, Q–R5; 10 P–KR3, P–KR4!. (B) 7 N–Q2, B–QB4; 8 O–O, O–O; 9 Q–B3, N–N5; 10 P × P, Q–Q3; 11 Q–N3, Q × Q = . Tartakover. 6 P–K5 is the Mieses Variation.

(b) Also 9 . . . B–R3; 10 P–QN3, P–N3; 11 N–K4, O–O–O; 12 B–N2, B–KN2; 13 P–B4, KR–K1; 14 Q–Q2, P–Q3! 15 Q–R5, B–N2; 16 O–O–O, P × P; 17 B–Q3, K–N1; 18 N–B5 = . Lutikov-Nezh netdinov, USSR Chp. 1952.

(c) 14 B–Q3, P–Q4; 15 P × P, P × P; 16 Q × Q, P × Q; 17 O–O, B–B3; drawn. Bednarski-Gligorić, Havana 1967.

(d) 7 B–Q3, P–Q3 (7 . . . Q–R5!? 8 O–O, B–B4; 9 N–Q2, O–O; 10 N–K4, B–K2; 11 R–K1, P–Q3; 12 P–QB4! N–N5; 13 N–B6†! B × N; 14 R–K4, N × B; 15 R × Q, B × R; 16 Q × N, P × P; 17 Q–K4, B–B3; 18 Q × BP, resigns. Kopayev-Polyak, Ukraine. Chp. 1946); 8 O–O, B–K2; 9 P × P, P × P; 10 B–K4, N–N5; 11 P–QR3, P–Q4 = .

(e) 14 B–N5, Q–N1; 15 QR–Q1, Q–N4 = . Padevski-Witkowski, Bulgaria 1955.

(f) (A) 11 . . . R–K1; 12 KR–K1 ∞ . (B) 11 . . . B–Q3; 12 B × N, Q × B; 13 Q × Q, P × Q; 14 N–K2, B–K3 = . Czerniak-Unzicker, Moscow 1956.

(g) 12 . . . P–KR3!? 13 B × P, P × B; 14 Q–K3, P–Q5; 15 Q × RP, Q–Q3! 16 Q–N5†, K–R1; 17 R × B, Q × R, with perpetual check, whereas attempts to win are risky, e.g. (A) 18 N–K4!? N–N1! 19 Q–R5†, K–N2; 20 P–KB4, P–KB4; 21 R–B3, N–R3! 22 R–N3†, N–N5 + + . (B) 18 N–K2!? R–Q1! 19 N–B4, R–Q4! 20 N × R, P × N + .

(h) 14 P–KR3, B–K3; 15 R–K2, with slight advantage. Spielmann-Yates, Semmering 1926.

(i) (A) 11 Q–B3, B–K2; 12 QR–K1, R–N1; 13 N–Q1, P–B4 = . (B) 11 N–N5, P–B4! 12 P–QB3! B–R4; 13 Q–R4, B–N3; 14 Q–R4, P–KR3; 15 B × P, P × B; 16 Q × P, P–B5; 17 Q–N5†, draw. Ivkov-Gligorić, Buenos Aires 1960.

(j) 14 K–R1, B–KN5; 15 P–KR3, B × N; 16 Q × B, R–K1 = . Alexander-Smyslov, England v. USSR 1954. Also see Four Knights' Game, cols. 16–20.

(k) 6 N × QN, N × N; 7 N × Q, N × Q; 8 N × BP, K × N; 9 B–B4†, K–B3; 10 K × N, P–B3 = . Euwe.

(l) Or 7 N–N5, Q × N†; 8 B–K2, B–N5†; 9 P–B3, B–R4; 10 O–O, O–O; Ilyich-Popov, corr. 1964; 11 B–K3! with pressure.

(m) Euwe prefers 11 P × P, O–O–O; 12 Q–B3—but 12 Q–K2, K–N1; 13 R–B3 disposes of Black most thoroughly. *Comments.*

(n) Also 11 . . . P–KB4; 12 P × P, P × P; 13 Q–K2, P–B4!

(o) 14 N–N3, B–B3; Popov-Hershman, corr. USSR 1965.

1 P-K4, P-K4; 2 N-KB3, N-QB3; 3 P-Q4, P×P

	11	12	13	14	15
4	B-QB4 (a)	... P-B3 (f)			
	B-B4 (b)	P-Q6	P-Q4	P×P	
5	P-B3 (c)	B×P	KP×P	B-QB4	N×P
	P×P (d)	P-Q3	Q×P	N-B3 (m)	P-Q3 (p)
6	N×P	P-KR3	P×P	N×P	B-QB4
	P-Q3	N-B3	B-KN5 (i)	B-N5	N-B3 (q)
7	B-KN5	O-O (g)	B-K2	P-K5	N-KN5
	Q-Q2	B-K2	B-N5† (j)	P-Q4 (n)	N-K4
8	Q-Q2	N-Q4	N-B3	P×N	Q-N3 (r)
	P-KR3	O-O	B×N	P×B	Q-Q2
9	B-R4	N-Q2	B×B	Q×Q†	B-N5
	KN-K2	R-K1	Q-B5	N×Q (o)	P-B3
10	O-O-O	P-KB4	B-K3 (k)	P×P	P-B4
	N-N3	B-B1	B×N†	R-KN1	N/4-N5
11	B-KN3	Q-B2	P×B	B-R6	P-KR3
	P-R3	P-KN3	Q×P†	N-K3	P×B
12	N-Q5	N/2-B3	K-B1	O-O-O	P×N
	P-N4 (e)	B-N2! (h)	Q-B5† (l)	B×N ∞	P-KR3 (s)

(a) The Scotch Gambit. If 4 B-QN5—The Relfsson Gambit—(A) 4 ... B-N5†; 5 P-B3, P×P; 6 O-O, KN-K2; 7 P×P, B-B4; 8 N-N5, P-Q3; 9 Q-R5, N-N3; 10 P-K5, N×P; 11 R-K1, Q-K2; 12 B-KB4, B-KN5; 13 Q-R4, B-Q2; 14 QN-Q2, O-O-O+. Kholmov-Shiyanovski, USSR Chp. 1961. (B) 4 ... B-B4!? 5 O-O, P-QR3; 6 B-R4, KN-K2; 7 P-B3, P×P; 8 N-N5, P-Q3; 9 Q-R5, N-N3 = .

(b) (A) 4 ... N-B3, see Two Knights' Defence. (B) If 4 ... B-N5†? 5 P-B3, P×P; 6 O-O! (1) 6 ... P-Q3; 7 P-QR3, B-QB4; 8 P-QN4, P-B7; 9 Q×BP, B-N3; 10 Q-N3, Q-K2; 11 N-B3, B-K3; 12 N-Q5± , or (2) 6 ... P×P; 7 B×P, N-B3; 8 P-QR3, B-B4; 9 N-N5, O-O; 10 N×BP, R×N; 11 B×R†, K×B; 12 P-K5 ± . *Comments.*

(c) (A) 5 O-O, P-Q3; 6 P-B3, B-KN5, see Giuoco Piano. 5 ... N-B3; 6 P-K5, see Max Lange. (B) 5 N-N5, N-R3; 6 N×BP, N×N; 7 B×N†, K×B; 8 Q-R5†, P-N3; 9 Q×B, P-Q3∓ .

(d) 5 ... P-Q6; 6 O-O, P-Q3; 7 P-QN4, B-N3; 8 P-QR4, P-QR3; 9 P-R5, B-R2; 10 Q-N3, Q-B3; 11 P-N5, N-K4; 12 N×N, P×N; (A) 13 B-K3, P×P; 14 B×NP†, P-B3; 15 B×B, R×B; 16 B×QP, N-K2 = . Zaitsev.(B) 13 P×P, P×P; 14 Q-R4†, B-Q2; 15 Q-Q1, N-K2; 16 Q×P, B-B1; 17 N-R3, O-O; 18 N-B2, N-N3; 19 N-N4, R-Q1; 20 Q-N3, R-K1; 21 B-KN5, Q-Q3; 22 KR-Q1, Q-B4; 23 B-Q5, R-N1; 24 B-K3, Q×BP; 25 N-R2, Q×P; 26 B×B, N-N5; 27 B-B4, R-N7; 28 Q-QB3, Q×Q; 29 N×Q, B-N5; 30 R/Q1-QB1, R-R1; 31 R×P, R-N5; 32 N-Q5, resigns. Sveshnikov-Petrosian, USSR Chp. 1974.

(e) 13 B-N3, B-N2 = . Lasker's analysis.

(f) The Göring Gambit, which after 4 ... P×P; 5 N×P becomes the "Semi" Danish Gambit.

(g) Or 7 B-KB4, B-K2; 8 QN-Q2, N-Q2; 9 N-B4, B-B3; 10 B-B3, O-O; 11 O-O, N/2-K4; 12 N-K3, B-K3; 13 N-Q2, P-QN4; 14 B-KN3, N-R4; 15 P-QR4, N/R4-B5 with equal risks. Ljubojević-Olafsson, Las Palmas 1974.

(h) 13 B-Q2, B-Q2; 14 QR-K1, P-QR3; 15 N-N5, R-K2; 16 P-K5, P×P; 17 N×N, B×N; 18 P×P, Q-Q4; 19 N-B3, N-Q2; 20 P-B4, Q-B4†; 21 B-K3, Q-R4; 22 B-Q2, Q-B4†; 23 B-K3, drawn. Velimirović-Keres, Suchumi 1966.

(i) Later attempts have not proved more successful, e.g. 6 ... N-KB3; 7 N-B3, B-QN5; 8 B-K2, O-O! 9 O-O, Q-Q1; 10 B-N5, P-KR3; 11 B-R4, B-K2; 12 R-B1, B-KN5; 13 N-K5,

B × B; 14 N × B, N–QN5; 15 Q–N3, P–QR4 (Velimirović-Kholmov, Sochi 1966); 16 KR–Q1! with pressure.

(j) (A) 7 . . . N–B3; 8 N–B3, Q–QR4; 9 O–O, B–Q3! 10 B–K3, O–O. (B) 7 . . . O–O–O!? 8 N–B3, Q–QR4; 9 B–K3, N–B3; 10 O–O, B–N5; 11 N–QR4, N–K5; 12 P–QR3 ± . Ghizdavu-Rozvan, Roumanian Chp. 1971.

(k) 10 Q–N3, Q × Q; 11 P × Q, KN–K2; 12 O–O, P–QR3; 13 R–R4, B–Q3; 14 B–N5, P–B3; 15 B–R5†, N–N3 = . Ljubojević-Ree, Amsterdam 1972.

(l) 13 K–N1, N–K2; 14 R–B1, Q × RP; 15 R–R1, Q–B5, drawn. Marshall-Capablanca, Lake Hopatcong, 1926.

(m) (A) 5 . . . P × P; 6 B × P, B–N5† (or 6 . . . P–Q3!); 7 N–B3! N–B3; 8 Q–B2, P–Q3; 9 O–O–O, O–O; 10 P–K5, N–N5; (Klovan-Suetin, Riga 1962); 11 N–Q5! B–QB4; 12 P × P, B × P∞. (B) 5 . . . B–B4; 6 B × P†, K × B; 7 Q–Q5†, K–B1; 8 Q × B†, Q–K2; 9 Q × BP, Q × P†; 10 B–K3 P–Q4; 11 QN–Q2†. (C) 5 . . . P–Q3 6 N × P, see col. 15. The column is Penrose's analysis.

(n) Keres mentions 8 B–N3, N–K5; 9 O–O, B × N; 10 B × P, B–B4; 11 P × B, N × QBP; 12 B × N†, P × B; 13 Q–K1 with initiative (but "initiative" still needs translation into a decisive advantage and a win).

(o) Black may capture with the knight or the king; e.g. 9 . . . K × Q; 10 P × P, R–K1†; 11 B–K3, B × N†; 12 P × B, K–K2; 13 O–O–O, K–B3; 14 KR–K1, B–K3; 15 N–Q4, K × P; 16 N × N, P × N; 17 B–Q4†, K–N3; 18 R–K3 (Ljubojević-Lombardy, Manila 1973), P–QR3 = .

(p) As none of the following side-lines was fully satisfactory for Black, he may best transpose into: (A) stratagems similar to colume 14, with first 5 . . . B–N5!? 6 B–QB4, P–Q3; 7 O–O, B × N; 8 P × B, B–N5; 9 Q–N3, B × N; 10 B × Pch, K–B1; 11 P × B, N–K4; 12 B × N, R × B; 13 P–KB4, N–B6†; 14 K–N2, N–R5†; 15 K–R1, Q–Q2 with an active game. Ciocaltea-Karaklajić, Vrnacka Banja 1971. (B) 4 . . . N–B3; 5 P–K5, N–K5; 6 P × P, B–N5†; 7 QN–Q2, P–Q3.

(q) Not so good is 6 . . . B–K3; 7 B × B, P × B; 8 Q–N3, Q–B1; 9 N–KN5, N–Q1; 10 P–B4, B–K2; 11 P–B5! P × P; 12 O–O ± (Liskov), but 11 . . . P–K4 is playable. Comments.

(r) 8 B–N3, P–KR3; 9 P–B4, P × N; 10 P × N, B–N5; 11 B–R4†, P–B3; 12 Q–N3 deserves attention.

(s) 13 N × BP! Q × N; 14 Q × P†, K–Q1; 15 P–N5 + . Comments.

Ruy Lopez

(1 P–K4, P–K4; 2 N–KB3, N–QB3; 3 B–N5)

White's initial three moves were recorded by the author of the historic Göttingen MS. in 1490 but it was not until 1561 that Lopez treated it systematically in his *Libro del Ajedrez*. On the eve of modern chess, its potential was explored in analyses by the Russians Jänisch and Chigorin. Then other experts followed suit until it finally became established as one of the major openings.

The basic concept is logical and simple—a once-removed attack on the King's pawn. Yet from this comes a bitter struggle for the centre and a hair-trigger balance between attack and defence. White secures a bind which may last well into the middle game and Black must beware of any false steps before he "gets his pieces out of the box." Some main lines have been exhaustively analysed for over twenty moves. Many tournament games really start from where these analyses end, saving both sides time on the clock—one of the many minor and major finesses of tourney tactics!

The Lopez used to be highly suitable for the competitor out to win with White and, for a while, Black could rarely hope for more than equality. However, it is exactly the very extensive depth and length of some analyses which has led to ultimately tenable positions with reduced material and little chance of winning. Thus both players have been either swayed away from the Ruy Lopez or forced to turn to new paths.

(*I*) The Systems *without* 3 . . . P–QR3 (cols. 1–19) are fewer in number and possibilities, but some have been revived.

(A) THE CORDEL DEFENCE, 3 . . . B–B4 (cols. 1–5) has proved safe enough.

(B) THE BERLIN DEFENCE 3 . . . N–KB3 (cols. 6–10) formerly also a "cramped" strategy, now a satisfactory reply to the once dreaded Spanish torture.

(c) The Old Steinitz Defence, 3 . . . P–Q3 (cols. 11–12); and

(d) The Cozio Defence 3 . . . KN–K2 (cols. 13–14) owe their sporadic appearance to their affinity with closed formations, now in vogue in tournament strategy; whereas

(e) Bird's Defence, 3 . . . N–Q5 (col. 15) deprives Black after 4 N × N of his one and only developed piece.

(f) The Schliemann Defence, 3 . . . P–B4!? (cols. 16–19) has, however, been frequently employed and widely scrutinized during the last three decades. Probably White's sound restraint, 4 P–Q3 (col. 19) provides a safe haven against Black's pawn wave, but it takes away the excitement.

The line deservedly attributed to Schliemann as its Western pioneer is on the Continent known as the Jänisch Defence, in just deference to the Russian's early research. However, the persistent exclusion of other analysts' credit is one of the many peculiar practices of regional rivalries.

The Schliemann Defence Deferred (col. 20) is not as effective with Black having played 3 . . . P–QR3 as it is without. In the columnar context, it now leads to the next section.

(*II*) The Closed Systems, with 3 . . . P–QR3 (cols. 21–90) give Black more elbow room inasmuch as "he can break the pin in one move (with . . . P–QN4) after White retreats his bishop to QR4" (Jänisch).

(a) The Exchange Variation 4 B × N (cols. 21–5) is a seemingly logical thought of cracking Black's solid pawn wall (. . . P–Q3) and, by P–Q4, building a pawn majority on the king's wing. But despite Fischer's success with this line, the exchange has lost some of its venom. However, the exchange can be invoked in several other ways, e.g. in cols. 26, 40, 83–5, and 130.

(b) The Modern Steinitz Defence employs 4 B–R4, P–Q3 (cols. 26–38) creating solid, stolid positions. The deferred exchange 5 B × N† (col. 26), is even tamer than 4 B × N, and 5 P–B3 (cols. 31–8) meets with adequate Black responses in cols. 33, 35, and 38. Cols. 39–40 (4 . . . N–B3; 5 O–O, P–Q3) are transpositions of cols. 81–2, but of independent character—as forerunners to Black's choice of the system 4 . . . N–B3, which we are dealing with next.

(c) The Chigorin Defence (cols. 41–52) is characterized by the moves shown in the respective heading up to and including 11 . . . Q–B2! which is essential to Chigorin's concept. He also, casually, touched upon earlier derivations, but they were later on researched in depth by younger masters. In cols. 41–5 and 50 Black tries to utilize the open queen's bishop file, otherwise he strives to keep the game closed in order to minimize the pivotal pressure of White's "Strong Point" structure, a term used by Fine. On the other hand, since Chigorin's analyses at the turn of the century, other elastic methods have been investigated.

(D) THE CLOSED DEFENCE branches off in several ways:

(1) 11 . . . B–N2 (cols. 53–4); (2) the aggressive return 11 . . . N–B3 (col. 55); (3) the manoeuvre 9 . . . N–Q2 and 11 . . . B–B3 (cols. 59–60); and, last not least, (4) 9 . . . P–R3 (cols. 61–5) advocated by Smyslov. All these lines offer lively defences. Bizarre and slower but well thought out is (5) 9 . . . N–N1 (cols. 66–70) the *Retreat Variation*, in some treatises called "Breyer" variation but without much documentation to support the term. Whereas the "Closed" Defence (and its outgrowth, the Chigorin System) keep the centre compact, Black can also employ more forcing methods.

(E) THE MARSHALL (COUNTER) ATTACK, introduced by him against Capablanca at New York in 1918 in a remarkable pawn-sacrifice, 8 . . . P–Q4! (cols. 71–8) which after exhaustive study has almost developed into a surefire agreement to draw! However, the double-edged dynamics of such explosions are bound to leave a few more aces to be played in the future.

The *Anti-Marshall* lines (cols. 79–80) might be employed by souls unfamiliar with the ramifications of the Marshall Attack proper but they would need some new inspirations.

(F) SUNDRIES are (1) the *Centre Variation* 6 P–Q4 (cols. 81–2); (2) the *Exchange Variation Double Deferred* 6 B × N (cols. 83–5); (3) the *Worral Attack* 6 Q–K2 (cols. 86–88), which was repopularized by Keres and allows White the option of R–Q1 instead of R–K1, if so desired, and (4) a doubtful deviation by Black, 5 . . . B–B4 (col. 90), practiced too long ago by Möller.

(*III*) The "Open" Defence with 3 . . . P–QR3 (cols. 91–118) which presents another formidable trunk of the Ruy Lopez, with intricate lines branching off.

After 1 P–K4, P–K4; 2 N–KB3, N–QB3; 3 B–N5, P–QR3; 4 B–R4, N–B3; 5 O–O, N × P; 6 P–Q4, P–QN4; 7 B–N3, P–Q4; 8 P × P, B–K3;

(A) 9 P–B3, Black may choose the classical 9 . . . B–QB4 (cols. 91–8) which offers him tactical mobility and pressure although it removes his king's bishop from the defence of his king side; or the speculative 9 . . . N–B4 (cols. 99–100); or the protective 9 . . . B–K2 (cols. 101–10) which also supports a king's side pawns attack, with 10 B–KB4, (col. 110), representing a less usual but quite consequential positional line to which Black must actively counteract, opening a combinational field.

(B) 9 Q–K2 (cols. 111–15) is the old-established *Howell Attack*, but invigorated by Keres in the 1940s, and we thus add his name to the line in justice to his systematic contemporary research. The cols. 116–18 represent earlier departures, now dormant.

(*IV*) The *Counter-Thrust Variations* (cols. 119–25) and the *accelerated* version (cols. 131–5) are clearly a modern backlash in reaction to the over-analysed standard lines. Dating back to Nezhmetdinov (and

Zukertort!) the line has recently been enriched by Matsukevich. The collective group term of "Archangelsk" Variation adopted in the Eastern hemisphere, strikes us as rather unstructural and we have chosen a more functional description.

The accelerated version was fathered by Taimanov, Furman and Johannessen. While restricted in scope, both treatments have added a new dimension to the Ruy Lopez defences and its . . . B–QN2 stratagems.

The individual variations in cols. 126–30 are without life until someone instils some.

1 P-K4, P-K4; 2 N-KB3, N-QB3; 3 B-N5, B-B4

	1	2	3	4	5
4	P-B3				O-O (*l*)
	P-B4	N-B3 (*g*)			Q-B3 (*m*)
5	P-Q4 ...... P × P?		P-Q4	O-O	P-B3
	P × KP (*a*)	P-K5	P × P	O-O	KN-K2
6	B × N (*b*)	P-Q4	O-O (*h*)	P-Q4	B × N
	QP × B	B-N3 (*e*)	N × P	B-N3	N × B
7	N × P!	N-K5!	P × P	B-N5 (*j*)	P-Q4
	B-Q3	N × N	B-N3	P-KR3	B-N3
8	Q-R5† (*c*)	P × N	Q-B2	B-KR4	P-Q5
	P-KN3	Q-R5	N-Q3!	P-Q3	N-N1
9	Q-K2	O-O	R-K1†	P-R4	P-Q6
	Q-R5	P-B3	N-K2	P-QR4	P × P
10	P-KR3	B-QB4	B-Q3	R-K1	N-R3
	B-K3 (*d*)	P-Q4 (*f*)	P-KR3 (*i*)	B-N5! (*k*)	N-R3 (*n*)

(*a*) 5 . . . P × QP; 6 P-K5, P × P; 7 N × P, KN-K2; 8 O-O, P-Q4; 9 P × P *e.p.*, Q × P; 10 Q-R4 ± .

(*b*) White can branch off with (A) 6 P × B, P × N; 7 Q × P, N-B3; 8 O-O, O-O; 9 B-N5, Q-K1; 10 N-Q2, P-Q3; 11 P × P, P × P; 12 N-K4, N × N; 13 Q × N, B-K3! = , Matulović-Nicevski, Skopje 1967. (B) 6 N-N5, B-N3! 7 P-Q5, P-K6! 8 N-K4! N-B3; 9 P × N, NP × P = .
(C) 6 N × P, N × N; 7 Q-R5†, N-B2; 8 B-QB4, Q-K2; 9 P × B, N-B3; 10 B × N†, K-B1! = .

(*c*) 8 O-O, Q-R5 also allows Black counterchances.

(*d*) 11 N-Q2, B × N; 12 P × B, Q-N4; 13 O-O, B × RP; 14 Q × P, B-B4; 15 Q-B3, O-O-O = . Vasyukov-Miagmasuren, Havana 1967.

(*e*) 6 . . . P × N; 7 P × B, Q-K2†; 8 B-K3, P × P; 9 R-N1, N-B3; 10 P-B3, P-Q4; 11 P × P *e.p.*, Q × P; 12 N-Q2, B-Q2; 13 Q × P, Q-K4; 14 B × N, P × B; 15 Q × NP, O-O-O; 16 O-O-O, B × P; 17 B-Q4, Q-K7; 18 Q-N3 ± . Zagorovski.

(*f*) 11 P × P *e.p.*, N-B3; 12 B-K6, B × B; 13 P × B, O-O; 14 B-K3, N-N5; 15 P-KR3, N × B; 16 P × N, B × P† ∓ . Mechkarov.

(*g*) 4 . . . KN-K2; 5 P-Q4, P × P; 6 P × P, B-N5†; 7 B-Q2, B × B†; 8 Q × B, P-QR3; 9 B-R4, P-Q4; 10 P × P, Q × P; 11 O-O ± . *Comments.*

(*h*) This is safer than 6 P-K5, N-K5; 7 O-O, P-Q4; 8 P × P *e.p.*, O-O! 9 P × BP, Q-B3; 10 B × N, P × B; 11 P × P, B-N3; 12 R-K1, B-KB4; 13 N-B3, KR-K1; 14 N × N, B × N; 15 B-N5, Q-Q3 = . J. Nielsen.

(*i*) 11 Q-K2, K-B1; 12 P-QN3, N-K1; 13 B-R3, P-Q3 = . *Archives.*

(*j*) (A) 7 R-K1, P-Q3; 8 P-KR3, N-K2 (or 8 . . . Q-K2); 9 N-R3, P-B3; 10 B-B1, N-N3; 11 N-B4, B-B2; 12 P × P, P × P; 13 Q-B2, N-R4! 14 B-KN5, P-B3; 15 QR-Q1, Q-K2; 16 B-QB1, B-N3 = . Robatsch-van Geet, Beverwijk 1967. (B) 7 P × P, KN × P; 8 Q-Q5, N-B4; 9 B-N5, N-K2; 10 Q-Q1, N-K5; 11 B-R4, P-Q4; 12 N-Q2, P-B3; 13 B-Q3, B-KB4; 14 Q-B2, N × N; 15 B × B, N × N†! 16 P × N, K-R1! = . Geller-Spasski, USSR 1963.

(*k*) (A) 11 P-Q5, N-QR2! (B) 11 N-R3, P × P; 12 B × QN, P × B; 13 P × P, R-K1; 14 Q-Q3, B × N; 15 P × B, P-N4; 16 B-N3; N-R4; 17 QR-B1, P-Q4! = . Suetin. 10 . . . P × P! allows good counterplay.

(*l*) 4 P-Q4, P × P; 5 O-O, see Scotch Game, col. 11, note (*a*) (B).

(*m*) Too chancy is 4 . . . N-Q5; 5 N × N, B × N; 6 P-B3, B-N3; 7 P-Q4, P-QB3; 8 B-R4, P-Q3; 9 N-R3, N-B3; 10 B-B2, B-K3; 11 B-N5, P-KR3; 12 B × N, Q × B; 13 P-Q5, B-Q2; 14 N-B4, B-B2; 15 Q-Q3 ± . Portisch-Spasski 1961.

(*n*) In the column, if 6 P-QN4, B-N3; 7 N-R3, P-QR3; 8 B × N, N × B; 9 N-B4, B-R2 = .

1 P–K4, P–K4; 2 N–KB3, N–QB3; 3 B–N5, N–B3; 4 O–O (*a*)

	6	7	8	9	10
	B–B4		N × P		
5	N × P		P–Q4		R–K1
	N × N! . . . . . . N × P		N–Q3 (*i*)		N–Q3
6	P–Q4	Q–K2 (*e*)	P × P . . . . B × N		N × P
	P–QR3 (*b*)	N × N	N × B	QP × B!	B–K2 (*m*)
7	P × N (*c*)	P–Q4 (*f*)	P–QR4	P × P	B–Q3
	P × B	B–K2	P–Q3	N–B4	O–O
8	P × N	P × N (*g*)	P–K6?!	Q × Q†	N–QB3
	Q × P	N–B4	P × P!	K × Q	N × N
9	N–B3	R–Q1	P × N	N–B3 (*k*)	R × N
	P–B3	O–O	N–K2	K–K1	B–B3
10	P–K5	B–QB4	N–N5	N–K2!	R–K3
	Q–N3	P–B3	N–B4	B–K3	P–KN3
11	R–K1	P–QR4	R–K1	N–B4	P–QN3
	O–O (*d*)	K–R1 (*h*)	B–K2 (*j*)	B–Q4 (*l*)	B–Q5 (*n*)

(*a*) 4 P–Q4, N × KP! 5 O–O, N–Q3, transposing into col. 8.

(*b*) (A) 6 . . . P–B3; 7 P × N, N × P; 8 B–Q3, P–Q4; 9 P × P *e.p.*, N–B3; 10 B–KN5! Q × P; 11 N–B3, B–K3; 12 B × N, P × B; 13 N–K4, Q–K4; 14 N × B, Q × N; 15 Q–B3, Q–KN4; 16 P–QR4, O–O–O; 17 P–R5, B–Q4; 18 B–K4 ± . Shamkovich-Aronin, Moscow 1962. (B) 6 . . . N × P; 7 P × B, Q–K2; 8 R–K1, N × P/7; 9 Q–K2 ± .

(*c*) 7 B–K2, N × P; 8 P × B, N × QBP; 9 P–QN4, N–K3; 10 B–N2, N–N3 ∞ .

(*d*) 12 N–K4, B–K2; 13 N–Q6, Q–K3. Van Scheltinga.

(*e*) (A) 6 N × BP, K × N (or 6 . . . N × BP!); 7 Q–R5†, P–N3; 8 Q–Q5†, K–N2; 9 Q × KN (9 B × N, R–K1! 10 B–R4, P–B3; 11 Q–Q3, Q–R5; 12 P–KN3, N × BP! 13 Q–B3†, Q–Q5 =), P–Q4; 10 Q–QR4, R–B1; 11 B × N, P × B; 12 Q × BP, Q–K2! 13 P–Q4, R × P! Draxl-Poschauko, Walchsee 1953. (B) 6 Q–N4! N–N4; 7 P–Q4, N × N; 8 R–K1, O–O; 9 R × N, P–Q3; 10 Q × N ± . Ostapenko-Fomenko, USSR 1970.

(*f*) 7 Q × N, Q–K2; 8 P–Q4, N–B3! 9 B × N, QP × B; 10 R–K1, Q × Q; 11 R × Q†, B–K2; 12 B–B4, B–B4; 13 R–K2, R–Q1 = . Comments.

(*g*) 8 Q × N, N–N3; 9 P–KB4, P–QB3! 10 B–Q3, P–Q4; 11 Q–K2, P–KB4 = . Comments.

(*h*) 12 R–R3! + O'Kelly-Dückstein, Zürich 1960.

(*i*) 5 . . . B–K2; (A) 6 Q–K2, N–Q3; 7 B × N, NP × B; 8 P × P, N–N2; 9 N–B3, O–O; 10 N–Q4! B–B4; 11 R–Q1, R–K1; 12 B–B4, B × N; 13 R × B, P–Q4; 14 P–QN4, P–QR3; 15 Q–R5, Q–Q2 = . Smrčka-Yudovich, corr. 1969. (B) 6 P × P, O–O; 7 Q–Q5, N–B4; 8 B–K3, N–K3; 9 N–B3, P–QR3; 10 B–QB4, P–Q3; 11 P × P ± .

(*j*) 12 P–N6, BP × P; 13 N × KP, B × N; 14 R × B, O–O; 15 Q–Q5, K–R1; with a minimal advantage for Black. Vasyukov-Neikirkh, Polanica Zdroj 1965.

(*k*) (A) 9 B–N5†, K–K1; 10 N–B3, P–KR3; 11 B–Q2, B–K2; 12 N–K4, B–K3; 13 P–QR3, P–QN3! = . (B) 9 P–QN3, P–KR3; 10 B–N2, B–K3; 11 N–B3!

(*l*) 12 N × B, P × N; 13 P–KN4, N–K2; 14 B–B4, P–QB3; 15 KR–K1, N–N3 = . Fischer-Bisguier, US Chp. 1963.

(*m*) 6 . . . N × N; 7 R × N†, B–K2; 8 B–Q3, O–O; 9 Q–B3, P–KN3; 10 N–B3! B–B3; 11 R–K3, R–K1; 12 P–QN3, R × R; 13 BP × R, B × N; 14 P × B, N–K1; 15 P–K4 ± . Lublinski-Bondarevski, Moscow 1944.

(*n*) 12 R–K2, P–QN3 = . Sherwin-Bisguier, US Chp. 1962.

1 P-K4, P-K4; 2 N-KB3, N-QB3; 3 B-N5

	Old Steinitz Defence		Cozio Defence		Bird's Defence
	11	12	13	14	15
	P-Q3		KN-K2		N-Q5 (j)
4	P-Q4		P-Q4 (g)		N×N (k)
	B-Q2		P×P		P×N
5	N-B3 (a)		N×P		O-O
	P×P (b)		N×N	P-KN3	P-QB3 (l)
6	N×P		Q×N	N-QB3	B-R4! (m)
	P-KN3		N-B3	B-N2	N-B3
7	B-K3	O-O	Q-Q5	B-K3	P-QB3
	B-N2	B-N2	N-N5!	O-O	B-K2
8	Q-Q2	B×N	Q-N3	Q-Q2	P-Q3
	N-B3	P×B	B-B4	P-Q4	P×P
9	P-B3 (c)	P-B4 (f)	P-QR3	O-O-O	N×P
	O-O	P-QB4	N-B3	P×P	P-Q3
10	B×N (d)	N/4-K2	Q-N3	N×P	P-Q4
	P×B	P-B4	O-O	N×N	O-O
11	O-O-O!	P-K5	B-N5	B×N	B-B2
	R-K1 (e)	B-QB3 ∞	P-B3 (h)	Q×B (i)	R-K1 (n)

(a) 5 P-B3, N-B3; 6 QN-Q2!? P-KN3; 7 P×P! P×P (7 . . . QN×P; 8 N×N, P×N; 9 Q-N3, R-QN1; 10 N-B4 ±); 8 B×N, B×B; 9 N×P, Q-Q3; 10 N×B ± . Kavalek-Donner, Amsterdam 1973—a position reached by transposition from 1 P-K4, P-Q3; 2 P-Q4, N-KB3; 3 N-Q2?! P-K4; 4 P-QB3, N-B3 (4 . . . QN-Q2; 5 KN-B3, P-B3 =); 5 KN-B3, P-KN3? etc. A fine example of the positional finesses in changing the order of moves advantageously.

(b) 5 . . . N-B3, dealt with at length and almost exclusively in former *MCO* editions; is outmoded as it allows White too many good choices, e.g. 6 O-O, B-K2; 7 R-K1, P×P! 8 N×P, O-O; 9 KN-K2, or 9 B-B1, or 9 B×N, P×B; 10 P-Q N3. The text, coupled with the deferred fianchetto, is a more dynamic attempt at counterplay.

(c) Müller and *Archives* consider 9 B×N, P×B; 10 B-R6, B×B; 11 Q×B, P-B4; 12 N/4-K2, B-B3 = . The text allows the opponent more options.

(d) 10 O-O-O, N×N; 11 B×N, N×P! 12 N×N! (12 P×N, KB×B; 13 Q×B, B×B; 14 N×B, Q-N4†!), QB×P; 13 B×B, K×B; 14 Q-B3†, P-B3 = .

(e) 12 B-R6, B-R1; 13 P-KR4, Q-N1; 14 P-R5, Q-N5! = . Zeitlin-Kimelfeld, USSR 1967. If 11 B-R6, P-Q4! *Comments.*

(f) Keres suggests 9 R-K1, N-K2; 10 B-B4, P-QB4; 11 N-B3, O-O; 12 P-K5, N-B4 and Black has a difficult time. The column is comment in *Archives* to analysis by Yudovich.

(g) If 4 P-B3, (A) 4 . . . P-QR3; 5 B-R4, P-Q3; 6 P-Q4, B-Q2; etc., as in col. 37. (B) 4 . . . P-Q3; 5 P-Q4, B-Q2; 6 O-O, P-KN3. Kupreichik.

(h) *12 B-B4†!* with a minimal advantage. Analyses in *Archives* by Mechkarov.

(i) 12 Q×Q, B×Q; 13 R×B, B-B4 = . Mechkarov.

(j) (A) 3 . . . P-KN3; 4 P-B3! (B) 3 . . . B-N5 (Alapin's Defence); 4 P-B3 and N-R3 ± .

(k) 4 B-R4, B-B4; 5 O-O, N×N†; 6 Q×N, Q-B3; 7 N-B3, P-B3 = . *Bilguer.*

(l) 5 . . . N-K2; 6 R-K1, P-KN3; 7 P-QB3, N-B3; 8 P-Q3, B-N2; 9 P-QB4! O-O; 10 N-Q2 ± . Panov.

(m) Or 6 B-B4, N-B3; 7 R-K1, P-Q3; 8 P-QB3, N-N5; 9 P-KR3, N-K4; 10 P-Q3!

(n) 12 P-B4, B-B1; 13 P-K5, N-Q4; 14 N×N, P×N; 15 K-R1 ± . Ivkov-Rossetto, Varna 1962.

1 P-K4, P-K4, 2 N-KB3, N-QB3; 3 B-N5

	16	17	18	19	20
	P-B4				P-QR3
4	P-Q4	N-B3		P-Q3 (*i*)	B-R4
	BP×P	P×P (*c*)		P×P	P-B4!?
5	N×P? (*a*)	QN×P		P×P	P-Q4 (*j*)
	N×N	P-Q4!		N-B3	KP×P
6	P×N	N×P		B-N5!	P-K5 (*k*)
	P-B3	P×N		B-K2	B-B4
7	N-B3	N×N		N-B3	O-O
	P×B	P×N (*d*)	Q-Q4	P-Q3	KN-K2
8	N×KP	B×P†	P-QB4	B-QB4	B-N3!
	P-Q4	B-Q2	Q-Q3	N-QR4	P-Q4
9	P×P *e.p.*	Q-R5†	Q-R5† (*g*)	Q-K2!	P×P *e.p.*
	N-B3	K-K2	P-N3	P-B3!	Q×P
10	N-N5	Q-K5†	Q-K5†	O-O-O	R-K1
	Q-R4†	B-K3	Q×Q	Q-B2	P-R3
11	B-Q2	B×R! (*e*)	N×Q dis†	P-KR3	QN-Q2
	P-N5! ∓ (*b*)	Q×B (*f*)	P-B3 (*h*)	N×B =	P-QN4 (*l*)

(*a*) 5 B×N, QP×B; 6 N×P and now (A) 6 . . . Q-R5! 7 Q-K2 (7 O-O, B-Q3! = or 7 N-QB3, B-QN5 =), B-K3! (7 . . . N-B3; 8 P-KR3!); 8 P-KR3, O-O-O = *Archives*. (B) 6 . . . N-B3; 7 B-N5, B-K2; 8 O-O, O-O; 9 P-QB3, B-KB4 ∞.

(*b*) Podgorný and Přibyl in *Ceskoslovenský Šach* 1969, p. 284.

(*c*) (A) 4 . . . N-B3; 5 P×P (1) 5 . . . P-K5; 6 N-N5, P-Q4; 7 P-Q3, B×P; 8 P×P, P×P; 9 Q-K2 ± . (2) 5 . . . B-B4; 6 N×P, O-O; 7 O-O, N×N; 8 P-Q4, B×P; 9 Q×B, P-Q3; 10 B-KB4 ± . (B) 4 . . . N-Q5!? (1) 5 B-R4, N-KB3; 6 P×P, B-B4; 7 N×P, O-O; 8 O-O, P-Q4; 9 N-K2, Q-Q3! 10 N×N, B×N; 11 N-B3, N-N5!; Mecking-Rodriguez, Las Palmas 1976. (2) 5 B-B4, P-B3; 6 O-O, P-Q3! 7 R-K1, N×Nch; 8 Q×N, P-B5 = Tautvilas. (3) 5 P×P, N×B; 6 N×N, P-Q3; 7 P-Q4, P-K5; 8 N-N5, B×P; 9 P-KB3, Q-Q2; 10 Q-K2, O-O-O; 11 P×P, R-K1 = . R. Byrne.

(*d*) The text is preferable to 7 . . . Q-N4; 8 Q-K2! N-B3; 9 P-KB4, Q-R5†; 10 P-N3, Q-R6; 11 N-K5†, P-B3; 12 B-B4, B-QB4; 13 P-Q3, N-N5; 14 N-B7! B-B7†; 15 K-Q1, P-K6; 16 Q-B3! + . Kavalek-Ljubojević, Amsterdam 1975. 9 . . . Q-QB4 has been tried.

(*e*) (A) 11 P-Q4, N-B3; 12 P-Q5! N×P; 13 B-N5†, N-B3; 14 B×R, Q×B; 15 Q×P†, K-K1; 16 O-O, B-K2. Ježek-Přibyl, corr. 1968. (B) 11 P-KB4?! P×P *e.p.*; 12 O-O! R-N1; 13 P-Q4 is sharp.

(*f*) 12 Q×BP†, K-B3; 13 O-O! B-K2; 14 P-KB4, P-KR3; 15 P×P dis †, K-N3; 16 P-Q3 with more elbow room. *Archives*. In the column, 6 N-N3 is a possibility; *e.g.* 6 . . . B-KN5; 7 P-KR3, B×N; 8 Q×B, N-B3; 9 O-O, B-Q3; 10 N-R5, P-K5; 11 N×N†, Q×N; 12 Q×Q, P×Q; 13 P-QN3, O-O-O = . Likterink-Böhm, Wijk aan Zee, 1980.

(*g*) (A) 9 P-B5!? Q×BP; 10 Q-R4, N-B3; 11 P-Q4, Q-Q3 = . *Archives*. (B) 9 N×P dis†, B-Q2; 10 B×B†, Q×B; 11 Q-R5†, P-N3; 12 Q-K5†, K-B2; 13 N-N5, P-B3; 14 Q-Q4! Balogh-Schardtner, corr. 1963.

(*h*) 12 B-R4 (12 N×BP, P-QR3!∓) 12 . . . B-N2 (*Archives* suggest 12 . . . B-Q3); 13 P-Q4, P×P *e.p.*; 14 B-B4, B-K3; 15 O-O-O, O-O-O = .

(*i*) (A) 4 O-O, P×P; 5 B×N, QP×B; 6 N×P, N-B3 and 7 . . . Q-Q5 ∓ . (B) 4 P×P, N-B3! 5 B×N, QP×B; 6 O-O, B-Q3; 7 R-K1, O-O; 8 N×P, B×P; 9 P-Q4, B×N; 10 P×B, N-N5 = . Pais-Tompa, Budapest 1962.

(*j*) 5 N-B3, P-QN4; 6 B-N3, P-N5; 7 N-Q5, P×P; 8 P-Q4, P×N; 9 Q×P, B-K2; 10 O-O, N×P; 11 N×P†, Q×N; 12 Q-B7†, K-Q1∓ . Lombardy-Sherwin, New York, 1971.

(k) 6 N × P, N × N; 7 Q × N, P–B4! 8 Q–K5†, Q–K2; 9 Q × Q†, B × Q; 10 B–N3! P × P; 11 N–B3, N–B3 = .

(l) 12 P–QR4, R–QN1; 13 P × P, P × P; Caputto-Zagorovski, corr. 1960; 14 N–B1! B–Q2; 15 P–B3! P–Q6; 16 B–K3 with a strong attack. *Comments.*

1 P-K4, P-K4; 2 N-KB3, N-QB3; 3 B-N5, P-QR3; 4 B × N, QP × B (a)

	21	22	23	24	25
5	O-O...				P-Q4 (q)
	P-B3		B-Q3	B-KN5 (l)	P × P
6	P-Q4		P-Q4	P-KR3	Q × P
	P × P	B-KN5	P × P	P-KR4!	Q × Q
7	N × P	P × P (e)	Q × P	P-Q3! (m)	N × Q
	P-QB4 (b)	Q × Q	P-B3	Q-B3	B-Q2 (r)
8	N-N3	R × Q	P-QN3 (i)	QN-Q2	B-K3
	Q × Q	P × P (f)	B-K3 (j)	N-K2 (n)	O-O-O
9	R × Q	R-Q3	B-R3	R-K1	N-Q2
	B-Q3 (c)	B × N (g)	N-R3	N-N3 (o)	N-K2
10	N-R5	R × B	B × B	P-Q4!	O-O
	P-QN4	N-B3	P × B	B-Q3	R-K1
11	P-QB4	N-B3	P-B4	P × B	KR-K1
	N-K2 (d)	B-N5 (h)	O-O (k)	RP × P (p)	N-N3 ∞

(a) 4 . . . NP × B; 5 P-Q4, P × P; 6 Q × P, Q-B3; (A) 7 P-K5, Q-N3; 8 O-O, B-N2; 9 N-B3 ± , (B) 7 Q-Q3, Q-N3; 8 O-O, B-K2. Fischer.

(b) Other attempts are (A) 7 . . . N-K2; (1) 8 B-K3, N-N3; 9 N-Q2, B-Q3; 10 N-B4, O-O; 11 Q-Q3, N-K4; 12 N × N, B × N; 13 P-KB4 ± . Fischer-Unzicker, Siegen 1970. (2) 8 N-B3, N-N3; 9 B-K3, B-Q3; 10 N-B5, O-O∞. (B) 7 . . . B-Q3; 8 Q-R5!? (8 B-K3 or 8 N-B5! Pytel), P-KN3; 9 Q-B3, P-KR4; 10 Q-Q3, Q-K2; 11 P-KB4! Pytel-Grabczenski, Poland 1971.

(c) (A) A recent strengthening is 9 . . . B-KN5; 10 P-KB3, B-K3; 11 B-K3, P-QN3; 12 N-B3 (12 P-QR4! B-Q3; 13 P-R5, O-O-O; 14 N-B3, K-N2; 15 N-R4 and Black needs to exercise utmost care in defending), B-Q3; 13 P-QR4, K-B2; 14 P-R5, P-B5; 15 N-Q4, P-QN4 = . Timman-Korchnoi, match 1976. (B) 9 . . . B-Q2 is a cautious answer with a few options for Black. In the column, also 10 . . . N-R3! may be tried.

(d) 12 B-K3, P-B4; 13 N-B3, P-B5; 14 P-K5! B × P; 15 B × QBP, B × N; 16 P × B, N-N3; 17 N-B6 (Fischer-Portisch, Havana 1966), B-Q2!

(e) 7 P-B3, B-Q3; 8 QN-Q2 (8 B-K3, N-K2; 9 QN-Q2, Q-Q2; 10 R-K1, O-O = . *Comments*) Q-K2; 9 R-K1, O-O-O; 10 P-QR3, N-R3; 11 P-N4, N-B2; 12 Q-R4, P × P; 13 P × P, B-B5; 14 P-R3, B-R4 = . Tatai-Pachman, Venice 1967.

(f) 8 . . . B × N; 9 NP × B, P × P; 10 P-KB4, N-B3; 11 P-KB3, B-Q3!

(g) Also playable is 9 . . . B-Q3; 10 QN-Q2, N-B3; 11 N-B4, N × P; 12 N/4 × P, B/5 × N; 13 N × B, O-O; 14 B-K3, P-QN4; 15 P-R4 (N-Q2!), QR-N1! 16 R-QB1, P × P; 17 R-Q4, KR-K1; 18 N-Q2, N × N; 19 R × N, K-R5; 20 P-KN3, B-K4; 21 R/1-B2, K-B2; 22 K-N2, R × P; 23 K-B3, P-B6; 24 K × R, P × R; 25 R × QP, R-N4; 26 R-B2, B-Q3; 27 R × P, R-QR4; 28 B-B4, R-R5†; 29 K-B3, R-R6†; 30 K-K4, R × RP; 31 B × B, P × B; 32 R × QP, R × P; 33 R × P, R × P; 34 K-B3 with a draw, is Fischer-Spasski, 16th match game, Reykjavik 1972.

(h) 12 B-N5, B × N; 13 P × B! R-KB1! 14 B × N, R × B; 15 R × R, P × R = . Fischer-Smyslov, Monte Carlo 1967.

(i) (A) 8 R-K1, N-K2; 9 P-K5, P × P; 10 N × P, O-O = , or (B) 8 P-K5, P × P; 9 N × P, Q-B3! have been tried.

(j) 8 . . . Q-K2; 9 R-K1, B-KN5 might be a shade more active.

(k) 12 N-B3 ± . Kagan-Zwaig, Hastings 1976-7.

(l) (A) Not so eccentric as it looks is 5 . . . Q-Q3, continued (1) 6 N-R3, P-QN4! (2) 6 P-B3, B-N5; 7 P-KR3, B × N; 8 Q × B, O-O-O; 9 Q × P, N-B3; 10 P-Q4 (if 10 Q-B4, P-QN4!), R-K1 = . (3) 6 P-Q4, P × P; 7 N × P, B-Q2; 8 B-K3, O-O-O; 9 N-Q2, N-R3; 10 P-KR3, Q-N3; 11 Q-B3, P-B4 = . Larsen-Portisch, Rotterdam 1977. (4) 6 P-Q3, P-B3; 7 B-K3, B-N5; 8 QN-Q2, O-O-O; 9 R-N1, N-K2; 10 P-N4, P-KN4; 11 P-QR4, N-N3; 12

P–N5, BP×P; 13 P×P, P×P; 14 R×P, Q–B3; 15 R–N2, B–QB4; 16 N–N3, B–N5; 17 KN–Q4! P×N; 18 Q×B†, Q–Q2; 19 Q×Q†, R×Q; 20 N×P, B–B6; 21 R–R2, R×N; 22 R–R3, R–N5; 23 R×B, R–K1; 24 P–B3, K–Q2; 25 R–R1, R–N4; 26 K–B2, K–Q3; 27 R/1–R3, P–R4; 28 R–R4, P–B3; 29 R/3–R3, P–N5; 30 R–R5, R/1–K4; 31 R×R, R×R; 32 P×P, P×P; 33 K–N3, R–N7; 34 R–B3, P–N4; 35 B–Q4, R–N8; 36 B×P, P–N5; 37 R–N3, R–KB8; 38 B–N5, P–B4; 39 P–B3, P×P; 40 R×P, R–Q8; 41 B–K3, P–B5; 42 P×P, resigns. Mecking-Korchnoi, match 1974. (B) 5 . . . B–Q3; 6 P–Q4, P×P; 7 N×P, N–B3; 8 N–QB3, B–KN5; 9 P–B3!

(*m*) 7 P–B3, Q–Q6! 8 P×B, P×P; 9 N×P, B–Q3! 10 N×Q, B–R2†; 11 K–R1, B–N6† with perpetual check.

(*n*) Alternatives are (A) 8 . . . P–KN4!? 9 N–B4! B×N; 10 Q×B, Q×Q; 11 P×Q, P–B3; 12 P–KR4, P×P; 13 P–B4±. (B) 8 . . . P–QN4; 9 R–K1 (or 9 N–N3), B–QB4; 10 P–B3, R–Q1; 11 Q–B2, N–K2 ∞. *Informator 11*.

(*o*) Black has also 9 . . . B×N; 10 N×B, P–B4 = .

(*p*) 12 N–R2, R×N! 13 Q×P! Q–R5; 14 Q×Q, R×Q; 15 N–B3, R–R4. Pachman-Lengyel, Vrnjačka Banja 1967.

(*q*) (A) 5 N–B3, P–B3! 6 P–Q4, P×P; 7 Q×P (7 N×P, P–QB4; 8 KN–K2, Q×Q†; 9 K×Q, B–K3=), Q×Q; 8 N×Q, B–Q3; 9 B–K3, N–K2; 10 O–O–O, B–Q2; 11 N–N3, O–O–O = . (B) For 5 P–Q3 see col. 130.

(*r*) (A) 5 . . . P–QB4; 8 N–K2, B–Q2; 9 N–Q2±. (B) 7 . . . B–Q3, 8 N–QB3, N–K2; 9 B–K3, B–Q2; 10 O–O–O, O–O–O; 11 P–B4, KR–K1; 12 N–N3 (Grünfeld-Schönmann, corr. 1918); 12 . . . P–B3 followed by . . . N–N3 = equalizes. The column is Peterson-Alekhin, Ørebro 1935.

1 P-K4, P-K4; 2 N-KB3, N-QB3; 3 B-N5, P-QR3; 4 B-R4, P-Q3

	26	27	28	29	30
5	B×N†	P-Q4	P-B4	O-O!	
	P×B	P-QN4	B-Q2 (f)	B-N5	
6	P-Q4	B-N3	N-B3	P-KR3	
	P-B3 (a)	N×P	P-KN3	B-R4	P-KR4
7	B-K3!	N×N	P-Q4	P-B3	P-B4 (j)
	N-K2	P×N	B-N2	N-B3!	Q-B3!?
8	N-B3	P-QB3 (d)	B-K3	P-Q4	Q-N3
	N-N3	P×P (e)	P×P (g)	N-Q2	O-O-O
9	Q-Q2 (b)	N×P	N×P	B-K3!	B×N
	B-K2	B-N2	KN-K2	B-K2	P×B
10	P-KR4	Q-K2	O-O	QN-Q2	P×B
	P-KR4	P-QB4	O-O	O-O	P×P
11	O-O-O	B-KB4	P-KR3	P-R3 (h)	N-R2
	B-K3 (c)	N-K2 =	N×N =	B-B3 (i)	P-Q4! (k)

(a) Likewise satisfactory is (A) 6 . . . N-B3; 7 O-O, B-K2; 8 P×P, N×P; 9 QN-Q2, N×N; 10 B×N, B-N5; 11 B-B3, P-Q4; 12 P-KR3, B-R4; 13 Q-Q3, P-QB4 = . Gurgenidze-Spasski, USSR Chp. 1961. If (B) 6 . . . B-N5; 7 P×P, P×P; 8 Q×Q†, R×Q; 9 KN-Q2! *Comments.*

(b) 9 Q-K2, B-K2; 10 O-O-O, B-Q2; 11 P-KR4, P-KR4; 12 P×P, BP×P; 13 N-KN5, Q-B1; 14 Q-B4, B×N; 15 P×B, Q-N2; 16 P-KN3, R-QN1; 17 P-N3, Q-N5; 18 Q-Q3, P-R4 = . Spasski-Ciocaltea, Havana 1962.

(c) 12 P×P, BP×P; 13 N-KN5, B×N; 14 B×B, Q-N1 = . Ivkov-Smyslov, 1956. Also good is 11 . . . B-N5. *Comments.* The column is the Exchange Variation Deferred-I.

(d) 8 B-Q5, R-N1; 9 B-B6†, B-Q2; 10 B×Q, Q×B; 11 Q×P, N-B3; 12 N-B3, B-K2; 13 O-O, O-O; 14 P-QR4, KR-K1; 15 Q-Q3, P-N5; 16 N-Q5, P-QR4; 17 P-QN3, N×N; 18 P×N, B-B3; 19 R-N1, P-B4 = . Hort-Keres, Oberhausen 1961.

(e) Black can decline the pawn with 8 . . . B-N2; 9 P×P, N-B3; 10 P-B3, B-K2; 11 O-O, O-O; 12 N-B3, P-B4 = . Yates-Bogolyubov, London 1930. The column is Stoltz-Flohr, match 1931.

(f) 5 . . . B-N5?! 6 P-KR3! B×N; 7 Q×B, N-B3; 8 N-B3 (8 P-Q4, P×P; 9 P-K5, N-Q2! =), B-K2; 9 P-Q3, O-O; 10 B-K3, N-Q2; 11 N-Q5, N-B4; 12 B×N/5, P×B; 13 B×N, P×B; 14 N×B†, Q×N = . Goldenov-Yudovich, 1947. Despite the tripled pawns, the position is quite blocked.

(g) 8 . . . KN-K2; 9 P-Q5! N-QN1; 10 P-B5! characteristic of a King's Indian. The column is Keres-Capablanca, Buenos Aires 1939, a version of the Duras Variation which is usually entered after prior 5 P-Q3.

(h) 11 P-Q5, N/3-QN1; 12 P-B4, P-R4; 13 B-B2, N-R3 = . Pachman.

(i) 12 P-KN4 (12 P-Q5, B×N; 13 N×B, N-K2 =), B-N3; 13 P-Q5, N/3-QN1; 14 B-B2 with more active play for White. Pachman. In the column (A) 5 . . . N-B3 see col. 39. (B) 5 . . . B-K2 (with the idea 6 P-B3, P-B4) can be thwarted by 6 B×N†, P×B; 7 P-Q4, P×P; 8 N×P, P-QB4; 9 N-B6, Q-Q2; 10 N-R5 ± . Karpov-Portisch, Milan 1975. (c) 5 . . . B-Q2; 6 P-B4 (Duras!), N-B3; 7 N-B3, B-N5 (For 7 . . . P-KN3 see col. 28); 8 P-KR3, B×N; 9 Q×B (Romanishin-Smyslov, Hastings 1976-7), N-Q2; 10 Q-N3, N-B4 = . Romanishin in *Informator 23.*

(j) (A) 7 B×N†, P×B; 8 P-Q4 (8 R-K1, Q-B3; 9 R-K3, P-N3; 10 P-Q4, P×P; 11 R-Q3, B×N; 12 R×B, Q-K4; 13 P-B3, B-N2; 14 P×P, Q×QP; 15 Q-N3, N-B3; 16 B-Q2, O-O! Analyses in *Československý Šach,* 1970, p. 46), Q-B3; (1) 9 QN-Q2, N-K2; 10 R-K1, B-Q2; 11 N-B4, Q-K3; 12 Q-Q3, P-B3; 13 P×P, QP×P; 14 B-K3, N-N3; 15 QR-Q1, B-K2 = . Matanović-Ciocaltea, Havana 1962. (2) 9 P×P, P×P; 10 QN-Q2, B-QB4 = . *Comments.* (B)

7 P–Q4, P–QN4 (7 . . . Q–B3; 8 P × P, P × P; 9 P × B, P × P; 10 B–KN5, Q–K3; 11 N–R4, B–K2; 12 B–N3 +); 8 B–N3, N × P; 9 P × B, P × P; 10 N–N5 (10 B × P†, K × B; 11 N–N5† is a gamble), N–R3; 11 P–KB4, P–Q4; 12 B × P, (1) 12 . . . P–B3 = . Zhuravlev. (2) 12 . . . B–B4; 13 B–K3, Q–Q3?! 14 P–N4, B–N3∞. Scholl-Kerkhoff, Dutch Chp. 1970.

(k) 12 N × P, Q–K3; 13 Q–N3, P × KP ∞ with a strong attack for the piece. *P/E*. In the column, v. den Berg's 7 . . . P–KN3 might be also considered, and also 7 P–Q4!

1 P–K4, P–K4; 2 N–KB3, N–QB3; 3 B–N5, P–QR3, 4 B–R4, P–Q3, 5 P–B3, P–B4

	31	32	33	34	35
6	P–Q4	P × P	(Siesta Variation)		
	P × KP	B × P			
7	N × P (*a*)	P–Q4		O–O	
	P × N	P–K5		B–Q6	
8	Q–R5†	N–N5 (*c*)		R–K1	
	K–K2!	P–Q4		B–K2	
9	B × N	P–B3!	P–QB4	P–B4	R–K3 (*j*)
	P × B	P–R3! (*d*)	P × P (*g*)	R–N1	P–K5
10	B–N5†	P × P	B × N†	Q–N3	N–K1
	N–B3	P × N	P × B	P–K5	B–KN4
11	P × P	P × B	Q–R4	N–Q4	R–R3 (*k*)
	Q–Q4	B–Q3	Q–Q2	N–B3	N–B3 (*l*)
12	B–R4	Q–N4 (*e*)	N–QB3	N–B5	N × B
	K–Q2 (*b*)	N–B3 (*f*)	N–B3 (*h*)	K–B2 (*i*)	P × N (*m*)

(*a*) 7 N–N5, P × P; 8 N × KP, B–B4; 9 Q × P, Q–K2; 10 P–B3, P–QN4; 11 Q–Q5, B–Q2; 12 B–N3, N–B3 ∓.

(*b*) 13 Q–N5, P–R3; 14 Q–B5†, K–K1; 15 Q–N6†, Q–B2; 16 Q × Q†, K × Q; 17 P × N, P × P ∓. Capablanca.

(*c*) (A) Andreas Steiner versus Capablanca, "Siesta" Tournament, Budapest 1928, played 8 B–KN5? B–K2; 9 N–R4, B–K3! 10 B × B, N × B; 11 Q–R5†, P–N3; 12 Q–R6, N–N1! 13 Q–B4, N–B3; 14 N–Q2, O–O; but the original appearance of this variation was in (B) Capablanca-Marshall, 14th match game 1909, with 8 Q–K2, B–K2; 9 KN–Q2, N–B3; 10 P–KR3, P–Q4; 11 N–B1, P–QN4; 12 B–B2, N–QR4; 13 N–K3, B–N3; 14 N–Q2, O–O; 15 P–QN4, N–N5; 16 QN × N, QP × N; 17 P–QR4, N–Q4; 18 N × N, Q × N; 19 P × P, P–K6! 20 O–O, R × P; 21 R × R, P × R†; 22 Q × P, P–KB1; 23 Q–K2, B × B; 24 Q × B/2, P × P; 25 B–K3, B–Q3; 26 B–B2, Q–N4; 27 Q–K4, P–R3; 28 R–K1, R × B; 29 K × R, B–N6†; 30 K–N1, B × R; 31 Q × B, draw. (C) 8 P–Q5, P × N; 9 P × N, P–QN4; 10 Q × P, B × N; 11 B–N3, B–N3; 12 O–O, N–B3; 13 B–N5, B–K2; 14 QR–K1, K–B1; 15 R–K3, P–R3; 16 B × N, B × B; 17 Q–Q5, P–KR4; 18 P–N3, Q–B1; 19 R–K6, Q–Q1; 20 R–K3, Q–B1; draw, Capablanca-Herman Steiner, New York 1931.

(*d*) 9 . . . P–K6; 10 P–KB4 (1) 10 . . . N–B3; 11 N–B3! or (2) 10 . . . B–Q3; 11 Q–R5†, P–N3; 12 Q–B3! *Comments.*

(*e*) (A) 12 N–Q2, Q–B3; 13 N–B3, P–N5; 14 Q–K2!† (B) 12 Q–K2†, K–B1; 13 P–KR3, P–N5; 14 Q × P, R–R5; 15 Q–N5, R–K5† ∓. Shapshnikov-Estrin, corr. 1963–4. (C) 12 Q–B3, P–N5! 13 Q–K3†, K–B1; 14 P–KN3, Q–B3; 15 O–O, R–K1 = . (D) 12 Q–Q3, K–B2; 13 N–Q2, N–B3; 14 K–Q1, R–K1; 15 B × N, P × B; 16 N–B1, P–B4 = . Estrin.

(*f*) 13 Q × P, K–B1; 14 B–B4, R–R4; 15 Q–N3, Q–K2† ∓. Baturinski-Estrin, Moscow 1947.

(*g*) Interesting is 9 . . . P–KR3; 10 P × P, Q × P; 11 B–N3, Q × P; 12 Q–R5†, P–N3; 13 B–B7†, K–K2; 14 B × P, B × B; 15 Q × B, P × N; 16 Q × P†, K–Q2; 17 Q–B5†, K–K1; 1 Q–N6†, K–Q2 = . *Comments.*

(*h*) 13 O–O, P–B4; 14 Q × Q†, K × Q; 15 B–K3, P × P; 16 B × P, B–Q3; 17 QR–Q1, K–B3 = . Shamkovich-Shiyanovski, USSR Chp. 1961.

(*i*) 13 N–R3, R–K1 = . Radtchenko.

(*j*) 9 Q–N3 (A) 9 . . . P–QN4; 10 Q–Q5, Q–Q2; 11 Q × B, P × B; 12 Q–B2, N–B3; 13 Q × QRP, O–O ± . Geller-Lutikov, USSR Chp. 1960. (B) 9 . . . R–N1; 10 Q–Q5, P–K5 ∞.

(*k*) 11 N–N3, B–R5! (11 . . . N–R3; 12 N × B, P × N; 13 Q–B3!); 12 Q–R5†, P–N3; 13 R × P, B × P†; 14 K–R1, P × R; 15 Q × R, K–B1; 16 N × B, P × N; 17 B × N, Q–K2 + . Harms-Kalish, corr. 1970.

(*l*) 11 . . . P–N4; 12 N × B, P × N; 13 B–N3, N–K4; 14 B–Q5, P–B3; 15 B–K4, N–B3 = .
Tandai-Kalish, corr. 1970.

(*m*) 13 R × QP, O–O; 14 R–R3, N–K5! 15 P–B3, Q–B3! Dannberg-Estrin, corr. 1965–6.

1 P–K4, P–K4; 2 N–KB3, N–QB3; 3 B–N5, P–QR3; 4 B–R4

	36	37	38	39	40
	(P–Q3)............................			N–B3	
5	(P–B3)			O–O	
	B–Q2			P–Q3 (*j*)	
6	P–Q4			R–K1 (*k*)	.... B × N†
	P–KN3?	..... KN–K2	...... N–B3	P–QN4 (*l*)	P × B
7	O–O	B–N3 (*d*)	O–O	B–N3	P–Q4
	B–N2	P–R3	B–K2 (*g*)	N–QR4	N × P!
8	P × P (*a*)	N–R4! (*e*)	R–K1	P–Q4	R–K1 (*n*)
	P × P	P × P	O–O	N × B	P–KB4
9	B–K3 (*b*)	P × P	QN–Q2	RP × N	P × P
	N–B3	N × P!	R–K1 (*h*)	B–N2!	P–Q4
10	QN–Q2	Q × N	P–QR3	B–N5!	N–Q4
	O–O	N–B3	B–KB1	P–R3	B–B4
11	P–QN4	Q–Q5!	P–QN4	B–R4	P–QB3
	R–K1 (*c*)	Q × N (*f*)	P–Q4! (*i*)	B–K2 (*m*)	Q–R5 (*o*)

(*a*) 8 P–Q5, QN–K2; 9 B × B†, Q × B; 10 P–B4, P–R3; 11 N–B3, P–KB4; 12 P × P, P × P; 13 N–KR4, N–KB3; 14 P–B4, P–K5; 15 B–K3, O–O; 16 P–KR3, P–B4 = . Fischer-Filip, Curaçao 1962.

(*b*) Also 9 B–KN5 (1) 9 . . . N–B3; 10 QN–Q2, Q–K2; 11 R–K1, P–R3; 12 B–R4, O–O; 13 N–B1 ± . Botvinnik. (2) 9 . . . KN–K2; 10 Q–B1! P–R3; 11 B–K3, N–R4; 12 R–Q1, P–QN4; 13 B–B2, N–B1; 14 QN–Q2 N–Q3; 15 P–QN4, N/4–N2; 16 P–QR4 ± . Evans-Bronstein, USA *v.* USSR, 1955.

(*c*) 12 B–N3, P–R3; 13 P–QR4, B–K3; 14 Q–K2, N–KN5; 15 B × B, R × B; 16 N–B4 with a slight advantage. Nikitin-Pitskaar, USSR 1958.

(*d*) (A) 7 O–O, N–N3; (1) 8 QN–Q2, B–K2; 9 R–K1, O–O; 10 N–B1, Q–K1! 11 B–N3, B–N5! ∓. Spasski-Larsen, match 1968. (2) 8 P–Q5; N–N1; 9 B × B†, N × B; 10 P–B4, B–K2; 11 N–B3, O–O; 12 B–K3, N–R5! ∓. *Comments.* (B) 7 B–K3, P–R3! (C) 7 QN–Q2, P–KN3; 8 P × P, P × P; 9 P–KR4, B–N2; 10 P–R5, N–B1 = . (D) 7 P–R4, P–R3; 8 P–R5, P × P; 9 N × P, N × N; 10 P × N, P–Q4; 11 P–K5, B × B; 12 Q × B†, N–B3! = . Quinteros-Larsen, Manila 1973. (E) 7 P × P! N × P! 8 N × N, P × N; 9 B–N3, Q–B1 = .

(*e*) (A) 8 Q–K2, N–N3; 9 Q–B4, Q–K2! 10 P–Q5, P–N4; 11 Q–K2, N–R4; 12 B–B2, P–QB3; 13 P–QN4, N–QB5 ∞. Simagin. (B) 8 QN–Q2, N–N3 (or 8 . . . P–KN3 or . . . P–KN4); 9 N–B4, B–K2; 10 N–K3, B–N4 = .

(*f*) 12 Q × P†, K–Q1; 13 N–B3, N–K4; 14 Q–Q5, Q–N5; 15 B–K3, B–B3; 16 Q–Q4, Q × NP; 17 O–O–O with initiative for the pawn. Keres.

(*g*) 7 . . . P–KN3; 8 QN–Q2, Q–K2; 9 B–B2, B–N2; 10 N–B4, O–O; 11 P × P, N × P; 12 N/3 × N, P × N; 13 B–N5, P–R3; 14 B × N, B × B; 15 N–K3, P–B3; 16 B–N3, QR–Q1 = . Kaplan-Ivkov. São Paulo 1973.

(*h*) Suspect is the "Kecskemét method" 9 . . . B–K1, with White having a variety of promising answers, e.g. 10 P–Q5 or 10 P–KR3, N–Q2; 11 P–Q5 or 10 B–N3 coupled with N to Q2–B1–N3.

(*i*) 12 B–N3, B–N5; 13 P–R3, B–R4; 14 P × KP, QN × KP; 15 P–N4, N × N†; 16 N × N, P × P; 17 P × B, P × N; 18 R × R, Q × R; 19 Q × P, Q–K8†; 20 K–N2, R–K1; 21 P–R6, P–B3 = . Fischer-Gligorić, Candidates Tournament 1959.

(*j*) For 5 . . . B–K2; 6 B × N or 6 N–B3 see cols. 83 and 89.

(*k*) 6 P–B3, N × P; 7 P–Q4, P–B4; 8 B × N†, P × B; 9 P × P, B–K2 = . Evans.

(*l*) Constricted but safe defences are (A) 6 . . . B–K2; 7 P–B3, O–O; 8 P–Q4, KN–Q2 (8 . . . B–Q2 transposes into col. 38); 9 B–K3, B–B3; 10 QN–Q2, R–K1 = . (B) 6 . . . B–Q2; 7 B × N, P × B; 8 P–Q4, P × P; 9 P–K5, P × P; 10 N × KP, B–K3; 11 N × QBP, Q–Q4; 12 Q–B3, Q × Q; 13 P × Q, B–QB4 = . Tal-Pytel, Lublin 1975. Compare also to cols. 81–2.

(*m*) 12 N–B3, N–Q2; 13 B × B, Q × B; 14 P × P, P × P; 15 N–Q5, Q–Q3 = . *Comments.*

(*n*) 8 Q–K2, P–KB4; 9 QN–Q2, N × N; 10 N × N, B–K2; 11 P × P, O–O; 12 Q–B4†, K–R1; 13 Q × BP, R–QN1 = . Euwe.

(*o*) 12 P–B3, N–B7; 13 P–KN3! Q–R4; 14 Q–K2, N–R6†; 15 K–N2, B × N; 16 P × B, P–B5 with sharp play. Belavenets.

1 P–K4, P–K4; 2 N–KB3, N–QB3; 3 B–N5, P–QR3; 4 B–R4, N–B3; 5 O–O, B–K2;
6 R–K1, P–QN4; 7 B–N3, P–Q3; 8 P–B3, O–O; 9 P–KR3, N–QR4; 10 B–B2, P–B4;
11 P–Q4, Q–B2; 12 QN–Q2, BP × P; 13 P × P

	41	42	43	44	45
	N–B3		B–N2		B–Q2
14	P–QR3!	N–N3	P–Q5	N–B1	N–B1
	B–Q2 (a)	P–QR4!	B–B1 (d)	QR–B1	QR–B1
15	N–N3	B–K3	R–N1	B–Q3 (f)	N–K3 (i)
	KR–QB1	P–R5	P–N5	N–Q2 (g)	KR–K1
16	B–K3	QN–Q2	N–B1	N–K3	P–Q5 (j)
	P–QR4	B–K3	N–N2	P × P	P–N3
17	R–B1	P–Q5	B–K3	N × P	P–QN3
	P–R5	N–QN5	B–Q2	B–KB3	N–N2
18	QN–Q2	B–N1	R–QB1	N/4–B5	P–QN4
	Q–N2	B–Q2	KR–B1	P–N3	N–KR4 =
19	B–N1	N–B1	Q–Q2	N–R6†	
	B–K1	KR–B1	Q–R4	K–R1	
20	Q–K2 ± (b)	Q–Q2	B–N1	R–N1?	B–N2 (h)
		N–R3 (c)	B–Q1 = (e)	B–N2 (h)	

(a) (A) 14 . . . P × P; 15 N–N3, R–K1; 16 KN × P ± *Comments.* (B) 14 . . . P–QR4; 15 B–Q3, B–R3; 16 P–Q5, N–Q1; 17 P–QN4 ± . Pachman-Blau, Hilversum 1947. (If 17 . . . Q–B6; 18 R–N1, Q × B; 19 R–K3 + + .)

(b) Keres-Borisenko, Moscow 1967. White maintains some pressure.

(c) 21 N–N3, P–R6 = . Geller-Ivkov, Havana 1965. In the column, worthy of note is also 17 P–R3, N–QR4! 18 N–N5! B–B1; 19 P–B4, N–Q2; 20 N/5–B3, B–B3; 21 BP × P, P × P; 22 P–Q5, B–K2 = . Wade, Blackstock and Booth.

(d) Another plan is 14 . . . QR–B1; 15 B–Q3 (15 B–N1, N–Q2; 16 N–B1, (A) 16 . . . N–B5; 17 R–K2, N/5–N3; 18 R–B2, Q–N1; 19 N–K3, P–N3; 20 B–Q2, N–R5; 21 P–QN3, N/5–B4; 22 P–QN4, N–R5; 23 P–R3, K–R1 = . Tal-Petrosian, USSR Chp. 1959), N–Q2; 16 N–B1, N–B5; 17 N–N3, N–B4; 18 B–B2, P–N3; 19 P–QN3, N–N3; 20 B–R6, R–K1; 21 R–B1, B–B1 = . Suetin-Krogius, Leningrad 1960. (B) 16 . . . P–B4; 17 P × P, B × P; 18 N–N5, B × N; 19 B × B, B–R1! = . Matera-Kane, match—Manhattan C.C.—Marshall C.C. 1973.

(e) Gligorić-Reshevsky, 4th match game 1952.

(f) (A) 15 R–K2, P–Q4! (If (1) 15 . . . N–R4; 16 P–Q5, N–KB5; 17 B × N, P × B; 18 P–QN3 ± . Pachman, or (2) 15 . . . N–Q2; 16 N–K3, KR–K1; 17 P–QN3, B–B1; 18 B–N2, N–QB3; 19 R–B1, Q–N1; 20 N–Q5, N–Q1; 21 B–N1, N–K3 (Szily-Keres, Budapest 1952); 22 P–R3 ±); 16 P × KP, N × P; 17 N–N3, P–B4; 18 P × P *e.p.*, B × P; 19 N × N, P × N; 20 B × P, B × B; 21 R × B, Q–B7! (1) 22 Q–K2, P–R3; 23 N–K1, Q–B3; 24 R–N1, KR–K1; 25 R × R†, R × R; 26 B–K5, N–N5; 27 P–QN3, N × B; 28 P × N, Q–K5 = . Ivkov-Matanović, Yugoslavia 1951. (2) 22 Q–Q5†?! K–R1; 23 N–K1! was worth consideration. (B) 15 B–N1, P–Q4; (If (1) 15 . . . KR–K1; 16 N–N3, B–B1; 17 B–Q2, N–B5; 18 B–B3, P–QR4; 19 P–R3, N × RP; 20 B × P, Q × B; 21 R × N, Q–N3; 22 P–Q5 ± . Fletcher-Euwe, Venice 1948 or (2) 15 . . . N–Q2; 16 N–K3 ±); 16 P × QP, P × P; 17 B–N5, KR–K1; 18 Q–Q3, Q–QB5; 19 R × B! R × R; 20 Q–R3, Q–B2; 21 P–Q6 ± . *Comments.*

(g) Too speculative is 15 . . . P–Q4; 16 P × KP, N × P; 17 N–N3, P–B4; 18 P × P *e.p.* B × P; 19 B × N, P × B; 20 N × P, B × N?! 21 R × B, Q–B7; 22 Q–Q5†, K–R1; 23 N–K1, Q–B2; 24 B–B4, Q–R2; 25 R–N1 ± . Aronin.

(h) Smyslov-Keres, Bled 1959, with Black's advantage, but 20 N/6–N4 maintains equilibrium. *Comments.* Fischer preferred 16 P–Q5, P–B4; 17 N–K3, P–B5; 18 N–B5, B–Q1; 19 B–Q2 ± .

(*i*) 15 R–K2, KR–K1; 16 N–N3, P–N3; 17 B–N5 seems strong. *Comments.*

(*j*) (A) 16 B–Q2, N–B3; 17 P–Q5, N–Q5; 18 B–Q3, N × N†; 19 Q × N, P–N3 = . Darga-Bisguier, Bled 1961. (B) 16 P–QN3, B–B1! The column is Robatsch-Bisguier, Hastings 1961–2.

1 P-K4, P-K4; 2 N-KB3, N-QB3; 3 B-N5, P-QR3; 4 B-R4, N-B3; 5 O-O, B-K2;
6 R-K1, P-QN4; 7 B-N3, P-Q3; 8 P-B3, O-O; 9 P-KR3, N-QR4; 10 B-B2, P-B4;
11 P-Q4, Q-B2; 12 QN-Q2

	46	47	48	49	50
	N-B3		B-Q2		R-Q1 (*l*)
13	P×BP (*a*)		N-B1 (*f*)		N-B1
	P×P		KR-K1		BP×P (*m*)
14	N-B1 (*b*)		P-QN3	N-K3	P×P
	B-K3!	B-Q3	P-N3 (*g*)	P-N3	P-Q4
15	N-K3	N-R4 (*d*)	B-N5	B-Q2 (*j*)	N×P
	QR-Q1	N-K2	N-R4 (*h*)	B-KB1	P×P
16	Q-K2	Q-B3	B×B	QR-B1	N-N3
	P-B5!	R-Q1	R×B	N-B3	B-Q3
17	N-B5!	N-K3	N-K3	N-Q5	B-B4
	B×N	Q-N2	N-KB3	N×N	B-N2
18	P×B	N-N4	N-N5!?	P×N	R-QB1
	KR-K1	N×N	BP×P	N-R4	Q-N3
19	B-N5!	P×N	P×P	P×KP	N×KP
	P-R3 (*c*)	N-N3 (*e*)	N-B3 (*i*)	P×P (*k*)	N×N (*n*)

(*a*) Rauzer's—now most popular—line. Static is (A) 13 P-Q5, N-Q1 (also 13 . . . N-QR4; 14 N-B1, N-B5; 15 P-QN3, N-N3; 16 N-K3, P-B5!); 14 P-QR4, R-N1! (1) 15 P-B4! P-N5! 16 N-B1, N-K1; 17 P-KN4, P-N3; 18 N-N3! N-N2; 19 K-R2, P-B3; 20 R-KN1, N-B2 = . Keres-Vidmar, Bad Nauheim 1936. (2) 15 P-QN4, P-B5; 16 N-B1, N-K1; 17 P×P, P×P; 18 N/3-R2, P-N3; 19 P-B4, P-B3 = . Harmless are (B) 13 N-B1, BP×P; 14 P×P, N×QP; 15 N×N, P×N; 16 N-N3, N-Q2; 17 N-B5, B-B3; 18 B-N3 (18 R-K2, Q-N3; 19 R-Q2, N-K4! ∓), Q-N3; 19 B-Q5, B-N2 = . (C) 13 B-N1, B-Q1; 14 P×KP, P×P; 15 N-B1, B-K2; 16 P-QR4, B-N2 = . (D) 13 P-QR4, B-Q2! = . (E) 13 P-QR3, BP×P (13 . . . B-Q2! 14 P-QN4, BP×QP; 15 P×P, QR-B1; 16 B-N3, P-QR4! =); 14 P×P, P×P; 15 N-N3, N-Q2; 16 QN×P, N×N; 17 N×N, B-B3; 18 B-K3, N-K4; 19 P-QN3, N-B3; 20 R-QB1 with a minimal plus. Tal.

(*b*) Interesting are (A) 14 P-QR4, R-N1 (14 . . . B-K3?! 15 N-N5, QR-Q1; 16 N×B, P×N; 17 P×P, P×P; 18 Q-K2, P-B5; 19 N-B3, B-B4; 20 B-K3, N-Q5?!); 15 P×P, P×P; 16 N-B1, B-Q3; 17 B-N5, N-K1; 18 N-K3, P-B3; 19 N-Q5, Q-B2; 20 B-K3, N-K2 = . Smyslov-Bolbochan, Moscow 1956. (B) 14 N-R2, P-B5! 15 QN-B1, B-QB4; 16 N-K3, N-K2 = . Suetin.

(*c*) If 19 . . . N-Q4; 20 B-K4, B×B; 21 B×N, B-B3; 22 B-K4 ± . In the column, if 17 N-N5, P-R3! 18 N×B, P×N; 19 P-QN3, B-B4 = . Suetin-Nei, Vilna 1967. The text is Parma's analysis.

(*d*) Possible is 15 B-N5, N-Q2; 16 P-QR4, R-N1; 17 N-K3, N-N3; 18 P×P, P×P; 19 N-Q5, N×N; 20 P×N, N-Q1 ∞ .

(*e*) 20 N-B5, B-K3; 21 P-N5 ± . Fischer-Filip, Curaçao 1962.

(*f*) (A) 13 P-QN4, P×NP; 14 P×NP, N-B3! 15 P-R3, QR-B1; 16 B-N3, KP×P; 17 B-N2, P-Q6; 18 N-B1, P-Q4 = . Boleslavski. (B) 13 P×KP, P×P; 14 N-R2, KR-Q1; 15 Q-B3, B-K3; 16 QN-B1, N-B5; 17 P-QN3, N-N3; 18 N-K3, P-B5; 19 N-B5, B-KB1 = . *Comments.*

(*g*) (A) 14 . . . BP×P; 15 P×P, N-B3; 16 B-N2, N×QP; 17 N×N, P×N; 18 R-QB1, Q-Q1; 19 Q×P, B-KB1; 20 QR-Q1 ± . Tal-Gligorić, Reykjavik 1964. (B) 14 . . . QR-Q1; 15 N-K3, B-B3; 16 N-B5 ± .

(*h*) 15 . . . K-N2; 16 N-K3, B-K3; 17 Q-Q2 ± . Keres-Zuidema, Beverwijk 1964.

(*i*) 20 P×P, P×P; 21 N-Q5, N×N; 22 P×N, N-Q5 ∞ . Ravinski. In the column, 18 R-QB1! might have more hidden punch.

(*j*) (A) 15 P × BP, P × P; 16 N-R2, QR-Q1; 17 Q-B3; B-K3; 18 N-N4, N × N; 19 P × N! N-B5! 20 N-Q5, B × N; 21 P × B, N-N3; 22 KR-Q1, R-Q2 = . Geller-Gligorić, Bled 1961. (B) 15 P-QR4, B-KB1; 16 P × NP, P × NP; 17 B-Q2, BP × P; 18 P × P, KR-B1 = . Keres.

(*k*) 20 P-QN3, B-N2; 21 P-B4, N-N2 = . Suetin. In the column, also playable is 14 P-Q5, N-N2; 15 N/3-R2, P-B5 = . Karpov-Petrosian, Milan 1975.

(*l*) Other choices are (A) 12 . . . B-N2; 13 N-B1, BP × P, see col. 43. (B) 12 . . . R-K1; 13 P-QN4! P × NP; 14 P × NP, N-B3; 15 B-R3 ± .

(*m*) 13 . . . P-Q4; 14 P × KP, QP × P; 15 QN-Q2, P × N; 16 P × N, B × P; 17 Q × P, B-K3; 18 N-K4, B-K2; 19 Q-R5 ± .

(*n*) 20 B × N, B × B; 21 R × B, Q-N2; 22 R-K1 ± . Tal-Gudmundson, Reykjavik 1964.

1 P–K4, P–K4; 2 N–KB3, N–QB3; 3 B–N5, P–QR3; 4 B–R4, N–B3; 5 O–O, B–K2;
6 R–K1, P–QN4; 7 B–N3, P–Q3; 8 P–B3, O–O; 9 P–KR3, N–QR4; 10 B–B2, P–B4;
11 P–Q4

	51	52	53	54	55
	(Q–B2) (*a*)		B–N2		N–B3
12	P–QN4	P–QR4	QN–Q2 (*h*)		QN–Q2 (*m*)
	P×NP	B–Q2 (*f*)	BP×P		Q–N3!
13	P×NP	B–N5	P×P		P×BP
	N–B5 (*b*)	KR–B1	N–B3	R–B1	P×P
14	QN–Q2	P×KP	P–Q5! (*i*)	P–Q5 (*k*)	N–B1
	B–N2 (*c*)	P×KP	N–QN5	N–R4	B–K3
15	N×N	P×P	B–N1	N–B1	N–K3
	P×N	B×NP	P–QR4	N–QB5	QR–Q1
16	P–Q5 (*d*)	QN–Q2	N–B1	P–QN3	Q–K2
	P–QR4	R–Q1	N–R3	N–N3	P–N3
17	P–N5	Q–B1	N–N3	B–K3	N–N5
	P–R5!	P–B5	B–B1	P–N3	P–B5
18	R–N1	N–B1	B–Q3	B–Q2	P–QR4
	N–Q2 (*e*)	N–N6 (*g*)	B–Q2 (*j*)	Q–B2 (*l*)	K–N2 (*n*)

(*a*) This move completes the "Chigorin" Defence as originally developed by the father of Russian Chess. He naturally experimented also with other earlier derivations of the "Closed" system but they were analysed in more depth by masters of this century.

(*b*) Also satisfactory is 13 . . . N–B3; 14 B–N2! N×NP; 15 B–N3, N–B3; 16 N–B3, P×P (16 . . . B–N2; 17 R–QB1, Q–Q1; 18 N–Q5, N–QR4; 19 N×B†, Q×N; 20 B–R3, N×B; 21 P×N, N×P = . Vasyukov-Kholmov, Tbilisi 1966); 17 N×QP, N×N; 18 Q×N, B–K3! 19 N–Q5, B×N; 20 B×B, QR–N1; 21 B–N3, N–K1; 22 QR–B1, Q–N3; 23 Q–Q5, Q–N2 = . Parma-Rinder, Bamberg 1962.

(*c*) (A) 14 . . . B–K3; 15 P–Q5, B–Q2; 16 N×N, Q×N = . Suetin. (B) 14 . . . P–Q4?! 15 P×QP, P×P; 16 N×N, P×N; 17 Q×P, B×NP = . Tal-Geller, Riga 1958.

(*d*) (A) 16 R–K3, KR–K1! (B) 16 P–QR4, QR–N1; 17 R–N1, P–Q4; 18 P×QP, N×P ∞.

(*e*) 19 B–K3, N–N3 = . *Comments*, our improvements on 18 B×P, Q–R4; 19 B–B2, Q×NP; 20 P–QR4, Q–R4; 21 B–R3, N–Q2; 22 R–N1, B–R3; 23 B–N4, Q–B2; 24 R–K3, QR–N1; 25 R–B3, Q–R2 ∓ . Tal-Sanguinetti, Munich 1958.

(*f*) 12 . . . P–N5; 13 P×NP, P×NP; 14 Q–Q2, B–N2 = . *Comments*.

(*g*) 19 B×N, P×B; 20 N/1–Q2, B–Q6; 21 N×NP, N×P = . L. Steiner-Gligorić, Budapest 1948.

(*h*) 12 P×KP, P×P; 13 Q×Q, QR×Q; 14 N×P, N×P is harmless. Black can also play first 11 . . . BP×P; 12 P×P, B–N2. The sequence is superficially similar to yet different from col. 43 where . . . Q–B2 has been played.

(*i*) (A) 14 N–N3, P–QR4; 15 P–QR4, P×RP; 16 R×P, N–QN5. Filip. (B) 14 N–B1, R–K1; 15 N–N3, P–N3; 16 B–R6, B–KB1; 17 Q–Q2, B×B; 18 Q×B, N×QP! 19 N×N, P×N; 20 QR–Q1, R–QB1; 21 B–N1, R–K3! 22 R×P, Q–K2 = . Tal-Petrosian, Moscow 1967.

(*j*) 19 B–K3, Q–N1; 20 R–QB1 ± . Fischer-Unzicker, Leipzig 1960.

(*k*) 14 N–B1, P–Q4! 15 P×QP, N×P; 16 N/1–Q2, N–B5 or 16 . . . P–B4 ∞ .

(*l*) 19 B–R5, B–Q1 = . Fuchs.

(*m*) (A) 12 P–Q5, N–QR4; 13 QN–Q2, Q–B2 = see Chigorin Defence. (B) 12 B–K3, N–Q2 (or 12 . . . Q–B2)' 13 QN–Q2, B–B3; 14 P×BP, P×P; 15 P–QR4, B–N2 = . Gufeld-Smyslov, USSR Chp. 1961. Black's 12th move was promoted by Borisenko, but is doubtful.

(*n*) 19 P×P, P×P; 20 R–N1, N–QR4; 21 N–B3, Q–B2; 22 N–Q5! ± . Tal-Bronstein, Tbilisi 1959.

1 P–K4, P–K4; 2 N–KB3, N–QB3; 3 B–N5, P–QR3; 4 B–R4, N–B3; 5 O–O, B–K2;
6 R–K1, P–QN4; 7 B–N3, P–Q3; 8 P–B3, O–O; 9 P–KR3

	56	57	58	59	60
	(N–QR4)		B–K3	N–Q2 (*j*)	
10	(B–B2)		P–Q4	P–Q4	
	P–B4		B × B	N–N3	B–B3
11	(P–Q4)		Q × B (*h*)	QN–Q2	P–QR4
	N–Q2		Q–N1	B–B3 (*k*)	N–R4
12	P × BP	QN–Q2! (*c*)	B–N5	N–B1	B–B2
	P × P	BP × P	N–QR4	R–K1	N–N3
13	QN–Q2	P × P	Q–Q1	N–N3	P × NP (*m*)
	P–B3! (*a*)	N–QB3 (*d*)	P–B3!	P–N3	P × NP
14	N–B1	N–N3 (*e*)	QN–Q2	B–R6	P × P
	N–N3	P–QR4	R–K1	P–R4	P × P
15	Q–K2	B–K3 (*f*)	P–QN4	P × P	B–K3
	R–R2	P–R5	N–N2	P × P	Q × Q
16	N–K3	QN–Q2	N–B1	Q–K2	R × Q
	B–K3 (*b*)	B–B3 (*g*)	P–N3 (*i*)	P–R5 (*l*)	N/4–B5 (*n*)

(*a*) 13 . . . Q–B2; 14 N–B1, N–N3; 15 N–K3, R–Q1; 16 Q–K2, B–K3; 17 N–Q5! N × N; 18
P × N, B × P; 19 N × P ± . Fischer-Keres, Curaçao 1962.

(*b*) 17 N–B5, R–K1; 18 N × R†, R/1 × N = . Ivkov-Quinones, Amsterdam 1964.

(*c*) 12 P–QN3, KP × P; 13 P × P, N–QB3; 14 N–B3, B–B3; 15 B–K3, P × P; 16 N × P,
N × N; 17 B × N, B–N2 = . Stein-Darga, Amsterdam 1964.

(*d*) 13 . . . B–B3; 14 P–Q5, N–N3; 15 P–QN3, N–N2, 16 N–B1, B–Q2; 17 B–Q2, Q–B2;
18 N–K3, KR–B1; 19 Q–K2 ± . Ostojić-Ciocaltea, Skopje 1969.

(*e*) (A) 14 N–B1, P × P; 15 N × P, N × N; 16 Q × N, N–K4; 17 Q–Q1, B–B3; 18 N–K3,
B–K3; 19 N–Q5, B × N; 20 Q × B, R–B1; 21 B–N3, N–B5 = . Ivkov-Keres, Beverwijk, 1964.
(B) 14 P–Q5, N–N5; 15 B–N1, P–QR4; 16 P–R3, N–R3; 17 P–QN4, N–N3; 18 Q–N3,
B–Q2 = . Suetin-Tal, Kiev 1964.

(*f*) 15 B–Q3, B–R3; 16 P–Q5, N–N5; 17 B–B1, P–R5; 18 P–R3, N × QP; 19 Q × N, P × N;
20 B × P, N–B3; 21 Q–Q3, B × B = . Kavalek-Gheorghiu, Tel Aviv 1964.

(*g*) 17 N–B1, P × P; 18 N × P, N × N; 19 B × N, N–K4; 20 N–K3, B–K3; 21 Q–Q2 ± .

(*h*) Stronger is 11 P × B, P × P; 12 P × P, N–QN5 (12 . . . P–Q4; 13 P–K5, N–K5; 14
N–B3, P–B4; 15 P × P *e.p.*, B × P; 16 N × N, P × N; 17 R × P, Q–Q4; 18 R–N4 ±); 13 P–Q5,
P–B4; 14 P × P *e.p.*, P–Q4; 15 P–K5, N–K5; 16 N–B3 with some advantage.

(*i*) 17 B × N, B × N; 18 P–Q5, P–B4 = . Gipslis-Nei, Leningrad 1963.

(*j*) 9 . . . B–N2; 10 P–Q4. (A) 10 . . . P × P; 11 P × P, P–Q4; 12 P–K5, N–K5; 13 N–B3,
N–R4; 14 B–B2, P–KB4; 15 P × P *e.p.*, B × P; 16 N × N, P × N; 17 B × P, B × B; 18 R × B,
P–B4; 19 R–N4 ± . (B) 10 . . . N–QR4; 11 B–B2, N–B5; 12 P–QN3, N–N3; 13 QN–Q2, P × P;
14 P × P, P–B4 ∞ . Fischer. (C) 10 . . . N–Q2; 11 QN–Q2, B–B3; 12 N–B1, N–K2; 13 N/1–R2,
P–B4; 14 N–N4, N–KN3; 15 P–QR4 ± . Balashov-Keres, Tallinn 1973. (D) 10 . . . R–K1; 11
QN–Q2 (11 N–N5, R–KB1; 12 P–KB4, P × BP; 13 B × P, N–R4; 14 B–B2, N–Q4! =),
B–KB1 = .

(*k*) 11 . . . P × P; 12 P × P, P–Q4; 13 B–B2, B–K3; 14 P–K5, Q–Q2; 15 N–N3, 15 . . .
N–R5; 16 B–N5. (1) P–B3; 17 P × P, B × P; 18 Q–N1, P–R3; Darga. (2) 16 . . . B–QN5! 17
R–K2, KR–K1 = . Spasski-Tal, Monaco 1959.

(*l*) 17 QR–Q1, B–Q2 = . Lepeshkin-Kuzmin, Tallinn 1965.

(*m*) Also 13 P–QN4! N/4–B5! 14 P–R5, N–Q2! 15 N–R3! N × N; 16 B × N, P–N3; 17
Q–Q3 ± . Geller-Portisch, Wijk aan Zee 1969.

(*n*) 17 R × R, N × R; 18 B–B5 with a better ending. Fuchs-Kostro, Vrnjačka, Banja 1967.

1 P–K4, P–K4; 2 N–KB3, N–QB3; 3 B–N5, P–QR3; 4 B–R4, N–B3; 5 O–O, B–K2;
6 R–K1, P–QN4; 7 B–N3, P–Q3; 8 P–B3, O–O; 9 P–KR3 (*a*), P–R3

	61	62	63	64	65
10	P–Q4 (*b*)				
	R–K1 (*c*)				
11	B–K3	QN–Q2			
	B–B1	B–B1			
12	QN–Q2	N–B1	P–R3		
	B–N2 (*d*)	B–N2 (*g*)	B–N2		
13	N–B1 (*e*)	N–N3	B–B2		B–R2
	N–QR4 (*f*)	N–QR4	N–N1	P–Q4	N–QR2
14	B–B2	B–B2	P–QN4	P × KP	P–QN4
	N–B5	N–B5	QN–Q2	QN × P	P × P
15	P–QR4	B–Q3 (*h*)	B–N2	N × N	N × P
	P–N3	N–N3	Q–N1!	R × N	P–B4
16	P–QN3!	B–Q2	P–B4	P–KB4	N–B5
	N–N3 =	P–B4 (*i*)	P × BP (*j*)	B–B4† (*k*)	P–N3 (*l*)

(*a*) The alternatives are less systematic and assuming but contain latent dangers just because of the lack of "guide lines"; e.g. (A) 9 P–QR4, P–N5; 10 P–Q4, P × QP; 11 P × QP, B–N5 = . (B) 9 B–B2, R–K1; 10 P–Q3, B–B1; 11 QN–Q2, P–Q4; 12 Q–K2, B–N2; 13 N–B1, P–KR3 ∞. Lein-Lengyel, Novi Sad 1972. (C) 9 P–Q3, N–QR4; 10 B–B2, P–B4; 11 QN–Q2, R–K1 = . (D) 9 P–Q4, B–N5! (1) 10 P–Q5, N–QR4; 11 B–B2, P–B3! 12 P × P (or 12 P–KR3!?), Q–B2; 13 QN–Q2, Q × P; 14 N–B1, KR–K1; 15 P–KR3, B–K3. (2) 10 B–K3, P × P; 11 P × P, N–QR4; 12 B–B2, P–B4; 13 QN–Q2, P × P; 14 B × P, N–B3; 15 B–K3, P–Q4! = . Unzicker-Keres, match 1956.

(*b*) 10 P–Q3, N–QR4; 11 B–B2, P–B4 transposes into note (*a*) (C).

(*c*) Black's 9th move prevents 10 N–N5; and 10 P–QR4, N–QR4; 11 B–B2, P–B4 may transpose into note (*a*). Also 10 . . . R–K1 is normal. *Comments.*

(*d*) Black did not choose the best course in 12 . . . B–Q2; 13 B–B2, Q–N1; 14 P × P, P × P; 15 N–R4, Q–Q1; 16 P–QR4, Q–K2? 17 N–B5, B × N; 18 P × B, P–N5; 19 B–K4! ± . Petrosian-Matanović, Skopje 1969.

(*e*) Probably the best continuation. Another leaf in the book is 13 Q–N1. (A) 13 . . . N–N1; 14 P–QR4, P × QP; 15 B × QP, N/1–Q2 (15 . . . P–B4! =); 16 B × N, Q × B; 17 P × P ± . Parma-Medina, Mallorca 1969. (B) 13 . . . Q–N1; 14 P–QR4, N–Q1; 15 Q–Q3, B–B3; 16 P–Q5 (16 P–B4! Gligorić), B–Q2; 17 P–B4, P × BP; 18 B × P, P–B3; 19 N–R2, P–QR4; 20 KR–QB1, P × P; 21 P × P, N–N2 = . Spasski-Gligorić, Skopje 1969.

(*f*) 13 . . . P–KN3; (1) 14 B–B2, B–N2; 15 P–Q5, N–K2; 16 P–QN3, P–B3; 17 P–B4, P × QP; 18 BP × P, R–B1 = . Tukmakov-Smyslov, USSR Chp. 1969. (2) 14 N–KR4! P–Q4! 15 P × QP, N × QP; 16 Q–N4, N–QR4 (Sigurjonsson-Padevski, Reykjavik 1970); 17 P × P! The column is Evans-Lombardy, match 1962.

(*g*) 12 . . . B–Q2; 13 N–N3, N–QR4; 14 B–B2, P–B4; 15 P–N3, N–B3! (1) 16 B–K3, BP × P; 17 P × P, P × P; 18 P–B1! N–QN5; 19 B–N2, P–Q4; 20 P–K5 ± . Fischer-Gheorghiu, Vinkovci 1968. (2) 16 P–Q5, N–K2; 17 P–B4! N–N3; 18 N–B5, N–B5 = . Spasski-Portisch, Lugano 1968.

(*h*) Partings of the way! (A) 15 P–QR4, P–Q4! (1) 16 P × NP, RP × P; 17 R × R, B × R; 18 P–N3, QP × P; 19 N × P/4, B × N; 20 B × B, P × P; 21 B–B2! R × R†; 22 Q × R, P–Q6; 23 Q–Q1, P–Q7! 24 N × P, N–R6, drawn. Unzicker-Gligorić, Lugano 1968. (2) 16 P–N3, QP × P; 17 N × P/4, N × N; 18 R × N, B × R; 19 B × B, N–N3; 20 B × R, N × B; 21 RP × P, RP × P; 22 B–K3, P × P = . Stein-Reshevsky, Los Angeles 1968. (B) 15 P–N3, N–N3; 16 B–N2, P–B4; 17 P × KP! P × P; 18 P–B4! Q–B2; 19 Q–K2, P–N5! = . Analysis by Gligorić.

(i) 17 P–Q5, B–B1! 18 N–R2, N–R2; 19 R–KB1, B–K2; 20 P–KB4, P×P; 21 B×BP, B–N4; 22 Q–B3, R–R2; 23 N–N4, B×B; 24 Q×B, B×N; 25 Q×B, Q–N4 = . Hecht-Gligorić, Büsum 1969.

(j) 17 P×P, N×P/4; 18 N×N, P×N; 19 N×P, P–B4! = . Matanović-Hecht, Raach 1969.

(k) 17 K–R2, R×P; 18 N×R, N×N; 19 B–K3, Q–B3; 20 P–KN3, B–Q3! = .

(l) 17 N–KN3, P–B5; 18 B–N1, N–B3; 19 P–B4, P–QR4 = .

1 P-K4, P-K4; 2 N-KB3, N-QB3; 3 B-N5, P-QR3; 4 B-R4, N-B3; 5 O-O, B-K2;
6 R-K1, P-QN4; 7 B-N3, P-Q3; 8 P-B3, O-O; 9 P-KR3, N-N1

	66	67	68	69	70
10	P-Q3	P-Q4 (g)			
	QN-Q2 (a)	QN-Q2 (h)			
11	QN-Q2	N-R4		P-B4	QN-Q2 (n)
	B-N2	P × P!	R-K1	P-B3 (k)	B-N2
12	N-B1 (b)	P × P	QN-Q2	P-B5 (l)	B-B2
	N-B4	N-N3	B-N2	Q-B2	R-K1 (o)
13	B-B2	N-KB3	N-B5	P × QP	P-QN3 (p)
	R-K1	P-B4	B-B1	B × P	B-KB1
14	N-N3 (c)	B-KB4	N-B3	B-N5	B-N2
	B-KB1	B-N2	P × P	P × P	P-N3
15	N-R2 (d)	P × P	N-N5	B × N	P-QR4!
	P-Q4 (e)	P × P	P-Q4	P × B	P-B4 (q)
16	Q-B3	Q × Q	BP × P	Q × P	P-Q5
	R-K3 (f)	B × Q (i)	N × P (j)	N-K4 (m)	P-B5 (r)

(a) 10 . . . P-B4; 11 QN-Q2, N-B3; 12 N-B1, P-R3; 13 N-N3, R-K1; 14 P-QR4, B-Q2;
15 N-B5, B-KB1; 16 P-N4, N-QR4; 17 B-B2, P-N5 = . Ciocaltea-Ree, Skopje Olympics
1972.

(b) Tamer is 12 B-B2, R-K1; 13 N-B1, B-KB1; 14 N-N3, P-B4; 15 N-B5, P-Q4; 16
N-R2, P × P; 17 P × P, P-B5; 18 Q-B3, Q-N3; 19 B-N5, P-R3; 20 B-K3, Q-K3; 21 QR-Q1,
QR-Q1 = . Ciocaltea-Filip, Harrachov 1966.

(c) Or 14 N-K3, B-KB1; 15 P-QN4, N/4-Q2; 16 N-B1, P-R3; 17 P-B4, P-B4; 18 P-R3,
BP × P; 19 RP × P, B-Q4! = .

(d) 15 P-N4?! N/4-Q2; 16 P-Q4, N-N3! 17 B-Q3, P-N3; 18 B-Q2, B-N2; 19 Q-B2,
R-QB1; 20 QR-Q1, Q-K2; 21 N-R2, N/B3-Q2; 22 P-Q5, P-B4 ∓. Krauss-Korn, corr. 1975.

(e) 15 . . . N-K3; 16 N-B5, P-R3; 17 N-N4, N × N; 18 Q × N, K-R2 = . Matanović-
Ivkov, Palma 1966.

(f) 17 N-B5, K-R1; 18 P × P, B × P; 19 Q-N3, N-R4 = .

(g) 10 P-QR4, B-N2; 11 P-Q3, QN-Q2; 12 P × P, P × P; 13 R × R, B × R; 14 N-R3,
B-B3; 15 N-B2, N-B4; 16 N-N4, B-N2; 17 B-R2, N/4-Q2; 18 B-N1, R-K1 = .

(h) Unrewarding is 10 . . . B-N2; 11 P × P, N × P; 12 P-K6! P × P; 13 B × P†, K-R1; 14
B-Q5, N-B4; 15 B × B, N × B; 16 P-QR4 ± .

(i) 17 B-Q6, R-K1; 18 B × QBP, N/N3-Q2; 19 B-Q4 (Fischer-Robatsch, Vinkovći 1968),
R × P = .

(j) 17 Q-R5, N × N; 18 B × N, P-KB3; 19 B-Q2, N-N3; 20 B-B2, P-N3; 21 N-R6†,
K-N2! 22 Q-R4, N-B5; 23 R × R, Q × R; 24 R-K1, N × B! 25 R × Q, R × R; 26 P-B3, B-B1;
27 N-N4, B × N; 28 Q × B, B-Q3; 29 K-B2, N-B5; 30 Q-Q7†, R-K2; 31 Q-B6, N-K6; 32
P-KN4, R-K3! 33 Q-Q7†, R-K2; drawn. Analysis by Dueball.

(k) Preferable to (A) 11 . . . P-N5; 12 P-B5! B-N2; 13 Q-B2, P × QP; 14 P-B6! or (B) 11
. . . B-N2; 12 N-B3, P-B3; 13 P-R3! or (C) 11 . . . P-B4; 12 P × KP, N/2 × P; 13 N × N,
P × N = .

(l) Occasional diversions are (A) 12 P-QR4, or (B) 12 QN-Q2, B-N2; 13 B-B2, N-K1; or
(C) 12 P × NP, RP × P; 13 N-B3, B-R3 or 13 . . . B-N2.

(m) 17 QN-Q2, R-Q1; 18 Q-K3, N-Q6; 19 Q-R6, B-B5; 20 Q × P, R-Q3; 21 Q-B3,
N × R; 22 R × N, Q-Q1∞. Fischer-Portisch, Santa Monica 1966. In the column, 16 . . .
B-B4; 17 Q-B3, P-QR4; 18 QN-Q2, P-R5; or also 16 . . . P-QB4 are useful alternatives.
Comments.

(n) Drawish is the fierce-looking 11 B-N5, B-N2; 12 QN-Q2, R-K1 (12 . . . P-R3; 13
B-R4, R-K1 =); 13 B-B2, P-R3; 14 B-R4, P-N3; 15 P-QN4, N-R4; 16 B × B, Q × B; 17
N-N3, N-N3 = . Novák-Kovacs, Harrachov 1967.

(*o*) Gligorić's favourite was 12 . . . P–B4; e.g. (A) 13 P–Q5, P–KN3 (or 13 . . . N–K1!); 14 N–B1, N–R4; 15 B–R6, R–K1; 16 P–QN3, B–KB3; 17 P–QR4, B–N2; 18 B–N5, Q–B2; 19 P–N3, N/4–B3; 20 Q–Q2, N–N3; 21 N–K3, P–KR4; 22 P–R5, QN–Q2; 23 N–N2, N–R2; 24 B–K3, QN–B3; 25 P–B4, B–QB1; 26 K–R2, P × P; 27 P × P, B–Q2; 28 N–N1, QR–N1; 29 KR–N1, K–R1; 30 P–B3, N–N1; 31 N–K2, drawn. Hartston-Gligorić, Bath 1973. (B) 13 N–B1, R–K1; 14 N–N3, B–KB1; 15 P–Q5, P–N3; 16 B–N5, P–R3; 17 B–K3, B–N2. Also compare col. 70, note (*r*).

(*p*) One of the many frequent crossroads of recent practice; e.g. (A) 13 P–QN4, B–KB1; 14 P–QR4 (14 B–N2, N–N3; 15 P–R3, KN–Q2 = . Kavalek-Matanović, Sousse 1967), and now (1) 14 . . . P–QR4; 15 NP × P, R × P; 16 R–N1, B–R3; 17 P × P, R × P ∞. (2) 14 . . . N–N3; 15 P–R5, QN–Q2; 16 B–N2, R–N1 (if 16 . . . Q–N1; 17 R–N1! P–B4; 18 NP × P, QP × P; 19 P × KP, QN × P; 20 N × N (better 20 P–B4!), Q × N = . Fischer-Spassky, 10th match game 1972); 17 R–N1, B–R1; 18 B–R1, P–N3; 19 P–B4, KP × P; 20 P × P, P × P; 21 N × P, P–Q4; 22 N/4–B3, P × P; 23 N–N5, P–K6 = . Planinć-Spasski, Amsterdam I, 1973. (B) 13 N–B1, B–KB1; 14 N–N3, P–N3; 15 B–Q2, P–B4; 16 P–Q5! B–N2; 17 P–N3 ± . Balashov-Zuidema, Beverwijk 1973.

(*q*) Also 15 . . . B–N2; 16 B–Q3, P–B3; 17 Q–B2; 18 P–QN4, N–N3 = .

(*r*) 17 B – N5, P – R3; 18 B – K3, P – KR4 = .

1 P–K4, P–K4; 2 N–KB3, N–QB3; 3 B–N5, P–QR3; 4 B–R4, N–B3; 5 O–O, B–K2;
6 R–K1, P–QN4; 7 B–N3, O–O; 8 P–B3, P–Q4!; 9 P × P

	71	72	73	74	75
	P–K5			N × P	
10	P × N		N–N5	N × P (*g*)	
	P × N		B–KN5	N × N	
11	P–Q4 (*a*)		Q–B2 (*e*)	R × N	
	B–KN5	P × P	N–K4	N–B3 (*h*)	. . . . P–QB3!
12	P–KR3	B–N5 (*c*)	N × KP	P–Q4	P–Q4
	B–R4	B–KN5	N × N	B–Q3	B–Q3
13	P–N4	Q–Q3	Q × N	R–K1 (*i*)	R–K1
	N × P	R–K1!	B–Q3	N–N5	Q–R5
14	Q × P	N–Q2	P–Q4	P–KR3	P–N3
	N–B3	N–R4	P–KB4	Q–R5	Q–R6
15	Q–N2	N–B3	Q–B2	Q–B3	B–K3 (*l*)
	R–K1	B–B3	N–B6† (*f*)	N × P	B–KN5
16	B–N5	R–K5	P × N	B–Q2 (*j*)	Q–Q3 (*m*)
	B–N3 (*b*)	Q–Q3 (*d*)	Q–R5	B–N2 (*k*)	

(*a*) 11 Q × P, B–KN5; 12 Q–N3, R–K1; 13 P–Q4, B–Q3; 14 P–KB4, N–R4; 15 R × R†,
Q × R; 16 Q–B2, Q × P; 17 P–KR3, B–K3; 18 B–K3, R–K1; 19 N–Q2, B × B; 20 P × B,
P–N4 = . Matanović-Milić, Beverwijk 1958.

(*b*) 17 N–Q2, N–R4; 18 N–B3, B × B; 19 Q × B, Q × Q†; 20 N × Q, N–B5 = . Suetin.

(*c*) Interesting is 12 Q–B3, B–K3; 13 B–KB4, N–Q4! 14 B–N3, P–QR4 ∞.

(*d*) 17 Q–K4, R × R; 18 Q × B, R × B; 19 N × R, B × N; 20 Q × N, Q–N3 = . Strand-Dalko,
corr. 1963.

(*e*) 11 P–B3, P × P; (A) 12 N × P/3!? N–QR4; 13 B–B2, R–K1; 14 P–Q4, Q × P; 15 Q–Q3,
B–Q3! returns Black's pawn, and is better than sudden death in (B) 12 P × P?? N × P; 13
N × RP (1) 13 . . . B–KB4; 14 N × R, B–Q6!! 15 R–K4, B × N; 16 P–QB4, B–B4†; 17 K–R1,
N–B3; 18 R–R4, N–K4; 19 N–B3, N–N3; 20 Q–K1, N × R; 21 Q × N, Q–K2; 22 P × P,
P × P + ; but not (2) 13 . . . B–Q3; 14 B × N, B × P†; 15 K × B, Q–R5†; 16 K–N2, Q–R6†; 17
K–N1, Q–N6†; 18 K–R1, K × N; 19 P × B, R–R1; 20 B–N2, K–N1†; 21 K–N1 and White can
defend himself.

(*f*) 17 P × B (also 17 R–K5, B–KR6!), Q × RP†; 18 K–B1, P × P ∓. In the column, 14
P–KB4, N–N3! is very promising (Gutman and Vitouski).

(*g*) (A) 10 P–QR4, B–N2; 11 P × P, P × P; 12 R × R, B × R; 13 N × P, N × N; 14 R × N,
N–B5; 15 P–Q4, N × P! ∓. Vinter (B) 10 P–Q4! P × P; 11 N × P, N × N; 12 Q × N!.

(*h*) This is the parent variation, now discarded. But there is also merit in 11 . . . B–N2; 12
P–Q4, Q–Q2; 13 P–QR4! B–KB3; 14 R–K1, P–N5; 15 P–QB4, N–K2; 16 P–Q5, P–B3! 17
P–Q6, N–B4; 18 P–B5, QR–K1 = . Ciocaltea-Tsaitlin, Kragujevać 1975.

(*i*) Wolf showed 13 R–K2! (A) 13 . . . N–R4; 14 Q–Q3, Q–R5; 15 P–N3, Q–R6; 16 B–Q5,
B–KB4; 17 Q–K3, QR–Q1; 18 B–N2 ± . or (B) 13 . . . N–N5; 14 P–KR3, Q–R5; 15 N–Q2 ± to
be equally satisfactory.

(*j*) (A) 16 R–K2? B–KN5? (16 . . . N–N5! 17 R–K8, N–B3; 18 R × R†, K × R; 19 N–Q2,
R–N1; 20 N–B1 = Tartakover); 17 P × B, B–R7†; 18 K–B1, B–N6; Capablanca-Marshall,
New York 1918; 19 K–K1 + . (B) 16 Q × N, B–R7† (16 . . . B–N6? 17 Q × P† + +); 17 K–B1,
B–N6! + .

(*k*) 17 Q × B, N–Q6; 18 R–K2, Q–N6; 19 K–B1, Q–R7; 20 P–N4! + .

(*l*) 15 R–K4!? (1) 15 . . . P–N4; 16 Q–B3, B–KB4; 17 B × N, P × B; 18 R–K3, B–K5; 19
R × B, P × R; 20 Q–B6, B–B5; 21 B × B, P × B; 22 Q × P/B4, P–B4 = . (2) 15 . . . B–Q2; 16
P–QB4, N–B3; 17 R–R4, Q–B4 = . Ken Smith.

(*m*) (A) 16 . . . QR–K1; 17 N–Q2, R–K3; 18 P–QR4, Q–R4; 19 P × P, RP × P; 20 P–QB4, P × P; 21 N × P, B–N5; 22 KR–QB1, B–K7; 23 B–Q1, B × Q = . (B) 16 . . . N × B; 17 R × N, P–QB4; 18 B–Q5, QR–Q1; 19 N–Q2, B–B2; 20 B–N2, Q–R3; 21 N–B3, B–N3; 22 N–K5, B–K3; 23 N–B3, B–N5 = . Adorjan.

1 P–K4, P–K4; 2 N–KB3, N–QB3; 3 B–N5, P–QR3; 4 B–R4, N–B3; 5 O–O, B–K2; 6 R–K1, P–QN4; 7 B–N3, O–O (a)

	76	77	78	79	80
8	(P–B3)	....		P–QR4	P–Q4 (m)
	(P–Q4)	Emery–Horowitz Variation		P–Q4 (j)	P–Q3
9	(P×P)	....		P×QP (k)	P–B3
	(N×P)		P–Q4 (f)	N–Q5	B–N5
10	(N×P)		P–K5	N×P	B–K3 (n)
	(N×N)		N–K5	B–N2	P×P
11	(R×N)		P×P (h)	B–R2	P×P
	(P–QB3)		B–KN5	N×QP	N–QR4
12	B×N	P–N3	N–B3	P–QB3	B–B2
	P×B	B–B3	N×N	N–B5	P–B4
13	P–Q4	R–K1	P×N	P×N	QN–Q2
	B–Q3	P–B4	Q–Q2	N×P	P×P
14	R–K3 (b)	P–Q4	P–KR3	P–Q5	B×P
	Q–R5	P×P	B–R4	N×R	N–B3
15	P–KR3 (c)	P×P	P–N4	Q×N	B–K3
	P–N4 (d)	B–N2 (e)	B–N3 (i)	B–B4 (l)	P–Q4 =

(a) 7 . . . B–N2; 8 P–B3, P–Q4; 9 P×P, N×P; 10 N×P, N×N; 11 R×N, N–B5; 12 P–Q4, N×P; 13 Q–K2 ± .

(b) Kevitz's improvement over the older 14 R–K1.

(c) 15 P–KN3, B–KN5; 16 P–B3, B×NP; 17 Q–K2, B–B5; 18 P×B, P–B4† ∓ . E.C.O.

(d) 16 Q–B3, B–K3; 17 Q–B6, KR–K1; 18 N–Q2, Q–B5; 19 Q×Q, B×Q; 20 R–K1, B×P! 21 N–B3, R×R† = . Zagorovski–Neiman, corr. 1966–8.

(e) 16 N–B3, N×N; 17 P×N, Q–Q2; 18 B–K3, KR–K1 = . A game Fischer-Spasski, Santa Monica 1966, ran 12 . . . B–B3; 13 R–K1, N–B3; 14 P–Q4, B–KN5; 15 Q–Q3, P–B4 (15 . . . Q–B2!); 16 P×P (16 B–B2!?), B×BP = .

(f) Disinterred and analysed in *Chess Review* 1968 by Horowitz (and Bisguier) in response to a suggestion by Thomas Emery.

(g) (A) After 9 . . . N×KP the text resembles the "Open Defence" (see there) where Black has not yet castled and White has played Q–K2 instead of R–K1, thus retaining the choice of R–Q1. If White continues 10 P×P, B–K3; 11 N–Q4, N×P; 12 P–B3, B–Q3, he arrives at the "Breslau Variation" (col. 107). (B) 9 . . . B–KN5; 10 KP×P, P–K5; 11 P×N, P×N; 12 P–KR3, is col. 71. (C) 9 . . . P×KP; 10 N×P, N×N; 11 P×N, Q×Q; 12 B×Q ± .

(h) 11 N×P? N×KP! 12 P–B3, P–QB4; 13 P×N, P×N; 14 B×P, P×P; 15 N×P barely maintains equality for White.

(i) 16 N–N5 ∞. Horowitz claims White for choice but practical proof is lacking.

(j) Positionally sound are also (A) 8 . . . B–N2; 9 P–Q3, (1) 9 . . . P–Q3; 10 B–Q2! P–N5! 11 P–B3, P–Q4; 12 BP×P, R–K1; 13 N–B3, N×NP; 14 N×KP, B–Q3; 15 P–Q4, P–B4; 16 B–N5, BP×P; 17 N–N4, B–K2 = . Geller-Jansa, Budapest 1970. (2) 9 . . . N–QR4; 10 B–R2, P–Q3; 11 B–Q2 (or 11 P–B3, P–B4; 12 QN–Q2, Q–B2; 13 N–B1, P–B5; 14 B–N5, N–R4 = . Bronstein-Pachman, Moscow 1946), N–B3; 12 N–B3, N–Q2 = . Keres-Ivkov, match USSR-Yugoslavia 1956. (B) 8 . . . P–N5; 9 P–B3, P–Q3; 10 P–R5, R–N1; 11 B–B4, P×P; 12 N×B, N×BP, B–N5; 13 P–R3, B×N; 14 Q×B, N–Q5; 15 Q–Q1, P–B3; 16 N–K2, N–N4 = . Tal-Smyslov, Moscow 1966.

(k) *Archives* suggests 9 B×P, but with 9 . . . B–N2! 10 N×P, N×N; 11 B×B, R–R2 Black creates problems at no risk to himself. *Comments.*

(l) 16 P–Q4, B/4×P; 17 N–KB3, P–QB4; 18 N×B, P×N; 19 B–KB4, B×QP; 20 B×B, Q×B ∓ . Zaitsev-Martinov, Moscow 1968. This and the next column are the "Anti-Marshall" variants, designed to bypass the attack.

(m) 8 P–KR3, B–N2; 9 P–Q3, P–Q3 (or 9 . . . P–R3); 10 QN–Q2, R–K1; 11 P–B3, B–KB1; 12 N–B1, N–QR4; 13 B–B2, P–Q4; 14 P × P, Q × P = . Compare the text move also with note *(b)* to cols. 61–5.

(n) (A) 10 P–QR4, Q–Q2; 11 Q–Q3, B × N. (B) 10 Q–Q3, B × N; 11 P × B, N–QR4; 12 P–KB4, N × B = . (C) 10 P–KR3, B × N; 11 P × B, N–QR4; 12 P–KB4, N × B; 13 P × N, P–B4 = . (D) 10 P–Q5, N–QR4; 11 B–B2, P–B3; 12 P × P, Q–B2! 13 QN–Q2, Q × P = .

1 P-K4, P-K4; 2 N-KB3, N-QB3; 3 B-N5, P-QR3; 4 B-R4, N-B3; 5 O-O, B-K2

	81	82	83	84	85
6	P-Q4(Centre Variation)		B × N	⎰ Exchange Variation	
	P × P		QP × B	⎱ Double Deferred	
7	P-K5	R-K1	P-Q3	Q-K1	N-B3
	N-K5	P-QN4 (c)	N-Q2 (e)	P-B4!	B-KN5 (j)
8	N × P	B-N3	QN-Q2	N × P	P-KR3
	N × N (a)	P-Q3	O-O	Q-Q5	B-R4
9	Q × N	B-Q5	N-B4	N-Q3 (h)	P-KN4?! (k)
	N-B4	B-Q2	P-B3!	Q × KP	B-N3
10	N-B3!	B × N	N-R4 (f)	Q × Q	N × P
	O-O	B × B	N-B4	N × Q	N × KP
11	B-KN5	N × P	N-B5 (g)	R-K1	R-K1 ± (l)
	B × B	B-Q2		P-B5	
12	Q × N	N-QB3		N-B4	
	B-K2 (b)	O-O (d)		N-B3 (i)	

(*a*) (A) Equally satisfactory is 8 . . . O-O; 9 N-B5 (9 P-QB3, P-B4!), P-Q4; 10 B × N, P × B; 11 N × B†, Q × N; 12 R-K1, P-B3; 13 P-KB3, N-N4; 14 N-B3, B-B4; 15 P × P, Q × P = . (B) 8 . . . N-B4; 9 N-B5! O-O; (9 . . . B-B1; 10 R-K1, N × B; 11 Q-N4, N-B4; 12 N × P†, B × N; 13 Q × B, R-B1; 14 Q × P, N-K3; 15 N-B3 ±); 10 Q-N4, P-KN3; 11 B × N ± .

(*b*) 13 Q-K3, P-Q4; 14 QR-Q1, P-QB3; 15 N-K2, Q-R4; 16 B-N3, B-KN5 = . Honfi-Krogius, Hamburg 1965. Compare cols. 81–2 and col. 39.

(*c*) More sedate is 7 . . . O-O; 8 P-K5, N-K1! 9 B-B4, P-B3; 10 B × N, QP × B; 11 Q × P, Q × Q; 12 N × Q, P × P; 13 B × P, P-B4 = .

(*d*) 13 B-B4, R-K1 = . Matulović-Hecht, Hamburg 1965. Probably better is 8 P-K5, N × P; 9 R × N, P-Q3; 10 R-K1!

(*e*) Black unnecessarily gives up the Bishop pair after 7 . . . B-KN5; 8 P-KR3, B × N (8 . . . B-R4; 9 P-KN4!); 9 Q × B, N-Q2; 10 N-Q2, O-O; 11 N-B4, B-B4; 12 B-K3, Q-K2; 13 Q-N4!

(*f*) Quite playable is 10 P-Q4?! P × P; 11 N × P, N-K4; 12 N-K3, B-QB4; 13 P-QB3, R-K1; 14 Q-K2, K-R1; 15 B-Q2, P-QR4; 16 P-KB4, N-B2; 17 N-Q1, P-QN3; 18 R-K1, B-R3; 19 Q-B3 and White maintains subtle pressure. *Misl.* 1970/5.

(*g*) 11 . . . B-K3! 12 Q-N4, P-KN3 = ; or 11 . . . B × N; 12 P × B, Q-Q2; 13 Q-N4, P-QN4; 14 N-K3, KR-K1; 15 P-KR3, Q-Q5; 16 R-Q1, QR-Q1; 17 R-N1, Q × Q; 18 P × Q, P-K5; 19 P-Q4, N-R5; 20 N-B1, P-B4 = . Hort-Reshevsky, Los Angeles 1968.

(*h*) 9 N-KB3, Q × KP; 10 Q × Q, N × Q; 11 R-K1, N-B3; 12 N-B3, P-R3; 13 P-Q4, P × P; 14 N × P, P-B4; 15 N-N3, B-K3; 16 N-R5, O-O-O = . *Misl.* 1970/5.

(*i*) 13 P-QN3, P × P; 14 RP × P, K-B1; 15 B-N2, B-KB4; 16 P-Q3, B-Q3; 17 B × N, P × B; 18 N-K2, R-K1; 19 N-Q2, B-QN5 = . Hecht-Szabó, Kecskemét 1964.

(*j*) Another main line is 7 . . . N-Q2; 8 P-Q4, (1) 8 . . . P-B3; 9 N-K2, O-O; 10 P-B3, B-Q3; 11 N-R4, R-K1; 12 Q-B2! (2) 8 . . . P × P; 9 Q × P, O-O; 10 B-B4, N-B4; 11 Q-K3, N-K3! 12 QR-Q1, Q-K1; 13 B-N3, B-QB4; 14 Q-K2, P-B3 = . Tal-Szabó, Leipzig 1960.

(*k*) (A) 9 Q-K2, Q-B1; 10 P-Q3, P-R3; 11 N-Q1, N-R2; 12 P-KN4, B × P; 13 P × B, Q × P†; 14 K-R2, Q-R4† = . Tal-Keres, Bled 1961. (B) 9 P-Q3, B-Q3; 10 Q-K2; Q-Q2; 11 N-Q1, O-O-O; 12 N-K3, P-KN4, 13 P-KN4, B-N3; 14 N-R2, P-KR4 ∞. Robatsch-Jimenez, Varna 1962.

(*l*) Analysis by L. Pickett.

1 P-K4, P-K4; 2 N-KB3, N-QB3; 3 B-N5, P-QR3; 4 B-R4, N-B3; 5 O-O

	86	87	88	89	90
	(B-K2)				B-B4
6	Q-K2 (Worrall Attack)			N-B3	P-B3
	P-QN4 (a)			P-QN4	B-R2
7	B-N3			B-N3	P-Q4
	P-Q3	O-O		P-Q3	N × KP (k)
8	P-QR4 (b)	P-B3 (f)		N-Q5	R-K1
	B-N5	P-Q4		N-QR4 (j)	P-B4
9	P-B3	P-Q3!		N × B	QN-Q2
	O-O (c)	R-K1	B-N2 (h)	Q × N	O-O
10	P-KR3	R-K1	R-Q1	P-Q4	N × N
	N-QR4? (d)	B-N2	R-K1	B-N2	P × N
11	B-B2	QN-Q2	QN-Q2	B-N5!	B-KN5
	B-K3	Q-Q2	B-KB1	N × B	Q-K1
12	P × P	N-B1	N-B1	RP × B	R × P
	P × P (e)	QR-Q1 (g)	N-QR4 (i)	O-O =	P-Q3 ±

(a) The customary treatment; doubtful is the restrained 6 . . . P-Q3; 7 P-B3 (or 7 B × N†, P × B), O-O; 8 P-Q4, P × P; 9 N × P, B-Q2; 10 R-Q1 ± .

(b) 8 P-B3, (A) N-QR4? 9 B-B2, P-B4; 10 P-Q4 (10 P-QR4, R-QN1; 11 P × P, P × P; 12 P-Q4, N-B3 =), Q-B2; 11 R-Q1, O-O; 12 B-N5, BP × P; 13 P × P, B-N5 = . Euwe. (B) 8 . . . O-O; 9 P-Q4, B-N5; 10 R-Q1, P × P; 11 P × P, P-Q4! 12 P-K5, N-K5; 13 N-B3, N × N; 14 P × N, N-R4 = . *P/E.*

(c) 9 . . . P-N5; 10 P-Q3, O-O; 11 QN-Q2 with more space for White.

(d) Less complicated is 10 . . . B × N; 11 Q × B, N-QR4; 12 B-B2, P-B4; 13 P-Q3, N-K1; 14 N-Q2, N-B2; 15 R-K1, B-N4 = . Unzicker-Eliskases, Buenos Aires 1960.

(e) 13 P-Q4, B-B5; 14 B-Q3, B × B; 15 Q × B, N-B5; 16 R × R, Q × R; 17 P-QN3, Q-R7! 18 P × N, P × BP; 19 Q-K3, Q × N; 20 P × P, N × P; 21 R-K1, N-B4; 22 B-R3, Q-N3; 23 Q-Q4, R-R1; 24 P × P, B × P; 25 Q-Q5, Q-N2; 26 Q × P, Q-N6 = . Cuellar-Szabó, Moscow 1965.

(f) 8 P-QR4, P-N5! 9 P-R5, P-Q3, 10 P-B3, R-N1; 11 B-QB4, P-Q4!. Tringov-Smyslov, Amsterdam 1964.

(g) 12 B-N5, N-QR4; 13 B-B2, P × P; 14 P × P, N-B5 = . Filip, Black's 8 . . . P-Q4 is Schlechter's move—memories of Marshall!

(h) 9 . . . P-Q5; 10 P × P, N × QP; 11 N × N, Q × N; 12 B-K3, Q-Q3 = .

(i) 13 B-B2, P-B4; 14 B-N5, P-R3; 15 B-Q2, Q-B2; 16 N-N3, QR-Q1 = . Hübner-Geller, Palma de Mallorca 1970.

(j) Into consideration comes 8 . . . B-N2! 9 N × N†, B × N; 10 B-Q5, Q-B1; 11 R-K1, O-O; 12 P-B3, N-R4 = . The column is *P/E.*

(k) 7 . . . P-QN4; 8 B-N3, Q-K2; 9 B-Q5! Suetin. 5 . . . B-B4 is the dubious Möller Variation; the column is Capablanca's analysis.

1 P–K4, P–K4; 2 N–KB3, N–QB3; 3 B–N5, P–QR3; 4 B–R4, N–B3; 5 O–O, N × P;
6 P–Q4, P–QN4; 7 B–N3, P–Q4; 8 P × P, B–K3; 9 P–B3, B–QB4; 10 QN–Q2,
O–O; 11 B–B2

	91	92	93	94	95
	P–B4		N × N	N × KBP (*k*) . .	B–B4
12	P × P *e.p.*	N–N3	Q × N	R × N	N–N3
	N × P/3 (*a*)	B–N3	P–B3	P–B3	B–KN5 (*n*)
13	N–N3	KN–Q4 (*d*)	P × P (*i*)	P × P	P–KR3 (*o*)
	B–N3	N × N	R × P	B × R† (*l*)	B–R4
14	N–N5 (*b*)	N × N (*e*)	N–N5!	K × B	P–N4
	B–N5 (*c*)	B × N (*f*)	B–B4	Q × P	B–N3
15	B × P†	P × B	P–QR4!	K–N1	B × N
	K–R1	P–B5	N–K2	QR–K1	P × B
16	Q–B2	P–B3	B × B	N–B1!	N × B
	Q–Q3	N–N6	N × B	N–K4	P × N
17	K–R1	P × N	Q–Q3	B–K3	B–B4
	N–K4 =	P × P (*g*)	P–R3 (*j*)	N × N† (*m*)	Q × Q (*p*)

(*a*) 12 . . . N × P/7; 13 Q–K2 (13 R × N! see col. 94), N–R6†; 14 R–K1, Q × P; 15 N–N3,
N–B7†; 16 R × N, B × R; 17 Q × B, QR–K1 = . *Comments.*

(*b*) 14 QN–Q4, N × N; 15 P × N (15 N × N, B–N5; 16 Q–Q3, P–B4; 17 N–B5, Q–Q2! =
Radtchenko), Q–Q3 = . *Comments.*

(*c*) Just tenable is (A) 14 . . . B–B1; 15 Q–Q3, N–K4; 16 Q–N3, N–B2; 17 N–Q4, B × N;
18 P × B, P–B3; 19 B–B4, R–R2. Jimenez-Ortega, Havana 1964 or (B) 14 . . . Q–Q2; 15
N × B, Q × N; 16 N–Q4 (16 B–N5!?), N × N; 17 P × N, QR–K1 = . Larsen.

(*d*) 13 P–QR4, Q–Q2; 14 QN–Q4, N × N; 15 N × N, P–B4! 16 N–K2, P–Q5; 17 P × P,
P × P; 18 N–B4, B–B5; 19 N–Q3, QR–K1; 20 P × P, P × P; 21 R–K1. Suetin-Nei, Tbilisi 1966.

(*e*) In Boey-Estrin, corr. 1972–5, White played 14 P × N, P–B5; 15 P–B3, N–N6; 16
P × N, P × P; 17 Q–Q3, B–KB4; 18 Q × B, R × Q; 19 B × R, Q–R5; 20 B–K6†, K–R1; 21
B–R3, B × P† with immense activity for Black. The text-move shows similar features.

(*f*) 14 . . . Q–Q2; 15 P–B3, N–B4; 16 K–R1! leaves Black strategically disorganized.

(*g*) 18 Q–Q3, B–B4; 19 Q × B, R × Q; 20 B × R, Q–R5; 21 B–R3, Q × P†; 22 K–R1,
Q × KP ∞ .

(*h*) 12 B × N, P–Q5; 13 N–N5, P–Q6; 14 Q–R5, B–B4; 15 B–N3, B–KN3 = . Pachman.

(*i*) Simagin suggested 13 Q–Q3, P–N3; 14 P × P, B–B4; 15 Q–K2, R–K1; 16 Q–Q1, B × B;
17 Q × B, Q × P = .

(*j*) 18 P × P, P × P; 19 R × R, Q × R; 20 Q × NP, Q–KB1; 21 P–QN4, P × N; 22 P × B,
P–B3; 23 Q–N4, R–K3; 24 B × P, R–K5; 25 Q–N6, Q–K1; 26 Q–N1, Q–N3; 27 P–R4, Q–K3;
28 P–N3, P–Q5; 29 P–QB4, Q–K4; 30 Q–Q3, R–N5; 31 K–N2, N–K6†; 32 B × N, P × B; 33
P–B4, Q–K2; 34 K–B3, Q–K3; 35 R–K1, R–N3; 36 R × P, resigns. Suetin-Antoshin, Sochi
1974.

(*k*) This daring complication, disinterred in Weird-Dilworth, Irish Corr. Chp. 1941, has
been known since as the Dilworth Attack. It was extensively analysed by Spanish and Latin-
American players, as well as in *MCO*, 7th and later editions.

(*l*) Insufficient is 13 . . . Q × P; 14 Q–B1 (A) 14 . . . B–KN5; 15 P–KR3, P–KR4?! 16
P × B, P × P; 17 Q–Q3, B × R†; 18 K × B, P × N; 19 Q–R7†, K–B2; 20 Q–R5†, P–N3; 21
Q–R7†. Majstrović-Karaklajić, Yugoslavia 1947. (B) 14 . . . N–K4; 15 N–Q4, Q–R5; 16
QN–B3, N × N†; 17 R × N, B–N5; 18 R–B2, QR–K1; 19 B–B4 ± . Pinkus.

(*m*) 18 Q × N, Q × Q; 19 P × Q, R × P; 20 B–B2, B–R6; 21 N–N3, P–N3; 22 R–Q1, P–B3;
23 R–Q3, R–B5; 24 R–Q2, R/1–KB1 = . K. Smith-Samarian, corr. 1958–60.

(*n*) 12 . . . B–KN3; 13 KN–Q4, B × N; 14 P × B, P–QR4; 15 B–K3, N–N5; 16 B–N1,
P–R5; 17 N–Q2, P–R6; 18 Q–B1, P × P; 19 Q × P ± .

(*o*) 13 N × B, N × N; 14 R–K1, R–K1; 15 B–K3, N–K3; 16 Q–Q3, P–N3; 17 B–R6, N–K2; 18 N–Q4, B–B4; 19 N × B, N × N; 20 B–Q2, Q–R5 = . Fischer-Larsen, Santa Monica 1966.

(*p*) 18 QR × Q, N–Q1 = . 14th match game Karpov-Korchnoi, 1978.

1 P-K4, P-K4; 2 N-KB3, N-QB3; 3 B-N5, P-QR3; 4 B-R4, N-B3; 5 O-O, N × P; 6 P-Q4; 7 B-N3, P-Q4, P-QN4; 8 P × P, B-K3; 9 P-B3

	96	97	98	99	100
	(B-QB4).............................			N-B4	
10	Q-K2.......	Q-Q3 { Motzko		B-B2	B-N5 (k)
	O-O	O-O { Variation		B-N5	Q-Q2
11	B-K3 (a)	B-K3	QN-Q2	R-K1	B-B2
	P-B3	P-B4 (d)	P-B4	B-K2 (h)	P-R3
12	P × P (b)	P × P e.p.	P × P e.p.	QN-Q2	B-B4
	Q × P	Q × P	N × P/3	P-Q5 (i)	B-N5
13	QN-Q2	B × P (e)	N-N5	N-N3	QN-Q2
	B-Q3	QR-Q1	N-K4!	P-Q6	N-K3! = (l)
14	P-QR4	B × B†!	Q-N3	B-N1	
	N × N	Q × B	Q-Q3	N × N	
15	Q × N	N-Q4!	R-K1	P × N	
	N-K4	N × N	KN-N5!	B-KB4	
16	N × N	P × N	QN-K4	B-K3	
	Q × N = (c)	B × P (f)	P × N (g)	O-O (j)	

(a) 11 QN-Q2 (or 10 QN-Q2, O-O; 11 Q-K2), B-B4; 12 N × N, P × N; 13 N-N5, N × P; 14 N × KP, Q-Q6; 15 Q × Q, N × Q; 16 N × B, N × N; 17 B-K3, N × B = . Vasyukov-Khasin, USSR Chp. 1961.

(b) 12 N-Q4, B × N; 13 P × B, P × P; 14 P × P, Q-K2; 15 N-B3, N × N; 16 P × N, N × P; 17 B-Q4, N-B5; 18 B × N, QP × B, drawn. Gligorić-Unzicker, Oberhausen 1961.

(c) 17 P-KB4, Q-R4 = . Bertok-Geller, Stockholm 1962.

(d) Worth a try are (A) 11 . . . Q-K2; 12 QN-Q2, B × B; 13 Q × B, N × N; 14 N × N, N-R4; 15 B-B2, N-B5! and (B) 11 . . . B × B; 12 Q × B, N-K2! 13 B-B2, B-B4; 14 N-R4, P-KB3! = .

(e) Simpler is 13 QN-Q2, N-K4; 14 N × N, Q × N; 15 B-Q4, B × B; 16 P × B, Q-Q3; 17 QR-B1, KR-K1 = .

(f) 17 B × B, P-B4; 18 Q-QN3, Q × Q; 19 P × Q, P × B; 20 P-B3, N-B4 = . The column is based on Ericson's analysis.

(g) 17 B × B†, K-R1; 18 B-K3! N × BP! 19 Q-R4, P-R3; 20 N × P, N × N; 21 Q × N, QR-K1 ∓ . Schelfout-Euwe, Amsterdam 1942.

(h) 11 . . . P-Q5; 12 P-KR3, B-R4; 13 P-K6! P × KP; 14 P × P, B × N; 15 Q × B, N × P; 16 Q-R5†, P-N3; 17 B × P†, P × B; 18 Q × R, N-B7; 19 B-R6, Q-K2; Unzicker-Lehmann, Berlin 1953; 20 N-B3! Pachman.

(i) Acceptable (are (A) 12 . . . O-O; 13 N-N3, Q-Q2; 14 N × N, B × N; 15 Q-Q3, P-N3; 16 B-N5, B-K2. (Lloyd-Lehmann, Bognor Regis 1961) 17 B-B4! (B) 12 . . . Q-Q2; 13 N-N3, N-K3; 14 P-KR3, B-R4 ∞ . Karpov-Korchnoi, 28th match game, 1978.

(j) 17 N-Q4, N × N; 18 P × N, B-QN5; 19 R-B1, P-B4; 20 B × P, P × P; 21 B-KB4, B × B; 22 Q × B, Q-Q4 = . Larsen. Interposing 13 P-KR3, B-R4 might be better.

(k) (A) 10 N-Q4, N × P; 11 P-KB4, N-B5; 12 R-K1, N-K5; 13 P-B5, B-Q2; 14 B × N, NP × B; 15 N-Q2 ± . (B) 10 QN-Q2, P-Q5; 11 N-N5, P × P; 12 N × B, P × N; 13 P × P, Q-Q6; 14 N-B3, Q × Q; 15 B × Q, B-K2 = . Karpov-Korchnoi, 10th match game, 1978.

(l) *MCO*'s improvement over 13 . . . R-Q1; 14 P-KR3!

1 P–K4, P–K4; 2 N–KB3, N–QB3; 3 B–N5, P–QR3; 4 B–R4, N–B3; 5 O–O, N × P;
6 P–Q4, P–QN4; 7 B–N3, P–Q4; 8 P × P, B–K3; 9 P–B3, B–K2

	101	102	103	104	105
10	QN–Q2			Q–K2	B–B2
	O–O!			N–B4 (*e*)	O–O (*g*)
11	Q–K2		B–B2	B–B2	Q–K2
	N × N	N–B4 (*b*)	P–B4!	P–Q5	Q–Q2!
12	Q × N (*a*)	N–Q4	N–N3	R–Q1	R–Q1
	N–R4	N × B	Q–Q2	B–B5	P–B4
13	B–B2	N/2 × N	QN–Q4	Q–K1	P × P *e.p.* (*h*)
	N–B5	Q–Q2	N × N	P–Q6	N × P
14	Q–Q3	N × N	N × N	N–R3	N–N5
	P–N3	Q × N	P–B4	Q–B1	B–KN5
15	N–Q4	B–K3	N × B (*d*)	B–N1	P–B3
	N × KP	B–KB4	Q × N	B–Q4	B–B4†
16	Q–N3 ∞	KR–Q1	P–B3	B × P	K–R1
		KR–Q1 (*c*)	N–N4 =	B × N (*f*)	QR–K1 =

(*a*) 12 B × N, N–R4; 13 B–B2, N–B5 (or 13 . . . P–QB4); 14 B–B1, Q–Q2; 15 P–QN3,
N–N3; 16 Q–Q3, P–N3; 17 B–R6, R–K1; 18 Q–Q2, Hecht-Langeweg, Hengelo 1968,
B–KB4 = . The column is Pachman's analysis.

(*b*) 11 . . . B–KB4; 12 R–Q1, N–B4; 13 N–B1, N × B; 14 P × N, B–K5; 15 B–B4! Suetin.

(*c*) 17 P–B3, B–KB1; 18 Q–KB2, P–QR4; 19 R–Q2, P–N5 = . Botwinnik-Euwe,
Leningrad 1934. In the column, even stronger is 16 . . . Q–KN3! 17 P–B3, P–QB3; 18 Q–B2,
KR–K1!

(*d*) 15 N–K2, QR–Q1; 16 N–B4, Q–B3; 17 P–QR4, B–B1 = . Fischer-Unzicker, Santa
Monica 1966. The column is Chajes-Tarrasch, Carlsbad 1923. *ECO* gives 13 . . . N–R4! 14
N × B, Q × N; 15 N–Q4, Q × P; 16 P–B3, B–Q3; 17 P–KN3, P–B5; 18 P × N, P × NP; 19
N–B3, P–N7; 20 K × P, R × N "with equality", but it is a question how Black draws after 21
R × R, Q × P†; 22 K–B1. *Comments*.

(*e*) Also 10 . . . O–O; 11 R–Q1, Q–Q2; 12 P–B4, NP × P; 13 B × P, P–B3! 14 B × QP,
B × B; 15 Q × N, B × Q; 16 R × Q, QR × Q1 with counter-chances. *Comments*.

(*f*) 17 P × B, N × B; 18 R × N, Q–B4! Euwe.

(*g*) Involved is (A) 10 . . . B–KN5; (1) 11 P–KR3, B–R4; 12 P–KN4, B–N3; 13 B–N3,
N–R4; 14 B × P, P–QB3; 15 B × N, B × B; 16 Q × Q†, R × Q; 17 QN–Q2, B–Q4 ∞.
Boleslavski. (2) 11 R–K1, N–B4; 12 QN–Q2 etc. as in column 99 (*i*) (B).(3) 11 B–N3, B–K3; 12
B–B2, B–BN5; 13 B–N3, etc.; forces a draw. *Comments*. (B) 10 . . . N–B4; 11 P–KR3, O–O;
12 R–K1, Q–Q2; 13 N–Q4, N × N; 14 P × N, N–N2 ∞. Karpov-Korchnoi, 24th match game,
1978.

(*h*) 13 QN–Q2, K–R1; 14 N–N3, B–B2; 15 QN–Q4, B–R4! Tal-Keres, Moscow 1966. The
column is Suetin's choice.

1 P–K4, P–K4; 2 N–KB3, N–QB3; 3 B–N5, P–QR3; B–R4, N–B3; 5 O–O, N × P; 6 P–Q4, P–QN4; 7 B–N3, P–Q4; 8 P × P, B–K3; 9 P–B3, B–K2

	106	107	108	109	110
10	P–QR4 (a)	R–K1 (d)	B–K3		B–KB4
	P–N5!	O–O	O–O	N–B4 (j)	P–N4! (l)
11	N–Q4	N–Q4	QN–Q2	B–B2	B–K3
	N × KP	N × KP!	N × N (f)	B–N5	P–KN5
12	P–KB4	P–B3	Q × N	QN–Q2	KN–Q2
	B–N5! (b)	B–Q3!	N–R4 (g)	N–K3!	N–B4!
13	Q–B2	P × N	B–B2 (h)	Q–N1!	Q–K2
	P–QB4	B–KN5	N–B5	B–R4	Q–Q2
14	P × N	Q–B2	Q–Q3	P–QR4	R–Q1
	P × N	P–QB4	P–N3	P–N5	N × B
15	P × QP	B × P	B–R6	P–R5	N × N
	O–O	P × N	R–K1!	B–N3	N × P
16	N–Q2	B × R	Q–Q4	N–N3	N–Q2
	B–K7 (c)	Q–R5 (e)	P–KB3 (i)	P × P (k)	B–Q3 (m)

(a) Dating back to Perlis-Lasker, St. Petersburg 1909 and re-used by Alekhin.

(b) 12 . . . N–B5? 13 Q–K2! N–B4; 14 B–B2, O–O; 15 N–Q2 + . Ryumin.

(c) 17 R–K1, R–B1; 18 Q–N1, B–R4; (1) 19 Q–Q3, B–N3; 20 N × N, P × N; 21 Q–Q1, B–R5; 22 R–B1, B–N4 = . Evans-Hanauer, New York 1949. (2) 19 N × N, B–N3; 20 N–B6†, B × N; 21 Q–R2, B–R5; 22 P–N3, B–K5 with attack. *Comments.*

(d) A move preparing 11 N–Q4, but enabling Black to initiate the dangerous "Breslau Variation" (12 . . . B–Q3?!). As all the excitement seems to peter out in due course, the line has fallen into disuse. 10 . . . N–B4 might transpose into col. 99, but does not have to.

(e) 17 R–B1, P–Q6; 18 Q–B2, Q × Q†; 19 R × Q, R × B; 20 B–B4, P–B3 ∓. *Comments.*

(f) 11 . . . Q–Q2; 12 B–B2, P–B4; 13 P × P *e.p.*, N × P; 14 Q–N1, B–KN5; 15 P–KR3, B × P! 16 N–N5! Keres.

(g) About even is 12 . . . Q–Q2; 13 B–N5! QR–Q1; 14 KR–K1, KR–K1. *Archives.*

(h) 13 N–Q4 see next column and note (j).

(i) Larsen's suggested improvement (over Suetin's 16 . . . P–QB4; 17 Q–B4, P–B3; 18 Q–N3 ±), continued 17 P × P, B × P; 18 Q–B4, B–B2 (or 18 . . . B–Q2) = .

(j) 10 . . . N–R4; 11 N–Q4, O–O; (1) 12 N–Q2, N × N; 13 Q × N, P–QB4; 14 N × B, P × N; 15 B–B2, N–N3; 16 P–KB4, P–Q5 = . Clark-Cortlever, England *v.* Holland, 1958. (2) 12 P–B3, N–B4; 13 B–B2, N–B5; 14 B–B1, N × KP; 15 P–QN4, N–N2; 16 P–KB4, N–B5; 17 Q–Q3, P–N3; 18 P–B5 with attacking chances. Kuhnert-Ohls, corr. 1931.

(k) 17 P × P, Q–N1; 18 Q–R2, O–O; 19 B × B, RP × B; 20 KR–N1 ± . *Archives.*

(l) Less energetic is 10 . . . O–O; 11 N–Q4, N–R4; 12 P–B3 or 12 B–B2 ± . *Comments.*

(m) 17 B–Q4, P–KB3; 18 N–B5, B × N; 19 B × B, K–B2 ∞. Averbakh-Korchnoi, USSR Chp. 1958.

1 P-K4, P-K4; 2 N-KB3, N-QB3; 3 B-N5, P-QR3; 4 B-R4, N-B3; 5 O-O, N × P;
6 P-Q4, P-QN4; 7 B-N3, P-Q4; 8 P × P, B-K3; 9 Q-K2 (Howell Attack)

		111	112	113	114	115
		B-K2			B-QB4	N-B4 (i)
10		R-Q1 (a)			B-K3	R-Q1
		N-B4		O-O	Q-K2	N × B
11		B × P	P-B4 (c)	P-B4	QN-Q2 (h)	RP × N
		B × B	P-Q5!	NP × P	B × B	Q-B1! (j)
12		N-B3	P × P	B × P	Q × B	P-B4 (k)
		B-B5!	N × B	Q-Q2 (e)	N × N	N-N5
13		R × Q†	NP × N	N-B3!	Q × N	P × NP
		R × R	N × N	N × N	O-O	P × P
14		Q-K3	N × P	P × N	KR-K1	R × R
		P-N5	Q-B1	P-B3	QR-K1	Q × R
15		P-QN3	N-B3	P × P	QR-Q1	B-Q2!
		B-K3	O-O	B × P	N-R4	P-QB3
16		N-K4	B-K3	B-KN5 (f)	Q-B1	N-Q4
		R-Q8† (b)	P-B3 (d)	B × P (g)	N-B5 ∞	N-R3 (l)

(a) Controversial is the sharp 10 P-B4!? (A) 10 . . . NP × P; 11 B-R4, B-Q2; 12 N-B3, N-B4; 13 P-K6, P × P; 14 B × N, B × B; 15 N-K5, Q-Q3; 16 Q-R5†, P-N3; 17 N × NP, P × N; 18 Q × R†, K-Q2; 19 Q-N7, P-Q5 with ample compensation for the exchange. Abroshin-Radtchenko 1954. (B) 10 . . . N-B4; 11 P × QP, B × P; 12 R-Q1, N × B; 13 P × N, O-O; 14 N-B3, B × N; 15 P × B, Q-B1; 16 N-Q5, B-Q1.

(b) 17 N-K1, N-Q5; 18 B-N2, N × BP; 19 Q-K2, R × R; 20 B × R, N × B; 21 N × N, B × N; 22 N-Q3, B-N3; 23 N × P, O-O; 24 N-B6, P-B3; 25 P-KR4—the "penultimate" position, which in practical experience mostly ends in a draw, e.g. 25 . . . P × P; 26 Q × P, R-B3; 27 N-Q4, B-B2; 28 N-B3, N-B7; 29 Q-K4, B-N3; 30 Q-Q5†, K-B1; 31 P-R5, B-K1; 32 Q-K4, B × P = . Suetin-Boleslavski, Riga 1958.

(c) Alternatives are (A) 11 B-K3, O-O; 12 P-B4, NP × P; 13 B × P, N-R4; 14 B × QP! B × B; 15 N-B3, B × N; 16 Q × B, Q-K1; 17 P-QN4, N-R5; 18 N × N? (18 N-Q5! Jansa), Q × N; 19 P × N, QR-Q1; 20 P-N3, Q × P/4; 21 Q-QB6, Q × P; 22 Q × RP, Q-K5 = . Jansa-Milev, Tel Aviv 1964. (B) 11 N-B3, N × B; 12 BP × N, O-O; 13 B-Q2, Q-Q2; 14 B-N5, QR-Q1; 15 QR-B1, KR-K1; 16 P-KR3, B × B; 17 N × B, P-Q5; 18 P-B4, B-B4; 19 QN-K4, P-Q6. Jovčić-Samarian, corr. 1969-70.

(d) 17 P × P, B × BP; 18 R × N, Q-K1 ∓. Keres and Suetin. Compare note (k).

(e) Ekström's move, further explored by Nilsson in *Fernschach*, 1966. Another line is 12 . . . B-QB4; 13 B-K3, B × B; 14 Q × B, Q-N1; 15 B-N3, N-R4; 16 QN-Q2, Q-R2! 17 Q × Q, R × Q; 18 N-Q4, N × N; 19 R × N, P-QB4; 20 N-K2, N × B; 21 P × N, P-Q5; 22 P-QN4, P-Q6; 23 N-B4, P-B5; 24 R-QB1, R-B2; 25 P-QN3, R-K1, drawn. Kuypers-Langeweg, Hoogoven 1968.

(f) 16 N-N5, B × N; 17 B × B, P-R3; 18 B-K3, N-K4; 19 B-N3, Q-Q3; 20 R-Q4, P-B4; 21 R-KB4, N-Q2; 22 R-K1, B-B2; 23 R-Q1, N-B3; 24 B-B2, QR-B1; 25 Q-Q3, KR-K1 = . Jansa-Martens, Göteborg 1968.

(g) 17 QR-B1, B-B3; 18 Q × B† (18 B × B, R × B; 19 N-N5, N-K2; 20 R-K1, P × B; 21 N × B, N-Q4 ∞), Q × Q; 19 B × QP, Q × B; 20 R × Q, N-N5; 21 R-Q7, KR-Q1; 22 KR × BP, N × P; 23 B × B, P × B = . Hartoch-Scholl, Hoogoven 1968. 16 . . . K-R1! = . *ECO*.

(h) If 11 R-Q1, R-Q1; 12 P-QR4! B × B; 13 Q × B, N-B4 = . *ECO*.

(i) Relaxing Black's counter-pressure is 9 . . . N-R4; 10 N-Q4! P-QB4; 11 N × B, P × N; 12 P-QB3, N × B; 13 P × N, P-B5; 14 P-QN4, P-KR4; 15 P-B3 ± . *Comments*.

(j) 11 . . . B-K2; 12 P-B4, O-O; 13 N-B3, N-N5; 14 B-K3, P-QB4?! is feasible. Also compare to col. 112, with 11 . . . N-B4 instead of 11 . . . P-Q5.

(*k*) (A) 12 N–B3?, N–N5; 13 N–Q4! B–K2; 14 N × B, P × N; 15 B–N5, B × B; 16 Q–R5†, P–N3; 18 Q × B, O–O = . Browne-Kaplan, San Juan 1969. (B) 12 B–N5, P–R3; 13 B–R4, B–QB4; Keres-Reshevsky, World Championship Team Tournament 1948; 14 P–QB4!?, QP × P; 15 P × P, B × P; 16 Q–K4, N–K2 ∞. *Comments.*

(*l*) 17 P–QN4, N–B2; 18 R–QB1, B–Q2; 19 Q–Q3 ± . Pisěk-Ratolistka, Prague 1957.

1 P–K4, P–K4; 2 N–KB3, N–QB3; 3 B–N5, P–QR3; 4 B–R4, N–B3; 5 O–O

	116	117	118	119	120
	(N × P)			P–QN4	(Counterthrust
6	(P–Q4) (a)			B–N3	Variation)
	(P–QN4)	Riga	P × P	P–Q3 (j)	
7	(B–N3)	Variation	R–K1	P–B3	N–N5
	(P–Q4)	P × P	P–Q4	B–K2	P–Q4
8	N × P (b)	R–K1	P–B4 (h)	P–Q4 (k)	P × P
	N × N	P–Q4	P × P e.p.	B–N5	N–Q5
9	P × N	N–B3	N × P	P–KR3 (l)	R–K1 (m)
	P–QB3	P × N (e)	B–K3	B × N	B–QB4
10	B–K3 (c)	B × P (f)	N–Q4	Q × B	R × P†!?
	B–K2	B–N2!?	Q–Q2	P × P	K–B1
11	N–Q2	N–N5!	N × QN	Q–N3	P–QB3
	B–KB4	P–B4	N × N	Q–Q2	N–N5
12	N × N	N–B7	P × N	Q × NP	P × N
	B × N (d)	Q–B3 (g)	P × N (i)	O–O–O ∞	B × P (n)

(a) Ineffective are (A) 6 R–K1, N–B4; 7 N–B3 (7 N × P, B–K2; 8 B × N, QP × B; 9 P–Q4, N–K3 =), B–K2; 8 B × N, QP × B = . (B) 6 Q–K2, N–B4; 7 B × N, QP × B; 8 P–Q4, N–K3, 9 P × P, N–Q5 = .

(b) (A) 8 N–B3, N × N; 9 P × N, P–K5; 10 N–N5, B–KB4; 11 P–B3, P–K6; 12 P–KB4, Q–Q2; 13 Q–B3, R–Q1; 14 Q × P†, B–K2 = . (B) 8 P–QR4, N × QP! = .

(c) 10 P–QB3, B–QB4; 11 N–Q2, N × N; 12 B × N, B–B4; 13 Q–B3, Q–Q2; 14 B–K3, B × B = . Petrosian-Teschner, Oberhausen 1961.

(d) 13 Q–N4, Q–Q2! 14 Q × P, O–O–O ∞ . Klovan-Zhuravlev, Riga 1963.

(e) 9 . . . B–K3; 10 N × N, P × N; 11 R × P, B–K2; 12 B × B, P × B; 13 N × P, O–O; 14 Q–N4, N × N; 15 R × N, Q–B1; 16 R–K4, R–B3; 17 B–K3 ± . Fischer-Trifunović, Bled 1961.

(f) 10 Q × P, Q × Q; 11 B × Q, B–N2; 12 R × N†, B–K2; 13 N–K5, O–O–O = . Schweitzer-Rohliček, corr. 1960.

(g) 13 B × N†, Q × B; 14 N × R, B–B4; 15 B–K3 ± . Sapundzher in *Misl.* 1966/1. In the column, 11 N–N5 may be answered 11 . . . B–K2; but it still leaves White better off; so does 11 B × N, B–K2; 12 Q–K2 ± . If 9 B × P? Q × B; 10 N–B3, Q–KB4 = .

(h) Other branches are (A) 8 B–KN5!? B–K2; 9 B × B, K × B! 10 B × N, P × B; 11 N × P, K–B1; 12 P–KB3, N–B3; 13 N × P, Q–Q3 = . Krause. (B) 8 N × P! B–Q3; 9 N × N, B × P†; 10 K–R1, Q–R5; 11 R × N†, P × R; 12 Q–Q8† ± . Capablanca-Ed. Lasker, New York 1915. (C) 8 N–K5, B–Q3! 9 N × N, B × P† ∞ .

(i) 13 P–QB4, with a powerful attack. Janetschek-Schaffler, Vienna 1961.

(j) 6 . . . B–K2; (A) 7 B–Q5, N × B; 8 P × N, N–N5; 9 N × P, O–O! 10 N–QB3, B–N2 = . *Comments.* (B) 7 P–QR4, B–N2! = . Columns 119–20 deal with the position where White omits transposition into main lines by R–K1 or Q–K2.

(k) Keres prefers 8 P–KR3, N–QR4; 9 B–B2, P–B4; 10 P–Q4, Q–B2; 11 P–QR4! B–N2; 12 RP × P, RP × P; 13 N–R3 ± , Szabó-Filip, Prague 1955. Better is first 8 . . . B–N2; e.g. 9 R–K1, N–QN1; 10 B–B2, QN–Q2; 11 P–Q4, N–N3 with an elastic position. *Comments.*

(l) Upon 9 B–K3 as given by Keres. (A) 9 . . . O–O; 10 P–KR3, B–R4; 11 QN–Q2, P–Q4; 12 P–N4, B–N3; 13 N × P, N × N; 14 P × N, N × P; 15 P–KB4 is too slow, compared to the immediate (B) 9 . . . N–QR4; 10 B–B2, P × P and . . . N–B5 or even (C) 9 . . . P × P; 10 P × P, N–QR4; 11 B–B2, N–B5. *Comments.*

(m) 9 P–QB3, N × B; 10 Q × N, B–Q3! 11 P–Q3, B–KB4; 12 P–QB4, O–O; 13 P × P, R–N1 = Kupper-Lombardy, Zürich 1960.

(n) Black has a strong attack for the piece (Kholmov), but White also has 10 P–QB3, N × B; 11 R × P†; K–B1; 12 P × N, N–N5; 13 P–Q4.

1 P–K4, P–K4; 2 N–KB3, N–QB3; 3 B–N5, P–QR3; 4 B–R4, N–B3; 5 O–O,
P–QN4; 6 B–N3, B–N2

	121	122	123	124	125
7	P–Q3	P–Q4	P–B3	R–K1!	
	B–K2	N × QP	N × P (f)	B–B4	
8	P–B3 (a)	B × P† (c)	P–Q4! (g)	P–B3	
	O–O	K × B	N–R4!	O–O	P–Q3!
9	R–K1	N × P†	B–B2 (h)	P–Q4	P–Q4
	P–R3!	K–N1	P × P	B–N3	B–N3
10	QN–Q2	Q × N	N × P	B–N5 (j)	P–QR4 (l)
	R–K1	P–B4	P–QB4	P–R3	O–O
11	P–Q4	Q–Q1 (d)	B × N	B–R4	B–N5
	B–KB1!	Q–K1	B × B	R–K1	P–R3
12	P–QR3 (b)	N–N4	R–K1	Q–Q3	B–R4
	P–Q3!	N × N (e)	P–Q4 (i)	P–Q3 (k)	R–K1 (m)

(a) 8 R–K1, O–O; 9 QN–Q2, P–R3! 10 N–B1, R–K1; 11 P–B3, B–KB1; 12 N–N3,
N–QR4; 13 B–B2, P–Q4; 14 Q–K2, P × P; 15 P × P, N–B5 with a comfortable game for Black.

(b) 12 P–Q5, N–QR4; 13 B–B2, P–B3! 14 P × P, B × P; 15 N–B1, Q–B2; 16 N–N3, P–Q4!
Unzicker-Planinc, Ljubljana 1969.

(c) 8 N × N, P × N; 9 P–K5, N–K5; (A) 10 P–QB3, P–Q6; 11 Q–B3, Q–K2; 12 B–K3,
Q × P; 13 B × P†, K–Q1; 14 B–KB4, Q–B3; 15 R–K1, B–Q3 ∓. Astashin-Golenishev, Kazan
1963. (B) 10 Q–B3, Q–K2; 11 N–Q2, N–B4; 12 Q–N3, P–N3; 13 N–B3, N × B; 14 RP × N,
B–N2; 15 B–N5, Q–B4 = . (c) 10 R–K1, Q–R5 (or 10 . . . P–QB4); 11 P–N3, N × NP; 12
BP × N, Q–R6; 13 Q–K2, B–B4; 14 Q–B1, Q–R4; 15 P–KR3, O–O; 16 K–R2, QR–K1; 17
B–KB4, P–Q3! ∞.

(d) 11 Q–K3, Q–K1; 12 Q–N3†, P–Q4; 13 P–KB4, N × P; 14 N–Q2, P–B5! 15 Q–KB3,
B–B4†; 16 K–R1, N–Q3 = . Analysis by Matsukevich in his summary of the 6 . . . B–N2 line in
Byulleten 1968.

(e) 13 Q × N, P–KR4; 14 Q–K2, Q × P; 15 Q × Q, B × Q; 16 P–QB3, P–R5; 17 P–KR3,
R–R4; 18 R–Q1, B–B3; 19 B–K3, R–K1 = . Gragger-Matsukevich, corr. 1967.

(f) Worthy of study is 7 . . . P–R3; 8 P–Q4, P–Q3; 9 R–K1, P–N3; 10 QN–Q2, B–N2; 11
P–QR3, O–O; 12 B–B2, N–Q2 = . Kinnmark-Zinn, Halle 1967, especially as the column so far
favours White's initiative!

(g) 8 R–K1, N–B4; 9 B–Q5, B–K2; 10 N × P, N × N; 11 B × B, N/K–Q6! 12 B × R, N × R;
13 Q × N, Q × B; 14 Q–K2, O–O; 15 P–Q4, N–K3; 16 N–Q2, R–K1! = . Lutikov-Planinc,
Skopje 1969.

(h) 9 N × P, N × B; 10 Q × N, Q–B3; 11 P–QR4, P–Q3; 12 N–B3, Q–K3 = .

(i) 13 N–B5, Q–Q2; 14 N–N3, B–K2; 15 N × B, P × N; 16 Q × Q†, K × Q; 17 R × P,
KR–K1 = . Matsukevich.

(j) 10 P–QR4, P–Q3; 11 P × NP, P × NP; 12 R × R, B × R; 13 P–Q5, N–K2; 14 B–N5,
N–N3; 15 N–R4, N × N; 16 B × N, P–R3; 17 N–R3, P–N4; 18 B–N3, Q–Q2 (Bednarski-Lewi,
Polish Chp. 1969); 19 Q–Q3, P–B3; 20 R–Q1, B–B4 = . *Archives.*

(k) 13 QN–Q2, N–QR4; 14 B–B2, P–B4; 15 P–Q5, P–B5; 16 Q–K2, K–R2; 17 P–QN4 ± .
Savon-Gipslis, USSR Chp. 1970.

(l) (A) 10 P–QR3, Q–K2! 11 Q–Q3, N–QR4; 12 B–B2, P–QB4; 13 QN–Q2, N–B3; 14
P–Q5, P–B5 ∓. (B) 10 B–KN5, P–KR3; 11 B–R4 (1) 11 . . . Q–K2; 12 P–QR4, O–O; 13
P × NP, P × NP; 14 R × R, R × R; 15 N–R3, P–N5 = . Aronin. (2) 11 . . . O–O; 12 P–QR4,
R–K1! (12 . . . Q–K2; 13 P–Q5!); 13 P × NP, P × NP; 14 R × R, B × R; 15 Q–Q3, P × P (15
. . . N–QR4; 16 B–B2, P–N4; 17 P × P ±); 16 P × P, N–QR4! 17 B × N! Q × B; 18 B–B2,
N–B3; 19 P–K5, P × P; 20 N–B3! ± .

(m) 13 P × NP, P × NP; 14 R × R, B × R; 15 P–Q5, N–QR2; 16 QN–Q2, K–R2; 17 N–B1,
R–N1; 18 N–K3, P–N4; 19 B–N3, B–N2 = . Gufeld-Bagirov, Leningrad 1963.

1 P–K4, P–K4; 2 N–KB3, N–QB3; 3 B–N5, P–QR3; 4 B–R4

	126 Nimzowitsch Variation	127 Wormald Variation	128	129 Anderssen's Line Duras Var.	130 Exchange Variation Deferred-II
	N–B3				
5	N–B3	Q–K2	P–Q3		B × N
	P–QN4 (a)	P–QN4	P–Q3		QP × B
6	B–N3	B–N3	P–B3	P–B4	P–Q3 (j)
	B–K2 (b)	B–K2 (e)	P–KN3	P–KN3	B–Q3
7	O–O	P–QR4	O–O (g)	P–Q4	QN–Q2
	P–Q3	R–QN1	B–N2	P × P	B–K3
8	N–Q5	P × P	P–Q4	N × P	Q–K2
	N–QR4 (c)	P × P	O–O	B–Q2	N–R4
9	N × B	P–Q4	P–Q5	N × N	N–B4
	Q × N	P–Q4	N–K2	P × N	B × N
10	P–Q4	P–B3	R–K1	O–O	P × B
	B–N2 (d)	N × KP	P–B3	B–N2	Q–B3
11	B–N5	N × P	P × P	P–B5	P–KN3
	O–O! =	N × N (f)	P × P (h)	O–O (i)	Q–K3 (k)

(a) (A) 5 . . . B–N5; 6 N–Q5, N × N; 7 P × N, P–K5!? 8 P × N, QP × P is speculative. (B) 5 . . . P–Q3; 6 B × N†, P × B; 7 P–Q4, N–Q2; 8 O–O, B–K2 = .

(b) (A) 6 . . . B–B4; 7 N × P, N × N; 8 P–Q4, B–Q3; 9 P × N! B × P; 10 P–B4, B × N†; 11 P × B, B–N2; 12 P–K5, N–K5; 13 O–O, P–Q4; 14 Q–N4, Q–K2! = . Bisguier-Turner, New York 1955. (B) 6 . . . P–Q3; 7 N–KN5, P–Q4; 8 N × QP, N–Q5! 9 N–B3! = . Keres and Suetin.

(c) Equally safe is 8 . . . B–N2; (1) 9 N × N†, B × N; 10 B–Q5, Q–B1; 11 R–K1, O–O; 12 P–B3, N–K2 = or (2) 9 N × B, Q × N; 10 R–K1, N–QR4; 11 P–Q4, N × B; 12 RP × N, N × P; 13 Q–Q3, P–KB4 = . Nei-Portisch, Beverwijk 1964.

(d) Or 10 . . . O–O; 11 B–N5, B–N5; 12 P × P, P × P; 13 Q–K2, P–R3; 14 B–KR4, KR–Q1; 15 Q–K3, B × N; 16 Q × B, R–Q3 = . Ciocaltea-Euwe, Varna 1962. The column is Keres-Euwe, match 1939–40.

(e) (A) 6 . . . N–QR4? 7 N × P, N × B; 8 RP × N, Q–K2; 9 P–Q4, P–Q3; 10 N–B6, Q × P; 11 Q × Q, N × Q; 12 O–O, B–B4; 13 P–QB4! ± . Novitski-Kamenetski, corr. 1968. (B) 6 . . . B–B4; 7 P–QR4, R–QN1; 8 P × P, P × P; 9 N–B3, O–O; 10 P–Q3, P–Q3; 11 B–N5, P–R3; 12 B × N, Q × B = .

(f) 12 P × N, O–O; 13 O–O, B–KB4 = . Spasski-Kholmov, Leningrad 1954. In the column, a novel try is 5 . . . B–B4; 6 B × N, NP × B; 7 N × P, O–O; 8 O–O, R–K1; 9 N × KBP, Q–K2; 10 N–N5, P–Q4; 11 P–Q3, B–KN5 ∓ . Kholmor-Polgar, Budapest 1979.

(g) The classical lines 7 P–Q4 and 7 QN–Q2 lead to no advantage either.

(h) 12 P–B4, Q–B2; 13 N–B3, B–K3; 14 Q–K2, P–B4 = . Stein-Korchnoi, Kiev 1964.

(i) 12 N–B3, Q–K2; 13 P × P, P × P; 14 P–B3, P–Q4 = . Duras-Cohn, Carlsbad 1911.

(j) 6 N–B3, B–KN5; 7 P–KR3, B–R4; 8 P–KN4, B–N3; 9 N × P, N × P! 10 N × N, B × N; 11 Q–K2, Q–Q4 ∓ . For 6 P–Q4 compare col. 25.

(k) 12 B–K3, P–QB4 = . Flohr-Reshevsky, Kemeri 1937.

1 P–K4, P–K4; 2 N–KB3, N–QB3; 3 B–N5, P–QR3; 4 B–R4, P–QN4; 5 B–N3, N–R4

	131	132	133	134	135
6	O–O...				B × P†?
	P–Q3				K × B
7	P–Q4				N × P†
	N × B	P–KB3		P × P	K–K2
8	RP × N	B × N	Q–K2	N × P	P–Q4 (*i*)
	P–KB3	R × B	P–N3	B–N2	N–KB3
9	N–B3 (*a*)	N–R4	R–Q1	B–Q2 (*e*)	Q–B3
	B–N2	Q–Q2	B–Q2	N × B (*f*)	B–N2
10	N–KR4	P–R4	N–B3	RP × N (*g*)	P–QN4
	N–K2	P–N5	N × B	P–N3	N–B5
11	P × P	P–QB3	RP × N	P–QB4	Q–K2
	QP × P	R–N1	B–N2	P–QB4	N × N
12	Q–B3	N–Q2	B–K3	N–KB3	P × N
	Q–B1 (*b*)	P–N3 (*c*)	P × P (*d*)	P–N5 (*h*)	N × P (*j*)

(*a*) 9 P–B4, B–N2; 10 N–B3, N–K2; 11 Q–K2, P–B3; 12 R–Q1, Q–B2; 13 B–K3, N–N3; 14 QR–B1, P–N5; 15 N–QR4 and now Pachman's precarious (A) 15 . . . P × P; 16 N × P, P–QB4; 17 N–K6, Q–K2; 18 N × B, R × N ∞, or (B) 15 . . . N–B5?! 16 B × N (16 Q–K1, P–QB4 =), P × B and Black regroups for a strong King side attack. *Comments.*

(*b*) 13 R–Q1, P–KR4! 14 P–R3, Q–K3; 15 N–Q5, O–O–O = . Adamski–Zwaig, Raach 1969.

(*c*) 13 N/4–B3, P–QB4; 14 P × BP, QP × P; 15 Q–K2, R–KN2; 16 N–K1, P–N6; 17 P–N3, Q–B3 ∓ . Hecht–Zwaig, Raach 1969.

(*d*) 13 N × P, N–K2; 14 P–QN4, O–O; 15 Q–Q2, N–B3; 16 N × N, B × N; 17 B–Q4, B–N2; 18 N–Q5, R–B2; 19 R–K1, Q–KB1 = . Tringov–Ostojić, Belgrade 1969.

(*e*) 9 (A) P–QB4 (Suetin) (1) 9 . . . P–QB4; 10 N–B5, P–N3; 11 N–K3! (2) 9 . . . N × P; 10 B × N, P × B; 11 N–QB3, N–KB3; 12 B–N5, B–K2; 13 N–B5 ± . Petrosian. (B) 9 Q–K1, P–QB4; 10 B–Q2, N × B; 11 N × N with pressure.

(*f*) 9 . . . P–QB4! 10 B–Q5! B × B; 11 P × B, P × N; 12 Q–K1†, Q–K2; 13 B × N, Q × Q; 14 R × Q†, N–K2; 15 N–Q2, K–Q2; 16 N–N3, P–Q6; 17 P–QB3, N × P (Smyslov–Evans, Havana 1964); 18 KR–Q1! = .

(*g*) 10 N × N! N–K2; 11 N–R5, (A) 11 . . . B–B1; 12 R–K1, P–QB4; 13 P–QN4, Q–B2; 14 P–QR4, N–B3; 15 RP × P, RP × P; 16 N–B3, N × N; 17 N–Q5, Q–Q1; 18 P–K5, B–K3; 19 B–N5! Black resigns. Kapengut–Alburt, USSR 1967. (B) 11 . . . B × P; 12 R–K1, B–Q4! 13 N–B3, B–K3 = .

(*h*) 13 B–B4, Q–B2; 14 P–K5, O–O–O = . Pachman. In the column, 10 N × N, B–K2; 11 N–R5 gives White some advantage.

(*i*) 8 N–QB3 (A) 8 . . . B–N2; 9 N–Q5†, B × N; 10 P × B, Q–K1; 11 O–O, K–Q1; 12 R–K1, N–KB3 = . (B) 8 . . . Q–K1; 9 N–Q5†, K–Q1; 10 Q–B3, B–N2; 11 N–B7†, K–B1; 12 O–O, N–KB3; 13 N × R, B × N; 14 P × B, B–Q3 ∓ . Pachman.

(*j*) 13 P–KB3, K–K1! ∓ . Taimanov.

Giuoco Piano

(incorporating the Evans Gambit)

(1 P–K4, P–K4; 2 N–KB3, N–QB3;
3 B–B4, B–B4)

According to some authorities the Giuoco Piano (Italian for "quiet game") is the oldest recorded opening. It is mentioned in the Göttingen manuscript of 1490, by Damiano in 1512 and Greco in 1600. As a consequence it has suffered the fate of being exhaustively analysed—so much so that only a few international masters still play it.

The characteristics of White's plan are prevention of . . . P–Q4 and attack against Black's weakest link on KB2. The trouble is that Black catces up in development and can exchange too many minor pieces for White to maintain the tension beyond the opening. But the Giuoco has many faces, ranging from the dull and drawish to the wild and woolly.

The variations resulting from 4 P–B3 (cols. 1–8) are extraordinarily volatile, but the fireworks fizzle out if Black reacts aggressively with 4 . . . N–B3. White's pawn sacrifice with 5 P–Q4, P × P; 6 P × P, B–N5†; 7 N–B3!? yields nothing against correct defence (cols. 1–4), while 7 B–Q2 simplifies into equal chances, e.g. in note (m). An important body of theory has crystallized in these variations and it is necessary for the competent player to familiarize himself with them.

4 . . . B–N3 (cols. 6–8) is a positional treatment which avoids early conflict and tries to secure equality but note (h) still looks precarious.

4 P–Q3 (cols. 9–10) is the quiet face of Janus. It creates no immediate threats and leads to an apparently dullish formation where both players rely on their natural ability to detect a chink in the opponent's armour.

Evans Gambit

(4 P–QN4!?)

Captain W. D. Evans introduced his gambit in 1830. Once described as "a gift of the gods to a languishing chess world," the pundits are little nearer deciding whether or not it is sound. This brash pawn-sacrifice (once warmly embraced by Labourdonnais, Morphy, and Chigorin) is just too speculative for modern tastes.

Like all gambits, the Evans offers material in return for rapid mobilization. Modern principles hold that Black should return it in order to reach an end-game where he can exploit the self-inflicted gash in White's pawn structure. Holding the pawn is a more direct attempt at refutation where Black experiences difficulty castling and White obtains nothing more tangible than temporary pressure. The play is tactical and tricky with both sides getting in their licks. All in all, the Evans is still the theoretician's problem child.

THE EVANS GAMBIT ACCEPTED 4 . . . B × P (cols. 11–17) conforms to the principle that the best way to refute a gambit is to accept it. After 5 P–B3 Black has two approaches: (A) 5 . . . B–R4; 6 P–Q4, P × P; 7 O–O, B–N3 (7 . . . P × P, col. 13, is a little too greedy) leads to the Normal Variation where White obtains fair compensation for his pawn; 6 . . . P–Q3 (cols. 14–15) prepares for the famous *Lasker Defence* (note (h)) which leads to a rather barren equality, if White decides to exchange queens in order to regain his pawn. 7 Q–N3 is more dynamic, but Black has adequate resources. (B) 5 . . . B–K2 (cols. 16–17) is a modern concept where Black returns the pawn in order to "win" the two bishops. It is a satisfactory alternative to the wild way of 5 . . . B–R4.

THE EVANS GAMBIT DECLINED 4 . . . B–N3 (cols. 18–20) is a gentle way of backing out of trouble and securing equal chances.

1 P-K4, P-K4; 2 N-KB3, N-QB3; 3 B-B4, B-B4; 4 P-B3, N-B3; 5 P-Q4, P×P; 6 P×P (a), B-N5†

	1	2	3	4	5
7	N-B3				B-Q2 (l)
	N×KP			P-Q4	B×B† (m)
8	O-O			P×P	QN×B
	B×N		N×N	KN×P	P-Q4! (n)
9	P-Q5 (b)		P×N	O-O	P×P
	B-B3	N-K4	P-Q4 (h)	B-K3	KN×P
10	R-K1	P×B (f)	P×B	B-KN5	Q-N3
	N-K2	N×B	P×B	B-K2	QN-K2
11	R×N	Q-Q4	R-K1† (i)	N×N	O-O
	P-Q3 (c)	P-KB4?	N-K2	B×N	O-O
12	B-N5 (d)	Q×N	Q-K2	KB×B	KR-K1
	B×B	P-Q3	B-K3	Q×B	P-QB3
13	N×B	N-Q4	B-N5	B×B	QR-B1
	O-O (e)	O-O (g)	Q-Q4 (j)	N×B (k)	Q-N3 (o)

(a) (A) 6 P-K5, P-Q4; 7 B-QN5 (7 P×N, P×B; 8 Q-K2†, B-K3; 9 P×NP, R-KN1), N-K5; 8 P×P, B-N5† = . (B) 6 O-O, N×P; 7 P×P, P-Q4; 8 P×B, P×B = .

(b) The Möller Attack. If 9 P×B, P-Q4; 10 B-R3, P×B; 11 R-K1, B-K3; 12 R×N, Q-Q4 = . Steinitz-Lasker, match 1896.

(c) If 11 . . . O-O (A) 12 P-Q6, P×P; 13 B-N5! N-N3; 14 Q-Q5 ± . (B) 12 P-KN4, P-Q3; 13 P-N5, B-K4; 14 N×B, P×N; 15 R×P, N-N3; 16 R-K1, Q-Q2! 17 B-K3, P-N4 ∓ . *Debyut.*

(d) Ineffectual seems Schlechter's "Bayonet" attack 12 P-KN4, O-O; 13 P-N5, B-K4; 14 N×B, P×N; 15 R×P, N-N3; 16 R-K1, Q-Q3! and White has positional weaknesses.

(e) (A) 13 . . . B-B4; 14 Q-B3! Q-Q2; 15 B-N5! Q×B; 16 Q×B + + . (B) 13 . . . P-KR3 (1) 14 B-N5†, B-Q2; 15 Q-K2, B×B; 16 Q×B†, Q-Q2; 17 Q-K2, K-B1 . Barczay-Portisch, Budapest 1969. (2) 14 Q-K2, P×N; 15 R-K1, B-K3; 16 P×B, P-KB3! and 17 . . . P-B3 = . (3) 14 Q-R5, O-O; 15 QR-K1, N-B4 ∓ . The column is drawn after 14 N×RP, K×N (14 . . . B-B4; 15 R×N =); 15 Q-R5†, K-N1; 16 R-R4, P-KB4; 17 Q-R7†, K-B2; 18 R-R6, R-KN1! 19 R-K1, Q-B1; 20 B-N5, R-R1! (20 . . . P-R3; 21 R/1-K6!) 21 Q×R, P×R; 22 Q-R7†, K-B3; 23 R×N, Q×R; 24 Q×RP†. If 14 Q-K2, N-B4; 15 Q-R5, P-KR3; 16 N-K6, P×N + . *Comments.*

(f) 10 Q-K2, N×N†; 11 P×N, B-B3; 12 P×N, P-Q3; 13 P-K5, P×P; 14 P-B4, P-K5 ∓ .

(g) 14 P-B3, N-B4; 15 R-K1, K-R1; 16 B-R3, P-QN3; 17 N-B6, B-R3; 18 Q-Q4, Q-N4; 19 B×N, QP×B; 20 Q-K5 ± . Romanov-Kotkov, corr. 1964. Larry Evans prefers 11 . . . O-O! = .

(h) 9 . . . B×P?! (A) 10 10 B-R3! and now (1) 10 . . . P-Q4; 11 B-N5, B×R; 12 R-K1†, B-K3; 13 Q-R4, or (2) 10 . . . P-Q3; 11 R-B1, B-R4; 12 Q-R4, P-QR3; 13 B-Q5, B-N3; 14 R×N! B-Q2; 15 R-K1†, K-B1; 16 R×QP, or (3) 10 . . . N-K2; 11 Q-N3, P-Q4; 12 Q×B, P×B; 13 KR-K1, B-K3; 14 B×N, K×B; 15 P-Q5! Q×P; 16 QR-Q1, Q-QB4; 17 R-K5, Q-N3; 18 R×B† + . (B) 10 Q-N3, P-Q4 (10 . . . B×R? 11 B×P†, K-B1; 12 B-N5, N-K2; 13 N-K5, B×P; 14 B-N6! P-Q4; 15 Q-B3†); 11 B×P, O-O; 12 B×P†, R×B; 13 N-N5, B-K3! 14 Q×B/3 (14 Q×B/6, Q-Q2!), R-B3; 15 N×B, R×N; 16 Q-B4, Q-B3; 17 B-N2 (Panov), Q-B2, with counterchances.

(i) Sokolski gives 11 P-N5, N-K2; 12 B-R3, O-O; 13 Q-K2, R-K1 = .

(j) 14 B×N, K×B; 15 Q-B2, P-KB3! 16 N-N5! P×N; 17 R-K5, Q×P; 18 QR-K1, QR-K1; 19 R×B†, K-Q2; 20 R-Q1, Q×R†! 21 Q×Q†, K×R; 22 Q-N4†, K-B3 = . Bogolyubov. In the column, 12 B-N5! is preferable.

(k) 14 R–K1, P–KB3; 15 Q–K2, Q–Q2; 16 QR–Q1 ± . Panov. (But not 16 QR–B1—Steinitz-Bardeleben, Hastings 1895—16 . . . K–B2! =).

(l) The Cracow Variation is 7 K–B1, P–Q4; 8 P × P, KN × P; 9 N–B3, B–K3; 10 Q–K2, O–O! = . Keres.

(m) (A) 7 . . . P–Q4; 8 P × P, KN × P; 9 B × B, QN × B; 10 Q–N3! ± . (B) 7 . . . N × KP; 8 B × B, N × B; 9 B × P† (9 Q–N3, P–Q4; 10 Q × N, P × B; 11 O–O, Q–Q3; 12 Q × BP, O–O =), K × B; 10 Q–N3†, P–Q4; 11 N–K5†, K–K3! 12 Q × N, P–B4! 13 Q–R3, P × P = .

(n) 8 . . . N × KP; 9 Q–K2, P–Q4; 10 N × N, O–O; 11 O–O–O, B–N5; 12 P–KR3, B × N; 13 P × B, P × B; 14 Q × P, Q–R5; 15 K–N1, Q–B5; 16 P–Q5, N–K4; 17 Q × P, QR–B1; 18 Q–Q6!. Mednis-Fischer, US Chp. 1964.

(o) 14 Q–R3, B–K3; 15 N–K4, QR–Q1; 16 N/4–N5 ± . Rossolimo-O'Kelly, Hastings 1950–1.

1 P–K4, P–K4; 2 N–KB3, N–QB3; 3 B–B4, B–B4

	6	7	8	9	10
4	(P–B3)			P–Q3 (j)	
	B–N3			N–B3	
5	P–Q4			N–B3 (k)	
	Q–K2		P×P	P–Q3	
6	O–O (a)		P×P	B–KN5 (l)	
	N–B3 . . . . . . P–Q3		P–Q3	P–KR3! N–QR4	
7	R–K1	P–QR4 (f)	N–B3	B×N	B×N (p)
	P–Q3	P–QR3	N–B3	Q×B	Q×B (q)
8	P–KR3 (b)	N–R3	P–KR3 (h)	N–Q5	N–Q5
	O–O	B–N5	N×KP (i)	Q–Q1 (m)	Q–Q1
9	N–R3 (c)	N–B2	B×P†	P–B3	P–QN4
	K–R1 (d)	B×N	K×B	N–K2 (n)	P–QB3!
10	N–B2 (e)	P×B	N×N	P–QN4 (o)	P×B
		Q–B3 (g)	P–Q4 =		N×B (r)

(a) 6 P–Q5, N–Q1; 7 P–QR4, P–QR3; 8 P–Q6!? Q×P; 9 Q×Q, P×Q; 10 N–N5 (10 B–Q5, N–QB3; 11 N–R3, QN–K2 =), N–R3 = .

(b) 8 P–QR4, P–QR3; 9 N–R3, B–N5; 10 N–B2, B×N; 11 P×B, N–KR4 = . Keres.

(c) 9 P–QR4, P–QR3. (A) 10 B–KN5, P–R3; 11 B–K3, Q–Q1! 12 B–Q3, B–R2! = . Tarrasch-Alekhin, Baden-Baden 1925. (B) 10 P–QN4, K–R1; 11 B–K3, P×P; 12 P×P, N×P; 13 QN–Q2, P–B4!; Klovan-Aronin, USSR Chp. prelims. 1963. (C) 10 N–R3 (Estrin).

(d) 9 . . . N–Q1; 10 B–B1, N–K1; 11 N–B4, P–KB3; 12 P–QR4, P–B3; 13 N×B, P×N; 14 Q–N3†, N–K3; 15 Q×P + . Tartakover-Euwe, Venice 1948.

(e) Weaker is 10 P–Q5, N–Q1; 11 B–B1, P–B3; 12 N–B4, B–B2 = . Ragozin-Panov, USSR Chp. 1948. The column is Bouwmeester-Euwe, Dutch Chp. 1952, which continued: 10 . . . N–Q1; 11 P–QN3, B–K3; 12 B–B1, N–N1; 13 N–K3, P–KB3; 14 N–Q5, Q–B2; 15 P–B4, B–R2 ± .

(f) 7 P–KR3, N–B3; 8 R–K1, P–KR3 (8 . . . O–O; 9 N–R3, K–R1; 10 N–B2, N–Q1; 11 P–QN3, B–K3; 12 B–B1, N–N1; 13 N–K3, P–KB3; 14 N–Q5, Q–B2 =); 9 P–QR4, P–R3; 10 N–R3, O–O; 11 B–N3, R–K1. Sherwin-Lombardy, US Chp. 1958.

(g) 11 N–K3, KN–K2 = . Keres.

(h) Also 8 B–K3, B–N5; 9 B–N3, O–O; 10 Q–Q3, R–K1; 11 O–O, B–KR4; 12 N–Q2, N–KN5; 13 N–Q5 ± . Becker-Mattison, Carlsbad 1929. 12 QR–K1 ± is better.

(i) 8 . . . O–O; 9 B–KN5, P–KR3; 10 B×N, Q×B; 11 N–Q5, Q–N3 ∞. The column is Paoli-Bisguier, Vienna 1952/3.

(j) 4 O–O; P–Q3 (4 . . . N–B3! =); 5 P–B3, B–KN5; 6 P–Q4, P×P; 7 Q–N3, Q–Q2 (or 7 . . . B×N; 8 B×P†, K–B1; 9 P×B, N–B3; 10 B–KB4, P×P; 11 P×P, N–QR4; 12 Q–K6, Q–K2 = . Keres); 8 B×P†, Q×B; 9 Q×P, K–Q2; 10 Q×R, B×N; 11 P×B, N–K4; 12 N–Q2, N×P†; 13 K–N2 (13 N×N, Q×N; 14 Q–Q5, draws), ∞ . Keres.

(k) 5 P–B3, P–Q3 (5 . . . P–Q4; 6 P×P, N×P; 7 O–O ±); 6 O–O (6 P–QR4, P–QR3; 7 N–R3, P–Q4; 8 P×P, N×P; 9 B–N3, O–O; 10 N–B4, Q–B3; 11 O–O, N–N5 = . Najdorf-Reshevsky, match 1952), B–N3; 7 P–QR4, P–QR3; 8 N–R3, O–O; 9 B–R2, B–R2; 10 N–B2, B–K3; 11 B–K3, B×B; 12 R×B, P–Q4; 13 Q–K2, P×P; 14 P×P, Q–K2 = . Rossolimo-Donner, Beverwijk 1953. Including move 5, this is the "Giuoco Pianissimo".

(l) The Canal Variation. (A) 6 B–K3, O–O! (B) 6 O–O, B–KN5! 7 P–KR3, B–R4 = .

(m) Satisfactory is 8 . . . Q–N3; 9 Q–K2, B–KN5; 10 P–B3, B–N3; 11 P–QR4, P–B4 = . Foltys-Keres, Munich 1936.

(n) 9 . . . P–QR3! 10 P–QN4, B–R2; 11 P–QR4, B–K3; 12 Q–N3, O–O; 13 N–K3, Q–Q2 = . Cortlever-Flores, Dubrovnik 1950. (B) 9 . . . N–R4; 10 P–QN4 see col. 10.

(*o*) Or 10 P–Q4, P×P; 11 P×P, B–N3; 12 N×B, RP×N = . The column is dead even, after 10 . . . N×N; 11 P×B, N–B5; 12 P–KN3, N–K3 = .

(*p*) 7 N–Q5, N×B; 8 P×N, P–B3; 9 N×N†, P×N; 10 B–K3, Q–N3; 11 Q–Q2, B–K3; 12 O–O–O, O–O–O = . Korchnoi-Bronstein, USSR Chp. 1952.

(*q*) 7 . . . P×B; 8 N–KR4, N×B; 9 P×N, P–B4; 10 N×P, B×N; 11 P×B, Q–R5; 12 Q–B3! Q×BP; 13 Q×P, K–Q2; 14 Q–N3 + . Cortlever-Trifunović, Holland *v.* Yugoslavia 1950.

(*r*) 11 P×N, P×N; 12 BP×P/5, Q–R4†; 13 Q–Q2, Q×BP, Q×BP/4; 14 O–O, O–O; 15 QR–N1, P–QN3 ∓ . Blau-Euwe, Lenzerheide 1956.

1 P–K4, P–K4; 2 N–KB3, N–QB3; 3 B–B4; B–B4; 4 P–QN4, B × P; 5 P–B3, B–R4;
6 P–Q4

	11	12	13	14	15
	P × P			P–Q3 (g)	
7	O–O			Q–N3 (h)	
	B–N3		P × P (e)	Q–Q2 (i)	
8	P × P		Q–N3	P × P	
	P–Q3		Q–B3	B–N3	P × P
9	N–B3	P–Q5 (c)	P–K5	B–QN5 (j)	O–O (k)
	B–N5 (a)	N–R4	Q–N3	KN–K2	B–N3 (l)
10	B–QN5	B–N2	N × P	P × P	R–Q1
	K–B1	N–K2	KN–K2 (f)	P × P	Q–K2
11	B–K3	B–Q3	B–R3	B–R3	P–QR4
	KN–K2	O–O	O–O	Q–N5	N–R3
12	P–QR4	N–B3	QR–Q1!	O–O	P–R5
	P–QR4	N–N3	R–K1	N–N3	B × P
13	B–QB4	N–K2	B–Q3 ±	B × P	B–R3
	B–R4 (b)	P–QB4 (d)		N–B5 =	Q–B3 (m)

(a) 9 . . . N–R4; 10 B–N5 (Göring's Attack), P–KB3; 11 B–K3, N–K2 (11 . . . N × B; 12 Q–R4†); 12 P–KR3, B–Q2; 13 B–N3 ± . Maróczy.

(b) 14 R–B1! ± . Cafferty-Cadden, corr. 1967–8.

(c) 9 B–N2, N–B3; 10 P–Q5, N–QR4; 11 B–Q3, O–O   . Sokolski.

(d) 14 R–B1, R–N1; 15 Q–Q2, P–B3 + . Anderssen-Zukertort, Berlin 1868.

(e) *MCO5* suggested 7 . . . KN–K2 (7 . . . P–Q3; 8 Q–N3, Q–B3; 9 P–K5, P × P; 10 R–K1!); 8 P × P (8 N–N5, P–Q4; 9 P × P, N–K4; 10 Q × P, P–KB3!); P–Q4; 9 P × P, KN × P; 10 B–R3, B–K3 = . Or 10 Q–N3, N/3–K2 = . *P/E*.

(f) (a) 10 . . . B × N? 11 Q × B, KN–K2; 12 N–N5, O–O; 13 B–Q3 + . (b) 10 . . . P–N4; 11 N × P, R–N1; 12 Q–K3, KN–K2; 13 Q–K2, Q–R4; 14 B–R3 ± . The column is Bilguer's.

(g) 6 . . . Q–K2; 7 O–O, B–N3; 8 B–R3, Q–B3; 9 P × P, N × P; 10 N × N, Q × N; 11 Q–N3, N–R3; 12 N–Q2, B–R4 = . Ragozin-Levenfish, USSR Chp. 1949.

(h) (a) 7 O–O, B–Q2; 8 Q–N3, Q–K2; 9 P × P, P × P; 10 R–Q1, O–O–O; 11 QN–Q2, N–R3 = is the old Sanders-Alapin line; Lasker's Defence gives Black a better end-game, however, after 7 . . . B–N3! 8 P × P, P × P; 9 Q × Q†, N × Q; 10 N × P, B–K3. (b) 7 B–KN5, P–B3 (7 . . . Q–Q2; 8 O–O, P–KR3; 9 B–R4, KN–K2; 10 P–Q5, N–QN1; 11 B × N, K × B is ∞); 8 Q–N3, KN–K2! 9 B–B7†, K–B1; (10 B–R5, 10 B–Q2 P–KN3; 11 B–R6†, K–K1; 12 B–N7, R–B1!) B–N3; 11 P–QR4, B–N5 + .

(i) (a) 7 . . . N × P!? 8 N × N, P × N; 9 B × P†, K–B1; 10 O–O, Q–K2; 11 B–QB4, N–B3; 12 P × P, N × P; 13 Q–B3†, N–B3; 14 N–B3, B × N; 15 Q × B, B–B4; 16 R–K1 ± . Thomas-Unzicker, Hastings 1950. (b) 7 . . . Q–K2; 8 P–Q5, N–Q5; 9 N × N (9 Q–R4†, Q–Q2! 10 Q × B, P–QN3; 11 N × N, P × Q; 12 B–QN5, P × N; 13 B × Q†, K × B =), P × N; 10 Q–R4†, B–Q2; 11 Q × B, Q × P†; 12 K–B1, P–Q6 = .

(j) (a) 9 P × P, N–R4; 10 Q–N4, N × B; 11 Q × N, Q × P; 12 B–R3, B–K3; 13 Q–N5†, Q–Q2; 14 Q–N4, P–QB4; 15 Q–N2, Q–Q6; 16 QN–Q2, O–O–O = . Mnatsakanian-Korelov, USSR Chp. 1963. (b) 9 QN–Q2, P × P (good is 9 . . . N–R4; 10 Q–R3, N × B; 11 N × N, B–B4; 12 Q–N3, N–K2); 10 B–R3, N–R4; 11 Q–N4, P–QB4; 12 Q–N2, N × B; 13 N × N, P–B3 (or Q–K3); 14 R–Q1, Q–B3; 15 N–Q6†, with attacking chances. Sokolski-Schumacher, corr. 1954. The column is analysis by G. Wood.

(k) (a) 9 P–QR4, N–R3! (b) 9 B–R3, B–N3; 10 O–O, N–R4; 11 N × P, N × Q; 12 P × N, Q–K3! 13 B × Q, B × B ∓ . Sokolski.

(l) 9 . . . N–R3; 10 B–R3, N–N3; 11 R–Q1, Q–N5; 12 B–N5, P–B3; 13 P–R3, Q × KP; 14 B–Q3, Q–KB5; 15 Q–Q5 ∞ . Hájek-Richter, Prague 1949.

(m) 14 B–N5, B–Q2; 15 P–B4! Aronin.

1 P–K4, P–K4; 2 N–KB3; N–QB3; 3 B–B4, B–B4; 4 P–QN4

	16	17	18	19	20
	(B × P)		B–N3 (*g*)		
5	(P–B3)		P–QR4	P–N5	B–N2
	B–K2 (*a*)		P–QR3	N–R4 (*m*)	P–Q3
6	P–Q4 (*b*)		N–B3 (*h*)	N × P (*n*)	P–QR4
	N–R4 (*c*)		N–B3 (*i*)	N–R3	P–QR3
7	N × P	B–Q3 (*e*)	N–Q5	P–Q4	P–N5
	N × B	P–Q3	N × N (*j*)	P–Q3	P × P
8	N × N	P × P	P × N	B × N	P × P
	P–Q4	B–N5 (*f*)	P–K5	P × N (*o*)	R × R
9	P × P	P × P	P × N	B × P	B × R
	Q × P	P × P	P × N (*k*)	R–KN1	N–Q5
10	N–K3	O–O	Q × P	B × P†	B × N
	Q–QR4 (*d*)	N–KB3 =	Q–K2† (*l*)	K × B +	P × B (*p*)

(*a*) (A) 5 . . . B–B4; 6 P–Q4, P × P; 7 P × P, B–N3, see col. 11. (B) 5 . . . B–Q3; 6 O–O, Q–K2; 7 P–Q4, N–B3; 8 QN–Q2, P–QN3; 9 B–Q3, N–QR4; 10 N–R4! P–N3; 11 P–KB4, P × QP; 12 P × P + . Khalilbeili-Shishov, USSR Chp. prelims 1958.

(*b*) 6 Q–N3; N–R3; 7 P–Q4, N–R4; 8 Q–R4 (or 8 Q–N5, N × B; 9 B × N, P × B =), N × B; 9 Q × N, P × P; 10 B × N, P × B; 11 P × P, P–Q3; 12 O–O, O–O; 13 N–B3, P–B3; 14 QR–K1, K–R1 = .

(*c*) Cordel's move. If (A) 6 . . . P × P; 7 Q–N3, N–R4; 8 B × P†, K–B1; 9 Q–R4, K × B; 10 Q × N, P–Q3; 11 P × P ± Lehmann–Donner, Munich 1954. Further study deserves (B) 6 . . . N–KB3; 7 P × P, N–KN5; 8 Q–Q5, O–O; 9 P–KR3, N–R3 = .

(*d*) Or 10 . . . Q–Q1, followed by N–B3 and O–O = . Euwe. The column is Porreca-Euwe, Bern 1957, which continued: 11 O–O, N–B3; 12 R–K1, B–K3; 13 P–QB4, P–B3; 14 B–N2, O–O–O; 15 Q–B1, K–N1 ∓ .

(*e*) 7 B–K2, P–Q4; 8 P × KP, P × P; 9 Q–R4†, P–B3; 10 Q × P, Q–Q4; 11 Q–QR4, B–K3; 12 QN–Q2 ± . *Comments.*

(*f*) Or (A) 8 . . . P × P; 9 N × P, N–KB3; 10 O–O, O–O; 11 Q–B2, B–K3; 12 R–Q1, Q–B1 = . Sokolski-Shishov, USSR Chp. prelims 1958. (B) Fischer gives 8 . . . N–QB3; 9 B–QB4, N × P; 10 N × N, P × N; 11 Q–R5! The column is Klovin-Ravinski, Leningrad 1959.

(*g*) The Evans Gambit Declined. (A) 4 . . . N × P; 5 P–B3, N–QB3;; 6 P–Q4, see col. 11. (B) 4 . . . P–Q4; 5 P × P, N × P; 6 O–O, N–KB3; 7 N × P, QN × QP; 8 P–Q4, B–K2, is playable.

(*h*) (A) 6 B–N2, P–Q3, see col. 20. (B) 6 B–R3, N–B3; 7 P–N5, N–QR4; 8 N × P, P–Q4 = . *Comments.*

(*i*) 6 . . . P–Q3; 7 N–Q5, N–B3; 8 N × B, P × N; 9 P–Q3 ± . Alexander-Broadbent, Nottingham 1946.

(*j*) 7 . . . N × P; 8 O–O, O–O; 9 P–Q3, N–B3; 10 B–KN5, P–Q3; 11 N–Q2! + . Kan-Botvinnik, Moscow 1929.

(*k*) 9 . . . O–O; 10 B–N2, P × N; 11 Q × P, QP × P; 12 Q–B3, R–K1†; 13 K–B1, Q–N4; 14 P–R4, Q–R3; 15 P–QR5 + . Sokolski-Goldenov, Kiev 1945.

(*l*) 11 K–Q1, QP × P; 12 R–K1, B–K3 = . Panov.

(*m*) Satisfactory is 5 . . . N–Q5; 6 N × N (6 N × P? Q–N4), P × N! = .

(*n*) Best is 6 B–K2, P–Q4; 7 P–Q3, N–KB3 = .

(*o*) 8 . . . P × B; 9 N × P, Q–B3; 10 Q–R5, O–O; 11 N × RP†, K–N2; 12 N–N4, B × N; 11 Q × B†, K–R1 + + . Max Lange.

(*p*) 12 P–Q3, N–B3; 13 QN–Q2, P–Q4 ∞ . Purdy.

Two Knights' Defence

(incorporating the Max Lange Attack)

(1 P–K4, P–K4; 2 N–KB3, N–QB3;
3 B–B4, N–B3)

The lineage of the Two Knights' begins with Polerio (1580) and runs past Bilguer in the *Handbuch* (1839) and Albert Pinkus' thorough analysis in *Chess Review* (1943–4) down to Estrin's and Petrosian's preoccupation with this colourful début. Black's third move opens a Pandora's box of complications and averts the well-mapped Giuoco Piano and Evans Gambit. The defence remains a favourite of tactical players who desire to wrest an early initiative albeit at the cost of a pawn.

The crucial lines spring from 4 N–N5, which has been branded everything from "a duffer's move" (Tarrasch) to "primitive" (Panov). Despite this calumny (the move violates the principle of never moving the same piece twice in the opening) Black is hard-pressed to justify the virtually forced loss of a pawn.

4 . . . P–Q4; 5 P × P, N–QR4; 6 B–N5†, P–B3; 7 P × P, P × P; 8 B–K2, P–KR3; 9 N–KB3, P–K5; 10 N–K5 is the main line (cols. 1–5) where White holds his pawn or else returns it under favourable conditions. Black has counterplay and White is thrown on the defensive, but his resources are adequate with correct play. 8 Q–B3 as in cols. 6–8 gives rise to unclear complications, whereas Morphy's 6 P–Q3 again holds the pawn but does permit Black equality (cols. 9–10).

After 4 N–N5, P–Q4; 5 P × P the exceptional lines where Black varies on move five are covered in columns 11–15. 5 . . . N × P permits White the choice of an easy advantage with 6 P–Q4 (col. 11, *a*) or a speculative attack with 6 N × BP!? col. 11). The *Fritz Variation* 5 . . . N–Q5 (cols. 12–13) was tested by Berliner, by Estrin, by Jovćić, and others and is still an open question. *Ulvestad's line* 5 . . . P–N4 (cols. 14–15) is imaginative but virtually refuted by 6 B–B1! However, it is closely linked to the Fritz Variation of which it is an acceleration and any new developments in either line will affect the other.

The tricky *Wilkes Barre Variation* (cols. 16–17) arises after 4 N–N5, B–B4!? and is so named because of extensive analyses accompanying the Wilkes Barre Club correspondence games in the 1920–30s (and later by Ken Smith and K. Williams), giving rise to a revival of this line which was also examined in depth by the Czech masters Traxler (in 1869) and Rohlíček (in the 1950s).

1 P-K4, P-K4; 2 N-KB3, N-QB3; 3 B-B4, N-B3; 4 N-N5, P-Q4; 5 P × P, N-QR4;
6 B-N5†, P-B3; 7 P × P, P × P; 8 B-K2, P-KR3; 9 N-KB3 (a), P-K5; 10 N-K5

	1	2	3	4	5
	B-Q3		B-QB4	Q-Q5	Q-B2
11	P-Q4	P-KB4 (f)	P-QB3 (l)	P-KB4	P-KB4 (p)
	P×P e.p. (b)	P×P e.p. (g)	B-Q3!	B-QB4	B-QB4 (q)
12	N×QP	N×P/3	P-KB4	R-B1	P-B3
	Q-B2	O-O (h)	Q-B2	Q-Q1	N-N2
13	P-QN3 (c)	P-Q4	P-Q4	P-B3 (m)	P-QN4
	O-O	P-B4 (i)	P×P e.p.	N-Q4	B-N3
14	B-N2	P×P (j)	Q×P	Q-R4!	P-QR4
	N-Q4 (d)	B×BP	O-O	O-O	P-QR4
15	N-B3	Q×Q	O-O	Q×KP (n)	P-N5
	N-B5	R×Q	O-O	Q-R5†	O-O
16	N×N	B-Q2	B-B3	K-Q1	P×P
	B×N (e)	N-B3 (k)	R-Q1 =	R-Q1 (o)	N-Q3 (r)

(a) A rare try is Steinitz's 9 N-KR3, B-QB4; 10 O-O, O-O; 11 P-Q3, N-Q4; 12 B-B3, N-N2; 13 N-B3, B-N3; 14 K-R1, N-B4; 15 B-K3, R-N1 = . Ciocaltea-Szabó, Sinaia 1964.

(b) 11 . . . Q-B2; 12 B-Q2! N-N2; 13 O-O, O-O; 14 N-R3 ± .

(c) Introduced by Honfi, this move concedes White a better hold than (A) 13 N-Q2, O-O; 14 N-B3 (14 P-QN4, N-Q4! 15 B-N2, N × P; 16 N × N, B × N; 17 O-O, R-Q1 ∓), P-B4; 15 O-O, B-N2; 16 N/Q-K1, QR-Q1 ∓. (B) 13 N-B3, O-O; 14 P-KN3, R-N1; 15 O-O, B-R6; 16 R-K1, KR-Q1; 17 B-K3, P-B4; 18 Q-B1, N-B5; 19 N-B4, N × B; 20 N × B, N-B4; 21 N-QN5, R × N ∓. Ivanov-Khan, Tashkent 1971.

(d) Deceptive is 14 . . . B-KB4; 15 B × N? P × B; 16 N-B3, QR-Q1; 17 Q-Q2, KR-K1 ∓.

(e) 17 P-N3, R-Q1; 18 B-Q3, R-K1†; 19 N-K2, B-N4; 20 O-O? (20 P-KR4! B-K2; 21 Q-Q2, P-QB4 =), B-N5; 21 P-KB3, B-R6; 22 K-R1 (22 R-K1, Q-N3†; 23 K-R1, Q-B7 + +), B × R + + . Honfi-Tal, Sarajevo 1966. Altogether, White's most solid line is 16 O-O!

(f) (A) 11 N-N4, N × N; 12 B × N, Q-R5; 13 B × B, R × B; 14 Q-K2, O-O; 15 N-B3, QR-K1 ∓. (B) 11 N-B4, N × N; 12 B × N, N-N5; 13 Q-K2, O-O; 14 P-KR3, Q-R5! ∓.

(g) (A) 11 . . . P-N4; 12 P-Q4, P × P; 13 B × P, N-Q4; 14 O-O! B-K3; 15 N-Q2, N × B; 16 R × N, Q-N3; 17 K-R1 + . Estrin. (B) 11 . . . Q-B2; 12 O-O (or 12 P-Q4), O-O; 13 N-QB3, B × N; 14 P × B, Q × P; 15 P-Q4, P × P e.p.; 16 Q × P ± . Fine-Reshevsky, US Chp. 1940.

(h) 12 . . . N-N5; 13 O-O, Q-B2; 14 P-KR3, B-R7†; 15 K-R1, P-R4. (A) 16 N-B3! (so as to answer 16 . . . B-N6; 17 N-K4!), B-B4; 17 P-Q4, O-O-O; 18 B-Q3 + . (B) 16 P-Q4, B-N6; 17 B-Q3, B-K3; 18 Q-K2, O-O-O; 19 P-N4, N-N2; 20 P-B4! Estrin.

(i) Bisguier's favourite. An alternative is 13 . . . Q-B2; 14 O-O, P-B4; 15 N-B3, P-R3; (1) 16 P-Q5, R-K1; 17 K-R1, R-N1; 18 P-QR3, N-N5 with an attack for the pawn. (2) 16 K-R1, B-N2; 17 B-K3, QR-Q1; 18 B-N1, KR-K1 ∞ . Spasski-Geller, Göteborg 1955.

(j) If 14 O-O, P × P; 15 K-R1, B-QB4; 16 P-B3, P × P; 17 N × P = .

(k) 17 N-B3, N-KN5! 18 N-K4, B-N3; 19 P-KR3, N-K6; 20 B × N, B × B; 21 B-Q3, R-QN1; 22 P-QN3, N-N5; 23 K-K2, B-N3; 24 KR-Q1, B-N2; 25 N-B2, N-Q4; 26 R-K1, N-K6; 27 R-KN1, R-K1; 28 K-Q2, N-Q4! 29 N-Q1, B × R; 30 N × B, N-N5; 31 P-N3, N × B; 32 P × N, R-K3; 33 N-QB3, R-Q1; 34 N/3-K2, B-R3; 35 P-Q4, R/1-K1; 36 N-B4, R-K6; 37 P-KN4, R/6-K5; 38 Resigns. Hartoch-Bisguier, Sombor 1975.

(l) (A) 11 P-KB4, Q-N3; 12 R-B1, B-N8! (B) 11 O-O, Q-Q5; 12 N-N4, N × N; 13 B × N, O-O = . The move 10 . . . B-QB4 was introduced and practiced by Herman Steiner.

(m) 13 P-Q4, B-N3; 14 P-QN4, N-Q4; 15 P × N, Q-R5†; 16 P-N3, Q × RP, etc.

(n) 15 P–QN4, Q–R5†; 16 K–Q1, R–Q1; 17 K–B2, Q × RP! 18 P × B, Q × P! with a furious attack. Romanov-Baturinski, corr. 1965.

(o) 17 P–Q4, P–B3; 18 B–Q3 ± . Nestorenko-Mosin, USSR 1963.

(p) (A) 11 N–N4, B × N; 12 B × B, B–B4; 13 B–K2, R–Q1; 14 P–QB3, N–N2; 15 O–O, P–KR4; 16 P–Q4, P × P e.p. ∓ . (B) 11 P–Q4 might transpose into cols. 1 or 3

(q) For Tenner's move 11 . . . B–Q3 see note f(B).

(r) With positional equivalent for the minus material. Belov-Solovyev, USSR 1968.

1 P–K4, P–K4; 2 N–KB3, N–QB3; 3 B–B4, N–B3; 4 N–N5, P–Q4; 5 P × P, N–QR4

	6	7	8	9	10
6	(B–N5†)			P–Q3	
	(P–B3)			P–KR3	
7	(P × P)			N–KB3	
	(P × P)			P–K5 (i)	
8	Q–B3 (a)			Q–K2 (j)	
	P × B	Q–B2	R–QN1 (e)	N × B	
9	Q × R	B–Q3	B × P† (f)	P × N	
	B–QB4 (b)	P–KR3 (d)	N × B	B–QB4	B–K2 (m)
10	O–O	N–K4	Q × N†	KN–Q2 (k)	N–Q4 (n)
	O–O	N–Q4	N–Q2	O–O	P–B3
11	P–QN4	QN–B3	P–Q3 (g)	N–N3	N–QB3
	B × P	N–KB5	B–K2	B–N5	O–O
12	N–QB3 (c)	B–B1 ±	N–K4 (h)	Q–B1 (l)	O–O (o)

(a) (A) B–R4, P–KR3; 9 N–KB3, P–K5; 10 Q–K2, B–K3; 11 N–K5, Q–Q5; 12 B × P†, N × B; 13 Q–N5, B–QB4! (B) 8 B–Q3, is best met by 8 . . . B–K2, or . . . N–N5. But inferior is 8 . . . N–Q4; 9 N–K4, P–KB4; 10 N–N3, N–KB5; 11 B × P! ± . Broun.

(b) Very complicated is (A) 9 . . . P–KR3! 10 N–K4, N–Q4; 11 Q–N8, N–B3! 12 Q × NP, N/4–N5; 13 N–R3, B–R3; 14 Q–R4, Q–Q5! 15 N–B3, B–B4; 16 P–Q3, Q × P†; 17 K–Q1, O–O; 18 R–K1, Q × P; 19 B–Q2, B–B7; 20 N–K2, B × R; 21 B × B, B–B1! 22 B × N, B–N5; 23 K–Q2, Q × N†; 24 K–B3, R–B1; 25 N–B4, N–Q5; 26 B–K7, B–K3; White resigned. Estimo-Balinas, Manila 1968. (B) 9 . . . Q–Q2; 10 Q–B3 (or 10 P–QN4, B × P; 11 P–QB3, B–B4; 12 B–R3 ±), B–N2; 11 Q–K2, N–B3; 12 O–O, B–K2; 13 P–QB3, P–KR3; 14 N–KB3, P–K5; 15 N–K1, N–K4; 16 P–Q4, N–B6†; 17 P × N, P × P; 18 Q–K5, N–K5; 19 B–B4 + . Vasilyev-Morosov, Omsk 1951. (C) 9 . . . N–N2; 10 P–Q4 (or 10 P–Q3, B–QB4; 11 B–K3, B × B; 12 P × B, N–Q4; 13 N × BP, Q–R4†; 14 P–N4, Q × P†; 15 P–B3 ± . Donovan-Santasiere, New York 1948), P × P; 11 O–O, B–K2; 12 P–QR4, P × P; 13 Q × P, O–O; 14 N–KB3 ± . O'Kelly-Milić, Bled 1950.

(c) 12 . . . B–QB4; 13 Q–B3, P–QR3; 14 QN–K4, B–N2; 15 Q–B5 ± . Zukharov-Kopayev, Lvov 1951.

(d) (A) 9 . . . B–Q3; 10 N–B3, O–O; 11 B–B5, B × B; 12 Q × B, P–KR3; 13 N–K4, N–Q4; 14 P–Q3, N–K2; 15 N–B6† ± . Kottnauer-Taimanov, Szczavno Zdroj 1950. (B) 9 . . . B–KN5; 10 Q–N3, B–Q2; 11 P–N3, B–Q3; 12 B–R3 ± . (C) 9 . . . B–K2; 10 N–B3, O–O; 11 B–B5, P–KR3; 12 KN–K4, N–Q4; 13 N–N3 ± .

(e) The Colman Variation. (A) Out of favour is Staunton's 8 . . . Q–N3; 9 B–Q3, B–Q3; 10 P–KR3, P–KR3; 11 N–K4, N × N; 12 B × N, O–O; 13 P–KN4 ± . Dr. Paoli-Sefc, Tren-ćanské Teplice 1949. But Black's 10th and 11th moves are open to further analysis. (B) 8 . . . P–KR3; 9 N–K4! N–N5; 10 P–KR3, P–R4; 11 P–QN4! N–N2; 12 B–B4 ± . Estrin.

(f) Still important is 9 B–Q3, P–KR3! 10 N–K4, N–Q4; 11 N–N3, P–N3; 12 O–O, B–KN2, and now: (A) 13 P–B3, P–KB4; 14 N–B2, O–O; 15 P–Q3, P–B4; 16 Q–Q1, Q–B2! 17 N–Q2, B–R3; 18 N–N3, KR–Q1 = . Estrin-Sellhofer, corr. 1960. (B) 13 N–B3, O–O; 14 B–K2, R–N5; 15 N × N, P × N; 16 Q–R3, N–B3; 17 P–Q3, P–KR4; 18 R–K1, P–R5; 19 N–B1, R–K1; 20 P–QB3, R–N3; 21 Q–R4, R–R3; 22 Q–Q1, P–Q5; Estrin-Ragozin, Moscow 1955; 23 P–QB4! Estrin considers 12 . . . P–KR4!? without further analysis.

(g) (A) 11 P–Q4, B–K2; 12 N–K4, R–N3; 13 Q–R4; O–O; 14 O–O, P–B4; 15 KN–B3, B–N2 ⨦ . Kallgren-Axelsson, Ørebro 1949. (B) 11 N–KB3, B–N3; 12 Q–K4, B–N2; 13 Q–K2, P–K5; 14 O–O, B–K2; 15 N–K1, O–O ⨦ . Kertesz-Gurskaya, Hungarian Chp. 1953.

(h) (A) 12 P–KR4, P–KR3; 13 N–KB3, O–O = . (B) 12 N–KB3, O–O; 13 Q–K4, R–N5; 14 Q–K2, P–K5! 15 P × P, N–B4; 16 N–B3, B–R3; 17 Q–Q1, Q–R4; 18 N–Q2, N × P, with pressure. Sickerl-Krišnik, Yugoslavia 1956. The column is Howland-Brown, corr. 1952, which continued: 12 . . . R–N3; 13 Q–R4, P–B4; 14 N–N3, O–O, with a good attack for the pawns.

(*i*) 7 . . . N×B; 8 P×N, B–Q3; 9 P–KR3, O–O; 10 N–B3, P–B3 (Rossetto-Gligorić, Buenos Aires 1955); 11 B–K3 ± .

(*j*) 8 P×P!? N×B; 9 Q–Q4, P–QN4 = . Flohr. If 9 . . . N–Q3, 10 KN–Q2!, P–B3; 11 P–B4 ± .

(*k*) (A) 10 P–KR3, O–O; 11 N–R2, P–K6 (Euwe recommends 11 . . . P–QN4); 12 B×P, B×B; 13 P×B, N–K5; 14 O–O, N–N6; 15 Q–B3, N×R; 16 N×N = . (B) 10 B–B4, O–O; 11 KN–Q2, B–KN5; 12 Q–B1, P–B3! 13 N–QB3, R–K1 = .

(*l*) 12 . . . B–N5† (A) 13 P–B3, B–K2; 14 P–KR3, B–R4; 15 P–N4, B–N3; 16 B–K3, N–Q2! 17 QN–Q2, N–K4; 18 O–O–O, P–N4 ∓ (Salwe-Marshall, Ostend 1908). (B) If 13 B–Q2, B×B†; 14 QN×B, R–K1; 15 P–KR3, P–K6! (C) 13 N–B3, P–B3 (or P–QN4); 14 P–KR3, B–KR4; 15 P–N4, B–N3; 16 P×P, P×P; 17 B–Q2 (better is B–K3), P–K6! + . Luckis-Keres, Buenos Aires 1939.

(*m*) 9 . . . B–Q3; 10 P–KR3, O–O; 11 N–Q4, R–K1; 12 B–K3, B–K4; 13 Q–Q2, B–Q2; 14 N–QB3, P–B3; Grob-Lundin, Ostend 1936; 15 O–O–O ± . Here, 11 . . . P–B3 = was better.

(*n*) 10 KN–Q2, O–O; 11 O–O, B–KN5; 12 Q–K3, B–KB4; 13 N–QB3, B–Q3; 14 P–KR3, R–K1; 15 N–N5, B–K4; 16 N–Q4, B–R2; 17 R–K1, N–Q2 = .

(*o*) 12 . . . P×P; 13 P×P, B–KN5; 14 Q–K3 (or Q–N5), N×P; 15 Q×KP, N×N; 16 P×N, Q–Q2 = . *Debyut*.

1 P–K4, P–K4; 2 N–KB3, N–QB3; 3 B–B4, N–B3; 4 N–N5, P–Q4, 5 P × P

	11	12	13	14	15
	N × P?	N–Q5 (Fritz's Variation)		P–N4 (Ulvestad's Variation)	
6	N × BP!? (a)	P–QB3 (e)		B–B1!.	B × P (m)
	K × N	P–N4		N × P (j)	Q × P
7	Q–B3†	B–B1!		B × P	B × N† (n)
	K–K3	N × P (f)		B–N2	Q × B
8	N–B3	N–K4 (g)		P–Q4	O–O
	N–N5 (b)	N–K3	Q–R5	P–B3 (k)	B–N2
9	Q–K4 (c)	B × P†	N–N3	O–O	Q–B3
	P–B3	B–Q2	B–KN5 (h)	Q–Q2 (l)	P–K5
10	P–QR3	B × B†	P–B3	P–QB4	Q–QN3
	N–R3	Q × B	P–K5?!	N–N3	O–O–O
11	P–Q4	O–O	P × N	P–Q5	Q–R3†
	N–B2	B–K2!	B–Q3	P × N	K–N1
12	B–B4	P–Q4	B × P†	P × N	N–QB3
	K–B2 (d)	P × P =	K–Q1 (i)	B × P	R–Q2 (o)

(a) The flamboyant "Fegatello" or "Fried Liver" attack in answer to Black's meek try to avoid the complexities of 5 . . . N–QR4. White can arrive at solid pressure by the direct moves 6 P–Q4, B–K3; 7 N × B, P × N; 8 P × P, N × P; 9 Q–R5†, N–B2; 10 O–O, Q–Q2; 11 R–K1, O–O–O; 12 Q–N4, R–K1; 13 N–B3, B–N5; 14 B–Q2 ± . *Debyut.* For side lines see more specialized literature. After 6 P–Q4, if 6 . . . B–N5† 7 P–B3, B–K2; 8 N × BP!!, K × N; 9 Q–B3†, K–K3; 10 Q–K4 ± .

(b) 8 . . . N–K2; 9 P–Q4, P–B3; 10 B–KN5, P–KR3; 11 B × N, B × B; 12 O–O–O, R–B1; 13 Q–K4! R × P; 14 KR–B1 with strong attack. *Comments.*

(c) Or 9 P–QR3, N × P†; 10 K–Q1, N × R (if 10 . . . N–Q5; 11 Q–K4! P–B3; 12 R–K1 + , Panov); 11 N × N, K–Q3; 12 P–Q4, P–B3; 13 B–B4, P × B; 14 Q × P†, K–Q2; 15 R–K1! + . Lisitsyn.

(d) 13 B × P, B–K3; 14 O–O, N × N; 15 Q–B3†, K–K2; 16 B × N, Q × B; 17 KR–K1, N–Q4; 18 B × N, P × B; 19 Q × P, Q–B3; 20 R × B†, Q × R; 21 Q × NP†, winning.

(e) 6 P–Q6, Q × P; 7 B × P†, K–K2; 8 B–N3, N–K6; 9 RP × N, P–KR3; 10 N–KB3, P–K5; 11 N–N1, K–B2 ∞. Bogolyubov-Rubinstein, Stockholm 1919.

(f) 7 . . . P–KR3; 8 P × N, P × N; 9 P × P, N × P; 10 B × P†, B–Q2; 11 B × B†, Q × B; 12 N–B3, N–B5; 13 P–Q4 ± , (instead of 12 P–Q4, B–N5†; 13 B–Q2, B × B†; 14 N × B, R–R5; 15 O–O, O–O–O =). *Comments.*

(g) (A) 8 N × BP, K × N; 9 P × N, P × P. (1) 10 Q–B3†, N–B3! 11 Q × R, B–QB4; 12 B × P, R–K1†; with strong attack. (2) 10 B × P, Q–K2†; 11 Q–K2, Q × Q†; 12 B × Q, N–N5; 13 B–B4†, B–K3; 14 B × B†, K × B = . (B) 8 P × N, Q × N; 9 B × P†, K–Q1; 10 O–O, B–N2; 11 Q–B3, P × P; 12 P–Q3, Q–K4! 13 Q × P, B–K2 = . Paoli-Robatsch, Venice 1967. (c) 8 P–KR4, P–KR3; 9 N–K4, N–K3; 10 B × P†, B–Q2; 11 Q–R4, N/3–B5 (or 11 . . . P–KB4); 12 P–Q4, N × P† = .

(h) 9 . . . B–N2; 10 P × N, O–O–O; 11 P–Q3, N–B5; 12 B × N, P × B; 13 Q–R5, Q–K2†; with pressure. Radtchenko; but 14 N–K2, P–N4; 15 N–Q2, R × P; 16 O–O–O leaves White in a better position.

(i) 13 O–O! P × P; 14 R × P (14 Q–N3!?, N–N5; 15 R × P, P–QB3! Berliner. R–QN1 (Estrin-Berliner, corr. 1966–7); 15 P–R4 ± . Jovčić-Kohnitsky, corr. 1969.

(j) 6 . . . N–Q5, transposes into the somewhat safer cols. 12–13.

(k) 8 . . . P × P; 9 O–O, B–K2; 10 N × BP! ± .

(l) 9 . . . P × N; 10 P–QB4, P–QR3; 11 P × N, Q × P; 12 N–B3, Q × P; 13 B–R4, Q × Q; 14 R × Q, B–B4; 15 N–K4 ± . Yanofsky.

(*m*) (A) 6 B–K2, N–Q5; 7 N–QB3, N × QP; 8 N–B3, N–B5 = . (B) 6 B–N3, N–Q5; 7 O–O, N × QP = .

(*n*) 7 B–K2, B–N2; 8 P–Q3, N–Q5; 9 B–KB3, is Euwe's suggestion.

(*o*) 13 R–K1, B–N5; 14 P–Q3, P × P; 15 P × P, R–K1 = . Kan-Konstantinopolski, Moscow 1945. In the column, also 8 Q–B3, P–K5; 9 Q–QN3, B–QB4; 10 Q × P†, K–Q1 ∓ .

1 P–K4, P–K4; 2 N–KB3, N–QB3; 3 B–B4, N–B3

	16	17	18	19	20
4	(N–N5).................		O–O (h)	P–Q4	
	B–B4 (a)		B–B4	P×P	
5	P–Q4	N×BP (d)	P–Q4	P–K5	O–O (k)
	P–Q4! (b)	B×P†	B×P (i)	P–Q4	N×P (l)
6	B×P	K–B1 (e)	N×B	B–QN5	R–K1
	N×QP	Q–K2	N×N	N–K5	P–Q4
7	N×BP	N×R	B–KN5	N×P	B×P (m)
	Q–K2	P–Q4	P–Q3	B–QB4	Q×B
8	N×R	P×P	P–B4	B–K3	N–B3
	B–KN5	B–N5! (f)	Q–K2	O–O	Q–QR4 (n)
9	P–KB3	B–K2	P×P	B×N	N×N!
	N×B	B×B†	P×P ∞	P×B	B–K3 (o)
10	P×B	Q×B		P–KB3	
	Q–R5† (c)	N–Q5 (g)		B×N (j)	

(a) The Wilkes Barre (or Traxler) Variation. If 4 . . . N×P? 5 B×P†, K–K2; 6 P–Q4, P–KR3 (6 . . . P–Q4; 7 N–QB3, N×QN; 8 P×N, Q–Q3; 9 P–QR4, K–Q1; 10 B–N8!); 7 N×N, K×B; 8 P–Q5, N–K2; 9 Q–R4†, P–N3; 10 Q×KP + .

(b) 5 . . . B×P? 6 N×BP, seems analogous to col. 17(e)(A), but for the superior alternative here of 11 Q–Q3! ± , instead of 11 Q–R5.

(c) 11 P–N3, Q–R6 + . In 1954, Ken Williams suggested 10 . . . N–N5.

(d) 5 B×P†, K–K2; 6 B–N3, R–B1; 7 O–O, P–Q3; 8 N–B3, Q–K1; 9 N–Q5†, K–Q1; 10 P–QB3, P–KR3; 11 P–Q4, P×P; 12 P–K5! ± . Also 6 B–Q5, R–B1; 7 N–KB3 is good.

(e) Another course is 6 K×B, N×P†! (A) 7 K–N1, Q–R5; 8 P–KN3 (stronger than 8 Q–B1? as in Perrins–Wilkes-Barre Chess Club, corr. 1930), N×NP; (1) 9 N×R, P–Q4; 10 Q–B3, Q–Q5†; 11 K–N2, N–B4; 12 P–B3, Q×B = . (2) 9 P×N, Q×P†; 10 K–B1, R–B1; 11 Q–R5, P–Q4; 12 B×P, N–N5; 13 B–B4, P–QN4! Rohlíček. (B) 7 K–K3, Q–R5 (7 . . . Q–R2; 8 P–B3, Q–B4†; 9 P–Q4, P×P†; 10 P×P, Q–K2; 11 K–Q3 ± . Estrin); (1) 8 P–KN3, N×NP; 9 P×N, Q–Q5†; 10 K–B3, P–Q4; 11 R–R4, P–K5†; 12 K–N2, R–B1 (12 . . . O–O; 13 Q–R5! B–K3; 14 B–N3! R×N; 15 Q×P†, K–B1; 16 R–B4 ± . Evans); 13 Q–R5, R×N = . R.C. Whitney. (2) 8 Q–B3, N–N4; 9 N×N, Q×N†; 10 K–Q3, P–Q4; 11 B×P, B–B4†! 12 K–B3, N–Q5 ∓ . Rohlíček.

(f) 8 . . . N–Q5; (A) 9 P–KR3? B–N6! 10 P–B3, N–B4; 11 Q–R4† (11 P–Q4, B–Q2; 12 B–KN5, Q–B1 +), B–Q2; 12 B–N5, Q–B4; 13 B×B†, N×B + + . (B) 9 P–Q6, P×P; 10 P–B3, B–N5; 11 Q–R4†, K–B1! 12 P×N, P×P! 13 K×B, N–K5† = . Grebenshikov-Grigoryev, corr. 1964. For extensive analysis of the Wilkes Barre see *Bibliography* under "Williams."

(g) (A) 11 Q×B, O–O–O!; 12 N–R3, R–B1; 13 K–K1, N–K5; 14 Q–K3, Q–R5†; 15 P–KN3, N×NP! 16 Resigns. Braun (DDR)–Walter (USA), corr. 1969–70. (B) Williams prefers 11 Q–Q1! In the column, if 8 B–K2, B–N3! 9 P–Q3, Q–B4! = . Keres) or 9 P×P (Williams).

(h) 4 N–B3, B–QN5; 5 O–O, O–O; 6 P–Q3, B×N; 7 P×B, P–Q4; 8 P×P, N×P; 9 P–KR3, N×P; 10 Q–Q2, N–Q4 = . See also note (a) (D) on page 94.

(i) 5 . . . P×P; leads into the Max Lange Attack. The column is Freiman-Bernstein, Wilna 1912.

(j) 11 Q×B, P–QB4; 12 Q–R4, P–Q5 = . *Informator* 5. 8 O–O is playable.

(k) (A) 5 N–N5, P–Q4; 6 P×P, Q–K2†; 7 K–B1, N–K4; 8 Q×P, N×B; 9 Q×N, P–KR3∞. (B) 5 N×P, N×P; 6 B×P†, K×B; 7 Q–R5†, P–N3; 8 Q–Q5†, K–N2; 9 N×N, NP×N; 10 Q×N, Q–K1! 11 Q×Q, B–N5† = .

(l) 5 . . . P–Q3; 6 N×P, B–K2; 7 N–QB3, O–O; 8 P–QN3, R–K1; 9 B–N2, B–B1; 10 R–K1, B–Q2; 11 Q–Q2, N–K4; 12 B–KB1, P–KN3; 13 P–KR3, B–N2; 14 QR–Q1, N–B3; 15 N–B3 ± . Corden-Smyslov, Hastings 1969–70.

(m) 7 N–B3, P × N (or 7 . . . P × B; 8 R × N†, B–K2; 9 N × P, P–B4; 10 R–B4, O–O; 11 N × N, Q × Q†; 12 N × Q, P × N; 13 R × QBP, B–Q3 =); 8 B × P, B–K3; 9 B × N, Q × Q; 10 R × Q, P × P; 11 B × P, P–B3; 12 R–K1, K–B2; 13 N–Q4, N × N = . 7 N–B3 is the Canal Variation.

(n) Two other substantial choices are (A) 8 . . . Q–KR4; 9 N × N, B–K3; 10 B–N5, B–QN5; 11 N × P, Q × Q; 12 KR × Q, N × N = ; Karaklajić-Blatny, Yugoslavia 1967; and (B) 8 . . . Q–Q1; 9 R × N†, B–K2; 10 N × P, P–B4; 11 B–R6, P × R; 12 B × P, N × N; 13 Q–R5†, K–Q2; 14 R–Q1, B–B3; 15 Q–Q5†, with a perpetual at best.

(o) The possible follow-up is (A) 10 QN–N5, O–O–O; 11 N × B, P × N; 12 R × P, B–Q3; (1) 13 B–N5, QR–B1; 14 B–R4, Q–R4 = . (2) 13 Q–K2, Q–R4; 14 P–KR3, QR–K1; 15 B–Q2, N–K4! = . (B) 10 B–N5, P–KR3; 11 B–R4, B–QN5!; 12 R–K2, P–KN4; 13 P–QR3, B–K2 = . (C) 10 B–Q2, Q–Q4; 11 B–N5, B–K2; 12 B × B, K × B; 13 P–B4, P × P e.p.; 14 Q–B2! KR–Q1! ∞. Keres.

1 P–K4, P–K4; 2 N–KB3, N–QB3; 3 B–B4, N–B3; 4 P–Q4 (*a*), P×P; 5 O–O, B–B4; 6 P–K5

	21	22	23	24	25
	N–KN5		P–Q4!		
7	B–B4	R–K1 (*d*)	P×N (*f*)		
	P–Q3 (*b*)	P–Q6!	P×B		
8	P×P	B×P†	P×P	R–K1†	
	B×P	K–B1!	R–KN1	K–B1	B–K3
9	R–K1†	Q×P	B–N5	B–N5	N–N5
	K–B1	B×P†	B–K2	P×P	Q–Q4
10	B×B†	K–B1	B×B	B–R6†	N–QB3
	Q×B	B×R	K×B	K–N1	Q–B4
11	P–B3†	Q–B5!	R–K1†	N–B3	QN–K4
	Q–B4	N–B3!	B–K3	B–B1	O–O–O!
12	N×P! (*c*)	P×N	R–K4	B×B	KN×B
	N×N	Q×P	P–Q6	K×B	P×N
13	Q×N	Q×Q	N–B3	N–K4	P–KN4
	Q×Q =	P×Q (*e*)	R×P =		Q–K4 (*g*)

(*a*) (A) 4 P–Q3, B–B4 (also 4 . . . B–K2; 5 B–N3, O–O etc., see Hungarian Defence); or (B) 4 O–O, B–B4; or (C) 4 N–B3, B–B4; see Giuoco Piano, or 4 . . . N×P! 5 N×N, P–Q4 = . (D) Upon White's attempt to reach the Max Lange via 4 O–O, B–B4; 5 P–Q4, P×P; 6 P–K5, Black can spoil the plan by 5 . . . B×P! 6 N×B, N×N; 7 P–B4, P–Q3; 8 P×P, P×P; 9 B–KN5, Q–K2 ∓ . See also note (*h*) to col. 18.

(*b*) Insufficient is 7 . . . O–O; 8 P–KR3, N–R3; 9 B×N, P×B; 10 P–B3, P–Q4; 11 B–N3, P×P; 12 N×P, P–Q5; 13 N–Q5 ± .

(*c*) 12 N/1–Q2, P–Q6; 13 N–Q4, N×N; 14 P×N, Q×P; 15 Q–B3, Q–B3; 16 Q–Q5, B–K3 = . Estrin.

(*d*) 7 B×P†, K×B; 8 N–N5†, K–N1; 9 Q×N, P–Q4 + .

(*e*) Gavrilov-Perfilyev, corr. 1951. Black is on thin ice but gets home after (A) 14 B–N3, B–N5; 15 B–R6†, K–K2; 16 B–N7, R–K1; 17 P–B3, B–B4; 18 QN–Q2, P–Q3; 19 R–K1†, N–K4. Or (B) 14 B–QB4, B–N5; 15 B–R6†, K–K2; 16 P–B3, B–B4; 17 QN–Q2, P–Q3; 18 R–K1†, N–K4; 19 B–N7, B–B4!

(*f*) 7 B–QN5, N–K5; 8 N×P, O–O! 9 N×N, P×N; 10 B×P, B–R3! 11 Q×P (11 B×R, B×R; 12 Q×P, B–B5!), 11 . . . B×R; 12 Q×N, B–N4! *Comments.*

(*g*) (A) 14 P×P, KR–N1; 15 B–R6, P–Q6; 16 P–B3, P–Q7; 17 R–K2, R–Q6! = . Leibold. (B) 14 B–N5 (1) 14 . . . B–N5; 15 P–B4! Q–R4; 16 P×P, KR–N1; 17 B×R, N×B; 18 Q×P! Q–N3; 19 Q×Q, BP×Q; 20 P–B3, B–K2; 21 P–B5! P×P; 22 P×P, R×P†; 23 K–R1, B–B1; 24 QR–Q1. Black resigned. Murei-Azaritis, corr. 1966. (2) 14 . . . P–KR3; 15 N×B (15 P×P, P×B; 16 P×R(Q), R×Q; 17 N–N3, Q–Q3!), Q×N; 16 P×P, P×B; 17 P×R(Q), R×Q; 18 R×P ± . Cafferty-Sombor, Bognor Regis 1965. (3) 14 . . . P–KN3; 15 P–B7, B–K2; 16 P–B4, Q–N2; 16 B×B, N×B; 17 N–N5, P–Q6; 18 N×KP, Q×BP; 19 N×R, R×N, with mobility for the exchange.

Four Knights' Game

(1 P–K4, P–K4; 2 N–KB3, N–QB3;
3 N–B3 or 1 P–K4, P–K4; 2 N–QB3,
N–QB3; 3 N–B3)

Tarrasch and Maróczy used to play the Four Knights' with every expectation of winning. But that was long ago! Nowadays the opening is still considered solid and sound, but somewhat conservative; yet it is used sporadically for psychological and tactical effect upon a suitable opponent, as actually applies to any choice of opening! White banks on his extra move and straight-forward development to gain a slight initiative in the middle-game. Black has the choice of copying moves and then breaking the symmetry at just the right moment, or of promptly and soundly sacrificing a pawn for fluent counterplay.

THE SYMMETRICAL VARIATION (cols. 1–9) is the oldest and best-known sequence. With 8 . . . Q–K2, the *Metger Unpin* (cols. 1–2), Black keeps the draw in hand. But other eighth moves also secure equality. *Svenonius'* line (col. 5) is no longer satisfactory, as shown by Keres. Black's bid for a Ruy Lopez in col. 10 just falls short.

THE RUBINSTEIN VARIATION (cols. 11–15) violates the principle that the same piece should not move twice in the opening. However, 4 . . . N–Q5 hits hard at the centre and throws White off balance. White can try to force a quick draw with 5 N × N (col. 14) but gets into trouble if he holds on to the pawn.

THE SCOTCH FOUR KNIGHTS' GAME 4 P–Q4 (cols. 16–20) is open to the theoretical objection that the early opening of lines resulting in wholesale exchanges is favourable to the second player and generally dissipates White's initiative. After 4 . . . P × P White may well transpose into the Scotch Game with 5 N × P instead of the dubious, though enterprising, 5 N–Q5!? (cols. 16–18). 4 . . . B–N5 (cols. 19–20) is not adequate in the line 5 . . . Q–K2 but there have been improvements for Black as shown in the notes.

95

1 P-K4, P-K4; 2 N-KB3, N-QB3; 3 N-B3, N-B3; 4 B-N5, B-N5; 5 O-O, O-O; 6 P-Q3, B × N (a); 7 P × B

	1	2	3	4	5
	P–Q3				P–Q4 (l)
8	B–N5				P × P (m)
	Q–K2		N–K2	P–KR3 (i)	Q × P
9	R–K1		B × N (g)	B–KR4	P–B4
	N–Q1 (b)		P × B	Q–K2	Q–Q3
10	P–Q4		N–R4	Q–Q2 (j)	B × N
	N–K3	B–N5	P–KB4	N–Q1	P × B
11	B–QB1	P–KR3	P–KB4	P–Q4	B–N2
	P–B4 (c)	B–R4	N–N3	B–N5	R–K1
12	P × KP (d)	P–N4	N × P	P–Q5	Q–K1
	P × P	B–N3	B × N	B × N	B–N5
13	B–QB4	P–Q5!	P × B	P × B	N × P
	R–Q1	P–B3	N × P	N × KP	N–Q2
14	B–Q5	B–KB1	P–N3	Q × P	P–B4
	N–B2	P × P	Q–N4	P × Q	P–B3
15	P–B4	P × P	Q–B3	B × Q	Q–N3 + (n)
	B–N5 (e)	Q–B2 (f)	P–QB3 (h)	N × QBP (k)	

(a) (A) 6 . . . N–K2; 7 B–N5 (7 N × P, P–Q4; 8 P × P? B × N; 9 P × B, Q × P + +), P–B3; 8 B–QB4, N–N3; 9 N–KR4 ±. Keres. (B) 6 . . . N–Q5! (1) 7 B–QB4, P–B3; 8 N × N, P × N; 9 N–K2, B–B4; 10 B–KN5, P–KR3; 11 B–R4, P–KN4 =. Duras. (2) 7 N × N, P × N; 8 N–K2, P–B3; 9 B–R4, P–Q4; 10 P–K5, N–N5; 11 P–QB3, P × P; 12 P × P ±. Perlis-Alekhin, Carlsbad 1911.

(b) 9 . . . P–QR3; 10 KB × N, P × B; 11 Q–Q2 ±. Keres. Or 11 N–Q2. Pachman. Moves 8 to 10 in the column constitute the "Metger Unpin."

(c) (A) 11 . . . P–B3; 12 B–B1, Q–B2; 13 P–N3, R–Q1; 14 B–N2, followed by N–R4 and P–KB4 ±. Not 14 N–R4, P–Q4! 15 P–KB4, N × KP ∓. (B) 11 . . . R–Q1; 12 N–R4 (12 B–B1, P–B4 =), P–KN3; 13 P–N3, P–Q4 =.

(d) (A) Keres suggests 12 P–Q5, N–B2; 13 B–Q3, P–QN4; 14 B–N5, P–KR3; 15 B–R4, B–Q2 =. (B) Upon 12 B–B1 we prefer 12 . . . N–B2! but double-edged is 12 . . . Q–B2!? 13 P–Q5! N–Q1; 14 N–R4, N–K1; 15 P–N3, Q–K2; 16 N–B5, B × N; 17 P × B, Q–B3; 18 Q–N4 ±. Petrosian-Lilienthal, Moscow 1949.

(e) 16 P–KR3, N/2 × B; 17 BP × N, B × N =. Alexander-Pachman, Dublin 1957.

(f) 16 B × N, P × B; 17 R–K3, P–N3; 18 N–R4, N–N2; 19 B–Q3, N–B4 =. Altshuler-Veltmander, corr. 1957–9.

(g) Sufficient is 9 N–R4, B–N5 (9 . . . P–B3; 10 B–QB4, P–Q4; 11 B–N3, Q–Q3; 12 P–B4! ±); 10 P–B3, B–Q2; 11 B–QB4, B–K3; 12 B–N3, B × B; 13 RP × B, N–Q2 =. Soultanbeieff-O'Kelly, 1934.

(h) 16 B–B4, P–Q4; 17 B–N3, P–B3; 18 K–R1, N–R4; 19 P–B4 ±. Debyut. In the column, 11 Q–R5 may maintain even more pressure.

(i) Safe too is 8 . . . B–Q2; 9 Q–Q2, P–KR3; 10 B–KR4, B–N5; 11 Q–K3, B × N; 12 Q × B, P–N4; 13 B–N3, K–N2 =.

(j) Keres prefers 10 R–K1.

(k) 16 B × R, K × B; 17 B–B4, P–N4; 18 B–N3, N–N2 =. Debyut. Black's Knight's pawn and better pawn-formation compensate for the exchange.

(l) The Svenonius Variation. Also playable is 7 . . . Q–K2; 8 B–QB4, P–Q3; 9 B–KN5, P–KR3; 10 B–R4, N–QR4; 11 N–Q2, N × B =. Levenfish-Alatortsev, match 1940.

(m) Or 8 B × N, P × B; 9 N × P, Q–Q3; 10 B–B4, R–K1; 11 P × P, R × N; 12 P–Q4, R–K8; 13 B × Q, R × Q; 14 KR × R, P × B; 15 P × P, B–K3; 16 QR–N1, R–QB1; 17 R–N7! with pressure. Keres.

(n) Korn-Frydman, corr. 1938.

1 P–K4, P–K4; 2 N–KB3, N–QB3; 3 N–B3, N–B3; 4 B–N5

	6	7	8	9	10
	(B–N5)				P–QR3 (i)
5	(O–O) (a)				B × N!
	(O–O)				QP × B
6	(P–Q3) (b)				N × P (j)
	P–Q3				N × P
7	B–N5			N–K2	N × N
	N–K2		B–N5	N–K2	Q–Q5
8	N–KR4	B × N	N–Q5	P–B3	O–O
	P–B3	P × B	N–Q5	B–R4	Q × N/4
9	B–QB4	N–KR4	N × B	N–N3	R–K1
	N–N3 (c)	N–N3 (e)	N × B	P–B3	B–K3
10	N × N	N × N	N–Q5	B–R4	P–Q4
	P × N	RP × N	N–Q5	N–N3	Q–KB4
11	P–B4	P–B4	Q–Q2	P–Q4	B–N5
	B–B4†	B–B4†	P–B3	R–K1	P–R3
12	K–R1	K–R1	N × N†	B–N3	Q–Q3
	B–K6 (d)	K–N2 (f)	P × N (g)	P × P (h)	Q–R2 (k)

(a) (A) 5 N–Q5, N × N; 6 P × N, P–K5; 7 P × N, QP × P ∓. (B) 5 P–Q3, N–Q5; 6 B–R4, P–QN4; 7 B–N3, P–Q4; 8 N × P, Q–K2; 9 P–B4, O–O ∓.

(b) 6 B × N (the Nimzowitsch Variation), QP × B; 7 N × P (7 P–Q3, Q–K2; 8 Q–K2, R–K1; 9 P–KR3, P–KN3; 10 Q–K3, N–R4; 11 N–K2, B–QB4; 12 Q–R6, P–B4 ∓. Capablanca-Jaffe, New York 1913), B × N; 8 QP × B, N × P; 9 Q–B3, N–Q3; 10 B–K3, Q–R5; 11 Q–B4, Q–R4; 17 KR–K1, Q–B4 = . *Debyut*.

(c) Also 9 . . . P–Q4; 10 B–N3, Q–Q3; 11 Q–B3 (Keres), B–N5; 12 Q–N3, B–Q2; 13 N–B3, N–N3; 14 B × N, Q × B; 15 P × P, B × N; 16 P × B, P × P; 17 KR–K1, P–K5; 18 N–Q4, B–B3 ∞. *Comments.*

(d) 13 Q–B3, B × P; 14 B × B, P × B; 15 Q × P, Q–K2; 16 Q–N3, B–K3 = .

(e) Or 9 . . . P–B3; 10 B–B4, P–KB4 = . Plater-O'Kelly, Hilversum 1947.

(f) 13 P–B5, P × P; 14 P × P, R–R1 = .

(g) 13 B–R4, B × N; 14 Q–R6, N–K7†; 15 K–R1, B × P†; 16 K × B, N–B5†; 17 K–R1, N–N3; 18 R–KN1, R–K1; 19 . . . R–K3; and 20 . . . Q–B1 = .

(h) 13 P × P, B–K3; 14 N–N5, B × B; 15 Q × B, Q–Q2; 16 P–B3, P–KR3; 17 N–R3, B–N3 = .

(i) The text endeavours to reach a Ruy Lopez where White's Queen's Knight is misplaced. A less desirable alternative is 4 . . . B–B4; 5 O–O, O–O (5 . . . P–Q3; 6 P–Q4, P × P; 7 N × P, B–Q2; 8 N–B5! ±); 6 N × P, N × N (6 . . . R–K1; 7 N–B3, N × P); 7 P–Q4, B–Q3 (7 . . . B–N5; 8 P × N, B × N; 9 P × B, N × P; 10 Q–Q4 ±. Najdorf-Pilnik, New York 1948); 8 P–B4, N–B3; 9 P–K5, B–N5; 10 P–Q5! P–QR3 (10 . . . B × N; 11 P × B, N–K5; 12 Q–K1!); 11 B–K2, B–B4†; 12 K–R1, N × QP; Shaposhnikov-Borisenko, corr. 1956; 13 Q × N ±.

(j) For 6 P–Q4, P × P; 7 Q × P, Q × Q; 8 N × Q see Ruy Lopez, Exchange Variation.

(k) 13 B–R4, B–Q3; 14 R–K3, B–KB5; 15 Q–R3, B–N4; 16 N × B, P × N; 17 B–N3, O–O–O; 18 Q–R5, R–Q2; 19 R–QB1 ±. Belavenets in *Debyut*. White threatens 20 P–QB4 and 21 P–Q5. In the column, not 12 . . . P × B?? 13 N–Q6†.

1 P–K4, P–K4; 2 N–KB3, N–QB3; 3 N–B3; N–B3; 4 B–N5, N–Q5

	11	12	13	14	15
5	N×P	B–R4		N×N	B–B4 (*j*)
	Q–K2	B–B4 (*c*)		P×N	B–B4
6	P–B4	N×P (*d*)		P–K5	N×P
	N×B	O–O		P×N	Q–K2
7	N×N	N–Q3		P×N	N–B3
	P–Q3	B–N3		Q×P	P–Q4
8	N–KB3	P–K5	O–O (*f*)	QP×P	N×P
	Q×P†	N–K1	P–Q4	Q–K4†	Q×P†
9	K–B2	O–O	N×P	Q–K2	N–K3
	N–N5†	P–Q3	N×N	Q×Q†	B–KN5
10	K–N1	P×P	P×N	K×Q	B–K2
	Q–B3	N–B3	Q–R5 (*g*)	P–QB3	N×B
11	QN–Q4 (*a*)	P–Q7	K–R1 (*h*)	B–Q3	Q×N
	Q–B4 (*b*)	B×P (*e*)		P–Q4 (*i*)	O–O–O (*k*)

(*a*) 11 Q–K2†, B–K2; 12 P–KR3, Q–N3†; 13 P–Q4, N–B3; 14 K–R2, B–Q2 ∓.

(*b*) 12 P–KR3, N–KB3; 13 K–R2, B–K3; 14 R–K1, O–O–O; 15 N×B, with strong pressure for the exchange. Bisguier-Soltis, Speed Tourn., New York, 1971.

(*c*) Alternatives are (A) 5 . . . N×N†; 6 Q×N, P–B3; 7 P–Q3, P–Q3; 8 O–O, B–K2; 9 N–Q5! ± . (B) 5 . . . P–B3; 6 O–O (or 6 N×P, P–Q4; 7 O–O, B–Q3; 8 P–B4, O–O =), P–QN4!; 7 B–N3, P–QR4; 8 N×P, Q–K2; 9 N–Q3; P–R5; 10 P–K5!, P×B!; 11 P×N, Q×P; 12 BP×P, B–K2 = .

(*d*) 6 O–O, O–O; 7 P–Q3, P–Q3; 8 N×N, B×N; 9 B–KN5, P–B3; 10 Q–Q2, P–KR3 = . Bagirov-Shamkovich, USSR Chp. 1961.

(*e*) 12 B×B, Q×B; 13 N–K1, QR–K1; 14 P–Q3, N–N5; 15 P–KR3, P–KB4! with a sharp position. If 16 P×N, P×P; threatening 17 . . . N–B6†. Keres.

(*f*) 8 N–B4, P–Q4; 9 P–Q3, B–N5; 10 P–B3, N–R4; 11 N×N! B×N; 12 N×P, P–QB3! 13 N×B, P×N; 14 B–N3, Q–R5†; 15 K–B1, N×B; 16 BP×N, P–KB4. Keres.

(*g*) Ravinski recommends 10 . . . Q×P; 11 N–B4 (if 11 P–QB3, Q–K5!), Q–N4; 12 P–Q3, B–N5; 13 N–Q5, Q–R4; 14 N–K7†, K–R1; 15 Q–Q2, B–QB4 = .

(*h*) (A) 11 . . . B–KB4; N–K5; P–KB3: 13 N–B3, N×N; 14 Q×N, Q–QB5; 15 R–K1, B×QBP with equality, Ravinski; however, (1) 16 B×B, Q×B; 17 Q–B3 ± . *Comments.* Not (2) 16 B–Q7, Q–Q5; 17 K–N1, P–KB4 ∓. No better are (B) 11 . . . B–N5; 12 P–KB3, B×P; 13 P×B, N–B4; 14 P–N4! (C) 11 . . . P–QB3?! 12 P–KN3, Q–K5†; 13 P–B3, Q×QP; 14 N–B4, Q–Q3; 15 P–B3, N–B4; 16 P–Q4 ± . Gordeyev-Cherpanov, Leningrad 1964.

(*i*) 12 B–KB4, B–N5†; 13 P–B3, B–K3; 14 K–B2, O–O; 15 KR–K1, B–B4†; B–K3, P–Q5; 17 P×P, B×QP, drawn. Kholmov-Keres, USSR Chp. 1961.

(*j*) (A) 5 B–K2, N×N†; 6 B×N, B–B4; 7 P–Q3, O–O; 8 B–N5, P–B3; 9 Q–Q2, P–QR4; 10 O–O, P–Q3 = . Aronin-Korelov, USSR Chp. 1963. (B) 5 O–O, N×B; 6 N×N, P–B3; 7 N–B3, P–Q3; 8 P–Q4, Q–B2; 9 P–KR3, P–QN4! 10 P–R3, P–QR3 = .

(*k*) 12 P–Q3, Q–K3 with compensation for the pawn. Krause.

1 P-K4, P-K4; 2 N-KB3, N-QB3; 3 N-B3, N-B3; 4 P-Q4 (*a*)

	16	17	18	19	20
	P×P			B-N5	
5	N-Q5!? (*b*)		N×P	N×P	P-Q5 (*l*)
	N×P	B-K2 (*f*)	B-N5	N×KP (*j*)	N-K2
6	Q-K2 (*c*)	B-QN5 (*g*)	N×N	Q-N4	N×P
	P-B4	P-Q3	NP×N	N×QN	P-Q3! (*m*)
7	N-N5 (*d*)	N×P	B-Q3	Q×P	B-N5†
	P-Q6!	B-Q2	P-Q4	R-B1	K-B1 (*n*)
8	P×P	O-O	P×P!	P-QR3	N-B3
	N-Q5	KN×N	Q-K2†	B-R4	N×KP
9	Q-R5†	P×N	Q-K2	N×N	Q-Q4
	P-N3	N×N	N×P	QP×N	N×N
10	Q-R4	B×B†	Q×Q†	Q-K5†	P×N
	P-B3!	Q×B	K×Q	Q-K2	B-QB4
11	P×N	Q×N	P-QR3	Q×Q†	Q-KR4
	P×N (*e*)	O-O = (*h*)	B-R4 (*i*)	K×Q (*k*)	B-Q2 ∓

(*a*) Also see Scotch Game, cols. 8–10. Alternatives are: (A) 4 P-QR3, P-Q4! (B) 4 B-B4, B-B4 see Giuoco Piano. (C) 4 B-K2, B-N5; 5 N-Q5, B-K2; 6 P-Q3, P-Q3; 7 N×B, Q×N; 8 O-O, O-O = . Blackburne-Tarrasch, Ostend 1905.

(*b*) Trajković "Belgrade Gambit." 5 N×P transposes into the Scotch Game.

(*c*) (A) 6 B-QB4, N-B4; 7 B-KN5! P-B3; 8 N-R4, P-KR4; 9 N-KN6, R-R2; 10 Q-B3! is a new revival. Trajković-Henriksen, corr. 1966-7. Also (B) 6 B-KB4, P-Q3; 7 Q-K2.

(*d*) 7 B-KB4, P-Q3; 8 O-O-O, B-K3! 9 N×QP, N×N; 10 R×N, P-QB3!

(*e*) 12 P×QP, (A) 12 . . . Q-R4†; (1) 13 K-Q1, Q×QP! 14 B-QB4, Q×B; 15 R-K1†, B-K2; 16 R×B†, K×R; 17 N-K4†, K-K3; 18 Q-B6†, K-Q4; 19 N-B3†, K-B4; 20 P-N4†, K×P; 21 Q-Q6†, K-R4; 22 Q-R3†, K-N3; 23 Q-Q6†, K-R4; drawn. Varady-Larsson, corr. 1961. (2) 13 B-Q2, Q-R5! 14 Q-N3! N-B7†; 15 K-Q1, N-K6††; 16 K-K2, P-B5; 17 Q-B3, Q-B5†; 18 K-K1, N×B; 19 R×N, B-N5; 20 Q-K4† ± . Keres. (B) 12 . . . B-N2! 13 Q-N3, O-O = .

(*f*) 5 . . . N×N; 6 P×N, N-N5?! 7 N×P (7 B-QB4, Q-K2†; 8 K-Q2, P-KN3!∞), N×QP; 8 N-B5, N-K2; 9 B-KN5, P-KB3; 10 B×P, P×B; 11 Q-R5†, N-N3; 12 O-O-O, P-Q3; 13 N-R4, B-N2; 14 B-B4, Q-Q2! = . Bellon.

(*g*) 6 B-KB4, P-Q3; 7 N×P, O-O = .

(*h*) Šefc-Szabó. Trenčanské Teplice 1949.

(*i*) 12 P-QN4 ± , *Informator* 5. In the column, if 8 . . . P×P; 9 O-O, O-O; 10 B-N5.

(*j*) (A) 5 . . . O-O is a double-edged experiment of Zaitsev's. (B) 5 . . . Q-K2; 6 Q-Q3, N×N; 7 P×N, Q×P; 8 B-Q2, O-O; 9 O-O-O, P-Q3 (if 9 . . . B×N; 10 B×B, Q-B5†; 11 R-Q2! ±); 10 P-B3, B-Q2; 11 P-N4, B-B3; 12 N-Q5 ± Kažić-Samarian, corr. 1961-4.

(*k*) 12 B-Q2, B-B4; 13 B×N, B×B†; 14 P×B, B×P; 15 K-Q2, B-N3 = . Bogolyubov.

(*l*) 5 P×P, KN×P; 6 Q-Q3, P-Q4; 7 P-QR3, B×N†; 8 P×B, B-B4 ∓.

(*m*) *Informator* 4 touches on 6 . . . O-O; 7 B-Q3, N/2×P; 8 P×N, R-K1; 9 O-O, R×N; 10 P-Q6, B×P; 11 N-N5, B-B1; 12 B-KB4, R-QB4 = .

(*n*) 7 . . . P-B3; 8 P×P, O-O; 9 N-Q7! Persitz. The column is Euwe.

Three Knights' Game

(1 P–K4, P–K4; 2 N–KB3, N–QB3;
3 N–B3 or 1 P–K4, P–K4; 2 N–QB3,
N–QB3; 3 N–B3)

This opening is an attempt by Black to avoid the equalizing but dull possibilities of the Four Knights' Game after 3 . . . N–B3. There are two main lines, other alternatives on Black's third move being considered in note *(i)*, at Black's disposal, i.e.:

(a) 3 . . . B–N5, advantageously met by 4 N–Q5 (cols. 1–2). White's edge is small but undeniable in all variations.

(b) 3 . . . P–KN3, an old Steinitz pet frequently adopted by Alekhin and Keres. After 4 P–Q4, P × P; 5 N–Q5! (cols. 3–4) secures the initiative, whereas 5 N × P (col. 5) simmers into equality.

1 P–K4, P–K4; 2 N–KB3, N–QB3; 3 N–B3

	1	2	3	4	5
	B–N5		P–KN3 (i)		
4	N–Q5 (a)		P–Q4		
	N–B3 (b)		P × P		
5	N × B	B–B4	N–Q5!		N × P
	N × N	O–O (f)	B–N2		B–N2
6	N × P (c)	P–B3	B–KN5		B–K3
	Q–K2 (d)	B–K2	QN–K2		N–B3 (o)
7	P–Q4	N × N† (g)	N × P	B–QB4 (m)	P–B3 (p)
	P–Q3	B × N	P–QB3 (j)	P–QB3	O–O
8	P–QR3	P–Q3	N–QB3 (k)	N × N	B–QB4
	P × N	P–Q3	P–KR3	N × N	P–Q3
9	P × N	P–KR3	B–KB4 (l)	O–O	Q–Q2
	N × P (e)	P–KR3 (h)		O–O (n)	N × N =

(a) (A) 4 B–N5, N–B3, leads into the Four Knights' Game. (B) 4 P–QR3(?) B × N; 5 QP × B (better is NP × B), P–Q3; 6 B–QB4, N–B3; 7 Q–Q3, B–K3; 8 P–R3, P–QR3 = . Flohr-Alekhin, Prague 1931.

(b) (A) 4 . . . B–K2; 5 P–Q4, P × P; 6 N × P, N × N; 7 Q × N, N–B3; 8 N × B, Q × N; 9 B–Q3, P–B4; 10 Q–K3, P–Q4; 11 P × P, N × P; 12 Q × Q† ± . Alekhin-Tartakover, New York 1924. (B) 4 . . . B–R4; 5 P–B3, N–B3; 6 P–QN4 and 7 Q–R4 ± .

(c) Weaker alternatives are: (A) 6 P–B3, N–B3; 7 P–Q4, P × P; 8 P–K5, N–K5; 9 P × P, P–Q4. (B) 6 P–Q4, P–Q4! 7 N × P, P × P; 8 P–QB3, QN–Q4. (C) 6 B–B4, P–Q4! 7 P × P, P–K5; 8 N–K5, O–O; 9 O–O, B–B4.

(d) 6 . . . P–Q3; 7 N–B3 (7 N–Q3, N–B3), N × P; 8 P–B3, N–QB3; 9 P–Q3, N–B3; 10 P–Q4 ± . Tartakover.

(e) 10 P × P, Q × P; 11 Q–K2, Q–K3; 12 P–KB3 ± . Fine.

(f) 5 . . . N × P; 6 O–O, N–B3; 6 P–Q4 see Four Knights' Game.

(g) 7 N × B†, Q × N; 8 O–O, P–Q3; 8 Q–K2, N–QR4; 10 B–Q3, N–R4!

(h) 10 O–O, B–Q2; 11 B–N3, N–K2 = . Maróczy-Grünfeld, Vienna 1920.

(i) (A) 3 . . . N–B3 see Four Knights' Game. (B) 3 . . . P–B4!? 4 P–Q4, P × KP; 5 KN × P, N–B3; 6 B–QB4, P–Q4; 7 N × QP! N × N; 8 Q–R5†, P–N3; 9 N × P, P × N; 10 Q × P†, K–Q2; 11 B × N, with strong attack. Balla-Breyer, Pistyan 1912. (C) 3 . . . B–B4; 4 N × P! N × N; 5 P–Q4, B–Q3; 6 P × N, B × P; 7 P–B4! B × N†; 8 P × B, P–Q3; 9 Q–Q4 ± . Comments.

(j) 7 . . . P–KR3; 8 B–K3, N × N; 9 P × N, N–B3; 10 P–QB4 (B–QB4!), O–O; 11 B–K2, P–QB3 = . Clemens-Darga, Bad Pyrmont 1961.

(k) Simple and good is 8 N × N, N × N; 9 Q–Q2. (A) 9 . . . P–Q4; 10 O–O–O, P × P; 11 Q–K3, Q–R4; 12 B × N, K × B; 13 N–N5! + . Fichtl-Udovčić, Berlin 1962. (B) 9 . . . P–KR3; 10 B–R4, P–Q4; 11 O–O–O (11 P × P, Q × P =), P–KN4; 12 B–N3, P × P; 13 Q–K3, Q–N3; 14 B–Q6 ∞. Szmetan.

(l) 9 B–R4, P–Q4; 10 P × P, Q–N3; 11 N–N3, Q–N5. Or 10 Q–Q2, P × P; 11 O–O–O, P–KN4; 12 B–N3, N–B4 = . Keres. The column is Lehmann-Keres, Hamburg 1960, which continued: 9 . . . P–Q4; 10 Q–Q2, N–B3; 11 O–O–O, N × P; 12 N × N, P × N; 13 B–B4, N–B4; 14 N–N3, Q × Q†; 15 N × Q = .

(m) 7 P–K5, P–KR3; 8 B × N, N × B; 9 Q × P, N × N; 10 Q × N, P–Q3!; 11 O–O–O, O–O! with good counterplay. Keres.

(n) 10 N × P, P–KR3; 11 B–R4, P–KN4; 12 B–KN3, P–Q4; 13 P × P, N × P; 14 P–QB3, Q–B3; 15 B × N, P × B (Honfi-Radović, Kecskemét 1962); 16 R–K1 ± .

(o) 6 . . . P–Q3; 7 Q–Q2, N–B3; 8 O–O–O (or 8 B–QN5), N–KN5; 9 N × N, P × N; 10 B–Q4, B × B; 11 Q × B, Q–B3 = . Bellon-Karpov, Las Palmas 1977.

(p) No better are: (A) 7 B–QB4, O–O; 8 N × N, NP × N; 9 P–K5, N–K1; 10 P–K6, BP × P; 11 B × P†, K–R1 ∓. Prameshuber-Keres, Munich Olympics 1958. (B) 7 B–K2, O–O; 8 O–O, R–K1; 9 N × N, NP × N = . Bagirov-Keres, USSR 1963. (C) 7 N × N, NP × N; 8 P–K5, N–N1; 9 P–B4, P–Q3 (or P–B3) = .

Vienna Game

(1 P–K4, P–K4; 2 N–QB3)

The Vienna is an introverted brother of the King's Gambit, into which it may transpose at several points. It is played with a view to a quick attack; but Black has a number of good equalizing defences and frequently gets an advantage. "The strength of this move (2 N–QB3)—paradoxically—is that it threatens nothing," writes Tartakover. And Weaver Adams, whose name might well be affixed to it because he has based his "White to Play and Win" system on it, writes that "2 N–QB3 conforms most to principles, develops naturally, prepares P–KB4, prevents . . . P–Q4, keeps the Q1–R5 diagonal open, and fortifies the king's pawn." But the "strength" of 2 N–QB3 is also its weakness—it lacks impetus.

    2 . . . N–KB3 (cols. 1–9) is the most forceful defence. After 3 B–B4, N × P! is logical and aggressive. Black's sacrifice of the exchange in col. 2 has never been exhaustively analysed, but his compensation is so obvious that the White side has virtually been abandoned, finally even by Adams who later advocated the equally dubious line in note (b).

    3 P–B4 (cols. 6–9) was one of Spielmann's favourites. With 3 . . . P–Q4 Black assures himself of at least an even game.

    3 P–KN3 (note (a)) leads to a positional struggle, favoured by Smyslov.

    Alternatives on Black's second move are considered in cols. 10–15. 2 . . . B–B4 allows White a slight edge. The Vienna Gambit after 2 . . . N–QB3 (cols. 12–15) is spectacular but speculative. Many of these lines provide an analytical feast, but anticipated revivals never seem to materialize. The Steinitz Gambit (col. 15) is definitely "out."

1 P–K4, P–K4; 2 N–QB3, N–KB3; 3 B–B4

	1	2	3	4	5
	N×P			N–B3	
4	Q–R5			P–Q3 (h)	
	N–Q3			B–N5 (i)	
5	Q×KP†	B–N3		B–KN5	B–Q2 (j)
	Q–K2	N–B3	B–K2	P–KR3	P–Q3
6	Q×Q†	N–N5 (b)	N–B3 (f)	B×N	N–Q5
	B×Q	P–KN3	N–B3	B×N†	B×B†
7	B–N3	Q–B3	N×P	P×B	Q×B
	N–B4	P–B4 (c)	O–O!	Q×B	O–O
8	N–B3	Q–Q5	N–Q5	N–K2	N–K2
	P–QB3	Q–K2 (d)	N–Q5	P–Q3	N×N
9	O–O	N×P†	O–O	O–O	B×N
	P–Q4	K–Q1	N×B	P–KN4	N–K2 =
10	R–K1	N×R	RP×N	P–Q4	
	O–O (a)	P–N3 (e)	N–K1 (g)	N–K2 =	

(a) Sämisch-Rubinstein, Hanover 1926. If 11 P–Q4, B–B3; 12 N–K2, B–K3 = . For 4 N–B3 see Petrov's Defence, col. 10. Also 8 N–Q5 is quite playable.

(b) Finally ineffective is Adams' Gambit 6 P–Q4!? N×P! 7 N–Q5, N–K3; 8 Q×KP, P–QB3! 9 N–B4, Q–K2; 10 N–B3, N–QB4; 11 O–O, Q×Q; 12 N×Q, B–K2; 13 R–K1, N–K3 + .

(c) 7 . . . N–B4; 8 P–KN4! P–K5 (8 . . . N–R3; 9 P–N5, N–B4; 10 Q–Q5); 9 Q–B4! B–Q3; 10 Q×P†, Q–K2; 11 Q×Q†, KN×Q; 12 N×P† + .

(d) Involved is 8 . . . Q–B3; 9 N×P†, K–Q1; 10 N×R, P–N3; 11 Q–B3, B–QN2; 12 P–KR4, N–Q5; 13 Q–R3 = . Vyakhirev-Verlinski, St. Petersburg 1909.

(e) (A) 11 P–Q3, B–QN2; 12 P–KR4, P–B5! 13 Q–B3, N–Q5; 14 Q–N4! B–KR3; 15 N–R3, N/3–B4; 16 N–N5, B × KN; 17 P × B, P–B6; 18 P–N3, P–K5 = . Nielsen-Altshuler, corr. 1966. (B) 11 N–B3, B–QN2; 12 P–Q4, N × P; 13 B–N5, N × N†; 14 Q × N, Q × B; 15 B–Q5, B–QR3! (15 . . . P–K5; 16 Q–QN3, B–QR3; 17 Q–R4! B–N4; 18 Q–Q4, N–K1; 19 N × P, B–KR3; 20 B–B4, Q × P; 21 R–KB1, B–B3; 22 N × P +); 16 R–Q1 (16 Q–B3, N–N4; 17 Q–B4, B–B4; 18 O–O, N–B2; 19 Q–N3, B × R; 20 R × B, Q–Q7 ∓), 16 . . . Q–B5! 17 Q × Q, P × Q; 18 R–Q4, K–B1; 19 R–R4, B–QN2; 20 R × RP, B × B; 21 N × P†, K–N1; 22 R–R4, B × NP; 23 R–N1, B–B3; 24 R–QN4, K–B2; 25 R–QN3, N–K5; 26 N–B4, B–Q4, White resigns. Koch-Šefc, Prague 1958.

(f) 6 Q × KP, O–O; 7 P–Q4, N–B3! 8 Q–B4, P–QN4! 9 N–B3, B–N2; 10 B–K3, N–R4; 11 O–O–O, P–N5; 12 N–K2, N/3–B5 ∞. Adams.

(g) 11 P–Q4, P–Q3; 12 N–KB3, B–K3 = . Alekhin.

(h) (A) 4 P–B4, N × P; 5 N–B3, N–Q3; (1) 6 B–N3, P–K5; 7 N–KN5, P–KR3; 8 KN × KP, N × N; 9 Q–K2, N–Q5; 10 Q × N†, Q–K2 = . (2) 6 B–Q5! P–K5; 7 N–K5, Q–R5†; 8 P–N3, Q–R6 = . (B) 4 KN–K2, N × P! = .

(i) (A) 4 . . . B–B4; 5 P–B4, P–Q3, see King's Gambit Declined. (B) 4 . . . N–QR4; (1) 5 Q–B3, N × B; 6 P × N, B–N5; 7 N–K2, P–Q3; 8 P–KR3, B–K3 = . Adams-Pinkus, New York 1944. (2) 5 B–N3, N × B; 6 RP × N, P–Q4; 7 P × P, B–QN5; 8 N–B3, N × P = . (3) 5 KN–K2! N × B; 6 P × N, B–K2; 7 O–O, P–Q3; 8 P–QN3, O–O = . Larsen-Portisch, Porech 1968.

(j) (A) 5 N–K2, P–Q4; 6 P × P, N × P; 7 B × N, Q × B; 8 O–O, Q–R4; 9 P–QR3, O–O; 10 B–K3, B × N; 11 N × B, N–Q5 = . Spielmann-Réti, Dortmund 1928. (B) 5 N–KB3, P–Q3; 6 O–O, B × N; 7 P × B, N–QR4; 8 B–N3, N × B; 9 RP × N! O–O; 10 P–B4, P–QN3 = . Larsen-Gligorić, Amsterdam 1964. The column is Santa Cruz-Wade, Havana 1964.

1 P-K4, P-K4; 2 N-QB3

	6	7	8	9	10
	(N-KB3)	. . . .			B-B4
3	P-B4 (a)				N-B3!
	P-Q4				P-Q3 (k)
4	P×KP	. . . .		P-Q3 (i)	P-Q4!
	N×P			P×BP	P×P
5	N-B3	P-Q3!	Q-B3	B×P!	N×P
	B-K2	Q-R5† (d)	P-KB4 (g)	B-QN5	N-KB3
6	P-Q4 (b)	P-N3	P-Q3	P×P	B-N5
	O-O	N×P	N×N	N×P	P-KR3
7	B-Q3	N-B3	P×N	B-Q2	B-R4
	P-KB4	Q-R4	P-Q5	B×N	N-B3
8	P×P e.p.	N×P!	Q-N3	P×B	N×N
	B×P!	B-N5 (e)	N-B3	O-O	P×N
9	O-O	B-N2	B-K2	N-B3	B-Q3
	N-B3	N×R	B-K3	R-K1†	Q-K2
10	N×N	N×P†	B-B3	B-K2	O-O
	P×N (c)	K-Q2 (f)	Q-Q2 (h)	Q-K2 (j)	Q-K4 (l)

(a) (A) 3 P-KN3, P-Q4; 4 P×P, N×P; 5 B-N2, B-K3; 6 N-B3! N-QB3; 7 O-O, B-K2; 8 R-K1, B-B3; 9 N-K4, O-O; 10 P-Q3, B-K2; 11 P-QR3, N-N3; 12 P-QN4, B-N5; 13 P-B3, P-QR3 = . Smyslov-Polugayevski, USSR Chp. 1961. (B) 3 N-B3, see Petrov's Defence and 3 . . . N-B3 is the Four Knights' Game.

(b) (A) 6 P-Q3, N×N; 7 P×N, O-O; 8 P-B4, P-KB3! 9 B-K3, P×P; 10 N×P, B-KB4 = . Spielmann-Kaufmann, 1917. (B) 6 Q-K2, P-KB4! or 6 . . . N×N; 7 QP×N, P-QB4!

(c) 11 B×P, N×P; 12 N-N5, B-B4! 13 P-B3, B×N; 14 QB×B, Q×B = . Spielmann-Réti, Vienna 1922. In the column, if 5 . . . B-QB4; 6 P-Q4, B-QN5; 7 B-Q2, P-QB4; 8 B-Q3!

(d) The text initiates "Würzburger's Trap". Two substantial choices are (A) 5 . . . B-QN5; 6 P×N, Q-R5†; 7 K-Q2, B-N5†; 8 N-B3, B×N; 9 P×B, P×P; 10 Q-Q4, B-R4; 11 K-K3, B×N; 12 B-N5†, P-B3; 13 P×B, P×B; 14 Q×KP, Q×Q†; 15 K×Q, with minimal advantage. (B) 5 . . . N×N; 6 P×N, P-Q5! (6 . . . B-K2; 7 P-Q4! O-O; 8 B-Q3, P-KB3; 9 Q-R5, P-KN3; 10 B×P, P×B; 11 Q×P†, K-R1; 12 N-B3! Q-K1; 13 Q-R6†, K-N1; 14 O-O, P×P; 15 B-KN5 + . Chess 1969/4); 7 N-B3, P-QB4 (7 . . . N-B3! might be safest); 8 B-K2, B-K2; 9 O-O, O-O; 10 Q-K1, P-B3. Milner-Barry-Alexander, Cambridge 1932. If 11 Q-N3, N-B3! = .

(e) 8 . . . N×R? 9 N×P†, K-Q1; 10 N×R, B-K2; 11 B-N2, B-R4†; 12 K-B1, N-B3; 13 P-Q4! B-N5; 14 B-K3, K-Q2; 15 P-Q5, N-K2; 16 P-K6† + .

(f) 11 N×R, N-B3; 12 B-K3, P-B3; 13 P-Q4, P×P; 14 P-Q5! ± . Milner-Barry-Sergeant, Margate 1938.

(g) 5 . . . N-QB3; 6 B-N5, N×N; 7 NP×N, Q-R5†; 8 P-N3, Q-K5†; 9 Q×Q, P×Q; 10 B×N†, P×B; 11 N-K2, B-K2! 12 R-B1, O-O; 13 R-B4, P-B3! with very active play for the pawn minus. Hromadka-Spielmann, Trenčanské Teplice 1928.

(h) 11 N-K2, B-B4! 12 P-B4, O-O; 13 O-O, B×P! 14 N-B4, B-K3 ∓ . Spielmann-Romanovski, Moscow 1925. If 15 R-N1, N-Q1.

(i) 4 P×QP, N×P (4 . . . P×P, see King's Gambit Accepted); 5 N×N, Q×N; 6 P×P, N-B3; 7 N-B3, B-KN5; 8 B-Q2, N×P = .

(j) 11 P-B4, N-KB3; 12 B-N5 (Spielmann-Lasker, St. Petersburg 1909), B-N5 ∓ .

(k) 3 . . . N-QB3; 4 N×P! see Three Knights' Game.

(l) 11 N-R4, B-N3; 12 B-N3 ± . Horowitz-Kupchik, Syracuse 1934.

1 P–K4, P–K4; 2 N–QB3, N–QB3

	11	12	13	14	15
3	B–B4	P–B4 (d)			
	B–B4 (a)	P × P (e)			
4	Q–N4 (b)	N–B3			P–Q4?! (m)
	P–KN3	P–KN4 (f)			Q–R5†
5	Q–B3	P–Q4		P–KR4 (k)	K–K2
	N–B3	P–N5!		P–N5	P–Q3 (n)
6	KN–K2	B–B4!?		N–KN5	N–B3
	P–Q3 (c)	P × N		P–KR3	B–N5
7	P–Q3	O–O		N × P	B × P
	B–N5	P–Q4 (g)		K × N	P–B4!
8	Q–N3	P × QP		P–Q4	P × P
	B × N	B–KN5		P–Q4 (l)	O–O–O
9	N × B	R–K1†	Q–Q2!	B × P	B–N3
	N–QR4	KN–K2	N/3–K2 (i)	B–N5	B × N†
10	B–N3 ±	N–K4	Q × BP	P–K5	K × B
		B–N2 (h)	Q–Q2 (j)	B–K3 +	N × P† (o)

(a) (A) 3 . . . N–B3, see col. 4. (B) 3 . . . Q–N4? 4 N–B3! Q × P; 5 R–KN1, Q–R6; 6 B × P† + .

(b) 4 P–Q3, N–B3; 5 P–B4, P–Q4; 6 P × QP, N–Q5; 7 P × P, B–KN5; 8 Q–Q2, Q–K2; 9 Q–B4, N × P†; 10 K–B1, O–O! 11 R–N1, QR–K1 + . Adams-H. Lyman, corr. 1962.

(c) 6 . . . B–B1; 7 P–Q4, B–N2! The column is Estrin-Ravinski, 1964.

(d) The Vienna Gambit. (A) 3 N–B3, see Three Knights' Game. (B) 3 P–KN3, B–B4; 4 B–N2, P–Q3; 5 N–R4, KN–K2; 6 N × B, P × N; 7 P–Q3, O–O = .

(e) 3 . . . B–B4; 4 N–B3, transposes into the King's Gambit Declined.

(f) The Pierce Gambit. 4 . . . N–B3, or 4 . . . P–Q3, or 4 . . . P–KR3, see King's Gambit Accepted.

(g) Also 7 . . . N × P! 8 B × P†, K × B; 9 B × P, P–B4 has merit. Dr. E. Schmidt.

(h) 11 P × P, N–R4; 12 B–B1, B–R4; 13 P–B4, R–KN1; 14 K–B2, P–N4; 15 N–B5, K–B1 ∓ . Bardeleben.

(i) 9 . . . N–R4; 10 B–N5†, B–Q2; 11 Q × P, B–Q3; 12 Q × P + .

(j) 11 P–Q6, N–N3; 12 Q–K4†, K–Q1 = .

(k) The Hamppe-Allgaier Gambit.

(l) Also good is 8 . . . P–B6; 9 B–B4†, P–Q4; 10 B × P†, K–K1; 11 P × P, B–K2; 12 B–K3, B × P†; 13 K–Q2, B–N4; 14 P–B4, B–B3; 15 P–K5, B–N2; 16 Q–K2, KN–K2 + .

(m) The Steinitz Gambit.

(n) Another effective riposte is 5 . . . P–Q4; 6 P × P, B–N5†; 7 N–B3, O–O–O; 8 P × N, B–QB4; 9 Q–K1, Q–R4! 10 P × P†, K–N1; 11 K–Q1, B × P; 12 B–Q2, B × N ∓ . Steinitz-Liverpool Chess Club 1899.

(o) 11 K–B2, Q–B3; 12 B–Q3, N × KBP; 13 Q–N4, P–KN3 ∓ .

Centre Game

(1 P–K4, P–K4; 2 P–Q4, P × P; 3 Q × P*)

The Centre Game is one of the oldest and most logical continuations of White's attack. Despite its inherent logic, however, the early development of White's Queen is such a serious breach of principle that the opening began to disappear from master practice long before 1900. After 3 . . . N–QB3 Black gains a free move and this solves all his theoretical problems. Further play usually finds White somewhat congested and on the defensive.

Col. 1 is the main line and, starting with the 9th move, the ensuing positions are replete with tricks and traps. But Black can thread his way through the maze and emerge with the initiative. Possibly the salvation of this opening lies in note *(b)*, where White retreats his queen to QR4 instead of K3. In any event, the only attraction of this opening today is surprise value. Tartakover, Spielmann, and Mieses were the last great players to give up on it.

¹ For the alternative 3 P–QB3 see the Danish Gambit. For 3 N–KB3, N–QB3 see Scotch Game.

1 P–K4, P–K4; 2 P–Q4, P × P; 3 Q × P (*a*), N–QB3; 4 Q–K3 (*b*)

	1	2	3	4	5
	N–B3		B–K2		P–KN3 (*l*)
5	N–QB3 (*c*)		N–QB3		B–Q2
	B–N5		N–B3		B–N2
6	B–Q2		B–Q2	B–B4	N–QB3
	O–O		P–Q4	O–O (*j*)	N–B3!
7	O–O–O		P × P	KN–K2	P–K5!? (*m*)
	R–K1		N × P	N–KN5!	N–KN5!
8	B–B4 (*d*)		N × N	Q–Q2	Q–K2 (*n*)
	P–Q3 (*e*)		Q × N	B–B4	KN × KP
9	N–R3	P–B3	N–K2	N–Q1	P–B4
	N–K4 (*f*)	N–QR4 (*h*)	B–KN5	Q–K2	N–Q5
10	B–N3	B–Q3	N–B4	P–KB3	Q–K4
	B–K3	P–Q4!	Q–Q2	Q–R5†	P–Q4
11	P–B4	Q–N5	P–KB3	N–B3	Q × QP
	N–B5	P–KR3	O–O–O!	KN–K4!	N × P†
12	B × N	Q–R4	O–O–O	P × Q	K–Q1
	B × B (*g*)	P–Q5 (*i*)	B–KB4 ∓	N × P† (*k*)	N × R ∓

(*a*) 3 N–KB3, B–B4; 4 N × P, N–KB3; 5 N–QB3, P–Q4; 6 P × P, O–O; 7 B–KN5, Q–Q3; 8 B × N, Q × B; 9 N–B3, B–KN5! 10 B–K2, B × N; 11 B × B, R–K1† ∓.

(*b*) (A) 4 Q–R4! is a Centre Counter Defence with colours reversed, with White having a move in hand. 4 . . . B–B4; or 4 . . . P–KN3 are in order, not 4 . . . P–Q4; 5 B–QN5. (B) 4 Q–B4, N–B3; 5 N–QB3, P–Q4! 6 N × P, N × N; 7 P × N, N–N5 = .

(*c*) 5 P–K5, N–KN5; 6 Q–K4, P–Q4; 7 P × P *e.p.*†, B–K3; 8 P × P, Q × P ∓.

(*d*) 8 Q–N3, R × P! (8 . . . N × P; 9 N × N, R × N; 10 P–QB3, B–B1; 11 B–Q3); 9 B–KN5 (9 N × R, N × N; 10 Q–K3, B × B†; 11 R × B, N × R ∓), B × N; 10 Q × B, P–KR3; 11 P–B3, R–K1; 12 B–R4, P–Q3 + . Glickman-Fuderer, Zagreb 1959.

(*e*) 8 . . . B × N; 9 B × B, N × P; 10 Q–B4, N–B3; 11 N–B3, P–Q3; 12 N–N5, B–K3; 13 B–Q3, P–KR3; 14 P–KR4, N–Q4; 15 B–R7†, K–R1; 16 R × N, B × R; 17 B–K4 (Winawer-Steinitz, Nuremberg 1896), R × B! 18 N × R, N–K4; 19 R–Q1, B × N = . (B) 8 . . . N–QR4! Reshevsky.

(*f*) 9 . . . N–QR4; 10 B–Q3, P–Q4; 11 Q–N3! P–Q5; 12 B–KN5! ∓.

(*g*) 13 P–K5, with divided chances. Kupreichik-Estrin, Leningrad 1965.

(*h*) 9 . . . N–K4; 10 B–N3, P–B3 (10 . . . B–K3; 11 N–Q5!); 11 P–N4, B–QB4; 12 Q–B4, P–QN4; 13 P–N5, N–N3 = .

(*i*) 13 QN–K2, B × B†; 14 R × B, P–B4; 15 P–QB4, B–K3 ∓, Feilitzsch-Keres, corr. 1932–33.

(*j*) Also 6 . . . N–QN5; 7 Q–K2, P–Q4 = . Sokolski.

(*k*) 13 K–B1, P–Q4! 14 K–N2, N × Q; 15 B × P, B–KN5; 16 B × N, B × N + . Troianescu-Spasski, Budapest 1953.

(*l*) 4 . . . B–N5†; 5 N–B3, KN–K2; 6 B–Q2, O–O; 7 O–O–O, P–Q3; 8 Q–N3, K–R1; 9 P–B4, P–B4, only equalizes.

(*m*) 7 O–O–O, O–O; 8 P–B3, P–Q4; 9 Q–B5, P × P; 10 B–KN5, Q–K1; 11 B × N, B × B; 12 N × P, B–N2 ∓. Blackburne-Lasker, match 1892.

(*n*) 8 Q–K4, P–Q4; 9 P × P *e.p.*†, B–K3; 10 P × P, Q × P ∓.

Danish Gambit

(1 P–K4, P–K4; 2 P–Q4, P × P; 3 P–QB3*)

The Danish is an offshoot of the Centre Game, and equally outmoded. Like all gambits, it is a violent attempt to wrest the initiative. Black gets into hot water only if he reacts with unbecoming greed or passivity. White's idea is to sacrifice one or two pawns for an open game and a quick, slashing attack based on splendid diagonals for his two bishops. Black is in the enviable situation of being able to secure an even game by declining it, or the preferable game by accepting! The theoretical antidote is Schlechter's line in col. 3, where Black returns all the material in order to reach a better ending. But an examination of older games reveals that even without this counterattack Black can accept both pawns and submit to the storm (note [e]). Alekhin recommended 3 . . . P × P; 4 N × P, a "half" Danish (cols. 4 and 5), but Black's prospects are more than adequate though not without hazard, as recent games show.

Black can safely decline the gambit with 3 . . . P–Q4 which completely neutralizes White's attack (cols. 1 and 2). The chances are balanced. Satisfactory alternatives on Black's third move are discussed in note *(a)*. In general, however, the best way to refute a sacrifice is to accept it.

* For 3 Q × P see Centre Game.

109

1 P-K4, P-K4; 2 P-Q4, P × P; 3 P-QB3

	1	2	3	4	5
	P-Q4 (a)		P × P		
4	KP × P		B-QB4	N × P	
	Q × P	N-KB3	P × P (d)	N-QB3	
5	P × P	N-KB3	B × P	B-QB4 (g)	
	N-QB3	N × P	P-Q4! (e)	B-N5 (h)	
6	N-KB3	Q × P	B × QP	N-B3	
	B-N5	N-QB3	N-KB3	N-B3	
7	B-K2	B-QN5	B × P†	O-O	P-K5 (l)
	N-B3	B-K2	K × B	B × N	P-Q4!
8	N-B3	O-O	Q × Q	P × B	P × N
	Q-QR4	O-O	B-N5†	P-Q3 (i)	P × B
9	O-O	B × N	Q-Q2	P-K5	Q × Q†
	O-O-O	P × B	B × Q†	N × P (j)	N × Q
10	B-K3	R-K1	N × B	N × N	P × P
	B-QB4 (b)	B-N2 (c)	P-B4! ∓ (f)	P × N (k)	R-KN1 (m)

(a) This and the other variations here and in cols. 1–2 are the Danish Gambit Declined. Satisfactory alternatives are (A) 3 . . . P-Q6; 4 B × P, B-B4; 5 N-B3, P-Q3; 6 Q-B2, N-QB3; 7 QN-Q2, P-QR3; 8 N-N3, B-R2; 9 QN-Q4, KN-K2; 10 O-O, O-O = . (B) 3 . . . Q-K2; 4 P × P, Q × P†; 5 B-K3, N-KB3; 6 N-KB3, B-N5†; 7 N-B3, O-O; 8 B-Q3, Q-K2; 9 O-O, P-Q4 ∓ .

(b) Or 10 . . . K-N1; 11 P-QR3, N-Q4 = .

(c) 11 N-R3, R-K1; 12 N-B4, P-QB4; 13 Q-Q1, R-N1 = . Keres.

(d) (A) 4 . . . N-QB3; 5 N-B3, B-B4; 6 N × P, P-Q3; 7 B-KN5, see Scotch Gambit. If 7 Q-N3, Q-Q2; 8 N-Q5, KN-K2; 9 Q-B3, O-O = . (B) 4 . . . P-Q3; 5 N × P, see Scotch (Göring) Gambit.

(e) Schlechter's antidote. Harder to handle are (A) 5 . . . N-KB3; 6 P-K5, N-N5; 7 B × P†, K × B; 8 Q × N, P-Q4! 9 Q-B4†, K-N1 = . (B) 5 . . . P-Q3; 6 N-KB3, N-QB3; 7 O-O, B-K3; 8 B × B, P × B; 9 Q-N3, Q-B1; 10 N-N5, N-Q1; 11 P-B4, B-K2 = .

(f) With mobilization of the queen-side pawns.

(g) 5 N-B3, B-N5; 6 B-KN5, KN-K2; 7 Q-B2, P-Q3; 8 O-O-O, B × N; 9 Q × B, O-O ∓ . Gufeld-Stein, USSR Chp. Prelim. 1959.

(h) For (A) 5 . . . P-Q3; or (B) 5 . . . B-B4, see Scotch Game and Gambit.

(i) Or 8 . . . O-O (A) 9 P-K5, P-Q4! or (B) 9 B-R3, P-Q3; 10 P-K5, N-K1 or (C) 9 Q-B2, P-Q3; 10 P-K5, N × P; 11 N × N, P × N; 12 B-R3, R-K1; 13 QR-Q1, N-Q2; 14 B × P†!?∞ .

(j) 9 . . . P × P; 10 N-N5, B-K3! 11 B × B, P × B; 12 Q-N3, Q-Q4; 13 N × KP, Q × Q; 14 P × Q, K-B2; 15 N × BP, QR-Q1! (Aronin) is a strong alternative.

(k) (A) 11 Q × Q†, K × Q; 12 B × P, K-K2; 13 B-N3, B-K3 ∓ . Yukhtman-Furman, USSR Chp. 1959. (B) 11 Q-N3, Q-K2; 12 B-R3, P-B4; 13 B-N5†! (13 Q-N5†, N-Q2; 14 QR-K1, O-O; 15 P-B4, P-QR3! ∓ . Penrose-Unzicker, Leipzig 1960). (1) 13 . . . K-B1; 14 P-B4, B-K3; 15 Q-R4, P × P; 16 Q × BP, P-KR4; 17 QR-K1, QR-B1; 18 B-Q3, R-R3, with a complicated game. Sorokin-Razdobarin, USSR 1960; or (2) 13 . . . B-Q2; 14 B × B†, Q × B; 15 B × P, N-K5! = . Mikhalchishin-Kluger, Debreczen 1967.

(l) 7 B-KN5, P-KR3; 8 B-R4, O-O; 9 Q-B2, R-K1; 10 O-O-O ∞ .

(m) 11 B-KR6, B × N†; 12 P × B, N-K3; 13 O-O-O! N × P; 14 N-Q4, N-K3; 15 KR-K1, B-Q2 = .

Bishop's Opening

(1 P–K4, P–K4; 2 B–B4)

White's purpose is to develop speedily and institute an attack without weakening his own king as in the King's Gambit. At one time the American master Weaver Adams claimed it as a forced win; while he was alone in this claim, later abandoning it in favour of the Vienna Game, his analyses helped to clarify the theory of the opening.

Black's most aggressive reaction is the Berlin Defence 2 . . . N–KB3 (cols. 1–4). White cannot afford to ignore the counterattack on his king's pawn. With 3 P–Q4 (cols. 1–3) White alters his plan and sacrifices a pawn for rapid development. Panov's suggestion in note *(e)* also dissipates all his attacking hopes. Attempts by White to steer for favourable variations of the King's Gambit Declined with 3 P–Q3 (col. 4) do not work out.

The alternative 2 . . . B–B4 (col. 5) produces equality, but without the potential counterplay offered by the Berlin Defence. 2 . . . P–QB3 (note *(i)*) is not quite adequate either.

111

1 P–K4, P–K4; 2 B–B4

	1	2	3	4	5
	N–KB3				B–B4 (*i*)
3	P–Q4 (*a*)			P–Q3	P–QB3 (*j*)
	P×P			P–B3! (*g*)	P–Q4 (*k*)
4	N–KB3			Q–K2	B×P
	N×P		P–Q4	B–K2	N–KB3
5	Q×P		P×P	P–B4	Q–B3
	N–KB3	N–B4	B–N5†	P–Q4!	O–O
6	B–KN5	B–KN5	P–B3	KP×P	P–Q4
	B–K2	P–KB3	Q–K2†	KP×P	P×P
7	N–B3	B–K3	K–B1 (*e*)	B×P	B–N5
	P–B3 (*b*)	P–B3	P×P	O–O	P×P
8	O–O–O	N–B3	N×P	P×P	B×N
	P–Q4	P–Q4	O–O	N×P	P–B7!
9	Q–R4	O–O–O	B–KN5	N–QB3	N–B3
	B–K3 (*c*)	B–K2 (*d*)	P–KR3 (*f*)	N–Q5 (*h*)	Q × QB =

(*a*) Ponziani's Gambit. (A) Upon Greco's 3 P–B4, both 3 . . . P×P, see King's Gambit, and 3 . . . N×P; 4 P–Q3, N–Q3; 5 B–N3, N–B3; are good. (B) 3 N–KB3 see Petrov's Defence and for 3 . . . N–B3, see Two Knight's Defence. (c) 3 N–QB3, see Vienna Game.

(*b*) Also 7 . . . N–B3; 8 Q–R4, P–Q3; 9 O–O–O, B–K3; 10 B–Q3, Q–Q2; 11 B–N5, O–O; 12 N–K5, Q–B1! = . Neishtadt.

(*c*) 10 B–Q3, QN–Q2; 11 N–Q4, N–B4; 12 P–B4, N–N1; 13 KR–K1, K–B1; 14 P–QN4, N×B†; 15 R×N, Q–Q3 = . *Comments.* 4 . . . N–B3 leads into a Two Knights' Defence. 4 N–KB3 is the Urusov Gambit.

(*d*) 10 Q–R4, QN–Q2; 11 N×P, P×N; 12 Q–R5†, P–N3; 13 Q×P + . Estrin-Taimanov, USSR 1949.

(*e*) Panov recommends also 7 B–K2, P×P; 8 N×P, O–O; 9 O–O without further follow-up. But 9 . . . P–B3! equalizes. The column is as good.

(*f*) 10 B–R4, B–KB4; 11 Q–Q4! QN–Q2 = . *Comments.*

(*g*) (A) 3 . . . N–B3; 4 N–QB3, B–B4 or 4 . . . B–N5, see Vienna Game. (B) 3 . . . B–B4; 4 N–QB3, N–B3; 5 P–B4, P–Q3, see King's Gambit Declined. (c) 3 . . . B–K2; 4 N–QB3, O–O; 5 P–B4, P×P; 6 B×P, P–B3; 7 P–K5, N–K1; 8 Q–B3, P–Q4; 9 P×P *e.p.*, N×P; 10 O–O–O, B–N4; 11 B–N3, N–R3; 12 P–Q4, N–B2; 13 KN–K2, B–K3 = . *Comments.*

(*h*) 10 Q–Q2, B–QN5; 11 P–QR3, R–K1†; 12 K–B1, B–R4 ∓ . Adams-Levin, Ventnor City, 1941. In the column, interesting is 4 N–KB3!? P–Q4; 5 B–N3, B–N5†; 6 P–B3, B–Q3; 7 B–N5 ∞ .

(*i*) The Classical Defence (A) 2 . . . P–QB3; 3 P–Q4, P–Q4; 4 P×QP, BP×P; 5 B–N5†, B–Q2; 6 B×B†, N×B; 7 P×P, N×P; 8 N–K2! N–KB3; 9 O–O ± . (B) 2 . . . P–KB4? 3 P–Q3, N–KB3! 4 P–B4, P–Q3; 5 N–KB3, BP×P; 6 QP×P, B–N5; 7 P×P, B×N; 8 Q×B + . *Debyut.*

(*j*) (A) 3 N–QB3 or 3 Q–N4 transposes into the Vienna Game. (B) 3 N–KB3, N–QB3 is the Giuoco Piano. (c) 3 P–QN4, B×P; 4 P–B4, P–Q4; 5 P×QP, P–K5; 6 N–K2, N–KB3; 7 O–O, O–O; 8 QN–B3, P–B3; 9 P×P, N×P ∓ . McDonnell-Labourdonnais, London 1834. (D) 3 P–Q3, N–KB3; 4 Q–K2, O–O = .

(*k*) The Lewis Counter Gambit. Another variant is 3 . . . N–KB3; 4 P–Q4, P×P; 5 P–K5, P–Q4; 6 P×N, P×B; 7 Q–R5, O–O! 8 Q×B, R–K1†; 9 N–K2, P–Q6; 10 B–K3, P×N; 11 N–Q2, N–R3; 12 Q×P/B4, Q×P = . Fine. The column is *Comments.*

1 P–K4, P–K4

	Alapin's Opening 1	Hungarian Defence 2	Inverted Hanham 3	Queen's Pawn Counter Gambit 4	5
2	N–K2	N–KB3 (c)			
	N–KB3 (a)	N–QB3		P–Q4 (l)	
3	P–KB4	B–B4	B–K2 (j)	P × P (m)	. . . . N × P
	N × P (b)	B–K2 (d)	N–B3	P–K5 (n)	Q–K2 (q)
4	P–Q3	P–Q4 (e)	P–Q3	Q–K2	P–Q4
	N–B4	P–Q3 (f)	P–Q4	P–KB4 (o)	P–KB3
5	P × P	P–Q5 (g)	QN–Q2	P–Q3	N–Q3
	P–Q4	N–N1	P–KN3	N–KB3	P × P
6	P–Q4	B–Q3	P–B3	P × P	N–B4
	N–K3	N–KB3 (h)	B–N2	P × P	Q–B2?
7	N–B4	P–B4	Q–B2	N–B3	N–Q2
	P–QB4	QN–Q2	Q–O	B–K2	B–KB4
8	N–B3	N–B3	N–B1	N × P	P–KN4!
	P × P	O–O	P–N3	O–O	B–N3
9	QN × P	P–KR3	N–N3	N × N†	B–B4
	N–B3 ∓	N–B4 (i)	B–N2 (k)	B × N (p)	Q–Q2 (r)

(a) (A) For 2 . . . P–QB4 see Sicilian Defence. (B) For 2 . . . B–B4; 3 P–Q4, P × P; 4 N × P see Scotch Game. This section covers only unusual opening systems by White and rarely encountered defences by Black. (c) 2 . . . N–QB3; 3 QN–B3, B–B4; 4 N–R4, B–K2; 5 P–Q4, P–Q3; 6 P–Q5, N–N1; 7 Q–Q3, P–KB4; 8 P × P, Q–Q2; 9 QN–B3, Q × P = . Alapin-Marco, Vienna 1898.

(b) Also strong is 3 . . . P × P; 4 N × P, Q–K2! Or simply 3 . . . P–Q4.

(c) 2 P–QR3 is Mengarini's Opening which allows Black to initiate a number of King's Pawn Openings in reverse (except for the Ruy Lopez); but it leaves White with a move in hand in defence. H. Meyers calls it a *Reversed Pawn Opening*.

(d) The characteristic move of the Hungarian Defence. If 3 . . . P–Q3; 4 P–Q4, B–N5 (For 4 . . . P × P; 5 N × P, N–B3 see Two Knights' Defence) 5 P–B3, Q–Q2 = .

(e) 4 P–Q3, N–B3; 5 B–N3, O–O; 6 QN–Q2, P–Q3 (6 . . . P–Q4!?); 7 P–B3, N–QR4; 8 B–B2, P–B4; 9 O–O, B–K3; 10 R–K1, N–B3 = . *Informator* 23.

(f) 4 . . . P × P; 5 N × P, P–Q3; 6 O–O, N–B3; 7 N–QB3, O–O; 8 P–KR3, N × N; 9 Q × N, B–K3; 10 B × B, P × B; 11 P–K5, N–Q2; 12 P × P ± . Tarrasch-Taubenhaus, Ostend 1905.

(g) (A) 5 P × P, P × P; (1) 6 Q × Q†, B × Q; 7 N–B3, N–B3; 8 B–K3, B–N5; 9 O–O–O, O–O = . Rossolimo-S. Bernstein, US 1954. (2) 6 B–Q5, B–Q2; 7 QN–Q2, N–B3; 8 N–B4, O–O = . Timman-Ivkov, Banja Luka 1975. (B) 5 P–KR3, N–B3; 6 N–B3, O–O; 7 O–O (7 B–K3, P × P; 8 N × P, P–Q4!), (1) 7 . . . P–KR3; 8 R–K1, R–K1; 9 B–K3, P × P; 10 N × P, B–B1; 11 B–B4, N × N; 12 Q × N, B–K3; Tal-Filip, Miskolc 1963. (2) 7 . . . N × QP; 8 N × N, P × N; 9 Q × P, P–B3; 10 P–QR4, N–Q2; 11 B–K3, P–QN3; 12 QR–Q1, Q–B2; 13 P–B4, P–QR3; 14 R–B3, P–QN4; 15 B–N3, K–R1; 16 R–N3, P–B3; 17 B–K6, N–B4; 18 B × B, KR × B; 19 B–B2, QR–N1; 20 P–N3, B–B1; 21 R–B3, drawn, as both camps are impenetrable; a modern example of unorthodox manoeuvring. Spasski-Hort, Reykjavik 1977.

(h) 6 . . . P–QB4; 7 P–KR3, N–KB3; is more active for Black. Konstantinopolski-Alatortsev, USSR Chp. 1952.

(i) 10 B–B2, P–QR4; 11 B–K3, P–QN3; 12 P–KN4 ± . Leonhardt-Hromádka, Pistyan 1912. Compare position with Old Indian Defence to the Queen's pawn.

(j) The ubiquitous King's Indian Attack (or Barcza System) crops up after 3 P–Q3, N–B3; 4 P–KN3, P–Q4; 5 QN–Q2, etc.

(k) 10 P–KR4, P–KR4 = . Tartakover-Bogolyubov, London 1922.

(l) (A) 2 . . . P–KB3 (Damiano's Defence); 3 N × P! Q–K2 (3 . . . P × N? 4 Q–R5†, P–N3; 5 Q × KP†, Q–K2; 6 Q × R +); 4 N–KB3, P–Q4; 5 P–Q3, P × P; 6 P × P, Q × P†; 7 B–K2, N–B3; 8 O–O + . (B) For 2 . . . P–KB4 see Latvian Gambit.

(m) 3 N–B3, P–Q5; 4 N–K2, B–Q3; 5 N–N3 = . Voellmy-Leiser, Basel 1944.

(n) (A) 3 . . . Q × P; 4 N–B3, Q–R4; 5 B–B4 gives White a strong variation of the Centre Counter Game. (B) 3 . . . B–Q3; 4 P–Q4, P–K5; 5 N–K5, N–K2; 6 B–N5, O–O; 7 B–R4, P–KB3; 8 B–B4, K–R1! = .

(o) 4 . . . N–KB3; 5 P–Q3! (5 N–B3, B–K2; 6 N × P, O–O; 7 P–Q3, R–K1; 8 B–Q2, N × P; 9 O–O–O, B–K3; 10 K–N1, N–QB3; 11 N–B3, B–B3; 12 N × N, Q × N; 13 P–B4, Q–Q3; 14 B–K3, P–QN4; 15 Q–B2, N–N5; 16 Q–B1, P × P; 17 P × P, Q–R3; 18 P–QR3, B–B4†; 19 K–R1, Q × P mate. Gligorić-Holze, simul. Hamburg 1970), Q × P; 6 KN–Q2, B–K2; 7 N × P, O–O; 8 QN–B3, Q–QR4; 9 B–Q2 + . Keres-De Agustin, Madrid 1943.

(p) 10 P–B3, Q × P; 11 Q–B4 with initiative. Keres.

(q) (A) 3 . . . P × P; 4 B–B4 (4 P–Q4, B–Q3 = . MCO 9th edition), Q–N4; 5 B × P† (5 N × P, Q × P; 6 R–B1, B–KN5; 7 P–KB3, B × P; 8 R–B2, Q–N8†; 9 R–B1, Q–N5. Keres), K–K2; 6 P–Q4, Q × P; 7 R–B1, B–KR6; 8 B–QB4, N–KB3; 9 B–B4, QN–Q2; 10 Q–Q2, N–N3; 11 B–K2, QN–Q4; 12 N–QB3 ± . Von Feilitzsch-Keres, corr. 1935. (B) 3 . . . B–Q3; 4 P–Q4, P × P; 5 B–QB4, B × N; 6 Q–R5! Q–K2; 7 P × B ± .

(r) 10 Q–K2, Q × QP; 11 N–K6, Q–N3; 12 N × P, N–Q2; 13 B–B4, N–K4; 14 O–O–O, B–B2; 15 N(4)–N5! P × N; 16 B × N, B × N; 17 B × BP! resigns. Boleslavski-Lilienthal, match tournament 1941.

Alekhin's Defence

(1 P–K4, N–KB3)

This defence is completely hypermodern in spirit and yet it was well known for more than a hundred years before Alekhin launched it into twentieth-century master competition with a spectacular success at Budapest in 1921. Its history can be traced from Allgaier's *Lehrbuch* (1811) to Alexandre's *Encyclopédie* (1837), down to Schallop's condescending remarks in the 7th edition of Bilguer's *Handbuch*. It was warmly embraced by Réti and the hypermoderns as a means of shocking the dogmatic Dr. Tarrasch and the sneering classical school. When Em. Lasker used it to defeat Maróczy in the great 1924 New York Tournament, it had really arrived. With the tremendous onrush of the Sicilian Defence in recent years, it receded backstage. Today it is reinstated, and the defence bearing his name became a favourite weapon of Mikenas, Smyslov, Korchnoi, Larsen, and of many U.S. masters.

The idea is to provoke the premature advance of White's centre pawns, immobilize them, and then use them as targets. As Tartakover says, "White has his initiative to defend." But if Black is to accomplish his purpose, he must allow his king's knight to be driven clear across the board to where it is not particularly well placed on QN3. The course of the game depends upon just how much White "provokes." Whereas theory definitely gives him the nod, practice is sometimes another matter.

The FOUR PAWNS ATTACK, 2 P–K5, N–Q4; 3 P–QB4, N–N3; 4 P–Q4, P–Q3; 5 P–B4 (cols. 1–9) sometimes called the "chase variation," is White's most violent attempt at refutation. Although it does confer the initiative and a marked space advantage, most moderns distrust this overextended centre. With 5 . . . P×P; 6 BP×P, N–B3; 7 B–K3, B–B4; 8 N–QB3, P–K3 Black can operate strategically behind the trenches for a long period of siege (cols. 1–6). Cols. 3 and 9 are probably Black's soundest continuations. Cols. 7–8 show interesting ways for Black to wriggle out of his theoretical strait-jacket on move 5 or 6. It may be that the salvation of this defence will ultimately rest in the correctness of one of these lines, but other trends have in the meantime been developed in the . . . P–KN3 variations, all of which should be studied in conjunction (e.g. cols. 13, 14, 20, 21, and various notes).

Cols. 10–17 investigate White's variance from the classical pattern, e.g. the *Exchange Variation* (cols. 11–14), which is too unassuming; *The Accelerated Chase Variation* 2 P–K5, N–Q4; 3 P–QB4, N–N3; 4 P–B5 (cols. 15–17), which may, however, fizzle out against best defence; *The Modern Variation* 3 P–Q4, P–Q3; 4 N–KB3 (cols. 18–23), which is possibly White's most "solid" positional approach, but here again flexible strategies have been invented by Black, resembling the Pirć Defence.

3 N–QB3 (cols. 24–5) contains sporadic revivals in some sidelines of some of the very early, original lines used in the 1920s. It does, however, provide proof of the constantly ongoing scrutiny of "out-dated" lines in the light of advanced technique and the search for surprise and improvement.

1 P-K4, N-KB3; 2 P-K5, N-Q4; 3 P-QB4, N-N3; 4 P-Q4, P-Q3; 5 P-B4, P×P; 6 BP×P, N-B3; 7 B-K3, B-B4; 8 N-QB3, P-K3; 9 N-B3 (*a*)

	1	2	3	4	5
	Q-Q2?	N-N5	B-K2		B-KN5
10	B-K2 (*b*)	R-B1	B-K2	P-Q5	B-K2
	O-O-O	P-B4	O-O	P×P	Q-Q2 (*k*)
11	O-O	B-K2 (*f*)	O-O	P×P	O-O (*l*)
	P-B3	B-K2	P-B3	N-N5	B-K2
12	P-Q5!? (*c*)	O-O	P×P (*h*)	N-Q4	Q-Q2
	Q-K1 (*d*)	O-O	B×P	B-N3?	O-O-O
13	B×N	P-QR3	Q-Q2	B-N5†	QR-Q1
	RP×B	P×P	R-B2 (*i*)	K-B1	B×N
14	Q-R4	N×P	QR-Q1	O-O	R×B
	N-N1	N-B3	R-Q2	K-N1	P-B3
15	Q-R8	N×B	P-B5	N-B5	R-N3
	P×KP	P×N	N-Q4	B×N	P-N3
16	N×P	R×P	N×N	R×B	Q-B2 ±
	B-Q3 (*e*)	P-N3 (*g*)	P×N =	N/5×QP (*j*)	

(*a*) First 9 B-K2 prevents 9 . . . B-KN5 but leads back into col. 2 after 9 . . . N-N5; 10 R-B1, P-B4; 11 N-B3.

(*b*) 10 P-Q5!? P×P; 11 P×P, N-N5; 12 N-Q4, N/3×P; 13 N×N, N×N (also risky is 13 . . . Q×N; 14 N×B, Q×KP; 15 R-B1, Q×N; 16 R×P, Q-K3; 17 B-N5†, N-B3; 18 O-O! B-K2∞. Tagman-Benko, corr. 1948); 14 N×B, B-N5†; 15 B-Q2, Q×N; 16 Q-R4†, P-B3; 17 B×B, Q-K5† ∓ .

(*c*) Adam's risky move. Safer is 12 P×P, P×P; 13 P-Q5!? Q-N2; 14 B×N, RP×B or 14 N-KR4, R-N1 = . In the column, instead of 11 . . . P-B3, Gipslis tried to revive the sharper 11 . . . B-KN5!? 12 P-B5! N-Q4; 13 N×N, Q×N; 14 N-N5! B×B; 15 Q×B, N×QP; 16 B×N, Q×B†; 17 K-R1, Q-Q7; 18 Q×Q, R×Q; 19 R×P, B×P; 20 N×KP, B-Q5; 21 N×B, R×N; 22 R×P, R-K5; 23 R-QB1, P-B3; 24 R-B1, P-KR4 = .

(*d*) 12 . . . N×KP; N×N, P×N; 14 P-QR4, K-N1; 15 P-R5! N-B1; 16 Q-N3 ± .

(*e*) 17 P-B5, B×P†! 18 K-R1, B-Q3; 19 B-N5, Q-R4; 20 B-B6 (with win for White–W. Adams– but), P×B; 21 P×BP, QR-B1 22 KR-Q1, B-Q6!! Analysis by Carvalho, São Paulo, 19 N-N5 ± is best.

(*f*) (A) 11 P-Q5, P×P; 12 P×P, N/5×QP; 13 B-KN5, B-K2; 14 B-N5†, K-B1! Pachman. (B) 11 B-N5, P-B3! 12 KP×P, NP×P; 13 B-R4, B-K2 = . *Comments.* (C) 11 P-QR3, P×P; 12 B-N5, P×N; 13 B×Q, P×P; 14 B-N5, P×R(Q); 15 B×Q, N-B7†; 16 K-B2, R-Q1; 17 Q-K2, B-B4†; 18 K-N3, O-O = . Znosko-Borovski's analysis.

(*g*) 17 R-B1, B-N4; 18 B-B5, R-K1 = . Petrov-Fine, Kemeri 1937.

(*h*) (A) 12 N-KR4, P×P; 13 N×B, P×N; 14 P-Q5, N-Q5! 15 B×N, P×B = . (B) 12 Q-K1 is playable, e.g. 12 . . . P×P; 13 P×P, N-Q2; 14 R-Q1, Q-K1 = .

(*i*) More of many Black's choices are (A) 13 . . . Q-K2; 14 QR-Q1, QR-Q1; 15 Q-K1, N-N5; 17 P-QR3, N-B7; or (B) 13 . . . Q-K1; 14 QR-Q1 (or 14 B-N5! Ljubojević), R-Q1; 15 Q-B1, Q-N3; 16 K-R1, R-Q2; 17 P-Q5, N-K2; 18 P×P, R×R; 19 R×R, B×P = . This and the column is *MCO* 11.

(*j*) 17 B×N, N×B; 18 Q-N3, B-B4†; 19 K-R1, Q-K2; 20 N-R4! N. Weinstein.

(*k*) Or (A) 10 . . . N-R4; 11 P-QN3, B-N5 = , Konstantinopolski. (B) 10 . . . B×N; 11 P×B, Q-R5†; 12 B-B2, Q-B5; 13 P-B5, N-Q2; 14 Q-B1 ± . In the column, for 9 . . . B-QN5 see page 97 (*c*)(B).

(*l*) 11 O-O, O-O-O; 12 P-B5! N-Q4; 13 N×N, Q×N; 14 N-N5 ± . Ghizhdavu.

1 P-K4, N-KB3; 2 P-K5 (a), N-Q4; 3 P-QB4, N-N3; 4 P-Q4, P-Q3

	6	7	8	9	10
5	(P-B4)				N-KB3
	(P×P)		B-B4		B-N5
6	(BP×P)		N-QB3		B-K2
	(N-B3)	P-N3 (c)	P-K3		P×P
7	N-KB3!?	N-QB3	P×P (e)	B-K3	P-B5 (i)
	B-N5	B-N2	P×P	P×P (g)	P-K5
8	P-K6!?	P-B5	N-B3	BP×P	P×N
	P×P	N-Q4	B-K2	B-K2	P×N
9	P-B5	B-QB4	B-Q3	N-B3	B×P
	N-Q4!	B-K3	B-N5	O-O	B×B
10	B-QN5	Q-N3	O-O	B-K2	Q×B
	Q-Q2	N×N	N-B3	P-KB3	N-B3 (j)
11	QN-Q2	B×B	B-K3	O-O	O-O
	P-KN3	P×B	B-B3	P×P	N×P!
12	N-B4	P×N	B-K2	N×P	Q×P
	B-N2 (b)	Q-Q4 (d)	O-O (f)	QN-Q2 (h)	RP×P (k)

(a) 2 N-QB3 may force 2 . . . P-K4 transposing into a Vienna game, or 2 . . . P-Q3 resulting in a Pirć Defence. More intriguing is 2 . . . P-Q4 with similarities to the Center Counter Defence, e.g. (A) 3 P-K5, P-Q5! (3 . . . KN-Q2; 4 P-K6! P×P; 5 P-Q4, N-KB3—5 . . . P-B4; 6 B-Q3 ± —; 6 N-KB3, P-KN3; 7 N-K5, B-N2; 8 P-KR4 ± Suttles-Mecking, Sousse 1967); 4 P×N, P×N; 5 P×NP, P×P† = Opočenský-Abramavicius, Folkestone 1933. (B) 3 P×P, N×P; 4 KN-K2, B-N5 (or 4 . . . N-QB3 =); 5 P-KR3, N×N; 6 NP×N, B×N; 7 B×B, P-QB3; 8 P-Q4, P-K3; 9 R-QN1, Q-B2; 10 B-K3, N-Q2; 11 P-QB4, B-K2 = . Lisitsyn-Mikenas, Riga 1968.

(b) 13 N-R5, O-O ∓ . Czerniak-Penrose, Amsterdam 1954.

(c) (A) 6 . . . P-QB4?; 7 P-Q5! P-K3; 8 N-QB3, P×P; 9 P×P, P-B5! 10 N-B3, B-KN5! 11 Q-Q4, B×N; 12 P×B, B-N5; 13 B×P, O-O; 14 R-KN1, P-N3; 15 B-KN5! Q-B2; 16 B-N3, B-B4; 17 Q-KB4, R-K1; 18 B-B6 ± . O'Kelly. (B) 6 . . . B-B4; 7 N-QB3, P-K3; 8 N-B3, B-QN5; 9 B-Q3! B-N5; 10 O-O, N-B3; 11 P-B5, B×QN; 12 P×B + .

(d) 13 N-B3, O-O; 14 O-O, N-B3; 15 B-N5, P-N3 = . Brasket-Berliner, US Open Chp. 1959.

(e) Foreclosing the possible counter . . . P-B4 as is possible in note (g). If 7 N-B3, P×P, see col. 9.

(f) 13 P-QN3 with some preponderance. Matanović-Olafsson, Bled 1961.

(g) Trifunović's system. Black keeps open the options of either . . . N-R3 or . . . N-Q2. Weaker is at once 7 . . . N-R3; 8 N-B3, P-B4! 9 B-K2, B-K2; 10 O-O, O-O; 11 Q-Q2, Q-K1; 12 P×QP ± . Donner-Schmid, Moscow Olympics 1956.

(h) 13 N-B3, P-B3; 14 Q-Q2, Q-K1; 15 QR-Q1, R-Q1 = . Shiyanovski-Smyslov, USSR Chp. 1961.

(i) Unsound is 7 N×P, B×B; 8 Q×B, Q×P; 9 O-O, QN-Q2; 10 N×N, Q×N; 11 N-B3, P-K3; 12 B-K3, B-K2; 13 QR-Q1, Q-B3; 14 Q-N4, O-O; 15 P-QN3, P-B4 + . Thomas-Flohr, Antwerp 1932.

(j) 10 . . . RP×P; 11 Q×P, N-Q2; 12 B-B4, P-K4; 13 B×P, N×B; 14 P×N, B-N5†; 15 N-B3, B×N†; 16 P×B, O-O ∞. Alekhin-Euwe, match 1935. Black just managed to draw.

(k) 13 B-K3, R-QN1; 14 Q-K4, N-N4 ∓ . *MCO* 11.

1 P–K4, N–KB3; 2 P–K5, N–Q4; 3 P–QB4, N–N3

	11	12	13	14	15
4	(P–Q4)				P–B5
	(P–Q3)				N–Q4
5	P × P (Exchange Variation)				B–B4
	KP × P		BP × P		P–K3 (j)
6	N–QB3 . . . . . . N–KB3		N–QB3		P–Q4
	B–K2 (a)	B–K2	P–N3?!		P–Q3
7	B–K2	B–K2	P–KR4 (f) B–Q3		BP × P
	O–O	O–O	P–KR3	B–N2	P × P
8	B–K3 (b)	O–O	B–K3	N–B3 (h)	Q–K2
	N–B3	B–B3	B–N2	B–N5	P × P
9	N–B3	N–B3	Q–Q2	B–K2	P × P
	B–N5	R–K1	N–B3	N–B3	N–QB3
10	P–QN3	P–KR3 (d)	P–Q5	P–QN3	N–KB3
	B–B3	N–B3	N–K4	O–O	N–R4 = (k)
11	O–O	B–B4	P–QN3	O–O	
	P–Q4! (c)	B–B4 (e)	QN–Q2 (g)	P–K4 (i)	

(a) (A) 6 . . . P–N3; 7 N–B3, B–N2; 8 B–N5! P–KB3; 9 B–K3, O–O! 10 P–B5, P × P; 11 P × P, N/3–Q2; 12 Q–Q5†, K–R1; 13 O–O–O, N–B3; 14 P–KR4 with some initiative. Rauzer-Mazel, USSR 1936. (B) 6 . . . B–K2; 7 B–K3, N–B3 (Black's 6th move here and in the column can be transposed); 8 R–B1?! O–O; 9 P–KR4, B–B3; 10 P–KN4, R–K1; 11 B–K2, B × NP with an intricate game. Suttles-Korchnoi, Sousse 1967.

(b) Other attempts are (A) 8 P–KR3, B–B4; 9 N–B3, N–B3; 10 O–O, P–KR3; 11 P–QN3 and (B) 8 N–B3, N–B3; 9 P–QN3, B–N5; 10 O–O, B–B3; 11 B–K3, P–Q4; 12 P–B5, N–B1; 13 P–KR3! B–K3! = .

(c) 12 P–B5, N–B1; 13 P–N4, N1–K2; 14 P–N5, N–R4 with somewhat more elasticity for Black. Gipslis-Larsen, Sousse 1967. Also (10 P–QN3), P–B4!

(d) White may also protect his B's pawn by 10 P–QN3! and only after 10 . . . B–N5 play 11 P–KR3, e.g. 11 . . . B × N; 12 B × B. Comments.

(e) 12 R–B1, P–KR3; 13 P–QN3, R–K2; 14 Q–Q2, Q–Q2; 15 KR–Q1, QR–K1; 16 B–B1, P–N4! ∓ . Matanović-Larsen, Mallorca 1968.

(f) A tamer alternative is 7 B–K3, B–N2; 8 N–B3, N–B3! 9 P–KR3, O–O; 10 B–K2, P–Q4; 11 P–B5, N–B5; 12 B × N, P × B; 13 O–O, P–N3 = (Schwarz).

(g) 12 P–B3, N–B4; 13 N–R3 ± , Ciocaltea-Fischer, Havana 1965. In the column, 7 . . . P–KR4! was good.

(h) 8 KN–K2, N–B3; 9 B–K3, O–O; 10 O–O, P–K4; 11 P–Q5, N–N5; 12 P–QN3, N × B; 13 Q × N, N–Q2; 14 Q–Q2, P–B4 = . Fischer-Berliner, US Chp. 1963.

(i) 12 P–Q5 (12 P × P!), N–K2; 13 N–K4, N–B4 = . Seidman-Fine, Hollywood 1945.

(j) Sokolski proposes 5 . . . P–QB3; 6 N–QB3, P–Q3; 7 BP × P (7 Q–N3, N–Q2!), P × P; 8 Q–N3, P × P; 9 N × N, P × N = .

(k) Gurgenidze-Mikenas, USSR 1968. The column is the Accelerated Chase Variation, dating back to Lasker.

1 P–K4, N–KB3; 2 P–K5, N–Q4

	16	17	18	19	20
3	(P–QB4)...............		P–Q4		
	(N–N3)		P–Q3		
4	(P–B5)		N–KB3 (d)	(Modern Variation)	
	(N–Q4)		B–N5		P–KN3
5	(B–B4)		B–K2	P–KR3	B–K2
	(P–K3)		P–K3 (e)	B × N	B–N2
6	N–QB3		O–O (f)	Q × B	O–O
	P–Q3	N × N (b)	B–K2 (g)	P × P	O–O
7	N × N	QP × N	P–B4	P × P	P–B4
	P × N	N–B3	N–N3	P–K3	N–N3
8	B × P	B–B4	N–B3	P–R3 (j)	P × P
	P–QB3	B × P	O–O	N–QB3	BP × P
9	B × KBP†	Q–N4	P–KR3 (h)	Q–K4	P–KR3 (l)
	K × B	P–KN4	B–R4	N/4–K2	N–B3
10	BP × P	B × NP!	B–K3	B–K3	N–B3
	Q–K1 (a)	R–KN1 (c)	P–Q4 (i)	N–B4 (k)	B–B4 (m)

(a) 11 Q–B3†, K–N1; 12 Q–K3, B–K3; 13 N–K2, N–Q2; 14 N–B4 is promising.

(b) (A) 6 . . . N–QB3; 7 P–Q4, N × N; 8 P × N, P–Q3; 9 BP × P, P × P; 10 P × P, B × P; 11 N–B3, O–O = . (B) 6 . . . B × P; 7 P–Q4, B–N5; 8 B × N, P × B; 9 Q–N4, Q–K2; 10 Q × P, Q–B1; 11 Q–N3, R–N1; 12 Q–B3, P–QB3; 13 N–K2, P–Q3 ∞ .

(c) 11 N–R3, B–K2! 12 B × B (12 P–B4, N × P; 13 P × N, B × B; 14 Q–R5, P–KR3; 15 O–O, R–N2 =), R × Q; 13 B × Q, K × B; 14 P–B4, R × NP! 15 O–O–O, K–K2 = .

(d) (A) 4 B–QB4? N–N3; 5 B–N3, P × P; 6 Q–B3, P–K3; 7 P × P, P–QR4! 8 P–B3, P–R5; 9 B–B2, B–Q2! 10 Q–N3, B–N4; 11 B–N5, Q–Q4; 12 N–Q2, N–B3; 13 P–KB4, N–B5 ∓ . Gufeld-Vasyukov, Kislovodsk 1968. (B) 4 P–QB4 see cols. 1–14.

(e) (A) 5 . . . P–KN3; 6 B–QB4, B–K3; 7 N–B3, B–N2; 8 N–K4 ± . (B) 5 . . . P–QB3?! (1) 6 O–O, B × N; 7 B × B, P × P; 8 P × P, P–K3; 9 Q–K2, N–Q2; 10 R–K1, Q–B2; 11 P–QR3, N–K2; 12 P–QN3, N–N3; 13 B–N2, O–O–O = . Kotov-Kopylov, Volgograd 1964. (2) 6 N–N5, B × B! 7 Q × B, P × P; 8 P × P, P–K3; 9 O–O, N–Q2; 10 P–QB4 (10 P–KB4, B–K2; 11 N–K4, N–B4; 12 QN–Q2, Q–B2 =), N–K2; 11 QN–B3, N–KB4; 12 N–B3, Q–B2; 13 R–K1, B–N5; 14 B–Q2, O–O and 15 . . . B–K2 = . Bagirov. In this last line, the strongest answer is 9 Q–R5! P–KN3; 10 Q–K2, N–Q2; 11 O–O ± . Sax-Shamkovich, Hastings 1977–78.

(f) A somewhat belated afterthought is now 6 P–QB4, N–N3; 7 P × P, P × P; 8 O–O, B–K2; (1) 9 B–K3, O–O; 10 N–B3 (but if 10 QN–Q2, P–B4! ∓), P–Q4! 11 P–B5, B × N! 12 B × B, N–B5; with more flexibility for Black. Janošević-Korchnoi, Sarajevo 1969, or (2) 9 QN–Q2, QN–Q2 or (3) 9 P–KR3, B × N; 10 B × B, N–B3; 11 P–Q5, P × P; 12 B × P, N × B ∓ . Penrose-Bobotsov, Mallorca 1969.

(g) 6 . . . N–QB3; 7 P–B4, KN–K2 (7 . . . N–N3! 8 P × P, P × P; 9 P–QN3, B–K2 =); 8 P × P, Q × P; 9 N–B3, N–N3; 10 P–Q5, P × P; 11 P × P, B × N; 12 P × B! ± .

(h) This is a frequent interpolation. White also has 9 P × P, P × P; 10 B–K3, N–B3; 11 P–Q5 (11 P–QN3! is quite playable), P × P; 12 N × P, N × N; 13 Q × N, B–B3; 14 KR–Q1, R–B1! 15 R–Q2, Q–R4; 16 Q–QN5! with a slight advantage.

(i) 11 P–B5, and now (A) 11 . . . N/3–Q2; 12 P–QN4, P–QN3; 13 R–B1, P–QB3; 14 N–QR4, P–R4 ∞ . Kavalek-Martz, U.S. Chp. 1973. (B) 11 . . . B × N; 12 B × B, N–B5; (1) 13 B–B4, N–B3; 14 P–QN3, N/5–R4; 15 Q–Q2, P–QN3; 16 QR–B1, P × P; 17 P × P, R–N1 = . (2) 13 P–QN3, N × B; 14 P × N, P–QN3; 15 P–K4! P–QB3; 16 P–QN4, NP × P; 17 NP × P, Q–R4; 18 N × P, B–N4! 19 B–R5, BP × N; 20 B × P†, R × B; 21 R × R, Q–Q7! = . Spasski-Fischer, 19th match game 1972.

(*j*) (A) 8 Q–KN3, N–Q2; 9 B–K2, P–QB3; 10 N–R3, N–K2; 11 O–O, N–KB4 = Pachman. (B) 8 Q–KN3, P–KR4 = . (C) 8 B–QB4, N–QB3; 9 Q–K4, N/4–K2; 10 B–K3, N–B4; 11 O–O, Q–R5 ∓ .

(*k*) Mikenas. In the column, better is 9 B–N5!, therefore 8 . . . N–Q2 or 8 . . . P–QB3 are preferable.

(*l*) 9 N–B3, B–N5! 10 B–K3, N–B3; 11 P–QN3, Q–Q2; 12 P–B5, N–B1; 13 P–N4! P–QR3; 14 R–N1, B×N; 15 B×B, P–K3; 16 P–QR4, N/1–K2; 17 P–N5, RP×P ∓ , Janošević-Kavalek, Sarajevo 1967. The varied history of the 3 P–Q4, P–Q3 line tends to favour Black.

(*m*) (A) 11 P–QN3, P–Q4! 12 P–B5, N–Q2; 13 B–N2, B–K5! 14 N–QR4, P–K4; 15 P×P, N/2×KP; 16 N×N, N×N; 17 P–B3, B–B4; 18 P–B4, N–B3; 19 B×B, K×B; 20 B–B3, Q–B3 ∓ . Minev-Bobotsov, Varna 1968. (B) 11 B–B4, P–K4; 12 B–N5, P–B3 = . O'Kelly. (C) 11 B–K3, P–Q4; 12 P–B5, N–B5?! 13 B×N, P×B = . Grabczewski-Jansa, Lugano 1968.

1 P-K4, N-KB3; 2 P-K5 (a), N-Q4

	21	22	23	24	25
3	(P-Q4)			N-QB3 (i)	
	(P-Q3)			N × N (j)	
4	(N-KB3)			NP × N	QP × N
	(P-KN3)		P × P (e)	P-KN3 (k)	N-B3 (n)
5	N-N5	B-QB4	N × P	P-Q4	N-B3
	P-KB3 (b)	N-N3 (c)	P-K3 (f)	P-Q3	P-Q3
6	P-QB4	B-N3	Q-B3 (g)	P-KB4	B-QN5
	N-N3	B-N2	Q-B3	B-N2	B-Q2
7	P × BP	N-N5 (d)	Q-N3	B-Q3	Q-K2
	P × P	P-Q4	P-KR3	P-QB4	P-K3
8	N-KB3	P-QR4	N-QB3	N-B3	B-KB4
	B-N5	P-KB3	N-N5	O-O	P-QR3 =
9	B-K2	P × P	B-N5†	P × BP (l)	
	B-N2	P × P	P-B3	P × KP	
10	O-O	Q-K2†	B-R4	P × P	
	O-O =	Q-K2 =	N-Q2 (h)	B-B4 (m)	

(a) Upon 2 N-QB3, Black may transpose into the Vienna Game (2 . . . P-K4) or the Pirć Defence (2 . . . P-Q3). Involved is 2 . . . P-Q4. For 2 . . . P-K3; 3 P-QB4! see English Opening, col. 21.

(b) 5 . . . P × P (5 . . . P-QB3 or 5 . . . P-KB3 may lead back into the column or into note (c)); 6 P × P, B-N2; 7 B-QB4, P-QB3; 8 N-QB3 (8 Q-K2, P-KR3; 9 N-B3, B-N5; 10 P-KR3, B × N; 11 P × B, P-K3; 12 B-N3, N-Q2 =), P-KR3; 9 N-B3, B-N5! = . Cols. 20-22 show different tactics but related strategies. The column is Krogius-Korchnoi, USSR 1958.

(c) Unwieldy, though tough to break, is 5 . . . P-QB3; 6 O-O (6 N-N5, B-N2; 7 Q-K2, O-O; 8 O-O, P-KR3 =), B-N2; 7 P × P, Q × P; (A) 8 R-K1! O-O; 9 B-KN5, B-N5; 10 QN-Q2, R-K1; 11 B-N3, P-KR3; 12 B-KR4, N-Q2; 13 P-B4, N-B5; 14 P-B5! Q × QP; 15 R-K4, B × N; 16 P × B ±. Tal-Ljubojević, Beverwijk 1973. (B) 8 P-KR3, O-O; 9 QN-Q2, N-Q2; 10 B-N3, Q-B2; 11 R-K1, N/2-B3; 12 N-B4!, P-QR4; 13 P-R3, P-R5; 14 B-R2, P-QN4 = . Kavalek-Ljubojević, Las Palmas 1973.

(d) (A) 7 O-O, O-O; 8 P-QR4, P-QR4; 9 P-R3, N-B3; 10 Q-K2, P-Q4; 11 N-B3, B-K3; 12 B-B4, Q-Q2; 13 QR-Q1, N-Q1! = . Keres. (B) (7 N-N5! P-Q4 = 7 . . . O-O? 8 P-K6!); 8 P-KB4, N-B3; 9 P-B3, P-B3; 10 N-B3, B-B4; 11 O-O, (1) 11 . . . Q-Q2 ∞. Karpov-Torre, Leningrad International 1973. (2) 11 . . . N-R4; 12 B-B2, B × B; 13 Q × B, Q-Q2; 14 QN-Q2, P-KB4; 15 N-K1, P-K3; 16 N/2-B3, B-B1; 17 N-Q3, B-K2; 18 P-QR4, O-O; 19 P-QN3, KR-Q1; 20 Q-R2, Q-K1; 21 B-R3, B × B; 22 Q × B, N-Q2; 23 N-Q2, Q-B1; 24 P-QN4, N-QB3; 25 P-R5, P-QR3; 26 N-N3, K-B2; 27 N/N-B5, N × N; 28 N × N, R-R2! 29 Q-R4, Q-K1; 30 P-N5, P × P; 31 Q × P, N × RP; 32 R × N, R × R; 33 Q × R, P-N3; 34 Q-R7, P × N; 35 Q × P†, Q-K2, drawn. Matanović-Martz, Malaga 1973.

(e) (A) 4 . . . N-QB3; 5 P-B4; N-N3; 6 P-K6, P × P; 7 P-KR4 (7 B-Q3, P-K4; 8 P × P, B-N5 =), P-K4; 8 P-Q5, N-Q5; 9 N × N, P × N; 10 B-Q3, Q-Q2; 11 B-N5, P-KR3; Tal-Larsen, match 1969; 12 B-QB1 ± . (B) 4 . . . N-N3?! 5 B-K2, P-N3; 6 O-O, B-N2; 7 P × P, BP × P; 8 P-QR4, O-O; 9 P-R5, N-Q4 = . Honfi-Schmid, Monte Carlo 1969. Or 5 P-QR4, P-QB3; or 5 N-B3, P-N3; 6 B-KB4, B-N2 = . (D) 4 . . . P-Q4 with a type of French set-up and a mobile QB (Koltanowski).

(f) 5 . . . N-Q2! 6 N × P?! K × N! 7 Q-R5†, K-K3; 8 Q-N4†, K-B2; 9 Q-R5† draws. (If 8 P-KN3, P-QN4! Larsen.)

(g) 6 Q-R5, P-KN3; 7 Q-B3, Q-K2; 8 N-B3, N-Q2; 9 B-QB4 (9 N/3 × N, P × N; 10 Q × P, P-KB3! ∓), N/4 × N; 10 N × N, Q × N; 11 P × N, B-N2 = . Ivkov-Larsen, match 1965.

(h) 11 O–O ± . Tal-Larsen, match 1965.

(i) Innocuous is 3 B–4, N–N3, 4 B–N3, P–QB4; 5 Q–K2, N–B3; 6 N–KB3, P–Q4; 7 P × P, e.p. 7 P–K3; 8 N–B3, B × P; 9 N–K4, B–K2; 10 P–Q3, N–Q4 ∓ . Yates-Rubinstein, Dresden 1926.

(j) 3 . . . P–K3; 4 N × N, P × N; 5 P–Q4, P–Q3; 6 N–B3, N–B3; 7 B–K2, B–K2; 8 B–KB4, O–O = . Sämisch-Alekhin, Budapest 1922.

(k) Again following the latest trend. (A) The "historical" line is 4 . . . P–Q3; 5 P–KB4, and now (1) 5 . . . P × P; 6 P × P, B–B4; 7 Q–B3, Q–B1; 8 B–B4, P–K3; 9 N–K2, B–K2; 10 O–O, O–O = . Comments. Or (2) 5 . . . N–B3; 6 N–B3, P × P; 7 P × P, Q–Q4; 8 P–Q4, B–N5; 9 B–K2, P–K3; 10 O–O, B–K2; 11 P–B4 (or 11 N–N5!) 11 . . . Q–Q2; 12 P–B3! Pachman. (B) 4 . . . P–QN3? 5 Q–B3! N–B3; 6 P–K6! (C) 4 . . . P–K3!? 5 P–KB4, P–QN3; 6 N–B3, B–N2; 7 P–Q4, B–K2; 8 B–Q3, P–Q3; 9 O–O, N–B3 ∞. Padevski-Larsen, Lugano 1968.

(l) Until now this "modern" game has been identical with Grob-Grünfeld, Meran 1926, which went 9 O–O, Q–B2; 10 Q–K1, BP × P; 11 BP × P, with a little more elbow-room. The column merely reflects contemporary technique.

(m) 11 B–K3, P–N3; 12 Q–K2, P–K3; 13 QR–Q1, Q–B2; 14 N–N5, N–B3; 15 P–N4! B × B = . Dückstein-Johansson, Lugano 1968.

(n) Again (A) 4 . . . P–KN3; 5 N–B3, B–N2; 6 B–KB4, P–Q3; 7 Q–Q2, N–B3; 8 O–O–O, B–N5 = . Bannik-Korchnoi, USSR 1954. Or (B) 4 . . . P–Q3; 5 N–B3, P × P; 6 Q × Q†, K × Q; 7 N × P, K–K1; 8 B–K3, P–KB3; 9 N–B3, P–K4; 10 N–Q2 ± . Hübner.

Caro-Kann Defence

(1 P–K4, P–QB3)

Mentioned by Polerio in 1590, this defence was little understood and scarcely played until H. Caro of Berlin and M. Kann of Vienna took up the cudgels in the 1890s. Capablanca adopted it for the first time against Atkins at London, 1922, and it remained highly regarded during his reign as World Champion. Nimzowitsch, Tartakover, and Flohr became permanent converts. More recently, Petrosian. But most masters could not warm to its dullness until Botvinnik fashioned it into a precise weapon in his title matches against Smyslov and Tal. (Ironically, it was his Panov-Botvinnik attack which nearly put the Caro-Kann out of commission in the 1930s.) Currently it is considered safe, a possible means of reaching an early end-game, though lacking the dynamic imbalance which produces winning chess. Its drawish reputation remains undiminished.

The Caro-Kann is characterized by 1 . . . P–QB3 preparing 2 . . . P–Q4 which in turn challenges the centre without imprisoning Black's queen's bishop. White enjoys greater mobility, and often a slight initiative, but Black's porcupine-like position is difficult to penetrate.

The Panov-Botvinnik Attack 1 P–K4, P–QB3; 2 P–Q4, P–Q4; 3 P × P, P × P; 4 P–QB4, N–KB3; 5 N–QB3 (cols. 1–15) is still critical, though, for the moment, the sting has been taken out of this involved and dangerous system. Its complexity requires that the main ramifications retain their place in any comprehensive overview of the Caro-Kann. White threatens to transpose into favourable variations of the Queen's Gambit Accepted, or to establish a lasting bind with P–QB5 at some stage. Black can equalize, but he must know how. I have retained the original classical treatment in cols. 1–7 as an illustration of the developments and the spirit of this attack; but the preferred sequence for Black lately has been with an early 5 . . . P–K3 (cols. 8–12) instead of 5 . . . N–B3; thus, incidentally, making 6 B–N5 even less desirable.

124

THE EXCHANGE VARIATION, without 4 P-QB4 (cols. 16–18), is meeker and now rarely played, just as the *Fantasy Variation* with 3 P-KB3 (cols. 19–20), loses impetus against a sensible defence.

THE ADVANCE VARIATION 1 P-K4, P-QB3; 2 P-Q4, P-Q4; 3 P-K5 (cols. 21–5) was given new life by Tal, but with care Black can avoid any disadvantage. The locked pawn structure gives Black strategical opportunities, if he can avoid a quick knock-out.

THE MAIN LINE 1 P-K4, P-QB3; 2 P-Q4, P-Q4; 3 N-QB3, P × P; 4 N × P (cols. 26–43) still remains the most persistent and elastic strategy. The defence 4 . . . B-B4; 5 N-N3, B-N3 (cols. 26–33) seems most endangered in cols. 32–3, but the move 4 . . . N-B3 has been the subject of revived interest; 5 N × N† (cols. 34–8), wherein the eccentric looking 5 . . . NP × N—originated by Nimzowitch—is the more imaginative answer, although it requires superior tactical skill. 4 . . . N-Q2 (cols. 39–43) is lately met by 5 B-QB4 but the wheels of fortune and of new attempts are constantly turning.

THE TWO KNIGHTS' VARIATION 1 P-K4, P-QB3; 2 N-QB3, P-Q4; 3 N-B3 (cols. 42–51) produces fancy footwork where Black can hold his own. However, it has been infrequently employed in the last few years.

Unusual approaches for White are handled in cols. 44–5.

In the search for novelty, the old Spielmann line 3 Q-B3 has been unearthed (col. 58) and new attention focused on 2 P-Q3 with possible transposition into a King's Indian in reverse (cols. 59–60). The positional manoeuvers of these strategems still preclude hasty judgment of their ultimate values.

1 P–K4, P–QB3; 2 P–Q4, P–Q4; 3 P × P, P × P; 4 P–QB4, N–KB3; 5 N–QB3, N–B3

	1	2	3	4	5
6	B–N5				
	P–K3		P × P	Q–N3	Q–R4!
7	P–B5	P × P (*d*)	P–Q5 (*f*)	P × P	B × N (*l*)
	B–K2	P × P	N–K4 (*g*)	QN × P	KP × B!? (*m*)
8	B–N5 (*a*)	B–N5	Q–Q4	B–K3 (*j*)	P × P
	O–O	B–K2	N–Q6†	P–K4	B–QN5
9	N–B3	KN–K2	B × N	P × P *e.p.*	Q–Q2!
	N–K5	O–O	P × B	B–B4	B × N
10	B × B	O–O	N–B3	P × P† (*k*)	P × B
	N × B (*b*)	B–K3	P–KN3 (*h*)	K–K2	Q × QP
11	R–QB1	N–B4	B × N	KN–K2	N–B3
	P–QN3!	Q–Q3	P × B	Q × P	B–R6!
12	N × N	KB × N	O–O	R–B1	P–B4
	P × N	Q × B	B–K2	R–Q1	Q–K5†
13	N–K5	R–K1	QR–Q1	N × N	Q–K3
	P × P (*c*)	P–KR3 (*e*)	O–O (*i*)	B × N =	B–B4

(*a*) 8 N–B3, O–O; 9 R–B1, N–K5; 10 B × B, Q × B; 11 B–K2, P–B3! 12 O–O, N × N; 13 P × N (or 13 R × N), R–Q1; 14 R–K1, P–K4; 15 B–B1, B–N5 ∞. *Comments.*

(*b*) 10 . . . Q × B; 11 B × N (better than 11 Q–B2, N–N4; 12 N × N, Q × N; 13 B × N, P × B; 14 O–O, P–K4; 15 P × P, Q × P with equality. Keres–Alekhin, AVRO 1938), N × N; 12 P × N, P × B; 13 O–O ± .

(*c*) 14 R × P, Q–R4†; 15 Q–Q2, Q × P ∓ . Boleslavski.

(*d*) Unimpressive is 7 N–B3, P × P! 8 B × P, B–K2; 9 O–O, O–O; 10 R–B1, P–QR3; 11 B–Q3, P–R3; 12 B–R4, R–K1; 13 P–QR3, N–Q4 = . Weiss–Podhorzer, Vienna 1934. Compare the . . . P × P lines with the Semi-Tarrasch Defence and the Queen's Gambit Accepted.

(*e*) 14 N × B, P × N; 15 B–R4, QR–K1; 16 R–QB1 with slight advantage. Lengyel–Filip, Havana 1966.

(*f*) 7 B × P, Q × P (7 . . . N × P; 8 N–B3, N × N†; 9 Q × N ±); 8 Q × Q, N × Q; 9 O–O–O, N–K3 ∞. *Comments.*

(*g*) Insufficient is 7 . . . N–QR4; 8 P–QN4, P × P *e.p.*; 9 P × P ± .

(*h*) If (a) 10 . . . B–B4; 11 O–O, P–KR3; 12 B × N, NP × B; 13 Q–KB4, B–Q2; 14 R–Q1, Q–N1; 15 Q–K3 ± . O'Kelly–Bobotsov, Zevenaar 1961. (b) 10 . . . P–K3; 11 O–O–O, B–K2; 12 R × P. (c) 10 . . . P–KR3; 11 B × N, KP × B; 12 O–O, B–K2; 13 N–K4 ± .

(*i*) 14 R × P, B–KB4; 15 R–Q2, B–Q3; 16 P–KN4, B–B1; 17 N–K4 + + .

(*j*) Fine suggests 8 KN–K2, N–B4; 9 Q–Q2, N–Q3; 10 B–K3, Q–R4; 11 N–N3 but practical proof is missing.

(*k*) 10 Q–R4†, K–K2; 11 P–QN4, B × NP; 12 KN–K2, R–Q1; 13 R–B1 (Estrin–Bagirov, Baku 1958), N–N5 = . The column is Pachman's analysis.

(*l*) 7 Q–Q2. (a) 7 . . . P–K4! 8 B × N, P × B; 9 N × P, Q × Q†; 10 K × Q, B–R3†; 11 K–Q1 (if 11 K–B3, P × P; 12 K–N3, O–O; 13 B–Q3, P–N4! ∓), O–O; 12 N × P†, K–N2 = . Pachman. (b) 7 . . . B–B4; 8 B × N, KP × B; 9 P × P, N–N5; 10 B–N5†, K–Q1; 11 K–B1, N × P = .

(*m*) Taken for granted so as to initiate Black's counter 8 . . . B–QN5. But with White's QB off, the risky looking NP × B; deserves attention, e.g. (a) 8 Q–N3, B–B4 = . (b) 8 P × P, N–N5; 9 B–B4, B–B4; 10 B–N3 (10 R–B1, B–R3; 11 P–QR3, B × R; 12 P × N, Q–R8 ∓), N–Q6†! (or 10 . . . P–QR3 but not 10 . . . R–Q1? 11 B–R4†) 11 K–B1, N × NP; 12 B–R4† (12 Q–Q2? B–R3! or 12 Q–K1, N–Q6), N × B ∓ . *Comments.*

1 P-K4, P-QB3; 2 P-Q4, P-Q4; 3 P × P, P × P; 4 P-QB4, N-KB3; 5 N-QB3

	6	7	8	9	10
	(N-B3)................		P-K3		
6	N-B3		N-B3 (g)		
	B-N5	P-K3	B-N5	B-K2	
7	P × P	P-B5	B-Q3 (h)	P-B5	
	KN × P	N-K5 (d)	P × P	O-O	
8	Q-N3 (a)	B-QN5	B × BP	B-Q3 (i)	
	B × N	B-Q2 (e)	Q-B2	P-QN3	
9	P × B	O-O	Q-Q3	P-QN4	
	P-K3!	B-K2	O-O	P-QR4 (j)	
10	Q × P	R-K1	O-O	N-QR4	
	N × P	N × N	P-QN3	QN-Q2	KN-Q2
11	B-N5†	P × N	N-QN5	P-QR3 (k)	Q-B2! (m)
	N × B	O-O	Q-Q1	RP × P	N-R3
12	Q-B6†!	B-KB4	B-B4	RP × P	B × P†
	K-K2	P-QN3 = (f)	P-QR3	P × P	K-R1
13	Q × N/N5 (b)		N-B3	NP × P	P-N5
	Q-Q2 (c)		B-N2 =	P-K4 (l)	N-N5 (n)

(a) The initiative has faded out of one of the "parent" variation 8 B-QN5, R-B1; 9 P-KR3, (A) 9 . . . B × N; 10 Q × B, P-K3; 11 O-O, P-QR3; 12 N × N, Q × N; 13 Q × Q, P × Q; 14 B-R4, B-K2; 15 B-K3, B-Q3; 16 B-N3, N-K2 = . Krause-Nimzowitsch, corr. 1925 and the recent (B) 9 . . . B-R4; 10 O-O, P-K3; 11 R-K1, B-K2; 12 R-K5, N × N; 13 P × N, B-N3 = . Khasin-Bagirov, USSR chp. 1961.

(b) 13 N × N is less persistent, e.g. (A) 13 . . . P-B3; 14 O-O, K-B2; 15 B-K3! or (B) 13 . . . P-QR3; 14 N-Q4, K-B3! 15 P-KR4, P-R3; 16 P-B4, P-N3; 17 R-KN1, Q-R4†; 18 B-Q2, B-N5 ∞. *Comments.*

(c) 14 N × N†, Q × N! 15 Q × Q, P × Q; 16 B-K3, K-K3; 17 O-O-O, R-B1†; 18 K-N1, B-B4; 19 KR-K1, K-Q3; 20 R-Q3, KR-Q1; 21 P-QR3, P-KR3; 22 P-KR4, P-KR4; 23 R-N1, P-N3; 24 B-N5, R-K1; 25 R/1-Q1, B × BP; 26 R × P†, K-B3; 27 R/5-Q2, R-K8 with equality. A game Rogoff-Kavalek, US Chp. 1975, continued 28 R × R, B × R; 29 R-K2, B-R4; 30 P-B4?, B-N3; 31 P-B5, P × P; 32 R-K5, P-B3! 33 R-K6†, K-Q4; 34 R × P, K-K5; 35 R-B7, R-B2; 36 R-B8, B-B4; 37 R-B6, B-Q5; 38 R-B8, B-N2; 39 R-K8†, K-B6; 40 R-K1, B-Q5; 41 P-N4, K-N5; 42 R-Q1, B-B7; 43 R-Q5, R-B2; 44 K-B2, P-B5; 45 K-Q1, P-B6; 46 P-R4, B-N6; 47 R-Q4†, K-R6; 48 B-K3, P-B7; 49 B × P, B × B; 50 R-K4, B × P; 51 P-R5, B-B7; 52 P-N5, P-R5; 53 K-K2, K-N7; 54 P-N6, P × P; 55 P × P, P-R6; 56 R-N4†, B-N6; 57 Resigns.

(d) 7 . . . B-K2; 8 B-QN5, B-Q2; 9 O-O, O-O; 10 R-K1, P-QR3; 11 B-Q3, P-QN3; 12 P × P, Q × P; 13 N-K5 ± . Shamkovich-Hort, Leningrad 1968.

(e) 8 . . . Q-R4! also deserves further exploration.

(f) Kholmov-Milić, Belgrade 1968. Also 12 . . . N-K4! = .

(g) (A) 6 P-B5 can transpose into col. 9, or continue with the immediate fianchetto 6 . . . P-QN3!; e.g., 7 P-QN4, P-QR4; 8 N-R4, KN-Q2; 9 B-QN5, NP × P; = . (B) 6 B-N5, B-K2; 7 N-B3, O-O; 8 R-B1, P-QN3; 9 B-Q3, N-B3; 10 O-O, N-QN5 = .

(h) 7 P-B5, N-K5; 8 B-Q2, B × N. The column is Benko-Filip, Curaçao 1962. It can also arise from the Nimzo-Indian Defence, col. 35.

(i) The text seems a little more consistent than (A) 8 P-QN4, P-QN3; 9 B-KN5, N-K5! (B) 8 B-KN5, P-QN3; 9 P-QN4, N-K5; 10 B × B, Q × B; 11 N-QR4, B-Q2; 12 B-Q3, N-QB3; 13 P-N5, N-N5; 14 O-O, P × P; 15 P × P, N × B; 16 Q × N, P-QR3; 17 P-B6, P × P; 18 N-N6, R-R6; 19 Q × NP, N-B6; 20 Q-N2, B × P; 21 N-Q4, B-R1; 22 N-B2, R-R3; 23 P-QR4,

Q–R2; 24 P–R5, R × P; 25 R × R, N–K7†; 26 K–R1, Q × R; 27 R–R1, Q–Q7; 28 N × B, P–Q5; 29 Q–N3, N–B8; 30 Q–N4, Q × N; 31 P–R3, P–Q6; 32 N–N6, P–Q7; 33 Resigns. Barlov-Christiansen, Tjentiste 1976.

(*j*) 9 . . . P × P; 10 NP × P, N–B3! 11 O–O, B–Q2; 12 P–KR3, N–K1; 13 B–KB4, B–B3; 14 B–QN5, N–B2; Fischer-Ivkov, Buenos Aires 1960; 15 R–K1 with a bind.

(*k*) (A) 11 B–KB4, P × NP; 12 P–B6, N–B4! 13 P × N, P × P; 14 O–O, Q–R4; 15 N–N2, B–R3 ∓. Prins-E. Richter, Teplice-Šanov 1949. (B) 11 Q–B2!? Q–B2?! = . Panov.

(*l*) 14 N × P, (1) 14 . . . N × N; 15 P × N, N–K5; 16 O–O! N × QBP; 17 B–B2, B–R3 ∞ or (2) 14 . . . B × P; 15 O–O, N × N; 16 P × N, N–K5! (or 16 . . . N–N5) = .

(*m*) (A) 11 P–KR4, P × BP; 12 NP × BP, B–R3! (B) 11 P–N5, P × P; 12 P × P, P–K4; 13 P–B6, P–K5; 14 P × N, N × P; 15 O–O, P × N; 16 Q × P, N–K4; 17 Q–K2, N × B; 18 Q × N, B–Q3; 19 B–R3 ± . Botvinnik-Pomar, Munich 1958.

(*n*) 14 Q–N1, P × N; 15 P–QR3, P–B5; 16 P × N, P × P; 17 B–B2, P–N6; 18 B × P, P × B; 19 Q × P ± . Liberzon-Opočenský, Leipzig 1965.

1 P-K4, P-QB3; 2 P-Q4; 3 P × P, P × P; 4 P-QB4

	11	12	13	14	15
	(N-KB3) (*a*)				
5	(N-QB3)				
	(P-K3)		P-KN3 (*g*)		
6	(N-B3)		P × P		
	(B-K2)		B-N2		
7	(P-B5)	P × P	Q-N3 (*h*)		
	P-QN3	N × P (*d*)	O-O		
8	P-QN4	B-Q3	B-K2	KN-K2	N-B3 (*n*)
	P-QR4	N-QB3 (*e*)	QN-Q2	R-K1! (*k*)	QN-Q2
9	N-QR4 (*b*)	O-O	B-B3	B-N5 (*l*)	B-KN5
	QN-Q2	O-O	N-N3	P-K3	N-N3
10	B-QN5 (*c*)	R-K1	B-N5 (*i*)	P × P	B-QB4
		B-B3 (*f*)	B-B4 (*j*)	B × P (*m*)	B-B4 (*o*)

(*a*) 4 . . . N-QB3; 5 N-KB3 (5 N-QB3, P-K4!), B-N5; 6 P × P, Q × P; 7 B-K2, P-K3; 8 O-O, N-B3; 9 N-B3, Q-QR4; 10 P-KR3, B-R4; 11 P-R3 ± . Capablanca-Czerniak, Buenos Aires 1939.

(*b*) Inconsequential is 9 B-N5†, B-Q2; 10 Q-R4, O-O; 11 B-KB4, N-K5; 12 N-K2, Q-K1; 31 B × B, N × B ∓ .

(*c*) 10 . . . O-O; 11 B-KB4, NP × P; 12 NP × BP, B-R3; 13 B × B, R × B; 14 Q-Q3, Q-R1; 15 O-O, N-K5; 16 QR-N1 + .

(*d*) Pachman's 7 . . . P × P!? 8 B-N5†, N-B3; 9 N-K5, B-Q2; 10 O-O, O-O; 11 R-K1, N-K5!? 12 N × QP, N × N; 13 P × N, B × B; 14 R × N, B-QB3; 15 N × B†, Q × N is precarious.

(*e*) Also 8 . . . N × N; 9 P × N, Q-B2; 10 O-O, N-Q2; 11 Q-B2, P-QN3; 12 R-K1, B-N2; 13 N-N5, N-B3; 14 B-N5†, B-B3; 15 B-KB4, Q-Q2 = . Lehmann-Karaklajić, Bognor Regis 1962.

(*f*) Continued 11 B-K4, QN-K2; 12 Q-B2, (1) 12 . . . P-KN3; 13 B-R6, B-N2; 14 B-N5, P-B3; 15 B-Q2, B-Q2; 16 Q-N3, B-B3 = . Spassky-Petrosian, 9th match game 1966 or (2) 12 . . . N-KN3; 13 Q-N3, N/4-K2; 14 N-K5, Q-N3; 15 Q-B2, P-KR3 = . Portisch-Pomar, Malaga 1964. Risky are (A) 10 . . . N-B3; 11 B-KN5, P-QN3; 12 P-QR3, B-N2; 13 B-B2, B-R3; 14 Q-Q2, R-B1; 15 Q-B4 ± . Szabó-Unzicker, Amsterdam 1954. (B) 10 . . . B-Q2; 11 N × N, P × N; 12 N-K5, N × N; 13 R × N! B-Q3?! 14 R × P, Q-B2; 15 R-KR5 + . Keres-Donner, Bled 1961.

(*g*) 5 . . . P × P; 6 B × P, P-K3; 7 N-B3, P-QR3; 8 O-O, B-K2; 9 Q-K2, P-QN4; 10 B-N3, O-O; 11 B-N5 ± .

(*h*) Powerful is 7 B-QB4, as in Tarjan-Czom, Plain Dealer International Tourn., Cleveland 1974, which continued 7 . . . O-O; 8 KN-K2, N-R3; 9 O-O, N-B2; 10 P-Q6!! Q × P; 11 B-R4, Q-Q1; 12 Q-N3, N/2-K1; 13 B-K5, N-Q3; 14 B-Q3, B-K3; 15 Q-R4, B-Q2; 16 Q-N3, B-K3; 17 Q-R4, B-Q2; 18 Q-Q1, N/B-K1; 19 Q-Q2, B-B4; 20 QR-Q1, Q-Q2; 21 KR-K1, R-Q1; 22 N-B4, B × KB; 23 Q × B, N-B4; 24 B × B, K × B; 25 P-Q5, N-B3; 26 P-KR3, Q-Q3; 27 P-KN3, R-Q2; 28 N-N5, Q-N3; 29 P-KN4, N-R5; 30 P-Q6, P × P; 31 P-N5, N-R4; 32 N-Q5, Q-Q1; 33 Q-Q4†, K-N1; 34 Q × N, R-K1; 35 R × R†, Q × R; 36 Q × N and White won.

(*i*) Sterile are (A) 10 B-B4, B-N5 (or 10 . . . B-B4; 11 R-Q1, Q-Q2; 12 P-KR3, P-KR4 =); 11 B × B, N × B; 12 N-B3, N-B3 ∞ . (B) 10 KN-K2, B-B4! 11 N-B4, P-N4! 12 N/4-K2, P-N5; 13 N-N3, B-N3; 14 B-K2, QN × P. *Archives*.

(*j*) (A) 10 . . . P-QR4; 11 B × N, KP × B; 12 KN-K2, B-B4; 13 R-Q1 is still an open question, just as (B) 10 . . . B-N5; 11 B × N, B × KB; 12 N × B, B × B; 13 P-QR4. The text 10 . . . B-B4; 11 R-Q1, P-QR4! 12 KN-K2, P-R5; 13 Q-N5, N-B1; 14 N-N3, N-Q3 ∞ is Orev-Bronstein, Kislovodsk 1968.

(*k*) 8 . . . N–R3; 9 P–N3, Q–N3; 10 Q × Q, P × Q; 11 B–N2, N–QN5; 12 O–O, R–Q1; 13 P–Q6! Tal-Botvinnik, Moscow 1966.

(*l*) Here the fianchetto fails: 9 P–KN3, P–K3; 10 P × P, B × P; 11 Q × P, QN–Q2; 12 B–N2, R–N1; 13 Q × P, B–B5; 14 B–B3, N–Q4 ∓ .

(*m*) 11 Q × P, QN–Q2; 12 O–O–O, Q–R4; 13 Q–N5, Q × Q; 14 N × Q, B × P = . Boleslavski.

(*n*) (A) 8 P–N3, N–B3! (B) 8 B–QB4, QN–Q2; 9 KN–K2, N–N3; 10 O–O, N × B; 11 Q × N, P–N3 = . Compare Grünfeld Defence, also for 8 B–KB4.

(*o*) 11 B × N, B × B; 12 R–Q1, R–B1; 13 B–Q3, B–N5; 14 B–K4, N–B5 = . *Comments.*

1 P–K4, P–QB3; 2 P–Q4, P–Q4

	16	17	18	19	20
3	P×P			P–KB3 (*h*) (Fantasy Variation)	
	P×P (Exchange Variation)			P×P	P–KN3 (*i*)
4	B–Q3 (*a*)			P×P	P–B3
	N–QB3			P–K4	B–N2
5	P–QB3			N–KB3	N–QR3
	N–B3	P–KN3	Q–B2	B–K3!	N–Q2
6	B–KB4 (*b*)	N–B3	N–B3	P–B3!	B–K3
	P–KN3 (*c*)	B–N5	N–B3	N–B3	P×P
7	N–B3	Q–N3!	O–O	B–Q3	P×P
	B–N2	B×N	B–N5	QN–Q2	KN–B3
8	P–KR3 (*d*)	Q×NP	R–K1	Q–K2	Q–B3
	B–B4	Q–B1	P–K3	B–Q3	O–O
9	O–O	Q×Q†	QN–Q2	QN–Q2	O–O–O
	B×B	R×Q	B–Q3	Q–K2	Q–R4
10	Q×B	P×B	N–B1	O–O	N–R3
	O–O (*e*)	N×P?! (*f*)	O–O = (*g*)	O–O–O =	P–QN4 =

(*a*) Played to restrict Black's QB, yet it is a lame line just as 4 P–QB3, N–QB3; 5 B–KB4, B–B4; 6 N–B3, P–K3; 7 Q–N3, Q–B1 (White permitted . . . B–B4 so as to create his Q-side attack!); 8 QN–Q2, N–B3; 9 B–K2, B–K2; 10 O–O, N–K5; 11 QR–B1, N×N = . Larsen-Spasski, San Juan 1969.

(*b*) Less forceful is 6 P–KR3, P–K4; 7 P×P, N×P; 8 N–B3, N–QB3! 9 O–O, B–K2 = .

(*c*) 6 . . . B–N5; 7 N–B3, P–K3; 8 Q–N3, Q–B1; 9 QN–Q2, B–K2; 10 O–O, O–O; 11 N–K5, B–R4; 12 Q–B2! B–N3; 13 N×B, RP×N; 14 N–B3, N–KR4; 15 B–K3, Q–B2; 16 P–KN3, QR–B1; 17 Q–K2, P–R3; 18 QR–K1, KR–K1; 19 B–B1, N–B3; 20 N–N5, B–Q3; 21 P–KB4, N–Q2; 22 N–B3, N–B1; 23 N–K5, N–K2; 24 K–N2, P–B3; 25 N–B3, R–N1; 26 P–KR4, P–QN4; 27 P–R3, N–B3; 28 Q–B2, N–K2; 29 Q–K2, Q–B3; 30 R–R1, P–QR4; 31 P–R5, P–N5; 32 BP×P, P×P; 33 P–R4! Q×P; 34 N–R4, P×P; 35 Q×P, KR–B1; 36 P–B5! Q–N6; 37 P×P, N×P; 38 Q–R7†, K–B2; 39 Q–R5†, K–B1; 40 N–N6†, K–K1; 41 R×N, K–Q2; 42 R×N†, B×R; 43 Q–B5†, resigns. Browne-Larsen, San Antonio 1972.

(*d*) 8 O–O, B–N5; 9 P–KR3, B×N; 10 Q×B, Q–N3; 11 P–QN4, O–O; 12 R–K1, KR–K1; 13 N–Q2, QR–B1; 14 P–QR4, N–KR4 = .

(*e*) 11 QN–Q2, Q–N3; 12 QR–N1, QR–B1 = . Bohatirchuk-Tartakover, Moscow 1925.

(*f*) 11 B–K3! N–QB3; 12 B–QN5, P–K4; 13 B×P, B–Q3; 14 B×N† ± . Rossolimo-Bronstein, Monte Carlo 1969. Black's fianchetto is an insecure line, refuted by White's 7th move. Less incisive is 7 B–KB4, B–N2; 8 QN–Q2, N–B3; 9 P–KR3, B × N; 10 N × B, O–O = .

(*g*) Tartakover-Flohr, Bled 1931.

(*h*) An isolated try is 3 N–Q2, P–KN3; 4 B–Q3! B–N2; 5 P–QB3, P×P; 6 N×P, B–B4; 7 N–B5, P–N3; 8 N–N3, B×B; 9 Q×B, N–B3; 10 N–B3 with a freer game although it ended in a draw. Geller-Botvinnik, Moscow 1968. The column is Kasparian-Kholmov, USSR Chp. prelim. 1949.

(*i*) 3 . . . P–K3; 4 B–K3, N–B3! (not (A) 4 . . . Q–N3; 5 N–Q2, Q×NP; 6 N–N3± or (B) 4 . . . P×P; 5 N–Q2! P×P; 6 KN×P ±); 5 N–B3, Q–N3; 6 R–N1, P–B4! 7 KP×P, BP×P = . The column is Vinogradov-Kopylov, USSR 1946.

1 P–K4, P–QB3; 2 P–Q4, P–Q4; 3 P–K5, B–B4 (*a*)

	21	22	23	24	25
4	B–Q3	P–KR4	P–QB4	N–K2	QN–B3 (*m*)
	B × B	P–KR4 (*d*)	P × P (*f*)	P–K3	P–K3
5	Q × B	P–QB4 (*e*)	B × P	N–N3 (*h*)	P–KN4
	P–K3	P–K3	P–K3	B–N3 (*i*)	B–N3
6	N–QB3 (*b*)	N–QB3	N–QB3	P–KR4	KN–K2
	Q–N3	N–Q2	N–Q2	P–KR3 (*j*)	P–QB4
7	KN–K2	P × P!	KN–K2!	P–R5	P–KR4
	Q–R3!	BP × P	N–K2	B–R2	P–KR4
8	N–B4!	B–KN5	O–O	B–Q3	N–B4
	Q × Q	B–K2	N–QN3	B × B	B–R2
9	N × Q	Q–Q2	B–N3	P × B (*k*)	N × RP
	N–Q2	B × B	Q–Q2!	N–K2	P × P
10	B–K3	Q × B	P–QR4!	N–B3	Q × P
	N–K2	Q × Q	P–QR4	N–R3	N–QB3
11	P–KB4	P × Q	N–N3	O–O	B–QN5
	N–KB4 (*c*)	P–QR3 =	B–N3 (*g*)	Q–Q2 (*l*)	B × P =

(*a*) (A) 3 . . . P–K3 shuts in the QB and creates a French Defence where Black now will lose a tempo with . . . P–QB4, which, however, is playable at once, e.g. (B) 3 . . . P–QB4; 4 P × P and now (1) 4 . . . P–K3; 5 Q–N4, N–QB3; 6 N–KB3, Q–B2; 7 B–QN5, B–Q2; 8 B × N, Q × B; 9 B–K3, N–K2; 10 QN–Q2, N–B4 = . (2) 4 . . . N–QB3; 5 N–KB3, B–N5; 6 B–QN5, Q–R4†; 7 N–B3, P–K3; 8 B–K3, N–K2 = . *Comments.*

(*b*) (A) 6 N–KB3, Q–R4†; 7 QN–Q2, Q–R3; 8 P–B4, N–Q2! 9 O–O, B–K2; 10 N–K1, P–KR4; 11 P × P, Q × Q; 12 N × Q, BP × P = (12 . . . KP × P?! is wilder); (B) 6 P–KB4, Q–R4†! 7 P–B3, Q–R3 = .

(*c*) 12 B–B2, P–KR4; 13 K–K2, P–QN3; 14 P–QN4, P–R4 = . Boleslavski.

(*d*) Upon (A) 4 . . . P–KR3; 5 B–Q3 is solid and avoids the questionable complications of 5 P–KN4, B–Q2! If (B) 4 . . . P–QB4; 5 P × P, Q–B2; 6 N–KB3, N–QB3; 7 N–B3, R–Q1; 8 N–QN5, Q–B1; 9 P–B3! ± .

(*e*) (A) 5 N–QB3, P–K3; 6 N–B3, B–KN5; 7 B–K2, P–QB4; 8 B–K3, N–QB3; 9 P × P, B × N = . Aronin-Smyslov, USSR 1961. (B) 5 N–K2, P–K3; 6 N–N3, P–KN3; 7 N × B, NP × N; 8 P–QB4, P–B4; 9 P × QP, Q × P; 10 N–QB3, Q × QP; 11 Q–B3, N–QB3 ± . Tal-Botvinnik, match 1961. Compare col. 24.

(*f*) 4 . . . P–K3; 5 N–QB3, N–Q2; 6 P × P, BP × P is equally playable.

(*g*) 12 B–B2, B × B; 13 Q × B, KN–Q4; 14 KN–K4, N–N5; 15 Q–K2, N/3–Q4; 16 P–B4, P–KN3; 17 R–R3, B–K2; 18 B–Q2, N–B7 = . Tal-Golombek, Munich 1958.

(*h*) Stereotyped is 5 N–B4 (1) 5 . . . P–B4; 6 P × P, KB × P; 7 B–Q3, N–K2; 8 O–O, O–O; 9 P–B3! N–Q2; 10 Q–K2, Q–B2; 11 R–K1, QR–B1 = or (2) 5 . . . B–K2; 6 B–Q3, B × B; 7 N × B, P–KR4; 8 N–Q2, N–Q2; 9 O–O, P–KN3; 10 N–B3, N–R3; 11 B × N, R × B; 12 Q–Q2, R–R2; 13 P–QR4, K–B1 = . Szabó-Barcza, Hungarian Chp. 1959.

(*i*) 5 . . . N–K2; 6 N × B, N × N; 7 P–QB3, P–B4; 8 B–Q3, P–KN3 = . Larsen.

(*j*) 6 . . . P–KR4; 7 B–K2, P–QB4! 8 B × P, B × B; 9 N × B, P–KN3; 10 B–N5, B–K2; 11 B × B, Q × B; 12 N–N3, R × P; 13 R × R, Q × R = . Brzuzka-Veresov, Poland *v.* Byelorussia 1958, might be more consequential and imaginative but is also even.

(*k*) 9 Q × B, Q–R4† (or 9 . . . P–QB4!); 10 P–B3, Q–R3; 11 K–K2, Q × Q† = .

(*l*) 12 QN–K2, N–KB4 = . Matulović-Pachman, Sarajevo 1961.

(*m*) (A) 4 P–KN4, B–Q2! 5 P–QB4, P–K3; 6 N–QB3, N–K2 = . (B) 4 KN–B3, P–K3; 5 B–Q3, N–K2; 6 O–O, N–Q2; 7 P–B3, B × B; 8 Q × B, N–N3 = .

1 P-K4, P-QB3; 2 P-Q4, P-Q4; 3 N-QB3, P × P; 4 N × P, B-B4; 5 N-N3, B-N3

	26	27	28	29	30
6	P-KR4				KN-K2 (i)
	P-KR3				P-K3
7	N-B3		KN-K2	P-R5 (g)	N-B4
	N-Q2		P-K3	B-R2	B-Q3
8	B-Q3	P-R5!	N-B4	N-B3	P-QB3
	B × B	B-R2	B-R2	N-Q2	N-B3
9	Q × B	B-Q3	B-B4	B-Q3	P-KR4
	Q-B2	B × B	N-B3	B × B	Q-B2
10	B-Q2	Q × B	O-O	Q × B	P-R5
	KN-B3	Q-B2	B-Q3	Q-B2	B × N
11	O-O-O (a)	B-Q2 (d)	R-K1 (f)	B-Q2	B × B
	P-K3	P-K3	O-O	P-K3	Q × B
12	K-N1 (b)	Q-K2!	P-B3!	O-O-O	P × B
	O-O-O (c)	KN-B3 (e)	N-Q4! =	O-O-O (h)	BP × B (j)

(a) Also 11 O-O, P-K3; 12 P-B4, B-Q3; 13 N-K4, N × N; 14 Q × N, O-O; 15 B-B3, P-QR4; 16 P-Q5, R-K1 = . Fischer-Donner, Varna 1962.

(b) If 12 KR-K1, O-O-O; 13 Q-K2, N-Q4! 14 N-K5, N × N; 15 P × N, B-K2! 16 P-R5! KR-K1; 17 Q-N4, B-B1; 18 P-KB4, P-QB4! ∓ .

(c) 13 P-B4, P-B4; 14 Q-K2, B-Q3; 15 N-K4, N × N! 16 Q × N, N-B3; 17 Q-K2, P × P; 18 N × P, P-R3; 19 B-B3, R-Q2 = . Smyslov-Botvinnik, match 1958.

(d) (A) 11 R-R4, P-K3; 12 B-B4, B-Q3; 13 B × B, Q × B; 14 N-K4, Q-K2; 15 O-O-O, KN-B3; 16 N × N†, P × N! 17 Q-Q2, N-N3; 18 Q-R5, Q-Q3; 19 R-Q3, Q-Q4! Gligorić-Petrosian, Candidates Tournament 1959. (B) 11 Q-K2, P-K3; 12 B-Q2, KN-B3; transposes into note (e).

(e) 13 O-O-O, O-O-O; 14 N-K5, (A) 14 . . . N × N; 15 P × N, (1) 15 . . . N-Q4! 16 P-KB4, P-QB4! 17 P-B4, N-N5; 18 B × N, R × R†; 19 R × R, P × B; 20 N-K4 ± . Spasski-Botvinnik, Moscow 1966. (2) 15 . . . N-Q2; 16 P-KB4, B-K2; 17 N-K4, N-B4; 18 N-B3, P-B3; 19 P × P, B × P; 20 Q-B4, Q-N3; 21 P-QN4 (Spasski-Petrosian, World Chp. 1966), Q-R3! = Reshevsky. (B) 14 . . . N-N3; 15 B-R5, R-Q4; 16 P-N4, R × B; 17 P × R, N-R5; 18 R-Q3, N-Q4; 19 R-N3 ± . Pegarero-Elystrand, Helsinki 1969.

(f) 11 N × P!? P × N; 12 B × P, QN-Q2! (12 . . . Q-B2; 13 N-R5 ±); 13 R-K1, Q-B2; 14 B-N8 dis. †, K-B1; 15 B × B, R × B; 16 N-B5! P-KN3; 17 B × P†, K-N1; 18 N × B, Q × B; 19 B-N5, R-K2; 20 Q-Q3, K-N2 (Tal-Botvinnik, Match 1960); 21 P-KB4! QR-K1; 22 R-K5, P-B4; 23 P-B3, P × P; 24 P × P = (Tal).

(g) (A) 7 N-R3! P-K4! 8 P × P, Q-R4†; 9 B-Q2, Q × P†; 10 B-K2, Q × P = . (B) 7 B-Q3, B × B; 8 Q × B, N-B3 = . Matanović-Pomar, Mallorca 1966.

(h) White has several choices, i.e. (A) 13 N-K4, KN-B3; 14 P-KN3, N × N; 15 Q × N, B-K2; 16 K-N1, KR-K1; 17 P-QB4, P-QB4 = . Geller-Hort, Skopje 1968. (B) 13 Q-K2, KN-B3; 14 N-K5, N-N3; 15 B-R5, R-Q4; 16 B × N, RP × B; 17 P-QB4, R-Q1; 18 N-K4, N × N = . Mecking-Pomar, Lugano 1968. Or, so far strongest, (c) 13 P-B4, KN-B3; 14 B-B3! B-Q3; 15 N-K4, B-B5†; 16 K-B2, N-K4; 17 N × N, B × N; 18 N-B5! B-Q3; 19 N-N3 ± . Bronstein-Kotov, Amsterdam 1968. Also compare col. 31, note (c).

(i) (A) If 6 P-KB4, P-K3; 7 P-KR4, P-KR3; 8 N-B3, N-Q2; 9 B-B4, B-K2; 10 B-K3, Q-B2; 11 P-R5, B-R2; 12 B-Q3, KN-B3 ∓ . Krauss-Korn, corr. 1974. (B) 6 N-R3, N-B3; 7 N-B4, P-K3! 8 B-B4, B-Q3; 9 N × B, RP × N; 10 B-KN5, QN-Q2; 11 O-O, Q-R4 = . Tal-Botvinnik, match 1960. 8 P-QB3 reverts to the column.

(j) 13 Q-Q2, Q × Q†; 14 K × Q, QN-Q2 = . Boleslavski-Petrosian, Zürich 1953.

1 P–K4, P–QB3; 2 P–Q4, P–Q4; 3 N–QB3, P × P; 4 N × P

	31	32	33	34	35
	(B–B4)			N–B3	
5	(N–N3) (a)			N × N†	
	(B–N3)			NP × N!	
6	N–B3	B–QB4		P–QB3	
	N–Q2	P–K3		B–B4	
7	B–Q3	KN–K2		B–QB4	N–K2
	KN–B3	N–KB3 (d)		P–K3	P–KR4 (k)
8	O–O	N–B4!	O–O!?	N–K2 (j)	P–KR4 (l)
	P–K3	B–Q3 (e)	B–Q3 (h)	B–Q3	N–Q2
9	P–B4	B–N3 (f)	P–B4	B–B4	N–N3
	B–K2	Q–B2	Q–B2	Q–B2	B–N5
10	B × B (b)	Q–B3	K–R1 (i)	B × B	B–K2 (m)
	RP × P	QN–Q2	B–KB4	Q × B	B × B
11	Q–K2	P–KR4!	N × B	N–N3	Q × B
	Q–B2	P–K4!	P × N	B–N3	Q–R4
12	R–Q1	N × B	P–QN3! ±	P–KR4	O–O
	O–O (c)	RP × N (g)		P–KR4 =	O–O–O (n)

(a) Too speculative is 5 B–Q3!? Q × P; 6 N–KB3, Q–Q1; 7 Q–K2, B × N = .

(b) 10 R–K1, (A) 10 . . . B × B; 11 Q × B, Q–B2; 12 B–Q2, O–O; 13 B–B3, QR–Q1; 14 Q–K2, KR–K1; 15 QR–Q1, P–B4 = evens out, and so does (B) 10 . . . O–O; 11 B × B, RP × B; (1) 12 B–B4, R–K1; 13 Q–B2, P–B4; 14 QR–Q1, P × P; 15 N × P, B–N5; 16 B–Q2, B × B; 17 Q × B, P–QR3 = . Najdorf-Kotov, Zürich 1953 or (2) 12 P–N3, Q–R4; 13 Q–K2, P–B4; 14 B–Q2, Q–B2 = . Evans.

(c) 13 P–Q5!? BP × P; 14 P × P, N–B4; 15 P–N4!? N × P; 16 R × N, P × R; 17 P × N, B–B3 ∞ . Matulović-Hort, Vinkovci 1968. In the column, 9 . . . B–Q3; 10 P–N3, O–O; 11 B–N2, Q–B2; 12 B × B, RP × B; 13 Q–K2, KR–K1; 14 N–K4, N × N = is Spasski-Karpov, 6th match game, 1974.

(d) The best sequence. If 7 . . . B–Q3; 8 P–KR4, P–KR3; 9 N–B4, B × N (else 9 . . . B–R2? 10 N/4–R5!); 10 B × B, N–KB3; 11 P–R5, B–R2; 12 Q–K2, QN–Q2; 13 O–O–O ± .

(e) The sequence of moves is again subtle and important as can be seen from cols. 32–33 and the notes. A lesser alternative here is 8 . . . N–Q4?; 9 N × B, RP × N; 10 N–K4!, Q–R5; 11 Q–K2 ± .

(f) If now 9 O–O, N–Q4! 10 N/3–R5 (if now 10 N × B, RP × N with pressure on the R-file), O–O; 11 B–N3, N–Q2; 12 N × B, RP × N; 13 N–N3, Q–R5 ∓ .

(g) 13 B–K3, O–O–O; 14 O–O–O, P × P = . Boleslavski.

(h) Other suggestions are 8 . . . QN–Q2; or after, 8 . . . B–Q3; 9 P–B4, Q–Q2! = (Pachman) in preference to the column.

(i) 10 P–B5, P × P; 11 N × P, B × N! 12 R × B, QN–Q2 = . Informator VI. The column is Westerinen-Kagan, Ybbs 1968.

(j) 8 N–B3, B–Q3! 9 N–R4, B–N3; 10 Q–K2, Q–K2; 11 B–R6, N–Q2 = . Comments. The column is Sanguinetti-Panno, Mar del Plata 1957.

(k) 7 . . . N–Q2; 8 N–N3, B–N3; 9 P–KR4, P–KR3; 10 P–R5, B–R2; 11 B–Q3, B × B; 12 Q × B, Q–B2; 13 Q–B3, P–K3; 14 B–B4, Q–R4; 15 O–O, Q–Q4; 16 Q–K2, B–Q3; 17 B × B, Q × B; 18 QR–Q1, O–O–O = . Adorjan-Hübner, Candidates' Match 1980.

(l) 8 N–N3, B–N5; (A) 9 P–B3, P–R5 = . Or (B) 9 B–K2, B × B; 10 Q × B, Q–Q4!

(m) 10 P–B3, Q–B2! 11 K–B2, B–K3.

(n) 13 P–QB4, P–K3; 14 P–R3, Q–B2! 15 N × P, P–QB4! 16 B–K3, P × P; 17 B × P, B–B4 with counterattack. P/E. In the column, 9 . . . B–N3!? 10 B–K2, Q–R4; 11 P–N4, Q–B2; 12 N × P, P–R4 = is Bellon-Larsen, Las Palmas 1976.

1 P–K4, P–QB3; 2 P–Q4, P–Q4; 3 N–QB3, P × P; 4 N × P

	36	37	38	39	40
	(N–B3)			N–Q2	
5	(N × N†) (a)			B–QB4! (l)	
	(NP × N)		KP × N!?	KN–B3	
6	B–K2 (b)	. . . . B–QB4	B–QB4 (i)	N–N5	
	N–R3 (c)	B–B4	N–Q2 (j)	P–K3 (m)	
7	N–B3	B–B4 (e)	N–K2	N–K2	Q–K2!
	B–N5	Q–N3 (f)	B–Q3	P–KR3	N–N3
8	O–O	B–QN3	O–O	N–B3	B–Q3 (o)
	N–B2	P–QR4	O–O	B–Q3	P–KR3
9	P–B4	P–QR4	B–B4	O–O	N/5–B3
	Q–Q2	N–Q2 (g)	N–N3	Q–B2	P–B4
10	B–K3 (d)	N–B3	B–Q3	R–K1	P × P! (p)
	B–N2	Q–R3	B–K3	O–O	B × P (q)
11	N–R4	N–R4	P–QB3	N–B3	N–K5
	B × B	B–N3	N–Q4	P–QN4!	QN–Q2!
12	Q × B	Q–N4	B × B	B–Q3	KN–B3
	KR–N1 =	P–R3 (h)	Q × B (k)	B–N2 (n)	N × N (r)

(a) Tepid is 5 N–N3, P–K4; 6 N–B3, P × P; 7 N × P, B–K2; or 5 . . . P–QB4 or 5 . . . P–KN3.

(b) (A) 6 N–B3 may lead into col. 34, note (j), or into col. 56, note (a)(B). (B) 6 B–KB4, Q–N3 (or 6 . . . B–N2; 7 B–K2, or 6 . . . B–B4; 7 B–B4); 7 N–B3, Q × NP 8 B–Q3; Q–B6† ∞ (c) 6 N–K2, and now (1) 6 . . . B–N5; 7 P–KB3, B–R4; 8 P–B3, N–Q2; 9 N–N3, B–N3 = . Pachman. (2) 6 . . . P–KR4; 7 P–KR4, B–N5; 8 Q–Q3, P–K4; 9 B–K3, N–Q2; 10 N–N3, Q–R4† = . Comments.

(c) Now the waiting move 6 . . . B–N2 might be considered, and after 7 N–B3, B–N5; 8 B–KB4, following up with 8 . . . N–Q2; 9 O–O, P–K4, Black has various ways to secure tactical counterplay.

(d) Yangarber-Kopilov, corr. 1968. The text allows the options of . . . O–O; and/or . . . P–K4, but questionable is 10 . . . O–O–O; 11 R–B1, P–KR4; 12 Q–Q2! (against . . . B–R3). Comments.

(e) Or 7 N–K2, P–K3; 8 O–O, P–KR4; 9 B–Q3, B × B; 10 Q × B, B–Q3; 11 B–B4, P–R5; 12 P–KR3, Q–B2; 13 B × B, Q × B; 14 Q–QN3, P–N3; 15 P–QB4, N–Q2; 16 QR–B1, O–O–O; 17 P–B5, P × P; 18 P × P, Q–B2; 19 Q–R4, R–R4; 20 P–QN4, R–Q4; 21 P–N5, N × P; 22 Q–R3, P × P; 23 N–B3, R–Q6; 24 Q–N4, R/6–Q5; 25 Q × P, P–R3; 26 Q–N1, R–QB5; 27 N–K2, N–Q6; 28 R × R, Q × R; 29 Q–N6, Q–N4; 30 Q–R7, Q–N2; 31 Q–K3, P–B4; 32 N–B1, P–B5; 33 Q–Q2, Q–N7; 34 Q–R5, Q–N4; 35 Q–R3, P–B6; 36 N × N, Q × N; 37 R–B1†, drawn. Browne-Donner, San Juan 1969.

(f) 7 . . . P–K3; 8 N–B3, R–N1; 9 O–O, B–Q3; 10 B × B, Q × B; 11 N–R4, B–N3 = .

(g) 9 . . . R–N1; 10 N–K2, R × P? 11 B–N3 ± .

(h) 13 B–B7, P–KB4; 14 Q–B4, B–N2 (Tal-Larsen, Las Palmas 1977); 15 O–O–O ± , Tal.

(i) White has many lines to choose from against 5 . . . KP × N, e.g. (A) 6 P–QB3, B–Q3; 7 B–Q3, O–O; (1) 8 Q–R5, P–KN3; 9 Q–R4, P–QB4; 10 N–K2, N–B3; 11 B–KR6, R–K1; 12 P × P, B × P = . Comments. (2) 8 Q–B2! P–KN3; 9 N–K2, R–K1; 10 P–KR4, N–Q2; 11 P–R5, N–B1; 12 B–R6! Spasski-Barcza, Leipzig 1960. (B) 6 N–B3, B–Q3; 7 B–K2 (7 B–K3, O–O; 8 Q–Q2, R–K1 =), O–O; 8 O–O, R–K1; 9 B–K3, B–KN5; 10 R–K1, N–Q2 = . Comments. (c) 6 P–KN3, Q–Q4; 7 N–B3, B–Q3; 8 B–N2, O–O; 9 O–O, Q–KR4; 10 P–B4, B–KN5; 11 Q–Q3, N–R3 = . Comments.

(j) Not so safe alternatives are (A) 6 . . . B–Q3; 7 Q–K2†, Q–K2; 8 Q × Q†, K × Q; 9 N–K2, B–K3; 10 B–Q3, R–Q1; 11 O–O, P–QR4; 12 P–QB4, P–R3; 13 B–Q2, P–R5; 14

KR–K1, N–R3; 15 P–QR3, K–B1; 16 B–B3 ± . Sergievski-Matokhin, USSR 1961. (B) 6 . . . B–K2; 7 N–K2, O–O; 8 O–O, N–Q2; 9 B–N3, R–K1; 10 N–B4, N–B1; 11 R–K1, B–Q3; 12 R × R, Q × R; 13 B–K3, Q–K5; 14 Q–Q2, N–N3; 15 P–B3, Q–B4; 16 N × N, RP × N; 17 P–QB4 ± . Boleslavski.

(*k*) 13 Q–Q2, QR–Q1; 14 KR–K1, P–KN3; 15 QR–Q1, K–N2; 16 B–K4, N–B2; 17 P–QN3, KR–K1; 18 B–N1, B–N5; 19 P–KR3, B × N; 20 R × B, R × R; 21 Q × R, N–Q4; 22 Q–Q2, N–KB5; 23 B–K4, P–KB4; 24 B–B3, P–KR3 = . Karpov-Korchnoi, 20th match game, 1978.

(*l*) If 5 N–KB3, KN–B3; 6 N × N†, N × N; 7 N–K5!? (played to contain Black's QB), N–Q2; 8 B–KB4, N × N; 9 B × N, B–B4 = .

(*m*) 6 . . . N–Q4; 7 KN–B3, P–KR3; 8 N–K4, QN–N3; 9 B–N3, B–B4; 10 N–N3, B–R2; 11 O–O, P–K3; 12 N–K5, N–Q2; 13 P–QB4, N/4–B3; 14 B–B4, N × N; 15 B × N, B–Q3; 16 Q–B3 ± (16 Q–K2? B–Q6! =).

(*n*) 13 N–K4, N × N; 14 R × N, P–QB4 ∞ . Boleslavski.

(*o*) 8 B–N3, P–QR4! ± . (8 . . . P–KR3; 9 N/5–B3, P–B4; 10 B–K3, Q–B2 =).

(*p*) 10 B–K3, N/N3–Q4; 11 N–K5, N × B; 12 P × N, B–Q3 = .

(*q*) The immediate 10 . . . QN–Q2; 11 N–K5, N × N; 12 Q × N, Q–R4†; 13 B–Q2, Q × BP; 14 N–B3, Q × Q; 15 N × Q leaves Black with a confined position. Parma-Smyslov, Lugano 1968.

(*r*) 13 N × N, O–O; 14 O–O, (A) 14 . . . B–Q3; 15 B–KB4 with more mobility, but hardly sufficient to break Black's solid defences. Matulović-Pfleger, Lugano 1968. (B) 14 . . . P–QN3; 15 R–Q1, Q–K2; 16 P–KN4? N–Q2! ∓ . Ciocaltea-Christiansen, Torremolinos 1976.

1 P–K4, P–QB3

	41	42	43	44	45
2	(P–Q4).			P–QB4	
	(P–Q4)			P–Q4	
3	(N–QB3)			KP × P	
	(P × P) (a)			P × P	
4	(N × P)			P × P (k)	
	(N–Q2)			N–KB3.	P–QR3!
5	N–KB3			Q–R4† (l)	N–QB3
	KN–B3			B–Q2 (m)	N–KB3
6	N–N3 (b)			Q–N3	Q–N3
	P–K3 (c)			N–R3!	QN–Q2
7	B–Q3 (d)			P–Q4	B–K2
	P–B4	B–K2		Q–N3	N–B4
8	O–O (e)	O–O		B–QB4	Q–B4
	P × P	O–O.	P–QB4!	R–B1	P–K3
9	N × P	Q–K2 (h)	P–QB3	N–QB3	B–B3
	B–B4 (f)	P–B4	O–O	Q × Q (n)	P × P
10	N–B3	P × P	Q–K2	P × Q ±	N × P
	O–O (g)	N × P (i)	P–QN3 (j)		B–K3 =

(a) (A) Utterly "closed" is 3 . . . P–KN3; 4 P–K5 (or 4 P–KR3!?), B–N2; 5 P–B4, P–KR4; 6 N–B3, B–N5; 7 P–KR3, B × N; 8 Q × B, P–K3; 9 P–KN3, Q–N3; 10 Q–B2, N–K2; 11 B–Q3, N–Q2; 12 N–K2, O–O–O; 13 P–B3, P–B3; 14 P–N3, N–KB4; 15 R–KN1, P–B4; 16 B × N, NP × B; 17 B–K3, Q–R3! 18 K–B1! P × QP∞. Fischer-Petrosian, World match, Belgrade 1970. (B) An adventurous but probably shortlived thrust is 3 . . . P–QN4!? 4 P–QR3 (or simply 4 P × P, P–N5; 5 N–R4, P × P; 6 N–KB3∞), P × P; 5 N × KP, B–B4 (not 5 . . . N–B3; 6 N × N†, KP × N; 7 P–QR4, P–N5; 8 B–QB4! Klovan-Gurgenidze, Alma Ata 1969); 6 B–Q3, B × N (6 . . . Q × P? 7 N–KB3 +); 7 B × B, N–B3, 8 B–Q3 (Tal-Gurgenidze, Alma Ata 1969), Q × P; 9 N–B3, Q–Q4; 10 O–O, P–K3; 11 R–K1, QN–Q2∞.

(b) (A) Treacherous is 6 N × N†, N × N; (1) 7 N–K5, B–K3 (7 . . . N–Q2; 8 B–KB4, N × N; 9 B × N, Q–Q4; 10 P–QB4 or 10 B–K2); 8 B–K2, P–KN3; 9 O–O, B–N2 = . Browne-Rogoff, US Chp. 1975. (B) An unexpected return to the square QB3 was the successful feature of 6 N–B3, P–K3; 7 B–Q3, P–B4; 8 Q–K2, P × P; 9 N × P, B–B4; 10 N–N3, B–Q3; 11 B–KN5, P–QR3; 12 O–O–O, Q–B2; 13 K–N1, O–O; 14 N–K4, B–K4; 15 P–KB4, B × BP; 16 N × N†, N × N; 17 B × N, P × B; 18 Q–N4†, K–R1; 19 KR–B1, B–K4; 20 B × KRP, P–B4; 21 Q–KR4, K–N2; 22 R–B3, R–K1; 23 P–N4, P–B5; 24 P–N5, K–B1; 25 R × P!! B × R; 26 Q–R6†, K–K2; 27 Q–B6†, K–B1; 28 P–N6, B–R3; 29 R–KB1, resigns. Tal-Shamkovich, USSR Chp. 1972.

(c) 6 . . . P–KN3; 7 B–QB4, B–N2; 8 O–O, O–O; 9 R–K1, P–QN4; 10 B–N3, P–QR4; 11 P–QR4, P–K3 = . Simagin-Smyslov, Moscow 1959.

(d) 7 B–QB4, N–N3; 8 B–N3, P–B4; 9 P–B3, Q–B2; 10 P × P, B × P; 11 O–O, O–O = .

(e) 8 P–QB3, B–K2; 9 O–O, O–O is similar to col. 43.

(f) 9 . . . N–B4!? 10 B–QB4, B–K2; 11 P–QN3, O–O; 12 B–N2, B–Q2; 13 Q–K2, Q–N3 allows Black less elasticity. Bradvarović-Trifunović, Yugoslavia 1964.

(g) 11 Q–K2, Q–B2; 12 N–K4, B–K2 = .

(h) 9 P–B4, P–B4; 10 P–N3, P–QN3; 11 B–N2, B–N2; 12 Q–K2, R–K1; 13 QR–Q1, Q–B2; 14 B–N1, Q–B3! P/E.

(i) 11 B–QB4, P–QN3; 12 R–Q1, Q–B2; 13 N–K5 with a free game.

(j) 11 N–K5, B–N2; 12 B–K3 with unresolved problems. Inferior is 12 P–KB4!? P × P; 13 P × P, N × N; 14 QP × N, N–N5! ∓ . Flohr.

(k) 4 P–Q4 simply transposes into the Panov-Attack.

(*l*) 5 B–N5†, QN–Q2; 6 N–QB3, (1) P–KN3; 7 N–B3 (7 P–Q4, P–QR3! =), B–N2; 8 P–Q6, P×P; 9 O–O, O–O = . Alekhin-Feigin, Kemeri 1937 is solid. (2) 6 . . . P–QR3; 7 B×N†, Q×B; 8 Q–N3, Q–N5; 9 KN–K2, P–QN4! is interesting.

(*m*) 5 . . . QN–Q2; 6 N–QB3, P–KN3; 7 P–KN3, B–N2; 8 B–N2, O–O; 9 KN–K2, N–N3; 10 Q–N3, B–B4, Wade-Zemgalis, Oldenburg 1949, is somewhat riskier.

(*n*) 9 . . . Q×P; 10 B×N! and White should win.

1 P–K4, P–QB3; 2 N–QB3, P–Q4; 3 N–B3, B–N5; 4 P–KR3, B × N; 5 Q × B, P–K3

	46	47	48	49	50
6	P–Q4	P–Q3			
	N–B3 (*a*)	N–B3			Q–B3
7	B–Q3 (*b*)	P–KN3	P–R3	B–Q2 (*j*)	Q–K2
	P × P	B–N5	QN–Q2	QN–Q2	B–N5
8	N × P	B–Q2	P–KN3	P–KN4	B–Q2
	Q × P (*c*)	P–Q5	P–KN3	B–N5	N–Q2
9	P–B3 (*d*)	N–N1	B–N2	P–R3	P–R3
	Q–Q1	Q–N3 (*f*)	B–N2	B–R4	B–R4
10	O–O	P–N3 (*g*)	O–O	O–O–O	P–KN3
	B–K2 (*e*)	P–QR4 (*h*)	O–O (*i*)	O–O (*k*)	P–Q5 (*l*)

(*a*) 6 . . . P × P; 7 N × P, Q × P; 8 B–Q3, N–Q2; 9 B–K3, Q–R5 (or Q × P) comes into consideration.

(*b*) 7 P–K5, KN–Q2 leads to a French Defence where Black has eliminated his bad queen's bishop.

(*c*) The Gambit can safely be declined with 8 . . . QN–Q2; 9 P–B3, N × N; 10 Q × N, N–B3; 11 Q–K2, Q–Q4; 12 O–O, Q–KR4; 13 Q × Q, N × Q = . Boleslavski-Bronstein, match 1950.

(*d*) 9 B–K3, Q–Q1; (A) 10 O–O–O, QN–Q2; 11 B–QB4, Q–R4 = . (B) 10 N × N†, Q × N; 11 Q–N3, threatening Q–B7.

(*e*) 11 R–Q1, QN–Q2; 12 Q–N3, N × N; 13 B × N, P–KN3; 14 B–B4, Q–N3; 15 B–B7, Q × P; 16 Q–B3, R–QB1; 17 QR–N1, Q × R; 18 B × Q, R × B; 19 Q–N3, R–QB1; 20 Q–K3, N–B4 = . Korchnoi-Spasski, USSR Chp. 1959.

(*f*) Simpler is 9 . . . B × B†; 10 N × B, P–K4; 11 B–N2, P–B4; 12 O–O, N–QB3 = . Fischer-Petrosian, candidates' tournament 1959.

(*g*) Intriguing is 10 P–B3, B–B4; 11 B–B1, QN–Q2; 12 Q–K2, P–K4; 13 N–Q2, P–QR4; 14 B–N2, O–O ∞. A real regrouping typical of the "closed" trend.

(*h*) 11 P–R3, B × B† (11 . . . B–K2; 12 P–QR4); 12 N × B, QN–Q2; 13 B–N2, Q–B4; 14 Q–Q1, P–R4 = . Fischer-Benko, candidates' tournament 1959.

(*i*) 11 Q–K2, N–K1; 12 K–R2, P–KB4; 13 P–B4, N–Q3∞; Matanović-Petrosian, Yugoslavia *v.* USSR, 1959. In the column 7 . . . B–K2; 8 P–KN4, P × P! 9 P × P, KN–Q2 is also playable.

(*j*) 7 B–K2, QN–Q2; 8 Q–N3, P–KN3; 9 O–O, B–N2; 10 B–B4, Q–N3; 11 QR–N1, O–O = . Smyslov-Botvinnik, match 1958.

(*k*) 11 P–KR4, P–QN4; 12 P–N5, N–K1 = . Darga-Gereben, Bordeaux 1964.

(*l*) 11 N–N1, B × B†; 12 N × B, N–K2; 13 P–KR4, O–O–O = . Unzicker-Pomar, Varna 1962.

1 P-K4, P-QB3; 2 N-QB3, P-Q4; 3 N-B3

	51	52	53	54	55
	(B-N5)		N-B3	P×P	
4	(P-KR3)		P-K5	N×P	
	(B×N)	B-R4	N-K5	N-B3	
5	(Q×B)	P×P	B-K2 (g)	N×N†	
	N-B3	P×P	B-B4	KP×N	
6	P-Q4 (a)	B-N5†	O-O	P-KN3	B-B4
	P×P	N-B3	P-K3	B-KN5 (i)	B-K2
7	Q-K3	P-KN4	N-N1	B-N2	O-O
	QN-Q2	B-N3	B-K2	Q-K2†	O-O
8	N×P	N-K5	P-Q3	Q-K2	P-Q4
	N×N (b)	R-B1	N-B4	Q×Q†	B-Q3!
9	Q×N	P-Q4 (e)	B-K3	K×Q	B-N3
	N-B3	P-K3	N/4-Q2	N-R3	QN-Q2
10	Q-Q3	Q-K2	P-Q4	P-B3	R-K1
	Q-Q4 (c)	B-N5	O-O	O-O-O	Q-B2
11	P-QB4	P-KR4 (f)	QN-Q2	P-Q4	P-B4
	Q-Q3 (d)		P-B4 (h)	N-B2	P-QB4 (j)

(a) More confining, yet resilient, is 6 P-Q3, P-K3; 7 P-QR3, QN-Q2; 8 P-KN4, P-KN3; 9 Q-N3, B-B4; 10 P-KR4, P-KR4; 11 P-N5, N-N5; 12 N-Q1, P×P; 13 P×P, Q-N3; 14 P-N4, B-Q5; 15 P-QB3, B-K4; 16 P-KB4, B-N2; 17 P-K5, O-O-O; 18 R-QR2, Q-B2; 19 B-K2, N-N3 = . Ljubojević-Hort, Petropolis 1973.

(b) Also 8 . . . P-K3; 9 N×N†, Q×N; 10 B-Q2, B-Q3; 11 P-QB3, O-O; 12 Q-N5, P-B4; 13 B-N5, KR-Q1; 14 B×N, Q×Q; 15 B×Q, R×B; 16 P×P, B×P; draw. Nezhmetdinov-Keres, USSR Chp. 1961.

(c) Provoking White's next move which commits White's position, yet 10 . . . Q-Q3! at once looks positionally stronger (11 P-KN3, P-K4! *Comments*).

(d) 12 B-K2, P-K4; 13 P-Q5, P-K5; 14 Q-B2, B-K2; 15 P×P, Q×P; 16 O-O, O-O; 17 B-K3, B-B4; 18 Q-B3, P-QN3; 19 KR-Q1 ± . Fischer-Keres, Bled 1961.

(e) Without effect is 9 P-KR4, P-B3; 10 N×B, P×N; 11 P-Q4, P-K3; 12 Q-Q3, K-B2; 13 P-R5, P×P; 14 P×P, KN-K2 = Fischer-Smyslov, Yugoslavia 1959.

(f) (A) 11 . . . Q-N3? 12 O-O, N-B3; 13 N-R4, Q-R4; 14 P-R5, B-K5; 15 P-B3 + . (B) 11 . . . N-K2! 12 P-R5, B-K5; 13 P-B3, O-O; 14 N×N, N×N; 15 B-K3, Q-B3! 16 P×B, N×P; 17 B×N, Q×B; 18 R-Q1, B×N†; 19 P×B, Q×P†; 20 R-Q2, P×P; 21 O-O, R-B4; 22 B-Q7, R-KN4; 23 R/1-Q1, Q-KR6; 24 Resigns. Grefe-Commons, US Chp. 1975.

(g) (A) 5 P-Q4, B-B4; 6 N-KR4, P-K3; 7 N×B, P×N; 8 N-K2, P-B4 = . Shapiro-Porath, Israel 1961. (B) 5 N-K2, B-N5; 6 KN-N1, B×N; 7 B×B, P-K3; 8 P-Q3, N-B4; 9 N-B3, N/4-Q2; 10 O-O, P-QB4; 11 P-B3, N-QB3 = .

(h) 12 P-B4! ± . Bronstein-Kirilov, USSR Chp. 1948.

(i) 6 . . . B-K2; 7 B-N2, O-O; 8 O-O, B-KN5; 9 P-Q4, N-Q2; 10 P-B4, N-N3; 11 P-N3, Q-Q2; 12 R-K1, KR-K1; 13 Q-Q2, P-QR4; 14 B-N2, P-R5; 15 B-B3 ± . Byvshev-Ratner, USSR, Chp. 1949.

(j) 12 B-K3, R-Q1; 13 Q-B2, P-QN3; 14 QR-Q1, N-B1; 15 P-KR3, N-N3 = . Boleslavski.

1 P–K4, P–QB3

	56	57	58	59	60
2	(N–QB3)	....	....	P–Q3 (j)	
	(P–Q4)			P–Q4 (k)	
3	(N–B3)	....	Q–B3	N–Q2	
	(P×P)		P×P (e)	P–K4	P–KN3
4	(N×P)		N×P	KN–B3 (l)	P–KN3 (n)
	(N–B3	B–N5 (c)	N–Q2	N–Q2 (m)	B–N2
5	(N×N†)	P–KR3	P–Q4 (f)	P–KN3	B–N2
	NP×N	B×N	KN–B3 (g)	P×P	P–K4 (o)
6	B–B4 (a)	Q×B	B–QB4	P×P	N–KB3
	B–N2	P–K3	P–K3 (h)	Q–B2	N–K2
7	P–KR3	P–B3	B–KN5	B–N2	O–O
	B–B4	N–B3	B–K2	B–B4	O–O
8	O–O	P–Q4	O–O–O	O–O	P–B3 (p)
	P–K3	N×N	N×N	N–K2	N–Q2
9	R–K1	Q×N	B×B	P–N3	P–QN4
	O–O!	B–Q3	Q×B	N–KN3	P–N3
10	P–Q4	Q–N4	Q×N	B–N2	B–N2
	N–Q2 (b)	Q–B3 (d)	N–B3 (i)	O–O =	B–N2 (q)

(a) (A) 6 P–KN3? B–N5; 7 B–N2, Q–Q2! 8 O–O, B–R6 or 8 P–KR3, B–K3; (B) 6 P–Q4, B–N5; 7 B–K2, Q–B2; 8 N–R4, B×B; 9 Q×B, N–Q2; 10 O–O, P–K3; 11 P–KN3, P–KR4; 12 P–QB4, O–O–O; 13 P–Q5, R–K1; 14 B–B4, B–Q3 = . Gurgenidze-Savon, USSR Chp. 1961. Compare cols. 34–6 where the king's knight has not yet moved.

(b) White has some minimal advantage. P/E.

(c) 4 . . . N–Q2; 5 B–B4, KN–B3; 6 QN–N5, P–K3; 7 Q–K2, N–Q4; 8 P–Q4, P–KR3; 9 N–K4, B–K2; 10 O–O, Q–B2; 11 B–N3, O–O; 12 P–B4 ± . Smyslov-Golombek, Venice 1950. Compare cols. 39–43.

(d) 11 B–Q3, P–KR4; 12 Q–K4, N–Q2; 13 P–KR4, Q–Q1 = . Simagin-Köberl, Szczavno Zdroj. Also compare with col. 46, with similar features.

(e) 3 Q–B3 is Spielmann's device, aimed at restricting Black's QB. If 3 . . . P–Q5? 4 B–B4, N–B3; 5 P–K5, P×N; 6 P×N, KP×P; 7 Q×QBP.

(f) 5 P–QN3!, QN–B3; 6 N×N, N×N; 7 B–N2, B–N5; 8 Q–N3, P–K3; 9 B–K2, B–KB4; 10 B–Q1 (In this variation Black succeeds in developing his QB but no longer effectively. 10 O–O–O! e.g. . . . N–K5; 11 Q–K3 was more dynamic), B–N3; 11 N–B3, B–Q3; 12 Q–R4, B–K2 = . Csom-Navarovsky, Kecskemét 1968.

(g) 5 . . . QN–B3; 6 P–B3, N×N; 7 Q×N, N–B3; 8 Q–B2, B–N5; 9 N–K2, P–K3; 10 N–N3, Q–Q4; 11 P–B3, B–R5; 12 N×B, Q×N; 13 B–KB4, N–Q4 = . Lutikov-Petrosian, USSR Chp. 1960.

(h) 6 . . . N–N3; 7 B–Q3, Q×P; 8 N–K2, Q–Q1; 9 N×N†, KP×N; 10 B–KB4 with quicker deployment.

(i) 11 Q–B3, O–O; 12 N–R3, P–B4 or 12 . . . P–QN4 = . Müller.

(j) Sporadically played are (A) 2 P–QN3, P–Q4; 3 P×P, P×P; 4 B–N2, N–QB3; 5 P–N3, P–K4; 6 B–N2, N–B3 = . (B) 2 N–K2, P–Q4; 3 P–K5, P–QB4; 4 P–Q4, N–QB3; 5 P–QB3, P–K3; 6 N–Q2, KN–K2 N–K2; 7 N–B3 results in a French Defence.

(k) 2 . . . P–K4! 3 P–KN3, N–B3; 4 B–N2, P–Q4; 5 N–Q2, B–QB4; 6 KN–B3, O–O! Stein-Jimenez, Havana 1968.

(l) 4 P–KN3, N–B3; 5 B–N2, B–QB4; 6 KN–B3, O–O! 7 O–O, R–K1; 8 P–B3, QN–Q2; 9 P–QN4, B–B1∞ . Stein-Jimenez, Havana 1969.

(m) Also 4 . . . B–Q3; 5 P–KN3, N–K2; 6 B–N2, O–O; 7 O–O, N–Q2; 8 P–N3, B–N5; 9 B–N2, P–Q5; 10 N–B4, N–KN3; 11 P–QR3, B–K2; 12 P–QN4, P–QN3; 13 P–B3, P–QB4; 14

BP × P, BP × QP; 15 P–KR4, P–B3; 16 Q–N3, R–B2; 17 N × QP, P × N∞. Ciocaltea-Bilek, Bath 1973. The column is Olafsson-Eliskases, Buenos Aires 1960.

(n) 4 KN–B3, B–N2; 5 P–KN3, P × P; 6 P × P, N–B3; 7 B–N2, O–O; 8 O–O, B–N5; 9 P–KR3, B × N; 10 Q × B, QN–Q2; 11 Q–K2, Q–B2! = . Monnier.

(o) (A) 5 . . . N–B3? 6 P–K5! (B) 5 . . . P × P! 6 P × P, N–B3; 7 KN–B3, O–O; 8 O–O, B–N5; 9 P–KR3, B × N; 10 Q × B, QN–Q2; 11 Q–K2, Q–B2 = .

(p) (A) 8 P–QN4!? P–QR4 (Stein-Cobo, Havana 1968, went 8 . . . Q–B2; 9 B–N2, P–QR4; 10 P × RP, R × P; 11 P–QR4, P–R3; 12 R–K1, P–Q5! =); 9 P × RP, Q × P; 10 B–N2, N–Q2 = . (B) 8 R–K1, P–Q5; 9 P–QR4, P–QB4; 10 N–B4, QN–B3; 11 P–B3, B–K3; 12 P × P, B × N; 13 P × B, KP × P; 14 P–K5, Q–Q2 = . Fischer-Hübner, Mallorca 1970.

(q) 11 R–K1, R–K1; 12 B–KR3, Q–B2 = . Stein-Hort, Los Angeles 1968. The differences in column and notes are only subtle. A lengthy analysis of White's "King's Indian" reply 2 P–Q3 can be found in *Chess Digest Magazine*, 1976/No. 11.

French Defence

(1 P–K4, P–K3)

The French derives its name from a correspondence game between London and Paris in 1834, even though Lucena had examined it in 1497. Variously disparaged over the years, it is nevertheless sensibly motivated and one of the most important close openings. It lists among its adherents Burn, Rubinstein, and Winawer, who invented their own variations, Nimzowitsch, Ståhlberg, Steinitz, Czerniak, R. Byrne, Guimard, Uhlmann, and its ultravirtuoso Botvinnik. A defence which offers scope for the imagination and numerous subtle resources, it appeals to rock-ribbed temperaments. French players are a breed apart. They are willing to submit to cramp and countless indignities in order to reach an end-game where the pawn structure definitely favours Black.

The concept of this sturdy defence is to barricade the position and build, hopefully, an impregnable wall against which White's attack will be dashed. The counter-punches with . . . P–QB4 and . . . P–KB3 are characteristic. On the minus side the French is defensive from the start; it not only cedes the centre temporarily, but locks in the queen's bishop as well.

THE CLASSICAL VARIATION (cols. 1–7) 1 P–K4, P–K3; 2 P–Q4, P–Q4; 3 N–QB3, N–KB3; 4 B–KN5, B–K2; 5 P–K5, KN–Q2; 6 B × B, Q × B has been extensively analysed for a century. White has a hard time getting a pull, but his best chance is an early Q–Q2 coupled with P–KB4, reinforcing the centre. Veering off with 4 . . . P × P, Burn's Variation (cols. 16–20) or still earlier with 3 . . . P × P (cols. 36–40), Rubinstein's Variation, releases the pressure on White's centre too soon.

THE ALEKHIN-CHATARD Attack 6 P–KR4 (cols. 8–12) has been shorn of its terror. Taking the pawn is difficult yet tenable (col. 8), but the immediate blow at the centre with 6 . . . P–QB4 (cols. 11–12) is theoretically adequate.

143

BURN'S VARIATION with 4 . . . P × P (cols. 14–20) releases the pressure on White's centre but Black's solid formation allows him time for varied defensive manoeuvres and has therefore retained interest.

THE MACCUTCHEON VARIATION 4 . . . B–N5 (cols. 21–30) is employed more rarely but has not been refuted.

In THE STEINITZ VARIATION (cols. 31–4), 4 P–K5 leaves White more vulnerable to . . . P–QB4 than in the Tarrasch Variation (see below) and almost commits him to P–KB4. Therefore the attempt 5 QN–K2 in col. 31 is intriguing.

RUBINSTEIN'S VARIATION 3 . . . P × P (cols. 36–40) releases the tension in the centre even earlier than the Burn Variation and, as White has not yet played B–N5, he has the greater choice of moves which need Black's utmost care. Hence, it is one of Black's least elastic weapons.

THE WINAWER VARIATION 1 P–K4, P–K3; 2 P–Q4, P–Q4; 3 N–QB3, B–N5 (cols. 41–78) is a game in itself and in constant flux. The bold pin on White's knight threatens to win a pawn and gives rise to highly intricate situations, especially in the lines with 7 Q–N4 (cols. 41–51) and equally so in cols. 59, 60 and 64 and also in col. 69. It is advisable to study thoroughly the suitable differences and transpositions in Black's playing either Q–B2 or . . . KN–K2 first.

THE EXCHANGE VARIATION 3 P × P (cols. 79–80) is for special occasions of surprise, but mostly an invitation to a draw.

TARRASCH'S VARIATION 3 N–Q2 (cols. 81–105) belies his purported dogmatism (just as his hypermodern approach to the *Chigorin Variation* does, see cols. 113–4). It sidesteps the Winawer, keeps the queen's bishop pawn mobile, and obstructs the queen's bishop only temporarily. Black's possibilities are no less and no more varied than in other lines of the French, but the stratagems available to both sides are more numerous. It proved its nine lives in this last decade when it was the most favoured of all French lines, most prominently so for Korchnoi and East Germany's Uhlmann.

THE NIMZOWITSCH (or ADVANCE) VARIATION is too limited in its much-analysed scope to command more than occasional use, but the sacrifice of White's centre can still catch an opponent unawares.

Diverse second moves are dealt with in cols. 111–15 and are of importance to players who are adept in turning closed positions to sudden positional advantage.

1 P-K4, P-K3; 2 P-Q4, P-Q4; 3 N-QB3, N-KB3; 4 B-N5, B-K2; 5 P-K5, KN-Q2; 6 B × B, Q × B

	1	2	3	4	5
7	Q-Q2.................		P-B4		
	O-O		P-QR3	O-O!	
8	P-B4	N-Q1 (c)	N-B3	N-B3	
	P-QB4	P-KB3	P-QB4	P-QB4	
9	N-B3	P-KB4	P×P	P×P	B-Q3 (h)
	N-QB3	P-QB4	N-QB3	N-B3 (f)	P-B4 (i)
10	O-O-O (a)	P-B3	Q-Q2	B-Q3	P×P e.p.
	P-B5 (b)	N-B3	Q×P	P-B4!	Q×P (j)
11	P-B5	N-B3	P-QR3 (d)	P×P e.p.	P-KN3 (k)
	R-N1	P×QP	P-QN4	Q×KBP	P-B5 (l)
12	Q-N5	P×QP	Q-B2	P-KN3	B-K2
	Q×Q†	P×P	B-N2	N×P	N-B3
13	N×Q	QP×P	Q×Q	O-O	O-O
	N-N3	Q-N5	N×Q	P-QN3	P-QR3
14	P×P	P-KN3	O-O-O	Q-Q2	N-K5
	P×P	N-B4	O-O	B-N2	R-K1
15	B-K2	Q×Q	B-Q3	QR-K1	B-B3
	P-KR3 =	N×Q =	QR-B1 (e)	QR-K1 (g)	N/2×N (m)

(a) Other lines are (A) 10 P × P, N × BP; 11 O-O-O, P-QR3; 12 B-Q3, P-QN4 = . (B) 10 P-KN3, P-QR3; 11 B-N2, N-N3; 12 P-N3, B-Q2; 13 N-K2, P×P; 14 N/2×P; Q-B4; 15 O-O, N-B1; 16 K-R1, N/1-K2 = . L. Steiner-Yanofsky, Karlovy Vary 1968.

(b) Also playable is (A) 10 . . . N-N3; 11 P-KR4, B-Q2; 12 R-R3, N-R4 = or (B) 10 . . . P-QR3 followed by . . . P-QN4. The column is L. Steiner-Purdy, Adelaide 1947.

(c) 8 QN-K2, P-QB4; 9 P-QB3, P-B3; 10 P-KB4, P × QP; 11 P × QP, P×P; 12 BP×P, N-QB3; 13 N-KB3, N-N3; 14 N-N3, Q-N5 = . The column is Sir G. Thomas-Lilienthal, Budapest 1934.

(d) 11 B-Q3, P-QN4; 12 Q-B2, B-N2; 13 Q × Q, N × Q; 14 B-K2, P-Q5! = .

(e) 16 KR-K1, KR-Q1; 17 N-K2 and N/2-Q4 ± .

(f) Also 9 . . . P-B4; 10 P×P e.p., Q × KBP; 11 P-KN3, N-B3; 12 Q-Q2, N×P; 13 O-O-O, R-Q1! 14 Q-K1! P-QR3 = .

(g) 16 Q-B2, N × B; 17 P × N, B-R3; 18 R-Q1, P-K4 = . Vasyukov-Gusev, USSR 1951.

(h) 9 N-QN5, P × P! 10 N-B7, N × P; 11 N × R, N × N†; 12 Q × N, Q-N5† = (Keres).

(i) 9 . . . P-B3; 10 QP×P, Q × P; 11 N-Q4! Q-N3; 12 N-R4, Q-R4†; 13 P-B3 ±

(j) 10 . . . R × P; 11 Q-Q2, N-B3; 12 P × P, N×P; 13 P-KN3! ± .

(k) 11 N-KN5! Q × BP! 12 B × P†, K-R1; 13 Q-Q2 ± .

(l) 11 . . . N-B3; 12 P×P, N×P; 13 O-O, B-Q2; 14 Q-Q2, B-K1; 15 QR-K1 ± .

(m) 16 BP×N, Q-N4; 17 N-K2 (17 N×P, P×N; 18 B×P†, B-K3 holds the game), N-K2; 18 N-B4, N-B4 ∞ .

1 P–K4, P–K3; 2 P–Q4, P–Q4; 3 N–QB3, N–KB3; 4 B–N5, B–K2; 5 P–K5, KN–Q2

	6	7	8	9	10
6	(B × B)		P–KR4 (Alekhin-Chatard Attack)		
	(Q × B)		B × B	P–QR3	
7	Q–N4	N–N5 (c)	P × B	Q–N4	
	O–O	N–N3!	Q × P	P–KB4 (k)	
8	N–B3	P–QB3 (d)	N–R3	Q–R5†	Q–N3!
	P–QB4	P–QR3	Q–K2 (f)	P–N3	P–B4
9	B–Q3	N–QR3	N–B4 (g)	Q–R6	B–K3
	P–B4	P–QB4	P–QR3 (h)	B × B!	O–O
10	P × P e.p.	N–B2	Q–N4	P × B	KN–K2
	R × P (a)	N–R5	P–KN3 (i)	K–B2	N–QB3!
11	Q–R4	R–N1	O–O–O	KN–K2	N–B4
	N–B1	P–QN4	N–N3	N–B1	N/2–N1
12	P × P	P–KB4	B–Q3	NB4	QN–K2
	Q × P	N–B3	QN–Q2	R–N1	P–B5
13	O–O	N–B3	R–R6	O–O–O	O–O–O
	N–B3 (b)	B–Q2 (e)	N–B1 (j)	R–N2 =	Q–K1 (l)

(a) Also 10 . . . N × P; 11 Q–R4, N–B3; 12 P × P, Q × P; 13 O–O–O, Q–N5!

(b) 14 QR–K1, B–Q2; 15 N–K5, N × N = . Bernstein-Lasker, Zürich 1934.

(c) 7 B–Q3, O–O; 8 P–B4 leads into col. 5.

(d) 8 P–QR4, P–QR3; 9 P–R5, P × N; 10 P × N, R × R; 11 Q × R, O–O; 12 P × P, Q × P; 13 B–Q3, N–B3; 14 P–QB3, P–N5 = . Maróczy.

(e) 14 Q–Q2 (Lasker-Lilienthal, Moscow 1936), R–QN1 = .

(f) 8 . . . Q–R3; 9 N–QN5! NR3; 10 P–KB4. Keres.

(g) 9 Q–N4, P–KB4 (9 . . . K–B1; 10 N–B4 see note (k)); 10 Q–R5†, P–N3; 11 Q–R6, N–B1; 12 N–B4, P–B3 = . Keres.

(h) 9 . . . P–KN3! 10 Q–N4, N–QB3; 11 O–O–O, N–N3; 12 R–R6, B–Q2 = . Westman-Westerinen, Helsinki 1961.

(i) 10 . . . K–B1; 11 Q–B3! (threatening 12 N–N6†) K–N1; 12 –Q3, P–R3 leaves Black vulnerable.

(j) 14 QR–R1, B–Q2; 15 N–R3, B–N4; 16 N–KN5, B × B; 17 P × B, N/3–Q2; 18 N × RP, O–O–O. Roider-Müller, corr. 1931.

(k) 7 . . . K–B1; 8 P–B4, P–QB4; 9 B × B†, Q × B; 10 N–B3, N–QB3; 11 O–O–O P–QN4; 12 P × P, N × BP; 13 B–Q3, followed by N–K2–Q4 ± . P/E.

(l) 14 N–N1, N–Q1; 15 B–K2. Black is in a bind—he had to defend against 13 P × P, or 14 N–R5, but will now face a mounting K-side attack. *Comments.*

FRENCH DEFENCE

1 P–K4, P–K3; 2 P–Q4, P–Q4; 3 N–QB3, N–KB3; 4 B–N5

	11	12	13	14	15
	(B–K2).............................			P×P ⎫ Burn's	
5	(P–K5)			N×P! ⎬ Variation	
	(KN–Q2)................		N–K5 (g)	B–K2	
6	(P–KR4)		B×B (h)	B×N	
	P–QB4 (a)		N×N	B×B	
7	B×B........	N–N5	Q–N4	N–KB3	
	K×B	P–B3	Q×B	N–Q2	
8	Q–N4 (b)	B–Q3	Q×NP	Q–Q2.......	P–B3 (k)
	K–B1	P–QR3!	Q–N5	P–QN3	P–QN3
9	N–B3 (c)	Q–R5†	Q×R†	B–N5	N×B†
	P×P	K–B1	K–Q2	B–N2	P×N!
10	Q×QP	R–R3	R–Q1	N×B†	B–Q3
	Q–N3	P×N	N×R†	P×N	B–N2
11	Q×Q	B–R6	K×N	Q–B3	Q–K2
	P×Q	Q–R4† (e)	Q×P†	P–QR3	P–QB4
12	B–N5	B–Q2	B–Q3	B–B6	O–O–O
	N–QB3 (d)	Q–B2 (f)	Q×NP (i)	B×B (j)	Q–B2 (l)

(a) Inferior are (A) 6 . . . P–KB3; 7 Q –R5† (7 B–Q3, P–QB4; 8 Q–R5†, K–B1; 9 KP×P, N×P; 10 B×N, B×B; 11 P×P, Q–R4; 12 N–K2, N–B3! =), K–B1 (7 . . . P–N3; 8 P×P, N×P; 9 Q–K2±); 8 P×P, N×P; 9 Q–B3 (also 9 Q–K2, P–B4; 10 P×P, N–R3; 11 N–B3, N×P; 12 O–O–O, P–N4; 13 Q–K3± refutes Black's line), P–B4; 10 P×P, QN–Q2; 11 O–O–O, N×P; 12 N–R3, B–Q2; 13 N–B4±. (B) 6 . . . P–KR3; 7 B×B! (7 Q–R5, P–KN3; 8 B×B, Q×B =) Q×B; 8 P–B4, P–QR3; 9 Q–N4, K–B1; 10 O–O–O±. P/E.

(b) 8 P–B4, Q–N3; 9 N–B3, Q×P; 10 N–QN5, Q–N5†; 11 K–B2! N–QB3; 12 P–B4 with somewhat more play for the minus pawn, keeping matters even.

(c) (A) 9 P×P, N×KP; 10 Q–N3, QN–B3! =. Comments. (B) 9 N–R4! is good.

(d) 13 B×N, P×B; 14 K–Q2, K–K2 =. Euwe.

(e) 11 . . . P×B; 12 Q×P†, K–K1; 13 Q–R5†, K–B1 with perpetual check.

(f) 13 R–N3, P×QP; 14 N–B3, N×P; 15 R×P! P–R3; 16 B–R7, K×R; 17 Q×P†, K–B2; 18 Q–R5†, drawn. Rossetto-Ståhlberg, Vina del Mar 1947.

(g) Nimzowitsch's "bizarre" 5 . . . N–N1!? does have some basis, e.g. (A) 6 B–KB4, P–KN4! followed by . . . P–KR4 and . . . N–KR3–B4. (B) 6 P–KR4, B×B; 7 P×B, Q×P; 8 N–R3, Q–K2; 9 Q–N4 (9 N–B4, P–KN3; 10 Q–N4, N–Q2; 11 B–Q3, N–B1∞), P–KB4; 10 Q–N3, N–Q2 =. Dennehy-Heidenfeld, Dublin 1964. (C) 6 B–K3, P–QN3; 7 P–KR4.

(h) 6 N×N, B×B; 7 N×B, Q×N; 8 P–KN3, P–QB4; 9 P–QB3, N–B3; 10 P–KB4, Q–K2; 11 N–B3, B–Q2; 12 Q–Q2 O–O =. 5 . . . N–K5 is Tartakover's suggestion.

(i) 13 Q×P, Q×KP; 14 Q×P†, K–B3; 15 P–KR4! with more leverage.

(j) 13 Q×B, R–R2; 14 O–O–O, Q–R1; 15 Q–B3, Q–Q4; 16 K–N1, P–QR4; 17 Q–K3±. Persitz-Czerniak, Israel 1961.

(k) 8 B–B4, O–O; 9 Q–K2, N–N3; 10 B–N3, B–Q2; 11 O–O, Q–K2; 12 KR–K1 is good.

(l) 13 P–KN3, P×P; 14 B–N5, P–QR3! 15 B×N†, Q×B; 16 R×P, Q–N4; 17 Q–K3, K–K2 =. Comments.

1 P–K4, P–K3; 2 P–Q4, P–Q4; 3 N–QB3, N–KB3; 4 B–N5, P×P; 5 N×P, B–K2
(*a*); 6 B×N, P×B

	16	17	18	19	20
7	N–KB3............................			B–B4	P–KN3
	P–N3		P–KB4	P–B3	B–Q2 (*h*)
8	Q–K2.......	B–QB4	N–B3	P–QB3	N–B3
	B–N2 (*b*)	B–N2	B–B3 (*e*)	P–KB4	B–B3
9	O–O–O	Q–K2	Q–Q2	N–N3	Q–K2
	P–B3	P–B3	P–B4!	N–Q2	P–B4
10	P–B4	O–O–O	O–O–O	Q–K2	N/4–Q2
	Q–B2	Q–B2	P×P	Q–B2	B–B3
11	K–N1	K–N1	N×P	N–B3	P–B3
	N–Q2	N–Q2	N–B3	N–N3	N–Q2 =
12	N–B3	KR–K1	B–N5 (*f*)	B–N3	
	O–O–O (*c*)	O–O–O (*d*)		N–Q4 (*g*)	

(*a*) 5 . . . QN–Q2 (A) 6 N×N†, N×N; 7 N–B3 leads into col. 38, and (B) 6 N–B3, B–K2; 7
N×N†, B×N into col. 39.

(*b*) Actually, Black has quite a number of hard defences rendering White's conduct
doubtful; e.g. 8 . . . P–KB4; 9 N–B3, P–B3. Or 8 . . . B–R3; 9 P–B4, –B3; 10 O–O–O, Q–B2;
etc. The premature . . . P–QB4 would, however, be met by P–Q5.

(*c*) O'Kelly–Kramer, Beverwijk 1952; 13 P–KN3 ± .

(*d*) White is at a crossroad. (A) 13 B–R6, B×B; 14 Q×B†, K–N1; (1) 15 Q–R4, Q–N2; 16
P–B4, P–QB4; (2) 15 P–KN3, KR–K1; or (3) 15 Q–K2, KR–N1; 16 P–KN3, K–N2! 17 P–B4,
P–KB4; 18 N–B3, B–B3 = (Minev). (B) 13 B–N3 (Korchnoi's move), K–N1; 14 P–QR3,
KR–N1; 15 P–N3, P–KB4; 16 N/4–Q2, B–B3! 17 N–K5, N×N; 18 P×N, B–K2! = .
Sokolov–Krusichnik, Zenica 1963.

(*e*) (A) 8 . . . P–B4; 8 P–Q5! (B) 8 . . . P–QB3! 9 P–KN3, N–Q2; 10 B–N2, Q–B2; 11
Q–K2, P–N3 = .

(*f*) 12 . . . B–Q2; 13 N×BP, P×N; 14 Q–Q6, B–K4; 15 KR–K1, Q–N4†; 16 K–N1,
O–O–O; 17 R×B, B–K3; 18 Q–B5, R×R†; 19 N×R, R–Q1; 20 N–B3, Q×P; 21 R–K1,
K–N1; 22 B×N, Q×B; 23 Q–K5†, Q–B2; 24 Q×Q†, K×Q; 25 N–K2, R–KN1; 26 R–N1,
R–N5; 27 P–KB3, R×R†; 28 N×R, K–Q3; 29 P–N3, K–K4; 30 K–B1, B–Q4; 31 K–Q2,
P–N4; 32 P–QR3, P–B5; 33 K–Q3, drawn; Liberzon–Botvinnik, USSR 1966. Post-mortem
analysis also considers 12 . . . B×N; 13 Q×B, Q×Q; 14 R×Q, B–Q2 = .

(*g*) 13 N–K5, N–B5; 14 Q–B3, N–N3; 15 O–O, N×N; 16 P×N, B–Q2; 17 KR–K1,
O–O–O. Parma–Kramer, Varna 1962.

(*h*) 7 . . . P–KB4; 8 N–QB3, (A) 8 . . . P–QB3; 9 B–N2, B–B3 = . (B) 8 . . . B–B3; 9
KN–K2, N–B3; 10 P–Q5, P×P; 11 N×P, B×P; 12 B–N2, O–O; 13 O–O, B–R1; 14 KN–B4,
N–K4 = . Fischer–Petrosian, 3rd match game 1971. The column is comment to game
Fischer–Minev, Havana 1966.

1 P-K4, P-K3; 2 P-Q4, P-Q4; 3 N-QB3, N-KB3; 4 B-N5, B-N5; 5 P-K5, P-KR3; 6 B-Q2

	21	22	23	24	25
	KN-Q2	B × N			
7	Q-N4	P × B (c)			
	B-B1!	N-K5			
8	N-B3 (a)	Q-N4			
	P-QB4	K-B1			P-KN3
9	N-QN5	P-KR4	B-Q3	B-B1	B-Q3
	P-KN3	P-KB4 (d)	N × B	P-QB4	N × B
10	B-Q3	P × P *e.p.* (e)	K × N	N-K2	K × N
	R-KN1	Q × P	Q-N4† (g)	P × P	P-QB4
11	P-B4	N-B3	Q × Q	P-B3 (i)	R-N1 (j)
	P × QP	N-B3	P × Q	N × P	Q-B2
12	P × P	Q-B4	P-KB4	N × P	N-B3
	N-B4	N × B	P × P	Q-R4	P × P
13	Q × QP	Q × N	R-KB1	B-Q2	P × P
	P × P (b)	P-K4 (f)	N-B3 (h)	Q-B4! =	N-B3 (k)

(*a*) 8 P-B4, P-QB4; 9 N-B3, N-QB3; mostly ends in Black's favour.

(*b*) 14 N-Q6†, B × N; 15 P × B, Q × P; 16 O-O, N × B; 17 Q × N, N-B3; 18 KR-K1† with some prospects. Nezhmetdinov-Chistyakov, USSR 1956. 6 ... KN-Q2 is Tartakover's suggestion.

(*c*) 7 B × B, N-K5; 8 B-R5 (8 B-N4, P-QB4; 9 B × P, N × B ∓), O-O; 9 B-Q3, N-QB3; 10 B-B3, N × B; 11 P × N, P-B3, 12 P-KB4, P × P; 13 BP × P, N-K2; 14 N-B3, P-B4; 15 O-O, Q-R4 ∓ . Fischer-Petrosian, Curaçao 1962.

(*d*) The older-established line is 9 ... P-QB4; 10 R-R3 (10 B-Q3, N × B; 11 K × N, Q-R4; etc.), Q-R4; 11 B-Q3, N × B; 12 R-N3, P-KN3; 13 K × N, P × P, 14 Q × QP, N-B3; 15 Q-KB4, P-Q5; 16 N-B3, Q × P†; 17 K-K2 with strong attack for the pawn.

(*e*) 10 Q-B4, P-B4; 11 P-KN4, P-KN3! = .

(*f*) 14 B-N5, P × P; 15 B × N, P × P; 16 Q × QP, P × B; 17 Q-B5†, Q-K2† = . Liberzon-Prokhorovich, Moscow Chp. 1959.

(*g*) 10 ... P-QB4; 11 P-KR4, Q-R4; 12 R-R3, P × P; 13 R-N3, Q × P†; 14 K-K2, R-N1; 15 R-K1 ± . Fuchs.

(*h*) 14 R × P, B-Q2; 15 N-R3, K-K2 = . *Comments.*

(*i*) 11 P × P, Q-R4†; 12 P-B3, N-B3; 13 P-B3, P-R4; 14 Q-R3, N × P; with a position to be explored.

(*j*) So far somewhat stronger than (A) 11 Q-B4, P × P! (11 ... N-B3, 12 N-B3, B-Q2; 13 QR-QN1 ±); 12 P × P, Q-R4†; 13 P-B3, N-Q2; 14 N-K2, P-N3! ∞; or (B) 11 N-B3, P × P; 12 P × P, N-B3, 13 QR-QN1 (13 P-KR4, Q-B2), Q-B2 (13 ... Q-R4†; 14 K-K2!); 14 P-KR4, B-Q2 (14 ... P-KR4; 15 Q-N3, Q-R4†; 16 K-K2, Q × P; 17 R-R1, Q-N7; 18 KR-QN1, Q-B6; 19 Q-B4 ±); 15 P-R5, P-KN4 = (16 N × P? P × N; 17 Q × P, N-K2 + + . Richter-Korn, corr. 1944).

(*k*) 14 K-K2! ± . Matulović-Sofrevski, Skopje 1968.

1 P–K4, P–K3; 2 P–Q4, P–Q4; 3 N–QB3, N–KB3; 4 B–N5, B–N5

	26	27	28	29	30
5	(P–K5)..................		P×P	N–K2	B–Q3
	(P–KR3)		Q×P	P×P	P×P
6	(B–Q2)......	B–K3 (c)	B×N	P–QR3	B×P
	(B×N)	N–K5	P×B	B–K2	P–B4
7	(P×B)	N–K2	Q–Q2	B×N	P×P
	(N–K5)	P–QB4	Q–QR4	P×B	Q×Q†
8	(Q–N4)	P–QR3	KN–K2	N×P	R×Q
	(P–KN3)	N×N	N–Q2	P–N3	QN–Q2
9	B–B1	N×N	P–QR3 (d)	KN–B3	B×N
	P–QB4 (a)	B×N†	N–N3	B–N2	N×B
10	B–Q3	P×B	R–Q1	Q–B3	B–B3
	N×QBP	Q–R4	B–K2	P–B3	B×P
11	P×P	Q–Q2	N–N3	O–O–O	KN–K2
	Q–R4	P–B5	B–Q2 =	P–KB4	K–K2 = (f)
12	B–Q2	P–N3		N–N3	
	Q–R5! (b)	N–B3		N–Q2 (e)	

(a) 9 . . . N×QBP; 10 B–Q3, (1) 10 . . . Q–K2; 11 B–Q2! (not 11 P–QR4, N–Q2!) N–R5 (or 11 . . . N–K5; 12 B–N, P×B; 13 R–N1! ±); 12 R–N1 ±. (2) 10 . . . P–QB4; 11 B×NP, R–N1; 12 B×P†, K×B; 13 Q–B3†, K any; 14 Q×N ±. *P/E.*

(b) 13 P–KR3, P–KR4! 14 Q×Q, N×Q = . Keres.

(c) Without bite are (A) 6 B–R4, P–KN4; 7 B–N3, N–K5; 8 N–K2, P–KB4! 9 P×P *e.p.*, Q×P; 10 Q–Q3, N–B3; 11 O–O–O, N×B; 12 N×N, B–Q2; 13 B–K2, O–O–O ∓. Purdy–Miller, Australia 1955. (B) 6 B–B1 (Dr. Olland), N–K5; 7 Q–N4, K–B1! 8 N–K2, P–QB4; 9 P–QR3, B–R4; 10 P–N4, N×N ∓. Rauzer–Belavenets, Leningrad 1937. (c) 6 P×N, P×B; (Steinitz–MacCutcheon, New York 1885); 7 P×P, R–N1; 8 P–KR4, P×P; 9 N–B3, R×P; 10 R×P, B–Q2; 11 Q–Q2, Q–B3; 12 O–O–O, N–B3; 12 N–K5, O–O–O! = . 6 B–K3 is Janowski's move.

(d) 9 N–B1, N–N3; 10 N–N3, Q–KN4; 11 P–QR3, Q×Q†; 12 K×Q, B–K2; 13 B–N5†, P–B3 ∓. Capablanca–Bogolyubov, New York 1924. In the column, 7 N–K2! is stronger, but Black can avoid the variation altogether by transposing into the Exchange Variation, cols. 79–80, with 5 . . . P×P.

(e) 13 B–B4, Q–B2 = . Te Kolsté–Torre, Baden-Baden 1925.

(f) Lasker-Tarrasch, match 1908.

1 P–K4, P–K3; 2 P–Q4, P–Q4; 3 N–QB3

	31	32	33	34	35
	(N–KB3)				P–QB4? (j)
4	P–K5 (a)				KP×P
	KN–Q2				KP×P
5	QN–K2	P–B4		Q–N4	P×P
	P–QB4	P–QB4		P–QB4	P–Q5
6	P–QB3	N–B3 (f)		N–B3	B–N5†
	N–QB3	N–QB3		N–QB3	N–B3
7	P–KB4	B–K3		P×P	B×N†
	Q–N3 (b)	P×P	Q–N3	P–B4	P×B
8	N–B3 (c)	KN×P	N–QR4!	P×P e.p.	QN–K2!
	P–B3	B–B4	Q–R4†	N×KBP	B×P
9	P–KN3 (d)	Q–Q2	P–B3	Q–N3	N–KB3
	P×QP	O–O	P×P	B×P!	Q–R4†
10	P×QP	O–O–O	P–QN4!	B–KN5	B–Q2
	B–N5†	Q–K2	N×NP	O–O	Q–N3
11	N–QB3	B–N5	P×N	B–Q3	O–O
	O–O (e)	N×N (g)	B×P† (h)	B–Q3 (i)	Q×P (k)

(a) Steinitz's move. Ineffective is Svenonius's 4 P×P, P×P; 5 B–N5, B–K2; 6 B–Q3, N–B3; 7 KN–K2, B–K3; 8 O–O, P–KR3; 9 B×N, B×B; 10 B–N5, Q–Q3; 11 B×N†, Q×B; 12 N–B4, O–O–O = . Spielmann–Alekhin, San Remo 1930.

(b) Good tries are (A) 7 . . . P–QN4; 8 N–B3; Q–N3; 9 P–QR3, P–QR4; 10 P–B5, P×QP! 11 P×KP, P×KP; 12 P×P, B–K2; 13 N–B4, N–Q1; 14 B–Q3, N–B2; 15 P–KR4, P–N5 = . Enevoldsen–Czerniak, Helsinki 1952. (B) 7 . . . P–B4; 8 N–B3, B–K2; 9 N–N3, P×P; 10 P×P, O–O; 11 B–K2, Q–N3; 12 O–O, P–N4 = .

(c) 8 P–KN3 at once might be stronger.

(d) 9 P–QR3, B–K2! 10 N–N3, O–O; 11 B–Q3, P×QP; 12 P×QP, P×P; 13 BP×P, P–QR4 = .

(e) 12 P×P, N×BP; 13 P–QR3, B–Q3 = . 11 B–Q2 is also playable.

(f) 6 P×P, (A) 6 . . . B×P; 7 Q–N4, O–O; 8 B–Q3, (1) 8 . . . P–B4; 9 Q–R3, B×N?! 10 R×B, N–B4; 11 B–Q2, N–B3 = . Fischer–Benko, Curaçao 1962. (2) 8 . . . N–QB3; 9 N–B3, P–B4; 10 Q–R3, N–Q5; 11 B–Q2, P–QR3 = . (B) 6 . . . N–QB3; (1) 7 P–QR3, B×P; 8 Q–N4, P–KN3; 9 N–B3, P–QR4; 10 B–Q3, N–N3; 11 B–Q2, B–Q2; 12 O–O–O, P–R5; 13 N–QN5, N–R4 = . Santasiere–Evans, US Open Chp. 1949. (2) 7 N–B3, B×P; 8 B–Q3, P–B3! 9 P×P, N×P; 10 Q–K2, O–O = . Tringov–Fuchs, Sofia 1958.

(g) 12 B×N, P–QR3; 13 B×N, B×B; 14 N–K2, P–QN3; 15 KR–B1, QR–B1 = . Liberzon–Chistyakov, USSR 1964. In the column, Korchnoi's recommendation is 8 . . . Q–N3.

(h) 12 B–Q2, B×B†! 13 N×B, P–QN3! 14 R–QN1, B–R3; 15 Q–N3, R–QB1 (Bronstein–Portisch, Amsterdam 1964); 16 B×B, Q×B; 17 Q–N4! Q–Q6; 18 R–N3, with White's advantage (Timman); however, 17 . . . N–B4; 18 N×N, R×N; 19 N–N3, R–QB1 is one of many other possibilities.

(i) 12 Q–R4, P–KR3 = . The column is one sort of the "Gledhill variation."

(j) (A) Unusual is 3 . . . N–QB3; 4 N–B3, N–B3; (1) 5 B–KN5, B–K2; 6 P–K5, N–K5; 7 B×B, Q×B; 8 B–Q3, N×N; 9 P×N, O–O; 10 O–O, N–R4 ∞. Or (2) 5 P–K5, N–K5; 6 B–Q3, B–N5; 7 B–Q2, N×B; 8 Q×N, P–B3 = . (3) 5 P×P, P×P; 6 B–QN5, B–K2; 7 N–K5, B–Q2 ∞. (B) Romanishin, and the Australians Fuller and Kellner, explored also 3 . . . B–K2; which is, however, more relevant against 3 N–Q2 (see Tarrasch Variation, cols. 81–5, note (a)).

(k) 12 R–K1, N–K2; 13 N/2×P! and Black is tied up.

1 P–K4, P–K3; 2 P–Q4, P–Q4; 3 N–QB3 (or N–Q2), P×P; 4 N×P, N–Q2 (*a*); 5 N–KB3 (*b*), KN–B3; 6 N×N† (*c*), N×N

	36	37	38	39	40
7	B–Q3		B–N5		N–K5
	P–QN3?	B–K2 (*f*)	P–B4	B–K2	Q–Q4
8	O–O (*d*)	Q–K2	B–QB4 (*h*)	B–Q3 (*k*)	B–K3 (*n*)
	B–N2	O–O	P×P	P–B4	B–Q3
9	P–B3	B–KN5	O–O	Q–K2 (*l*)	N–B3
	B–K2	P–B4	B–K2	O–O	B–Q2
10	Q–K2	P×P	Q–K2	O–O–O	B–K2
	O–O	Q–R4†	P–KR3 (*i*)	Q–R4	P–QN4
11	B–KB4	P–B3	B–B4	K–N1	O–O
	P–B4	Q×BP	O–O	P×P	B–B3
12	P×P	O–O	QR–Q1	P–KR4	P–QR4
	P×P (*e*)	P–KR3 (*g*)	B–Q2 (*j*)	B–Q2 (*m*)	P–QR3 (*o*)

(*a*) The only move that matters, compared with (A) 4 . . . N–KB3; 5 N×N†, P×N! 6 N–B3, P–N3; 7 B–KB4, B–QN2; 8 B–N5†, P–B3; 9 B–Q3, B–Q3; 10 B–N3, Q–B2; 11 Q–K2, N–Q2; 12 O–O–O ± . H. Steiner–Tartakover, Groningen 1946, or (B) 4 . . . B–K2; 5 N–KB3, N–KB3; 6 N×N†, B×N; 7 P–B3 ± , or 6 B–Q3, QN–Q2; 7 Q–K2, O–O! 8 O–O, N×N; 9 Q×N, N–B3; 10 Q–R4! ± .

(*b*) 5 P–KN3, KN–B3; 6 N×N†, N×N; 7 B–N2, P–K4! 8 N–B3, P×P; 9 Q×P, B–K3 = . *Comments.*

(*c*) (A) 6 B–Q3, N×N; 7 B×N, N–B3 as in the column, or 7 . . . P–QB4?! (B) 6 B–KN5, B–K2 also reverts to the main line.

(*d*) 8 Q–K2, B–N2; 9 B–N5, B–K2; 10 O–O–O (10 O–O, O–O; 11 QR–Q1, P–KR3; 12 B–KB4, B–Q3 = . *Comments*), O–O; 11 P–KR4, (1) 11 . . . Q–Q4; 12 K–N1, P–B4; 13 KR–K1, Q–Q3; 14 P–B3, QR–Q1∞ ; or (2) 11 . . . P–B4; 12 P×P, P×P = .

(*e*) 13 KR–Q1, Q–N3; 14 N–K5 ± . Keres–Foltys, Szczavno Zdroj 1950.

(*f*) Black remains cramped after 7 . . . P–B4; 8 P×P, B×P; 9 B–N5, B–K2; 10 Q–K2 (or also 10 O–O, O–O; 11 Q–K2), O–O; 11 O–O–O, Q–R4; 12 K–N1, P–KR3; 13 P–KR4 ± . Spielmann–Petrov, Margate 1938.

(*g*) 13 B–R4 (13 B–B4, Q–KR4), B–Q2; 14 N–K5, KR–Q1; 15 N×B (else . . . B–K1), R×N = . Ritson–Morry's recipe.

(*h*) Again White can choose several concepts which need razor-sharp defence, e.g. (A) 8 B–N5† (Simagin), B–Q2; 9 B×B†, Q×B; (1) 10 Q–K2, B–K2; 11 O–O–O, O–O; 12 P×P, Q–B2; 13 N–K5, Q×P; 14 B×N, B×B, 15 N–Q7, Q–N4†; 16 K–N1, KR–Q1! Pachman. (2) 10 B×N, P×B; 11 P–B3, P×P; 12 N×P, B–B4; 13 Q–B3, O–O; 14 O–O–O, P–B4! = . Kottnauer; but not 14 . . . Q–K2? 15 N–N3, B–N3; 16 P–N4 + . Spasski–Petrosian, Moscow 1967. (B) B–Q3; 8 B–K2, see col 39. Faulty is (c) 8 Q–Q3, B–K2; 9 B×N, B×B; 10 Q–N5†, B–Q2; 11 Q×NP, R–QN1; 12 Q×P, R×P; 13 B–Q3, P×P; 14 O–O, B–B3; 15 Q–R3, Q–N3 + . Tal–Petrosian, Curaçao 1962.

(*i*) Another solid defence is 10 . . . P–QR3; 11 QR–Q1, N–Q2; 12 B×B, Q×B; 12 N×P, O–O; 14 N–B5, Q–B3; 15 N–Q6, N–K4; 16 B–N3, N–N3 = . Matanović–Barcza, Varna 1962.

(*j*) 13 R×P, Q–N3; (A) 14 R–Q3, B–N4 = . Tal–Benko, Curaçao 1962. (B) 14 Q–Q2, B–B3; 15 B×RP, N–K5; 16 Q–B4, P×B; 17 R×N! B×R; 18 Q×B, R–Q1; 19 P–QN3∞ . Tal–Portisch, 1965. White has a pawn and a powerful attack for the exchange.

(*k*) (A) 8 B–QB4, O–O; 9 Q–K2, P–QN3; 10 O–O–O, B–N2; 11 K–N1, P–QR4?! 12 P–KR4! P–R5; 13 P–R3, N–K5; 14 B–Q3 with some initiative. Spasski–Sakharov, Sochi 1966. (B) 8 P–KR4! P–B4; 9 Q–Q2! P–KR3; 10 B×B, B×B; 11 O–O–O, O–O (Gligorić–Balashov, Skopje 1970); 12 B–N5!. Variations in cols. 38 and 39 before the 10th move are frequently transposed.

(*l*) 9 P×P, Q–R4†; 10 P–B3, Q×BP; 11 Q–K2, B–Q2; 12 N–K5, B–B3; 13 P–KR4, R–Q1; 14 O–O–O, N–Q2; 15 N×B, B×B†; 16 P×B, Q×NP†; 17 K–B2, P×N; 18 R–R5∞, with more play for the pawn. Spasski–Petrosian, Chp. match 1966.

(*m*) 13 N×P, B–B3; 14 KR–K1, KR–K1; 15 P–KN4, Q–N3; 16 N–N3, N–Q4; 17 P–QB4, N–N5 = . Spasski–Bronstein, USSR 1959.

(*n*) Also 8 B–K2, P–B4; 9 B–K3, P×P; 10 B×P, B–B4 = . *Comments.*

(*o*) 13 N–K1, P–K4 = . Fine–Snethlage, corr. 1940.

1 P-K4, P-K3; 2 P-Q4, P-Q4; 3 N-QB3, B-N5; 4 P-K5, P-QB4; 5 P-QR3, B×N†; 6 P×B, N-K2; 7 Q-N4

	41	42	43	44	45
	N-B4			O-O	Q-B2
8	B-Q3		N-B3	N-B3	B-Q3 (i)
	P-KR4		P-KR4	QN-B3	P×P
9	Q-B4	Q-R3	Q-B4	B-Q3	N-K2
	N-B3 (a)	P×P	P-B5	P-B4	P×P
10	N-K2 (b)	N-B3 (d)	B-K2 (g)	P×P e.p.	Q×NP
	QN-K2	Q-B2 (e)	N-B3	R×P	R-N1
11	N-N3	QR-N1	O-O	B-KN5	Q×P
	N-N3 (c)	P×P	Q-R4	R-B2	QN-B3!
12	Q-Q2	P-N4	Q-Q2	B×N	P-B4! (j)
	B-Q2	N-K2	QN-K2	R×B	B-Q2
13	R-QN1	P×P	QR-N1	Q-R4	R-QN1
	R-QN1 =	QN-B3 (f)	Q-B2 =	P-KN3 (h)	O-O-O =

(a) 9 . . . Q-R5? 10 N-K2 (10 Q-Q2, N-B3), Q×Q; 11 N×Q, N-K2; 12 B-K3±. Bisguier–Fine, New York 1948–9.

(b) 10 B×N, P×B; 11 Q-N3, Q-R4! 12 N-K2, B-K3; 12 O-O, O-O-O∓. Teschner–Uhlmann, Wageningen 1957.

(c) Schwarz considers 11 . . . P-B5; 12 N×N, P×N = to be better. The column is Stein–Petrosian, USSR 1961.

(d) (A) 10 N-K2! is recommended by *P/E*. (B) 10 P-N4, N-K2 (10 . . . Q-R4; 11 K-K2, N-K2; 12 B-Q2! P×P; 13 B×P; Q-R5; 14 P×P, B-Q2; 15 K-Q2, QN-B3; 16 N-B3, O-O-O is rather ambiguous); 11 P×QP, Q-B2; 12 N-K2, QN-B3; 13 R-QN1, N×QP; 14 N×N, Q-B6†; 15 B-Q2, Q×N; 16 P-KB4 is also good. Keres.

(e) Still valid is 10 . . . N-B3; 11 P-N4, KN-K2; 12 P×RP, Q-B2; 13 B-KB4, N-N3; 14 Q-N4, N×B; 15 Q×N, Tal–Petrosian, USSR Chp. 1957, 15 . . . R×P! = . *Comments.*

(f) 14 B-KB4, N-N3; 15 B-N3, N/N3×P; 16 K-B1, P-B3; 17 B-N5∞. Comments to Tal–Korchnoi, USSR Chp. 1958, which went 16 N×N, N×N; 17 K-B1, B-Q2∓.

(g) 10 P-QR4, N-B3; 11 B-K2, QN-K2; 12 O-O, Q-R4∓. *Comments.*

(h) 14 O-O, P-B5; 15 B-K2, B-Q2; 16 KR-K1, Q-R4; 17 N-K5, QR-K1; 18 N-N4, Q×BP; 19 Q-B6, R-N2 = . Korchnoi–Bronstein, USSR 1958.

(i) 8 Q×NP transposes into other variations of the line with . . . Q-B2 which is often played on the 6th or later moves and interchanged with the move . . . N-K2.

(j) If 12 B-KB4, B-Q2; 13 O-O, O-O-O; 14 Q-R5, P-Q5; 15 B-N3, B-K1; 16 Q-B3, N×P + . Unzicker–Uhlmann, Varna Olympics 1962. The column is *Comments.*

1 P–K4, P–K3; 2 P–Q4, P–Q4; 3 N–QB3, B–N5; 4 P–K5, P–QB4; 5 P–QR3,
B × N†; 6 P × B, N–K2; 7 Q–N4, P × P; 8 Q × NP, R–N1; 9 Q × P, Q–B2

	46	47	48	49	50
10	N–K2...............................			K–Q1	
	P × P	QN–B3		N–Q2	
11	P–B4	P–KB4		R–N1	N–B3!
	B–Q2 (*a*)	B–Q2!		N–QB4!	N × P
12	Q–Q3 (*b*)	Q–Q3 (*d*)		B–Q3	B–KB4
	N–B4 (*c*)	P × P		P × P	Q × P
13	N × P	P–KR4	Q × BP (*f*)	N–B3	N × N
	N–R3!	N–B4	N–B4	B–Q2	Q × R†
14	N–N5	P–R5	R–QN1 (*g*)	B–KN5!	B–B1
	Q–R4†	O–O–O	P–Q5	B–B3 (*i*)	R–B1
15	B–Q2	P–R6	Q–B4!		B–Q3!
	Q–R5 =	R–N3 (*e*)	Q–R4† (*h*)		B–Q2 (*j*)

(*a*) (A) 11 ... P–N3; 12 N–N3! B–Q2; 13 N–R5! ± . Ivkov–Rossetto, Belgrade 1962. (B) 11 ... QN–B3; see col. 47.

(*b*) (A) 12 N–Q4, P–R3; 13 Q–Q3, QN–B3; 14 Q × BP, QR–B1 = . (B) 12 R–QN1 see col. 69, note (*g*).

(*c*) Parma–Bronstein, Belgrade 1964.

(*d*) Or 12 P–R3, P × P; 13 P–N4, O–O–O; 14 Q–Q3, P–Q5; 15 QR–N1, N × P∞ . R. Byrne–Uhlmann, Monte Carlo 1968.

(*e*) 16 P–R7, R–R1; 17 R–QN1, P–B3; 18 P × P, B–K1; 19 Q × BP, R × RP; 20 R × R, Q × R; 21 R–N3 ± . Vasyukov–Doroshkevich, Moscow 1967.

(*f*) A variety of strategies and transpositions has been tried at this juncture, i.e. (A) 13 N × P, P–R3; 14 R–QN1, (1) 14 ... R–QB1; 15 P–KR4! N–R2! 16 R–R3, N–N4; 17 R–QN3, N–B4 = . Bednarski–Uhlmann, Mariánské Lázně 1965, or (2) 14 ... N–R4; 15 P–KR4, N–B4; 16 R–R3, O–O–O! 17 P–R5, R–N5! = . (B) Keres's idea 13 N–N3! O–O–O; 14 B–K2, N–B4; 15 N × N, P × N; 16 O–O, P–Q5; 17 B–B3, R–N3; 18 R–K1, B–K3; 19 R–N1∞ . Less effective are (c) 13 B–K3, N–B4; 14 B–B2 (or 14 N–Q4, KN × N; 15 B × N, O–O–O; 16 P–N3, P–B3! ∓), O–O–O; 15 R–QN1, P–Q5; 16 N–N3, P–B3! 17 N × N, P × N; 18 P × P, Q × P; 19 B–N3, Q–R3. Fuchs–Uhlmann, Dresden 1956, and (D) 13 QR–N1, O–O–O; 14 N × P, N–R4; 15 N–N5, B × N; 16 R × B, N–B5 . Kotkov–Slepov, USSR 1959.

(*g*) 14 B–Q2, Q–N3! 15 P–QR4, R–QB1 ∓ . Bogdanović–Uhlmann, Sarajevo 1963.

(*h*) 16 B–Q2, Q × RP; 17 R × P, N–K6! 18 B × N, P × B; 19 Q–B3, Q × Q; 20 N × Q, N–Q5; 21 N–K4, B–B3 = . Portisch in *Informator* 5.

(*i*) (Yanovsky–Uhlmann, Havana 1966) 15 R–N4! ± . However, Black had a better move in 13 ... N × B†; and an earlier 10 ... QN–B3; 11 N–B3, P × P; 12 N–N5, N × P; 13 P–B4, R × N; 14 P × R, N/4–N3 = . Hansen–Wirth, corr. 1973.

(*j*) (A) 16 R–K1, N–B3! 17 N × P, R × N; 18 B–N6! O–O–O! 19 Q × R! P–K4; 20 K–K2, P–K5; 21 K–B1, Q–B6; 22 B–B5 = . Fuchs. (B) 16 K–K2, (1) 16 ... N–B4; 17 R–K1, Q–B6; 18 B–KN5! N–K2; 19 N–N4! (Yodovich), or (2) 16 ... O–O–O; 17 N × P, R × N; 18 Q × R, N–B3; 19 R–Q1!

1 P-K4, P-K3; 2 P-Q4, P-Q4; 3 N-QB3, B-N5; 4 P-K5, P-QB4; 5 P-QR3,
B × N†; 6 P × B, N-K2

	51	52	53	54	55
7	(Q-N4)......	N-B3	P-QR4.................		P-KR4
	(P × P)	B-Q2!? (c)	QN-B3		Q-R4!
8	(Q × NP)	P-QR4! (d)	N-B3		B-Q2
	(R-N1)	Q-R4	Q-R4		Q-R5!
9	(Q × P)	Q-Q2	B-Q2	Q-Q2	N-B3
	(Q-B2)	QN-B3	B-Q2	B-Q2	QN-B3
10	(K-Q1)	B-K2	B-K2	B-Q3 (f)	P-R5
	QN-B3	R-QB1	P-B5	P-B3!	P × P
11	N-B3	P × P	P-R4	O-O	R-R4
	P × P	N-N3	P-B3	P × KP	N-B4
12	N-N5	O-O	P-R5	P × KP (g)	R-B4
	R-B1 (a)	O-O	P × P	O-O	P-B3
13	B-KB4	Q-K3 ±	P-R6	R-K1	P × BP (i)
	B-Q2 (b)		P × RP (e)	P-KR3 (h)	

(a) (A) Better 12 . . . N × P, answered by (1) 13 P-B4, R × N! (or 13 . . . P-B3! 14 B-N5†,
K-Q1 =); 14 P × R, N/4-N3; 15 B-K2, P-K4; 16 R-B1, B-K3; 17 B-N5†, K-Q1 = .
Matulović-Tatai, Venice 1969. (2) 13 B-KB4, Q-N3; 14 B × N, R × N; 15 P-KR4, R-KN1; 16
K-K1, B-Q2; 17 R-R3, R-N5 ∓ . Matulović-Uhlmann, Budapest 1967. (B) Korchnoi suggests
to try 12 . . . Q × P; 13 Q × P†, K-Q2 ∞ .

(b) 14 R-QN1, N-R4; 15 B-Q3 (15 Q-Q3, O-O-O; 16 P-KR4, P-Q5 = .
Petrusyak-Uhlmann, Halle 1967), Q-B4; 16 Q-R3, B-B3; 17 Q-K3, P-Q5; 19 N-K4! R.
Byrne.

(c) White's "decoy" is more precisely countered by (A) 7 . . . Q-B2; transposing into col.
56 etc. Risky is (B) 7 . . . Q-R4; 8 B-Q2, P-B5; 9 P-QR4, N-Q2; 10 N-N5.

(d) Spasski, versus Korchnoi, match 1977, frequently employed 8 P × P, Q-B2; e.g. 9
B-Q3, B-R5! 10 R-QN1! N-Q2; 11 R-N4, B-B3; 12 O-O, N × BP! 13 R-N4, N-N3; 14
N-Q4, O-O-O = . 10th match game. The column is Smyslov-Uhlmann, Mar del Plata 1966.

(e) 14 N × P, N × N; 15 P × N, O-O-O; 16 R × P, N-N3 = . Fischer-Padevski, Varna
1962, which continued too sharply: 17 B-N5!? (17 P-B4! =), Q × P†; 18 K-B1, QR-B1; 19
B-B6, R × B!

(f) (A) 10 B-R3 (or 10 B-K2 or P-R4), P × P; 11 P × P, Q × Q†; 12 K × Q, P-QN3; 13
B-Q3 (Safvat-Silva, Varna 1962), N-B4 = . (B) 10 B-K2, O-O; 11 O-O, P-B3; 12 KP × P,
R × P; 13 P × P, B-K1; 14 P-B4, Q-B2; 15 B-N2, R-R3; 16 Q-N5, R-N3; 17 Q-Q2, R-R3 = .
Minić-Uhlmann, Zagreb 1965. (C) 10 B-QN5, N × KP; 11 N × N, B × B; 12 B-R3, B-R3; 13
B × P, P-B3 = . Mnatsakanian-Korchnoi, Erevan 1965.

(g) Deviating from 12 N × P, N × N; 13 P × N, O-O; 14 P-QB4, Q × Q; 15 B × Q, B-B3;
16 P-R5, QR-Q1; 17 B-K3, P-Q5; 18 B-Q2, N-N3 = . Fischer-Uhlmann, Stockholm 1962.

(h) 14 B-R3, B-K1; 15 Q-K3, P-QN3; 16 N-Q2, N-B4 = . Smyslov-Uhlmann, Havana
1964.

(i) (A) 13 . . . NP × P; 14 P-N4, P-K4; 15 R × N, B × R; 16 P × B, P × P; 17 B × P,
O-O-O = . (B) 13 . . . P-K4; 14 P × NP, R-KN1 = . Salm-Koch, corr. 1956.

1 P-K4, P-K3; 2 P-Q4, P-Q4; 3 N-QB3, B-N5; 4 P-K5, P-QB4; 5 P-QB3, B×N†; 6 P×B, Q-B2

	56	57	58	59	60
7	N-B3			Q-N4	
	N-K2!		N-Q2 (f)	P-B3!	P-B4
8	B-K2	P-QR4 (c)	B-Q3	N-B3	Q-N3
	P-QN3 (a)	P-QN3 (d)	N-N3	P-B5 (h)	N-K2 (j)
9	O-O	B-N5†	O-O	B-K2	Q×P
	B-R3	B-Q2	P-B5	N-B3	R-N1
10	B-Q3 (b)	B-Q3	B-K2	O-O	Q×P
	B×B	QN-B3	N-R5	Q-B2	P×P
11	P×B	O-O	B-Q2	Q-R3	K-Q1
	O-O	P-KR3!	B-Q2	KN-K2	B-Q2 (k)
12	P-QR4	R-K1(e)	R-K1	P-R4	Q-R5†
	N-Q2 =		N-K2	B-Q2	K-Q1!
13			N-N5	B-R3	N-K2!
			P-KR3 (g)	O-O-O (i)	P×P (l)

(a) 8 . . . B-Q2; 9 P-QR4, QN-B3; 10 O-O, P-B3; 11 R-K1, P×KP; 12 P×KP, O-O-O; 13 B-R3, N-R4; 14 N-Q4 ± . Keres.

(b) 10 B×B, N×B; 11 Q-K2, QN-N1; 12 P-QR4, QN-B3 = . *Comments.*

(c) (A) 8 B-Q3, B-Q2! (8 . . . P-QN3; 9 O-O, B-R3; 10 B×B, N×B; 11 Q-K2, Q-N2; 12 P-QR4!); 9 P-QR4, QN-B3; 10 Q-Q2, P-R3; 11 O-O, P-B5; 12 B-K2, O-O! = . (B) 8 P-KR4, QN-B3; 9 P-R5, P-KR3 = . Keres.

(d) Varying from the older 8 . . . QN-B3; 9 B-K2, P-QN3; 10 O-O, B-Q2; 11 B-R3, N-R4; 12 Q-B1, O-O; 13 Q-N5, N-N3; 14 P×P, P×P; 15 Q-K3, QR-B1; 16 B-R6, N-QB5! 17 Q-K2, R-Q1 = . Kuypers-Corral, Berlin 1965.

(e) There may follow (A) 12 . . . N-R4; 13 N-Q2, O-O; 14 Q-N4, P-B4; 15 P×P e.p. R×P; 16 N-B3, QR-KB1; 17 Q-N3!, or (B) 12 . . . O-O! 13 B-R3, N-R4! 14 P×P, P×P; 15 N-Q2, N-N3; 16 Q-R5, B-K1; 17 Q-K2, P-B4; 18 P×P e.p., R×P = . Portisch.

(f) Cols. 56-7 dispose of these riskier choices (A) 7 . . . B-Q2; 8 P-QR4, N-QB3; 9 B-R3, P-QN3; 10 B-Q3, N-R4; 11 O-O, N-K2; 12 R-K1, P-B5; 13 B-KB1, P-R4; 14 P-N3 ± , and (B) 7 . . . P-QN3; 8 P-QR4, B-R3; 9 B×B, N×B; 10 Q-K2, N-N1; 11 P-R5, Q-B3 ∞; Bogdanović-Krogius, Sarejevo 1968; and 11 . . . P×RP; 12 B-R3, N-Q2; 13 P×P, N-K2; 14 P-B6! ± . Tal-Donner, Wijk aan Zee 1968.

(g) 14 N-R3, O-O-O; 15 N-B4 with a bind.

(h) 8 . . . N-B3; 9 Q-N3, P×KP! 10 P×KP, Q-B2 = is also quite satisfactory.

(i) 14 P-R5, P-R4; 15 N-Q2! . Matulović-Byrne, Sousse 1967.

(j) 8 . . . P×P; 9 P×P, N-K2; 10 B-Q2, O-O; 11 B-Q3, P-QN3; 12 N-K2, B-R3; (1) 13 N-B4, Q-Q2; 14 B×B, N×B; 15 Q-Q3, N-N1; 16 P-KR4 ± . Reshevsky-Botvinnik, Moscow 1948. (2) 13 B-N4, B×B; 14 P×B, N/1-B3; 15 B-Q6, Q-Q2; 16 O-O, R-B2; 17 P-QR4, N-B1; 18 B-R3 ± . *Comments.*

(k) The only riposte. If 11 . . . QN-B3; 12 N-B3, N×P; 13 B-KN5! N/4-N3; 14 B-B6 and P-KR4-5.

(l) 14 Q-B3! QN-B3! 15 Q×QBP, N×P; 16 Q×Q†, K×Q; 17 N-Q4, N-N5; 18 K-K1, P-K4; 19 P-KB3, P×N; 20 P×N, P×P = . Collins-Lobdell, corr. 1971-72.

1 P–K4, P–K3; 2 P–Q4, P–Q4; 3 N–QB3, B–N5; 4 P–K5, P–QB4; 5 P–QR3

	61	62	63	64	65
	P×P	B–R4			
6	P×B (*a*)	P–QN4.............	....	Q–N4	B–Q2
	P×N	P×NP	P×QP	N–K2	P×P
7	Q–N4! (*b*)	N–N5	Q–N4 (*d*)	P×P	N–N5
	K–B1	N–QB3	N–K2	B×N†	B–B2
8	N–B3	KN–B3	P×B (*e*)	P×B	P–KB4
	Q–B2	P–QR3	P×N	N–Q2 (*h*)	N–KR3
9	B–Q3	N–Q6†	Q×NP	N–B3 (*i*)	Q–R5
	N–QB3	K–B1	R–N1	Q–B2	N–B4
10	O–O	B–Q3	Q×P	Q×NP	N–KB3
	P–B4	P–N6†	QN–B3	R–KN1	P–KN3
11	Q–B4 ±	K–B1	N–B3 (*f*)	Q×P	Q–R3
		B–B2 (*c*)	Q–B2 (*g*)	N×KP (*j*)	N–B3 (*k*)

(*a*) 6 Q×P, N–QB3; 7 Q–N4, B×N†; 8 P×B, KN–K2; 9 Q×NP, R–KN1; 10 Q×P, N×P∓. *Comments.*

(*b*) (A) 7 P×P, Q–B2! 8 N–B3, N–K2∓. (B) 7 N–B3, and now (1) 7 ... P×P; 8 B×P, P–B4; 9 P×P *e.p.*, N×P; 10 B–Q3, O–O; or (2) 7 ... Q–B2; 8 Q–Q4, N–K2 (8 ... P×P; 9 B×P, N–K2; 10 B–Q3 ± *P/E*); 9 B–Q3, N–Q2; 10 O–O, P–B4∞. *Comments.*

(*c*) 12 N×B, P×P; 13 B×BP, R×N; 14 P–KR4, B–N3; 15 B–K3, Q–B2; 16 P–R5, P–R3; 17 B–Q3, N–R4; 18 R–R4, N–B5; 19 B–B1, N–K2 =. Boleslavski–Katalimov, USSR Chp. 1960.

(*d*) 7 N–N5, B–B2; (1) 8 P–KB4, N–K2; 9 N–KB3, B–Q2! =. Smyslov–Botvinnik, match 1954. (2) 8 N–KB3, N–QB3; 9 N×B†, Q×N; 10 B–QN5, N–K2; 11 B–N2, B–Q2; 12 B×N, N×B; 13 Q–K2, O–O; 14 O–O, P–B3; 15 P×P, P×P∞.

(*e*) 8 N–N5, B–B2; 9 Q×NP, R–N1; 10 Q×P, P–R3; 11 N×B†, Q×N; 12 N–K2, B–Q2 and ... P–R4 =. Euwe.

(*f*) 11 P–B4, Q×P; 12 N–B3, B–Q2; 13 N–N5, R–KB1; 14 R–QN1, O–O–O; 15 N×BP, R×N; 16 Q×R, B–K1; 17 Q×P†, B–Q2; 18 Q–B6, B–B4; 19 B–K2, Q–B4. Taimanov.

(*g*) (A) Fischer–Tal, Leipzig 1960, continued 12 B–QN5, B–Q2; 13 O–O, O–O–O; 14 B–N5, N×KP! 15 N×N, B×B; 16 N×P! B×R; 17 N×R, R×B; 18 N×KP, R×P†; 19 K–R1! Q–K4; 20 R×B, Q×N; 21 K×R, Q–N5†; draw. (B) An alternative to Black's 11th move is 11 ... Q×P; 12 R–QN1, Q–B2; 13 P–KB4, B–Q2; 14 B–N3, O–O–O =. Damjanović–Udovćić, Yugoslav Chp. 1963.

(*h*) For alternatives compare with col. 69, where White's pawn is still on QR2.

(*i*) 9 Q×NP, R–KN1; 10 Q×P, N×KP.

(*j*) 12 Q–R5, N×N†; 13 Q×N, B–Q2; 14 B–KB4, Q×P∞. White exerts pressure. The lines in cols. 62–64 cast doubt on 5 ... B–R4!?

(*k*) 12 B–Q3, P–KR4; 13 P–KN4, N–K6; 14 R–KN1 K–Q2! =. *Comments.*

1 P–K4, P–K3; 2 P–Q4; P–Q4; 3 N–QB3, B–N5; 4 P–K5, P–QB4

	66	67	68	69	70
5	B–Q2		P × P	Q–N4	
	N–QB3	N–K2	Q–B2 (f)	N–K2	
6	N–N5 (a)	N–N5 (c)	N–B3	N–B3 (g)	. . . . P × P
	B × B†	B × B†	N–K2	P × P (h)	QN–B3 (i)
7	Q × B	Q × B	B–Q3	N × P	B–Q2 (j)
	N × QP	O–O	N–Q2	Q–B2	N–B4 (k)
8	N × N	P–QB3	O–O	B–N5†	N–B3
	P × N	QN–B3 (d)	B × N	QN–B3	B × P
9	N–B3	N–B3	P × B	O–O	B–Q3
	N–K2	P–QR3	N × BP	B × N	P–KR4
10	Q × P	N–Q6	B–K3	P × B	Q–KB4
	O–O	P × P	N × B =	B–Q2	QN–K2
11	B–Q3	P × P		B × N	P–KR3
	N–B3	P–B3		P × B	P–QR3
12	Q–K3	N × B		B–R3	O–O–O
	P–B4 (b)	R × N (e)		Q × P =	N–N3 =

(a) Another try is 6 N–B3, P × P! 7 N–QN5, B–B4; 8 P–QR3, KN–K2; 9 P–QN4, B–N3; 10 B–Q3, N–N3; 11 Q–K2, B–B2; 12 B–N5, Q–Q2; 13 B × N, BP × B! Keres' suggestion to Christoffel–Botvinnik, Groningen 1946.

(b) 13 O–O, B–Q2 = . Aronin–Petrosian, USSR, Chp. prelims. 1949.

(c) 6 P–QR3, B × N; 7 B × B leaves Black too much choice, e.g. (1) 7 . . . P × P; 8 B × P (8 Q × P, N–B4! 9 Q–N4, P–KR4; 10 Q–B4, P–KN4; 11 B–N5†, N–B3; 12 Q–Q2, P–Q5; 13 B–N4, Q–Q4 ± . Sakharov–Petrosian, USSR Chp. 1958), QN–B3; 9 N–B3, Q–B2; 10 P–B3, N–N3; 11 B–N5, B–Q2 = ; or (2) 7 . . . QN–B3; 8 N–B3, P–B5; 9 B–K2, P–QN4; 10 O–O, B–Q2; 11 Q–Q2, P–QR4 = ; Bernstein–Nimzowitsch, Zürich 1934; or (3) 7 . . . P–QN3; 8 P–QN4, Q–B2; 9 N–B3, P × NP; 10 B × P, B–R3; 11 B–Q3, B × B; 12 Q × B, QN–B3; 13 B–Q6, Q–Q2 = . Sanguinetti–Fuchs, Munich 1958.

(d) 8 . . . N–B4; 9 B–Q3, B–Q2; 10 N–B3 (10 N–K2, N–R5!), B × N; 11 B × B, Q–N3; 12 B–Q3, N–B3; 13 P × P, Q × BP is just about equal. Stoltz–Nimzowitsch, match 1934.

(e) 13 P × P, R × P; 14 B–Q3, N–N3 = . Unzicker–O'Kelly, Oldenburg 1949.

(f) 5 . . . N–K2; 6 N–B3, QN–B3; (1) 7 B–Q2! B × P! 8 N–KR4! B–N5; 9 P–QR3 ± , *P/E*, but not (2) 7 B–Q3, P–Q5; 8 P–QR3, B–R4; 9 P–QN4, N × NP; 10 P × N, B × P; 11 O–O, B × N; 12 R–N1, P–KR3 = .

(g) (A) A gamble is 6 Q × NP, R–N1; 7 Q–R6, P × P; 8 P–QR3, B × N†; 9 P × B, Q–B2; 10 N–K2, P × P; 11 P–B4, B–Q2; 12 R–QN1, QN–B3; 13 N–N3, O–O–O; 14 B–Q3, N–Q5; 15 Q–R5, Q–B4∞ . Sigurjonsson–Uhlmann, Hastings 1975–76. Also refer to col. 46, note (b) (B). (B) If at once 6 P–QR3, Q–R4! 7 P × B, Q × R; 8 K–Q1, P × QP; 9 N–N5, O–O; 10 N–KB3, QN–B3; 11 B–Q3, N–N3; 12 R–K1, N × NP ∓ . Jansa–Korchnoi, Luhačovice 1969.

(h) Also 6 . . . QN–B3; 7 B–Q2, O–O; 8 B–Q3, P–B4; 9 P × P e.p., R × P; 10 Q–R5, P–N3 was tried in Sax–Mednis, Budapest 1976. The column is Spasski–Uhlmann, Manila 1976.

(i) Also 6 . . . B × N†; 7 P × B, N–N3; 8 N–B3, N–Q2; 9 B–K3, Q–R4 = . Euwe.

(j) 7 N–B3, P–Q5! 8 B–QN5, Q–R4; 9 B × N†, P × B; 10 Q × QP, N–B4 ∓ .

(k) (A) 7 . . . B × P; 8 N–B3, O–O; 9 B–Q3, P–B4∞ . *P/E*. (B) 7 . . . O–O; 8 N–B3, P–B4; 9 Q–R4! P–Q5; 10 N–K2, B × B†; 11 N × B, Q–Q4; 12 N Q2–N3, Q2–N3, N–N3; 13 Q–R3! ± . Estrin. The column is *Comments*. 5 Q–N4, for a while a dreaded "refutation" of 4 . . . P–QB4, has lost most of its impetus.

1 P-K4, P-K3; 2 P-Q4, P-Q4; 3 N-QB3, B-N5

	71	72	73	74	75
4	(P–K5)		P–QR3	B–Q2	
	P–QN3 (a) . . .	Q–Q2 (d)	B × N†	P × P	
5	P–QR3	B–Q3 (e)	P × B	Q–N4	
	B × N†	P–QN3	P × P	Q × P	
6	P × B	N–B3	Q–N4	O–O–O!? (g)	
	Q–Q2 (b)	N–QB3	N–KB3	P–KB4	P–KR4
7	Q–N4 (c)	O–O	Q × NP	Q–N3	Q–N5! (i)
	P–KB4	B–N2	R–N1	B–Q3	B–K2
8	Q–N3	N–K2	Q–R6	B–KB4	Q–N3
	B–R3	O–O–O	QN–Q2 (f)	B × B†	B–Q3
9	B × B	P–B3	N–K2	Q × B	B–KB4
	N × B	B–K2	P–B4	Q–B4	P–R5!
10	N–K2	N–N3	N–N3	P–B3	Q–N4 (j)
	N–N1!?	N–R3	Q–B2!	N–K2	N–KB3
11	N–B4	N–R5	Q–K3	P × P	Q–N5
	N–QB3 =	N–B4 =	Q–B3 =	O–O (h)	B × B† ∓

(a) Nimzowitsch's suggestion, to develop Black's QB, but difficult to implement successfully.

(b) 6 . . . N–K2 (in place of the older 6 . . . P–QB4); 7 Q–N4! N–N3; 8 P–KR4, P–KR4; 9 Q–Q1 (9 Q–N3, B–R3; 10 N–K2, Q–Q2 =), B–R3; 10 B × B, N × B; 11 B–N5, Q–Q2; 12 N–K2 ± . Ivkov–R. Byrne, Varna 1962.

(c) 7 N–R3! B–R3; 8 B–Q3, P–QB4 (8 . . . N–K2; 9 Q–N4, B × B; 10 P × B, N–B4; 11 O–O, P–KR4; 12 Q–B3, P–B4 is more solid); 9 Q–N4, P–B4; 10 Q–R5†, del Corral–Keene, Barcelona 1975. The column is Gligorić's analysis.

(d) 4 . . . N–K2 was played for a while so as to avoid 5 Q–N4 as in col. 69 and to transpose into the usual main lines another move or two later. Different treatments arise after (A) 5 B–Q2, P–QN3; 6 N–N5, B × B†; 7 Q × B, B–R3 ∞ ; or (B) 5 Q–N4, N–B4; 6 B–Q3, P–KR4; 7 Q–B4, N–B3; 8 P–QR3, B–K2; 9 B × N (9 N–B3, P–KN4; 10 N × NP, N/3 × QP = . R. Byrne), P–KN4; 10 Q–Q2, P × B; 11 P–KR4, P × P ∓ . Calvo–Petrosian, Las Palmas 1973.

(e) 5 P–QR3, B–B1; 6 N–R3 (6 Q–N4 P–KB4 =), P–QN3; 7 N–B4, B–R3; 8 B × B, N × B; 9 Q–K2, N–N1; 10 B–K3, N–QB3; 11 P–KN4, O–O–O; 12 O–O–O, N–R4! = Schmid–Yanofsky, Lone Pine 1975.

(f) (A) The older line is 8 . . . P–B4; 9 N–K2, R–N3! 10 Q–Q2! (10 Q–K3, N–B3; 11 P × P, P–QR4! or 11 . . . Q–R4!∞), QN–Q2; 11 B–N2, Q–B2 = . Botvinnik. (B) 8 . . . P–N3; 9 B–N5, R–N3; 10 Q–R4, B–N2; 11 N–K2! P–KR3; 12 B × P, R–N5 = . (c) 8 . . . R–N3; 9 Q–K3, B–Q2!? (or 9 . . . N–B3; 10 B–N2, N–K2) 10 B–N2, B–B3 ∞ . Persitz–Sheldrick, England 1966. The column is Fischer–R. Byrne, USA Chp. 1966–67, but there, 9 . . . P–N3; 10 B–N5, Q–K2; 11 Q–R4, B–N2; 12 N–N3, P–KR3 would have given Black a very good game.

(g) Recent, but not quite solid. The only tenable move seems 6 N–B3, N–KR3! 7 Q × P†, B × Q; 8 N × Q, B–Q2; 9 N × P = .

(h) 12 N–B3, N–Q2; 13 P × P! ∞ P/E.

(i) Risky is 7 Q–N3, B–Q3; 8 P–B4, P × P e.p.; 9 Q × P ∞ .

(j) 10 Q–N5, Q–B3; 10 Q × Q, N × Q; 11 B × B, P × B; 12 N–N5, N–R3 ∓ .

1 P-K4, P-K3; 2 P-Q4, P-Q4

	76	77	78	79	80
3	(N-QB3)	. . . .		P×P (j)	Exchange Variation
	(B-N5)			P×P	
4	N-K2 (a)	. . . . B-Q3 (d)		B-Q3	
	P×P	P×P	. . . . P-QB4	N-QB3	. . . . . . N-KB3
5	P-QR3	B×P	P×QP	N-KB3 (k)	N-KB3
	B-K2 (b)	N-KB3	Q×P	B-Q3	B-Q3
6	N×P	B-B3 (e)	B-Q2	O-O	O-O
	N-QB3	O-O	B×N!	B-KN5	O-O
7	B-K3	N-K2	B×B	P-B3	B-KN5
	N-B3	P-K4	P×P	KN-K2	B-KN5
8	KN-B3	O-O (f)	B×QP	R-K1	QN-Q2
	N×N (c)	B×N	Q×NP	Q-Q2	QN-Q2
9	N×N	N×B	Q-Q2 (h)	QN-Q2	P-B3
	P-K4	P×P	N-KB3	O-O-O	P-B3
10	P×P!	N-N5	O-O-O	P-N4	Q-B2
	Q×Q† =	P-B4 (g)	N-B3 (i)	QR-K1 (l)	Q-B2 (m)

(a) 4 Q-N4, N-KB3; 5 Q×P, R-N1; 6 Q-R6, P-B4! 7 P-QR3, R-N3; 8 Q-K3, B-R4; 9 B-Q2, N-N5! ∓.

(b) Upon 5 . . . B×N†; 6 N×B comes (A) 6 . . . N-QB3! B-QN5, N-K2; 8 N×P! P-QR3 = ; but not (B) 6 . . . P-KB4; 7 P-B3! P×P; 8 Q×P, Q-R5† (8 . . . Q×P; 9 Q-N3 ±); 9 P-N3, Q×QP; 10 B-KB4, P-B3; 11 Q-K2, Q-N3; 13 O-O-O ±.

(c) 8 . . . O-O; 9 N-N3, P-QN3; 10 B-K2, B-N2; 11 O-O, Q-Q2; 12 Q-Q2, QR-Q1; 13 KR-Q1, Q-B1 = . Alekhin-Euwe, match 1935.

(d) Without bite is the "Pseudo"-Exchange Variation 4 P×P, P×P; 5 B-Q3, N-QB3; 6 N-K2, KN-K2; 7 O-O, B-KB4; 8 N-N3, B×B; 9 Q×B, O-O; 10 B-N5, P-B3; 11 B-Q2, B×N; 12 Q×B, Q-Q2; 13 KR-K1, N-B4; 14 N×N, Q×N; 15 Q-B5, Q-Q2 = . Bisguier-R. Byrne, US Chp. 1960. But Larsen tried 5 Q-B3.

(e) If 6 B-N5, QN-Q2; 7 N-K2, P-KR3; 8 B×N, N×B; 9 B-B3, P-B4 = .

(f) Another idea is 8 P×P, Q×Q†; 9 K×Q, N-N5; 10 B×N, B×N with more action for the pawn.

(g) 11 B-B4, P-QR3; 12 N-Q6, N-B3; 13 P-B3, B-K3; 14 B×N, P×B; 15 P×P, P×P; 16 Q×P, N-K1 = . Gipslis-Geller, USSR Chp. 1958.

(h) 9 Q-B3, Q×Q; 10 N×Q, P-B3; 11 O-O-O! N-B3; 12 B-N5, B-Q2; 13 R-KN1, P-K4; 14 B-B5, P-KN3; 15 N-Q2 and 16 N-B4 ∓ .

(i) 11 N-K2, Q-Q4 = . Sax-Bodo, Hungary 1968.

(j) The Exchange Variation, which has no meat left. Col. 80 is a classic model of symmetrical "best play."

(k) An early draw resulted from 5 P-QB3, B-Q3; 6 N-K2 (6 Q-B3, QN-K2!), Q-R5; 7 N-R3, P-QR3; 8 Q-Q2, KN-K2; 9 N-B2, B-KB4; 10 B×B, N×B; 11 Q-N5, Q×Q; 12 B×Q draw. Seidman-R. Byrne, US Chp. 1962.

(l) If Black castles long, White can possibly wrest the initiative upon inaccurate play of Black's, as for instance 11 N-N3, N-N3? 12 B-K3, N-R5; 13 B-K2, B×N; 14 B×B ± . Maróczy-Spielmann, Bad Sliać 1932. Correct is 11 . . . P-B3 (12 N-B5, B×N; 13 NP×B, N-Q1 =).

(m) 11 KR-K1, KR-K1; 12 B-R4, B-R4 = . Capablanca-Maróczy, Lake Hopatcong 1926.

1 P-K4, P-K3; 2 P-Q4, P-Q4; 3 N-Q2, N-QB3 (*a*); 4 KN-B3 (*b*), N-B3; 5 P-K5 (*c*), N-Q2

	81	82	83	84	85
6	N-N3!		P-B3	P-B4 (*h*)	P-QN3
	B-K2	P-B3	P-B3	P-B3 (*i*)	P-B3
7	B-QN5	B-QN5	B-Q3 (*f*)	BP×P	B-N2
	P-QR3	P-QR3	P×P	KP×P	B-K2
8	B×N	B×N	P×P	B-N5	P-QR3
	P×B	P×B	QN×P	P-QR3	O-O
9	O-O	O-O	N×N	B-R4	B-N5
	P-QB4	P-QB4	N×N	P×P	P-QR3
10	N-R5	P-B4!	Q-R5†	N×P	B×N
	N-N1	P×BP	N-B2	N/2×N	P×B
11	P×P	N-R5	B×P	P×N	P×P
	B×P (*d*)	N-N3 (*e*)	B-Q2 (*g*)	P-QN4 (*j*)	B×P (*k*)

(*a*) (A) 3 . . . P×P; 4 N×P see cols. 36–40. (B) Precarious is 3 . . . P-KB4; 4 P×BP, P×P; 5 KN-B3, N-KB3; 6 P-B4, B-Q3; 7 P×P, O-O; 8 B-K2, N×P; 9 O-O, K-R1; 10 R-K1, B-K3; 11 B-QB4, B-N1 = . Geller-Benko, Curaçao 1962. (C) 3 . . . P-QN3; 4 KN-B3, N-KB3; 5 P-K5, KN-Q2; 6 P-B3, P-QB4∞. Janosević-Bilek, Harrachov 1966. (D) Fuller, Kellner and Romanishin explored 3 . . . B-K2; (1) 4 B-Q3! (4 P-QB3? P×P! or 4 P-K5, P-QB4– or also 4 . . . P-QN3– 5 P×P, N-QB3; 6 KN-B3, Q-B2; 7 B-N5, B×P; 8 N-N3, B-N3; 9 O-O, N-K2 = . Harding in *Chess*, 1978/10), N-QB3; 5 KN-B3 (also 5 P-QB3!? P×P; 6 B×P, N-B3; 7 B-B3, O-O; 8 N-B4 ±), N-N5 – for 5 . . . N-B3 see next section– 6 B-K2, P×P; 7 N×P, N-KB3! 8 N×N†, B×N; 9 O-O, P-B3! ± . (2) 4 KN-B3, N-KB3; 5 P-K5, KN-Q2; 6 B-Q3, P-QB4; 7 P-B3, N-QB3 (or 7 . . . P-QN3); 8 O-O, Q-N3 (compare col. 91, note (*b*)); 9 P×P (9 R-K1, P×P; 10 P×P, N×QP; 11 N×N, Q×N; 12 N-N3, Q-QR5!), N×BP; 10 B-B2, P-QR4 = . Estrin-Zagorovski, corr. 1976–7. For 4 . . . P×P see Rubinstein Variation.

(*b*) 4 P-QB3, P-K4; 5 P×QP, Q×P; 6 KN-B3, P×P! 7 B-B4, Q-KR4; 8 O-O, N-B3; 9 Q-K1†, B-K2; 10 N×P, O-O = . Fischer-R. Byrne, US Chp. 1965–6.

(*c*) 5 P×P, P×P see col. 100. If 5 . . . KN×P; 6 N-N3.

(*d*) 12 P-B4! O-O; 13 B-N5, Q-Q2; 14 N-N3, B-R2; 15 R-B1, B-N2; 16 P-B5, P-B3; 17 B-B4 ± . Estevez-Huebner, Leningrad 1973.

(*e*) 12 KP×P, NP×P (12 . . . Q×BP; 13 P×P, N-Q4; 14 N×P, B×P; 15 B-N5 +); 13 N-K5! P×N; 14 Q-R5†, K-Q2; 15 P×BP, B×P; 16 B-K3, B-Q3; 17 QR-Q1! Bronstein.

(*f*) (A) 7 B-N5, P×P; 8 P×P, B-K2; 9 O-O, O-O, 10 R-K1, Q-K1∞. (B) 7 N-R4, Q-K2; 8 B-Q3, P×P! 9 Q-R5† = . *P/E.*

(*g*) 12 N-B3, Q-B3; 13 N-N5, B-B4 = . Vinogradov-Villard, Estonia 1951.

(*h*) No advantage accrues from a number of other attempts, e.g. (A) 6 B-K2, P-B3; 7 P×P, Q×P! 8 N-B1, P-K4; 9 N-K3, P-K5; 10 N×P, Q-Q3; 11 P-B4, P×N; 12 B-B4, P×B; 13 Q×P†, N/2-K4; 14 P×N, Q-Q1; 15 O-O-O, B-KB4; 16 KR-K1, B-QN5 = . *Comments.* (B) 6 B-N5, P-QR3; 7 B×N, P×B; 8 P-B4 (for 8 N-N3 see Col. 81), 8 . . . P×P; 9 O-O, B-K2; 10 N×B, N-N3; 11 N-R5, Q-Q4 = . (C) 6 P-KN3, B-K2; 7 B-R3, P-KR4; 8 B-N2, P-R5; 9 O-O, P-R6; 10 B-R1, P-KN4; 11 P-B3, P-N5; 12 N-K1, P-B4; 13 P×P *e.p.*, N×BP; 14 N-N3, P-K4 = .

(*i*) Evans suggests 6 . . . P×P; 7 N×P, N-N3; 8 P-QR3(?), B-K2; 9 P-KR4, B-Q2.

(*j*) 12 B-N3, N-Q5; 13 O-O, P-B4; 14 N-B3, B-N5 = . Trifunović-Szabó, Hilversum 1947. Keres now suggests 15 P-K6, B×P; 16 R-K1∞ .

(*k*) 12 O-O, P-B4; 13 R-K1, Q-K2 = . Mednis-R. Byrne, US Chp. 1964.

1 P-K4, P-K3; 2 P-Q4, P-Q4; 3 N-Q2, N-KB3; 4 P-K5, KN-Q2; 5 P-KB4, P-QB4; 6 P-B3

	86	87	88	89	90
	N-QB3..				P-QN3
7	QN-B3!				QN-B3
	Q-N3!......P×P.................B-K2 (h)				B-R3
8	P-KN3	P×P		B-Q3	B×B
	P×P	N-N3......P-KR4		Q-R4	N×B
9	P×P	B-Q3	B-Q3 (e)	K-B1	N-K2
	B-N5†	B-Q2	N-N3	P×P?	P-QN4
10	K-B2	N-K2	N-R3	P×P	O-O
	P-B3 (a)	P-KR4	B-Q2	P-QN3	N-N3
11	K-N2	O-O	O-O	B-Q2	P-B5!
	Q-Q1 (b)	B-K2	P-N3	B-N5	B-K2
12	B-Q3	P-QR3	P-R3! (f)	B-K3	N-B4
	N-N3 (c)	P-R4 (d)	P-R4 (g)	B-R3 (i)	N-B2 (j)

(a) If 10 . . . P-B4; 11 K-N2, (A) 11 . . . N/2-N1; 12 N-R3! B-Q2; 13 N-B2, N-R3 14 QR-N1! N-B2; 15 N-Q3, B-K2; 16 B-K3 ± . Suetin–Uhlmann, Sarajevo 1965. (B) 11 . . . Q-Q1?! 12 B-Q3, N-N3; 13 N-K2, B-Q2; 14 P-KR3, B-K2; 15 P-KN4, P-N3; 16 N-B3, P-KR3 = . Liberzon–Uhlmann, Sarajevo 1965.

(b) 11 . . . O-O; 12 B-Q3, R-B2; 13 N-K2, N-B1; 14 P-KR4, B-Q2; 15 P-R5, B-K2; 16 N-R4 ± . Sarkarov–Geller, Leningrad 1961. Compare with Steinitz Variation, col. 31.

(c) 13 Q-B2, P-B4; 14 N-K2, B-K2; 15 P-QR3, B-Q2; 16 P-N3, R-QB1 = . Bronstein–Uhlmann 1961.

(d) 13 B-Q2, P-QR5; 14 R-B1; P-N3; 15 Q-K1, K-B1! Matanović–Uhlmann, Skopje 1968. 7 . . . P×P is a variant of the Leningrad System, col. 94. In the column, 9 P-KN4 was better.

(e) Also good is first 9 P-QR3, N-N3; 10 B-Q3, B-Q2; 11 N-K2, P-R4; 12 O-O, P-QR5; 13 Q-K1, N-R4; 15 P-B5! P × P; 16 Q-N3! with pressure. Wade–Uhlmann, Skopje 1968.

(f) (A) Better than 12 B-Q2, N-B5! 13 B × N, P × B; 14 N/R-N5, N-K2; 15 Q-K2, Q-N3; 16 P-QR4, R-QB1 = . Matulović–Uhlmann, Skopje 1968. (B) 12 N/R-N5 can also be played at once.

(g) 13 Q-K2, B-K2; 14 N/R-N5, P-QR5; 15 Q-KB2 with initiative. Marić–Uhlmann, Skopje 1968.

(h) Inferior are (A) 7 . . . P-B5; 8 N-K2, B-K2; 9 P-KN3! or at once 8 P-QN4! (B) 7 . . . P-B4; 8 B-Q3, Q-R4; 9 K-B2, B-K2; 10 N-K2, P-QN4; 11 B-Q2 ± . Penrose–Uhlmann, Hastings 1966-7. But interesting is (c) 7 . . . Q-R4; (1) 8 P × P, Q × P/4; 9 B-Q3, B-K2; 10 N-K2, Q-N3; 11 N/2-Q4, N × N; 12 N × N, B-B4; 13 B-B2, N-N1 = . Minić–Udovćić, Zagreb 1970. (2) 8 K-B2, P-QN4; 9 B-Q3, P-N5; 10 N-K2, N-QN3 ∞.

(i) 13 N-K2, B-K2; 14 P-QR3, B × B; 15 Q × B, P-QN4; 16 K-B2, P-B4; 17 P-R3 P-N3 = . Botvinnik–Uhlmann, Varna 1962. Better was 9 . . . P-QN4; 10 P × P, P-N5 = .

(j) 13 N-R5 ± . Korn–Rausch, corr. 1960.

1 P-K4; P-K3; 2 P-Q4, P-Q4; 3 N-Q2, N-KB3; 4 P-K5, KN-Q2; 5 B-Q3 (*a*),
P-QB4; 6 P-QB3

	91	92	93	94	95
	N-QB3..				P-QN3
7	KN-B3......	N-K2			N-K2 (*i*)
	Q-N3	P-B3	Q-N3.......	P × P	B-R3
8	O-O	N-KB4	N-B3	P × P	B × B
	P × P	Q-K2	P × P	N-N3 (*g*)	N × B
9	P × P	KP × P	P × P	O-O	O-O
	N × QP	Q × P	P-B3 (*d*)	B-Q2	N-B2
10	N × N	N-B3	P × P	P-B4 (*h*)	P-KB4
	Q × N	P × P	N × BP	P-N3	P-B4!
11	N-B3	O-O	O-O	N-KB3	N-B3
	Q-N3	N/2-K4	B-Q3	P-KR4	B-K2
12	Q-R4	N × N	B-KB4 (*e*)	B-Q2	B-K3
	Q-N5 (*b*)	N × N (*c*)	B × B (*f*)	B-N2 =	P-B5! (*j*)

(*a*) (A) For 5 KN-B3, N-QB3 see cols. 81, etc., and for 5 . . . P-QB4 see cols. 96, etc. (B)
Too meek is 5 P-QB3, P-QB4; 6 KN-B3? N-QB3; 7 B-K2? P × P; 8 P × P, Q-N3! 9 N-N3,
P-QR4; 10 P-QR4, B-N5†; 11 K-B1, P-B3 = .

(*b*) 13 Q-B2, Q-B4; 14 Q-K2 with a minute advantage. The text 12 . . . Q-N5 prevents
Q-KN4 as after 12 . . . B-K2; 13 Q-KN4! P-N3; 14 B-KR6 ± . Shaplinski-Dommes, USSR
1956. In the column, for 8 . . . B-K2 compare note (*a*) (D) to cols. 81-5.

(*c*) 13 B-N5†, N-B3 = ; or 13 . . . B-Q2; 14 B × B†, K × B; 15 R-K1; R-K1; 16 P-B4!
Comments.

(*d*) (A) 9 . . . B-N5†; 10 B-Q2, B × B†; 11 Q × B, Q-N5; 12 R-QB1, Q × Q†; 13 K × Q ± .
Keres-Flores, Buenos Aires 1939. (B) 9 . . . B-K2; 10 O-O, O-O; 11 N-B4! ± .

(*e*) 12 N-B3, O-O (12 . . . B-Q2; 13 B-KN5, O-O-O = . Makagonov); 13 B-K3, Q-Q1
(13 . . . Q × NP? 14 Q-QN5, B-K2; 15 R-N1, Q × RP; 16 R-R1! Q-N7; 17 R-R4 and 18
B-B1 +); 14 B-KN5, B-Q2; 15 R-K1 ± . Karpov-Hort, Budapest 1973.

(*f*) 13 N × B (A) Q × NP; 14 R-K1, O-O; 15 N × KP, B × N; 16 R × B, QR-K1; 17 R × R,
R × R; 18 Q-QB1! Q × Q 19 R × Q, R-QB1 = . Platz-Uhlmann, Berlin 1962. (B) 13 . . . O-O;
14 Q-Q2! B-Q2; 15 KR-K1, QR-K1; 16 QR-Q1, K-R1; 17 B-N1, B-B1; 18 Q-B3, K-N1; 19
N-N5, N-Q1, 20 Q-B2, Q-B3; 21 Q × P† N × Q; 22 B × N†, K-R1; 23 N-N6 mate. Lombardy-Sherwin, New York, 1959.

(*g*) The Leningrad System. Another possibility is 8 . . . P-B3; 9 P × P (9 N-KB4, N × QP;
10 Q-R5†, K-K2; 11 N-N6†, P × N; 12 P × P†, N × P! - 12 . . . K × P? 13 Q × R, K-B2; 14
Q-R3, N-K4; 15 N-N3! ± - 13 Q × R, K-B2; 14 O-O, P-K4 ∓), N × BP; 10 O-O, B-Q3; 11
N-KB3, Q-B2; 12 N-B3, P-QR3; 13 B-KN5, N-KN5; 14 P-KR3 ± . Hutchings-Keene,
Barcelona 1975.

(*h*) 10 N-KB3, B-K2; 11 N-B4, P-N3 = .

(*i*) Palliatives have been found against (A) 7 Q-R4, P-QR4; 8 N-K2, B-R3 = ; or (B) 7
KN-B3, B-R3; 8 B × B, N × B; 9 Q-K2, N-B2; 10 O-O, B-K2; 11 R-K1, P-KR3; 12 N-B1,
Q-B1; 13 N-N3, Q-R3; 14 Q-K3, P-N3; 15 P-N3, P-B5 = . Browne-Petrosian, Zagreb 1970.
(C) 7 P-KB4, B-R3; 8 B × B, N × B; 9 QN-B3, B-K2; 10 N-K2, O-O = ; or (D) 7 Q-N4, B-R3;
8 B × B, N × B; 9 N-K2, N-B2; 10 O-O, P-N3 = .

(*j*) 13 K-R1, P-QN4; 14 R-KN1! Bednarski-Petrosian, Lugano 1968, P-KR4! 15 N-N5,
N-B1 = . *Informator* 6. In the column, quietly stronger is 10 N-KB4! B-K2; 11 R-K1, O-O;
12 Q-N4 (Keres).

1 P–K4, P–K3; 2 P–Q4, P–Q4; 3 N–Q2, P–QB4

	96	97	98	99	100
4	KN–B3	P × QP			
	N–QB3	Q × P	KP × P		
5	B–N 5	KN–B3	KN–B3	B–N5†	
	P × KP (*a*)	P × P!	P–QR3	N–B3 (*f*)	
6	N × P	B–B4	P × P (*d*)	Q–K2†	KN–B3
	Q–R4†	Q–Q3	B × P	B–K2 (*g*)	B–Q3
7	N–B3	O–O	N–N3	P × P	O–O
	P × P	N–KB3	B–R2	N–B3	N–K2
8	N × P	N–N3	B–Q3 (*e*)	N–N3	P–B4
	B–Q2	N–B3	Q–K2†	O–O	O–O
9	N × N	R–K1	B–K2	B–K3 (*h*)	P × BP
	P × N	P–QR3	N–KB3	R–K1	B × P
10	Q–B3	P–QR4	O–O	O–O–O	N–N3
	R–B1	B–K2	O–O	P–QR4	B–Q3 (*j*)
11	B–Q3	KN × P	B–KN5	P–QR4	B × N
	B–N5 (*b*)	N × N (*c*)	N–B3 =	B–Q2 (*i*)	P × B (*k*)

(*a*) (A) 5 . . . P–QR3; 6 P × QP, P × B; 7 P × N, P × BP; 8 P × P, B × P; 9 O–O, N–B3; 10 N–N3! Q × Q; 11 R × Q, B–N3 = . (B) 5 . . . P × QP; 6 N × P, B–Q2; 7 N × N, P × N; 8 B–Q3, Q–B2; 9 Q–K2, N–K2; 10 N–B3, N–N3; 11 P–K5, R–QN1; 12 O–O, B–K2 = . Tal–Korchnoi, Moscow 1971.

(*b*) 12 O–O, B × N; 13 P × B, N–B3; 14 P–B4, O–O; 15 B–N2, P–K4; 16 Q–N3, KR–K1 = . Gipslis–Liebert, Lublin 1972.

(*c*) 12 Q × N, Q × Q; 13 N × Q, B–Q2; 14 B–B4, QR–B1 = . Averbakh–Stahlberg, Zürich 1953.

(*d*) 6 B–K2, P–B5; 7 O–O, B–Q3; 8 R–K1, N–K2; 9 P–QN3, P × P; 10 RP × P, QN–B3; 11 N–B1, O–O; 12 N–K3, B–B5; 13 B–Q3, B–K3; 14 B–R3, R–K1 = .

(*e*) 8 B–N5, N–KB3; 9 KN–Q4, O–O; 10 B–K2, Q–Q3; 11 O–O, N–K5 = . Keres–Botvinnik, Moscow 1948. The column is *MCO*11.

(*f*) 5 . . . B–Q2 has recently been *en vogue*; e.g. 6 Q–K2†, (A) 6 . . . B–K2; 7 P × P, N–KB3; 8 N–N3, O–O; 9 B–K3, R–K1; 10 N–B3, (1) 10 . . . P–QR3; 11 B × B, QN × B; 12 O–O, N × P = . (2) 10 . . . B × P; 11 N × B, Q–R4†, 12 Q–Q2, Q × B; 13 O–O–O, P–QN3 = . Karpov–Korchnoi, 22nd match game 1978. (B) 6 . . . Q–K2; 7 B × B†, N × B; 8 P × P, N × P; 9 N–N3, Q × Q†; 10 N × Q, N × N; 11 RP × N, B–B4; 12 B–Q2, N–K2; 13 N–B4, O–O = . Karpov–Korchnoi, 16th match game 1978.

(*g*) 6 . . . Q–K2; 7 P × P, Q × Q†; 8 N × Q, B × P; 9 N–QN3, B–N3; 10 P–QR4, N–K2; 11 P–R5, B–B2; 12 B–KB4! Szabó–Barcza, Stockholm 1952; or 10 . . . P–QR3; 11 B × N†. P × B 12 P–R5, B–R2 = .

(*h*) 9 N–B3, R–K1; 10 B–K3, P–QR3; 11 B–Q3, B–N5 (11 . . . N–Q2; 12 O–O–O, N × P; 13 N × N, B × N; 14 B × P†, K × B; 15 Q–Q3†. Byrne); 12 O–O–O, N–K4; 13 P–KR3, B × N; 14 P × B, Q–B2; 15 K–N1, N/4–Q2; 16 P–QB4 ± . Smyslov–Uhlmann, Cienfuegos 1973.

(*i*) 12 N–B3, N–R2; 13 N/B3–Q2, N–K5! = . Gligorić.

(*j*) 10 . . . B–N3; 11 B × N, P × P (11 . . . P × B reverts to the column); 12 B–R4, Q × Q; 13 R × Q, P × N; 14 B × P, B–N5 = .

(*k*) 12 P–B5, B–B2; 13 QN–Q4, P–KR3 (13 . . . P–QR4; 14 R–K1, B–R3; 15 B–Q2, R–R2; 16 QR–B1, Q–Q2 ∞); 14 R–K1, B–N5; 15 P–KR3, B–KR4 = .

1 P–K4, P–K3; 2 P–Q4, P–Q4; 3 N–Q2, P–QB4; 4 P × QP, KP × P; 5 B–N5†,
N–B3; 6 KN–B3, B–Q3; 7 P × P, B × BP; 8 O–O, N–K2; 9 N–N3, B–Q3

	101	102	103	104	105
10	QN–Q4		B × N†	B–N5	
	O–O (a)		P × B	O–O	
11	P–B3	B–N5 (e)	Q–Q4	R–K1	B–KR4!
	B–KN5	P–B3	O–O	Q–B2	Q–N3 (i)
12	Q–R4 (b)	B–K3	B–B4	P–B3	B–Q3
	B–R4	N–K4	N–B4	B–KN5	P–QR4
13	R–K1 (c)	R–K1	Q–Q2	P–KR3	P–R4 (j)
	Q–B2	P–QR3	Q–N3	B–R4	N–B4
14	P–KR3	B–KB1	B × B	B–K2!	B × N (k)
	B–N3	K–R1	N × B	P–KR3	B × B
15	B–N5	P–KR3	P–QR4	B × N	B–N3
	P–QR3 (d)	B–Q2 (f)	N–K5 (g)	N × B (h)	B × B (l)

(a) The same position can be reached by the transposition at White's 7th move, i.e. 7
O–O, P × P; 8 N–N3, N–K2; 9 N/N3 × P, O–O, with one move less in total count. The
"missing" move was absorbed by the omission of the apparent win and loss of tempo in the
manoeuvres 7 . . . B × BP; and 9 . . . B–Q3. The difference shows up only in regard to the
numbering of moves, showing one more move as having been played in those game scores
where this particular position after QN–Q4 has been arrived at by these two different routes.
Our tabulation here consolidates the transpositions just as some other openings manuals have
done; some differ.

(b) 12 B–K2, R–K1; 13 R–K1, P–QR3; 14 B–KN5, P–R3; 15 B–R4, Q–N3! 16 Q–N3,
B–QB4 = . Karpov–Korchnoi, 4th match game 1974.

(c) (A) 13 B–K3, Q–B2; 14 P–KR3, N–R4; 15 B–Q3, N–B5! 16 N–QN5, Q–Q2; 17 B × N,
P × B; 18 KR–Q1, N–B4; 19 Q × BP! (19 P–KN4? P–QR3; 20 P × B, P × N; 21 Q–N4, Q–B3;
22 R × B, N × R + ; or 19 B–B4, B × N; 20 P × B, N–R5; 21 B–N3, N × P†; 22 K–N2, Q–B3; 23
R × B, N–K8† +), B × N; 20 P × B, N × B; 21 P × N, Q × P; 22 N × B, Q–N6†; 23 K–B1,
Q × P†; 24 K–K1, Q–N6†; drawn. Karpov–Korchnoi, 12th match game 1974. (B) 13 B–Q3,
B–B4! (or first 13 . . . P–KR3); 14 R–K1, P–KR3; 15 B–K3, B–QN3; 16 P–KR3, Q–Q3; 17
B–K2, KR–K1 (in the 14th match game came 17 . . . QR–K1 =); 18 QR–Q1, Q–B3 = .

(d) 16 B–KB1, P–R3; 17 B × N, N × B; 18 QR–Q1, N–B3; 19 B–Q3, B–R4; 20 P–KN4,
B–N3; 21 Q–B2! B × B; 22 Q × B, QR–Q1 = . Karpov–Korchnoi, 8th match game 1974.

(e) (A) 11 B–K3, B–KN5; 12 Q–Q2! Q–B2; 13 P–KR3, B–R4; 14 N–R4, B–N3; 15 N × B,
RP × N; 16 B × N, P × B; 17 P–QB4, Q–Q2! = . Matulović–Suetin, Belgrade 1974. (B) 11
P–QN3, B–KN5; 12 B–N2, Q–N3; 13 N × N, P × N; 14 B–Q3, P–QB4 = .

(f) 16 P–B3, R–B1; 17 P–QR4, R–K1; 18 N × N, P × N; 19 N–B3, B–K3∞.
Geller–Uhlmann, Amsterdam 1970.

(g) 16 Q–Q4, B–K3! 17 P–R5, Q–N4; 18 Q–Q3, Q–N5 with an active game for Black.
Velimirović–Vaganian, Kragujevać 1974. Karpov suggested 14 KR–K1 as giving White a
better chance of developing an initiative.

(h) 16 KN–Q4, B × B; 17 Q × B, P–R3; 18 Q–B3 with some advantage, but a final draw.
Karpov–Korchnoi, 18th match game 1974.

(i) 11 . . . B–KN5; 12 B–K2, (1) 12 . . . B–R4; 13 R–K1, Q–N3; 14 KN–Q4, B–N3; 15
P–QB3! KR–K1; 16 B–B1, B–K5; 17 B–N3, B × B; 18 RP × B (Karpov–Uhlmann, Madrid
1973), QR–Q1 = . (2) 12 . . . R–K1; 13 R–K1, Q–N3; 14 KN–Q4, N–N3; 15 N × N, R × B; 16
R × R, P × N = . Vogt–Uhlmann, Potsdam 1974. The treatment in the column was revived by
Gulko.

(*j*) No better advantage offer (A) 13 P–B3, P–R5; 14 QN–Q4, N–N3; 15 N–QN5, B–B5; 16 B–N3, B × B; 17 P × B, B–N5 = . Zhidkov–Gulko, USSR 1974. (B) 13 P–B4, P–R5; 14 P × P, N–N5; 15 QN–Q4, N × B; 16 Q × N, R–R4 ∓ . Vaganian.

(*k*) 14 B–QN5, N × B; 15 N × N, B–K4; 16 P–B3, R–Q1; 17 N–B3, B–N5 = .

(*l*) 16 P × B, B–K5 ± . Balashov–Gulko, Moscow Chp. 1974.

1 P–K4, P–K3; 2 P–Q4, P–Q4(*a*); 3 P–K5, P–QB4

	106	107	108	109	110
4	P–QB3		N–KB3	P × P	Q–N4
	N–QB3 (*b*)		P × P	N–QB3	P × P (*j*)
5	N–B3		B–Q3	N–KB3	N–KB3
	Q–N3		N–QB3	B × P	N–QB3 (*k*)
6	B–K2	P–QR3 (*e*)	O–O	B–Q3	B–Q3
	P × P	P–B5!	KN–K2 (*g*)	KN–K2!	Q–B2 (*l*)
7	P × P	B–K2! (*f*)	B–KB4	B–KB4!	Q–N3
	N–R3 (*c*)	B–Q2	N–N3	Q–N3	P–B3
8	P–QN3	O–O	B–N3	O–O	P × P
	N–B4	KN–K2	B–K2	N–N3 (*h*)	Q × Q
9	B–N2	QN–Q2	R–K1	B–N3	P–B7†
	B–N5†	N–R4	Q–N3	Q × P	K × P
10	K–B1	R–K1	QN–Q2	QN–Q2	RP × Q
	P–KR4	P–KR3	B–Q2!	N/N3 × P	P–K4 ±
11	N–B3	R–N1	N–N3	N × N	
	O–O	N–N3	R–QB1	N × N	
12	N–QR4	Q–B2	P–QR3	R–N1	
	Q–Q1 (*d*)	B–K2	P–QR3 =	Q–B6 (*i*)	

(*a*) (A) For 2 . . . P–QB4!? see Queen's Pawn Games, col. 9 (Franco–Benoni Defence). (B) Unusual may be the "Queen's Fianchetto Defence" 2 . . . P–QN3; 3 P–KB4, B–N2; or 3 P–QR3; or 3 P–QB4, B–N2; 4 P–B3, B–N5†, or 3 N–QB3, B–N5∞. Compare Larsen Defence, Queen's Pawn Games, col. 10, note (*k*) (E).

(*b*) 4 . . . Q–N3; 5 B–Q3, B–Q2; 6 P × P, B × P; 7 Q–K2, N–K2; 8 P–QN4 + .

(*c*) Another alternative is 7 . . . KN–K2; 8 N–R3 (8 P–QN3 see text), N–B4; 9 N–B2, B–K2! 10 R–QN1, P–QR4 = . Here also 5 . . . B–Q2; 6 B–K2, P–B3; 7 O–O, P × P; 8 P × P. Q–K2; 9 R–K1 .

(*d*) 13 P–KR3, P–R5; 14 B–Q3, P–QN3; 15 Q–B1, B–Q2; 16 Q–KB4, B–K2; 17 P–KN4, P × P *e.p.*; 18 R–KN1, P–B3; 19 B × N, P × B; 20 R × P, N–N5 = . Wade–Uhlmann, Buenos Aires 1960.

(*e*) Complicated but questionable is 6 B–Q3!? P × P; 7 P × P, B–Q2; 8 O–O, N × QP; 9 N × N, Q × N; 10 N–B3, P–QR3! (A) 11 Q–K2, N–K2; 12 R–Q1, Q–N3; 13 B–K3, Q–B2; 14 P–B4, N–B3; 15 B–KB2, with minimal compensation for the pawn minus, and likewise in (B) 11 K–R1, N–K2; 12 P–B4, P–KN3∞.

(*f*) 7 P–KN3, B–Q2; 8 B–R3 (A) 8 . . . N–R4; 9 QN–Q2, N–K2! 10 O–O, N–N3; 11 R–N1, R–B1; 12 Q–B2, Q–B2; and White is in a bind. E. Richter–Korn, corr. 1961. (B) 8 . . . O–O–O; 9 N–N5, N–R3; 10 O–O, K–N1; 11 P–B4, K–R1; 12 R–B2, P–B3; 13 N–B3, P–B4; 14 N–N5, B–K2; 15 N–Q2, N–R4!∞. Velimirović–Basman, Harrachov 1967. (C) 8 . . . B–K2; 9 QN–Q2, N–R4; 10 O–O, P–KR4; 11 N–K1, O–O–O; 12 N–N2, P–N3; 13 N–K3, N–R3∞.

(*g*) (A) 6 . . . P–B3; 7 B–QN5, B–Q2; 8 B × N, P × B; 9 Q × P, Q–N3! = . (B) 6 . . . B–B4; 7 QN–Q2, KN–K2; 8 N–N3, B–N3; 9 B–KB4, N–N3; 10 B–N3 ± .

(*h*) 8 . . . Q × P; 9 QN–Q2, Q–N3; 10 N–N3, N–N3; 11 B–N3, B–K2; 12 P–KR4 ± . Nimzowitsch–Spielmann, San Sebastian 1912.

(*i*) 13 R–N3, Q–Q5; 14 B–N5†, N–Q2; 15 B × N†, B × B; 16 R × P, K–K2∞. The column is the Keres variation.

(*j*) 4 . . . N–QB3; 5 N–KB3, KN–K2; 6 P–B3, N–B4; 7 P × P! *Comments.*

(*k*) Also 5 . . . P–B4; (A) 6 Q–N3, (1) 6 . . . KN–K2; 7 B–Q3, KN–B3; 8 O–O, N–Q2; 9 QN–Q2, N–B4; 10 P–KR4, N–K5∞; or (2) 6 . . . Q–N3; 7 B–Q3, N–Q2; 8 O–O, N–K2; 9

P–B3, P × P! (B) 6 Q–B4, N–QB3; 7 QN–Q2, Q–B2; 8 N–N3, B–N5†; 9 B–Q2, B × B†; 10 QN × B, KN–K2; 11 B–N5, B–Q2; 12 B × N, N × B; 13 N–N3 = . Korn-Clark, corr. 1977.

(*l*) In addition 6 . . . KN–K2; 7 O–O, N–N3; 8 R–K1, B–K2! is also strong. The text is Fine's analysis.

1 P–K4, P–K3

	111	112	113	114	115
2	P–Q3		Q–K2		N–KB3 (g)
	P–Q4 (a)		P–QB4	B–K2	P–Q4
3	N–Q2		P–KB4 (e)	P–QN3	N–B3
	N–KB3 (b)		N–QB3	P–Q4	P–Q5
4	P–KN3		N–KB3	B–N2	N–K2
	P–QB4 (c)		KN–K2	B–B3	P–QB4
5	B–N2		P–KN3	P–K5	P–B3
	N–B3		P–KN3	B–K2	N–KB3
6	KN–B3	N–R3	P–Q3	Q–N4	P–K5
	B–K2	B–K2	B–N2	B–B1	KN–Q2
7	O–O	O–O	N–B3	N–KB3	P×P
	O–O	O–O	N–Q5	P–QB4	P×P
8	R–K1	P–KB4	N×N	B–N5†	Q–R4
	P–QN4!	P–QN4	P×N	B–Q2	N–QB3
9	P–K5	N–B2	N–Q1	B×B†	N/2×P
	N–Q2 (d)	B–N2! =	P–N3 =	Q × B (f)	N/2 × P (h)

(a) (A) 2 . . . P–QN3; 3 P–KN3, B–N2; 4 B–N2, B–K2; 5 N–KB3, P–Q3; 6 O–O, N–KB3; 7 P–B4, O–O; 8 N–B3, P–B4; 9 P–KR3, N–B3; 10 P–Q4, P×P; 11 N×P±. Evans–Foguelman, Buenos Aires 1960. (B) 2 . . . P–QB4; 3 N–Q2, N–QB3; 4 P–KN3, P–KN3; 5 B–N2, B–N2; 6 KN–B3 (or 6 N–K2), KN–K2; 7 O–O, O–O; 8 P–B3, P–Q3; 9 P–QR4, P–B4 = . Smyslov–Botvinnik, match 1954. The position may also arise from the Sicilian Defence, Closed System (and actually dates back to Staunton!).

(b) (A) Too cramped is 3 . . . N–Q2; 4 P–KN3, P–QN3; 5 B–N2, B–N2; 6 Q–K2, Q–K2; 7 N–R3, P–N3; 8 P–QB3, B–N2; 9 P–KB4, R–Q1; 10 P–K5, N–R3; 11 O–O, B–R3; 12 N–B2, O–O; 13 R–K1, KR–K1; 14 N–B3±. Elowitch–Coudari, Portland 1966. (B) 3 . . . P–QN3; 4 KN–B3, P–QB4; 5 P–KN3, N–KB3.

(c) 4 . . . P×P; 5 P×P, P–K4; 6 KN–B3, B–QB4; 7 B–N2, N–B3; 8 O–O, O–O; 9 P–B3, P–QR4! = . Csom–Fuchs, Berlin 1968. The début resembles a Philidor Defence Reversed, with a tempo ahead for White. All lines where . . . P–QB4 is played transpose into a Sicilian Defence.

(d) 10 N–B1, P–QR4; 11 B–B4, P–N5; 12 N–K3, B–R3; 13 P–KR4, P–R5; 14 P–R3, B–N4! = . Damjanović–Uhlmann, Monte Carlo 1968. 4 . . . P–QB4 transposes into a King's Indian in reverse. Also compare with King's Fianchetto and Réti–Barcza System (col. 13), which also arrives at the position after 8 R–K1. For 8 . . . Q–B2 see there. Also compare Sicilian Defence, cols. 166–70, note (a).

(e) (A) 3 P–KN3, N–QB3; 4 N–KB3, KN–K2; 5 B–N2, P–KN3; 6 N–B3, B–N2; 7 P–Q3, P–Q4 = . 2 Q–K2 is the Chigorin Variation. (B) 3 P–QN3, N–QB3; 4 B–N2, P–Q3 = .

(f) 10 N–B3, N–QB3; 11 O–O, KN–K2 = . Chigorin–Tarrasch, match 1893.

(g) Other meek alternatives are (A) 2 P–QN3, P–Q4; 3 B–N2, N–KB3; 4 P–K5, KN–Q2; 5 P–KB4, P–QB4; 6 N–QB3, N–QB3; 7 N–B3, B–K2 = ; Cruz–Uhlmann, Havana 1964. (B) 2 P–QB4, P–Q4; 3 BP×P, P×P; 4 P×P, N–KB3; 5 B–N5†, QN–Q2 = . (c) 2 P–KB4, P–Q4; 3 P–K5, P–QB4 = . (D) 2 P–KN3, P–Q4; 3 B–N2, P×P; 4 B×P, N–KB3; 5 B–N2, N–B3 = . (E) For 2 P–Q4, P–QB4 see Franco–Indian Defence (1 P–Q4, P–K3; 2 P–K4, P–QB4). (F) For 2 P–QB3 see Sicilian Defence, col. 183.

(h) 10 B–N5, B–Q2 = . Gufeld–Korchnoi, USSR Chp. 1959. In the column, instead of 2 . . . P–Q4, also playable is 2 . . . P–QB4; 3 P–Q3, N–QB3; 4 P–KN3, P–Q4; 5 Q–K2, N–B3 = . Torre–Gizhdavu, Lone Pine 1975.

Sicilian Defence

(1 P–K4, P–QB4)

Mentioned by Polerio in 1594, given its name by the Italian master Greco in the seventeenth century, the Sicilian received its earliest practical tests and a big boost in popularity in the MacDonnell–La Bourdonnais match (1834), Staunton *v.* St. Amant match (1843), and the great London Tournament of 1851. Since then it has experienced repeated refutations and rehabilitations. But age cannot wither nor custom stale its infinite variety. Barely a year passes which does not cause us to re-evaluate some variation. Today the defence is a regular in every tournament, and one should refrain from 1 P–K4 unless prepared to confront it.

The Sicilian owes most of its effectiveness to the semi–open queen's bishop's file produced after White plays P–Q4 and the inevitable exchange of pawns. With 1 . . . P–QB4 Black immediately puts pressure on the queen's flank and plans complete liberation with . . . P–Q4. The move also strikes at Q5 and QN5, half opens a file and frees the queen. From the strategical point of view the Sicilian has the advantage of allowing a large choice of pawn configurations. Moreover, it avoids prepared variations and certain drawing openings like the Giuoco Piano and Four Knights' Game. The dominant theme is struggle—in the opening, in the middle-game—hardly suitable for those who wish to play for a draw. The greatest danger is that White will get the upper hand in the centre and then break through with a winning attack on the king's side. By and large the end-game tends to favour Black since White often weakens his position by early, ambitious king's-side pawn advances. The Sicilian is Black's most dynamic, asymmetrical reply to 1 P–K4. It produces the psychological and tension factors which denote the best in modern play and gives notice of a fierce fight on the very first move.

The Sicilian section has been arranged in categories mainly governed by Black's choice of second move after 2 N–KB3 (. . . P–Q3; . . . P–K3;

171

. . . P–QR3; . . . N–QB3, etc.) and overlapping transpositions have as far as possible been cross referenced. It is advisable always to take in the full sequence of all typical moves of a given variation so as to visualize—or separate—its characteristics within the framework of all the different systems given herein.

As against previous editions, the structure has been revamped and tightened and is divided into:

(A) Black's reply (2 N–KB3) 2 . . . P–Q3, which creates four distinct strategies:

(1) THE NAJDORF SYSTEM, characterized by 3 P–Q4, P×P; 4 N×P, N–KB3; 5 N–QB3, P–QR3 (cols. 1–25). It was originally researched by Opočenský but practised and popularized by Najdorf especially with and against the ambitious thrust 6 B–N5 (cols. 1–18). The latest off-shoot here is the "Poisoned Pawn Variation" with 6 . . . P–K3; 7 P–B4, Q–N3; 8 Q–Q2, Q×P?! (cols. 1–10), with much of the findings effectively recapitulated by a group of younger British players, Botterill, Harding, Hartston, Keene and senior master Wade.

The now overplayed knight's-pawn capture is avoided in cols. 11–18. In regard to replies other than 6 B–N5, the modest 6 B–K2, P–K4! (cols. 19–20) is Opočenský's first patent. *The Sicilian King's Bishop's Variation* 6 B–QB4 (cols. 24–5) has been often employed by Fischer and was also analysed by Sozin as a pendant to the same line in the . . . N–QB3 complex dealt with later.

(2) THE YUGOSLAV ATTACK (in some compendia called the *Rauzer Attack*) differs from the above with 5 . . . P–KN3, continued 6 B–K3, B–N2; 7 P–B3, O–O; 8 Q–Q2, N–B3 (cols. 26–30). It is important to note that the order of the 6th–8th moves may often be transposed. White plays P–B3 to safeguard his centre and prevent . . . N–KN5, then castles queen's side and strives for a strong king-side attack. White's successes induced Black to avoid an early . . . P–Q3 and force an immediate . . . P–Q4, but enough other defences have been developed in the meantime.

(3) THE DRAGON VARIATION is the most formidable line of the series with . . . P–Q3 and . . . P–KN3, whereby Black intends to fianchetto his king's bishop and exert pressure on the diagonal, at the same time creating an impenetrable porcupine-like perimeter for the defence of his king. Secondary 6th moves (cols. 31–5) are best answered by an immediate . . . N–B3. The main line arises after 6 B–K2 (cols. 36–45) and it seems to allow White some steady, persistent, lasting pressure. This may account for a passing preference, on Black's part, for the Najdorf System or some of the "Non-Dragon" lines with 2 . . . N–QB3.

Odds and ends are found in cols. 46–55. Cols 47–8 are a departure from the maxim not to expose the queen, yet it can here become very strong and the line offers an occasional variety. Col. 49 is closely linked to the other forms of the *Tartakover–Morra Gambit* in cols. 172 and 185 and the

Sicilian Centre Gambit (col. 184). Col. 50 is inferior for Black; the *Wing Gambit* (col. 55) is good for skittles. Altogether, cols. 51–5 are *Semi-closed Variations*.

(4) THE NIMZOWITSCH–ROSSOLIMO ATTACK, 3 B–N5 may apply after both 2 . . . P–Q3 (cols. 56–7) or 2 . . . N–QB3 (cols. 58–60), which is the next main sector of Black's Sicilian defences. There has been resurgent interest in this attack but mainly as a surprise and probing weapon, as the line is intrinsically narrow in scope. Khachaturov (1937) also takes credit for its development.

(B) Black's reply (2 N–KB3), 2 . . . N–QB3 differs from Section (A) in at least the one aspect that a contemplated . . . P–KN3—in conjunction with . . . P–Q3—is deferred, thus allowing White to avoid or prevent the Dragon's tactics if he chooses. This is the reason that for cols. 61–90 the term "Anti–Dragon" may be used; they serve to hinder Black from fianchettoing his king's bishop, or neutralize its sting.

(1) THE RICHTER (–RAUZER) ATTACK, (2 N–KB3) 2 . . . N–QB3; 3 P–Q4, P × P; 4 N × P, N–B3; 5 N–QB3, P–Q3; 6 B–KN5 (cols. 61–82) originated with Richter's follow-up 7 N × N (col. 81). It has since been further developed, next by Rauzer, and most recently with Larsen's added defence 6 . . . B–Q2 (61–70). This has helped to sustain this complex weapon in the fore-front of tournament practice. The attack prevents both the Dragon and the Boleslavski Variations by threatening to double Black's king's bishop pawn with B × N.

Other sixth moves for White are handled in cols. 83–93.

(2) THE LEONHARDT–SOZIN ATTACK 6 B–QB4 (cols. 86–90) has also undergone an up-surge in Fischer's hands, with later analytical support by Nikitin and the Yugoslavs Marić and Velimirović.

(3) THE BOLESLAVSKI VARIATION 6 B–K2, P–K4?! (cols. 91–2) is as controversial and full of fight and resilience as ever. Since the Russian grandmaster, a latter-day hypermodern and prolific theoretician, showed that Black's "backward" queen's pawn could not be exploited and rather becomes a pivotal pillar of support, the system is now regarded as thoroughly sound and dynamic—another argument against 6 B–K2.

(4) THE PELIKÁN VARIATION 5 . . . P–K4 (cols. 93–5) demonstrates just about equality—but on a tightrope. Its analysis has recently been amplified by Sveshnikov.

(5) THE FOUR KNIGHT'S VARIATION 5 . . . P–K3 (cols. 96–100) has also remained quite neo-modern and 6 KN–N5 has not yet shaken it.

(6) THE ACCELERATED DRAGON 4 . . . P–KN3 has become a legitimate term and theme since the Maróczy Bind (see further below) has lost some of its terror and new territory has been explored instead with 5 N–B3 (cols. 100–5). While Black seems to force the fianchetto with precipitate haste so as to arrive at an otherwise frustrated Dragon, his attempts have not been clearly refuted.

THE MARÓCZY BIND 5 P–QB4 (cols. 106–10) is of course closely related, and used to be the only authentic and logical move to punish Black's audacity; but slow positional stubbornness took the venom out of the dreaded strangle. Nevertheless, new forceful discoveries for White in other systems might again question this precarious equality. The Maróczy is often reached via the English opening.

(7) THE LÖWENTHAL VARIATION 4 . . . P–K4 (cols. 111–15) is a kind of hyper-accelerated Boleslavski-Pelikán-pawn-push dating back to 1836. It has likewise retained its feasibility.

(8) THE TAIMANOV VARIATION 4 . . . P–K3; 5 N–QB3, Q–B2 (cols. 116–25) is a more recent, viable and elastic battle plan which is also coupled with the preventive . . . P–QR3, and thus has some affinity with the Paulsen Defence, see col. 168. However, the systems are kept separately identifiable. Replacing 5 . . . N–B3 with 5 . . . Q–B2 also avoids any complications of cols. 96–100.

White's deviations on the fifth move (cols. 126–30) do not upset Black's equilibrium. Col. 130 was also originated by Taimanov.

(c) Black's reply (2 N–KB3) 2 . . . P–K3 is one of Black's oldest schemes, strongly linked to the earlier Paulsen treatment with . . . P–QR3, and represented in the Scheveningen Variation (1923) of the transition period from classical to modern chess.

(1) THE SCHEVENINGEN VARIATION 3 P–Q4, P × P; 4 N × P, N–KB3; 5 N–QB3, P–Q3; 6 B–K2, B–K2; 7 O–O, N–B3; (cols. 131–41) keeps Black in a restricted position which yet contains latent power. White's initiative, while not telling, is durable, but if he falters with his customary king's side action, the counter-attack sets in quickly with . . . P–Q4. For cols. 142–5 see further below.

(2) THE MODERN SCHEVENINGEN VARIATION 7 . . . B–K2 (cols. 146–50) postpones 2 . . . N–QB3 and, in col. 146 and 150 is countered by O–O–O instead of O–O. The same feature is shown in col. 141.

(3) THE MODERN PAULSEN DEFENCE evolves as in cols. 142–5 after 6 B–K2, P–QR3 or 6 B–K3, P–QR3, as also in cols. 152–4 after 6 P–KN3 or 6 P–KN4 followed by 6 . . . P–QR3—which is the thematic move if played early. 6 P–KN3 is too slow, but the Keres Attack 6 P–KN4 is dangerous in enterprising hands.

(4) THE SICILIAN COUNTER-ATTACK 5 . . . B–N5 (cols. 156–8) has become subject to doubt in the wake of stable analysis (in col. 158) by Albert Becker, "master emeritus" of the Sicilian. If it stands up, Black may have to resort instead to 5 . . . N–QB3 (cols. 96–100).

(5) THE PAULSEN VARIATION, 4 . . . P–QR3 (cols. 159–70) is still based more or less on the early Paulsen recipes but for the fact that the once typical . . . QN–Q2 had virtually been dropped. It allows White too much leeway by failing to subject his centre to pressure. Considerable new thought was added to this line in the 1950s by the Russian master

Kan. The treatment is similar to Taimanov's except Black has not yet developed with . . . N–QB3. Cols. 161–2 are an alternative form of the *Maróczy Bind* (II).

(D) Other Black's replies (2 N–KB3) 2 . . . P–QR3; or 2 . . . N–KB3; or 2 . . . P–KN3:

(1) THE TARTAKOVER–O'KELLY VARIATION 2 . . . P–QR3 (cols. 171–2) utilizes this preventative move at the earliest moment but abdicates the use of other defence systems where . . . P–QR3 is superfluous and replaceable by a more dynamic choice. Col. 172 is also a variant of the Tartakover–Morra Gambit.

(2) THE NIMZOWITSCH VARIATION 2 . . . N–KB3 (col. 173) just about holds its own but has become a stereotype, robbing it of its usefulness as a versatile tournament weapon.

(3) THE "ULTRA" FIANCHETTO, 2 . . . P–KN3 (cols. 174–5) also known as the Hyper-accelerated Dragon—as different from the "accelerated" 4 . . . P–KN3, see paragraph (B-6)—merely has "ultramodern" features and appears well defensible in col. 175.

(E) CLOSED SYSTEMS, other than 2 N–KB3 are sporadically employed, i.e.

(1) The system with 2 N–QB3 (cols. 176–80), one of the oldest, safest, and possibly slowest methods.

(2) THE KERES VARIATION, 2 N–K2 (col. 181) which is out of favour.

(3) THE WING GAMBIT, 2 P–QN4 (col. 182) which is too impetuous.

(4) THE ALAPIN VARIATION, 2 P–QB3 (col. 183)—2 . . . P–Q4! = , but it can transpose into many independent, closed lines, dissected in *Chess Digest Magazine* 1977/10 and 11, by the Kiev master Bannik.

(5) THE SICILIAN CENTRE GAMBIT, 2 P–Q4!? (col. 184–5), followed up if so selected, by 3 P–QB3 the *Morra Gambit*, declined or accepted. Lately, the American Ken Smith, editor of *Chess Digest Magazine*, laid claim to a résumé of this line in conjunction with the related cols. 49 and 172 all of which at one time or another might flow into each other.

1 P–K4, P–QB4; 2 N–KB3, P–Q3; 3 P–Q4, P×P; 4 N×P, N–KB3; 5 N–QB3, P–QR3; 6 B–KN5, P–K3; 7 P–B4, Q–N3; 8 Q–Q2, Q×P; (Poisoned Pawn Variation); 9 R–QN1, Q–R6

	1	2	3	4	5
10	P–K5			B×N	
	P×P (*a*)			P×B	
11	P×P			B–K2	
	KN–Q2			B–N2	N–B3
12	N–K4	B–QB4 (*d*)		O–O (*h*)	N×N?
	P–R3!	B–N5	Q–R4	P–B4	P×N
13	B–R4 (*b*)	R–N3	B×KP	KR–Q1	O–O
	Q×P	Q–R4	P×B	N–B3 (*i*)	Q–R4
14	R–N3	O–O (*e*)	N×P	N×N	K–R1
	N–QB3	O–O	N×P!	B×N	B–K2
15	N×N	B–B6	N–Q5	Q–K3	P–B5
	P×N	N×B	Q×Q†	P×N	P×P
16	N–Q6†	P×N	K×Q	R–N3	P×P
	B×N (*c*)	R–Q1 (*f*)	K–Q2 (*g*)	Q–B4 (*j*)	B×P (*k*)

(*a*) 10 . . . P–R3; 11 B×N, P×B; 12 N–K4, BP×P; 13 R–N3! Q–R5; 14 P×P, P×P; 15 N–B6†, K–K2; 16 N–B5†! K×N; 17 Q–Q8†, K×N; 18 B–Q3†, P–K5; 19 O–O†, K–K4 (19 . . . K–N3; 20 Q–B6†, K–R2; 21 R–B4! B–N2; 22 R×KP! + +); 20 Q–B6†, K–Q3; 21 Q×R, N–Q2! 22 R×BP, P×B; 23 R×P†, K–B3; 24 R×B, N×R; 25 Q×N, K–N3; 26 Q–B2†, K–B2; 27 Q–N3 with perpetual check. Analyses by Prieditis, Prins, and Fischer.

(*b*) 13 B–N5, P×KB (Hartston suggests 13 . . . P×QB?! 14 R–N3, Q×P; 15 O–O ∞); 14 N×NP, P×B; 15 N×Q, R×N; 16 R–N5, N–QB3; 17 O–O, B–K2; 18 N–Q6†, B×N; 19 P×B, P–B3; 20 R–K1, N/3–K4; 21 Q–N4, R–QR3; drawn. Platonov-Minić, Sochi 1968.

(*c*) 17 P×B, P–QR4; 18 B–K2, P–R5; 19 R–QB3, Q–R8†; 20 B–Q1, P–R6; 21 O–O, P–R7; 22 Q–K3; O–O + + . Boey-O'Kelly, Belgian Chp. 1957.

(*d*) 12 R–N3, Q–R4; 13 B–K2, Q×KP; 14 N–K4, N–B4; 15 N×N, B×N; 16 N×P, Q–R8†! drawn.

(*e*) 14 P–QR3! B–B4; 15 N×P, P×N; 16 B×KP, P–R3! 17 B–B7†, K×B; 18 Q–Q5†, K–N3; 19 Q–K4†, K–B2; 20 Q–Q5†, drawn. Zaitsev and Khasin.

(*f*) 17 R×B, Q×R; 18 Q–N5, P–KN3; 19 R–B4, P–N3 (19 . . . R×N; 20 Q–R6, Q–B1; 21 Q×Q†, K×Q; 22 R×R, B–Q2; O'Kelly); 20 R–R4, Q–B1; 21 K–B1, R–R2 = . Mazzoni-Lee, Havana 1966.

(*g*) 17 N/6–B7, R–R2; 18 KR–K1, N–B5† and . . . P–QN4 ∓ .

(*h*) 12 P–B5, B–R3; 13 Q–Q3, Q–B4; 14 P×P, P×P; 15 B–N4, R–N1; 16 B×P, R×P; 17 B×B, R–Q7; 18 Q–R3, Q×N/5; 19 N–K2, Q×P; 20 Q–R5†, Q–N3; 21 Q×Q, P×Q; 22 B×P, R–R2; 23 B–K4, drawn. Ivkov-Sakharov, Yugoslavia–USSR 1966.

(*i*) 13 . . . O–O; 14 P×P, P×P (14 . . . N–B3; 15 N×N, P×N; 16 P–B6!); 15 N–Q5, N–B3; 16 N×N, P×N; 17 N–K7†, K–R1; 18 N×B, KR×N = . Parma-Fischer, Zagreb 1970.

(*j*) 17 Q×Q, P×Q; 18 R×B, P×P; 19 R×P, B–Q2; 20 R–K5, P–KB4; 21 P–N4, R–KN1; 22 K–B2, P×P; 23 R×KP, P–KR4; 24 K–N3, K–K2 ∞. Parma-Fischer, Havana 1965.

(*k*) 17 B×P! Q×B; 18 R×B, P–Q4; 19 R–K1, Q–N2; 20 Q–R6, O–O–O; 21 Q–R3, Q–Q2; 22 N–R4! Matanović. In the column, 11 . . . N–B3 is better answered with 12 N–N3! B–N2; 13 P–B5, O–O; 14 O–O, N–K4; 15 N–Q4, P–N4; 16 K–R1, B–Q2; 17 B–R5 ± . Parma-Fischer, Bled 1961.

1 P-K4, P-QB4; 2 N-KB3, P-Q3; 3 P-Q4, P×P; 4 N×P, N-KB3; 5 N-QB3, P-QR3; 6 B-KN5, P-K3; 7 P-B4, Q-N3; 8 Q-Q2, Q×P

	6	7	8	9	10
9	(R-QN1)		N-N3		
	(Q-R6)		QN-Q2	N-B3 (f)	
10	P-B5		B×N	B-Q3	R-QN1
	N-B3!		P×B	P-Q4	Q-R6
11	P×P		B-K2	B×N	B×N
	P×P		P-KR4 (e)	P×B	P×B
12	N×N		O-O	N-R4	B-Q3
	P×N		Q-R6	Q-R6	B-N2
13	P-K5!		QR-Q1	N-N6	O-O
	P×P	N-Q4 (b)	B-K2	P-Q5!	O-O! (h)
14	B×N	N×N (c)	K-R1	O-O	R-B3
	P×B	BP×N	N-B4	QR-N1	K-R1
15	N-K4	B-K2	B-B3	P-B5	R-R3
	B-K2	P×P	R-QR2	Q-N5	N-K2
16	B-K2	O-O (d)	N×N	Q×Q	P-B5
	P-KR4 (a)		Q×N! =	B×Q (g)	P×P (i)

(a) (A) 17 P-B4, P-KB4; 18 R-N3, Q-R5; 19 O-O, P × N (Kavalek–Fischer, Sousse 1967); 20 K-R1, P-B4; 21 Q-B3, Q-B3; 22 Q × P, R-KB1! = . Heemsoth in *Fernschach* 1978. (B) 17 R-N3!, Q-R5; 18 N × P† B × N; 19 P-B4! B-R5†; 20 P-N3, B-K2; 21 O-O, B-Q2 .

(b) 13 . . . N-Q2; 14 P × P, Q × KP; 15 B-Q3, Q-K4†; 16 N-K4, B-Q3; 17 P-N3, R-QN1; 18 R-Q1, R-N5; 19 O-O, B-B4†; 20 N × B, Q × N†; 21 B-K3 + .

(c) 14 N-K4, P × P; 15 B-K2, B-N5; 16 R × B, Q × R; 17 Q × Q, N × Q; 18 O-O, N-Q4; 19 N-Q6†, K-Q2; 20 N-B4, K-K1; 21 N-Q6†, K-Q2; drawn.

(d) (A) 16 . . . R-R2; 17 K-R1, Q-B4; 18 P-B4, P-Q5 (Bednarski–Sakharov, Varna 1968); 19 B-R5† (or 19 Q-Q3! B-K2; 20 Q-KB3, B × B =), P-N3; 20 B-Q1, B-K2; 21 B-R4†, K-Q1; 22 R-B7, P-R3; 23 B × P, P-K5! = . Heemsoth. (B) 16 . . . B-B4†; 17 K-R1, R-B1; 18 P-B4, R × R†; 19 R × R, B-N2; 20 B-Q1! Black's position is very precarious but if 20 Q-B2, B-K2; 21 Q × P, B × B; 22 Q-R5†, K-Q2; 23 Q × B, K-Q3; 24 Q × P, R-QN1; 25 P-R4, P-Q5; 26 R-B7, Q-R6†; 27 K-N1, Q-K6†; 28 K-R2, Q × B; 29 R × B, R × R; 30 Q × R, Q × BP = .

(e) 11 . . . Q-R6; 12 O-O, N-B4; 13 P-B5, B-Q2; 14 P × P (or 14 B-R5), P × P; 15 B-R5†, K-Q1 (better is 15 . . . K-K2); 16 N-Q4, B-K2! ∞ .

(f) Also 9 . . . Q-R6 at once, with the queen trying to return speedily into centre action, e.g. (A) 10 B × N, P × B; 11 B-K2, (1) 11 . . . B-N2; 12 O-O, N-B3; 13 R-B3, B-Q2; 14 P-B5, P-KR4; 15 R-N3, B-R3; = . (2) 11 . . . N-B3; 12 O-O, B-Q2; 13 P-B5 (13 K-R1), N-K4; 14 P × P, P × P; 15 B-R5†, K-Q1; 16 QR-N1, R-B1; 17 N-K2, B-K2; 18 N-B4, K-B2 = . Tal–Portisch, Varese 1976. (3) 11 . . . P-KR4; 12 O-O, N-B3; 13 K-R1, B-Q2; 14 Q-K3, R-B1; 15 N-N1, Q-R5; 16 P-B4, N-R4; 17 Q-QB3, N × P; 18 Q × P, R-R3; 19 Q-Q4, R-R2; 20 P-B5, P × P! 21 N-B3, B-N2; 22 N × Q, B × Q; 23 N × B, B × N; 24 QR-B1! P-N4; 25 R × P, R-B4; 26 B × N, P × B? 27 R × R, P × R; 28 R × P, B-Q2; 29 R × P, R-R3; 30 P-KR3, R-Q3; 31 N-B3, R-Q8†; 32 K-R2, R-R8; 33 R-R5, B-N4; 34 N-Q4, B-B8; 35 N-N3, R-K8; 36 R-KB5, B-B5; 37 R × RP, B × N; 38 P × B, R × P; 39 R-R5, R-K6! 40 P-QN4, R-K5; 41 R × P, R × P; 42 R-R8†, K-K2; 43 R-KN8, P-B4! drawn. Tal–R. Byrne, Dubna 1973. (B) 10 B-Q3, B-K2; 11 O-O, P-R3; 12 B-R4, N × P; 13 N × N, B × B; 14 P-B5, P × P; 15 B-N5†, P × B; 16 N × P†, K-B1; 17 N × B, N-B3; 18 N-Q6, R-Q1; 19 N × P/N5, Q-K2 ∓ . Spasski–Fischer, 7th match game 1972.

(g) 17 N × B, R × N; 18 P × P, P × P; 19 R × P, K-K2; 20 QR-KB1, N-K4 = . Minić-Barczay, Varna 1967. In the column, playable is 10 B × N, P × B; 11 N-R4, Q-R6; 12 N-N6, R-QN1; 13 N-B4. Q-R5; 14 K-B2. P-K4 = . Ligterink-Barzay, Wijk aan Zee, 1977.

(h) *Archives* prefer 13 . . . B-Q2 and K-K2, to avoid White's King's side assault. Also 12 . . . B-K2 is feasible.

(i) 17 P × P, B × P; 18 B × B, N × B; 19 N-Q5 ± . Matulović-Kavalek, Sousse 1967.

1 P-K4, P-QB4; 2 N-KB3, P-Q3; 3 P-Q4, P×P; 4 N×P, N-KB3; 5 N-QB3, P-QR3; 6 B-KN5, P-K3; 7 P-B4

	11	12	13	14	15
	(Q-N3).................		B-K2	P-N4	P-R3 (n)
8	N-N3		Q-B3	P-K5	B-R4
	Q-K6†	QN-Q2	Q-B2	P×P	Q-N3
9	Q-K2	Q-B3	O-O-O	P×P	Q-Q3 (o)
	Q×Q†	B-K2 (c)	QN-Q2	Q-B2	Q×P
10	B×Q	O-O-O	P-KN4 (f)	P×N!? (j)	R-QN1
	QN-Q2	Q-B2	P-N4	Q-K4†	Q-R6
11	P-QR4 (a)	B-Q3	B×N	B-K2	P-K5
	B-K2	P-R3	N×B (g)	Q×B	N-Q4
12	O-O-O	B-R4	P-N5	Q-Q3	N×N
	P-R3	P-KN4! (d)	N-Q2	R-R2 (k)	Q×Q
13	B-R4	P×P	P-QR3 (h)	N-K4	B×Q
	P-K4	N-K4	R-QN1!	Q-K4	P×N
14	P-B5	Q-K2	P-KR4	N-KB3 (l)	P-K6! +
	P-QN3 (b)	N/3-N5 (e)	P-N5 (i)	Q×NP (m)	

(a) Alternatives are 11 B-B3, B-K2! or 11 O-O-O, P-QN4! *Archives.*

(b) 15 B-B3 (15 B-QB4! Rabar), B-N2 ∓. Joppen–Bronstein, Belgrade 1954.

(c) 9 . . . Q-B2; 10 P-QR4, B-K2; 11 B-Q3, P-R3; 12 Q-R3, N-B4; 13 N×N, Q×N; 14 B-R4, O-O; 15 B-B2, Q-B3; 16 Q-B3, P-QN3; Haag–Barczay, Salgotarian 1967. (B) 10 O-O-O, P-N4; 11 P-QR3, B-N2; 12 B×N, N×B; 13 P-B5, P×P; 14 Q×P, B-K2; 15 N-Q5, N×N; 16 P×N, B-KB3! = .

(d) This is better than 12 . . . N×P; 13 N×N, B×B; 14 Q-N4! Boleslavski.

(e) 15 N-Q4, P×P; 16 B-N3, B-Q2; 17 N-B3, Q-B4! Rajković–Udovćić, Yugoslav Chp. 1962.

(f) (A) 10 B-K2, P-N4 (10 . . . P-R3; 11 B-R4, R-QN1; 12 KR-K1 Hort); 11 B×N, N×B; 12 P-K5, B-N2; 13 P×N, B×Q; 14 B×B, B×P; 15 B×R, P-Q4; 16 B×P, B×N; 17 R×B, P×B; 18 R-K1†, K-B1; 19 R-K5, P-R3; 20 N×QP, Q-R2! ∞. Analysis by Dueball and Zuckerman. (B) 10 Q-N3, P-R3; 11 B-R4, P-KN4; 12 P×P, R-KN1; 13 Q-K1, P×P; 14 B-N3, N-K4; 15 N-B3, B-Q2; 16 B×N, P×B; 17 Q-N3, O-O-O; 18 Q×KP, N-N5 = . (c) 10 B-Q3, (1) 10 . . . P-N4; 11 KR-K1, B-N2; 12 N-Q5, P×N; 13 N-B5, B-B1; 14 B×N, P×B; 15 P×P†, K-Q1; 16 Q-K4, Q-B4! ∞. Jimenez–Mecking, Mallorca 1970. Safer may be 12 Q-N3, P-N5; 13 N-Q5, P×N; 14 P×P, K-Q1 = . (2) 10 . . . P-R3; 11 Q-R3, N-N3 (or 11 . . . N-B1; 12 P-B5, N/1-R2); 12 P-B5, P-K4; 13 KN-K2, B-Q2; 14 K-N1, B-B3; 15 B-K3, QN-Q2; 16 P-KN4, O-O-O; 17 Q-B3, N-B4; 18 B×N! Browne–Grefe, Lone Pine 1976. Here, also 11 B-R4, P-KN4; 12 P-K5, P×B; 13 P×N, N×P, 14 P-B5!? (Soltis).

(g) Both 11 . . . B×P; 12 B×P! and 11 . . . P×B; 12 P-B5, N-K4; 13 Q-R3! are inferior.

(h) 13 P-B5, N-B4! 14 P-B6, P×P; 15 P×P, B-B1; 16 Q-R5! comes out even.

(i) 15 P×P, R×P; 16 B-R3, O-O! 17 N×P, P×N; 18 B×P†, K-R1; 19 N-Q5, Q-B5! 20 B-B5! R×B! 21 P×R, B-N2; 22 KR-K1, B-KB1 = . Fischer and Vuković.

(j) Worth consideration is 10 Q-K2, KN-Q2; 11 O-O-O, B-N2; 12 Q-N4, Q×P; 13 B-Q3 (13 B-K2, B-B4), P-R3; 14 B-R4, P-N4; 15 B-N3, Q-K6† = . Spasski.

(k) Or 12 . . . Q×BP; 13 R-KB1, Q-K4; (A) 14 O-O-O, R-R2; 15 N-B3, Q-B5† = . (B) 14 R-Q1, R-R2; 15 N-B3, Q-B2; 16 N-K5, B-K2; 17 N×BP ± .

(l) (A) 14 O-O-O!, R-Q2; 15 Q-B3, Q-B2, 16 Q-R5 ± has more punch. If (B) 14 O-O, R-Q2; 15 N-KB3, Q×NP; etc. as in note (m).

(m) 15 O-O, R-Q2; 16 Q-K3, B-N2; 17 QR-N1, Q×BP; 18 N/3-N5, Q-B2! 19 P×P, B×P ∓ ; Parma–Tatai, Athens 1968.

(*n*) (A) 7 . . . QN–Q2; (1) 8 Q–B3, Q–B2; 9 O–O–O, P–N4; 10 B–Q3, B–N2; 11 KR–K1, P–R3; 12 Q–R3, O–O–O; 13 B × N, N × B; 14 N–Q5, N × N; 15 P × N, B × QP: 16 P–R4 with an attack for the pawn (Kavalek). Compare note (*f*) (C). (2) 8 B–QB4, P–N4; 9 B × KP, P × B; 10 N × KP, Q–R4; 11 N × B, R × N; 12 Q × P, Q–N3; 13 O–O–O, Q × Q; 14 R × Q, P–N5; 15 N–K2, P–R3 ∞. Matulović–Tringov, Vrnačka Banja 1973. (3) 8 Q–K2, Q–B2; 9 P–KN4, P–N4; 10 O–O–O, B–N2; 11 B–N2, N–N3 = . (B) 7 . . . Q–B2; 8 B–Q3 (or 8 Q–K2, QN–Q2; 9 O–O–O, P–N4; 10 P–KN4!), QN–Q2; 9 Q–K2, P–N4; 10 O–O–O, B–N2; 11 KR–K1, B–K2; 12 P–K5 + . Spasski.

(*o*) If 9 P–QR3, B–Q2; 10 B–B2, Q–B2! (risky is 10 . . . Q × P; 11 N/4–K2, N–N5; 12 B–N1, and 13 B–N6); 11 Q–B3, B–K2; 12 B–Q3, N–B3; 13 O–O, O–O; 14 QR–K1, KR–Q1 = . The column is Mikenas–Tal, Riga 1959.

1 P-K4, P-QB4; N-KB3, P-Q3; 3 P-Q4, P×P; 4 N×P, N-KB3; 5 N-QB3, P-QR3

	16	17	18	19	20
6	(B-KN5)			B-K2	⎫ Opocenský
	(P-K3)		QN-Q2	P-K4 (*h*)	⎭ Variation
7	Q-B3 .... Q-Q2?!		B-QB4!	N-N3 (*i*)	
	QN-Q2 (*a*)	N-B3 (*d*)	Q-R4	B-K2 (*j*)	
8	O-O-O	O-O-O	Q-Q2	O-O	
	Q-B2	P-R3	P-K3	O-O (*k*)	
9	Q-N3	B-R4	O-O-O!	P-B4	B-K3 (*n*)
	P-N4 (*b*)	N×P	P-N4!	P-QN4	QN-Q2 (*o*)
10	B×P	Q-B4	B-N3!	P-QR3 (*l*)	P-QR4
	P×B	N-N4	B-N2	B-N2	P-QN3
11	N/4×NP	N×N	KR-K1	B-B3	Q-Q2
	Q-N1	P×N	R-B1 (*f*)	QN-Q2	B-N2
12	N×P†	Q-R4	P-K5!	P-N3	P-B3
	B×N (*c*)	Q-N3 (*e*)	N×P (*g*)	R-B1 (*m*)	Q-B2 (*p*)

(*a*) Black may also defend with 7 . . . P-KR3; 8 B-R4, QN-Q2; 9 O-O-O, N-K4; 10 Q-K2, P-KN4; 11 B-N3, B-Q2 = .

(*b*) 9 . . . R-QN1; 10 P-B4, P-N4; 11 B-Q3, P-N5; 12 N/3-K2, B-N2; 13 Q-B3, P-Q4 = .

(*c*) 13 Q×B, Q×Q; 14 R×Q, P-R3; 15 B×N, N×B; 16 KR-Q1, B-N2; 17 P-B3! ∞. Fichtl–Doležal, ČSSR 1954.

(*d*) 7 . . . P-R3; 8 B×N, Q×B; 9 P-KN3, N-B3; 10 O-O-O, N×N; 11 Q×N, Q×Q; 12 R×Q, B-Q2 = . Schmidt–Evans, US Open Chp., Rochester 1959.

(*e*) 13 P-B4, N-R2; 14 P-B5, R-QN1; 15 P×P, B×P; 16 B-B4, Vasyukov–Zukharov, USSR 1960, with a strong attack.

(*f*) (A) 11 . . . B-K2; 12 P-B4, N-N4; 13 B×N! (13 P-K5, P×P; 14 B×N! P×B; 15 P×P, O-O-O =), P×B; 14 Q-K3, O-O-O; 15 P-QR3 ± . Matsukevich. (B) 11 . . . N-B4; 12 P-K5! P×P; 13 B×P! P×B; 14 N×KP, N/4-Q2; 15 B×N, N×B; 16 R×P, K-B2; 17 Q-K3! P-R3 (17 . . . B-B1; 18 N-N5†, K-N1; 19 R-K8! + . O'Kelly; 18 N×B, KR×N; 19 R-K7†, K-N1; 20 R×B, P-N5; 21 N-Q5! N×N; 22 Q-K5! R-B3; 23 R×N, resigns. Matsukevich–Voorema, corr. 1966. (C) 11 . . . O-O-O; (1) 12 P-QR3, K-N1; 13 P-B4, R-B1; 14 R-K3 (or 14 P-K5?!), N-B4; 15 B×N, P×B; 16 B-R2, Q-N3 = . Matulović–Baretić, Yugoslav Chp. 1977. (2) 12 P-B4, P-R3; 13 B×N, N×B; 14 P-QR3 ± .

(*g*) 13 N×KP, P×N; 14 R×N, P×R; 15 B×N + + . *P/E*.

(*h*) The text was originated by Opočenský and other Czech masters, but also popularized by Najdorf. If (A) 6 . . . P-K3 see Modern Paulsen or Scheveningen Variation, and (B) 6 . . . P-KN3 see Dragon Variation. An occasional variant is (C) 6 . . . QN-Q2; (1) 7 B-K3, P-K3; 8 P-QR4, P-QN3; 9 P-B4, B-N2; 10 B-B3, R-B1; 11 O-O, R×N; 12 P×R, N×P; 13 N-K2, Q-B2; 14 Q-K1, P-Q4 = . Mednis–Browne, Oberlin 1975. (2) 7 P-B4, P-K4; 8 N-N3, N-N4; 9 B-B3, Q-N3; 10 P-B5, B-Q2; 11 R-QN1, B-B3! ± . Olafsson–Quinteros, Lanzarote 1974. (3) 7 P-QR4, P-KN3; 8 O-O (8 P-R5, P-QN4; 9 P×P e.p., N×NP =), B-N2; 9 B-K3, O-O; 10 Q-Q2, N-B4   . (4) 7 O-O, P-KN3! 8 P-B4, B-N2; 9 B-K3, O-O = . Lyangov in *Byulleten*, 1978/7.

(*i*) (A) 7 N-B3, B-K2 (7 . . . P-R3; 8 B-QB4, B-K3; 9 B-N3, B-K2; 10 O-O, QN-Q2); 8 O-O, O-O; 9 B-KN5, QN-Q2; 10 P-QR4, P-R3; 11 B-K3, Q-B2; 12 N-Q2, P-QN3; 13 B-QB4, B-N2; 14 Q-K2, N-B4; 15 P-B3, KR-Q1; 16 N-Q5, N×N = . Bannik–Krogius, USSR Chp. 1963. (B) 7 N-B5, P-Q4! = .

(*j*) If at once 7 . . . B-K3? 8 P-B4! Q-B2; 9 P-KN4, P×P; 10 P-N5, KN-Q2; 11 B×BP, N-QB3; 12 O-O ± . Adorjan.

(*k*) Again 8 . . . B–K3; 9 P–B4, Q–B2; 10 P–QR4?! QN–Q2; (A) 11 K–R1, O–O; 12 B–K3, P × P; 13 R × P, N–K4; 14 P–R5, KR–N1 (14 . . . QR–B1! Byrne); 15 B–N6, Q–Q2; 16 R–R4, R–QB1; 17 R–Q4 ± . Karpov–Polugayevski, 8th match game 1973. (B) 11 P–B5, B–B5; 12 P–R5, O–O; 13 B–K3, P–QN4; 14 P × P *e.p.*, N × P/3; 15 K–R1! Geller–Fischer, Curaçao 1962. For the time being, this treatment has superseded the earlier B–K3 as in col. 20.

(*l*) More enterprising is 10 P–QR4, B–N2 (or P–N5); 11 RP × P, RP × P; 12 R × R, B × R; 13 P × P, Q–N3†; 14 Q–Q4, Q × Q; 15 N × Q, P × P = . Sherwin–Evans, US Open Chp. 1952.

(*m*) 13 Q–K1, N–N3; 14 K–R1, N–B5; 15 N–Q2, Q–Q2; 16 N × N, R × N; 17 B–Q2, P–Q4 ∞. A perfect position for Black. Yanofsky–Bolbochan, Stockholm 1962.

(*n*) (A) 9 B–KN5, B–K3; 10 B × N, B × B; 11 N–Q5, N–Q2; 12 Q–Q3, R–B1; 13 P–QB3, B–N4 = . Averbakh–Petrosian, USSR Chp. 1959. (B) 9 P–QR4, N–B3! 10 B–N5, B–K3; 11 B × N, B × B; 12 N–Q5, R–B1 = . Vogt–Ftáčnik, Trenčanské-Teplice 1979.

(*o*) (A) 9 . . . Q–B2; 10 P–QR4, (1) 10 . . . B–K3; 11 P–R5, Q–B3; 12 Q–Q3, R–B1; 13 KR–Q1, QN–Q2; 14 N–Q5, B × N; 15 P × B, Q–B2; 16 P–QB4 ± , (2) 10 . . . P–QN3; 11 Q–Q2, B–K3; 12 KR–Q1, QN–Q2; 13 P–B3, KR–Q1; 14 N–B1 ± . Boleslavski. (B) 9 . . . B–K3; 10 P–B4, P × P; 11 R × P, N–B3!

(*p*) 13 KR–Q1, KR–B1; 14 N–B1 ± . The column is Geller's analysis.

1 P-K4, P-QB4; 2 N-KB3, P-Q3; 3 P-Q4, P×P; 4 N×P, N-KB3; 5 N-QB3, P-QR3

	21	22	23	24	25
6	P-KN3......	P-B4	B-K3	B-QB4 (g) ⎰	King's Bishop
	P-K4 (a)	P-K3 (c)	P-K4?! (d)	P-K3 (h) ⎱	Variation
7	KN-K2	Q-B3	N-N3 (e)	O-O........	B-N3
	B-K2	Q-N3	B-K3	B-K2 (i)	P-QN4 (l)
8	B-N2	N-N3	Q-Q2	B-N3	P-B4 (m)
	O-O	N-B3	QN-Q2	O-O (j)	B-N2
9	O-O	B-Q3	P-B3!	P-B4	P-B5
	P-QN4	B-K2	B-K2	P-QN4	P-K4
10	P-KR3	B-K3	P-N4	P-QR3	KN-K2
	B-N2	Q-B2	P-QN4	B-N2	QN-Q2
11	N-Q5	O-O	P-N5	P-B5!	O-O (n)
	N×N	O-O	N-R4	P-K4	B-K2
12	P×N	QR-K1	O-O-O	QN-K2	N-N3
	N-Q2 (b)	N-QN5 =	O-O (f)	QN-Q2! (k)	R-QB1 (o)

(a) (A) 6 . . . P-K3; see Scheveningen Variation. (B) 6 . . . P-KN3; see Dragon Variation. (C) 6 . . . B-N5; 7 P-B3, B-Q2; 8 B-K3! N-B3; 9 Q-Q2, P-K3; 10 O-O-O ±. (D) 6 . . . P-QN4; 7 B-N2, B-N2; 8 O-O, P-K3; 9 Q-K2, QN-Q2; 10 P-QR3 and P-KB4, P-KN4 ±. *P/E.*

(b) 13 P-QR4, N-B4; 14 N-B3! Q-Q2; 15 P × P, P × P; 16 R × R, R × R ∓. *Comments.*

(c) (A) 6 . . . Q-B2; 7 B-Q3, QN-Q2; 8 O-O, P-QN4; 9 P-QR3, B-N2; 10 Q-K2, P-K3; 11 K-R1, N-B4 = ; with White deploying his forces on the king's wing, Black on the queen's wing. (B) 6 . . . N-B3; 7 B-K2, Q-N3; 8 N-N3, P-K3; 9 B-B3, B-K2; 10 Q-K2, O-O; 11 B-K3 ±. (C) 6 . . . P-K4; 7 N-B3 (7 N-N3 see col. 19), Q-B2; 8 B-Q3, QN-Q2; 9 O-O, P-QN4; 10 K-R1, B-N2; 11 Q-K1, P-N3 = . (D) 6 . . . Q-N3; 7 B-B4, N-B3; 8 N × N, P × N; 9 Q-Q3, P-K3; 10 B-N3. (E) 6 . . . P-KN3; 7 B-K2, B-N2; 8 N-N3, N-B3; 9 B-K3, O-O; 10 P-N4, P-QN4; 11 P-N5, N-Q2; 12 Q-Q2, B-N2; 13 P-KR4 ±. Nezhmetdinov–Aronin, USSR 1950. The column is Keres–Smyslov, Moscow 1959.

(d) (A) For 6 . . . P-K3 see Modern Scheveningen Defence with 6 B-K3. (B) 6 . . . N-N5; 7 B-N5! (C) 6 . . . QN-Q2; 7 B-K2, N-B4; 8 B-B3, B-Q2; 9 P-KN4, P-R3; 10 Q-K2, P-KN3 = .

(e) 7 N-B3, P-R3; 8 B-QB4, B-K3; 9 N-Q5, QN-Q2; 10 N × N†, Q × N; 11 B × B, Q × B = . *Comments.*

(f) 13 R-N1, R-B1; 14 N-K2! ±. *Comments.*

(g) 6 P-QR4 mostly invites Black to play the Dragon Variation.

(h) 6 . . . N-B3? 7 N × N, P × N; 8 P-K5, N-N5 (8 . . . P × P; 9 B × P†!); 9 B-B4, Q-N3; 10 Q-B3, B-B4; 11 P × P ±.

(i) (A) Risky is the pawn grab 7 . . . P-QN4; 8 B-N3, P-N5; 9 N-R4, N × P; 10 P-KB4, B-N2; 11 P-B5, P-K4; 12 N-K6! with exciting possibilities. *P/E.* (B) Earlier lines, analysed in the 1930s, arise after 7 . . . N-B3; e.g. 8 B-K3, Q-B2; 9 B-N3, N-QR4; 10 P-B4, P-QN4; 11 P-B5, and now 11 . . . P-K4; 12 N/4-K2, B-N2; 13 N-N3, N-B5; 14 B × N, Q × B; 15 Q-B3, P-KR4; 16 P-KR4, P-Q4 might equalize.

(j) 8 . . . P-QN4; (A) 9 P-QR4, P-N5; 10 N-R2, Q-N3! = . (B) 9 Q-B3, Q-N3; 10 B-K3, Q-N2; 11 Q-N3, B-Q2! 12 KR-K1, N-B3; 13 P-B4, P-N5! (C) 9 P-B4, O-O! 10 P-K5, P × P = . *Informator* 24.

(k) 13 N-N3, N-B4; 14 B-Q5, B × B; 15 P × B, R-B1; 16 B-N5, N/4-Q2; 17 B × N, N × B; 18 N/B3-K4, R-B5 ∓. Kotkov–Polugayevski, USSR 1959.

(*l*) Or (A) 7 . . . B–K2; (1) 8 P–B4, O–O; 9 Q–B3, Q–B2; 10 O–O, P–QN4 = . Fischer –Tal, Zürich 1959. (2) 8 P–N4, Q–R4; 9 Q–B3, N–B3; 10 N × N, P × N; 11 B–Q2, Q–B2; 12 P–N5, N–Q2; 13 O–O–O ± . (B) 7 . . . N–B3 see Leonhardt–Sozin Attack.

(*m*) Alternatives are (A) 8 O–O, B–K2; 9 B–K3, O–O; 10 P–QR4, P–N5; 11 N–R2, N × P; 12 N × NP, B–N2; 13 P–R5, P–Q4; 14 N–Q3, N–Q2; 15 P–KB4, R–B1; 16 P–B3, B–Q3; 17 Q–N4, B–B2; 18 R–B3, B × RP; 19 N–K5, P–B4; 20 Q × P†, K × Q; 21 N × KP†, K–B3; 22 N × Q, KR × N; 23 N × N†, R × N; 24 R × B, P–Q5; 25 P × P, R–KN1; 26 B × R, resigns. Watson–Jacobs, US Students Chp. 1970. (B) 8 Q–K2, B–K2; 9 P–N4 ∞ .

(*n*) 11 B–N5, B–K2; 12 N–N3, R–QB1; 13 B × N! (13 O–O? P–KR4!), N × B; 14 N–R5! O–O ∞ .

(*o*) 13 B–KN5, O–O = . Ciocaltea–Minić, Bucharest 1966.

1 P–K4, P–QB P–QB4, 2 N–KB3, P–Q3, 3 P–Q4, P×P; 4 N×P, N–KB3; 5 N–QB3, P–KN3; 6 B–K3, B–N2; 7 P–B3, O–O (*a*); 8 Q–Q2, N–B3

	26	27	28	29	30
9	O–O–O	B–QB4 (*f*)			
	P–Q4 (*b*)	B–Q2!			
10	P×P	O–O–O			P–KR4
	N×P	Q–R4 (*g*)			R–B1 (*n*)
11	N/4×N	B–N3			B–N3
	P×N	KR–B1			N–K4
12	N×N (*c*)	P–KN4	P–KR4	K–N1!?	P–R5
	P×N	N–K4	N–K4	N–K4	N×RP (*o*)
13	Q×P	P–KR4 (*h*)	P–R5	P–KR4 (*l*)	O–O–O
	Q–B2	N–B5	N×RP	N–B5	N–QB5
14	Q×R (*d*)	B×N	B–R6	B×N	B×N
	B–B4	R×B	N–Q6† (*j*)	R×B	R×B
15	Q×R†	N–N3	K–N1!	N–N3	P–KN4
	K×Q (*e*)	Q–R3 (*i*)	N×P (*k*)	Q–B2 (*m*)	N–B3 (*p*)

(*a*) At times, Black transposes with 7 . . . N–B3; 8 Q–Q2, B–Q2!? 9 B–QB4, postponing castling; but this independent version has not yet proved any greater success.

(*b*) More sober, but unrefuted is the simplifying 9 . . . N×N! 10 B×N, B–K3; 11 K–N1 (11 N–Q5, R–B1! =), P–QR3; 12 P–KR4, P–QN4; 13 P–R5, P–N5; 14 N–Q5, B×N; 15 P×B, Q–R4 = . Geller–Horowitz, USSR–USA 1954.

(*c*) 12 B–Q4, P–K4; 13 B–B5, B–K3; (A) 14 B–B4, R–K1; 15 N×N, P×N; 16 B×P, B×B; 17 Q×B, Q–N4†; 18 Q–Q2, Q–B3; 19 P–B3, QR–QB1 = . Milev–Geller, Moscow 1956. (B) 14 N–K4, R–K1; 15 P–KR4, R–N1; 16 P–KN4, P–B4; 17 P×P, P×P; 18 N–Q6, B–KB1?. (Sigurjonsson–Miles, Wijk aan Zee 1977); 19 N–B4! Correct was 18 . . . R–B1! = .

(*d*) 14 Q–QB5, Q–N2; 15 Q–R3, B–B4; 16 B–QR6, Q–B2; 17 Q–B5, Q–N3; 18 Q×Q, P×Q; 19 B–QB4, KR–QB1; 20 B–N3, QR×P! = . Averbakh.

(*e*) 16 R–Q2, P–KR4; 17 B–K2, K–N1; 18 P–QR3, Q–N1 = .

(*f*) Another wrinkle is 9 P–KN4, (A) 9 . . . N×N; 10 B×N, B–K3; 11 O–O–O, Q–R4; 12 K–K1, KR–B1; 12 P–QR3, QR–N1; 14 P–N5, N–R4; 15 N–Q5, Q×Q; 16 R×Q, B×N; 17 P×B, P–QR3; 18 R–N1, P–N4; 19 P–B3, P–R4; 20 B–R7, R–N2; 21 B–K3, B–K4 = . Karpov–Dueball, Skopje Olympics 1972. (B) 9 . . . B–Q2; 10 P–KR4, Q–R4; 11 P–R5, N×N; 12 B×N, KR–B1; 13 P–R6? B–R1 ∓.

(*g*) (A) 10 . . . R–B1; 11 B–N3, N–K4; 12 P–KR4, N–B5; 13 B×N, R×B; 14 P–R5, N×RP; 15 P–KN4, N–B3; 16 QR–N1, R–K1; 17 P–N5, N–R4; 18 R×N, P×R; 19 N–Q5, K–R1 = .(B) 10 . . . Q–N1; 11 P–KR4, R–B1; 12 N–Q5! KN×N; 13 B×N, P–K3!? Levy.

(*h*) (A) 13 Q–K2, R×N! 14 P×R! Q×BP; 15 P–N5, N–R4 = . Kupreichik–Gufeld, USSR Chp. 1973. (B) 13 K–N1, N–B5 (13 . . . P–QN4; 14 P–N5!); 14 B×N, R×B; 15 N–N3, Q–Q1; 16 B–Q4, B–K3; 17 Q–K3, P–QR4; 18 B–N6 is promising.

(*i*) 16 P–R5, R×N; 17 P×R, B–K3; 18 K–N1; R–QB1; 19 B–Q4, R–B5; 20 P×P, RP×P. Bikhovski–Gik, Moscow 1968.

(*j*) 14 . . . B×B; 15 Q×B, R×N; 16 P×R. (A) 16 . . . Q×BP; 17 N–K2, Q–B4; 18 P–N4, N–KB3; 19 P–N5, N–R4; 20 R×N, P×R; 21 R–R1, Q–K6†; 22 K–N1, Q×BP; 23 R×P. (B) 16 . . . R–QB1; 17 K–N1, and Q–B1.

(*k*) 16 K×N, B×B; 17 Q×B, R×N! (Zaitsev's recipe against Khasin's 15 K–N1); 18 P–N4, N–B3; 19 P–N5, N–R4 = .

(*l*) (A) 13 Q–K2, P–QN4! 14 N/3×P, QR–N1; 15 P–QB4, P–QR3; 16 N–R3, B–K1 = . (B) 13 B–N5!? N–B5 (13 . . . Q–Q1; 14 KR–K1, N–B3; 15 P–B4!); 14 B×N/4, R×B; 15 N–N3, Q–K4; 16 KR–K1, R×N; 17 P×R, B–K3! 18 B–K3, R–B1; 19 B–Q4, Q–N4 with a slight advantage to White—analysis by Moles, Lilienthal and Tal.)

(*m*) 16 P–R5, R × N! 17 Q × R, Q × Q; 18 P × Q, N × RP; 19 B–Q4, B–K3; 20 KR–K1, N–B3; 21 P–K5, P × P; 22 B × KP, N–Q4; 23 K–N2, R–QB1 ∞. Ostojić–Honfi, Monte Carlo 1968.

(*n*) (A) 10 . . . P–KR4; 11 O–O–O, N–K4; 12 B–N3, R–B1; 13 B–N5, R–B4; (1) 14 K–N1? P–N4; 15 KR–K1, P–R4; 16 P–B4, N–B5; 17 B × N, P × B!. Barczay–Sosonko, Wijk aan Zee 1977. (2) 14 KR–K1, P–N4; 15 P–B4, N–B5; 16 B/3 × N, P × B; 17 B × N, B × B; 18 P–K5, B–N2; 19 P–K6, B–B1; 20 P × P†, R × P; 21 N–K6 ±. Karpov–Sosonko, Tilburg 1979. (3) 14 P–B4, N–B5; 15 Q–Q3, P–N4; 16 P–K5, Q–N3; 17 B × N/B6, P × B; 18 P × P, B × P; 19 N–K4, B–N2; 20 P–B3, R–Q4 ±. Rodriquez–Gufeld, Barcelona 1979. (B) 10 . . . N–K4; 11 B–N3, P–KR4; 12 B–R6!

(*o*) 12 . . . N–B5?! 13 B × N, R × B; 14 O–O–O, Q–R4; 15 N–N3, Q–B2 = .

(*p*) 16 N/4–K2, Q–R4; 17 B–R6, B × B; 18 Q × B, KR–B1; 19 R–Q3! R/5–B4; 20 P–N5! R × P; 21 R–Q5, R × R; 22 N × R, R–K1; 23 N/2–B4, B–B3; 24 P–K5, B × N; 25 P × N, P × P; 26 Q × RP†, K–B1; 27 Q–R8†, K–K2; 28 N × B†, resigns. Karpov–Korchnoi, 2nd match game 1974.

1 P–K4, P–QB4; 2 N–KB3, P–Q3; 3 P–Q4, P×P; 4 N×P, N–KB3; 5 N–QB3, P–KN3

	31	32	33	34	35
6	P–KN3	B–N5	P–B4 P–B4! (*d*) (Levenfish Variation)		
	N–B3! (*a*)	B–N2	N–B3 (*e*)		QN–Q2
7	B–N2	Q–Q2	N×N	B–N5	B–K2
	N×N!	N–B3	P×N	Q–B2! (*i*)	B–N2
8	Q×N	O–O–O	P–K5	N–Q5	B–K3
	B–N2	O–O	P×P (*f*)	N×N	O–O
9	O–O	N–N3	Q×Q†	P×N	B–B3
	O–O	R–K1	K×Q	P–QR3	N–N3 (*k*)
10	Q–Q3 (*b*)	P–B3	P×P	B×N†	Q–K2
	B–K3	P–QR3	N–N5 (*g*)	P×B	P–K4
11	N–Q5	K–N1	B–KB4	N×P	N–N3
	N×N	P–N4	B–K3	B–KN2	N–N5
12	P×N	P–KR4	N–K4	B–K3	B×N/4
	B–B4 =	B–K3 (*c*)	N–B2 (*h*)	B–N2 (*j*)	Q–R5† (*l*)

(*a*) If 6 . . . B–N2; 7 B–N2, O–O; 8 P–KR3, N–B3; 9 N/4–K2! B–Q2; 10 O–O, R–B1; 11 N–Q5, N×N; 12 P×N, N–K4; 13 P–QR4! ± .

(*b*) 10 P–KR3, B–K3; 11 Q–Q1, Q–R4; 12 N–Q5, B×N; 13 P×B, N–Q2; 14 P–QB3, B–B3 = . Janosević–Martinović, Smederevska Palanka 1978. The column is *Comments*.

(*c*) 13 P–N4, N–K4 = . Poulsen–Cortlever, Buenos Aires 1939. For 8 B–K2 see col. 44.

(*d*) (A) 6 N–Q5, B–N2; 7 B–N5†, B–Q2; 8 O–O, O–O; 9 R–K1, N–B3 = . (B) Solid is 6 B–QB4, B–N2; 7 O–O, N–B3; 8 B–K♯, O–O; 9 P–KR3, B–Q2; 10 B–N3, Q–R4; 11 R–K1, KR–K1; 12 Q–K2, Q–R4 = .

(*e*) (A) 6 . . . B–N2; 7 P–K5, P×P; 8 P×P, KN–Q2; 9 P–K6, N–K4; 10 B–N5†, QN–B3; 11 P×P†, K×P; 12 O–O† ± . (B) 6 . . . P–QR3! 7 B–QB4, B–N2; 8 B–N3, O–O; 9 B–K3, N–B3; 10 P–KR3, B–Q2; 11 Q–Q3 (or 11 Q–B3!?), P–QN4; 12 O–O–O (or 12 O–O!?), R–B1; 13 P–N4, P–N5; 14 N/3–K2, P–QR4 ∞ . Hübner–Hort, Baguio 1978.

(*f*) 8 . . . N–Q2; 9 P×P, P×P; 10 B–K3, Q–K2? 11 Q–Q4, N–B3; 12 O–O–O, P–Q4; 13 R–K1, B–K3; 14 P–KN4! B–K2 (14 . . . B×N2; 15 B–B2, B–K3; 16 P–B5, P×P; 17 B–R4, B–N2; 18 R–N1†); 15 P–B5, O–O; 16 P–N5! B×P; 17 P×N, B×KBP; 18 Q–B5, KR–K1; 19 Q×Q, R×Q; 20 B–Q2, B–K5; 21 N×B, P×N; 22 B–QB4, B–Q5; 23 B–KN5, resigns. Peters-Zaltsman, U.S. Chp. 1980.

(*g*) 10 . . . N–Q4; 11 N×N, P×N; 12 B–KN5, P–KR3; 13 B–R4, P–N4; 14 B–B2 ± . *Comments*.

(*h*) 13 N–B5, B×KP; 14 O–O–O†, K–B2; 15 N×B†, P×N; 16 B×B†, N×B; 17 R–K1, K–Q3; 18 P–KN3, N–N5; 19 B–B4, P–K4; 20 R–K2 with a minimal pull. Boleslavski.

(*i*) An older try is 7 . . . B–Q2; 8 B×N, B×B; 9 P–K5, P×P; 10 P×P, N–K5; 11 N×N, B×N; 12 O–O, B–N2 (Penrose-Barden, Hastings 1957–8); 13 B–B4 = . *Comments*.

(*j*) 13 B–Q4, B×B; 14 Q×B, O–O; 15 O–O, B×N = . Schmid–Parma, Malaga 1963.

(*k*) 9 . . . P–QR3; 10 O–O, Q–B2; 11 K–R1, P–K4! (Boleslavski); 12 N–N3, P–QN4 = .

(*l*) 13 P–N3, Q×B; 14 Q×B, B×Q ∞ . Keene.

1 P–K4, P–QB4; 2 N–KB3, P–Q3; 3 P–Q4, P×P; 4 N×P, N–KB3; 5 N–QB3, P–KN3; 6 B–K2, B–N2; 7 B–K3, N–B3; 8 O–O, O–O

	36	37	38	39	40
9	N–N3		Q–Q2	P–B4 (*g*)	Zollner
	B–K3		N–KN5 (*d*)	Q–N3	Gambit
10	P–B4		B×N	Q–Q3!	P–K5
	N–QR4	Q–B1	B×B	N–KN5	P×P
11	P–B5	Q–K1 (*b*)	P–B4 (*e*)	N–Q5	P×P
	B–B5	N–KN5	N×N	B×N!	N×P
12	N×N	B×N	B×N	B×N	N–B5
	B×B	B×B	P–K4	B×B†	Q×P
13	Q×B	P–B5	B–K3	Q×B	N×P†
	Q×N	P×P	P×P	Q×P	K–R1
14	P–KN4	P–KR3	R×P	B×B	B–Q4
	QR–B1	B×P	B–K3	QR×B	Q–N5!
15	P–N5	P×B	R–B2	QR–N1	B×N
	R×N	P×P	B–K4	Q×RP	Q×N/2
16	P×N	Q–R4	B–Q4	R×P	Q–Q4
	R×B (*a*)	P–B4 (*c*)	R–B1 (*f*)	P–K3 ±	N–K1 (*h*)

(*a*) 17 Q×R, B×P; 18 P–B3, R–B1; 19 P–QR3, R–B5; 20 QR–K1, P–QN4! Simagin.

(*b*) 11 P–KR3, R–Q1 (Flohr's move); 12 B–B3, B–B5; 13 R–B2, P–K4! 14 P–B5, P×P = . Steinmeyer–Benko, US Chp. 1963. 11 . . . P–QR4 is a good precaution.

(*c*) 17 K–R1! R–B2; 18 R–KN1, N–K4; 19 N–Q5, Q–Q2; 20 N–Q4, N–N3; 21 R×N! P×R; 22 R–KN1, P–K4; 23 R×P! Q–Q1; 24 B–N5, Q–R4; 25 N–B6†, K–B1; 26 N–K6† + . Domnitz–Kraidman, Tel Aviv 1964.

(*d*) Doubtful is the over-rated defence 9 . . . P–Q4? e.g. (A) 10 N×N, P×N; 11 P–K5, N–K5!. If 11 . . . N–Q2; 12 P–B4, P–K3; 13 N–R4, P–B3; 14 N–B5, N×N; 15 B×N, R–B2; 16 Q–K3 ± . Korn–Winter, London 1949. (B) 10 KR–Q1! N×N; 11 Q×N, N×P; 12 Q×QP, N–Q3; 13 Q–N3, B–K3; 14 N–Q5, B×N (14 . . . P–N3; 15 B–KB4); 15 R×B ± . *Comments*. If (c) 10 P×P, N×P; 11 N/3×N, N×N; (1) 12 B–QB4, B–K3 (12 . . . N–B4; 13 B–B5, P–K3; 14 N–K7†, N×N =); 13 B×N, B×N; 14 B×B/7, B×B; 15 Q–R6, B×R; 16 B×R, Q×B; 17 Q×Q†, K×Q; 18 K×B, drawn. Honfi–Trifunović, Kecskemét 1968. (2) 12 P–QB4, P–K4; 13 P–B4, B–K3; 14 P×P, N×B†; 15 Q×N, B×N; 16 QR–Q1, Q–K2 = . Gufeld and Lazarev in *Byulleten* 1969.

(*e*) (A) 11 N–Q5, B–Q2! 12 P–QB4, N–K4; 13 P–QN3, P–K3 = . (B) 11 P–B3, B–Q2; 12 QR–Q1, R–B1; 13 R–B2, Q–R4; 14 N–N3, B×N! = .

(*f*) 17 R–Q1, Q–R4; 18 P–QR3, R–B5; 19 N–K2, Q×Q; 20 R×Q, drawn. Unzicker–Geller, W. Germany–USSR, 1960.

(*g*) If 9 K–R1, P–Q4! but not 9 . . . B–K3; 10 P–B4, Q–B1; 11 B–B3, B–B5; 12 R–KN1 ± . McKelvie–Soltis, Manhattan C. C. 1969. The column is *Comments*.

(*h*) 17 B×B†, N×B; 18 B–Q3, B–K3 ∞ . Levy.

1 P–K4, P–QB4; 2 N–KB3, P–Q3; 3 P–Q4, P×P; 4 N×P, N–KB3; 5 N–QB3, P–KN3; 6 B–K2, B–N2

	41	42	43	44	45
7	(B–K3)...........			O–O.......	N–N3
	(N–B3)			N–B3	N–B3
8	P–KR4......	N–N3		N–N3(g)	P–N4
	P–KR4 (a)	O–O		O–O	P–N3
9	P–B3	P–B4		P–B4 (h)	P–B4
	O–O	N–QR4 (c)		P–QN4!	B–N2
10	Q–Q2	P–KN4!?		B–B3	B–B3
	P–Q4	P–N3!.......	B–K3	P–N5	O–O
11	N×N	P–N5	P–N5 (e)	N–Q5	P–KR4
	P×N	N–Q2	N–Q2	N×N	P–QR4
12	P–K5	O–O	B–Q4	P×N	P–R4
	N–K1	B–N2	P–B3	N–R4	N–N5
13	P–B4	B–Q3	P–KR4	N×N	P–R5
	P–B3	R–B1	P×P	Q×N	P–Q4
14	O–O–O	N×N	B×B	R–K1	P–K5
	P×P (b)	P×N (d)	K×B (f)	R–K1 =	N×NP! (i)

(a) 8 . . . O–O; 9 P–R5, P–Q4; 10 RP×P, RP×P; 11 N×N! P×N; 12 P–K5, N–K5; 13 N×N, P×N; 14 B–Q4, Q–R4†; 15 B–B3, Q–Q4; 16 Q–B1 ± . Botvinnik.

(b) 15 P×P, B×P; 16 P–KN4, B×NP; 17 B×B, P×B; 18 P–R5, P–N4 = . Smyslov–Botvinnik, match 1958.

(c) (A) 9 . . . P–QR4; 10 P–QR4, B–K3; 11 O–O! (1) 11 . . . Q–B1; 12 N–Q4, B–N5; 13 N/4–N5, B×B; 14 Q×B, Q–N5; 15 Q–B2, QR–B1; 16 P–R3, Q–K3; 17 Q–B3, N–QN5; 18 R–B2 ± , or (2) 11 . . . R–B1; 12 P–B5, B×N; 13 P×B, N–QN5; 14 B–QB4, N–Q2; 15 Q–K2! Liberzon–Pavlenko, USSR 1968. (B) 9 . . . P–QR3; 10 P–N4, P–K4; 11 P–N5, P×P; 12 B×BP, N–K1 ∞ (c) 9 . . . P–K4; 10 O–O, P–QR4; 11 P–QR4, P×P = . Pachman.

(d) 15 Q–K1, N–B4; 16 P–B5, B–K4; 17 Q–R4, P–K3; 18 P–B6, P–KR4; 19 B–K2, K–R2; 20 B×P, R–KR1∞ . Van den Burg–Rajković, Ørebro 1966.

(e) 11 P–B5, B–B5; 12 P–K5, B×B! 13 Q×B, N–Q2; 14 P–B6, KP×P; 15 P×QP∞ .

(f) 15 N–Q4, B–N1; 16 P–B5, Q–N3! = . Gufeld and Lazarev.

(g) 8 B–KN5, O–O; 9 N×N!? (9 N–N3 is usual), P×N; 10 Q–Q2, R–N1; 11 QR–N1, R–K1; 12 B–R6, B–R1; 13 P–QN4!? B–K3; 14 P–KR3, P–Q4!? (14 . . . N–Q2 to N3 to B5! or . . . B–B5 was positionally called for — perhaps Black intended to "confuse" the program); 15 P×P (15 P–K5, N–Q2; 16 P–B4, P–B3∞), N×P; 16 N×N, Q×N; 17 Q×Q, P×Q; 18 B–KB4, QR–B1; 19 B–QN5, KR–Q1; 20 B–Q3, B–B6; 21 B–QR6, R–B3; 22 B–QN5, R/3–B1 = . Computer 4.9 — P. Benjamin (2050), Stanford U., August 1980.

(h) (A) 9 B–KN5, B–K3 (or 9 . . . P–QR4; 10 P–QR4, B–K3; 11 Q–Q2, R–B1; 12 QR–Q1, N–K4; 13 N–Q4, B–B5; 14 N/4–N5, B×N = . Vitolins–Georgadze, USSR Chp. prelims, 1976); 10 K–R1, N–Q2; 11 P–B4, N–N3; 12 P–B5, B–B5 = . Torre–Sosonko, Bad Lauterberg 1977. (B) 9 K–R1, B–K3; 10 P–B4, Q–B1; 11 B–B3, B–B5; 12 R–B2, R–Q1; 13 N–Q5, P–K3; 14 N×N†, B×N = . Sigurjonsson–Miles, Hastings 1975–6. The column is H. Steiner–Evans, match 1952.

(i) 15 N–Q4! N–KR3; 16 P×P, BP×P! 17 N–K6, Q–Q2; 18 N×R, R×N; 19 N–N5, P–Q5 = . Smyslov–Korchnoi, Moscow 1960. The sequence in cols. 44 and 45 usually arises after 1 P–K4, P–QB4; 2 N–KB3, N–QB3; 3 P–Q4, P×P; 4 N×P, N–B3; 5 N–QB3, P–Q3; 6 B–K2, P–KN3; and by 7 N–N3. White evasively prevents exchanges. *Comments.*

1 P–K4, P–QB4; 2 N–KB3, P–Q3; 3 P–Q4

	46	47	48	49	50
	P×P				N–KB3
4	(N×P)	Q×P		P–B3	P×P (n)
	(N–KB3)	N–QB3	P–QR3	P×P	N×P
5	P–KB3	B–QN5	B–K3	N×P	P×P
	P–K4! (a)	B–Q2 (d)	N–KB3	N–QB3	P–K3
6	B–N5† (b)	B×N	N–B3	B–QB4	Q–Q3
	B–Q2 (c)	B×B	N–B3	P–K3 (j)	N×QP
7	B×B†	P–B4 (e)	Q–N6	O–O	N–B3
	QN×B	N–B3	Q×Q	P–QR3? (k)	N–B3
8	N–B5	N–B3	B×Q	Q–K2	B–B4
	P–Q4	P–K3 (f)	P–N3	N–B3 (l)	P–B3
9	P×P	B–N5 (g)	O–O–O	R–Q1	O–O–O
	Q–R4†	B–K2	B–R3†	Q–B2	P–K4
10	N–B3	O–O	K–N1	B–KN5?	N–QN5 ±
	N–N3 ∓	O–O (h)	O–O (i)	B–K2 (m)	

(a) Black has too many good choices, including (A) 5 . . . N–B3; 6 P–QB4, P–K3; 7 N–B3, B–K2; 8 B–K3, O–O; 9 N–B2, P–Q4! 10 BP×P, P×P; 11 N×P, N×N; 12 Q×N, Q–B2 ∞. Lombardy–Fischer, US Chp. 1961. (B) 5 . . . P–K3; 6 P–QB4, N–B3; 7 N–B3, B–K2; 8 B–K3, O–O; 9 B–K2, P–Q4 = .

(b) If 6 N–N3, P–Q4; 7 B–N5, B–K3! 8 P×P, Q×P; (A) 9 N–B3, B–QN5; 10 B–Q2, Q–Q1; 11 B–N5†, N–B3; 12 Q–K2, O–O; 13 B×N, P×B; 14 O–O–O, Q–B2 = . (B) 9 QN–Q2, B–K2; 10 B–QB4, Q–B3; 11 Q–K2, O–O; 12 O–O, P–KR3; 13 B–R4, QN–Q2; 14 B×B, Q×B = . Lombardy–Evans, New Jersey Open 1959.

(c) 6 . . . QN–Q2; 7 N–N3! P–QR3; 8 B–K2, P–QN4; 9 P–QR4, P×P; 10 R×P, N–N3; 11 R–R1, P–Q4 = . The column is Euwe's analysis.

(d) Novel is 5 . . . P–K3; 6 O–O, KN–K2; 7 P–B4, P–QR3; 8 B×N†, N×B; 9 Q–Q3, B–K2; 10 N–B3, O–O; 11 R–Q1, Q–B2; 12 B–K3, N–K4 ∞.

(e) 7 N–B3! N–B3; 8 B–N5, P–K3; 9 O–O–O, B–K2; (A) 10 P–K5, P×P; 11 Q×P, Q–N1; 12 Q–K2, O–O; 13 N–K5, Q–B2; 14 R–Q3, N–Q4; 15 B–Q2, QR–B1; 16 R–R3! N×N; 17 B×N, B–KR1 ∞. (B) 10 KR–K1, O–O; 11 K–N1, Q–R4; 12 Q–Q2, Q–N3; 13 N–Q4, KR–Q1; 14 P–B3, B–K1; 15 P–KN4, Q–B2; 16 P–KR4, P–N4 = . E.C.O.

(f) 8 . . . P–KN3; 9 B–N5, B–N2; 10 O–O = . Archives. If 10 N–Q5, B×N! = .

(g) 9 O–O, B–K2; 10 P–QN3, O–O; 11 B–N2, P–QR3 = .

(h) 11 KR–K1, P–KR3; 12 B–R4, P–R3; 13 QR–Q1, Q–R4; 14 Q–Q2, Q–N3; 15 N–Q4, QR–B1; 16 R–K3, KR–K1 ∞. Schweber–Najdorf, Buenos Aires 1970.

(i) 11 N–Q4, B–Q2; 12 P–B3, N–K4; 13 N–N3 (Benko–Vukcević, Telematch New York–Cleveland 1977), KR–B1; 14 N–R5, B–B3; 15 N–Q5, B×N; 16 P×B, N/3–Q2; 17 B–Q4, P–N3 = . Comments.

(j) (A) 6 . . . P–QR3, threatening N–B3 and B–N5, forcing White to lose a tempo with P–KR3 is noteworthy. For (B) 6 . . . P–KN3 see col. 185. (c) 6 . . . N–B3; 7 P–K5!

(k) Instead of this move, with lines similar to col. 172, Black may also branch off with (A) 7 . . . KN–K2; 8 B–KN5, P–QR3 (8 . . . Q–Q2; 9 Q–K2, N–N3; 10 QR–Q1); and now (1) 9 P–QR4, P–R3; 10 B–K3, N–N3; 11 N–Q2, B–K2; 12 P–B4, B–B3; 13 N–N3, O–O; 14 P–R5, B×N; 15 P×B (Capello–Saidy, Venice 1969), P–Q4! 16 P×P, P×P; 17 B×P, Q–B3! ∞. Archives. (2) 9 Q–K2, P–R3; 10 B–K3, B–Q2; 11 QR–Q1, N–N3; 12 N–Q4, N×N; 13 B×N, P–K4 = . (B) 7 . . . N–B3; 8 Q–K2, B–K2; 9 R–Q1, P–K4; 10 P–KR3, O–O; 11 B–K3! (11 P–QN3, P–QR3; 12 B–R3, Q–R4! ∓), B–K3; 12 P–QN4, R–B1 = . Marić.

(*l*) 8 . . . B–K2; 9 R–Q1, Q–B2; 10 B–B4, N–K4; 11 B × N, P × B; 12 B–N5†, P × B; 13 N × NP, Q–R4; 14 QR–B1, P–B3 (better 14 . . . N–B3); 15 R–B7, Q–R5; 16 Q–Q3, P–QN3; 17 P–QN3, Q × RP; 18 Q–Q8†, resigns. Tilette–Giacomelli, corr. 1968.

(*m*) 11 QR–B1, O–O; 12 B–N3, P–R3; 13 B–KB4, P–K4; 14 B–K3, Q–Q1; 15 N–Q5, N × N; 16 B × N, B–Q2 = . Fischer–Korchnoi, Buenos Aires 1960. 10 B–B4! ± was stronger. The column is the Tartakover–Morra Gambit with Matulović, Ken Smith *et al.* sharing in the research. Also compare cols. 172 and 185.

(*n*) (A) 4 N–B3, B–N5! (4 . . . P × P see main lines); 5 B–K2, N–B3; 6 B–N5, Q–R4; 7 Q–Q2, P × P; 8 B × N, NP × B; 9 N × P, B × B; 10 N/4 × B, O–O–O; 11 O–O, P–K3 = . *Comments.* (B) 4 B–N5†, B–Q2; 5 B × B†, Q × B; 6 N–B3, P × P; 7 N × P, P–KN3; 8 O–O, B–N2 = . (C) 4 P–Q5 would lead into the Old Benoni, but here the sequence would be antipositional and to no advantage. The column is Cortlever–Kottnauer, Beverwijk 1947, but 5 . . . Q × P! would have been better than 5 . . . P–K3? in the text.

1 P–K4, P–QB4; 2 N–KB3, P–Q3

	51	52	53	54	55
3	P–B3		P–KN3 (*e*)	N–B3	P–QN4 (*l*)
	N–KB3		P–KN3	N–KB3! (*i*)	P×P (*m*)
4	B–Q3	P–Q3	B–N2	P–K5	P–Q4
	N–B3	P–KN3	B–N2	P×P	N–KB3
5	B–B2 (*a*)	P–KN3	O–O	N×P	B–Q3
	B–N5 (*b*)	B–N2	N–QB3	P–QR3	P–Q4 (*n*)
6	P–KR3	QN–Q2	P–B3	B–K2 (*j*)	QN–Q2
	B–R4	O–O	P–K4! (*f*)	P–K3	P×P
7	P–Q3	B–N2	P–Q3 (*g*)	O–O	N×P
	P–Q4	P–K4	KN–K2	Q–B2	QN–Q2
8	Q–K2	O–O	N–R4!	N–B4	N/4–N5
	P–K3	N–B3	O–O	P–QN4	Q–B2
9	QN–Q2	P–QR4	P–KB4	N–K3	P–B4
	B–K2 (*c*)	P–KR3 (*d*)	P×P (*h*)	B–Q3 (*k*)	P–KR3 (*o*)

(*a*) 5 O–O, P–KN3; 6 B–B2, B–N5; 7 P–KR3, B×N; 8 Q×B, B–N2; 9 Q–K2, O–O; 10 P–Q3, P–QN4; 11 B–K3, R–B1 = . Czerniak–Ståhlberg, Mar del Plata 1943.

(*b*) Or (A) 5 . . . P–K4; 6 P–Q4, Q–B2; 7 P×KP, P×P; 8 N–R3, P–QR3; 9 N–B4, P–KN3; 10 B–N5, B–K2; 11 B×N, B×B; 12 B–N3, O–O; 13 N–K3, P–QN4; 14 B–Q5, B–Q2; 15 P–KR4! QR–Q1; 16 P–R5, N–K2; 17 P×P, RP×P; 18 Q–K2, K–N2; 19 O–O–O, R–KR1 = . Lombardy–Evans, match 1962. (B) 5 . . . P–KN3; 6 O–O, B–N2; 7 P–KR3, O–O; 8 P–Q4, P×P; 9 P×P, N–QN5; 10 N–B3, N×B. Kopec.

(*c*) 10 N–B1, Q–R4 = . Pfeiffer–Kottnauer, Helsinki 1952.

(*d*) 10 N–R4, P–Q4 = . Brasket–Evans, US Open Chp. 1960. Also compare Alapin's Line, col. 183, Réti Opening, col. 24 and Fianchetto Opening, col. 2.

(*e*) 3 P–Q3, P–K3; 4 P–KN3, P–Q4; see Réti Opening, Barcza System, col. 31.

(*f*) 6 . . . P–K3 (with transposition); 7 P–Q3, KN–K2; 8 R–K1, O–O; 9 P–Q4, P×P; 10 P×P, P–Q4; 11 P–K5, B–Q2; 12 N–B3, R–B1; 13 B–B4, N–R4; 14 R–QB1, P–QN4∞. Fischer–Panno, Buenos Aires 1970.

(*g*) 7 R–K1, KN–K2; 8 P–Q3, O–O ∞. Compare Réti Opening and Fianchetto Opening.

(*h*) 10 P×P, P–B4; 11 N–Q2, K–R1; 12 N/2–B3 ± . Ciocaltea–Fischer, Varna 1962.

(*i*) As usual, knights before bishops; as long as White does not waste time on P–KR3, . . . B–KN5 can wait. If at once 3 . . . B–N5; B–K2!, but not 4 P–KR3, B × N; 5 Q × B, N–QB3.

(*j*) 6 P–QR4, Q–B2; 7 P–Q4, P–K3; 8 B–K3, B–K2; 9 N–B4, QN–Q2; 10 P–Q5, P×P; 11 N×P, N×N; 12 Q×N, O–O; 13 B–Q3, N–B3; 14 Q–B3, B–N5; 15 Q–N3, Q×Q; 16 RP×Q, P–R3; 17 P–KB3, B–K3; 18 N–N6, QR–Q1; 19 K–B2, N–Q4; 20 N×N, B×N; 21 P–KN4, QR–K1 = . Gilden–R. Byrne, US Chp. 1973.

(*k*) 10 P–KR3, N–B3; 11 P–QR4, P–N5; 12 N–N1, B–N2; 13 P–Q3, N–Q5; 14 N–Q2, O–O; 15 N–B3, N×B†; 16 Q×N, KR–K1; 17 N–B4, P–K4; 18 N–N5, P–K5; 19 N×B, Q×N; 20 N×KP, N×N; 21 P×N, B×P; 22 B–K3, Q–QB3 with a promising game for Black. Tarjan–Mednis, US Chp. 1973.

(*l*) The Wing Gambit Deferred.

(*m*) Safe but timid is 3 . . . N–KB3; 4 P×P, N×P; 5 P×P, P–K3 (5 . . . N×QP/3; 6 B–N2 ±); 6 B–N2, Q–N3; 7 B–Q4, Q×P = .

(*n*) Also 5 . . . P–K3; 6 O–O, B–K2; 7 QN–Q2, P–Q4; 8 P–K5, KN–Q2; 9 N–K1, N–QB3; 10 Q–N4, O–O; 11 QN–B3, P–B4 ∓ . Corden–Gligorić, Hastings 1970–1.

(*o*) 10 N–R3, P–KN4; 11 N/R–N1, B–N2; 12 N–K2, P–K4; 13 N–N3, P–K5!; 14 Q–K2, O–O ∓ . Medina–Pomar, Santander 1947.

1 P–K4, P–QB4; 2 N–KB3

	56	57	58	59	60
	(P–Q3)	. . . .	N–QB3		
3	B–N5†		B–N5		
	B–Q2	N–B3 (f)	P–K3	P–KN3 (k)	
4	B×B†	O–O	N–B3 (h)	O–O (l)	
	Q×B(a)	P–QR3	KN–K2 (i)	B–N2	
5	O–O (b)	B×N†	O–O	P–B3	R–K1
	N–QB3 (c)	P×B	P–QR3	N–B3	P–K4
6	R–K1 (d)	P–Q4	B×N	R–K1	P–B3
	N–B3	P×P	N×B	O–O	KN–K2
7	P–B3	Q×P	P–Q4	P–Q4	P–Q4 (n)
	P–K3	P–K4	P×P	P×P	BP×P
8	P–Q3	Q–Q3	N×P	P×P	P×P
	B–K2	P–B3!	P–Q3	P–Q4	P×P
9	P–QR4	P–B4	N×N	P–K5	B–KB4
	O–O (e)	B–K3 (g)	P×N (j)	N–K5 (m)	P–QR3 (o)

(a) 4 . . . QN×B; 5 P–B4, KN–B3; 6 N–B3, P–KN3; 7 P–Q4, P×P; 8 N×P, B–N2; 9 O–O, O–O; 10 B–K3, P–QR3; 11 R–B1, R–B1; 12 P–QN3, Q–R4; 13 P–B3, P–K3!? 14 N/4–K2 (Shamkovich–Browne, U.S. Chp. 1980), Q–B2 = .

(b) 5 P–B4, (A) 5 . . . N–QB3; 6 N–B3, (1) 6 . . . P–KN3; 7 P–Q4, P×P; 8 N×P, B–N2 = . (2) 6 . . . N–B3; 7 P–Q4, P×P; 8 N×P, Q–N5; 9 O–O, Q×Q; 10 R×Q, N×N; 11 R×N, R–B1; 12 P–QN3, P–KN3; 13 B–N2, B–N2; drawn. Benko–Browne, U.S. Chp. 1980.

(c) 5 . . . N–KB3; 6 P–K5, P×P; 7 N×P, Q–B1; 8 P–Q4, P–K3; 9 N–QB3, N–B3; 10 N×N, Q×N; 11 B–N5, O–O–O; 12 B×N, P×B; 13 P–Q5, P×P; 14 Q–B3, R–Q3= . Gurgenidze–Petrosian, Moscow 1967.

(d) Also 6 P–B3, N–B3; 7 P–Q4, P×P; 8 P×P, P–Q4; 9 P–K5, N–KN1 = . Gurgenidze.

(e) 10 QN–Q2, Q–B2 = . del Corral–Benko, Mallorca 1968.

(f) 3 . . . N–Q2; 4 P–Q4, P×P; 5 Q×P, N–B3; (A) 6 B–N5, P–K3; 7 O–O, B–K2; 8 N–B3, O–O; 9 QR–Q1, Q–B2 = . *Comments.* Also the "Boleslavski–Pelikan" counter-thrust 5 . . . P–K4 or 6 . . . P–K4 has been employed, but might be positionally risky; e.g. (B) 6 O–O, P–K4; 7 Q–Q3, P–KR3; 8 P–B4, B–K2; 9 N–B3, O–O; 10 B×N, B×B; 11 P–QN3, P–R3; 12 P–QR4, Q–B2; 13 N–R4, KR–Q1; 14 B–K3, P–QN3; 15 P–B3, Q–N2; 16 KR–Q1, B–KB1; 17 P–KN4, B–K2; 18 N–N5, B×N; 19 NP×B, QR–N1; 20 K–R1, K–R2; 21 R–R2, Q–B3; 22 N–Q5, N–N1; 23 N–N4, Q–B1; 24 Q–Q5, R–B1; 25 R–KN1, N–B3; 26 Q–Q2, R–N1; 27 Q–KN2, P–QR4; 28 N–Q3, N–Q2; 29 Q–R3, B–B3; 30 Q–R5, Q–B1; 31 R/2–KN2, R–KR1; 32 N–B2, Q–K2; 33 N–N4, K–N1; 34 N×B†, Q×N; 35 B–B2, resigns. Peters–van Baarle, London 1978.

(g) 10 N–B3, Q–B2 ∞. Radovich–Lombardy, Leipzig 1960.

(h) 4 O–O, KN–K2; (A) 5 R–K1, P–QR3; 6 B–B1, P–Q3; 7 P–B3, N–N3; 8 P–Q4, B–Q2; 9 P×P, P×P = . (I) 5 P–B3, P–QR3; 6 B–R4, P–QN4; 7 B–B2, B–N2; 8 Q–K2, P–Q4 = . (C) 5 P–QN3, P–QR3; 6 B×N, N×B; 7 B–N2, P–Q3; 8 P–Q4, P×P; 9 N×P, B–Q2 = . Karaklajić–Cvetković, Yugoslav Chp. 1977.

(i) 4 . . . N–Q5; 5 O–O, P–QR3; 6 B–Q3, N–K2; 7 N×N, P×N; 8 N–K2, N–B3; 9 P–B3, B–B4; 10 P–QN4, B–R2; 11 P–QR4, O–O = . Gurgenidze–Dzhindzhihashvili, Gorki 1971.

(j) 10 Q–N4, P–KN3; 11 P–K5!? P–Q4! 12 B–N5, B–K2 = . Gurgenidze–Osnos, Alma Ata 1969.

(k) 3 . . . Q–N3; (A) 4 Q–K2, P–K3; 5 O–O, N–B3; 6 P–K5, N–Q4; 7 N–B3 (Gufeld–Korchnoi, USSR Chp, 1961), B–K2! = . (B) 4 N–B3, P–K3; 5 O–O, KN–K2; 6 R–K1, N–Q5; 7 B–QB4, N/2–B3; 8 P–Q3, B–K2; 9 N×N, P×N; 10 N–K2, O–O; 11 P–QB3, B–B3 = . Boehm–Miles, Amsterdam 1977.

(*l*) 4 P–B3, N–B3; 5 P–K5, N–Q4; 6 O–O, B–N2; 7 P–Q4, P × P; 8 P × P, O–O; 9 N–B3, N–B2; 10 B–QB4, P–Q3 peters out into equality. Nezhmetdinov.

(*m*) 10 N–B3, N × N; 11 P × N, N–R4; 12 B–N5, B–B4; 13 N–Q2, R–K1 = . Or 12 B–R3, B–Q2; 13 B–Q3, R–B1 = . Barendregt–Damjanović, Amsterdam 1969.

(*n*) 7 P–QR3, O–O; 8 P–QN4, P × P; 9 RP × P, P–Q4 = . Botvinnik–Veresov, USSR 1963.

(*o*) 10 B–R4, P–QN4; 11 B–QN3, P–Q3! = . *Archives*.

1 P–K4, P–QB4; 2 N–KB3, N–QB3; 3 P–Q4, P×P; 4 N×P, N–B3; 5 N–QB3, P–Q3; 6 B–KN5 (*a*), B–Q2 (Larsen's Variation)

	61	62	63	64	65
7	B×N	N–N3 (*d*)	.... P–B4	Q–Q3 (*h*)	
	NP×B	P–KR3	Q–N3 (*f*)	N×N (*i*)	
8	N–N3 (*b*)	B–R4	N–N3	Q×N	
	R–KN1	R–B1	N–KN5!	Q–R4	
9	P–N3	B–K2	Q–K2	P–B4	B–Q2
	P–B4	P–KN4	N–Q5	P–K4	P–K4 (*k*)
10	Q–K2	B–N3	N–Q5	Q–Q3	Q–Q3 (*l*)
	B–N2	P–KR4	N×Q	B–K2	Q–B2
11	P×P	P–KR4	N×Q	O–O–O	B–N5!
	B×P	P–N5	P×N	B–B3	B–K2
12	B–N2	B–KB4	K×N	K–N1	B×N
	Q–Q2	N–K4	P–R3	P×P	B×B
13	O–O	Q–Q4	B–R4	B×P	O–O–O
	B×N (*c*)	N–N3 (*e*)	P–KN4 (*g*)	O–O (*j*)	B–K2 (*m*)

(*a*) The thematic move of this attack, designed to prevent Black from veering into the Dragon Variation . . . P–KN3 when that is his intention. Thus the system is dubbed the "Anti-Dragon." The immediate threat is B × N and 6 . . . P–K3 used to be taken as the best and only answer. The text 6 . . . B–Q2 tries otherwise. For 6 P–B4 see col. 33.

(*b*) Discredited is 8 N–B5, Q–R4! 9 B–N5, P–QR3; 10 B–K2, B × N; 11 P × B, Q × BP: 12 N–Q5, R–B1; 13 O–O, R–KN1; 14 R–K1, P–K3; 15 P–QB4, B–K2; 16 N × B, K × N. *Archives.*

(*c*) 14 P × B, B–R6; 15 B × B, Q × B = . Barczay–Szilagyi, Hungarian Chp. 1969.

(*d*) 7 B–K2, (A) 7 . . . P–QR3; 8 O–O, P–K3; 9 Q–Q3, B–K2; 10 QR–Q1, N × N; 11 Q × N, B–B3; 12 R–Q3, Q–R4; 13 R–N3, Q–K4; 14 Q–Q2, N × P; 15 N × N, Q × N; 16 B × B, K × B = . (B) 7 . . . Q–R4; 8 B × N, NP × B; 9 N–N3, Q–KN4; 10 N–Q5, O–O–O = .

(*e*) 14 B–KN5, B–N2 (Damjanović–Stein, Tallinn 1969); 15 O–O = .

(*f*) If 7 . . . N–KN5; 8 N/4–N5, Q–N3; 9 Q–Q2 ± .

(*g*) 14 B–N3, P × P; 15 B × P, B–N2; 16 P–B3, B–QB3 = . Matulović–Masić, Sombor 1968.

(*h*) Obviously the sharpest move trying to forestall (7 Q–Q2), R–B1! Inferior is 7 N–N3, P–KR3 or P–K3.

(*i*) (A) 7 . . . P–QR3!? 8 O–O–O, P–N4; 9 N × N, B × N; 10 Q–K3! Q–N1; 11 B–Q3, P–R3; 12 B × N, NP × B; 13 P–B4 ± . (B) 7 . . . R–B1; 8 N × N, B × N; 9 O–O–O!

(*j*) 14 B–K2, KR–K1; 15 B–B3, B–B1; 16 N–Q5, N–Q2; 17 Q–Q2, Q × Q; 18 R × Q, QR–B1; 19 KR–Q1, N–K4; 20 P–QN3, drawn. Liberzon–Stein, USSR Chp. 1969–70.

(*k*) (A) 9 . . . Q–B2; 10 N–Q5! (10 B–QB4, P–K3; 11 B–N3, B–K2; 12 P–B4, O–O; 13 R–KB1, P–QN4! = . R. Byrne–Benko, US Chp. 1969), N × N; 11 P × N, Q × P (11 . . . Q–B4!); 12 R–B1, Q–KB4; 13 B–Q3, Q–K4†; 14 Q × Q, P × Q; 15 R–B7, R–QN1! 16 O–O, P–K3; 17 P × P, B × P; 18 B–N5† ± . *Misl* 1970/6. (B) 9 . . . R–B1; 10 O–O–O, P–QR3 = . See col. 66.

(*l*) 10 Q–K3, R–B1; 11 B–Q3, P–QR3; 12 O–O, B–K2; 13 Q–N3, N–R4; 14 Q–B3, N–B3; 15 P–QR4, B–K3; 16 Q–K2, Q–B2; 17 K–R1, O–O; 18 P–B4, P × P = .

(*m*) 14 N–N5, B × N; 15 Q × B†, Q–B3; 16 Q–Q5, Q × Q; 17 R × Q ± . Bronstein–Stein, USSR 1969. There is room for Black improvements.

1 P–K4, P–QB4; 2 N–KB3, N–QB3; 3 P–Q4, P×P; 4 N×P, N–B3; 5 N–QB3, P–Q3; 6 B–KN5, B–Q2; 7 Q–Q2, R–B1; 8 O–O–O (*a*), N×N; 9 Q×N

	66	67	68	69	70
	Q–R4!				R×N!?
10	B–Q2	B–K3	P–B4		Q×R
	P–QR3	P–QR3	P–K3	R×N (*e*)	N×P
11	B–QB4	P–B3	P–K5	P×R	Q–K3
	Q–QB4	P–K3	P×P	P–K4	N×B
12	Q×Q	Q–N6	P×P	Q–N4	Q×N
	R×Q	Q×Q	R×N	Q×Q	Q–N3
13	B–N3	B×Q	B–Q2	P×Q	B–B4
	P–KN3	B–B3	Q×RP	N×P (*f*)	P–K3
14	B–K3	B–B4	B×R		Q–N3
	R–B1 (*b*)	B×P (*c*)	P–KN3 = (*d*)		P–KN3 (*g*)

(*a*) Safe, but limited in scope, are (A) 8 P–B4, P–KR3; 9 B×N, NP×B; 10 O–O–O, N×N; 11 Q×N, Q–R4; 12 B–B4, Q–B4; 13 B–N3, Q×Q; 14 R×Q, P–K3; 15 B–R4, B×B; 16 R×B, P–R3; 17 R–B1, P–KR4 = . Platonov–Stein, USSR Chp. 1969. (B) 8 N–N3, (1) 8 . . . P–K3; 9 O–O–O, P–QR3; 10 P–B4, B–K2 = . Or (2) 8 . . . P–KR3 = . (c) 8 P–B3, P–QR3; 9 O–O–O, N×N; 10 Q×N, Q–R4 = .

(*b*) 15 B–Q4, B–N2; 16 N–Q5, N–R4; 17 B×B, N×B; 18 P–K5, R–B3; 19 N–N4, R–N3 = . Benko–R. Byrne, US Open Chp. 1968. In the column, if 10 . . . P–K4; 11 Q–Q3, P–QR3; 12 K–N1 (also 12 P–QR3), P–R3; 13 P–B3, Q–B2; 14 P–KN3, B–K2; 15 P–KR4, P–QN4 = . Polgar–Nagy, Hungarian Chp. 1972.

(*c*) 15 B×KP, P×B; 16 N×B, N×N; 17 P×N, B–K2; 18 KR–B1, B–N4†; 19 K–N1, K–K2; 20 P–B3, KR–B1; 21 K–B2, R×R; 22 R×R, R–B1; drawn. Suetin–Gheorghiu, Hastings 1967/8.

(*d*) Analysis by Markland.

(*e*) This, and Black's 13th move in the column are crucial in this line. If (A) 11 B×N, R–B2! 12 B×NP, P–K4!   ; or (B) 11 Q×R? Q×Q; 12 P×Q, N×P; 13 B–R4, P–KN3! ∓. O'Kelly–Radulov, Havana 1969.

(*f*) The modern revival started with (A) 14 B–B4, (1) 14 . . . P–N4; 15 B–Q5, N–B6; 16 P×P, P–KR3; 17 B–R4, P–N4; 18 B–KN3, N–K7†; 19 K–N2, N×B; 20 P×N, B–N2; drawn. Janošević–Larsen, Belgrade 1964. (2) 14 . . . P–B4; 15 KR–K1, N×B; 16 P×N, P–KN3; 17 B–Q5, B–B1; 18 P–B4, P–K5; 19 P–N3, P–KR3; 20 P×P, B×P†; 21 K–B2, K–K2; 22 K–N3, B–N2; 23 R–K2, P–N3 = . Matsukevich–Furman, Leningrad 1969. (B) 14 R–K1, N×B; 15 P×N, B–K2; 16 P–KR4, P–KR3; 17 P×P, R×P! 18 P–R5, B–N4†; 19 K–N1, B–Q7; 20 R–K4, P–B4; 21 R–QB4, K–Q1; 22 P–B3, B–KN4; 23 P–N5, B×P; 24 R–QN4, B–QB3; 25 R–R3, K–B2; 26 P–B4 = . Zuidema–Pickett, Holland 1969. (c) 14 B–R4, P–KN4; 15 P×P, B–K2; 16 R–K1, P–Q4; 17 B–Q3, P–KR3; 18 P–B4, P×NP; 19 P×P, R×B; 20 R×N, R×R; 21 B×R, P–B4; 22 B–B2, B×P; 23 P–KR4, P×P; 24 R×P, B–R6†; 25 K–Q2, K–K2; drawn. Unzicker–Gheorghiu, Ljubljana 1969.

(*g*) 15 B–N3, B–K2; 16 P–KR4, P–KR4; 17 KR–K1, Q–N5; 18 Q–K3, P–R4; Bednarski–Simagin, Polanica Zdroj 1968; 19 Q–Q4 ± .

1 P-K4, P-QB4; 2 N-KB3, N-QB3; 3 P-Q4, P×P; 4 N×P, N-B3; 5 N-QB3, P-Q3; 6 B-KN5, P-K3; 7 Q-Q2, B-K2; 8 O-O-O

	71	72	73	74	75
	N×N		O-O		
9	Q×N		N-N3		KN-N5
	O-O		Q-N3	P-QR3	Q-R4
10	P-B4 (a)		P-B3	B×N	B×N
	P-KR3?	Q-R4	P-QR3 (h)	P×B	B×B
11	B-R4	B-B4	P-N4	B-K2	N×QP
	Q-R4	B-Q2	R-Q1	K-R1	R-Q1
12	B-QB4 (b)	B-N3 (e)	B-K3	B-R5	P-B4
	P-K4 (c)	B-B3 (f)	Q-B2	B-Q2	P-K4
13	P×P	KR-B1	P-KR4	P-B4	Q-Q5
	P×P	P-N4!?	P-QN4	P-N4	Q-B2
14	Q-Q3	B×N	P-N5	K-N1 (j)	P-B5
	Q-B4 (d)	B×B (g)	N-Q2 (i)		N-Q5 (k)

(a) Black's early exchange of Knights (which can also be postponed or avoided) allows White here the choice (A) 10 P-K5, P×P; 11 Q×KP, B-Q2! 12 P-KR4, R-B1; 13 R-R3, Q-B2 (13 . . . R-B4; 14 Q-K3, Q-B1; 15 R-N3, R-Q1; 16 P-R5, Q-B3; 17 P-R6, P-KN3 =); 14 Q×Q, R×Q; 15 N-N5, B×N; 16 B×B, P-KR3; with minimal advantage for White. (B) 10 P-B3, Q-R4; 11 B-R4, B-Q2; 12 P-QR3, KR-B1; 13 Q-N4, Q-B2; 14 B-N3, P-QR4; 15 Q-N3 (15 Q-Q4, P-K4; 16 Q-Q2, B-K3; 17 B-K2 =), Q-B4 ∓. Pilnik–Euwe, Munich 1958.

(b) 12 P-K5, P×P; 13 Q×P, Q×Q! 14 P×Q, N-Q4; 15 B×B, N×B; 16 B-Q3, P-QN3! 17 B-K4, R-N1; 18 KR-K1, B-N2; 19 R-Q7, B×B; 20 R×B, N-B3; 21 N-N5, KR-Q1; drawn. Unzicker–Darga, Madrid 1967.

(c) 12 . . . R-Q1; 13 KR-B1, Q-R4; 14 P-KN3, B-Q2; 15 P-B5, P×P; 16 P×P, B×P; 17 QR-K1, P-Q4; 18 R×B/7, P×B; 19 Q-B2! B-R6; 20 P-KN4 +.

(d) 15 B×N (or 15 B-N3), B×B; 16 N-Q5 ±. Boleslavski.

(e) (A) 12 P-K5, P×P; 13 P×P, B-B3; 14 B-Q2, N-Q2; 15 N-Q5, Q-Q1; 16 N×B†, Q×N; 17 KR-K1, KR-Q1 ∞. *Archives.* (B) 12 K-N1, B-B3; 13 KR-B1, P-KR3 (or 13 . . . QR-Q1; 14 P-B5, P-Q4); 14 B-R4, Q-R4; 15 B-KN3, Q-QB4; 16 B-R4; drawn. R. Byrne–Larsen, US Open Chp. 1968. (C) 12 KR-K1, KR-Q1; 13 B-N3, P-KR3; 14 B-KR4, Q-R4! *Comments.*

(f) Also 12 . . . KR-Q1; 13 KR-B1, QR-B1; 14 P-B5, Q-B4 =. Kotkov.

(g) 15 Q×QP, B×N; 16 Q×B, QR-B1; 17 Q-Q7 (Polugayevski–Osnos, USSR Chp. 1969), QR-Q1; 18 Q-K7, B-Q7†; 19 K-N1, B×P; 20 R×R, Q×R! ∞. 13 . . . KR-Q1 seems safest.

(h) 10 . . . R-Q1; 11 B-K3, Q-B2; 12 Q-B2 (or 12 P-N4! *P/E*), N-Q2; 13 N-N5, Q-N1; 14 P-N4, P-QR3; 15 N/5-Q4 ±. Fischer–Benko, US Chp. 1960.

(i) Black is about to gain the initiative and White counters with 15 P-N6! BP×P (or 13 . . . RP×P); 16 P-R5, P×P; 17 R×P, N-B3; 18 R-N5, N-K4; 19 Q-N2, B-B1; 20 P-B4 (20 B-K2, B-N2; 21 P-R3, P-Q4), N-B5; 21 B×N, P×B; 22 N-Q4, R-N1; 23 R-N1, R-N2 ∞. Boleslavski.

(j) Tal–Larsen, match 1969. Black continued 14 . . . Q-N3 but 14 . . . N-R4 or 14 . . . P-N5 or 14 . . . B-K1 (Lutikov) are to be considered.

(k) 15 N/6-N5, Q-R4; 16 Q-B4, B×P! 17 P-QN4, Q-R3 =.

1 P-K4, P-QB4; 2 N-KB3, N-QB3; 3 P-Q4, P×P; 4 N×P, N-B3; 5 N-QB3, P-Q3; 6 B-KN5, P-K3; 7 Q-Q2

	76	77	78	79	80
	(B-K2)		P-QR3		P-KR3
8	(O-O-O)		O-O-O		B×N
	(O-O)		B-Q2	P-R3	P×B
9	P-B4		P-B4	B-R4 (i)	O-O-O
	P-KR3	P-Q4 (c)	P-R3 (f)	N×P	P-R3
10	B-R4	P-K5	B-R4	Q-B4	P-B4
	P-K4	N-Q2	N×P (g)	N-N4	B-Q2
11	N-B5	P-KR4 (d)	Q-K1	N×N	B-K2
	B×N	N-N3	N-B3	P×N	P-KR4
12	P×B	Q-K3	N-B5	Q-R4	K-N1
	Q-R4	B-Q2	Q-R4	Q-N3	Q-N3
13	K-N1	B×B	N×P†	P-B4	N-N3
	QR-Q1	Q×B	B×N	N-R2	O-O-O
14	B×N (a)	P-R5	R×B	P-B5	KR-B1
	B×B (b)	N-R4 (e)	O-O-O (h)	B-K2 (j)	B-K2 (k)

(a) 14 P-KN4, P×P; 15 Q×BP, P-Q4; 16 B-Q3, P-Q5; 17 B×N, B×B; 18 N-K4, B-K4; 19 Q-B3, N-N5; 20 P-QR3, N-Q4 = .

(b) 15 N-Q5, Q×Q; 16 N×B†, P×N; 17 R×Q, P×P = . Spasski–Larsen, Santa Monica 1966.

(c) (A) For 9 . . . N×N see col. 71. (B) 9 . . . P-K4; 10 N-B5, B×N; 11 P×B, Q-R4; 12 K-N1, QR-B1; 13 B-B4! ± . Tal–Calvo, Havana 1966.

(d) 11 B×B, Q×B; 12 N-B3! N-N3; 13 Q-K1! B-Q2; 14 B-Q3, P-B4; 15 P×P *e.p.* ± . O'Kelly–Tal, Mallorca 1966.

(e) 15 N-N3 N/4-B5; 16 Q-Q4, KR-B1; 17 K-N1, P-R4; 18 P-B5, P-R5; 19 P-B6, Q-B1; 20 R-R3, N×P/7; 21 K×N, N-B5†; 22 B×N, R×B; Kujpers–Minev, Halle 1967; 23 Q-Q2 ± .

(f) (A) 9 . . . R-B1; 10 N-B3, Q-R4; 11 K-N1, P-N4; 12 P-K5! P-N5; 13 P×N, P×N; 14 P×P/7, B×P; 15 Q×P/6, R-B2; 16 B-B4 ± . (B) 9 . . . B-K2; (1) 10 P-B5, R-QB1; 11 P×P, P×P; 12 B-QB4, N×N; 13 Q×N, Q-R4; 14 B×N, P×B; 15 B-N3 ± . (2) 10 B-K2, Q-B2; 11 B-B3, O-O-O; 12 N-N3, B-K1; 13 Q-K1, N-Q2; 14 B×B, N×B; 15 Q-B2, N-QN3; 16 R-Q3, B-B3; 17 N-Q4, P-K4; 18 N/4-K2, P×P? (18 . . . K-N1; 19 KR-Q1, P-B3 = . Byrne); 19 N-Q5, B×N; 20 P×B, N-R5; 21 Q-Q4, Q-Q2; 22 N×P, N-KB4; 23 Q-R7, N-R5; 24 N-K6, P×N; 25 P×P, Q-QB2; 26 Q-R8†, Q-N1; 27 B×P†, K-B2; 28 Q×P, Q×B; 29 Q×N, resigns. R. Byrne–Liberzon, Biel 1976. (c) 9 . . . P-N4; (1) 10 N×N, B×N; 11 P-K5!? P×P; 12 Q×Q†, R×Q; 13 R×R†, K×R; 14 P×P, P-R3; 15 B×N†, P×B; 16 P×P, R-N1; 17 N-K2, B-Q3 ∓ ; but 11 B-Q3 might be more cautious. (2) 10 B×N, P×B; 11 K-N1 Q-N3; 12 N×N, B×N; 13 B-Q3, Q-B4 = . (3) 10 P-QR3, B-K2; 11 N-B3, P-N5; 12 P×P, N×NP; 13 B-B4, Q-B1; 14 P-QN3, Q-B4; 15 P-K5, P-Q4; 16 P×N, P×P; 17 N-K4, Q-R4; 18 N×P†, K-Q1; 19 Q-Q4, N-B3; 20 Q-K3, K-B1; 21 N×B, B-N5; 22 N-N6†, K-B2; 23 B-B6, P-Q5; 24 N×R†, R×N; 25 QB×P, N×B; 26 Q×N, resigns. Evans–N. Weinstein, Portimao 1975.

(g) 10 . . . R-B1; 11 N-B3, Q-R4; 12 K-N1, P-QN4; 13 P-K5, P-N5; 14 P×N, P×N; 15 BP×P, P×Q; 16 P×R(Q), N-N5; 17 P-QR3, N×P; 18 N×P, N×P†; 19 P×N, P-K4; 20 N-B4, R-N1†; 21 K-R2, B-K3; 22 R×P ± .

(h) 15 R-Q1, P-K4; 16 B-B4, P×P; 17 N-K4, B-K3; 18 B×B†, P×B; 19 N-Q6† K-N1; 20 Q×P, KR-B1 = . Comments.

(*i*) (A) 9 B–KB4, B–Q2! (1) 10 N × N, B × N; 11 P–B3, P–Q4! 12 Q–K1, B–N5; 13 P–QR3, B–R4! Kostro–Simagin, Varna 1966. (2) 10 B–N3, R–B1; 11 P–B3, B–K2; 12 P–KR4, O–O; 13 B–K1, P–Q4! Simagin. (B) 9 B–K3, B–Q2; (1) 10 P–B3, Q–B2; 11 P–KN4, P–QN4; 12 R–N1, N–K4 = . (2) 10 P–B4, Q–B2; 11 K–R1, B–K2; 12 B–Q3, R–QB1 = . Timman–Hort, Tilburg 1977.

(*j*) 15 N–K4! R–QN1; 16 Q–R3, Q–N5! = . O'Kelly–Simagin corr. 1964.

(*k*) 15 N–R4, Q–R2; 16 P–B4, N–Q5 = . Di Camillo–R. Byrne, US Open Chp. 1958.

1 P-K4, P-QB4; 2 N-KB3, N-QB3; 3 P-Q4, P×P; 4 N×P, N-B3; 5 N-QB3, P-Q3

	81	82	83	84	85
6	(B-KN5)		P-KR3	B-K3	N/4-K2 (j)
	(P-K3)		P-KN3	N-KN5 (g)	P-K3
7	N×N	Q-Q3 (c)	B-K3	B-QN5	P-KN3
	P×N	B-K2 (d)	B-N2	N×B	P-Q4!
8	P-K5	R-Q1	Q-Q2 (f)	P×N	P×P
	P×P (a)	O-O	O-O	B-Q2	N×P
9	Q-B3	B-K2	O-O-O	O-O	B-N2
	B-K2!	B-Q2	N×N	P-K3	N×N
10	Q×P†	O-O	B×N	B×N	Q×Q†
	B-Q2	N×N	Q-R4	P×B	K×Q
11	Q-B3	Q×N	K-N1	P-K5	N×N
	P-K5	B-B3	P-K4	B-K2 (h)	B-Q2
12	N×P	K-R1	B-K3	Q-R5	B-Q2
	N×N (b)	Q-R4! (e)	B-K3	O-O (i)	B-K2

(a) Also 8 . . . Q-R4; 9 B×N, P×B; 10 P×QP, Q-K4†; 11 Q-K2, B×P; 12 O-O-O, R-QN1; 13 Q×Q, B×Q∓.

(b) 13 B×B, Q-R4†∓. *P/E.* The column (7 N×N) is the original Richter Attack. Playable, but riskier than 6 . . . P-K3, are (a) 6 . . . P-KR3; 7 B-R4, P-K3; 8 N×N, P×N; 9 P-K5, P×P; 10 Q-B3, B-K2 = ; or (b) 6 . . . Q-N3; 7 N-N3, P-K3; 8 Q-Q2, B-K2; 9 P-KR4∞.

(c) Discarded attempts are (a) 7 B-N5, B-Q2; 8 O-O, P-KR3; 9 B-KR4, P-R3; 10 B-K2, B-K2; 11 N-N3, Q-B2; 12 P-B4, P-KN4! = . Alekhin-Foltys, Margate 1937. (b) 7 B-K2, P-QR3; 8 O-O, B-Q2; 9 K-R1, B-K2; 10 P-B4, N×N; 11 Q×N, B-B3; 12 QR-Q1, O-O; 13 P-B5, Q-B1 = . *Comments.*

(d) Not quite so safe is 7 . . . P-QR3; 8 R-Q1, B-Q2; 9 B-K2, B-K2; 10 O-O, O-O; 11 Q-N3, Q-B2; 12 K-R1, K-R1; 13 P-B4, N×N; 14 R×N, B-B3; 15 Q-R4 ± .

(e) 13 P-B4, KR-K1 = . Boleslavski.

(f) 8 P-KN4, O-O; 9 P-N5, N-K1; 10 P-KR4, N-B2; 11 P-B4, P-K4; 12 N/4-K2 (Lasker-Napier, Cambridge Springs 1904), 12 . . . B-N5! = . 6 P-KR3 is Weaver W. Adams' patent.

(g) 6 . . . P-K4!? 7 N/4-N5, P-QR3 (or 7 . . . B-K2); 8 N-R3, P-QN4; 9 N-Q5, N×N; 10 P×N, N-K2; 11 P-QB4, P-N5; 12 N-B2, N-B4; 13 B-Q2, P-QR4; 14 B-Q3, P-N3 = . R. Byrne). Compare cols. 91-4.

(h) If 11 . . . P×P; 12 Q-R5, P-KN3; 13 Q×KP ± . *Comments.*

(i) 13 P×P, B×P; 14 N-K4, B-K2; 15 QR-Q1, Q-B2. Karaklajić-Taimanov, Yugoslavia-USSR, match 1956; 16 N-QN3, P-KR3 = .

(j) (a) 6 P-B3, P-KN3; 7 B-K3, B-N2; etc. see Yugoslav Attack. (b) 6 N-N3, P-QR3! 7 P-QR4, P-KN3 = . (c) 6 P-B4, P-KN3 see col. 33.

1 P–K4, P–QB4; 2 N–KB3, N–QB3; 3 P–Q4, P×P; 4 N×P, N–B3; 5 N–QB3, P–Q3, 6 B–QB4

	86	87	88	89	90
	P–K4 (*a*)	Q–N3	P–K3		
7	N/4–K2	N–N3 (*d*)	B–K3 (*f*)		
	B–K3	P–K3	Q–B2	B–K2	
8	B×B	O–O	Q–K2	Q–K2 (*h*)	
	P×B	B–K2	P–QR3	P–QR3	O–O
9	O–O	B–K3 (*e*)	B–N3	O–O–O	O–O–O
	B–K2	Q–B2	N–QR4	O–O (*i*)	N×N (*n*)
10	P–B4	P–B4	P–N4	B–N3	B×N
	O–O	O–O	P–QN4	Q–B2 (*j*)	Q–R4
11	N–N3 (*b*)	B–Q3	P–N5	P–N4 (*k*)	P–K5
	P×P	P–QR3	N–Q2	N×N (*l*)	P×P
12	R×P	Q–B3	O–O–O	R×N (*m*)	B×P/5
	Q–N3† (*c*)		N–B4 (*g*)		P–QN3 (*o*)

(*a*) 6 . . . B–Q2; 7 B–N3, P–KN3; 8 P–B3 (Fischer–Gligorić, Zürich 1959), (A) 8 . . . B–N2; 9 B–K3, R–QB1 is admissible. *Comments.* (B) 8 . . . N×N; 9 Q×N, B–N2; 10 B–N5, O–O; 11 Q–K3, P–N4; 12 P–KR4, P–QR4; 13 P–R4, P×P∞. Ciocaltea–Stein, Caracas 1970.

(*b*) If 11 P–B5, P–Q4! 12 N–N3, P–Q5; 13 N/B3–K2, P×P; 14 R×P, Q–Q2 = .

(*c*) 13 K–R1, QR–Q1; 14 P–N3, P–Q4, 15 P×P, N×P; 16 R×R, B×R; 17 N×N, R×N; 18 Q–K1, N–Q5; 19 B–K3, B–B4 = . Garcia–Pomar, Havana 1969.

(*d*) (A) 7 N/4–K2, P–K3; 8 O–O, B–K2; 9 B–N3, O–O; 10 K–R1, N–QR4; 11 B–N5, Q–B4; 12 P–B4, P–N4; 13 N–N3 (Fischer–Benko, Zürich 1959), N×B = . (*Archives*); or 13 . . . B–N2! (B) 7 N×N, P×N; 8 O–O, P–K4! = . (C) 7 B–K3, P–QR3; 8 Q–K2, Q–B2; 9 O–O–O, N–QR4; 10 B–Q3, P–QN4 = . Tisdall–Dorfman, Mexico 1977. (D) 7 N/4–N5, P–QR3; 8 B–K3, Q–R4; 9 N–Q4, N–KN5; 10 N×N! P×N; 11 B–Q2, P–N3; 12 Q–K2, B–N2; 13 O–O, O–O = . *Informator* 24. So far, 7 N–N3 in the column is the preferred answer to Benko's original invention 6 . . . Q–N3.

(*e*) 9 P–QR4, O–O (9 . . . P–QR3; 10 B–Q3; Q–B2; 11 P–B4, P–QN3; 12 K–R1, B–N2; 13 Q–B3 ±); 10 P–R5, Q–B2; 11 B–Q3, B–Q2; 12 P–B4, N–QN5 = . Romanishin–Karpov, Leningrad 1977. The rest of the column is Espig–Hort, Polanica Zdroj 1977.

(*f*) (A) 7 B–N3 is Fischer's waiting move, with (1) 7 . . . P–B4!, or (2) 7 . . . B–K2; 8 P–B4, O–O; 9 B–K3, N×N; 10 B×N, P–K4! = ; or 8 O–O, etc., leading into conventional lines. (B) For 7 O–O, P–QR3 see also Najdorf System, col. 24, note (*g*). Last not least, compare cols. 87–8 with cols. 24–5, for a complete picture.

(*g*) Marić' suggestion. Otherwise 12 . . . P–N5; 13 N–R4, N×B; 14 RP×N, N–B4; 15 N×N, P×N; 16 N–B5, P–QR4; 17 K–N1, P–R5; 18 P×P, R×P; 19 Q–N5†, B–Q2; 20 R×B, Q×R; 21 Q–N8†, drawn.

(*h*) 8 B–N3, O–O; 9 O–O. (A) 9 . . . P–QR3; 10 P–B4, N×N; 11 B×N, P–QN4; (1) 12 P–K5, P×P; 13 P×P, N–Q2; 14 N–K4, B–N2; 15 N–Q6, B×N; 16 P×B, Q–N4; 17 Q–K2, P–K4; 18 B–K3, Q–N3; 19 QR–Q1, K–R1 = . Browne–Donner, Wijk aan Zee 1974. (2) 12 P–QR3, B–N2; 13 Q–Q3, P–QR4! 14 P–K5, P×P; 15 P×P, N–Q2; 16 N×P, N–B4; 17 B×N, B×B†; 18 K–R1, Q–R5∞. Fischer–Spasski, 4th match game 1972. Here 19 Q–N3 would have been strong. (B) 9 . . . B–Q2; 10 P–B4, N×N; 11 B×N, B–B3; 12 Q–K2, P–QN4; 13 N×P, B×N; 14 Q×B, N×P; 15 P–B5! B–B3! 16 Q–Q3! P–Q4; 17 B×B, N×B; 18 P–B4! Q–N3†; 19 K–R1, P×QBP; 20 Q×P, P×P; 21 R×P, QR–Q1. Nikitin.

(*i*) 9 . . . N–QR4?! 10 B–N3, Q–B2; 11 P–N4, P–QN4; 12 P–N5, N×B†; 13 RP×N, N–Q2; (A) 14 N–B5 (KR–N1, P–N5 ∓), P×N; 15 N–Q5, Q–Q1; 16 P×P, B–N2; 17 P–B6, P×P; 18 KR–K1, B×N = . (B) 14 P–R4, P–N5; 15 N–R4, N–B4; 16 P–R5, N×P∞.

(*j*) One other tack (A) 10 . . . Q–R4; and now (1) 11 KR–N1, N × N; 12 B × N, P–QN4; 13 P–N4, P–N5; 14 P–N5, N–K1! (Hartston–Langeweg, Vlissingen 1966); 15 N–Q5±. (2) 11 P–B4! B–Q2; 12 P–N4, N × N; 13 R × N, P–K4; 14 R–Q5! N × R; 15 N × N, B–Q1; 16 P–B5, Q–N4; 17 Q–B3, P–QR4; 18 P–QR4, Q–R3. Bogdanović. (B) 10 . . . Q–K1; 11 KR–N1, N–Q2; 12 P–N4, N–B4; 13 P–N5, P–N4; 14 K–N1, B–Q2; 15 Q–R5, N × B; 16 BP × N∞. Gizhdavu.

(*k*) Extensively analysed have been also 11 KR–N1, P–QN4; 12 P–N4, P–N5; 13 N–Q5, P × N; 14 N × N, Q × N; 15 P–N5, P × P; 16 P × N, B × P; 17 B–Q5, Q–R5; all with a good game for White after either 18 B–Q4, or 18 B × R, or 18 B–N5, making note (*i*) or col. 90 the safer defence.

(*l*) But here 11 . . . N–Q2; 12 P–N5, N × N; 13 R × N, P–QN4; 14 P–KR4, N–B4; 15 P–R5, P–B4! (Perennyi–Tompa, Hungarian Chp. 1977) looks promising for Black.

(*m*) In this variation, Black may continue (A) 12 . . . P–K4; 13 R–B4, Q–Q1; 14 P–N5, N–K1; 15 R–N1, B–Q2! 16 N–Q5, B–N4; 17 B–N6! Q–Q2! 18 Q–N4! B–Q1; 19 Q × Q, B × Q; 20 R–B3, B–K3; 21 B × B, R × B; 22 N–K3, R–Q2; 23 B–R4, R–B2; drawn. Spasjević–Ostojić, Belgrade 1966. Or (B) 12 . . . P–QN4; (1) 13 R–N1, P–K4; 14 P–N5, P × R; 15 P × N, B × P; 16 N–Q5, Q–Q1; 17 B–R6, P–N3; 18 Q–B3, B–KN2; 19 B–N5, Q–Q2; 20 R–N3, B–N2; 21 N–B6†, B × N; 22 B × B! (2) 13 P–N5, N–Q2! (*i*) 14 Q–R5! R–Q1! 15 P–K5 (15 N–Q5, P × N; 16 B × P, N–K4! =), P × P; 16 N–Q5, P × N; 17 B × P, P × R; 18 Q × BP†, K–R1; 19 B × P, B × P†; 20 K–N1, Q–K4! 21 B × Q, N × B! with sufficient defence. Yugoslav analysis. Successful was the immediate pawn storm (ii) 14 P–KR4, N–B4; 15 P–B4, R–N1; 16 P–N6!? BP × P; 17 P–R5, P–KN4; 18 P × P, P–R4; 19 P–R6, P–N3; 20 N × P! Q–B3; 21 N–B3, R–N5; 22 R/1–Q1, Q–N2; 23 B–QB4! Q–N1; 24 P–N3, B–Q2; 25 Q–Q2, B–B1; 26 R × P, R × B; 27 P × R, Q–N5; 28 Q–Q4, R–B2; 29 Q × N, Q × N; 30 R–Q8†, B–B1; 31 B–Q4, resigns. Bradford–Tarjan, US Open 1978.

(*n*) (A) 9 . . . Q–B2; 10 B–N3, P–QR3; see col. 88. (B) 9 . . . Q–R4; 10 B–N3, N × N; 11 B × N, B–Q2; 12 K–N1, B–B3; 13 P–B4, QR–Q1; 14 KR–B1 (14 P–B5, P–K4; 15 B–B2, P–Q4 has been played too), P–QN4; 15 P–B5, P–N5; 16 P × P, P × N (Fischer–Geller, Skopje 1967) 17 R × N! P × R; 18 P × P†, K–R1; 19 R–KB1! +. Mureya. (C) 9 . . . B–Q2; 10 B–N3, R–B1 (10 . . . N × N; 11 B × N, Q–R4; 12 R–Q3!); 11 P–KB4, N–QR4; 12 P–K5, P × P; 13 P × P, N × B†; 14 RP × N, N–Q4: 15 N × N, P × N; 16 P–KN4, R–K1 =. Boleslàvski. (D) 9 . . . P–QR3 see col. 89. (E) 9 . . . P–Q4; 10 N–B3!

(*o*) 13 N–N5, B–R3; 14 B–B3, Q–R5; 15 R–Q4, B × N; 16 B × B, Q × P; 17 KR–Q1, KR–Q1; 18 R–QR4, R × R†; 19 Q × R, Q–Q4; 20 Q × Q, N × Q; 21 B–Q4, B–N4†; 22 K–N1, P–KR4; 23 B–B6, R–Q1; 24 R × P, N–N5; 25 B–Q7, N–B3 =. Bogdanović–Shamkovich, Sarajevo 1963.

1 P–K4, P–QB4; 2 N–KB3, N–QB3; 3 P–Q4, P × P; 4 N × P, N–B3; 5 N–QB3

	91	92	93	94	95
	(P–Q3)		P–K4 (Pelikán's Variation)		
6	B–K2 ⎰Boleslavski		KN–N5		
	P–K4 ⎱Variation		P–Q3		
7	N–N3	N–B3 (f)	B–N5		N–Q5 (o)
	B–K2 (a)	B–K2 (g)	P–QR3		N × N
8	O–O (b)	O–O	N–R3 (j)		P × N
	O–O	O–O	P–N4 (k)		N–K2 (p)
9	P–B4 (c)	B–KN5 (h)	N–Q5	B × N (m)	P–QB4
	P–QR4 (d)	B–K3	B–K2	P × B	N–N3 (q)
10	P–QR4	B × N	B × N	N–Q5	Q–R4
	N–QN5	B × B	B × B	P–B4!	B–Q2
11	K–R1	N–Q5	P–QB3	P–QB3!	Q–N4
	B–K3	B × N	O–O	B–KN2	Q–N1
12	P–B5	Q × B	N–B2	P × P	B–K3
	B–Q2 (e)	Q–N3 (i)	R–N1 =	B × P (n)	P–N3 (r)

(a) 7 . . . P–KR3; 8 O–O, B–K3; 9 B–B3, B–K2; 10 B–K3, P–R3 = . *Comments.*

(b) (A) 8 B–KN5, N × P; 9 B × B, N × N; 10 B × Q, N × Q; 11 R × N, K × B; 12 R × P†, K–K2 = . Böök–Bronstein, Saltsjöbaden 1948. (B) 8 P–B3, P–Q4; 9 N × P, N × N; 10 P × N, N–N5; 11 P–QB4, B–KB4; or 11 B–N5†, K–B1 = . *P/E.*

(c) (A) 9 B–K3, B–K3; 10 B–B3, N–QR4; 11 N × N, Q × N; 12 Q–Q2, KR–B1; 13 KR–Q1, Q–N5; 14 QR–N1, P–KR3; 15 P–QR3, Q–B5; 16 QR–B1, P–R3; 17 B–K2, Q–B2; 18 P–B3, N–Q2; 19 B–B1, P–QN4 = . Boleslavski–Euwe, Zürich 1953: Euwe defending against White's own variation. (B) 9 P–B3, Q–N3†; 10 K–R1, R–Q1 ∓. Pachman.

(d) Another good reply is 9 . . . P × P; 10 B × P, Q–N3†; 11 K–R1, B–K3; 12 N–Q5, B × N! 13 P × B, N–K4; 14 P–B4, N–K5! = .

(e) 13 B–KN5, R–B1; 14 B–B3, B–B3; 15 Q–K2, P–R3; 16 B–R4, Q–B2 = ; or 14 . . . P–R3; 15 B–R4, K–R2 = . *P/E.*

(f) 7 N × N, P × N; (A) 8 Q–Q3, B–K2; 9 O–O, O–O; 10 R–Q1, N–Q2; 11 B–K3, N–N3; 12 P–QR4, P–QR4; 13 P–QN3, P–KB4; 14 P–B3, K–R1 = . Ortega–Smyslov, Havana 1964. (B) 8 P–B4, Q–B2; 9 O–O, B–K2; 10 Q–Q3, O–O; 11 P–B5, P–Q4 = . Bialas–Boleslavski, Hamburg 1960.

(g) 7 . . . P–QR3; 8 O–O, B–K2; 9 B–K3, O–O; 10 Q–Q2, B–K3; 11 QR–Q1, R–B1! = .

(h) 9 B–K3, P–QR3; 10 Q–Q2, B–K3; 11 QR–Q1, Q–Q2; 12 P–KR3, KR–K1 = . Euwe. (B) 9 P–QN3!? P–KR3; 10 B–N2, B–K3; 11 Q–Q2, P–QR3 = .

(i) 13 Q–N3, N–Q5; 14 N × N, P × N; 15 Q × Q, P × Q; 16 B–B4, KR–B1; 17 B–N3 ± . Smyslov–Hort, Tilburg 1977.

(j) 8 B × N, P × B; 9 N–R3, P–Q4!? 10 N × P, B × N; 11 P × B, B–K3; 12 B–B4, Q–R4†; 13 Q–Q2, Q × Q†; 14 K × Q, O–O–O; 15 QR–Q1, P–B4 = . Najdorf–Pelikán, Argentine Chp. 1955.

(k) 8 . . . B–K3; 9 N–N4, R–B1; 10 N–K3, B–K2; 11 B × N, B × B; 12 N/B3–Q5, B–N4; 13 P–QB3, O–O; 14 P–KN3, P–KN3; 15 P–KR4, B × N; 16 N × N, P–QN4 = . Gheorgiu.

(l) Smyslov–Shveshnikov, USSR Chp. 1977. The follow-up is *Comments.*

(m) A satisfactory subsitute is 9 N/R3–N1, B–K2; 10 B × N, B × B; 11 N–Q5, B–N4; 12 P–QR4, P–N5; 13 B–B4, O–O; 14 O–O, B–K3 = . Mnatsakanian–Aleksandria, Tbilisi 1977.

(n) 13 N–B2 ± . *Informator* 24.

(o) 7 B–K3, P–QR3; 8 N–R3, R–QN1; 9 B–N5, B–K3; 10 N–B4, P–N4; 11 N–K3, B–K2; 12 B × N, B × B = .

(*p*) Also 8 . . . N–N1; 9 P–QB4, P–QR3; 10 N–B3, B–K2 (or 10 . . . P–KN3?!); 11 B–K2, O–O; 12 O–O, P–B4; 13 P–B4, B–B3 = . Tal–Tseshkovski, U.S.S.R. Chp. 1979.

(*q*) 9 . . . N–B4!? 10 B–Q3, B–K2; 11 O–O, O–O = .

(*r*) 13 P–KR4, P–KR4; 14 P–KN3 with pressure. Westerinen–Barle, Esbjerg 1977. Compare col. 84.

1 P–K4, P–QB4; 2 N–KB3, N–QB3; 3 P–Q4, P×P; 4 N×P, N–B3; 5 N–QB3, P–K3 (*a*)

	96	97	98	99	100
6	B–K2	N×N	P–KN3	KN–N5	
	B–N5	NP×N!	B–N5 (*h*)	B–N5	
7	O–O!	P–K5	B–N2	P–QR3	B–KB4
	B×N (*b*)	N–Q4	P–Q4	B×N†	N×P
8	P×B	N–K4 (*e*)	P×P	N×B	N–B7†
	N×P	P–KB4 (*f*)	N×P	P–Q4	K–B1 (*k*)
9	B–Q3	P×P *e.p.*	O–O	P×P	Q–B3
	P–Q4 (*c*)	N×P	N×N/6	P×P	N×N
10	B–R3	N–Q6†	P×N	B–Q3	P×N
	N×N	B×N	B×P	P–Q5	Q–B3
11	P×N	Q×B	N×N	N–K2	B–Q2
	Q–R4	Q–N3	Q×Q	O–O	Q–K4†
12	Q–B1 (*d*)	B–Q3	R×Q	O–O	Q–K3
		P–B4 (*g*)	B–Q2 (*i*)	P–KR3 (*j*)	Q×N (*l*)

(*a*) The same position arises after 1 P–K4, P–QB4; 2 N–KB3, P–K3; 3 P–Q4, P×P; 4 N×P, N–B3; 5 N–QB3, N–QB3. Whichever the sequence, the variation is risky. See col. 93. Unstable is also 4 . . . P–K4? 5 N–N5, P–QR3, 6 N–Q6†, B×N; 7 Q×B, Q–B3; 8 Q–B7, KN–K2; 9 N–B3, N–N5; 10 B–Q3, P–Q4; 11 O–O, P–Q5; 12 N–R4! Parma–Bleimann, Netanya 1971. Also see col. 112. For the sequence 5 . . . P–KN3; etc., see next page, note (*b*).

(*b*) 7 . . . Q–B2; 8 N/4–N5, Q–N1; 9 P–QR3, B–K2; 10 B–K3, P–QR3; 11 N–Q4, Q–B2; 12 P–B4, P–Q3; 13 Q–K1 is a kind of Scheveningen.

(*c*) 9 . . . N×QBP; 10 Q–N4, O–O; 11 B–N2, P–B4; 12 N×BP, P×N; 13 Q–B4†, P–Q4; 14 Q×N/3, P–Q5; 15 Q–N3†, K–R1; 16 B–R3, R–K1; 17 KR–K1. *Comments.*

(*d*) (A) 12 . . . B–Q2; 13 R–N1, B–B3; 14 P–KB3, N–B3; 15 R–N3 (or 15 B–N4, Q–B2; 16 B–B5), P–KR3; 16 Q–N2, N–Q2; 17 B–Q6, Q–Q1 ∞. Korelov–Peterson, Riga 1964. (B) 12 . . . P–B3 is recommended in *Archives.*

(*e*) 8 N×N, BP×N; 9 B–Q3! P–N3; 10 O–O, B–KN2; 11 B–KB4, O–O; 12 Q–K2, P–Q3! = . Evans–Seidman, US Chp. 1954.

(*f*) 8 . . . Q–R4†; 9 B–Q2, N–N5; 10 P–KB4, Q–Q4; 11 N–B3, Q–Q5; 12 R–B1, B–B4; 13 Q–B3 ± . *Comments.*

(*g*) 13 B–KB4 (or 13 Q–N3, O–O; 14 O–O, B–N2), B–N2; 14 O–O, R–QB1; 15 P–B4, Q×Q; 16 B×Q, R–B3 = . Hennings–Zinn, Zinnowitz 1966.

(*h*) 6 . . . P–Q4; 7 P×P, N×P; 8 B–N2, N×N; 9 P×N, N×N; 10 Q×N, Q×Q; 11 P×Q, B–N5†; 12 K–K2 ± . Czerniak–Vizantiadis, Athens 1968.

(*i*) 13 R–N1, B×N; 14 B×B†, P×B; 15 B–R3! P–QR4! 16 R–N7, B–N5; 17 B×B, P×B; 18 R/1–Q7, O–O; 19 R×NP, R×P; 20 R–QB4, R–R3 = . *Comments.*

(*j*) 13 B–KB4, R–K1; 14 R–K1, Q–Q4; 15 Q–Q2, B–B4; 16 B×B, Q×B = . Schmidt–Browne, San Juan 1969. In the column, for 6 . . . P–Q3; 7 B–KB4, P–K4! 8 B–N5, P–QR3; 9 N–R3, P–N4; see col, 93—the same position with one full move less.

(*k*) Enterprising is 8 . . . K–K2; 9 Q–B3, P–Q4; 10 O–O–O, B×N; 11 P×B, P–KN4; 12 B–N3, P–B4; 13 P–B4 (or 13 B–QB4, B–Q2; 14 KR–K1!), P–B5; 14 N×R (R. Becker).

(*l*) 13 P×B, P–QN3 ∞. Milić.

1 P-K4, P-QB4; 2 N-KB3, N-QB3; 3 P-Q4, P×P; 4 N×P, P-KN3 (a); 5 N-QB3, B-N2 (b); 6 B-K3, N-B3

	101	102	103	104	105
7	N×N..................		B-QB4		
	NP×N		P-Q3!	Q-R4?!	O-O! (m)
8	P-K5		P-B3	O-O	B-N3!
	N-N1	N-Q4	Q-N3	O-O	P-QR4!
9	B-Q4	N×N	N-B5 (h)	N-N3! (k)	P-QR4 (n)
	P-QB4 (c)	P×N	Q×P	Q-B2	N-KN5
10	B×P	Q×P	N×B†	P-B4	Q×N
	Q-B2	R-QN1	K-B1	P-Q3	N×N
11	B-Q4	B-QB4 (f)	N-Q5	B-K2	Q-Q1
	B×P	O-O	N×N	P-N3	N×B
12	B-K2 (d)	P-B4!	B×N	P-N4	P×N
	B-QN2!	P-Q3	K×N	B-N2	P-Q3
13	B×B	B-N3	R-QN1 (i)	P-N5	N-Q5
	Q×B	P-QR4	Q-B6†	N-Q2	R-R3
14	O-O	O-O	K-B2	R-B2	Q-Q2
	N-B3 (e)	B-N2 (g)	Q-R4 (j)	KR-K1 (l)	P-K3 (o)

(a) Black's 2nd and 4th moves are designed to bypass the Richter (–Rauzer) Attack, while still allowing the Maróczy Bind which—for the time being—is held to be tamed. But this is still questionable.

(b) 5 . . . N-B3? 6 N×N, (1) 6 . . . QP×N; 7 Q×Q†, K×Q; 8 B-QB4, K-K1; 9 B-B4! or 9 P-K5! ± , (2) 6 . . . NP×N; 7 P-K5, N-N1; 8 B-QB4! or 8 Q-B3! ± .

(c) 9 . . . P-B3; 10 P-B4, Q-R4; 11 Q-K2, P×P; 12 B×KP, B×B; 13 Q×B, Q×Q†; 14 P×Q ± .

(d) 12 P-B4, B×B; 13 Q×B, N-B3; 14 P-KN4 (14 O-O-O, O-O; 15 B-B4, B-N2; 16 R-Q2, P-Q4! =), B-N2; 15 R-KN1, O-O; 16 O-O-O, KR-B1; 17 R-Q2, QR-N1; 18 R-N3, P-QR4; 19 R-K3, P-Q4! Dückstein-Stein, Sarajevo 1967.

(e) 15 B-B3, B×B; 16 Q×B, O-O; 17 KR-K1, Q-QB4; 18 QR-Q1, QR-N1; 19 P-KR3, KR-K1; 20 P-QN3, drawn. Bradvarević-Pirc, Yugoslav Chp. 1957.

(f) 11 B×P, R×P; 12 B-Q4, R×BP; 13 B-Q3, P-K3; 14 Q-R8! R-B3; 15 O-O, B-QR3! = . Black has good play for the pawn sacrifice.

(g) 15 Q-B4, R-QB1; 16 Q-Q3 (Gheorghiu-Forintos, Ljubljana 1969), P×P!∞ .

(h) Equally intriguing is 9 B-QN5, Q-B2; 10 P-KN4! B-Q2! 11 P-N5, N-KR4; 12 N-Q5, Q-Q1! (Yudovich); or 12 . . . Q-R4†; 13 P-B3, P-K3; 14 B×N, P×B; 15 N-N3, Q-Q1; 16 N-B6†, N×N = . Zaitsev-Gufeld, USSR 1964.

(i) Another try is 13 O-O, Q-B6; 14 R-K1, P-B3; 15 R-N1, Q-R4; 16 P-KB4, Q-B2; 17 P-B5, B-Q2; 18 R-N3, QR-QB1 = . Tal-Shamis, USSR Chp. 1967.

(j) 15 Q-QB1, P-R4; 16 R-Q1, Q-B2; 17 R-N3, P-B3; 18 Q-N2, N-Q1; 19 B-Q4, R-B1! = . Shashin.

(k) 9 B-N3, P-Q3; 10 P-KR3, B-Q2; 11 P-B4, N×N; 12 B×N, B-B3; 13 Q-Q3, QR-Q1; 14 QR-Q1, N-Q2; 15 B×B, K×B; 16 N-Q5 (16 K-R1, Q-QB4 =), P-K3; 17 Q-Q4†, P-K4; 18 P×P, P×P; 19 Q-Q3, N-B4 = . Tal-Matanović, Mallorca 1967.

(l) 15 P-KR4, N-R4; 16 N-Q4, P-QR3∞. Zaitlin-Gheorgadze, USSR 1969. In the column 12 B-B3, B-N2; 13 N-Q5 is better according to Boleslavski, but 12 . . . P-QR3?! might be best for Black.

(m) 7 . . . N-QR4; 8 B×P†! K×B; 9 P-K5, P-Q4; 10 P×N, B×P; 11 Q-B3, P-K3; 12 O-O-O, N-B3; 13 P-KR4, P-KR4; 14 KR-K1 ± .

(n) 9 P-B3, P-Q3; 10 Q-Q2, N-K4; 11 O-O-O is more consequential.

(o) 15 N-B3, P-K4; 16 O-O, B-K3 ∓ . *Comments.*

1 P–K4, P–QB4; 2 N–KB3, N–QB3; 3 P–Q4, P × P; 4 N × P, P–KN3; 5 P–QB4 (*a*)

	106	107	108	109	110
	N–B3	B–N2			
6	N–QB3	N–B2	B–K3		
	N × N	P–Q3	N–B3 (*g*)		
7	Q × N	B–K2	N–QB3		
	P–Q3	N–B3	O–O		N–KN5
8	B–K3 (*b*)	N–B3	B–K2		Q × N
	B–N2	N–Q2!	P–Q3		N × N
9	P–B3! (*c*)	B–Q2 (*e*)	O–O		Q–Q1 (*k*)
	O–O	O–O	P–QR3	B–Q2 (*i*)	P–K4 (*l*)
10	Q–Q2	O–O	R–K1	Q–Q2 (*j*)	B–Q3 (*m*)
	B–K3	N–B4	N–KN5	N × N	O–O
11	R–B1	P–QN3	B × N	B × N	O–O
	Q–R4	P–QR4	B × N	B–B3 ∞	P–Q3
12	N–Q5 (*d*)	R–N1	B × B/8		Q–Q2
		P–B4 (*f*)	B × B (*h*)		B–K3 (*n*)

(*a*) 5 N × N, NP × N; 6 Q–Q4, N–B3; 7 P–K5, N–Q4! ∓. The text may also arise from an English, or Réti, Opening, e.g. 1 N–KB3, P–QB4; 2 P–B4, P–KN3; 3 P–Q4, P × P; 4 N × P, N–QB3; 5 P–K4, or from the Benoni or King's Indian, e.g. 1 P–Q4, N–KB3; 2 P–QB4, P–B4; 3 N–KB3, P–KN3; 4 N–B3, B–N2; 5 P–K4, etc. See col. 93.

(*b*) 8 B–K2, B–N2; (A) 9 O–O, O–O; 10 Q–K3! N–Q2; 11 K–R1, N–B4; 12 P–B4, P–B4 = . Gligorić. (B) 9 B–N5, P–KR3; 10 B–K3, O–O; 11 Q–Q2, K–R2; 12 O–O, B–K3, 13 P–B4, R–B1; 14 P–QN3, Q–R4; 15 P–QR3, B–Q2; 16 P–B5 ± . Larsen–Fischer, match 1971. (C) 9 B–Q2, O–O; 10 Q–K3, P–K3 = .

(*c*) Also 9 B–K2, O–O; 10 Q–Q3, N–Q2; 11 B–Q4!

(*d*) (A) 12 . . . Q × Q†; 13 K × Q, B × N; 14 BP × B, KR–B1; 15 R × R† (or 15 B–K2, P–QR3; 16 P–QN4 K–B1; 17 P–QR4), R × R; 16 P–KN3! R–B2; 17 B–R3! ± Polugayevski-Ostojič, Belgrade 1969. (B) 12 . . . Q × P; 13 N × P†, K–R1; 14 B–Q4, KR–K1; 15 Q–B3, N–R4; 16 B × B†, N × B; 17 P–QN3, Q–R3! = . Gipslis.

(*e*) (A) 9 O–O, N–B4; 10 P–B3, B × N = . (B) 9 Q–Q2 is for choice. (C) 9 B–K3, B × N†; 10 P × B, Q–R4 = .

(*f*) 13 P × P, B × P; 14 B–N4, B–Q6; 15 B–K2, B–B4; draw. Korchnoi–Matulović, Sarajevo 1969.

(*g*) 6 . . . P–Q3; 7 B–K2, N–R3; 8 O–O, O–O; 9 Q–Q2, N–KN5; 10 B × N, B × B; 11 N–B3, Q–R4; 12 QR–B1, KR–B1; 13 P–QN3, P–QR3 ∞. Geller–Larsen, Monte Carlo 1967. In here, 12 P–B4! was strong.

(*h*) 13 R × B, R × B; 14 Q–Q2, Q–R4; 15 R–Q1, KR–K1; 16 R–R3 ± . R. Byrne–Formanek, Atlantic Open, New York 1970.

(*i*) 9 . . . N × N; 10 B × N, B–K3; 11 K–R1, Q–R4; 12 Q–Q3, KR–B1; 13 P–QN3, P–QR3; 14 P–B4 ± . Smyslov–Gheorghiu, Moscow 1967.

(*j*) 10 R–B1, P–QR3; 11 N–N3, N–K4; 12 N–Q5, N × N; 13 BP × N, B–N4; 14 B–Q4, Q–Q2 = . Darga–Taimanov, Havana 1964. Watch transpositions from the King's Indian Defence, col. 16 (*a*).

(*k*) 9 O–O–O, N–B3!? is double-edged.

(*l*) Or 9 . . . N–K3; (A) 10 Q–Q2, Q–R4; 11 R–B1, P–Q3; 12 B–K2, B–Q2; 13 O–O, B–QB3; 14 P–B3, O–O; 15 KR–Q1, QR–QB1 ∓. McKelvie–S. Byrne, Marshall C.C. 1971. (B) 10 R–B1, P–Q3! 11 B–Q3, O–O; 12 O–O, N–B4; 13 B–N1, P–QR4; 14 Q–Q2, B–Q2; 15 B–Q4, B × B; 16 Q × B, B–B3; 17 Q–Q2, P–B3; 18 KR–Q1, R–B2; 19 B–B2, Q–N3; 20 R–N1, R–Q1; 21 N–Q5, Q–R2; 22 P–QN3, P–K4! = . Portisch–Petrosian, match 1974.

(*m*) 10 N–N5! O–O; 11 Q–Q2, Q–R5; 12 B–Q3, P–Q4; 13 BP × P, N × N; 14 B × N, Q × KP; 15 O–O! R–Q1; 16 KR–Q1, B–K3; 17 P–B3 ± . Penrose.

(*n*) 13 KR–Q1, Q–R5; 14 N–K2, N × N†; 15 Q × N ± . Geller–Barczay, Sousse 1967.

1 P-K4; P-QB4; 2 N-KB3, N-QB3; 3 P-Q4, P×P; 4 N×P, P-K4 (a); 5 N-N5, P-QR3; 6 N-Q6†, B×N; 7 Q×B, Q-B3

	111	112	113	114	115
8	Q×Q......	Q-B7.......	Q-Q1!.................		Q-R3 (j)
	N×Q	KN-K2	Q-N3		KN-K2
9	N-B3	N-B3	N-B3		N-B3
	N-QN5	N-N5 (c)	KN-K2		R-QN1
10	B-Q3	B-Q3	P-KR4......	B-K3	B-K3
	N×B†	P-Q4	P-KR4	P-Q4	P-QN4
11	P×N	O-O (d)	B-N5	N×P (h)	N-Q5
	P-R3	P-Q5	P-Q4	N×N	N×N
12	B-K3	N-K2	P×P (f)	Q×N	P×N
	P-Q3	O-O	N-N5	O-O	P-N5
13	P-Q4	P-KB4	B×N	Q-Q2	Q-Q3
	B-K3 (b)	B-N5 (e)	K×B (g)	Q×KP (i)	N-K2 (k)

(a) (A) This thematic move was originated in a game MacDonnell–Labourdonnais in 1834 and later enlarged upon by Löwenthal. (B) The systems involving . . . P-K3 are handled in later columns. (C) 4 . . . P-Q3; 5 P-QB4, N-B3; 6 N-QB3, P-KN3; or 6 . . . N×N; 7 Q×N, P-KN3 see Maróczy Bind. (D) 4 . . . P-QR3; 5 P-QB4 (5 N-QB3, see Taimanov Variation), P-K4! 6 N-B2, B-B4; 7 N-B3, N-B3; 8 B-K3, P-Q3; 9 B-K2, O-O; 10 Q-Q2, B-K3; 11 O-O, R-B1 = . Pilnik–Euwe, New York 1948/9. (E) 4 . . . P-Q4!? (Nimzowitsch) is best met by 5 P×P, Q×P; 6 B-K3, B-Q2; 7 N-B3, Q-K4; 8 Q-Q2! P-K3; 9 O-O-O, N-B3; 10 N/4-N5, O-O-O; 11 B-KB4 + + . Benko–Sandrin, US Open Chp. 1963 or by Kashdan's 5 B-QN5. (F) For 4 . . . Q-B2 see Taimanov Variation, p. 175, note (a).

(b) 14 O-O-O, QR-B1 = . Baumbach's analysis in *Schach* 1968.

(c) If 9 . . . Q-K3 (Bialas–Joppen, Bad Pyrmont 1961); 10 B-KN5! P-Q4; 11 B×N, N×B; 12 O-O-O, P-Q5; 13 B-B4 ± . Ravinski.

(d) More energy is displayed by 11 P×P?! N/2×P; 12 N×N, N×N; 13 Q-R5.

(e) 14 P×P, Q-B3; 15 Q×N, N×B = . Perfors–Baumbach, corr. 1962-4.

(f) 12 B×N! P-Q5! (Vlagsma's interpolation) 13 B-KN5 (13 B-B5, P×N; 14 P-B3, P×P; 15 R-QN1, P-N3! 16 B×NP, O-O; 17 R×P, R-N1!), P×N; 14 P×P, Q×P†; 15 B-K2, P-B3; 16 B-K3, B-N5; 17 Q-Q3, Q×Q; 18 P×Q, B×B; 19 K×B, O-O-O = . Fischer–Tal, Curaçao 1962.

(g) 14 B-Q3, N×B†; 15 Q×N, Q×Q; 16 P×Q, P-QN4; 17 O-O-O, R-Q1; 18 KR-K1 with a slight advantage. Zuckerman.

(h) 11 P×P, N-N5; 12 B-Q3, N×B†; 13 Q×N, Q×Q; 14 P×Q, B-B4 = .

(i) 14 P-KB3, Q-N3; 15 B-Q3, B-B4; 16 B×B, Q×B; 17 O-O, QR-Q1 = , Cirić-Szabó, Belgrade 1964.

(j) 8 Q-Q2, Q-N3; 9 N-B3 (A) 9 . . . P-Q4; 10 N×P, Q×P†; 11 B-K2, Q×NP; 12 R-B1, R-QN1; 13 N-B7†, K-K2 = . Gipslis. (B) 9 . . . KN-K2; 10 P-KR4, N-Q5 = .

(k) 14 P-Q6, N-B4; 15 B-B5, O-O; 16 O-O-O, R-K1 ∞ . Baumbach.

1 P-K4, P-QB4; 2 N-KB3, N-QB3; 3 P-Q4, P × P; 4 N × P, P-K3 (a); 5 N-QB3,
Q-B2; 6 B-K3, P-QR3; 7 B-Q3

	116	117	118	119	120
	N-B3 (b)				
8	O-O...				Q-K2 (j)
	P-QN4 (c)		B-Q3!	N-K4	B-Q3
9	N-N3.......	N × N!	K-R1 (f)	P-KR3	P-KN3
	B-K2	Q × N	B-B5	P-QN4 (g)	B-K4
10	P-B4	P-QR3	B × B	P-B4	N × N
	P-Q3	B-N2	Q × B	N-B5	NP × N
11	Q-B3	Q-K2	KN-K2	B × N	B-Q2
	O-O!	P-N5	Q-R5!	Q × B	P-Q4
12	P-QR4	P × P	P-KR3	Q-Q3 (h)	P-B4
	P-N5	B × P	O-O	P-Q4	B-Q5 =
13	N-K2	R-R4	P-B4	P-K5	
	P-K4!	P-QR4	P-Q3 =	N-Q2	
14	P-B5	B-QN5		Q × Q	
	P-Q4 (d)	Q-B2 (e)		QP × Q (i)	

(a) Black may initiate the "Taimanov" by playing . . . Q-B2 one move earlier, but
remains with somewhat fewer choices after 4 . . . Q-B2; 5 N-N5 (5 P-QB4, N-B3; 6 N-QB3,
N × P; 7 N × N, Q-K4; 8 N-N5, Q × N†; 9 B-K2, Q-K4; 10 P-B4, Q-N1 ∞. Nikitin-Furman,
USSR Chp. 1959), Q-N1; 6 P-QB4, N-B3; 7 N/5-B3 (7 N/1-B3, P-QR3; 8 N-R3, P-K3; 9
N-B2, P-QN4 =), P-K3; 8 P-B4, P-Q3; 9 B-K2, P-QN3; 10 O-O, B-N2 = . Boleslav-
ski-Korchnoi, USSR Chp. 1960.

(b) 7 . . . P-QN4; 8 N × N, P × N; 9 O-O, B-N2; 10 P-QR4, P-N5! ∞. *Comments.*

(c) (A) 8 . . . P-Q3; 9 P-B4, B-K2; 10 Q-B3, B-Q2; 11 QR-K1, O-O; 12 P-QR3,
P-QN4; 13 Q-N3, K-R1; 14 N × N, B × N; 15 P-K5! ± . Tal-Olafsson, Bled 1961. (B) 8 . . .
N × N; 9 B × N, B-B4; 10 B × N, P × B; 11 Q-N4 ± . Keres.

(d) 15 N-N3, B-N2; 16 P × P, N-N1; 17 N-K4, N/1-Q2; 18 P-B4, P × P *e.p.*; 19 N × P,
P-K5; 20 B × KP, B-Q3; 21 QR-B1, QR-K1 = . Tal.

(e) 15 B-Q4 with White pressure.

(f) (A) 9 N × N, NP × N; 10 P-B4, P-K4; 11 P-B5, B-K2! 12 Q-B3, B-N2; 13 B-QB4,
P-Q4! 14 P × P, P × P; 15 N × P, Q × B; 16 N × N†, B × N; 17 Q × B, O-O; 18 Q-N3,
Q-K5 = . Grabczewski-Doda, Polanica Zdroj 1968. (B) 9 P-KR3, B-B5; 10 Q-Q2, B × B; 11
Q × B, Q-N3; 12 N-B5, Q × Q; 13 N × Q, P-QN4; 14 QR-K1 (Radulov-Anderson, Hastings
1972-3), B-N2 = . The column is Boleslavski's suggestion.

(g) 9 . . . B-B4; 10 Q-K2 (or 10 K-R1, P-Q3; 11 Q-K2, P-QN4; 12 P-B4, N/4-Q2; 13
N-N3, B × B; 14 Q × B, B-N2; 15 QR-K1, P-K4; 16 N-K2, O-O; 17 N-N3, P-Q4! =), P-Q3
(10 . . . N-N3; 11 N-N3, B × B; 12 Q × B, P-Q3; 13 QR-Q1 ± . Kaplan-Suetin, Hastings
1968); 11 P-B4, N-N3; 12 N-N3, B × B†; 13 Q × B, O-O; 14 QR-K1 ± .

(h) Explorable is 12 P-K5, N-Q4; 13 N × N, Q × N; 14 Q-N4, B-N2; 15 QR-Q1, Q-K5;
16 Q-N3, B-K2; 17 R-Q2, O-O = . Hort-Mecking, Mallorca 1969.

(i) 15 P-B5, N × P; 16 P × P, B × P; 17 QR-K1, N-Q2; 18 N × B, P × N = .
Fischer-Petrosian, Santa Monica 1966. Black has a plus pawn, White the play.

(j) 8 Q-Q2, N-KN5; 9 B-KB4, P-K4; 10 N × N, QP × N = . *Archives.*

1 P-K4, P-QB4; 2 N-KB3, N-QB3; 3 P-Q4, P×P; 4 N×P, P-K3; 5 N-QB3, Q-B2

	121	122	123	124	125
6	(B-K3)................		B-K2!		P-KN3
	(P-QR3)		P-QR3		P-QR3!
7	P-QR3......N-N3		P-B4 .... O-O (f)		B-N2
	P-QN4 (a)	N-B3	B-B4	N-B3	N-B3
8	N×N	P-B4	B-K3!	B-K3	O-O
	Q×N (b)	B-N5	P-Q3	B-N5	B-K2 (i)
9	B-K2	B-Q3	Q-Q2	N-R4 (g)	R-K1
	B-N2	O-O	KN-K2	N-K2	N×N
10	Q-Q4 (c)	O-O	O-O-O	P-QB4!	Q×N
	R-B1	B×N	O-O	N×P	B-B4
11	O-O-O	P×B	N×N	P-B5	Q-Q1
	N-B3	P-Q3	N×N	N-Q4	P-Q3
12	R-Q2	R-B3	B×B	N-N3	B-K3
	B-B4 =	P-K4 (d)	P×B (e)	O-O (h)	P-K4 (j)

(a) 7 . . . N-B3; 8 P-B4, N×N; 9 Q×N, N-N5; 10 B-Q2, Q-B4; 11 Q×Q, B×Q; 12 N-Q1, P-Q3; 13 B-K2, N-B3; 14 N-B3, B-Q5 = . Yanofsky–Olafsson, Stockholm 1962.

(b) The other example is 8 . . . P×N; 9 B-K2, B-N2; 10 O-O, P-QB4; 11 P-B4, B-K2; 12 B-B3, N-B3; 13 P-K5, R-Q1; 14 Q-K1, N-Q4 = . Spasski–Darga, Varna 1962.

(c) If 10 B-B3, Q-B2; 11 P-K5, R-B1; 12 O-O, B×B; 13 Q×B, P-Q3; 14 P×P, B×P; 15 R-Q4, N-B3 = ! *Comments.*

(d) 13 P-B5, P-Q4; 14 R-N3, K-R1; 15 P×P, N-K2; 16 B-B5, with considerable pressure, Spasski–Suetin, Moscow 1967. Further tests are required to find improvements for Black; e.g. 13 . . . N-K2; 14 R-N3, K-R1; 15 B-KN5, P-Q4; 16 N-Q2, N/2-N1 = . Suetin.

(e) 13 P-K5, R-Q1; 14 Q-K3, N-Q5; 15 B-B3 ± . In the column, Black might play 7 . . . N×N; 8 Q×N, N-K2; 9 O-O, P-QN4; 10 K-R1, N-B3; 11 Q-B2, B-K2; 12 B-K3, P-Q3; 13 QR-Q1, R-QN1∞ . Tal–Taimanov, USSR Chp. 1974.

(f) Besides 7 P-B4, the text entails another sharp counter to the Taimanov, possibly requiring Black to change plans and transpose into the Scheveningen Variation by 7 . . . N-B3; 8 . . . P-Q3 and 9 . . . B-K2; or vice versa. Moreover, White also has 7 P-QR3, P-QN4; 8 N×N, Q×N; 9 O-O, B-N2; 10 B-B3, Q-B2; 11 P-K5, QR-B1; 12 B×B, Q×B; 13 B-KB4! ± . Kholmov. Compare col. 130.

(g) Also 9 N×N, NP×N! 10 Q-Q4! (10 B-Q3, P-Q4!), P-B4; 11 Q-B4, B-N2; 12 P-QR3 (12 B-B3, Q-K4!), B×N; 13 Q×B, N×P; 14 Q×NP, O-O-O ∞ . *Archives.*

(h) 13 Q-Q4, P-B4; 14 B-QB4, N×B; 15 P×N, P-Q3; 16 B×P†, B×B; 17 Q×B, P×P∞ . Moiseyev. In the column, in place of 9 . . . N-K2; Black may try 9 . . . O-O; 10 N×N, NP×N; 11 N-N6, R-N1; 12 N×B, KR×N; 13 B×P, R-Q1; 14 B-Q3, B-Q3; 15 K-R1, B-K4∞ . Smejkal–Karpov, Leningrad 1973.

(i) (A) 8 . . . P-Q3; 9 R-K1, B-Q2; 10 N×N, P×N; 11 N-R4, P-K4; 12 P-QB4, B-K2; 13 P-B5, O-O; 14 P×P, B×P; 15 B-N5, B-K2; 16 Q-B2 ± . Tal–Najdorf, Belgrade 1970. (B) It is safer for Black to take first, e.g. 8 . . . N×N; 9 Q×N. *Comments.*

(j) 13 Q-Q2, B-K3; 14 P-KR3, R-QB1; 15 P-R3, K-K2; 16 P-B4, P-QN4∞ . Sax–Matulović, Vraca 1975.

1 P–K4, P–QB4; 2 N–KB3, N–QB3; 3 P–Q4, P × P; 4 N × P *(a)*, P–K3

	126	127	128	129	130
5	P–QB4	N–N5			N–QB3
	N–B3	P–Q3 *(d)*			P–QR3
6	N–QB3 *(b)*	B–KB4		P–QB4	B–K2
	B–N5	P–K4 *(e)*		N–B3!	KN–K2
7	N × N	B–K3		QN–B3	P–B4 *(l)*
	NP × N *(c)*	P–QR3	N–B3	P–QR3	P–QN4
8	B–Q3	N/5–B3 *(f)*	B–N5	N–R3 *(i)*	O–O
	P–K4	N–B3	B–K3!	B–K2	B–N2
9	O–O	B–QB4 *(g)*	QN–B3	B–K2	N–N3?!
	O–O	N–QR4!	P–QR3	O–O	N–N3
10	B–Q2	B–N3	B × N	O–O	B–K3
	B–K2	N × B	P × B	P–QN3 *(j)*	B–K2
11	Q–K2	RP × B	N–R3 *(h)*	B–K3	Q–K1
	P–Q3 =	B–K3 =		B–N2 *(k)*	O–O *(m)*

(a) 4 P–B3, P × P; 5 N × P, P–Q3; see cols. 49, 172 and 185.

(b) The column can also arise from the English Opening after 1 P–QB4, P–QB4; 2 N–KB3, N–QB3; 3 N–B3, N–B3; 4 P–Q4, P × P; 5 N × P, P–K3; 6 P–K4, and it is also a relative of the Maróczy Bind, but 6 . . . B–N5 spoils it all!

(c) Full equality results also from 7 . . . QP × N; 8 Q × Q†, K × Q; 9 B–Q2, P–K4; 10 O–O–O, K–K2; 11 P–B3, B–K3; 12 B–K3, N–Q2; 13 N–Q5†, P × N; 14 BP × P, B–QB4; 15 B × B, N × B; 16 P × B, N × P/3 = . Konstantinopolski. The column is Czerniak–Najdorf, Mar del Plata 1942.

(d) 5 . . . N–B3; 6 QN–B3, see col. 99 and col. 158.

(e) To an inferior ending leads 6 . . . N–K4; 7 QN–R3, B–K2! 8 Q–Q4, N–KB3; 9 O–O–O, O–O; 10 N × QP, Q × N; 11 Q × Q, B × Q; 12 R × B, N–N3; 13 B–K3, N × P; 14 R–Q1 (or 14 R–Q4) ± . Euwe.

(f) 8 N/5–R3, P–QN4; 9 P–QB4, P–N5; 10 N–B2, N–B3; 11 B–K2, B–K2; 12 O–O, O–O; 13 N–Q2, R–N1 = . Fischer–Reshevsky, Buenos Aires 1960.

(g) The other favourites are (A) 9 N–R3, R–QN1; 10 B–KN5, P–QN4; 11 N–Q5, Q–R4†; 12 B–Q2, Q–Q1; 13 B–N5, drawn. Aronin–Taimanov, USSR Chp. 1962. (B) 9 B–KN5, B–K2; 10 B × N, B × B; 11 N–Q5, B–N4; 12 B–B4, O–O; 13 QN–B3, B–K3; 14 O–O, P–N4; 15 B–N3, N–Q5; 16 N–K2, N × B; 17 RP × N, Q–N1 = . Kapengut–Furman, USSR Chp. 1967. The column is Fischer's suggestion.

(h) Apparently the mutual loss of tempo, . . . P–K3–K4 and B–K3–N5 has no ill effects. The column may continue (A) 11 Q–N3; 12 N–B4, Q–Q5; 13 N–K3, O–O–O; or (B) 11 . . . N–Q5; 12 N–B4, R–B1; 13 N–K3, B–R3 = ; or (C) 11 . . . P–Q4; 12 P × P, B × N; 13 NP × B, Q–R4; 14 Q–Q2, O–O–O; 15 B–B4, KR–N1; 16 R–Q1, B–B4 ∞ . Fischer–Petrosian, 1st match game 1971.

(i) 8 N–Q4, B–K2; 9 B–K2, O–O; 10 O–O, B–Q2; 11 B–K3, N × N; 12 Q × N, B–B3; 13 P–B3, Q–N1; 14 P–QR4, P–Q4! 15 BP × P, P × P; 16 P × P, R–Q1; 17 B–QB4, P–QN4 = .

(j) 10 . . . B–Q2; 11 B–K3, R–N1; 12 Q–Q2, Q–R4; 13 KR–Q1, KR–Q1 = . Gufeld–Doda, Leningrad 1967.

(k) Possible continuations are (A) 12 Q–Q2, N–K4; 13 P–B3, P–Q4; 14 KP × P, P × P; 15 P × P, N × P; with no life left. Browne–R. Byrne, San Juan 1969. Or (B) 12 Q–N3, N–Q2; 13 P–B3, N–B4; 14 Q–Q1, B–B3; 15 Q–Q2, B–K4; 16 R–B2, P–B4; 17 P × P, R × P = . Or at once (C) 12 P–B3! R–K1; 13 Q–N3, N–Q2; 14 KR–Q1, N–R4 = .

(l) This recent combination of an earlier . . . N–QB3; . . . P–K3; and . . . P–QR3; allows also (A) 7 B–KB4, N–N3; 8 N × N (or 8 B–N3), NP × N; 9 B–Q6, B × B; 10 Q × B, Q–K2; 11

O–O–O, Q × Q; 12 R × Q, K–Q1; 13 KR–Q1, K–B2 = . (B) 7 O–O, N × N; 8 Q × N, N–B3; 9 Q–K3, B–Q3! 10 P–B4, O–O = . Kuzmin–Taimanov, Leningrad 1977. (C) 7 B–K3, N × N; 8 Q × N, P–QN4! 9 P–B4, N–B3; 10 Q–Q2, B–K2; 11 O–O, O–O = .

(m) 12 R–Q1, P–Q3; 13 Q–B2 = . Mariotti–Taimanov, Leningrad 1977. Structurally, col. 130 might as well rank behind col. 125 as part of a "Neo–Taimanov" line. In the column, a further finesse comes in with 6 P–B4, Q–B2; 7 N–B3, P–QN4; 8 B–Q3, B–B4; 9 Q–K2, P–Q3; 10 B–K3, KN–K2; 11 O–O, B–N2 = . *Comments.*

1 P-K4, P-QB4; 2 N-KB3, P-K3 (*a*); 3 P-Q4, P×P; 4 N×P, N-KB3 (*a*); 5 N-QB3, P-Q3 (*a*); 6 B-K2, B-K2; 7 O-O, N-B3 (*a*); 8 B-K3, P-QR3 (*a*); 9 P-B4

	131	132	133	134	135
	O-O (*b*)	Q-B2			
10	Q-K1 (*c*)	Q-K1		P-QR4	K-R1 (*l*)
	N×N	B-Q2	N×N (*i*)	O-O	N-QR4
11	B×N	R-Q1 (*e*)	B×N	N-N3	Q-K1
	P-QN4	O-O	P-QN4	B-Q2	N-B5
12	R-Q1	Q-N3 (*f*)	Q-N3	P-R5	B-B1
	B-N2	N×N (*g*)	O-O	QR-B1	P-QN4
13	B-B3	B×N	P-QR3	B-B3	P-QN3
	N-K1	B-B3	B-N2	N-QN5	N-N3
14	P-QR3	B-Q3	K-R1	B-N6	B-B3
	Q-B2	N-R4	KR-Q1	Q-N1	B-N2
15	Q-B2	Q-R3	B-Q3	R-B2	P-QR3
	B-QB3	P-K4	N-K1	B-B3	P-N3 =
16	P-K5	N-Q5	QR-K1	N-Q4	N-Q4
	B×B (*d*)	B×N (*h*)	B-KB1 (*j*)	P-Q4 (*k*)	

(*a*) The position after Black's seventh move is the typical "Scheveningen" build-up. By mutual consent, Black's 2nd, 4th, 5th and 7th moves can be variously transposed. Black's 8 . . . P-QR3 is Paulsen's legacy and in later columns reoccurs at earlier stages. Cols. 136–7 deal with the Scheveningen Variation without or with a late . . . P-QR3. However, if 2 . . . P-QR3; 3 P-B4! is also good.

(*b*) A mobilization slightly speedier than by 9 . . . Q-B2 (see next column) is attempted by 9 . . . B-Q2; 10 Q-K1, P-QN4; 11 P-QR3, O-O; 12 Q-N3, N×N; 13 B×N, B-B3 = . Bellon–Larsen, Las Palmas 1977.

(*c*) 10 K-R1, B-Q2; 11 Q-K1, P-QN4; 12 P-QR3, Q-N1; 13 Q-N3, P-N5; 14 P×P, Q×P; 15 N×N, B×N = .

(*d*) 17 Q×B, R-B1; 18 K-R1, Q-B3; 19 Q-K3, P×P; 20 P×P, N-B2; 21 N-K4, N-Q4; 22 Q-KN3, Q×P; 23 N-B6†, K-R1; 24 N×N, P×N; 25 B-B3, Q-N3; 26 R×P, KR-Q1; 27 Q-R3, Q-K3; 28 R×R†, R×R; 29 Q-B3, Q-Q4; 30 Q×Q, R×Q; 31 P-KN3, drawn. Diesen–Hort, Polanica Zdroj 1977.

(*e*) (A) 11 K-R1, O-O! 12 B-B3, K-R1; 13 P-QR4, QR-B1; 14 R-Q1, N×N; 15 B×N, P-K4 = . Gligorić–Najdorf, Prague 1946. (B) 11 Q-N3, O-O; 12 N-B3, P-Q4; 13 P-K5, N-KR4; 14 Q-B2, P-KN3 = . Trifunović–Najdorf, Stockholm 1948. (c) 11 P-QR4, O-O; 12 Q-N3, QR-N1; 13 K-R1, K-R1; 14 B-B3, P-KN3?! 15 N×N, P×N? (15 . . . B×N! =); Soltis–Quinteros, Cleveland 1975. (D) 11 R-K1, O-O; 12 Q-N3, N×N; 13 B×N, B-B3∞. R. Byrne–Fraguela, Las Palmas 1976.

(*f*) 12 B-B3, N-QR4; 13 Q-B2, N-N5; 14 B-B1, P-K4 = . Sozin–Botvinnik, Moscow 1931.

(*g*) Also 12 . . . K-R1; 13 K-R1, P-QN4; 14 P-QR3, P-N5; 15 P×P, N×NP; 16 P-K5, KN-Q4; 17 N×N, N×N; 18 B-Q3, N-N5 = . Alexander–Trifunović, Staunton Memorial 1951.

(*h*) 17 P×B, P×B; 18 Q×N, P-KN3; 19 Q-B3 = . Bondarevski–Kotov, USSR Chp. 1951.

(*i*) 10 . . . O-O (A) 11 R-Q1, N×N; 12 B×N, P-QN4; 13 B-Q3, P-N5; 14 N-K2∞ . (B) 11 P-KN4, N×N; 12 B×N, P-K4; 13 P×P, P×P; 14 Q-N3, B-QB4; 15 B×B, Q×B†; 16 K-R1, B-K3 = . *Comments.* (c) 11 Q-N3! N×N; 12 B×N, P-QN4; 13 P-QR3, B-N2; 14 K-R1, KR-Q1; 15 B-Q3! ± .

(*j*) 17 P–K5, P–N3 = . Smyslov–Kotov, USSR 1951.

(*k*) 17 N × B, P × N; 18 B–K3 = . Pinkus–Kaufman, New York 1954.

(*l*) 10 B–B3, (A) 10 . . . N–QR4; 11 Q–K2, B–Q2; 12 QR–Q1, R–QB1; 13 Q–B2, N–B5; 14 B–B1, O–O; 15 P–KN4, K–R1; 16 P–N5, N–N1; 17 P–B5, P–Q4 = . Michel–Najdorf, Mar del Plata 1944. (B) 10 . . . B–Q2; 11 K–R1, N × N; 12 B × N, P–K4; 13 B–K3, B–B3; 14 Q–K1, O–O; 15 Q–N3, P × P; 16 B × P, N–Q2 = .

1 P–K4, P–QB4; 2 N–KB3, P–K3; 3 P–Q4, P×P; 4 N×P, N–KB3; 5 N–QB3, P–Q3; 6 B–K2, B–K2; 7 O–O, N–B3

	136	137	138	139	140
8	(B–K3)...............................			K–R1	
	O–O			O–O (*i*)	
9	P–B4			P–B4	
	B–Q2 (*a*)			Q–B2	
10	Q–K1......	K–R1	N–N3	B–B3	N–N3
	N×N (*b*)	N×N	P–QR3 (*g*)	P–QR3	P–QR3
11	B×N	B×N	B–B3	P–KN4!	P–QR4
	B–B3	B–B3	R–N1	N×N!	P–QN3
12	B–Q3 (*c*)	B–B3 (*e*)	P–KN4	Q×N	B–B3
	N–Q2	N–Q2	B–K1	N–Q2	R–N1! (*k*)
13	QR–Q1	P–QR4	P–N5	P–N5	Q–K1
	P–K4 (*d*)	P–K4 (*f*)	N–Q2 (*h*)	P–QN4 (*j*)	KR–Q1 (*l*)

(*a*) Other choices are (A) 9 . . . P–QR3; 10 Q–K1, (1) 10 . . . N×N; 11 B×N, P–QN4; 12 P–QR3, B–N2 = . Or (2) 10 . . . Q–B2; 11 P–QR4, R–K1; 12 N–N3, P–QN3; 13 B–B3, B–N2; 14 Q–K2, N–Q2. (B) 9 . . . P–K4!? 10 N–N3, P–QR4; 11 P–QR3, P–R5; 12 N–B1, P×P; 13 R×P, B–K3; 14 N–Q5, B×N; 15 P×B, N–K4; 16 R–QN4, Q–B1; 17 N–R2, N/3–Q2; 18 P–B4 (18 N–B3!), B–Q1; 19 K–R1, R–K1; 20 B–Q4, N–B4; 21 B×N/B4, Q×B; 22 N–B3, B–R4; 23 N–K4, Q–B2; 24 R×RP, N–Q2; 25 P–B5, N×P; 26 N×N, P×N; 27 B–N5, KR–Q1; 28 P–QN4, B–N3; 29 R×R, R×R; 30 P–Q6, Q–Q1; 31 P×P, B×P; 32 P–Q7, Q–K2; 33 P–QR4, R–Q1; 34 Q–Q5, P–QN3?; 35 R–KB1, Q–K3; 36 Q×Q, P×Q; 37 B–B4, P–R3; 38 B×P†, K–R2; 39 P–N3, B–K2; 40 R–QB1, K–N3; 41 R–B6, resigns. Peters–Kavalek, US Chp. 1975.

(*b*) Black also equalizes with 10 . . . Q–B2; 11 Q–N3, N×N; 12 B×N, B–B3; 13 K–R1, QR–Q1; 14 P–K5, P×P; 15 B×P, Q–N3; 16 P–B5, P×P; 17 R×P, B–Q3! = . Nikitin.

(*c*) 12 Q–N3, P–KN3! 13 B–Q3, N–R4; 14 Q–B2, N×P; 15 Q×N, P–K4; 16 Q–B2, P×B; 17 Q×P, Q–R4; 18 K–R1, Q–K4 = . Zhdanov–Kapengut, Latvian Chp. 1966.

(*d*) 14 P×P, P×P; 15 B–B2, B–B4; 16 B–B4, Q–N3; 17 B–N3, N–B3 = .

(*e*) 12 B–Q3, N–Q2; 13 Q–K2, P–K4 (also playable are (1) 13 . . . N–B4; 14 B×N, P×B; 15 P–K5, Q–N3; or (2) 13 . . . P–QR3; 14 QR–Q1, P–QN4; 15 R–B3, P–K4; 16 B–K3, B–B3! 17 R–R3, P×P; 18 P–K5, P–N3 =); 14 B–K3, P×P; 15 B×BP N–K4; 16 B×N, P×B; 17 B–B4, P–KN3 = . Nikitin.

(*f*) 14 B–K3, P×P; 15 B×BP, N–K4 = . Ćirić–Krogius, Sochi 1965.

(*g*) (A) 10 . . . Q–B2; 11 P–KN4! P–Q4; 12 P×P, N×P; 13 N×N, P×N; 14 B–B3! ± . (B) 10 . . . P–QR4; 11 P–QR4, N–QN5; 12 B–B3, B–B3; 13 N–Q4! P–KN3; 14 R–B2, P–K4; 15 N×B, P×N; 16 P×P, P×P; 17 Q–KB1! Q–B1; 18 P–R3, N–Q2; 19 B–N4, P–R4; 20 B×N, Q×B; 21 Q–B4, B–R5; 22 R–Q2, Q–K2; 23 R–KB1, KR–Q1; 24 N–N1, Q–N2; 25 K–R2, K–N2; 26 P–B3, N–R3; 27 R–K2, R–KB1; 28 N–Q2, Q–Q1; 29 N–B3, P–B3; 30 R–Q2, B–K2; 31 Q–K6, QR–Q1; 32 R×R, B×R; 33 R–Q1, N–N1; 34 B–B5, R–R1; 35 R×B, resigns. Karpov–Spasski, 9th match game 1974.

(*h*) 14 B–N4, P–QN4; 15 P–KR4, N–N3; 16 P–B5, N–N5; 17 Q–K2, B–Q2 = . Nikitin.

(*i*) (A) 8 . . . B–Q2; 9 P–B4, Q–B2; 10 N–N3, P–QR3; 11 P–QR4, R–QB1; 12 B–B3, N–QN5; 13 B–K3, B–B3; 14 R–B2, P–Q4; 15 P–K5, N–K5; 16 B×N! ± . (B) 8 . . . P–QR3! see cols. 131–5.

(*j*) 14 B–K3, B–N2; 15 P–B5, N–K4; 16 B–N2, KR–K1; 17 P–B6, B–KB1 = .

(*k*) The parent game of this variation went 12 . . . B–N2; 13 B–K3! Maróczy–Euwe, Scheveningen 1923.

(*l*) 14 B–K3, N–QR4; 15 R–Q1, N–B5; 16 B–B1, P–QN4 = . Foltys–Benko, Budapest 1948.

(6 . . . P – QR3)

1 P–K4, P–QB4; 2 N–KB3, P–K3; 3 P–Q4, P×P; 4 N×P, N–KB3; 5 N–QB3, P–Q3

	141	142	143	144	145
6	(B–K2)	....		B–K3 *(l)*	
	(B–K2)	P–QR3		P–QR3	
7	B–K3	O–O		P–B4 *(m)*	
	N–B3	Q–B2	QN–Q2?	QN–Q2 *(n)*	
8	Q–Q2	P–B4 *(c)*	P–B4 *(i)*	Q–B3 *(o)*	B–K2 *(r)*
	O–O	B–K2 *(d)*	P–QN4	Q–B2 *(p)*	P–QN4
9	O–O–O *(a)*	B–B3 *(e)*	B–B3	P–KN4	P–KN4
	P–QR3	QN–Q2? *(f)*	B–N2	P–QN4	P–R3
10	P–B4	K–R1	P–K5 *(j)*	P–N5	P–N5?!
	Q–B2	O–O *(g)*	B×B	P–N5	P×P
11	P–KN4	P–KN4	N×B	P×N	P×P
	P–QN4	R–Q1	P–N5	P×N	R–R6!? *(s)*
12	P–N5	P–N5	P×N	P×NP	B–B2 *(t)*
	N–Q2 *(b)*	N–K1 *(h)*	P×N *(k)*	B×P *(q)*	R×N *(u)*

(a) 9 P–B4, N×N; 10 B×N, B–Q2; 11 O–O–O is to be considered.

(b) 13 N×N, Q×N; 14 B–B3, B–N2; or 14 . . . R–N1 ∓ . Suetin.

(c) 8 P–QR4, N–B3; 9 B–K3, B–K2; 10 N–N3, P–QN3; 11 P–B4, O–O; 12 B–B3, R–N1 = .

(d) 8 . . . QN–Q2 (Paulsen's move); 9 P–KN4! P–QN4; 10 P–QR3, B–N2; 11 B–B3, N–B4; 12 Q–K2, P–K4; 13 N–B5 ± . Nezhmetdinov–Tal, USSR Chp. 1961.

(e) (A) 9 B–K3, N–B3 (if 9 . . . P–QN4; 10 P–K5!) = . (B) 9 P–QR4 has often been tried here or later. Compare with other compatible sequences.

(f) The Paulsen touch again, but the correct course is 9 . . . N–B3! = transposing into col. 135, note *(i)* of the Scheveningen Variation.

(g) 10 . . . N–B1; 11 P–KN4, P–R3; 12 P–B5, P–K4; 13 N/4–K2, B–Q2; 14 N–N3, P–QN4; 15 P–QR3, B–B3; 16 K–N2, N/1–Q2; 17 P–KR4, N–R2; 18 R–R1, with attack.

(h) 13 B–N2, N–N3; 14 P–B5, P–K4; 15 N/4–K2, Nikitin–Nei, USSR 1952.

(i) Neglected in recent practice yet strong is 8 P–QR4, P–QN3; 9 P–B4, B–N2; 10 B–B3, Q–B2; followed by 11 K–R1 or 11 P–B5 or 11 P–KN4.

(j) 10 P–QR3, B–K2! and . . . O–O, as in the Scheveningen.

(k) 13 P–B5, Q–N3†; 14 K–R1, P×NP; 15 B×P, Q×B; 16 P×KP, P×KP; 17 P–B7†, K–Q1; 18 N–Q4, N–B4; 19 R–QN1 ± . Simagin.

(l) 6 B–K3 and 6 B–K2 may easily be interchanged in this system without . . . N–QB3 and must be studied in conjunction with the system where . . . N–QB3 has been or is going to be played, 5 . . . P–QR3 and 6 . . . P–QR3 are also often transposed.

(m) 7 B–K2 is now tame and would precipitate action by White so as to forestall Black's secure build-up, e.g. 7 . . . B–K2; 8 P–KN4!? P–QN4; 9 P–N5, KN–Q2; 10 P–B4, P–N5; 11 N–R4, B–N2; 12 B–B3, N–QB3; 13 P–KR4, O–O; 14 O–O, N×N; 15 B×N, P–K4! ± . Byrne–Polugayevski, Montilla 1975.

(n) (A) 7 . . . P–QN4! 8 Q–B3, B–N2; 9 B–Q3, QN–Q2; 10 P–KN4, P–N5; 11 QN–K2, N–B4! = . Savon–Petrushin, USSR Chp. prelims. 1977. Weaker is 7 . . . B–K2; 8 Q–B3, Q–B2; 9 P–KN4! (c) 7 . . . N–B3 is the straightest answer.

(o) (A) 8 B–Q3, P–QN4; 9 P–QR3, B–N2; 10 Q–B3, B–K2; 11 O–O, O–O; 12 QR–K1, R–B1; 13 Q–R3, N–B4; 14 B–B2, P–N3 = . (B) 8 P–QR4 or 8 B–K2 transpose into conventional lines.

(p) 8 . . . P–K4; 9 N–N3.

(q) 13 P–N3, B–N2; 14 R–KN1, B–KB3; 15 B–Q3, P–QR4; 16 Q–R5, K–K2; 17 N–N5 ± . Korn–Krausz, corr. 1976.

(r) 8 B–K2, P–QN4; 9 P–QR4, P–N5; 10 N–B6, Q–B2; 11 N × P, P–Q4; 12 Q–Q4!? (12 N–Q3 =), B–B4; 13 N/4 × QP, P × N; 14 N × P, N × N; 15 Q × P, N × B ∞. Belyavski–Stean, Alekhine Memorial Tournament, Moscow 1975.

(s) A strategy of mutal mix-up, unbalancing and unexpected daring. If 11 . . . N–KN1; 12 P–N6!

(t) 12 B–KB4 (or 12 Q–Q2, P–N5; 13 P × N, P × N; 14 Q × P, N × P ∓) was refuted by 12 . . . P–N5; 13 N–Q5, P × N; 14 P × N, N × P; 15 N–B6, Q–N3; 16 P × P, N–K5! 17 Q–Q4, Q × Q; 18 N × Q, P–N4; 19 B–QB1, B–KN2; 20 N–B6, N–N6; 21 R–KN1, N × B; 22 R × P, N–Q5; 23 R × B, N × P†; 24 K–Q1, N × R; 25 R–N8†, K–Q2; 26 R–B8, R–Q6†; 27 B–Q2, R × P; 28 N × P, R–KB4; 29 B–B3, P–R4; 30 N–Q3, P–R5; 31 resigns. Byrne–Brown, US Chp. 1975.

(u) 13 P × N! (not 13 P × R, N × KP) R–KR6; 14 N × P! Q–R4†; 15 P–B3, P × N; 16 P × P, B × P; 17 Q × P, R–R3; 18 R–KN1 with a winning stranglehold despite less material.

1 P–K4, P–QB4; 2 N–KB3, P–K3; 3 P–Q4, P×P; 4 N×P, N–KB3; 5 N–QB3, P–Q3; 6 B–K3, N–B3; 7 P–B4, B–K2

	146	147	148	149	150
8	Q–B3				B–K2
	O–O	P–K4	P–QR3		O–O
9	O–O–O	N×N	B–Q3		Q–Q2
	Q–B2 (*a*)	P×N	Q–B2		P–QR3
10	N/4–N5	P×P	O–O	N–N3	O–O–O
	Q–N1	P×P	O–O	P–QN4	Q–B2
11	P–KN4	B–QB4	QR–K1 (*d*)	O–O	P–KN4
	P–QR3	O–O		B–N2 (*e*)	P–QN4
12	N–Q4	P–KR3 (*c*)		Q–R3	P–N5 (*g*)
	N×N (*b*)			O–O (*f*)	

(*a*) (A) 9 . . . B–Q2; 10 R–N1, N×N; 11 B×N, B–B3; 12 P–KN4, Q–R4; 13 P–N5, N–Q2; 14 Q–R5! KR–B1; 15 R–N3, N–B1; 16 P–B5, P×P; 17 P×P, Q×BP; 18 B–R3, Q–B5†; 19 B–K3, Q–B5; 20 B×R± . (B) 9 . . . N×N; 10 B×N, Q–R4; 11 P–K5, P×P; 12 P×P (12 B×P, N–Q2!), N–Q2; 13 B–QN5, B–N5; 14 B×N± . Stein–Kuzmin, Tallinn 1965.

(*b*) 13 B×N (A) 13 . . . P–K4; 14 P–N5, B–N5; 15 Q–N2, P×B; 16 P×N, P×N; 17 P×B, P×P†; 18 K–N1, B×R; 19 P×R (Q)†, Q×Q; 20 B–B4, B–R4; 21 Q–R3, P–KN3 ∞. (B) 13 . . . P–QN4; 14 P–N5, N–Q2; 15 B–Q3, P–N5; 16 N–Q5?! P×N; 17 P×P, P–N3; 18 QR–K1, B–Q1; 19 Q–R3, N–K4; 20 Q–R6, B–N3 ∞.

(*c*) (A) 12 . . . N–K1? 13 O–O, N–Q3; 14 B–Q3, Q–R4; 15 P–R3, B–K3; 16 P–QN4, Q–B2; 17 N–R4, P–KB4; 18 N–B5± . (B) 12 . . . B–K3! 13 B–N3, P–R3; 14 B×B, P–B5; 15 Q–K2, P–B5; 16 Q×P, N–R4; 17 Q×P†, K–R1; 18 N–Q5, B–R5†; 19 K–Q2, N–N6: 20 KR–Q1, Q–R4†; 21 K–B1, N–K7†; 22 K–N1, QR–N1 ∓. Nikitin. In the column, the strongest move is 10 P–B5, R–QN1; 11 B–B4! Q–R4; 12 B–N3, N–Q2? 13 O–O–O (13 Q–R5, O–O) and Black is in a squeeze. Of uncertain value is the hasty 9 P×P, N×P! 10 B–N5†, KN–Q2; 11 Q–K2, O–O; 12 O–O, N–N3; 12 N–B5, B–K3 = . Ree–Hort, Wijk aan Zee 1971.

(*d*) (A) 11 Q–R3 (or 11 P–KN4), N×N; 12 B×N, P–K4! = . (B) 11 K–R1, B–Q2! 12 QR–K1, P–QN4; 13 P–QR3, QR–N1; 14 N×N, B×N; 15 Q–R3! QR–Q1! 16 B–Q4, P–K4! 17 P×P, P×P; 18 N–Q5, B×N; 19 B×KP, Q×B; 20 P×B, Q×NP; 21 R×N, P–N3! = . Novopashin–Korchnoi, USSR 1962.

(*e*) 11 . . . O–O; 12 P–KN4! P–N5; 13 N–K2, P–Q4; 14 P–K5, N–K5; 15 N–N3± . Moiseyev. The position may arise from 1 P–K4, P–QB4; 2 N–KB3, P–K3; 3 P–Q4, P×P; 4 N×P, P–QR3—"Kan" Variation—5 N–QB3, Q–B2; 6 B–Q3, N–QB3; 7 B–K3, N–B3; 8 O–O, P–QN4; 9 N–N3, B–K2; 10 P–B4, P–Q3; 11 Q–B3. Crosschecking is advisable.

(*f*) 13 QR–K1, QR–Q1! 14 P–N4, N–QN5! 15 P–N5, N–Q2; 16 P–B5, N×B; 17 P×N, P–N5; 18 N–K2, P×P = .

(*g*) (A) 12 . . . N×N; 13 B×N, N–Q2; 14 P–QR3, B–N2; 15 P–B5, N–K4! ∞. (B) 12 . . . N–Q2; 13 N×N, Q×N; 14 B–B3, B–N2! 15 KR–B1, N–N3; 16 B×N, Q×B; 17 P–B5, K–R1; 18 B–R1, P–N5; 19 N–K2, Q–R4; 20 P–B6, B–Q1 = . Osnos–Kirilov, USSR 1966.

1 P–K4, P–QB4; 2 N–KB3, P–K3; 3 P–Q4, P×P; 4 N×P, N–KB3; 5 N–QB3, P–Q3

	151	152	153	154	155
6	P–KN3			P–KN4 (f)	
	N–B3	P–QR3 (Modern Paulsen		P–QR3	P–KR3 (h)
7	B–N2	B–N2 Defence-II)		P–N5	P–N5 (i)
	B–Q2	Q–B2		KN–Q2	P×P
8	O–O	O–O		B–N2	B×P
	B–K2	B–K2 (b)		P–N4	N–B3
9	N/4–K2!	N/4–K2	P–B4	P–B4	Q–Q2
	P–QR3	QN–Q2	O–O! (d)	B–N2	Q–N3
10	P–KR3	P–KR3	P–KN4	P–B5	N–N3
	Q–B2	O–O	N–B3	P–K4	P–QR3
11	K–R1	P–KN4	N×N	N/4–K2 (g)	O–O–O
	P–QN4	R–Q1	P×N	B–K2	B–Q2
12	P–R3	N–N3 (c)	P–N5	P–B6! ±	B–K3
	O–O (a)		N–Q2 (e)		Q–B2 (j)

(a) 13 P–KN4, K–R1; 14 N–N3, P–N5; 15 P×P, N×QNP; 16 P–N5, N–N1; 17 P–B4, P–Q4! = . Bondarevski.

(b) 8 . . . N–B3; 9 N/4–K2, B–K2; 10 P–N3, O–O; 11 B–N2, P–QN4 = .

(c) (A) 12 . . . P–QN4; 13 P–K5, P×P; 14 B×R, N–N3; 15 Q–K2 (15 Q–B3, N×B; 16 Q×N/8, B–N2!), N×B ∞ = . (B) 12 . . . R–N1; 13 P–N5, N–K1; 14 P–B4, P–QN4; 15 P–QR3, B–N2 = .

(d) 9 . . . N–B3; 10 N×N, P×N; 11 P–K5! P×P; 12 P×P, N–Q2; 13 B–B4, O–O; 14 N–K4, B–N2; 15 Q–R5 with chances.

(e) 13 P–B5, R–K1; 14 P–B6, B–B1; 15 K–R1, P–KN3; 16 P–KR4, N–K4; 17 B–B4, P–QR4; 18 B×N, P×B; 19 P–R5, B–R3; 20 R–B3 ± . Fuchs–Vasyukov, Polanica Zdroj 1965.

(f) The Keres Attack. For (A) 6 B–QB4, P–QR3; 7 B–N3 or 7 O–O see cols. 24–5. For (B) 6 P–B4, P–QR3; and 7 . . . P–KN3 see col. 22. (c) 6 B–N5, B–K2; 7 Q–Q2 (7 P–B4, P–KR3; 8 B–R4, N×P; 9 B×B, N×N; 10 B×Q, N×Q; 11 R×N, K×B; 12 N–N5, N–B3; 13 N×QP, K–K2; 14 N×B†, QR×N ∓ . Zuckerman), P–QR3; 8 O–O–O, P–N4; 9 P–QR3, B–N2; 10 P–B3, QN–Q2 = . Berger–Spasski, Amsterdam 1964.

(g) 11 N–N3, N–QB3; 12 B–K3, N–R4; 13 N×N, Q×N; 14 O–O, N–N3; 15 Q–B3, P–N5; 16 N–Q5, N×N; 17 P×N, B–K2; 18 P–QR3, with a minimal advantage. Ćirić–Langeweg, Beverwijk 1968. The column is Nikitin's analysis.

(h) A third resource is 6 . . . N–B3; 7 P–N5, N–Q2; 8 B–K3, (8 N/4–N5, N–N3; 9 B–KB4, N–K4; 10 Q–R5, N–N3; 11 B×P, B×B; 12 R–Q1, O–O; 13 N×B, Q–K2 =), B–K2 (or 8 . . . N–N3!); 9 P–KR4, O–O; 10 Q–Q2, P–QR3; 11 O–O–O, N×N; 12 B×N, P–N4; 13 P–QR3, B–N2 = . Ivkov. 8 P–KR4 is sharp.

(i) The present preference, as against 7 B–N2, (A) 7 . . . N–B3; (1) 8 P–KR3, B–K2; 9 B–K3, B–Q2; 10 N/4–K2, O–O; 11 O–O, N–QR4; 12 P–N3, P–QN4; 13 P–K5, P×P; 14 B×R, Q×B with counterplay for the exchange (Nikitin); (2) 8 P–N5! P×P; 9 B×P, Q–R4; 10 P–KR4! (B) 7 . . . P–QR3; 8 P–KR3, B–Q2; 9 B–K3, N–B3; 10 P–B4, B–K2; 11 N/4–K2, O–O; 12 O–O, with pressure. Whatever the individual choice, 6 P–KN4 remains dangerous, requiring discovery of further defences.

(j) 13 P–B4, P–QN4; 14 B–N2, R–B1 = . Stein–Krogius, USSR Chp. 1966.

1 P–K4, P–QB4; 2 N–KB3, P–K3; 3 P–Q4, P × P; 4 N × P

	156	157	158	159	160
	(N–KB3)			P–QR3 (Paulsen Variation)	
5	(N–QB3)			N–Q2	
	B–N5 (a) (Sicilian Counter Attack)			P–Q3	N–K2!?
6	P–K5		N–N5	B–Q3	B–Q3 (k)
	N–Q4	N–K5	N–QB3 (g)	N–KB3	P–QN4
7	B–Q2 (b)	Q–N4	B–KB4 (h)	O–O	O–O
	B × N!	Q–R4!	N × P	B–K2	B–N2
8	P × B	Q × N (e)	N–B7†	P–QB4	P–QR4!
	Q–B2 (c)	B × N†	K–K2 (i)	O–O	P × P
9	P–KB4	P × B	Q–B3	P–QN3	R × P
	O–O	Q × P†	P–Q4	B–Q2!	N–N3
10	P–B4	K–Q1	O–O–O	B–N2	N/2–N3
	Q–N3!	Q × R	B × N	N–B3	N–QB3
11	P–B3	N–N5	P × B	Q–K2 ∞	R–K1
	N–K2 (d)	P–Q4 (f)	P–KN4 (j)		N × N (l)

(a) (A) For 5 . . . N–QB3; see cols. 96–100. (B) If 5 . . . P–QR3? 6 P–K5 ± .

(b) 7 Q–N4, P–B4; (A) 8 P × P e.p, N × P; 9 Q × P, R–N1; 10 Q–R6, R–N3 = . (B) 8 Q × NP, R–B1; 9 B–K2, Q–R5! 10 O–O, R–B2; 11 Q–R6, Q × Q ∓ . Andreyev in *Misl* 1967/2.

(c) 8 . . . Q–K2; 9 Q–N4, K–B1; 10 B–Q3, P–Q3; 11 P–KB4 ± .

(d) 12 B–Q3, P–Q3; 13 Q–R5, N–B4 with some counterplay, Mahel–Ericson, corr. 1959.

(e) Interesting is 8 Q × P, B × N†; 9 P × B, Q × P†; 10 K–K2, P–N3! 11 Q × R†, K–K2; 12 B–R3†, P–Q3; 13 N–B6†, Q × N; 14 P × P†, K–Q2; 15 Q–N2! ∞ . Fuchs–Kauder, Leipzig 1960.

(f) 12 P × P e.p., N–R3; 13 P–Q7†, B × P! 14 N–Q6†, K–K2; 15 B × N, B–B3! 16 N–B5†, K–K1; 17 Q–QN4, R–Q1†; 18 N–Q6†, K–K2; 19 K–K2, Q–K4†; 20 N–K4†, K–K1; 21 B × P, B × B; 22 Q × B, P–B4; 23 B–N5! with a favourable ending. Ćirić–Kelečević, Sarajevo 1968.

(g) 6 . . . P–Q4; 7 P–K5, KN–Q2; 8 Q–N4, B–B1; 9 B–N5, Q–R4; 10 Q–QR4!

(h) The older try is 7 P–QR3, B × N†; 8 N × B, P–Q4; 9 B–Q3, P × P; 10 N × P, N × N; 11 B × N, Q × Q†; 12 K × Q, B–Q2 = . Robatsch–Ståhlberg, Havana 1964.

(i) 8 . . . K–B1; 9 Q–B3, P–Q4; 10 O–O–O, B × N; 11 P × B, R–QN1; 12 N × P! P × N; 13 Q × N! P × Q; 14 R × Q†, N × R; 15 B × R, P–QR3 (15 . . . N–B3; 16 B–Q6†, K–K1; 17 B–QB4! ±); 16 B–K2! Becker.

(j) 12 B–N3, P–B4; 13 P–B4! P–B5; 14 N × P†, P × N; 15 P × P ± . Becker.

(k) 6 P–KN3, P–Q4! 7 B–N2, P–K4! = .

(l) 12 N × N, B–Q3; 13 Q–R5, N–B5; 14 B × N, B × B; 15 N–N3, Q–B2; 16 P–K5 ± . Vasyukov–Savon, Budapest 1965.

1 P-K4, P-QB4; 2 N-KB3, P-K3; 3 P-Q4, P × P; 4 N × P, P-QR3 (a)

	161	162	163	164	165
5	P-QB4 ⎱ Maróczy		B-Q3		
	N-KB3 ⎰ Bind—II.		B-B4	N-QB3 (j)	
6	N-QB3		N-N3	N × N	
	B-N5		B-R2	NP × N	QP × N
7	B-Q3	Q-B3 (e)	O-O (g)	O-O	O-O
	N-B3	Q-B2	N-QB3	P-Q4	P-K4
8	N × N (b)	N-B2	Q-K2 (h)	P-QB4 (k)	N-Q2
	QP × N	B-Q3	KN-K2	N-B3	Q-B2
9	P-K5	B-K2	B-K3	N-B3	P-QR4
	N-Q2 (c)	N-B3	B × B	B-K2	N-B3
10	P-B4	Q-K3	Q × B	BP × P	Q-B3
	N-B4	P-QN3	P-Q4	BP × P	B-QB4 (m)
11	B-B2	B-Q2	P-K5	P × P	Q-N3
	Q × Q† (d)	O-O (f)	Q-B2 (i)	P × P (l)	O-O

(a) Porges–Paulsen, Dresden 1892, continued 5 B-Q3, N-KB3; 6 N-QB3, Q-B2; 7 B-K3, B-B4; 8 O-O, O-O; 9 Q-Q2, P-QN4 ∓ but see note (j).

(b) Less promising are 8 N-B2 or 8 N-K2 or 8 B-B2, as shown in detail in Moiseyev's monograph on the Paulsen Variation.

(c) 9 . . . Q-R4? 10 P × N, B × N†; 11 P × B, Q × P†; 12 B-Q2, Q × B; 13 P × P, R-KN1; 14 B-R6! Q-B6†; 15 K-B1, Q × P†; 16 K-N1, Q-Q4; 17 Q-K2 ± . Boleslavski.

(d) 12 K × Q, B × N; 13 P × B, K-Q1; 14 B-K3, P-QN3; 15 R-QN1, K-B2; 16 K-K2, R-QN1; 17 KR-Q1, P-QR4 = . Müller. In the column, also 6 . . . P-Q3; 7 B-K2, B-K2; 8 P-KN4! P-Q4! ∞ .

(e) Other options are (A) 7 B-Q2, O-O; 8 P-K5, B × N; 9 B × B, N-K5; 10 B-N4, P-Q3; 11 Q-K2, Q-N3 = . (B) 7 P-K5, N-K5; 8 Q-N4, N × N; 9 P-QR3, B-B1; 10 P × N, Q-R4; 11 Q-N3, P-Q3; 12 P × P, B × P; 13 Q × B, Q × P†; 14 B-Q2, Q × R†; 15 K-K2, Q-N7 ∓ .

(f) 12 P-KN4, B-B4; 13 Q-N3, P-Q3 = . Smyslov–Olafsson, Cand. tournament 1959.

(g) (A) 7 P-QB4, N-QB3; 8 O-O, KN-K2 = . (B) 7 Q-K2, N-QB3; 8 B-K3, B × B; 9 Q × B, KN-K2; 10 QN-Q2 (10 O-O leads into the column), O-O; 11 O-O-O, P-Q3; 12 P-KB4, N-N5! = . Moiseyev.

(h) (A) 8 Q-N4, N-B3; 9 Q-N3, P-Q3; 10 K-R1, O-O; 11 B-KN5, N-KR4; 12 Q-R4, P-B3; 13 B-Q2, P-KN3 = . Matanović–Velimirović, Yugoslavia 1964. (B) 8 QN-Q2, N-B3; 9 N-B4, P-Q4; 10 P × P, P × P; 11 Q-K2†, B-K3; 12 N-K5, N × N; 13 Q × N, B-N1; 14 Q-N5, O-O = .

(i) 12 R-K1, B-Q2; 13 QN-Q2, P-B3 = . Parma–Korchnoi, Zagreb 1964.

(j) (A) Back in favour is 5 . . . N-KB3; 6 O-O, P-Q3; 7 P-QB4, B-K2; 8 N-B3, O-O; 9 K-R1, P-QN3 = . For 6 N-QB3 see note (a). (B) 5 . . . P-KN3?! 6 P-KB4, B-N2; 7 N-KB3, P-Q3; 8 O-O, N-K2; 9 K-R1, QN-B3; 10 N-B3, P-QN4; 11 Q-K1, N-N5 ∞ . Boudy.

(k) 8 Q-K2, N-B3; 9 B-KN5, B-K2; 10 N-Q2, O-O; 11 QR-K1, R-K1; 12 K-R1, B-N2; 13 P-KB4, N-Q2 = .

(l) (A) 12 B-K3, O-O; 13 B-Q4, B-K3; 14 KR-K1 ± . Matanović–Ree, 1966. (B) 12 Q-R4†, Q-Q2; 13 R-K1, Q × Q; 14 N × Q, B-K3; 15 B-K3, O-O; 16 B-QB5, KR-K1; 17 B × B, R × B; 18 P-QN4 ± . Fischer–Petrosian, 7th match game 1971.

(m) Better than 10 . . . P-KR4; 11 N-B4, B-K3; 12 N-K3, B-QN5, 13 Q-N3. The column is *Comments*.

1 P-K4, P-QB4; 2 N-KB3, P-K3; 3 P-Q4 (*a*), P × P; 4 N × P, P-QR3

	166	167	168	169	170
5	B-Q3)	N-QB3 (*d*)			. . . . . N-Q2
	(N-QB3)	P-QN4	Q-B2		N-KB3!
6	(N × N)	B-Q3 (*e*)	P-KN3	B-K2	B-Q3 (*k*)
	(QP × N)	B-N2	P-QN4	N-KB3	P-K4
7	P-KB4	O-O	B-N2	O-O	KN-N3
	P-K4 (*b*)	N-K2	B-N2	B-N5	N-B3
8	P × P	B-K3! (*f*)	O-O	Q-Q3 (*i*)	O-O
	Q-R4†	KN-QB3	N-KB3	N-B3	B-K2
9	N-Q2	N-N3	R-K1	P-QR3	P-KB4
	B-K3	P-Q3	P-Q3	B × N	O-O
10	O-O	P-B4	N-Q5	P × B	Q-K2
	N-K2	B-K2	P × N	O-O	P-Q3
11	K-R1	P-B5	P × P†	P-KB4	N-B3
	N-N3 (*c*)	O-O (*g*)	K-Q1 (*h*)	P-Q4 (*j*)	P-QR4 (*l*)

(*a*) (A) Compare the lines of the "Modern Closed" Sicilian (cols. 176–180) for similar stratagems after 3 P-Q3?! N-QB3; 4 P-KN3, e.g., (1) 4 . . . P-KN3; 5 B-N2, B-N2; 6 O-O, KN-K2; 7 R-K1, O-O; 8 P-K5, P-N3! 9 QN-Q2, P-Q3; 10 P × P, Q × P; 11 N-B4, Q-Q1 = . Garcia–Najdorf, Mar del Plata 1968. It can also arise from or transpose into the French Defence, col. 111 (*a*) and dates back to Staunton, 1851. (2) 4 . . . KN-K2; 5 B-N2, P-Q3; 6 P-B3, P-KN3 = ; or (3) 4 . . . P-Q4; 5 QN-Q2, N-B3; 6 B-N2, B-K2; 7 O-O, O-O; 8 Q-K2, P-QN4   ; or 8 R-K1, etc., exactly as in the French Defence, col. 111, or Réti Opening, Barcza system, col. 13. (B) 3 N-B3, N-QB3; 4 B-N5 (see col. 58), or 4 Q-K2, KN-K2; 5 P-KN3, P-Q4; 6 B-N2, P-Q5; 7 N-Q1, P-K4; 8 O-O, P-B3 = . Smyslov–Larsen, Hastings 1972–3. See also col. 78, note (*g*). (*c*) 3 P-B3, P-Q4! (but if 3 . . . N-KB3; 4 P-K5, N-Q4; 5 P-Q4, P × P; 6 P × P, P-Q3; 7 B-QB4! ± . Evans.); 4 B-Q3, N-QB3 5 P-K5 (1) 5 . . . B-Q2; 6 O-O, KN-K2; 7 B-B2, R-B1; 8 R-K1, Q-N3; 9 P-Q3, N-B4; 10 QN-Q2, B-K2 = . Kopec–Commons, New York 1974. (2) 5 . . . P-Q5; 6 Q-K2, KN-K2; 7 O-O, N-N3; 8 Q-K4, B-K2 (8 . . . P × P; 9 QP × P, KN × P; 10 N × N, N × N; 11 B-N5†, N-Q2; 12 R-Q1 ±); 9 N-R3, O-O; 10 P × P, P × P; 11 N-B2, Q-B2! 12 R-K1, R-Q1; 13 P-KR4, P-KR4; 14 P-KN4, P × P; 15 P-R5, QN × P; 16 N × N, P-B4; 17 Q-K2, N-B5; 18 Q-B1, P-QN4!; resigns. Sax-Ljubojević, Yugoslavia 1980.

(*b*) 7 . . . P-QB4; 8 O-O, N-K2; 9 B-K3, N-B3; 10 N-Q2, B-K2. Müller.

(*c*) 12 N-B4, Q-B2; 13 P-QR4, B-K2; 14 N-Q6†, B × N; 15 P × B, Q × P; 16 Q-R5, Q-K4; 17 Q-K2, O-O; 18 P-R5, KR-K1 = .

(*d*) These variations were further explored by Russian master Kan in the 1950s. Throughout cols. 161–70 and whenever the move . . . N-QB3 is, or seems, feasible in conjunction with . . . Q-B2, reference is necessary to the Taimanov variation, cols. 121–5.

(*e*) 6 B-K2, B-N2; 7 B-B3, N-QB3; 8 B-KB4, P-Q3; 9 N × N, B × N; 10 O-O, B-K2 = .

(*f*) White may vary with 8 B-N5, P-R3; 9 B-K3, KN-B3! 10 N-N3, P-Q3; 11 P-B4, B-K2; 12 P-B5, with attack. Less energetic are 8 R-K1, 8 P-K5 or 8 Q-R5.

(*g*) 12 Q-R5, N-K4; 13 N-Q4, N × B; 14 P × N, P-K4; 15 P-B6, P × N; 16 P × B, Q × P; 17 B × P, N-Q2 ∞. Moiseyev.

(*h*) 12 B-N5, QN-Q2; 13 P-QB4 ± .

(*i*) Ineffective is 8 B-Q2, N-B3! 9 N × N, NP × N; 10 B-Q3, P-QR4; 11 Q-K2, P-Q4; 12 P × P, BP × P; 13 N-N5, Q-Q1 = .

(*j*) 12 P-K5, N-K5; 13 B-B3, N-B4 = . Keres–Khasin, USSR Chp. 1957. The stability of this Paulsen Variation is borne out by its recurrence in (5 N-QB3, Q-B2;) 6 B-Q3, N-KB3; 7 O-O, N-B3; 8 N × N, NP × N; 9 P-B4, P-Q4; 10 Q-B3, B-N2; 11 K-R1, B-K2; 12 P-QN3,

P–Q5; 13 N–Q1, P–B4; 14 N–B2, O–O; 15 Q–R3, N–Q2; 16 B–Q2, P–QR4; 17 P–K5, P–N3; 18 N–N4, P–R5; 19 P–B5! ± . Karpov–Cobo, Skopje 1972. The whole sequence is identical with Winawer–L. Paulsen, Berlin 1881!

(*k*) 6 P–K5, N–Q4; 7 B–QB4, P–Q3; 8 P × P, N–KB3; 9 O–O, B × P; 10 N/2–B3, O–O; 11 Q–K2, Q–B2 = . Geller–Gipslis, Moscow 1967.

(*l*) 12 B–K3, P–R5; 13 N–B1, N–Q2; 14 P–B3, N–B4; 15 B–QB2, B–K3 = . Gershman–Suetin, USSR 1965.

1 P-K4, P-QB4; 2 N-KB3

	171 Tartakover- O'Kelly Var.	172 Morra Gambit-I	173 Nimzowitsch Variation	174 The Hyper-accelerated Dragon	175
	P-QR3!	. . . .	N-KB3	P-KN3	
3	P-Q4 (a)		P-K5! (f)	P-Q4 (h)	
	P×P		N-Q4	B-N2	P×P
4	N×P	P-B3	N-B3	N-B3! (i)	Q×P
	N-KB3!	P×P	P-K3	N-QB3	N-KB3
5	N-Q2 (b)	N×P	N×N	B-K3	P-K5
	N-B3	N-QB3	P×N	Q-R4	N-B3
6	N×N	B-QB4	P-Q4	Q-Q2	Q-QR4
	QP×N!	P-Q3	N-B3	N-B3	N-Q4
7	B-Q3	O-O	P×P	P×P	Q-K4
	P-K4	N-B3	B×P	N-KN5	N/4-N5?!
8	O-O	P-KR3 (d)	Q×P	B-QB4	P-QR3 (k)
	B-KN5	P-K3	Q-N3	Q-N5	P-Q4
9	Q-K1	Q-K2	B-QB4	B-N3	Q-K2
	B-QB4 (c)	B-K2 (e)	B×P† (g)	N×B (j)	N-R3∞

(a) (A) 3 P-KN3, P-KN3; 4 B-N2, B-N2; 5 O-O, N-QB3; 6 P-B3, P-Q3; 7 P-Q3 (7 P-Q4, P×P; 8 P×P, Q-N3!), N-B3; 8 N-R3, O-O = . Réti-Tartakover, match, Vienna 1919. (B) 3 P-B3, P-Q4 (or 3 . . . P-Q3!); 4 P×P, Q×P; 5 P-Q4, P×P (or 5 . . . B-N5; 6 B-K2, P-K3; 7 O-O, QN-Q2 =); 6 P×P, N-KB3; 7 N-B3, Q-Q3! 8 B-QB4 (or 8 B-KN5), P-K3; 9 O-O, B-K2; 10 N-K5, N-B3 = . Unzicker-Taimanov, Leningrad 1960. Compare col. 184. (c) 3 P-B4, N-QB3; 4 P-Q4, P×P; 5 N×P, N-B3; 6 N-QB3, P-K4; 7 N-N5, P-Q4; 8 BP×P, B×N; 9 P×B, N-Q5; 10 B-Q3! N×QP; 11 O-O, B-N5; 12 B-K4, N×N; 13 P×N, B×P; 14 R-N1, O-O; 15 Q-N4, Q-Q3; 16 R-Q1 (Kupper-Tordion, Bern 1956), QR-B1∞ . *(Schach-Echo* 1956).

(b) 5 N-QB3, P-K4; 6 N-B3, B-N5; (A) 7 B-QB4, Q-B2; 8 Q-Q3, P-QN4; 9 B-N3, B-N2; 10 B-Q2, B×N; 11 B×B, P-Q3 = . Alexander-Prins, Bern 1962. (B) 7 B-Q2, P-Q3; 8 B-Q3, QN-Q2; 9 P-QR3, B×N; 10 B×B, N-B4; 11 B-N4, Q-B2; 12 N-Q2, B-K3 = . Schmidt-O'Kelly, Beverwijk 1949.

(c) 10 N-N3! B-R2; 11 B-K3, Q-B2 = . Spielmann-Tartakover, match, Vienna 1921.

(d) (A) 8 Q-K2, B-N5; 9 R-Q1, P-K3; 10 B-B4, Q-B2 = . Devault-Ludvik, corr. 1968. (B) 8 B-KN5, P-K3; 9 Q-K2, B-K2; 10 KR-K1, Q-B2 = ; see col. 49 and 185.

(e) 10 B-B4, (A) 10 . . . B-Q2 = . Devault-Ken Smith, Austin 1967. (B) 10 . . . Q-B2; 11 KR-Q1, O-O; 12 B-QN3, Q-N1; 13 QR-B1, N-K4; 14 N-Q4, B-Q2 = . *Byulleten* 1971, No. 6. Also see cols. 49 and 185.

(f) Effective is the delaying treatment 3 N-B3! (A) 3 . . . P-Q4? 4 B-N5†, B-Q2; 5 P-K5, P-Q5; 6 P×N, P×N; 7 P×NP, P×P†; 8 Q×P, B×P; 9 B-Q3. (Fischer-Sherwin, US Chp. 1963), Q-N3! = . (B) 3 . . . N-B3; 4 P-Q4, P-Q4; 5 P×QP, N-QB3; 6 P-B4, N-N3; (1) 7 P-QN4, N×NP; 8 B-N2, B-K2; 9 P-KR4 ± . Gurgenidze-Mnatsakanian, Tbilisi 1977. Or (2) 7 P-QN3, B-K2; 8 B-N2, O-O; 9 B-K2, P-B3; 10 P×P, P×P; 11 O-O ± . Moreover, White also has 5 P×QP, KN×P; 6 N×N, Q×N; 7 B-K3, P×P; 8 N×P, Q-R4†; 9 P-B3, N×N; 10 P-QN4 ± . Spasski-Pribyl, Tallinn 1973.

(g) 10 K-K2, O-O; 11 R-N1, B-B4; 12 N-N5, N-Q5†; 13 K-Q1! N-K3; 14 N-K4, P-Q3; 15 P×P, R-Q1; 16 B-Q3, B×P ∞.

(h) Features of the "Robatsch" Defence are exhibited by 3 P-B4, B-N2; 4 P-Q4, P-Q3 (4 . . . Q-R4†; 5 B-Q2, Q-N3; 6 B-B3, N-KB3; 7 P-Q5, O-O; 8 QN-Q2, P-Q3; 9 B-K2, P-K4 = . Gufeld/Lazarev); 5 N-B3, N-QB3 (6 P-Q5, N-Q5!); 6 B-K3, Q-N3; 7 N-Q5,

Q-R4†; 8 Q-Q2, Q×Q†; 9 B×Q, K-Q1; 10 P×P, P×P; 11 O-O-O, B-N5; 12 N-KN5, B×R; 13 N×P†, K-Q2; 14 K×B, B×P; 15 N×R, B×N; 16 P-N3, P-K3; 17 B-R3, N-Q5! Schwarz. The position can also arise after 1 N-KB3, P-KN3; 2 P-K4, P-QB4; etc.

(*i*) 4 P×P, Q-R4†; 5 N-B3, N-KB3; 6 N-Q2! Q×BP; 7 N-B4, O-O; 8 P-K5, N-N5; 9 Q×N, P-Q4; 10 B-K3, Q-N5; 11 Q-N3 (11 Q-R4, P×N; 12 O-O-O, B-K3; 13 N-Q5, B×N; 14 R×B, Q-K8†; 15 R-Q1, Q-R4 =), P×N; 12 O-O-O, B-K3; 13 P-B4, N-B3; 14 B-K2, QR-Q1 = . Vasyukov-Hort, Havana 1967.

(*j*) 10 Q×N, N-Q5; 11 P-K5, N-B4; 12 Q-K4, Q×P; 13 Q-Q5, with a somewhat better endgame. Damjanović-Filipović, Yugoslavia 1966.

(*k*) 8 B-QN5, Q-R4; 9 N-B3, B-N2; 10 O-O, O-O; 11 B-KB4, P-Q4; 12 P×P *e.p.*, B-B4 ∓ . The column is Steinberg-Shidkov, USSR 1968.

1 P–K4, P–QB4; 2 N–QB3

	176	177	178	179	180
	N–QB3.................		P–Q3 (g)		
3	P–B4	P–Q3	P–KN3!		
	P–KN3 (a)	... P–Q3 (f)	N–QB3		
4	B–B4 (b)	P–KN4	B–N2		
	B–N2	P–K4	P–KN3		
5	N–B3	B–N2	P–Q3		
	P–K3	KN–K2	B–N2		
6	P–B5	P–KR4	B–K3	KN–K2......	P–B4
	NP × P (c)	N–N3	P–K4!	P–K4! (i)	P–K3
7	P–Q3	P–R5	Q–Q2	O–O	N–B3
	P–Q4 (d)	N–B5	KN–K2	KN–K2	KN–K2
8	P × QP	B × N	P–KR4	B–K3	O–O
	B × N†	P × B	P–KR3	O–O	O–O
9	P × B	N–Q5	N–R3	P–B4	B–Q2
	P × P (e)	P–KN4 =	N–Q5 (h)	N–Q5 (j)	R–N1 (k)

(a) 3 . . . P–K3; 4 N–B3, P–Q4; 5 B–N5, KN–K2; (1) 6 Q–K2, P × P; 7 N × P, P–QR3; 8 B × N†, N × B; 9 P–QN3, B–K2; 10 B–N2, O–O = . Rossolimo–Zuckerman, US Chp. 1967. (2) 6 P × P! N × P (6 . . . P × P; 7 Q–K2, Q–N3; 8 B × N†, P × B; 9 O–O, B–B4; 10 P–Q4! Zinn); 7 O–O! B–K2; 8 B × N†, P × B; 9 N–K5, Q–B2; 10 P–Q3, O–O; 11 Q–K1! ± . Zinn–Richardson, Budva 1963.

(b) 4 N–B3, B–N2; (A) 5 B–N5, P–Q3; 6 O–O, B–Q2; 7 B × N (7 Q–K1, N–Q5! =), B × B; 8 P–Q3, N–B3; 9 Q–K1, N–Q2; 10 B–K3, P–QN4! = . Pietzsch–Eliskases, Leipzig 1960. Also compare col. 58. (B) 5 B–B4, P–Q3; 6 O–O, P–K3 (6 . . . N–B3); 7 P–B5, KP × P; 8 P–Q3, KN–K2; 9 Q–K1! ± . Tarjan–Rattinger, San Juan 1971.

(c) 6 . . . KP × P; 7 P–Q3, KN–K2; 8 O–O, O–O; 9 Q–K1, P–QR3 = .

(d) Or first 7 . . . KN–K2; 8 O–O, P–Q4; 9 P × QP, P × P; 10 B–N3, B–K3 ∞ .

(e) 10 Q–K2†, KN–K2; 11 B–QN5, B–K3; 12 O–O, P–QR3∞. A timely return of the pawn might improve Black's counter chances.

(f) Also 3 . . . P–KN3; 4 P–QN3, B–N2; 5 B–N2, R–N1; 6 P–N3, P–Q3; 7 KN–K2, P–K3 = . The column is Suttles–Reshevsky, US Open Chp. 1965.

(g) Deferring . . . N–QB3, or rather transposing with 2 . . . P–Q3, reduces White's conventional choices after 2 . . . N–QB3; 3 N–KB3 (and 4 P–Q4), and still retains a "closed" strategy. Also possible is 2 . . . P–K3; as in cols. 166–70, note (a).

(h) 10 N–Q1, B–N5; 11 N–N1, P–Q4 = . Redolfi–Sanguinetti, Mar del Plata 1959. In the column, 5 N–B3, B–N2; 6 O–O, B–N5; 7 P–KR3, B × N; 8 Q × B, P–K3 is Romanishin–Gulko, USSR Chp. 1977.

(i) 6 . . . P–N3; 7 O–O, B–N2; 8 B–K3 and 9 Q–Q2!

(j) 10 Q–Q2, B–K3; 11 QR–K1, Q–Q2; 12 N–B1, QR–Q1; 13 N–Q5, P–N3; 14 P–B3, N/5–B3 = . Kholmov–Tal, USSR Chp. 1969.

(k) 10 R–N1, P–QN4; 11 P–QR3, P–B4! 12 B–K3, Q–B2; 13 B–B2, K–R1; 14 R–K1, P–N5∞. Spasski–Larsen, match 1968.

1 P-K4, P-QB4

	181 Keres' Line	182 Wing Gambit	183 Alapin's Line	184 Sicilian Gambit	185 Centre Morra Gambit-II
2	N-K2......	P-QN4!?	P-QB3......	P-Q4 (j)	
	P-Q3 (a)	P×P	P-Q4 (e)	P×P	
3	P-KN3	P-QR3	P-Q4 (f)	P-QB3 (k)	
	P-KN3	P-Q4 (c)	P-K3	P-Q4 (l).....P×P	P×P
4	B-N2	P×QP	KP×P (g)	KP×P	N×P
	B-N2	Q×P	KP×P	Q×P	N-QB3
5	O-O	N-KB3	N-KB3	P×P	N-B3
	N-QB3	P-K4	N-QB3	N-QB3	P-KN3 (n)
6	P-QB3	P×P	B-K3	N-KB3	B-QB4
	P-K4	B×P	P×P (h)	P-K4	B-N2
7	P-Q3	N-R3	B×QP	N-B3	P-K5 (o)
	KN-K2	B×N	N×B	B-QN5	Q-R4 (p)
8	P-QR3	B×B	Q×N	B-Q2	O-O
	O-O	N-QB3	N-B3	B×N	N×P
9	P-QN4	P-B4	B-N5†	B×B	N×N
	P-N3 (b)	Q-Q1 (d)	B-Q2 (i)	P×P (m)	B×N (q)

(a) (A) 2 . . . N-QB3; 3 P-KN3, P-Q4! (B) 2 . . . N-KB3; 3 QN-B3, P-Q4; 4 P×P, N×P; 5 N×N, Q×N; 6 P-Q4! P-K4!∞. Noting Black's sixth move, the variation could also arise from 1 P-K4, P-K4; 2 N-K2!? (Alapin) 2 . . . P-QB4!?

(b) 10 P-KB4, P×BP; 11 P×KBP, P-Q4; 12 P-K5, B-N5; 13 P-KR3, B×N; 14 Q×B, P-B3 = . Keres–Fischer, Stockholm 1962.

(c) 3 . . . P×P! 4 N×P, P-Q3; 5 B-N2, N-QB3; 6 P-Q4, N-B3; 7 B-Q3, P-K3; 8 N-B3, B-K2; 9 O-O, O-O = . Marshall–Sämisch, 1925.

(d) 10 Q-N1, KN-K2; 11 B-Q3 (Bronstein–Benko, match Moscow–Budapest 1949), P-KR3; and . . . O-O = . Comments.

(e) Black may also choose the formation (A) 2 . . . P-KN3; 3 P-Q4, P×P; 4 P×P, P-Q4; 5 P-K5, N-QB3; 6 N-QB3, B-N2; 7 B-K2! Or (B) 2 . . . P-QN3; 3 P-Q4, B-N2; 4 B-Q3 (or 4 P-Q5!?), N-KB3; 5 N-Q2 (or 5 P-B3). Or (c) 2 . . . P-Q3; 3 P-Q3 (or 3 B-Q3?!), N-KB3; see col. 51. (D) 2 . . . P-K3, 3 N-KB3, N-KB3; see cols. 166–70 notes (a). (E) 2 . . . N-KB3; 3 P-K5, N-Q4; 4 P-Q4, P×P; 5 N-B3, N-QB3; 6 P×P, P-Q3; 7 B-QB4 (or 7 N-B3 =), P-K3!? (7 . . . N-N2?!); 8 O-O, B-K2; 9 Q-K2, O-O; 10 N-B3, N×N; 11 P×N, P×P = . Comments.

(f) 3 P×P, Q×P (or 3 . . . N-KB3!); 4 P-Q4, N-KB3; 5 N-B3, N-B3; 6 P×P, Q×BP; 7 B-K3, Q-QR4; 8 P-QN4, Q-B2 = .

(g) 4 P-K5, N-QB3; 5 N-B3, Q-N3; 6 P-QR3, P-B5 = . (Silmar–Mrs. Kushnir, Lone Pine 1975) has French features.

(h) After 6 . . . P-B5 Black's position remains frozen, whereas the text allows him some mobility. White now exchanges his immobile bishop.

(i) 10 B×B†, Q×B; 11 O-O, B-K2; 12 QN-Q2, O-O; 13 KR-K1, B-Q3 = . Sveshnikov–Tal, USSR Chp. 1973.

(j) (A) 2 P-Q3, N-QB3 (or 2 . . . P-K3); 3 P-KN3 see Réti–Barcza System, or Flank Openings, King's Fianchetto Opening. The sequence chosen here allows 2 . . . P-Q4?! 3 P×P, N-KB3; 4 N-QB3, P-KN3; 5 B-N5, B-N2; 6 Q-Q2, P-KR3; 7 B-R4, N-R3 ∞. (B) 2 P-KN3, P-Q4! 3 P×P, Q×P; 4 N-KB3, B-N5; 5 B-N2, Q-K3† (or 5 . . . N-QB3; 6 P-KR3, B-B4; 4 O-O, Q-Q2; 8 K-R2, O-O-O; 9 P-Q3, P-K4 =); 6 K-B1, B-R6; 7 N-B3, N-QB3; 8 P-Q3, Q-Q2 = . For 2 . . . P-KN3 see King's Fianchetto Opening. (c) 2 P-KB4, N-QB3; 3 N-KB3, P-K3; 4 B-N5, N-K2; 5 O-O, P-Q4 = .

(*k*) 3 N–KB3, (1) 3 . . . N–QB3! 4 P–B3, P × P; 5 N × P, P–Q3; transposing into col. 49; or (2) 3 . . . P–K4; 4 P–B3? P × P; 5 N × P, N–QB3; 6 B–QB4, B–N5; 7 O–O, N–B3 ∞. Grechkin–Shamayev, USSR 1946.

(*l*) Declining the gambit, which can also be affected by (A) 3 . . . N–KB3; 4 P–K5, N–Q4; 5 Q × P, P–K3; 6 B–QB4, N–QB3; 7 Q–K4, P–Q3; (1) 8 N–B3, P × P; 9 N × P, B–Q3; 10 N × N, P × N; 11 O–O, O–O; 12 N–Q2, P–B4 = . Leonidov–Moiseyev, USSR 1967. (2) 8 P × P, N–B3; 9 Q–K2, B × P; 10 B–KN5, P–QR3; 11 P–QR4, N–K4; 12 N–Q2, N × B = . Champion–Tiemann, corr. 1977–8.

(*m*) 10 N × P, KN–K2; 11 N × N, Q × N = . Knežević–Matulović, Kraljevo 1967.

(*n*) Now Black is well advised to transpose into the safer cols. 49 or 172 by playing 5 . . . P–Q3 as the strategy in the column leads him downhill.

(*o*) 7 O–O, P–Q3! but not 7 . . . N–R3; 8 B–B4, O–O; 9 P–KR3, K–R1; 10 Q–Q2, N–KN1; 11 P–K5, or 11 N–KN5 ± .

(*p*) Probably Black should risk 7 . . . N × P; 8 N × N, B × N; 9 Q–B3, B × N†; 10 P × B, N–B3; 11 B–N5, O–O; 12 B × N (otherwise . . . N–R4), P × B; 13 O–O, R–N1; 14 QR–N1, P–QR3; 15 P–QR4, Q–R4, with Black two pawns up. *Comments.*

(*q*) 10 N–Q5, P–K3; 11 R–K1, P–B3; 12 B–N3! K–B2; 13 R × B, P × R; 14 Q–B3†, K–K1; 15 B–R6 + . Sokolov–Pete, Kikinda 1954 (if 15 . . . N × B; 16 Q–B6 wins). White also has a forced win after 10 . . . N–B3; 11 R–K1, P–Q3; 12 B–KR6, B–K3; 13 R × B! P × R; 14 B–N5†, N–Q2; 15 R–B1, B × N; 16 Q × B, Q–Q1; 17 R–Q1 (S. E. Jones).

Centre Counter Defence

(1 P–K4, P–Q4; 2 P × P)
*If 2 P–K5? B–B4. For 2 N–QB3,
N–KB3 see Alekhin's Defence.

The Centre Counter is better than its reputation, and its unpopularity is largely undeserved. Attempts to rehabilitate it have come from such varied quarters as Bronstein and Nona Gaprindashvili in Russia, Karaklajić in Yugoslavia, and Seidman in the USA. Black does not hem in his bishop, and White is forced to adopt an open game in order to sustain the initiative. There are two main branches, depending upon whether Black plays 2 . . . Q × P or 2 . . . N–KB3.

   2 . . . Q × P is open to the theoretical objection that the early development of the queen is a violation of principle, that the centre is abandoned to White with gain of tempo after 3 N–QB3. Still, there is no outright refutation of 3 . . . Q–QR4 (cols. 1–3), and White can obtain only a minimal edge against 3 . . . Q–Q1 (cols. 4–5). However, Black's margin of safety has narrowed in cols. 1–5, and therefore 2 . . . N–KB3 (cols. 6–10) has gained in popularity.

   Apparently 3 P–Q4, N × P; 4 P–QB4 (col. 10) with features similar to the Caro–Kann still represents the most sustained effort by White to maintain pressure in an otherwise periodically rehabilitated defence.

229

1 P-K4, P-Q4; 2 P×P, Q×P; 3 N-QB3

	1	2	3	4	5
	Q-QR4			Q-Q1	
4	P-Q4 (a)			B-B4	P-Q4
	N-KB3.................		P-K4	P-KN3	N-KB3
5	N-B3		N-B3 (g)	N-B3	B-KB4 (j)
	B-N5	N-B3 (d)	B-QN5	B-N2	P-KN3
6	P-KR3	B-QN5 (e)	B-Q2!	P-Q4	Q-Q2
	B×N (b)	B-Q2	B-N5	N-KB3	B-N2
7	Q×B	O-O!	P-QR3	O-O	O-O-O
	P-B3	O-O-O	B-Q3	O-O	P-B3
8	B-QB4	B-K3	B-QB4	P-KR3	B-R6
	P-K3	N-Q4	P×P	P-B3	O-O
9	O-O	P-QR4	Q-K2†	R-K1	P-KR4
	QN-Q2 (c)	N×B (f)	Q-K4 (h)	QN-Q2 (i)	Q-R4 (k)

(a) (A) 4 N-B3, N-KB3; 5 P-Q4, B-KN5; as in the column. (B) 4 P-QN4 (The Kotrc–Mieses Gambit), Q×NP; 5 R-N1, Q-Q3; 6 N-B3, N-KB3; 7 P-Q4, P-QR3; 8 B-QB4, P-K3; 9 O-O, B-K2; 10 R-K1, P-QN4 ∓. Sir G. Thomas–DuMont, Tunbridge Wells, 1912.

(b) 6 . . . B-R4; 7 P-KN4, B-N3; 8 N-K5, P-B3; 9 P-KR4 QN-Q2; 10 N-B4, Q-B2; 11 P-R5, B-K5; 12 R-R4 ± .

(c) 10 B-B4, B-K2; 11 KR-K1, O-O; 12 P-QR3, KR-K1; 13 B-KN3, QR-Q1; with an as yet unresolved position.

(d) 5 . . . P-B3; 6 N-K5! e.g. 6 . . . B-B4; 7 P-KN4! ± .

(e) Restrictive but not fully convincing is 6 P-Q5?! N-QN5; 7 B-N5†, P-B3; 8 P×P, P×P; 9 B-R4, B-Q2 (but not 9 . . . B-R3? 10 P-QR3! R-Q1; 11 B-Q2 + + . Fischer–Seidman, US Chp. 1960).

(f) 10 P×N, P-B3; 11 N-Q2, P-K3; 12 N-R2, N-K4; 13 P-QN4, Q-N3; 14 P-B4, P-B3; 15 P-B5 ± . Mednis–Seidman, US Chp. 1962.

(g) 5 P×P, N-QB3; 6 N-B3, B-QN5; 7 B-Q2, B-N5; 8 B-QN5, KN-K2; 9 P-QR3, QB×N; 10 P×B, B×N; 11 B×N†, N×B; 12 B×N, Q-R5; 13 Q-Q5, Q×BP∞. Mechkarov.

(h) 10 Q×Q†, B×Q; 11 N×B, P×N; 12 B×P† ± . Veselý–Krocian, ČSSR 1956.

(i) 10 B-KN5, P-KR3; 11 B-K3 ± . Comments.

(j) Tamer but also good is 5 B-QB4, B-N5; 6 P-B3, B-B1; 7 B-KN5, P-K3; 8 P-B4, QN-Q2; 9 N-B3, N-N3; 10 B-N3, P-QR4; 11 P-QR4 ± . Fuderer–Bronstein, Yugoslavia v. USSR 1959.

(k) 10 P-R5! + . Fischer–Robatsch, Varna Olympics 1962.

1 P–K4, P–Q4; 2 P × P, N–KB3

	6	7	8	9	10
3	B–N5†	. . . .	. . .	P–Q4 (j)	
	B–Q2			N × P	
4	B–K2	. . . . B–B4		N–KB3	. . . . . . P–QB4
	N × P	P–QN4!?	. . . . B–N5 (f)	B–N5! (k)	N–KB3 (m)
5	P–Q4	B–K2 (d)	P–KB3	B–K2	N–KB3
	P–KN3	N × P	B–B4	P–K3	P–KN3
6	P–QB4 (a)	B–B3	N–B3 (g)	O–O	N–B3
	N–N3	B–B3	QN–Q2	N–QB3	B–N2
7	N–QB3	N–K2	Q–K2 (h)	P–B3	P–KR3
	B–N2	N–KB3	N–N3	B–Q3	O–O
8	P–B5	B × B†	B–N3	N–K5	B–K3
	N–B1	N × B	Q–Q2	B × B	QN–Q2
9	B–KB4 (b)	O–O	P–Q6!	Q × B	Q–Q2
	O–O (c)	P–K3 (e)	Q × P (i)	B × N (l)	P–B3 (n)

(a) 6 N–KB3, B–N2; 7 O–O, O–O; 8 P–B3, B–N5! = .

(b) 9 P–Q5, P–QB3; 10 Q–N3, P–N3; 11 B–B3, O–O; 12 B–K3, P × QP; 13 B × P, N–B3; 14 R–Q1, Q–B2; 15 N–N5, Q–N2; 16 N–Q4, P–K4! = .

(c) 10 B–B3, N–B3; 11 KN–K2, P–K4; 12 P × P, N × P; 13 B–K4, P–QB3; 14 O–O, B–K3 = . Suetin–Lutikov, USSR 1959.

(d) Solid is also 5 B–N3! B–N5; 6 N–KB3, N × P; 7 N–B3, N × N; 8 N–K5!

(e) 10 P–Q4, B–K2 = . Suetin–Bronstein, USSR 1965.

(f) No safe alternative is 4 . . . P–KN3; 5 N–QB3, B–N2; 6 P–Q4, P–B3: 7 KN–K2 and Black is cramped.

(g) A parting of ways, choosing between the text and (A) 6 P–B3, P–QR3; 7 P–QR4, QN–Q2 and . . . N–N3. *Bilten.* (B) 6 N–K2, N × P; 7 N–N3, B–N3; 8 O–O, P–K3; 9 P–B4, N–QB3; 10 P–Q4, QN–K2; 11 B–N3, P–KR4; 12 Q–K2, P–R5 = . Bergraser–Schmid, corr. 1955. (C) 6 P–KN4?! B–B1; 7 N–B3, (1) 7 . . . QN–Q2; 8 P–N5, N–N3; 9 B–N5†, KN–Q2; 10 P–B4, N × P; 11 N × N, P–QB3; 12 B–B4, P × N; 13 B × P, P–K4! 14 N–B3, Q–R4, 15 B–N3, P–K5; 16 Q–K2, N–B4 = . O'Kelly on Fischer–Bergraser, Monte Carlo 1967 (2) 7 . . . P–B3; 8 P × P, N × BP; 9 P–Q3, P–K4; 10 P–N5, N–KR4; 11 N–K4, B–K2; 12 N–K2, O–O; 13 P–B3, N–R4; 14 B–K3, N × B = . Alexandria–Gaprindashvili, Women's World Chp., Tbilisi 1976.

(h) (A) 7 KN–K2, N–N3; 8 P–Q3, QN × P; 9 N × N, N × N; 10 N–N3, P–KN3; 11 P–B4, Q–Q3; 12 Q–B3, O–O–O = . (B) 7 P–KN4, see note (g) (C).

(i) 10 N–N5, Q–Q2; 11 Q–K5, O–O–O; 12 N × P†, K–N1; 13 N–N5, KN–Q4; 14 P–QR4, P–KB3; 15 Q–K2, P–K4 = . Schwarz.

(j) Immediately underpinning the pawn plus by 3 P–QB4 leads nowhere, e.g. 3 . . . P–B3! (A) 4 P × P, N × P; 5 P–Q3, P–K4! 6 N–QB3, with (1) 6 . . . B–KB4; 7 N–B3, B–QN5 (Schwarz gives 7 . . . B–B4; 8 B–N5; 9 Q–Q2, O–O–O); 8 B–K2, P–K5; 9 N–KR4, B–K3; 10 O–O, P × P = ; Boleslavski; or (2) 6 . . . B–QB4; 7 B–K3, B × B; 8 P × B, Q–N3; 9 Q–Q2, B–K3; 10 P–K4, N–KN5 ∞ . (B) 4 P–Q4, P × P; see Caro–Kann Defence, Panov-Attack. (C) 4 N–QB3, P × P; 5 P × P, N × P; 6 N–B3, N–QB3; (1) 7 B–B4, P–K3; 8 P–Q4, N × N; 9 P × N, B–K2; 10 O–O, O–O; 11 B–Q3, P–QN3 ∞ . Timman–Seidman, US Open Chp. 1974. (2) 7 P–Q4, B–N5; 8 Q–N3, B × N; 9 P × B, N–N3; 10 P–Q5, N–Q5; 11 Q–Q1, P–K4; 12 P × P, P × P; 13 B–K3, B–B4; 14 P–N4! Q–B3! 15 P × B, N × P†; 16 K–K2, O–O; 17 P × N, QR–Q1 ∓ . Hermlins–Piskins, corr. 1976.

(k) 4 . . . P–KN3; 5 B–K2! B–N2; 6 P–B4, N–N3; 7 N–B3, O–O; 8 B–K3, N–B3; 9 Q–Q2, P–K4; 10 P–Q5, N–K2, 11 O–O–O and P–B5! ± . Sokolski.

(l) 10 P × B, Q–R5! = . White's P–B4 on the 5th, 6th or 7th move leads into col. 5.

(*m*) Slightly safer than 4 . . . N–N3; 5 N–KB3, P–N3 (5 . . . B–N5; 6 P–B5!); 6 N–B3, B–N2! (6 . . . B–N5; 7 B–K2, B–N2; 8 O–O, O–O; 9 B–K3, N–B3; 10 P–Q5, B × N; 11 B × B, N–K4; 12 P–B5! N/3–B5; 13 B–B1, N × B†; 14 Q × N, P–N3; 15 Q–K4, N–K4; 16 P–B6! + . Bondarevski).

(*n*) 10 B–K2, R–K1; 11 R–Q1, Q–R4; with a restricted but solid position for Black. Tal–Bronstein, USSR 1967. The nuances in the transposition and timing of White's N–KB3 or P–QB4 and Black's . . . P–KN3 or . . . B–N5 or . . . N–KB3 in cols. 9–10 are important to note in close conjunction.

Nimzowitsch Defence

(1 P–K4, N–QB3)

To be facetious and formal, the first outstanding characteristic of this bizarre defence is its unfathomably widespread misspelling as "Nimzovitch" Defence. It defies the Baltic master's own Indo-Germanic version of his name—which, if transcribed into English would correctly sound "Nimtsovich." The defence was first advocated by the German master Eduard Fischer (b.1831) in the last century. Nimzowitsch subjected it to deep study and came to the conclusion that it was sound. Czerniak, Rosetto, Mikenas and Lutikov have also experimented with it. But Alexander Kevitz of the Manhattan Chess Club has probably played and analysed it more than anyone—including its originator! Most masters, however, believe that the defence is too cramped, requiring too patient handling. Still, Black's move contains novelty value and appeals to players desiring to avoid well-trodden paths.

2 P–Q4, seizing the centre, is a healthy and aggressive reaction. Black can either counter with 2 . . . P–Q4 (cols. 1–2) which is best met by 3 P–K5, or with 2 . . . P–K4 which gives White a space advantage after 3 P × P (col. 3) or 3 P–Q5 (col. 4). White retains the initiative, but Black's position is certainly playable and solid.

2 N–KB3 (col. 5) and other second moves would indicate White's willingness to forgive and forget should Black oblige with 2 . . . P–K4. But we are here concerned only with independent lines which arise out of the Nimzowitsch proper. In view of note *(n)* White probably does best to avoid transposing into Alekhin's Defence after 2 . . . N–KB3. 3 N–B3 (instead of P–K5), P–K4 leads to the Four Knights' Game whereas 3 . . . P–Q4 leads to the Centre Counter.

233

1 P–K4, N–QB3

	1	2	3	4	5
2	P–Q4				N–KB3
	P–Q4	P–K4 (i)			P–Q3 (o)
3	P–K5	N–QB3 (c)	P × P	P–Q5	P–Q4
	P–B3 (a)	P–K3 (d)	N × P	QN–K2	B–N5 (p)
4	P–KB4 (b)	N–B3 (e)	P–KB4 (j)	B–Q3	B–QN5
	B–B4	N–B3 (f)	N–N3	N–N3 (l)	P–QR3
5	N–K2	B–KN5 (g)	B–K3	B–K3	B–R4
	P–K3	B–K2	B–N5†	N–B3? (m)	P–QN4
6	N–N3	P–K5	N–Q2	P–KR4	B–N3
	P × P	N–K5	N–B3	P–KR4	N–B3 (q)
7	BP × P	B × B	P–B3	P–KB3	P–B3
	Q–Q2	Q × B	B–R4	B–K2	P–K3
8	N × B	B–Q3	B–Q3	Q–Q2	Q–K2
	P × N	Q–N5	Q–K2	P–Q3	B–K2
9	P–B3 ±	O–O	Q–B3	P–QB4	O–O
		N × N (h)	P–Q4 (k)	P–B4 (n)	O–O (r)

(a) 3 . . . B–B4; 4 P–QB3, P–K3; 5 N–K2, KN–K2; 6 N–N3, B–N3; 7 B–Q3 (7 N–Q2, P–QR3), Q–Q2; 8 Q–B3, B × B; 9 Q × B, N–N3; 10 P–KR4 ± .

(b) If 4 N–KB3, B–N5; 5 B–K2, P–K3; 6 P × P, N × BP; 7 P–B3, B–Q3; 8 B–KN5 (Tartakover), B × N! 9 B × B, O–O = . Ward. The column is Alekhin's improvement 9 P–B3! to the game Te Kolsté–Nimzowitsch, Baden-Baden 1925, but 7 . . . B–N3 is safer.

(c) 3 P × P, Q × P; 4 N–KB3, B–N5; 5 B–K2, O–O–O; 6 N–B3, Q–QR4; 7 B–K3, N–B3; 8 N–Q2! B × B; 9 Q × B, Q–KB4; 10 N–N3, P–K4! = . *Misl.*

(d) Or 3 . . . P × P followed by (A) 4 P–Q5! N–K4; (1) 5 Q–Q4, N–N3; 6 Q–R4†, B–Q2; 7 Q–N3 ± (Fine), in preference to (2) 5 B–KB4, N–N3; 6 B–N3, P–QR3; 7 B–QB4, N–B3; 8 Q–Q4, P–B4! = ; *Archives:* or (3) 5 P–B3, P–K3; 6 Q–Q4, B–Q3; 7 P–B4, P–QB4; 8 Q × KP, N–KB3; 9 Q–R4†, B–Q2; 10 B–N5, N–N3 ∞. Unusual but solid is Nimzowitsch's 4 . . . N–N1; 5 B–KB4, N–KB3; 6 B–B4, P–QR3; 7 Q–K2, P–QN4; 8 B–QN3, P–B4; 9 P × P e.p., N × P = . If (B) 4 B–QN5, B–Q2; 5 B × N, B × B; 6 P–Q5, B–Q2; 7 B–B4, N–B3; 8 Q–K2, P–B3; 9 O–O–O, Q–R4 = .

(e) Also 4 P–K5, (A) 4 . . . B–N5; 5 N–B3, P–QN3; 6 B–Q3, Q–Q2; 7 B–Q2, B–N2; P–QR3, B–KB1; 9 O–O, O–O–O (Myers). (B) 4 . . . KN–K2; 5 N–B3 (5 QN–K2, P–QN3; 6 N–B4, N–N3; 7 N–R5, R–KN1 (Myers), P–QN3; 6 N–K2, B–R3; 7 P–KN3, P–R4 ∞. (C) 4 . . . P–B3; 5 P × P, N × BP; 6 N–B3, B–Q3; 7 B–KN5, O–O; 8 B–Q3, N–QN5; 9 O–O, N × B; 10 Q × N, P–B4 = . Vinogradov.

(f) 4 . . . B–N5; 5 P–K5, B × N† (5 . . . KN–K2; 6 Q–Q3!); 6 P × B, N–R4; 7 P–QR4, N–K2; 8 B–Q3, P–QN3; 9 N–Q2, P–QB4 = . Becker–Nimzowitsch, Breslau 1925.

(g) 5 P–K5, N–K5; 6 B–K2, B–K2; 7 Q–Q3, N × N; 8 P × N, N–R4; 9 N–Q2, O–O is open to further testing.

(h) 10 P × N, Q × BP; 11 R–N1, Q–R6; 12 N–N5, Q–K2 = . Lehmann–Lohsse, Germany 1964. The variation is akin to the French Defence.

(i) Another thematic reply. If (A) 2 . . . P–Q3; (1) 3 P–Q5?! N–K4; 4 N–QB3, P–QB4; 5 P–B4, N–Q2! 6 N–B3, P–KN3; 7 P–K5, B–N2; 8 P–K6! P × P; 9 P × P, N–N1; 10 P–B5! ± . Bogdanović–Nikolić, Yugoslavia 1965. (2) 3 N–KB3, B–N5; 4 N–B3 (4 B–QN5!), N–B3; 5 B–K3, P–K4; 6 P–Q5, N–QN1; 7 B–K2 = . (B) 2 . . . P–K3; 3 N–KB3, P–Q4; 4 P–K5, P–QN3; 5 P–B3, QN–K2; 6 B–Q3, P–QR4; 7 Q–K2, N–B4; 8 P–KR4, P–R4; 9 N–N5, KN–K2 = . Alekhin. Also compare col. 2.

(*j*) (A) 4 N–QB3, B–B4 (or 4 . . . B–N5!); 5 P–B4, N–QB3! 6 N–B3, P–Q3; 6 B–N5, N–B3; 7 Q–K2 = . (B) 4 N–KB3, B–N5†; 5 P–B3, B–Q3 = . Kevitz. In view of the text, these lines are preferable.

(*k*) 10 P–K5, N–N5; 11 N–N3, N × B; 12 N × B, N–R5 ∓. Schwarz.

(*l*) 4 . . . P–Q3; and . . . P–KN3 achieves a safe King's Indian set up.

(*m*) (A) 5 . . . B–N5†! 6 N–Q2, P–Q3! secures equality more easily. (B) 5 . . . B–K2 is also satisfactory.

(*n*) 10 N–B3, P–R3; 11 P–R3 ± . Szabó–Rossetto, Buenos Aires 1960.

(*o*) Best is (A) 2 . . . N–B3; 3 P–K5, N–Q4; 4 P–Q4, P–Q3; 5 P–B4, N–N3; 6 P–K6, P × P; 7 N–N5, P–KN3; 8 B–Q3, N–N5! = , *Comments*, or (B) 2 . . . P–K4, which is also the answer to 2 N–QB3.

(*p*) 3 . . . N–KB3; 4 N–B3, B–N5; 5 B–K3, P–K4; 6 P–Q5 (6 B–N5, P × P; 7 Q × P, B–K2 =), N–QN1; 7 P–KR3, B–R4; 8 P–KN4, B–N3; 9 N–Q2, B–K2; 10 B–N2, P–B3 = . Karklins–Myers, Chicago 1972.

(*q*) 6 . . . P–K4 *á la* Ruy Lopez is tenable, e.g. 7 B–Q5, Q–Q2; 8 B–K3, KN–K2; 9 P–B3, R–QN1; 10 QN–Q2, P–N3 = . Burns–Korn, corr. 1958.

(*r*) 10 QN–Q2 (Fine–Mikenas, Hastings 1938), P–Q4! 11 P–K5 (11 P × P, P × P), N–Q2; 12 P–QR4, P–N5 ∞.

Pirć Defence

(1 P–K4, P–Q3; 2 P–Q4, N–KB3;
3 N–QB3, P–KN3)

Since the 1940s, this system has been known variously as the "Pirć Defence"—after its pioneer Vasja Pirć and a group of his compatriots; whence the other often used description of "Yugoslav Defence"—or also "Ufimtsev Defence" in recognition of the Russian master's independent researches.

Our 10th edition placed it as "Pirć–Robatsch" Defence among the Queen's Pawn games as it has many structural similarities with the Indian complex. However, many contemporary writers classify this system as "Semi-Open" and we have fallen in line so as to facilitate for our readers comparisons with other reference books.

White's first two moves are interchangeable and . . . P–KN3 may be played even sooner, but if either N–QB3 or . . . N–KB3 are omitted at an early enough stage we no longer have a conventional Pirć but rather a King's Fianchetto Defence (Robatsch), now dealt with separately in the next chapter.

The Pirć is not a fighting defence. It is fluid and slippery, with the object of closing the game and slowly equalizing, whether White opens 1 P–K4 or 1 P–Q4.

The Pirć proper is characterized by the order 1 . . . P–Q3 and 2 . . . N–KB3, practically provoking 3 N–QB3. Too committed is 3 B–Q3, whereas 3 P–B3, P–KN3 will lead to the Sämisch variation of the King's Indian, or into col. 3, with 3 N–QB3, P–KN3; 4 P–B3.

3 N–QB3, (. . . P–KN3) blocks White's queen's bishop's pawn and thus rules out the strict transposition into the King's Indian which requires the typical P–QB4 at the earliest moment. The question whether White has saved a tempo by holding back his queen's bishop's pawn and gains an advantage by mobilizing a piece instead or whether he has failed to

236

establish a grip on the centre is one to be decided by the player's predilections.

The determining choices arise after White's fourth move.

4 B–N5 and castling queen's side is shown in cols. 1–2, but a too rapid advance of pawns as in note *(b)* (A) seems ineffective here just as in similar variations on the same theme.

4 P–B3 (cols. 3–5) is a preventive underpinning which slightly pays off only in col. 4.

4 P–B4, followed by . . . B–N2; 5 N–B3 (cols. 6–16) is the more forceful treatment but Black has developed antidotes in both 5 . . . P–B4 (cols. –9) and 5 . . . O–O (cols 9–16)—a line dating back to the game Weiss–Paulsen, Nürnberg 1883! White reaches endgames that are better, but not enough to realize a win.

4 B–QB4, 4 B–K3, 4 P–KN3, 4 P–KR4, 4 KN–K2 and 4 B–KB4 are rarer approaches (cols. 17–20).

4 N–B3 (cols. 21–30) aims at White's developing all pieces naturally, without a forthright effort at a quick breakthrough and refutation. White's main alternatives on the 5th move are 5 B–QB4 (cols. 21–5) or 5 B–K2 (cols. 16–30), both of which are being constantly explored, with 5 B–K2 now enjoying the greater exposure. White's quiet and solid build-up without positional weakness on either wing can only be broken by somewhat risky strategems on the part of Black or by his "sitting it out" and hoping that White might overreach himself.

1 P-K4, P-Q3; 2 P-Q4, N-KB3; 3 N-QB3, P-KN3

	1	2	3	4	5
4	B-KN5................. P-B3				
	B-N2 (a) P-B3	P-B3			
5	Q-Q2 (b)	P-B3 (f)	B-K3		
	P-KR3 (c)	B-N2 (g)	QN-Q2 ..... Q-N3 .... B-N2 (m)		
6	B-K3 (d)	Q-Q2	Q-Q2	Q-B1	Q-Q2
	N-N5	Q-R4	Q-B2	B-N2	O-O
7	B-KB4	O-O-O	N-R3 (i)	B-Q3 (k)	O-O-O
	P-K4	P-KR3!	P-QN4	O-O	R-K1
8	P×P	B-K3	N-B2	KN-K2	K-N1
	N×KP	QN-Q2	N-N3	QN-Q2	P-QN4
9	O-O-O	K-N1	P-QN3	P-KR4	B-R6
	QN-B3	P-QN4	P-QR3	R-K1	B-R1
10	P-KR3	Q-K1	P-QR4	P-K5	QN-K2
	B-K3	R-QN1	B-QN2	N-Q4	QN-Q2
11	B-K3	P-QN3	B-K2	N×N	P-KR4
	N-B5 (e)	Q-B2 (h)	B-N2 (j)	P×N (l)	P-K4 (n)

(a) (A) 4 . . . QN-Q2; 5 P-B4, P-KR3; 6 B-R4, B-N2; 7 Q-B3, O-O; 8 O-O-O, allows White a strong attack. Suetin-Kampenis, USSR 1959. (B) Tenable but dubious is 4 . . . P-KR3; (1) 5 B-R4, B-N2; 6 B-K2, B-N2; 6 B-K2, P-B4; 7 P-K5, N-R4! or (2) 5 B-K3! N-N5; 6 B-KB4, N-QB3; 7 N-B3, P-K4; 8 P×P, N/5×P; 9 N×N, N×N; 10 B×N, P×B; 11 Q×Q†, K×Q; 12 O-O-O†, B-Q2; 13 B-B4, P-KB3 ∞.

(b) (A) Inconsequential is here 5 P-B4, O-O; 6 P-K5, N-N5! 7 P-B5, P-KB3 ∓. (B) Prematurely relaxing pressure is 5 P-K5!? (1) 5 . . . KN-Q2; 6 P×P, BP×P; 7 N-B3, O-O = ; or creating counterchances by (2) 5 . . . P×P; P×P, Q×Q†; 7 R×Q, KN-Q2; 8 N-Q5; 6 P×P, B×P; 9 N-KB3, B-Q3 . (c) Colourless is 5 N-B3, O-O; 6 Q-Q2, P-B3 = .

(c) (A) 5 . . . QN-Q2; 6 O-O-O, P-K4; 7 P×P, P×P; 8 N-B3, P-KR3; 9 B-R4, P-KN4; 10 B-N3, Q-K2 = . Fischer-Ault, US Chp. 1960. (B) 5 . . . P-B3; 6 N-B3, Q-R4; 7 B-Q3, B-N5 = .

(d) 6 B-R4, P-KN4; 7 B-N3, N-R4. In the column, White plays N-KB3 rather late, as different from note (a)(B)(2).

(e) 12 B×N, B×B; 13 N-B3 (Zaitsev-Savon, USSR 1963), Q-B3 = .

(f) 5 Q-Q2, P-N4; 6 B-Q3, B-KN2; 7 P-B4, Q-N3! = . Kurajica.

(g) Possibly also 5 . . . Q-N3; 6 R-N1, B-N2; 7 Q-Q2, O-O; 8 KN-K2, R-K1; 9 P-KN4, QN-Q2; 10 P-KR4, P-K4; 11 P-Q5, P×P; 12 N×P, N×N; 13 Q×N, P-KR3; 14 B-Q2, N-B4 = . Witkowski-Fuderer, Yugoslavia 1955.

(h) 12 KN-K2, (Damjanović-Etruk, Tallinn 1969), P-QR3! 13 P-KN4, P-B4 = . Gufeld's comment.

(i) 7 KN-K2, B-N2 (or 7 . . . P-QN4); 8 P-QR4! O-O; 9 P-KR4, P-K4; 10 O-O-O, P-Q4! 11 P-KR5 = .

(j) 12 O-O, O-O; 13 N-Q3, (Ciocaltea-Benoit, Monte Carlo 1969) QN-Q2 = .

(k) 7 KN-K2, O-O; 8 N-B4, Q-R4; 9 B-K2, P-K4; 10 P×P, P×P; 11 N-Q3, QN-Q2; 12 O-O, R-K1; 13 P-QR4, N-B1 = . Lipnitski-Bronstein, USSR 1951.

(l) 12 P-K6, N-B3; 13 P×P† with an edge. *Informator.*

(m) 5 . . . P-QN4; 6 Q-Q2, QN-Q2; 7 N-R3, B-QN2; 8 O-O-O, P-QR3; 9 K-N1, Q-B2; 10 P-KN4, P-K4; 11 P-N5, N-R4; 12 N-K2 ± . Ritson-Morry.

(n) 12 P-R5, P-Q4; 13 RP×P. BP×P = . Gipslis-Smyslov, USSR 1961.

1 P-K4, P-Q3; 2 P-Q4, N-KB3; 3 N-QB3, P-KN3; 4 P-B4, B-N2; 5 N-B3 (a)

	6	7	8	9	10
	P-B4			O-O	
6	B-N5†	P×P		P-K5 (h)	
	B-Q2	Q-R4		KN-Q2 (i)	
7	P-K5	B-Q3 (d)		P×P?!	P-KR4
	N-N5	Q×BP		P-QB4!?	P-QB4
8	P-K6 (b)	Q-K2		P×KP (i)	P-R5
	B×B	O-O	B-N5	Q×P†	P×QP
9	P×P†	B-K3	B-K3	B-K2	Q×P (m)
	K×P	Q-QR4	Q-QR4	P×P	QP×P
10	N×B	O-O	P-KR3?!	N-QN5 (k)	Q-B2
	Q-R4†	QN-Q2 (e) ...	N-KR4!	N-QB3	P-K5!
11	N-B3	P-KR3 (f)	Q-B2	O-O	N-KN5?! (n)
	P×P	P-QR3	B×QN	P-QR3	N-KB3
12	N×P	Q-B2	P×B	QN×QP	P×P
	B×N (c)	P-K4 =	Q×P† (g)	N×N (l)	RP×P (o)

(a) 5 P-K5, (A) 5 . . . KN-Q2 may transpose into col. 9. (B) Playable is 5 . . . P×P; and now (1) 6 BP×P, N-Q4! ∞; or (2) 6 QP×P, Q×Q; 7 K×Q (7 N×Q, N-Q4 =), N-N5; 8 K-K1, P-KR4 (e.g. 9 P-KR3, N-KR3) = .

(b) (A) 8 B×B†! Q×B; 9 P-Q5, N-QR3; 10 P-KR3, N-R3; 11 P-KN4, O-O-O; 12 B-K3, P-K3; 13 Q-K2 ± . Filipowicz-Heiberg, Gansdal 1977. (B) 8 P-KR3, (1) 8 . . . P×QP; 9 Q×P, N-KR3; 10 B-Q2! (2) 8 . . . B×B; 9 N×B, P×KP; 10 P×N, Q-R4†; 11 P-B3, P-K5 = . Fedorov-Tseitlin, USSR 1977.

(c) 13 Q×B, N-QB3; 14 Q-Q5† Q×Q = . Zuidema-Suttles, Havana 1966.

(d) (A) 7 Q-Q3, Q×BP; 8 B-K3, Q-QR4; 9 B-K2, O-O; 10 O-O, P-QR3; 11 K-R1, QN-Q2 = . Geller-Nicolayevski, USSR 1958. (B) 7 B-N5†, B-Q2; 8 B×B†, QN×B; 9 O-O, Q×BP; 10 K-R1, O-O = .

(e) (A) 10 . . . N-B3; 11 P-KR3! P-K4 (11 . . . B-Q2; 12 P-R3, KR-B1; 13 Q-B2, B-K1; 14 P-B5 ± . Olafsson-Benko, Wijk aan Zee 1969); 12 P×P, N×P/4 = . Comments. (B) 10 . . . B-N5; 11 QR-Q1, N-B3; 12 B-B4, N-R4; 13 B-N3, B×QN; 14 P×B, Q×BP; 15 P-B5! N-B3! = Spasski-Fischer, 17th match game, Reykjavik 1972.

(f) 11 Q-K1 tries to speed up the attack by Q-R4. The column is Ree-Benko, Wijk aan Zee 1969. If 6 P-K5, P×KP; 7 QP×P, Q×Q†; 8 K×Q, N-N5; 9 K-K1, N-QB3; 10 B-N5, B-Q2; 11 P-KR3, N-R3; 12 B-K3, P-N3; 13 R-Q1 (Peretz-Domnitz, Netanya 1969), N-B4; 14 B-B2 is also ± .

(g) 13 K-B2, P-K4; 14 P×P, P×P = . Botterill and Keene.

(h) 6 B-K3, P-B4! 7 P×P, Q-R4; 8 B-Q3, N-N5; 9 B-Q2, Q×BP = . Balashov-Timman, Bugajno 1978.

(i) 6 . . . P×P? 7 QP×P! Q×Q†; 8 K×Q (8 N×Q, N-Q4), R-Q1†; 9 K-K1, N-Q4; 10 N×N, R×N; 11 B-B4, R-Q1; 12 N-N5, P-K3; 13 B-K2! Honfi-Barcza, Hungary, 1967.

(j) 8 P×BP, N×P; 9 B-K2, P×P! 10 O-O, N-B3 ∞.

(k) 10 N×P? R-K1; 11 O-O, Q-B4; 12 N-N5, P-QR3 + .

(l) 13 N×N, B×N†! 14 Q×B, Q×B; 15 B-Q2, Q-N4! 16 B-N4, Q-N3! 17 Q×Q, N×Q; 18 B×R, K×B ∓ . Pfleger-Torre, Manila 1974.

(m) An intricate gambit line is initiated with 9 P×NP!? P×N (forced); 10 P×BP†, R×P; and presented in detail in Byulleten 1969/10. With best play it ends in a deadlock. One typical main line is 11 B-B4! N-B1! 12 B×R†, K×B, 13 N-N5†, K-N1; 14 Q-R5, P-KR3! 15 Q-B7†, K-R1; 16 Q-N3, Q-R4; 17 N-B7†, K-R2; 18 N-N5† = . Moiseyev.

(n) 11 N×P, Q-N3; 12 Q-R4, Q-R4†; 13 P-B3, Q×KRP; 14 Q×Q, P×Q; 15 R×P, might secure White a superior endgame. Comments.

(o) 13 Q-R4, Q-Q5 ∞ . Padevski-Matanovic, Havana 1966.

1 P–K4, P–Q3; 2 P–Q4, N–KB3; 3 N–QB3, P–KN3; 4 P–B4, B–N2; 5 N–B3, O–O

	11	12	13	14	15
6	(P–K5)	B–Q3			
	(KN–Q2)	N–B3		QN–Q2	B–N5 (i)
7	B–B4	P–K5	O–O (f)	Q–K2! (h)	P–KR3
	N–N3	P × P	B–N5	P–B4	B × N
8	B–N3	QP × P (b)	P–K5	P–Q5	Q × B
	N–B3	N–Q4	P × P	N–N3	N–B3
9	B–K3	N × N (c)	QP × P	O–O	B–K3
	N–R4	Q × N	N–Q4	P–QR3	N–Q2 (j)
10	Q–K2	Q–K2	N × N	P–QR4	P–K5
	N × B	B–B4 (d)	Q × N	Q–B2	N–N5
11	RP × N	B × B	P–KR3	Q–K1 ±	O–O–O
	P–KB3 (a)	P × B (e)	B × N (g)		P–QB4 (k)

(a) 12 P–R3 (12 O–O, B–N5; Botterill in *Chessman Quarterly*), P–B3; 13 O–O, Q–B2 (or 13 . . . B–K3!?) ∞. Comments.

(b) 8 BP × P, (ᴀ) 8 . . . N–KN5; 9 B–K4, P–B3; 10 P × P, P × P; 11 O–O, K–R1; 12 B–Q3, B–K3 = . Or (ʙ) 8 . . . N–KR4; 9 B–K4, B–N5; 10 B–K3, P–B3; 11 P × P, P × P (or 11 . . . B × P!); 12 Q–Q3, N–K2 = .

(c) 9 B–Q2!? (ᴀ) 9 . . . B–N5; 10 B–K4, N–N3; 11 P–KR3, B × N; 12 Q × B, N–Q5; 13 Q–Q3, P–KB3; 14 O–O–O, P × P; 15 P × P, P–B4 = . Parma. (ʙ) 9 . . . N/3–N5; 10 B–K4, P–QB3; 11 N × N, P × N; 12 B × N, P × B; 13 N–Q2, B–B4; 14 O–O–O ± ! (c) 9 . . . N–N3; 10 Q–K2, N–N5; 11 B–K4, P–KB4; 12 B–Q3, N × B = .

(d) Also 10 . . . B–N5; 11 B–K4, Q–R4†; 12 B–Q2, Q–N3 = .

(e) 12 B–K3, QR–Q1; 13 P–KR3, P–KR3 = . Pachman.

(f) (ᴀ) 7 B–K3, P–K4; 8 BP × P, P × P; 9 P–Q5, N–Q5; 10 N × N, N–N5! 11 N–B5, P × N; 12 B–B5, P–B5! 13 Q–B3, Q–R5†; 14 P–N3, N × P ∞. (ʙ) 7 P–B5, N–QN5; 8 O–O P × P; 9 P × P, P–B4; 10 B–KN5, P × P; 11 B × N, B × B; 12 N–K4, P–K4! = .

(g) 12 Q × B, Q × Q; 13 R × Q, QR–Q1 = . Bagirov–Averbakh, USSR 1963.

(h) White also has (ᴀ) 7 P–K5, N–K1; 8 N–K4, P–QB4; 9 P–B3, Q–N3; 10 N/4–Q2, P × QP; 11 N–B4, Q–B3; 12 BP × P! (ʙ) 7 O–O, P–K4; 8 BP × P, P × P; 9 P–Q5, P–B3; 10 P × P, P × P; 11 K–R1, Q–B2 with initiative for White. Matulović. The column is Kavalek's analysis.

(i) Playable is also (ᴀ) 6 . . . P–B3; 7 O–O, P–QN4; 8 P–K5, N–K1; 9 N–K4, P–QR4; 10 Q–K1, N–B2; 11 Q–R4, N/1–R3 = . (ʙ) 6 . . . N–R3; (1) 7 O–O, P–B4; 8 P–Q5! R–N1; 9 K–R1, N–B2; 10 P–QR4, P–N3; 11 Q–K1, P–QR3; 12 Q–R4, P–QN4; 13 P × P, P × P; 14 P–K5, P × P ∞. (2) 7 P–K5 (1) 7 . . . N–Q2; 8 P–KR4, P–QB4; 9 P–R5, P × QP; 10 RP × P, RP × P; 11 N–KN5, P × P; 12 P–B5, N–B3; 13 P × P, B–N5 = . Borkowski–Nunn, Groningen 1974. Also compare col. 10. (2) 7 . . . P × P, 8 QP × P, N–Q4; 9 N × N, Q × N; 10 Q–K2, B–K3; 11 B–K4, Q–R4†; 12 B–Q2, Q–N3; 13 B–B3, N–N5 = . *New York Times.*

(j) 9 . . . P–K4; 10 QP × P, P × P; 11 P–B5! N–Q5! 12 Q–B2! P × P; 13 P × P ± .

(k) 12 P × BP, Q–R4; 13 BP × P, P × P; 14 P–R3, P × P; 15 P × N, Q–R8†; 16 K–Q2, Q × P; 17 N–Q5, P × P; 18 Q × P, QR–Q1; 19 R–QN1, Q–K4; 20 Q × Q, N × Q; 21 N–B4, KR–K1; 22 B–B2, P–QR3; 23 KR–KB1, R–Q2; 24 R–N3, R–QB1; 25 B–N1, P–N3; 26 K–K2, R–K1; 27 K–B2, P–QN4; 28 K–N3, N–B3; 29 K–R2, B–B1; 30 B–QB5, B × B; 31 P × B, R–K4; 32 R–QR1, R × P; 33 R × RP, N–Q5; 34 R–N2, R–B6; 35 R/6–R2, K–N2; 36 N–K2, N × N; 37 B × N, P–N5; 38 B–Q3, R–N2; 39 R–N3, resigns. R. Byrne–Korchnoi, Alekhin Memorial Tournament, Moscow 1975.

1 P–K4, P–Q3; 2 P–Q4, N–KB3; 3 N–QB3, P–KN3

	16	17	18	19	20
4	(P–B4)	B–QB4	B–K3	P–KN3	P–KR4 (i)
	(B–N2)	P–B3	B–N2	B–N2	B–N2
5	(N–B3)	Q–K2	B–K2 (f)	B–N2	B–QB4 (j)
	(O–O)	B–N2	O–O	O–O	N–B3
6	B–K2 (a)	P–K5 (c)	Q–Q2	KN–K2	N–B3
	P–B4	P × P	P–K4	QN–Q2 (g)	B–N5
7	P × P	P × P	P × P	O–O (h)	P–Q5
	Q–R4	N–Q4	P × P	P–K4	N–K4
8	O–O	N–B3 (d)	O–O–O	P–B4	B–K2
	Q × P†	B–N5	Q × Q†	P × QP	KN–Q2
9	K–R1 (b)	O–O	B × Q	N × P	B–K3
		O–O (e)	N–B3 =	R–K1	P–QB3

(a) 6 B–B4 offers good long-range prospects as well.

(b) (A) 9 . . . QN–Q2; and now (1) 10 N–Q2, P–QR3; 11 N–N3, Q–B2 = ; Wade–Shamkovich, Mallorca 1966; or (2) 10 Q–Q3, P–QR3; 11 B–K3, Q–B2; 12 B–Q4, P–K4; 13 P × P, P × P; 14 B–K3, P–QN4; 15 QR–Q1, B–N2; 16 Q–Q6, QR–B1; 17 B–KN5, KR–K1 = . Older continuations are (B) 9 . . . N–N5; 10 N–Q5! N–QB3; 11 P–B3, P–QR4; 12 Q–Q3, P–N3; 13 N–Q4! Pachman. (C) 9 . . . P–QN4; 10 P–K5, P × P; 11 P × P, N–N5; 12 Q–Q5! Q–N3! 13 P–KR3, N–KR3; 14 Q × R, B–N2; 15 N–Q5, Q–R3; 16 N–N4, Q–N3; Vlagsma–Bobikiewicz, Beverwijk 1962; 17 B–K3, Q × B; 18 Q × B, Q × B; 19 Q × RP, N–B4; 20 Q–B2 ± . (D) 9 . . . N–B3; and (1) 10 N–Q2, P–QR4; 11 N–N3, Q–N3; 12 P–QR4, N–QN5; 13 B–B3, B–K3 = ; Comments; or (2) 10 Q–K1, B–N5; 11 B–Q3, B × N: 12 R × B, N–Q5; 13 R–B1, Q–KR4! = . Broberg–Kollberg, corr. 1966. In the column 6 . . . P–B3 may be tried.

(c) 6 N–B3 transposes into column 22.

(d) Yudovich suggests 8 B–Q2! with quiet pressure.

(e) 10 Q–K4, B × N; 11 Q × B, P–K3 = . Klovski–Gufeld, Riga 1968.

(f) 5 B–QB4, O–O; 6 KN–K2, QN–Q2; 7 P–B3; P–QR3 = . Comments.

(g) Also (A) 6 . . . P–K4; 7 O–O, N–B3; 8 P × P, P × P = ; Buljovčić–Matulović, Sombor 1968; or (B) 6 . . . P–B3 so as to counteract the influence of White's fianchettoed Bishop.

(h) 7 P–B4, P–K4; 8 BP × P, P × P; 9 P–Q5, P–QR4; 10 P–N3, P–R3; 11 B–Q2, N–B4; 12 B–K3, Q–K2; 13 Q–Q2, K–R2; 14 O–O–O, N–K1; 15 P–KR3, P–N3 (or . . . P–B4?!); with a complex game Rejfir–Korn, corr. 1953–4. The column is Broun–Koshnitsky, Australia 1952.

(i) Ineffective is (A) 4 KN–K2, B–N2 5 P–KN3, O–O; 6 B–N2, P–K4; 7 O–O, N–B3! = . Ivkov. (B) 4 B–KB4, B–N2; 5 Q–Q2, N–B3; 6 P–Q5, P–K4; 7 P × P e.p., P × P; 8 B–QN5, O–O; 9 KN–K2, P–QR3 = . Schmidt–Botvinnik, Moscow Olympics 1966.

(j) If 5 B–K2, (A) 5 . . . P–B4; 6 P × P, Q–R4; 7 K–B1! Q × BP; 8 B–K3, Q–QR4; 9 P–R5, P × P = . (B) 5 . . . N–B3; 6 B–K3, P–K4; 7 P–Q5, N–Q5!; 8 B × N, P × B; 9 Q × P, O–O; 10 Q–Q2, R–K1; 11 P–B3, N–R4! = . Keres–Bouwmeester, Varna Olympics 1962. The column is Nezhmetdinov–Vasyukov, USSR 1961.

1 P–K4, P–Q3; 2 P–Q4, N–KB3; 3 N–QB3, P–KN3; 4 N–B3, B–N2; 5 B–QB4

	21	22	23	24	25
	P–B3			O–O	
6	O–O	Q–K2	B–N3 (e)	B–N3	O–O (i)
	P–Q4	O–O	O–O!	B–N5 (g)	N–B3!
7	P × P (a)	B–KN5 (c)	P–KR3!	B–K3	B–K3
	P × P	P–N4 (d)	P–QR4! (f)	N–B3	P–QR3
8	B–N5†	B–Q3	P–R3	P–KR3	P–QR4
	B–Q2	Q–B2	P–R5	B × N	N × KP
9	B × B†	P–K5	B–R2	Q × B	N × N
	QN × B	P × P	QN–Q2	P–K4	P–Q4
10	R–K1	Q × P	O–O	P × P	B–Q3
	O–O	Q–Q1!	P–K4	P × P	P × N
11	B–B4	Q–B4	B–K3	N–Q5	B × KP
	R–B1	N–R3	Q–K2 =	N–Q5	Q–Q3 =
12	Q–Q3	P–QR4		N × N†	
	N–N3 (b)	N–B2 =		B × N (h)	

(a) 7 B–Q3, B–N5; 8 P–K5, KN–Q2; 9 P–KR3, B × N; 10 Q × B, P–K3; 11 N–K2, P–QB4; 12 P–B3, N–QB3 = . v. Scheltinga–Botvinnik, Wagenigen 1958.

(b) 13 P–QN3, Q–Q2 = . Marić–Portisch, Skopje 1968.

(c) Too rash is 7 P–K5, N–Q4; 8 O–O, N × N; 9 P × N, P × P! (9 . . . B–N5; 10 B–B4, P × P; 11 P × P, P–K3 =); 10 P × P, B–N5 ∓ . Comments.

(d) 7 . . . P–KR3; 8 B × N, P × B; 9 O–O–O, N–Q2; 10 P–QR4, P–R3; 11 B–N3, P–QN4; 12 P–R4, P × P; 13 N × P, N–N3 ∞ . The column is Balogh–O'Kelly, corr. 1961.

(e) The most positional treatment, but also not decisive. Remaining alternatives are (A) 6 P–QR4, P–Q4; 7 P × P, P × P; 8 B–N3, B–N5 = ; or (B) 6 P–K5, P × P, 7 N × P, O–O; 8 O–O, QN–Q2; 9 B–KN5! N–N3! 10 B–N3, P–QR4; 11 P–QR4, N/B–Q4; 12 N × N, P × N; 13 B–KB4, P–B3; 14 N–Q3, R–K1 = . Perez–Tringov, Havana 1965.

(f) 7 . . . N–R3; 8 O–O, N–B2, 9 B–K3, P–QR4; 10 P–QR4, P–Q4; 11 P–K5, KN–Q2 (Poali–Bronstein, Szombathely 1966); 12 R–K1∞ . The column is Csom–Uhlmann, Zinnowitz 1967.

(g) 6 . . . N–B3; 7 P–KR3, N–QR4; 8 B–K3, P–B3; 9 Q–Q2 = .

(h) 13 Q–N4, with a very slim advantage. Spasski–Kotov, Sochi 1967.

(i) (A) 6 Q–K2, P–B3; as in col. 22 (B) 6 P–K5, P × P; 7 N × P, QN–Q2; 8 O–O, P–B4; 9 B–K3, P × P; 10 B × P, N × N; 11 B × N, B–N5; 12 P–B3, B–B4 = . Malisov–Tarve, Khomel 1968. The column is Filip–Larsen, Havana 1967.

1 P–K4, P–Q3; 2 P–Q4, N–KB3; 3 N–QB3 (*a*), P–KN3; 4 N–B3, B–N2; 5 B–K2 (*b*),
O–O; 6 O–O (*c*)

	26	27	28	29	30
	QN–Q2	B–N5	N–B3	P–B3 (*k*)	
7	P–K5	B–K3!	P–KR3 (*i*)	B–KN5	P–QR4 (*m*)
	N–K1	N–B3	P–K4	P–KR3	Q–B2 (*n*)
8	B–KN5 (*d*)	Q–Q2 (*e*)	P × P	B–KB4	P–KR3
	P–KB3	P–K4	N × P/4	N–R4	P–K4
9	P × BP	P × P? (*f*)	N × N	B–K3	P × P
	P × P	P × P	P × N	P–K4	P × P
10	B–K3	KR–Q1	Q × Q	Q–Q2	B–K3
	P–B3	Q × Q (*g*)	R × Q	K–R2	N–R4
11	P–Q5	R × Q	B–K3	N–K1	P–R5
	P–QB4 =	KR–Q1 (*h*)	P–B3 (*j*)	N–B5 (*l*)	N–B5 (*o*)

(*a*) 3 N–Q2? P–K4; 4 P–QB3, N–Q2; 5 KN–B3, P–B3 = becomes a favourable Philidor
Defence. 3 . . . P–KN3; 4 P–QB4, P–B4 creates a good King's Indian Defence, e.g. 5 KN–B3,
B–N5; 6 B–K2, Q–R4!

(*b*) Rarely used are (A) 5 P–KR3, O–O; 6 B–K3, P–B3; 7 Q–Q2, Q–R4; 8 O–O–O, P–K4;
9 B–KR6, P–QN4 = . Prins–Kramer, Beverwijk 1954. (B) 5 B–K3, O–O (or 5 . . . QN–Q2; 6
Q–Q2, N–N5; 7 B–KB4, P–K4 =); 6 Q–Q2, B–N5, and 7 . . . N–B3 = .

(*c*) If here (A) 6 B–K3, B–N5; 7 Q–Q2, N–B3; 8 P–Q5, N–QN1 and 9 . . . P–B3 = ; or (B) 6
B–KB4, N–B3; 7 P–Q5, P–K4! 8 P × P *e.p.*, B × P; 9 O–O, R–K1; 10 R–K1, P–KR3; 11
P–KR3, P–KN4; 12 B–K3, P–Q4; 13 P × P, N × P; 14 N × N, Q × N = . Unzicker–Botvinnik,
Varna Olympics 1962.

(*d*) (A) A noteworthy attempt at greater initiative was 8 B–KB4, N–N3; 9 R–K1, P–QB3
(= , Filip–Petrosian, Curaçao 1962); followed by 10 Q–B1?! If (B) 8 R–K1, P–QB3! but not 8
. . . P–B4; 9 B–KN5! The column is Spasski–Hodos, USSR 1963.

(*e*) (A) 8 P–KR3, B × N; 9 B × B, N–Q2; 10 Q–Q2, N–N3; 11 B–K2, P–K4; 12 P × P, P × P;
13 Q × Q, QR × Q; 14 B–B5, KR–K1; 15 B–N5, R–K3 = . Ćirić–Botvinnik Beverwijk 1969.
(B) 8 P–Q5, N–N1; 9 P–KR3, B × N; 10 B × B, QN–Q2; 11 P–QR4, P–QR4 = .

(*f*) 9 P–Q5! N–K2; (1) 10 P–QR4! N–K1; 11 P–R5! (2) 10 QR–Q1, B × N; 11 B × B, N–Q2
(Spasski's original suggestion); 12 P–KR3, K–R1; 13 B–K2, P–KB4; 14 P–B4 (Karpov–Keene,
Moscow 1977), P–QR3; 15 BP × P, N × P = . Friedstein.

(*g*) The text easily results in an inferior endgame. Worth trying is 10 . . . Q–B1! 11 Q–K1,
R–Q1; 12 R × R†, Q × R; 13 R–Q1, Q–KB1; 14 P–KR3, B × N; 15 B × B, P–QR3! = Timman–Matulović, Wijk aan Zee 1974.

(*h*) 12 QR–Q1, R × R; 13 R × R, N–K1; 14 N–Q5?! B × N; 15 P × B, N–Q5; 16 B–Q1,
N–K3; 17 P–B3, B–B1; 18 B–R4, K–N2! = . Reshevsky–Ivkov, Santa Monica 1966.

(*i*) (A) 7 B–N5, P–KR3; 8 B–KB4, P–R3; 9 P–QR4, Q–K1! = . Haag–Gufeld, Tallinn
1969. (B) 7 P–Q5 N–N1; 8 R–K1, P–B3; 9 B–B1, R–K1 (or 9 . . . B–N5! 10 P–KR3, B × N; 11
Q × B, QN–Q2; 12 B–K3, Q–R4; 13 P–R3, QR–B1 =); 10 P–KR3, P–QR3; 11 P–QR4, P × P;
12 N × P, P–N3; 13 P–B3, B–N2; 14 N × N†, B × N; 15 B–N5, N–Q2; 16 B × B, N × B; 17
P–K5, P × P; 18 N × P, Q × Q? 19 KR × Q, KR–Q1; 20 N–B4 ± . Liberzon–Ervin, Lone Pine
1975.

(*j*) 12 QR–Q1, R × R; 13 R × R, B–K3 = . Hort–Bronstein, Krems 1967.

(*k*) Experimental are (A) 6 . . . N–R3?! 7 R–K1, P–B4; 8 B × N (for 8 P–Q5 see Benoni
Defence), P × P; 9 B × P, B × B; 10 N × P∞ Smyslov–Larsen, Monte Carlo 1967. (B) 6 . . .
B–N5; 7 B–K3, N–B3; 8 P–Q5 (8 Q–Q2, P–K4! 9 P–Q5, N–K2; 10 QR–Q1, B–Q2! 11 N–K1,
P–QN4! =), B × N; 9 B × B, N–K4; 10 B–K2, P–B3; 11 P–QR4, Q–R4; 12 R–R3, KN–Q2; 13
R–K1, KR–B1; 14 B–B1, P–QR3 (Liberzon–Timman, Bad Lauterberg 1977); 15 R–N3 ± . (c)
6 . . . P–QR3; 7 R–K1, N–B3; 8 P–K5 (8 P–KR3, N–Q2!), N–K1; 9 B–KB4, P–B4 = .

Larsen. (D) Too reckless, allowing White a progressive stranglehold, was 6 . . . P–B4; 7 P–Q5! N–R3 (7 . . . B–N5!?); 8 B–KB4, N–B2; 9 P–QR4, P–N3 (9 . . . B–N5?!); 10 R–K1, B–N2? (10 . . . P–QR3; . . . B–Q2; and then . . . R–N1 might offer a chance to hold on); 11 B–B4, N–R4? 12 B–N5, N–B3; 13 Q–Q3, P–QR3; 14 QR–Q1, R–N1; 15 P–R3, N–Q2; 16 Q–K3, B–QR1; 17 B–R6, P–QN4; 18 B × B, K × B; 19 B–B1, N–B3; 20 P × P, P × P; 21 N–K2, B–N2; 22 N–N3, QR–R1; 23 P–B3, R–R5; 24 B–Q3, Q–R1; 25 P–K5, P × P; 26 Q × KP, N × P; 27 B × QNP, R–R2; 28 N–R4, B–B1; 29 B–K2, B–K3; 30 P–QB4, N–N5; 31 Q × P, Q–N1; 32 B–B1, R–B1; 33 Q–KN5, K–R1; 34 R–Q2, N–B3; 35 Q–R6, R–N1; 36 N–B3, Q–KB1; 37 Q–K3, K–N2; 38 N–N5, B–Q2; 39 P–N4, Q–R1; 40 P–N5, N–QR4; 41 P–N6, resigned. Karpov–Korchnoi, 32nd match game 1978, with Karpov retaining the World Championship. An amazing anti-climax just after Korchnoi had levelled the score to 5:5.

(*l*) 12 P × P, N × B†; 13 Q × N, P × P; 14 N–Q3, N–Q2 = . Trifunović–Eising, Dortmund 1961.

(*m*) (A) 7 B–KB4, QN–Q2! (B) 7 R–K1, Q–B2! 8 B–KB4 (or 8 P–K5, P × P; 9 N × P, R–Q1; 10 B–QB4, N–Q4; 11 Q–B3, B–K3 =), N–R4! 9 B–K3, P–K4; 10 P × P, P × P = . (C) 7 P–KR3, P–QN4; 8 P–K5, N–K1; 9 B–KB4! B–N2; 10 Q–Q2, N–Q2; 11 KR–K1, N–N3; 12 B–R6, Q–B2 = .

(*n*) (A) A lesser choice is 7 . . . B–N5; 8 N–Q2, B × B; 9 Q × B, KN–Q2; 10 N–N3, N–R3; 11 B–KN5 ± . Haag–Polugayevski, Budapest 1965. (B) Cautious is 7 . . . P–QR4, but it also loses a tempo needed for counter-action; e.g. 8 P–R3, N–R3; 9 B–KB4!

(*o*) 12 N–Q2, B–K3; 13 N–B4, R–Q1 = . Shashin in *Byulleten* 1968/9.

Robatsch (or King's Fianchetto) Defence

(1 P–K4, P–KN3; 2 P–Q4, B–N2)

or

(1 P–Q4, P–KN3, 2 P–K4, B–N2)

The King's Fianchetto Defence was extensively used by L. Paulsen a hundred years ago. It now is an offspring of the Pirć Defence which provided the Austrian master Robatsch with the stimulus to analyse and practise this system, an effort in which he was joined by Averbakh, Larsen and others.

Its hallmark is the omission of Black's early attack . . . N–KB3, leaving Black the option of developing . . . N–KR3 or . . . KN–K2, and keeping the KB–diagonal open longer. Likewise, White might in the absence of . . . N–KB3 abstain from an immediate N–QB3 and develop the piece only after P–QB4. Transpositions are possible into the Benoni Defence.

(A) 3 P–QB4 (cols. 1–8) is therefore the most "logical" follow-up to Black's "Hyper-accelerated King's Fianchetto" as I once dubbed this line in *Chess Review's* "Spotlight."

(B) 3 P–KB4 (cols. 9–10) once considered incontrovertibly the most advantageous continuation, has since been eroded and other varieties have been tried, i.e.:

(C) 3 N–QB3 (cols. 11–14) may in some variations transpose into variations dealt with the Pirć Defence—whereas in this section we are concerned with independent lines, one of them dating back to 1879!

(D) 3 N–KB3 (cols. 15–19) followed by 4 P–B3 seemed a smasher in the game Geller–Ree, but the shock has worn off.

(E) 3 P–QB3 (col. 20) is a safe defensive stonewall opening a king-side attack (4 P–KB4), but it does not gain momentum.

Although the Robatsch is now also located among the asymmetrical King's Pawn Games, it has strong affiliation with the Flank Openings (the Réti, the English, the Fianchettoes, the King's Indian, and reversed Indian system) and should be studied in conjunction with the respective sections.

245

The basic position in the Diagram may also be arrived at by transposing White's first two moves. Col. 10 of the "Queen's Pawn Games" section applies to sequences that arise from answers other than (1 P–Q4, P–KN3) 2 P–K4.

Some opening books call the Robatsch the "Modern Defence."

ROBATSCH (or KING'S FIANCHETTO) DEFENCE 247

1 P-K4, P-KN3; 2 P-Q4, B-N2; 3 P-QB4, P-Q3; 4 N-QB3

	1	2	3	4	5
	N-QB3.................................			P-QB3......	P-QB4 (j)
5	P-Q5.......	B-K3		N-B3	B-K3 (k)
	N-Q5	P-K4		B-N5 (h)	Q-N3
6	B-K3	KN-K2 (c)	...P-Q5	B-K3	KN-K2
	P-K4 (a)	P-B4! (d)	N-Q5! (f)	N-Q2	N-QB3
7	P×P e.p.	P-B3	KN-K2	B-K2	N-Q5
	N×P	N-B3	N×N	B×N	Q-R4†
8	B-K2	P-Q5	B×N	B×B	B-Q2
	N-K2	N-K2	P-KB4	KN-B3	Q-Q1
9	Q-Q2	Q-Q2	P-B3	O-O	B-B3
	P-KB4 (b)	O-O (e)	N-B3 (g)	P-QR3 (i)	P-K4 (l)

(a) 6 . . . P-QB4; 7 KN-K2, Q-N3; 8 Q-Q2, (A) 8 . . . P-B4; 9 O-O-O, N × N; 10 B × N, N-B3; 11 P × P ± . Ivkov-Hübner, Dortmund 1975. (B) 8 . . . B-N5; 9 P-B3, B-Q2 ∞.

(b) 10 B-R6, B × B; 11 Q × B, P × P; 12 N × P, N-KB4; 13 Q-Q2, Q-R5; 14 N-QB3, O-O ∞. Mikov-Kotov, USSR 1960.

(c) If (A) 6 P × P, P × P; 7 Q × Q†, N × Q! (B) 6 P-Q5, QN-K2; 7 P-KN4, P-KB4; 8 NP × P, P × P! 9 Q-R5†, K-B1; 10 B-R3, N-KB3; 11 Q-B3, P-B5; 12 B-Q2, P-B3; 13 KN-K2, B × B; 14 Q × B, Q-Q2; 15 Q × Q, N × Q; 16 N-B1, R-B1; 17 N-N3 (Portisch–Minić, Ljubljana/Portoroz 1973), K-B2 = .

(d) Risky is 6 . . . N-R3; 7 P-Q5! (7 P-B3, P-B4; and now (1) 8 Q-Q2, N-B2; 9 O-O-O, O-O; 10 K-N1, P-QR3 = ; Hottes–Kotov, Hamburg 1960; or (2) 8 P-Q5, N-K2; 9 Q-Q2, N-B2; 10 N-B1, O-O =), N-QN1; 8 P-B3, P-KB4; 9 Q-Q2, N-B2; 10 O-O-O, O-O; 11 K-N1, P-B4; 12 KP × P, P × P; 13 P-B4, with a minimal plus in space. *Archives.*

(e) (A) 10 O-O-O, P-QR3; 11 P-B5, P-QN4! Bobotsov-Kottnauer, Hastings 1959-60; or (B) 10 N-B1! with an equal game.

(f) 6 . . . QN-K2; (A) 7 P-KN4, P-KB4 (7 . . . N-B3, 8 P-B3!); 8 NP × P, P × P; 9 Q-R5†, K-B1; 10 B-R3! ± . (B) 7 P-KN4, N-KB3; 8 B-K2, O-O; 9 P-KR4, N-K1; 10 P-R5 ± .

(g) 10 Q-Q2, O-O; 11 P × P, P × P; 12 O-O-O, P-QR3; with a precarious balance. In the column, even stronger is 9 P × P, P × P; 10 B-R5†, K-B1; 11 P-B4 ± .

(h) 5 . . . P-QR3? 6 B-K2, P-QN4; 7 O-O, B-N5; 8 B-K3 ± . Hort-Larsen, Lugano 1968.

(i) 10 P-KN3, P-KR4; 11 P-KR3, P-K4; 12 B-N2, O-O; 13 Q-Q2 (Schmid–Bronstein, Monte Carlo 1969), P × P; 14 B × P, P-QN4 = . Marić.

(j) 4 . . . P-KB4; (A) 5 P × P, B × BP; 6 N-B3! N-KR3; 7 B-K2, O-O; 8 O-O, N-R3; 9 P-Q5, P-B4; 10 N-KN5, N-B2 = . Polugayevski-Bilek, Lugano 1968. (B) 5 KN-K2, P-K4; 6 P-Q5, N-K2; 7 N-N3, P-B3 = .

(k) (A) 5 P × P, P × P; 6 Q × Q, K × Q; 7 B-N5†, P-B3; 8 R-Q1†, N-Q2; 9 B-K3, P-B3; 10 P-KN3, K-B2; 11 B-N2, B-R3; 12 P-B4, N-K2 = . Kmoch. (B) 5 P-B4, Q-N3! 6 N-B3, B-N5; 7 P-Q5, N-B3; 8 P-KR3, B × N; 9 Q × B, N-R3; 10 R-QN1, N-Q2 ∓. Uhlmann–Olafsson, Reykjavik 1968.

(l) 10 P × BP, P × P; 11 N-B1. Olafsson-Barendregt, Beverwijk 1959. White has some tactical advantage.

1 P-K4, P-KN3; 2 P-Q4, B-N2

	6	7	8	9	10
3	(P-Q4).............................			P-KB4	
	(P-Q3)			P-QB4 (j)....	P-Q3
4	(N-QB3)		N-KB3	P-Q5 (k)	N-KB3 (n)
	P-K4	N-Q2	N-Q2 (h)	P-K3 (l)	P-QB4 (o)
5	P-Q5 (a)	N-B3 (d)	N-B3	N-QB3 (m)	P-Q5 (p)
	P-QB4 (b)	P-K4	P-K3	P-QR3	N-KB3 (q)
6	B-K2	B-K2	B-K2	P-QR4	B-N5†
	N-KR3!?	N-K2!? (e)	N-K2	P-Q3	B-Q2
7	P-KR4!	B-K3 (f)	B-K3	N-B3!?	B × B†
	P-B3	O-O	P-N3	P × P	QN × B
8	B-K3	Q-Q2	O-O	N × P	P-K5
	N-B2	P-KB4	B-N2	B-K3 =	N-K5
9	N-R3	B-R6	Q-B2		Q-K2
	N-QR3 (c)	B × B (g)	P-KR3 = (i)		Q-R4† (r)

(a) 5 P × P, P × P; 6 Q × Q†, K × Q; (A) 7 B-N5†, P-B3; 8 R-Q1†, N-Q2; 9 B-K3, P-B3; 10 P-KN3 or (B) 7 P-B4, N-QB3; 8 N-B3, B-N5; 9 P × P, B × N; 10 P × B, B × P; 11 B-N5†, K-K1! 12 O-O-O, Tarjan–Matulović, Novi Sad 1975, give White a better endgame but it has proved difficult to transform into a clear win.

(b) There are no really reliable defences to be found in this 4 . . . P-K4 line but it is sufficiently outbalancing so as to account for possible surprises of Black's; e.g. 5 . . . N-K2; 6 P-KR4, P-KR4; 7 B-K2, N-Q2; 8 N-R3, P-R4; 9 P-B3, N-QB4; 10 N-B2, N-N1; 11 B-N5 ± . Averbakh–Kottnauer, Hastings 1959–60. (B) 5 . . . N-KR3; 6 P-KR4! P-R4; 7 B-Q3, N-R3; 8 KN-K2, N-QB4; 9 B-B2 ± . (C) 5 . . . N-Q2; 6 B-K2, KN-B3; 7 B-K3, N-B4; 8 B-B3, O-O; 9 P-KN4! ± . (D) 5 . . . P-KB4; 6 P × P, B × P; 7 B-Q3, N-K2; 8 B-N5! ± . All *Comments*. (E) 5 . . . N-Q2; (1) 6 B-K3, P-QR4; 7 B-Q3, B-R3(?); 8 Q-Q2, B × B; 9 Q × B, N-B4; 10 O-O-O, B-Q2; 11 B-B2 (Westerinen–Larsen, Helsinki 1969), Q-B3 = . (2) 6 B-K2! KN-B3; 7 B-K3, N-B4; 8 B-B3, O-O; 9 P-KN4 ± . *Comments*. Compare the column and the Benoni Defence.

(c) 10 P-R3, B-Q2; 11 R-QN1, P-B4; 12 P × P ± ! Uhlmann–Barendregt, Beverwijk 1961. In the column, simply 6 . . . N-KB3!? might help maintain equal chances.

(d) 5 P-KB4 transposes into the King's Indian Defence—see there.

(e) Again best is 6 . . . N-KB3; 7 B-N5, P × P; 8 N × P, P-KR3; 9 B-R4, N-B4; 10 Q-B2, P-QR4 = . *Comments*.

(f) Without bite is 7 O-O, O-O; 8 P-Q5 (Udovčić–Minić, Zagreb 1969), P-QR4 = .

(g) 10 Q × B, KP × P; 11 N × P, N-K4; 12 P-B4, N-B2 = . Hort–Suttles, Lugano 1969.

(h) Equally effective against White's tame move are (A) 4 . . . B-N5; 5 B-K2, N-QB3; 6 B-K3, P-K4; 7 P-Q5, B × N; 8 B × B, N-Q5; 9 P-KR4! P-KR4; 10 N-B3, P-QB4! = . Pachman. (B) 4 . . . P-K4; 5 B-K3, N-QB3; 6 B-K2, N-B3; 7 P-Q5, N-K2; 8 KN-Q2! O-O; 9 N-QB3, N-K1! = .

(i) Petrosian–Spassky, 12th match game 1966 (by transposition).

(j) 3 . . . P-Q4?! 4 P-K5, N-KR3; 5 N-KB3; O-O; 6 B-K2, P-QB4; 7 P × P, Q-R4†; 8 N-B3, R-Q1; 9 O-O, Q × P†; 10 Q-Q4, Q-R4; 11 B-Q3, N-QB3; 12 Q-B2, B-B4 = . Romanovski–Kostyuchenko, USSR 1963.

(k) More aggressive than the—oldest known—line 4 P × P, Q-R4†; 5 B-Q2, Q × BP; 6 B-B3, N-KB3; 7 Q-Q4 (Lasker–Bardeleben, Berlin 1890), Q × Q; 8 B × Q, N-B3 = .

(l) Or 4 . . . P-Q3; 5 N-KB3, N-KB3; 6 N-B3 (6 B-N5†, QN-Q2!), O-O; 7 B-K2, P-QR3; 8 P-QR4, P-K3 = .

(m) 5 P-B4, P × P; 6 BP × P, P-Q3; see Modern Benoni. The column is Euwe's analysis, but 7 P × P?! is a possible improvement.

(n) (A) Upon 4 N-QB3, N-KB3 transposes into the Pirć Defence, note (a) to cols. 6–10 but (B) 4 . . . P-QB3; 5 N-B3, B-N5; 6 B-K2, N-Q2; 7 B-K3, P-K4; 8 BP×P, P×P; 9 P-Q5! gives White an edge. For (B) 4 . . . P-QB3 see col. 20.

(o) Feasible alternatives are (A) 4 . . . P-QR3; 5 P-QR4, P-N3; 6 B-K2 (6 P-R5, P-QN4! =), P-K3; 7 O-O, N-Q2; 8 P-Q5, P-K4! 9 N-K1, N-K2; 10 N-Q3; O-O; 11 P-B4, P×P; 12 B-P, P-R3 = ; Westerinen–Ivkov, Bamberg 1968; or (B) 4 . . . N-KB3; with a kind of King's Indian Defence, e.g. (A) 5 P-K5, KN-Q2; 6 B-B4, N-N3; 7 B-N3, P-Q4; 8 P-B3†. (B) 5 B-Q3, P-K4; 6 P-B3, P × BP; 7 B × P, O-O; 8 O-O, P-B4; 9 QN-Q2, P × P; 10 P × P, N-R4; 11 B-K3, P-Q4 = .

(p) 5 P×P, Q-R4†; 6 P-B3, Q×BP; 7 B-Q3, N-KB3; 8 Q-K2, O-O; 9 QN-Q2, P-K4 = . Bogdanović–Kotov, Sarajevo 1966.

(q) A critical point of decision, with 5 . . . P-K3 followed by 6 . . . N-K2 (and if 7 N-QB3, B × N!) probably preferable. Compare col. 9.

(r) 10 QN-Q2, N×N; 11 B×N, Q-N3; 12 O-O, P×P; 13 P×P, O-O (Dückstein–Alexander, Munich 1958); 14 B-B3! Euwe.

1 P–K4, P–KN3; 2 P–Q4 (*a*), B–N2 (*b*)

	11	12	13	14	15
3	N–QB3..				N–KB3
	P–QB4	P–Q3 (*e*)			P–Q3
4	P–Q5	B–K3	P–B4 (*h*)		B–K2
	P–Q3	P–QR3	P–QR3	N–QB3 (*k*)	P–K3 (*m*)
5	B–K2	P–B3 (*f*)	N–B3	B–K3	P–B3
	B × N† (*c*)	N–Q2	P–QN4 (*i*)	N–B3	N–Q2
6	P × B	Q–Q2	B–K3	B–K2	O–O
	N–KB3	P–QN4	B–N2	O–O	N–K2
7	Q–Q3	P–QR4!	B–Q3	N–B3	QN–Q2
	Q–R4	P–N5	P–N5	B–N5	P–N3
8	B–Q2	N–Q1	N–QN1	P–K5	P–QR4
	Q–R5	R–QN1	N–KB3	P × P	P–QR3
9	P–QB4	P–R5!	QN–Q2	QP × P	R–K1
	P–QN4 (*d*)	P–K4 (*g*)	QN–Q2 (*j*)	N–Q2 (*l*)	B–N2 (*n*)

(*a*) 2 P–KN3, P–Q3; 3 B–N2, B–N2; 4 P–Q3, P–QB4; see Flank Openings, King's Fianchetto variations.

(*b*) Stubborn is 2 . . . P–QB3; 3 P–QB3; B–N2; 4 B–Q3, P–Q3; 5 P–KB4, P–K4; 6 QP × P, P × P; 7 P × P, Q–R5† 8 P–N3, Q–K2! 9 N–B3, B–N5 = . Uhlmann.

(*c*) 5 . . . N–KB3 leads into the Pirć Defence.

(*d*) 10 P–KB3, P × P; 11 Q × P, Q × Q; 12 B × Q, B–R3 = . Pérez–Haag, Havana 1962.

(*e*) Safe and of hidden resilience is also (A) 3 . . . P–QB3; 4 P–B4, P–Q4; 5 P–K5, P–KR4; 6 N–B3, N–KR3; 7 B–K3, B–N5; 8 B–K2, P–K3; 9 Q–Q2, N–Q2; 10 P–KN3, N–KB4; 11 B–B2, P–QN4! 12 P–KR3, B × N; 13 B × B, N–N3! (Zinn–Ciocaltea, Lugano 1968) 14 P–N3 with equilibrium. (B) For 3 . . . P–QB4; 4 N–B3, P × P; see Sicilian Defence. "Ultra-modern" is (c) 3 . . . P–N3; 4 B–K3, B–N2!? 5 B–Q3, P–K3; 6 Q–Q2, P–Q3; 7 KN–K2, N–Q2; 8 O–O, N–K2; 9 P–B4, O–O ∞. Minckwitz 1879!!

(*f*) 5 Q–Q2, N–Q2; 6 O–O–O, P–QN4; 7 P–B3, B–N2; 8 P–KR4, P–N5; 9 QN–K2, P–QB4; 10 N–R3, Q–B2; 11 N–N5, KN–B3; 12 K–N1, R–QB1! = . Teufel–Ivkov, Bamberg 1968.

(*g*) 10 P–Q5, P–KB4; 11 R–R4, P–N6; 12 P × NP, KN–B3 = . Balinas–Ivkov, Lugano 1968.

(*h*) (A) 4 B–KN5, P–QB3; 5 Q–Q2, P–QR4!? (5 . . . N–B3); 6 N–B3, P–R5; 7 B–K2, Q–R4; 8 O–O, B–N5; 9 QR–Q1, N–QR3; 10 P–K5, P–R3 ∞. Soltis–Suttles, San Juan 1971. (B) 4 N–B3, N–B3; see Pirć Defence, cols. 21–30.

(*i*) 5 . . . N–Q2; 6 B–B4, P–K3! 7 P–QR4, N–K2; 8 O–O, O–O; 9 B–K3, P–N3; also equalizes. *Comments.*

(*j*) 10 P–KR3, O–O; 11 O–O, P–B4; 12 P–Q5, Q–B2! = . Dückstein–Ivkov, Bamberg 1968.

(*k*) This is a risky variation, just as 4 . . . P–QB3; 5 N–B3! (5 B–K2, Q–N3; 6 P–K5, N–KR3 =); 5 . . . B–N5; 6 B–K3, Q–N3; 7 Q–Q2! B × N; 8 P × B, Q × NP; 9 R–QN1, Q–R6; 10 R × P! ± . Marić.

(*l*) 10 P–KR3, B × N; 11 B × B, N–N3; 12 O–O ± . R. Byrne–Keene, Hastings 1972. Compare Pirć Defence, cols. 11 and 27.

(*m*) (A) 4 . . . N–Q2; 5 O–O, KN–B3; 6 P–K5, N–Q4; 7 P–B4, N–N3; 8 Q–N3, P × P; 9 P–B5, P × P; 10 P × N, RP × P = . Antoshin–Steinberg, Kharkov 1968. (B) 4 . . . N–KB3; 5 N–B3, O–O; 6 O–O, P–N3! 7 R–K1, B–N2; 8 P–K5.

(*n*) 10 B–Q3, O–O; 11 N–B4, Q–K1; 12 B–Q2, P–KB3; 13 Q–K2, K–R1; 14 K–R1, Q–B2 = . Petrosian–Spasski, 16th match game 1966. Black's moves in col. 15 are typical for the stodgy and passive but solid "Hippopotamus" Defence—also called the Ujtelky System.

1 P-K4, P-KN3; 2 P-Q4, B-N2

	16	17	18	19	20
3	(N-KB3)				P-QB3
	(P-Q3) (a)				P-Q3 (o)
4	P-B3		B-QB4 (h)		P-KB4
	P-QB3	N-Q2 (e)	N-KB3 (i)	... P-QB3 (m)	N-KB3
5	QN-Q2 (b)	B-Q3 (f)	Q-K2 (j)	B-N3	P-K5 (p)
	N-B3 (c)	P-K4!	O-O (k)	P-QN4	N-Q4 (q)
6	B-K2	O-O	O-O	O-O	N-B3
	O-O	KN-B3	P-B3	N-QR3	O-O
7	O-O	P-QR4	B-N3	P-B3	B-B4
	QN-Q2	P-QR4	B-N5	N-B3	P-QB3
8	R-K1	R-K1	QN-Q2	P-K5	O-O
	Q-B2	O-O	P-Q4	N-Q4	P-QR4 (r)
9	B-B1	P-R3	P-B3	P×P	P-QR4
	P-K4 (d)	R-K1 (g)	QN-Q2 (l)	Q×P = (n)	N-R3 =

(a) (A) 3 . . . N-KB3; 4 QN-Q2, P-Q3; 5 B-K2, O-O; 6 O-O, N-B3; 7 R-K1! R-K1; 8 P-B3, P-K4; 8 P×P!? N×P; 10 N×N, R×N = *Informator* 11. (B) 3 . . . P-QB4?! 4 P-B4, P×P; 5 N×P, N-KB3; 6 N-QB3, P-Q3; 7 B-K2, N-QB3 may transpose into the Sicilian Defence, 106-10 if both players cooperate—else compare also Sicilian Defence, col. 174, note (h). (c) 3 . . . P-QB3; 4 B-K2, P-Q4; 5 P-K5, B-N5; 6 O-O, P-K3 = .

(b) 5 B-Q3, B-N5; 6 P-KR3, B × N; 7 Q × B, N-Q2; 8 O-O, P-K4 = .

(c) 5 . . . N-Q2; 6 B-K2, N-R3; 7 O-O, P-QB4! = . *Comments.*

(d) 10 P-QR4. Geller-Ree, Beverwijk 1969. Black is somewhat cramped.

(e) (A) 4 . . . B-N5; 5 QN-Q2, N-Q2; 6 P-KR3, B × N; 7 N × B, P-K4; 8 B-Q3, N-K2; 9 O-O, O-O; 10 B-KN5, P-KB3; 11 Q-N3†, K-R1; 12 B-K3, P-N3; 13 QR-Q1, Q-K1 = . (B) 4 . . . N-KB3! 5 QN-Q2, O-O; 6 B-K2, (1) 6 . . . P-B4; 7 P×P, P×P; 8 O-O, N-B3; 9 Q-B2, P-N3 = Petrosian-Mecking, Mallorca 1969. (2) 6 . . . QN-Q2; 7 O-O, P-K4 = .

(f) 5 B-K3, KN-B3; 6 B-Q3, P-B3; 7 QN-Q2, P-K4; 8 N-B4, Q-B2; 9 P-KR3 (9 P-QR4, N-N5), P-QN4 = . *Comments.*

(g) 10 N-R3, P-KR3; 11 Q-B2, N-B1 = . Ivkov in *Informator* 5.

(h) (A) 4 B-K2, N-KB3; 5 N-B3, see Pirć Defence. (B) 4 P-B4, P-K3; 5 B-Q3, P-N3; 6 O-O, B-N2; 7 R-K1, N-Q2; 8 P-QR4, P-QR4; 9 N-R3, N-K2, 10 R-N1, O-O; 11 N-B2, P-K4; 12 P-Q5, N-QB4; 13 N-R3, P-B4 = . Friedlaender-McLeod, Western US Open Chp. 1901. Black's Double Fianchetto has been utilized also against the Réti, English or Fianchetto Openings.

(i) (A) 4 . . . P-K3 is good. Or (B) 4 . . . P-QB4; 5 P × P (or 5 O-O), Q-R4†; 6 P-B3, Q × BP; 7 Q-N3, P-K3; 8 B-K3, Q-B2; 9 QN-Q2, N-KB3; 10 N-Q4, P-QR3 = . Minić-Timman, Wijk aan Zee 1970.

(j) 5 QN-Q2, O-O; 6 O-O, N-B3; 7 P-K5, P×P; 8 P×P, N-Q4 = .

(k) 5 . . . N-B3; 6 P-K5, P×P; 7 P×P, N-KN5; 8 B-QN5, B-Q2 is a sharp response.

(l) 10 P-K5, N-K1; 11 P-KR3, B × N; 12 N × B, N-B2; 13 P-KR4 ± . Savon-Shamkovich, USSR Chp. 1971.

(m) Preparing either . . . P-QN4 or . . . P-Q4. Also 4 . . . P-QB4 is playable.

(n) Ostojić-Smyslov, Monte Carlo 1969. 9 P-QR4! is sharper. Compare also col. 9.

(o) (A) 3 . . . P-Q4; (1) 4 N-Q2, P-QB4; 5 P × BP, N-KB3; 6 P × P, Q × P; 7 KN-B3 (7 N-N3!), Q × BP; 8 B-K2, O-O = . Hennings-Gulko, USSR 1968. (2) 4 P × P, Q × P; 5 N-B3, P-QB4 = . If (B) 3 . . . P-N3; 4 B-K3, B-N2; 5 N-Q2, P-Q3; 6 KN-B3, P-K4∞. Steinitz-Montgredien, London 1863.

(p) 5 B-Q3 see col. 10, note *(p)*(A).

(q) If 5 . . . P×P; 6 BP×P, N–Q4; 7 N–B3, O–O; 8 B–QB4, P–QB4; 9 O–O, P×P; 10 Q×P, P–K3; 11 B–KN5, N–QB3! = .

(r) Or 8 . . . P–K3; 9 Q–K1, P–QB4! 10 K–R1, N–QB3 = . Kurajica–Udovčić, Zagreb 1969. The column is Bogdanović–Kotov, Sochi 1967

Queen's Pawn Openings

Queen's Gambit Accepted

(1 P–Q4, P–Q4; 2 P–QB4, P × P)

The fearless acceptance of this gambit is additional proof of the strengthening of Black's defensive armour. In 1512 Damiano wrote that Black gets an inferior game, in 1536 Ruy Lopez showed how White regains the gambit pawn, and in the eighteenth century Philidor reaffirmed his predecessors' opinions. Staunton had his ideas too—one of which was that . . . P–KR3 is a must for Black. Coming to more modern times, Steinitz was happy in the role of second player because he could isolate White's queen's pawn and manoeuvre his Knight to a blockade on Q4. The virtuosi of this defence were Alekhin, Fine, Flohr, Gligorić, and Reshevsky. But the strategical ideas are limited, due to the symmetrical pawn structure (4–4 and 3–3 on the queen's side). A sharp battle rages when Black can establish a queen's-side majority with P–QB5 at a favourable moment (col. 1), but such opportunities are rare. The current view is that the slight initiative White reaps from the opening is difficult to maintain in the hurly-burly of practical chess. Black can play for a draw provided that he avoids myriad pitfalls.

The strategy of the Queen's Gambit Accepted is designed to avoid the cramped formations of the Orthodox Defence and its problem child, the invalid queen's bishop, which can here obtain a fine diagonal on QN2. Black surrenders the centre temporarily with the conviction that . . . P–QB4 will restore the balance. White's first objective is P–K4, through the immediate 3 P–K4 (col. 37) is under constant debate. This pawn-thrust often involves a sacrifice, but it is sometimes needed to offset Black's tactics on the queen's side. In reply, both 7 . . . N–B3 (cols. 1–5) and 7 . . . P–QN4 (cols. 6–11) are legitimate. Attempts for White to vary on the 7th move (cols. 12–14) or the 6th move (col. 15) are generally innocuous.

On the other hand, Black often varies successfully from the main. It is hard to make headway against Smyslov's idea of establishing a Grünfeld-like pattern with 4 . . . P–KN3 (cols. 16–17); noteworthy is 4 . . . B–K3 (col. 18), as favoured by Winawer and Flohr and still not decisively refuted; and 4 . . . B–N5 (cols. 19–24) which should be studied in conjunction with cols. 34–5.

4 N–B3 (cols. 25–7) is somewhat meek, whereas the *Manheim Variation* 4 Q–R4† (cols. 28–31) is a durable line, mostly due to the frequent possibility of transposition into more (or less!) favourable lines of the Queen's Catalan (with P–KN3).

Alekhin's Variation 3 . . . P–QR3 (cols. 32–5) is subject to periodic revival, thus testifying to the World Champion's intuition. The fianchetto of Black's queen's bishop seems as satisfactory as the development . . . B–N5 with a subsequent . . . B × N.

3 P–K3 (col. 36) and 3 P–K4 (col. 37–40) are more dangerous than has been believed and require a most careful defence.

1 P-Q4, P-Q4; 2 P-QB4, P × P; 3 N-KB3, N-KB3; 4 P-K3, P-K3; 5 B × P, P-B4;
6 O-O, P-QR3; 7 Q-K2, N-B3

	1	2	3	4	5
8	R-Q1	P-QR4		N-B3	
	P-QN4	B-K2 (e)		P-QN4	
9	B-N3 (a)	R-Q1	P × P	B-N3	
	P-B5 (b)	Q-B2	N-K5!	B-N2	P-B5 (m)
10	B-B2	N-B3	R-Q1 (h)	R-Q1	B-B2
	N-QN5!	O-O	Q-B2	Q-B2 (j)	B-N2
11	N-B3	P-R3 (f)	P-QN3	P-Q5	P-QR4
	N × B	R-Q1	N × QBP	P × P	P-N5
12	Q × N	P-Q5!	B-N2	N × P (k)	N-K4
	B-N2 (c)	P × P	O-O	N × N	N-QR4
13	P-Q5	B × QP	QN-Q2	B × N	N × N†
	Q-B2	N-QN5	B-Q2	B-K2	P × N
14	P-K4	P-K4	P-K4	P-QN3	P-K4
	P-K4 (d)	KN × B (g)	KR-Q1 (i)	O-O (l)	Q-B2 (n)

(a) (A) If 9 B-Q3, P-B5. (B) Important is 9 P × P, Q-B2; 10 B-N3 (10 B-Q3, N-QN5! 11 P-QR4, P × P; 12 R × P, R-QN1! = Alekhin), B × P; 11 P-QR4, P-N5; 12 QN-Q2 O-O = . Pirc-Kashdan, Bled 1931. Also compare col. 14.

(b) Black does not have this resource of depriving White of the Bishop-pair after 8 N-B3; whereas 8 . . . B-N2, or . . . Q-N3, or . . . Q-B2, or . . . P × P transposes into cols. 2-5 respectively.

(c) Alternatives are (A) 12 . . . N-Q4; 13 P-K4, N-N5; 14 Q-K2, N-Q6; 15 P-QR3! (B) 12 . . . B-K2; 13 P-Q5, Q-B2; 14 P-K4, P-K4 = . (c) 12 . . . Q-B2; 13 P-K4, B-N2; 14 P-Q5, P × P; 15 P-K5, N-K5; 16 N × QP, B × N; 17 R × B, N-B4 = . Comments.

(d) 15 B-N5, N-Q2; 16 QR-B1, B-Q3; 17 N-K2, O-O; 18 N-N3 (Stáhlberg-Alexander, Staunton Memorial 1951), QR-B1; 19 N-B5, KR-K1 = . Comments.

(e) A still open question is 8 . . . P × P; 9 R-Q1, B-K2 (Pachman presents 9 . . . P-Q6! 10 B × QP, Q-B2; 11 P-K4, N-KN5 ∞); 10 P × P, O-O; 11 N-B3, N-Q4! 12 B-Q3, N/3-QN5; 13 B-N1, B-Q2; (1) 14 N-K5, QB-B3; 15 R-R3! N-B3; 16 B-N5, P-KN3; 17 B-R6, R-K1; 18 R-K1, B-B1 ∞ ; or (2) 14 Q-K4, P-KN3; 15 N-K5 = . The line is important in view of the column.

(f) Flat is 11 P-QN3, B-Q2! 12 B-N2, QR-Q1; 13 P-Q5, P × P; 14 N × P, N × N; 15 B × N, B-N5! 16 QR-B1, R-Q2; 17 P-R3, B-R4; 18 P-K4, KR-Q1 = . Gligorić.

(g) (A) 15 N × N, N × N; 16 P × N! Langeweg-Filip, Beverwijk 1966. (B) 15 P × N? B-B4; 16 B-B4, Q × B; 17 Q × B, B × P! = .

(h) 10 N-Q4, N × QBP; 11 N × N, P × N ∞ is Bronstein's tack.

(i) 15 Q-K3, B-K1; 16 B-K2, P-QR4 = . Petrosian-Portisch, Zagreb 1965.

(j) 10 . . . Q-N3; 11 P-Q5 (11 P-QR4, P-B5; 12 P × P, P × P =), P × P; 12 P-K4! O-O-O; 13 N × QP, N × N; 14 B × N, N-N5; 15 B × P ± . Comments.

(k) 12 P-K4! (compare note (j)), P-Q5! 13 P-K5, O-O-O! 14 P × N, P × N; 15 R × R†, N × R; 16 P × BP, P × P = . Fuderer-Andrić, Yugoslav Chp. 1951.

(l) 15 B-N2! KR-Q1 = . Euwe-Kramer, New York 1948-9.

(m) 9 . . . P × P; 10 R-Q1, B-K2; 11 P × P, N-QR4! 12 N-K5, O-O! = . R. Byrne-Burger, US Chp. 1966.

(n) 15 B-K3 (15 P-Q5, O-O-O), B-Q3; 16 QR-B1, R-KN1; 17 KR-Q1, P-B4 = . Gligorić-Troianescu, Sofia 1947.

1 P-Q4, P-Q4; 2 P-QB4, P×P; 3 N-KB3, N-KB3; 4 P-K3, P-K3; 5 B×P, P-B4;
6 O-O, P-QR3; 7 Q-K2, P-QN4; 8 B-N3, B-N2

	6	7	8	9	10
9	R-Q1				P-QR4
	QN-Q2				QN-Q2
10	N-B3			P-QR4	RP×P (h)
	Q-B2?	Q-N1!	B-K2 (d)	B-K2	RP×P
11	P-K4 (a)	P-Q5	P-K4	P×BP (f)	R×R
	P×P	N×P	P×P	O-O	Q×R
12	N-Q5!? (b)	N×N	N×QP	N-K5	N-B3
	P×N	B×N	Q-B2	Q-B2	P-N5
13	P×P†	B×B	B-N5	P-B6	N-QN5
	B-K2	P×B	P-N5	N×N	Q-R4 (i)
14	R×P	R×P	N-R4	P×B	P-K4!
	K-B1!	B-K2 (c)	Q-K4 (e)	N/4-N5 (g)	B-K2! (j)

(a) 11 P-KR3, B-K2; 12 B-Q2, O-O; 13 QR-B1, QR-B1; 14 P-K4, P-K4! = *Comments.*

(b) (A) Strong is 12 N×QP, (1) 12 . . . B-Q3; 13 P-N3, B-K4; 14 P-B3, O-O; 15 B-K3 + . Reshevsky-Najdorf match 1952. (2) *Archives* 1952 gave 12 . . . B-B4 = . (B) 12 P-K5! P×N; 13 P×N, N×P; 14 N-K5, B-B4; 15 B-KB4, Q-N3; Spasski-Suetin, USSR 1963; "with a sharp game—Sokolski." But (1) 16 P×P, N-Q4 (16 . . . O-O; 17 N×P, K×N; 18 R-Q6!); 17 B×N, B×B; 18 R×B, P×R; 19 N-N6 dis. †, Q-K3; 20 Q×Q†, P×Q; 21 N×R + . If (2) 16 N×P, Q-B3! 18 N-Q6†, K-B1! 18 N×B, Q×N (18 . . . P×P; 19 QR-N1, Q×N; 20 Q×KP +); 19 P×P, N-K5; 20 K-B1, R-K1; 21 QR-B1, P-N4 ∞. The column is Geller-Fuderer, Göteborg 1955.

(c) 15 P-K4, N-N3! 16 R-B5, O-O; 17 B-B4, Q-N2 = . Suetin.

(d) Older tries are (A) 10 . . . P-N5; 11 N-QR4, Q-R4; 12 B-Q2! P×P; 13 N×P, B-K2; 14 P-QR3, O-O; 15 P×P, Q-KN4; 16 P-B3. (B) 10 . . . B-B3; 11 P-K4, P×P; 12 R×P! B-B4; 13 R-Q3, Q-N3 ∞. *Comments.*

(e) 15 B×N, N×B; 16 N-N6, R-Q1; 17 B-R4†, K-B1; 18 B-B6, Q-B2; 19 B×B, Q×B = . Smyslov-Keres, Budapest 1950.

(f) (A) 11 RP×P, RP×P; 12 R×R, Q×R; 13 QN-Q2, P-B5; 14 B-B2, N-K5! N-K5! = . (B) 11 B-B2, O-O; 12 P-K4, P×RP; 13 N-B3, P×P; 13 N×QP (Evans-Winser, Hastings 1949-50), P-R6 = .

(g) 15 P-B4, Q×NP; 16 P×P, P×P; 17 R×R, R×R; 18 Q-B3, Q×Q; 19 P×Q, N-R3 = . Guimard-Bazan, Buenos Aires, 1960.

(h) (A) 10 QN-Q2, P-B5! 11 B-B2, N-N3 ∞. (B) 10 P-K4!? P×QP; 11 N×P (11 P-K5, N-N5; 12 P×P, B-B4; 13 P×P, O-O! =), B-B4; 12 R-Q1, Q-N3 = . Ståhlberg-Najdorf, Buenos Aires 1941.

(i) Also good is 13 . . . Q-N1; 14 P-K4, P×P; 15 KN×P, N-B4; 16 P-K5, KN-Q2; 17 B-KB4; N×B, 18 N×N, B-K2; 19 R-Q1, B-R3 = .

(j) 15 P-K5, N-K5 (or 15 . . . N-Q4; 16 B-N5, B-B3; 17 B×N, B×N; 18 B-QB4, B×B; 19 Q×B, N-N3 = ; Maderna-Ståhlberg, Mar del Plata 1947); 16 B-B2, B-QB3; 17 B×N, Q×N ∓ . Uhlmann-Benko, Buenos Aires 1960.

1 P-Q4, P-Q4; 2 P-QB4, P×P; 3 N-KB3, N-KB3; 4 P-K3, P-K3; 5 B×P, P-B4

	11	12	13	14	15
6	(O-O)				Q-K2 (j)
	(P-QR3)				P-QR3 (k)
7	(Q-K2).	P-K4		B-N3 (g)	P×P
	(P-QN4)	N×P	P-QN4	N-B3 (h)	B×P
8	B-Q3	P-Q5 (c)	B-Q3	Q-K2	O-O
	P×P!	B-K2	B-N2	P×P	N-B3!
9	P×P	P×P	R-K1 (e)	R-Q1	P-K4
	B-N2 (a)	B×P	P×P	B-K2	P-QN4
10	QN-Q2	Q×Q†	P-QR4	P×P	P-K5
	B-K2	B×Q	P×P	N-QR4 (i)	P×B
11	N-N3	B×B	R×P	B-B2	P×N
	QN-Q2	P×B	KN-Q2	P-QN4! =	P×P
12	B-KB4	R-K1	N×P		Q×P
	O-O (b)	N-KB3 (d)	B-K2 (f)		Q-N3 (l)

(a) Black also fares well after 9 . . . N-B3; 10 P-QR4, P×P; 11 R×P, N-QN5; 12 B-N5†, B-Q2; 13 B×B†, Q×B; 14 N-B3, B-K2; 15 B-N5, Q-N2 = .

(b) 13 KR-B1, R-B1; 14 R×R, Q×R; 15 P-QR4, P×P; 16 R×P, N-Q4 = . R. Byrne-Turner, US Chp. 1962.

(c) 8 Q-K2, N-KB3; 9 P-Q5! P-QN4! 10 P×P, P×B; 11 R-Q1, Q-N3! 12 P×P, dis. †, K×P; 13 Q×P† with attack is to be considered.

(d) 13 R×P†, B-K2; 14 B-K3, K-Q2; 15 R-N6, K-B2; 16 R-N3, N-Q4; 17 B-N5, N-QB3 = . Archives.

(e) 9 P-K5, N-Q4; 10 QN-Q2, N-QB3; 11 N-K4, P×P; 12 P-QR4, P×P; 13 B-KN5, Q-Q2; 14 B-B2, P-R3; 15 B-R4, N-N3; 16 Q-Q2, P-Q6; 17 B×QP, N-N5; 18 B-N1, Q×Q; drawn. Szabó-Olafsson, Mariánské Lázne 1961.

(f) 13 B-B2, N-QB3; 14 N×N, B×N; 15 R-Q4, B-B4; 16 R-Q2, Q-B2; 17 B-R4, R-Q1; 18 B×B, Q×B; 19 Q-B2, R-QB1; 20 Q-B3, N-B3; 21 R/2-K2, drawn. Portisch-Petrosian, Stockholm 1962.

(g) (A) 7 P-QR4 see cols. 2-3. (B) If 7 N-B3, P×P; 8 P×P, P-QN4; 9 B-N3, B-N2; 10 B-N5, B-K2 = .

(h) 7 . . . P-QN4; 8 P-QR4, P-B5; 9 B-B2, B-N2; see col. 1. This column handles the lines where an early . . . P-QN4 is omitted, but always compare with cols. 6-10.

(i) 10 . . . O-O; 11 N-B3, N-QN5; 12 N-K5, QN-Q4; 13 R-Q3, B-Q2; 14 R-N3, P-KN3; 15 B-R6, R-K1; 16 P-KR4 + . Filip-Conrady, Varna 1962. The column is Botvinnik-Petrosian, 20th match game 1963.

(j) No real threat poses yet 6 N-B3, with the replies (1) 6 . . . P-QR3; 7 P-QR4, N-B3; 8 O-O, B-K2; 9 N-K5!?, B-Q2! = ; or (2) 6 . . . P×P; 7 P×P, B-K2; 8 O-O, O-O; 9 Q-K2 (9 P-QR3 or 9 P-Q5 could be explored in practice), N-B3; 10 B-K3, N-QR4! = . Spasski-Petrosian, 3rd match game 1966.

(k) An alternative is 6 . . . P×P; 7 P×P, N-B3; 8 B-K3! (8 O-O!? N×P; 9 N×N, Q×N; 10 R-Q1, Q-N3; 11 B-N5†, B-Q2; 12 N-B3, B×B; 13 Q×B†, Q-B3! 14 B-K3, B-K2; 15 QR-B1, O-O; 16 Q×Q, P×Q = . Lutikov-Flohr, Minsk 1952), B-K2; 9 O-O, O-O; 10 N-B3, P-QR3; 11 KR-Q1, N-QN5! 12 QR-B1, QN-Q4 ∞. White has an "isolani" but more active play after 13 N-K5.

(l) 13 N-B3, Q-N5; 14 Q×Q, B×Q; 15 N-K4, B-K2; 16 R-Q1, B-N2; 17 B-B4, R-KN1; 18 N-K1, N-N5; 19 N-Q6†, B×N; 10 B×B, N-Q4 = . Averbakh-Suetin. USSR 1960.

1 P-Q4, P-Q4; 2 P-QB4, P × P; 3 N-KB3, N-KB3; 4 P-K3

	16	17	18	19	20
	P-KN3		B-K3	B-N5	
5	B × P		N-R3 (d)	B × P	
	B-N2		P-B4	P-K3	
6	O-O		N × P	Q-N3	
	O-O		N-B3	B × N	
7	N-B3		B-K2 (e)	P × B	
	KN-Q2 (a)		P-KN3	QN-Q2! (g)	
8	Q-K2	P-K4	O-O	Q × P!	
	N-N3	N-N3	P × P	P-B4!	
9	B-N3	B-K2	P × P	N-B3	O-O!
	P-QR4	B-N5	B-N2	P × P	P × P
10	P-QR4	B-K3	QN-K5	P × P	R-Q1
	N-B3	N-B3	O-O	B-Q3!	B-B4!
11	R-Q1	P-Q5	N × N	B-Q2 (h)	P × P
	B-N5 (b)	B × N (c)	P × N (f)	O-O (i)	B-N3 =

(a) This position including White's 7th move might also arise from the Grünfeld Defence, e.g. 1 P-Q4, N-KB3; 2 P-QB4, P-KN3; 3 N-QB3, P-Q4; 4 N-B3, B-N2; 5 P-K3, P × P; 6 B × P, O-O; 7 O-O, continued as in this column or (A) 7 . . . N-B3; (1) 8 P-K4, B-N5; 9 P-Q5, N-QR4; 10 B-K2, P-B3; 11 P-KR3, B × N = . (2) 8 P-KR3! P-QR3; 9 P-K4, P-QN4; 10 B-N3, N-Q2 = . Minev-Smyslov, Moscow 1959. (B) 7 . . . P-B4; 8 P-Q5, B-N5 = . These deviations are of importance in view of a possible 8 P-K4 (col. 17). On White's part, instead of 7 N-B3, another positional strategy is 7 P-QN3, e.g. 7 . . . P-B3 (stonewalling; otherwise playable are also 7 . . . P-QB4 or 7 . . . P-K4); 8 B-N2, B-N5; 9 QN-Q2, QN-Q2; 10 P-KR3, B-B4; 11 R-K1, N-N3; 12 B-KB1, N-K5; 13 N × N, B × N; 14 N-Q2, B-B4; 15 R-B1 with minimal pressure. Karpov-Korchnoi, 24th match game 1974.

(b) 12 P-R3, B × N; 13 Q × B, P-K3; 14 B-Q2, Q-K2; 15 B-K1, Geller-Plater, Szczawno Zdroj 1957, 15 . . . KR-Q1; 16 QR-B1, QR-N1; 17 Q-K2, N-Q4; with a solid game. *Comments.*

(c) (A) 12 P × B, N-K4; 13 R-N1, P-QB3 (13 . . . Q-Q2; 14 P-B4, N/4-B5; 15 B-Q4!); 14 B × N ± . (B) 12 B × B, N-K4; 13 B-K2, N/4-B5; 14 B-KB4! P-QB3 (14 . . . N × NP; 15 Q-N3, B × N; 16 Q × B, N/7-R5; 17 Q-R5, P-QR3; 18 KR-Q1 +); 15 P × P, Q × Q (15 . . . P × P; 16 Q-N3, N × NP? 17 B-QR6! +); 16 QR × Q, P × P; 17 B-B1, P-QR4 ∞.

(d) (A) 5 N-N5, B-Q4; 6 N-QB3, P-K3 (6 . . . P-KR3!? 7 P-K4 ∞); 7 Q-B2, P-KR3 = . But critical is also (B) 5 N-B3, P-B3; 6 P-QR4, P-KN3; 7 P-K4, N-R3, 8 N-KN5! N-B2; 9 P-K5, N/3-Q4 ∞.

(e) 7 Q-R4, P × P; 8 QN-K5, B-Q2; 9 N × B, N × N; 10 N × P, N × N; 11 Q × N, P-K4; 12 Q-QR4, Q-N3 = . Van Scheltinga-Flohr, Beverwijk 1960.

(f) 12 Q-R4, B-Q4 = . Sherwin-Berliner, US Chp. 1961.

(g) No better are (A) 7 . . . P-QN3; 8 N-B3, B-K2; 9 P-Q5, P × P; 10 N × P, O-O; 11 N × B†!, Q × N; 12 B-Q2 ± , Zaitsev-Spasski, USSR Chp. 1961; or (B) 7 . . . P-B4; 8 P × P!

(h) (A) 11 P-B4, O-O; 12 B-N3, N-R4! = . (B) 11 N-K4, N × N; 12 P × N, O-O; 13 P-K5, N-N3; 14 B-Q3, B-N5†; 15 K-K2, Q × P; 16 Q-K4, Q × Q†; 17 B × Q QR-N1 = .

(i) 12 N-N5, N-N3; 13 B-N3, P-QR3; 14 N × B, Q × N = . Gadalinski-Porebski, Poland 1963.

1 P–Q4, P–Q4; 2 P–QB4, P × P; 3 N–KB3, N–KB3

	21	22	23	24	25
4	(P–K3)				N–B3
	(B–N5)				P–B4
5	(B × P)				P–Q5 (*i*)
	(P–K3)				P–K3
6	(Q–N3)	P–KR3		O–O (*g*)	P–K4
	(B × N)	B–R4		P–QR3	P × P
7	(P × B)	N–B3		Q–K2	P–K5!
	(QN–Q2)	QN–Q2	P–QR3 (*e*)	N–B3	N–K5
8	(Q × P)	O–O	O–O	R–Q1	N × P
	(P–B4)	B–Q3!	N–B3	B–Q3	B–K3
9	P × P (*a*)	P–K4	B–K2	P–KR3	B × P
	B × P	P–K4	B–Q3	B–R4	Q–R4†
10	P–B4	B–K2 (*c*)	P–R3	P–K4	B–Q2
	O–O	B–N3	O–O	B × N	N × B
11	N–B3	P × P	P–QN4 (*f*)	Q × B	Q × N
	R–N1 (*b*)	N × P/4 (*d*)		P–K4 (*h*)	Q × Q† (*j*)

(*a*) 9 R–N1, P–N3; 10 N–B3, B–K2; 11 P × P, N × P; 12 Q–B6†? (12 Q–N5†! =) 12 . . . K–B1! 13 P–B4, N/3–K5! ∓ . Hodos–Tal, USSR Chp. 1961.

(*b*) 12 Q–B3, Q–B2; 12 B–N3, B–N5; 14 B–Q2, N–B4; 15 B–B2, B–R4; 16 R–QN1, KR–Q1; 17 Q–K2, N/3–K5! 18 B × N, R × B! 19 Q × R, N × B; 20 Q–Q3, B × N†; Tal–Shiyanovski, USSR Chp. 1961; 21 P × B, R × R†; 22 Q × R, Q × P†; 23 K–K2, Q–Q7†; 24 K–B3, P–B4 = .

(*c*) If 10 P × P, N × P/4; 11 B–K2, N × N†; or (11 . . . B × N; 12 B × B, Q–K2?! 13 B–K2, O–O–O ∞ . Marić); 12 B × N, B × B; 13 Q × B, Q–K2 = . Spasski–Szabó, Belgrade 1964. For 6 . . . B × N; see col. 34 (*h*).

(*d*) 12 N–KR4, B–QB4; 13 N × B, RP × N; 14 B–N5, P–B3; 15 Q × Q†, R × Q, 16 KR–Q1, O–O; 17 K–B1 with only a slight advantage. Korchnoi–Szabó, Belgrade 1964.

(*e*) 7 . . . N–B3 has also been found quite safe here, just as 7 . . . P–B4.

(*f*) (A) 11 . . . Q–K2; 12 B–N2, QR–Q1 = . Geller–Sakharov, USSR 1963. (B) 11 . . . Q–K1; 12 P–N5, P × P; 13 N × P, N–R4; 14 P–QR4, Q–N1; 15 B–N2, R–Q1; 16 N–Q2; B × B; 17 Q × B, B–N5 = . Uhlmann–Matulović, Sarajevo 1965.

(*g*) (A) 6 QN–Q2, QN–Q2; 7 Q–N3, R–QN1; 8 O–O, P–B3 = is also harmless. (B) 6 N–B3, QN–Q2; 7 P–KR3, B–R4; 8 B–K2, B–Q3; 9 O–O, O–O; 10 P–K4, P–K4; 11 P × P, N × P/4; 12 N–Q4, B × B; 13 Q × B, N–N3; 14 N–B5, B–K4; 15 P–B4, B × N; 16 P × B, R–K1 = . Quinteros–Ghitescu, Polanica Zdroj 1977. Also compare col. 22.

(*h*) 12 Q–KN3, Q–K2; 13 P–Q5, N–Q5; 14 N–B3, P–QN4 = .

(*i*) 5 P–K4, P × P; 6 Q × P, Q × Q; 7 N × Q, P–QR3 = . *MCO* 10.

(*j*) 12 K × Q, N–R3! 13 B–N5†, K–Q1; 14 N–B4, N–B2 = .

1 P–Q4, P–Q4; 2 P–QB4, P × P; 3 N–KB3, N–KB3

	26	27	28	29	30
4	(N–B3) . . . . Q–R4† (Mannheim Variation)				
	P–QR3 (a)		N–B3 . . . . P–B3		
5	P–K4 (b)		N–B3	Q × BP	
	P–QN4		N–Q4 (f)	B–B4 . . . . B–N5	
6	P–K5		P–K4	P–KN3	QN–Q2 (k)
	N–Q4		N–N3	QN–Q2	QN–Q2! (l)
7	P–QR4		Q–Q1	B–N2	P–KN3
	N × N		B–N5	P–K3 (h)	Q–R4
8	P × N		P–Q5	O–O	B–N2
	Q–Q4! B–N2		N–K4	B–K2	P–K4
9	P–N3	P–K6?!	B–KB4	N–B3 (i)	O–O
	B–K3! (c)	P × KP!	N–N3	O–O	P–K5!
10	B–KN2	B–K2	B–K3	B–B4	N–K5
	Q–N2	Q–Q4	P–K3	P–QR4	B–K3!
11	O–O	N–N5	P–QR4	P–QR4 (j)	Q–B2
	B–Q4 (d)	Q × NP (e)	P × P! (g)	Q–N3 =	N × N (m)

(a) (A) Quite defensible is also 4 . . . N–B3, 5 P–K3, B–N5; 6 B × P, P–K3; 7 B–N5, B–N5! 8 Q–R4, B × KN; 9 P × B, Q–Q3; 10 B–Q2, O–O; Boleslavski. (B) 4 . . . P–KN3; 5 B–N5 (5 P–K4!), B–N2; see Grünfeld Defence.

(b) 5 P–QR4, N–B3! 6 P–K4, B–N5; 7 B × P! B × N; 8 P × B, Q × P! 9 Q–N3, O–O–O (also 9 . . . N–K4, 10 B–K2, Q–N3! 11 Q × Q, P × Q; 12 B–K3, N/4–Q2 = . Pachman); 10 B × BP, P–K4; 11 O–O, Q–N5; 12 P–B4, Q × Q; 13 B × Q, B–Q3; 14 P × P, B × P = . Geller–Gurgenidze, Moscow 1963.

(c) 9 . . . B–N2; 10 B–KN2, Q–Q2; 11 B–QR3! P–K3; 12 B × B, K × B; 13 O–O, P–N3; 14 N–R4 ± . Bronstein–Korchnoi, Moscow 1964.

(d) 12 B–QR3, P–K3; 13 B × B, K × B; 14 N–R4, B × B; 15 N × B, N–Q2; 16 N–K3, P–N3; 17 P–B4, N–N3; 18 Q–N1, N–Q4 = . Ivkov–Filip, Zagreb 1965.

(e) 12 R–B1, B–Q4; 13 B–N4 (13 B–B4, P–N5! 14 B–N4, P–R3! 15 B–R3, Q × N! Polugayevski–Szabó, Budapest 1965), P–QR4; 14 P–R4, P–N5 ∞ . Pachman.

(f) 5 . . . B–N5 is also practical; e.g. 6 N–K5, B–Q2; 7 Q × BP, P–K3; 8 B–N5, B–K2; 9 B × N, B × B; 10 N × B, Q × N; 11 P–K3, B–K2! 12 P–QR3, O–O; 13 B–K2, N–R4; 14 Q–R2, P–QB4 = . Petrosian–Korchnoi, Curaçao 1962.

(g) 12 P–R5, P × P; 13 Q × Q†, R × Q; 14 P × N, P × N = . Up to and including Black's tenth move, the column is Botvinnik–Petrosian, match 1963.

(h) 7 . . . N–K5; 8 N–B3, N × N; 9 P × N, N–N3; 10 Q–N3, B–K5; 11 O–O, Q–Q4 = . *Comments.*

(i) 9 Q–N3, Q–N3! 10 QN–Q2, O–O; 11 R–K1, KR–Q1; 12 Q–R4, P–QR4; (Tamanov–Geller, USSR Chp. 1963). 13 N–R4, B–N3.

(j) 11 Q–N3, N–Q4! 12 B–Q2, N × N; 13 B × N, B–K5 = . Filip–Tringov, Tel Aviv 1964.

(k) 6 N–K5? B–K3; 7 Q–Q3, QN–Q2; 8 N × N, B × N; 9 N–B3, Q–N3; 10 B–Q2, P–K4! 11 P × P, N–N5; 12 Q–N3, O–O–O ∓ . Pytlakowski–Smyslov, Helsinki 1952.

(l) (A) 6 . . . P–KN3? 7 P–KN3, B–N2; 8 B–N2, O–O, 9 O–O, N–R3; 10 N–K5! B–K3; 11 Q–R4 ± . (B) 6 . . . Q–Q4; 7 P–K3, Q × Q; 8 B × Q, QN–Q2 ∞ . Pachman.

(m) 12 P × N, Q × KP; 13 N × P, N × N; 14 B × N, Q–QB4 = . Mikenas.

1 P–Q4, P–Q4; 2 P–QB4, P × P; 3 N–KB3

	31	32	33	34	35
	(N–KB3)	.... P–QR3 (d)	(Alekhin Variation)		
4	(Q–R4†)	P–K4?!	..... P–K3		
	QN–Q2 (a)	P–QN4	P–QN4!	..... B–N5	
5	N–B3 (b)	P–QR4	P–QR4	B × P (h)	
	P–K3	B–N2	B–N2	P–K3	
6	P–K4	P–QN3	P–QN3 (f)	Q–N3	.... P–KR3 (j)
	P–B4	B × P	P–K3	B × N	B–R4
7	P–Q5	N–B3	P × BP	P × B	N–B3
	P × P	B–N2	P × BP	P–QN4	N–Q2
8	P–K5	RP × P	B × P	B–K2	P–K4
	P–QN4	RP × P	N–Q2	P–QB4	P–QB4
9	Q × NP	R × R	O–O	P × P	P–Q5
	R–QN1	B × R	KN–B3	B × P	P–K4
10	Q–R4	P × P	QN–Q2	R–N1	P–QR4
	P–Q5 (c)	P × P (e)	P–B4 (g)	B–B1! (i)	B–Q3 =

(a) Another defence is 4 . . . Q–Q2; 5 Q × BP, Q–B3; 6 N–R3, Q × Q; 7 N × Q, P–K3; 8 P–QR3, P–QR4; 9 B–B4, P–QN4 = .

(b) (A) For 5 P–KN3 see Catalan System. (B) 5 P–K3, P–QR3; 6 B × P, R–QN1 = .

(c) 11 P × N, P × N; 12 B × P, R–N5! 13 Q–Q1! P × BP; 14 P–QN3 = . *Comments.*

(d) This line has undergone many changes in reputation from one decade to another. For 3 . . . P–QB3 see Slav Defence.

(e) 11 P–Q5! ± . Neishtadt. Or 11 N–K5! ± . Taimanov.

(f) (A) 6 N–B3, P–N5; 7 B × P, P–K3; 8 Q–N3, N–QB3; 9 P–R5, P × N; 10 Q × B, N–N5; 11 N–K5 (11 B × RP? R–N1!), P × P (11 . . . N–B7†; 12 K–Q1, N × P; 13 P × N, Q × P†; 14 K–B2!); 12 B × NP, R–N1; 13 Q–K4, N–K2; 14 O–O, N/2–Q4 = . (B) 6 P × P, P × P; 7 R × R, B × R; 8 P–QN3! P–K3; 9 P × P, P × P; and now (1) 10 N–K5, N–Q2; 11 Q–R4, KN–B3; 12 N–B6, N–N3! 13 Q–N5, Q–Q2; 14 N–R7, Q × Q† = ; or (2) 10 B × P, N–KB3; 11 Q–R4†, QN–Q2; 12 O–O, B–Q3; 13 N–K5, O–O; 14 N–B6, N–N3; 15 N × Q, N × Q = . Haberditz.

(g) 11 B–R3, B–K2; 12 Q–B2, P × P; 13 N × P (Weiner–Haberditz, Vienna 1948), B × B; 14 R × B, Q–K2 = . Euwe prefers 8 B–R3.

(h) This line is similar to cols. 19–22 but for the omission of . . . N–KB3. If 5 P–KR3, B × N; 6 Q × B, N–QB3; 7 B × P, P–K3; 8 N–B3, N–N3; 9 O–O, B–Q3; 10 R–Q1, O–O; 11 P–R3, P–K4 = . Geller–Sajtar, Helsinki 1952.

(i) 11 N–B3, N–KB3; 12 B–Q2 and 13 O–O–O with chances for both sides.

(j) 6 P–Q5, P × P; 7 B × QP, Q–K2; 8 Q–N3 (or 8 N–B3!), P–QB3; 9 B–B4, Q–N5†; 10 Q × Q, B × Q†; 11 QN–Q2, N–Q2 = . Polugayevski–Smyslov, Havana 1962.

1 P–Q4, P–Q4; 2 P–QB4, P × P

	36	37	38	39	40
3	P–K3	P–K4			
	P–K4!	P–K4	P–QB4		
4	B × P (a)	N–KB3	N–KB3	P–Q5	
	P × P	P × P (d)	P × P	P–K3	
5	P × P (b)	B × P	Q × P	B × P	
	B–N5†	B–N5† (e)	Q × Q	N–KB3	P × P!?
6	N–B3	B–Q2	N × Q	N–QB3!	B × P!?
	N–KB3	B × B†	B–Q2	P × P	B–Q3
7	N–B3	QN × B	B × P	N × P	P–K5!
	O–O	N–KB3 (f)	P–QR3	B–K3	B × P
8	O–O	P–K5	B–K3	B–KN5!	B × P†
	B–N5	N–N5!	P–K3	Q–R4†	K–K2
9	B–KN5	P–KR3	N–Q2	P–QN4!	Q–N3
	N–B3	N–R3	N–QB3	P × P	N–QB3
10	N–Q5	O–O	N × N	B–N5†	N–KB3
	B–K2 (c)	O–O (g)	B × N (h)		P–QR3 (i)

(a) 4 P × P, Q × Q†; 5 K × Q, B–K3; 6 N–Q2, N–QB3 = .

(b) (A) 5 N–KB3, B–N5†! 6 K–B1, Q–K2; 7 P × P, N–KB3; 8 N–B3, O–O; 9 B–KN5, B–K3 = . (B) 5 Q–N3!? Q–K2; 6 N–KB3, Q–N5†; 7 B–Q2, Q × Q; 8 P × Q, P × P; 9 B × KP, B–N5†; 10 N–B3, N–QB3; 11 O–O with tactical compensation for the pawn minus.

(c) 11 N × B†, Q × N; 12 P–KR3, B × N; 13 Q × B, N × P; 14 Q × P, Q–B4; 15 B × N, Q × B = . Trifunović.

(d) 4 . . . B–N5†; 5 B–Q2, exchanging Bishops' first, is still safer.

(e) 5 . . . N–QB3; 6 O–O, B–K3?! 7 B × B, P × B; 8 Q–N3, Q–Q2; 9 Q × P, R–N1; 10 Q–R6, N–B3; 11 QN–Q2, B–K2; 12 P–QR3, O–O; 13 P–QN4 ± .

(f) (A) 7 . . . N–QB3; 8 O–O, N–B3! 9 P–K5, N–KN5! 10 P–KR3, N–R3; 11 N–N3, O–O; reverts into the column. (B) 7 . . . N–KR3; 8 O–O, P–QR4; 9 N–N3, Q–K2; 10 R–B1, P–QN3 = . Partos–Miles, Biel 1977.

(g) 11 N–N3, N–B3; 12 QN × P, N × N; 13 Q × N, Q × Q; 14 N × Q, N–B4 = . Pachman–Tringov, Havana 1965.

(h) 11 P–B3, N–B3; 12 K–B2, B–K2 = . Réti–Rubinstein, Bad Kissingen 1928.

(i) 11 O–O, N–Q5; 12 N × N, B × N; 13 N–B3, with somewhat better game. Veresov–Neishtadt, Moscow 1965.

Queen's Gambit Declined

(1 P–Q4, P–Q4; 2 P–QB4)

Like many another famous old opening, this dates back to the 1490 Göttingen Manuscript. For a long time it was considered to be unenterprising, cautious, and dull—not an honourable weapon for the daring combatant. This tide of thinking persisted until the 1873 Vienna Tournament where players seemed to weary of the over-analysed King's Pawn game. Ever since then the Queen's Gambit has been on the upsurge and has become the workhorse of the leading masters.

This gambit—a gambit in name only—evolves a further complex of lines which continue to grow in substance and frequency: Albin Counter Gambit, Cambridge Springs Variation, Chigorin's Defence, Exchange Variation, Lasker Defence, Manhattan Variation, Orthodox Defence, Ragozin System, Tarrasch Defence, Tartakover Defence, Vienna Variation, and several unorthodox defences which each have their own peculiar character. The Slav and Semi-Slav formations are summarized separately in the last section of the Queen's Gambit.

White's second move begins the action: he seeks some living space in the centre by hammering at the barricade on Black's Q4. It leads to sound formations, active minor piece play, few weaknesses, a safe king, the avoidance of early exchanges, a steady increase of pressure, and an enduring initiative giving rise to crisp combinations as well as refined positional manoeuvres. A little thing, from which great systems flow, is that after 1 P–Q4 this pawn is protected, whereas after 1 P–K4 the king's pawn is not. White's main strategical objective is to force P–K4 as soon as possible in order to establish a dominating centre and completely demolish the blockade which Black sets up with 1 . . . P–Q4. That he can successfully carry this out with any hope of significant advantage is doubtful.

263

Black must struggle against becoming cramped, entangled, and slowly squeezed to death. As usual, he must solve the problem of where to develop his queen's bishop. He must be precise and strive for counter-play with either . . . P–QB4 or . . . P–K4. He has good practical defences at his disposal and, theoretically, can twist and turn, break our of his difficulties, and step into the middle-game on an equal footing. The only reason the Gambit Declined is not seen more often is that it is too passive—even when Black breaks his bonds and emerges from the opening he can hope for little more than a drawish equality. On the other hand, this enforced defensive posture, whereby Black bides his time, makes it very palatable for contemporary players.

THE ORTHODOX DEFENCE (cols. 1–12) gives Black a temporary cramp, although without any organic weaknesses, with the probability of withstanding White's persistent positional pressure and emerging with equal chances. White's hopes are for a King's-side attack, based on his superior centre; Black tries to utilize his pawn-majority on the Queen's side.

Cols. 1–3 represent the best-known variation. White is unable to demonstrate any advantage on his 13th move. 11 N–K4 (cols. 4–5) is no better or worse than the usual O–O. 8 Q–B2 (col. 8) or 8 P–QR3 (col. 9) are good for variety but Black can still equalize. Varying with 7 . . . P–QN3 (col. 10) weakens QB3 and incurs a slight disadvantage. Henneberger's 7 . . . P–QR3 (col. 10) is doubtful.

7 Q–B2 (cols. 11–12) appears to be answered equally well by 7 . . . P–B4 (col. 11) and 7 . . . P–B3 (col. 12).

LASKER'S DEFENCE (cols. 13–15) is a sound way of forcing early exchanges in order to ease the pressure on Black's game. Black can hold his own in all variations, but with all the simplification the best he can hope for is a draw with good play.

TARTAKOVER'S DEFENCE (cols. 16–20) makes use of the moves leading up to Lasker's Defence but substitutes the fianchetto of the queen's bishop for 7 . . . N–K5. 6 . . . P–KR3 is required by the modern method, a good, practical defence—lately quite fashionable—with White unable to demonstrate a clean-cut edge. Col. 21 represents the deviation with 6 R–B1 in order to combat both the Lasker and the Tartakover systems. White's chances are a little more promising inasmuch as it permits him more flexibility with his king's knight, which remains free to develop on K2. Column 22 investigates what happens when Black eschews early castling and continues with 5 . . . QN–Q2 instead. Again the critical move is . . . N–K5!

THE CAMBRIDGE SPRINGS VARIATION (cols. 23–5) is a time-honoured attempt of Black to profit from the absence of White's queen's bishop on the queen's side after it develops at KN5. Indeed, the Cambridge is so well respected that it is often avoided by the adoption of Exchange Variation. White can demonstrate no clear-cut theoretical advantage.

THE MANHATTAN VARIATION (cols. 26–7) is named after the strong chess club in New York City where Black's surprise . . . B–N5 was scrutinized in the 1920s. It is a cross between the Queen's Gambit Declined and the Nimzo–Indian Defence. Again, it is difficult for White to make tangible progress.

THE EXCHANGE VARIATION (cols. 28–35) can be played from the third move on. White has the choice of a minority attack on the queen's side (after castling) or a king's-side attack (after castling long). Both plans provoke crucial situations. White has a slight grip but he allows Black to solve the problem of his queen's bishop although, as always, the line contains a slight drop of poison.

Black's violent reaction with 4 . . . P–B4 (cols. 36–8) before White has a chance to exchange is probably sound; especially since improvements have been found in the formerly dubious line 5 . . . Q–N3 (after 5 P × QP). In cols. 39–40, Portisch's equalizing analyses still hold good.

THE RAGOZIN SYSTEM (cols. 41–5) has a lot in common with the Nimzo–Indian Defence, into which it can frequently transpose. Robert Fischer has been a firm advocate and his games tend to show that Black can pull even, but it is tricky and intricate.

THE SEMI-TARRASCH (or *Semi Classic*) DEFENCE (cols. 46–50) is an attempt to discourage 4 N–B3 (in place of 4 B–N5). Against 5 P × QP, N × P! avoids the liability of the isolated queen's pawn so common in the Tarrasch proper. White's best chance is 6 P–K3 (cols. 48–50) where he enjoys greater mobility and chances for the initiative. But it is a hard game!

THE TARRASCH DEFENCE (cols. 51–68) has long been judged wanting despite Keres' attempts to rehabilitate it. Tarrasch believed that Black's freedom compensated for the isolated queen's pawn. He wrote: "The future will decide who has erred in estimating this defence—I or the chess world." For a long time it has been held that White can obtain a slight edge but in recent years the defence has gained in favour. The main branches are: (A) The Rubinstein Variation, (B) The Swedish Variation, (C) Other.

(A) The *Rubinstein Variation* (cols. 51–5) is characterized by an early P–KN3 for White followed by the fianchetto of his king's bishop bearing down on Black's weak queen's pawn but Black's counterplay is sufficient.

(B) The *Swedish Variation* (cols. 56–9) is characterized by Black's 6 . . . P–B5. 7 P–K4 (col. 59) has been shorn of its terror. Despite reams of analysis, one gets the feeling that the last word has hardly been uttered on this complicated strategical treatment.

(C) Other methods for White, not involving the fianchetto of his king's bishop, are handled in cols. 60–2. They do not net him any appreciable edge.

Both the *Marshall Gambit* (col. 63) and the ancient *Tarrasch Gambit* (col. 64) have undergone revival and will doubtlessly be further explored. The *Hennig–Schara Gambit* (col. 65) is speculative but unsound. White's positional treatment 4 P–K3 (cols. 65–8) is safe and less ambitious, but full of dangerous "wait and see." Black's preventive 3 . . . B–K2 (avoiding the pin 4 B–N5) (cols. 69–70) is void of active counterplay and drawish.

THE VIENNA VARIATION (cols. 71–3) presents an argument against 3 N–KB3. It spells a fight with Black getting in his full share of the blows. The main line 7 P–K5 (col. 71) was previously considered inferior, but there have been notable improvements and it is now considered crucial. Black can avoid these complications by the simple expedient of 6 . . . P–KR3 (cols. 72–7) which makes it difficult for White to get anything. It is noteworthy that Black can also equalize with the simple 4 . . . P–KR3 or 4 . . . P × P (cols. 74–5).

CHIGORIN's DEFENCE (cols. 76–8) does not quite equalize, but is better than its reputation and crops up from time to time in the tournament games of players who are not afraid to take a chance. Characterized by 2 . . . N–QB3, it spells an unorthodox contest.

THE SYMMETRICAL DEFENCE (cols. 79–80) contains grist for the theorist's mill—it poses the crucial question of whether Black can imitate White although a move behind. However, at best, it is good for no more than a draw. The antidote is sound development and common sense.

ALBIN's COUNTER GAMBIT (cols. 81–5) is a vigorous attempt to break the hammer-lock of the Queen's Gambit at the cost of a pawn. A clear refutation has not been found, but theorists and masters continue to regard the gambit with a jaundiced eye. White does best to return the pawn at an appropriate moment, playing to win the two bishops and steer the struggle into positional channels.

1 P–Q4, P–Q4; 2 P–QB4, P–K3; 3 N–QB3, N–KB3; 4 B–N5, B–K2; 5 P–K3, O–O; 6 N–B3, QN–Q2; 7 R–B1, P–B3; 8 B–Q3, P × P; 9 B × P, N–Q4; 10 B × B, Q × B

	1	2	3	4	5
11	O–O............................			N–K4	
	N × N			N/4–B3 (*g*)	
12	R × N			N–N3	
	P–K4			Q–N5†......	P–K4
13	P × P	Q–B2	Q–N1 (*e*)	Q–Q2	O–O!
	N × P	P–K5 (*b*)	P × P	Q × Q†	P × P?!
14	N × N	N–Q2	P × P	K × Q	N–B5
	Q × N	N–B3	N–N3	P–B4	Q–Q1
15	P–B4	R–B1 (*c*)	B–N3	B–N5	N/3 × P (*h*)
	Q–K5	B–Q2	Q–B3	P–QN3	N–K4
16	Q–K2	B–N3	R–K1	P × P	B–N3
	B–B4	K–R1	B–K3	N × P	B × N
17	B–Q3	R–B5	B × B	K–K2	N × N
	Q–Q4	B–K3	P × B	B–N2	P–KN3 =
18	P–K4	R–K5	QR–K3	KR–Q1	
	Q–Q5† (*a*)	B × B (*d*)	QR–K1 (*f*)	KR–Q1 =	

(*a*) 19 K–R1, KR–K1; 20 R–B4, Q–Q2 = . *Comments.* Most of the conventional long-established lines are analysed in detail in *Byulleten* 1967/7 and other treatises.

(*b*) 13 . . . P × P; 14 P × P, (A) 14 . . . N–N3; 15 R–K3, Q–Q1; 16 B–N3, N–Q4; (16 . . . B–N5; 17 N–K5, B–K3; 18 B × B, P × B; 19 KR–K1); 17 B × N, Q × B; 18 R–K5, Q–Q3; 19 N–N5, Q–N3 = . Analyses by Müller, Neishtadt and Schwarz. (B) 14 . . . N–B3; 15 R–K1, Q–Q3; 16 N–N5, B–N5; 17 R–KN3, B–R4; 18 R–KR3, Q–N5! = .

(*c*) 15 B–N3, B–N5! 16 R–K1, K–R1; 17 P–QR3, QR–Q1 = . *Comments.*

(*d*) 19 R × Q, B × Q; 20 R × B, QR–N1; 21 N–N3, N–Q4; 22 R–Q7, N–N3; 23 N–B5, N × R; 24 N × N, K–N1 = . Gligorić–Alvarez, Havana 1962.

(*e*) Other alternatives (A) 13 P–K4, or (B) 13 B–N3, or (C) 13 P–Q5, or (D) 13 R–K1, all equalize as shown in earlier *MCO* editions.

(*f*) 19 R–K5, N–Q2; 20 R/5–K3, N–N3 = . *Comments.*

(*g*) If (A) 11 . . . P–K4; 12 O–O, P × P; 13 Q × P, N/2–N3; 14 B–N3, B–N5; 15 N–N3, B × N; 16 P × B ± . Najdorf–Ståhlberg, Zürich 1953. (B) 11 . . . P–QN3; 12 O–O, B–N2; 13 N–K5! KR–B1! ∞.

(*h*) (A) 15 B–N3, P × P; 16 Q–Q6 is an intriguing possibility. If (B) 15 N/5 × P, N–N3; 16 B–N3, B–N5; 17 Q–B2, Q–K2; 18 P–KR3, B × N = .

1 P-Q4, P-Q4; 2 P-QB4, P-K3; 3 N-QB3, N-KB3; 4 B-N5, B-K2; 5 P-K3, O-O;
6 N-B3, QN-Q2; 7 R-B1 (*a*)

	6	7	8	9	10
	(P-B3)				P-QR3
8	(B-Q3)		Q-B2	P-QR3	P-B5! (*k*)
	P-KR3 (*b*)		N-K5 (*h*)	N-K5	P-B3
9	B-B4	B-R4	B × B	B × B	P-QN4 (*l*)
	N-R4	P × P (*d*)	Q × B	Q × B	P-QR4
10	B-K5	B × P	N × N	Q-B2	P-QR3
	N × B	P-QN4	P × N	N × N	RP × P
11	P × N	B-Q3	Q × P	Q × N	RP × P
	P × P	P-R3	Q-N5†	R-K1	P-QN3
12	B × P	B-N1 (*e*)	N-Q2	R-Q1	B-Q3 (*m*)
	Q × Q†	B-N2 (*f*)	Q × NP	P × P	P × P
13	R × Q	Q-B2	R-QN1	B × P	NP × P
	P-KN3	R-K1	Q-R6	P-QN3	R-R6
14	P-KN4	N-K5	Q-B2	O-O	O-O
	N-N2 (*c*)	P-B4 (*g*)	P-K4 (*i*)	B-N2 (*j*)	Q-R4 (*n*)

(*a*) An old favourite of Botvinnik's was 7 B-Q3, e.g. 7 . . . P × P; 8 B × P (à la Queen's Gambit Accepted), P-B4; 9 O-O, P-QR3; 10 P-QR4, P × P; 11 P × P, N-N3; 12 B-N3, B-Q2; 13 N-K5, B-B3; 14 B-B2, QN-Q4; 15 B-N1, N-QN5? 16 R-K1, P-KN3; 17 B-R6, R-K1; 18 R-R3, Q-Q3; 19 N-K2, QR-Q1; 20 R-R3, Q-Q4? (20 . . . B-K5!); 21 N-KB3, Q-QR4; 22 N-B3, QN-Q4; 23 N-K5, N × N; 24 P × N, B × RP; 25 Q-K2, B-Q2; 26 B-N5, N-Q4; 27 N × BP, B × B; 28 R × P, N-B3; 29 B × P, N × R; 30 Q-R5, Q × P; 31 Q × N†, K-B1; 32 R-KB1, Q × P; 33 N-K5, Q-KB5; 34 N × B†, R × N; 35 Q-R8†, K-K2; 36 Q × R†, K-B3; 37 Q × R, K × B; 38 Q × P†, B-B3; 39 Q-K8†, K-R3; 40 P-N3, Q-QN5; 41 R-K1, P-R4; 42 R-K6, Q-N7; 43 Q-B7, K-N4; 44 P-R4†, K-N5; 45 Q-N6†, K-R6; 46 Q-B5 mate. Vaganian–Gulko, USSR 1975.

(*b*) Also playable is 8 . . . P-QR3; and now (A) 9 O-O, P × P; 10 B × P, P-N4; 11 B-Q3, P-B4∞. *Comments.* (B) 9 P × P, KP × P; 10 O-O, R-K1; 11 Q-B2, N-B1; 12 R-N1, P-KN3 = . Pachman. Compare col. 10, note (*j*).

(*c*) 15 N-K4 with more elbow room. Fine–Maróczy, Zandvoort 1936. An earlier 6 . . . P-KR3 avoids this line.

(*d*) 9 . . . N-K5; 10 B × B, N × N; 11 P × N, Q × B; 12 P × P, KP × P; 13 N-Q2! is a less desirable choice of a Lasker's Defence.

(*e*) 12 P-R4, P × P; 13 N × P, Q-R4†; 14 N-Q2, B-N5; 15 N-B3, P-B4 = .

(*f*) 12 . . . P-B4; 13 P × P, N × P; 14 Q-B2, R-K1; 15 B × N, B × B; 15 Q-R7†, K-B1; 17 P-QN4, N-Q2; 18 N-K4! N-N3! 19 N × B, Q × N; 20 R-B7, B-Q2 = . *Archives*.

(*g*) 15 R-Q1 with good prospects of attack.

(*h*) Here and in col. 9, another riposte reminiscent of Lasker's Defence. Also strong is 8 . . . P-QR3; 9 P-QR3, P-R3; 10 B-R4, R-K1; 11 B-Q3, P × P; 12 B × P, P-QN4; 13 B-R2, P-B4! Compare note (*a*).

(*i*) 15 B-Q3, P × P; 16 B × P†, K-R1; 17 O-O, Q-Q3 = . Alekhin.

(*j*) 15 P-K4, P-QB4 = . Fine–Stȧhlberg, Stockholm 1937.

(*k*) 8 P × P, P × P; 9 B-Q3, R-K1; 10 O-O, P-B3; 11 Q-B2, N-B1; 12 P-KR3, N-K5! 13 B-KB4, P-KB4; 14 N-K5, N-Q2 = . An ultimate draw. Petrosian–Bisguier, Stockholm 1962. Also compare note (*a*).

(*l*) 9 B-Q3, P-QN3; 10 P × P, P-B4; 11 O-O, P-B5; 12 B-B2, N × P; 13 N-K5, B-N2; 14 P-B4, R-N1; 15 P-B5, QN-Q2; 16 B-B4, R-B1; 17 Q-B3, P × P; 18 B × P, N × N; 19 P × N, N-K5; 20 N × N, P × N; 21 Q-R3, P-N3; 22 QR-Q1, Q-N3; 23 R-Q7, QR-K1; 24 P-K6,

P × B; 25 R × KB, R × R; 26 Q–N3†, K–R1; 27 B–R6, P × P; 28 B × R, R–Q2; 29 B–R6, Q–R4; 30 Q–QN8†, Q–Q1; 31 Q–K5†, K–N1; 32 Q × P†, R–B2; 33 R × P, resigns. Portisch–Petrosian, Palma de Mallorca 1974.

(*m*) 12 B–KB4, P × P; 13 NP × P, R–R6! 14 B–Q3, Q–R4; 15, Q–Q2, B–R3 + . Neishtadt.

(*n*) 15 N–N1! White has a solid hold on all strategic points.

1 P-Q4, P-Q4; 2 P-QB4, P-K3; 3 N-QB3, N-KB3; 4 B-N5, B-K2; 5 P-K3, O-O; 6 N-B3

	11	12	13	14	15
	QN-Q2	....	P-KR3		
7	Q-B2!	....	B-R4	Lasker Defence	
	P-B4 (a)	P-B3	N-K5		
8	O-O-O	R-Q1	B×B		
	P×QP	R-K1	Q×B		
9	R×P?!	P-QR3	P×P	Q-B2	R-B1
	Q-R4	P×P!	N×N	N×N (g)	N-KB3
10	B-Q3	B×P	P×N	Q×N	B-Q3
	P-KR3	N-Q4	P×P	P×P	QN-Q2
11	P×P?!	B×B	Q-N3	B×P	O-O
	P×B	Q×B	R-Q1 (d)	P-QN3	P×P
12	N×P	O-O	P-B4	O-O	B×P
	R-Q1	N×N	B-K3 (e)	B-N2	P-B4
13	N×BP	Q×N	Q×P	B-K2	P×P
	K×N (b)	P-QN3 (c)	P×P (f)	R-B1 (h)	N×P (i)

(a) Rubinstein's 7 Q-B2 still requires a razor-sharp defence of a precarious nature, e.g. (A) 7 ... P-KR3; 8 P-KR4! P-B4; 9 O-O-O, Q-R4; 10 P-KN4, P×BP; 11 B×BP, N-N3; 12 B-K2, B-Q2; 13 B×N, P×B; 14 P-N5, P×QP; 15 R×P, KR-B1; 16 P×RP + . Barcza. (B) 7 ... P-QR3; 8 P×P! P×P; 9 B-Q3, P-B3; 10 P-KN4! and O-O-O ± .

(b) 14 P×P†, K-B1! 15 P×N, B×P! ∓ . Neishtadt.

(c) Because of this move, Black passes up the customary "tempo" 9 ... P-QR3; 10 B-Q3, P×P. Keres-Ståhlberg, Zürich 1953, continued 14 N-K5, B-N2; 15 P-B4, N×N; 16 BP×N, P-QB4 = .

(d) Also 11 ... P-QB3; 12 P-B4, B-K3; 13 R-QN1, N-Q2! = .

(e) 12 ... P×P; 13 B×P, N-B3; 14 B-K2, R-Q3; 15 O-O, B-K3! 16 Q-B3, B-Q4; 17 KR-B1, R-QB1; 18 N-K1, P-B4; 19 N-Q3, P-KN4 = . Korelov-Kholmov, USSR Chp. 1963. The text is Cotlar's variant.

(f) 14 Q×R, Q-R6; 15 R-QN1, B-Q4! 16 Q×B, R×Q; 17 R×N†, K-R2; 18 R-QN1, R-KB4; 19 B×P, R×N; 20 P×R, Q-B6†; drawn.

(g) 9 ... N-KB3 is old and solid.

(h) 14 KR-Q1, P-QB4; 15 Q-R3, N-Q2! 16 R-Q2, P-K4 = . Van Scheltinga-Grau, Buenos Aires 1939.

(i) 14 N-K5, N/4-Q2; 15 Q-Q4, N×N; 16 Q×N, B-Q2; 17 N-Q5, N×N; 18 B×N, B-N4. Kotov-Najdorf, Groningen 1946.

1 P–Q4, P–Q4; 2 P–QB4, P–K3; 3 N–QB3, N–KB3; 4 B–N5, B–K2; 5 P–K3, O–O; 6 N–B3, P–KR3 (*a*)

	16	17	18	19	20
7	B × N	B–R4			
	B × B	P–QN3			
8	Q–Q2 (*b*)	P × P		B–K2	B–Q3 (*i*)
	P–QN3	N × P (*d*)		B–N2	B–N2
9	P × P	B × B		B × N	O–O
	P × P	Q × B		B × B	QN–Q2 (*j*)
10	P–QN4	N × N		P × P	R–B1
	B–N2	P × N		P × P	P–B4
11	R–QN1	B–K2	R–B1 (*f*)	O–O	Q–K2
	N–Q2	B–K3	B–K3	Q–K2	R–B1
12	P–N5	O–O	Q–R4	Q–N3	P × QP
	R–K1	P–QB4	P–QB4	R–Q1	N × P
13	P–QR4	N–K5!	Q–R3	QR–Q1	B × B
	N–B1 (*c*)	N–Q2 (*e*)	R–B1 (*g*)	P–B4 (*h*)	Q × B (*k*)

(*a*) Black can immediately enter this defence with 6 . . . P–QN3; e.g. (A) 7 P–QR3, B–N2; 8 R–B1, N–K5; 9 B × B, Q × B; 10 P × P, P × P; 11 N × N, P × N; 12 N–Q2, R–B1! = . Evans–Reshevsky, US Chp. 1969–70. However, this position arose, more naturally, from a Queen's Indian Defence 1 P–Q4, N–KB3; 2 P–QB4, P–K3; 3 N–KB3, P–QN3; 4 N–B3, B–N2; 5 P–QR3, P–Q4; 6 B–N5, B–K2; 7 P–K3, O–O. The sequence with 6 as given in the column P–QN3 allows the alternative (B) 7 B × N, B × B; 8 B–Q3 (8 P × P, P × P; 9 B–Q3, B–K3 ∓), B–N2; 9 P × P, P × P; 10 P–KR4, P–B4! 11 B × P†, K × B; 12 N–N5†, K–R3! 13 Q–Q3, P–N3; 14 P–R5!? ∞ .

(*b*) 8 R–B1, P–B3; 9 B–Q3, N–Q2; (A) 10 O–O, P × P; 11 B × P, P–K4; 12 N–K4, Q–K2 = . Kottnauer. (B) 10 P × P, BP × P; 11 O–O, P–R3; 12 Q–K2! P–QN4; 13 P–K4, B–K2 ∞ . Sokolov.

(*c*) 14 P–N3! with initiative Korchnoi–Ćirić, USSR–Yugoslavia 1966.

(*d*) 8 . . . P × P; 9 B–Q3, B–K3; 10 O–O, QN–Q2; 11 R–B1, P–B4; 12 B–N1! ± .

(*e*) 14 P–B4, N × N; 15 BP × N, QR–Q1 = . Pachman–Darga, Varna 1962.

(*f*) (A) 11 B–Q3, B–K3; 12 O–O, P–QB4; 13 P × P, P × P; 14 P–K4, R–Q1 = . (B) 11 Q–N3, B–K3; 12 R–B1, R–B1; 13 B–Q3, P–QB4; 14 Q–R3, K–B1; 15 P–QN3, P–QR4 = . Browne–Grefe, US Chp. 1975.

(*g*) (A) 14 B–K2, K–B1! Van Scheltinga–Donner, Beverwijk 1953. (B) 14 B–N5, P–R3; 15 P × P! P × P; 16 O–O (Furman–Geller, USSR Chp. 1970), Q–N2 ∞ ; or 14 . . . Q–N2!

(*h*) 14 P × P, B × N; 15 Q × B, P × P; 16 R–B1, N–Q2 ∞ . Korchnoi–Geller, match 1971.

(*i*) (A) 8 Q–B2 (1) 8 . . . P–B4; 9 R–Q1, P × QP; 10 KN × P, B–N2; 11 B–K2, QN–Q2; 12 O–O, P × P; 13 B × P, Q–B1 = . *Comments.* (2) 8 . . . B–N2; 9 B × N, B × B; 10 P × P, P × P; 11 O–O–O, P–B4; 12 P–KN4, P × P; 13 P × P, N–B3 = . Uhlmann–Spasski, Moscow 1967. (B) 8 Q–N3?! B–N2; 9 B × N, B × B; 10 P × P, P × P; 11 R–Q1, R–K1 = . Gulko–Radashkovich, USSR 1971. (c) 8 R–B1, B–N2; (1) 9 B × N, B × B; 10 P × P, P × P; 11 P–QN4 (Korchnoi–Spasski, 7th match game 1977), R–K1 = . (2) 9 B–Q3, P–B4! = .

(*j*) Also plausible is 9 . . . P–B4; 10 P × QP, N × P; 11 B × B, Q × B; 12 N × N, P × N; 13 P × P, P × P; 14 R–B1, N–Q2 = . *Comments.*

(*k*) 14 N × N, B × N; 15 B–R6, R–B2 = . Gligorić–Benko, Hollywood, 1963.

1 P-Q4, P-Q4; 2 P-QB4, P-K3; 3 N-QB3, N-KB3; 4 B-N5

	21	22	23	24	25
5	(B-K2)		QN-Q2		
	(P-K3) (a)		P-K3	Cambridge	
	(O-O)	QN-Q2	P-B3	Springs	
6	R-B1	N-B3	N-B3	Variation	
	P-KR3	N-K5!	Q-R4		
7	B-R4	B×B	N-Q2	B×N	P×P
	P-QN3	Q×B	B-N5	N×B	N×P (j)
8	P×P (b)	P×P	Q-B2	B-Q3	Q-Q2 (k)
	N×P	N×N	O-O (f)	B-N5	B-N5
9	B×B	P×N	B-R4 (g)	Q-N3	R-B1
	Q×B	P×P	P-B4	P×P!	P-B3
10	N×N	Q-N3	N-N3	B×BP	B-R4
	P×N	N-N3	Q-R5	O-O	O-O
11	B-K2 (c)	B-Q3	B×N	O-O	P-K4
	P-QB4	B-K3	N×B	B×N	N×N
12	B-B3	O-O	QP×P	P×B	P×N
	B-N2 (d)	O-O = (e)	B×N† (h)	P-QN3 (i)	B-R6 (l)

(a) (A) 5 P×P, P×P; see Exchange Variation. (B) 5 Q-B2, P-KR3; 6 B-R4, O-O; 7 P-K3, P-B4; 8 P×BP, P×P; 9 B×P, Q-R4 = . (c) 5 N-B3, O-O; (1) 6 Q-B2, N-K5; 7 B×B, Q×B; 8 R-B1, N×N; 9 Q×N, P-QB3 = . (2) 6 P-K3 see cols. 16-20. (3) 6 R-B1, P-KR3; 7 B-R4, P-QN3; 8 B×N, B×B; 9 P×P, P×P; 10 P-KN3, P-B3; 11 B-N2, B-B4; 12 O-O, Q-Q3; 13 P-K3, N-Q2; 14 N-K1, KR-K1; 15 N-Q3, P-N3 = . Korchnoi-Karpov, 13th match game 1978.

(b) 8 B×N, B×B; 9 P×P, P×P; 10 Q-B3, B-N2 = . *Comments.*

(c) Equal weight carries 11 N-K2, B-N2; 12 N-B4, P-QB4; 13 P×P, R-Q1! 14 B-N5, P×P; 15 O-O, N-R3; 16 Q-R5, Q-B3 = .

(d) 13 N-K2, N-Q2! 14 O-O, N-B3 = . Euwe.

(e) Stahlberg-Liebstein, Mar del Plata 1944.

(f) 8 . . . P×P; 9 B×N, N×B; 10 N×P, B×N†! (10 . . . Q-B2; 11 P-QR3, B-K2; 12 B-Q3, O-O; 13 O-O, B-Q2; 14 P-QN4, KR-Q1; 15 KR-B1, with the freer game. Evans-Whitaker, US Chp. 1948).

(g) 9 B-K2, (A) 9 . . . N-K5?! 10 N/2×N, P×N; 11 B-R4, P-KN4; 12 B-N3, P-KB4!?∞. Pallwitz-Jahn, Mecklenburg 1951. (B) 9 . . . P-K4; 10 O-O, KP×P; 11 N-N3, Q-B2; 12 N/N×P, P×P; 13 B×P, Q-R4 = . Sämisch-Kashdan, Frankfurt 1930.

(h) 13 Q×B, N-K5; 14 Q-R5, Q×Q = . Alekhin.

(i) 13 N-K5, B-N2; 14 B-K2, P-B4 = . Capablance-Ed. Lasker, New York 1924.

(j) Also 7 . . . KP×P; 8 B-Q3, N-K5; 9 O-O, N×B; 10 N×N, B-K2; 11 P-B4, N-B3 = . Janowski-Bogolyubov, New York 1924.

(k) 8 Q-N3, B-N5; 9 R-B1, P-K4; 10 B-QB4, P×P; 11 B×N, P×B = .

(l) 13 R-QN1, P-K4 = . *Comments.*

1 P-Q4, P-Q4; 2 P-QB4, P-K3; 3 N-QB3, N-KB3; 4 B-N5, QN-Q2

	26	27	28	29	30
	Manhattan Variation				
5	(P-K3)	N-B3	P×P	Exchange Variation	
	B-N5	B-N5	P×P		
6	P×P	P×P	P-K3		
	P×P	P×P	P-B3		
7	B-Q3	Q-R4	B-Q3		
	P-B4	Q-K2 (b)	B-K2 (c)		
8	N-B3	P-QR3	Q-B2 (d)		
	Q-R4	B×N†	O-O	N-B1	
9	O-O (a)	P×B	KN-K2	N-B3	N-B3
	P-B5	O-O	R-K1 (e)	R-K1	P-KN3
10	B-B2	P-K3	O-O-O	O-O (h)	O-O
	B×N	P-B4	N-B1	N-B1	N-K3
11	P×B	B-Q3	P-KR3	QR-N1 (i)	B-R4
	N-K5!	Q-K3	K-R1 (f)	N-K5	O-O
12	Q-K1	B×N	P-KN4	B-KB4!	QR-N1
	Q×BP =	Q×B =	N-N1 (g)	N-Q3! =	N-N2 (j)

(a) 9 Q-B2, P-B5; 10 B-B5, N-N3! 11 B×N, B×B; 12 Q×B, B×N†; 13 P×B, Q×P†; 14 K-K2, N-Q2; 15 B-R4 ± (Taimanov), but the line can be opposed by first 8 . . . P-B5 (and if 9 B-B2, Q-R4). *Comments.* In the column, if 11 . . . Q×BP; 12 R-B1, Q-R6; 13 N-K5, P-N4; 14 N×N, N×N; 15 P-K4 ± . Pafnutieff-Bisguier, Hollywood 1952.

(b) Also 7 . . . P-B4; 8 P×P, B×N†; 9 P×B, O-O; 10 P-B6, Q-B2! = . Reinfeld.

(c) The column is Colle-Vuković. Kecskemét 1927. Feasible is the immediate 7 . . . P-KN3.

(d) 8 N-B3, N-K5! 9 B×B, Q×B; 10 B×N, P×B; 11 N-Q2, P-KB4 = .

(e) Viable is 9 . . . P-KR3; 10 B-R4, N-K1; 11 B-N3, QN-B3; 12 O-O, B-Q3 = . *Comments.*

(f) Or 11 . . . Q-R4; 12 K-N1, B-K3; 12 P-B4, QR-B1 = . Neishtadt.

(g) 13 B×B, R×B; 14 P-N5, R-B2; 15 QR-N1, B-Q2; 16 P-KR4, B-K1! = . Müller-Chalupetsky, corr. 1953.

(h) If 10 P-KR3, N-B1; 11 B-KB4, B-K3; 12 O-O, R-B1; 13 QR-B1, P-B4∞ ; or 11 . . . N-N3; 12 B-N3, B-Q3!∞.

(i) 11 B×N, B×B; 12 P-QN4, B-N5; 13 N-Q2, P-QR3, 14 P-QR4, Q-Q3; or at once 13 . . . Q-Q3 allows Black at least equality. The stunning 31st match game Korchnoi-Karpov, 1978, whereby White tied the score 5:5 (before losing the next, deciding, game of the match), went 13 . . . R-B1; 14 B-B5, B×B; 15 Q×B, Q-Q2; 16 Q×Q, N×Q; 17 P-QR4, B-K2; 18 KR-N1, N-B3; 19 P-R5, P-QR3; 20 N-R4, B-B1; 21 N-B5, R-K2; 22 K-B1, N-K1; 23 K-K2, N-Q3; 24 K-Q3, R/1-K1; 25 R-K1, P-KN3; 26 R-K2, P-B3; 27 R/1-K1, B-R3; 28 N/2-N3, B-B1; 29 N-Q2, B-R3; 30 P-R3, K-B2; 31 P-N4, B-B1; 32 P-B3, R-Q1; 33 N/2-N3, N-N4; 34 R-KB1, B-R3; 35 P-B4, B-B1; 36 N-Q2, N-Q3; 37 R/1-K1, P-R3; 38 R-KB1, R-N1; 39 R-QR1, R/1-K1; 40 R/1-K1, R-N1; 41 P-K4, P×P†; 42 N/2×P, N-N4; 43 N-B3, R×R; 44 R×R, B×N; 45 NP×B, B-N7; 46 N×N, RP×N; 47 P-B5, P×P; 48 P×P, R-KN1; 49 K-B3, R-K1; 50 R-Q2, R-K5; 51 K-N4, K-K1; 52 P-R6, P×P; 53 K-R5, K-Q2; 54 K-N6, P-N5; 55 P-Q5, P×P; 56 R×P†, K-B1; 57 R-Q3, P-QR4; 58 R-KN3, P-N6; 59 K-B6, K-N1; 60 R×P†, K-R2; 61 R-N7†, K-R3; 62 R-N6†, K-R2; 63 K-N5, P-R5; 64 R×P, R-KB5; 65 R×P, P-R6; 66 R-R6†, K-N1; 67 R×P, R×P; 68 R-KN3, R-B3; 69 R-N8†, K-B2; 70 R-N7†, K-B1; 71 R-KR7, resigns.

(j) 13 P-QN4, B-KB4; 14 P-QR4, P-QR3; 15 B×B, N×B; 16 B×N, B×B = . Polugayevski-Milev, Havana 1962.

1 P-Q4, P-Q4; 2 P-QB4, P-K3; 3 N-QB3, N-KB3; 4 B-N5 (a), P-B3; 5 P×P, KP×P

	31	32	33	34	35
6	P-K3			N-B3	
	P-KR3?	B-K2	Q-N3	B-KB4	B-K2
7	B-R4	Q-B2	B×N (g)	Q-N3	Q-B2
	B-KB4	B-KN5 (e)	Q×NP	Q-N3	P-KN3
8	Q-B3 (b)	B-Q3	Q-B1	B×N	P-K3
	Q-N3?!	QN-Q2	B-R6	P×B	B-KB4
9	Q×B	P-KR3	B×P	P-K3	B-Q3
	Q×NP	B-K3	R-N1	N-R3	B×B
10	Q-B8†	B-KB4	KN-K2	Q×Q	Q×B
	K-K2	N-R4	Q×Q†	P×Q	QN-Q2
11	R-N1! (c)	B-R2	N×Q	K-Q2	O-O
	Q×N† (d)	P-KN3 (f)	B-N7 (h)	K-Q2 (i)	O-O (j)

(a) 4 P×P, P×P at once leads into cols. 28–30 without allowing Black the alternative 4 B-N5, P-B3; 5 P×P, BP×P; with a "Slav" Exchange variation; but, on the other hand, the early capture permits 4 . . . N×P, see Semi-Tarrasch Defence, cols. 46–50.

(b) Black has no problems after 8 B-Q3, B×B; 9 Q×B, B-K2; 10 KN-K2, QN-Q2; 11 O-O, O-O; 12 P-B3, R-K1; 13 B-B2, P-B4! 14 P×P, B×P; 15 QR-Q1, N-K4; 16 Q-N5, Q-N3; 17 Q×Q, P×Q = . Botvinnik-Geller, USSR Chp. 1955.

(c) (A) 11 N×P†, P×N; 12 Q-B1, Q-N5†; 13 K-K2, P-KN4! 14 B-N3, N-K5 = . Smyslov. (B) 11 N-Q1, Q-N5†; 12 K-K2, P-KN4; 13 B-N3, Q-B5† = .

(d) 12 K-Q1, P-KN4; 13 B-N3! N-K5 (13 . . . B-N2; 14 Q-B7†, QN-Q2; 15 B-Q6†, K-K3; 16 B-N4 +); 14 N-B3, B-N2; 15 R×P†, K-B3; 16 B-K5†, K-N3; 17 N-R4†, P×N; 18 Q-K6†!! Zaitsev.

(e) Safe is also 7 . . . O-O; 8 N-B3, N-K5; 9 B×B, Q×B; 10 N×N, P×N = .

(f) 12 KN-K2, N-N2; 13 P-KN4, N-N3; 14 O-O-O, B-Q3 = . Reshevsky-Gligorić, match 1952.

(g) (A) 7 Q-N3 is playable. (B) 7 Q-B2, N-K5! 8 N×N, P×N; 9 Q×KP†, B-K3∓. Stark-Zinn, E. Germany 1965.

(h) 12 N-Q1, B×N; 13 B-K5, B-R6 = . Titenko-Terentev, USSR 1966.

(i) 12 P-KN3, P-N4 = . Stein-Fischer, Stockholm 1962.

(j) 12 QR-B1, R-K1; 13 N-Q2, K-N2; 14 N-N3, B-Q3 = . Taimanov-Korchnoi, USSR 1963.

1 P-Q4, P-Q4; 2 P-QB4, P-K3; 3 N-QB3, N-KB3

	36	37	38	39	40
4	(B-N5)...........................			N-B3	
	P-B4 (a)			B-K2	
5	P×QP			B-B4	P-K3
	BP×P		Q-N3?!	O-O	O-O
6	Q×P		P×KP (e)	P-K3	P-QN3
	B-K2		P×QP	P-B4 (h)	P-QN3 (l)
7	P-K4		P×P†	QP×P	B-Q3
	N-B3		K×P	Q-R4 (i)	B-N2
8	Q-Q2........	Q-K3	N-R4	Q-B2 (j)	O-O
	N×QP?! (b)	N-QN5	B-N5†	R-Q1	QN-Q2
9	P×N	Q-Q2!	B-Q2	R-B1	B-N2
	B×B	P×P	Q-R4 (f)	P×P	N-K5
10	P-B4	B×N	Q-N3†	B×P	Q-B2
	B-R5† (c)	B×B (d)	N-Q4 (g)	Q×BP (k)	P-KB4 (m)

(a) 4 . . . B-N5; (A) 5 N-B3, *see* Vienna Variation col. 71. (B) 5 P-K3, P-B4! 6 Q-N3, P-KR3; 7 B×N, Q×B; 8 BP×P, KP×P; 9 B-N5†, N-B3 = . *Comments.*

(b) 8 . . . N×KP; 9 N×N, P×P, 10 B×B, Q×B; 11 Q×P, O-O; 12 P-B3, N-N5; 13 Q-QB5, Q×Q; 14 N×Q, N-B7†; 15 K-Q2, N×R; 16 B-Q3, R-Q1 = . Donner-Ståhlberg, Göteborg 1955.

(c) 11 P-N3, P×P?! 12 P×B, Q×P†; 13 Q-B2, Q-K2†; 14 Q-K2, B-K3; 15 O-O-O (15 N-B3, P-Q5; 16 N-QN5, O-O; 17 N×QP, N×N; 18 N×N, KR-Q1; 19 O-O-O, QR-B1†; 20 N-B2, B-B4! Furman), P-Q5; 16 N-QN5, P-QR3∞. Gipslis.

(d) 11 B-N5†, B-Q2; 12 B×B†, Q×B; 13 N×P, N×N; 14 P×N, O-O; 15 N-K2, QR-B1; 16 O-O, KR-Q1; 17 KR-Q1, R-B3; 18 N-B3, B×N; 19 P×B, R-B4! Black will regain the "isolani," and with positional pressure. *Comments.*

(e) Long under a cloud, Canal's 5 . . . Q-N3 still warrants attention. No advantage results from (A) 6 N-R4, Q-N5†; 7 B-Q2, Q×QP; 8 N-QB3, N-K5∞. or (B) 6 Q-N3, BP×P; 7 Q×Q, P×Q; 8 B×N, P×B; 9 N-N5, B-N5†; 10 K-Q1, R-R4! = ; or (c) 6 N-B3, Q×P; 7 R-B1 (7 N-QR4, Q-N5†; 8 B-Q2, Q-R6; 9 P×KP, B×P; 10 P-K3, N-K5 =), N×P! 8 N-QR4, Q-R6; 9 N×P, N-Q2 = . Unclear is (D) 6 B×N, Q×P; 7 Q-B1, Q×Q; 8 R×Q, P×B; 9 N-B3! K-Q1! 10 P-K4, BP×P; 11 N×P, B-R6; 12 N-N3, B-R6; 13 R-B2, P-QR3; 14 B-K2, N-Q2∞. Furman-Kavalek, Harrachov 1966.

(f) Neishtadt suggests 9 . . . B×B†; 10 Q×B, Q-N4; 11 P-QN3, N-B3; 12 N-KB3, R-K1! = .

(g) 11 B×B, Q×B†; 12 ×Q×Q, N×Q; 13 R-Q1, B-B4! = .

(h) (A) Another one of Black's many defences against 5 B-B4 is here 6 . . . QN-Q2; (1) 7 R-B1, P-B4; 8 P×BP, N×P; 9 B-K2, P×P; 10 B×P, P-QR3; 11 N-K5, Q×Q†; 12 R×Q, P-QN4! = . Larsen-Portisch, Mallorca 1967. (2) 7 Q-B2, P-B3; 8 B-Q3. But weaker is (B) 6 . . . P-QN3; 7 P×P, P×P; 8 B-K2! B-N2; 9 P-KR3, P-B4; 10 O-O, N-B3; 11 N-K5 ± .

(i) A decade ago, Portisch analysed 7 . . . B×P; 8 P-QR3, N-B3; 9 Q-B2, Q-R4; 10 R-Q1, B-K2; 11 N-Q2, P-K4; 12 B-N5, Q-Q5; 13 N-N3, Q-N3! = . The 23rd match game Korchnoi-Karpov, 1978, continued 14 B×N, B×B; 15 N-Q5, Q-Q1; 16 B-Q3, P-KN3; 17 P×P, N×P; 18 N×N, P×N; 19 N×B, Q×N; 20 O-O, B-K3; 21 KR-K1, QR-B1; 22 P-QN3, KR-Q1; 23 B-K4, R-B2; 24 Q-Q2, B-N5; 25 P-B3, B-K3; 26 P-QR4, P-N3; 27 P-R5, P-QN4; 28 P×P, B×P; 29 R-N1, B-Q4; 30 P-N6, P×P; 31 R×P, R-B3; 32 R×R, B×R; 33 B-Q3, B-Q2; 34 P-R6, B-B4; 35 Q-B4, K-N2; 36 B×B, Q×B; 37 Q×Q, P×Q; 38 R-R1, P-Q6; 39 K-B2, R-K1; 40 R-R2, R-K2; 41 R-Q2, R-K3; drawn.

(j) 8 P-QR3, P×P; 9 B×P, Q×BP; 10 Q-K2, P-QR3; 11 P-K4, P-QN4; 12 B-Q3, B-N2; 13 QR-B1, Q-R4 = . Lengyel-Ivkov, Beverwijk 1965.

(*k*) 11 B–N3, P–QN4; 12 O–O, B–N2; 12 Q–K2! allowed some initiative, Larsen–Kujpers, Beverwijk 1967. In the column, for 4 . . . P×P; 5 P–K4, B–N5; 6 B–N5, P–B4; see col. 71.

(*l*) Other strategies with Queen's Indian features, are (A) 6 . . . B–N5; 7 B–Q2, Q–K2; 8 B–Q3, P–QN3; 9 O–O, P–B4; 10 Q–K2, B–N2, and (B) 6 . . . P–B4; 7 B–N2, N–B3.

(*m*) 11 QR–K1, P–B3; 12 N–K2, B–Q3; 13 N–K5, B×N; 14 P×B, N/2–B4; 15 B×N, BP×B; 16 N–B4, R×N; 17 P×R, N–Q6 = . Najdorf–Bisguier, Bled 1961.

1 P-Q4, P-Q4; 2 P-QB4, P-K3; 3 N-QB3, N-KB3; 4 N-B3, B-N5

	41	42	43	44	45
5	P×P		Q-R4†	P-K3 (g)	
	P×P		N-B3	O-O	
6	B-N5 (a)		P-K3 (e)	B-Q2	B-Q3
	P-KR3 (b)		O-O	N-B3	N-B3 (j)
7	B-R4		B-Q2	P-QR3 (h)	O-O (k)
	P-KN4	P-B4	P-QR3	B×N	P×P
8	B-N3	P-K3	Q-B2	B×B	B×P
	N-K5	O-O	P×P	N-K5	B-Q3
9	N-Q2!	P×P	B×P	Q-B2	N-QN5 (l)
	N×QN	QN-Q2	B-Q3	P-QR4	B-K2
10	P×N	B-K2	P-QR3	P-QN3	P-KR3
	B×P	Q-R4	P-K4	P-QN3!	P-QR3
11	R-B1	O-O	P-Q5	B-N2	N-B3
	B-R4!	B×N	N-K2	B-R3	B-Q3
12	Q-B2	P×B	P-R3	B-Q3	P-K4
	N-B3 (c)	Q×P/4 (d)	P-QN4 (f)	P-B4 (i)	P-K4 =

(a) 6 Q-R4†, N-B3; 7 B-N5, P-KR3; 8 B×N, Q×B; 9 P-K3, O-O; (A) 10 B-K2, B-K3; 11 O-O, P-R3; 12 KR-B1, B-Q3; 13 Q-Q1, N-K2; 14 N-QR4, P-QN3; 15 N-B3, KR-Q1; 16 Q-B1, P-B3 = . Taimanov–Kotov, Zürich 1953. (B) 10 R-B1, P-R3; 11 P-QR3, B×N†; 12 R×B, Q-Q3; 13 Q-B2, B-K3; 14 B-K2, KR-B1; 15 O-O, N-K2; 16 R-B1, B-B4! Gheorghiu–Zuckerman, Cleveland 1975.

(b) Solid is 6 . . . Q-Q3; 7 N-Q2, P-B3; 8 P-K3, O-O; 9 B-Q3, QN-Q2; 10 O-O, R-K1 = . Ståhlberg–Taimanov, Stockholm 1952.

(c) 13 P-K3, O-O; 14 P-KR4, P-N5 ∞. Korchnoi–Khasin, USSR 1961.

(d) 13 R-B1, N-K5; 14 P-B4, N-N3; 15 P×P, Q×QP = . *Comments.*

(e) Other established lines are (A) 6 P×P, N×P; 7 B-Q2, N-N3; 8 Q-N5, P-QR3; 9 Q-Q3, B-K2; 10 R-Q1, P-K4! (B) 6 N-K5, B-Q2; 7 N×B, Q×N; 8 P-QR3, B×N†; 9 P×B, O-O; 10 P-K3, P-QR3, 11 B-K2, P-QN4; 12 P×NP; P×P; 13 Q×P, KR-N1; 14 Q-Q3, N-QR4 = . Tolush–Sokolski, Leningrad 1938.

(f) 13 B-R2, Q-Q2! 14 P-K4, P-QR4 = . Reshevsky–Ragozin, Semmering 1937.

(g) For (A) 5 Q-N3, N-B3; 6 P-K3, see Nimzo–Indian Defence. (B) 5 B-N5, see Vienna Variation. Also compare this column and col. 66.

(h) 7 Q-B2, P×P, 8 B×P, Q-Q3; 9 B-N5, P-K4 = . *Comments.*

(i) 13 R-QB1, R-B1; 14 O-O (Pachman–Fischer, Santiago 1959), N-K2 = . *Comments.*

(j) 6 . . . P-QN3; or 6 . . . P-B4; or 6 . . . QN-Q2; are dealt with under the Nimzo–Indian Defence.

(k) 7 P-QR3, B×N†; 8 P×B, N-QR4; 9 N-Q2, P-B4; 10 O-O, P-QN3; 11 P×QP, KP×P; 12 P-B3, R-K1 = . Reshevsky–Fischer, match 1961.

(l) (A) 9 Q-B2, P-K4; 10 P-KR3, Q-K2; 11 B-Q2, B-Q2; 12 QR-K1, QR-K1 = . Ragozin. (B) 9 B-N5, P-K4; 10 B×N, P×P! 11 B×P, B×B; 12 N×P, Q-Q2; 13 N/4-N5, Q-B3; 14 P-B3, B-K4! = . The column is Taimanov–Fischer, Buenos Aires 1960

1 P–Q4, P–Q4; 2 P–QB4, P–K3; 3 N–QB3, N–KB3; 4 N–B3, P–B4

	46	47	48	49	50
5	P × QP				
	N × P (a)				
6	P–K4		P–K3 (f)		
	N × N		N–QB3		
7	P × N		B–B4	B–Q3	
	P × P		P × P	B–K2	
8	P × P		P × P	O–O	
	B–K2!	B–N5†	B–K2	O–O	
9	B–K2	B–Q2	O–O	P–QR3	
	O–O	B × B† (c)	O–O	P × P	N × N (j)
10	O–O	Q × B	R–K1 (g)	P × P	P × N
	P–QN3	O–O	P–QR3	B–Q2	P–QN3
11	Q–Q2	B–B4!	B–Q3	Q–B2	Q–B2 (k)
	B–N2	N–B3 (d)	N–B3	P–KN3	P–N3
12	Q–K3	O–O	B–KN5	B–KR6	R–Q1
	N–Q2 (b)	P–QN3 (e)	P–N4 (h)	R–K1 (i)	P × P (l)

(a) Less resilient is 5 . . . BP × P; 6 Q × P! P × P; 7 P–K4! N–B3; 8 B–QN5, N × P; 9 O–O, N–B3; 10 N–K5, B–Q2; 11 N × B! Q × N; 12 B × N, P × B; 13 B–R6, O–O–O; 14 KR–B1, K–N1; 15 N–R4 ± .

(b) 13 B–N2, R–B1; 14 QR–B1, N–B3; 15 B–Q3, R × R; 16 R × R, Q–R1 = . Lilienthal–Flohr, Moscow 1935. In the column, however, also energetic is 8 . . . N–B3; 9 B–QB4, P–QN4; 10 B–K2, B–N5†; 11 B–Q2, B × B†; 12 Q × B, P–QR3; 13 O–O, O–O; 14 P–QR4, P × P; 15 R × P, B–N2; 16 P–Q5, P × P; 17 P × P, N–K2; 18 P–Q6, N–N3; 19 R–Q1, Q–Q2; 20 R–R5, KR–K1 = . Martz–Bisguier, US Chp. 1973.

(c) 9 . . . Q–R4; 10 R–QN1! B × B†; 11 Q × B, Q × Q†; 12 N × Q, O–O; 13 B–N5! ± . Rubinstein–Schlechter, San Sebastian 1912.

(d) (A) Out of favour is 11 . . . N–Q2; 12 O–O, P–QN3; 13 QR–Q1, B–N2; 14 KR–K1, R–B1; 15 B–N3, N–B3; 16 Q–B4, Q–B2; 17 Q–R4, KR–Q1 (Keres–Fine, Ostend 1937); (1) 18 P–K5! N–Q2; 19 N–N5 ± . (2) 18 P–Q5! (B) 11 . . . P–QN3; 12 O–O, N–B3; 13 QR–Q1! B–N2; 14 KR–K1, R–B1; 15 P–Q5! ± . Spasski–Petrosian, match 1969.

(e) 13 QR–Q1! (13 KR–Q1, B–N2; 14 Q–B4, Q–B3! 15 Q–K3, KR–Q1 = . Reshevsky–Fine, Hastings 1937–8), N–R4; 14 B–Q3, B–N2; 15 KR–K1, R–B1; 16 P–Q5! P × P; 17 P–K5, N–B5; 18 Q–B4 ± . Polugayevski–Tal, Moscow 1969.

(f) 6 P–KN3, P × P; 7 N × N, Q × N; 8 Q × P, Q–QN4; 9 P–K4, Q–N5†; 10 Q × Q, B × Q† = . Benko–Korchnoi, Curaçao 1962.

(g) 10 N–K4, N–B3; 11 B–Q3, N–Q4; 12 Q–K2, P–QN3; 13 R–Q1, N–QR4; 14 B–B2, N–N5; 15 B–N1, B–R3 = . Spasski–Tal, USSR Chp. 1963.

(h) 13 R–QB1, B–N2; 14 B–N1, R–B1; 15 P–QR3, N–QR4 = . Spasski–Korchnoi, USSR Chp. 1963.

(i) 13 N–K4, QR–B1; 14 Q–K2, P–B4; 15 N–B3, B–B3; 16 B–QB4 = . R. Byrne–Bisguier, New York Chp. 1963. In the column 9 R–K1, P × P; 10 P × P, N–B3; 11 B–KN5, P–QN3; 12 R–QB1, B–N2 equalizes.

(j) 9 . . . P–QN3; 10 Q–B2, P–N3; 11 P–QN4, N × N; 12 Q × N, B–Q2 (Portisch–Tal, Mallorca 1966); 13 P–N5, N–R4; 14 B–N2 ± . *Archives.*

(k) 11 B–N2, B–B3; 12 N–Q2, B–N2; 13 N–K4, B–K2; 14 P–KB4, P × P; 15 KP × P, P–N3; 16 Q–K2, R–B1; 17 R–B3, N–R4; 18 R–R3, B × N; 19 B × B, N–N5; drawn. Averbakh–Moiseyev, Moscow Chp. 1970.

(l) 13 KP × P, B–N2 = . Antoshin–Moiseyev, USSR Chp. 1970.

(Rubinstein Variation)

1 P-Q4, P-Q4; 2 P-QB4, P-K3; 3 N-QB3, P-QB4; 4 BP×P, KP×P; 5 N-B3, N-QB3; 6 P-KN3, N-B3; 7 B-N2, B-K2!; 8 O-O, O-O

	51	52	53	54	55
9	P×P	B-K3	B-N5 (d)		
	P-Q5 (a)	N-KN5	P×P (e)		
10	N-QR4	B-B4	KN×P		
	B-B4	B-K3	P-KR3		
11	B-B4	P×P	B-K3		
	B-K5! (b)	B×P	R-K1	B-KN5	
12	R-B1	N-KN5?!	R-B1	Q-R4	R-K1 (j)
	Q-Q4	P-KR3	B-B1 (f)	N-QR4 (h)	B-KB1
13	P-N3	N×B	N-N3	QR-Q1	N-N3
	QR-Q1	P×N	B-K3	N-B5	B-K3
14	Q-Q2	B-R3	N-N5	B-B1	N-N5
	Q-R4 =	N×BP (c)	B-KN5 (g)	Q-B1! (i)	B-N5 (k)

(a) 9 . . . B×P; 10 N-QR4! B-K2; 11 B-K3, R-K1; 12 R-B1, B-KN5; 13 P-QR3 Q-Q2; 14 R-K1, or 13 . . . B-Q2; 14 N-B3 ± .

(b) Just a shade tamer but safe is 11 . . . Q-Q2; 12 P-QN4, QR-Q1.

(c) 15 B×P†, K-R1; 16 Q×P∞ .

(d) (A) 9 B-B4, P×P! 10 N×P, Q-N3; 11 N×N, P×N = . (B) 9 P-N3, N-K5; 10 B-N2, B-B3; 11 N-QR4, R-K1; 12 R-B1, P×P; 13 N×P, B×N; 14 B×B, B-B4; 15 P-K3, Q-Q2 = . Uhlmann-Spasski, Siegen 1970.

(e) (A) 9 . . . B-K3 seems effectively met by (1) 10 R-B1! P-QN3! 11 P×P (11 N-K5, N×N; 12 P×N, N-N5; 13 B-B4, P-KN4! 14 B-Q2, P-Q5! =), P×P; 12 N-QR4! N-K5; 13 N×P!! + . (2) 10 P×P, B×P; 11 B×N, Q×B; 12 N×P, Q×P; 13 N-B7, QR-Q1; 14 Q-B1, Q×Q; 15 QR×Q, P-QN3; 16 N×B, P×N; 17 R-B4! N-Q5∞. Petrosian-Spasski, 16th match game 1969. (B) If 9 . . . P-B5; 10 N-K5, B-K3; 11 P-B4!

(f) 12 . . . B-KN5; 13 N-N3, B-K3; 14 B-Q4! Gligorić.

(g) 15 P-KR3, B-KB4; 16 N/5-Q4, N×N; 17 N×N, B-Q2; with fully active counterplay. Petrosian-Spasski, 18th match game 1969.

(h) 12 . . . Q-Q2; 13 B×QP, N×B; 14 N×N, B-R6; 15 N×N, P×N; 16 Q×BP ± .

(i) 15 Q-B2, R-Q1; 16 P-N3, N-K4; 17 B-N2, Q-Q2 = . Petrosian-Spasski, 12th match game 1969.

(j) (A) 12 N-N3, B-K3; 13 R-B1, R-K1; (1) 14 N-N5, Q-Q2; 15 N/5-Q4, B-KR6; 16 N×N, P×N; 17 Q-Q3, B×B; 18 K×B, P-QR4! = . Petrosian-Spasski, 2nd match game 1969. (2) 14 N-B5, B×N; 15 B×B, Q-R4! 16 B-QR3, QR-Q1 = ; (3) 14 R-K1, Q-Q2; 15 B-B5, QR-B1; 16 B×B, Q×B; 17 P-K3, KR-Q1; 18 Q-K2, B-N5! = . (B) 12 P-KR3, B-K3; 13 R-B1, Q-Q2; 14 K-R2, N-K4; 15 Q-R4, Q×Q; 16 N×Q, N-B5; 17 B-B4, P-KN4 = .

(k) 15 P-KR3, B-KB4; 16 N/5-Q4, N×N; 17 N×N, B-Q2; 18 Q-N3, Q-R4 = .

1 P–Q4, P–Q4; 2 P–QB4, P–K3; 3 N–QB3, P–QB4; 4 BP×P, KP×P; 5 N–B3,
N–QB3

	56	57	58	59	60
6	P–KN3 ⎱	Swedish....................................			B–B4
	P–B5 ⎰	Variation			N–B3 (*h*)
7	B–N2			P–K4	P–K3
	B–QN5			P×P	B–K2 (*i*)
8	O–O			N–KN5	B–K2
	KN–K2			Q×P (*f*)	O–O
9	N–K5	P–K4	P–QR3	B–B4	P×P
	O–O	P×P (*b*)	B–R4 (*d*)	B–QN5	B×P
10	N×N	N×P	P–K4	Q×Q	O–O
	P×N	O–O	O–O	N×Q	B–K3
11	N–R4!	Q–B2!	P×P	B×P	R–B1
	N–B4	Q–Q4	N/2×P	B–K3	R–B1
12	P–N3	B–K3	N×N	N×B	N–K5
	R–K1	B–KB4	Q×N	B×N†	B–Q3
13	P×P	N–R4	N–N5	P×B	N×N
	B–R3 (*a*)	B×N (*c*)	Q×P (*e*)	N×N (*g*)	P×N =

(*a*) 14 R–N1, B–KB1; 15 R–K1, B×P; 16 P–QR3 ± . Smyslov–Barcza, Bucharest 1953. If
11 P–K4, B×N! = .

(*b*) 9 . . . O–O; 10 P×P, N/2×P; 11 B–N5! B–K2 (11 . . . QN–K2 may be examined); 12
N×N, B×B; 13 N×B, Q×KN; 14 N–K3 ± , *Comments*.

(*c*) 14 B×B, N×P; 15 B×P†, K–R1; 16 Q–K4, Q×Q; 17 B×Q, N/5–B3 = .

(*d*) 9 . . . B×N; 10 P×B, O–O; 11 P–QR4, R–K1; 12 N–Q2, B–B4 = .

(*e*) 14 Q–R4, B–Q1; 15 R–Q1, Q–K4; 16 B–B4, Q–QB4 = . Szabó–Bronstein, Amsterdam
1956.

(*f*) 8 . . . B–K2; 9 B×P, B×N; 10 Q–R5, P–KN3; 11 Q×B, N–B3; 12 O–O, (A) 12 . . .
N×P; 13 Q–K5†, B–K3; 14 B–N5†, N×B; 15 B–N5! Panov. (B) 12 . . . O–O, 13 R–Q1,
B–N5!? 14 N×P! B×R; 15 N×N†, K–R1; 16 B–K3, N×P; 17 B–Q5, N–B6†; 18 B×N,
B×B; 19 Q–R4, B–R4; 20 B–Q4 + + .

(*g*) 14 B–N5†, K–K2 = . Analysis by Ståhlberg.

(*h*) 6 . . . B–N5; 7 Q–N3! but not 7 P×P, P–Q5 = .

(*i*) Also 7 . . . P×P; 8 N×P, B–QN5; 9 B–QN5, B–Q2 = . The column is Tal–Keres,
USSR Chp. 1959.

1 P–Q4, P–Q4; 2 P–QB4, P–K3; 3 N–QB3, P–QB4; 4 BP × P

	61	62	63 Marshall Gambit	64 Tarrasch Gambit	65 Hennig-Schara Gambit
	(KP × P)				BP × P!?
5	(N–B3)		P–K4	P × P!	Q × P (g)
	(N–QB3)		QP × P	P–Q5	N–QB3
6	P–K3		P–Q5	N–R4	Q–Q1
	N–B3		P–B4!	P–N4!	P × P
7	B–N5	B–K2	B–KB4	P × P e.p.	Q × P
	B–Q3 (a)	P–QR3 (c)	B–Q3	P × P	B–K3
8	P × P	O–O	B–N5†	P–QN3!	Q × Q†
	B × BP	P–B5	K–B2	N–KB3	R × Q
9	O–O	N–K5!	N–R3	P–K3	P–K3 (h)
	O–O	Q–B2	N–KB3	B–Q2!	N–N5 (i)
10	P–QN3	N × N	B–B4	Q × P!	B–N5†
	B–K3	Q × N	P–QR3	N–B3	K–K2
11	B–N2	P–QN3	P–R4	Q–N2!	K–B1
	Q–K2 (b)	B–QN5 (d)	R–K1 (e)	N–K5 (f)	N–KB3 (j)

(a) (A) Doubtful is 7 . . . P–QR3; 8 B × N†, P × B; 9 Q–R4! Q–N3; 10 O–O, B–K3, 11 P–K4! P × KP; 12 P × P, B × BP; 13 N × P, N × N; 14 Q × N, P–R3; 15 P–QN4! ± . Fridshtein–Estrin, Moscow 1957. (B) Playable is 7 . . . P × P; 8 N × P, Q–N3; or 8 P × P; B–QN5 = .

(b) 12 N–K2, QR–B1; 13 P–QR3, KR–Q1; 14 N/2–Q4, B–KN5; 15 B–K2, N–K5 = . Petrosian–Botvinnik, match 1963.

(c) (A) 7 . . . P × P! 8 N × P, B–Q3; 9 O–O, O–O (identical with col. 50 after 7 . . . P × P, etc., with reversed colours and White (Black) being a move ahead); 10 N–B3, P–QR3; 11 P–QN3, R–K1; 12 B–N2, B–KN5; 13 P–KR3, B–R4 = . Larsen–Gheorghiu, Mallorca 1968. (B) Avoiding an isolated pawn and setting up a queen-side pawn majority, yet very controversial is 7 . . . P–B5!? 8 N–K5, B–QN5; 9 O–O, O–O; 10 N × N, P × N; 11 Q–B2, P–N3; 12 B–Q2, B–KB4; 13 Q–R4, B–Q3!? (according to R. Byrne, 13 . . . Q–N3; 14 P–QN3, P × P; 15 Q × NP would have left White's pawn-structure backwardly rigid); 14 Q × P/B6 R–N1; 15 P–QN3, R–N3; 16 Q–R4, B–Q2; 17 Q–R5, B–QN5; 18 Q × RP, B–B1; 19 P × P, R–R3; 20 Q–N8, Q–R4; 21 P × P, B × N; 22 B × B, Q × B; 23 QR–B1, Q–Q7; 24 R × B, resigns. Kavalek–Calvo, Montilla 1976.

(d) 12 B–Q2, P–QN4; 13 P × P, NP × P = . Petrosian.

(e) 12 Q–Q2, Q–K2 = . Tolush–Furman, USSR Chp. 1957.

(f) 12 P–QR3! Analysis by Haberditz, and an important point in reviving this line.

(g) Or 5 Q–R4†, B–Q2; 6 Q × QP, P × P; 7 Q × QP, N–KB3! 8 Q–Q1, N–B3; 9 P–K3, (9 N–B3! B–QN5; 10 B–Q2, O–O; 11 P–KN3!), Q–N3; 10 N–B3; O–O–O; 11 B–Q2, Q × P; 12 QR–N1, Q–R6; 13 B–B4! ± .

(h) 9 P–K4, N–Q5; or 9 . . . B–QN5; or 9 . . . B–QB4; are all good replies.

(i) 9 . . . P–QR3; 10 P–QR3, P–KN3; 11 N–B3, B–N2; 12 B–K2, KN–K2; 13 O–O, O–O; 14 P–K4, N–Q5 ∞. Trifunović–Kozomara, Sarajevo 1957.

(j) 12 N–B3, N–B7; 13 R–QN1, B–B4; 14 B–Q2! Smyslov–Estrin, USSR 1951.

1 P–Q4, P–Q4; 2 P–QB4, P–K3; 3 N–QB3

	66	67	68	69	70
	(P–QB4)............................			B–K2	
4	P–K3			B–B4	P×P (j)
	N–KB3			N–KB3	P×P
5	N–B3			P–K3	B–B4
	N–B3			O–O	P–QB3
6	P×BP	P–QR3 (c)		R–B1	P–K3
	B×P	B–Q3	P–QR3 (f)	P–B4	B–KB4
7	P–QR3	P×BP	P×BP (g)	QP×P	P–KN4 (k)
	P×P (a)	B×BP	B×BP	N–B3	B–K3
8	Q×Q†	P–QN4	P–QN4	N–B3	P–KR3
	K×Q	B–Q3	B–Q3	B×P	B–Q3 (l)
9	B×P	B–N2	B–N2	P–QR3	KN–K2
	B–Q2	O–O	O–O	P–Q5	N–K2
10	P–QN4	P×P (d)	P×P	P×P	Q–N3
	B–Q3	P×P	P×P	N×P	B–B1 =
11	N–QN5	N–QN5	B–K2	N–K5	
	B–N1 (b)	B–N1 (e)	B–K3 (h)	P–QN3 (i)	

(a) 7 . . . O–O; 8 P–QN4, B–Q3; is a tempo ahead of col. 62. Compare this and col. 54.

(b) 12 N/5–Q4, N×N; 13 N×N, K–K2; 14 B–N2, R–B1 = . Pachman–Spasski, Amsterdam 1964.

(c) (A) 6 P×QP, see cols. 61–62. (B) 6 B–Q3, P×BP; 7 B×BP, see Queen's Gambit Accepted. With the text, White foregoes the strategy of settling Black with an "isolani."

(d) 10 Q–B2, P–QR4 ∞. Tal.

(e) 12 B–K2, Botvinnik–Tal, match 1960, 12 . . . Q–K2 and . . . R–Q1 = .

(f) (A) 6 . . . N–K5; 7 Q–B2! N×N! is a safe alternative. Petrosian–Fischer, 8th match game 1971, continued 8 P×N, B–K2; 9 B–N2, O–O; 10 B–Q3, P–KR3; 11 O–O, N–R4; 12 N–Q2, P×BP; 13 N×P, N×N; 14 B×N, P–QN3; 15 P–K4, B–N2 = . (B) Risky is 6 . . . P×QP; 7 KP×P, B–K2; (1) 8 P–B5! (the same position is arrived at in the Caro–Kann, Panov Attack, after 1 P–K4, P–QB3; 2 P–Q4, P–Q4; 3 P×P, P×P; 4 P–QB4, N–KB3; 5 N–QB3, P–K3; 6 N–B3, B–K2; 7 P–QR3, N–B3; 8 P–B5), N–K5; 9 Q–B2, P–B4; 10 B–QN5, B–B3; 11 B–KB4, O–O; 12 B×N, P×B; 13 O–O, B–Q2; 14 B–K5, B–K1; 15 P–QN4! Reshevsky–Sarapu, Sousse 1967. Less punch has (2) 8 B–Q3, P×P; 9 B×BP, O–O; 10 O–O, P–QR3! 11 B–KN5, P–N4; 12 B–R2, B–N2; 13 R–B1 = .

(g) Also 7 P–QN3, B–Q3! (A) 8 B–K2, O–O; 9 O–O, P–QN3; 10 B–N2, B–N2 = . Bronstein–Padevski 1956. The same sequence may also arise from the English Opening, Symmetrical Variation, (B) 8 B–Q3, O–O; 9 O–O, P–QN3; 10 B–N2, ×QP; 11 KP×P, B–N2 = .

(h) 12 O–O, Q–K2; 13 Q–Q2, QR–Q1 = . Kholmov–Suetin, USSR 1956.

(i) 12 B–Q3, B–N2; 13 O–O, P–KR3 (13 . . . N–B3! =). Petrosian–Bykhovski, Moscow Chp. 1968.

(j) Black's 3 . . . B–K2 is a finesse to bypass the pin 3 . . . N–KB3; 4 B–N5 and White's development of B–KB4 tries to be logical, but need not be more effective. 4 P–K4, P×P; 5 N×P, N–KB3; 6 N×N†, B×N; 7 N–B3 is akin to the Rubinstein Variation of the French.

(k) 7 KN–K2, N–B3; 8 N–N3, B–K3; 9 B–Q3, P–KN3 = ; or 7 . . . N–Q2; 8 P–KR3, KN–B3.

(l) Also 8 . . . N–B3; 9 N–B3, QN–Q2; 10 B–Q3, N–N3; 11 Q–B2, N–B5 = . Botvinnik–Petrosian, match 1963. The column is Korchnoi–Spasski, match 1968.

1 P-Q4, P-Q4; 2 P-QB4, P-K3; 3 N-KB3, N-KB3 (*a*); 4 B-N5 (*b*)

	71	72	73	74	75
	B-N5†!	(Vienna Variation)		P-KR3	P×P
5	N-B3			B×N (*h*)	N-B3 (*l*)
	P×P	P-KR3!		Q×B	P-B4
6	P-K4 (*c*)	B×N		Q-N3 (*i*)	P-K4
	P-B4	Q×B		P-B3	P×P
7	P-K5 (*d*)	P×P!		QN-Q2 (*j*)	Q×P
	P×P†	P×P		N-Q2	Q×Q
8	Q-R4†	Q-N3	R-B1	P-K4	N×Q
	N-B3	P-B4	O-O	P×KP	P-QR3
9	O-O-O	P-K3	P-QR3	N×P	B×P
	B-Q2	O-O!	B×N†	Q-B5	P-N4
10	N-K4	P×P	R×B	B-Q3	B-Q3
	B-K2	B×N†	P-B3	B-K2	B-N2
11	P×N	Q×B	P-K3	O-O	P-B3
	P×P (*e*)	Q×Q† (*f*)	R-K1 (*g*)	O-O (*k*)	QN-Q2 =

(*a*) 3 . . . P-QB4? 4 BP×P, KP×P; 5 P-KN3, N-QB3; 6 B-N2, P-B5; 7 O-O, B-QN5; 8 P-N3! P×P; 9 Q×P, KN-K2; 10 B-Q2! Korchnoi.

(*b*) (A) 4 P-KN3, see Catalan System. (B) 4 P-QN3, P-B4; 5 P×QP, KP×P; 6 P-K3, N-B3; 7 B-K2, P×P; 8 N×P, B-N5†; 9 B-Q2, B-Q3; 10 N×N, P×N; 11 N-B3, O-O = . Bronstein–Shamkovich, USSR 1960.

(*c*) 6 Q-R4†, N-B3; 7 P-K4, B-Q2; 8 Q-Q1, P-N4! 9 P-K5, P-KR3; 10 B-R4, P-N4; 11 KN×P, N-Q4! = .

(*d*) Less clear is 7 B×P, P×P; 8 N×P, Q-R4; 9 B×N, B×N†; 10 P×B, Q×P†; 11 K-B1, Q×B†; 12 K-N1, O-O; 13 Q-N4, P-KN3; 14 Q-B4, N-Q2; 15 P-K5, N×B; 16 P×N, K-R1; 17 R-QB1, P-K4; 18 Q-R6, Q×R†; 19 Q×Q, P×N; 20 P-KR4, B-B4; drawn. Trifunović–Gligorić, Mar del Plata 1953.

(*e*) 12 B-R4, QR-B1! 13 K-N1, and Black has no good continuation, e.g. 13 . . . P-N4; 14 Q×NP, P-B6; 15 KN×P! Q-B2; 16 B-N3, P-K4; 17 Q-N3! or 13 . . . N-R4; 14 Q-B2, P-K4; 15 N×QP, P×N; 15 R×P, Q-N3; 17 R×B! K×R; 18 B-K2 + .

(*f*) 12 P×Q, N-Q2; 13 R-Q1, N×P; 14 R×P, P-QN3; 15 R-Q2, B-N2; 16 B-K2, KR-B1! = .

(*g*) 12 B-K2, P-QR4; 13 O-O, B-N5 = . In the column, for 8 Q-R4†, see col, 41(*a*).

(*h*) 5 B-R4? B-N5†! 6 N-B3, with (1) 6 . . . P×P; 7 Q-R4†, N-B3; 8 P-QR3, B×N†; 9 P×B, Q-Q4; 10 B×N, P×B; 11 Q-B2, P-B4∓ ; Pachman; or (2) 6 . . . P-KN4; 7 B-N3, N-K5; 8 R-B1, P-KR4!

(*i*) Possibly more forceful than 6 N-B3, P-B3; (A) 7 P-K4, P×KP; 8 N×P, B-N5†; (1) 9 N-B3, P-B4; 10 R-B1, O-O; 11 P×P, P-K4! = , Pavey–Bisguier, New York 1954; or (2) 9 K-K2, Q-Q1! 10 P-KN3, O-O; 11 B-N2, N-Q2; 12 Q-Q3, B-K2; 13 KR-Q1, Q-B2; 14 N-B3, R-Q1 = . Uhlmann–Pachman, Moscow 1956. (B) 7 P-K3, N-Q2; 8 B-Q3, B-N5! 9 P-QR3! (9 O-O, Q-K2; 10 R-B1, O-O; 11 P-QR3, B-Q3; 12 P-B5, B-N1!∞ . Pachman), B×N†; 10 P×B, P-K4; 11 P-K4! P×KP; 12 B×P, Q-B5 = .

(*j*) A revival of an idea of Alekhin's. The current variation was 7 N-B3, N-Q2 (also 7 . . . P×P; 8 Q×BP, N-Q2; 9 P-K4, P-K4; 10 P-Q5, N-N3 = ; or 9 R-Q1, P-KN3); 8 P-K4, P×KP; 9 N×P, Q-B5; 10 B-Q3, P-K4! = .

(*k*) 12 KR-K1, P-QB4 (12 . . . R-Q1; 13 QR-Q1 ±); 13 QR-Q1! Lengyel–Szily Hungary 1966.

(*l*) 5 P-K4, P-KR3; 6 B×N, Q×B; 7 P-K5, Q-Q1 = . The column is Kamenetski–Murei, USSR 1966.

1 P–Q4, P–Q4; 2 P–QB4

		Chigorin's Defence		Symmetrical Defence	
	76	**77**	**78**	**79**	**80**
	N–QB3........................			P–QB4	
3	N–QB3......	N–KB3 (c)		P × QP	N–KB3
	P × P	B–N5		N–KB3	N–KB3
4	N–B3 (a)	Q–R4	P × P (e)	P × P (g)	P × QP
	N–B3 (b)	B × N	B × N	Q × P	P × P
5	P–K4	KP × B	NP × B (f)	Q × Q	N × P
	B–N5	P–K3	Q × P	N × Q	N × P
6	B–K3	N–B3	P–K3	B–Q2!	P–K4
	B × N	N–K2 (d)	P–K4	P–K4	N–KB3 (i)
7	P × B	P × P!	N–B3	N–QR3	N–QB3
	P–K4	P × P	B–N5	N–QB3!	P–K4
8	P–Q5	B–QN5	B–Q2	N–N5	N/4–N5
	N–K2	P–QR3	B × N	P–QR3	P–QR3
9	Q–R4†	B × N†	P × B	P–K4	Q × Q†
	N–Q2	N × B	P × P	P × N	K × Q
10	O–O–O	O–O	BP × P	P × N	N–R3
	N–N3	Q–Q2 =	N–B3 ∞	N–Q5 (h)	P–QN4 =

(a) 4 P–Q5, (A) 4 . . . N–QR4; 5 B–B4! P–K3! 6 P–K4, N–KB3; 7 Q–R4†, P–B3; 8 P × BP, N × BP might be tenable. (B) 4 . . . N–K4! 5 B–B4, N–N3; 6 B–N3, P–K4! 7 P × P *e.p.*, B × P; 8 N–KB3, N–B3; 9 N–Q4, B–Q2; 10 P–K3, B–QN5; 11 B × P/4, O–O = . Gligorić–Smyslov, Amsterdam 1971.

(b) 4 . . . P–QR3; 5 Q–R4, B–K3; 6 N–K5, B–Q2; 7 N × B, Q × N; 8 P–K3, P–K4; 9 B × P, P × P; 10 P × P, with initiative. *Comments.*

(c) 3 P × P, Q × P; 4 N–KB3, P–K4! 5 N–B3, B–QN5; 6 B–Q2, B × N; 7 B × B, P–K5 = .

(d) 6 . . . B–N5; 7 P–QR3, B × N†; 8 P × B, N–K2; 9 B–Q3, P × P; 10 B × BP, O–O; 11 O–O ± . The column is Panov's analysis. Portisch's try is 5 NP × B, e.g. 5 . . . N–B3; 6 N–B3, P–K3; 7 P–K3, P–QR3; 8 B–Q2, P × P; 9 Q × BP, B–K2, but the position remains actually equal. Earlier in the column, another thematic idea "à la Albin" is 3 . . . P–K4?! 4 QP × P, P–Q5 (see there), or 4 N × P! N × N; 5 P × N, P–Q5; 6 P–K4!

(e) Other options are (A) 4 N–B3, P–K3; 5 P × P (5 P–K3, KN–K2; 6 P–KR3, B × N; 7 Q × B, P–QR3; 8 P × P, P × P; 9 R–QN1, Q–Q3; 10 B–Q2, P–KN3 = . Ivkov–Rosetto, Buenos Aires 1960), P × P; 6 B–N5, P–B3; 7 B–B4, B–N5; 8 P–K3, KN–K2; 9 P–KR3, B–KB4 = . Milev–Spasski, Havana 1962. (B) 4 P–K3, P–K3; 5 QN–Q2, N–B3; 6 B–K2, B–K2; 7 O–O, O–O; 8 P–QN3 ∞ .

(f) 5 P × N, B × BP; 6 N–B3, N–B3! 7 P–B3, P–K4! 8 P × P, Q × Q†; 9 N × Q, N–Q2; 10 B–B4, O–O–O ∞ . *Comments.* The column is Bisguier–Littlewood, Hastings 1961–2.

(g) 4 P–K4?! N × KP; 5 P × P! N × QBP; 6 N–KB3, P–K3; 7 N–B3, B–K2! 8 B–KB4!

(h) 11 R–B1, R × P; 12 N–B3! Euwe.

(i) 6 . . . N–B2!? 7 N–QB3, P–K4; 8 N/4–N5, Q × Q†; 9 K × Q, N × N; 10 N × N! N–R3; 11 B–QB4!, B–QB4; 12 K–K2. Pinkus. The column is Kmoch's analysis; if 4 P–K3!? P × QP; 5 KP × P, P–KN3; 6 N–B3, B–N2; 7 B–K2, O–O; 8 O–O, N–B3; 9 P–KR3, P–N3; 10 N–K5, B–N2; 11 B–B3, N–QR4 ∓ . Smejkal–Ree, Wijk aan Zee 1976.

1 P–Q4, P–Q4; 2 P–QB4, P–K4; 3 P × KP, P–Q5

	81	82	83	84	85
4	N–KB3...				P–K4
	N–QB3				N–QB3
5	QN–Q2		P–QR3	P–KN3	P–B4
	B–KN5!		B–N5!	B–KN5 (*f*)	P–KN4 (*g*)
6	P–KR3	P–KN3 (*c*)	Q–N3!	B–N2	P–KB5 (*h*)
	B × N	Q–Q2	Q–Q2	Q–Q2	N × P
7	N × B	B–N2	Q × P	O–O	N–KB3
	B–N5†	O–O–O	R–N1	O–O–O	B–N5†
8	B–Q2	P–KR3	Q–R6	Q–N3	QN–Q2
	Q–K2	B–KB4	P–B3	B–R6	N–QB3
9	P–R3 (*a*)	P–R3	P–K6	P–K6!	B–Q3
	B × B†	P–B3	Q × P		P–N5
10	Q × B	P × P	QN–Q2		O–O (*i*)
	O–O–O (*b*)	N × P (*d*)	KN–K2 (*e*)		P × N (*j*)

(*a*) 9 B × B, Q × B†; 10 Q–Q2, Q × Q†; 11 K × Q, KN–K2; 12 P–K4, P × P *e.p.*†; 13 K × P, N–N3; 14 B–Q3! KN × P; 15 N × N, N × N; 16 P–B4, N × B; 17 K × N, O–O–O†; 18 K–B3, R–Q2 = . Füster–Balogh, corr. 1944.

(*b*) 11 O–O–O, N × P; 12 N × N, Q × N; 13 P–K3, P–QB4; 14 P × P = . Toth–Balogh, corr. 1944.

(*c*) 6 P–QR3, KN–K2 (or . . . Q–K2); 7 P–KN3, N–N3; 8 B–N2, Q–Q2; 9 P–N4, O–O–O; 10 B–N2, QN × KP; 11 N × N, N × N = .

(*d*) 11 P–QN4, R–K1; 12 B–N2, B–Q6; 13 O–O! B × KP; 14 Q–R4, B × R; 15 R × B, K–N1; 16 P–N5, N–Q1; 17 N × P, with attacking chances. Bondarevski–Mikenas, USSR 1950.

(*e*) Bogolyubov–Helling, Berlin 1937, 11 Q–R4.

(*f*) (A) 5 . . . B–KB4; 6 P–QR3! (B) 5 . . . B–K3; 6 P–N3 (or 6 Q–R4), Q–Q2; 7 B–KN2, O–O–O; 8 O–O, B–KR6; 9 P–K3 ± . The column is Spasski–Forintos, Gorki 1965, with wild possibilities.

(*g*) Another possibility is 5 . . . P–B3; 6 N–KB3, P × P; 7 B–Q3, B–N5†; 8 QN–Q2, P × P; 9 O–O, N–B3; 10 N–N3, O–O; 11 P–B5, Q–K2 = .

(*h*) 6 N–KB3, P × P; 7 B × P, B–KN5; 8 B–Q3, KN–K2; 9 O–O, N–N3; 10 Q–B1, B × N; 11 R × B, QN × P; 12 B × N, N × B = . Jonasson.

(*i*) Possible is 10 N–N1, N–K4; 11 Q–B2, N–K2 ∞. *Comments.*

(*j*) 11 N × P, B–Q3; 12 P–K5, N × P; 13 R–K1 ± .

Queen's Gambit— Slav and Semi-Slav Defence

(1 P–Q4, P–Q4; 2 P–QB4, P–QB3)

The Slav genealogy is the largest on the Queen's Gambit tree. Originated by Alapin, and popularized in the 1935–7 world title matches between Alekhin and Euwe, it provides Black with a solid and, often, a surprisingly active defence. Characterized by 2 . . . P–QB3, the Slav aims at bolstering Black's queen's pawn without hemming in his perennial "problem child" (the queen's bishop) which is free to develop at KB4 or QN2. The Semi-Slav is identified by an early . . . P–K3, creating a phalanx-like formation of Black's centre pawns. It is a tough nut to crack and Black retains the option of reverting into the Stonewall Variation of the Dutch Defence if he delays . . . N–KB3. Nothing revolutionary has happened since the last editions to alter traditional evaluations, but almost every line has been studded with subtle refinements.

For reference and convenience the branches are broken down into: (A) Semi-Slav: Meran Variation. (B) Semi-Slav: Various. (C) Semi-Slav: Anti-Meran Variations and the Anti-Meran Gambit. (D) Semi-Slav and Slav with 3 N–QB3. (E) Slav: Dutch Variation. (F) Slav: Various. (G) Exchange Variation.

(A) THE SEMI SLAV: MERAN SYSTEM (cols. 1–15) is characterized by 3 N–KB3, N–B3; 4 N–B3, P–K3; 5 P–K3, QN–Q2; 6 B–Q3; P × P; 7 B × BP, P–QN4. Black shuts in his queen's bishop temporarily, but this is balanced by the rapid grouping of his pieces on the queen's wing and the liberating . . . P–QB4. White must seize the opportunity of acting in the centre or renounce his chance of gaining the initiative. A close examination of the line shows that it is an improved version of the Queen's Gambit Accepted. White loses a tempo by 6 B–Q3, but later Black gives it back by playing . . . P–QB4 (after having played 2 . . . P–QB3). The main lines are tricky and intricate, White barely retaining the upper hand.

286

Reynolds' Variation (cols. 9–10) narrowly misses being a positional refutation. It is still theoretically crucial and all the problems have not been resolved, as Black's defence hinges on note (g) and on col. 10. A variety of defences, in cols. 11–14 are enterprising but easily precarious.

(B) THE SEMI-SLAV: VARIOUS (cols. 16–18) offers a rich mixture of developing patterns for White and Black after 5 P–K3. The *Chigorin Variation* 6 . . . B–Q3 (col. 16) is no longer considered a sound equalizing method whereas 6 . . . B–K2 (col. 17) is only sporadically being tried.

The *Romih Variation* 6 . . . B–N5 (col. 18) also fights to break loose with . . . P–K4 by exerting indirect pressure on White's centre *à la* Nimzo-Indian. It leads to a refined positional struggle with White retaining the slightly freer position.

(C) THE SEMI-SLAV ANTI-MERAN VARIATIONS AND ANTI-MERAN GAMBIT (cols. 19–25) are complex and still not fully investigated. The Anti-Meran inventions of Stoltz, 6 Q–B2 (col. 19), and Rubinstein, 6 N–K5 (col. 20), fail to achieve any advantage.

The *Anti-Meran Gambit* was popularized by Botvinnik against Denker in the USSR *v.* USA radio-match of 1945. It arises after White varies with 5 B–N5, P × P; 6 P–K4, P–N4; 7 P–K5, P–KR3; 8 B–R4, P–N4 (cols. 21–5). The main lines seem to unravel to approximately even chances, but it is a sharp fight with Black often coming out on top.

(D) THE SEMI-SLAV with 3 N–QB3 (cols. 26–30) covers the complicated *Abrahams Variation* (col. 26) and the speculative *Marshall Gambit* (cols. 27–8), which Black does best to accept. The play is rough-and-tumble where White gets lively play and open lines in return for his pawn. Cols. 29 and 30 already belong in the Slav system, due to the omission of an early . . . P–K3. Col. 29 and Col. 30 note (j) are the antidote. White's plan is logical, but not dangerous to Black.

(E) THE SLAV: DUTCH VARIATION (cols. 31–5) has held stage centre since the Alekhin-Euwe title match in 1937. It has appealed to technicians such as Smyslov and Petrosian. After 3 N–KB3, N–B3; 4 N–B3, P × P; 5 P–QR4, B–B4 (6 P–K3, P–K3; 7 B × P, B–QN5) White does well to complete his development and press for P–K4. Although he maintains more options, the prospects are drawish.

(F) THE SLAV: VARIOUS (cols. 36–45) includes all attempts by White to obtain more than he gets in the Dutch Variation by varying earlier from the Main Line. The *Krause Attack*, 6 N–K5 (cols. 36–7), is one of the sharpest weapons at his disposal. It involves Black's readiness to sacrifice a piece for three pawns (col. 37), but current opinion gives him at least equality. Note (b) indicates that the older 6 . . . QN–Q2 is unsatisfactory.

6 N–R4 (col. 36 with note (a)) leads to a draw by repetition or otherwise and is a fascinating divergence—in Black's favour. Column 38 exploits the omission of 5 . . . B–B4 but cols. 39–40 show a different strategy of successfully supplanting 5 . . . N–R3?!

Geller's Variation 5 P–K4!? (col. 41) involves a pawn sacrifice and gives Black a solid position if he exercises some defensive skill.

Alekhin's Variation 5 P–K3 (col. 42) attempts to dispense with the weakening and wasted (?) 5 P–QR4, but Black can gain equality by launching an all-out queen's-side offensive with 5 . . . P–QN4.

(G) THE SLAV: EXCHANGE VARIATION (cols. 43–5) contains a drop of poison after 4 P × P, P × P. Previously labelled anything from a refutation to a dead draw, endorsed by Botvinnik and Reshevsky, it now seems fairly settled that Black has well-balanced equalizing chances. The symmetrical pawn-structure makes it difficult for either side to stir up winning chances against best play. White's extra tempo does not mean much in this type of closed position. A player seeking to win with Black at all costs should avoid the Slav, because of this simple exchange line, if White is only playing for a draw. Yet the Slav is here to stay and represents a basic body of modern theory.

1 P-Q4, P-Q4; 2 P-QB4, P-QB3; 3 N-KB3, N-B3; 4 N-B3, P-K3; 5 P-K3, QN-Q2; 6 B-Q3, P×P; 7 B×BP, P-QN4 (Meran System); 8 B-Q3, P-QR3; 9 P-K4, P-B4; 10 P-K5, P×P; 11 N×NP. (*Blumenfeld's Continuation*)

	1	2	3	4	5
	P×N	....	N×P		
12	P×N		N×N		
	Q-N3!		P×N		
13	P×P		Q-B3	O-O	
	B×P		B-N5† (*f*)	Q-Q4!	
14	O-O	Q-K2	K-K2	Q-K2	
	N-B4 (*a*)	B-N2 (*d*)	R-QN1	B-R3	B-N2?!
15	B-KB4!	B×NP	Q-N3!	B-N5	B×P†
	B-N2	Q-Q3	Q-Q3	B-K2	K-Q1
16	R-K1	O-O	N-B3	P-B4	P-B3
	B-Q4?! (*b*)	O-O	Q×Q	O-O	B-B4
17	B-K5	B-Q2	BP×Q	R-B3	K-R1
	B×B	P-K4	B-Q3	B-N2	K-K2
18	N×B	N-N5	B-KB4	R-R3	B-QB4
	R-KN1 (*c*)	N-B3 (*e*)	B×B (*g*)	P-R3 (*h*)	Q-Q3 (*i*)

(*a*) Usual but less vigorous is 14 . . . O-O; 15 B-KB4! B-N2; 16 R-K1, B-Q4; 17 Q-K2! P-N5; 18 QR-B1, QR-B1; 19 N-N5! ∞. Szabó-Szily, Trenčanské-Teplice, 1949.

(*b*) Paul Schmidt's controversial move which has more fight than (A) 16 . . . N×B; 17 Q×N, B×N; 18 Q×B, O-O; 19 QR-B1, QR-B1; 20 Q-KN3, K-R1; 21 P-KR4, KR-K1; 22 P-R5! or (B) 16 . . . R-Q1; 17 R-QB1, R-Q4; 18 B-K5! O-O; 19 B×P†, K×B; 20 P-QN4!

(*c*) (A) 19 P-KN3, R-N2; 20 Q-R5, Q-N2! (B) Euwe's 19 B-B1 needs proper testing.

(*d*) For choice are (A) 14 . . . B-QR3; 15 P-QN4, O-O; 16 O-O, Q-Q3; 17 P-QR3, B-N2; or (B) 14 . . . O-O; 15 O-O, N-B4; 16 B×P†, K×B; 17 N-N5†, K-N3; 18 Q-N4, P-B4; 19 Q-N3, R-B2; 20 B-B4, P-K4!

(*e*) 19 B-Q3, P-K5! *Comments.*

(*f*) 13 . . . Q-R4†; 14 K-K2, B-Q3; 15 Q-Q2, Q-R3; 16 P-QR4! *Comments.*

(*g*) 19 P×B, B-Q2; 20 N×P, K-K2; 21 QR-B1, KR-QB1 = . Szabó-Ståhlberg, Saltsjöbaden 1948. 15 Q-N3! was Reshevsky's idea.

(*h*) 19 R-KB1, KR-B1; 20 B×N, B×B; 21 N-N4, K-B1! = . Polland-Kashdan, Boston 1938.

(*i*) 19 P-QN4, B×NP; 20 R-QN1, KR-QN1 = . Freiman.

1 P–Q4, P–Q4; 2 P–QB4, P–QB3; 3 N–KB3, N–B3; 4 N–B3, P–K3; 5 P–K3,
QN–Q2; 6 B–Q3, P × P; 7 B × BP, P–QN4; 8 B–Q3, P–QR3; 9 P–K4, P–B4

	6	7	8	9	10
10	(P–K5)			P–Q5	(Reynolds'
	(P × P)	N–N5!		P–K4 (g)	Variation)
11	(N × NP)	B–K4	N–N5 (d)	P–QN3 (h)	
	N–N5	R–R2	P × P	P–B5!?	B–Q3!
12	Q–R4!	N–N5	Q × N (e)	P × P	O–O
	B–N2 (a)	P × P	N × P	P × P	O–O
13	QN × P	Q × N	Q–N3	B–B2	P–QR4 (j)
	Q–N3	P × N	P × N	B–N5	P–B5!
14	O–O	O–O	B–K4	B–Q2	NP × P
	B–B4	N × P	P × P	Q–R4	P–N5
15	P–KR3	Q–N3	B × NP	N–K2	N–K2
	N × BP (b)	P × P	N–B5!	N × KP	N–B4
16	R × N	B × NP	B × R	B × N	N–N3
	QB × N	N–B5 =	Q–Q7†	P–B6	Q–B2
17	R × B		K–B1	N × P	B–N5
	B × N† (c)		B–Q3 (f)	B × N (i)	N–K1 =

(a) (A) 12. . . N–B4; 13 N–Q6†, K–K2; 14 Q × QP, Q–R4†; 15 B–Q2, N × B†; 16 Q × N, N × KP; 17 Q–K3, N × N†; 18 P × N! + . *Archives* (B) 12 . . . N/5 × KP? 13 N × N, N × N; 14 N–B7†, K–K2; 15 Q–N4†! K–B3; 16 N–K8†! Q × N; 17 Q × P, B–N5†; 18 K–K2 + + .

(b) Another critical line is 15 . . . QB × N; 16 P × N! B–Q4; 17 N–B3! ∞, or 16 . . . B–N2; 17 N–B3.

(c) 18 K–R1, R–R2; (A) 19 B–KB4, K–K2 = . Vécsey. (B) 19 B–Q2?! is Euwe's recommendation. 11 . . . N–N5 is Rabinovich's suggestion.

(d) Also 11 B–KB4, P × P; 12 N–K4, B–N5†; 13 K–B1, B–N2; 14 P–KR3, N–R3; 15 R–B1, Q–N3 = . Vécsey–Korn, corr. 1953.

(e) 12 N × BP! Q–R5! 13 P–KN3, Q–R4; 14 N × R, QN × P; 15 N–K4, B–N5†; 16 K–B1, N–K6† = .

(f) 18 B–B6†, K–K2; 19 Q–QB3, Q × B; 20 Q × Q, N × Q ∞ .

(g) (A) Wanting is 10 . . . P × P; 11 P–K5, N–N5; 12 B–N5, P–B3; 13 P × P, N/2 × P; 14 P–KR3, N–R3; 15 N × QP, Q × N; 16 B × QN, Q–K3†; 17 B–K5, B–N2; 18 O–O, O–O–O; 19 R–K1! + . (B) Probably the best, and satisfactory, fighting chance provides 10 . . . P–B5! 11 P × P! (11 B–B2, P–K4! 12 O–O, B–B4; 13 P–QN3, P × P; 14 B × P, O–O = . Ornstein–Nei, Tallinn 1977), P × P (11 . . . P × B; 12 P × N†, Q × P; 13 N–K5, Q–K2; 14 B–B4, N × P! 15 N × N, Q–N5† also is promising); 12 B–B2, B–N2! 13 O–O, Q–B2; 14 N–N5 (14 Q–K2, O–O–O; 15 P–K5, N–Q4), N–B4; 15 P–B4, P–R3; 16 P–K5, P × N; 17 B–N6†, K–K2 ∞. Ftacník–Panchenko, Sochi 1977.

(h) 11 O–O, P–B5! 12 B–B2, B–Q3; 13 N–KR4, N–B4; 14 P–B4, P × P! 15 P–K5, B × P; 16 R–K1, N–N5; 17 N–B3, N–Q6! Pachman.

(i) 18 O–O, B × B; 19 N × B, O–O; 20 N–B4, Q–N5; 21 Q–B2 ± . Uhlmann–Pomar, Stockholm 1962.

(j) 13 R–K1, R–N1; 14 B–B1, N–K1; 15 P–QR4, N–B2; 16 P × P, N × NP; 17 N × N, P × N; 18 B–N2, R–K1 = . Averbakh–Nikitin, USSR 1959. The column is Kotov-Gutierrez, Santiago 1957.

1 P-Q4, P-Q4; 2 P-QB4, P-QB3; 3 N-KB3, N-B3; 4 N-B3, P-K3; 5 P-K3, QN-Q2; 6 B-Q3, P × P; 7 B × BP, P-QN4

	11	12	13	14	15
8	(B-Q3)................................				B-K2 (j)
	(P-QR3).................		B-N2	P-N5	P-QR3 (k)
9	(P-K4)......	O-O	P-K4 (d)	N-K4!	P-K4
	P-N5	P-B4	P-N5	N × N	P-N5
10	N-QR4	P-QR4	N-QR4	B × N	P-K5
	P-B4	P-N5	P-B4	B-N2	P × N
11	P-K5	N-K4	P-K5	O-O (h)	P × N
	N-Q4	B-N2	N-Q4	B-K2	P × NP!? (l)
12	O-O	N × N† (c)	N × P (e)	P-QN3	P × P
	B-N2	N × N	B × N (f)	O-O	B × P
13	B-KN5 (a)	P × P!	P × B (g)	B-N2	B × NP
	B-K2 (b)	B × P =		N-B3 (i)	Q-R4† (m)

(a) 13 R-K1, P-B3; 14 B-Q2, R-B1; 15 Q-K2, Q-R4; 16 N × P, B × N; 17 P × B, N × BP; is enterprising (Portisch-Wade, Havana 1964), but 18 P × P should win.

(b) 14 B × B, Q × B; 15 R-B1, P × P; 16 R-K1, O-O; 17 B-K4, KR-Q1; holds Black's game together (Levenfish).

(c) 12 QN-Q2, B-Q3! (12 . . . B-K2; 13 Q-K2, O-O; 14 R-Q1, P-QR4; 15 N-B4, Q-B2 = is Grünfeld-Rubinstein, Meran 1924, the parent game of this system); 13 N-B4, B-B2 ∓ .

(d) 9 O-O, P-N5; 10 N-K4, B-K2; 11 N × N, N × N; 12 P-K4, O-O; 13 Q-B2 (also 13 P-K5, N-Q2; 14 Q-B2, P-KR3; 15 B-R7†, K-R1; 16 B-K4, Q-N3; 17 B-K3, P-QB4; 18 P × P, B × P (18 . . . B × B!); 19 QR-Q1 ± , Korchnoi- Polugayevski, 3rd match game 1977), P-KR3; 14 B-K3, R-B1; 15 KR-Q1, P-B4; 16 P × P, N-N5; 17 B-Q4, P-K4; 18 P-KR3, P × B; 19 P × N, R × P; 20 Q-Q2, P-QR4; 21 QR-B1, Q-Q2 (Q-R1!); 22 R × R, B × R; 23 P-N5, P × P; 24 Q × P/5, Q-K2; 25 Q-R5, P-N3; 26 Q-R6, Q-B3; 27 B-B4, P-Q6! 28 P-K5, Q-B4; 29 R × P, B-K5; 30 R-Q6, Q-N5; 31 R-KB6, B-B4; 32 B-N3, B-Q5; 33 N × B, Q × N; 34 R × P†, B × R; 35 Q × B†, K-R1; 36 Q-R6†, K-N1; 37 P-K6, Q-K5; 38 P × P†, R × P; 39 Q-KB6, QN8†; 40 K-R2, Q-R2†; 41 K-N3, Q-Q6†; 42 P-B3! Q × B; 43 Q-Q8†, resigns. 7th match game, Korchnoi-Polugayevski, Evian 1977.

(e) 12 O-O, P × P; 13 R-K1, P-N3; 14 B-KN5, B-K2; 15 B-K6, B-KB1; 16 B-KN5, Q-R4 = . Tukmakov-Sveshnikov, USSR Chp. 1977.

(f) (A) . . . N × N; 13 P × N, B × P; 14 B-N5†, K-K2?! 15 O-O, Q-N3; 16 B-Q3, P-KR3; 17 Q-K2, KR-Q1∞. Uhlmann-Larsen, match 1971. (B) 12 . . . Q-R4 = .

(g) (A) 13 . . . P-QR3; 14 O-O, N × BP; 15 B-B2, R-QB1; 16 Q-Q4 ± . (B) 13 . . . N × BP; 14 B-N5†, K-K2 (14 . . . K-B1; 15 O-O ±); 15 Q-N4, Q-N3; 16 B-QB4, N-Q2; 17 Q-R4† = .

(h) (A) 11 B-Q2, B-K2; 12 P-QR3, P-QR4; 13 Q-R4, Q-N3; 14 P × P, P × P; 15 Q × R†, B × Q; 16 R × B†, B-Q1; 17 O-O, O-O; 18 KR-K1, Q-N4! (Uhlmann-Zinn, Dresden 1959); 19 R-B1, P-QB4; 20 R-N8, Q-R3; 21 R-B6, Q-R5∞. (B) 11 Q-R4, Q-N3; 12 N-Q2, R-B1; 13 P-QR3! P × P; 14 N-B4! Q-R3; 15 Q-N3, Q-N4; 16 Q × Q, P × Q; 17 B × B, R-B2∞. Portisch-Ree, Wijk aan Zee 1975.

(i) 14 B-Q3, P-B4; 15 P × P, B × P; 16 R-B1, B-K2; 17 N-K5, Q-Q4 = . Panno-Olafsson, Portorož, 1958.

(j) 8 B-N3? P-N5! (8 . . . B-N2 leads—unnecessarily—into the Queen's Gambit Accepted); 9 N-K2, B-N2; 10 O-O, B-Q3∓ .

(k) (A) Another version of Wade's variation, 8 . . . B-N2; 9 P-QR3, P-QR3; 10 P-QN4, P-QR4, 11 R-QN1, P × P; 12 P × P, N-Q4; 13 N × N, KP × N; 14 O-O, B-Q3; is playable.

Szabó–Wade, Haifa 1958. (B) 8 . . . B–K2; 9 O–O, P–QR3; 10 P–K4, P–N5 = ; and (C) 8 . . . P–N5; 9 N–QR4, B–N2; 10 O–O, B–K2; 11 B–Q2, O–O = are further choices.

(*l*) 11 . . . N × P; 12 P × P, B–Q3 is another possibility.

(*m*) 14 N–Q2, R–QN1; 15 Q–B2, P–QB4; 16 B–QB3, with more mobility.

1 P–Q4, P–Q4; 2 P–QB4, P–QB3; 3 N–KB3, N–B3; 4 N–B3 (*a*), P–K3 (*b*); 5 P–K3, QN–Q2

	16	17	18	Anti-Meran Variations	
				19	20
6	(B–Q3)............................			Q–B2	N–K5
	B–Q3	B–K2	B–N5	B–Q3 (*j*)	N × N
7	P–K4 (*c*)	O–O (*e*)	P–QR3!	P–K4 (*k*)	P × N
	P × KP	P × P (*f*)	B–R4	P × KP	N–Q2
8	N × P	B × P	Q–B2	N × P	P–B4
	N × N	P–QN4	O–O (*h*)	N × N	B–N5
9	B × N	B–Q3	B–Q2	Q × N	B–Q2
	O–O	P–N5	B–B2	P–K4	O–O =
10	O–O	N–K4	O–O	P–B5	
	Q–B2	N × N	P × P	B–K2	
11	B–B2	B × N	B × P	N × P	
	P–KR3	B–N2	P–K4	N × N	
12	R–K1	P–QN3	B–R2!	Q × N	
	R–Q1 (*d*)	O–O (*g*)	P–KR3 (*i*)	O–O ∞	

(*a*) Too reticent is 4 P–K3, P–K3; 5 B–Q3, QN–Q2; 6 QN–Q2, P–QN3; 7 O–O, B–K2; 8 P–QN3, B–N2; 9 B–N2, O–O; 10 P–K4, P × KP; 11 N × P, P–B4 = . R. Byrne–S. Bernstein, US Chp. 1962.

(*b*) For the Schlechter Variation 4 . . . P–KN3; 5 B–B4, see Grünfeld Defence.

(*c*) Also 7 O–O, O–O; 8 P–K4, P × BP; 9 B × P, P–K4; 10 B–K3, Q–K2; 11 P–KR3, P × P; 12 N × P, N–K4; 13 B–N3 ± . Müller.

(*d*) 13 B–Q2, P–QB4; 14 P × P, N × P; 15 Q–K2 ± . Alekhin.

(*e*) At once 7 P–QN3! might be more precise.

(*f*) 7 . . . O–O; 8 P–QN3! P–QN3; 9 B–N2, B–N2; 10 Q–K2, P–B4; 11 QR–Q1, N–K5; 12 P × BP, N × N; 13 B × N, NP × P; 14 P × P ± .

(*g*) 13 B–N2, N–B3 = . Petrosian–Botvinnik, Moscow 1967.

(*h*) Also satisfactory is 8 . . . P × P; 9 B × P, O–O; 10 O–O, B–B2; 11 P–R3 P–K4; 12 B–R2, P × P; 13 P × P, N–N3; 14 R–K1, QN–Q4; 15 B–N5, Q–Q3 = . Evans–Minev, Varna Olympics 1962.

(*i*) 13 QR–K1, R–K1; 14 P × P, N × P; 15 N × N, R × N; 16 P–B4, B–B4 = . The column is the somewhat shaky Romih Variation.

(*j*) Solid is 6 . . . B–K2; 7 P–QN3, O–O; 8 B–N2, P–QN3; 9 B–Q3, B–N2; 10 N–K5, P–B4! = .

(*k*) (A) If 7 B–Q2, O–O; 8 O–O–O, P–B4! 9 P–K4, BP × P; 10 KN × P, P × BP; 11 B × P, N–N3; 12 B–K2, B–Q2 = ; but not 8 . . . P–QN4; 9 P × NP, P–B4; 10 P–K4, B–N2; 11 KP × P, KP × P: 12 Q–B5! ± . (B) 7 P–QN3, O–O; 8 B–K2, P × P; 9 P × P, P–K4; 10 O–O, R–K1; 11 P–QR4, Q–K2; 12 R–N1, P–K5; 13 N–Q2, N–B1; 14 P–B3, P × P; 15 N × P, P–B4 = . Rogoff–Mednis, US Chp. 1978. This and the next column is *Comments*, as based on analyses by Stoltz and by Rubinstein.

1 P–Q4, P–Q4; 2 P–QB4, P–QB3; 3 N–KB3, N–B3; 4 N–B3, P–K3; 5 B–N5 (Anti-Meran Gambit), P × P (*a*); 6 P–K4 (*b*), P–N4; 7 P–K5, P–KR3; 8 B–R4, P–N4

	21	22	23	24	25
9	N × KNP	. . . .		P × N	
	P × N			P × B	
10	B × NP			N–K5	
	QN–Q2			Q × BP	
11	P–KN3	. . . .	Q–B3 (*e*)	P–KN3 (*h*)	. . . B–K2
	B–QN2	. . . . . . N × P	B–QN2	N–Q2	N–Q2!
12	B–N2	P × N	B–K2	Q–K2!	O–O
	Q–N3 (*c*)	Q × Q†	Q–N3 (*f*)	N × N	N × N
13	P × N	R × Q	B × N	P × N	P × N
	O–O–O	N–Q4	P–B4	Q–K2	Q × P
14	O–O	N–K4	N–K4	B–N2	B–B3
	N–K4	B–N5†	R–KN1	B–QN2	B–QN2
15	Q–K2	K–K2 ±	Q–B4	O–O–O	R–K1
	Q × P		P × P	R–Q1	Q–B2
16	B–K3		B–R5	R × R†	B–R5
16	B–K3		B–R5	R × R†	B–R5
		Q–Q6 (*d*)	N–B4 (*g*)	K × R (*i*)	Q–Q2 (*j*)

(*a*) 5 . . . P–KR3; 6 B × N, Q × B; 7 P–K3, N–Q2; 8 B–Q3, B–N5; 9 O–O, Q–K2; 10 P–QR3, B × N; 11 P × B, P × P = . Geller.

(*b*) 6 P–QR4, B–N5; 7 P–K4, P–QN4; 8 P–K5, P–KR3; 9 B–R4, P–N4; 10 N × P, N–Q4; 11 Q–R5! Q–B2; 12 N–K4, N–Q2 = . Van Scheltinga–Stumpers, 1947.

(*c*) 12 . . . R–KN1; 13 B × N, N × B; 14 P × N, Q × BP; 15 P–QR4, P–N5; 16 N–K4, Q–B4; 17 Q–K2, O–O–O; 18 Q × P, B–N2 = . Smyslov–Bronstein, Budapest 1950.

(*d*) 17 KR–Q1, Q × Q; 18 R × R†, K × R; 19 N × Q, N–Q6 = . Smyslov–Botvinnik, match 1954.

(*e*) 11 P × N, B–QN2; (A) 12 B–K2, Q–N3; 13 P–QR4! (Denker v. Botvinnik, 1945, played 13 O–O?), P–N5; 14 P–R5, Q–R3; 15 N–K4, O–O–O; 16 Q–B2, P–B4; 17 B × P, P–B3; 18 B–Q3, P–N6 = . Pachman. (B) 12 P–KN3! Q–N3; 13 B–N2, P–B4; 14 P–Q5! O–O–O; 15 O–O, P–N5; 16 P × P! Euwe.

(*f*) Müller's 12 . . . Q–B2; 13 P × N, O–O–O; 14 B–B4, Q–N3; 15 P–QR4, P–B4 deserves attention.

(*g*) 17 B × P†, K–Q2! ∞ . Zöllner–Junge, Warsaw 1942.

(*h*) 11 P–R4, P–N5; 12 N–K4, Q–B4! = .

(*i*) 17 N–K4 followed by 18 R–Q1(†), and 19 N–B6, or 19 Q–K3 + . *Comments.* Possibly 15 . . . B–N2; 16 P–B4, O–O; 17 R–Q6, QR–Q1 offers a better defence.

(*j*) 17 Q × Q†, K × Q; 18 B × P, B–Q3 = . Pachman.

1 P–Q4, P–Q4; 2 P–QB4, P–QB3; 3 N–QB3 (*a*)

	26	27	28	29	30
	P–K3			P × P	...... P–K4 (*j*)
4	N–B3 .... P–K4 (Mars hall Gambit)			P–K4	P × QP
	P × P	P × KP		P–K4	BP × P
5	P–QR4 (*b*)	N × P		N–B3	P–K4
	B–N5	B–N5†		P × P	P × KP
6	P–K3	B–Q2!		Q × P	B–N5†
	P–QN4	Q × P!		Q × Q	B–Q2
7	B–Q2	B × B		N × Q	P × P
	P–QR4	Q × N†		B–QB4	B × B
8	P × P	B–K2 .... N–K2		B–K3	Q × Q†
	B × N	N–QR3 (*d*)	N–QR3 (*g*)	N–B3	K × Q
9	B × B	B–Q6 (*e*)	B–B3 (*h*)	P–B3	N × B
	P × P	P–QN3	N–K2	O–O	B–N5†
10	P–QN3	N–B3	B × P	B × P	K–K2
	B–N2 (*c*)	B–N2 (*f*)	N–N5 (*i*)	QN–Q2 =	P–QR3 (*k*)

(*a*) 3 P × P, P × P; 4 P–KN3, N–KB3; 5 B–N2, P–KN3; see Grünfeld Defence.

(*b*) 5 P–K3, P–QN4; 6 P–QR4. (A) 6 . . . P–N5; 7 N–K4, B–R3; 8 Q–B2, Q–Q4; 9 N/4–Q2! P–B6 = . *Comments*. (B) 6 . . . B–N5 reverts to the column.

(*c*) (A) 11 P × P, P–N5; 12 B–N2, N–KB3; 13 B–Q3, B–K5; 14 B × B, N × B; 15 Q–B2, P–B4 = . *Comments*. (B) 11 P–Q5! N–KB3; 12 P × BP, P–N5; 13 B × N! Q × B! 14 Q–R4†, K–B1! 15 N–Q4, P × P; 16 Q–N5, B–B3; 17 Q–B5†, Q–K2; 18 R × P, Q × Q; 19 R × Q, K–K2! ∞ . The column is the Abrahams (or Noteboom) Variation.

(*d*) An involved scenario follows 8 . . . P–QB4! 9 B × P, Q × NP; 10 B–B3, Q–N4; 11 B–Q6! N–K2; 12 N–K2, N–B4! 13 R–KN1, Q–Q1! *Comments*.

(*e*) 9 B–B3, N–K2! 10 B × P, R–KN1; 11 B–B3, N–Q4! 12 P × N, Q × NP; 13 P × KP! B × P! 14 B–B6! Q × R; 15 Q–Q6, R × N†; 16 K–Q2, Q–Q4†; 17 Q × Q, B × Q; 18 R × R, K–Q2; 19 B × N, P × B = . Yudovich.

(*f*) 11 N–K5, P–B3; 12 O–O, P × N; 13 B–R5†, P–N3; 14 R–K1, Q–R5; 15 B–N4, R–Q1; 16 R × P, N–B4! = .

(*g*) Also 8 . . . N–Q2; 9 Q–Q6, P–QB4! 10 B × P, N × B; 11 Q × N, B–Q2 = .

(*h*) 9 B–Q6, or B–R3 may be tried. *Comments*.

(*i*) 11 Q–Q6! N–Q6†; 12 K–Q2, N–KB4; 13 Q × N, Q × Q†; 14 K × Q, N × B = . Kholmov.

(*j*) The Winawer Gambit. 3 . . . N–KB3; 4 P–K3, P–KN3; 5 P–B4 (5 N–B3 see Grünfeld Defence), B–N2; 6 N–B3, O–O; 7 B–K2, B–B4; 8 O–O, QN–Q2; 9 N–K5 is still even.

(*k*) 11 N–Q4, N–K2; 12 K–K3 ± . Alekhin's analysis.

1 P–Q4, P–Q4; 2 P–QB4, P–QB3; 3 N–KB3, N–B3; 4 N–B3, P×P; 5 P–QR4, B–B4; 6 P–K3, P–K3; 7 B×P, B–QN5; 8 O–O

	31	32	33	34	35
	O–O............................			QN–Q2	
9	Q–K2			Q–N3 (*g*)	N–R4
	B–N5?		QN–Q2	P–QR4	O–O
10	R–Q1	P–R3!	P–K4	N–R2	P–B3
	QN–Q2	QB×N (*c*)	B–N5 (*e*)	B–K2!	B–N3
11	P–K4	Q×B	R–Q1	N–R4!	P–K4 (*i*)
	Q–K2	QN–Q2	Q–R4	B–KN5	P–K4 (*j*)
12	P–K5 (*a*)	R–Q1	P–K5	P–B3	N×B
	N–Q4	P–K4	N–Q4	N–Q4	P×N
13	P–KR3	P–Q5	N–K4	P×B	B–K3
	B–KR4	B×N	P–B3	B×N	Q–N3!
14	N–K4	P×P	P×P	P–K4	K–R1
	P–KB4	P–K5	N/2×P = (*f*)	KN–N3	QR–Q1
15	P×P *e.p.*	Q–K2		B–Q3 ± (*h*)	P×P
	QN×P (*b*)	B–K4 (*d*)			Q×B (*k*)

(*a*) 12 B–KN5, P–KR3; 13 B–R4, P–K4; 14 P–Q5, Q–B4 = . *Comments.*

(*b*) 16 B–KN5, Q–B2; 17 N–N3, B×N; 18 Q×B, QR–K1; 19 QR–B1 ± . Spasski–Cobo, Havana 1962.

(*c*) 10 . . . B–KR4; 11 R–Q1, Q–K2; 12 P–K4, QN–Q2; 13 P–R5! (Barendregt) or 13 P–KN4 ± (Gligorić).

(*d*) 15 P×N, Q–K2; 17 R–R2 ± . Levenfish–Alatortsev, USSR Chp. 1948.

(*e*) 10 . . . B–N3; 11 B–Q3 (11 B–KN5, Q–R4; 12 B–Q3, P–B4; 13 P×P, B×N; 14 P×B, Q×P/4 =), B–QR4 = .

(*f*) Filip–Smyslov, Bucharest 1953.

(*g*) 9 Q–K2, B–N3; 10 P–K4, O–O! (10 . . . B×N? 11 P×B, N×P; 12 B–R3, Q–B2; 13 Q–K3! N–N3; 14 N–K5! Gligorić).

(*h*) *Archives* line, with a somewhat better position for White.

(*i*) 11 N×B! RP×N; 12 Q–B2! is strong. Borisenko.

(*j*) Romanovski prefers 11 . . . Q–R4; 12 N–R2, N–N3; 13 B–K2, KR–Q1!

(*k*) 16 P×N, N×P; 17 Q–N3, B×N ∓ . *Comments.*

1 P–Q4, P–Q4; 2 P–QB4, P–QB3; 3 N–KB3, N–B3; 4 N–B3, P × P

	36	37	38	39	40
5	(P–QR4)				
	(B–B4)		P–K3	N–R3?! (*k*)	
6	N–K5 (*a*) (Krause Attack)		P–K4!	P–K4	P–K3 (*m*)
	P–K3 (*b*)		B–N5	B–N5	B–N5
7	P–B3 (*c*)		P–K5	B × P	B × P
	B–QN5		N–K5 (*i*)	P–K3	P–K3
8	B–N5	P–K4 (*f*)	Q–B2	B–K3	O–O
	P–KR3!	B × P	Q–Q4	B–K2	N–N5
9	B × N (*d*)	P × B	B–K2	O–O	Q–K2
	P × B	N × P	P–QB4	O–O	B–K2
10	N × P/4	B–Q2 (*g*)	O–O	R–B1 (*l*)	R–Q1
	P–QB4	Q × P	N × N	N–N5	O–O
11	P × P	N × N	P × N	Q–K2	P–R5
	Q × Q†	Q × N†	P × P	P–KR3	Q–B1
12	R × Q	Q–K2	P × P	KR–Q1	P–K4
	B–B7 (*e*)	B × B† (*h*)	P–B6 (*j*)	Q–R4 =	P–B4 (*n*)

(*a*) (A) 6 N–R4, B–B1! 7 N–B3! B–B4 would force an early draw (hardly acceptable under present tournament rules), as 8 N–R4, B–B1; 9 P–K3, P–K4 (or rather 6 N–R4, B–B1; 7 P–K3, P–K4) is better for Black, White would have to play 8 N–K5 at this stage, and thus might as well choose N–K5 on the 6th move. (B) P–K3, P–K3; 7 B × P, B–QN5; 8 O–O, O–O; 9 N–R4, B–N5 = . Botvinnik–Smyslov, match 1954.

(*b*) 6 . . . QN–Q2; 7 N × P/4, Q–B2; 8 P–KN3, P–K4; 9 P × P, N × P; 10 B–B4, KN–Q2; 11 B–N2, P–B3; 12 O–O, R–Q1; 13 Q–B1, B–K3; 14 N–K4 ± . Euwe–Alekhin, match 1937.

(*c*) 7 B–N5, B–QN5! 8 N × P/4 (8 P–B3 see column), 8 . . . Q–Q4; 9 Q–N3, N–R3; 10 O–O–O maintains the balance. *Comments.*

(*d*) 9 B–R4, P–B4; 10 P × P, Q–Q4; 11 Q × Q, N × Q; 12 O–O–O, P–KN4?! 13 N × N, P × N; 14 B–B2, B–K3; 15 P–R4 ± . *Comments.*

(*e*) 13 R–QB1, B–N6! = . *P/E.*

(*f*) Black holds his own against 8 N × P/4, O–O; 9 B–N5, P–KR3; 10 B–R4, P–B4; 11 P × P, Q × Q†, 12 R × Q, B–B7; 13 R–B1, B–R2! 14 N–Q6, P–QN3 = . *Comments.*

(*g*) 10 Q–B3, Q × P; 11 Q × P†, K–Q1; 12 B–N5†, N × B! 13 Q × KNP, B × N†; 14 P × B, Q × P†; 15 K–K2, Q–B7†; 16 K–K1, draw. *Comments.*

(*h*) 13 K × B, Q–Q4†; 14 K–B2, N–Q2; 15 N × P/4! O–O–O; 16 Q–K3, P–QB4 = . *Comments.*

(*i*) 7 . . . N–Q4; 8 B–Q2, B × N! 9 P × B, P–QN4; 10 N–N5, P–B3; 11 P × BP, N × KBP; 12 B–K2, P–QR3; 13 B–B3, with a strong attack. Alekhin–Bogolyubov, match 1929.

(*j*) 13 B–Q2, N–B3; 14 B × P, B × B; 15 Q × B, O–O; 16 P–R5 ± . Alekhin.

(*k*) Something old, yet something new originates from 5 . . . B–N5; (A) 6 P–K3, P–K3; 7 B × P, QN–Q2; 8 P–R3, B–R4; 9 Q–K2, B–QN5; 10 O–O, Q–K2; 11 P–K4, P–K4; 12 P–Q5, P–R4; 13 R–Q1, O–O; 14 P–N4, B–N3; 15 N–R4, P × P; 16 N × B, BP × N; 17 B × P†, K–R1; 18 B × P, QR–N1; 19 B–Q5, N–B4; 20 B–N5, P–R3; 21 B–R4, N–K3 = . Hort–Bronstein, Petropolis 1973. (B) 6 N–K5, B–R4; 7 P–B3, KN–Q2; 8 N × P/B4, P–K4; 9 N × P, N × N; 10 P × N, Q × Q†; 11 K × Q, N–R3; 12 P–K4, O–O–O†; 13 K–B2, N–N5†; 14 K–N3, P–B3; 15 P–K6! ± . Dzhindzhikhashvili–Podgayets, USSR Chp. 1973.

(*l*) 10 P–R3, B–R4; 11 P–KN4, B–N3; 12 N–K5, N–N5; 13 R–B1, P–B4! = . Bronstein–Smyslov, Moscow 1961 and *Comments* in the column.

(*m*) (A) 6 N–K5, N–KN5! 7 N × P/4, P–K4! 8 N × P, N × N; 9 P × N, Q × Q†; 10 N × Q, N–N5; 11 N–K3, B–QB4; 12 B–Q2, B–K3 = . Vladimirov–Shamkovich, USSR Chp. 1964. (B)

6 P-KN3! N-QN5; 7 B-N2, P-QR4; 8 O-O, P-KN3; 9 N-K5, B-K3; 10 P-K4, B-N2; 11 P-B4, O-O∞, with an involved "Catalonian" character. Balcerowski–Grabczewski, Poland 1971.

(n) 13 P-K5, KN-Q4 = . Uhlmann–Teschner, Stockholm 1962.

1 P–Q4, P–Q4; 2 P–QB4, P–QB3; 3 N–KB3, N–B3

	41	42	43	44	45
4	(N–B3)		P × P ⎱	Exchange	P–K3 (*l*)
	(P × P)	Alekhin's Variation	P × P (*e*) ⎰	Variation	B–B4
5	P–K4	P–K3	N–B3		P × P (*m*)
	P–QN4	P–QN4	N–B3		P × P!
6	P–K5	P–QR4	B–B4		Q–N3
	N–Q4	P–N5	B–B4	P–K3 (*i*)	Q–B1
7	P–QR4	N–R2 (*b*)	P–K3	P–K3	N–R3
	P–K3	P–K3	P–K3 (*f*)	N–KR4 (*j*)	P–K3
8	P × P	B × P	B–QN5 (*g*)	B–KN5	B–Q2
	N × N	B–N2 (*c*)	B–QN5	Q–N3	N–B3
9	P × N	O–O	N–K5	P–QR3	R–B1
	P × P	B–K2	Q–R4	P–KR3	N–Q2!
10	N–N5	Q–K2	B × N†	B–R4	B–N5
	B–N2	O–O	P × B	P–N4	B–K2
11	Q–R5	R–Q1	O–O	B–N3	Q–R4
	P–N3 (*a*)	P–QR4 (*d*)	B × N (*h*)	N × B (*k*)	O–O (*n*)

(*a*) 12 Q–N4, B–K2; 13 B–K2, N–Q2; 14 B–B3, Q–B2! (14 . . . Q–B1; 15 P–KR4! ±); 15 N–K4, N–N3; 16 B–R6, is about even. 5 P–K4 is Geller's move.

(*b*) 7 N–QN1, (A) 7 . . . B–R3! 8 Q–B2, P–K3; 9 B × P, B × B; 10 Q × B, Q–Q4; 11 QN–Q2, QN–Q2; 12 Q–K2, N–K5; 13 N × N, Q × N; 14 O–O, B–K2; 15 B–Q2, O–O; 16 KR–B1, P–QB4! 17 Q–N5, KR–N1! 18 Q × N, R–N2; 19 N–N5, B × N; 20 Q–Q6, P × P; 21 R–B4, P–K4 = . *Comments.* (B) 7 . . . P–K3; 8 B × P, P–QR4; 9 O–O, B–K2 = . Flohr.

(*c*) Also adequate are (A) 8 . . . QN–Q2; 9 O–O, B–N2; or 9 . . . B–Q3; and (B) 8 . . . P–QR4; 9 O–O, QN–Q2; 10 B–Q2, B–K2; 11 Q–K2, O–O = .

(*d*) 12 B–Q2, QN–Q2; 13 N–B1, P–B4; 14 N–N3, Q–N3; 15 B–K1, KR–Q1 = . Reshevsky–Smyslov, USA *v.* USSR 1945. The line is similar to the Queen's Gambit Accepted.

(*e*) 4 . . . N × P; 5 P–K4, N–N3; 6 P–KR3, P–N3; 7 B–K2 ± .

(*f*) Less satisfactory is (A) 7 . . . Q–N3; 8 P–QR3! Q × NP; 9 N–QR4, Q–B7; 10 Q × Q, B × Q; 11 N–B5 ± . Müller. Playable is (B) 7 . . . P–QR3; 8 N–K5, R–B1; 9 P–KN4, B–Q2; 10 B–N2, P–K3; 11 O–O, P–R3; 12 B–N3, B–K2! 13 P–B4, N × N! 14 BP × N, N–R2 = . *Comments.*

(*g*) Or 8 Q–N3, B–QN5; 9 B–QN5, Q–K2; 10 P–QR3, B × N†; 11 Q × B, O–O = .

(*h*) 12 P × B, Q × BP = . Botvinnik–Tal, match 1961.

(*i*) (A) 6 . . . P–KN3; see Grünfeld Defence. (B) 6 . . . Q–R4; 7 P–K3, B–B4; 8 Q–N3, Q–N5! = is solid.

(*j*) (A) 7 . . . B–K2; 8 B–Q3, O–O; 9 P–KR3, B–Q2; 10 O–O, Q–N3! 11 Q–K2, KR–B1; 12 QR–B1, B–K1 = . Botvinnik–Smyslov, USSR Chp. 1952. Also (B) 7 . . . B–Q3; 8 B–N3, O–O; 9 B–Q3, P–QR3! 10 R–QB1, Q–K2! = . *Comments.*

(*k*) 12 RP × N, B–N2 = . Petrosian–Botvinnik, USSR 1962.

(*l*) (A) 4 P–KN3, see Réti or Queen's Catalan Opening. (B) 4 Q–B2, P–KN3! (C) 4 Q–N3, P–K3; or also 4 . . . P–KN3.

(*m*) Tame is 5 B–Q3, P–K3; 6 N–B3, B × B; 7 Q × B, B–N5; 8 O–O, O–O; 9 B–Q2, N–R3!.

(*n*) 12 B × N, P × B; 13 Q × BP, Q × Q; 14 R × Q, QR–N1; 15 B–B1, B × N; 16 P × B, KR–B1 = . *Comments.*

Catalan Opening

(A) Queen's Catalan
(1 P–Q4, P–Q4; 2 P–QB4, P–K3;
3 P–KN3)

(B) Indian Catalan
(1 P–Q4, N–KB3; 2 P–QB4, P–K3;
3 P–KN3)

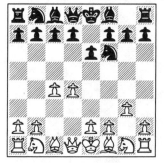

The Catalan opening is a hyper-positional approach towards obtaining an advantage by the early fianchetto of White's king's bishop. White hopes to exert consistent pressure on Black's centre and the diagonal without otherwise compromising his own positional structure.

The Catalan combines features of the Queen's Gambit and the Réti opening and it may arise also from:

(c) 1 N–KB3, P–Q4; 2 P–QB4, P–K3; 3 P–KN3, N–KB3; 4 P–Q4.

(d) 1 P–QB4, N–KB3; 2 P–Q4, P–K3; 3 P–KN3, P–Q4.

(e) 1 P–Q4, N–KB3; 2 P–QB4, P–K3; 3 P–KN3, P–Q4.

The variations where Black omits 3 . . . P–Q4 are found in section (B) which thus provides a link between the Queen's Gambit and its Indian adjunct.

The Neo–Catalan system, where White omits an early P–Q4, is still classified under the Réti opening, as the delayed pawn push results in a different strategy.

THE QUEEN'S CATALAN with 4 N–KB3 (cols. 1–10) generally runs to equality. The most White can get is pressure along the diagonal, often striking at airy nothing. But considering the Catalan's tendency to manoeuvre closely, and also due to a revival of the Queen's Indian, this line has recently regained some favour.

THE ACCELERATED CATALAN (cols. 11–13) is distinguished by 4 B–N2, a slight but often significant deviation which aims at keeping the long diagonal open as long as possible before developing with N–KB3. The pressure is, however, so slight and possibilities have been so much explored that this system has lost most of its popularity. The same applies to cols. 14–16.

THE ANTI-CATALAN (cols. 17–20) summarizes various replies to White's fianchetto, sometimes more active but also riskier.

THE INDIAN CATALAN (cols. 21–25) is a sequence of moves more in line with modern strategy and, as shown under paragraph (E), will lead into the main lines of the Queen's Catalan after 3 . . . P–Q4, but the given lines deal with the replies different from the "orthodox" treatment. Except for the hazardous col. 21, Black generally achieves full satisfaction with a variety of other defences.

1 P-Q4, P-Q4; 2 P-QB4, P-K3; 3 P-KN3, N-KB3; 4 N-KB3, B-K2; 5 B-N2, O-O
(*a*); 6 O-O, QN-Q2

	1	2	3	4	5
7	N-B3		Q-B2 (*g*)		
	P-B3	P × P	P-QN3	P-B3	
8	P-N3 (*b*)	P-K4 (*d*)	P × P	P-N3	QN-Q2 (*l*)
	P-QN3	P-B3	N × P	P-QN3 (*j*)	P-QN3
9	B-N2	P-QR4	N-B3	B-N2	P-K4
	B-N2	P-QR4 (*e*)	B-N2	B-N2	B-N2!
10	Q-B2	Q-K2	N × N	N-B3	P-N3
	R-B1	N-N3	B × N!? (*h*)	R-B1	R-B1
11	QR-Q1	R-Q1	P-K4	QR-Q1	R-Q1
	Q-B2	B-N5	B-N2	P-QN4!	Q-B2
12	P-K4	N-K5	R-Q1	P-B5	B-N2
	P × KP	Q-K2	P-QB4!	P-N5	KR-Q1
13	N × P	B-K3	P-Q5	N-N1	QR-B1
	N × N (*c*)	B-Q2 (*f*)	P × P (*i*)	N-K5 (*k*)	Q-N1 (*m*)

(*a*) 5 . . . P-B4; 6 P × QP, KP × P; 7 N-B3, N-B3; 8 O-O, O-O; see Queen's Gambit, Tarrasch Defence, cols. 56–60.

(*b*) (A) 8 Q-B2, P × P; 9 R-Q1, N-Q4; 10 P-QR3, P-QN4; 11 P-K4, N × N; 12 P × N, B-N2 ⤤. (B) 8 Q-Q3, P-QN3; (1) 9 P × P, BP × P; 10 B-B4, P-QR3; 11 P-K4, P × P; 12 N × P, B-N2; 13 KN-N5, N × N; 14 N × N, N-B4; 15 N × N, B × B; 16 K × B, P × N; 17 KR-Q1, Q-N3; draw. Szabó–Eliskases, Buenos Aires 1960 (2) 9 P-K4, B-R3; 10 P-N3, R-B1; 11 B-B4, RK1! 12 KR-Q1, N-B1; 13 P-QR4, B-N5; 14 P-K5, N/3-Q2; 15 B-Q2, N-N1; 16 Q-B2! B-N2, ∞. Korchnoi-Petrosian 1975.

(*c*) 14 Q × N, P-QB4; 15 P-Q5, B-B3; 16 Q-B2, P × P! 17 P × P, B × B; 18 Q × B, QR-Q1 = . Kramer–Fichtl, Varna Olympics 1962.

(*d*) Upon 8 Q-B2 Black may defend with either (1) 8 . . . P-B4; 9 R-Q1, Q-N3; 10 P × P, Q × BP; 11 N-KN5, P-KR3; 12 B-K3, Q-B4; 13 KN-K4, N-Q4; 14 B-Q4, R-Q1 = ; or (2) 8 . . . P-B3; 9 P-K4, P-QN4; 10 B-B4, P-N5; 11 N-K2, P-QR4; 12 Q × P, P-B4; 13 KR-Q1, Q-N3; 14 Q-B2, B-N2 = . Tolush–Goldenov, USSR 1947.

(*e*) 9 . . . Q-R4 or 9 . . . P-QN3 have also been employed.

(*f*) 14 N × P/4, N × N; 15 Q × N (Botvinnik–Lasker, Nottingham 1936), P-K4; 16 P × P, N-N5 = .

(*g*) 7 QN-Q2, P-QN3; 8 P-N3, B-N2; 9 B-N2, P-B4; 10 P-K3, R-B1; 11 R-B1, R-B2; 12 Q-K2, Q-R1; 13 KR-K1, R/1-B1; 14 P × QP, B × P; 15 P-K4, B-N2; 16 P-Q5, P × P; 17 P × P (Bronstein–Keene, Teeside 1975), N × P; 18 N-K4, R-B1 = . R. Byrne.

(*h*) Another possibility (which may be improved upon) is 10 . . . P × N; 11 R-Q1, B-Q3 (11 . . . P-QB4, 12 P × P!, P × P; 13 N-K1, N-B3; 14 P-N3 ±); 12 B-N5, P-KB3; 13 B-B4, B × B; 14 P × B, R-B2; 15 P-N4, N-B1; 16 P-K3, Q-Q3; 17 P-N5, P-QR4; 18 P-KR4, K-R1; 19 QR-B1, R-K1; 29 B-R3, P-N3; 21 R-Q3, R-N2; 22 R-B3, R/1-K2; 23 K-B1, Q-Q1; 24 K-K2, P-R3; 25 R-KN1, Q-Q3; 26 K-Q2, Q-Q1; 27 R-KN3, R-N1; 28 N-R2, Q-Q3; 29 P-R3, R/1-N2; 30 K-B1, R/K2-B2; 31 K-N2, Q-Q1; 32 N-B3, Q-K1; 33 B-B1, R-K2; 34 B-Q3, K-N1; 35 Q-N3, K-R1; 36 R-B1, P-B3; 37 K-R2, P × P; 38 B × QNP, Q-Q1; 39 B-Q3, R-N1; 40 R-QN1, R-K3; 41 P-B5, P × P; 42 R × R↑, K × R; 43 B × P, R-Q3; 44 P-K4, P-R5; 45 Q-K3, P × P; 46 Q × RP, K-B2; 47 R-KN1, B-Q4↑; 48 K-N2, K-K1; 49 R-N7, B-B2; 50 B × P, Q-Q2; 51 B-Q3, Q-B3; 52 Q-K3↑, R-K3; 53 Q-B4, N-Q2; 54 Q-B5, R-K2; 55 B-N5, Q-Q3; 56 R-R7, K-Q1; 57 R-R8↑, resigns. Kavalek–Medina, Montilla 1975.

(*i*) 14 P × P, B-KB3; 15 P-KR4, P-KR3 = . Geller–Medina, Beverwijk 1965.

(*j*) Also 8 . . . P-QN4; 9 QN-Q2, NP × P; 10 P × P, B-R3; 11 B-N2, R-N1; 12 QR-N1, Q-R4; 13 B-B3, B-N5 = . Geller–Larsen, match 1966.

(*k*) 14 N–K1, P–B4; 15 N–Q3, P–QR4; 16 N–B4, R–B3; 17 P–B3, N–N4 = . Geller–Bisguier, Bled 1961.

(*l*) 8 R–Q1, N–K5! 9 QN–Q2, P–KB4; with a "Dutch" formation.

(*m*) 14 Q–N1, P–QR4; 15 N–K5, Q–R1 = . Benko–Pachman, Budapest 1948.

1 P–Q4, P–Q4; 2 P–QB4, P–K3; 3 P–KN3, N–KB3; 4 N–KB3

	6	7	8	9	10
	(B–K2)......	P–B4	P×P		
5	(B–N2)	P×QP (c)	B–N2		Q–R4†
	(O–O)	N×P	P–B4	P–QN4! (h)	QN–Q2
6	(O–O)	B–N2	O–O (e)	P–QR4	B–N2
	P–B3 (a)	P×P	N–B3 (f)	P–B3	P–QR3 (i)
7	N–B3	O–O	Q–R4	O–O	Q×BP (j)
	P–QN3	B–B4	N–Q2	B–N2	P–B4
8	N–K5	N×P	P×P!	N–K5	P×P
	P–QR4 (b)	O–O	B×P	Q–B1	B×P
9	Q–B2	P–QR3	Q×BP	P–N3	O–O (k)
	B–R3	N–QB3	O–O	BP×P	P–QN4
10	R–Q1	N×N	N–B3	Q×P	Q–KR4
	P–QN4 =	P×N	P–QR3	P–N5	B–N2
11		P–QN4	N–K4	P–R5	QN–Q2
		B–K2 (d)	B–K2 (g)	KN–Q2∞	B–K2 (l)

(a) Less promising are (A) 6 . . . P–QN3; 7 P×P! (1) 7 . . . P×P; 8 N–B3, B–N2; 9 B–N5! or (2) 7 . . . N×P; 8 P–K4, N–KB3; 9 N–B3, B–N2; 10 N–K5, P–B4; 11 P–Q5! ± . Drawish is (B) 6 . . . P×P; (1) 7 N–K5, N–B3; 8 B×N, P×B; 9 N×P/B6, Q–K1; 10 N×B†, Q×N; 11 Q–R4, P–B4; 12 Q×BP, P×P; 13 Q×QP, P–K4; 14 Q–KR4, R–N1; 15 B–N5, R×P; 16 N–B3, Q–K3; 17 B×N, Q×B; 18 Q×Q, P×Q; 19 QR–N1, R×R; 20 R×R, B–K3; 21 P–B3, R–B1; 22 R–QB1, R–N1; 23 R–B2, R–QB1; 24 K–B2, B×P; 25 R×B, drawn. Korchnoi–Karpov, 15th match game 1978 (with transposition). Or (2) 7 Q–B2, P–QR3; 8 P–QR4 (or 8 Q×P, P–QN4; 9 Q–B2, B–N2; 10 B–B4, N–Q4; 11 N–B3, N×B; 12 P×N, N–Q2; 13 KR–Q1, Q–B1; 14 N–K4, P–QB4 =). N–B3! 9 Q×P, Q–Q4; 10 QN–Q2, R–Q1; 11 P–K3, Q–KR4; 12 P–K4, B–Q2; 13 P–N3 (Korchnoi–Tal, USSR 1968), QR–B1 = . (3) 7 Q–R4 see col. 15. Or (c) 6 . . . P–B4; 7 P×QP, N×P; 8 P–K4! (8 N–B3? N–QB3; 9 N×N, P×N; 10 P×P, B×P =), N–N3; 9 N–B3, P×P; 10 N×P, P×N; 11 N×N, P×N; 12 Q–B2, B–R3; 13 R–Q1, Q–B2; 14 P–N3 ± . Compare also Queen's Gambit, Tarrasch Defence. (D) 6 . . . N–B3; 7 P×P, P×P; 8 B–N5, N–K5 = is playable.

(b) 8 . . . B–N2; 9 P–K4, P×BP; 10 N×P/4, B–R3; 11 P–N3, P–QN4; 12 N–K3 ± .

(c) 5 B–N2, P×QP; 6 N×P, see Indian Catalan.

(d) 12 B–N2, B–B3; 13 Q–B2, B×B; 14 Q×B, P–QR4 = . Evans–Poschel, US Jr. Chp. 1947.

(e) If 6 Q–R4†, B–Q2! 7 Q×BP, B–B3; 8 P×P, QN–Q2.

(f) 6 . . . QN–Q2; (A) 7 N–K5, N×N; 8 P×N, Q×Q; 9 R×Q, N–Q4; 10 N–B3, N×N; 11 P×N, B–K2 = . *Comments.* (B) 7 N–R3!? N–N3; 8 N×P, N×N; 9 Q–R4†, B–Q2; 10 Q×N. (Furman–Calvo, Madrid 1974), 10 . . . P–QN4; 11 Q–B2, R–B1∞ . *Comments.*

(g) 12 B–K3, N–N3; 13 Q–N3, N–Q4; 14 KR–Q1, Q–B2 = . O'Kelly–Euwe, New York 1951.

(h) (A) 5 . . . P–QR3; (1) 6 P–QR4, P–B4; 7 O–O, N–B3; 8 P×P! Q×Q; 9 R×Q, B×P; 10 QN–Q2 ± . (2) 6 O–O, P–QN4; 7 N–K5, N–Q4 (7 . . . R–R2, P–QR4!); 8 N–QB3, P–QB3 (8 . . . B–N2!); 9 N×N, KP×N! 10 P–K4, B–K3; 11 P–QR4, P–N5; 12 P×P, B×P; 13 Q–N4, P–KR4? 14 B×B, P×B (14 . . . P×Q; 15 B×KBP†, K–K2; 16 B–N5† ±); 15 Q–B5, QR–R2; 16 R–K1, R–K2; 17 B–N5, P–N3; 18 B×R, P×Q; 19 B×Q K×B; 20 N×P†, resigns. Sosonko–Hübner, Tilburg, 1980. A game wherein some enterprising innovations lend to rapid disaster even in an innocuously slow, closed opening. (B) 5 . . . P–B4; 6 O–O (for 6 Q–R4 see col. 10), N–B3; 7 Q–R4, B–Q2! (1) 8 P×P, B×P; 9 Q×BP, Q–K2; 10 N–B3, B–N3; 11 P–K4, R–QB1; 12 Q–K2, P–KR3; 13 B–K3, B×B; 14 Q×B, O–O; 15 P–K5,

N–Q4; 16 N × N, P × N; 17 QR–Q1, P–Q5 = . Schmidt–Pomar, Skopje Olympics 1972. (2) 8 Q × BP, P × P; 9 N × P, R–B1; 10 N–QB3, N × N; 11 Q × N, B–B4 = . The column is Krogius–Furman, Moscow 1967.

(*i*) (A) 6 . . . P–B3; 7 Q × P/4, B–Q3; 8 N–B3, O–O; 9 O–O, P–K4 = . *Comments.* (B) 6 . . . P–QN3; 7 Q × BP, B–N2; 8 O–O, P–B4; 9 R–Q1, P–QR3; 10 P × P, B × P; 11 P–QN4, B–K2; 12 B–N2, P–QN4; 13 Q–Q4, R–QB1; 14 QN–Q2, O–O with more counter-action on the queen-side than in the column. Karpov–Korchnoi, 22nd match game 1974.

(*j*) 7 N–B3, B–K2; 8 N–K5, R–QN1; 9 N × N, B × N; 10 Q × BP, P–QN4 = . *Comments.*

(*k*) 9 Q–KR4, O–O; 10 O–O, N–Q4; 11 Q × Q, R × Q; 12 QN–Q2, P–QN4; 13 N–N3, B–N3; 14 B–N5, P–B3 (14 . . . R–K1; 15 B–Q2 ±); 15 B–Q2, N–B4 = . Analysis by Neikirkh and Tsvetkov.

(*l*) 12 N–N3, R–QB1; 13 Q–Q4, O–O; 14 B–Q2, N–B4 = . Keres–Korchnoi, Curaçao 1962.

1 P–Q4, P–Q4; 2 P–QB4, P–K3; 3 P–KN3, N–KB3

	11	12	13	14	15
4	B–N2 ⎱ (Accelerated	. . . .		N–QB3	
	P×P ⎰ Catalan)			P×P	B–K2
5	Q–R4†			Q–R4†	B–N2
	QN–Q2	B–Q2		N–B3!	O–O
6	N–Q2! (*a*)	Q×BP		B–N2	N–B3
	P–B3 (*b*)	B–B3 (*c*)		B–Q2	P×P
7	Q×BP/4	N–KB3 (*d*)		Q×BP	Q–R4
	P–K4	B–Q4	QN–Q2	N–QN5!	P–QR3
8	KN–B3	Q–Q3	N–B3	Q–N3	Q×BP
	N–N3	P–B4!	N–N3	P–B4	P–QN4
9	Q–Q3	N–B3	Q–Q3	N–B3	Q–Q3
	P×P	B–B3	B–N5	P×P	B–N2 = (*h*)
10	N×P	O–O	O–O	N×P	
	B–K2	QN–Q2	O–O	P–K4	
11	O–O	R–Q1	R–Q1	N–B3	
	O–O =	Q–N3! (*e*)	P–KR3 (*f*)	B–K3 = (*g*)	

(*a*) 6 N–KB3, P–QR3; 7 N–B3, (A) 7 . . . R–QN1; 8 Q×BP, P–QN4 = . Petrosian–Panno, Los Angeles 1963. (B) 7 . . . P–B4; 8 O–O, R–QN1; 9 P×P, B×P = .

(*b*) (A) 6 . . . P–QR3; 7 N×P, P–QN4; 8 Q–B2, N–Q4; 9 N–K3! (B) 6 . . . P–B4; 7 N×P, P×P (7 . . . P–QR3; 8 B–Q2); 8 B–B4, B–K2; 9 N–Q6†, K–B1; 10 N–B3, Q–N3; 11 N–B4! ± . The column is *Comments*.

(*c*) Unrefuted is 6 . . . N–B3; 7 N–KB3, N–QR4; 8 Q–Q3, P–B4; 9 O–O (A) 9 . . . N–B3; 10 P×P, B×P = . Kashdan–Horowitz, New York 1949–50. Not so good is (B) 9 . . . B–K2; 10 N–QB3, R–QB1; 11 P×P, B×P; 12 N–K5 ± .

(*d*) 7 P–B3, QN–Q2; 8 P–K4, P–K4; 9 P–Q5, N–N3; 10 Q–B3, B–N4; 11 Q×P†. B–K2 = .

(*e*) 12 P–K4, P×P; 13 N×P, B–B4; 14 N×B, B×P†; 15 K–B1, P×N; 16 N–R4, Q–R4; 17 K×B, Q×N; 18 Q–Q6, with counterplay for the pawn. Müller–Ratzek, Vienna 1951. Compare with col. 18.

(*f*) 12 B–Q2, Q–K2; 13 P–QR3, B×QN; 14 Q×B, KR–Q1 = . Smyslov–Keres, USSR Chp. 1948.

(*g*) 12 Q–R4†, B–Q2 = . "Keres," according to Neishtadt. Up to move 7, also compare note (*c*).

(*h*) Stoltz–Vidmar, Groningen 1946. This sequence differs from col. 6, note (*a*–B).

1 P-Q4, P-Q4; 2 P-QB4, P-K3; 3 P-KN3

	16	17	18	19	20
			Anti-Catalan		
	(N–KB3)	.... P–QB4	...... P × P	.... B–N5†	
4	N–Q2	P × QP	Q–R4†	B–Q2	
	P–B4 (a)	KP × P	B–Q2	B × B†	B–K2 (g)
5	QP × P	N–KB3	Q × BP	Q × B (f)	B–N2
	B × P	N–QB3 (c)	P–QB4	N–KB3	N–KB3
6	B–N2	B–N2	P × P	N–KB3	N–KB3
	N–B3	N–B3	B–B3	O–O	O–O
7	KN–B3	O–O	N–KB3	B–N2	Q–N3
	O–O! (b)	B–K2	N–Q2	Q–K2	P–QN3
8	O–O	P × P	B–K3	O–O	P × P
	P–QR4	B × P	KN–B3	N–B3	P × P
9	P × P	QN–Q2	B–N2	R–B1 ±	N–B3
	P × P	O–O	Q–B2		B–N2
10	N–N3	N–N3	O–O		O–O ± (h)
	B–N3 =	B–N3	B–Q4		
11		QN–Q4	Q–QR4		
		R–K1 (d)	B × BP (e)		

(a) 4 . . . N–K5; 5 N–KB3, P–KB4! 6 B–N2, B–K2; and possibly . . . P–QN3, is a solid answer.

(b) 7 . . . P–QN3; 8 O–O, B–N2; 9 P–QR3, O–O; 10 P–QN4, B–K2; 11 B–N2, R–B1; 12 Q–N1! ± . Smyslov. The column is Korchnoi–Matanović, Belgrade 1964.

(c) The actual course was 1 P–Q4, P–Q4; 2 P–QB4, P–K3; 3 N–KB3, P–QB4; 4 P × QP, KP × P; 5 P–KN3, N–QB3.

(d) 12 P–N3, N × N; 13 N × N, B × N; 14 Q × B, R × P = . Mikenas–Aronin, USSR Chp. 1963. Compare Tarrasch Defence, Col. 51.

(e) 12 B × B, Q × B; 13 N–B3, B–B3 = . Neishtadt. Compare with col. 13.

(f) 5 N × B, N–KB3; 6 K–NB3, O–O; 7 B–N2, QN–Q2; 8 O–O, R–K1 = .

(g) 4 . . . Q–K2; 5 B–N2, B × B†? 6 Q × B, N–KB3; 7 N–KB3, O–O; 8 O–O, N–B3; 9 R–B1! ± . Bondarevski–Ilivitski, USSR Chp. 1948. By transposition, this is identical with column 19. See also note (h).

(h) The more usual sequence in cols. 19 and 20 is via 1 P–Q4, N–KB3; 2 P–QB4, P–K3; 3 P–KN3, B–N5†, etc. 4 N–B3 will then transpose into the Nimzo-Indian Defence, and . . . P–Q4 back into col. 19.

1 P–Q4, N–KB3; 2 P–QB4, P–K3; 3 P–KN3

	21	22	23	24	25
	P–K4!?	P–B4		B–N5†	
4	N–KB3 (a)	N–KB3 (b)		N–Q2	B–Q2 (k)
	P×P	P×P (c)		P–B4 (h)	B×B† (l)
5	N×P	N×P		P×P! (i)	Q×B (m)
	P–Q4	P–Q4	N–B3 (e)	B×P	N–K5 (n)
6	B–N2	B–N2	B–N2	B–N2	Q–B2
	P×P	P–K4!	Q–N3 (f)	N–B3	P–KB4
7	Q–R4†	N–KB3 (d)	N–B2!	KN–B3	P–B3
	P–B3	P–Q5	B–B4	P–QN3	N–KB3
8	Q×P/4	O–O	P–K3	O–O	P–K4
	B–K2	N–B3	O–O	B–N2	P×P
9	O–O	P–K3	N–B3	P–QR3	P×P
	O–O	B–K2	Q–R3	O–O	P–K4
10	R–Q1 ±	P×P	Q–K2	P–QN4	
		P×P	R–Q1 (g)	B–K2 (j)	

(a) Also 4 B–N2, P×P; 5 Q×P, N–B3; 6 Q–Q1, B–N5†; 7 N–Q2 ± .

(b) For 4 P–Q5, P×P! 5 P×P, P–Q3; 6 B–N2, P–KN3; 7 N–QB3, see Benoni Defence, col. 1.

(c) For . . . P–Q4 see Queen's (or Anti-) Catalan.

(d) 7 N–B2, P–Q5; 8 O–O, N–B3; 9 N–Q2, B–KN5; 10 N–B3, P–QR4; 11 B–N5, B–QB4 = . Petrosian–Keres, Zürich 1953. The column is Saigin–Tal, USSR 1954.

(e) Good is also 5 . . . Q–B2! 6 N–QB3 (6 B–N2, B–N5†), Q×P; 7 P–K4, Q–N5; 8 P–QR3, Q–N3; 9 P–K5, N–B3 = .

(f) 6 . . . B–N5†; 7 N–B3 (also 7 B–Q2, B×B; 8 Q×B, Q–N3; 9 N–N3, Q–N5; 10 N–R3, O–O∞), Q–N3; 8 P–K3, B×N† = . *Comments.*

(g) 11 P–QR3, P–Q4; 12 P–QN4, P–Q5; 13 N–K4 ± . Neishtadt.

(h) Safe are (A) 4 . . . O–O; 5 P–QR3, B–K2 = ; or (B) 4 . . . N–K5; 5 N–B3, P–KB4; 6 B–N2, O–O; or possibly . . . P–QN3; all according to taste.

(i) (A) 5 P–QR3, B×N†; 6 Q×B, P×P; 7 N–KB3, N–B3; 8 N×P, N–QR4! 9 P–N3, P–Q4 ∓ . (B) 5 N–KB3, P×P; 6 P–QR3, B–K2; 7 N×P, N–B3; 8 N×N, NP×N; 9 B–N2, P–Q4 = .

(j) 11 B–N2, R–B1; 12 Q–N1, with initiative. Smyslov–Petrosian, Moscow 1967.

(k) (A) For 4 N–B3 see Nimzo-Indian Defence. (B) Also compare with the Bogo-Indian Defence.

(l) 4 . . . Q–K2; 5 B–N2, N–B3! 6 N–KB3, B×B; 7 QN×B, O–O; 8 O–O, P–Q3; 9 P–K4, P–K4 = . Compare with the Bogo-Indian Defence.

(m) 5 N×B, (A) 5 . . . P–Q3; 6 KN–B3, N–B3; 7 B–N2, O–O; 8 O–O, P–K4; 9 P–Q5, N–K2; 10 P–K4, N–Q2 = . (B) 5 . . . P–QN3; 6 KN–B3, B–N2; 7 B–N2, O–O; 8 O–O, P–B4; 9 R–B1, P–Q3; 10 N–N1, Q–K2; 11 N–B3, N–B3; 12 P–K3, KR–Q1; 13 R–K1, QR–B1; 14 P–N3 = . Hort–Larsen, Montreal, 1979.

(n) 5 . . . P–QN3; 6 N–B3, B–R3; 7 Q–B2 (or 7 P–QN5), P–B4; 8 P–K4, P×P; 9 N×P, O–O; 10 N–QB3, B–N2; 11 O–O–O, P–QR3 (or 11 . . . N–R3!); 12 R–KN1. Belyavski–Razuvayev, U.S.S.R. 1978. For various . . . P–QN3 moves compare also Queen's Indian Defence.

Queen's Pawn Games

(1 P–Q4 . . .)

This is a comprehensive heading for all games which begin with 1 P–Q4 except the Queen's Gambit and Indian Systems, and those which are not substantial enough in content to require a separate section.

Many of the aforementioned complexes are often reached by transposition but this section deals only with lines that flow in unique channels. The first two sections deal with variations after 1 P–Q4, P–Q4 without White's P–QB4.

(A) THE COLLE SYSTEM 1 . . . P–Q4; 2 N–KB3 (cols. 1–3) which bears the name of the Belgian master who scored many brilliant victories with it, begins rather tamely by stifling the queen's bishop with 3 P–K3 but often erupts dangerously against indifferent defence. It is a powerful line for experienced White players against opponents who are unaware of its pitfalls. Although a properly "booked" Black player has nothing to fear, Koltanowski of San Francisco has remained a knowledgeable advocate of the system.

(B) THE STONEWALL SYSTEM, 1 . . . P–Q4; 2 P–K3 (col. 6) is closely related to the Colle System. The column is self-explanatory.

(C) THE FRANCO-INDIAN DEFENCE, 1 . . . P–K3 (col. 7), combines the French and the Nimzo-Indian. It is open to experimentation and appears to be sufficiently elastic, with possible transpositions especially into a type of Benoni as shown in the next section.

(D) THE FRANCO-BENONI SYSTEM, can be reached via col. 7 but not customarily via the Benoni or French proper.

(E) THE KING'S FIANCHETTO VARIATION, 1 . . . P–KN3 (col. 9) turns sooner or later into a Pirć, a Robatsch, or Double Fianchetto, or related defences. THE OWEN DEFENCE (col. 10) is so named after the strong British amateur John Owen who employed this early fianchetto in his match (at odds of pawn and move) against Morphy in 1858 — thus often making it a Fianchetto Attack! A full century later, 1 . . . P–QN3 (just as 1 P–QN3) has frequently been Bent Larsen's favoured son.

The following columns deal with the incidental openings which arise after 1 . . . N–KB3 but do not strictly conform to any of the schematic Indian defences. Any of them might transpose into a King's Indian Defence when followed up with P–QB4 and transpositions must be watched.

(F) THE RICHTER–VERESOV ATTACK (cols. 11–12), the *Ruth Opening*, or *Trompovsky Attack* (col. 13) and the *Torre Attack* (cols. 14–15) are typical for the Queen's Gambit move B–N5 being employed one way or the other in these Indian-like lines. Altogether, Black can hold his own against all these strategies. The *Neo-Indian Attack* (col. 21) also falls into this category.

(G) THE POLISH DEFENCE (col. 16) neglects the centre but has not been refuted and allows for occasional surprise. It can also arise from the Réti system.

(H) THE BLACKMAR (-DIEMER) GAMBIT (cols. 17–18), produces exciting chess. Black can secure at least even chances by declining, but acceptance of the pawn gives him a promising game. Diemer, Gunderam and Müller were the leading connoisseurs of this gambit, pro and con.

(I) THE KEVITZ–TRAJKOVIĆ DEFENCE (cols. 19–20) is a kind of Alekhin's Defence against the queen's pawn, with the same conception of luring White to establish a far-flung centre which may later be undermined. A recent co-champion of this defence is the Russian Lutikov.

(J) THE DÖRY DEFENCE (col. 22), characterized by the unabashed 3 . . . N–K5, used to be adopted by Keres. There is no outright refutation and the variant often becomes a Queen's Indian defence.

(K) THE BLUMENFELD (COUNTER) GAMBIT (cols. 23–5) has by now lost most its tactical novelty and, in col. 25, tends in White's favour.

(L) THE BUDAPEST (COUNTER) GAMBIT (cols. 26–30) is a daring thrust (2 . . . P–K4) which made its tournament début in Esser–Breyer, Budapest 1916. It is tricky and psychological, but unstable against Rubinstein's solid positional 4 B–B4 in reply to 3 . . . N–N5 (col. 26–8). However, a thorough survey by Glasscoe, Staker and Stayert has opened up new vistas in this vitriolic gambit.

The *Fajarowicz Variation* (cols. 29–30) with 3 . . . N–K5 is distinguished by the absence of an immediate threat but contains dormant dangers which are best met in col. 29. The whole complex was well summarized in a pamphlet published in 1972 by *Chess Digest Magazine* (but without the author's name).

1 P–Q4, P–Q4; 2 N–KB3

Colle System

	1	2	3	4	5
	N–KB3				N–QB3
3	P–K3			B–B4 (h)	B–B4 (j)
	P–B4		B–B4 (f)	P–B4	B–N5
4	QN–Q2 (a)		B–Q3	P–K3	P–K3
	N–B3	QN–Q2	P–K3	N–B3	P–K3
5	P–B3	P–B3	B × B	P–B3	B–K2
	P–K3	P–KN3 (d)	P × B	Q–N3	N–B3
6	B–Q3	B–Q3	Q–Q3	Q–B1	N–K5
	B–Q3	B–N2	Q–B1	B–B4	B × B
7	O–O	O–O	P–QN3	P × P	Q × B
	O–O	O–O	N–R3	Q × BP	N × N
8	P × P (b)	P–QN4!	O–O	QN–Q2	B × N
	B × P	P × NP	B–K2	R–B1	P–B3
9	P–K4	P × P	P–B4	N–Q4	O–O
	P–K4 (c)	N–K1 (e)	O–O (g)	N × N (i)	B–K2 (k)

(a) 4 P–QN3, P–K3; 5 B–N2, N–B3; 6 B–Q3, B–Q3; 7 O–O, O–O; 8 P–QR3, Q–K2 (or 8 . . . P–QN3 =); 9 N–K5 R–Q1 = . Zukertort.

(b) 8 Q–K2, N–Q2! 9 P–K4, BP × P; 10 BP × P, N–N5; 11 B–N1, P–QN3 = . *Comments*.

(c) 10 P × P, N × P; 11 N–K4, B–K2; 12 N–N3, P–B4 = . Colle–Euwe, match 1928.

(d) Effective are also (A) 5 . . . Q–B2; 6 B–Q3, P–KN3 = ; or (B) 5 . . . P–K3; 6 B–Q3, B–Q3; 7 O–O, O–O; 8 R–K1, Q–N3; 9 P–QN3, P–K4 = . Fine–Keres, Kemeri 1937.

(e) 10 B–N2, N–Q3; 11 Q–N3, N–N3; 12 P–QR4, B–B4!; 13 B × B, P × B; 14 P–N5, QN–B5 = . Prins–Landau, Zandvoort 1936.

(f) (A) 3 . . . P–KN3; 4 B–Q3 (4 P–B4, B–N2; 5 N–B3, see Grünfeld Defence), B–N2; 5 QN–Q2, O–O; 6 P–QN3, B–B4! 7 B × B, P × B; 8 B–N2, N–K5 = . (B) 3 . . . P–K3; 4 P–QR3! P–B4; 5 P × P, B × P; 6 P–B4. (c) 3 . . . P–B4; 4 P × P, Q–R4†; 5 B–Q2, Q × BP; 6 N–R3. Dünhaupt.

(g) 10 N–B3, P–B3; 11 B–N2, N–K5; 12 KR–B1, R–Q1 = . Alekhin–Euwe, match 1935.

(h) If 3 B–N5, N–K5 (or 3 . . . P–KR3; 4 B–R4, B–B4! = ; or 3 . . . P–B4; 4 P–K3, P–K3; 5 P–B4, Q–R4† =); 4 B–R4, P–QB4; 5 P × P (5 P–B3, Q–N3!), Q–R4† = .

(i) 10 KP × N, Q–N3; 11 P–QR4, P–QR3; 12 P–R5, Q–B3 = . O. Bernstein–H. Steiner, London 1946.

(j) For 3 P–B4 see Kevitz–Trajković Defence and Queen's Gambit cols. 77–78 (Chigorin's Defence).

(k) 10 N–Q2, O–O; 11 B × N, B × B; 12 P–QB4, B–K2 = . DeGreiff–Spasski, Havana 1962.

1 P-Q4

	Stonewall System 6	Franco–Indian 7	Franco–Benoni 8	King's Fianchetto 9	Owen Defence 10
1	(P-Q4)......	P-K3		P-KN3 (k) ...	P-QN3!?
2	P-K3 (a)	P-QB4 (c) ...	P-K4 (g)	N-KB3 (l)	P-K4! (n)
	N-KB3	B-N5† (d)	P-QB4	B-N2 (m)	B-N2
3	B-Q3	N-QB3	P-Q5	P-B3	B-Q3! (o)
	P-B4	P-QB4 (e)	P×P	P-Q3	P-K3
4	P-QB3	P×P	P×P	P-K4	N-KB3
	N-B3 (b)	B×N†	P-Q3	N-Q2	P-QB4
5	P-KB4	P×B	N-KB3 (h)	B-Q3	P-B3!
	B-N5	Q-R4	N-KB3 (i)	P-K4	N-KB3
6	N-B3	N-B3	B-N5†	O-O	O-O
	P-K3	N-KB3	QN-Q2	KN-B3!	N-B3
7	O-O	P-K3	O-O	P-QR4!	QN-Q2 (p)
	B-Q3	O-O	B-K2	P-QR4 =	B-K2
8	Q-K1	N-Q4	P-QR4		R-K1
	O-O	N-K5	O-O		Q-B2
9	N-K5	B-N2	R-K1		P-QR3
	B-B4! =	N×P/4 (f)	R-K1 (j)		P-Q4 (q)

(a) White aims at an inverted Dutch Stonewall. For (A) 2 B-B4, see col. 4. (B) 2 P-KN3, N-KB3; 3 B-N2, B-B4; 4 N-KB3, P-K3; 5 O-O, QN-Q2; 6 P-B4, P-B3; see Réti Opening. (c) 2 P-K4? (Blackmar Gambit), P×P; 3 P-KB3? (for 3 N-QB3 see col. 17) P-K4! 4 QP×P, Q×Q†; 5 K×Q, N-QB3; 6 B-KB4, KN-K2 ∓.

(b) Also 4 ... QN-Q2; 5 P-KB4, P-KN3; 6 N-B3, B-N2; 7 O-O, O-O; 8 N-K5, Q-B2 = . This and the column is *Comments*. Evans suggested 8 B-Q2, followed by B-K1.

(c) 2 N-QB3, P-QB4 (2 ... P-Q4; see French Defence. If 2 ... P-KB4; 3 P-K4!); 3 P-Q5, N-KB3; 4 P-K4, P-Q3; leads into the Benoni and so does 2 P-K4, P-QB4; 3 P-Q5.

(d) (A) 2 ... P-KB4 transposes into the Dutch and avoids the Staunton Gambit but allows the Staunton Gambit Deferred p. 271 (h) (B). (B) 2 ... P-QB4; see Benoni col. 31, with ... N-KB3. Without, see next section (c) 2 ... P-QB4; 3 P-Q5, P×P; 4 P×P, P-Q3; 5 N-KB3, P-KN3; 6 N-B3, B-N2; 7 P-K4, N-K2!? 8 B-N5†, B-Q2 = . (D) 2 ... P-QN3 see note (n).

(e) Again (A) 3 ... P-KB4, reverts to the Dutch, and for (B) 3 ... N-KB3, see Nizmo-Indian. (c) 3 ... B×N†; 4 P×B, P-KB4!

(f) 10 N-N3, Q-B2; 11 N×N, Q×N; 12 P-QR4! with some promise. *Comments.*

(g) (A) 2 N-KB3, P-QB4; 3 P-KN3, P×P; 4 N×P, Q-N3! Pomar–Larsen, Mallorca 1969. (B) 2 P-KN3, P-QB4; 3 N-KB3, Q-R4; 4 QN-Q2, P×P = . The column can arise from the French Defence, after 1 P-K4, P-K3; 2 P-Q4, P-QB4, etc.

(h) This is more flexible than (A) 5 P-QB4 (see Benoni), or (B) 5 N-QB3, N-KB3; 6 N-B3, B-K2; 7 B-K2, O-O; 8 O-O, N-R3; 9 B-KB4, N-B2; 10 R-K1, P-QN3; 11 P-KR3, R-K1; 12 P-QR4, B-B1; 13 Q-Q2, P-KR3; 14 N-KR2, P-R3; 15 N-N4, B-B4 = . Unzicker–Larsen, Lugano 1970.

(i) 5 ... B-N5!? 6 B-K2, B×N; 7 B×B, B-K2; 8 O-O, N-KB3; 9 N-R3 ± . Gligorić–Barcza, Ljubljana 1969.

(j) 10 N-B3, P-QR3; 11 B-B1, P-QN3 = . Gligorić–Larsen, Büsum 1969.

(k) (A) For 1 ... N-KB3; 2 N-KB3, P-N3, see note (m) below and with 2 P-KN3, P-KN3; 3 B-N2, B-N2; 4 P-K4, P-Q3; 5 N-QB3, O-O a position is reached allowing transpositions into and from the King's Indian Attack, e.g. 6 KN-K2, P-K4; 7 O-O, N-B3! 8

R–K1, B–Q2; 9 P × P, P × P; 10 N–Q5, B–K3; 11 B–N5, N–N1 = . Kotov. (B) 1 . . . N–QB3; 2 P–QB4; N–B3, see Kevitz–Trajković Defence, or 2 P–K4, see Nimzowitsch Defence. (C) 1 . . . P–QN4; 2 N–KB3, see Polish Defence. Eccentric is (D) 1 . . . P–K4 (The Englund Gambit); 2 P × P, N–QB3; 3 N–KB3, Q–K2; 4 B–KB4, Q–N5†; 5 B–Q2, Q × P; 6 N–B3, B–N5; 7 R–QN1, Q–R6; 8 R–N3, Q–R4; 9 P–QR3 ± . *Comments.*

(*l*) 2 P–K4, see Pirc or Robatsch Defence, all in character with this column.

(*m*) 2 . . . N–KB3 becomes a pseudo King's-Indian without P–QB4 and it can also be arrived at with 1 P–Q4, N–KB3; 2 N–KB3, P–KN3. Feasible continuations are (A) 3 P–QN3, B–N2; 4 B–N2, O–O; 5 P–N3, P–B4; 6 P × P, Q–R4†; 7 Q–Q2, Q × BP; 8 N–B3, P–Q4 = . Yudovich–Kholmov, USSR 1966. Compare Réti Opening, cols. 34–35. (B) 3 B–B4, B–N2; 4 P–K3, P–Q3; 5 P–KR3, O–O; 6 QN–Q2, QN–Q2; 7 B–B4, P–K3; 8 P–B3, Q–K2 = . (C) 3 P–KN3, (1) 3 . . . B–N2; 4 B–N2, P–Q3; 5 O–O, O–O; 6 N–B3 (faulty would be now to follow in the path of line (A) by 6 P–N3? P–K4!! 7 P × P, P × P; 8 B–N2, P–K5 ∓ . Geller), QN–Q2; 7 P–K4, P–K4; 8 P–KR3! R–K1; 9 R–K1, P–B3; 10 B–N5, P–KR3; 11 B–K3, P–QN4; 12 P–R3, B–N2; 13 Q–Q2, K–R2; 14 QR–Q1, P–R3; 15 N–KR2, P–B4 = . Vuković. (2) 3 . . . P–QN3, compare Unorthodox Flank Openings, col. 10, note (*m*). (3) 3 . . . P–Q4; 4 B–N2, B–N2; 5 QN–Q2 (D) 3 P–B3, B–N2; 4 B–B4, O–O; 5 QN–Q2, P–Q3; 6 P–K4, N–B3; 7 B–QN5, P–QR3; 8 B–R4, P–QN4; 9 B–QN3, N–QR4; 10 B–B2, N–B5, 11 P–QN3, N–N3; 12 P–B4, KN–Q2; 13 O–O, P–K4 = . Bisguier–Gligorić, Stockholm 1962. (E) 3 QN–Q2, B–N2; 4 P–K4, P–Q3; 5 B–B4, O–O; 6 O–O, N–B3! 7 P–B3, P–K4; 8 P × P, N × P; 9 N × N, P × N; 10 Q–B2, Q–K2; 11 R–K1, R–Q1; 12 N–B3, P–KR3 = . Bisguier–Reshevsky, New York Chp. 1963.

(*n*) Slightly different is the approach with 2 P–QB4!? P–K3; e.g. (A) 3 N–KB3, N–KB3; 4 P–K3, etc., a Queen's Indian Defence, col. 21. (B) 3 P–Q5! (1) 3 . . . N–KB3; 4 P–QR3 (4 N–QB3, B–N5; 5 Q–N3, B × N†; 6 Q × B, P × P; 7 P × P, B–N2; 8 P–Q6, P × P; 9 B–N5, N–B3; 10 B × N, Q × B; 11 Q × Q, P × Q =), B–N2; 5 N–QB3, P–QR4; 6 P–K4, P × P; 7 KP × P, B–K2; 8 N–B3, N–R3; 9 B–K3, O–O; 10 B–K2, P–Q3; 11 O–O, B–B1! = . *Comments.* (2) 3 . . . B–R3; 4 P–K4, P × P; 5 KP × P, N–KB3; 6 N–QB3, B–N5; 7 Q–K2† B–K2! 8 Q–B2, P–B3 = . Browne–Christiansen, US Chp. 1977. (C) 3 P–K4, see French Defence, cols. 106–10, note (*a*) 1 . . . P–QN3 is also known as the Larsen Defence, employed by him against 1 N–KB3 as well.

(*o*) The omission of 3 N–QB3 is almost a virtual refutation of this Queen's Fianchetto. Also 3 N–Q2, P–N3; 4 P–QB3 serves as an effective bulwark; if 3 . . . P–K3; 4 KN–B3, P–KB4; 5 B–Q3 ± .

(*p*) 7 Q–K2, B–K2; 8 P–QR3, P–Q3; 9 P–QN4, Q–B2; 10 QN–Q2, P–K4; 11 NP × P, NP × P; 12 P × BP, P × P; 13 B–B4 ± . Farago–Szabó, Hungarian Chp. 1977.

(*q*) 10 P–K5, N–Q2; 11 P–QN4, P–B5; 12 B–B2, O–O–O; 13 N–B1 ± . Torre–Larsen, Geneva 1978.

1 P-Q4, N-KB3

	Richter–Veresov Attack		Trompovsky Attack (Ruth Opening)	Torre Attack	
	11	**12**	**13**	**14**	**15**
2	N-QB3		B-N5	N-KB3	
	P-Q4 (a)		P-Q4 (g)	P-K3 (j)	
3	B-N5 (b)		N-Q2 (h)	B-N5	
	P-KR3 (c)		P-KN3	P-KR3	P-B4
4	B-B4	B×N	P-K3	B-R4	P-K3
	P-QR3	KP×B (e)	B-N2	P-KN4	P×P (l)
5	N-B3	P-K3	B-Q3	B-N3	P×P
	QN-Q2	P-B3	O-O	N-K5	B-K2
6	P-K3	B-Q3	P-KB4	KN-Q2	QN-Q2
	P-K3	B-Q3	P-B4	N×B	P-Q3
7	B-K2?	Q-B3	P-B3	RP×N	P-B3
	B-K2	O-O	P×P	P-Q4	QN-Q2
8	O-O	KN-K2	KP×P	P-K3	B-Q3
	P-B4 (d)	R-K1! (f)	Q-N3 (i)	P-QB4 (k)	P-QN3 (m)

(a) (A) 2 . . . P-KN3; or 2 . . . P-Q3; 3 P-K4, P-KN3; see Pirć Defence. (B) 2 . . . P-K3; 3 P-K4, P-Q4; see French. (C) 2 . . . P-B4; 3 P-Q4, P-Q3; 4 P-K4, P-KN3, see Benoni.

(b) 3 P-K4, P×P; 4 P-B3 see col. 17.

(c) 3 . . . P-B3, 4 P-K3, or 4 Q-Q2, or 4 Q-Q3, QN-Q2; 5 P-K4, P×P; 6 N×P, N×N; 7 Q×N, P-KR3 = . (B) 3 . . . QN-Q2! 4 N-B3, (1) 4 . . . P-K3; 5 P-K3 (5 P-K4, P-KR3; 6 B-R4, B-K2 =), B-K2; 6 B-K2, O-O; 7 O-O, P-QN3! = . Taimanov–Gligorić, Copenhagen 1965. (2) 4 . . . P-B3; 5 P-K3, Q-R4; 6 B-Q3, N-K5; 7 O-O, N×N; 8 P×N, Q×P! = . (3) 4 . . . P-KR3; 5 B-R4, P-B4; 6 P-K3, P-K3 = . (4) 4 . . . P-KN3; 5 P-K3, B-N2; 6 B-Q3, O-O; 7 O-O, P-B4 = . (C) 3 . . . P-KN3; 4 B×N, P×B; 5 P-K4, B-QN5! = . (D) 3 . . . B-B4; 4 B×N, KP×B; 5 P-K3, B-QN5; 6 B-Q3, B×B; 7 Q×B, N-B3; 8 KN-K2, Q-Q2; 9 O-O-O, O-O-O = . Veresov–Bronstein, Moscow 1959. (E) 3 . . . P-B4; 4 B×N, NP×B; 5 P-K4, QP×P; 6 P×P, Q-R4; 7 Q-Q2, Q×BP; 8 O-O-O, B-Q2; 9 N×P, Q-B2; 10 Q-K3 ± .

(d) 9 P-KR3, O-O = . Rossetto–Taimanov, Havana 1967. 7 B-Q3 is more active.

(e) 4 . . . NP×B; 5 P-K3, P-B3; 6 Q-R5, B-N2; 7 N-B3, Q-Q3; or 7 KN-K2, Q-Q3; 8 N-N3, P-K3; 9 Q-N4! *Comments.*

(f) Preparing for the defensive retreat . . . B-B1, or . . . N-Q2-B1. There comes 9 O-O-O, P-QN4; (A) 10 QR-N1, P-N5; 11 N-R4, N-Q2; 12 P-N4, N-N3 (we prefer 12 . . . Q-R4!); 13 N-N5, B×N; 14 P×B, N-Q2; 15 P-KR4 (Kaikamdzhozov–Karasmoichev, Varna 1963), N×P! Rattmann; or (B) 10 P-KN4, N-Q2! (10 . . . P-N5; 11 N-R4, N-Q2; 12 P-R4, N-N3; 13 N×N, P×N; 14 P-N5, BP×P; 15 P×P, R×RP; 16 K-N1—Rattmann's suggestion, with the intention 17 QR-N1, and 18 P×P ± —16 . . . R-R2! 17 P×P, P-N3; 18 QR-N1, K-R2∞) 11 P-KR4 (11 QR-N1, P-N5; 12 N-Q1∞, but not 12 N-R4, Q-R4; 13 P-N3, N-N3∓; or 13 Q-B5, P-N3!), P-N3; 12 P-N5, P-KR4; 13 P×BP (else 13 . . . P-KB4), N×P; 14 QR-N1, P-N5! ∓ . But most of these analyses may become obsolete if the alternative 7 . . . P-KN3 (as against 7 . . . O-O in the column) stands up, e.g. 8 P-KN4, P-KR4; 9 P×P, R×P; 10 KN-K2, P-KB4; 11 N-N3, R-R5; 12 O-O-O, Q-B3; 13 K-N1, B-K3; 14 P-K4! R-B5 (or 14 . . . QP×P; 15 N/N3×KP, Q-K2; 16 N×B†, Q×N; 17 P-Q5!?); 15 Q-K3, BP×P; 16 B×P, N-Q2∞. J. Adams in *Chess* 1978/11.

(g) (A) 2 . . . N-K5; 3 B-B4, (1) 3 . . . P-Q4; 4 P-KB3, N-Q3; 5 P-K3, N-B3 = . Trompovsky–Eidelman, Rio de Janeiro 1952. (2) 3 . . . P-QB4; 4 P-KB3, Q-R4†; 5 P-B3,

N–KB3; 6 P–Q5, P–Q3; 7 P–K4, P–KN3; 8 N–KR3, B–N2; 9 Q–Q2, O–O; 10 B–R6, QN–Q2 = . Alburt–Dorfman, USSR Chp. 1977. (B) 2 . . . P–K3; 3 P–K4, P–KR3; 4 B × N, Q × B; 5 N–KB3, P–Q3; 6 N–B3, P–KN3; 7 Q–Q2, Q–K2; 8 O–O–O, P–R3; 9 P–KR4, B–N2; 10 P–KN3, P–QN4; 11 B–R3, P–N5! = . Korchnoi–Karpov, 19th match game 1974. (C) 2 . . . P–B4; (1) 3 B × N, NP × B; 4 P–Q5, Q–N3; 5 Q–B1, P–Q3 = . (2) 3 P–Q5, Q–N3; 4 N–QB3, Q × P; 5 B–Q2, Q–N3; 6 P–K4, P–Q3 (6 . . . P–K4?!); 7 P–B4, P–N3; 8 P–K5, KN–Q2 = . Vaganian–Jansa, Kragujevać 1975; or 3 . . . P–N4; 4 N–B3, B–N2; etc., see Old Benoni note (a). (D) 2 . . . P–KN3; 3 B × N, P × B; 4 P–K3, B–N2; 5 N–K2, P–Q3 = .

(h) (A) 3 N–KB3, see col. 4 (h). (B) 3 N–QB3, see cols. 11–12.

(i) 9 R–QN1, Q–K3†; 10 Q–K2, Q × Q; 11 N × Q (Rakić–Bukić, Novi Travnik 1969), N–B3; 12 P–QN4, P–KR3; 13 B–R4, B–N5 = . Marić.

(j) 2 . . . P–B4; 3 P–Q5—the Old Benoni again— 3 . . . B–QN4!? 4 B–N5!—Shades of the Benko or the Blumenfeld Gambit—and now (A) 4 . . . B–N2; 5 B × N (1) 5 . . . KP × B; 6 P–K4, P–QR3; 7 B–K2, B–Q3; 8 P–QR4, Q–N3; 9 P × P, P × P; 10 R × R, B × R; 11 N–B3, P–N5; 12 N–QN5, O–O; 13 O–O, B–N2; 14 N × B, Q × N; 15 B–B4, R–K1; 16 Q–Q3, N–R3; 17 N–Q2, N–B2 = . Browne–Korchnoi, Wijk aan Zee 1980. Compare with Old Benoni, note (b). (2) 5 . . . NP × B; 6 P–K4, Q–N3; 7 P–B4, P–N5; 8 N–R4, Q–Q3; 9 N–Q2, Q–K4; 10 Q–B2! Prokes–Hromádka, Czechoslovak Chp. 1928. (B) 4 . . . P–N3; 5 P–Q6, P × P; 6 N–B3, P–KR3; 7 B–B4, Q–N3; 8 P–K4, P–N5; 9 N–QN5, N × P; 10 N–Q2, Q–B3; 11 Q–K2, P–B4; 12 N × N! ± (If 12 P–KB3, B–QN2). Balashov–Alburt, U.S.S.R. Chp. 1977. (C) 4 . . . P–Q3; 5 P–K3, P–QR3; 6 P–QR4, P–N5; 7 B × N, KP × B; 8 QN–Q2, P–QR4?; 9 B–N5†, N–Q2; 10 O–O, P–B4; 11 P–K4!

(k) 9 P × P, B–N2! 10 P–QB3, Q–B2; 11 P–K4, O–O = . Kan–Antoshin, USSR 1955. In the column, for 2 . . . P–KN3; see King's Fianchetto Defence, col. 10.

(l) As this type of attack gained recognition, another line continued 4 . . . Q–N3; e.g. (A) 5 B × N, P × B; 6 Q–B1, N–B3; 7 P–B3, P–Q4; 8 QN–Q2, B–Q2; 9 B–K2, R–B1 = . (B) 5 N–B3?! Q × P; 6 N–N5, Q–N5†; 7 P–B3, Q–R4; 8 N–Q2, P–QR3!; 9 N–B4, Q × N!; 10 N–Q6†, B × N; 11 B × Q, P × B ± . Bisguier–Sherwin, N.Y. 1954. (C) 5 Q–B1! N–K5; 6 B–KB4, P–Q4; 7 B–Q3, P–B4; 8 P–B3, B–K2; 9 QN–Q2, N–QB3; 10 P–KR3, O–O; 11 O–O . (D) 5 QN–Q2, Q × P; 6 B–Q3 (1) 6 . . . Q–N3; 7 O–O, N–B3; 8 R–N1 (or 8 B × N!?), Q–Q1; 9 P–K4, P × P; 10 P–K5, P–KR3 = . (2) 6 . . . P–Q4; 7 P–B4, Q–B6! 8 N–K5 (or 8 Q–K2!?), N–B3; 9 R–QB1, Q–R6; 10 N × N, P × N; 11 Q–B2, R–QN1; 12 QR–N1, R × R = . Spasski–Miles, Tilburg 1978 (and analysis by J. Adams).

(m) 9 N–B4, B–N2; 10 Q–K2, Q–B2; 11 O–O, O–O = . Torre–Lasker, Moscow 1925.

1 P–Q4, N–KB3

	Polish Defence	Blackmar (–Diemer) Gambit		Kevitz–Trajković Defence	
	16	**17**	**18**	**19**	**20**
2	(N–KB3)	P–KB3		P–QB4	
	P–QN4	P–Q4		N–B3 (h)	
3	P–KN3 (a)	P–K4		N–QB3	N–KB3
	P–K3	P × P		P–Q3 (i)	P–Q3
4	B–N2	N–B3		N–B3 (j)	P–Q5
	P–B4	B–B4	P × P	P–K4	N–K4
5	N–K5	P–KN4 (c)	N × P (e)	P–Q5	N–B3
	P–Q4	B–N3	B–N5 (f)	N–K2	N × N†
6	O–O	P–N5	P–KR3	P–K4	KP × N
	B–N2	N–Q4	B × N	N–N3	P–K4
7	P × P	N × P	Q × B	B–K2	B–Q3
	B × P	P–K3	P–B3	B–K2	B–K2
8	N–Q3	P–QB4	B–K3	P–KR4	Q–B2
	B–K2 (b)	N–K2 (d)	P–K3 (g)	P–KR3 (k)	O–O (l)

(a) The reticent treatment. Good is also (A) 3 P–QR4! or (B) 3 P–K3, P–QR3; 4 P–QR4. For (c) 3 B–N5, P–B4; 4 P–Q5 etc. see col. 13, note (g) and old Benoni, note (a).

(b) 9 P–QR4, P–N5 = . Udovčić–Portisch, Havana 1964.

(c) 5 P × P, N × P; 6 Q–B3, (A) 6 . . . N–Q3; 7 B–KB4, P–K3; 8 O–O–O, P–QB3; 9 P–Q5, BP × P; 10 N × P, B–K5; 11 Q–K3, P × N; 13 R × P, B–K2 (or 12 . . . P–B4); 13 B–N5†, N–B3; 14 B × N†, P × B; 15 R × N, B × R; 16 Q × B†, K–B1; 17 N–B3, B × B†; 18 Q × B, Q–B3; 19 Q–N4†, Q–K2 + . Analysis by Diemer, Gunderam and Müller. (B) 6 . . . N × N; 7 P × N, Q–B1; 8 B–Q3, B × B; 9 P × B, P–QB3 ∓ . Hoey–Lyon, US Forces Chp. 1970.

(d) 9 N–N3, QN–B3; 10 B–K3, N–B4; 11 N × N, B × N ∓ . Tartakover–Simonovich, Paris 1954.

(e) Or 5 Q × P! P–B3; 6 B–Q3, B–N5; 7 Q–B2, P–K3; 8 P–KR3, B–R4; 9 KN–K2, QN–Q2; 10 O–O, B–K2; 11 P–KN4, B–N3; 12 P–N5! ± . Honfi Jr.–Füster, Hungarian Chp. 1950.

(f) Also (A) 5 . . . P–KN3; 6 B–QB4, B–N2; 7 N–K5, O–O; 8 B–KN5, QN–Q2; 9 O–O, P–B4; and Black gains the upper hand; or (B) 5 . . . P–B4; 6 P–Q5, P–KN3.

(g) 9 B–Q3, QN–Q2; 10 O–O, B–K2; 11 R–B2, Q–R4; 12 P–KN4, O–O = . Callaghan–Bisguier, Washington 1966.

(h) (A) 2 . . . P–B4; see Benoni. (B) 2 . . . P–Q4?; 3 P × P, N × P; 4 P–K4, N–N3; 5 N–QB3, P–K3; 6 N–B3 ± .

(i) (A) 3 . . . P–K3; 4 P–Q5! (B) 3 . . . P–Q4; see Queen's Gambit, Chigorin Defence. (c) 3 . . . P–K4; 4 P–Q5, N–K2; 5 P–K4 (or 5 P–Q6!?), P–Q3; 6 P–KN3, P–KN3 ∞. Vano–Kevitz, Manhattan CC 1954.

(j) 4 P–Q5, N–K4; 5 P–B4, N–N3; 6 P–K4, P–K3; 7 N–B3, P × P; 8 BP × P, B–K2; 9 B–Q3 gives White more space, but some players prefer to hold out for Black.

(k) 9 P–R5, N–B1; 10 N–KN1, N/1–Q2; 11 B–B3, P–B3; 12 N/1–K2, P–QR4 = . Trapl–Lutikov, Warsaw 1969.

(l) 9 B–K3, P–B3; 10 P–KN4, P × P; 11 P × P, Q–R4; 12 O–O–O, K–R1; 13 Q–N3, R–QN1 = . Nedeljković–Trajković, Belgrade 1952.

1 P-Q4, N-KB3; 2 P-QB4, P-K3

	Neo–Indian Attack	Döry Defence	Blumenfeld (Counter) Gambit		
	21	22	23	24	25
3	B–N5 (a)	N–KB3			
	B–N5† (b)	N–K5 (e)	P–B4		
4	N–Q2 (c)	P–K3	P–Q5 (g)		
	P–KR3	P–QN3	P–QN4!?		
5	B × N	B–Q3	P × KP		B–N5
	Q × B	B–N5†	BP × P		P × QP? (j)
6	P–QR3	QN–Q2	P × P		P × QP
	B × N†	B–N2	P–Q4		P–KR3
7	Q × B	P–QR3	P–K3	B–B4	B × N
	P–Q3	B × N†	B–Q3	B–Q3	Q × B
8	P–K3	N × B	N–B3	B × B	Q–B2
	P–K4	P–KB4	O–O	Q × B	P–Q3
9	N–B3	N × N	B–K2?	QN–Q2	P–K4
	B–N5 (d)	P × N (f)	B–N2 (h)	O–O (i)	P–R3 (k)

(a) 3 N–QB3, P–Q4 leads into the Queen's Gambit (see there), and is now the preferred sequence to reach it.

(b) (A) 3 . . . P–KR3; see note (d). (B) 3 . . . P–Q4; see Queen's Gambit. (C) 3 . . . P–B4; 4 P–Q5, P–N4; 5 N–KB3, see Blumenfeld Counter Gambit.

(c) Only this move provides individual character. If 4 N–QB3, see Nimzo–Indian Defence, or, after 4 . . . P–Q4, Queen's Gambit.

(d) 10 B–K2, N–B3 (10 . . . O–O!); 11 O–O–O? O–O–O; 12 P–Q5, N–K2 ∞. *Comments.*

(e) (A) 3 . . . P–QN3; see Queen's Indian Defence. (B) 3 . . . B–N5†; see Bogolyubov–Indian.

(f) 10 Q–R5†. I. Fairhurst–Keres, Hastings 1937–8.

(g) (A) 4 P–KN3, see Indian Catalan. (B) 4 N–B3, see English opening.

(h) 10 P–QN3, QN–Q2; 11 B–N2, Q–K2 ∞. Tarrasch–Alekhin, Pistyan 1922. 9 P–K4, P × P; 10 N–KN5 is stronger.

(i) 10 P–K3, P–QR3; 11 P × P, B × P; 12 B–K2, N–B3; 13 O–O, KR–N1; 14 P–QN3, P–K4 = .

(j) 5 . . . P × BP! 6 P–K4, Q–R4†; 7 Q–Q2, Q × Q†; 8 QN × Q, B–K2! = .

(k) 10 P–QR4, P–N5; 11 QN–Q2, B–N5; 12 B–K2, N–Q2; 13 N–KN1! = . L. Svensson–L. Karlsson, corr. 1964.

1 P-Q4, N-KB3; 2 P-QB4, P-K4; 3 P × P!

	26	27	28	29	30
	N-N5			N-K5	
4	P-K4	B-B4 (d)		N-KB3 (k)	
	N × KP	N-QB3 (e) . . .	P-KN4	N-QB3 (l)	
5	P-B4	N-KB3	B-Q2 (h)	P-QR3	QN-Q2
	KN-B3 (a)	B-N5†	N × KP	P-Q3	N-B4
6	N-KB3 (b)	QN-Q2 (f)	B-B3 (i)	Q-B2	P-KN3
	B-B4	Q-K2	B-N2	P-Q4 (m)	P-KN3
7	N-B3	P-QR3	P-K3	P × P	N-N3
	P-Q3	KN × KP	P-N5	Q × P	N-K3
8	B-Q3	N × N	N-K2	N-B3	B-Q2
	B-KN5	N × N	P-Q3	N × N	B-N2
9	P-KR3	P-K3	N-B4	Q × N	B-B3
	B × N	B × N†	P-KR4	B-KN5	P-QR4
10	Q × B	Q × B	N-Q2	B-B4	B-N2
	N-Q5 (c)	P-Q3 (g)	P-QR4 (j)	O-O-O =	P-R5 (n)

(a) Also 5 . . . N-N3; (A) 6 N-KB3, (1) 6 . . . B-N5†; 7 N-B3, P-Q3 (or 7 . . . Q-B3!?); 8 Q-N3, N-B3; 9 B-Q2, O-O; 10 O-O-O, R-K1; 11 B-Q3, B-N5 = . Mititelu–Kitkovski, Sofia 1955. (2) 6 . . . B-B4? 7 P-B5, N-K2; 8 N-B3! Good is (3) 6 . . . N-B3! first. (B) 6 B-K3, B-N5†; 7 N-B3, B × N†; 8 P × B, Q-K2; 9 B-Q3, P-KB4; 10 Q-B2, P × P; 11 B × P, N × P!; 12 B × N, P-Q4; 13 P × P, B-B4; 14 O-O-O, B × B = . *Spotlight* 1956.

(b) 6 B-K3, B-N5†; 7 N-B3, Q-R5†; 8 P-KN3, B × N†; 9 P × B, Q-K2; 10 B-Q3, N-R3; 11 N-B3, N-B4; 12 O-O, O-O; 13 R-K1, P-QN3 = . Pachman.

(c) 11 Q-N4, O-O; 12 B-Q2, P-QR3; 13 O-O-O, P-QN4 = . Minev.

(d) A novel shocker is 4 P-K6?! QP × P! 5 Q × Q†, K × Q; 6 N-QB3, B-N5; 7 B-Q2 (Panteleyev–Segal, Bulgaria 1970), P-KB3! 8 P-QR3, B × N; 9 B × B, N-Q2 ∞. Bukić.

(e) 4 . . . B-N5†; 5 N-Q2 (5 N-B3, see next note (e), P-Q3!? 6 P × P, Q-B3; 7 N-R3! ± (not 7 B-N3, Q × NP; 8 N-B3, B-KB4 ∓).

(f) 6 N-B3, Q-K2; 7 Q-Q5, P-B3 (7 . . . B × N†; 8 P × B, Q-R6; 9 R-QB1 ±); 8 P × P, N × P; 9 Q-Q3, O-O; Wade–Gligorić, Dundee 1967; 10 B-Q2 ± .

(g) 11 B-K2, (A) 11 . . . N-N3; 12 B-N3, O-O; 13 O-O, P-KB4; 14 B-B3, R-N1 = *Comments.* (B) 11 . . . B-Q2 (1) 12 P-K4, B-B3; 13 P-B3, P-QR4; 14 P-QN3 = (2) 12 Q-B3, O-O; 13 O-O, KR-K1; 14 QR-Q1, B-B3. Glasscoe, Staker, Stayert. 4 B-B4 is Rubinstein's treatment.

(h) Double-edged is 5 B-N3, N-QB3; 6 N-KB3, B-N2; 7 N-B3, KN × KP; 8 N × N, B × N; 9 B × B, N × B; 10 Q-Q4, P-Q3; 11 P-B5, O-O; 12 O-O-O, B-K3 = . Khasin–Drimer, match Moscow–Bucharest 1969.

(i) 6 N-KB3, B-N2; 7 N × N, B × N; 8 Q-B1, P-KR3; 9 N-B3, P-Q3; 10 P-KR4, P-N5; 11 P-KN3, N-B3; 12 B-N2, B-K3 = . Tartakover–Korn, Mandrake C.C. 1949.

(j) 11 P-KN3 leaves White with the better development and diagonal pressure, but 6 . . . QN-Q3! should be considered in the column. 4 . . . P-KN4 is Balogh's impetuous idea.

(k) 4 Q-B2, P-Q4; 5 P × P *e.p.*, B-B4; 6 N-QB3! N × QP; 7 P-K4, N × KP; 8 B-Q3! N × P; 9 B × B, N × R; 10 N-B3, B-Q3! 11 N-K4, B × P = .

(l) In consequential gambit style is 4 . . . P-Q3?! (1) 5 Q-B2, B-B4; 6 N-B3, P-Q4; 7 P × P, B-QN5; 8 B-Q2, B × N; 9 B × B, Q × P ∞; or (2) 5 QN-Q2, B-B4; 6 N × N. B × N; 7 P-K3, N-B3 = . Vasconcellos.

(m) Also 6 . . . B-B4; 7 N-B3, N-N6; 8 P-K4, N × R; 9 P × B, QN × P! = ; the column was suggested by Vasconcellos.

(n) 11 QN-Q2, P-Q3; 12 P × P, B × B; 13 P × B, Q × P; 14 N-K4, Q-K2 = .

Indian Defence Systems

Queen's Indian Defence

(1 P–Q4, N–KB3; 2 P–QB4, P–K3;
3 N–KB3, P–QN3 or
1 P–Q4, N–KB3; 2 P–QB4, P–QN3 or
1 P–Q4, N–KB3; 2 N–KB3, P–QN3 or
1 P–QB4, N–KB3; 2 P–Q4, P–QN3; or
1 N–KB3, N–KB3; 2 P–Q4, or 2 P–QB4,
or 2 P–KN3—, P–QN3 and similar
transpositions).

The Queen's Indian, in Russia dubbed "Neo–Indian," was popularized by Nimzowitsch and the other hyper-moderns. It has become more or less "stock" against 3 N–KB3. Masters are becoming prone to avoid it altogether by playing 3 N–QB3, and this tacit compliment accounts for its infrequency in tournaments rather than any defect in the defence, which is more persistent than the Bogolyubov–Indian.

The basic strategy for Black is control of his K5 square. This is accomplished largely with his queen's bishop and king's knight, rather than pawns, and is feasible because 3 N–KB3 lacks vigour (compared to 3 N–QB3 which strikes at the vital square and threatens P–K4). While Black's goal is seldom carried out in its entirety, his play remains aggressive. The ensuing simplifications are drawish in character due to the balanced pawn structure. For a long while White's best theoretical chances were thought to lie in countering with a king's-side fianchetto and working for pawn-wedges at K4 and Q5. Lately the quieter course with P–K3 followed by B–Q3 has become fashionable. It is doubtful, however, that either system confers any appreciable advantage.

THE MAIN VARIATION (cols. 1–10) demonstrates a variety of resources for both sides with the practical chances evenly divided. The standard order of moves is: 1 P–Q4, N–KB3; 2 P–QB4, P–K3; 3 N–KB3, P–QN3; 4 P–KN3, B–N2; 5 B–N2, B–K2; 6 O–O, O–O and now the breakdown depends upon how White continues on his seventh turn.

(a) 7 N–B3 (cols. 1–6) is best met by 7 . . . N–K5, followed later by P–KB4, with a Dutch-like formation.

(b) 7 P–Q5!? (col. 7) is Pomar's sharp prescription. It must be met precisely and leads to lively gambit play. If anyone succeeds in reinforcing

White's play, this line gives him a chance at a tactical refutation of the Queen's Indian.

(c) Lacking vigour are 7 R–K1, 7 Q–B2 and 7 P–N3 (cols. 8–10).

DIVERGENCES FOR BLACK on move four and five are interesting. Several of these offer hope of equality or better. 6 N–B3 (note (a)-(b)) was utilized in the match Korchnoi–Karpov in 1974.

(a) 5 . . . B–N5† (cols. 11–12) is playable, particularly after 6 B–Q2, with Alekhin's retreat 6 . . . B–K2.

(b) 5 . . . P–B4 and 5 . . . Q–B1 on the other hand leave something to be desired. Black voluntarily accepts cramped quarters, but retains various chances to break out.

(c) The step-child without a name, which Euwe christened the *Exaggerated Fianchetto*, 4 . . . B–R3, has proved so interesting that attempts have sometimes been made to abandon 4 P–KN3 altogether and seek a more natural tack. Exerting pressure on the QR3–KB8 diagonal instead of the customary QR1–KR8 diagonal is an odd but logical Alekhin idea which has received new attention during the last few years. Black seeks to profit by the absence of White's king's bishop from its normal diagonal after it steps to KN2. Column 15 is crucial to the theory of this curious sideline.

THE CLOSED VARIATIONS (cols. 16–23) are a return to old-fashioned methods. 4 N–B3, B–N2; 5 B–N5 (cols. 17–20) can be adequately defended in cols. 21–3. White abandons the king's bishop fianchetto and strives for a straightforward B–Q3, N–B3, and P–K4. Black's counter-chances are adequate.

THE MARIENBAD SYSTEM (cols. 24–5) remains an effective equalizing method against 2 N–KB3. Both 3 P–KN3 (reverting to Main Line-like formations) and 3 P–K3 (akin to the Colle System) are unable to procure any advantage.

Transpositions via 1 P–QB4, or 1 N–KB3, or 1 P–KN3 may often end up in Queen's Indian Defence lines, provided that at some point White follows up with the thematic P–Q4. Even in its absence, the reader is advised to watch the comparable Flank Openings for Queen's Indian-like features.

1 P–Q4, N–KB3; 2 P–QB4, P–K3; 3 N–KB3, P–QN3; 4 P–KN3, B–N2; 5 B–N2,
B–K2; 6 O–O, O–O; 7 N–B3, N–K5! 8 Q–B2 (*a*), N × N; 9 Q × N

	1	2	3	4	5
	P–KB4 . . . . P–QB4 . . . . . . B–K5 (*g*)				
10	P–N3	B–K3	P–Q5 (*c*)	R–Q1	N–K1 (*h*)
	B–KB3	B–KB3	P × P (*d*)	P–Q3	B × B
11	B–N2	Q–Q2	N–K1	P–N3	N × B
	P–QR4 (*b*)	P–Q3	P–Q5	B–KB3	P–QB3
12	Q–Q2	KR–Q1	Q × P	B–N2	P–Q5
	N–R3	Q–K1	B × B	Q–K2	BP × P
13	QR–Q1	QR–B1	N × B	Q–Q2	P × P
	Q–K1	B–K5	N–B3	R–Q1	N–R3
14	N–K1	N–K1	Q–Q5†	N–K1	N–B4
	B × B	B × B	R–B2	B × B	Q–B1
15	N × B	N × B	B–K3	N × B (*f*)	Q–B3
	P–KN4	N–Q2	B–B3	N–Q2 =	Q–B2
16	KR–K1	Q–B2	Q–Q2		P–K4
	Q–N3 =	P–QR4 =	N–K4 = (*e*)		N–B4! =

(*a*) (A) 8 N × N, B × N; 9 N–K1, (1) 9 . . . B × B; 10 N × B, P–Q4; 11 Q–R4, P × P; 12
Q × P, P–QB4; 13 P × P, B × P = . Averbakh–Furman, USSR Chp. 1964. (2) 9 . . . P–Q4; 10
B × B, P × B; 11 N–B2, P–QB4; 12 P–N3, P × P = . (B) 8 B–Q2, B–KB3; 9 Q–B2, N × B; 10
Q × N, P–Q3; 11 P–K4, N–Q2; 12 P–Q5, N–K4 = .

(*b*) Other choices are (A) 11 . . . P–Q3; 12 QR–Q1, Q–B1! 13 Q–Q2, B–K5! 14 N–K1,
B × B; 15 N × B, N–Q2; 16 Q–B2, R–K1; 17 KR–K1! Benko–Filip, Portoroz 1958. (B) 11 . . .
N–B3! 12 QR–Q1 (or 12 Q–Q2), N–K2; 13 N–K1, B × B; 14 N × B, P–KN4 = . Pirc–Euwe.
Amsterdam 1954. The column is Petrosian–Bronstein, USSR Chp. 1951. The next column is
Comments.

(*c*) (A) 10 N–K5, B × B; 11 K × B, B–B3; 12 Q–B3, P–B3; 13 B–B4, Q–K1 = . (B) 10 R–Q1,
B–KB3; 11 Q–K3, Q–B1! = . *Comments.*

(*d*) Also safe is 10 . . . N–R3; 11 P × P, P × P; 12 N–N5, B × B; 13 N × KP, B–KB3!

(*e*) Mühring–Kupper, Vevey 1953. Also 13 . . . N–R3 is playable.

(*f*) Gheorghiu–Korchnoi, Mallorca 1968, continued 15 . . . P × P? 16 B × P, B × B; 17
Q × B ± . 11 B–K3? was Larsen-Karpov, Amsterdam, 1980.

(*g*) 9 . . . P–Q4!?; 10 N–K5, N–R3; 11 B–Q2, P–KB3; 12 N–Q3, P–QB4; 13 BP × P,
KP × P; 14 P × P, P × P; 15 QR–Q1?, R–N1; 16 P–N3, Q–Q2; 17 B–B4, QR–K1 ∞. Mychess
B-Chess Challenger 8, Microcomputer chess Chp., San José 1980.

(*h*) (A) 10 R–Q1, P–Q3; 11 Q–K3, P–Q4 = . (B) 10 P–N3, P–KB4; 11 B–N2, B–KB3; 12
QR–Q1, N–B3; 13 Q–B1, N–K2; 14 N–K1, B × B; 15 N × B, N–N3; 16 P–Q5, B × B; 17 Q × B,
P–K4 = . Unzicker–Matanović, Bad Pyrmont 1951. (C) Critical is, however, 10 B–B4! P–QB3;
11 KR–Q1, P–Q4; 12 P × P, Q × P; 13 N–K1! B × B; 14 N × B, with a shade better for White.
The column is Lilienthal's suggestion.

1 P-Q4, N-KB3; 2 P-QB4, P-K3; 3 N-KB3, P-QN3; 4 P-KN3, B-N2; 5 B-N2, B-K2; 6 O-O (a), O-O

	6	7	8	9	10
7	(N-B3) ...... P-Q5 .... P-N3 .... Q-B2 .... R-K1				
	P-Q4?	P×P	P-B4 (g)	P-B4	P-Q4
8	B-B4 (b)	N-Q4	B-N2	P×P	N-B3
	P-B3	B-B3!? (d)	P×P	P×P	QN-Q2
9	N-Q2	P×P	Q×P	N-B3	N-K5
	QN-Q2	B×P	N-B3	P-Q3	N-K5
10	P-K4	B×B	Q-B4	R-Q1	P×P
	R-B1	N×B	P-Q4	Q-N3	N×N/6
11	Q-B2	P-K4	R-Q1	P-N3	P×N
	P-B4	N-N5 (e)	Q-B1	N-B3	N×N
12	KP×P	N/1-B3	N-B3	B-N2	P-Q6
	KP×P	N/1-B3	P×P	P-KR3	B×B
13	N-N5	N-B5	Q×P	P-K3	P×B
	P-QR3 (c)	N-K4 (f)	N-QN5 =	KR-K1 (h)	Q×P (i)

(a) (A) 6 P-Q5, P×P; 7 N-Q4, O-O; 8 N-B5, B-N5†; 9 N-B3, R-K1 = . (B) 6 N-B3 (1) 6 ... O-O, 7 Q-Q3 (7 Q-B2, P-B4; 8 P-Q5, P×P; 9 N-KN5, N-B3; 10 N×QP, P-N3; 11 Q-Q2! N×N; 12 B×N, R-N1!? 13 N×RP! R-K1; 14 Q-R6± . Korchnoi–Karpov, 21st match game 1974), P-Q4; 8 P×P, N×P; 9 N×N, P×N; 10 O-O, N-Q2; 11 R-Q1, R-K1; 12 B-K3, B-Q3; 13 QR-B1, P-QR4 = . Korchnoi–Karpov, 13th match game 1974. The 11th match game continued 11 B-B4, P-QB4; 12 P×P, P×P with a classical position of hanging pawns in a fluid set-up. (2) 6 ... N-K5! 7 B-Q2, B-KB3 (7 ... N×N; 8 B×N, B-K5 =); 8 O-O, O-O; 9 Q-B2, N×B; 10 Q×N, P-Q3; 11 QR-Q1, N-Q2; 12 N-K1, B×B; 13 N×B, Q-K2; 14 N-K1, P-B4; 15 N-B2, QR-B1; 16 P-N3, KR-Q1; 17 P-K4, N-N1; 18 KR-K1, P×P; 19 N×P, Q-N2; 20 R-K3, P-QR3; 21 Q-K2, N-B3; 22 N×N, Q×N; 23 R/3-Q3, P-R3; 24 P-QR4, Q-B4; 25 Q-Q2, P-QN4; 26 RP×P, B×N; 27 Q×B, P×P; 28 R-Q4, Q-B2; 29 Q-N4, P-K4; drawn. Korchnoi–Karpov, 23rd match game 1974.

(b) 8 N-K5, (A) 8 ... Q-B1! 9 P×P, N×P; 10 N×N, P×N; 11 B-B4! (11 Q-N3, Q-K3! =) Q-K3; 12 Q-B2, P-B3; 13 P-K4! (B) 8 ... N-R3; 9 Q-R4, P-B4; 10 P-K3, Q-B1; 11 BP×P, BP×P = .

(c) 14 N-Q6, B×N; 15 B×B± . *Comments*.

(d) A quite solid riposte is 8 ... P-B3! e.g. 9 P×P, N×P; 10 B×N, P×B; 11 N-QB3, B-N5 = .

(e) 11 ... N-KB3; 12 P-K5, N-K1; 13 Q-B3, P-QB3; 14 R-Q1, P-Q4! 15 P×P e.p., N×P; 16. N-B5, N-Q2! 17 Q-N4! P-N3; 18 N-R6†, K-R1; 19 B-B4, with a dangerous attack. *Archives*.

(f) 14 P-B4, N-N3; 15 Q-N4, K-R1; 16 P-QR3, N-B3 = . Uhlmann–Padevski, Monte Carlo 1968.

(g) Also 7 ... P-Q4; 8 N-K5, Q-B1; 9 P×P, B×P; 10 B×B, N×B; 11 B-N2, P-B4! = . Vidmar–Yanofsky, Groningen 1946. The column is Pachman's analysis.

(h) 14 QR-B1, P-R3; 15 Q-K2, Q-B2 = . Grünfeld–Eliskases, Vienna 1935.

(i) 14 K×B, N-B3; 15 Q-R4, Q-Q2 = . Keres–Botvinnik, AVRO 1938. Voronkov suggests 8 P×P, P×P; 9 N-B3, P-B3; 10 B-B4, QN-Q2 = .

1 P-Q4, N-KB3; 2 P-QB4, P-K3; 3 N-KB3, P-QN3; 4 P-KN3

	11	12	13	14	15
4					
	(B-N2)			B-N5†	B-R3
5	(B-N2)			B-Q2	Q-R4!? (i)
	B-N5†		Q-B1 (f)	B×B†	B-K2 (j)
6	B-Q2 (a)		O-O	Q×B	B-N2 (k)
	B×B†	B-K2 (c)	P-B4	B-R3	O-O
7	Q×B	O-O	P-Q5!? (g)	P-N3 (h)	N-B3
	O-O	O-O	P×P	P-B3	P-B3
8	N-B3	N-B3	P×P	B-N2	B-B4
	P-Q3	P-Q4	N×P	P-Q4	P-Q3 (l)
9	Q-B2	P×P	P-K4	O-O	R-QB1
	Q-K2	P×P (d)	N-B2	O-O	Q-K1
10	O-O	Q-B2	N-B3	R-B1	P-B5!
	QN-Q2	QN-Q2	B-K2	QN-Q2 =	NP×P
11	P-K4	QR-B1	R-K1		P×P
	QR-B1 (b)	R-K1 (e)	O-O ∞		P-K4 (m)

(a) 6 QN-Q2, O-O; 7 O-O, P-Q4; 8 P-QR3. B-K2; 9 P-QN4, P-B4 = . Rubinstein–Alekhin, Semmering 1936.

(b) 12 KR-K1, P-K4; 13 QR-Q1, P-B3; 14 Q-R4, R-B2. Reshevsky–Keres, Semmering 1937. White has a slight pull. Black's . . . P-Q4 instead of . . . P-Q3 at anytime is mostly answered by N-K5, followed by N-Q3.

(c) (A) 6 . . . P-QR4; 7 O-O, B×B; 8 Q×B, O-O = . (B) 6 . . . Q-K2; 7 O-O, B×B; (1) 8 KN×B, B×B; 9 K×B, P-B4 = . (2) 8 Q×B, O-O; 9 N-B3, P-Q3 = .

(d) Or 9 . . . N×P; 10 R-K1, P-QB4; 11 P-K4, N-B2. Müller.

(e) 12 B-B4, P-B3; 13 KR-Q1, QR-B1 = . Comments.

(f) (A) 5 . . . P-N3; 6 O-O, B-N2; 7 N-B3, N-K5; 8 N×N, B×N; 9 B-N5, P-KB3; 10 B-K3, N-B3; 11 P-Q5, N-K2 = . Kavalek–Spasski, 2nd match game 1977. (B) 5 . . . P-B4; 6 N-B3 (the Benoni move 6 P-Q5 is too risky now), P×P; 7 Q×P, P-QR3 (or 7 . . . B-K2; 8 O-O, O-O; 9 R-Q1, P-Q3 =); 8 O-O, P-Q3; 9 P-N3, QN-Q2; 10 B-N2, B-K2 = . Uhlmann–Ljubojević, Amsterdam 1975.

(g) 7 P-N3, P×P; 8 B-N2, B-K2; 9 N×P, B×B; 10 K×B, O-O; 11 N-QB3, Q-N2†; 12 P-B3, P-QR3; 13 P-K4, N-B3; 14 Q-Q2, QR-B1 = . Pachman.

(h) (A) 7 Q-B2, P-B4; 8 B-N2, N-B3; 9 P×P, P×P; 10 O-O, O-O; 11 R-Q1, R-N1 = . Cobo–Szabó, Varna Olympics 1962. (B) 7 N-R3, P-B4; 8 B-N2, N-B3 = . The column is Bronstein–Polugayevsky, USSR Chp. 1961. For 5 . . . P-QR4? see Bogolyubov–Indian Defence.

(i) The alternatives are (A) 5 QN-Q2, P-B4; (1) 6 B-N2, N-B3; 7 P×P, KB×P; 8 O-O, O-O; 9 P-N3, B-K2; 10 B-N2, B-N2; 11 N-K5, Q-B2 = . (2) The sacrificial attempt at initiative 6 P-K4?! P×P; 7 P-K5, N-N1; 8 B-N2, N-QB3; 9 O-O ∞. Uhlmann–Keres, Moscow 1967. (B) 5 P-N3, P-Q4; 6 B-KN2, P×P; 7 N-K5, B-N5†; 8 B-Q2, Q×P ∞.

(j) (A) 5 . . . P-B3; 6 N-B3, P-QN4!? 7 P×P, P×P; 8 N×P, Q-N3; 9 N-B3, with a small plus. (B) 5 . . . P-B4; 6 B-N2, B-N2; 7 O-O, Q-B1; 8 B-B4, P×P = .

(k) As good or bad is 6 N-B3, B-N2; 7 B-N2, O-O; 8 B-N5! P-Q4; 9 B×N, B×B; 10 P×P, P×P; 11 O-O, R-K1 = .

(l) (A) 8 . . . P-QN4; 9 P×P, P×P; 10 N×P, N-Q4; 11 O-O! (B) 8 . . . Q-B1; 9 R-QB1, P-Q3; 10 O-O, QN-Q2; 11 KR-Q1, B-N2; 12 P-K4, N-R4 ∞. (C) 8 . . . B-N2; 9 O-O, N-R4; 10 B-Q2, P-B4 = .

(m) 12 P×P, KB×P; 13 B-N5, N-Q4; with almost equal play. This variation is the "Exaggerated Fianchetto" (4 . . . B-R3).

1 P-Q4, N-KB3; 2 P-QB4, P-K3; 3 N-KB3, P-QN3

	16	17	18	19	20
4	P-QR3	N-B3 (c)			
	P-B4! (a)	B-N2			
5	P-Q5	B-N5 (d)			
	P×P	P-KR3			
6	P×P	B-R4			
	P-N3!?	B-K2			P-KN4
7	N-B3	P-K3 (e)			B-N3
	B-KN2	P-B4	N-K5		B-N5 (j)
8	B-N5	B-K2	N×N	B-N3	P-K3
	O-O	P×P	B×N	O-O (h)	N-K5
9	P-K3	N×P	B-N3 (g)	B-Q3	Q-B2
	P-Q3	O-O	O-O	P-Q4	B×N†
10	N-Q2	O-O	N-Q2	Q-B2	P×B
	P-KR3 (b)	N-B3 (f)	B-N2 =	N×B (i)	P-Q3 (k)

(a) (A) 4 . . . B-N2; 5 N-B3, P-Q4; 6 B-N5, see Queen's Gambit Declined, Tartakover Variation. (B) 4 . . . P-Q4; 5 N-B3 see note (d).

(b) 11 B-R4 (Petrosian-Larsen, Mallorca 1968), B-R3! Larsen also weighs 8 P-Q6?!

(c) 4 B-N5, B-N2; 5 N-B3, P-KR3 leads into this column. (B) 4 B-B4, B-N2; 5 P-K3 (1) 5 . . . B-K2; 6 P-KR3, O-O; 7 N-B3, P-Q4; 8 P×P, P×P; 9 B-Q3, P-B4; 10 O-O, N-B3; 11 N-K5, P-QR3 = . Miles-Spasski, Buenos Aires 1978. (2) 5 . . . N-K5; 6 N/3-Q2, B-K2; 7 N×N, B×N; 8 N-B3, B-N2; 9 B-Q3, O-O; 10 P-Q5, P-KB4; 11 P-KR3, B-N5; 12 Q-N3, N-R3 = . Day-Keene, Buenos Aires 1978. (c) 4 P-KN3, B-N2; 5 B-N2, (1) 5 . . . B-K2; 6 O-O, O-O; 7 N-B3, N-K5; 8 Q-B2, N×N; 9 Q×N, P-QB4; 10 R-Q1, P-Q3 = . Brown-Grefe, U.S.A. 1977. (2) 5 . . . P-Q4; 6 O-O, B-K2; 7 N-K5, O-O; 8 N-B3, N-R3 (Byrne's idea); 9 P×P, P×P; 10 N-Q3!, P-B4!; 11 P×P, P×P; 12 B-N5, R-N1; 13 Q-R4, P-B5; 14 B×N, B×B; 15 N-B4, N-B4!; 16 Q×P!, Q-Q3; 17 QN×P, B×P; 18 QR-Q1, N-Q2; 19 N-K3, Q-QN3; 20 Q-R4, N-B4; 21 Q×P, B-R3; 22 Q-B2, KR-B1; 23 Q-B5, P-N3; 24 Q-N4, R-K1; 25 R-N1, Q-R2; 26 B-Q5, K-R1; 27 N-B4, B×N; 28 B×B, N-K5; 29 N-Q3, P-B4; 30 Q-B4, Q-Q5; 31 R×B, R×R; 32 N×R, Q×N; 33 R-Q1, Q-N3; 34 R-Q7, Q-B4; 35 R-QB7, Q-Q5; 36 B-Q3, Q-R8†; 37 K-N2 winning. Kavalek-Ljubojević, Montreal 1979. In line (D), 4 B-B4, compare also the treatment in Queen's Gambit, col. 39.

(d) (A) 5 P-QR3, (1) 5 . . . B×N (5 . . . B-K2, 6 P-Q5!); 6 NP×B, B-K2; 7 P-B4, P-Q4; 8 P-KB5, KP×P; 9 N-N2, O-O; 10 P×P, B-Q3 = . Petrosian-Spasski, match 1966. (2) 5 . . . P-Q4; 6 P×P, N×P; 7 P-K3, B-K2; 8 B-N5†, P-B3; 9 B-Q3, O-O 10 P-K4, N×N; 11 P×N, P-QB4; 12 O-O, P×P; 13 P×P, N-B3; 14 B-K3, B-B3; 15 B-N1, R-B1; 16 Q-Q3, P-N3; 17 B-R2, Q-Q2; 18 QR-Q1, N-R4? (18 . . . KR-Q1!); 19 B-R6, KR-K1; 20 N-N5, Q-K2; 21 P-B4, Q-B2; 22 P-B5, B×N; 23 B×N, Q-B6; 24 P×KP, P×P; 25 Q-K2, Q×P; 26 Q-KB2, R-B2; 27 R-Q3, Q-Q3; 28 B-KB4, Q-K2; 29 B×R, B-R3; 30 B-Q6, resigns. Furman-Panno, Madrid 1974. The game won White the Brilliancy Prize. (ii) 6 . . . P×P; 7 B-KN3, QN-Q2; 8 B-N2, P-QR3; 9 B-B4, N-R4; 10 B-N5, B-K2; 11 B×B, Q×B; 12 N-KR4!, N/4-B3; 13 N-B5, Q-B1; 14 Q-N3, O-O-O; 15 O-O, N-QN1; 16 QR-B1, N-B3; 17 N×QP, N×N; 18 B×N, N×P; 19 Q-B4!, N×P†; 20 Q×N, B×B; 21 Q×P†, K-N1; 22 R×P, K×R; 23 Q-R7†, K-B3?!; 24 R-B1†, Q-B4; 25 R×Q†, P×R; 26 P-QN4, P×P; 27 P×P, KR-K1; 28 N-K7†, K-Q3; 29 Q-B5†, K-K3; 30 N×B, R×N; 31 Q-B6†, resigns. Kasparov-Antoshin, Baku 1980. A quiet road to utter demolition. (B) For 5 B-B4 see Queen's Gambit Declined, col. 39.

(e) 7 Q-B2, P-B4 (for 7 . . . P-Q4 see Queen's Gambit Declined); 8 P-K4, P×P; 9 N×P, N-B3! 10 N×N, B×N; 11 O-O-O, Q-B2; 12 B-N3, Q-N2; or 12 . . . P-Q3 = . Comments.

(f) 11 R–B1, N × N; 12 Q × N, N–K5; 13 B × B, N × N; 14 R × N, Q × B = . Spasski–Keres, match 1965.

(g) 9 B × B, Q × B; 10 B–K2, O–O = . The column is Uhlmann–Padevski, Havana 1964.

(h) 8 . . . B–N5; 9 Q–B2, B × N†; 10 P × B, P–Q3; 11 N–Q2! (Korchnoi–Matanović, Belgrade 1964), N × N; 12 Q × N, P–KB4 = .

(i) 11 RP × N, P–QB4; 12 BP × P, KP × P; 13 P × P, P × P; 14 R–Q1, N–Q2∞. Korchnoi–Zuidema, Belgrade 1964.

(j) Also 7 . . . N–R4; 8 Q–B2! N–QB3; 9 O–O–O, N × B; 10 RP × N, P–N5; 11 N–K1, Q–N4†! 12 P–K3, O–O–O; 13 P–R3, B–N2; 14 K–N1, K–N1; 15 N–Q3, P–KR4 = . Uhlmann–Taimanov, Havana 1964.

(k) 11 B–Q3, N × B; 12 RP × N, N–Q2 = . Cobo–Smyslov, Havana 1965. Compare note (h).

1 P–Q4, N–KB3

	21	22	23	24	25
2	(P–QB4)			N–KB3 ⎱	The Marienbad
	(P–K3) (a)			P–QN3 (i) ⎰	System
3	(N–KB3)			P–KN3	P–K3!
	(P–QN3)			P–KN3 (j)	P–B4!
4	P–K3			B–N2	QN–Q2
	B–N2			B–QN2	P–K3
5	B–Q3			P–B4	B–Q3
	B–K2?	P–B4 (e)		B–N2	B–N2 (l)
6	N–B3!	N–B3	O–O	O–O	O–O
	P–Q4	B–K2	B–K2	O–O	N–B3
7	Q–R4†! (b)	O–O	P–QN3	N–B3	P–B3
	P–B3 (c)	P × P	O–O	N–K5	B–K2
8	P × P!	P × P	B–N2	N × N	P–K4
	P × P	P–Q4	P × P	B × N	P × P
9	O–O	P–QN3 (f)	P × P	B–B4	N × P
	O–O (d)	O–O (g)	P–Q4 (h)	P–Q3 (k)	N–K4 (m)

(a) If 2 . . . P–QN3, (A) 3 P–B3! P–Q4; 4 P × P, N × P; 5 P–K4, or (B) 3 N–QB3, B–N2!? 4 P–B3, P–Q4; 5 P × P, N × P; 6 N × N, Q × N; 7 P–K4, Q–Q2; 8 B–QB4, P–N3; 9 Q–N3, P–K3; 10 N–K2, B–N2 = . Agdamus–Fischer, Buenos Aires 1970.

(b) Ståhlberg's sleeper, yet a potent answer to Black's fifth move. Good for White is also 7 O–O, O–O, 8 P–QN3, QN–Q2; 9 B–N2, N–K5; 10 Q–K2. P–KB4; 11 P × P, P × P; 12 QR–Q1, P–QR3; 13 N–K5, B–Q3; 14 P–B4! Romanovski.

(c) (A) 7 . . . Q–Q2; 8 Q–B2, O–O; 9 P × P, P × P; 10 O–O, P–B4; 11 P–QN3, N–B3; 12 N–K5! (B) 7 . . . QN–Q2; 8 P × P, P × P; 9 N–K5!

(d) 10 Q–B2, P–B4; 11 P–QN3, N–B3; 12 P–QR3, P–KR3 (Ståhlberg–Bronstein, Zürich 1953); 13 N–K2, R–B1; 14 Q–N1! ± .

(e) (A) 5 . . . B–N5†; 6 QN–Q2 (6 N–B3, see Nimzo-Indian Defence, cols. 49–50), O–O; 7 O–O P–Q4; 8 P–QN3, QN–Q2; 9 B–N2, N–K5! 10 P–QR3, B–Q3; 11 Q–B2, P–KB4! 12 P–QN4, P–B4! 13 NP × P, NP × P; 14 BP × P, KP × P ∞ . (B) 5 . . . P–Q4! 6 O–O, B–Q3! 7 N–B3, O–O; 8 P–QN3, QN–Q2; 9 B–N2, P–QR3 = .

(f) 9 P × P, N × P; 10 B–N5†, B–B3! 11 Q–R4! Q–Q2! Darga–Olafsson, Hastings 1956.

(g) 10 B–N2, N–B3! 11 R–B1, R–B1; 12 R–K1, R–K1; 13 N–K5, P × P = . Keres–Darga, Bled 1961.

(h) 10 QN–Q2, N–B3; 11 Q–K2, R–K1; 12 QR–B1, R–QB1; 13 KR–Q1, B–B1; 14 N–B1, P–N3; 15 N–K3, (Hort–Langeweg, Beverwijk 1968), N–KR4 ∞ .

(i) Upon 2 P–QB4, P–QN3 White has (A) 3 P–B3! P–Q4; 4 P × P, N × P; 5 P–K4, or (B) 3 N–QB3, B–N2!? 4 P–B3! In the column, a "triple-fianchetto," the 2nd and 3rd moves can be transposed.

(j) (A) 3 . . . B–N2; 4 B–N2, P–B4; 5 P × P, P × P; 6 O–O, P–N3; 7 P–B3, B–N2; 8 Q–N3, Q–N3; 9 N–K5, Q × Q; 10 P × Q, B × B; 11 K × B, P–Q3; 13 N–Q3, N–B3 = . Tartakover–Balogh, Prague 1931. (B) 3 . . . P–K3; see Kevitz–Trajković Defence.

(k) 10 Q–Q2, N–Q2; 11 B–R6, P–K3; 13 B × B, K × B = . Guimard–Euwe, Groningen 1946.

(l) 5 . . . B–R3; 6 P–B4! The column resembles the Colle System.

(m) 10 B–B2 B–R3; 11 P–KB4, N–B3 = . *Comments.*

Bogolyubov- (or Bogo-) Indian Defence

(1 P–Q4, N–KB3; 2 P–QB4, P–K3;
3 N–KB3, B–N5†)

The Bogolyubov–Indian, colloquially called "Bogo–Indian," has a distinctive character. Yet it frequently transposes into several other openings, namely the Nimzowitsch–Indian Defence, the Catalan Opening, the Queen's Gambit Declined or the Queen's Indian. It is not often seen because White usually plays 3 N–QB3.

The forcing check, and the exchange of minor pieces which ordinarily follows—except in col. 5—somewhat avoids tension and offers Black equalizing chances.

After the interposition 4 B–Q2 (cols. 1–3), Black in addition to the three old-established choices of (A) 4 . . . B × B†, (B) 4 . . . Q–K2 and (C) 4 . . . B–K2, also has (D) 4 . . . P–QR4!?

(A) The capture 4 . . . B × B† (col. 1) is the most consistent choice. If White recaptures with 5 Q × B then 5 . . . P–Q4 with a formation akin to the Queen's Gambit levels, and if 5 QN × B, then 5 . . . P–Q3 also equalizes.

(B) The protective 4 . . . Q–K2 (col. 2) also holds up.

(C) The retreat 4 . . . B–K2 (note f) which duplicates Alekhin's manoeuvre in the Dutch Defence, is likewise sufficient to stay on even terms.

(D) The supporting 4 . . . P–QR4!? (col. 3) aims at preserving the bishop till it may choose to capture White's queen's knight rather than his queen's bishop, and after an eventual . . . P–R5 paralyse his queen's side. But the tactic is called into question after P–KN3. Otherwise, for variations with P–KN3 the Catalan Opening should be referred to.

The Interposition 4 QN–Q2 (cols. 4–5) preserves material as it does not invite an exchange, but it lacks punch.

327

1 P-Q4, N-KB3; 2 P-QB4, P-K3; 3 N-KB3, B-N5†

	1	2	3	4	5
4	B-Q2			QN-Q2 (i)	
	B×B†	Q-K2	P-QR4 (f)	O-O (j)	
5	Q×B (a)	P-KN3 (d)	P-KN3! (g)	Q-B2	P-K3 (m)
	P-Q4 (b)	O-O	P-QN3	P-Q4	P-QN3
6	P-K3	N-B3	B-N2	P-QR3	B-Q3
	O-O	P-Q3	B-N2	B-K2	B-N2
7	N-B3	B-N2	O-O	P-K3	O-O
	QN-Q2	P-K4	O-O (h)	P-QN3? (k)	P-Q4
8	B-Q3	O-O	B-B4	P×P!	Q-B2
	P-B3	B×N	B-K2	P×P	QN-Q2
9	QR-B1 (c)	B×B	N-B3	P-QN4	P-QN3
	Q-K2	P-K5	N-K5	P-B4	P-B4
10	O-O	N-K1	N×N ±	NP×P	
	P×P	P-Q4		P×P	
11	B×P	P×P		P×P	
	P-K4 =	N×P (e)		Q-R4 (l)	

(a) 5 QN×B, P-Q3; 6 P-K4, O-O; 7 B-Q3, P-K4; 8 P×P, P×P; 9 N×P, N-B3; 10 N/2-B3, N×N; 11 N×N, Q-Q5 = . *Comments.*

(b) (A) 5 . . . P-QN3; 6 P-KN3, see Queen's Indian Defence. (B) 5 . . . N-K5; 6 Q-B2, P-KB4; 7 P-KN3, or (C) 5 . . . P-Q3; 6 N-B3, O-O; 7 P-KN3 creates a Catalan Opening, but 7 P-K3, N-B3; 8 B-K2, Q-K2; 9 O-O is better.

(c) (A) 9 O-O, P×P; 10 B×P, P-K4! 11 B-N3, P×P = . Johner–Grünfeld, Pistyan 1922. (B) 9 P-K4, P×KP; 10 N×P, N×N; 11 B×N, Q-K2 = . Compare Queen's Pawn games. The column is *Comments.*

(d) Also 5 N-B3, P-QN3; 6 P-K3, B-N2; 7 B-Q3, KB×N; 8 B×B, N-K5; 9 B×N, B×B; 10 O-O, O-O = . Marshall–Kashdan, New York 1927.

(e) 12 Q-N3, P-QB3; 13 N-B2, N-R3 = . Panno–Petrosian, Los Angeles 1963.

(f) 4 . . . B-K2; 5 N-B3, P-Q4; 6 Q-B2 (6 B-N5, see Queen's Gambit Declined), QN-Q2; 7 P-K4, P×KP; 8 N×P, P-B3; 9 O-O-O, P-QN3; 10 B-Q3, B-N2; 11 B-B3, N×N; 12 B×N, N-B3; 13 B-Q3, Q-B2; 14 Q-K2, O-O-O! = . Lilienthal–Pinkus, USSR v. USA, 1945.

(g) 5 N-B3, O-O; 6 P-K3, (A) 6 . . . P-Q3; 7 Q-B2, QN-Q2; 8 P-QR3, B×N; 9 B×B, Q-K2 = . Glioric–Tal, Belgrade 1968. (B) 6 . . . P-QN3; 7 B-Q3, B-N2; 8 O-O, P-Q3; 9 Q-B2, QN-Q2; 10 P-QR3, KB×N; 11 B×B, R-K1 = . Porath–Bronstein, Amsterdam 1964.

(h) 7 . . . B×B; 8 Q×B, O-O; 9 N-B3 ± . Black's QRP is now a weakness.

(i) 4 N-B3, N-K5; 5 Q-B2, P-KB4; see Nimzo–Indian Defence.

(j) 4 . . . P-QN3; 5 P-QR3, B×N†; 6 Q×B, P-QR4; 7 P-QN3, B-N2; 8 P-K3, O-O; 9 B-K2, P-Q3 is an acceptable stratagem.

(k) At this moment it might be safer to steer into a Queen's Gambit with 7 . . . QN-Q2; 8 B-Q3, P×P; or 8 . . . P-B4.

(l) 12 B-N2, Q×BP; 13 Q×Q, B×Q; 14 B×N, P×B; 15 N-N3, B-N3; 16 B-N5 ± . Korchnoi–Bannik, USSR Chp. 1963.

(m) (A) 5 P-QR3, B×N†; (1) 6 Q×B, P-QN3; 7 P-QN4, B-N2; 8 P-K3, P-Q3; 9 B-K2, QN-Q2 = . Malich–Havansi, Lugano 1968. (2) 6 B×B, N-K5; 7 B-B4, P-Q3; 8 P-KN3, P-KB4; 9 B-N2, N-Q2; 10 N-Q2, QN-B3; 11 N×N, N×N = . Bisguier–Popel, US Open 1958. (B) 5 Q-R4, N-B3; 6 P-QR3, B×N†; 7 B×B, P-Q3 = . The column is Uhlmann–Ortega, Havana 1964.

Nimzowitsch (or Nimzo)- Indian Defence

(1 P–Q4, N–KB3; 2 P–QB4, P–K3;
3 N–QB3, B–N5)

Blessed with a catchy prefix, Nimzowitsch has lent his name to one of Black's most active and sound defences. With a slight inversion of moves it was introduced in Steinitz–Englisch, Vienna 1882, but the dogmatic author of the monumental *My System* did all the spadework and realized its hidden possibilities. When Tarrasch charged that Nimzowitsch's moves were ugly, he replied: "The beauty of a chess move lies not in its appearance, but in the thought behind it."

The Nimzowitsch–Indian—Nimzo–Indian for short—although not strictly an "Indian" structure since it involves no fianchetto, is one of the corner-stones and turning points of modern opening theory. Characterized by the pinning sortie 3 . . . B–N5, it exerts pressure on the queen's side and centre by restraining P–K4. Black must sometimes be prepared to exchange a bishop for a knight, but he obtains compensation by rapid development and/or the doubling of White's queen's bishop's pawn. Botvinnik was probably correct in maintaining that it is doubtful whether there is any refutation to this defence. It permits Black to equalize and keep alive some winning chances without taking too much risk of losing. It is hard to think of any modern master who at one time or another has not resorted to this defence.

THE CLASSICAL VARIATION, marked by 4 Q–B2 (cols. 1–15) leads to a drab game without chances for either side, though sometimes White is a little freer. It is now regarded as an old system, somewhat played out. Black can equalize with 4 . . . P–Q4 (cols. 1–5), 4 . . . P–B4 (cols. 6–8), 4 . . . N–B3 (cols. 9–11), 4 . . . P–Q3 (col. 12) and 4 . . . O–O (cols. 13–15). The absence of a threat (other than P–K4, if that can be regarded as one), as well as the premature development of White's queen, holds little future for this system if White wants to avoid drawish set-ups.

THE RUBINSTEIN VARIATION, typified by 4 P–K3 (cols. 16–55) is by far and away the most fashionable answer to the Nimzo–Indian. White sometimes gets a slight edge, but this is infinitesimal and requires patience and positional manoeuvring. Black's resources have kept the defence on a sterling level.

The standard replies are the interchangeable moves 4 . . . O–O; 5 . . . P–Q4; and 6 . . . P–B4; with 7 . . . N–QB3 (8 P–QR3, B × N) to follow (cols. 16–22). Retreating the bishop by 8 . . . B–R4 (cols 23–5) is rendered doubtful so far in col. 25.

THE NEO–RUBINSTEIN VARIATION (cols. 26–30), which has as its hallmark the substitution 8 . . . P × BP, has also established a place in chess theory.

The GLIGORIĆ VARIATION (cols. 31–40) we have so dubbed on account of the Yugoslav champion's extensive practice with the line 7 . . . P × BP and 7 . . . QN–Q2 to which he has added some valuable analysis in the past, and the strategy is still being applied on occasions.

Odd lines, by no means inferior and indeed very *en vogue*, are contained in cols. 41–4. It was the "oddness" of 5 N–K2 which may have prompted Korchnoi to adopt it in his 1978 match versus Karpov (col. 45). In a way, 5 N–K2 forces Black to exchange, whereas White's P–QR3 forces Black to exchange or retreat, but also loses tempi for White. Black's first important deviation from the "standard" replies, that is 4 . . . P–QN3, also comes off favourably (cols. 46–50). Certain deviations from the main lines that might arise from the earlier moves 4 . . . P–B4 or 4 . . . P–Q4 are shown in cols. 51–5.

The SÄMISCH VARIATION 4 P–QR3 (cols. 56–70) is undoubtedly the most clear-cut attempt at outright refutation. White loses a move in order to force Black to carry out his strategy! White's most consequential follow up is with P–B3 with the stage set for sharp attack (cols. 56–63); or he may quietly continue with the "stonewall"-like 6 P–K3 (cols. 64–6). Black's resilience is demonstrated with his further possibilities 5 . . . P–QN3 and 5 . . . N–K5 (cols. 67–79), all well defensible.

THE SPIELMANN VARIATION 4 Q–N3 (cols. 71–2) was popularized by its namesake at Carlsbad 1929, but despite its soundness it has fallen from favour as too sterile.

Diverse fourth moves for White in cols. 73–5 are capable of further experimentation.

1 P–Q4, N–KB3; 2 P–QB4, P–K3; 3 N–QB3, B–N5; 4 Q–B2, P–Q4

	1	2	3	4	5
5	P–QR3		P × P (g)		
	B × N†		Q × P	P × P	
6	Q × B		N–B3 (h)	B–N5 (j)	
	N–B3	N–K5	P–B4	P–KR3	P–B4 (k)
7	N–B3 (a)	Q–B2	B–Q2	B × N!	P–QR3 (l)
	N–K5	P–QB4 (c)	B × N	Q × B	B × N†
8	Q–N3 (b)	P × BP	B × B	P–QR3	P × B
	N–R4	N–QB3	P × P!	B × N†	N–B3
9	Q–R4†	P × P (d)	N × P	Q × B	N–B3
	P–B3	P × P	O–O	O–O	P–KR3
10	P × P	N–B3	P–K3	P–K3	B × N
	P × P	B–B4	P–K4	P–B3	Q × B
11	P–K3	P–QN4	N–B3	N–B3	P–K3
	B–B4	O–O (e)	N–B3	B–B4	O–O
12	B–Q2	B–N2	B–K2	N–K5	B–K2
	N × B =	P–QN3! (f)	B–N5 (i)	N–Q2 =	B–B4 =

(*a*) 7 P–K3, P–K4; 8 P × KP, N–K5 (8 . . . P–Q5; 9 Q–Q3, N–KN5; 10 N–B3, P × P; 11 Q × Q†, K × Q =); 9 Q–Q3, N–B4; 10 Q–B2, P × P; 11 B × P, N × P, 12 B–N5†, P–B3; 13 Q × N, Q–R4† = . Kotov–Szabó, Budapest 1950.

(*b*) 8 Q–B2, P–K4! 9 P–K3, B–B4; 10 B–Q3, KP × P; 11 KP × P, O–O; 12 O–O, R–K1 = .

(*c*) (A) 7 . . . O–O; 8 N–R3, and 9 P–B3 ± . (B) 7 . . . N–QB3; 8 P–K3, P–K4; 9 P × QP, Q × P; 10 B–B4, Q–R4†; 11 P–N4, N × NP; 12 Q × N, N–B7†; 13 K–K2! Q–K8†! 14 K–B3, N × R; 15 B–N2! O–O; 16 K–N3, B–Q2! 17 N–B3, Q × R; 18 N–N5, P–KN3; 19 Q × KP! QR–K1; 20 Q–B6, R × P†! 21 P × R, Q–K8†; 22 Q–B2, N–B7! 23 Q × Q, N × Q; 24 K–B2, P–N4; 25 B–K2, N–B7; 26 B–Q1, N × RP; 27 B × N, R–R1; 28 B–N3, B–K1 = . *Comments.*

(*d*) (A) 9 P–K3, Q–R4†; 10 B–Q2, N × B; 11 Q × N, P × P; 12 Q × Q, N × Q; 13 R–B1, P–QN4; 14 P × P *e.p.*, B–N2; 15 N–B3, K–K2! Tolush–Sokolski, Leningrad 1934. (B) 9 N–B3, Q–R4†; 10 N–Q2, N–Q5; 11 Q–Q3, P–K4; 12 P–QN4, Q–R5; 13 R–R2, N × N = .

(*e*) In reply to Bogolyubov's text 11 P–QN4, good is also 11 . . . N–N6?! 12 Q–N2, N × R; 13 Q × P, R–KB1; 14 B–R6, Q–K2; 15 Q × R†, Q × Q; 16 B × Q, K × B; 17 P–N3, B–K5; 18 B–N2, P–QR4 ∞ .

(*f*) 13 P–N5, P × P; 14 P × N, Q–R4†; 15 N–Q2, QR–N1! 16 R–Q1, P–Q5; 17 P–B7, Q × BP; 18 N × N, B × N; 19 Q–Q2, KR–K1; with pressure for the piece. Katĕtov.

(*g*) 5 P–K3, O–O; 6 P–QR3, B–K2; 7 N–B3, P–B4; 8 P × BP, B × P; 9 B–K2, N–B3 = .

(*h*) 6 P–K3, P–B4; 7 P–QR3, B × N†; 8 P × B, (1) 8 . . . O–O; 9 N–B3, P × P; 10 BP × P, P–QN3; 11 B–B4, Q–B3; 12 B–Q3, Q × Q; 13 B × Q, B–R3 = . (2) 8 . . . N–B3; 9 N–B3, O–O; 10 P–B4, Q–Q3; 11 B–N2, P × P; 12 P × P, P–QN3 = , both from match Alekhin–Euwe, 1937. (3) 8 . . . QN–Q2; 9 N–B3, P–QN3; 10 P–B4, Q–Q3; 11 B–N2, B–N2; 12 B–K2, P × P; 13 P × P, O–O; 14 O–O, N–N5 = . Botvinnik–Levenfish, match 1937.

(*i*) 13 P–KR3, B–R4; 14 O–O, KR–Q1 = . Flohr–Reshevsky, AVRO 1938.

(*j*) 6 P–QR3, B × N†; 7 P × B, P–B4; 8 P–B3, Q–B2; 9 R–R2, P–KR3 = . The column is Flohr–Euwe, match 1932.

(*k*) Also playable are (A) 6 . . . Q–Q3; 7 B × N, Q × B; 8 P–QR3, B × N†; 9 Q × B, O–O; 10 P–K3, P–B3 = . Capablanca–Euwe, match 1931. (B) 6 . . . O–O; 7 P–K3, R–K1; 8 B–Q3, P–KR3; 9 B–R4. P–B4; 10 N–K2, N–B3 = . Lisitsyn.

(*l*) 7 O–O–O is sharper. The column is Makarczyk–Gadalinski, Zopot 1951.

1 P-Q4, N-KB3; 2 P-QB4, P-K3; 3 N-QB3, B-N5; 4 Q-B2

	6	7	8	9	10
	P-B4			N-B3 (Milner-Barry Variation)	
5	P×P			N-B3	
	O-O	N-B3	N-R3 (e)	P-Q3 (g)	
6	P-QR3 (a)	N-B3	P-QR3	P-QR3	
	B×BP	B×P	Q-R4	B×N†	
7	N-B3	B-N5	B-Q2	Q×B	
	N-B3	P-QN3!	N×P	P-QR4	O-O
8	P-QN4 (b)	P-K3	O-O-O	P-QN3 (h)	P-QN4
	B-K2	B-N2	B×N	O-O	P-K4 (k)
9	P-K3	B-K2	B×B	B-N2 (i)	P×P
	P-QN3	R-QB1	Q-N3	R-K1	N-K5
10	B-N2	O-O	P-K3	R-Q1	Q-K3
	B-N2	B-K2	P-Q3	Q-K2	P-B4
11	B-Q3	QR-Q1	N-B3	P-Q5	B-N2
	R-B1	P-Q3	B-Q2	N-N1	B-K3 (l)
12	O-O	R-Q2	P-QN4	P×P	R-B1
	P-KR3 (c)	P-QR3 (d)	QN-K5 (f)	P×P (j)	Q-K2 (m)

(a) (A) 6 B-B4 (1) 6 . . . N-R3; 7 P-QR3 (7 B-Q6, R-K1; 8 P-QR3, Q-R4; 9 R-B1, B×N†; 10 Q×B, Q×Q†; 11 R×Q, N-K5=. Meyer-Flum, corr. 1966), B×N†; 8 Q×B, N-K5; 9 Q-Q4, QN×QBP; 10 P-QN4, N-QN6; 11 Q×N, N×R; 12 B-K5, P-QR4=. (2) 6 . . . B×P; 7 N-B3, (1) 7 . . . N-B3; 8 P-K3, P-Q4; 9 R-Q1 (9 P-QR3, Q-R4; 10 N-Q2, B-N5! 11 R-B1, B×N; 12 Q×B, Q×Q; 13 R×Q, P-K4; 14 B-N5, B-K3=), Q-R4; 10 P-QR3, R-Q1; 11 N-Q2, P-Q5; 12 N-N3, Q-N3; 13 N-R4, B-N5†; 14 P×B, Q×P†; 15 N-Q2, Q-R4; 16 P-QN3, N-QN5; 17 Q-N1, P-Q6∞. Taimanov. Black has some attack, but it may not be worth the material sacrificed. (II) 7 . . . P-QN3; 8 P-K3, B-N2=. (B) 6 N-B3, N-R3; 7 P-QR3, B×N†; 8 Q×B, N×P; 9 P-K3, P-QR4; 10 B-K2 (10 P-QN3! = Taimanov), P-R5; 11 O-O, P-QN3; 12 B-Q2, B-R3; 13 Q-B2, R-B1∞. Kholmov-Bondarevski, USSR Chp. 1948. (C) 6 B-N5, N-R3; 7 P-QR3, B×N†; 8 Q×B, N×P; 9 B×N, Q×B; 10 Q×Q, P×Q; 11 P-B3, P-QR4; 12 P-K4, P-N3; 13 R-Q1, P-R5=. Kotov-Averbakh, USSR Chp. 1951.

(b) 8 P-K3, P-Q4; 9 P-QN4, B-Q3; 10 B-N2, P-QR4! 11 P-N5, N-K4; 12 P×P, P×P; 13 B-K2, B-K3=. *Comments.*

(c) 13 KR-Q1, P-QR4! 14 P-N5, N-N1; 15 P-K4, Q-B2; 16 Q-K2, P-Q3; 17 N-QR4, QN-Q2=. Najdorf-Reshevsky, match 1952.

(d) 13 KR-Q1, O-O; 14 B-B4, N-K1=. Rubinstein-Sämisch, Berlin 1926.

(e) Another one of the many defences which put the 4 Q-B2 line out of business is here 5 . . . B×P; 6 N-B3, P-Q4; 7 P-K3, O-O; 8 B-K2, P×P; 9 B×P, QN-Q2; 10 O-O, P-QR3; 11 P-QR3, P-QN4; 12 B-K2, B-N2=.

(f) F. Krausz-Korn, corr. 1954. In the column, playable is 6 . . . B×N†; 7 Q×B, N×P; 8 P-QN4, N/4-K5; 9 Q-B2, P-Q4=.

(g) 5 . . . P-Q4; (A) 6 B-N5, P-KR3; 7 B×N, Q×B; 8 P-K3, O-O; 9 P-QR3, B×N; 10 Q×B, P-QR4=. (B) 6 P-K3! O-O; 7 P-QR3, B×N†; 8 Q×B, B-Q2; 9 P-QN3, P-QR4; 10 B-N2, P-R5; 11 P-QN4, P×P; 12 B×P, N-R2; 13 P-Q5! ±. Donner-Taimanov, Havana 1967.

(h) 8 B-N5, P-R3; 9 B-R4, Q-K2; 10 P-K3, P-K4; 11 P-Q5, N-QN1; 12 B-K2, QN-Q2; 13 O-O, P-R5=. Borowski-Sliwa, Warsaw 1952.

(i) 9 P-N3, Q-K2; 10 B-KN2, N-K5; 11 Q-B2, P-B4; 12 O-O, P-K4; 13 P-Q5 N-N1; 14 B-N2, Q-B2! =. *Comments.*

(*j*) 13 P–N3, P–QN3 = . Donner–Reshevsky, Amsterdam 1950.

(*k*) 8 . . . R–K1; 9 B–N2, P–K4; 10 P × P, N × KP; 11 N × N, P × N; 12 P–K3, B–B4 = .

(*l*) 11 . . . N × KP; 12 N × N, P × N; 13 P–N3, R–K1; 14 B–N2, N–B3; 15 O–O, P–B3; 16 Q–B5, Q–B2; 17 KR–Q1 ± . Denker–Evans, New York 1951.

(*m*) 13 P × P, Q × P; 14 P–KN3, QR–Q1   . Gadalinski–Szabó, Spindlerův Mlýn 1948.

1 P-Q4, N-KB3; 2 P-QB4, P-K3; 3 N-QB3, B-N5; 4 Q-B2

	11	12	13	14	15
	(N-B3)	P-Q3!	O-O		
5	(N-B3)	B-N5 (c)	P-QR3 (f)	B-N5	N-B3
	(P-Q3)	O-O (d)	B×N†	P-B4 (h)	P-B4
6	B-Q2!	P-K3 (e)	Q×B	P×P	P×P
	O-O (a)	P-K4	P-QN3!	N-R3	N-R3
7	P-QR3	N-K2	N-B3	P-QR3	P-QR3 (j)
	B×N	Q-K2	B-N2	B×N†	B×N†
8	B×B	P×P	B-N5	Q×B	Q×B
	Q-K2	P×P	P-Q3	N×P	N×P
9	P-QN4	P-QR3	P-K3	B×N	P-QN4 (k)
	P-K4	B×N†	QN-Q2	Q×B	QN-K5
10	P×P	N×B	Q-B2	Q×Q	Q-B2
	N×KP	P-B3 =	Q-K1	P×Q	P-QR4!
11	P-K3		N-Q2	P-B3	R-QN1
	B-N5 (b)		P-B4 (g)	P-QR4 (i)	P×P (l)

(a) 6 ... P-K4; 7 P×P, P×P; 8 O-O-O! B×N; 9 B×B, Q-K2; 10 P-K3, B-N5; 11 P-KR3, B-R4; 12 Q-N3, R-QN1; 13 P-KN4, B-N3; 14 N-R4±. Ragozin–Lisitsyn, USSR Chp. 1944.

(b) 12 N×N, P×N; 13 P-B3, B-R4; 14 B-K2±.

(c) 5 P-QR3, B×N†; 6 Q×B, QN-Q2; 7 N-B3, P-Q3; 8 P-KN3, B-N2; 9 B-N2, O-O; 10 P-QN4, P-QR4 =. O'Kelly–Pachman, Hilversum 1947. Also see col 13.

(d) 5 ... QN-Q2; 6 P-K3, P-B4; 7 B-Q3, Q-R4; 8 N-B3, P-KR3; 9 B-R4, P×P; 10 P×P, P-QN3; 11 O-O, B×N =. Pachman–Smyslov, Venice 1950.

(e) 6 N-B3, QN-Q2; 7 P-QR3, B×N†, Q×B, R-K1 =. Suetin.

(f) 5 P-K4, (A) 5 ... P-Q4; 6 P-K5, N-K5; 7 B-Q3, P-QB4; 8 P×BP, N-QB3; 9 B×N, P×B; 10 Q×P, B×N†; 11 P×B, Q-R4; 12 N-K2, Q×BP; 13 B-B4, N-R4 =. (B) 5 ... P-Q3; 6 P-K5, P×P; 7 P×P, N-N5; 8 N-B3, N-QB3; 9 B-B4, P-B3; 10 R-Q1, Q-K2; 11 P×P, Q×P∓. Ježek–Pachman CSSR 1953.

(g) 12 P-QN4, P-K4; 13 NP×P, NP×P =. Reshevsky–Keres, Moscow 1948.

(h) Also playable is 5 ... P-KR3; 6 B-R4, P-B4; 7 P×P, N-R3 (7 ... Q-R4; 8 B×N, P×B; 9 P-K4, B×N†; 10 P×B, Q×BP; 11 N-R3, K-N2; 12 Q-Q2, N-B3; 13 B-K2, R-R1; 14 N-B4, K-B1∞. Filip); 8 P-QR3! B×N†; 9 Q×B, P-KN4; 10 B-N3, N-K5 =. *Comments.*

(i) 12 P-K4, P-N3; 13 R-Q1, P-R5 =. Kotov–Averbakh, USSR Chp. 1951.

(j) (A) 7 P-K3, P-N3; 8 P-QR3, B×N†; 9 Q×B, P-QN3; 10 B-K2, B-R3; 11 P-QN4, N/4-K5; 12 Q-N3, P-Q4 =. Van Scheltinga–Gligorić, match 1949. (B) 7 B-N5, N×P; 8 P-QR3, B×N†; 9 Q×B, N/3-K5; 10 B×Q, N×Q; 11 B-K7, N-N6 =. B. H. Wood–Euwe, Hastings 1949–50.

(k) 9 P-KN3, P-QN3; 10 B-N2, B-R3! 11 N-Q2, B-N2; 12 P-B3, P-Q4 =. *Comments.*

(l) 12 P×P, P-Q4 =. Thomson–Zuidema, World Jun. Chp. The Hague 1961.

Rubinstein Variation

1 P–Q4, N–KB3; 2 P–QB4, P–K3; 3 N–QB3, B–N5; 4 P–K3, O–O; 5 B–Q3, P–Q4;
6 N–B3, P–B4; 7 O–O, N–B3; 8 P–QR3, B × N; 9 P × B, P × BP; 10 B × P, Q–B2

	16	17	18	19	20
11	P–QR4	R–K1	B–N5	B–Q3	B–N2 (h)
	P–K4 (a)	P–K4	B–Q2	P–K4	P–K4
12	B–R3	P–Q5	P–QR4	Q–B2	P–R3
	P–QN3	N–QR4	N–QR4	R–K1 (e)	B–B4 (i)
13	Q–B2 (b)	P–Q6	B–R3	P–K4 (f)	B–N5
	B–N5	Q–N3	P–QN3	P–B5	P–K5
14	N–N5	N × P	B–Q3	B × P	N–R4
	N–QR4	N × B	B–B3	P × P	B–Q2
15	B–R2	N × N	N–K5	P × P	P–QB4
	B–R4	Q–R3	B–K5	N–QR4	P × P
16	P–KB4	Q–Q3	B–K2	B–Q3!	P × P
	P × BP	R–Q1	KR–Q1	Q × Q	Q–B5
17	R × P	P–K4	R–B1	B × Q	P–N3
	B–N3 =	B–K3 = (c)	QR–B1 = (d)	N × P (g)	Q–Q3 (j)

(a) Also (A) 11 . . . R–Q1; 12 B–R3, P × P; 13 BP × P, P–QN3 = ; or (B) 11 . . . P–QN3; 12 B–R3, P–K4; 13 Q–B2, B–N2; 14 B–K2, P–K5 = . Najdorf–Reshevsky, match 1953.

(b) If 13 P × BP, N–QR4 = . The column is Reshevsky–Najdorf, match 1953.

(c) Kluger–O'Kelly, Bucharest 1954. In the column, 13 . . . Q–N1; or 13 . . . Q–Q1 are also effective.

(d) Donner–Van Scheltinga, Beverwijk 1959.

(e) (A) 12 . . . R–Q1; 13 P–R3, Q–K2 = . *Comments.* (B) 12 . . . Q–K2; 13 N × P, N × N; 14 P × N, Q × P; 15 P–B3!? N–Q4; 16 B × P†, K–R1 = . White must return the pawn.

(f) 13 N × P, N × N; 14 P × N, Q × P; 15 P–B3, B–Q2! 16 R–Q1, QR–Q1; 17 P–K4, B–B3; 18 B–N2, R–Q2 = . Evans–Rossolimo, US Chp. 1963.

(g) 18 R–K1, B–B4; draw. Averbakh–Karaklajić, USSR v. Yugoslavia 1956.

(h) Other alternatives, also allowing equality are (A) 11 B–R2, P–K4; 12 P–R3, P–K5; 13 N–R2, B–B4; 14 N–N4, B × N; 15 P × B, P–QR3; 16 Q–K2, KR–K1 = . (B) 11 B–K2, R–Q1 (11 . . . P–K4; 12 P–Q5, P–K5; 13 N–K1, N–K4; 14 P–KB4, P × P *e.p.*; 15 P × P ±). 12 Q–B2, P–K4; (1) 13 B–N2, B–N5; 14 P × KP, N × P; 15 P–B4, N × N†; 16 P × N, B–R6; 17 KR–Q1, R × R†; 18 R × R, R–Q1; 19 R–N1, Q–Q2; 20 K–R1 ± . (2) 13 P × KP, N × P; 14 N–K1 (or 14 P–KR3?!), P–B5; 15 P–K4, B–N5; 16 P–B3, Q–B4†; 17 K–R1, B–K3 = . Taimanov.

(i) 12 . . . P–K5; 13 N–Q2, N–QR4; 14 B–R2, P–B5; 15 P–B3, B × P; 16 N × P, N × N; 17 P × N, Q–N6; 18 Q–B3, Q × Q; 19 R × Q, B–Q2 = . Taimanov.

(j) 18 P–Q5, N–K4; 19 B × B, KN × B; 20 Q–Q4, P–B4; 21 P–B4, P × P *e.p.*; 22 N × P, Q–KN3! = . Uhlman–Szabó, Wageningen 1957.

Rubinstein Variation

1 P–Q4, N–KB3; 2 P–QB4, P–K3; 3 N–QB3, B–N5; 4 P–K3, O–O; 5 B–Q3, P–Q4;
6 N–B3, P–B4; 7 O–O, N–B3; 8 P–QR3

	21	22	23	24	25
	(B×N)		B–R4 (g)		
9	(P×B)		P×QP (h)		
	Q–B2?	P–QN3	KP×P		
10	P×QP (a)	P×QP (d)	P×P		
	KP×P	KP×P	B×N		
11	N–R4! (b)	P–QR4 (e)	P×B		
	Q–K2	P–B5	B–N5		Q–R4
12	P–B3	B–B2	P–B4	R–N1	Q–B2!
	N–K5	B–N5!	N–K4	Q–B1	Q×P/4
13	P–N3	Q–K1	P×P (i)	P–R3	P–QR4
	N×BP	N–K5!	B×N	B–R4	R–K1
14	Q–B2	B×N (f)	P×B	B–K2	R–N1 (k)
	P–B5	P×B	Q×P	R–Q1	B–N5
15	B×P	N–Q2	B–K2	B–N2	R–N5 ±
	P×B (c)	Q–Q4 =	Q×QBP =	N–K5 (j)	

(a) (A) 10 B–N2, P×BP; 11 B×P, P–K4; see col. 20. (B) 10 Q–B2, N–QR4! 11 P×QP, P–B5 = . Geller–Petrosian, Amsterdam 1956.

(b) 11 P–R3, P–B5 (11 ... N–K2; 12 P×P, Q×P; 13 Q–B2! ±); 12 B–B2, N–K2; 13 P–QR4! B–B4! 14 B–R3, N–K5; 15 N–R4! B–K3; 16 P–KB4, P–KB3 ∞ . Gligorić–Korchnoi, Mallorca 1968.

(c) 16 Q×N, B–R6; 17 N–N2, P–QN4; 18 B–N2 ± . Pachman–Milić, Sarajevo 1961.

(d) (A) 10 P–QR4, B–R3! (B) 10 N–K5, N×N; 11 P×N, P×P; 12 B×P, Q×Q; 13 R×Q, N–N5; 14 P–B4, B–N2 = . *Comments* (c) 10 B–N2! B–R3! 11 P×QP, B×B; 12 Q×B, Q×P! 13 P–B4, Q–K5! = .

(e) Other important tries: (A) 11 B–N2, P–B5; 12 B–B2, B–N5; 13 Q–K1, N–K5! 14 N–Q2, N×N; 15 Q×N, B–R4: 16 P–B3, B–N3; 17 P–K4, Q–Q2; 18 QR–K1, P–B4! 19 P×QP, Q×P; 20 P–QR4, KR–K1 = . Smyslov–Petrosian, Zürich 1953. (B) 11 P×P, P×P; 12 P–B4, P×P; 13 B×P, N–QR4; 14 Q–B2, N×B; 15 Q×N, Q–Q4 = . Reshevsky–Najdorf, match 1953. (c) 11 N–Q2, B–K3; 12 B–N2, P–B5; 13 B–B2, P–QN4; 14 P–B3, P–QR4; 15 R–K1, Q–N3; 16 N–N1, P–N5; 17 Q–Q2, P–N6; 18 B–N1, P–R5 = . Euwe–Averbakh, Zürich 1953. (D) 11 N–K5, N×N; 12 P×N, N–Q2; 13 P–KB4, P–B5; 14 B–B2, N–B4 = .

(f) 14 N–Q2, N×N; 15 B×N, P–B4; 16 P–B3, B–R4; 17 P–K4, BP×P; 18 P×P, R×R†; 19 Q×R, B–N3 = . Euwe.

(g) A recent revival is 8 ... P×QP; 9 KP×P, P×P; 10 B×P, B×N; 11 P×B, Q–R4; 12 Q–K2, Q×BP; 13 B–Q2, Q–B7; 14 B–Q3, Q–R5; 15 B–QN5, Q–B7; 16 B–Q3, Q–R5; 17 B–QN5, Q–B7 = . Szabó–Polugayevski, Hilversum 1973.

(h) (A) 9 P–KR3, P×QP; 10 KP×P, P×P; 11 B×P, B–N3; 12 B–K3, N–Q4! 13 B×N, P×B = . (B) 9 R–K1, P–QR3; 10 P×BP, P×P; 11 B×P, B×N; 12 P×B, Q×Q; 13 R×Q, N–K5 = . Kluger–Troianescu, Bucharest 1954. (c) 9 N–QR4, P×QP; 10 KP×P, P×P; 11 B×P, P–KR3; 12 P–QN4, B–B2; 13 B–N2, P–QN3; 14 N–K5, B–N2; 15 R–B1 = . Reshevsky–Levenfish, Moscow 1939.

(i) 13 B–N2, N×N†; 14 P×N, B–R6; 15 R–K1, N–K5! 16 B–K5, Q–N4†; 17 B–N3, N×B; 18 RP×N, P×P; 19 B×P, Q×BP = . Furman–Taimanov, USSR Chp. 1954. The column is Furman–Vladimirov, USSR Chp. 1954.

(j) 16 N–Q2, B×B; 17 Q×B, N×P/4; 18 P–QB4, P–Q5 = . Panno–Averbakh, Argentina *v.* USSR 1954.

(k) *Comments* to Flohr–Landau, Bournemouth 1939.

Neo-Rubinstein Variation

1 P–Q4, N–KB3; 2 P–QB4, P–K3; 3 N–QB3, B–N5; 4 P–K3, O–O; 5 B–Q3, P–Q4;
6 N–B3, P–B4; 7 O–O, N–B3; 8 P–QR3, P × BP; 9 B × P (*a*), B–R4 (*b*);

	26	27	28	29	30
10	B–Q3 (*c*)	.... Q–Q3			... B–Q3
	P–KR3 (*d*)	... P–QR3			P × P (*n*)
11	B–B2	N–K4 (*f*)	R–Q1!		P × P
	Q–K2	P–QN4	P–QN4		P–KR3 (*o*)
12	N–K5	B–R2 (*g*)	B–R2		B–B2
	R–Q1	P–B5	B–N2	P–B5 (*j*)	B–B2
13	N × N	Q–B2	P × P	Q–K2	R–K1
	P × N	N × N	B × N	Q–K1!	R–K1
14	Q–B3	Q × N	Q–B2	B–Q2! (*k*)	.... B–K3
	B–R3	B–N2	Q–K2	B–N3!	P–QN3
15	R–Q1	B–N1	Q × B	P–QN3?! (*l*)	Q–K2
	QR–B1 (*e*)	P–N3 (*h*)	KR–Q1 (*i*)	P × P (*m*)	B–N2

(*a*) 9 P × B, P × QP; 10 B × P, P × N; 11 P × P, Q–B2; 12 Q–K2, P–K4; 13 P–K4
(Gligorić–Wade, Skopje 1968), P–KR3 = .

(*b*) The older line 9 . . . P × P, 10 P × P, B–K2; 11 Q–Q3! P–QR3; or 11 . . . P–QN3 is
somewhat discredited.

(*c*) Recent tries are (A) 10 N–K2, B–N3; 11 P × P, B × P; 12 Q × Q, R × Q; 13 P–QN4,
B–K2; 14 B–N2, B–Q2; 15 KR–Q1, QR–B1 = . Visier–Kristinsson, Lugano 1968, (B) 10 B–R2,
P × P; 11 P × P, B–N3 = , and (c) 10 N–QR4! P × P; 11 P × P, N–Q4; 12 Q–Q3.

(*d*) Equality resulted from 10 . . . P × P; 11 P × P, B–N3; 12 B–K3, Q–Q3; 13 Q–Q2,
N–Q4; 14 N × N, P × N; 15 KR–K1, B–Q2; 16 QR–Q1, QR–B1 = . Donner–Lengyel, Amsterdam 1968.

(*e*) 16 N–K4, N × N; 17 B × N, B–N3 = . Ojanen–Johannsson, Lugano 1968.

(*f*) Prudent "quickies" resulted from (A) 11 P × P, Q × Q; 12 B × Q, B × N; 13 P × B,
N–QR4! (1) 14 R–N1, R–Q1; drawn. Gligorić–Larsen, Sousse 1967. (2) 14 B–B2, B–Q2; 15
P–K4, B–B3; 16 R–K1, KR–B1; 17 B–B4, N–Q2 = . Gligorić–O'Kelly, Dundee 1967. (B) 11
P–QR4, B–Q2; 12 P × P, Q–K2; 13 P–K4, Q × P; 14 B–K3, Q–R4; 15 B–B4, QR–B1; 16
QR–B1, KR–Q1 = . Portisch–Larsen, Poreć 1968.

(*g*) 12 N × N†, (A) 12 . . . Q × N; 13 Q–K4, B–N2; 14 B–Q3, P–N3; 15 P × P, N–N5! 16
Q–K5! Q × Q; 17 N × Q, N × B; 18 N × N, KR–Q1; 19 N–K5, B–B2; 20 N–N3, (1) 20 . . .
P–QR4! 21 N–Q4, R–Q4; 22 P–B6, B–B1; 23 B–Q2, P–K4; 24 N–B3, B–N5; 25 P–K4, R–Q3;
26 B–K3, R × P; draw. Gligorić–Unzicker, Ljubljana 1969. (2) 20 . . . B × N? 21 P × B,
P–QR4; 22 R–N1, P–N5; 23 P × P ± , Portisch. (B) 12 . . . P × N! 13 Q–K4, B–N2; 14 B–Q3,
P–B4; 15 Q–B4, P–B5 ∞ . Larsen.

(*h*) 16 Q–B4, B–B2; 17 Q–R6, Q–B3; 18 B–Q2, N–QR4 = . Rabar–Ivkov, Belgrade 1954.

(*i*) 16 B–Q2, N–K5; 17 Q–B2, N × QBP; 18 B–K1, N–R4! 19 QR–B1, R × R; 20 R × R,
R–QB1 = . Portisch–Larsen, Poreć 1968. Also refer to col. 30.

(*j*) Suspect—but not refuted—is 12 . . . B–N3; 13 Q–B2, P–B5! 14 N–K2, Q–B2! 15
N–N3, B–N2; 16 B–Q2, QR–Q1; and 17 . . . P–K4 ∞ . Portisch–Olafsson, Wijk aan Zee 1969.

(*k*) Weak are (A) 14 P–KR3, P–K4; 15 P–Q5, N–Q1; 16 P–K4, N–N2; 17 B–N1, N–Q2; 18
B–B2, N–Q3 ∓ ; or (B) 14 B–N1, P–K4; 15 P–Q5, B × N! 16 P × B, N–QR4; 17 P–K4, N–N6;
18 R–R2, N × B; 19 R × N, B–N5 ∓ . Gligorić–Tal, Belgrade 1968. Interesting is (c) 14 P–K4,
P–K4; 15 P–Q5, N–Q5; 16 N × N, P × N; 17 R × P, Q–K4; 18 B–K3, N–N5; 19 P–B4, Q–N1;
20 QR–Q1, N × B; 21 Q × N, B–N3; with complications. Gligorić–Gheorghiu, Skopje 1968.

(*l*) 15 B–N1, (A) 15 . . . B–N2; 16 P–QR4, N–QR4 = . Larsen. (B) 15 . . . P–K4!? 16 P × P,
N × P; 17 N–K4, N × N, 18 B × N, N–B3; 19 N–N5, P–R3; 20 Q–B3, B–Q2! = . Larsen.

(*m*) 16 B × P, B–N2; 17 B–K1, P–K4!? (17 . . . R–Q1!), 18 P–Q5, N–QR4; 19 B–B2
(Portisch–Haag, Hungarian Chp. 1969), R–B1! ∓ .

Neo-Rubinstein Variation

(n) A complex game resulted from 10 . . . B–N3; 11 P × P, B × P; 12 P–QN4, B–K2; 13 B–N2, P–QR3; 14 R–B1, B–Q2; 15 B–N1, R–B1; 16 Q–Q3, B–K1; 17 Q–B2, N–R2; 18 KR–Q1, Q–N3; 19 N–KN5, P–N3; drawn. Najdorf–Reshevsky, match 1953.

(o) 11 . . . B–N3; 12 B–K3, N–Q4; 13 N × N, P × N; 14 P–KR3, N–K2 = . Gligorić–Polugayevski, Vinkovci 1970. Also refer to col. 26. The column is Taimanov–Mecking, Mallorca 1970.

1 P–Q4, N–KB3; 2 P–QB4, P–K3; 3 N–QB3, B–N5; 4 P–K3, O–O; 5 B–Q3, P–Q4;
6 N–B3, P–B4; 7 O–O, P × BP (*a*) (Gligorič Variation); 8 B × P

	31	32	33	34	35
	Q–K2....................................				QN–Q2
9	B–Q3!	Q–K2	P–QR3		Q–Q3 (*j*)
	N–B3	B–Q2 (*c*)	B–R4		P–QR3
10	N–K4	P–QR3	Q–K2 (*e*)		P–QR4
	P × P	B × N	R–Q1!	N–B3 (*h*)	P × P (*k*)
11	P × P	P × B	B–Q2	R–Q1	P × P
	P–KR3	B–B3	P × P	R–Q1	R–K1
12	Q–K2	N–K5	N × P	B–R2	R–Q1
	R–Q1	B–Q4	B–N3 (*f*)	B–N3	N–N3
13	B–K3	B–Q3	N/4–N5!	N–QR4	B–N3
	P–K4	B–K5	B–Q2	B–Q2	B–Q2
14	P × P	P–QR4	KR–Q1	N × B	N–K5
	N × P (*b*)	R–B1 (*d*)	B × N (*g*)	P × N (*i*)	B–B3 (*l*)

(*a*) (7 . . . N–B3); (A) 8 P × QP, KP × P; 9 N–K5, R–K1; 10 N × N, P × N; 11 Q–R4, B–Q2! or 11 . . . Q–R4 = . (B) 8 P × BP, B × P; 9 P–QR3, P–QR3; 10 P–QN4, B–R2; 11 B–N2, P × P = . Miles. (C) 8 P–QR3, P × QP; 9 KP × P, P × P; 10 B × P, B–K2; 11 Q–Q3, P–QN3; 12 QB–N5, B–N2; 13 B–N3, N–Q4; 14 B–B2, P–N3; 15 B–R6, R–K1; 16 KR–K1, R–QB1; 17 B–N3, N × N; 18 P × N, B–B3; 19 QR–Q1, N–R4 ± . Hakanen-Kovn, corr. 1954. Refer also to cols. 26–30.

(*b*) 15 N × N, Q × N; 16 N × N†, Q × N; 17 B–K4, B–Q3; 18 P–KN3, B–KR6; 19 KR–Q1, QR–N1; 20 Q–R5 ± . Olafsson–O'Kelly, Dundee 1967.

(*c*) 9 . . . N–B3; 10 R–Q1, R–Q1; 11 P–QR3, B–R4; transposes into col. 34.

(*d*) 15 B–R3, QN–Q2; 16 QR–N1, B × B ∞ . *Comments.*

(*e*) (A) 10 B–Q3, QN–Q2; 11 N–K4, N × N; 12 B × N, B–N3! 13 B–B2, R–Q1! 14 Q–K2, N–B1; 15 P × P, Q × P; 16 P–QN4, Q–KR4; 17 B–N2, B–Q2 = . Gligorić–Smyslov, Moscow 1967. (B) 10 Q–B2, B–Q2: (1) 11 B–Q2, R–B1! 12 B–Q3, P × P; 13 P × P, P–KR3; 14 KR–K1, Q–Q1; 15 Q–B1, Q–B1; 16 N–K5, N–B3! = . Portisch–Smyslov, Moscow 1967. (2) 11 B–R2, R–B1; 12 B–Q2, P × P; 13 P × P, B–B3; 14 P–Q5! B × N; 15 QP × B, B × B; 16 P × P, Q × NP; 17 Q × B, N–B3; 18 QR–B1, with a slight advantage, but difficult to exploit. Portisch–Gheorghiu, Skopje 1968. (C) 10 Q–Q3, QN–Q2! (D) 10 B–Q2, N–B3; 11 R–B1, R–Q1; 12 P × P, Q × P; 13 B–K2, Q–K2; 14 Q–B2, B–Q2; 15 P–QN4, B–B2 = . Najdorf–Unzicker, Lugano 1968.

(*f*) 12 . . . P–K4; 13 N–N3, B–N3; 14 N–R4, and 15 B–N4 ± . Gligorić.

(*g*) 15 B × B, N–B3; 16 B–K1, R × R; 17 R × R, R–Q1; 18 R–B1 ± . Polugayevski–Portisch, Budapest 1969.

(*h*) 10 . . . B–Q2; 11 B–Q2, P × P; 12 P × P, N–B3; 13 B–KN5, B × N; 14 P × B, Q–Q3; 15 B–Q3, N–Q4; 16 P–B4, N–N5; 17 B × N, Q × B; 18 Q–K3, Q × Q; 19 P × Q, P–QN3 = . Gligorić.

(*i*) 15 B–Q2, B–K1; 16 B–K1 ± . Kraidman–Boutteville, Havana 1966.

(*j*) (A) 9 P–QR3, P × P! 10 P × P, B × N; 11 P × B, Q–B2; 12 Q–Q3, P–QN3 = . (B) 9 Q–K2, P–QR3; 10 P–QR4, P × P; 11 P × P, N–N3 = . (C) 9 B–Q3, P–QN3; 10 Q–K2, B–N2; 11 R–Q1, P × P; 12 P × P, R–B1; 13 B–Q2, B–K2; 14 B–KN5, R–K1 = . Gligorić. (C) 9 Q–N3, P–QN3; 10 P–Q5, B × N; 11 P × P, B–R4; 12 P × N, Q × P; 13 R–Q1, Q–K2 = .

(*k*) 10 . . . P–QN3; 11 N–R2, P–QN4!? 12 RP × P, RP × P; 13 B × NP, B–N2; 14 B–Q2, B × N; 15 P × B, B × B; 16 Q × B, N–K4 = . Taimanov.

(*l*) 15 B–N5, B–K2 = . Furman–Kholmov, USSR Chp. 1957. In the column, 9 . . . P × P; 10 P × P, P–QN3; or 9 . . . P–QN3 might be played, but not 9 . . . P–QR3; 10 P–QR4!

1 P-Q4, N-KB3; 2 P-QB4, P-K3; 3 N-QB3, B-N5; 4 P-K3, O-O; 5 B-Q3, P-Q4;
6 N-B3, P-B4; 7 O-O (Gligorić Variation)

	36	37	38	39	40
	(P × BP)			QN-Q2 (i)	
8	(B × P)			P-QR3 (j)	
	B-Q2	P-QN3 (c)		B-R4	
9	B-Q3 (a)	Q-K2 (d)		Q-B2 (k)	
	B-B3	B-N2		P × BP	BP × P
10	P-QR3	R-Q1		B × P	KP × P
	P × P	P × P	QN-Q2 (g)	Q-K2	P × P
11	P × P	P × P	P-Q5	P × P	B × P
	B-K2	QN-Q2	B × N	Q × P	B × N
12	R-K1	P-Q5 (e)	P × P	N-QR4	P × B (m)
	QN-Q2	B × N!	B-R4	Q-B2	P-QN3
13	B-B2	P × P	P × N	Q-K2	R-K1
	P-QR3	B × N (f)	Q-K2	P-QR3	B-N2 =
14	Q-Q3		P-K4	P-QN4	
	R-K1 (b)		QR-Q1 (h)	P-QN4 (l)	

(a) Again various points of departure or transposition are presented in (A) 9 Q-K2, B-B3 (9 . . . Q-K2; see col. 32); 10 R-Q1 (10 P-QR3, B × QN; 11 P × B, QN-Q2; 12 B-N2, P × P; 13 BP × P, N-N3; 14 B-Q3, N-R5; 15 N-K5, B-Q4 = . Evans–Wade, Buenos Aires 1960), B × KN; 11 Q × B, N-B3; 12 P-QR3, B × N; 13 P × B, Q-B2; 14 B-N5, P-QR3; 15 B × N, Q × B; 16 Q × Q, P × Q; 17 R-N1, KR-N1; 18 B-Q2, N-K5 = . Barcza–Portisch, Stockholm 1962. (B) 9 P-QR3, B × N; 10 P × B, B-B3; 11 N-K5, B-Q4; 12 B-K2, P × P; 13 BP × P, N-B3; 14 N-Q3, N-QR4; 15 B-N2, R-B1 = . Taimanov–Wade, Buenos Aires 1960.

(b) 15 B-N5, P-N3 = . Gligorić–Najdorf, Los Angeles 1963.

(c) If 8 . . . P × P (instead of 8 . . . P-QN3); 9 P × P (9 N × P!?), P-QN3; 10 R-K1, B-N2; 11 B-Q3, N-B3; 12 B-B2, B-K2; 13 P-QR3, R-B1; 14 Q-Q3, P-N3; 15 B-R6, R-K1; 16 QR-Q1, B-B1; 17 B-N5, B-K2; 18 B-R4, P-QR3; 19 B × N, B × B; 20 P-Q5 ± . Tarjan–Browne, US Chp. 1977.

(d) (A) 9 Q-Q3, P-QR3; 10 P-QR4, QN-Q2; see col. 35, note (k). (B) 9 P-QR3, P × P! 10 P × B, P × N; 11 Q × Q, R × Q; 12 P × P, N-K5; 13 B-N2, B-N2; 14 KR-Q1, N-QB3; 15 R × R†, R × R; 16 N-Q4, P-QR4; 17 P-B3, N-Q3 = . Gligorić–Filip, Varna 1962.

(e) Well trodden are (A) 12 B-KN5, B × QN; 13 P × B, Q-B2; 14 N-Q2, KR-K1; 15 B-N5, P-QR3; 16 B × QN, N × B; 17 P-QB4, P-R3; 18 B-K3, N-B3 = . Rabar. (B) 12 B-Q3, R-B1; 13 B-Q2, B-K2; 14 B-KB4, N-R4; 15 B-K3, KN-B3; 16 B-KB4, drawn. Reshevsky–Unzicker, Buenos Aires 1960. (c) 12 N-K5, R-B1; 13 R-Q3, B × N; 14 P × B, R × B; 15 N × R, B-R3; 16 N-Q6, N-N1; 17 N-K4, N × N; 18 Q × N, B × R; 19 Q × B, N-B3 = . Gligorić–Toran, Torremolinos 1961.

(f) (A) 14 P × QB, P × P; 15 P × B, Q-B2; 16 B × P†, K-R1; 17 B-K3, N-B4; 18 B-Q5, N × B; 19 R × N, N-K3; 20 Q-Q3, N-N5; 21 B × N, Q × B; 22 K-N2, QR-Q1 = . Gligorić–Unzicker, Leipzig 1960. (B) 14 Q × B, N-K4! 15 Q-K2, Q-B2; 16 B-N3, N/4-N5! 17 P-N3, Q-K4; 18 Q × Q, B × Q; 19 P-KR3, N-R3; 20 P-N4, P × P; 21 P-N5, N-B2!∞ . Donner–Van den Berg, Beverwijk 1965.

(g) Enterprising is 10 . . . Q-B1; 11 N-QN5, P × P; 12 QN × QP, N-B3; 13 P-QR3, N × N; 14 N × N, B-K2; 15 P-QN4, P-QR4! 16 P-N5, P-K4; 17 N-B3, B × N; 18 P × B, P-K5. Najdorf–Olafsson, Los Angeles 1963.

(h) 15 B-KN5, Q × KP; 16 Q × Q, B × Q; 17 B × N, P × B = . Najdorf–Smyslov, Havana 1962.

(*i*) 7 . . . P–QN3? 8 P × QP, KP × P; 9 P × P, P × P; 10 N–K2, B–N5; 11 P–QN3, or 9 N–K5, B–N2; 10 B–Q2, N–B3; 11 P–QR3, or 9 . . . Q–B2; 10 B–Q2; all give White an advantage.

(*j*) 8 P × QP KP × P; 9 P–QR3, B–R4; 10 P–QN4, P × NP; 11 N–QN5! P–QR3; 12 Q–N3! P × P; 13 N–Q6, B–B2; 14 B × P/3, B × N; 15 B × B, R–K1; 16 KR–B1, R–K3 = . Gligorić.

(*k*) Explorable sidelines are (A) 9 Q–N3, B–N3; 10 N–K2, P–QR4; 11 P × BP, B × P∞. (B) 9 BP × P, KP × P; 10 P–QN4! P × NP; 11 N–QN5, P–QR3; 12 Q–N3! Q–K2; 13 B–Q2 ± . Gligorić–Yanofsky, Lugano 1968.

(*l*) 15 B–Q3, P × N; 16 P × B, N–B4; 17 B–Q2 (Portisch–Langeweg, Beverwijk 1968), N × B = .

(*m*) 12 Q × B, N–N3; 13 B–R2, QN–Q4; 14 Q–Q3, P–QN3 = .

1 P–Q4, N–KB3; 2 P–QB4, P–K3; 3 N–QB3, B–N5; 4 P–K3, O–O

	41	42	43	44	45
5	(B–Q3)...................			(Nimzo–Benoni)	N–K2
	(P–Q4)...................			P–B4	P–Q4
6	(N–B3).............		P–QR3	P–Q5	P–QR3
	P–QN3 (*a*)		B–K2 (*h*)	P–QN4	B–K2 (*l*)
7	O–O		N–B3	P × KP	P × P (*m*)
	B–N2 (*b*)		P × P	BP × P	P × P (*n*)
8	P–QR3......	P × P	B × P	P × P	N–B4 (*o*)
	B–Q3 (*c*)	P × P	P–B4	P–QR3 (*j*)	P–B3 (*p*)
9	P–QN4	B–Q2 (*e*)	O–O	KN–K2	B–Q3
	P × P	B–Q3 (*f*)	N–B3	P–Q4	R–K1
10	B × BP	N–K5	P × P	O–O	O–O
	QN–Q2	P–B4	Q × Q	P–K4	QN–Q2
11	B–N2	P–B4	R × Q	P–QR3	P–B3
	Q–K2	N–B3	B × P	P × P	N–B1
12	N–QN5	B–K1	P–QN4	B × P	P–QN4
	P–QR3 (*d*)	P × P (*g*)	B–K2 (*i*)	B × N (*k*)	N–N3 (*q*)

(*a*) Black can vary his 4th, 5th or 6th; White his 5th and 6th move. For (A) 6 . . . P–B3 see Semi-Slav Defence, Romih Variation. (B) 6 . . . N–B3; see Queen's Gambit, col. 45, Ragozin Variation.

(*b*) 7 . . . P–B4; 8 BP × P, KP × P; 9 N–K5, B × N = . Or 9 P × P! P × P; 10 N–K2, N–B3; 11 P–QN3, B–N5 (11 . . . B–K3!?) 12 B–N2, R–B1; 13 N–N3, P–Q5; 14 P–KR3! Kane-Peters, Saratoga 1980.

(*c*) Not necessarily an improvement over (A) 8 . . . B × N; 9 P × B, N–B3; 10 P × P, P × P; 11 P–QR4, N–QR4; 12 B–R3, R–K1; 13 N–Q2, N–K5; 14 N × N, P × N; 15 B–K2, B–Q4 = . Kottnauer. (B) 8 . . . B–K2; 9 P–QN3, QN–Q2; 10 B–N2, N–K5; 11 N–Q2, N × QN; 12 B × N, P–QB4; 13 P–QN4, P × QP = . Panno–Eliskases, Mar del Plata 1954. However, as sporadically the "best" lines become over-played for a while, masters and experts must seasonally search for new experiments of tactical surprise.

(*d*) 13 N × B, P × N; 14 P–N5, P–Q4; 15 B–Q3, P × P; 16 Q–N3, B–R3; 17 B–B3, with a little better position for White. Gligorić–Donner, 1968.

(*e*) 9 N–K5, (A) 9 . . . B–Q3; (1) 10 N–N5!? P–QR3! 11 N × B, P × N = . *Informator* 7. (2) 10 P–B4, P–B4; 11 Q–B3, N–B3; 12 Q–R3, N–QN5; 13 B–N1, N–K5; 14 P–R3, N–R3 ∞ . (B) 9 . . . QN–Q2; 10 P–B4, P–B4; 11 B–B5, P–N3; 12 B–R3 (12 B–B1!), B × N; 13 P × B, N × N; 14 QP × N, N–K5! 15 Q–B2 (15 Q–Q3!), B–R3; 16 R–Q1, Q–R5; 17 P–B4, B × P; 18 B–N2, P–QN4; 19 B–Q7, QR–Q1; 20 P–K6, Q–K2; 21 P × P† R × P; 22 B–KR3, R–K1; 23 P–N3, N × P; 24 R–K1, Q–K5; 25 Q × Q, N × Q; 26 P–R3, P–N4; 27 B–K5, N–B7; 28 K × N, R × B; 29 K–B3, P–Q5; 30 P × QP, R × P†; 31 K–N3, R × R; 32 R × R, R × P; 33 R–K5, P–KR3; 34 B–B5, K–N2; 35 R × P, K–B3; 36 B–B2, R–Q7; 37 B–R7, R–R7; 38 R–B6†, K–K4; 39 R–R6, P–QN5; 40 R–R5†, K–Q5; 41 P × P, R × R; 42 P × R, K–B4; 43 B–K4, K–N4; 44 K–N4, B–K3†; 45 K–R5, K × P; 46 K × P, P–N5; 47 K–N5, K–N5; 48 K–B6, B–B1; 49 K–K5, P–R4; 50 K–Q4, B–K3; 51 K–B3, K–N6; 52 K–Q2, K–N7; 53 B–B6, B–N6; 54, resigns. Portisch–Rogoff, Las Palmas 1976.

(*f*) (A) 9 . . . QN–Q2; 10 R–B1, P–QR3; 11 N–K5, N × N! 12 P × N, N–Q2 = . (B) 9 . . . P–QR3; 10 N–K5, B–Q3; 11 R–B1, P–B4; 12 P–B4, N–B3; 13 N–K2, P–QR4; 14 B–B3, N–K2; 15 P–B5, N–B3! = . Van den Berg–Korchnoi, Hamburg 1965.

(*g*) 13 P × P, N × P; 14 B–R4, N–K3; 15 B–QN5, K–R1; 16 N–Q7, R–KN1; 17 N–K4, B–K2; 18 N–K5, Q–KB1; 19 N–N5, N × N; 20 P × N, B–Q3 ∞ . Lehmann–Donner, Mallorca 1967.

(*h*) 6 . . . P × P; 7 B × P, B–Q3; 8 N–B3, QN–Q2 (in this constellation, 8 . . . P–QR3 is preferable); 9 P–QN4! P–K4; 10 B–N2. Botvinnik–Van Scheltinga, Wijk aan Zee 1969.

(*i*) 13 B–N2, B–Q2 = . Botvinnik–Kholmov, Moscow 1969.

(*j*) 8 . . . B–N2; 9 N–KB3, P–Q4; 10 O–O, QN–Q2; 11 N–K2, Q–K1; 12 N–N3, P–K4; 13 B–B5, P–N3; 14 B–R3, P–QR3; 15 N–N5, P × P; 16 N–K6, P–B5; 17 B–Q2 (Korchnoi–Karpov, 7th match game 1978), B–Q3! = . Larsen.

(*k*) 13 P × B, B–R3; 14 R–N1, Q–Q3; 15 P–QB4, P–Q5; 16 N–N3, N–B3; 17 P–QR4, N–QR4; 18 Q–Q3, Q–K3; 19 P × P, BP × P; 20 P–B5, KR–B1; 21 P–B4, R × P; 22 B × B, Q × B; 23 Q × Q, R × Q; 24 B–R3, R–Q4; 25 N–B5, K–B2; 26 P × P, R × P; 27 R–N5, N–B5; 28 R–N7†, K–K3; 29 N × QP†, K–Q4; 30 N–B3 (30 N–B2, R × P; 31 B–B8! +), N × B; 31 N × R, K × N; 32 R–K7†, K–Q5; 33 R × P? (R–B4†!), N–B5; 34 R–B4†, N–K5; 35 R–Q7†? (35 R × P!), K–K6; 36 R–B3†, K–K7; 37 R × P, QN–Q7; 38 R–QR3, R–QB3; 39 R–R1?? (39 P–N3 =), N–B6†; resigns. Korchnoi–Karpov, 17th match game 1978. An amazing anticlimax in a World Championship game. Also con.pare col. 51.

(*l*) (A) 6 . . . B–Q3; 7 P–B5, B–K2; 8 P–QN4, P–QN3; 9 N–B4, P × P; 10 NP × P, B–R3; 11 B × B, N × B; 12 O–O, N–N1; 13 B–Q2, N–B3; 14 Q–R4, Q–Q2; 15 N–Q3 ± . Saidy–Fischer, US Chp. 1961. (B) 6 . . . B × N† is the lesser evil.

(*m*) 7 N–N3, P–QB4; 8 QP × P, B × P; 9 P–QN4, B–K2; 10 B–N2, P × P; 11 Q–B2, P–QN4!; 12 N × P, P–QR4; B × P, P × P = .

(*n*) (A) 7 . . . N × P; 8 Q–B2, N–Q2; 9 P–QN4, P–B3; 10 B–Q2, N/4–N3!; 11 N–N3 ± . Reshevsky–Korchnoi, Amsterdam 1968. (B) 7 . . . N × P; 8 N × N, P × N; 9 P–KN3, N–Q2; 10 B–N2, N–B3; 11 O–O, B–Q3; 12 N–B3, N–B3; 13 P–QN4, P–QR3; 14 R–K1, R–K1 = . Reshevsky–Botvinnik, AVRO 1938.

(*o*) 8 P–KN3, P–B3; 9 B–N2, P–QR4; 10 O–O, N–R3; 11 N–B4, N–B2; 12 P–B3, P–B4; 13 N–R4, N–R3; 14 P–KN4, B–Q2; 15 N–B3, B–B3 = . Lutikov–Tal, USSR Chp. 1959.

(*p*) Active is 8 . . . P–QR4; 9 B–Q3, R–K1; 10 O–O, P–B3; 11 P–B3, N–R3; 12 Q–B2, P–KN3; 13 P–KN4, N–B2 = . Reshevsky–Evans, US Chp. 1959.

(*q*) 13 N/4–K2, P–QR4; 14 R–N1, P × P; 15 P × P, B–K3; 16 P–K4, P × P; 17 P × P, P–N4; 18 K–R1, B–B5 = . Evans–Unzicker, Buenos Aires 1960.

1 P–Q4, N–KB3; 2 P–QB4, P–K3; 3 N–QB3, B–N5; 4 P–K3, P–QN3

	46	47	48	49	50
5	N–K2			B–Q3 (*j*)	
	B–R3		B–N2	B–N2 (*k*)	
6	N–N3	P–QR3	P–QR3	N–B3	
	B × N† (*a*)	B–K2 (*d*)	B × N†	N–K5	O–O
7	P × B	N–B4 (*e*)	N × B	O–O	O–O
	P–Q4	O–O (*f*)	P–Q4	B × N	B × QN (*m*)
8	B–R3 (*b*)	P–QN3 (*g*)	P–QN4	P × B	P × B
	B × P	P–Q4	O–O	N × QBP	B–K5
9	B × B	B–N2	P × P	Q–B2	Q–B2 (*n*)
	P × B	P–B3	N × P	B × N	B × B
10	O–O	B–Q3	Q–B2	P × B	Q × B
	QN–Q2	B–Q3	P–QB4	Q–N4†	P–Q3
11	Q–R4	Q–B3	QP × P	K–R1	P–K4
	P–B4! (*c*)	QN–Q2 (*h*)	P × P (*i*)	Q–KR4 (*l*)	N–B3 (*o*)

(*a*) Or 6 . . . O–O; 7 P–K4, N–B3; 8 B–Q3, P–Q4! = .

(*b*) A deviation from the earlier 8 Q–B3, O–O; 9 P–K4, P × BP; 10 B–N5, P–R3; Saidy–Fischer, USA Chp. 1965, although 11 P–KR4! might have allowed pressure for White. In the column, sharp is 8 . . . P × P; 9 P–K4, Q–Q2; 10 B–K2, N–B3; 11 Q–B2, O–O–O = .

(*c*) 12 P × P, O–O! 13 P–B6, N–B4; 14 B × N, P × B; 15 QR–N1, R–B1 = . Saidy–Lombardy, Netanya 1969.

(*d*) 6 . . . B × N†; 7 N × B, P–Q4; (A) 8 P–QN3, O–O; 9 B–K2, P × P; 10 P × P, N–B3; 11 P–QR4, Q–Q2; 12 N–N5, KR–Q1; 13 B–N2, N–QR4; 14 Q–B2, P–B3 = . Botvinnik–Smyslov, match 1957. (B) 8 Q–B3, O–O; 9 B–K2, P–B4 = . (C) 8 P × P, B × B; 9 K × B, P × P; 10 P–B3, N–B3 (10 . . . P–B4! =); 11 K–B2, O–O; 12 R–K1, R–K1; 13 K–N1, Q–Q2; 14 P–QN3, QR–Q1; 15 R–R2, N–QR4; 16 R–Q2 ± . Mecking–Najdorf, Buenos Aires 1970.

(*e*) 7 P–QN3, P–Q4; 8 B–N2, O–O; 9 N–B4 reverts into the column.

(*f*) Also 7 . . . P–Q4; 8 P × P, B × B; 9 K × B, P × P; 10 P–KN4, P–KN4; 11 N–Q3, P–KR4; 12 P × P, R × P; 13 N–K5, P–B3 = .

(*g*) (A) 8 P–QN4, P–Q4; 9 P–N5, B–N2; 10 P × P, P × P; 11 B–N2, P–B4; 12 B–K2, P–B5 = . Botvinnik–Moiseyev, USSR Chp. 1951. (B) 8 P–K4, P–Q3; 9 B–Q2, QN–Q2 = .

(*h*) 12 O–O, B–N2 = . R. Byrne–Brasket, US Open, 1958.

(*i*) 12 N × N, Q × N; 13 P–N5, P–QR3; 14 P × P, B × P; 15 P–K4, Q–Q3; 16 B × B, Q × B; 17 Q–K2, N–B3; drawn. Bronstein–Spasski, USSR Chp. 1961.

(*j*) 5 P–QR3, B × N†; 6 P × B, B–N2; 7 P–B3, N–B3; 8 P–K4, P–Q3; 9 B–Q3, N–QR4; 10 N–K2, Q–Q2; 11 O–O, B–R3 = . Gligorić–Keres, Zürich 1953.

(*k*) Forceful is also 5 . . . P–B4; 6 N–B3, B–N2 (or 6 . . . O–O; 7 P–Q5! P–QN4!); 7 O–O, O–O; 8 N–QR4, P × P; 9 P × P, B × N; 10 Q × B, N–B3; 11 R–Q1, P–Q4 = . Visier–Keres, Kapfenberg 1970.

(*l*) 12 R–KN1, Q × BP†; 13 R–N2, P–KB4; 14 B–N2, N–K5; 15 R–KB1, N–QB3; 16 B–K2, Q–R6; 17 P–Q5, N–K2; 18 R × P, R–KN1; 19 R × R†, N × R; 10 P × P, O–O–O = . Euwe.

(*m*) (A) 7 . . . P–Q4; 8 P–QR3, B–Q3; 9 P–QN4, P × P; 10 B × P, QN–Q2; 11 B–N2, P–QR4; 12 P–N5, P–K4 = . Averbakh–Taimanov, USSR Chp. 1961. (B) 7 . . . P–B4; 8 N–QR4! P × P; 9 P × P, B–K2; 10 R–K1, P–Q3; 11 P–QN4, QN–Q2; 12 B–B2, P–QR4; 13 P–QR3, P × P; 14 P × P, P–QN4; 15 P × P, N–Q4! = . Kaplan.

(*n*) Or 9 B–K2, P–B4; 10 N–Q2, B–N3; 11 B–B3, N–B3; 12 B–R3, R–B1; 13 P × P, Q–K2; 14 N–N3, N–K4 = . Reshevsky–Fischer, Buenos Aires 1970.

(*o*) 12 B–N5, P–KR3; 13 B–R4, P–K4; 14 P–Q5, N–N1; 15 Q–K2, QN–Q2 = . Minev–Hecht, Varna 1962.

1 P–Q4, N–KB3; 2 P–QB4, P–K3; 3 N–QB3, B–N5; 4 P–K3

	51	52	53	54	55
	P–B4		P–Q4 (j)		
5	N–K2	B–Q3 (e)	P–QR3 (k)		
	P×P (a)	N–B3	B–K2		B×N†
6	P×P	N–B3 (f)	N–B3		P×B
	P–Q4 (b)	B×N†	O–O		P–B4 (n)
7	P–QR3 (c)	P×B	B–Q3	P–QN4	P×QP
	B–K2	P–Q3	P–QN3	QN–Q2	KP×P
8	P–B5	P–K4	O–O	B–N2	B–Q3
	O–O	P–K4	P–B4	P–B3	Q–R4!
9	P–QN4	P–Q5	Q–K2	B–Q3	Q–Q2
	P–QN3	N–K2	N–B3	P×P	O–O
10	P–N3	N–R4 (g)	P×BP	B×P	N–K2
	P×P	P–KR3	NP×P	B–Q3	P–QN3
11	QP×P	P–B3 (h)	R–Q1	N–K2	O–O
	P–QR4 (d)	P–KN4 (i)	B–N2 (l)	P–QR4 (m)	B–R3 =

(a) 5 . . . P–Q4; 6 P–QR3, B×N†; 7 N×B, P×QP; 8 KP×P, P×P; 9 B×P, N–B3; 10 B–K3, O–O; 11 O–O, P–QN3; 12 Q–Q3, B–N2; (1) 13 KR–Q1, P–KR3 = . Evans–Ken Smith, US Open 1951. (2) 13 QR–Q1, P–KR3; 14 P–B3, N–K2; 15 B–B2, KN–Q4; 16 B–R2, N–B5; 17 Q–Q2, N/5–N3; 18 B–N1, Q–Q2; 19 P–KR4 ± . This can also arise from 7 . . . B×N† in the column.

(b) A recent version of the Nimzo-Benoni (compare col. 44) is 6 . . . O–O; 7 P–QR3, B–K2; 8 P–Q5!, P×P; 9 P×P, R–K1; 10 P–KN3, B–B4; 11 B–N2, P–Q3; 12 P–R3, B–B4; 13 O–O, N/1–Q2(?) 14 P–KN4, B–K5; 15 N–N3, B×B; 16 K×B, N–B1; 17 P–N5, N/3–Q2; 18 P–KR4 ± . Kasparov-Csom, Baku 1980.

(c) 7 P–B5, N–K5! 8 B–Q2, N×B; 9 Q×N, P–QN3; 10 P–QR3, B×N; 11 N×B, P×P; 12 B–N5†, B–Q2; 13 P×P, P–QR4; 14 R–QB1, P–R5 = . Averbakh–Panno, Portoroz 1958.

(d) 12 R–QN1, P×P; 13 P×P, N–B3; 14 B–KN2, R–QN1; 15 B–QR3, B–Q2; 16 O–O, N–R2 = . Gligorić–Szabó, Helsinki 1952. On 11 NP×P Black must play for an early break with . . . P–K4.

(e) 5 N–B3 (A) 5 . . . O–O; 6 B–K2, B×N†; 7 P×B, P–Q3; 8 O–O, N–B3; 9 N–Q2, P–K4; 10 B–N2, P–QN3; 11 Q–B2, B–R3; 12 P–B4, KP×QP = . Taimanov–Evans, USSR *v.* USA 1954. (B) 5 . . . P–QN3! 6 B–Q3, B–N2.

(f) 6 KN–K2, P–Q4; 7 O–O, O–O; 8 P–QR3, P×QP; 9 KP×P, P×P; 10 B×P, B–K2 = . Pachman.

(g) 10 P–N3, P–KR3; 11 N–R4, P–KN4 = . Najdorf–Hübner, Wijk aan Zee 1971.

(h) 11 P–B4, N–N3; 12 N×N, P×N; 13 O–O! Q–K2; 14 Q–B3, O–O; 15 Q–N3, K–R2; 16 P–B5, P–KN4; 17 Q–R3, K–N1; Larsen–Ivkov, Manila 1973.

(i) 12 N–B5, N×N; 13 P×N, N–R4; 14 P–N3, N–N2 = . Donner–Langeweg, Wijk aan Zee 1971.

(j) 4 . . . N–B3; 5 N–K2! P–Q4; 6 P–QR3, (A) 6 . . . B–K2; 7 P×P, P×P; 8 N–B4, B–KB4; 9 Q–N3, N–QR4; 10 Q–R4†, P–B3; 11 B–Q2 + . *Archives.* (B) 6 . . . B–Q3; 7 P–B5, B–K2; 8 P–QN4, O–O; 9 P–B4, N–QN1; 10 P–KN3, N–K1 = . Zaitsev–Bronstein, USSR Chp. 1970.

(k) (A) 5 Q–R4†, see Queen's Gambit, Ragozin system. (B) 5 N–B3, see main lines.

(l) 12 P×P, P×P; 13 P–K4, P–Q5; 14 P–K5, N–K1; 15 Q–K4, P–B4 = .

(m) 12 P–N5, N–N3; 13 B–Q3, P×P; 14 B×P, B–Q2 = . Botvinnik–Reshevsky, The Hague 1948.

(n) 6 . . . P×P; 7 B×P, P–QN3; 8 N–K2, B–N2; 9 O–O, Q–Q3; 10 P–B3, P–B4; 11 P–K4, Q–B3; 12 B–Q3, is about even but thematically wrong would be 12 . . . P–B5? 13 B–B2, QN–Q2; 14 N–N3 ± . Kotov–Kagetsu, Toronto 1954. The column is Kramer–Evans, New York State Chp. 1949.

1 P–Q4, N–KB3; 2 P–QB4, P–K3; 3 N–QB3, B–N5; 4 P–QR3, B × N†; 5 P × B, P–Q4; 6 P–B3, P–B4; 7 P × QP, N × P

	56	57	58	59	60
8	P × P			Q–Q2.......	Q–Q3 (*m*)
	Q–R4.......	P–B4		Q–R4 (*i*)	P × P
9	P–K4	P–QB4......	P–K4 (*e*)	B–N2 (*j*)	P × P
	N–KB3 (*a*)	Q–R5† (*c*)	P × P	N–QB3 (*k*)	P–QN3 (*n*)
10	B–K3	P–N3	Q–B2	P–K4	P–K4
	O–O	Q × BP	P–K6 (*f*)	N–N3	B–R3
11	Q–N3	P–K4	B–Q3 (*g*)	P–QR4	Q–Q2
	N–B3	Q–B6†	N–Q2	O–O	B × B
12	B–QN5	B–Q2	P–QB4	B–Q3	K × B
	B–Q2 (*b*)	Q–K4 (*d*)	Q–R4† (*h*)	R–Q1 (*l*)	N–K2 =

(*a*) Also (A) 9 . . . N–B2, 10 Q–Q4 (10 B–K3, N–Q2 =), P–B3; 11 P–KB4 (11 B–QB4, P–K4; 12 Q–Q3, B–K3 ∓), N–B3; 12 Q–B4, P–K4; 13 P–B5 ± . (B) 9 . . . N × P; 10 Q–Q2, N–B3; 11 B–N2, N–R5; 12 B × P, R–KN1; 13 B–B6, Q × Q†; 14 K × Q, N × P; 15 K–K3 ± .

(*b*) 13 N–K2, N–K4; 14 B × B, N/3 × B; 15 O–O, Q–B2 = . *Byulleten* 1969.

(*c*) Dynamic is 9 . . . Q–B3; 10 B–Q2 (10 B–N5, Q × B; 11 P × N, P × P; 12 Q × P, N–B3 = . Taimanov), N–B6; 11 Q–B1, N–R5 = . Pachman.

(*d*) (A) 13 B–Q3, O–O; 14 R–B1, N–QB3; 15 N–K2, P × P = . *Comments*. (B) 13 B–N2, P × P; 14 P–B4, Q–B3; 15 B × P, Q–Q5! 16 B × N, Q × B; 17 N–B3, P–K4! = .

(*e*) (A) 9 Q–B2, P–B5!? 10 P–K4, P × P *e.p.*; 11 B–Q3, N–Q2; 12 P–QB4, Q–R4†; 13 K–B1, N/4–B3 = . Zaitsev. (B) 9 N–R3?! Q–R4 (9 . . . B–Q2; 10 P–K4, P × P; 11 N–N5, P × P; 12 Q × P, Q–B3; 13 Q × Q, N × Q; 14 B–QB4 ± . Schwartz); 10 N–B2, Q × P/4; 11 Q–Q4, Q × Q; 12 P × Q, N–QB3; 13 P–K3, P–B5; 14 P × P ± . Taimanov. The line can stand further testing.

(*f*) (A) Tamer is 10 . . . N–KB3; 11 P × P, QN–Q2; 12 B–QB4, Q–K2; 13 N–B3. *Comments*. (B) 10 . . . P × P; 11 N × P, Q–R4; 12 B–Q3, N–QB3; 13 B × P! R × B; 14 Q × R, Q × P†; 15 K–B2 ± .

(*g*) 11 B–N2, N–Q2; 12 O–O–O, Q–R4; 13 Q–K4, QN × P; 14 R × N, N × Q; 15 R × Q, N–B7; 16 R–K5, O–O; 17 N–R3, N × R; 18 R × P/3, P–K4 = . Shaposhnikov–Vladimirov, USSR 1961.

(*h*) 13 K–B1, N–B5; 14 B × KP, N × B; 15 Q × N, O–O = . Polugayevski.

(*i*) Good counterplay also evolves from (A) 8 . . . P × P; 9 P × P, P–B4; 10 P–K3, N–QB3; 11 B–Q3, O–O; 12 N–K2, Q–R5†; 13 P–N3, Q–R6; 14 B–N2, B–Q2 = . Portisch–Padevski, Budapest 1959; or (B) 8 . . . O–O; 9 P–K4, N–N3; 10 P–QR4, B–Q2; 11 B–N5, P–QR3; 12 B × B, N/1 × B; 12 N–K2, N–B5 = . Botvinnik–Smyslov, Moscow 1966.

(*j*) 9 P–K4, Q × BP; 10 B–N2, Q × Q†; 11 K × Q, N–K2; 12 P × P, O–O; 13 R–B1, KN–B3; 14 K–K3, B–Q2; 15 B–Q3, R–B1; 16 N–K2, B–K1; 17 P–B4, N–Q2; 18 R–B3, R–B2 = . R. Weinstein–Sherwin, US Chp. 1961.

(*k*) Also (A) 9 . . . P × P; 10 P × P, N–QB3; 11 P–K4, N–K6 = ; or (B) 9 . . . N–N3; 10 P–K3, N–R5 = . H. Steiner–Donner, Venice 1950.

(*l*) 13 N–K2, B–Q2 ∞. Tal–Barstatis, Riga 1961.

(*m*) 8 P–K3, O–O; 9 B–Q2, P–B4; 10 B–Q3, P–KB5; 11 P–K4, Q–R5† = . Šajtar–Barcza, Mariánské Lázné 1951.

(*n*) 9 . . . N–QB3; 10 P–K4, N–N3; 11 B–K3, O–O; 12 R–Q1, P–B4; 13 P × P, P × P; 14 P–Q5, N–K4; 15 Q–Q4, R–K1; 16 K–B2, B–Q2; 17 B–Q3, R–QB1; 18 N–K2. Müller. The column is O'Kelly–Van den Berg, Zürich 1960.

1 P–Q4, N–KB3; 2 P–QB4, P–K3; 3 N–QB3, B–N5; 4 P–QR3, B × N†; 5 P × B

	61	62	63	64	65
	(P–Q4)		P–Q3 (*e*)	P–B4	
6	(P–B3)		P–B3	P–K3	
	O–O		O–O	N–B3	Q–R4
7	P × P		P–K4	B–Q3	B–Q2
	P × P		P–K4	O–O	N–K5
8	P–K3		B–N5! (*f*)	N–K2	B–Q3
	B–B4 (*a*)		N–QB3	P–Q3 (*h*)	N × B
9	N–K2		N–K2	N–N3	Q × N
	QN–Q2 (*b*)		P–N3	P–QN3	P–Q3
10	N–N3	N–B4	P–KN4	B–N2	N–B3
	B–N3	P–B4	B–R3	B–R3	N–Q2
11	B–Q3	B–K2	N–N3	P–K4	O–O
	P–B4	R–B1	P–R3	R–B1	O–O
12	O–O	P–N4	B–K3	R–QB1	Q–B2
	R–K1 (*c*)	B–N3 (*d*)	N–R2 (*g*)	P × P (*i*)	P–KR3 (*j*)

(*a*) 8 . . . N–R4; (A) 9 N–K2, P–KB4, 10 P–N3, P–QN3; 11 B–N2, B–R3; 12 O–O, N–KB3; 13 R–K1, N–B3; 14 N–B4, Q–K1; 15 P–R3, R–Q1; 16 P–N4, P–KN4 = . Taimanov–Averbakh, USSR Chp. 1959. (B) 9 Q–B2, R–K1; 10 P–N4, N–B5; 11 P–KR4, P–QB4; 12 K–B2, N–N3; 13 B–Q3, N–B3 = .

(*b*) 9 . . . P–B4; 10 P–N4, B–Q2! but not 10 . . . B–K3; 11 N–N3, N–B3; 12 B–Q3, R–K1; 13 O–O, N–K2; 14 R–R2 ± , as given in *Byulleten* 1970.

(*c*) 13 N–B5 with some advantage according to Smyslov (but it is hardly substantial).

(*d*) 13 P–KR4, P × P! opens Pandora's box. *Comments*.

(*e*) The neutral 5 . . . O–O; causes a certain, not critical, delay in Black's development after 6 P–B3! N–K1! 7 P–K4, P–QN3; 8 B–Q3, B–R3; 9 P–QR4, N–QB3; 10 B–R3, P–Q3; 11 P–B4, N–R4; 12 Q–K2, P–KB4! 13 P–K5, Q–R5†; 14 P–N3, Q–N5 = .

(*f*) 8 B–Q3, N–B3; 9 N–K2, Q–K1! 10 O–O, P–QN3! (H. Müller's refutation, e.g.) 11 Q–R4, B–N2 (or 11 . . . N–QR4) + ; or 11 P–KN4, N–QR4; 12 N–N3, B–R3; 13 Q–K2, Q–R5 + . *Comments*.

(*g*) 13 B–Q3, N–R4; 14 Q–K2, with a ferocious attack. Pachman.

(*h*) Also 8 . . . P–K4; 9 P–Q5, N–QR4; 10 P–K4, P–Q3; 11 O–O, P–QN3 = .

(*i*) 13 P × P, P–K4; 14 Q–R4, N–QR4; 15 O–O, Q–K1 = . Botvinnik–Keres, AVRO 1938.

(*j*) 13 N–Q2, P–K4; 14 N–K4, Q–B2; 15 P–QR4, P–QR4; 16 QR–N1, P–B4; 17 N–N3, P–KN3, 18 R–N5, N–B3; 19 KR–N1, R–N1; 20 Q–N2, N–Q2; 21 Q–B2, P–N3 = . Vladimirov–Bronstein, USSR Chp. 1961.

1 P–Q4, N–KB3; 2 P–QB4, P–K3; 3 N–QB3, B–N5; 4 P–QR3, B × N†; 5 P × B

	66	67	68	69	70
	(P–B4)	P–QN3		N–K5	
6	(P–K3)	P–B3		P–K3	Q–B2
	P–QN3 (a)	B–R3		O–O! (h)	P–KB4!
7	B–Q3	P–K4		B–Q3	P–B3! (j)
	B–N2	N–B3	P–Q4	P–KB4	Q–R5†
8	P–B3	P–K5 (d)	BP × P (f)	Q–B2	P–N3
	N–B3	N–KN1	B × B	P–QN3!?	N × NP
9	N–K2	N–R3	K × B	B × N	P × N
	O–O (b)	P–B3 (e)	P × P	P × B	Q × R
10	P–K4	P–B4	B–N5!	Q × P	N–R3
	N–K1	N–R4	P × P	N–B3	Q–R7
11	B–K3	Q–R4	P × P	N–B3	B–B4
	P–Q3 (c)	P–QB4 =	P–KR3 (g)	B–R3 (i)	P–Q3 (k)

(a) 6 . . . N–B3; 7 B–Q3, P–Q3; 8 N–K2, P–QN3; 9 O–O, Q–Q2; 10 P–K4, B–R3; 11 B–N5, O–O–O; 12 N–B1! N–QR4; 13 N–N3 ± . Geller–Lisitsyn, USSR Chp. 1955. Even without White's restricting P–B3, Black is cramped.

(b) 9 . . . P–Q3; 10 O–O, P–K4; 11 P–K4, Q–K2; 12 P–B4, N–Q2; 13 BP × P, P × KP; 14 P–Q5, N–R4; 15 N–N3, P–N3; 16 B–R6 ± . Taimanov.

(c) 12 O–O, N–R4; 13 N–N3, Q–Q2 = . *Comments.* The early omission of . . . P–Q3 gives Black an important tempo.

(d) 8 B–N5, P–R3; 9 B–R4, N–QR4; (A) 10 Q–R4, Q–B1; 11 N–R3, N–R2 = . Geller–Smyslov, USSR Chp. 1949. Or (B) 10 P–K5, P–KN4; 11 B–B2 ∞ .

(e) 9 . . . N–R4; 10 Q–R4, N–K2; 11 B–Q3, O–O; 12 B–N5! The column is Averbakh's analysis.

(f) (A) 8 P–K5!? N–N1; 9 N–R3, P × P! 10 B–K2, Q–Q2; 11 B–N5, N–QB3; 12 O–O, KN–K2; 13 B × N, N × B; 14 P–B4, O–O; 15 B–B3, R–N1; 16 B–K4, P–R3; 17 Q–B3, B–N4! ∓ . Vladimirov–Mukhitdinov, USSR Chp. semi-finals 1955. (B) 8 B–N5, P–KR3; 9 B–R4, B × P; 10 B × B, P × B; 11 Q–R4†, Q–Q2; 12 Q × BP, Q–B3 = .

(g) 12 B × N, Q × B†; 13 Q–B3, N–Q2 ∞ .

(h) 6 . . . P–KB4; 7 Q–R5†, P–N3; 8 Q–R6, P–Q3; 9 P–B3, N–KB3; 10 P–K4, P–K4; 11 B–N5, Q–K2; 12 B–Q3, R–B1 (Botvinnik–Tal, match 1960); 13 Q–R4! ± .

(i) 11 N–Q2, N–R4 = . The column, with 8 . . . P–QN3, contains an enterprising pawn sacrifice in return for mobility.

(j) No better have proved to be (A) 7 N–R3, O–O; 8 P–B3, N–KB3; 9 P–B5, P–QN3; 10 P × P, BP × P! 11 P–K3, Q–B2; 12 B–Q2, N–K1; 13 P–QB4, B–R3; 14 R–B1, N–Q3; 15 Q–R4, Q–B3! = . Botvinnik–Tal, match 1960. Or (B) 7 P–K3, P–QN3; 8 B–Q3, B–N2; 9 N–K2, Q–R5; 10 O–O, O–O; 11 P–B3, N–N4! = . Vladimirov–Tarasov, USSR 1957.

(k) 12 O–O–O, O–O; 13 P–B5 = , *Comments,* rather than 12 P–N4, Q–R8! ∓ ; Crabbendam–De Graaf, Bevervijk 1963.

1 P–Q4, N–KB3; 2 P–QB4, P–K3; 3 N–QB3, B–N5

	71	72	73	74	75
4	Q–N3 . . (Spielmann Variation)		N–B3	P–B3	B–N5 (l)
	P–B4	N–B3 (d)	P–B4 (f)	P–Q4 (i)	P–KR3 (m)
5	P×P	N–B3	P–Q5 (g)	P–QR3	B–R4
	N–B3	P–Q4	P–Q3	B–K2 (j)	P–B4!
6	N–B3 (a)	P–K3 (e)	B–N5	P–K4	P–Q5
	N–K5	O–O	P–KR3	P×KP	B×N† (n)
7	B–Q2	P–QR3	B×N	P×P	P×B
	N×QBP (b)	P×P	Q×B	P–K4	P–K4
8	Q–B2	B×P	R–B1	P–Q5	P–B3
	O–O	B–Q3	O–O	B–QB4	P–Q3
9	P–QR3	N–QN5	P–K3	B–N5	Q–B2 (o)
	B×N	P–K4	P–K4	P–KR3	QN–Q2
10	B×B	N×B	B–K2	B–R4	P–K3
	P–QR4	P×N	P–K5	P–QR4	Q–K2
11	P–KN3	P×P	N–Q2	B–Q3	B–Q3
	P–B4 (c)	P×P =	Q–N3 (h)	Q–Q3 (k)	P–KN4 (p)

(a) (A) 6 B–Q2, B×P; 7 P–K3, O–O; 8 R–B1, P–QN3; 9 N–B3, (1) 9 . . . B–N2; 10 B–K2, Q–N1; 11 O–O, R–Q1; 12 KR–Q1, N–K4 = . Foguelman–Ivkov, Amsterdam 1964. (2) 9 . . . P–Q4; 10 P×P, P×P; 11 B–N5, B–N2 = . (B) 6 B–N5, P–KR3; 7 B–R4, B×P = .

(b) 7 . . . N×B; 8 N×N, P–B4; 9 P–N3, B×P; 10 B–N2, O–O; 11 O–O, P–QN3; 12 Q–R4, B–N2; 13 N–N3, Q–K2; 14 QR–Q1 ± .

(c) 12 B–N2, Q–B2; 13 O–O, P–R5; 14 N–Q2, P–QN3; 15 P–B4, B–R3 = . Euwe–Evans, Hastings 1949/50.

(d) 4 . . . Q–K2; 5 P–QR3, B×N; 6 Q×B, P–QN3; 7 P–B3, P–Q4; 8 P×P, N×P; 9 Q–B2, Q–R5†; 10 P–N3, Q×QP; 11 P–K4, N–K2; 12 B–KB4 ± .

(e) (A) 6 B–N5, P–KR3; 7 B×N, Q×B; 8 P–K3, P×P; 9 B×P, O–O = . (B) 6 P–QR3, P×P; 7 Q×P, Q–Q4; 8 Q×B, N×Q; 9 N×Q, N–B7†; 10 K–Q2! with most involved complications. The column is Trifunović–Barcza, Spindlerův Mlýn 1947. 4 . . . N–B3 is the "Zürich Variation," similar to the Queen's Gambit, Ragozin System.

(f) 4 . . . O–O; 5 B–N5, P–B4 (5 . . . P–Q4; see Queen's Gambit, Ragozin System); 6 R–B1!

(g) (A) Innocuous is 5 P–KN3, N–K5; 6 B–Q2, N×B; 7 Q×N, Q–R4; 8 B–N2, O–O; 9 O–O, P×P; 10 N×P, N–B3; 11 KR–B1, Q–QB4 = . For 5 . . . P×P; 6 N×P see English Opening, col. 26. (B) Best is 5 P–K3, leading into the Rubinstein Variation.

(h) 12 K–B1, B×N; 13 R×B, N–Q2! ∞ . Larsen–Kaplan, San Juan 1969.

(i) A singular deviation is (A) 4 . . . N–R4; 5 N–R3, P–KB4; 6 P–K4, P×P; 7 B–N5, N–KB3! 8 P×P, P–KR3 = . Benko–Shipman, Washington 1965. (B) 4 . . . P–B4. 5 P–Q5! N–R4! 6 P–KN3, P–B4; 7 B–Q2, O–O; 8 P–K3, P–Q3; 9 P×P, B×P; 10 N–Q5, B×N = . Portisch–Forintos, Hungary 1969. A modern combine of Catalan and Benoni features.

(j) Also effective is 5 . . . B–Q3; 6 P–K4, P–B4; 7 QP×P, B×BP; 8 P×P, P×P; 9 B–N5, B×N; 10 R×B, Q–N3 = . Archives.

(k) 12 N–B3, QN–Q2; 13 Q–Q2, P–B3 = . Portisch–Szabó, Hungarian Chp. 1960.

(l) No punch has 4 B–Q2, O–O; 5 P–K3, P–Q4; or 5 . . . P–QN3.

(m) Playable is 4 . . . P–B4; 5 P–Q5!? P–Q3; 6 R–B1, P×P; 7 P×P, O–O; 8 P–K3, QN–Q2; 9 N–K2, P–KR3; 10 B×N, Q×B = .

(n) A position of crucial choices, e.g. (A) 6 . . . P–QN4; 7 P×KP, BP×P; 8 P×P, O–O; 9 P–K3, (1) 9 . . . Q–R4; 10 N–K2, P–R3; 11 P×P, B×P; 12 B×N, R×B; 13 P–B3, N–B3∞. (2) 9 . . . P–Q4; 10 B–Q3, P–Q5; 11 P×P, P×P; 12 P–QR3, B–R4; 13 P–QN4, P×N; 14 P×B, B–N2; 15 N–B3, Q×P; 16 O–O, QN–Q2; 17 Q–K2, B×N = .

Spasski–Unzicker, Bath 1973. (B) 6 . . . P–Q3; 7 P–K3, P×P; 8 P×P, QN–Q2; 9 B–QN5, B×N†! 10 P×B, P–QR3; 11 B×N†, B×B; 12 N–K2, B–N4 = . *Comments*. (C) 6 . . . P×P; 7 P×P, O–O; 8 P–K3, R–K1 = . (D) 6 . . . B×N†; 7 P×B, Q–R4; 8 B×N, P×B; 9 Q–Q2, P–Q3; 10 P–K4, P–K4 = . Mrs. Karff–Miss Lane, US Women's Chp. 1966.

(o) 9 P–K4, QN–Q2; 10 B–Q3, N–B1; 11 N–K2, P–KN4; 12 B–B2, N–N3 = .

(p) (A) 12 B–N3, P–N3; 13 N–K2, P–K5! = . Bagirov–Estrin, USSR 1968. (B) 12 B–B2, P–K5; 13 P×P, N–K4; 14 P–KR4, N×B†; 15 Q×N, N×KP; 16 P×P, B–B4; 17 R×P, R×R; 18 P×R, Q–B3; 19 P–R7, O–O–O; 20 resigns. Merino–Bisguier, Orense 1974.

Grünfeld Defence

(1 P–Q4, N–KB3; 2 P–QB4, P–KN3;
3 N–QB3, P–Q4)

Incorporating the
Neo-Grünfeld Defence
(1 P–Q4, N–KB3; 2 P–QB4, P–KN3;
3 P–KN3, B–N2; 4 B–N2, P–Q4)
(or variations thereof, cols. 41–5)

Invented in 1922 by the Austrian master and theoretician, Ernst Grünfeld, this defence has been adopted by all shades of players with a profound strategical temperament.

Grünfeld claimed 2 . . . P–KN3 as characteristic and claimed authorship of that move. At that time the King's Indian had no specific name and was regarded as vaguely atrocious. So he gave 3 . . . P–Q4 an exclamation mark in order to distinguish what appeared to him as the only playable form of this defence. It is now the fianchetto of the king's bishop plus the followup with 3 . . . P–Q4 which is considered thematic.

Black's strategy is based on hypermodern principles: White is invited to establish a classical pawn steam-roller in the centre which later serves as a target as Black hammers away at it. Meanwhile White tries to solidify his space advantage and push Black against the wall. All this provokes positions where the question of who really controls the centre is not easily resolved, making the defence practical, lively and promising.

(1) White's sharpest continuation is 4 P × P, N × P; 5 P–K4 (cols. 1–10). However, it has declined in popularity, the opinion being that it

351

prematurely clarifies the centre and relieves the tension. Most of the lines resolve into equal chances. One way to play it for Black (cols. 9–10) is to omit or defer . . . P–QB4 until after . . . P–QN3, . . . B–N2, and . . . N–B3, the advantage of this being he will then be in a position to defend his pawn on QB4 instead of being forced to exchange it.

(2) 4 N–B3, B–N2; 5 Q–N3, P × P; 6 Q × BP, O–O; 7 P–K4, B–N5; 8 B–K3, KN–Q2! (col. 11–15) is Smyslov's brilliant innovation which maintains the tension and strikes at Q5. Black's minor pieces also become particularly active in the centre (which White is hard-pressed to maintain). It is doubtful whether this line confers White any advantage, although it is still regarded as theoretically crucial. Alternatives for Black on move 7 are considered in cols. 16–19 and are all perfectly satisfactory including the Prins Variation (col. 18–9). Deviations for White at an earlier stage (cols. 20–3) are generally passive and unpromising, though the search for more active lines has brought them into prominence, particularly 5 B–N5 (col. 22).

5 P–K3 (cols. 24–27) is a quiet method which aims at slow positional pressure. Black holds his own.

(3) 4 B–B4, B–N2; 5 P–K3 (cols. 31–5) at least has the merit of developing the queen's bishop to a good diagonal. The trouble is that Black can strike at the centre with . . . P–QB4 while, if White attempts to gain a pawn after 5 . . . O–O; 6 P × P, N × P; 7 N × N, Q × N; 8 B × P (cols. 31–2), Black's gambit secures him active counterplay. If White can find any improvement here he is advised to try it. 5 . . . P–B3 (col. 34) is less active and permits White a minimal space advantage.

(4) Alternatives for White at move 4 are handled in cols. 28–30, with the consequential attack 4 B–N5 (cols. 29–30) commanding most interest. It can be avoided by first 3 . . . B–N2 (see cols. 26–30, (a)) but only if Black wishes to invite—or risk—a King's Indian Defence.

(5) THE NEO-GRÜNFELD DEFENCE (or Kemeri variation since it was greatly practised at Kemeri, 1937) 1 P–Q4, N–KB3; 2 P–QB4, P–KN3; 3 P–KN3, B–N2; 4 B–N2, P–Q4 (cols. 36–40) sets delicate positional problems. The early fianchetto of White's king's bishop coupled with the delayed development of his queen's knight resulted from a search inspired by the advent of the Catalan Opening, for new and more aggressive lines against the Grünfeld. Its outstanding advocate in later years was Robert Byrne. Regardless, Black went right on playing an immediate or deferred . . . P–Q4 (when he didn't steer for the King's Indian with . . . P–Q3). This evoked paternity rights. Euwe and Grünfeld both claimed that they invented the Black pawn thrust. Some authors, Trifunović and Mikenas for instance, bolstered Grünfeld's claim by including this variation in their monographs on his defence. MCO 9th edition sought a compromise by creating a separate classification and section—Neo–Grünfeld—but by

now all systems involving . . . P–Q4 can be considered to belong to the Grünfeld Defence, including col. 23 of the English Opening.

The most relevant lines arise after 5 P × P, N × P; 6 P–K4, N–N5 (cols. 36–7) where Black holds his own in the rapid-fire complications.

A subtle positional struggle results from 6 N–KB3, O–O; 7 O–O, P–QB4 but the resulting simplifications are considered too drawish (col. 38). The other lines arising from 5 N–KB3, O–O; 6 O–O, P–B4 or 6 . . . P × P (cols. 39–40) are somewhat intricate and must be studied by any player wishing to specialize in this defence.

The lines where Black adopts . . . P–QB3 (cols. 41–3) are passive but again quite satisfactory for equality. It is hard for White to make progress against the stone wall in the centre.

(6) Alternatives for White on move three are analysed in cols. 44–5. After either Mengarini's 3 Q–B2 (note (g)) or 3 P–B3, Black of course has the option of transposing to the King's Indian Defence after White has already committed himself. Nevertheless, these systems for White do have some vitality and the advantage of novelty.

1 P-Q4, N-KB3; 2 P-QB4, P-KN3; 3 N-QB3, P-Q4; 4 P × P, N × P; 5 P-K4 (a),
N × N; 6 P × N, P-QB4; 7 B-QB4, B-N2; 8 N-K2

	1	2	3	4	5
	O-O				N-B3 (k)
9	O-O				B-K3
	P × P	N-B3 (c)			P × P
10	P × P	B-K3			P × P
	N-B3	Q-B2		N-R4 (h)	Q-R4†
11	B-K3	R-B1		B-Q3	B-Q2
	B-N5	R-Q1 (d)		P-N3	Q-R6
12	P-B3	P-B4	Q-K1 (f)	Q-Q2	R-QN1
	N-R4	B-N5	Q-R4	B-N2	O-O
13	R-B1 (b)	P-B5	R-Q1 (g)	QR-B1 (i)	O-O!
	N × B	P × BP (e)		R-B1 (j)	B-N5 (l)
14	R × N ±				

(a) (A) 5 P-K3, B-N2; 6 Q-N3, N × N; 7 P × N, O-O; 8 N-B3, P-QB4; 9 B-K2, N-B3; 10
O-O, P × P; 11 BP × P, P-N3 = . Zografakis–Cortlever, Dubrovnik 1950. (B) 5 P-KN3, B-N2;
6 B-N2, N × N; 7 P × N, P-QB4; 8 P-K3, O-O; 9 N-K2, N-B3; 10 O-O, B-Q2; 11 B-Q2,
R-B1; N-R4 = . García–Smyslov, Havana 1962.

(b) (A) 13 B × P†, R × B; 14 P × B, R × R†; 15 K × R, Q-Q2; 16 P-KR3, Q-K3; 17 Q-Q3,
Q-B5; 18 Q-Q2, Q-R3; 19 Q-B2, N-B5 = . Spasski–Korchnoi, USSR Chp. 1955. (B) 13
B-Q5, B-B1! 14 B-N5, P-KR3; 15 B-R4, P-R3 = . Ilivitski–Korchnoi, USSR Chp. 1955. (C)
13 B-Q3, B-K3; 14 P-Q5!? B × R; 15 Q × B, P-B3; 16 Q-N1, B-Q2 = .

(c) 9 . . . N-Q2? 10 B-KN5! P-KR3; 11 B-K3, Q-B2; 12 R-B1, P-R3; 13 Q-Q2, K-R2;
14 B-Q3, P-QN4; 15 N-B4, P-K4; 16 N-Q5, Q-Q3; 17 P × BP, N × P; 18 P-QB4, N × B; 19
Q × N ± . Bronstein–Botvinnik, match 1951.

(d) (A) 11 . . . N-R4; 12 B-Q3, P-N3; 13 Q-Q2, B-N2; 14 B-KR6, QR-Q1; 15 B × B,
K × B; 16 Q-K3, P-K4; 17 P-Q5, P-B5; 18 B-N1, B-B1; 19 P-B4, P × P; 20 R × P, Q-K4; 21
Q-N3, P-B3; 22 R/1-B1, B-Q2; 23 B-B2, N-N2 = . Furman–Taimanov, USSR Chp. 1959.
(B) 11 . . . P-N3? 12 P-B4 or 12 Q-Q2.

(e) (A) 14 B × P†! K × B! (14 . . . K-R1? 15 P × KBP, P × P; 16 P × P, B × N; 17 Q × B,
B × P; 18 B × B†, R × B; 19 Q-R5, Q-K4; 20 B-N6!! Q-N2; 21 QR-B3, QR-Q1; 22 R-KR3,
R-Q7; 23 P-B6! + . Clement); 15 Q-N3†, P-K3; 16 N-B4, Q-Q2; 17 KP × P, N-R4; 18
Q × P†, Q × Q; 19 N × Q; P × P! = . (B) 14 KP × P, Q-Q3 = .

(f) Another twist is (A) 12 Q-Q2, Q-R4; 13 Q-N2 (or 13 KR-Q1?!), P-N3; 14 B-Q5,
B-N2! 15 KR-Q1, P-K3; 16 B-N3, P × P; 17 P × P, QR-B1; 18 P-K5, B-B1 = .
Gligorić–Tukmakov, Leningrad 1937. (B) 12 B-B4, Q-Q2! 13 P-Q5, N-R4; 14 B-Q3,
P-QN4 = .

(g) (A) 13 . . . P × P; 14 P × P, Q × Q; 15 KR × Q, P-N3; 16 P-Q5, N-K4; 17 B-QN5,
B-Q2; 18 N-Q4! B × B; 19 N × B, R-Q2 ∞ . Gligorić–Hartston, Praia da Rocha 1969. (B) 13
. . . N-R4; 14 B-Q3, Q-Q2; 15 P-Q5, P × P = . Rashkovski–Tseshkovski, Odessa 1974.

(h) 10 . . . P × P; 11 P × P, B-N5 (11 . . . N-R4!? 12 B-Q3, N-B3; 13 B-QN5!); 12 P-B3,
see col. 1.

(i) 13 B-KR6, P × P; 14 B × B, K × B; 15 P × P, P-K3; 16 QR-B1, Q-K2 = . Filip.

(j) 14 B-KR6, P-K3; 15 B × B, K × B; 16 Q-K3, Q-K2 = . Banník–Simagin, USSR Chp.
1956.

(k) A novel addition is 8 . . . N-Q2?! 9 O-O (9 B-KN5, Q-R4!), Q-B2; 10 B-B4, P-K4;
11 P × KP, B × P; 12 B × B, N × B! 13 B-N5†, B-Q2; 14 B × B†, Q × B; 15 Q × Q†. K × Q ∞ .
Teschner–Smyslov, Monte Carlo 1959.

(l) 14 P-Q5, P-QN4; 15 R × P! N-K4; 16 B-N3, Q-R3; 17 P-QR4, QR-N1; 18 P-R3 ± .
Shamkovich. Also 15 B-B1 is good.

1 P–Q4, N–KB3; 2 P–QB4, P–KN3; 3 N–QB3, P–Q4; 4 P×P, N×P; 5 P–K4,
N×N; 6 P×N

	6	7	8	9	10
	(P–QB4).................		B–N2		
7	B–N5†	P–Q5	B–QB4 (d)		
	B–Q2	B–N2	O–O		
8	B×B† (a)	Q–N3	N–K2		
	Q×B	O–O	P–N3	N–B3	
9	N–B3	B–K3	O–O? (e)	B–KN5......	O–O (h)
	B–N2	Q–R4	B–N2	N–R4	P–N3
10	O–O	B–Q2	P–B3	B–N3	B–K3
	O–O	N–R3	P–QB4	P–N3!	Q–Q2 (i)
11	B–K3	R–B1	B–KN5	Q–Q3	R–B1
	P×P	P–B5	P×P	Q–Q2	B–N2
12	P×P	B×P	P×P	O–O	B–QN5
	N–B3	N–B4	N–B3	B–N2	P–QR3
13	R–B1	Q–N1 (c)	B–Q5	QR–Q1	B–R4
	KR–B1 (b)		Q–Q2 (f)	QR–B1 (g)	P–QN4 (j)

(a) (A) 8 P–QR4, B–N2; 9 N–K2, P×P; 10 P×P, N–B3 and . . . O–O =. (B) 8 B–QB4,
B–N2; 9 N–K2, O–O; 10 O–O, P×P =. *Comments.*

(b) 14 Q–Q2, P–N3; 15 R–B2, P–K3; 16 KR–B1, N–K2 =. Kashdan–Alekhin, London
1932.

(c) The column is a suggestion by Gunderam.

(d) 7 P–KB4, P–QB4; 8 B–K3, Q–R4; 9 K–B2, O–O; 10 Q–N3, P×P; 11 P×P, N–Q2 =.

(e) (A) 9 P–KR4! (1) 9 . . . P–K4; 10 P–R5, P×QP; 11 P×NP, RP×P; 12 P×P, Q–K2∞.
Euwe. (2) 9 . . . B–QR3; 10 B×B, N×B; 11 P–R5, P–QB4; 12 P×NP, RP×P; 13 Q–Q3,
Q–B1; 14 Q–N3, P×P; 15 P×P± (3) 9 . . . N–B3; 10 P–R5, N–R4 =. (B) 9 B–Q5, P–B3; 10
B–N3∞.

(f) 14 Q–Q2, P–K3; 15 B×N, B×B =. Botvinnik–Smyslov, match 1954.

(g) 14 P–QB4, P–K3; 15 B–Q2, N×B =. Portisch–Filip, Leipzig 1960.

(h) (A) 9 P–KR4, N–R4; 10 B–N3, P–QB4; 11 P–R5, N×B; 12 P×N, P×QP; 13 P×QP,
B–Q2; 14 P×P, RP×P; 15 Q–Q3, Q–N3 =. Spasski–Stein, USSR Chp. 1964. (B) 9 B–K3,
P–N3; 10 Q–Q2 (or 10 O–O, B–N2; 11 R–B1, P–K3), N–R4; 11 B–Q3, P–QB4; 12 B–KR6,
B×B; 13 Q×B, P×P; 14 P×P, N–B3; 15 P–KR4!? Gligorić.

(i) (A) 10 . . . B–N2; 11 R–B1! N–R4; 12 B–Q3, P–QB4; 13 P–Q5, P–B5; 14 B–B2,
(Portisch–Uhlmann, Zagreb 1965), P–K3; 15 P×P, P×P; 16 N–Q4, Q–K2; 17 Q–N4,
P–K4 =. (B) 10 . . . N–R4; 11 B–Q3, P–QB4; 12 Q–R4, P×P; 13 P×P, B–Q2 =. Hartston.

(j) 14 B–B2, QR–Q1; 15 P–QR4, P–K4 =. Toran–Larsen, Beverwijk 1956.

1 P-Q4, N-KB3; 2 P-QB4, P-KN3; 3 N-QB3, P-Q4; 4 N-B3, B-N2; 5 Q-N3, P×P; 6 Q×BP, O-O; 7 P-K4, B-N5; 8 B-K3, KN-Q2! (*a*)

	11	12	13	14	15
9	B-K2 (*b*)	.... R-Q1	Q-N3		
	N-N3	N-QB3	N-QB3	N-N3 (*i*)	
10	Q-Q3 (*c*)	R-Q1	Q-N3	R-Q1	P-QR4
	N-B3	N-N3 (*e*)	P-K4!	N-B3	P-QR4
11	R-Q1	Q-B5 (*f*)	P×P	P-Q5	P-Q5
	B×N	Q-Q3	B×N	N-K4	QB×N
12	B×B	P-KR3	P×B	B-K2	P×B
	P-K4	B×N	QN×P	N×N†	Q-Q3
13	P-Q5	P×B	B-R3	P×N	N-N5
	N-Q5	KR-Q1	N×P†	B-R4	Q-N5†
14	B×N	P-Q5	K-K2	P-B4 (*j*)	Q×Q
	P×B	N-K4	N/6-K4	B×B	P×Q
15	N-K2	N-N5	B×N	N×B	N×P
	P-QB4 (*d*)	Q-KB3 (*g*)	N×B (*h*)	Q-Q2 (*k*)	R×P (*l*)

(*a*) (A) Tamer is 8 . . . N-B3; 9 P-Q5, B×N (9 . . . N-QR4; 10 Q-R4, P-B3; 11 R-Q1 ±); 10 P×B, N-K4; 11 Q-K2, P-QN4; 12 R-Q1, P-N5 ∞. (B) 8 . . . QN-Q2; 9 Q-N3, N-N3; 10 N-KN5 ± .

(*b*) 9 O-O-O may be answered with 9 . . . P-K4! or 9 . . . N-N3; 10 Q-B5, P-K4 = .

(*c*) 10 Q-B5, P-QB3; 11 R-Q1, QN-Q2; Q-QR5, P-K4! 13 P-Q5, P×P; 14 N×P, N×N; 15 Q×N, B-K3; 16 Q-Q2, N-B3! 17 Q-N4, P-QR4= . Botvinnik-Smyslov, match 1958.

(*d*) 16 P×P *e.p.*, P×P; 17 O-O, P-QB4; 18 P-QN3, Q-B2 = . Turner-Benko, US Chp. 1962.

(*e*) Stronger might be 10 . . . B×N; 11 P×B, P-K4; 12 P×P, N/3×P; 13 Q-N3, Q-R5!

(*f*) 11 Q-Q3 reverts into col. 11.

(*g*) 16 P-B4, N/4-Q2 (Botvinnik-Fischer, Varna, 1962); 17 Q×BP, Q×NP = .

(*h*) 16 Q-N5, P-QB3; 17 Q×NP, R-N1; 18 Q×N, R×P†; 19 K-B1, Q×Q; 20 R×Q, B×N; 21 R×RP, R-K1; 22 R-R4 = . Evans-Fischer, US Chp. 1963.

(*i*) If 9 . . . B×N; 10 P×B, N-QB3; 11 O-O-O! (11 R-Q1, P-K4 see col. 13), P-K4; 12 P×P, QN×P; 13 B-R3, P-B4; 14 B×N! N×B; 15 Q-N5, B-Q5; 16 B×B, P-QR3; 17 Q-Q3, P×B; 18 Q×P± . *Comments.*

(*j*) 14 P-KR4, Q-Q2; 15 P-R4, B×N†! 16 Q×B, N×RP; 17 Q-Q4, P-KB3 = .

(*k*) 16 P-KR4, P-QB3; 17 P-R5, P×QP; 18 P×NP, RP×P; 19 B-Q4, B×B; 20 R×B, K-N2; 21 N-N3, R-KN1! 22 P-B5, R-R1 = . Lilienthal-Bronstein, Stockholm 1948. In the column, 10 . . . P-K3; 11 B-QN5, B×N; 12 P×B, Q-R5 = ; Forintos-Smejkal, Bar 1977.

(*l*) 16 R×R, N×R; 17 P-N3, N-B6; 18 B-R3, B-K4; 19 B-N6, N-R3; 20 N×N, P×N (20 . . . R-R1!); 21 B-QB5, B-Q3 = . Euwe.

1 P-Q4, N-KB3; 2 P-QB4, P-KN3; 3 N-QB3, P-Q4; 4 N-B3, B-N2; 5 Q-N3,
P×P; 6 Q×BP, O-O

	16	17	18	19	20
7	(P-K4) . . . . P-K3 (*m*)				
	P-B3 . . . . . . N-B3 . . . . N-R3 (*f*) The Prins Variation				P-N3
8	B-K2	P-Q5 (*d*)	B-K2 . . . . B-N5 (*j*)		B-K2
	P-QN4!	N-QR4	P-B4	P-R3	B-N2
9	Q-N3	Q-Q3	P-Q5	B-R4	O-O
	Q-R4 (*a*)	P-B3	P-K3	P-B4	QN-Q2
10	B-Q2	P×P (*e*)	O-O (*g*)	P-Q5	R-Q1
	P-N5	N×BP	P×P	P-K3 (*k*)	Q-B1
11	N-QR4	Q×Q	P×P	O-O-O	B-Q2
	N×P	R×Q	R-K1 (*h*)	Q-R4	P-B4
12	B×P	B-K2	B-N5	Q-N5!	Q-N3
	Q-Q1 (*b*)	P-N3	P-R3	Q×Q	Q-B2 =
13	O-O	O-O	B-B4	B×Q	
	B-K3 (*c*)	B-N2 =	B-B4 (*i*)	P×P (*l*)	

(*a*) 9 . . . P-QR4; 10 Q-B2, P-N5; 11 N-Q1, P-R5; 12 O-O, B-K3 = . Luckis-Benko,
Buenos Aires 1952.

(*b*) Enterprising are (A) 12 . . . Q-KB4; 13 O-O, B-K3; 14 Q-R3, B-Q4; 15 B×P,
R-K1 = and (B) 12 . . . Q-B2; 13 O-O, B-K3 ∞. Hort.

(*c*) 14 Q-K3, N-Q3; 15 KR-Q1, N-Q2; 16 N-B5, B-Q4 = . Florian-Bronstein, Budapest
1949.

(*d*) (A) 8 B-K2, B-N5 (1) 9 P-Q5, N-QR4, 10 Q-R4, B×N; 11 B×B, P-B3; 12 O-O,
P×P; 13 R-Q1, N-B3 = . Reshevsky-D. Byrne, US Chp. 1957. (2) 9 B-K3, B×N; 10 P×B,
P-K4; 11 P-Q5, N-Q5; 12 O-O-O, N-K1 = . (B) 8 B-K3, B-N5; see cols. 11-15.

(*e*) 10 P-QN4, P×P; 11 P×N, N×P; 12 B-Q2, B-B4 = . The column is
Uhlmann-Korchnoi, Stockholm 1962.

(*f*) 7 . . . P-QR3 and now (A) 8 P-QR4, P-QN4; 9 Q-N3, P-B4; 10 P×BP, B-K3 ∞. (B) 8
P-K5 (1) 8 . . . P-QN4; 9 Q-N3, N-N5; 10 P-KR3, N-R3; 11 B-KB4, B-N2; 12 B-K2,
N-B4; 13 R-Q1, N-Q2 = . Portisch-Adorian, Budapest 1970. Or (2) 8 . . . KN-Q2! 9 P-K6,
P×P; 10 Q×P†, K-R1; 11 N-KN5, N-QB3! 12 N-B7†, R×N; 13 Q×R, N×P∓. (c) 8
Q-N3, P-QN4; 9 P-K5, B-K3; 10 P×N?! B×Q; 11 P×B, K×P; 12 P×B, N-B3 ∞. Por-
tisch-Flatow, Adelaide 1971.

(*g*) 10 B-N5, P×P! 11 N×P, B-K3; 12 R-Q1, Q-R4† 13 B-Q2, B×N; 14 P×B, Q-N3;
15 B-B3 (Sosonko-Kalinin, Kharkov 1967), QR-Q1; 16 O-O, N-QN5! with a somewhat
better game for Black.

(*h*) 11 . . . B-B4; 12 R-Q1, R-K1; 13 P-QR3, N-K5; 14 B-K3, N-Q3; 15 Q-B4,
N-K5 = . Polugayevski-Korchnoi, USSR Chp. 1960.

(*i*) 14 QR-Q1, N-K5; 15 B-Q3, N-Q3; 16 B×N, B×B; 17 R×B, Q×B = .
Bolbochan-Pilnik, Mar del Plata 1950.

(*j*) 8 Q-R4, P-B4; 9 P-Q5?! Q-N3! 10 B×N, P×B; 11 O-O, P-K3; 12 P-Q6, B-N2; 13
P-K5, N-Q4; 14 N-K4, N-N5; 15 R-K1, N-Q6! ∞. Polugayevski.

(*k*) Aggressive, yet harmless is 10 . . . P-QN4?! 11 N×P, Q-R4†; 12 N-Q2, N×KP?! 13
Q×N, B×P! 14 R-Q1, B-B4; 15 Q-QB4, N-N5; 16 N-N3, Q×P; 17 N-R1, Q-R4 = .
Pachman.

(*l*) 14 P×P, P-N4; 15 B-N3, B-B4 = .

(*m*) 7 P-KN3, B-K3! 8 Q-R4, N-B3 = . The column is Reshevsky-Uhlmann, Buenos
Aires 1960.

1 P-Q4, N-KB3; 2 P-QB4, P-KN3; 3 N-QB3, P-Q4; 4 N-B3, B-N2

	21	22	23	24	25
5	(Q-N3)......	B-N5 (d)	B-B4	P-K3	
	P-B3	N-K5!? (e)	O-O	O-O (n)	
6	P×P (a)	P×P (f)	R-B1	Q-N3......	P×P
	P×P	N×B	P-B4 (i)	P-K3	N×P
7	B-N5	N×N	P×BP	B-Q2	B-B4
	P-K3	P-K3	P×P (j)	P-N3	N×N (p)
8	P-K3 (b)	Q-Q2	P-K4 (k)	R-B1	P×N
	O-O	P×P (g)	Q-R4	B-N2	P-QB4
9	B-Q3	Q-K3†	N-Q2 (l)	B-K2	O-O
	N-B3	K-B1	B-K3	QN-Q2	Q-B2
10	O-O	Q-B4	B×P	O-O	Q-K2
	P-KR3	B-B3	B×B	N-K5	N-B3 (q)
11	B-R4	P-KR4	N×B	KR-Q1	B-Q3 (r)
	P-KN4 (c)	P-B3 (h)	Q×BP (m)	P×P (o)	

(a) (A) 6 B-N5, N-K5; 7 P×P, N×B; 8 N×N, P-K3; 9 P×BP, N×P! (B) 6 B-B4, P×P; 7 Q×BP, B-K3; 8 Q-Q3, N-Q4; 9 B-Q2, N-N5; 10 Q-N1, P-QB4; 11 P×P, N/1-R3 = .

(b) 8 P-K4, P×P; 9 B-N5†, B-Q2; 10 N-K5, O-O; 11 N×KP, Q-R4†; 12 Q-B3, Q×Q†; 13 N×Q, B×B; 14 N×B, N-Q4 = . Trifunović.

(c) 12 B-N3, N-KR4; Keres-Frydman, Buenos Aires Olympics 1939.

(d) After 5 Q-R4†, Black equalizes in various ways, although this does not negate the raison d'être of White's move; e.g. (1) 5 . . . B-Q2; 6 Q-N3, P×P; 7 Q×BP, O-O; 8 P-K3, N-R3 = . Comments. (2) 5 . . . P-B3; 6 P×P, N×P; 7 P-K4, N-N3; 8 Q-B2, B-N5; 9 N-K5, B-K3 = .

(e) Experimental is 5 . . . P×P; (1) 6 P-K3, B-K3; 7 N-Q2 (7 B×P), P-B4; 8 P×P, N-Q4? 9 B×BP, N×N; 10 P×N, B×B; 11 Q-R4†, N-B3; 12 Q×B, O-O; 13 N-N3, N-K4; 14 Q-K2, N-Q6†; 15 K-B1, N-K4∞. Petrosian-Savon, USSR Chp. 1969. (2) 6 P-K4, P-B4; 7 P-Q5, P-N4; 8 P-K5, P-N5; 9 P×N, P×P; 10 Q-K2†, K-B1; 11 B-K3, P×N; 12 B×P†, K-N1; 13 P×P, P-KR4? (13 . . . B-QR3!); 14 Q×P, B-QR3; 15 Q-N3, N-Q2; 16 B-K3, Q-QB1; 17 B×B, Q×B; 18 P-B4, R-N1; 19 Q-Q3, N-K4; 20 N×N, P×N; 21 O-O, P-K5; 22 Q×P, B×R; 23 R×B, P-B4; 24 Q-K5, Q-N2; 25 R-QB1, K-R2; 26 P-KR3, KR-K1; 27 Q-B4, Q-N2; 28 P-B5, QR-B1; 29 P-Q6, R-K5; 30 Q-N5, R-KB1; 31 P-B3, R-K3; 32 Q-B4, R/1-K1; 33 B-Q2, R-Q1; 34 R-N1, K-N1; 35 Q-B4, Q-KB2; 36 K-R2, R-K4; 37 Q×Q†, K×Q; 38 B-N5, R-Q2; 39 R-QB1, R-K1; 40 B-B4, P-N4; 41 B×P, R-QB1; 42 K-N3, K-K3; 43 K-B4, K-Q4; 44 R-Q1†, K-B3; 45 K×P, R-QN1; 46 P-N4, P×P; 47 RP×P, R-B1†; 48 B-B6, K×P; 49 K-K6, resigns. Benko-Hartston, Hastings 1974-5.

(f) Attention deserves 6 B-R4, P-QB4; 7 BP×P, N×N; 8 P×N, Q×P; 9 P-K3, N-B3; 10 B-K2, P×P; 11 BP×P, (1) 11 . . . P-K4; 12 P×P, Q-R4†; 13 Q-Q2, Q×Q†; 14 K×Q, N×P; 15 QR-QN1, O-O = . (2) 11 . . . O-O; 12 O-O, B-B4; 13 N-Q2, QR-B1; 14 B-B3, Q-Q2; 15 N-N3, Q-K1∞.

(g) 8 . . . P-KR3; 9 N-R3, P×P; 10 Q-K3†, K-B1; 11 N-B4, N-B3; 12 R-Q1, N-K2 = . Taimanov-Borisenko, Leningrad 1960.

(h) 12 P-K4, P-KR3; 13 N-B3, K-N2; 14 O-O-O, B-K3; 15 B-Q3, N-Q2 = . Soos-D. Byrne, Varna 1962.

(i) (A) For 6 . . . P-B3 see lines with 4 B-B4. (B) 6 . . . P×P; 7 P-K3, B-K3; 8 N-KN5, B-Q4; 9 N×B, N×N; 10 B-N3, P-QB4! = ; or 9 P-K4, P-KR3; 10 P×B, P×N; 11 B×NP, N×P = .

(j) Or 7 . . . B-K3; 8 N-Q4, N-B3; 9 N×B, P×N; 10 P-K3, Q-R4; 11 B-K2, P-K4? (11 . . . QR-Q1! =); 12 P×P, P×B; 13 P×N, P×BP; 14 P×P, N-K5; 15 O-O, N×N; 16

P×N, R×P; 17 Q-N3†, K-R1; 18 Q-N7 (Tal–Mikenas, Lithuanian Chp. 1962), QR-KB1 = .

(k) 8 Q×Q, R×Q; 9 P-K3, N-R3; 10 P-B6, P×P; 11 B×P (Korchnoi–Stein, USSR Chp. 1963), N-QN5 = .

(l) 9 P-K5, N-R4; 10 B-K3, N-QB3; 11 B×P, N×P; 12 N×N, B×N = .

(m) 12 N-Q2, N-B3; 13 O-O, KR-Q1; 14 N-Q5, Q-Q5; 15 R×N! R×N! = . Comments to Reshevsky–Steinmeyer, US Chp. 1963.

(n) (A) For 5 . . . P×P see Queen's Gambit Accepted, col. 16. (B) 5 . . . P-B3; (1) 6 Q-N3, P-K3; 7 B-Q2; O-O; 8 B-Q3, QN-Q2; 9 O-O, P-N3 = . (2) 6 B-K2 is good. (c) For 5 . . . P-B4; 6 B-K2, P×QP; 7 KP×P, O-O see Queen's Gambit, Symmetrical Defence. col. 80.

(o) 12 Q×BP, N-Q3; 13 Q-N3, P-QB4! = . Polugayevski–Korchnoi, USSR Chp. 1958.

(p) If 7 . . . N-N3; 8 B-N3, P-QB4; 9 O-O, P×P; 10 P×P, N-B3; 11 P-Q5, N-R4; 12 B-N5, P-KR3; 13 B-K3, B-N5; 14 P-KR3, B×N; 15 Q×B, N/3-B5; 16 B-B1, N×B; 17 P×N, N-Q3; 18 R-K1, R-K1 = . Keres–D. Byrne, San Antonio 1972.

(q) 10 . . . B-N5; 11 B-R3, N-Q2; 12 QR-N1, N-N3 = .

(r) If 11 B-R3, P-N3; 12 QR-B1, N-R4! Simagin. The column is Primavera–Walsh, Munich 1958, ctd. 11 . . . R-K1; 12 B-N2, P-K4 = .

1 P-Q4, N-KB3; 2 P-QB4, P-KN3; 3 N-QB3, P-Q4 (a)

	26	27	28	29	30
4	(N-B3)		Q-N3	B-N5?! (l)	
	(B-N2)		P×P	N-K5!? (m)	
5	(P-K3)	P×P	Q×BP	P×P	B-R4 (o)
	(O-O)	N×P	B-K3 (h)	N×N (n)	N×N (p)
6	(P×P)	B-Q2 (e)	Q-N5† (i)	P×N	P×N
	(N×P)	P-QB4 (f)	N-B3 (j)	Q×P	P-QB4 (q)
7	(B-B4)	R-B1	N-B3	N-B3	P-K3
	N-N3	N×N	N-Q4	B-N2	N-B3 (r)
8	B-N3!	B×N	P-K4	P-K3	P×QP
	P-QB4 (b)	P×P	N-N5	P-QB4	Q×P
9	O-O	N×P	Q-R4	B-N5†	Q-B3!
	P×P	O-O	B-Q2	B-Q2	Q×Q?
10	N×P	P-K3	Q-Q1	P-B4	N×Q
	B-Q2 (c)	Q-Q4	P-K4	Q-K5	B-N2
11	Q-K2	N-N5	P-QR3	O-O	B-QN5
	N-B3 (d)	Q×Q† (g)	P×P (k)	B×B!	B-Q2 (s)

(a) The lines in cols. 11 through 35 with 4 N-B3, B-N2, or 4 B-B4, B-N2; are often arrived at by the more restrained transposition 3 . . . B-N2; and 4 N-B3 or 4 B-B4 is followed up with 4 . . . P-Q4. This requires Black to be prepared to defend a King's Indian if White now chooses 4 P-K4?! instead but it allows Black to bypass the lines in cols. 28–30 if for any reason he so prefers.

(b) 8 . . . N-R3; 9 N-K4, P-QB4; 10 N×P, N×N, 11 P×N, N-Q2 = . Tipary-Gereben, Hungary 1947.

(c) 10 . . . N-R3; 11 Q-K2, N-B4; 12 B-B2, B-Q2; 13 P-QR4, P-K4; 14 N-B3, B-K3 = . Najdorf-Benko, Los Angeles 1963.

(d) 12 N×N, B×N; 13 R-Q1, Q-B2; 14 P-K4, QR-Q1! = . Minev-Malich, Varna 1962. If 8 B-K2, P-QB4! In the column, White may vary with 6 B-Q2, P-B4; 7 P×BP, N-R3; 8 P×P, N×BP; 9 B-B4, B-B4; 10 O-O, R-B1; 11 Q-K2, N/3-K5; 12 N-Q4, N×B; 13 Q×N, N-K5; 14 N×N, B×N; 15 Q-N4, B×QP = . Smyslov-Ivkov, Petropolis 1973.

(e) (A) 6 P-KN3, O-O; 7 B-N2, P-QB4; 8 O-O, N×N; 9 P×N, P×P and 10 . . . P-K4 with wild complications. *Comments.* (B) 6 P-K4, N×N; 7 P×N, O-O; 8 B-K2, P-N3 = . (C) 6 Q-N3, N×N; 7 P×N, P-QB4; 8 P-K3, O-O; 9 B-R3, P×P; 10 N×P, N-B3 = . Romanishin-Tukmakov, USSR Chp. 1974. Compare with the columns where 5 Q-N3 is played.

(f) Safer is 6 . . . O-O; 7 R-B1, N-N3; 8 P-K3, N-B3; 9 B-N5, B-Q2; 10 O-O, P-K4; 11 P-Q5, N-QN5; 12 B×B, Q×B; 13 P-K4, P-KB4! = .

(g) 12 R×Q, N-B3; 13 B×B, K×B; 14 B-K2, B-B4; 15 P-KN4 with a seemingly preponderant position for White but Black successfully drew the end game. Petrosian-Fischer, World match, Belgrade 1970.

(h) (A) 5 . . . P-B3; 6 N-B3, B-N2; 7 P-KN3, B-K3; 8 Q-Q3, N-R3; 9 B-N2, B-B4 = . Pachman-Szabó, Varna 1962. (B) 5 . . . B-N2; see cols. 11–20.

(i) 6 Q-Q3, B-N2; 7 P-K4, P-B3; 8 N-B3, O-O; 9 B-K2, N-K1; 10 O-O, N-Q3; 11 Q-B2, B-B5; 12 B-B4, B×B; 13 Q×B, Q-N3; 14 QR-Q1, Q-R3 = . Reshevsky-Kashdan, match 1944.

(j) Boleslavski considers 6 . . . B-Q2; 7 Q×P, B-B3; 8 Q-N3, Q×P; 9 N-B3, Q-N3 with development to compensate for Black's isolated pawns.

(k) 12 N-QN1, N-R3; 13 P-QN4, N/R3×P; 14 P×N, B×P†; 15 B-Q2, Q-K2 = . Petrosian-Benko, Los Angeles 1963.

(*l*) A vigorous move, revived with a good deal of controversy. Meek alternatives are (A) 4 P–B3, B–N2; 5 P–K4, P × KP; 6 P × P, O–O; 7 N–B3, B–N5; 8 B–K3, P–K4 = . (B) 4 Q–R4†, B–Q2; 5 Q–N3, N–B3; 6 N–B3, N–QR4; 7 Q–N4, N × P = . (C) 4 P–KN3, P × P; 5 Q–R4†, KN–Q2; 6 B–N2, B–N2; 7 P–Q5, O–O; 8 Q × BP, N–N3; 9 Q–KR4, P–QB3 = .

(*m*) Much steam is taken out of the debate by the old answer 4 . . . P × P; 5 P–K4, B–N2; 6 B × P, O–O; 7 KN–K2, P–B4; 8 P–Q5, QN–Q2; 9 P–B3, N–K4 = . Kan–Ryumin, USSR 1939.

(*n*) Also 5 . . . N × B; 6 P–KR4, N–K5; 7 N × N, Q × P; 8 N–QB3, Q–QR4; 9 P–R5, B–N2; 10 P × P, RP × P; 11 R × R†, B × R; 12 P–K3, B–K3; 13 N–K2, B–B5 = . Lilienthal–Ilivitski, USSR 1955. The column is Alekhin–Grünfeld, Pistyan 1922.

(*o*) Weaker choices are (A) 5 B–B4, N × N; 6 P × N, B–N2; 7 N–B3, O–O; 8 P–B5, P–N3! = . (B) 5 N × N, P × N; (1) 6 Q–Q2, B–N2; 7 O–O–O, P–KR3; 8 B–B4, P–QB4; 9 P × P, Q × Q†; 10 B × Q, B–K3; 11 P–K3, N–Q2; 12 P–B3, N × P; 13 B–N4, R–B1 = . Alatortsev–Flohr, Leningrad 1939. (2) 6 P–K3, P–QB4! 7 Q–Q2, B–Q2; 8 P–Q5, Q–N3; 9 O–O–O, N–R3; 10 P–B3, N–N5 = . Flohr–Aronin, USSR Chp. 1951.

(*p*) 5 . . . . P–QB4; 6 P × QP, N × N; 7 P × N, Q × P; 8 P–K3, P × P; 9 Q × P, Q × Q; 10 BP × Q, P–K3; 11 R–N1, B–K2; 12 B–N5†, B–Q2; 13 B–N3 (13 B × B†, N × B; 14 B × B, K × B; 15 R × P, KR–QN1! ∓), N–B3 = . Donner–Hort, Amsterdam 1970.

(*q*) Also (A) 6 . . . B–N2! 7 P–K3, P–QB4; 8 N–B3 (8 P × QP, P × QP! but not 8 . . . Q × P; 9 Q–B3), N–B3; 9 P × QP, Q × P; 10 B–K2, P × P; 11 BP × P, O–O; 12 O–O, P–N3 = . Grohmann–Teschner, Berlin 1949. (B) 6 . . . B–R3; 7 Q–N3, P × P; 8 Q × BP, N–Q2; 9 Q–N3 (9 P–K4, N–N3; 10 Q–N3—or 10 Q–Q3—, B–K3; 11 Q–B2, B–N2; 12 P–QB4!? B × QP; 13 R–Q1, P–QB4; 14 P–R4, Q–Q2; 15 P–R5, Q–R5! =), P–B4; 10 B–N3, B–N2; 10 P–K3, Q–N3; 11 Q–B2 ± . *Comments.* (C) Experimental is 6 . . . P × P; (1) 7 N–B3, B–N2; 8 Q–R4†, P–B3; 9 Q × BP, B–K3; 10 Q–Q3, P–QN4; 11 P–K4, B–B5; 12 Q–K3, B × B; 13 K × B (or 13 R × B), N–Q2; 14 K–K2∞ . *Comments.* (2) 7 P–K3, B–K3; 8 R–N1, P–N3; 9 N–B3, B–N2; 10 N–Q2, O–O = or 9 B–K2, B–R3∞ .

(*r*) More precise is first 7 . . . P × QP; 8 BP × P/4, N–B3; 9 N–B3, B–N2 = as it helps Black avoid an unfavourable exchange of Queens. *Comments.*

(*s*) 12 O–O, R–QB1; 13 QR–N1, P–QR3; 14 B–K2, N–R4; 15 N–K5! B × N; 16 P × B, B–K3; 17 P–QB4, R–B2; 18 KR–B1, K–Q2; 19 P–B4, with a somewhat better end game. Müller suggests now 19 . . . P–KR4 = .

1 P-Q4, N-KB3; 2 P-QB4, P-KN3; 3 N-QB3, P-Q4; 4 B-B4, B-N2; 5 P-K3

	31	32	33	34	35
	O-O (Grünfeld Gambit)	. . . .		P-B3	P-B4
6	P×P	. . . .	R-B1 (e)	N-B3	P×BP
	N×P		P-B4	O-O	Q-R4
7	N×N		P×BP	Q-N3 (h)	R-B1 (j)
	Q×N		B-K3! (f)	Q-R4	P×P (k)
8	B×P		N-B3	N-Q2	B×P
	N-B3	. . . . . .	N-R3	N-B3	QN-Q2	O-O
9	N-K2	B×N (b)	N-Q4	B-K2	N-B3
	B-N5	Q×NP	Q-R4	N-R4	N-B3
10	P-B3	Q-B3	N-N3	B×N	O-O
	QR-B1!	Q×Q	Q-Q1	P×P	Q×QP
11	N-B3	N×Q	N-Q4	Q-Q1	B-QN3
	Q-K3	P×B	N×N	Q×B	Q-KR4
12	B-KB4	R-QB1 (c)	P×N	Q×Q	P-KR3
	N×P (a)	P-QR4 (d)	P×P (g)	P×Q (i)	R-Q1 (l)

(a) 13 P×B, KR-Q1; 14 B-Q3, N-B3; 15 Q-N1, N-K4 = . Simagin.

(b) 9 B-N3, B-B4; 10 P-QR3, KR-B1; 11 N-B3, R-B7; 12 P-N4, Q-N6; 13 B×N, Q-B6†; 14 K-B1, P×B = . Evans–Saidy, US Chp. 1969–70.

(c) No better are (A) 12 R-KN1, B-N2; 13 K-K2, P-B3; 14 KR-Q1, QR-B1; 15 QR-B1, B-Q4; or (B) 12 O-O, B-N2; 13 N-K5, QR-B1; 14 KR-B1, P-B3; 15 N-Q7, KR-K1 = . Evans–Gligorić, Amsterdam 1964.

(d) 13 KR-N1, P-R5 (also 13 . . . B-K3; 14 P-N3, P-R5 =); 14 R-N5, B-B4; 15 K-K2, KR-B1 = . Vuković. In the column, playable is 9 . . . P×B; 10 N-B3, B-B4! 11 O-O, KR-B1 = .

(e) Older lines are (A) 6 N-B3, P-B4; 7 P×BP, (1) 7 . . . N-K5; 8 B-K5, N×N; 9 B×N, B×B†; 10 P×B, Q-R4 = . Rabar–Barcza, Munich 1942. (2) 7 . . . Q-R4; 8 Q-N3 (or 8 R-B1!), N-K5; 9 B-K5, N×N; 10 B×N, B×B†; 11 Q×B, Q×Q†; 12 P×Q, P×P; 13 B×P, N-Q2; 14 P-B6, P×P = . Comments. (B) 6 Q-N3, (1) 6 . . . P-B3; 7 N-B3, Q-R4; 8 B-Q3, P×P; 9 B×BP, P-QN4; 10 B-K2, B-K3; 11 Q-B2, P-N5; 12 Q-R4, Q-N3 = . Pomar–Uhlmann, Varna 1962. Or (2) 6 . . . P-B4; 7 BP×P! P×P; 8 P×P, QN-Q2. Compare Caro–Kann Defence, col. 13.

(f) Better chances for White result from 7 . . . Q-R4; 8 P×P, R-Q1; 9 B-B4, B-K3; 10 P-K4! (10 P-QN4, Q×NP; 11 Q-N3, Q×Q; 12 B×Q, N×P; 13 N×N, R×N! 14 B×R, B×B; 15 N-B3, N-B3; 16 O-O, B×P∞. Podgorný–Průcha, Prague 1943), N×KP; 11 N-K2 + . Pomar–Tatai, Malaga 1969.

(g) 13 B-K5, P-N3; 14 N-N5, N-K1; 15 B×B, K×B = . Panno–Benko, Los Angeles 1963.

(h) (A) 7 R-B1, B-N5 (7 . . . P-N3; or 7 . . . P-K3; or 7 . . . B-K3; are all playable); 8 P-KR3, B×N; 9 Q×B, Q-R4; 10 B-Q3, QN-Q2; 11 O-O, P×P; 12 B×BP, P-K4; 13 P×P, N×P; 14 B×N, Q×B; 15 KR-Q1, QR-Q1; drawn. Najdorf–Flohr, Budapest 1950. Upon 7 . . . Q-R4 may follow 8 Q-N3, P×P (duller but solid is 8 . . . QN-Q2); 9 B×P, P-QN4; 10 B×P†! R×B; 11 B×N, R×B; 12 N-K5, P-K3; 13 N×BP, Q-N3; 14 N×R, Q×N; 15 Q×NP, R-N2; 16 Q-QR5, R×P?! (16 . . . B-Q2!?); 17 Q-Q8†, K-B2; 18 N-K4, Q-N5†; 19 K-B1, B-R3†; 20 K-N1, P-N4; 21 R-B7†, K-N3; 22 R×B†, K×R; 23 Q×N†, K-N1; 24 Q×NP†, K-R1; 25 Q-K5†, K-N1; 26 P-KR4, resigns. Martz–Chellstorp, Houston 1974. (B) 7 P-KR3, P-N3; 8 Q-N3, P-K3; 9 B-K2, B-N2; 10 P×P, KP×P; 11 O-O, QN-Q2; 12 KR-Q1, N-R4; 13 B-Q6, R-K1; 14 P-QR4, P-QR4; 15 QR-B1, R-K3; 16 B-R2, R-B1 = . De Greiff–Smyslov, Havana 1962.

(*i*) 13 N × P, N–N3; 14 N–R5, R–K1; 15 O–O–O, N–Q4; 16 N × N, P × N = . Pirć.

(*j*) (A) 7 Q–R4†, Q × Q; 8 N × Q, N–K5! (B) 7 Q–N3, see note (*e*).

(*k*) 7 . . . N–K5; 8 P × P, N × N; 9 Q–Q2, Q × RP; 10 P × N, Q–R4; 11 B–B4, N–Q2; 12 N–K2, N–K4; 13 B–R2 (Petrosian–Fischer, 2nd match game 1971), Q × P/4 = .

(*l*) 13 N–Q2, Q × Q; 14 KR × Q ± (Boleslavski), but in the column, 11 . . . Q–QR4 may be considered. *Comments.*

1 P–Q4, N–KB3; 2 P–QB4, P–KN3; 3 P–KN3, B–N2; 4 B–N2, P–Q4

	36	37	38	39	40
5	P × P			N–KB3	
	N × P			O–O	
6	P–K4		N–KB3!	O–O	
	N–N5		O–O	P–B4	P × P
7	P–Q5		O–O	P × BP	N–R3
	P–QB3		P–QB4 (*f*)	P × P!	QN–Q2
8	N–K2		P × P (*g*)	N–R3 (*i*)	N × P
	P × P!	O–O	N–R3	N–R3	N–N3
9	P–QR3 (*a*)	O–O	N–N5!	N × P	QN–K5
	Q–R4 (*b*)	P–K3	N/4–N5	B–K3	P–B3
10	O–O	P–QR3 (*d*)	N–QB3	QN–K5	P–K3
	P × P	KN–R3	P–KR3	N × P	B–B4
11	B–Q2	QN–B3	N–B3	B–K3	Q–K2
	QN–R3	BP × P	Q × Q	R–B1	B–K5
12	Q–K1	P × P	R × Q	R–B1	R–Q1
	P–B4 (*c*)	P × P (*e*)	B–K3 (*h*)	N/4–K5 (*j*)	KN–Q2 = (*k*)

(*a*) 9 P × P, B–B4; 10 O–O, O–O; 11 QN–B3, QN–R3; 12 B–B4, N–Q6; 13 P–Q6, N × B; 14 N × N, N–B4; 15 P × P, Q × P; 16 R–K1, Q–Q1; 17 Q–B3, R–B1 = . Ståhlberg–Pachman, Mariánské Lázne 1954.

(*b*) 9 . . . KN–B3; 10 P × P, N–K4; 11 P–B4, N–N5; 12 P–R3, N–KB3; 13 B–K3, O–O; 14 QN–B3, QN–Q2; 15 O–O, N–N3; 16 B–B2 ± . R. Byrne–Mednis, US Chp. 1960.

(*c*) 13 B × N, N × B; 14 Q × N, Q × Q; 15 P × Q, B × P; 16 R–R2, B–K4; drawn. R. Byrne–Benko, US Chp. 1963.

(*d*) 10 B–Q2, B × P; 11 B × N, B × R; 12 QN–B3, B × N; 13 N × B, R–K1; 14 Q–B1, P–K4; 15 B–QR3, N–Q2! 16 P–B4, N–B3; 17 P × KP, N–N5 = .

(*e*) 13 N × P, N–B3; 14 KN–B3 ± . Pachman–Filip, Czechoslovak Chp. 1954.

(*f*) Cramped alternatives are (A) 7 . . . N–N3; 8 N–B3, N–R3; 9 P–KR3, P–QB3; 10 B–B4, B–K3; 11 Q–B1, Q–Q2; 12 K–R2, KR–Q1; 13 R–Q1, Q–K1; 14 P–K4 + . Schweber–Stein, Stockholm 1962. (B) 7 . . . P–QB3; 8 QN–Q2! N–Q2; 9 N–B4, N/4–N3; 10 N–R5, Q–B2; 11 N–N3 ± . (C) 7 . . . N–QB3; 8 P–K4 (8 N–B3, N–N3; 9 P–K3, P–K4! 10 P–Q5, N–K2! 11 P–K4, B–N5 = . Keene–Uhlmann, Hastings 1970–1), N–N3; 9 P–Q5, N–N1; 10 N–B3, P–QB3; 11 Q–N3, P–K3! 12 P × BP, N × P; 13 R–Q1, Q–K2; 14 B–K3 ± .

(*g*) 8 P–K4, N–KB3; 9 P–K5, N–Q4; 10 P × P, N–N5; 11 N–B3, QN–B3; 12 Q–K2, Q–Q6; 13 R–Q1, Q × Q; 14 N × Q, B–N5! = .

(*h*) (A) 13 N–K1, N × BP; 14 B–K3, QR–B1; 15 N–N5 (Gligorić–Olafsson, Los Angeles 1963); 15 . . . P–QR4; 16 N–R7, R–B2; 17 N–N5, draw. (B) 13 B–K3! N–B7; 14 QR–B1, N × B; 15 P × N, N × P; 16 P–QN4! ±

(*i*) (A) 8 N–B3, N–B3; 9 Q–R4, N–Q4; 10 Q × BP, N × N; 11 P × N, P–K4 = . (B) 8 Q–B2, Q–Q4; 9 N–R3, Q × P; 10 Q × P, Q × Q; 11 N × Q, N–B3; 12 QN–K5, N × N; 13 N × N, N–N5! = . *Comments.*

(*j*) 13 Q–R4, P–QR3; 14 N–Q3, N–Q3; 15 N–B5, B–Q4 = . Pirć–O'Kelly, Bled 1950.

(*k*) Dodero–Gligorić, Mar del Plata 1955.

1 P–Q4, N–KB3; 2 P–QB4, P–KN3

	41	42	43	44	45
3	(P–KN3)...............................			P–B3 (g)	
	P–B3 (a)			P–Q4	
4	N–QB3......	B–N2		P × P	
	P–Q4	P–Q4		N × P	
5	P × P	N–KB3		P–K4	
	P × P	B–N2		N–N3	
6	N–R3	O–O		N–B3	
	B–N2	O–O		B–N2	
7	N–B4	P × P	N–R3 (e)	B–K3	
	O–O	P × P	N–K5	O–O	
8	B–N2	N–K5 (c)	B–B4	Q–Q2.......	P–B4
	P–K3	B–B4	Q–N3	N–B3	N–B3!
9	O–O	N–QB3	Q–B1	O–O–O	P–Q5
	N–B3	N–K5	B–K3	P–K4	N–N1
10	P–K3	Q–N3?	R–Q1	P–Q5	P–QR4
	P–N3 (b)	N–QB3 (d)	N–R3 (f)	N–Q5 (h)	P–QB3 (i)

(a) (A) 3 . . . B–N2; etc., without . . . P–Q4; see King's Indian Defence. (B) 3 . . . P–B4; 4 N–KB3, P × P; 5 N × P, see King's Indian Defence. (C) 3 . . . P–Q4; 4 P × P! N × P; 5 B–N2, see cols. 36–8.

(b) 11 P–N3, B–QR3; 12 R–K1, R–B1; 13 B–N2, R–K1 = . Najdorf–Gligorić, Zürich 1953.

(c) 8 N–B3, N–K5! 9 N × N, P × N; (1) 10 N–N5! Q × P; 11 N × KP! N–B3; 12 Q–N3, B–B4; 13 N–B3, Q–N3; 14 Q × Q, P × Q; 15 B–K3, R–R3 = . Petrosian–Geller, USSR Chp. 1958. (2) 10 N–K5, Q–Q4; 11 P–N3 is strong. Gufeld.

(d) 11 Q × QP, N × QN; 12 P × N, Q × Q; 13 B × Q, N × N; 14 P × N, B × P; 15 B–R6, KR–Q1; 16 B × QNP, QR–N1; 17 QR–Q1, B × BP; 18 R × R†, R × R; drawn. Benko–Fischer, US Chp. 1963. In the column, 10 B–B4, N–QB3; 11 N × N/6, P × N; 12 N–R4 is stronger.

(e) Also cogent is (A) 7 QN–Q2, B–B4; 8 P–N3, N–K5; 9 B–N2, Q–R4! 10 Q–K1! N × N; 11 Q × N, Q × Q; 12 N × Q, R–Q1; 13 KR–Q1. (B) 7 P–N3, B–B4; 8 B–N2, (1) 8 . . . P–QR4; 9 N–B3, N–K5; 10 R–B1, N × N = . Spasski–Uhlmann, Hastings, 1965–6. (2) 8 . . . QN–Q2; 9 QN–Q2, B–K5; 10 N × B, N × N; 11 N–K5, P–K3 ∞. Gligorić.

(f) 11 B–K5, P–B3; 12 B–B4, B–B2; 12 P–B5, Q–Q1 = . Botvinnik–Donner, Leipzig 1960.

(g) 3 Q–B2 (Mengarini's move), P–Q4; 4 P × P, N × P; 5 P–K4, N–N3; 6 N–QB3, B–N2; 7 B–K3, O–O; 8 N–B3, P–KB4 = .

(h) 11 N–N5, N × N; 12 B × N, B–Q2; 13 B–Q3, P–QB3; 14 P × P, Q–B2 = .

(i) 11 P–R5, N/3–Q2; 12 P–K5, P × P; 13 Q × P, N–QB3; 14 N–B3, N/2–N1; 15 Q–N5, N–R3 = . *Comments.*

King's Indian Defence

(1 P–Q4, N–KB3; 2 P–QB4, P–KN3)

(incorporating the
Old [Chigorin] Indian Defence)
(1 P–Q4, N–KB3; 2 P–QB4, P–Q3)

Strategically, the King's Indian and the old (Chigorin) Indian are closely intertwined, although Chigorin's version (2 . . . P–Q3, without . . . P–KN3, and often resembling a Philidor-Hanham Defence), is now rarely seen. It mostly transposes back into the King's Indian proper.

While the term "Old" Indian has in Russian been expanded to cover the King's Indian as well, most of the credit for 2 . . . P–KN3 belongs to neo-romanticists and the anti-classicists who flourished after World War I, Alekhin, Bogolyubov, Breyer, Euwe, Réti and Tartakover. Capablanca also employed it regularly.

Its use fell behind in the thirties, only to reappear in the forties when Boleslavski and later Bronstein hammered it into more definite patterns and "sold" it to their colleagues.

Obviously 3 . . . B–N2 permits White to seize the centre with P–K4, a hyper-modern concept of using the rigid pawn front as a target. The result is a highly complex struggle where White's chances lie chiefly in the queen's side, Black's on the king's side. The defence owes much of its effectiveness to the latent power of the fianchettoed king's bishop—as do the Grünfeld and Sicilian. The resulting formations are basic to modern chess since Black can apparently shut his eyes without regard to the order of White's initial moves.

However, the affinity of the King's Indian Defence and the Flank Openings, with their closed manoeuvring and intrinsic transpositions, still makes it imperative to have an intimate feel of all Indian fianchetto structures.

This author discussed most of the various systems of the full Indian complex in great detail in *Chess Review* of 1955 and it is somewhat debatable which, if any, is the "correct" sequence for Black. The "Old" Indian (with 2 . . . P–Q3) inhibits the Sämisch variation, but on the other hand runs into some difficulty resulting from the early exchange of queens after . . . P–K4; not to mention 3 N–KB3. Thus, the King's Indian with 2 . . . P–KN3 is more common. True, it allows White more leeway, but has the flexible advantage of keeping him guessing whether or not Black will switch into the Grünfeld, or the Double Fianchetto.

(*I*) The Classical Line (cols. 1–15) is characterized by 1 P–Q4, N–KB3; 2 P–QB4, P–KN3; 3 N–QB3, B–N2; 4 P–K4, P–Q3; 5 N–B3, O–O; 6 B–K2, P–K4 with White continuing 7 O–O, or otherwise. Black's foremost replies to 7 O–O are (A) 7 . . . N–B3 (cols. 1–7) and (B) 7 . . . QN–Q2 (cols. 8–10); for the moment the former is under a cloud as seen from the lines given, whereas the latter alternative still stands up; but these judgements must not be taken dogmatically, as proven by sporadic use of any of these lines.

Attempts to vary from 7 O–O are covered in cols 11–15; still earlier attempts for Black and White in cols 16–20.

(*II*) The Four Pawns Attack, 5 P–B4 (cols 21–5 dates back to Englisch-Tarrasch, Hamburg 1884. It is never without sting and after periods of dormancy revives every so often, as shown in the text.

(*III*) The Borisenko-Averbakh Variation (cols. 26–7) combining B–K2 and B–N5, has been subject to new experimentation in col. 26, but the old established cols. 27 still appears to be the solid defence. Columns 29 and 30 are nondescript.

(*IV*) The Sämisch Variation 5 P–B3 (cols. 31–50) is one of White's sharpest continuation. White intends to solidify his centre, then launch a porcupine attack with P–KN4, P–KR4, etc., with a potential queen's-side initiative up his sleeve as well.

After 5 . . . O–O (cols. 31–45) White's and Black's strategies have crystallized into standard patterns of equal opportunity. An original thought is the solid, yet very resilient treatment 5 . . . P–B3 and 6 . . . P–QR3, developed by R. Byrne and als∴ explored by Evans, Fischer and other American masters. 7 P–QR4 (col. 47) prevents the thematic . . . P–QN4 (cols. 48–50), but weakens White's queen's side.

(*V*) The Fianchetto System 1 P–Q4, N–KB3; 2 P–QB4, P–KN3; 3 P–KN3, B–N2; 4 B–N2, O–O; followed by:

(a) 5 N–QB3 (cols. 51–70) was in earlier editions called the "main" line, a general term now dropped in favour of a more functional description. It may also arise after first 3 N–QB3, B–N2; 4 P–KN3, O–O; 5 B–N2 but the sequence in the heading is more consequent. 5 . . . P–Q3; 6 N–B3, QN–Q2; 7 O–O, P–K4; 8 P–K4, P–B3; 9 P–KR3! (cols. 51–4) might still be called the standard "main line" of the system but time and again does Black find adequate counters except for col. 54. Other deviations from the "main" are cols. 55–7.

Two of the more prominent defensive tools are the *Yugoslav Variation*, 6 . . . P–B4 (cols. 58–60) and the *Panno Variation*, 6 . . . N–B3 (cols. 61–5) and there is not much to add to the self-explanatory course of the columns chosen.

The riposte 6 . . . P–B3 (cols. 66–7) is insecure. White's alternatives on the 6th move (cols. 68–70) are solid but barren.

(b) 5 N–KB3 (cols. 71–5) contains a few finesses due to the transpositions of White's Knights' moves—or rather an omitted or belated N–QB3. But generally, the lines merge with the 5 N–QB3 variations.

The possible interchanges with other openings in the notes should be carefully followed.

(*VI*) The Old (Chigorin) Indian, with 2 . . . P–Q3 (cols. 76–80) has been considerably narrowed down in versatility, but it still remains an effective weapon and Black has several chances to switch into the King's Indian.

Column 80 is a stratagem developed by Pirć, and also used frequently by the Grandmaster L. Schmid.

1 P-Q4, N-KB3; 2 P-QB4, P-KN3; 3 N-QB3, B-N2; 4 P-K4, P-Q3; 5 N-B3, O-O; 6 B-K2, P-K4; 7 O-O, N-B3; 8 P-Q5, N-K2

	1	2	3	4	5
9	N-K1	P-QN4	N-Q2 (Taimanov Variation) . . .		B-Q2
	N-Q2 (a)	N-R4	N-K1	N-Q2 (i)	N-K1
10	N-Q3 (b)	N-Q2	P-QN4	P-QN4	R-B1 (n)
	P-KB4	N-B5	P-KB4	P-KB4	P-KB4
11	B-Q2 (c)	P-B5 (e)	P-B5 (g)	N-N3 (j)	Q-N3 (o)
	N-KB3	P-B4	P-QR4	P × P (k)	P-N3
12	P-B3	P-B3	B-R3	N × P	P × P
	P-B5	P-KN4	P × NP	N-KB3	P × P
13	P-B5	N-B4	B × P	N-N3 (l)	N-KN5
	P-KN4	N/2-N3	P × BP	N-B4	N-KB3
14	R-B1	B-K3	B × P	N × N	P-B4
	N-N3	N × B†	P-N3	B × N	P-KR3
15	P × P	Q × N	B-QN4	B-K3	P × P
	P × P	P-B5	N-Q3	P-KR4	P × P
16	N-N5	B-B2	N-B4	Q-Q2	P-B5
	R-B2 (d)	R-B3 (f)	P × P (h)	R-B2 (m)	N/3 × P (p)

(a) 9 . . . P-B4; 10 N-Q3, P-QR3; 11 B-K3, P-QN4; 12 P × P, P × P; 13 P-QN4! ± .

(b) 10 P-B3, P-KB4; 11 P-KN4, N-KB3; 12 N-N2, P-B3! 13 R-N1, P × QP = .

(c) Larsen's temporizing improvement upon the immediate 11 P-B3!? P-B5; 12 B-Q2, P-KN4! 13 P-QN4, N-KB3; 14 P-B5, P-KR4 = .

(d) 17 Q-B2, P-N5; 18 N-B7, P × P; 19 P × P (19 B × P, R-N1; 20 N-K6, B × N; 21 P × B, R-K2), B-R6; 20 N-K6!∞ (20 N × R, N × KP; 21 P × N, Q-N4†; 22 K-B2, Q-R5†; draw).

(e) 11 P-QR4, P-KB4; 12 B-B3, P-KN4; 13 P × P, N × BP; 14 P-N3, N-Q5; 15 P × N, N × B†; 16 Q × N, P-N5 (Petrosian-Gligorić Zagreb 1970); 17 Q-Q3, B-B4 = .

(f) 17 P × P, P × P; 18 N-N5! Kevitz-Kramer, Manhattan C.C. Chp. 1966, is another serious challenge.

(g) Yudovich advocates 11 P-B3, P-B5; 12 P-B5, P-KN4; 13 N-B4, R-B2; 14 B-R3, N-N3; 15 P-N5, but 11 . . . B-R3; 12 N-N3, B × B; 13 R × B, N-KB3 may be considered.

(h) 17 N × N, P × N; 18 N × P, N-B4; 19 R-K1 ± . Taimanov-Portisch, Hungary 1969.

(i) (A) 9 . . . B-R3!? 10 P-QN4, P-R4; 11 P × P, R × P; 12 N-N3, B × B; 13 Q × B! R-R1; 14 P-QR4 (14 P-B4, P × P; 15 Q × P, N-Q2; 16 P-B5, N-K4! = . Gligorić in *Chess Life*), P-B4; 15 P-B4, P × P; 16 Q × P, N-K1; 17 P-K5, P × P; 18 Q × P, P-B3; 19 Q-B4, P-N3; 20 N-N5. Taimanov-Tatai, Venice 1969, with a freer game for White. (B) 9 . . . P-B4; 10 R-N1, N-K1; 11 P-QN4, P-N3; 12 P-QR4, P-B4; 13 P-R5, N-KB3 = . Gheorgiu in *The Chess Player*.

(j) Also important are (A) 11 P-QR4, N-B3; 12 P-B5, P-B5; 13 N-B4, P-KN4; 14 P × P, P × P; 15 P-N5, P-N5; 16 B-R3, P-B6 . (B) 11 P-B5, P × BP; 12 NP × P, N × P; 13 B-R3, N × KP; 14 N/2 × N, P × N; 15 N × P, B-B4; 16 P-Q6!∞ .

(k) 11 . . . N-KB3; 12 Q-Q3, P-B5; 13 P-B5, P-KN4; 14 P-B3, P-N5; 15 B-Q2, P-N6; 16 P × NP, N-R4; is also safe.

(l) *Archives* suggest to try 13 B-B3, N-B4; 14 B-N5 .

(m) 17 QR-K1, N-K5; 18 Q-B1, B-B3! 19 P-B3, N-N4; 20 P-B5, P-K5 ∓ . *Comments.*

(n) 10 P-QN4, P-KB4; 11 Q-N3, N-KB3; 12 P × P, P × P; 13 P-B5, K-R1; 14 P × P, P × P = . Korchnoi-Geller, match 1971.

(o) 11 P × P, P × P; 12 N-KN5, P-KR3; 13 N-K6 B × N; 14 P × B, Q-B1; 15 Q-N3, P-B3 ∓ . Taimanov-Fischer, 1st match game 1971.

(p) 17 N × N, N × N; 18 P × P, RP × P = . Taimanov-Fischer, 3rd match game 1971.

1 P–Q4, N–KB3; 2 P–QB4, P–KN3; 3 N–QB3, B–N2; 4 P–K4, P–Q3, 5 N–B3, O–O; 6 B–K2, P–K4; 7 O–O

	6	7	8	9	10
	(N–B3)		QN–Q2		
8	B–K3		P–Q5	B–K3	R–K1
	R–K1	N–KN5	N–B4?!	R–K1 (g)	P × P (i)
9	P × P (a)	B–N5	N–Q2	P–Q5	N × P
	P × P	P–B3 (d)	P–QR4	N–N5	N–B4
10	Q × Q	B–B1	Q–B2	B–N5	B–B1
	N × Q (b)	K–R1 (e)	B–R3	P–KB3	R–K1
11	N–QN5	P–Q5	N–N3	B–R4	P–B3
	N–K3	N–K2	B × B	N–B1	P–B3 (j)
12	N–N5	N–K1	QR × B (f)	N–Q2	B–K3
	R–K2!	N–R3	KN–Q2	P–KR4	P–QR4
13	KR–Q1	B–K3	QR–Q1	B × N	Q–Q2
	P–B3	P–KB4	N × N	P × B	KN–Q2
14	N × N	P–B3	Q × N	P–B4	B–B2
	B × N (c)	P–B5 =	N–B4 =	P × P e.p. (h)	P–R5 ∞

(a) 9 P–Q5, N–Q5! 10 N × N, P × N; 11 B × P, N × KP; 12 B × B, K × B; 13 N × N, R × N = .

(b) 10 . . . R × Q; 11 B–N5, R–B1; 12 KR–Q1, B–N5; 13 QR–B1, P–KR3; 14 B–K3, KR–Q1; 15 P–KR3, B × N; 16 B × B ± . Addison–R. Byrne, US Chp. 1969–70.

(c) 15 N–B3, R–Q2 = . Reshevsky–Fischer, 9th match game 1961.

(d) 9 . . . B–B3!? 10 B × B, N × B; 11 P–Q5, N–K2; 12 N–K1, N–Q2; 13 N–Q3, P–KB4; 14 P × P, P × P; 15 P–B4, N–KN3; 16 Q–Q2 ± . Reshevsky–Fischer, 1st match game 1961.

(e) (A) 10 . . . N–R3; 11 P × P! BP × P; 12 B–N5, Q–Q2; 13 N–Q5, K–R1; 14 P–QN4 ± . Reshevsky–Najdorf, match 1953. (B) 10 . . . P–B4; 11 B–N5, B–B3; 12 B × B, Q × B; 13 P–Q5, N–Q1; 14 N–K1 ± . Udovćić–Rabar, Yugoslav Chp. 1953.

(f) 12 N × N, B–R3! 13 N–Q3, N–Q2 = . Petrosian–Geller, USSR Chp. 1949.

(g) Riskier is at once 8 . . . N–N5; 9 B–N5, P–KB3; 10 B–R4, N–R3; 11 P–Q5,N–B2; 12 N–K1, P–QB4; 13 N–Q3 ± . Gligorić–Tringov, Titovo Užice 1966. Compare also col. 11 and note (a).

(h) 15 Q × P, N–R2 ∓ . Najdorf–Geller, Moscow 1967. Also 9 . . . N–Q5!

(i) (A) 8 . . . R–K1; 9 B–B1, P–B3; 10 P–Q5! (B) 8 . . . P–B3; 9 B–B1, P–QR4; 10 R–N1, R–K1; 11 P–Q5, N–B4; 12 N–Q2, B–R3; 13 N–N3, B × B; 14 R × B, N × N; 15 Q × N, P–B4 = . Boleslavski.

(j) 11 . . . KN–Q2; 12 B–K3, P–B3; 13 P–ON4!

1 P-Q4, N-KB3; 2 P-QB4, P-KN3; 3 N-QB3, B-N2; 4 P-K4, P-Q3; 5 N-B3, O-O; 6 B-K2, P-K4

	11	12	13	14	15
7	B-K3		P-Q5 (d)		
	P×P	Q-K2 (b)	QN-Q2	P-B4 (i)	N-R3
8	N×P	P-Q5	B-N5 (e)	B-N5 (j)	B-N5
	R-K1	N-K1	P-KR3	P-KR3	P-KR3
9	P-B3	P-KR4	B-R4	B-R4 (k)	B-R4
	P-B3	P-KB4	P-KN4	Q-B2	P-KN4
10	Q-Q2	P-R5	B-N3	N-Q2	B-N3
	P-Q4	P-B5	N-R4	N-K1	N-R4
11	KP×P	B-Q2	P-KR4 (f)	P-B3	N-Q2
	P×P	P-KN4	N-B5 (g)	P-B4	N-B5
12	O-O	P-R6	P×P	P-QR3	O-O (m)
	P×P (a)	B-B3 (c)	P×P (h)	B-B3 (l)	

(a) 13 QR-Q1, P-QR3 = . Reshevsky-Giligorić, Los Angeles 1963.

(b) (A) 7 . . . QN-Q2; 8 O-O, N-N5; 9 B-N5, P-KB3; (1) 10 B-R4 leads into col. 9–10. (2) 10 B-Q2, N-R3; 11 P×P, QP×P; 12 P-QN4, P-B3; 13 P-B5, Q-K2; 14 Q-N3†, N-B2; 15 KR-Q1, R-K1 = . (B) 7 . . . N-N5; 8 B-N5, P-KB3;9 B-R4, Q-Q2 (9 . . . N-B3; see col. 7); 10 P-Q5, P-KB4; 11 P×P, P×P; 12 N-KN5, Q-K1; 13 B×N, P×B; 14 N/5-K4, Q-N3; 15 O-O, B-B4 = . Taimanov-Spasski, USSR Chp. 1963.(C) 7 . . . P-B3; 8 O-O, P×P; 9 N×P, R-K1; 10 P-B3, P-Q4!? 11 BP×P, P×P; 12 Q-N3! ± . Nei-Stein, Tbilisi 1967. (D) 7 . . . N-B3; 8 P-Q5, N-K2; 9 N-Q2 ∞.

(c) 13 N-R2, K-R1; 14 B-N4, B×B; 15 N×B, N-Q2; 16 Q-B3 (or 16 Q-K2), R-KN1; 17 O-O-O, with a bind. Gligorić-Fischer, Monte Carlo 1967.

(d) (A) 7 B-N5, QN-Q2 (7 . . . P-KR3; see column); 8 Q-Q2, P-B3; 9 O-O (better O-O-O), P×P; 10 N×P, N-B4; 11 P-B3, KN×P! Adamski-Geller, Lugano 1968. (B) 7 P×P, P×P; 8 Q×Q, R×Q; 9 B-N5, R-K1; 10 O-O-O, N-R3; 11 N-K1, P-B3; 12 N-B2, N-B4: with a tenable position for Black.

(e) The Petrosian system. If 8 O-O, N-B4; 9 Q-B2, P-QR4; 10 B-N5 (10 N-Q2 see col. 8), 10 . . . P-KR3; 11 B-K3, KN-Q2; 12 N-Q2, P-B4; 13 P×P, P×P; 14 P-B4, P×P; 15 B×P, N-K4; 16 N-B3, N-N3; 17 B-K3, Q-K2 = . Petrosian-Gligorić, Varna 1962.

(f) Digressing from 11 O-O, N-B5; 12 N-Q2, N-B4! (A) 13 B-N4, N×KP; 14 N/2×N, P-KB4; 15 P-B3, P-KR4! (B) 13 P-QN4, N/4-Q6; 14 Q-N1, N×B ch; 15 N×N, N-B5; 16 N-QB3, P-KB4; 17 P-B3, Q-B3 with attacking chances on both sides. *E/P.*

(g) Further study deserves 11 . . . P-N5! 12 N-Q2, P-KB4; 13 P×P, QN-B3! 14 B×P, KN×B; 15 P×N, N×B; 16 Q×N, B×P; 17 Q-K2, P-K5! Balashov-Tukmakov, USSR 1966.

(h) A thematic position from which White might proceed (A) 13 B-B1, N-B4! or (B) 13 K-B1, P-KB4; 14 B×N, NP×B; 15 N-KR4, N-B4 = or (C) 13 Q-B2?! N×P ch (better than 13 . . . P-KB4; 14 B×N, KP×B; 15 O-O-O, N-B4; 16 R-R5); 14 K-B1, N-B5; 15 B×N, NP×B; 16 K-N2, P-KB4; 17 QR-KN1, N-B4; 18 K-B1 ± . Vukić-Brinck-Claussen, 1964.

(i) Ivkov's move, extensively employed at Bled 1961 and probably leading to equality. But 7 . . . P-QR4 is also good.

(j) 8 O-O, N-N5! 9 N-K1, N-KR3; 10 N-Q3, N-Q2; 11 P-B4, P-B4 = .

(k) 9 B-Q2, P-R3; 10 Q-B1, K-R2; 11 P-KR4 is Rabar's idea.

(l) 13 B-B2, Q-K2; 14 Q-B2, N-N2; 15 P-QN4, N-Q2; 16 N-N3, P-N3; 17 NP×P, N×P; 18 N×N, NP×N = . Najdorf-Matanović, Havana 1962.

(m) 12 . . . P-KB4 (for 12 . . . N-B4 see note (f)); 13 P×P, B×P; 14 B-N4, Q-B3; 15 QN-K4, Q-N3; 16 B×B, R×B; 17 P-N4, P-R4; 18 P-KR3, QN×P; 19 R-N1, P-R4; 20 P-R3, QN-Q6; 21 R×P, R-B2; 22 P-B3, QR-KB1; drawn. Petrosian-Geller Stockholm 1962.

1 P-Q4, N-KB3; 2 P-QB4, P-KN3; 3 N-QB3, B-N2; 4 P-K4, P-Q3; 5 N-B3, O-O

	16	17	18	19	20
6	(B-K2)	B-K3	P-KR3	P-KN3	B-N5
	B-N5 (a)	QN-Q2 (c)	P-K4 (f)	B-N5	P-B4
7	B-K3!	P-KR3 (d)	P-Q5	B-N2 (i)	P-Q5
	KN-Q2!	P-K4	QN-Q2	N-B3	P-QR3 (j)
8	R-QB1!	P-Q5	B-N5 (g)	P-KR3	P-QR4
	P-K4!	Q-K2	P-KR3	B × N	Q-R4
9	P-Q5	P-KN4	B-K3	B × B	B-Q2!
	P-QR4!	N-B4	Q-K2	P-K4	P-K3
10	P-KR3	N-Q2	P-KN4	P-Q5	B-K2
	B × N	P-QR4	N-B4	N-Q5	P × P
11	B × B	B-K2	B-Q3	B-N2	BP × P
	P-KB4	N-K1	N-R2	N-Q2	B-N5
12	R-QN1	N-N3	Q-K2	O-O	O-O
	N-B4 (b)	P-B4 (e)	N × B† (h)	P-KB4 =	B × N (k)

(a) 6 . . . P-B4; (A) 7 O-O, (1) 7 . . . P × P; 8 N × P, N-B3; see Sicilian Defence. Maróczy Bind. (2) 7 . . . P × P; 8 N × P, N-R3; 9 B-B3, N-B4; 10 N-N3! *Comments*, (B) 7 P-Q5, P-K3; 8 B-N5, P-KR3; 9 B-R4, P × P; 10 BP × P, see Benoni Defence, col. 9.

(b) 13 P-QN3, QN-Q2; 14 O-O (Hamann-Bobotsov, Vrnjačka Banja, 1967), Q-K2 = .

(c) (A) 6 . . . P-B4; 7 P-KR3, Q-R4 (7 . . . P × P; 8 N × P is again a Sicilian, Maróczy Bind); 8 Q-Q2, N-B3; 9 R-Q1, P-K4; 10 P × BP, P × P; 11 B-Q3, N-K1 = . *Archives*. (B) 6 . . . P-K4; 7 P × P, P × P; 8 Q × Q, R × Q; 9 N-Q5, R-Q2! 10 O-O-O, N-B3 = .

(d) Also, 7 N-Q2, P-K4; 8 P-Q5, N-K1; 9 B-K2, P-KB4; 10 P-B3, P-B5; 11 B-B2, P-QR4; 12 P-QR3, N/1-B3; 13 P-QN4, P-N3; 14 N-R4 (Sultan Khan-Flohr, Prague 1931), B-QR3 = .

(e) 13 N × N, P × N; 14 NP × P, P × P; 15 P × P, B × P; 16 Q-Q2 ± . Kavalek.

(f) 6 . . . P-B4; (A) 7 B-K3, Q-R4; 8 Q-Q2, N-B3; 9 P-Q5, N-Q5! = ; but (B) 7 P-Q5 poses problems. Also playable is (c) 7 B-K2, P × P; N × P, N-B3; 9 B-K3, B-Q2; 10 O-O, P-QR3; 11 Q-Q2, P-QN4∞. Larsen-Kavalek match 1970.

(g) 8 P-KN4?! N-B4; 9 Q-B2, P-QR4; 10 B-K2, P-B3 = .

(h) 13 Q × N, P-KB4; 14 NP × P, P × P = . Bartosek-Blatný, Czechoslovakia 1954.

(i) 7 P-KR3, B × N; 8 Q × B, N-B3; 9 P-Q5, N-Q5; 10 Q-Q3, N-Q2; 11 P-B4, P-K4 = . Sajtar-Boleslavski, Warsaw 1974. The column is Eigler-Benko, Hungarian Chp. 1952.

(j) For (A) 7 . . . P-K3; and (B) 7 . . . P-KR3, see note (a). Both transpositions are safer than the text.

(k) 13 B × B, QN-Q2 = . Tot-Gligorić, Yugoslavia 1955. Compare cols. 26 and 30.

1 P–Q4, N–KB3; 2 P–QB4, P–KN3; 3 N–QB3, B–N2; 4 P–K4, P–Q3; 5 P–B4, P–B4 (*a*)

	21	22	23	24	25
6	P × P	N–B3	P–Q5		
	Q–R4	O–O	O–O		
7	B–Q3	B–K2	N–B3		B–K2 (*j*)
	Q × BP	P × P	P–K3		P–K3
8	N–B3	N × P	B–K2		P × P
	N–B3	N–B3	P × P (*f*)		P × P (*k*)
9	Q–K2	B–K3 (*c*)	KP × P	P–K5	P–KN4
	B–N5	N × N (*d*)	N–R4	P × KP (*h*)	N–B3 (*l*)
10	B–K3	B × N	O–O!	P × KP	P–KR4
	Q–QR4!	P–K4	B × N	N–N5	N–Q5!?
11	O–O	P × P	P × B	B–N5	P–R5
	N–Q2 (*b*)	P × P	P–B4	P–B3	P–Q4 (*m*)
12		B–B5	N–N5	P × BP	P–K5
		R–K1 (*e*)	N–N2 (*g*)	B × P (*i*)	N–K5 (*n*)

(*a*) 5 . . . O–O? 6 N–B3 (A) 6 . . . P–K4; (1) 7 BP × P, P × P; 8 P–Q5! P–B4; 9 B–N5! P–KR3; 10 B–R4, Q–N3; 11 Q–Q2, N × R4; 12 B–B2, N–R3 ∞. Geller. (2) 7 QP × P, P × P; 8 Q × Q, R × Q; 9 N × P! R–K1 (9 . . . N × P; 10 N × N, P–KB3; 11 P–B5! ±); 10 B–Q3, N × P? 11 B × N, P–KB3; 12 B–Q5 + . (B) 6 . . . B–N5; 7 B–K2, KN–Q2; 8 B–K3, B × N; 9 B × B, N–QB3; 10 P–Q5, N–R4; 11 Q–Q3, P–QB3; 12 P–QN4 ± .

(*b*) If 11 . . . B × N; 12 R × B, N–KN5; 13 R–R3, N–Q5; 14 Q–Q2! Pafnutieff. After the text, White has two possibilities, (A) 12 Q–Q2, B × KN; 13 R × B, N–B4; 14 R–QB1, O–O; 15 B–N1, Q–N5; 16 P–QN3, P–QR4 = . Johannessen-Johannsson, Varna Olympics 1962; or (B) 12 QR–B1, O–O; 13 Q–KB2, B × KN; 14 P × B (Bisguier-Petrosian, USA *v*. USSR, 1954), N–B4; 15 B–N1, N–K3 = . In the column, 10 . . . Q–KR4; 11 O–O, N–Q2 has been tried, and, earlier, 7 . . . KN–Q2; 8 N–K2, N × P; 9 O–O, B–N5 = .

(*c*) 9 N–B2, B–K3! 10 O–O, R–B1; 11 R–N1, P–QR3; 12 P–QN3, P–QN4! 13 P × P, P × P; 14 B–B3, Q–R4; 15 B–Q2, P–N5; 16 N–R4, N–Q2 = . Korn-Richter, corr. 1958.

(*d*) A crucial position. There is (A) 9 . . . B–N5; 10 B × B (or 10 N × N), N × B; 11 Q × N, N × N; 12 Q–Q1, N–B3 = . (B) 9 . . . N–KN5; 10 B × N, N × N; 11 QB × B, B × B; 12 Q × B, N × B; 13 Q–Q1, N–B3; 14 O–O, P–B4 ∞. (C) 9 . . . P–K4; 10 N × N, P × N; 11 P × P, P × P; 12 Q–R4! B–N5; 13 R–Q1, Q–N1; 14 R–Q2. Safe is (D) 9 . . . B–Q2; 10 O–O, P–QR3; 11 R–B1, R–B1; 12 Q–Q2, R–K1; 13 KR–K1, P–K4; 14 N × N, B × N; 15 B–B3, P × P; 16 B × P, N–Q2! 17 B × P, N–K4.

(*e*) 13 Q × Q, R × Q; 14 R–Q1, R × R†; 15 K × R, B–K3; 16 P–QN3, N–Q2; 17 B–K3, N–N1! Tal-Petrosian, Portoroz 1958.

(*f*) 8 . . . P–QN4; 9 P–K5, P × KP; 10 KBP × P, N–N5; 11 B–KB4, P–N5; 12 N–K4, N–Q2; 13 P × P + .

(*g*) 13 B–B3, N–Q2; 14 R–K1, N–B3; 15 R–N1, R–K1; 16 R × R†, Q × R; 17 R–N2, B–Q2; 18 R × P, R–N1 = . Forintos-Gligorić, Ljubljana 1969. In the column, Black can switch into the Volga-Benko Gambit structure with 7 . . . P–QN4; 8 P × P, P–QR3; 9 P × P, Q–R4; 10 B–Q2, B × P; 11 B × B, Q × B = .

(*h*) 9 . . . KN–Q2! 10 BP × P, P × P; 11 O–O, P × P; 12 B × P, N–KB3; 13 Q–Q2, P–QR3 ∞.

(*i*) (A) 13 Q × P†, Q × Q; 14 N × Q, B × B; 15 N × B, N–QB3, 16 N–B7, R–N1 = . Nei-Kirillov, USSR 1966. (B) 13 B × B, N × B; 14 P × P, B–N5 = .

(*j*) 7 B–Q3, P–K3. (A) 8 N–B3, (see cols. 37–8) (B) 8 KN–K2, P × P; 9 KP × P, B–N5; 10 O–O, R–K1; 11 Q–B2, B × N; 12 B × B, QN–Q2; 13 B–Q2, P–QR3; 14 QR–K1, P–R3; 15 P–QR4, N–B1; 16 P–R3, R–B1; 17 B–B3, R–B2 = . Penrose-Gligorić, Hastings 1961–2.

(k) 8 . . . B × P is a safe equalizer. Gligorić.

(l) 9 . . . P–QN4; 10 P × P, B–N2; 11 B–B3, P–QR3; 12 P × P, N × RP∞; or 10 . . . P–QR3; is a dynamic response.

(m) The column is Gunderam's dangerous "Six-Pawn" Attack, to which he quotes (A) 11 . . . B–Q2; 12 P × P, P × P; 13 N–R3, B–B3; 14 N–KN5, Q–K2 (14 . . . P–Q4!); 15 Q–Q3, N–Q2; 16 Q–R3, with White pressure. (B) Gligorić gives 11 . . . P–QN4! and if 12 RP × P, P–N5!

(n) 13 RP × P, RP × P; 14 Q–Q3 ± . Mariotti–Gligorić, Praia de Rocha 1969.

1 P-Q4, N-KB3; 2 P-QB4, P-KN3; 3 N-QB3, B-N2

	26	27	28	29	30
4	(P-K4)			N-B3	P-K3 (*k*)
	(P-Q3)			P-Q3	O-O
5	B-K2 ⎞	Borisenko-	KN-K2	B-B4 (*h*)	N-B3 (*l*)
	O-O ⎟	Averbakh	O-O	P-B3	P-Q3
6	B-N5 ⎬	Variation	N-N3	P-K3	B-K2
	P-B4 (*a*) ⎠		P-K4	Q-R4!	R-K1!
7	P-Q5 (*b*)		P-Q5	B-Q3 (*i*)	O-O
	P-QR3!? P-K3		QN-Q2 (*g*)	N-R4	P-B3
8	P-QR4	N-B3	B-K2	B-N5	Q-B2
	Q-R4	P×P (*e*)	P-QR3	P-KR3	P-K4
9	B-Q2	BP×P	P-KR4	B-R4	P-QN3
	P-K3	P-KR3	P-KR4	P-KN4	QN-Q2
10	N-B3 (*c*)	B-R4!	B-N5	B-N3	B-N2
	P×P (*d*)	P-QN4 (*f*)	Q-K1 =	N-Q2 (*j*)	P-K5 (*m*)

(*a*) This column deals mainly with the strategies where White's N-KB3 is either omitted or significantly delayed. Otherwise White's 5th and 6th and Black's 5th and 7th move may easily transpose into other columns, e.g. cols 20 or 30. Comparisons are in order also with the Benoni, col. 17. As to the text, Black also has (A) 6 . . . P-KR3; 7 B-K3, P-B4; 8 P-Q5, P-K3; (1) 9 Q-Q2, P×P; 10 KP×P, K-R2; 11 P-KR3, N-R3; 12 N-B3, B-B4 = . Uhlmann-Fischer, Siegen 1970. (2) 9 P-KR3, P×P; 10 KP×P, R-K1; 11 Q-Q2, K-R2; 12 B-Q3, N-R3; 13 KN-K2, N-B2; 14 O-O, B-Q2 = . (B) 6 . . . QN-Q2; 7 B-B4! but not 7 Q-Q2, P-K4; 8 N-B3, P-B3! = . Weak is an early 5 B-N5? P-B4; 6 P-Q5, Q-R4; 7 B-Q3, N×KP!

(*b*) Uhlmann practised and analysed 7 P×P and 8 B-Q2, aiming at a Maroczy bind, e.g. 7 P×P, Q-R4; 8 B-Q2, Q×BP (8 . . . P×P? 9 P-K5, KN-Q2; 10 P-B4!); 9 N-B3, B-N5; 10 B-K3, Q-B1 (10 . . . Q-QR4! 11 Q-N3, QN-Q2! =); 11 QR-B1, N-B3; 12 P-QN3, Q-K3; 13 P-KR3, B×N; 14 B×B, QR-B1; 15 O-O, P-QR3; 16 R-K1; Q-K4; 17 N-Q5, KR-K1; 18 Q-Q2, K-B1; 19 QR-Q1, N×P; 20 Q-B1, P-B4; 21 B×N, P×B; 22 B-R6, K-N1; 23 B×B, Q×B; 24 R×P, P-K3; 25 Q-K3, P-K4; 26 P-B4, R-B1; 27 P-QB5, KP×P; 28 N×P, P-Q4; 29 N-K6, Q-K2; 30 R×P, R-B3; 31 N-Q8, R×N; 32 R×Q, R×R; 33 R×NP, R-K4; 34 Q-R6, resigns. Tarjan-Hulak, Skopje 1976.

(*c*) Problematical is the Pawn storm 10 P-KN4, P×P; 11 KP×P, Q-Q1; 12 P-KR4, R-K1; 13 K-B1, QN-Q2; 14 P-R5, N-K5; 15 N×N, R×N; 16 P×P, BP×P; 17 R-QR3, N-B3! ∞ . Ciocaltea-Gligorić, Moscow 1956.

(*d*) 11 BP×P (11 KP×P, Q-B2; 12 O-O, QN-Q2 =). R-K1; 12 O-O, Q-B2; 13 Q-B2, B-N5; 14 P-KR3, B×N; 15 B×B, QN-Q2; 16 P-R5, R-K2; 17 R-R4, R-K1; 18 P-KN3 ± . Toran-Walther, Bad Aibling 1968. Compare Benoni Defence, col. 9.

(*e*) Also 8 . . . P-KR3; 9 B-Q2, P×P; 10 KP×P, B-B4; 11 N-KR4, B-Q2; 12 O-O, N-R3; 13 N-B3, R-K1 = . Szabó-Larsen, Dallas 1957. But 8 Q-Q2! is best.

(*f*) 11 B×P, P-N4; 12 B-N3, N×KP; 13 N×N, Q-R4†; 14 Q-Q2, Q×B; 15 N×QP, Q×P; 16 Q×Q, B×Q = . Portisch-Szabó, Hungarian Chp. 1960. Also 10 . . . P-KN4; 11 B-N3, N-R4; 12 N-Q2, N×B; 13 RP×N can be defended.

(*g*) Or 7 . . . P-QB3; 8 B-K2, P×P; 9 BP×P, QN-Q2; 10 B-KN5, P-KR3; 10 B-K3, P-R3 = . Szabó-R. Byrne, Havana 1966.

(*h*) (A) 5 B-N5, P-B4 (for 5 . . . O-O; see note (*k*); 6 P-K3, P-KR3; 7 B-R4, P-KN4; 8 B-N3, N-R4; 9 P×P, N×B; 10 RP×N, P×P; 11 Q×Q†, K×Q; 12 O-O-O†, B-Q2! 13 B-K2, N-B3; 14 N-Q2, P-N3 = . Smyslov-Petrosian, Candidates Tournament 1959. (B) 5 P-KN3, see cols. 51-67.

(*i*) (A) 7 P-KR3, N-K5! (B) 7 Q-Q2, B-N5; 8 B-K2, N-R4 = . (C) 7 N-Q2, N-R4; 8 N-N3, Q-KB4; 9 B-Q3, Q-N5; with simplification.

(j) 11 R–QN1, P–QB4 = . Boleslavski.

(k) 4 B–N5, (A) 4 . . . O–O (1) 5 N–B3, P–KR3; 6 B–R4, P–Q3; 7 P–K4! P–B4; 8 P–Q5 might lead into cols. 20 or 26. (2) 5 P–K3, P–Q3; 6 B–K2, QN–Q2; 7 N–B3, P–B3; 8 Q–B2, P–K4; 9 R–Q1, P–KR3! = . Smyslov-Ivkov, Zagreb 1970. (B) 4 . . . P–Q3; 5 P–K3 (1) 5 . . . P–KR3; 6 B–R4, O–O; 7 N–B3, QN–Q2; 8 Q–B2, P–B3; 9 R–Q1 ± . (2) 5 . . . P–B3; 6 N–B3, Q–R4; 7 Q–Q2, B–N5; 8 B–K2, QN–Q2 = . (C) 4 . . . P–B4; 5 P–K3, Q–R4; 6 Q–Q2, P–Q3; 7 N–B3!

(l) 5 B–Q3, P–Q3; 6 KN–K2, P–K4; 7 O–O, KN–Q2; 8 P–B4, P–KB4; 9 B–B2, N–QB3; 10 P–QR3, P–QR4; 11 R–N1, N–K2 = . Aloni-Kotov, Amsterdam 1954.

(m) 11 N–Q2, P–Q4; 12 QR–B1, P–QR3 = . Vestol-Porath, Munich 1958.

1 P-Q4, N-KB3; 2 P-QB4, P-KN3; 3 N-QB3, B-N2; 4 P-K4, P-Q3; 5 P-B3, O-O; 6 B-K3, P-K4; 7 P-Q5

	31	32	33	34	35
	P-B3			P-B4!?	N-R4
8	B-Q3!	Q-Q2	KN-K2	P-KN4! (f)	Q-Q2
	P×P!	P×P	P×P	N-K1!	P-KB4
9	BP×P	BP×P	BP×P	P-KR4	O-O-O!
	N-K1	P-QR3	P-QR3	P-B4	P-QR3 (h)
10	Q-Q2	P-KN4 (b)	P-KN4	NP×P	B-Q3
	P-B4	QN-Q2	P-KR4	P×P	N-Q2
11	P×P	KN-K2	P-KR3	P×P	KN-K2
	P×P	P-KR4	QN-Q2! (d)	B×P	QN-B3
12	KN-K2	P-N5	B-N5	B-Q3	K-N1
	N-R3	N-R2	Q-N3	P-K5	P-QN4
13	O-O	P-KR4	Q-Q2	P×P	P×NP
	N-B4 (a)	P-B3 = (c)	N-R2 (e)	B-B1 (g)	P×KP =

(a) 14 KB-B2, P-QR4; 15 P-QN3 (15 P-QR3, P-R5! 16 B×N, P×B; 17 N×P, P-N3; 18 N/4-B3, N-Q3=), B-Q2; 16 P-QR3, P-N4; 17 P-N4, P×P; 18 P×P, with a small advantage. Boleslavski.

(b) (A) 10 KN-K2, P-QN4; 11 O-O-O, B-Q2; 12 R-K1! *Comments.* (B) 10 O-O-O, QN-Q2; 11 K-N1, P-QN4; 12 R-B1, N-B4; 13 P-KN4, N-K1; 14 P-KR4, P-B4 . Perez-Najdorf, Havana 1962.

(c) Szabó-Gligorić, match Hungary-Yugoslavia, 1959.

(d) 11 . . . N-R2; 12 P×P, Q-R5†; 13 B-B2, Q×P/4; 14 N-N3, Q-N4; 15 P-KR4, Q-B5; 16 B-N2, QN-Q2; 17 KN-K2, Q-B3; 18 B-K3± . Polugayevski.

(e) 14 B-R4, P×P! 15 RP×P, N-B4; 16 O-O-O, B-Q2 = . Attention must be paid to the subtle timing of the moves Q-Q2 (or KN-K2) and . . . N-R2 in cols. 32, 33 and note (d).

(f) 8 Q-Q2, N-R4; 9 O-O-O, P-B4; 10 P×P, P×P; 11 B-Q3, P-QR3; 12 KN-K2, P-QN4; 13 QR-KN1, P×P! 14 B-N1, R-R2! 15 P-KN4, P×P; 16 P×P, N-B5; 17 B×N, P×B; 18 N×P, B-Q5; 19 R-N2, K-R1∞ .

(g) 14 P-K5! B×P; 15 N-B3, B-N2; 16 N-KN5, N-KB3; 17 Q-Q2± . Boleslavski.

(h) Also 9 . . . N-Q2; (A) 10 B-Q3 (1) 10 . . . P×P; 11 P×P, N-B5; 12 KB-B2, N-B3; 13 N-B3, P-QN4; 14 N×P, B-QR3; 15 N-R3, R-N1∞ . Korchnoi-Stein, USSR Chp. 1965 (2) 10 . . . QN-B3; 11 P×P, P×P; 12 N-R3, P-B3; 13 KR-N1, P×P; 14 BP×P, K-R1; 15 K-N1. Portisch-Gligorić, Siegen 1970, P-B5! = . (B) 10 P×P, P×P; 11 B-Q3, P-QR4; 12 KN-K2, N-B4; 13 KB-B2, Q-R5; 14 P-KN3, Q-K2.

1 P–Q4, N–B3; 2 P–QB4, P–KN3; 3 N–QB3, B–N2; 4 P–K4, P–Q3; 5 P–B3, O–O;
6 B–K3

	36	37	38	39	40
	P–K4			QN–Q2?	P–N3
7	P×P	KN–K2		Q–Q2 (*f*)	B–Q3!
	P×P	P–B3	P×P!	P–B3 (*g*)	B–N2! (*i*)
8	Q×Q	Q–Q2!	N×P	KN–K2	KN–K2
	R×Q	P–QR3	P–B3	P–QR3	P–B4
9	N–Q5	O–O–O	Q–Q2 (*c*)	R–Q1	P–Q5 (*j*)
	N×N	QN–Q2	P–Q4	P–QN4	P–K3
10	BP×N	K–N1	BP×P (*d*)	N–B1	B–N5 (*k*)
	P–QB3	P–QN4	P×P	P×P	QN–Q2
11	B–QB4	N–B1	P–K5	B×P	P–QN3 (*l*)
	P–QN4	R–K1	N–K1	P–Q4	P–QR3
12	B–N3	P–Q5	P–B4	B–K2	P–QR4
	B–N2	P–N5	P–B3	P×P	P–R3
13	O–O–O	N/3–K2	B–N5	P×P	B–R4
	P–QB4 (*a*)	P×P (*b*)	P×P! (*e*)	Q–B2 (*h*)	R–K1 (*m*)

(*a*) 14 B–QB2, N–Q2; 15 N–K2, B–KB1; 16 N–B3, P–QR3; 17 P–QN3 = . Botvinnik–Tal, 13th match game 1961.

(*b*) 14 BP×P, N–N3; 15 Q×P, R–N1; 16 N–B3, P–QR4; 17 Q–R3, B–Q2 = . Khasin–Boleslavski, USSR Chp. 1954.

(*c*) 9 N–B2, R–K1; 10 Q–Q2, P–Q4; 11 O–O–O, Q–R4; 12 BP×P, P×P; 13 P×P, B–B4; 14 B–QB4! QN–Q2; 15 KR–K1, QR–B1; 16 B–N3, N–K4; 17 Q–K2, P–QR3; 18 K–N1, P–QN4 = . Aloni–Matulović, Netanya 1961.

(*d*) 10 KP×P, P×P; 11 B–K2 (11 O–O–O, etc., see note (*c*)), P×P! 12 B×P, P–QR3 = .

(*e*) 14 P×P, Q–R5†; 15 P–N3, Q–K2; 16 N×P, Q×P; 17 B–QB4, K–R1; 18 O–O–O, N–B3; 19 N×N, P×N; 20 N–B3 ± . Boleslavski.

(*f*) 7 N–R3, P–K4! 8 P–Q5, N–B4; 9 P–KN4, N–K1; 10 Q–Q2, P–B4; 11 NP×P, P×P; 12 B–N5, Q–Q2; 13 N–B2, P–B5; 14 N–N4, K–R1; 15 P–KR3, Q–B2; 16 B–R4, P–QR4; 17 O–O–O, B–Q2 = . R. Weinstein–Benko, US Chp. 1961.

(*g*) No better prospects offers 7 . . . P–B4; 8 KN–K2! P–QR3; 9 O–O–O, Q–R4; 10 K–N1! P–QN4; 11 QP×P, QP×P; 12 N–Q5, N×N; 13 Q×Q, N×B; 14 R–B1, N×BP; 15 R×N, P×R; 16 N–B3, R–N1; 17 P–B4! Saidy–Commons, US Chp. 1974.

(*h*) 14 P–K5, N–Q4; 15 N×N, P×N; 16 O–O, N–N3; 17 P–QN3, P–B3; 18 N–Q3 ± . Saidy–R. Byrne, US Open Chp. 1960.

(*i*) 7 . . . P–QR3; 8 KN–K2! P–B4; 9 P–K5! N–K1 (9 . . . KN–Q2! 10 P×QP, KP×P; 11 O–O, N–QB3; 12 B–K4, B–N2; 13 Q–Q2, R–K1; 14 KR–Q1, N–B3; 15 B–N5, N×B = . O'Kelly–Johannsson, Varna 1962); 10 P×QP, N×P; 11 P×P, P×P; 12 O–O, N–Q2; 13 P–QN3, N–N2; 14 R–B1 ± . Boleslavski.

(*j*) Into consideration comes 9 O–O, N–B3; 10 B–QB2, P–K4! 11 P×KP, P×P; 12 B–N5, Q×Q; 13 QR×Q, N–Q5; 14 B–QR4 ± .

(*k*) 10 O–O, P×P; 11 BP×P, QN–Q2; 12 R–N1, R–K1; 13 Q–Q2 (Hort–Bogdanović, Sarajevo 1964), N–K4 = .

(*l*) 11 O–O, B–QR3; 12 Q–R4!? Q–B1; 13 N–N3, P–R3; 14 B–Q2, P×P; 15 KP×P, B–N2 ∓ .

(*m*) 14 O–O, Q–B2; 15 Q–Q2, with a bind. Boleslavski.

1 P-Q4, N-KB3; 2 P-QB4, P-KN3; 3 N-QB3, B-N2; 4 P-K4, P-Q3; 5 P-B3 (a), O-O (b)

	41	42	43	44	45
6	B-K3 .... B-N5 (k)				
	N-B3			P-B4	QN-Q2
7	Q-Q2.......	KN-K2		P-Q5	KN-K2
	R-N1?	P-QR3?	R-N1	P-K3	P-B4
8	O-O-O	N-B1 (e)	Q-Q2 (h)	Q-Q2	Q-Q2 (l)
	P-QR3	P-K4	R-K1	P×P	Q-R4
9	P-KR4 (c)	P-Q5	R-Q1 (i)	N×P	O-O-O
	P-K4	N-Q5	P-QR3	B-K3	P-QR3
10	P-Q5	N-N3	N-B1	B-Q3	K-N1
	N-Q5	N×N	P-K4	B×N	R-K1
11	KN-K2	Q×N! (f)	P×P	KP×B	P×P
	P-B4!	P-B4	N×P	R-K1†	P×P
12	P×P e.p.	P×P e.p.	B-K2	N-K2	N-B1 ±
	P×P (d)	P×P (g)	P-QN4 (j)	Q-N3 =	

(a) 5 P-KR3, O-O; (A) 6 B-N5, P-B4! 7 P-Q5, P-N4; 8 P×P, P-QR3 (8 . . . Q-R4; 9 B-Q2, P-QR3; 10 P-QR4, Q-N5! =); 9 P×P, Q-R4; 10 B-Q2 Q-N5! = with a pseudo "Volga-Benko-Gambit" configuration of the Benoni Defence. (B) 6 B-K3, P-K4 (or 6 . . . P-B4); 7 P-Q5, QN-Q2; 8 N-B3, N-B4; 9 N-Q2, P-QR4; 10 B-K2, KN-Q2 = . Larsen-Reshevsky, Sousse 1967.

(b) Also into contention enter (A) 5 . . . N-B3; 6 B-K3, P-QR3; 7 KN-K2, R-QN1 (Shamkovich); and (B) 5 . . . P-K4; 6 KN-K2, P-B3; 7 B-N5, O-O; 8 Q-Q2, QN-Q2.

(c) 9 B-R6, P-K4; 10 KN-K2, P-QN4; 11 P-Q5, N-QR4; 12 N-N3, P-N5; 13 N-N1, B × B; 14 Q × B, N-N2; 15 P-KR4, K-R1; 16 P-R5, N-N1; 17 Q-Q2, N-B4 = .

(d) 13 N × N, P × N; 14 B × P, B-K3; 15 P-R5, P-B4; 16 B-B2, N × RP; 17 P-KN4, N-B3; 18 Q × P, N-Q2; 19 Q-R2, P-R3 = . Boleslavski.

(e) Just as good is the older 8 Q-Q2, R-N1; 9 R-Q1, P-QN4; 10 N-B1, P-K4; 11 P × KP, P-N5; 12 N-Q5, N × P/4; 13 N × N†, B × N; 14 B-K2. Best was 7 . . . B-Q2!

(f) 11 P × N, P-B4; 12 P-QN4, P × P; 13 N-R2, N-R4; 14 N × P, P-B4; 15 P × P, P × P; 16 B-K2, N-B5 ∓. Gunnarson-Ivkov, Vrnjačka Banja 1967.

(g) 13 O-O-O (Spasski-Korchnoi, match 1968), Q-K2; 14 R-Q2, with pressure.

(h) (A) 8 N-B1, P-K4; 9 P-Q5, N-Q5; 10 N-N3, P-B4; 11 P × P e.p., P × P; 12 B-K2, P-Q4; 13 KP × P, P × P; 14 N × N, N-N5; B × P, R × P ∓. Timman-Westerinen, The Hague 1968. (B) Boleslavski suggests to try 8 P-QR3, P-QR3; 9 P-QN4, B-Q2; 10 Q-Q2, P-QN4; 11 P × P, P × P; 12 P-Q5, N-K4; 13 N-Q4.

(i) If (A) 9 N-B1, P-K4; 10 N-N3, P × P; 11 N × P, P-Q4; 12 BP × P N × QP; 13 N/B3 × N, N × N; 14 B × N, Q × N; 15 B × B, Q × Q† = . Ree. (B) 9 R-QN1, P-QR4! = .

(j) 13 P × P, P × P (Gheorghiu-Kavalek, Amsterdam 1969); 14 O-O, N-B5; 15 B × N, P × B = .

(k) 6 KN-K2? P-B4! 7 B-K3! P-N3; compare col. 40. The column is from Boleslavski.

(l) 8 P-Q5, N-K4; 9 N-N3, P-KR3; 10 B-Q2, P-KR4; 11 B-K2, P-K3; 12 P-B4, N/4-N5; 13 P-KR3, N-R3; 14 O-O, P × P; 15 BP × P, R-K1; 16 B-B3, N-Q2; 17 KN-K2, R-N1; 18 P-QR4, P-R3; 19 R-N1, P-B4 = . Petrosian-Reshevsky, Los Angeles 1963. The column is Evans' suggestion.

1 P-Q4, N-KB3; 2 P-QB4, P-KN3; 3 N-QB3, B-N2; 4 P-K4, P-Q3; 5 P-B3

	46	47	48	49	50
	P-K4!?......	P-B3 ⎫			
6	P-Q5 (a)	B-K3 ⎬ R. Byrne's Defence System			
	N-R4	P-QR3 ⎭			
7	B-K3	P-QR4......	KN-K2......	B-Q3.......	Q-Q2
	P-KB4	P-QR4 (c)	P-QN4	P-QN4 (i)	P-QN4
8	Q-Q2	B-Q3	N-B1	P×P (j)	O-O-O
	P-B5	N-R3 (d)	O-O	RP×P	Q-R4! (l)
9	B-B2	KN-K2 (e)	P×P	KN-K2	K-N1
	B-B3	O-O (f)	BP×P	O-O	QN-Q2
10	KN-K2	O-O	P-QN4!	P-QN4	B-R6 (m)
	B-R5	P-K4	P-Q4	QN-Q2	B×B
11	P-KN3	Q-Q2	P-K5	O-O	Q×B
	B-N4	N-Q2	KN-Q2	N-N3 (k)	B-N2!? (n)
12	P-KN4	QR-Q1	B-K2	P-QR4	Q-Q2
	B×P (b)	P×P (g)	P-B3 (h)	P×P =	O-O-O (o)

(a) Quite effective is also 6 KN-K2, P-B3; 7 B-N5, O-O; 8 Q-Q2, Q-R4; 9 P-Q5, P×P; 10 BP×P, N-R3; 11 N-B1, B-Q2; 12 P-QR3! KR-B1; 13 P-KN4 ± . Korchnoi-Tal, USSR 1956. Compare also Chigorin Indian.

(b) 13 P×B, P-B6; 14 B-K3, B×B; 15 Q×B, P×N = . Porreca-Gligorić, Zagreb 1955.

(c) The logical reply to 7 P-QR4 which prevents . . . P-QN4 but weakens White's Queen's wing.

(d) The first point of decision, between the text and 8 . . . P-K4?! (A) 9 KN-K2, N-R3; 10 Q-Q2, N-QN5; 11 R-Q1, Q-K2; 12 B-QN1, O-O; 13 O-O, P×P; 14 B×P, B-K3; 15 P-QN3, P-Q4 = . Bronstein-Evans, Amsterdam 1964. (B) 9 P-Q5, N-R3; 10 KN-K2, O-O; 11 O-O, N-Q2; 12 B-N1, Q-K2; 13 P-KN4, N/2-B4; 14 N-N3, N-N5 = . Kende-Kupreichik, Riga, 1967.

(e) 9 R-B1, O-O; 10 KN-K2, N-Q2; 11 O-O, P-QB4; 12 P-B4, N-N5; 13 B-N1, P×P; 14 N×P, N-B4; 15 P-B5, B-Q2; 16 P-QN3, P-K3 ∞ . Gheorghiu-Szabó, Winnipeg 1967.

(f) Müller in *Archives* gives 9 . . . N-QN5; 10 B-N1, O-O; 11 O-O, P-N3∞ .

(g) The move was criticized, in favour of the immediate 12 . . . N-QN5, but without further evidence. The column may continue 13 N×P, (A) 13 . . . N/2-B4; 14 B-N1, Q-N3 = . Reshevsky-Stein, Los Angeles 1968. (Or (B) 13 . . . N/3-B4; 14 B-QB2, Q-N3; 15 P-QN3, Q-N5; 16 R-N1, R-K1; 17 KR-Q1, N-B1 = . Bobotsov-Stein, Odessa 1968.

(h) 13 P×P, P×P; 14 N-Q3, R-K1∞ . *Comments.*

(i) Another point of decision, as against 7 . . . O-O; 8 KN-K2, P-QN4! (8 . . . QN-Q2; 9 Q-Q2, P-QN4; 10 P-KR4! Hort-R. Byrne, Varna 1962); 9 O-O, QN-Q2; 10 R-B1, B-N2; 11 Q-Q2, P×P; 12 B×P, N-N3 = . Hort-Benko, Monte Carlo 1968.

(j) 8 KN-K2, QN-Q2; 9 P-QN3! O-O; 10 O-O (Portisch-R. Byrne, Monte Carlo 1968), P-K4; 11 P-Q5, BP×P; 12 BP×QP, N-R4 = .

(k) 11 . . . B-N2; 12 Q-Q2, P-K4; 13 KR-Q1, P×P; 14 N×QP, N-K4; 15 B-B1, KN-Q2; 16 P-QR4, with more freedom, Geller-Fischer, Havana 1965.

(l) Perhaps stronger than the original "copyright" 8 . . . P×P; 9 B×P, O-O; 10 P-KR4, P-Q4 (10 . . . B-K3!); 11 B-N3, P×P; 12 P-R5! ± . Spasski-Evans, Varna 1962.

(m) 10 N-R3, R-N1; 11 N-B2, N-N3; 12 P-K5, P×KP; 13 P×KP, B-B4†; 14 K-R1, KN-Q2 = . Pachman.

(n) Also 11 . . . P-K4; 12 P-Q5, P-N5; 13 QN-K2, P×P; 14 BP×P, K-K2; is still unrefuted.

(o) 13 P-Q5! P-N5; 14 N/3-K2, P×P; 15 BP×P (Gheorghiu-R. Byrne, Monte Carlo 1968). Q-N3 = .

1 P–Q4, N–KB3; 2 P–QB4, P–KN3; 3 P–KN3, B–N2; 4 B–N2, O–O; 5 N–QB3, P–Q3; 6 N–B3, QN–Q2; 7 O–O, P–K4; 8 P–K4;

	51	52	53	54	55
	P–B3				
9	P–KR3 (a)				N×P
	Q–N3	Q–R4	P–QR3	P×P	N–B4 (k)
10	R–K1 (b)	B–K3 (d)	B–K3	N×P	P–B3!
	P×P	P×P	P–QN4	N–B4	P–QR4!
11	N×P	N×P	P×NP	B–K3	B–K3
	R–K1	N–N3	RP×P	R–K1	P–R5
12	N–B2	Q–Q3	P×P	Q–B2	Q–B2 (l)
	N–B4	Q–R3	P×P	P–QR4	P–B3
13	R–N1	P–N3	P–QN4	QR–Q1	KR–Q1
	KN–Q2	P–Q4	R–K1	P–R5	KN–Q2
14	B–K3	Q–B2!	P–QR4	KR–K1	B–B2
	B×N	P–B4 (e)	P×P	KN–Q2 (h)	Q–R4
15	P×B	KP×P	R×P	P–B4 (i)	P–KR3
	Q–B2 (c)	P×N (f)	B–QR3 (g)	Q–R4 (j)	R–K1 (m)

(a) Other moves have not yet stood the test, e.g., (A) 9 P–N3, P×P; 10 N×P, N–B4; 11 B–N2, P–QR4; 12 Q–B2, P–R5; 13 KR–Q1, P×P; 14 P×P, R×R; 15 R×R, Q–N3; 16 N–R4, N×N; 17 R×N, N–Q2 ∓. Ståhlberg-Boleslavski, Budapest 1950. (B) 9 B–K3, N–N5! 10 B–N5, Q–N3! (10 . . . P–B3; 11 B–B1, P–KB4; 12 B–N5, Q–K1; 13 P–Q5, P–KR3; 14 QP×P, NP×P; 15 B–B1, Q–K3; 16 N–KR4! *Comments*), 11 P–KR3, P×P! 12 N–QR4, Q–R3; 13 P×N, P–N4; 14 N×P, P×N; 15 N×P, Q×N ∓. Botvinnik-Smyslov, match 1954. Only equality results from (c) 9 R–K1, Q–K2 = . (D) 9 R–N1, P–QR4; 10 P–N3, P×P = . (E) 9 P–Q5, P×P; 10 BP×P, N–B4 = .

(b) 10 P–Q5, N–B4; (A) 11 R–K1, P×P; 12 BP×P, B–Q2; 13 B–B1 (Reshevsky-Evans, Hollywood 1963), KR–B1 = . (B) 11 Q–B2, P×P; 12 BP×P, B–Q2; 13 B–K3, P–QR4; 14 KR–B1, KR–B1; 15 N–Q2, Q–Q1 = . Evans-Lombardy, match 1962.

(c) 16 B–R6, P–B3; 17 P–B4, N–K3; 18 P–KB5, N/3–B4; 19 N–K3, drawn. Ivkov-Sigurjonson, Raach 1969.

(d) 10 R–K1, P×P; 11 N×P, Q–QB4; 12 B–K3 (12 B–B1?! *Comments*), Q×P; 13 B–KB1, Q–N5; 14 N–B2, Q–R4; 15 Q×P, N–K4 = . Lengyel-Liptay, Hungarian Chp. 1963.

(e) (A) 14 . . . P×BP; 15 P–QN4! (B) 14 . . . P×KP; 15 N×KP, N×N; 16 Q×N ± .

(f) 16 B×P, B–B4; 17 Q–Q2, QR–B1∞ . *Comments*.

(g) 16 R–K1, Q–B2; 17 Q–R1, B–N2; 18 R–QB1, N–N3; 19 R–R2, B–KB1; 20 N–QN5, Q–Q1; 21 R×R, B×R; 22 N–R7, QN–Q2; 23 N×BP, B×N; 24 R×B, B×P = . Portisch-Penrose, Munich 1958.

(h) 14 . . . Q–R4; 15 B–B4, B–B1; 16 R–Q2, KN–Q2? (16 . . . N–R4! =); 17 R/1–Q1, N–K4; 18 P–N3, P×P; 19 P×P, Q–N3; 20 B–K3, R–R6; 21 R–N1, Q–R3; 22 K–R2, R–R8; 23 R×R, Q×R; 24 P–B4, Q–R6? (24 . . . N/K4–Q2?!); 25 P×N, P×P; 26 N–B3, N×NP; 27 R–Q3, N–B4; 28 B×N, Q×B; 29 N–QR4, Q–N5; 30 Q–N3, P–KB4; 31 Q×Q, B×Q; 32 R–N3, B–R4; 33 N–N6, B×N; 34 R×B, K–N2; 35 P–B5, R–K2; 36 K–N1, K–B3; 37 K–B2, B–K3; 38 K–K3, R–Q2; 39 R–N1, P–R3; 40 B–B1, B–R7; 41 R–N2, P–K3; 42 R–Q2, R–KB2; 43 R–Q6, resigns (e.g., 43 . . . P–KN4; 44 B–B4, R–K2; 45 P×P, K×P; 46 B×B†, R×B; 47 R–Q7, etc. with a won ending). Evans–Browne, Lone Pine 1975.

(i) 15 R–K2, Q–R4; 16 R/2–Q2, N–K4; 17 B–B1, P–R6; 18 P–N3, N–B6†; 19 N×N, B×N; 20 R×P, N×KP; 21 R/6–Q3, B–N2; 22 B–Q4, N–B4; 23 B×B, K×B; 24 R–Q4, B–B4; 25 Q–B1, N–K5; 26 P–KN4, P–B4; 27 R/4–Q3, B–K3; 28 Q–B4, N–B3; 29 N–N5, R–R3; 30 R–KB3, B–B1; 31 R–Q6, R×R; 32 Q×R, Q–Q1; 33 Q×P, R–K8; 34 R–K3, R–R8; 35 Q–K7, Q×Q; 36 R×Q, R×P; 37 R×P†, K–R3; 38 N–B3? (38 P–B4 =), R–R8? (38 . . .

N-K5!; 39 B-Q3, N-N4 ±); 39 P-N5†, K-R4; 40 P × N, R × B†; 41 K × R, B × P†; 42 K-K2, P-R7; 43 R × P†, K-N5; 44 R-R4†, K-B4; 45 N-Q4†, resigns. Diesen-Browne, Lone Pine 1976.

(*j*) 16 B-B2, N-N3; 17 B-B1, B-Q2 (or 17 . . . N-K3; 18 Q-Q2, N × N =); 18 P-R3, QR-Q1; 19 K-R2, B-QB1 = . Ståhlberg-Boleslavski, Candidates tournament, Zürich 1953.

(*k*) 9 . . . R-K1; 10 B-K3, N-K4 first might be preferable.

(*l*) Also 12 R-B2, P-B3; 13 N-B2, Q-K2; 14 R-Q2, KN-Q2; 15 R-B1 (15 R × P, P-R6!), B-K4; 16 B-B2, R-K1 = . Averbakh-Gligorić Candidates tournament, Zürich 1953. Many of the games quoted in these columns and notes arose by transposition, e.g. 1 N-KB3, N-KB3; 2 P-KN3, P-KN3; 3 B-N2, B-N2; 4 O-O, O-O; 5 P-B4, P-Q3; etc. Thus, compare also with the English or Réti, or Flank Openings.

(*m*) 16 K-R2, N-K4; 17 N/3-K2, Q-B2; 18 QR-N1, P-R6; 19 P-N3, N/K4-Q2; 20 B-K1, P-R4; 21 K-R1, N-B1; 22 B-B3, with a bind. Evans-Sherwin, US Chp. 1954.

1 P–Q4, N–KB3; 2 P–QB4, P–KN3; 3 P–KN3, B–N2; 4 B–N2, O–O; 5 N–QB3, P–Q3; 6 N–B3

	56	57	58	59	60
	(QN–Q2)		P–B4 (Yugoslav Variation)		
7	(O–O) (*a*)			O–O (*f*)	
	(P–K4)			N–B3	
8	P–K3 (*a*)	P×P	P×P	P–K3	P–Q5 (*i*)
	P–B3	N×P (*d*)	P×P	B–N5	N–QR4
9	P–N3	N×N	B–K3!	P–KR3	N–Q2
	P–K5 (*b*)	P×N	B–K3	B×N	P–K4!
10	N–KN5	B–N5	B×P	B×B	P–QR3!
	P–Q4	Q×Q	Q–R4	N–Q2	P–N3!
11	P×P	QR×Q	B–QR3	B×N	P–QN4
	P×P	P–B3	B×P	P×B	N–N2
12	P–B3	R–Q2	N–Q4	P–N3	R–N1 (*j*)
	P×P	B–K3	N×N	Q–R4	N–K1
13	Q×P	P–N3	Q×N	B–N2	N/2–K4
	P–KR3 (*c*)	KR–K1 (*e*)	QR–B1 (*g*)	P×P (*h*)	P–KR3 (*k*)

(*a*) The line of most consequence, apart from 7 P–Q5, as shown further below. (A) 8 P–KR3, P–B3; 9 B–K3, N–R4; and . . . P–KB4 = . (B) 8 Q–B2? P×P; 9 N×P, N–N3; 10 R–Q1 (or 10 Q–Q3, P–Q4; 11 P×P, QN×P =), N×P; 11 N/3–N5, P–QR3; 12 Q×N, P×N; 13 N×P, B–Q2 = . This line might be circumvented, or rather Q–B2 be played to greater advantage in the lines where White omits N–QB3, as the Queen then serves to protect the QB Pawn. (c) 8 P–N3, R–K1; 9 Q–B2, P×P! 10 N×P, N–B4; 11 B–N2, P–QR4; 12 R–Q1, with chances on both sides. Another consequential thrust (in the column, instead of 7 O–O) is 7 P–Q5!? P–K4; 8 P×P *e.p.*, P×P; 9 O–O, N–B4; 10 B–K3, N/4–K5; 11 N×N, N×N; 12 Q–B2, N–B3; 13 P–B5, B–Q2; 14 Q–N3, N–Q4; 15 N–N5? (15 B–N5! =), R–B4; 16 B–Q2, R×N; 17 B×R, Q×B; 18 Q×P, Q–Q1; 19 P×P, P×P; 20 B×N, R–N1; 21 B×P†, B×B; 22 Q–K4, Q–Q2; 23 QR–Q1, R×P; 24 Q–R8†, B–B1; 25 R–N1, Q–N4; 26 R×R, Q×R; 27 Q×P, Q×KP; 28 Q–K3, Q×RP; 29 P–R4, Q–Q4; 30 K–R2, Q–KB4; 31 R–Q1, P–Q4; 32 R–K1, Q–R6†; 33 K–N1, B–KB4; 34 Q–Q4, B–K5; 35 R×B, P×R; 36 Q–Q5†, K–N2; White resigns. Benko-Browne, US Chp. 1975.

(*b*) 9 . . . R–K1; 10 B–N2, P–K5; 11 KN–Q2, P–Q4; 12 P–B3, P×P; 13 Q×P, N–N3 = .

(*c*) 14 N–R3, N–N3; 15 B–R3, R–K1; 16 N–B4, B–N5; 17 Q–B2, B–B4! 18 P–R3,Q–Q2; 19 QR–B1, P–N4 = . Barcza-Uhlmann, Mariánské Lázne 1957.

(*d*) Still playable is 8 . . . P×P; 9 P–N3, R–K1; 10 B–QR3, P–B3; 11 Q–Q2, Q–R4; 12 N–QR4, Q×Q = . Bernstein-Boleslavski, Groningen 1946.

(*e*) 14 N–R4, N–N5! 15 N–B5, P–KR3; 16 N×B, R×N; 17 P–KR3, P×B; 18 P×N, drawn. Darga-Fischer, Bled 1961.

(*f*) (A) 7 P–Q5, See Benoni Defence, col 16. (B) 7 P×P, P×P; 8 Q×Q, R×Q; 9 B–K3, N–R3 = .

(*g*) 14 Q–B4, N–R4; 15 Q–K3, B×N; 16 Q×B, Q×Q; 17 P×Q, R–B2 = .

(*h*) 14 P×P, Q–KB4; 15 K–N2, P–Q4; 16 P–KN4, Q–B3; 17 P×P, N–N3; 18 P×P, Q×QBP†; 19 P–Q5, Q–N2; 20 Q–B3, QR–B1 = . Ilivitski-Taimanov, USSR Chp. 1955.

(*i*) 8 P–KR3, P×P; 9 N×P, N×N; 10 Q×N, B–K3! = . Böök.

(*j*) 12 B–N2, B–Q2; 13 N–N3, (A) 13 . . . N–K1; 14 P–K4, P–B4; 15 P×P, P×P, 16 P–N5, P–QR3 = . (B) 13 . . . N–KR4; 14 P–K4, P×P; 15 P×P, Q–B2; 16 N–Q2, P–QR4; 17 P×P, R×P; 18 R×R, N×R; 19 N–N5, B×N; 20 P×B, B–R3 = . Lombardy-Evans, match 1962.

(*k*) 14 P×P, NP×P; 15 Q–R4, P–B4; 16 N–Q2, R–B2 = . Boleslavski.

1 P–Q4, N–KB3; 2 P–QB4, P–KN3; 3 P–KN3, B–N2; 4 B–N2, O–O; 5 N–QB3, P–Q3; 6 N–B3, N–B3 (Panno Variation); 7 O–O (a)

	61	62	63	64	65
	P–QR3		B–N5	P–K4 (e)	
8	Q–Q3	R–K1	B–K3 (d)	P–Q5 (f)	
	R–N1	B–B4	P–K4	N–K2	
9	B–K3 (b)	P–K4	P × P	P–B5	P–K4
	P–QN4	B–N5	P × P	N–Q2	N–K1
10	N–Q2	P–Q5	Q × Q	P × P	P–QN4 (h)
	B–Q2	B × N	KR × Q	P × P	P–KR3
11	P–Q5	Q × B	QR–Q1	P–QR4	B–N2!
	N–QR4	N–Q5	B–K3	N–QB4	P–KB4
12	P × P	Q–Q1	P–N3	N–Q2	P × P
	P × P	P–QB4	P–KR3 =	P–N3	P × P
13	P–QN4	P × P e.p.		P–QN4	N–KR4
	N–N2 (c)	N × P =		N–N2 (g)	B–B3 (i)

(a) 7 P–Q5, N–QR4; 8 N–Q2, P–B4; 9 O–O, P–K4! see col. 60. Also compare with Benoni Defence, col. 16 (7 P–Q5).

(b) 9 P–K4, P–K4; 10 P–Q5, N–K2; 11 B–K3, N–R4; 12 N–KR4, B–B3; 13 N–B3, B–N2 = . Comments.

(c) 14 QR–B1, P–K3; 15 N/2–K4, N–K1; 16 Q–Q2, K–R1; 17 B–R6 ± . Smejkal-Portisch, Raach 1969. In the column, if 8 P–KR3, P–K4; 9 P–Q5, N–K2; 10 P–B5, P–QN4! 11 P × P e.p., P × P; 12 P–K4, P–QN4 = .

(d) (A) 8 P–KR3, B × N; 9 B × B, N–Q2; 10 B–N2, N × P; 11 B × P, R–N1; 12 B–N2, R–N5! 13 P–K3, N–K3 = . Najdorf-Geller, Zürich 1953. (B) 8 P–Q5, N–QR4; 9 N–Q2, P–B4; 10 P–KR3, B–Q2; 11 Q–B2, P–K4; 12 P–K4, N–R4; 13 P–R3 = . Gudmundsson-Pachman, Varna 1962. The column is Ståhlberg-Unzicker, Göteborg 1955. Black's 7th move was introduced by Simagin.

(e) Szabó's Variation. (A) 7 . . . R–N1 transposes into col. 61. If 8 P–Q5, N–QR4; 9 N–Q2. P–B4; 10 P × P e.p. (else see col. 60), P × P! ∓ . Black's rook on N1 prevents P–QN4, making the transposition important. (B) 7 . . . B–B4; 8 P–N3! N–K5; 9 B–N2, Q–Q2; 10 R–B1, N–N5; 11 N × N, B × N; 12 Q–Q2 ± .

(f) 8 P × P, N × P, see col. 57. The text is more ambitious.

(g) 14 Q–N3, B–Q2; 15 B–R3, P–QR3; 16 N–B4, P–QN4; 17 N–Q2, Q–N3; 18 B–N2 ± . Korchnoi-Fischer, Curaçao 1962.

(h) 10 N–K1, P–KB4; 11 N–Q3! N–KB3! 12 P–B3, P–KR4! 13 P–B4, P × KP; 14 N × P/4, N × N; 15 B × N, B–N5 ∓ . Pachman-Uhlmann, Leipzig 1960.

(i) 14 P–B4, B × N; 15 P × B, N–N3; 16 P × P ± . Pachman.

1 P-Q4, N-KB3; 2 P-QB4, P-KN3; 3 P-KN3, B-N2; 4 B-N2, O-O; 5 N-QB3, P-Q3 (a)

	66	67	68	69	70
6	(N-B3)		P-K3	P-K4	
	P-B3		QN-Q2	P-B4	P-K4
7	O-O		KN-K2	P×P (j)	KN-K2
	Q-R4 (b)		P-QR3	P×P	P×P
8	P-K4 (c)		P-N3	Q×Q	N×P
	Q-R4 (d)		R-N1	R×Q	N-B3
9	R-K1 (e)	.... P-K5	P-QR4	P-K5	N×N
	P-K4 (f)	P×P	P-K4	KN-Q2	P×N
10	P-N3	P×P	B-QR3	P-B4	O-O
	B-N5	N-N5	P-N3	N-QB3	N-Q2!
11	B-QR3	R-K1	O-O	B-K3	Q-B2
	R-Q1	N-Q2	B-N2	N/2×P!?	Q-B3
12	P-Q5	B-B4	P-Q5	P×N	N-K2
	N-K1 (g)	P-KN4 (h)	P-QR4 (i)	N×P (k)	R-K1 (l)

(a) 5 . . . P-B4; 6 N-B3, P×P; 7 N×P, N-B3; 8 O-O, (A) 8 . . . Q-R4; 9 N-B2, P-Q3; 10 B-Q2, Q-R4; 11 P-K4, Q×Q = ; or (B) 8 . . . N×N; 9 Q×N, P-Q3; 10 Q-Q3, B-K3; 11 B-Q2, Q-Q2; 12 QR-B1, QR-B1; 13 P-N3, B-R6; 14 N-Q5, B×B = . Reshevsky-Stein, Amsterdam 1964.

(b) The alternative 7 . . . P-QR3; 8 P-K4 (8 P-Q5, QN-Q2! 9 P-K4, P×P; 10 BP×P, N-B4; 11 R-K1, B-Q2; 12 B-Q2, N-Q6), P-QN4; 9 P-K5, N-K1; 10 Q-K2 (or 10 P×QP, P×QP: 11 P-N3 ±), P×BP; 11 Q×P, B-K3; 12 Q-R4, N-B2; 13 R-K1, P-KR3; 14 P×P, P×P; 15 B-B4, P-N4; 16 B-QB1, Q-Q2; 17 P-KR4, P-B3; 18 P-Q5. Suetin.

(c) Archives and Misl quote also (A) 8 P-KR3, (1) 8 . . . P-K4; 9 P-Q5, P×P; 10 P×P, P-QN4; 11 N-Q2, B-Q2! 12 P-R3, Q-B2; 13 Q-N3, Q-N3; 14 P-QR4, P×P (Donner-Kavalek, Amsterdam 1968); 15 Q-R3, R-B1 = ; (2) 8 . . . B-K3; 9 P-Q5, B-Q2; 10 P-K4, R-B1; 11 P-R3, P×P; 12 BP×P, Q-N3; 13 Q-K2, Q-R3! = . Smejkal-Jacobson, Raach 1969. (B) 8 P-Q5, Q-N5; 9 N-Q2, B-Q2; 10 P-QR3 (10 P-K4, P-QR4; 11 R-K1, N-R3; 12 P-QR3, Q-N3; 13 N-B3, N-B4; 14 B-K3, P×P! Sokolov), Q-N3; 11 Q-N3, R-B1 ∓ . Filip-Larsen, Zagreb 1965.

(d) 8 . . . B-N5; 9 P-KR3, B×N; 10 B×B, KN-Q2; 11 B-K3, P-QR3; 12 P-R3, P-QB4; 13 P-QN4 ± . Archives.

(e) Larsen gives 9 Q-N3, P-K4; 10 P-Q5, N-R3; 11 B-K3, N-KN5. The text, by simple development, exposes Black's manoeuvres as a waste of time.

(f) The threat was 10 P-K5, P×P? 11 R×P. If 9 . . . B-N5; 10 P-Q5, P-B4; 11 P-QR3, N-R3; 12 Q-Q3, N-B2; 13 N-KR4 ± .

(g) 13 Q-Q3, P-KB4; 14 N-Q2, N-Q2; 15 P-B3 ± . Comments.

(h) 13 B×P, QN×P; 14 B-R4, N-N3 . If 10 N×P, Q×Q; 11 R×Q, B-K3 = . Comments.

(i) 13 P-K4, N-B4; 14 Q-B2, P-R4 = . Botvinnik-Smyslov, match 1954.

(j) (A) 7 KN-K2, P×P; 8 N×P, see Sicilian Defence. (B) 7 P-Q5, N-R3; see Benoni Defence.

(k) 13 R-Q1, B-N5; 14 R×R†, R×R; 15 P-KB1, N-Q6†; 16 B×N, R×B = . Kramer-R. Weinstein, US Chp. 1962. Still better is 9 . . . N-K1; 10 P-B4, P-B3.

(l) 13 R-N1, Q-K2; 14 B-Q2, N-B4; 15 QR-K1, P-KR4 = . Najdorf-Bronstein, Budapest 1950.

1 P–Q4, N–KB3; 2 P–QB4 (a), P–KN3; 3 P–KN3, B–N2 (b); 4 B–N2, O–O

	71	72	73	74	75
5	N–KB3 (c)				
	P–B4	P–Q3			
6	O–O (d)	O–O (g)			
	P×P	QN–Q2 (h)...	B–B4	N–B3 (k)	.... (QN–Q2)
7	N×P	P–K3	N–B3	P–Q5	Q–B2
	N–B3 (e)	P–K4	Q–B1	N–QR4	P–K4
8	N–QB3	P–N3	R–K1	QN–Q2 (l)	R–Q1 (n)
	N×N	R–K1	R–K1	P–B4	R–K1
9	Q×N	N–B3	P–K4	P–K4	P–K4
	P–Q3	P–B3	B–R6	P–QR3	P–B3
10	Q–Q3	B–N2	P–K5	R–N1	N–B3
	P–QR3	P–K5	B×B	P–QN4	Q–K2!
11	B–Q2	N–Q2	K×B	P–N3	P–N3
	B–B4	P–Q4	KN–Q2	R–N1	P×P
12	P–K4	P–B3	P–K6	P×P	N×P
	B–K3 (f)	KP×P (i)	P×P (j)	P×P (m)	N–B4 (o)

(a) For 2 N–KB3, P–KN3; see Queen's Pawn's games.

(b) (A) 3 . . . P–B3; 4 B–N2, P–Q4; see (Neo-) Grünfeld Defence, col. 42. (B) 3 . . . P–B4; (1) 4 N–KB3, P×P; 5 N×P, Q–R4† (5 . . . B–N2; see other main lines, or also English Opening); 6 N–B3, N–K5; 7 Q–B2! N×N; 8 B–Q2, Q–QB4; 9 B×N, Q×P; 10 P–K4, Q–B4 ∞. (2) 4 P–Q5, P–QN4; 5 P×P, P–Q3; 6 B–N2, B–KN2; 7 N–B3, O–O = . Keres-Opočenský, Parnu 1937 a facsimile of the Volga Gambit. (c) 3 . . . P–Q4; see Neo-Grünfeld Defence, cols. 36–40.

(c) 5 P–K4, P–Q3; 6 N–K2, P–K4; 7 N–B3! see Col. 70.

(d) 6 P–Q5, see col. 58, or note ƒ Benoni Defence.

(e) 7 . . . P–Q4; 8 P×P, N×P; 9 N–QB3, N×N; 10 P×N, N–B3! 11 N×N, P×N; 12 Q–N3, Q–N3! 13 B–K3, Q×Q; 14 P×Q, B–K3; 15 B×BP, QR–B1; 16 B–N7 R×P = . *Comments.*

(f) 13 P–N3, N–Q2; 14 QR–B1, N–B4; 15 Q–K2, P–QN4! = . Portisch-Geller, Skopje 1968. Keene points out 15 Q–B2! ± .

(g) 6 P–K3, QN–Q2; 7 N–B3, P–K4; see col. 56.

(h) 6 . . . P–B4; 7 P×P, P×P; 8 N–K5, KN–Q2; 9 N–Q3, N–K4! 10 N×N, B×N; 11 N–B3, Q–R4; 12 B–N5, N–B3; 13 B×N, P×B; 14 B×P, R–K1; 15 B–N5, Q–N5! = . Donner-Gligorić, Buenos Aires 1951. Also compare col. 72.

(i) 13 Q×P, P×P; 14 N×P! N–N3; 15 N–K5, B–K3 ∓. Zak-Simagin, USSR Chp. 1952. Also compare col. 68.

(j) 13 N–KN5, N–B1; 14 Q–B3, N–B3; 15 Q–B7†, K–R1; 16 R–K4 + . Dueball-Westerinen, Raach 1969.

(k) The Panno Variation, but without N–QB3 having been played—providing some subtle difference in this and the next column.

(l) 8 KN–Q2, (A) . . . P–B4; 9 N–QB3, P–K4! see col. 60. (B) 8 . . . P–B3! 9 P–QR3, P×P; 10 P×P, N–N5 (or 10 . . . N–Q2; 11 R–R2, N–N3 =); 11 R–R2, N–K4; 12 P–N3, B–Q2; 13 P–R3, B–N4; 14 B–N2, R–B1 = . *Comments.*

(m) 13 P–QN4, (Korchnoi-Petrosian, USSR 1955), N–B5! = .

(n) If now 8 N–B3, P×P; 9 N×P, N–N3; 10 R–Q1! N×BP; 11 N–QN5, P–QR3; 12 Q×N, P×N; 13 N×NP, B–Q2!

(o) 13 P–B3, P–QR4; 14 B–N2, Q–B2! = . Boleslavski. Compare this and col. 72.

1 P–Q4, N–KB3; 2 P–QB4, P–Q3

	76	77	78	79	80
3	N–QB3..				N–KB3
	P–K4			B–B4 (g)	P–B3 (i)
4	P×P	N–B3 (c)		P–K4	N–B3
	P×P	QN–Q2	P–K5	P–B4	B–N5
5	Q×Q†	B–N5 (d)	N–KN5	P×P	P–K4
	K×Q	B–K2	B–B4	P×P	QN–Q2
6	N–B3	Q–B2	P–KN4	Q×Q†	B–K2
	QN–Q2 (a)	P–B3	B×P	K×Q	P–K4
7	P–KN3	P–K3	B–N2	B–N5	O–O
	P–B3	O–O	P–B3	P–B3	B–K2
8	B–R3	O–O–O	N/5×KP	P–K4	B–K3
	B–Q3	Q–R4	N×N	B–K3	B×N!
9	B–K3	B–Q3	B×N!	O–O–O†	B×B
	P–KR3	R–K1	N–Q2	K–B2	O–O
10	O–O	B–R4	Q–N3	P–QN3	Q–Q2 (j)
	R–K1 (b)	N–B1 (e)	Q–N3 (f)	B–R6† (h)	R–K1 (k)

(a) 6 . . . KN–Q2; 7 P–QN3, P–KB3; 8 B–N2, P–B3; 9 O–O–O, K–B2; 10 P–KN4, N–R3; 11 P–N5, KN–B4; 12 P–KR4, B–K3; 13 B–KR3 ± . Boleslavski.

(b) 11 N–KR4, B–B1; 12 P–N3, P–KN4; 13 N–B5, N–B4; 14 P–B3, K–B2 = . Bronstein-Panno, Amsterdam 1954. The exchange of queens diminishes any chances.

(c) (A) 4 P–Q5, P–KN3! (B) 4 P–K4 (1) 4 . . . P×P; 5 Q×P, N–B3! = (2) 4 . . . QN–Q2, N–Q2; 5 B–K3, P–KN3; 6 KN–K2, B–N2; 7 P–B3, P–KR4!? 8 Q–Q2, P–QR3; 9 P–Q5, Q–K2; 10 P–QN4, P–R5; 11 N–B1, N–R4; 12 N–N3, P–KB4, 13 O–O–O (13 P–B5!—R. Byrne in *The New York Times*), P–N3; 14 B–Q3, O–O; 15 B–N5, B–B3; 16 B×B, Q×B; 17 P×P, P×P; 18 P–N4, P×P; 19 P×P, N–B5; 20 P–KN5, Q–N2; 21 N–K4, P–R4; 22 P–QR3, P×P; 23 P×P, B–N2; 24 KR–N1, R–R6; 25 B–B2, P–N4; 26 K–N2, N–QN3; 27 N–B6†, K–B2; 28 Q–K1, N×P†; 29 K–N1, R/1–QR1; 30 Q×P, R×N†; 31 B×R, Q–N3†; 32 B–B2, N–R6†; 33 K–R1, N×B†; 34 K–N2, N×NP; 35 Q–R7†, Q×Q; 36 N×Q, B×P; 37 resigns. Holm-Rhode, Sandejiord 1975. (C) 4 P–KN3, P×P = .

(d) Another possibility is 5 P–K4, (1) 5 . . . P–KN3; 6 P×P, P×P; 7 B–K2, B–N2; 8 O–O, O–O; 9 B–N5, P–KR3; 10 B–R4, R–K1; 11 Q–B2, P–B3 = . (2) 5 . . . B–K2; 6 B–K2, P–B3; 7 O–O, P–QR3 (7 . . . O–O!); 8 N–KR4!, P–KN3 (8 . . . N×P; 9 N×N, B×N; 10 N×P†); 9 B–R6, Q–N3; 10 N–B3, N–N5; 11 B–B1, O–O; 12 P–KR3, N/5–B3; 13 P–B5!, Q–B2; 14 BP×P, Q×P; 15 B–K3, R–K1; 16 Q–B2 with an edge. Miles-Larsen, London 1980. White won on the 33nd move.

(e) 11 P×P, P×P; 12 B×N, B×B; 13 K–N1 = . Comments.

(f) 11 P–K3, N–B3; 12 B–N2, O–O–O ∞ . Comments.

(g) 3 . . . QN–Q2; 4 B–N5, P–KR3; 5 B–R4, P–KN4; 6 B–N3, N–R4; 7 P–K3, QN–B3 = . Uhlmann-Najdorf, Varna, 1962.

(h) 11 K–B2, N–R3; 12 KN–K2, KR–Q1 = . Evans-Ridout, Winnipeg 1958.

(i) (A) 3 . . . QN–Q2; 4 B–B4, P–KN3; 5 N–B3, B–N2; 6 P–K3, P–B3; 7 B–Q3, N–R4; 8 B–N5, P–KR3; 9 B–R4, P–KN4; 10 B–N3, Q–R4; 11 R–QN1, P–QB4 = . Boleslavski in the Russian *Yearbook* 1951-2. (B) 3 . . . B–N5; 4 N–B3, QN–Q2; 5 P–K4, P–K4; 6 B–K2, B–K2; 7 B–K3, O–O; 8 O–O, B×N; 9 B×B, R–K1; 10 Q–B2, P×P = . Comments.

(j) A crossroad. The other choice is 10 P–Q5, P×P; 11 N×P, N×N; 12 Q×N, Q–B2; 13 QR–B1, Q–B3; 14 KR–Q1, KR–B1; 15 Q–Q2, N–B3; 16 Q–Q3, P–KR3; 17 R–B2, R–B2; 18 R/1–QB1, QR–QB1 = . Szabó-Navarovsky, Budapest 1965. *Archives* point out that the position arose from the Caro-Kann after 1 P–K4, P–QB3; 2 P–QB4, P–K4?! 3 N–KB3, P–Q3;

4 P-Q4, B-N5; 5 B-K2, B × N; 6 B × B, B-K2; 7 O-O, QN-Q2; 8 N-B3, KN-B3; 9 B-K3, O-O; 10 P-Q5.

(*k*) 11 P-Q5, B-B1; 12 P-QN4?! (12 P × P, or 12 P-QN3, are safer) N-N3 = . Bukić-Pirć, Yugoslav Chp. 1968.

Benoni Defence

(Incorporating the Benko-Gambit)

(1 P–Q4, N–KB3; 2 P–QB4, P–B4)
    or
(1 P–Q4, P–QB4; 2 P–Q5—
the Classic Benoni)

This formerly obscure "BEN-ONI" counter gambit has undergone such formidable metamorphoses that it now commands its independent section.

Sprung on the chess world in systematic shape in a phamphlet published at Frankfurt in 1865 by A. Reinganum, Black's thrust was first adoped in serious tournament play by von de Lasa against Hanstein in 1841, and shortly after by St. Amant against Staunton, Paris 1843.

During the later period of classical style it remained dormant, to be fully revived in the 1930s. It now has developed into a Semi-Indian system mainly because its flexibility and richness in transpositions gives hope to both the attack and the defence!

In the MODERN and in the INDO-BENONI (cols. 1–15), Black aggressively plays . . . P–K3 followed by the pawn exchange and chances are still considered either even or further to be explored in Taimanov's line 8 B–N5† (col. 2) or with Mikenas's forceful 8 P–K5 (col. 3). The positional Fianchetto P–KN3 (col. 1 and also cols. 14, 16 and 30) does not create the same pressures as does 7 B–Q3 (cols. 4–6), introduced by Ojanen v. Keres at Helsinki, 1960; or Gligorić's strategy, later adapted by others, of 7 N–B3 and 8 B–K2 (cols. 7–8). The Queen's Gambit-like move 8 B–KN5 (cols. 9–10) or Uhlmann's 7 B–N5 (cols. 12–13) are always full of venom and still alive as ever, just like col. 19, which is part of the *Hromádka Variation* of older vintage, with 3 . . . P–Q3 and . . . P–KN3 to follow. Hromádka and his Czech team mates were among the first to systemize the newer version and some of the newest strategies (cols. 21–5) were again pioneered by the younger Czechs, especially in developing the variation with 5 . . . B–K2! However, 3 . . . P–K3 denies White the benefit of some dangerous turns that arise after the transposition 3 . . . P–Q3.

White's *Anti-Benoni* treatment with N–KB3 in notes (*a*) to cols. 1–5 and 16–20 causes Black no problem.

Cols. 26–30 are an outgrowth of the modest note (*a*) devoted to the "Volga Gambit" in the previous edition. Mostly due to Benko's tournament dynamics, the sacrificial move (3 P–Q5), P–QN4 has developed into a formidable system, with the same demolishing thrust now often lurking in the background or actively employed in similar formations in other Indian-like openings. Thus the former, nondescript term "Volga Gambit" is now universally recognized as THE BENKO GAMBIT, widely used and still under active investigation.

The CLASSIC or "OLD" BENONI does not leave Black enough options for manoeuvre, and 2 . . . P–B4 (Col. 32) is too much of a "mono-rail." But Schmid's 2 . . . P–Q3 so far firmly holds its ground.

Generally, transpositions to and from the English Opening, the Réti Opening, or the King's Indian Defence have to be constantly watched or utilized and comparison is the order of the day as in all contemporary openings.

All in all, the Benoni Defence opens new vistas for the second player.

1 P–Q4, N–KB3; 2 P–QB4, P–B4; 3 P–Q5 (*a*), P–K3; 4 N–QB3 (*b*), P × P; 5 P × P, P–Q3 (*c*)

	1	2	3	4	5
6	P–KN3	P–K4			
	P–KN3	P–KN3		(Ojanen-Penrose Variation)	
7	B–N2	P–B4	B–Q3		
	B–N2	B–N2		B–N2	
8	N–B3	B–N5†	P–K5?! (*i*)	KN–K2 (*k*)	
	O–O	KN–Q2	KN–Q2!	O–O	
9	O–O	B–Q3 (*e*)	N–N5!	O–O	
	Q–K2! (*d*)	O–O	P × P	P–N3!	N–R3
10	N–Q2	N–B3 (*f*)	N–Q6†	P–B4	B–KN5!
	QN–Q2	N–R3 (*g*)	K–K2!	B–QR3	N–B2
11	N–B4	O–O	N × B†	B × B	P–B4
	N–K4	N–B2	Q × N	N × B	P–KR3
12	N × N	N–Q2	B–B4	N–N3	B–R4
	Q × N =	R–N1 (*h*)	N–N3 (*j*)	P–B5! (*l*)	R–K1 (*m*)

(*a*) (A) No impact has 3 P × P, P–K3; 4 N–KB3, B × P; 5 N–B3, P–Q4; 6 P–K3, O–O; a Queen's Gambit accepted with reversed colours. (B) 3 N–KB3, P × P (3 . . . P–K3; 4 P–K3, P × P; 5 P × P, P–Q4 see Caro-Kann, Panov Attack); 4 N × P, P–K3; 5 N–QB3 (1) 5 . . . P–QR3; 6 B–N5, N–B3; 7 P–K3, B–K2 = . *Comments.* Also see English Opening, col. 33, note (*g*). (2) 5 . . . B–N5; 6 N–N5, P–Q4; 7 P × P (7 B–B4, O–O; 8 N–B7, N–R4!), P × P; 8 P–QR3, B × N†; 9 P × B, O–O; 10 P–K3, N–K5; 11 B–Q3, B–Q2 = . Interesting is (4 N × P) P–Q3; 5 N–QB3, P–K4; 6 N/4–N5, P–QR3; 7 N–R3, B–K3; 8 P–K4, N–B3; 9 B–K2? (9 N–B2!) N–Q5; 10 B–K3, N × B; 11 N × B, B–K2 = . Boris-Mychess, Micro-computer chess tourn., San José, 1980. The sequence was 1 P–QB4, P–QB4; 2 N–KB3, N–KB3; 3 P–Q4, P × P; 4 N × P etc. (C) For 3 P–K3 see note (*a*) to cols. 16–20, the Modern Benoni Declined.

(*b*) (A) The text may also be reached via 1 P–Q4, N–KB3; 2 P–QB4, P–K3; 3 N–QB3, P–B4; 4 P–Q5. (B) 4 N–KB3, etc., see Queen's Pawn Games. For 4 . . . P–QN4 see Blumenfeld Counter Gambit.

(*c*) 5 . . . P–KN3? 6 P–Q6! Q–N3; 7 B–B4! ± .

(*d*) (A) 9 . . . P–QR3; 10 P–QR4, QN–Q2; 11 N–Q2, R–K1 (11 . . . R–N1; 12 N–B4, N–K1; 13 P–R5, N–K4; 14 N–N6, N–B2; 15 P–R3 ±); 12 P–R5! P–QN4; 13 P × P *e.p.*, N × NP; 14 N–N3, with more elbow room. (B) 9 . . . R–K1; 10 B–B4, P–QR3; 11 P–QR4, Q–B2; 12 R–B1 ± .

(*e*) No better are (A) 9 N–B3, O–O; 10 O–O, P–QR3; 11 B–Q3, P–QN4 = . Cherepkov-Suetin, USSR 1961; or (B) 9 P–QR4, Q–R5†! 10 P–N3, Q–K2; 11 N–B3, O–O! 12 O–O, N–R3; 13 R–K1, N–N5; 14 B–B1, P–N3 = . Lutikov-Vasyukov, USSR Chp. 1959.

(*f*) Planning the manoeuvre N–Q2 and N–QB4.

(*g*) 10 . . . P–QR3; 11 P–QR4, N–KB3; 12 O–O, B–N5; 13 P–R3, B × N; 14 Q × B, QN–Q2; 15 B–Q2, Q–b2; 16 QR–K1, P–B5; 17 B–N1, P–QN4; 18 K–R1, KR–K1; 19 P × P, P × P; 20 N × P, Q–B4; 21 N–B3, QR–N1; 22 R–K2, Q–B2; 23 N–Q1, N–B4; 24 P–K5, KN–Q2; 25 P–K6, P × P; 26 P × P, N × P; 27 P–B5, P × P; 28 B × P, N–K4; 29 Q–R5, N–B1; 30 B–B3, N/4–N3; 31 R/2–KB2; B–K4; 32 B–K4, R–N4; 33 N–K3, R–K2; 34 N–Q5, Q–Q1; 35 N × R†, Q × N; 36 Q–N4, B × B; 37 R × N†, Q × R; 38 R × Q†, K × R; 39 P × B, resigns. Trefler-Rhode, World Open, N.Y. 1975. (C) 7 B–K2, B–N2; 8 P–KN4, O–O; 9 P–KR4? is the "Blitz-type" Bayonet Attack.

(*h*) 13 P–QR4, P–QR3; 14 N–B4, N–K1; 15 Q–B3, Q–B3; 16 P–R5, P–QN4 = . Saidy-Evans, US Chp. 1964.

(*i*) Compare with the Four Pawns Attack of the King's Indian Defence after (A) 8 B–Q3, or (B) 8 B–K2. If (C) 8 N–B3, O–O; 9 B–K2, R–K1; 10 P–K5, P × P; 11 P × P, N–N5; 12 B–KN5, Q–N3 = . Yudovich. Complicated is 12 . . . P–B3?!

(*j*) The text is *Comments*. An alternative is 12 . . . R–K1; 13 N–B3, K–B1; 14 O–O, N–N3; 15 B–N5, R–Q1; 16 P × P (or 16 P–Q6), R × P = . Mikenas-Suetin, USSR Chp. 1963.

(*k*) 8 N–B3, O–O; 9 P–KR3, R–K1; 10 O–O (10 B–KN5, Q–R4), QN–Q2 allows Black several options.

(*l*) 13 B–K3, N–B4; 14 B–Q4, R–K1; 15 P–B5, N–Q6; 16 Q–B3, N–K4; 17 B × N, R × B; 18 N–N5, Q–QB1; 19 P–N4, Q–Q2; 20 N–Q4, R–QB1; 21 P–N5, R–B4 = . Giterman-Suetin, USSR Chp. 1962.

(*m*) 13 P–R4, P–R3; 14 P–R3, R–N1; 15 B–KB2 ± . Ivkov-Jansa, Vrnjacka Banja 1967.

1 P-Q4, N-KB3; 2 P-QB4, P-B4; 3 P-Q5, P-K3; 4 N-QB3, P × P; 5 P × P, P-Q3;
6 P-K4, P-KN3

	6	7	8	9	10
7	(B-Q3)	N-B3			B-KB4
	(B-N2)	B-N2			P-QR3
8	(KN-K2)	B-K2		B-KN5	P-QR4
	(O-O)	O-O		P-KR3	B-N2
9	(O-O)	O-O		B-R4	N-B3
	P-QR3	R-K1 (*b*)		P-KN4	O-O
10	P-QR4	Q-B2	N-Q2	B-N3	B-K2
	Q-B2	N-R3	N-R3 (*e*)	N-R4	B-N5
11	P-R3	B-KB4 (*c*)	P-B3 (*f*)	B-N5† (*i*)	O-O
	QN-Q2	N-QN5	N-B2 (*g*)	K-B1!	R-K1
12	P-B4	Q-N1	P-QR4	B-K2!	N-Q2
	R-N1! (*a*)	N-R4! (*d*)	P-N3 (*h*)	N × B (*j*)	B × B (*k*)

(A) 13 N-N3, P-B5; 14 B-B2, P-QN4; 15 P × P, P × P; 16 B-K3, P-N5! 17 R-R7, Q-Q1∞. Bertok-Portisch, Stockholm 1962.

(*a*) (B) 9 . . . B-N5? 10 P-KR3, B × N; 11 B × B! (B) Interesting is 9 . . . P-QR3; 10 P-QR4, B-N5; 11 P-R3, B × N; 12 B × B, QN-Q2; 13 B-B4, N-K1; 14 B-K2, Q-B2; 15 R-B1, P-B5!

(*c*) One of many choices, e.g. (A) 11 R-K1, B-N5! (11 . . . N-B2; 12 N-Q2, N-Q2; 13 N-B4, N-K4; 14 N-K3 ± . Hort-Bouazis, Sousse 1967) 12 P-QR3, P-B5; 13 B-K3, R-QB1; 14 QR-Q1, N-B4 = . Polugayevski-Matulović, Skopje, 1968. (B) 11 P-QR3, N-B2; 12 R-K1, Q-K2 (Hartston gives 12 . . . R-N1; 13 B-KB4, N-R4 =); 13 B-KN5, P-KR3; 14 B-R4, P-KN4; 15 B-N3, N-R4∞. Korchnoi-Bilek, Sousse 1967.

(*d*) 12 B-KN5, P-B3; 14 B-K3, P-B4; 15 P-QR3, P-KB5; 16 B × QBP! ∞ .

(*e*) Another approach is 10 . . . QN-Q2 (A) 11 P-QR4, N-K4 (11 . . . P-QR3? 12 R-R3, R-N1; 13 P-R5, Q-B2; 14 P-R3, P-QN4; 15 P × P e.p. Petrosian-Quinteros Lone Pine); 12 R-R3, B-Q2; 13 Q-B2, P-KN4 = . (B) 11 Q-B2, N-K4 (11 . . . N-R4; 12 B × N, P × N; 13 N-B4, N-K4; 14 N-K3, Q-R5; 15 B-Q2, N-N5; 16 N × N, P × N; 17 B-B4, Q-B3 = . Spasski-Fischer, 3rd match game 1972); 12 P-QN3, P-KN4; 13 B-N2, P-N5! (1) 14 KR-K1, N-R4; 15 N-Q1, N-KB5; 16 B-N5, R-B1; 17 N-K3, Q-N4 = . Korchnoi-Mecking, Augusta 1974. (2) 14 P-B4? P × P e.p. 15 P × P, N-R4; 16 P-B4? N × P; 17 R × N, Q-N4† ∓ .

(*f*) Also playable is (A) 11 R-K1, N-B2; 12 P-QR4, P-N3; (1) 13 P-KR3, R-N1; 14 B-B1, P-QR3 (Boleslavski); or (2) 13 Q-B2, N-R3! (13 . . . N-N5, 14 B × N! B × B; 15 N-B4 ±); 14 B-N5, N-QN5 = . Risky is (B) 11 P-B4!? N-B2; 12 B-B3, R-N1! 13 N-B4, P-QN4; 14 N-R5, B-Q2; 15 P-K5, P × P; 16 P × P, R × P; 17 B-B4, R-B4; 18 B-N3, P-N5 ∓ . Zinser-Evans, Venice 1967.

(*g*) 11 . . . N-Q2; 12 N-B4, N-K4; 13 N-K3, P-B4; 14 P-B4, N-KB2; 15 P-QR3, N-B2; 16 P × P, P × P; 17 B-Q3, Q-B3; 18 R-B3, B-Q2; 19 Q-B2, N-KR3; 20 B-Q2, R-K2; 21 QN-Q1, QR-K1 = .

(*h*) (A) 13 N-B4, B-QR3; 14 B-N5, P-R3! 15 B-R4 (or 15 B-Q2), Q-Q2; 16 Q-Q2, K-R2 = . Boleslavski. (B) 13 K-R1, Q-K2!? 14 N-B4, B-R3 ∞ . In the column, there is also 12 . . . N-Q2; 13 K-R1, P-B4; 14 P × P, P × P = .

(*i*) 11 B-K2, P-R3; 12 P-QR4, O-O; 13 N-Q2, N × B; 14 RP × N, P-B4; 15 P × P, B × P; 16 N-B4, Q-K2; 17 N-N6, R-R2; 18 O-O, N-Q2 = . Bilek-Evans, Amsterdam 1964.

(*j*) 13 RP × N, P-R3! 14 Q-B2, N-Q2; 15 P-R4, Q-K2! 16 N-Q2, B-Q5 = . Mecking-Keene, Hastings 1966-7.

(*k*) 13 Q × B, N-R4; 14 B-K3, N-Q2; 15 P-R5, Q-B2; 16 P-KN4, KN-B3 = .

1 P–Q4, N–KB3; 2 P–QB4, P–B4; 3 P–Q5, P–K3; 4 N–QB3, P × P; 5 P × P, P–Q3; 6 N–B3, P–KN3

	11	12	13	14	15
7	N–Q2...... B–N2 (a)	B–N5 .... B–N2		P–KN3...... B–N2	B–B4 (j) B–N2
8	N–B4 O–O	P–K4 ...... P–KR3!	N–Q2?! P–KR3!	B–N2 O–O	Q–R4† B–Q2
9	B–B4 N–K1	B–R4 P–KN4 (d)	B–R4 P–KN4	O–O Q–K2 (h)	Q–N3 Q–B2
10	Q–Q2! P–N3 (b)	B–N3 N–R4	B–N3 N–R4 (f)	N–Q2 QN–Q2	P–K4 O–O
11	P–K3 B–QR3	B–N5† K–B1!	Q–R4† K–B1	N–B4 N–K4	B–K2 P–QN4 (k)
12	P–QR4 P–B4 (c)	P–K5! N × B (e)	Q–N3 N × B (g)	N × N Q × N (i)	N × P B × N (l)

(a) 7 . . . QN–Q2; 8 P–KN3, B–N2; 9 B–N2, O–O; 10 O–O, Q–K2; 11 P–KR3, P–N3; 12 P–QR4, B–QR3; 13 R–K1 = . Donner-Petrosian, Göteborg, 1955.

(b) Sharper than 10 . . . B × N; 11 Q × B, P–QN4; 12 N–Q2, P–N5; 13 Q–B2, Q–K2; 14 Q–K4, Q–B3; 15 O–O–O, followed by P–KR4!

(c) 13 B–K2, Q–B3; 14 B–N3, B × N; 15 B × B, P–QR3 = . Osnos-Forintos, Varna 1962.

(d) 9 . . . P–R3; 10 N–Q2! P–QN4; (A) 11 B–K2, O–O; 12 Q–B2, R–K1; 13 O–O! QN–Q2; 14 P–R4, P–N5; 15 N–Q1, P–N6; 16 Q–Q3, R–N1; 17 P–B4 ± . Taimanov-Boleslavski, USSR 1960. (B) 11 P–R4! P–N5; 12 N/3–N1, O–O; 13 B–Q3, P–QR4; 14 Q–B3, B–R3; 15 B × B, R × B; 16 N–B4, QN–Q2; 17 N/1–Q2, R–K1; 18 O–O ± . *Comments.*

(e) 13 RP × N, P–R3; 14 B–Q3, P–B5 ∞. Gulko-Savon, USSR Chp. prelims 1977.

(f) 10 . . . P–QR3; 11 P–QR4, N–R4; 12 N–B4, N × B; 13 RP × N, P–B4; 14 Q–N3 + .

(g) 13 RP × N, P–N4! ∞. Tal. In the column, *Informator* 24 suggests 8 P–K3, P–KR3; 9 B–R4, P–KN4; 10 B–N3, N–R4; 11 B–N5†, K–B1∞ .

(h) (A) 9 . . . P–QR3; 10 P–QR4, R–K1; 11 N–Q2, QN–Q2; 12 P–KR3, N–R4; Osnos-Tal, Alma Ata 1969; 13 N–B4! N–K4; 14 N–R3 ± , with a slightly better position (Suetin). (B) 9 . . . N–R3, 10 P–KR3! (10 N–Q2, R–N1; 11 P–QR4, N–B2; 12 N–B4, KN–K1; 13 B–B4, P–B4; 14 Q–Q2, P–N3 = . Addison-Evans, Hollywood 1963), N–B2; 11 P–K4! N–Q2; 12 R–K1 ± . Korchnoi-Tal, USSR Chp. 1962.

(i) 13 P–QR4, P–QR3; 14 P–R5, R–K1; 15 B–B4, Q–K2; 16 Q–N3, N–Q2 = . Gligorić-Petrosian, Zürich 1953.

(j) 7 P–K4, B–N2; 8 B–N5 see col. 12.

(k) (A) 11 . . . P–QR3; 12 P–K5! P × P; 13 B × KP, Q–B1∞ . (B) 11 . . . N–R4; 12 B–K3, B–N5; 13 P–KR3, B × N; 14 B × B, N–Q2; 15 B × N, P × B; 16 O–O, QR–K1; 17 Q–B2, P–QR3; 18 P–QR4, Q–Q1; 19 P–R5, K–R1; 20 R–R4, Q–B1; 21 N–Q1, P–N4; 22 P × P *e.p.*, N × P; 23 R–R2, P–B4; 24 Q–N3, Q–N2 ∞. Timman-Ljubojević, Amsterdam 1972.

(l) 13 B × B, N × KP; 14 O–O, P–QR3; 15 B–Q3, N–KB3 = . Evans-Perez, Amsterdam 1964.

1 P-Q4, N-KB3; 2 P-QB4, P-B4; 3 P-Q5 (*a*), P-Q3; 4 N-QB3, P-KN3

	16	17	18	19	20
5	P-KN3......P-K4				
	B-N2	B-N2			
6	B-N2	B-K2.............................B-Q3 (*k*)			
	O-O	O-O			P-K4
7	N-B3! (*b*)	N-B3...................B-KN5!			P-KR3
	P-K4 (*c*)	P-K4.......P-K3		P-N4 (*i*)	O-O
8	P × P *e.p.*	B-N5	O-O (*f*)	P × P	B-N5
	B × P	P-KR3	P × P	P-QR3	P-KR3
9	N-KN5	B-R4	BP × P	P × P	B-K3
	B × P!	P-KN4	B-Q2 (*g*)	B × P	N-R4! =
10	B × P	B-N3	N-Q2	N-B3	
	QN-Q2	N-R4	N-R3	Q-N3	
11	B × R	N-Q2	P-B3	QR-N1	
	Q × B (*d*)	N-B5 (*e*)	N-B2 (*h*)	QN-Q2 (*j*)	

(*a*) (A) Another "anti"-Benoni refusal of this defence is 3 P-K3!? P-KN3 (for 3 . . . P × P; 4 P × P, P-Q4; 5 N-QB3, see Caro-Kann Defence, cols. 3 and 8); 4 N-KB3, B-N2; 5 N-QB3, P-Q4; 6 B-K2, BP × P; (1) 7 P × P, O-O; 8 O-O, N-B3; 9 P-KR3, with a Queen's Gambit, Tarrasch Defence reversed. White's last move prevents . . . B-N5 but there is a question of how White can use his extra tempo. 9 . . . P × P; 10 B × P, N-QR4; 11 B-Q3, B-K3; gives Black a more solid position than 10 . . . P-N3!? 11 P-R3, P-K3; 12 B-B4. (2) 7 N × QP?, O-O; 8 O-O, P × P; 9 B × P, P-QR3; 10 Q-K2, P-K4! ∓ . Bisguier-Reshevsky, Buenos Aires 1970. (B) For other choices see note (*a*) of cols. 1-5.

(*b*) (A) 7 P-K4? P-QR3; 8 KN-K2, R-K1! 9 O-O, P-K3; 10 P-QR4, P × P; 11 BP × P, QN-Q2; 12 P-B4 (12 P-KR3, R-N1; 13 P-R5, P-QN4! ∓), Q-B2 ∓ . Thelen-Hromádka, Prague 1944. (B) 7 N-R3!, P-QR3; 8 N-B4, P-QN4; 9 P × P, P × P; 10 QN × P, B-QR3 = .

(*c*) 7 . . . N-R3, 8 O-O, N-B2; 9 P-QR4, R-N1; 10 R-R2 ± .

(*d*) 12 O-O, P-Q4; 13 R-K1 (or 13 P-B3), P-Q5; with compensation for the exchange. Eliskases-Garcia, Buenos Aires 1964.

(*e*) 12 O-O, N-Q2; 13 B-N4, N-B3; 14 B × B, Q × B; 15 P-B3, K-R1; 16 P-QR3, P-N3; 17 P-QN4, P-KR4; 18 B-B2, B-R3 = . Polugayevski-Vasyukov, USSR Chp. 1961.

(*f*) 8 B-N5, P-KR3; see King's Indian Defence, col. 62. If 7 B-KN5 at once (without N-KB3), the preventive counterattack . . . P-KR3 is no longer advisable.

(*g*) (A) 9 . . . B-N5? 10 P-KR3, B × N; 11 B × B, QN-Q2; 12 B-B4, N-K1; 13 Q-Q2, P-QR3; 14 B-N5! Gligorić-Matulović, Mallorca 1967. (B) 9 . . . R-K1! 10 N-Q2, N-R3; 11 P-B4, N-B2 = . Soos-Matulović, Skopje 1967.

(*h*) 12 P-QR4, P-N3 = . Gligorić-Matulović, Sousse 1967.

(*i*) An attempt at immediate refutation, reminiscent of the same manoeuvre in the King's Indian Defence. This line is crucial for the whole Hromádka variation as slower answers also pose problems for Black, e.g. (A) 7 . . . P-KR3; 8 B-B4! or (B) 7 . . . P-K3?! 8 P × P, B × P; 9 N-B3, N-B3; 10 B-B4, N-K1; 11 Q-Q2 (not 11 N-QN5, B × NP and . . . B-K4), Q-K2; 12 R-Q1, N-K4; 13 N × N, P × N; 14 B-K3, P-B4; 15 P-B3, P-B5; 16 B-B2, N-B3; 17 O-O, KR-Q1; 17 N-Q5, Q-KB2 ∞. Rejfir̆-Korn, corr. 1965. However (2) 12 O-O-O! might have left Black critically cramped.

(*j*) 12 O-O, KR-N1; 13 Q-B2, P-R3; 14 B-KB4, P-N4 = . Calvo-Benko, Mallorca 1968. Black has play for the pawn but not more. Also compare King's Indian Defence, col. 26.

(*k*) For 6 P-B4 see King's Indian Defence, col. 23. The column is Mititelu-Velimirović, Novi Sad 1969 (with transposition).

1 P-Q4, N-KB3; 2 P-QB4, P-B4; 3 P-Q5, P-K4 (*a*); 4 N-QB3, P-Q3; 5 P-K4 (*b*)

	21	22	23	24	25
	P-KN3			B-K2!	
6	B-Q3 (*c*)		P-KR3	N-B3 (*i*)	
	N-R3	B-N2	B-N2	O-O	
7	KN-K2	KN-K2	P-KN4 (*g*)	B-Q3	B-K2
	B-N2? (*d*)	O-O!	N-R3	N-K1	QN-Q2
8	P-B3	P-KR3!	B-Q3	P-KR3	O-O
	N-B2	P-QR3	N-B2	P-QR3	N-K1
9	B-K3	B-N5	B-K3	P-R3	P-QR3 (*l*)
	P-QR3	P-R3	B-Q2	N-Q2	P-KN3
10	P-QR3	B-K3	P-R3	P-KN4	B-R6
	O-O	K-R2	R-N1	N-B2 (*j*)	N-N2
11	Q-Q2	Q-Q2	P-N4	P-N4	Q-Q2 (*m*)
	KN-K1 (*e*)	QN-Q2 (*f*)	P-N3 (*h*)	P-QN4! (*k*)	

(*a*) For 3 . . . P-KN3; 4 N-QB3, P-Q3; 5 P-K4, B-N2; 6 P-B4 see King's Indian Defence, col. 23.

(*b*) 5 N-KB3, B-K2! or 5 P-KN3, B-K2! will revert to the above columns.

(*c*) 6 B-K2! B-N2; 7 B-N5! P-KR3?! 8 B-K3, N-R3; 9 Q-B1 deserves thorough testing, to prove the merits of 5 . . . P-KN3. *Comments.*

(*d*) Better 7 . . . N-QN5; 8 B-N1, B-N2; 9 P-KR3, B-Q2; 10 B-K3, O-O; 11 Q-Q2, N-R3; 12 B-Q3, N-N5; 13 B-N1, N-R3; 14 P-R3, N-B2; 15 B-Q3, R-N1! = . Spasski-Petrosian, Moscow 1969.

(*e*) 12 P-KN4, P-R3; 13 P-KR4, K-R2; 14 N-N3, B-Q2; 15 P-N4 ± . Evans-Sherwin, Montreal 1956.

(*f*) 12 P-KN4, N-K1; 13 P-KR4 ± , Olafsson-Gufeld, Moscow 1961.

(*g*) Also 7 KN-K2, N-R3; 8 B-N5, N-B2; 9 Q-Q2, P-QR3; 10 P-QR4, R-QN1, 11 P-R5, P-N4; 12 P × P *e.p.*, R × P; 13 P-KN4, with a minimal advantage.

(*h*) 12 KN-K2, K-B1; 13 N-N3, P-KR4; 14 P-KN5! N-R2; 15 P-KR4 ± . Taimanov-Doda, Leningrad 1966.

(*i*) (A) Upon 6 P-KN3, P-QN4! is aggressive, but harmless in 6 . . . O-O; 7 B-N2, N-K1! 8 KN-K2, N-Q2; 9 O-O, P-KN3 = . Osnos-Yukhtman, USSR 1969. (B) 6 KN-K2, P-QR3 (6 . . . O-O? 7 N-N3, N-K1; 8 P-KR4!); 7 N-N3, P-KN3; 8 B-Q3, P-KR4; 9 O-O, P-R5; 10 KN-K2, N-R4; 11 B-K3, B-N4! = . Mühring-Ciocaltea, Zinnowitz 1966.

(*j*) 10 . . . P-KN3; 11 B-R6, N-N2; 12 P-N4, P-N3 = . Bukić-Ciocaltea, Szombathely 1966.

(*k*) 12 P × NP, RP × P; 13 B-K3, B-R3; 14 O-O, Q-N1 = . Mecking-Matanović, Sousse 1967.

(*l*) 9 N-K1, B-N4; 10 P-QR3, P-KN3 = . Sanguinetti-Jansa, Lugano 1968.

(*m*) Black has two equalizers, (A) 11 . . . K-R1; 12 P-QN4, P-N3; 13 KR-Q1, P-R3; 14 QR-N1, R-R2; 15 R-N2, Q-K1! = . Malich-Polugayevski, Havana 1966; or (B) 11 . . . N-B3; 12 P-QN4, P-N3; 13 N-K1, K-R1; 14 P × P, NP × P; 15 P-B4, N-N1 = . Uhlmann-Vasyukov, Hastings 1965-6.

1 P-Q4, N-KB3; 2 P-QB4, P-B4; 3 P-Q5, P-QN4

	26	27	28	29	30
4	P×P (a)				
	P-QR3				
5	P×P	....		P-K3	N-QB3 (o)
	B×P (b)			P-N3 (k)	P×P
6	P-KN3	N-QB3		N-QB3	P-K4
	P-Q3	P-N3		B-N2	P-N5 (p)
7	B-N2	N-B3 (e)		N-B3 (l)	N-N5
	P-N3	P-Q3		O-O	P-Q3
8	P-N3 (c)	P-KN3	P-K4 (h)	P-QR4 (m)	N-KB3 (g
	B-KN2	B-KN2	B×B	P×P	QN-Q2
9	B-N2	B-N2 (f)	K×B	B×P	B-KB4
	O-O	O-O	B-N2	P-Q3	N-R4
10	N-KR3	O-O	P-KN3 (i)	P-K4	B-N5
	QN-Q2	QN-Q2	O-O	B-QR3	N/4-B3
11	O-O (d)	Q-B2	K-N2	B-Q2	P-K5
		Q-R4 (g)	QN-Q2 (j)	N-K1 (n)	R-R4 =

(a) 4 N-KB3 (the gambit declined, just as it might by 4 P-QR4, P×BP; 5 N-QB3, P-Q3; 6 P-K4, P-N3! 7 B×P, B-KN2; 8 N-B3, B-N5; 9 P-R3, B×N; 10 Q×B, O-O =), B-N2 (if 4 ... P-K3? 5 B-N5!, leading into a good variation of the Blumenfeld Gambit; see Queen's Pawn Games); 5 P-QR4, P-N5; 6 QN-Q2, P-Q3; 7 P-K4, P-K4; 8 P×P, P×P, *e.p.* P×P; 9 B-Q3, P-K4! = .

(b) (A) 5 ... P-N3; 6 P-KN3 (6 N-QB3, B×P; 7 P-KN3, P-Q3; 8 B-N2, QN-Q2; 9 N-B3, B-KN2, 10 O-O, N-N3; 11 R-K1, O-O; 12 N-Q2 ∞. Alburt); P-Q3; 7 B-N2, B-KN2; 8 P-K4, O-O; 9 N-K2, (1) 9 ... QN×P, N×P!? 10 O-O, Q-N3; 11 N-Q2, N-KN5; 12 QN-B4 ± . (2) 9 ... B×P; 10 O-O, QN-Q2; 11 QN-B3, N-K4 = . Or the original "Volga Gambit". (B) 5 ... P-K3; 6 N-QB3, N×P; 7 N×N, P×N; 8 Q×P, N-B3; (1) 9 P-K3, B-K2; 10 B-B4, O-O; 11 N-B3, B×P; 12 B-Q2, 12 QN-B4 ± . (2) 9 N-B3, B×P; 10 N-K5, N×N; 11 Q×N, B-K2. (3) 9 P-K4, B-K2; 10 B-QB4, O-O; 11 N-B3, B×P; 12 B-Q2, Q-N3; 13 O-O! Q×P; 14 P-K5, N-Q5; 15 N×N, Q×N; 16 Q×Q, P×Q = . Sodomski-Prokhovski, corr. 1974.

(c) 8 N-KR3, QN-Q2; 9 P-N3, B-KN2; 10 B-N2, O-O; 11 O-O, Q-N3; 12 B-QB3, R-R2; 13 N-B4, KR-R1 = . Pytel-Schaufelberger, Biel 1974.

(d) Followed by 11 ... Q-B2 and ... KR-N1; or 11 ... Q-N3 = .

(e) 7 P-B4, P-Q3; (A) 8 N-B3! B-KN2; 9 P-K4, B×B; 10 R×B! O-O; 11 K-B2, Q-N3; 12 K-N1, N-R3; 13 P-K5, KN-Q2; 14 Q-K1, P-B5† = . (B) 8 P-K4, B-N2; 9 B-K2, O-O; 10 N-B3, Q-N3; 11 O-O, KN-Q2 = .

(f) 9 B-R3, O-O; 10 O-O, QN-Q2; 11 R-K1, N-N3 = . Szabó-Bellon, Montilla 1975. If 11 Q-B2, Q-B2 = .

(g) (A) 12 R-K1, N-N3; 13 P-K4, KN-Q2 = . (B) 12 R-N1, N-N3; 13 R-Q1, N-N5; 14 N-Q2, N-Q2 = . (C) 12 R-Q1, KR-N1; 13 B-Q2, N-K1; 14 B-R3, B-QB1 = . Hort-Benko, US Open Chp. 1974. (D) 12 N-Q2, N-K1 (12 KR-B1—Schwarz); 13 N-N3, Q-B2; 14 R-N1, N-N3 = . (E) B-Q2!.

(h) 8 N-Q2, (A) 8 ... B-N2; 9 P-K4, (1) 9 ... B×B; 10 N×B, O-O; 11 N-K3, QN-Q2; 12 O-O, Q-N3; 13 Q-B2, KR-N1; 14 R-N1, N-K1; 15 B-Q2 (or 15 P-N3!?), Q-R3; 16 P-N3, N-K4 = . Benko. (2) 9 ... O-O; 10 B×B, N×B; 11 O-O, KN-Q2; 12 N-B4, N-N3; 13 N-K3, Q-B2 = . Benko. (B) 8 ... Q-R4; 9 P-K4, B×B; 10 K×B, B-N2; 11 P-KN3, QN-Q2; 12 N-B4, Q-R3; 13 Q-K2, O-O; 14 K-N2, N-N3 = .

(i) Also 10 P-KR3 and 11 K-R2, to prevent Black's manoeuvre ... N-N5 and ... N-K4.

(j) *Informator* 24. Or 11 . . . Q–R4; 12 R–K1, KN–Q2; 13 R–K2, N–R3; 14 B–B4, KR–N1; 15 R–B1, R–R2; 16 Q–Q2 (Tarjan-Webb, Hastings 1977–78), R/2–N2! with at least equality.

(k) 5 . . . P–K3; (A) 6 N–QB3, (1) 6 . . . PR × P; 7 B × P, Q–R4; 8 B–Q2, N–R3; 9 B–B4, N–QN5; 10 N–K2! B–R3; 11 B × B, Q × B; 12 O–O, KN × P; 13 N × N, N × N; 14 P–K4 (Balogh-Korpas, Hungarian Chp. 1974), N–N5 = . (2) 6 P × QP; 7 N × P, B–N2; 8 N × N†, Q × N; 9 N–B3, B–Q3; 10 B–Q2, Q × P; 11 R–B1, O–O ∞. Schwarz. (B) 6 P × KP, BP × P; 7 N–Q2, P–Q4; 8 KN–B3, P–B5; 9 P × P, N × P; 10 B–K2, N–B4; 11 O–O, B–Q3; 12 Q–B2, B–R3; 13 P–QN3!. Schwarz.

(l) (A) 7 P–K4, P–Q3; 8 N–B3, O–O; 9 P–QR4, P–K3 = . Farago-Filipowicz, Polanica Zdroj 1977. (B) 7 P × P, O–O; 8 P–K4 (8 N–B3, N × RP!), P–Q3; 9 N–B3 = . (C) 7 Q–N3, P–Q3; 8 P–QR4! QN–Q2; 9 R–R3, O–O; 10 B–QB4, P × P; 11 P × P, B–N2 = . Baumbach-Grünberg, Erfurt 1973.

(m) 8 P × P, P–Q3; 9 B–K2, (A) 9 . . . N × RP; 10 O–O, Q–N3; 11 N–Q2, N–B2; 12 N–B4, Q–R2; 13 P–K4, B–QR3; 14 Q–B2, KR–N1 = . (B) 9 . . . B × P; 10 O–O, QN–Q2; 11 B × B, R × B; 12 Q–B2, Q–R1; 13 P–K4, KR–N1 ∞. Arnandov-Popov, Bulgarian Chp. 1973.

(n) 12 O–O, N–B2   . Portisch-Barlov, Belgrade 1975.

(o) 5 P–B3?! P–N3; 6 P–K4, P–Q3; 7 N–QB3, B–KN2; 8 B–N5, O–O; 9 Q–Q2 (or 9 P × P), R–K1 = .

(p) 6 . . . Q–R4; 7 P–K5, N–K5; 8 B–Q2, N × N; 9 P × N, P–B5. The column is analysis by Zaitsev.

(q) 8 B–KB4, P–N4; 9 B × NP, N × KP; 10 B–R4, B–KN2; 11 B–Q3, N–KB3; 12 N–KB3, QN–Q2; 13 O–O, B–N2; 14 N–N5, P–R3; 15 N–K6, P × N; 16 P × P, O–O; 17 P × N, Q × P; 18 R–B1, B–B3 ∓. Halldorson-Benko, New York 1978.

1 P-Q4, P-QB4 (*a*); 2 P-Q5 (*b*)

	31	32	33	34	35
	P-K4		P-B4	P-Q3 (*i*)	
3	P-K4		P-K4	P-K4	
	P-Q3		P×P	P-KN3	
4	B-Q3	N-QB3 (*e*)	N-QB3	N-QB3	N-KB3
	N-Q2 (*c*)	N-K2 (*f*)	N-KB3	B-N2	B-N2
5	Q-K2	P-KN3	B-KN5	N-KB3 (*j*)	B-K2
	P-KN3	N-N3	P-Q3	N-KB3	N-QR3 (*n*)
6	N-QB3	P-KR4	Q-Q2	B-K2 (*k*)	O-O
	B-N2	B-K2	Q-R4	N-R3 (*l*)	N-B2
7	P-B4	P-R5	B×N	O-O	N-B3
	N-R3	N-B1	KP×B	N-B2	N-B3!
8	N-B3	B-N5†	P-B3	P-QR4!	N-Q2
	P-B3	QN-Q2	B-K2	P-QR3!	O-O
9	O-O	P-R4	P×P	N-Q2	P-QR4
	O-O	P-QR3	O-O	B-Q2	P-N3
10	K-R1	B-K2	N-B3	P-K5!	N-B4
	P×P (*d*)	P-R3 (*g*)	N-Q2 = (*h*)	P×P (*m*)	B-QR3 =

(*a*) 1 . . . P-KN3; 2 P-QB4, P-QB4; 3 P-Q5, P-K4; 4 P-K4, B-N2; 5 N-QB3, P-Q3; 6 B-K2, (A) 6 . . . P-B4; 7 P×P, P×P; 8 B-R5†, K-B1; 9 N-B3, B-B3! = . Bagirov-Razuvayev, USSR Chp. 1977. (B) 6 . . . N-KR3; 7 N-B3, O-O; 8 O-O, P-B4 = .

(*b*) (A) 2 P-K4, see Indian Defence (and for 2 . . . P×P; 3 P-QB3 see Morra Gambit). (B) 2 N-KB3, N-KB3; (1) 3 P-Q5, P-QN4; 4 B-N5! (4 P-B4, B-N2; 5 N-B3, P-N5; 6 Q-N3, Q-R4; 7 N-Q1, P-K3 = . Guimard-Keres, Göteborg 1955), B-N2; 5 B×N, KP×B (5 . . . NP×B!?); 6 P-K4!, P-QR3; 7 B-K2, B-Q3!?; 8 P-QR4, Q-N3; 9 P×P, P×P; 10 R×R, B×R; 11 N-B3, P-N5; 12 N-QN5, O-O; 13 O-O (Browne-Korchnoi. Wijk aan Zee 1980), 13 . . . R-K1! ∞. Compare Queen's Pawn Games, Torre Attack, note (*j*). (2) 3 P-K3, P-KN3; 4 N-QB3, see King's Indian Defence.

(*c*) A line still of undecided value. Upon (A) 4 . . . N-K2; 5 N-K2, P-KN3 is playable, but not 5 . . . N-Q2; 6 O-O, N-KN3; 7 P-QR4, B-K2; 8 N-Q2, P-QR3; 9 QN-B4, QR-N1; 10 P-R5, with some pressure. Filip-Lundquist, Mariánské Lázne 1961. (B) 4 . . . P-KN3; (1) 5 N-KB3, B-N2; 6 O-O, N-KR3; 7 N-B3, O-O; 8 P-QR4, N-Q2; 9 N-QN5, N-QN1; 10 P-B3, P-R3; 11 N-R3, P-B3; 12 N-B4, N-B2 = . Wexler-Trifunović, Amsterdam 1950. (2) 5 P-KB4?! P×P; 6 B×P, B-N2; 7 N-KB3, B×P; 8 QN-Q2, B×R; 9 Q×B, Q-B3; 10 Q×Q, N×Q; 11 B×P±. Krylov-Brix, Bratislava 1948. 5 . . . B-N2; 6 N-KB3, P-B3! 7 N-B3, P-QR3; 8 P-QR4, Q-R4; 9 O-O, P-QN4; 10 B-Q2, Q-B2! ±. Korn-E. Richter, corr. 1947-8.

(*d*) 11 ᵥB×P, N-B2; 12 P-QR4, P-KN4; 13 B-K3, R-K1; 14 N-Q2, QN-K4; 15 N-B4, B-N5 = . Sajtar-Basyuni, Mariánské Lázne 1954.

(*e*) (A) 4 P-KB4, P×P; 5 B×P, N-K2; 6 B-N5†, B-Q2; 7 B×B†, Q×B; 8 N-KB3, N-N3 = . Kmoch. (B) 4 P-QB4, B-K2; 5 N-QB3, B-N4; 6 N-B3, B×B; 7 R×B, N-KB3; 8 B-K2, O-O; 9 O-O, N-R3; 10 P-KR3, N-B2 = . *Comments*. (C) 4 P-KN3, P-B4; 5 B-N2, N-KB3; 6 N-QB3, B-K2; 7 KN-K2, P-QN4; 8 N×P, N×P; 9 B×N, P×B; 10 QN-B3, O-O; 11 O-O, B-R6; 12 R-K1, N-Q2; 13 N×P, N-B3 = . Pachman.

(*f*) Or (A) 4 . . . P-QR3; 5 P-QR4, P-KN3; 6 P-R4, P-KR4; 7 N-B3, B-N5; 8 B-K2, B×N; 9 B×B, N-Q2; 10 P-R5, B-R3; 11 B×B, N×B; 12 Q-Q2, P-B3; 13 N-Q1, P-B4∞. Antoshin-Belov, Moscow 1962; or (B) 4 . . . P-KN3; 5 B-K2 (5 P-B4?! P×P; 6 B×P, N-B3; 7 N-B3, B-N5! =), B-N2; 6 N-B3, N-KB3 = (6 . . . N-K2? 7 P-KR4! P-KR4; 8 N-Q2! Ghitescu-Larsen, Büsum 1969); or (C) 4 . . . B-K2! 5 B-Q3, B-N4; 6 N-B3, B×B; etc., as in col. 26, or finally (D) 4 . . . N-KB3; 5 N-B3, B-K2; 6 B-K2, O-O; 7 O-O, QN-Q2 = . Hort.

(g) 11 B–K3, B–N4; 12 Q–Q2, N–R2; 13 N–B3, B × B; 14 Q × B, O–O = . Alekhin-Castillo, Buenos Aires 1939.

(h) Hudy-Tompa, Hungary 1969. A "Dutch" type defence

(i) (A) 2 . . . N–KB3; 3 N–QB3, P–K4; 4 P–K4 see col. 29, note ((f)–(4)). If 4 P × P *e.p.*, BP × P; 5 P–K4, N–B3! = . For (B) 2 . . . P–K3; 3 P–K4 see Queen's Pawn Games, Franco-Benoni. For 2 . . . N–KB3; 3 B–N5 see Queen's Pawn Games, Trompovsky Attack.

(j) 5 P–B4, N–KB3; 6 B–N5†, KN–Q2; 7 P–QR4, O–O; 8 N–B3, N–R3; 9 B × QN, P × B; 10 P–R5, R–N1; 11 O–O, R–N5 ∞. Shachurov-Goldberg, Moscow Chp. 1963.

(k) 6 B–N5†, QN–Q2; 7 P–QR4, O–O; 8 O–O, P–QR3 = .

(l) 6 . . . O–O; 7 O–O, B–N5! 8 N–Q2, B × B; 9 Q × B, P–K3; 10 N–B4, P × P; 11 P × P, R–K1; 12 Q–B3, QN–Q2; 13 B–B4, N–K4; 14 B × N, P × B; 15 KR–K1, N–Q2; 16 P–Q6, N–N3; 17 N × N, Q × N; 18 P–Q7, R–K3 with excellent counter-play. Corral-Stein, Las Palmas 1973.

(m) 11 N–B4, P–QN4; 12 P × P, P × P; 13 R × R, Q × R; 14 N × KP, P–N5; 15 P–Q6! P × P! = . Larsen-Szabó, Büsum 1969.

(n) 5 . . . B–N5; 6 KN–Q2! B × B; 7 Q × B, N–Q2! Marić. The column is Larsen's comment in *Informator* 7.

Dutch Defence

(1 P–Q4, P–KB4)

Occasionally favoured by Morphy in the mid-nineteenth century, this aggressive defence caught on only after Botvinnik's success with it in his 1933 match with Flohr and at Nottingham in 1936. It was then adopted by Alekhin, Alexander, Bronstein, R. Byrne, Tartakover, and Guimard. But when Alekhin discarded it and Botvinnik's ardour cooled, it went under a cloud. Today it is considered sound but unfashionable—*pro tem!*

The main idea of the Dutch is control of Black's K5 coupled with the use of the king's bishop and king's knight files for a possible attack. White strives for P–K4 and penetration on the queen's wing. The result is imbalance, tension, and lively tactics. Whatever its intrinsic value, the Dutch works well in practice and has a real sting. Again, the idea of a timely KBP-push of Black's has inspired a few other Indian-system variations and Flank openings.

Development and pawn-chains are much influenced by the action of White's king's knight. When it is developed at KR3, in conjunction with the fianchetto of the king's bishop, Black counters best with . . . P–Q3 and . . . P–K4 because the Stonewall would permit White a rapid P–KB3 and P–K4. With the king's knight on KB3 Black may enter the typical Stonewall granite formation of the pawns on Q4, QB3, K3.

THE MODERN SYSTEM (cols. 1–10) arises after 2 P–KN3, and White's KNP-fianchetto effectively stops Black's king's side attack and deflects the strategy into positional lines.

The *Stonewall Formation* (cols. 1–3) comes about with 6 . . . P–Q4. The game remains closed and the ideas are clear-cut. Black just fails to equalize but White needs the utmost skill to exploit his spatial advantage.

The *Fluid Formation* (cols. 4–5) with 6 . . . P–Q3 is currently Black's better choice.

401

Black's early "Dutch Indian" counter fianchetto . . . P–KN3 is an attempt to break out of the conventional pattern in cols. 1–6 but also exists due to the fact that with the contemporary trend of "closed" openings, the Dutch Defence often occurs after, e.g. 1 P–KN3, P–KB4; 2 B–N2, N–KB3; 3 N–KB3 or 3 P–B4, thus precluding a Stonewall Formation and favouring . . . P–KN3 at some early stage. These lines are exemplified in the *Leningrad Variation* 2 . . . P–KN3; 3 B–N2 (cols. 7–8) which, however, still is under a cloud in col. 7. Again, as against a nondescript geographical denomination, we have chosen the functional term *Dutch-Indian.*

Based on the same strategic idea but more refined is the *Antoshin Variation* 2 . . . N–KB3; 3 B–N2, P–Q3 (cols. 9–10) and therefore merits attention as an alternative.

Cols. 7–10 must be scrutinized in close conjunction with the English Opening, the Robatsch, the Dutch Réti line of the Réti Opening, and also with the Unorthodox Flank Openings. They all contain their hidden nuances of favourable transpositions or hold-backs, awaiting the right moment to utilize either White's P–Q3 or P–Q4 pushes, or of . . . P–K3. Likewise, the appropriate choice of playing P–K3 or P–KN3 enters the picture.

THE CLASSICAL SYSTEM, with 2 P–QB4, (cols. 11–13) has, true to its name, become dormant and will only revive after new paths have been opened.

THE STAUNTON GAMBIT, 2 P–K4 (cols. 16–20) is without doubt fully sound as far as gambits go—and refutes at once the long-range objectives of the Dutch Defence. But Black's resources appear adequate for keeping the balance of the changed battle field.

Summing up, despite Black's added tactical ideas, and although the Defence as a whole now requires less space than in previous editions, it still contains unexpected resources which are ever so often being exploited as evidenced by recent games quoted in cols. 10, 15, etc.

1 P-Q4, P-KB4; 2 P-KN3, P-K3; 3 B-N2, N-KB3; 4 N-KB3, B-K2; 5 O-O, O-O; 6 P-B4

	1	2	3	4	5
	P-Q4 (Stonewall Formation)............			P-Q3 (f) (Fluid Formation)	
7	Q-B2.......	P-N3 (c)		N-B3	
	P-B3	N-B3.......	P-B3	Q-K1.......	P-QR4
8	QN-Q2 (a)	N-K5	B-QR3	P-N3 (g)	Q-B2 (h)
	Q-K1	B-Q2	P-QN3	P-QR4	N-B3
9	N-K5	P×P	B×B	B-N2	P-K4
	QN-Q2	P×P	Q×B	QN-Q2	N-QN5
10	N-Q3	N-QB3	N-K5	Q-B2	Q-K2
	K-R1	B-K1	B-N2	N-N5	P×P
11	R-N1	B-N5	N-Q2	P-KR3	N×P
	N-K5	N-K5	QN-Q2	N-R3	N×N
12	N-B3	B×B	N×N	P-K3	Q×N
	P-KN4	N×B	N×N	P-KN4 ·	P-K4 =
13	P-QN4	R-B1	P-K3	N-K2	
	B-B3 (b)	N-N3 (d)	QR-B1 (e)	P-B3 =	

(a) Another method is 8 N-B3, Q-K1; 9 B-B4, Q-R4; 10 QR-Q1, QN-Q2; 11 P-N3, K-R1; 12 P-K3, N-K5; 13 B-B7! ± .

(b) 14 N/B3-K5, N-Q3; 15 P-B5, N-B2; 16 P-B4, QN×N; 17 QP×N, B-N2; 18 P-QR4 ± . Reshevsky-Guimard, Buenos Aires 1960.

(c) 7 N-B3, P-B3; 8 R-N1, K-R1; 9 P×P, BP×P; 10 B-B4, N-B3; 11 N-K5, B-Q2; 12 R-B1, R-B1; 13 Q-Q3, N-KR4 = .

(d) 14 P-B4, N×N; 15 BP×N, B-R4; 16 Q-Q3, P-B3 = . Vladimirov-Smyslov, USSR Chp. 1961.

(e) 14 R-B1, P-B4; 15 Q-K2 (Botvinnik-Bronstein, match 1951), B-R3 = .

(f) (A) Out of fashion is Alekhin's 6 . . . N-K5; (1) 7 P-Q5! B-B3; 8 Q-B2, P-QR4; 9 QN-Q2, N×N; 10 N×N ± . (2) 7 QN-Q2, B-B3; 8 Q-B2, P-Q4; 9 P-N3, P-B3; 10 P-K3, N-Q2; 11 B-N2, K-R1 = . *Comments.* (B) Cramped is 6 . . . P-B3; 7 Q-B2, P-QN3; 8 QN-Q2, Q-B2; 9! N-K5, B-N2; 10 N-Q3! QN-Q2; 11 P-QN4 (Portisch-Radulov, Budapest 1969), B-Q3 = .

(g) (A) 8 Q-B2, N-B3; 9 P-Q5, N-QN5; 10 Q-N3, N-R3; 11 P×P, N-B4; 12 Q-B2, B×P; 13 P-N3, KN-K5 = . *Comments* (B) 8 R-K1, (1) 8 . . . N-K5; 9 Q-B2, Q-N3; 10 B-K3, N×N; 11 Q×N, N-B3; 12 P-QN4, B-B3; 13 P-N5, N-Q1; 14 P-B5, N-B2; 15 P×P, P×P; 16 N-Q2, P-K4 = . (2) 8 . . . Q-N3; 9 P-K4, N×P; 10 N×N, P×N; 11 R×P, N-B3; 12 R-K2 = .

(h) 8 R-K1, N-K5; 9 Q-B2, N-QB3 (or 9 . . . N×N?! *Comments*); 10 N×N, N-N5; 11 Q-N1, P×N; 12 Q×P, P-K4; 13 P-N4! P×P! 14 N×P, B-R5; 15 B-K3, R-K1; 16 Q-B4, R-B1; drawn. Reshevsky-Larsen, Santa Monica 1966. The column is Reshevsky-Udovćić, Maribor 1967.

1 P-Q4, P-KB4; 2 P-KN3

	6	7	8	9	10
	(P-K3)	P-KN3 Dutch-	....	N-KB3 Antoshin's	
3	(B-N2)	B-N2 Indian		B-N2 Variation	
	(N-KB3)	B-N2	N-KB3	P-Q3	P-KN3
4	N-KR3	N-KR3 (c)	N-KB3	P-QB4	N-KB3
	B-K2	N-QB3	B-N2	P-B3	B-N2
5	O-O	P-Q5	O-O (e)	N-QB3	P-QB4
	O-O	N-K4	O-O	Q-B2	O-O
6	P-QB4	N-B3	P-B4 (f)	N-B3 (k)	O-O (o)
	P-Q3	N-KB3	P-Q3	P-K4!	P-Q3
7	N-B3	P-K4	N-B3!	O-O (l)	P-Q5
	Q-K1	P-Q3	P-B3! (g)	P-K5 (m)	QN-Q2
8	P-K4 (a)	N-B4	P-Q5!? (h)	N-K1	N-B3
	P×P	P-B3	P-K4!	B-K2	N-B4 (p)
9	N-B4	O-O	P×P e.p. (i)	P-B3	Q-B2
	P-B3 (b)	O-O (d)	B×P (j)	P×P (n)	P-QR4 =

(a) 8 N-B4, B-Q1; 9 P-K4, P-K4; 10 QP×P, QP×P; 11 N-Q3, P×P; 12 N×P, N-B3; 13 R-K1, Q-N3 = . Levenfish-Ryumin, USSR Chp. 1934.

(b) 10 QN×P, N×N; 11 B×N, P-K4 = . Reshevsky-Botvinnik, The Hague 1948.

(c) 4 N-KB3, N-QB3; 5 P-N3, P-Q3; 6 B-N2, N-R3; 7 N-B3, P-K3; 8 Q-Q2, N-B2 might maintain a—precarious—balance. Cols. 7-8 are also called the "Leningrad Variation" but the move N-KR3 was already anticipated at Karlsbad (Karlovy Vary) in 1923.

(d) 10 KP×P, B×P; 11 QN-K2, P×P; 12 N-Q4, Q-Q2; 13 N×B, P×N; 14 N×P, P-K3; 15 N×N† ± . Pachman-Alexander, Hastings 1954-5. Also compare col. 10.

(e) If 5 P-N3!? P-K3 (5 . . . P-Q3; 6 B-N2, P-B3; 7 QN-Q2, Q-B2; 8 O-O, O-O; 9 P-B4 with a somewhat cramped "Antoshin" position.) 6 B-N2, P-Q4; 7 P-B4, P-B3; 8 O-O, O-O; 9 N-B3, QN-Q2; 10 P-K3, Q-B2; 11 N-K2, R-K1; 12 R-B1, N-K5 with a very fluid game on both wings.

(f) (A) *P/E* give 6 P-Q5, P-Q3 (6 . . . P-QN3; 7 N-B3, B-N2; or even first 6 . . . P-QR4 or 6 . . . P-B3 are safer); 7 N-Q4, Q-K1!? 8 N-QB3, P-B3; 9 B-N5, B-Q2; 10 B×N, B×B ∞. (B) 6 P-N3 (1) 6 . . . N-K5; 7 B-N2, P-B4; 8 P-B4, N-QB3; 9 P-K3 ± . (2) 6 . . . P-Q3! 7 B-N2, P-B4; 8 P-B4, N-B3; 9 P-K3, P-K4?!

(g) 7 . . . N-B3; 8 P-Q5! (A) 8 . . . N-K4; 9 N×N, P×N; 10 Q-N3, P-K3; 11 R-Q1, P×P; 12 P×P, K-R1; 13 B-K3 ± . (B) 8 . . . N-QR4; 9 Q-R4, P-B4; 10 P×P e.p., P×P; 11 N-Q4, B-Q2 = . Kuzminikh.

(h) Also (A) 8 R-K1, N-R3; 9 P-N3, B-Q2; 10 B-N2, Q-R4; 11 P-K4, P×P; 12 N×P, N×N; 13 R×N, QR-K1 = . Kuzminikh. (B) 8 Q-B2, K-R1 (or 8 . . . N-R4); 9 B-N5, B-K3 = . Mecking-Botvinnik, Hastings 1966.

(i) 9 P×P, P×P, 10 P-N3 is to be considered.

(j) 10 P-N3, N-R4 = . *Comments* to Kuzminikh's analysis.

(k) 6 P-Q5, P-KN3; 7 N-B3, B-N2; 8 O-O, O-O; 9 P-K4, P×QP! = .

(l) 7 P×P, P×P; 8 O-O, B-N5! 9 Q-B2, P-K5; 10 N-Q4, O-O; 11 B-B4, Q-B2 = . Seleznev-Antoshin, USSR 1961.

(m) 7 . . . B-K2; 8 P-B5! P-K5; 9 P×P, B×P; 10 N-K5 ± . Udovćić-Lombardy, Zagreb 1969.

(n) 10 B×P, O-O; 11 N-N2, QN-Q2; 12 B-B4, R-B2; 13 P-B5, N-B1 = . Antoshin.

(o) 6 N-QB3, P-Q3; (A) 7 N-B4, P-B3; 8 P-Q5, P-K4; 9 P×P e.p., N-R3; 10 O-O, Q-K2; 11 R-K1, P-KN4; 12 N-Q3, N-K5 = . Portisch-Naranja, Palma de Mallorca 1970. (B) 7 O-O, P-K4! 8 P×P, P×P; 9 Q×Q, R×Q; 10 N-Q5, R-Q2 ∞. (C) 7 P-Q5, P-B3! 8 O-O!

P–K4; 9 P × P *e.p.*, B × P; 10 P–N3, N–R3; 11 B–N2, Q–K2 = . Taimanov-Knežević, Slančev Brag 1974.

(*p*) Confined but solid is 8 . . . N–K4; 9 P–N3, P–B3; 10 B–N2, B–Q2; 11 N–B4, R–B1. Compare col. 8. This column is *Comments* to the Karlsbad-Antoshin Variation.

1 P–Q4, P–KB4

	11	12	13	14	15
2	P–QB4				N–QB3 (*k*)
	P–K3			P–KN3	P–Q4
3	P–KN3		N–KB3 (*h*)	N–QB3	B–N5
	N–KB3		P–Q4	N–KR3	N–KB3
4	B–N2		P–K3	P–K4	P–K3 (*l*)
	B–K2	B–N5†	P–B3	P–Q3	P–K3
5	N–QB3	B–Q2 (*d*)	B–Q3	P–QN3	B–Q3
	O–O	Q–K2 (*e*)	N–B3	B–N2	B–K2
6	P–K3 (*a*)	N–KB3 (*f*)	O–O	B–N2	N–B3
	P–Q4 (*b*)	O–O	B–Q3	O–O	O–O
7	KN–K2	O–O	P–QN3	N–B3	O–O
	P–B3	B × B	O–O	N–B3	N–K5
8	P–N3	Q × B	B–R3	B–K2	B × B
	B–Q3	N–K5	N–K5	P–K4	Q × B
9	O–O	Q–B2	B × B	P × KP	N–K5
	Q–K2 (*c*)	P–Q3 (*g*)	Q × B (*i*)	N × P (*j*)	N–Q2 (*m*)

(*a*) Equally tame are (A) 6 Q–N3; N–B3; 7 P–Q5, N–K4; 8 P × P, P × P; 9 B–B4, KN–Q2; 10 R–Q1, Q–K1; 11 N–N5, B–Q1; 12 N–KR3, P–QR3 = ; and (B) 6 P–Q5 P–K4! 7 P–K4, P–Q3; 8 KN–K2, P × P; 9 N × P, N × N; 10 B × N, N–Q2; 11 N–B3, N–B4; 12 B–N2, Q–K1 = .

(*b*) Also 6 . . . P–Q3; 7 KN–K2, P–B3; 8 O–O, P–K4; 9 P–Q5, Q–K1; 10 P–K4, N–R3 = .

(*c*) 10 Q–B2, N–K5; 11 B–N2 = . *Comments.*

(*d*) (A) 5 N–B3 is also playable. (B) N–Q2, O–O; 6 N–B3, P–Q4 = .

(*e*) 5 . . . B × B†; 6 Q × B, O–O; 7 N–QB3, P–Q3; 8 N–B3, N–B3; 9 O–O, P–K4; 10 B × B†; 6 Q × B, P–Q5, N–K2; 11 P–K4, N–N3; also equalizes, but inferior is (B) 5 . . . B–K2; 6 Q–N3, P–Q4 (6 . . . O–O; 7 N–QB3, P–QR4; 8 N–R3 ±); 7 B–N4, B × B†; 8 Q × B N–B3; 9 Q–R4, B–Q2; 10 P × P! P × P; 11 N–QB3, N–K2; 12 Q–N3 ± .

(*f*) 6 N–KR3, O–O; 7 O–O, B × B; 8 N × B, P–Q3; 9 Q–B2, QN–Q2 = .

(*g*) 10 N–B3, N × N; 11 Q × N, N–Q2 = . *Comments.*

(*h*) (A) 3 N–QB3, N–KB3; 4 N–B3, B–N5; 5 B–Q2, O–O; 6 P–K3, P–QN3; 7 B–Q3, B–N2; 8 O–O, KB × N; 9 B × B, N–K5 = . *Comments.* (B) 3 P–K4!? (the Staunton Gambit Deferred), P × P; 4 N–QB3, N–KB3; 5 P–B3! P × P; 6 N × P, P–QN3; 7 B–Q3, B–N2; 8 B–N5, B–K2; 9 Q–B2, N–B3; 10 P–QR3 ± .

(*i*) 10 N–K5, N–Q2; 11 P–B4, P–QN3; 12 N–Q2, P–B4 = . Pachman-Evans, Buenos Aires 1960. The column arose after 1 P–Q4, P–Q4; 2 P–QB4, P–K3; 3 N–KB3, P–QB3; 4 P–K3, P–KB4!

(*j*) 10 P × P, N × KBP; 11 O–O, B–Q2; 12 Q–Q2, drawn. Flohr-Euwe, Holland 1969.

(*k*) 2 N–KB3, P–K3; 3 P–B3, N–KB3; 4 B–N5, B–K2; 5 QN–Q2, N–K5! = .

(*l*) 4 B × N, KP × B (4 . . . NP × B! 5 P–K3, P–B3 = . *Comments*); 5 P–K3, B–K3! 6 B–Q3, P–KN3; 7 Q–B3! P–B3; 8 KN–K2, N–Q2; 9 P–KR3, Q–N3; 10 P–KN4! (Browne-R. Byrne, US Chp. 1977), P × P; 11 P × P, B–B2; 12 O–O–O, O–O–O! 13 N–B4, B–Q3 with White pressuring on the file. *Informator* 24.

(*m*) 10 N/5 × N, B × N; 11 N–K2, N–Q3; 12 Q–Q2, P–K4; 13 P × P, Q × P; 14 Q–B3, Q × Q; drawn. Smyslov-Guimard, Havana, 1962.

1 P-Q4, P-KB4 (*a*); 2 P-K4, P×P (*b*); 3 N-QB3, N-KB3 (*c*)

	16	17	18	19	20
4	P-B3	P-KN4	B-KN5		
	N-B3	P-KR3 (*e*)	N-B3	P-KN3	P-B3
5	P×P	P-N5	P-Q5	B-QB4! (*h*)	P-B3
	P-K4	P×P	N-K4	P-Q4	Q-R4
6	P×P	B×P	Q-Q4	B×N	B-Q2
	QN×P	P-Q4	N-B2	P×B	P-K6
7	N-B3	P-B3	B×N	B×P	B×P
	P-Q3	B-B4	KP×B	P-KB4	P-K4
8	B-KB4	B-N2	N×P	Q-K2	Q-Q2
	N×N† (*d*)	P×P	P-KB4	P-B3	B-N5
9	Q×N	N×P (*f*)	N-N3	B-N3	KN-K2
	B-K3	P-B3	P-KN3	Q×P	O-O
10	B-Q3	Q-Q2	O-O-O	N-B3	O-O-O
	B-K2 =	QN-Q2 (*g*)	B-R3† =	Q-B3 (*i*)	P×P =

(*a*) (A) 1 . . . P-K3; 2 P-QB4, (1) 2 . . . P-KB4 averts the Staunton Gambit. (2) 2 . . . B-N5†; 3 N-B3, P-KB4 is the Franco-Indian and for 3 N-KB3; see Nimzo-Indian Defence. (B) 1 . . . P-Q3; 2 P-K4 see Pirc (or Robatsch) Defence.

(*b*) 2 . . . P-Q3? (Balogh); 3 P×P, B×P; 4 Q-B3, Q-B1; 5 B-Q3, B-N5 .

(*c*) Black merely shirks the issue if he plays 3 . . . P-KN3; 4 P-B3! or 4 P-KR4! B-N2; 5 P-R5, N-KB3; 6 P-R6, B-B1; 7 B-KN5, P-Q4; 8 P-B3, Q-Q3; 9 Q-Q2, P×P; 10 P×P, with attack.

(*d*) Also 8 . . . N-N3; 9 B-N3, N-R4; 10 B-B2, N/4-B5; 11 B-Q4 ± . In the column, also 7 . . . B-Q3; 8 N-QN5, N×N†; 9 Q×N, B-K4 = . *Comments.*

(*e*) (A) 4 . . . P-K3; 5 P-N5, N-Q4; 6 N×P ± . (B) 4 . . . P-Q4; 5 P-N5, N-N1; 6 P-B3, P-K4; 7 QP×P, B-N5; 8 P×P, P-Q5; 9 P-QR3, B-R4; 10 P-N4, P×N = .

(*f*) 9 Q×P, P-K3; 10 KN-K2, B-K2 ± . Pachman.

(*g*) 11 O-O-O, Q-R4; 12 K-N1, O-O-O; 12 P-KR4, N-K5 . *Comments.*

(*h*) Also 5 P-KR4, P-Q4; 6 P-R5, B-B4; 7 B×N, P×B; 8 N-KR3 ± . Kuzminikh.

(*i*) 11 O-O-O, B-K2 ∞. Khachaturov.

Flank Openings

English Opening

(1 P–QB4)

The English derives its name from its association with Howard Staunton who played it against St. Amant in their match (1843) and again in the England *v.* France team match (1843) as well as the historic 1851 London Tournament. Staunton realized that White had a Sicilian Defence with a move in hand. "This way of opening the game, although not usual, is perfectly safe," he observed. Like many another début, however, it was unpopular at the beginning. Zukertort, Steinitz, Mason, and Rubinstein kept it alive. It was not until after World War I that Nimzowitsch, Réti, and Tartakover revived and moulded it into a definite weapon. Today it is accepted as routine—Botvinnik, Keres, and Smyslov can be added to its leading exponents.

The English is one of the "positional" openings—a typical product of the reversal in chess ideology produced by the hypermodern revolution. White concentrates on speedy development, striking at his Q5 square. The theory is that, if Black plays in the centre, White will counter there effectively; if not, a centre advance after both sides are fully developed will not be easy for Black to meet. In addition the numerous transpositional possibilities require both players to stay on their toes. A quick switch into the Grünfeld, Nimzo-Indian, King's Indian, Queen's Gambit, Dutch, Benoni or Réti is normal. Equally so can many lines be arrived at via the King's Indian Attack, or a Fianchetto opening. Nevertheless, Black has so many good systems at his disposal that often his only practical problem is which one to select! In Europe the opening is sometimes dubbed the "Sicilian Attack."

The Four Knights' Variation 1 P–QB4, P–K4; 2 N–QB3, N–KB3; 3 N–B3, N–B3 (cols. 1–5) leads to a Sicilian Defence with colours reversed. 4 P–Q4 is most logical. In the Sicilian, Black must fight hard for . . . P–Q4; once he plays it he obtains almost certain equality. Here the extra

411

tempo is naturally beneficial, but Black can achieve equality best by 4 . . . P×P as in col. 2, where he gives up one or two bishops in order to wreck White's pawn structure.

4 P–K4 was one of Nimzowitsch's favourites. White hopes to play P–Q4 later with some impact, but the temporary hole created there can be utilized in several ways to equalize (col. 3).

4 P–KN3 is an attempt to steer for the Dragon Variation with colours reversed. The trouble is Black can aim for simplicity (col. 4) in order to obtain even chances. Korchnoi used this device in 1978 against Karpov.

Another fourth move for White is 4 P–Q3 (col. 5). The pattern is similarly dull.

THE ACCELERATED FIANCHETTO with 3 P–KN3 (cols. 6–10), also known as *Carls' or Bremen System*, is less committal since White keeps the diagonal open before playing N–KB3. Keres' 3 . . . P–B3 is a dynamic and effective way of securing equality (cols. 8–10). This line too is still much alive, as is the Dutch pattern (cols. 11–12) which is a little "loose" but also secures even chances. Against 2 . . . N–QB3 (cols. 13–15) White can play a reversed Closed System of the Sicilian where he breaks with P–K3 and P–Q4, but actually no antidote has been found.

1 P–QB4, N–KB3; 2 N–QB3 (cols. 16–24) involves systems where Black refrains from breaking the symmetry with an early P–K4; 2 . . . P–K3 (cols. 16–22) can lead to a Nimzo-Indian pattern and col. 16 resembles a Queen's Indian; whereas 2 . . . P–Q4 (cols. 23–4) leads satisfactorily to a Grünfeld pattern, and 2 . . . P–B3 to a Slav pattern. All these lines entail jockeying for position; White can hope for no more than a minimal edge with little danger of complications. Where these lines are coupled with White's delayed move P–Q4, comparison with the Queen's Gambit and Queen's Pawn sections is called for: they are all solid.

THE SYMMETRICAL VARIATION proper, involving . . . P–QB4 either on the first or second move is handled in cols. 26–40. This system, which Tarrasch ridiculed as modest, unambitious, imitative, and a horror to all true friends of the noble game can lead to deadeye equality. On the other hand, this symmetry can be very deceiving. As scrutiny of the columns and notes will disclose, and as proved by the revised columns, the symmetrical "ouverture" allows a plethora of transposition from and into dangerous lines of the Sicilian Defence (Maróczy Bind), the Fianchetto Opening, the Benoni or the King's Indian Attack and constant referral to other sections is advisable.

1 P–QB4, P–K4; 2 N–QB3, N–KB3; 3 N–B3, N–B3

	1	2	3	4	5
4	P–Q4		P–K4	P–KN3	P–Q3 (*m*)
	P–K5	P × P	B–N5 (*g*)	B–B4 (*j*)	P–Q3
5	N–Q2 (*a*)	N × P	P–Q3	B–N2 (*k*)	P–KN3
	N × P (*b*)	B–N5 (*d*)	P–Q3	P–Q3	P–KN3
6	N/2 × P	B–N5 (*e*)	B–K2 (*h*)	O–O	B–N2
	N × N	P–KR3	O–O	O–O	B–N2
7	N × N	B–R4	O–O	P–Q3!?	R–QN1
	B–N5†	B × N†	B × N	B–K3	O–O
8	B–Q2	P × B	P × B	P–QR3	O–O
	B × B†	P–Q3	Q–K2	P–QR4	P–QR4 (*n*)
9	Q × B	P–B3	N–K1	B–N5	P–QR3
	N–K3 (*c*)	O–O (*f*)	N–K1 (*i*)	P–KR3 (*l*)	R–K1 (*o*)

(*a*) 5 N–KN5, P–KR3; 6 KN × KP, N × N; 7 N × N, Q–R5! 8 N–B3, Q × QP = .

(*b*) 5 . . . B–N5; 6 P–K3, B × N; 7 P × B, O–O; 8 B–R3, R–K1; 9 Q–B2, P–Q3; 10 P–B5, P–Q4; 11 P–R3, B–K3; 12 B–K2, Q–Q2 = . Steinmeyer-Benko, US Open 1959.

(*c*) 10 P–KN3, O–O; 11 B–N2, P–Q3 = . Botvinnik-Flohr, match 1933. Also 7 Q × N!

(*d*) 5 . . . B–B4; 6 N × N, NP × N; 7 P–KN3, P–KR4; 8 B–N2, P–R5; 9 O–O, P × P; 10 P × P, Q–K2; 11 B–B4, B–N2; 12 P–R3, N–R4; 13 P–K3 ± , or 12 Q–Q3!

(*e*) (A) 6 N–B2, B × N†; 7 P × B, P–Q4; 8 P–K3 B–K3; 9 P × P, N × P; 10 P–QB4, KN–N5 = . (B) 6 P–KN3, N–K4; 7 Q–N3, B × N†; 8 Q × B, P–Q4; 9 N–N5, N–N3; 10 P × P, O–O; 11 N × BP, N × P; 12 N × N, Q × N; 13 Q–B3, Q–QN4 = , or 13 . . . Q × Q!

(*f*) 10 P–K4, N–K4; 11 B–K2, N–N3; 12 B–B2, N–Q2; 13 Q–Q2, N–N3 = . Botvinnik-Pirć, Moscow 1935.

(*g*) 4 . . . B–B4; 5 N × P, N × N; 6 P–Q4, B–N5; 7 P × N, N × P; 8 Q–Q4, P–KB4; 9 P × P *e.p.*, B × N†; 10 P × B, N × P/3 = . Tartakover.

(*h*) 6 P–KN3, B–QB4; 7 P–KR3, B–K3; 8 B–N2, P–KR3; or 8 P–R3, P–QR4 = .

(*i*) 10 N–B2, P–B4; 11 P × P, B × P = . Fine-Dake, Mexico City 1935.

(*j*) (A) 4 . . . P–Q4; 5 P × P, N × P; 6 P–Q3, B–K3; 7 B–N2, B–K2; 8 O–O, O–O; 9 P–QR3, Q–Q2; 10 B–Q2, QR–Q1; 11 P–QN4, N × N = . Ragozin-Petrov, Semmering 1937. (B) 4 . . . N–Q5; 5 N–KR4, P–KN4; 6 N–B3, N × N; 7 P × N, B–B4; 8 Q–K2, P–Q3 = . *Informator* 24. (C) 4 . . . B–N5; 5 B–N2 (5 N–Q5, P–K5; 6 N–R4, O–O; 7 B–N2,R–K1 = . *Comments*), O–O; 6 O–O, P–K5; (1) 7 N–KN5, B × N; 8 NP × B, R–K1; 9 P–Q3, P × P; 10 P × P, P–Q3; 11 R–N1, P–KR3; 12 N–K4, N–K4 = . (2) 7 N–K1, B × N (or 7 . . . R–K1; 8 N–B2, B × N =); 8 QP × B, P–KR3 (8 . . . R–K1; 9 N–B2, N–K4 = . Schmidt-Lewi, Lublin 1969); 9 N–B2, R–K1; 10 N–K3, P–Q3; 11 Q–B2, P–QR4; 12 P–QR4, Q–K2; 13 N–Q5, N × N; 14 P × N, N–N1; 15 B–K3, B–B4; 16 P–R3, N–Q2; 17 P–QB4, P–QN3; 18 Q–B3, N–B4; 19 P–N3, Q–Q2; 20 K–R2, R–K2; 21 B–Q4, P–KB3; 22 QR–B1, Q–K1; 25 Q–K3, drawn. Karpov-Korchnoi, 6th match game 1978.

(*k*) 5 N × P, B × P†; 6 K × B, N × N; 7 P–K4, P–B4; 8 P–Q3, P–Q3; 9 P–KR3, O–O = .

(*l*) 10 B–R4 (Filip-Keres, Amsterdam 1956), N–Q5! = . 7 P–K3 is a strategic alternative.

(*m*) 4 P–K3, B–N5! 5 Q–B2, (A) 5 . . . O–O; 6 P–QR3, B × N; 7 Q × B, R–K1; 8 P–Q3, P–Q4; 9 P × P, Q × P; 10 B–K2, P–K5! = . Velitski-Smyslov, USSR 1964. (B) 5 . . . B × N; 6 Q × B, Q–K2; 7 P–QR3, O–O; 8 P–QR3, P–QR4; 9 B–K2, P–R5; 10 O–O, P–Q3; 11 N–Q2, B–N5; 12 P–B3, B–Q2; 13 N–K4, N–K1; 14 Q–K1, P–B4; 15 N–B3, N–B3; 16 B–Q2, N–QR4!?; 17 B–Q1, P–QN3; 18 N × P, P–K5 ∓ . Smysbv-Romanishin, Tilburg 1979.

(*n*) 8 . . . N–Q5; 9 P–QN4, R–K1; 10 N × N, P × N; 11 N–N5, N–N5; 12 P–KR3, P–B3! = . Stanev-Klundt, Students' Team Chp. Ybbs 1968.

(*o*) 10 P–QN4, P × P; 11 P × P, P–K5! 12 P × P, N × P; 13 N × N, R × N; 14 N–Q2, R–K1 = . Stolyar-Bannik, Moscow 1957. For the same line without an early . . . N–KB3, compare col. 14.

1 P–QB4, P–K4; 2 N–QB3 (*a*), N–KB3; 3 P–KN3

	6	7	8	9	10
	P–Q4	B–N5	P–B3		
4	P × P	B–N2 (*d*)	N–B3! (*h*)		
	N × P	O–O	P–K5 (*i*)		
5	B–N2	N–B3 (*e*)	N–Q4		
	N–K2 (*b*)	R–K1 (*f*)	P–Q4	Q–N3 (*m*)	
6	N–B3	O–O	P × P	N–N3	P–K3
	QN–B3	P–K5	P × P (*j*)	P–QR4!?	P–Q4
7	P–QN4	N–Q4	P–Q3	P–Q3	Q–B2!
	P–QR3	N–B3	Q–N3	P–R5	B–Q2
8	O–O	N–B2	P × P (*k*)	N–Q2	P–QR3
	N–B4	B × N	B–QB4	P–K6	B–K2
9	B–N2	QP × B (*g*)	P–K3	P × P	P–QN4
	B–K2 (*c*)	P–KR3 =	P × P (*l*)	N–N5 (*n*)	O–O (*o*)

(*a*) If (A) 2 P–KN3, N–QB3! but not 2 . . . P–KN3? 3 P–Q4! But compare King's Fianchetto. For (B) 2 P–QN3 see Queen's Fianchetto Opening, col. 8.

(*b*) 5 . . . N–N3; 6 N–B3, N–B3; 7 P–QR3, B–K3 (7 . . . B–K2! 8 P–Q3, O–O; 9 P–QN4, P–B3! =); 8 P–Q3, P–B3; 9 P–QN4, P–QR4? 10 P–N5, N–Q5; 11 N × N, P × N; 12 N–K4, P–R5; 13 B–Q2 ± . Furman-Korchnoi, USSR Chp. 1959. Better was 9 . . . B–K2; 10 O–O, P–B4! 11 B–K3, B–B3; 12 N–K1, QR–N1; 13 B × N, RP × B; 14 R–B1, P–KR4 = . Shatskes.

(*c*) 10 P–Q3, B–K3; 11 P–QR3, P–B3; 12 P–K3, O–O; 13 Q–B2, Q–Q2 = . Pachman-Cobo, Havana 1964.

(*d*) 4 Q–N3!? N–B3; 5 N–Q5, B–B4; 6 P–K3, O–O; 7 B–N2, N × N; 8 P × N, N–K2; 9 N–K2, P–Q3; 10 O–O, P–QB3; 11 P–Q4, KP × P, P × P; 12 KP × P, B–N3; 13 B–N5, B–Q2; 14 P–QR4, P–KR3; 15 B × N, Q × B; 16 B–B3, QR–N1; 17 P–R5 B–B2; 18 Q–B3, KR–B1; 19 N–B4, B–Q1; 20 KR–K1 (Korchnoi-Karpov, 25th match game 1978), with a minimal advantage for White, but the game ended in a draw at the 80th move.

(*e*) 5 P–K4, N–B3; 6 KN–K2, P–Q3; 7 O–O, B–QB4; 8 P–KR3, N–Q5; 9 P–Q3, P–B3; 10 K–R1 (Portisch-Ree, Wijk aan Zee 1969), P–QR3 = . Also 5 . . . P–B3 and . . . P–Q4!

(*f*) 5 . . . N–B3; 6 O–O, P–K5; 7 N–KN5, B × N; 8 NP × B, R–K1; 9 P–B3 (or 9 P–Q3, P × P; 10 P × P, P–KR3; 11 N–K4, P–QN3 =), P × P; 10 N × P/3, P–Q4; 11 P × P, Q × P! 12 N–Q4, Q–KR4; 13 N × N, P × N; 14 P–K3, B–N5; 15 Q–R4, R–K3; 16 R–N1? B–K7; 17 R–K1, N–N5! 18 P–KR3, Q–KB4; 19 R × B, Q × R; 20 Q × N, Q × B†; 21 K–R2, R–Q1; 22 Q–N4, P–KR3; 23 P–B4, Q–Q8; 24 R–B2, Q–K8; 25 resigns. Sigurjonsson-Smyslov, Reykjavik 1974.

(*g*) 9 NP × B!? P–Q3! 10 N–K3, N–K4; 11 P–Q3, P × P; 12 P × P, P–B3 ∞ . Tal-Kholmov, Tbilisi 1969.

(*h*) Ineffective are (A) 4 P–Q4, P × P; 5 Q × P, P–Q4; 6 B–N5, B–K2; 7 N–B3, O–O; 8 B–N2, P–KR3; 9 B–B4, P–B4; 10 Q–Q3, P–Q5; 11 N–QN5, N–B3; 12 B–B7, Q–K1; 13 O–O, B–N5! = . Rejfír-Keres, Moscow 1956. (B) 4 B–N2, P–Q4; 5 P × P, P × P; 6 P–Q3! N–B3; 7 N–B3, B–K2; 8 O–O, O–O; 9 P–Q4, P–K5; 10 N–K5, B–K3 = .

(*i*) A waiting tactic is 4 . . . P–Q3; 5 B–N2, P–KN3; 6 O–O, B–N2; 7 P–Q3 (7 P–Q4 might be timely), O–O; 8 R–N1, R–K1; 9 P–K4, P–Q4! = . *Informator* 8.

(*j*) Aggressive alternatives are (A) 6 . . . Q–N3?! 7 N–N3! P × P; 8 B–N2, N–B3! (or 8 . . . B–QN5); 9 O–O, B–QN5! = . Flohr, and (B) 6 . . . B–QB4, 7 N–N3, B–N3; 8 P–Q3 (8 P × P, N × P; 9 B–N2, B–KB4; 10 O–O, O–O), B–KB4; 9 B–N2, BP × P; 10 P × P, N × P; 11 N × N, B × N; 12 B × B, P × B = . Schmid-Popov, corr. 1962-4.

(*k*) 8 N–N3, N–N5! 9 P–Q4, B–K3; 10 P–B3, P × P; 11 P × P, N–KB3; 12 B–K3, N–B3 = . Korchnoi-Keres, Curaçao 1962.

(*l*) 10 B–N2, O–O; 11 O–O, B–KN5 = . Benko-Tringov, Varna 1962.

(*m*) 5 . . . B–B4; 6 N–N3, P–Q3; 7 B–N2, B–B4; 8 O–O, QN–Q2, N/–Q2; 9 P–Q3, P × P; 10 P × P, O–O; 11 B–B4, R–K1; 12 Q–Q2 ± ! Smyslov-Bronstein, Monte Carlo 1969.

(*n*) 10 N/2–K4, N × KP; 11 Q–Q2! N × B; 12 R × N, B–K2; 13 P–B5! Q–Q1; 14 Q–B4, O–O; Matera-Soltis, New York 1969; and now 15 N–Q6, B × N; 16 P × B, gives White the initiative, casting doubts on the early excursion 5 . . . Q–N3. In the column, 6 . . . P–Q3 has more elasticity. *Comments.*

(*o*) Najdorf-Rossetto, Buenos Aires 1968.

1 P-QB4, P-K4; 2 N-QB3

	11	12	13	14	15
	P-Q3		N-QB3		
3	P-KN3 (*a*)		P-KN3		N-B3
	P-KN3 (*b*)		P-KN3 (*g*)		P-B4 (*m*)
4	B-N2		B-N2		P-Q4
	B-N2		B-N2		P-K5
5	P-K3	P-K4 (*d*)	P-Q3 (*h*)		N-Q2 (*n*)
	N-KB3	N-K2 (*e*)	P-Q3		N-B3
6	KN-K2	KN-K2	R-QN1 (*i*)	. . . P-B4	P-K3
	O-O	QN-B3	B-K3	KN-K2	P-KN3 (*o*)
7	O-O	P-Q3	P-QN4	N-R3 (*k*)	P-QR3
	P-B3!	P-B4	Q-Q2	O-O	B-N2
8	P-Q4	N-Q5	P-N5	O-O	P-QN4
	R-K1	O-O	N-Q1	B-Q2	O-O
9	P-QN4	B-K3	P-QR4	B-Q2	P-KN3
	P-K5 (*c*)	B-K3 (*f*)	N-K2 (*j*)	Q-B1 (*l*)	P-Q3 =

(*a*) (A) 3 P-Q4, P×P (3 . . . N-Q2; 4 N-B3, KN-B3; 5 P-K3, see Old (Chigorin) Indian Defence); 4 Q×P, N-QB3; 5 Q-Q2, N-B3; 6 P-QN3, P-KN3; 7 B-N2, B-N2; 8 P-K3, O-O = . Barcza-Dely, Hungary 1963, or 8 P-KN3! (B) 3 N-B3, B-N5! 4 P-Q4, B×N (4 . . . N-KB3!); 5 NP×B, P×P; 6 Q×P, N-K2; 7 P-N3 ± .

(*b*) Or (A) 3 . . . N-KB3; 4 B-N2, P-KN3; 5 P-Q3, B-N2; 6 P-K4, O-O; 7 KN-K2, P-B3; 8 O-O, P-QR3; 9 P-KR3, P-QN4 = . Popov-Kavalek, Hoogoven 1975. (B) 3 . . . B-K3; 4 B-N2, P-QB3; 5 P-N3, P-Q4; 6 P×P, P×P = . (*c*) 3 . . . P-KB4; 4 B-N2, (1) 4 . . . N-KB3; 5 P-Q3 (5 P-Q4, B-K2; 6 P-K3, P-B3; 7 KN-K2, O-O; 8 O-O, Q-K1; 9 Q-B2, N-R3 = turns the variation into a Dutch Defence), and now (i) 5 . . . P-KN3; 6 N-R3, B-N2; 7 O-O, O-O; 8 B-Q2, P-B3 = . *Comments;* or (ii) 5 . . . B-K2; 6 N-B3, O-O; 7 O-O, K-R1; 8 P-QN4, P-QR4; 9 P-N5, QN-Q2; 10 B-QR3, Q-K1 = . Benko-Larsen, Winnipeg 1967, or (iii) 5 . . . N-B3, 6 N-R3, see col 15 (*m*). (2) 4 . . . N-QB3; 5 P-Q3, N-B3; 6 P-K3, B-K2; 7 KN-K2, O-O; 8 O-O, Q-K1; 9 P-B4, B-Q1; 10 P-QR3, R-N1; 11 P-QN4, B-K3; 12 N-Q5, P-QN4; 13 B-N2, NP×P; 14 QP×P, P-K5; 15 N×N†, B×N; 16 B×B, R×B; 17 R-B1, P-QR4; 18 P-N5, N-Q1; 19 R-KB2, N-N2; 20 B-B1, N-B4; 21 N-B3, B-B2; 22 N-Q5, B×N; 23 P×B, N-Q6; 24 B×N, P×B; 25 Q×P, Q×NP; 26 Q×Q, R×Q; 27 R×P, R-B2; drawn. Karpov-Korchnoi, 27th match game 1978

(*c*) 10 P-N5, B-B4; 11 P-QR4, QN-Q2; 12 B-QR3, P-B4 = . Spiridonov-Matulović, Athens 1969.

(*d*) (A) 5 P-N3, N-K2; 6 P-K3, P-QB4; 7 B-N2, QN-B3; 8 P-Q3, O-O; 9 Q-Q2, B-K3; 10 N-Q5, P-B4 = . *Informator* 6. (B) 5 P-Q3! N-K2; 6 P-B4, P-QB3; 7 N-B3, O-O; 8 O-O, N-R3 = . *Comments.* An early P-Q4 for White transposes into the King's Indian Defence.

(*e*) 5 . . . P-KB4; 6 P×P, P×P; 7 Q-R5†, K-B1; 8 P-Q3, N-KB3; 9 Q-K2, K-B2 = . D. Byrne-Fischer, US Chp. 1966.

(*f*) 10 Q-Q2, Q-Q2; 11 O-O, R-B2 ∞ . Benko-Botvinnik, Monte Carlo 1968.

(*g*) Viable is 3 . . . P-B4; 4 B-N2, N-B3; 5 P-Q3, (A) 5 . . . B-B4! 6 P-K3, P-B5?! 7 KP×P, O-O; 8 KN-K2, Q-K1; 9 O-O, P-Q3; 10 N-QR4, B-Q5; 11 N×B, P×N; 12 P-KR3, P-KR4! = . Saidy-Fischer, New York, 1969. (B) 5 . . . P-Q3; 6 N-R3?! B-K2; 7 P-B4! (White's 6th and 7th moves constitute Lombardy's "Paris Attack." Compare also King's Indian Attack), O-O; 8 N-B2, R-N1 = . *Comments.*

(*h*) (A) 5 P-K3, P-Q3; 6 KN-K2, KN-K2; (1) 7 P-Q4, B-R3! = ; or (2) 7 R-QN1, P-QR3; 8 P-QN4, P-B4; 9 P-Q3, O-O; 10 O-O, R-N1; 11 P-QR4?! P-QR4 (11 . . . N-R2! 12 N-Q5, B-K3 = . *Comments*); 12 P-N5, N-N5 (Spasski-Larsen, Lugano 1968); 13 B-QR3 + .

(B) 5 R–QN1, P–Q3; 6 P–QN4, P–QR3; 7 P–K3, P–B4; 8 KN–K2, N–B3! 9 P–Q3, O–O; 10 O–O, R–N1! = . (C) 5 P–K4, P–Q3; 6 P–Q3, KN–K2; 7 KN–K2; O–O; 8 O–O, P–B4 = .

(i) 6 N–B3, N–B3; 7 R–QN1, transposes into col. 5.

(j) 10 B–QR3, P–KR3; 11 N–B3, O–O; 12 O–O, P–KB4; 13 N–Q2, R–B1 = . Botvinnik-Liberzon, Moscow 1968.

(k) 7 N–B3, O–O; 8 O–O, P–KR3; 9 P–K4, P–B4; 10 N–Q5, N × N; 11 BP × N, N–Q5 = . Alekhin-Tarrasch, Vienna 1922. The column also is the "Paris Attack," characterized by White's 6th and 7th move.

(l) 10 N–B2, N–B4; 11 R–N1, P × P∞ . Lombardy-Rossolimo, US Chp. 1968.

(m) 3 . . . P–KN3; 4 P–Q4, P × P; 5 N × P, B–N2; 6 N × N, NP × N; 7 P–KN3, Q–K2; 8 B–N2 (8 B–Q2! Q–K3; 9 P–QN3!), Q–N5! 9 O–O! N–K2! = . Smyslov-Szabó, Buenos Aires 1970. The actual sequence was 1 P–QB4, P–KN3; 2 N–KB3, B–N2; 3 N–B3, P–K4; 4 P–Q4, P × P; 5 N × P, N–QB3; 6 N × N. Check against King's Fianchetto Defence, col 3, for transposition.

(n) (A) 5 N–K5, P–Q3; 6 N × N, P × N; 7 P–B3, N–B3 = . *Comments.* (B) 5 P–Q5, P × N; 6 P × N, P × NP; 7 P × P†, Q × P; 8 Q × Q†, B × Q; 9 B × P, P–B3; 10 O–O, N–B3; 11 B–K3, B–K3 = .

(o) Also 6 . . . B–N5; 7 B–K2, O–O; 8 O–O, R–K1; 9 P–B3, P × P = .

1 P–QB4, N–KB3; 2 N–QB3, P–K3 (*a*); 3 N–B3

	16	17	18	19	20
	P–QN3 (*b*)	. . . B–N5 (*e*)			
4	P–KN3	Q–B2	P–KN3	Q–N3 (*j*)	
	B–N2	P–B4 (*f*)	P–B4 (*h*)	P–B4	N–B3
5	B–N2	P–QR3	B–N2	P–QR3	P–KN3 (*m*)
	B–K2	B–R4	N–B3	B–R4	P–Q4
6	O–O	P–K3 (*g*)	O–O	P–KN3	B–N2
	O–O	N–B3	O–O	N–B3	O–O
7	P–N3 (*c*)	P–Q4	N–QR4!	B–N2	O–O
	P–Q4	P–Q3	Q–K2	P–Q4 (*k*)	P–Q5
8	P–K3	B–Q3	P–QR3	O–O	N–N1
	P × P	P–K4?	B–R4	B × N!	P–QR4
9	P × P	P × KP	P–Q4	Q × B	P–Q3
	P–B4 (*d*)	N × P ±	P–Q3 (*i*)	P–Q5 (*l*)	P–K4 =

(*a*) This is often preferred to . . . P–K4 as it denies White control of the square Q5. Compare also col. 23 (*f*). White need not reciprocate with his own fianchetto as in column 16, but can maintain centralization with 4 P–K4, B–N2; 5 Q–K2, B–N5!; 6 P–K5, N–N1; 7 P–Q4, N–K2; (A) 8 B–Q2, O–O; 9 O–O–O, P–Q4; 10 P–KR4, B × N; 11 B × B, P × P; 12 Q × P, B–R3; = Korchnoi-Karpov, 3rd match game 1974 (ending in a draw). (B) 8 Q–Q3, P–Q4; 9 P × P, P × P; 10 P–QR3, B × N†; 11 Q × B, O–O; 12 P–QN3, N–Q2 (Korchnoi-Karpov, 7th match game 1974), also ebbing out in a draw—altogether, two sterile lines merely utilized as a breather during a difficult match. For 2 . . . P–B4 mainly see cols. 26–30.

(*b*) An isolated attempt at a Queen's Indian Defence which arises if White now pushes P–Q4. But he prefers a Double-Fianchetto, and if now 4 P–K4 see col. 21, note (*a*–B).

(*c*) 7 P–Q4, P–B4; 8 P–N3, P × P; 9 Q × P, N–B3; 10 Q–B4, Q–N1 = . Petrosian-Portisch, match 1974. This sequence is identical with the Queen's Indian Defence, col. 4. Also refer to this section's col. 27.

(*d*) 10 Q–K2, N–B3; 11 R–Q1, R–B1 = . Portisch-Smyslov, Monte Carlo 1969.

(*e*) Feasible is 3 . . . P–B4; (A) 4 P–K3, B–K2; 5 P–QN3, O–O; 6 B–N2, P–QN3; 7 P–Q4, P × P; 8 P × P, P–Q4 = . Keres-Smyslov, Zürich 1953. Or (B) 4 P–KN3, P–QN3; 5 P–K4!? (5 B–N2, B–N2; 6 O–O, B–K2; 7 P–Q4, N–K5!∞) 5 . . . B–N2; 6 P–Q3, B–K2; 7 B–N2, O–O; 8 O–O, N–B3 = . The text shows similarities to the Nimzo-Indian.

(*f*) More "neutral" is first 4 . . . O–O; (A) 5 P–K4, P–K4; 6 P–QR3, B × N; 7 QP × B, P–QN3; 8 B–N5, P–Q3; 9 B–K2, B–N2; 10 N–Q2, QN–Q2 = . Hort-Sosonkó, Tilbury 1977. (B) 5 P–QR3, B × N; 6 Q × B, P–QN3; 7 P–QN3, B–N2; 8 P–N3, P–Q4; 9 B–KN2, P–Q5 = . Uhlmann-Augustin, Décín 1977. (c) 5 P–QN3, P–B4; 6 B–N2, Q–K2; 7 P–K3, N–B3; 8 B–K2, P–Q3; 9 O–O, B × N; 10 B × B, P–K4 = . Petrosian-Balashov, USSR Chp. 1977.

(*g*) Or the fianchetto-line again, 6 P–KN3, N–B3; 7 B–N2, O–O; 8 O–O, Q–K2; 9 R–Q1, P–K4; 10 P–Q3, P–Q3; 11 B–N5, B × N! = . Pachman-Matanović, Vrnjačka Banja 1967. The column is Larsen-Gheorghiu, Winnipeg 1967. Correct was 8 . . . O–O; 9 O–O, Q–K2 = .

(*h*) Safe are also (A) 4 . . . P–QN3; 5 B–N2, B–N2; 6 O–O, B × N! 7 NP × B, P–Q3! = . (B) 4 . . . O–O; 5 B–N2, P–Q4; 6 P–QR3, B × N = .

(*i*) 10 R–N1, P–K4! 11 P–QN4! P–K5! = . Ivkov-Gheorghiu, Beverwijk 1968.

(*j*) 4 P–QR3, B × N; 5 NP × B, P–QN3; 6 P–Q3, P–Q3; 7 P–N3, B–N2; 8 B–N2, QN–Q2; 9 P–K4, P–QR4; 10 O–O, P–KR3 = . Sliwa-Csom, Zinnowitz 1967.

(*k*) As good is 7 . . . O–O; 8 O–O, P–QR3; 9 P–Q3, R–N1! = . Pachman-Parma, Titovo Užice 1966.

(*l*) 10 Q–B2, P–QR4; 11 P–Q3, P–K4 = . Not 8 . . . P–Q5; 9 N–QR4! ± .

(*m*) (A) 5 P–QR3, B–K2; 6 P–Q4, P–Q4 = . (B) 5 P–Q4, see Nimzo-Indian Defence. The column is Langeweg-Bronstein, Beverwijk 1963.

1 P-QB4, N-KB3

	21	22	23	24	25
2	(N-QB3)	....			P-KN3
	(P-K3)	....	P-Q4 (f)		P-B3 (l)
3	P-K4		P×P		B-N2
	P-B4 (a)		N×P		P-Q4
4	P-K5		P-KN3 (g)		P-N3
	N-N1		N×N		P-K3 (m)
5	N-B3	P-Q4	NP×N		B-N2
	N-QB3	P×P	P-KN3		B-K2
6	P-Q4	Q×P	B-N2		P-Q3
	P×P	N-QB3	P-QB4	B-N2	QN-Q2
7	N×P	Q-K4	N-B3	R-QN1 (i)	N-KB3
	N×P	P-Q3	B-N2	N-Q2	O-O
8	B-B4 (b)	N-B3 (d)	O-O	N-B3 (j)	O-O
	P-Q3 (c)	Q-R4?	O-O	O-O	P-QN3
9	Q-Q2	P×P	R-N1	O-O	Q-B2
	N-KB3 =	B×P (e)	N-B3 (h)	P-QB4 (k)	B-N2 (n)

(a) (A) 3 . . . P-Q4; (1) 4 BP×P, P×P; 5 P-K5, N-K5; 6 N-B3, B-KB4! = . (2) 4 P-K5!, N-K5 (4 . . . P-Q5; 5 P×N, P×N; 6 QNP×P, Q×P; 7 P-Q4, P-B4; 8 N-B3, P-KR3; 9 B-Q3, P×P; 10 P×P, B-N5†; 11 K-B1±, Seirawan-Korchnoi, Wijk aan Zee 1980); 5 N×N, P×N; 6 Q-N4, B-Q2; 7 Q×KP, B-B3; 8 Q-K3, N-R3; 9 P-Q4, N-N5; 10 K-Q2!±. Seirawan-Timman, Wijk aan Zee 1980. (B) 3 . . . P-QN3; 4 N-B3, B-N2; (1) 5 P-Q3, P-Q3; 6 P-KN3, P-N3 (or 6 . . . B-K2); 7 B-N2, B-N2; 8 O-O, O-O; 9 N-K1, N-K1 = . Portisch-Spasski, Geneva 1977. (2) 5 B-Q3, P-B4; 6 O-O (or 6 B-B2, P-Q3; 7 P-Q4, P×P; 8 N×P, B-K2; 9 O-O, O-O; 10 P-QN3!—also 6 P-K5), N-B3; 7 P-K5, N-KN5; 8 B-K4, P-B4; 9 P×P e.p., N×P; 10 B×N, B×B = . Korchnoi-Polugayevski, 1st match game 1977. Also compare Reti Opening, col. 37, note (e-B). 5}B-Q3 is part of the Kopee Variation (see Index). (3) 5 Q-K2, (i) 5 . . . B-N5; 6 P-K5, etc., as on the preceding page, note (a). (ii) 5 . . . P-QB4? 6 P-K5, N-N1; 7 P-Q4, B×N; 8 Q×B, N-QB3; 9 P-Q5, N×P; 10 Q-N3±. Korchnoi-Petrosian, 3rd match game 1974.

(b) Furman suggests 8 N/4-N5, P-Q3; 9 P-B5 (9 N-K4, P-Q4; 10 P×P, P×P=), P-QR3; 10 N×P†, B×N; 11 P×B, B-Q2∞. But even better is 8 . . . P-B3; 9 B-K3, P-QR3; 10 N-Q6†, B×N; 11 Q×B, N-K2 = .

(c) Or 8 . . . N-N3; 9 B-N3, P-QR3? (9 . . . P-K4!); 10 Q-R4. Archives.

(d) 8 P-B4, P×P; 9 P×P, B-N5; 10 B-Q2, P-B4; 11 Q-K3, N-R3; 12 N-B3, O-O; 13 P-QN3, N-B2 = . Heemsoth-Koch, corr. 1954.

(e) (A) 10 Q-N4? N-K4! 11 N×N, B×N; 12 B-Q2, N-B3 = . Schwarz. (B) 10 B-Q2!±. In the column, better is 8 . . . P×P; 9 N×P, (1) 9 . . . B-Q2 10 N×B, Q×N; 11 B-N5, B-N5! = . Filip. Or (2) 9 . . . N-B3; 10 N×N, Q-N3; 11 Q-B3, P×N; 12 B-K2, B-N2; 13 O-O, P-B4 = . Korchnoi-Karpov, 29th match game 1978.

(f) (A) 2 . . . P-B3; 3 P-K4, P-Q4 (3 . . . P-K4; 4 N-B3, P-Q3; see King's Indian Defence); (1) 4 P-K5, P-Q5; 5 P×N, P×N; 6 NP×P, KP×P; 7 P-Q4, B-Q3; 8 B-Q3, O-O; 9 N-K2, R-K1 = . Nimzowitsch. (2) 4 KP×P, P×P; 5 P-Q4, etc. see Caro-Kann, Panov Attack. (B) 2 . . . P-KN3; 3 P-KN3, B-N2; 4 B-N2, O-O; 5 P-K4! P-B4 (or 5 . . . P-Q3).

(g) 4 P-Q4, N×N; 5 P×N, P-K4 (or 5 . . . P-QB4); 6 N-B3, P×P; 7 P×P, B-KB4; 8 P-K3, B-N5† (or 8 . . . B-Q3); 9 B-Q2, Q-K2; 10 B-K2, O-O; 11 O-O (D. Byrne-Prins, Varna Olympics 1962), B-Q3 = . Compare col. 30, note (n).

(h) (A) 10 P-B4, P-N3; 11 B-N2, B×B = . D. Byrne-Averbakh, USA v. USSR, 1954. (B) 10 Q-R4, N-R4; 11 P-Q3, P-N3; 12 Q-R4, B-N2; 13 B-R6, B×B; 14 Q×B, B×N; 15

B × B, R–B1; 16 B–N2, Q–Q2; 17 QR–K1, P–QN4 = . Karpov-Korchnoi, 30th match game 1978.

(*i*) (A) 7 P–KR4, P–KR3; 8 N–R3, O–O; 9 Q–N3, N–Q2; 10 N–B4, P–K3 = . *Comments.* (B) 7 Q–N3, N–B3; 8 N–B3, O–O; 9 O–O, N–R4; 10 Q–B2, P–QB4; 11 P–Q3, B–B4; 12 P–K4, B–Q2 = . Botvinnik-Smyslov, match 1958. (C) 7 P–KB4, P–B4; 8 N–R3!? O–O; 9 O–O, N–B3; 10 R–N1, N–R4; 11 N–B2, R–N1; 12 Q–B2, Q–B2; 13 P–Q3, P–QN4; 14 P–K4 (Wright-Schmidt, Dresden 1969), P–K4 = . White's 7th and 8th moves exemplify the "Paris Attack,"

(*j*) 8 Q–B2, R–QN1 = . Korchnoi-D. Byrne, Mallorca 1968.

(*k*) 10 P–B4, Q–B2; 11 P–Q3, R–N1 = . Portisch-Polugayevski, Hungary 1969. In the column, for 6 . . . P–Q4 see Grünfeld Defence.

(*l*) For 2 . . . P–KN3; 3 P–QN3, see also col. 34.

(*m*) (A) 4 . . . P × P; 5 P × P, Q–Q5; 6 N–B3, Q × P; 7 N–B3, P–K3 . (B) 4 . . . P–KN3; 5 B–N2, B–N2; (1) 6 N–QB3, O–O; 7 N–B3 ± . *Comments.* For 7 . . . B–N5?! compare Réti Opening, cols. 2, 17, and 19. (2) 6 N–KB3, B–N5; 7 O–O, O–O; 8 P–Q3, B × N; 9 B × B, QN–Q2; 10 B–N2, R–N1 = . Larsen-Uhlmann, match 1971.

(*n*) 10 P–K4, N–B4 = . Lewi-Witkowski, Lublin 1969. A "Double Fianchetto" strategy.

1 P-QB4, P-QB4 (a); 2 N-KB3 (b), N-KB3; 3 N-B3

	26	27	28	29	30
	P-K3		P-KN3	P-Q4	
4	P-Q4	P-KN3	P-KN3 (j)	P×P	
	P×P	P-QN3	B-N2	N×P	
5	N×P	B-N2	B-N2	P-K4	P-KN3 (n)
	N-B3 (c)	B-N2	N-B3	N-N5	P-KN3 (o)
6	N/4-N5	O-O (e)	P-Q4 (k)	B-B4	B-N2
	P-Q3	B-K2 (f)	P×P	N-Q6† (m)	B-N2
7	B-B4	P-QN3 (g)	N×P	K-K2	O-O
	P-K4!	O-O	N×N	N-B5†	O-O (p)
8	B-N5	B-N2	Q×N	K-B1	Q-N3
	P-QR3	P-Q4	O-O	N-B3	N-N5
9	B×N	N-K5 (h)	O-O	P-Q4	P-Q3
	P×B (d)	N-B3 (i)	P-Q3 (l)	P×P =	QN-B3 =

(a) A number of important transposition of tactical importance come into play after (A) 1 . . . P-KB4; 2 N-KB3 or 2 P-KN3, for which see Réti Opening cols. 27-9; or 2 P-Q4 see Dutch Defence, Classical System. (B) 1 . . . P-KN3; (1) 2 P-KN3, P-QB3; 3 B-N2, P-Q4; becomes a King's Fianchetto Opening. (2) 2 P-Q4, B-N2; 3 N-QB3, P-Q3; 4 N-B3 or 4 P-K4 leads into the Robatsch or King's Indian Defence. (3) 2 P-K4, P-K4!?; 3 P-Q4!?, N-KB3; 4 N-KB3, B-N5†; 5 B-Q2, B×B; 6 Q×B, N×P. Adorjan. (c) 1 . . . P-K3; (1) 2 P-Q4 is a Queen's Gambit or Nimzo-Indian, and (2) N-QB3 reverts to cols. 16-22. For (3) 2 P-KN3, P-Q4; 3 B-N2, N-KB3; 4 N-KB3 see Réti Opening, Neo Catalan. (D) Similar to the Kevitz-Trajković Defence is the stratagem 1 . . . N-QB3!? 2 P-Q4, P-K4 (2 . . . P-Q4 is a Queen's Gambit, Chigorin Var.); 3 P×P, N×P; 4 P-K4 (or 4 P-K3), Q-R5; 5 Q-B2, N-KB3; 6 N-QB3, B-N5; 7 B-Q2, B×N; 8 B×B, P-Q3; 9 B×N, P×B; 10 B-Q3, B-N5; 11 N-K2, O-O-O = . Comments. (E) 1 . . . P-QB3; 2 N-QB3, N-KB3.

(b) 2 P-QN3, N-KB3; 3 B-N2, P-KN3!? 4 B×N!? is Karpov-Browne, San Antonio 1972. Also see Unorthodox Flank Openings, col. 10, note (j).

(c) Somewhat untried is 5 . . . B-N5?!; 6 P-KN3, N-K5?!; 7 Q-Q3, Q-R4; 8 N-B2!, B×N† (8 . . . N×N; 9 N×B, N×RP; 10 R×N, Q×N†; 11 B-Q2, Q-N3; 12 B-N2! Belyavski-Alburt, U.S.S.R. Chp 1974); 9 P×B, N-B4!; 10 Q-Q2, P-QN3; 11 B-KN2, B-N2; 12 B×B, N×B; 13 B-R3, N-B3; 14 O-O, P-Q3; 15 QR-N1, Q-R5; 16 KR-Q1, O-O; 17 R-N5, Q×P; 18 R-N5, P-B3; 19 R-KR5, Q×RP; 20 R-R4, KR-Q1; 21 Q-Q3, P-B4; 22 P-QB4, N-B4; 23 Q-B3, Q-N6; 24 Q×Q, N×Q; 25 R×QP, R×R; 26 B×R, R-Q1; 27 resigns (as 27 B-B4, P-K4; 28 B-K3, R-Q8† and 29 . . . N/6-Q5 wins the ending). Lombard-Rogoff, Biel 1976. The variation can also be reached via the Nimzo-Indian Defence, col. 73, note (g).

(d) 10 N-R3, B-K3; 11 P-KN3, P-B4; 12 B-N2, B-N2; 13 Q-Q2, O-O ∞. Informator 8.

(e) For 6 P-Q4, P×P see Queen's Indian Defence, col. 13, note (f-B) and col. 4, this section. Further, compare this and col. 16.

(f) Subjected to question in two test games has been 6 . . . P-QR3; (A) 7 R-K1, P-Q3; 8 P-K4, QN-Q2; 9 P-Q3 (9 P-Q4! with a Sicilian Defence, Maroczy Bind), B-K2   . Portisch-Ljubojević, Milan 1975, and (B) 7 P-N3! P-Q3; 8 P-Q4! P×P; 9 Q×P, QN-Q2; 10 B-N2, B-K2; 11 KR-Q1, O-O; 12 N-K1, Q-N1; 13 P-K4! R-B1; 14 Q-K3! R-R2; 15 N-B3, N-N5; 16 Q-K2, N/5-K4; 17 N-K1, B-R1; 18 R-Q2, N-B4; 19 N-B2, N-B3; 20 P-B4, N-Q2; 21 N-K3, N-B3; 22 P-KN4, N-K1; 23 P-N5, R/2-B2; 24 P-KR4, P-N4; 25 P-KB5, NP×P; 26 P×KP, P×KP; 27 B-KR3, N-Q1; 28 N×P, R-B4; 29 R-KB1, P-N3; 30 Q-B2, N-KN2; 31 N-Q5, B×N; 32 P×B, P-K4; 33 B×R, Q×B; 34 N×KP, N-B4; 35 N-N4, N-B2; 36 Q-K2, N×RP; 37 Q×B, Q×N†; 38 K-R2, resigns. Korchnoi-Garcia, Alekhin Memorial, Moscow 1975.

(g) Solid is 7 P–Q4, P×P; 8 Q×P, O–O; 9 R–Q1, N–B3! 10 Q–B4, Q–N1; 11 Q×Q, QR×Q; 12 B–B4, QR–B1; 13 N–K5, P–Q3; 14 N×N, B×N; 15 B×P, KB×B; 16 R×B, B×B = . *Comments.*

(h) 9 P×P, N×P; 10 N×N, B×N; 11 Q–N1, N–Q2; 12 R–Q1, B–KB3 = . Larsen.

(i) Or 9 . . . QN–Q2; 10 P–B4, N×N; 11 P×N, N–N5; 12 P–K4, N×KP; 13 KP×P, B–KB3; 14 P–Q4, N–N3! = . Larsen-Donner, Havana 1967. The column continues 10 P–B4, R–B1; 11 P–K3, P–QR3; 12 P×P, P×P; 13 R–B1, P–QN4 = . Larsen-Matulović, Sousse 1967. The same sequence arises from 1 N–KB3, P–QB4; 2 P–QN3, etc.

(j) 4 P–Q4, P×P; 5 N×P, B–N2; 6 P–K3 (6 P–K4 transposes into the Sicilian Defence), N–QB3; 7 B–K2, O–O; 8 O–O, N×N; 9 Q×N, P–Q3; 10 Q–Q2, B–K3; 11 Q–B2, P–QR3 = . Danov-Fischer, Skopje 1967.

(k) (A) 6 P–Q3 is a choice. For (B) 6 P–N3, see Réti Opening.

(l) (A) 10 Q–Q3, B–K3! (10 . . . P–QR3; 11 B–K3!); 11 B–Q2! Q–Q2; 12 QR–B1, QR–B1; 13 P–N3, B–R6; 14 N–Q5, B×B; 15 K×B, N×N; 16 P×N, R×R; 17 R×R, R–B1 = . Reshevsky-Stein, Amsterdam 1964. (B) 10 B–N5, B–K3; 11 Q–B4, Q–R4; 12 QR–B1, QR–N1; 13 P–N3, KR–QB1; 14 Q–Q2, P–QR3; 15 B–K3, P–QN4; 16 B–R7, P×P; 17 B×R, R×B; 18 P×P, B×P; 19 KR–Q1, N–Q2; 20 N–Q5, Q×Q; 21 N×P†, K–B1; 22 R×Q, K×N; 23 R×B, R–N8†; 24 B–B1, N–B4; 25 K–N2, P–QR4; 26 P–K4, B–R8; 27 P–B4, P–B3; 28 R–K2, K–K3; 29 R/K2–QB2, B–N7; 30 B–K2, P–R4; 31 R–Q2, B–R6; 32 P–B5†, P×P; 33 P×P†, K–K4; 34 R/B4–Q4, K×P; 35 R–Q5†, K–K3; 36 R×P, K–K2; 37 R–B6, resigns. Fischer-Spasski, 8th match game 1972.

(m) 6 . . . B–K3! 7 B×B, N–Q6†; 8 K–B1, P×B; 9 N–KN5, Q–Q2; 10 Q–N4, N–B3 ∞. Shatskes.

(n) (A) 5 P–K3, P–K3; 6 P–Q4 with a Queen's Gambit, Semi-Tarrasch Defence. Or 5 . . . N–QB3; 6 B–N5, P–K3! Shatskes. (B) 5 P–Q4, P×P; 6 Q×P, N×N; 7 Q×N, N–B3; 8 P–K4!, B–N5; 9 B–QN5, R–B1; 10 B–K3!, B×N; 11 P×B, P–QR3; 12 R–Q1, Q–B2; 13 B×N†, Q×B; 14 Q–Q4, P–B3; 15 O–O, P–K4; 16 Q–R7. Portisch-Hübner, Montreal 1979.

(o) Or (A) 5 . . . N×N!; 6 NP×N, P–KN3; 7 Q–R4†, N–Q2; 8 P–KR4, P–KR4; 9 R–QN1, B–N2; 10 B–KN2, O–O; 11 P–B4! P–K4; 12 P–Q3, N–N3 ∞. Petrosian-Szabó, Bucharest 1953. (B) 5 . . . N–QB3; 6 B–N2, N–B2; 7 P–Q3, P–K4; 8 O–O, B–K2; 9 N–Q2, B–Q2; 10 N–B4, O–O; 11 B×N, B×B; 12 N×P, B–K1; 13 Q–N3, P–QN3; 14 B–K3, K–R1; 15 KR–Q1! (15 P–B4!), P–B3; 16 N–B3, B–B2; 17 Q–R4, N–Q4; 18 N×N, B×N; 19 P–QR3, P–QR3; 20 N–Q2, Q–B1; 21 P–B3, Q–K3; 22 K–B2, B–K3; 23 R–K1, B–KB3; 24 Q–B2, P–KB5; 25 B×KBP, P–KN4; 26 P–K4, P×P; 27 P×B, Q–R6, 28 N–B1, B–Q5†; 29 K–K2, QR–K1†; 30 K–Q1, R×R†; 31 K×R, R–K1†; 32 resigns. Commons—Gheorghiu, Lone Pine 1975.

(p) 7 . . . N–QB3!; 8 N×N, Q×N; 9 P–Q3, (A) 9 . . . Q–Q3; 10 B–K3! B×P; 11 R–N1, B–N2; 12 Q–R4, O–O; 13 KR–B1, P–N3; 14 P–Q4, N×P! 15 N×N, P×N, 16 B–B4, P–K4; 17 B×R, B–B4!; 18 Q×RP, B×R; 19 R×B, P×B; 20 B–K4, P–Q6! ∓. Doda-Kirov, Polanica Zdroj 1974. (B) 9 . . . O–O; 10 B–K3, B–Q2; 11 N–Q4?! Q–Q3; 12 N×N, B×N; 13 B×B, Q×B; 14 R–B1, Q–K3; 15 B×P, B×P; 16 R–N1, B–N2; 17 P–QR4, KR–Q1; 18 B–K3, P–N3; 19 Q–Q2, R–Q4; 20 R–N5? R×R ∓. Timman-Olafsson, Amsterdam 1974.

1 P–QB4, P–QB4; 2 N–KB3

	31	32	33	34	35
	(N–KB3) (*a*)				P–KN3
3	(N–B3)		P–KN3 (*g*)	. . . P–QN3	N–B3 (*l*)
	N–B3		P–QN3 (*h*)	P–KN3	B–N2
4	P–Q4 (*b*)		B–N2	B–N2	P–Q4 (*m*)
	P × P		B–N2	B–N2	P × P
5	N × P		O–O	P–KN3	N × P
	P–K3 (*c*)		P–KN3 (*i*)	O–O	N–QB3
6	P–K3	N/4–N5 (*e*)	P–N3	B–N2	N–B2 (*n*)
	B–K2	B–N5	B–N2	P–Q3	B × N†
7	B–K2	P–QR3	B–N2	P–Q4	P × B
	O–O	B × N†	O–O	N–K5!	N–B3
8	O–O	N × B	N–B3!?	O–O	P–B3
	P–Q3	P–Q4	P–Q4!	N–QB3	Q–R4
9	P–QN3	P × P	N × P	QN–Q2	B–Q2
	P–QR3 (*d*)	P × P (*f*)	N × N (*j*)	B–B4! (*k*)	P–Q4 =

(*a*) (A) 2 . . . P–KN3; 3 P–Q4, P × P; 4 N × P, N–QB3; 5 P–K4, see Sicilian Defence, Maróczy Bind. Also compare note (*c*). For 3 N–B3, see col. 35. (B) 2 . . . N–QB3; 3 P–Q4, P × P; 4 N × P, P–K3; 5 N–N5!.

(*b*) 4 P–K3, P–K3; 5 P–Q4, P–Q4; 6 P–QR3, P–QR3; 7 P × BP, B × P; 8 P–QN4 = . Benko-Lombardy, US Chp. 1969–70. See Queen's Gambit. Tarrasch Defence.

(*c*) 5 . . . P–KN3; 6 P–K4, see Sicilian Defence, Maróczy Bind. Also see note (*l*) and (*n*).

(*d*) 10 B–N2, B–Q2 = . Petrosian-Spasski, match 1966.

(*e*) Also 6 P–KN3, (A) 6 . . . Q–N3; (1) 7 N–B2! B–B4; 8 P–K3, O–O; 9 B–N2, Q–R3! 10 Q–K2, N–QN5 = . *Archives*. (2) 7 N–B3, N–K4; 8 P–K4, B–N5; 9 Q–K2, O–O; 10 P–B4, N–B3; 11 P–K5, N–K1; 12 B–Q2, P–B3; 13 P × P, N × P = . (B) 6 . . . B–B4; 7 N–B3, B–N5; 8 B–N2, P–Q4; 9 O–O, P × P; 10 N–Q2 + . Stean in *Informator* 24. But 7 . . . B–K2! equalizes.

(*f*) 10 P–K3, O–O; 11 B–K2, B–B4 = . Smyslov-Hort, Monte Carlo 1968. In the column, also 7 B–B4 and 7 B–N5 have been tried.

(*g*)(A) 3 P–Q4 transposes into the Benoni Defence col. 1 (*a*–B), or, after 1 P–Q4, N–KB3; 2 P–QB4, P–B4; 3 N–KB3, P–Q4, into the Queen's Gambit, col. 80. (B) 3 P–Q4, P × P; 4 N × P, P–QN3!; 5 N–QB3, B–N2; 6 P–B3, P–Q3; 7 P–K4, QN–Q2; 8 B–K2, P–K3; 9 O–O, B–K2; 10 B–K3, O–O; 11 Q–Q2 ± . Polugayevski-Ljubojevič, Baguio 1980.

(*h*) (A) 3 . . . P–KN3; 4 P–Q4, see King's Indian Defence. (B) 3 . . . P–K3; 4 B–N2, N–QB3; 5 O–O, P–Q4; 6 P–Q4, B–K2; 7 P × QP, KP × P = ; see Queen's Catalan, and 8 N–B3 arrives at a Queen's Gambit, Tarrasch Defence. (C) 3 . . . P–Q4; 4 P × P, N × P; 5 B–N2, N–QB3; 6 P–Q4, P × P; 7 N × P, N/4–N5; 8 N × N, Q × Q†; 9 K × Q, N × N = .

(*i*) 5 . . . P–K3; (A) 6 P–N3, B–K2; 7 B–N2, O–O; 8 P–K3, P–Q4; 9 Q–K2, N–B3 = . Kushnir-Gaprindashvili, Women's Chp., Tbilisi 1969. Compare this line and the column with the "Double Fianchetto" and the Réti Opening, Nimzowitsch Attack; (B) 6 N–B3, B–K2; 7 P–Q4, P × P; 8 Q × P, O–O; 9 R–Q1, P–Q3; 10 P–K4?! QN–Q2 = .

(*j*) 10 B × B, K × B; 11 P × N, Q × P; 12 P–Q4, N–R3 = . In the column, 8 P–Q4, or 8 P–K3! create otqher possibilities.

(*k*) 10 N–R4, N × N; 11 Q × N, P × QP; 12 N × B, P × N = . Keres. In the column, a better attempt towards an advantage than 7 P–Q4 is 7 O–O, P–K4; 8 N–B3, N–B3; 9 P–Q3, N–KR4; 10 N–Q5, B–N5; 11 P–QR3, B–R3; 12 P–N4!? (Petrosian-Portisch, 9th match game 1974).

(*l*) 3 P–Q4, P × P; 4 N × P, N–QB3; 5 P–K4, see Sicilian Defence, Maróczy Bind. Also compare notes (*c*) and (*n*).

(*m*) 4 P–K3, N–KB3; 5 P–Q4, O–O; 6 P × P, N–R3 = .

(*n*) (A) 6 N–B3, P–Q3; 7 B–Q2, P–QR4; 8 N–R4 ∞. *Archives*. The column is Stein-Matulović, Sousse 1967. (B) 6 P–K4, P–Q3 see Sicilian Defence, Maróczy Bind. Also compare notes (*c*) and (*l*).

1 P–QB4, P–QB4; 2 N–QB3

	36	37	38	39	40
	N–KB3......	N–QB3			
3	P–KN3	P–KN3			
	P–Q4	P–KN3			
4	P×P	B–N2			
	N×P	B–N2			
5	B–N2	N–B3......	P–Q3.......	P–K3......	P–QR3 (*i*)
	P–K3 (*a*)	P–QR3 (*c*)	P–QR3 (*e*)	P–K3 (*g*)	P–Q3 (*j*)
6	N–B3	P–Q3	P–QR4	KN–K2	N–B3
	N–QB3	R–N1	P–Q3	KN–K2	P–K4
7	O–O	O–O	P–K4	O–O	O–O
	B–K2	N–B3	N–B3	O–O	KN–K2
8	P–Q4	N–K1	KN–K2	P–Q4	R–N1
	N×N	O–O	B–Q2	P×P	B–K3
9	P×N	N–B2	P–R3	N×P	P–Q3
	O–O (*b*)	P–Q3 (*d*)	O–O (*f*)	N×N (*h*)	P–KR3 (*k*)

(*a*) 5 . . . N–B2; 6 N–B3, N–B3; 7 P–Q3, P–K4; (1) 8 B–K3, B–K2; 9 R–QB1, O–O; 10 N–Q2, B–Q2; 11 O–O, N–K3; 12 N–Q5, N/K3–Q5; 13 N–K4, P–QN3; 14 N/4–B3, R–B1; 15 B–Q2 (Dake-Rogoff, Lone Pine 1976), B–N5 = . (2) 8 O–O, B–K2; 9 P–QR3, O–O; 10 B–Q2, B–K3; 11 R–B1, P–B3; 12 N–K4, N–R3, Drawn. Evans-Diesen, U.S. Chp. 1980.

(*b*) 10 R–N1, Q–R4; 11 Q–N3, R–Q1 = . Geller-Keres, Curaçao 1962.

(*c*) 5 . . . P–K3; (A) 6 P–Q3, KN–K2; 7 O–O, O–O; (1) 8 B–N5?! P–KR3; 9 B–Q2, P–N3; 10 P–QR3, B–N2; 11 R–N1, P–Q4; 12 P–QN4, P × BP. Korchnoi-Karaklajić, Beverwijk 1968. (2) 8 B–Q2, P–N3; 9 Q–B1, B–N2; 10 B–R6, P–Q3; 11 P–QR3, Q–Q2; 12 B × B, K × B; 13 P–K3 and Black's position is vulnerable. Uhlmann-Larsen, match 1971. (B) 6 P–N3! KN–K2; 7 B–N2, O–O; 8 N–QR4, P–K4; 9 O–O, P–Q3; 10 P–K3, P–B4; 11 P–Q3, P–KR3 = . Smyslov-Fischer, Buenos Aires 1970. Compare note (*g*)-(C). For 5 . . . N–B3 see col. 28.

(*d*) 10 B–Q2, B–Q2; 11 P–QR4, N–K1; 12 R–N1, N–B2; 13 P–QN4, P × P; 14 N × P, N × N; 15 R × N, 16 RP × P, P × P; 17 P × P = . D. Byrne-Sherwin, US Chp. 1962.

(*e*) 5 . . . P–Q3; (A) 6 B–Q2 (6 P–K4 see note (*g*)) 6 . . . P–QR3; 7 R–N1, B–Q2; 8 P–QR3, R–N1∞ . Kholmov-Vasyukov, Moscow 1969, Truly "symmetrical" up to White's 8th move. (B) 6 N–KB3, B–Q2; 7 O–O, Q–B1; 8 R–N1, B–R6; 9 B–Q2, N–B3 = .

(*f*) 10 B–K3, P–K4; 11 O–O, R–N1; 12 R–N1, N–K1; 13 N–Q5, P–QN4 = . D. Byrne-Evans, US Chp. 1969–70.

(*g*) 5 . . . N–R3; 6 KN–K2, N–B4; 7 P–QR3, O–O; 8 R–QN1, P–QR4; 9 O–O, P–Q3; 10 P–Q3, R–N1; 11 B–Q2, P–K3; 12 N–B4, KN–K2; 13 Q–B2, P–N3; 14 QR–Q1, B–N2; 15 N–N5, Q–Q2; 16 B–QB3, N–K4. = . Fraguela-Karpov, Montilla 1976.

(*h*) 10 P × N, P Q4; 11 P × P, N × P; 12 Q–N3 (12 N × N, P × N; again "symmetric," was indeed Keller-Krausz, corr. 1969–70, with 13 Q–N3, B × P; 14 B–R6 B–N2; 15 B × B, K × B; 16 B × P =), N–K2; 13 P–Q5, P × P; 14 B–N5, P–KR3; 15 B × N, Q × B; 16 N × P, Q–K4 = . Forintos-Sapi, Hungary 1969.

(*i*) White also tries (A) 5 P–K4, N–B3; 6 KN–K2, O–O; 7 P–Q3, P–Q3; 8 O–O, N–K1; 9 B–K3, N–Q5; 10 P–B4, N–B2; 11 R–N1, P–QR4; 12 Q–Q2, R–N1 = . Meyer-Deutsch, New York 1970. Or (B) 5 N–R3, P–K3! = . *Comments.* Or (C) 5 P–N3, P–K3! 6 B–N2, KN–K2; 7 N–R4, B × B; 8 N × B, O–O; 9 P–K3, P–Q4!∞ . Smyslov-Fischer, Mallorca 1970. Compare also note (*b*)-(B).

(*j*) (A) 5 . . . P–K3; 6 R–N1, KN–K2; 7 P–QN4, P × P; 8 P × P, P–Q4 = . (B) 5 . . . P–QR3; (1) 6 N–R3, P–KR4; 7 N–B4, N–B3; 8 O–O, R–QN1; 9 P–QN4! P × P; 10 P × P, N × P; 11 P–Q4, O–O; 12 Q–N3, N–B3; 13 R–Q1! Sakharov-Schöneberg, Varna 1968. (2) 6 R–N1,

R–N1; 7 P–QN4, P × P; 8 P × P, P–QN4; 9 P × P, P × P; 10 N–B3, P–K4; 11 P–K4, KN–K2; 12 O–O, O–O = . Reshevsky-Petrosian, Los Angeles 1963.

   (*k*) 10 P–QN4, R–N1; 11 N–K1, O–O; 12 N–Q5, P × P; 13 P × P, P–QN4; 14 N–B2, K–R2 = . Reshevsky-Evans, Buenos Aires 1960.

Réti Opening

(1 N–KB3)

The variable nature of this opening is indicated by the variety of names under which parts of it have been baptized—Opening of the Future, Barcza System, Catalan, King's Indian Reversed, Nimzowitsch Attack, Réti Opening, Santasiere's Folly, Zukertort Opening, etc. Some of these names have been dropped and some other distinct patterns, for instance the Indian and Queen's Catalan, are now in separate sections but others have been added to this chapter.

1 N–KB3 was recorded by Lopez in 1561, Zukertort adopted it "incidentally" in 1845, Réti moulded it into a distinct pattern after World War I, and Barcza began the modern trend towards the King's Indian Reversed, but now renamed the "King's Indian Attack."

The Réti is hypermodern, subtle, and flexible. Réti himself said: "It directs pressure against the centre, prevents 1 . . . P–K4 and keeps open almost all the possibilities (of transposition) for the first player." The pawn-structure is elastic. Few or no pawns are placed on the fourth rank where they might obstruct their own pieces or become objects of attack. Once Black commits himself in the centre with . . . P–Q4 then White directs his attack not at the weakened K5 square, but at the target pawn itself by means of P–QB4, P–KN3, and B–N2.

This rather noncommittal system lacks sharpness in the opening but tends to produce rather profound middle-games, a delayed struggle. It requires sound judgement and a positional flair, little in the way of prepared analysis, but both players must be prepared to transpose into almost every other conceivable opening—the French, Sicilian, Catalan, English, Queen's Gambit, Slav etc.

THE ALFRED WOLF (or "Landstrasser") GAMBIT, the first important systematization of the Réti, appears in cols. 1–10, where Réti's 1 N–KB3 is coupled with the late Viennese master's Alfred Wolf's pseudo-gambit 2

P–QB4. This aims at immediate disruption of Black's centre push . . . P–Q4.

In reply, the *London System* (cols. 1–2), which allows Black's queen's bishop an active role, and the "Benoni Reversed" (cols. 4–5) which affords Black enough pressure on Q5, are quite safe for Black. The *Réti Accepted* (col. 3) gives White more leeway and does not always suffice for equality.

THE SEMI-CATALAN SYSTEM (cols. 6–10) or RÉTI-CATALAN, is a quiet drawing line, distinguished from the Queen's, Neo, and Indian Catalan System by the delay or avoidance of an early P–Q4 for White.

THE BARCZA SYSTEM with 2 P–KN3 (cols. 11–23), a son of the Réti, carries the idea of noncommittal moves a step further. White mobilizes his entire king's side with N–KB3, P–KN3, B–N2, O–O before he touches a centre pawn. Black has a variety of replies but as soon as he shows his hand White transposes into the most favourable opening available. A subjective yet subtle system, it involves a slow build-up with decisive action postponed until the middle-game. Black's simplest way of equalizing is merely to copy White's moves right down the line. If he chooses an equally passive method it is also difficult for White to get anything. Column 13 is a good example of White's king's-side attack *v.* Black's queen's-side counterplay, and cols. 14–15 have been among many recent choices. Miscellaneous systems for Black are handled in cols. 17–25. Most of them can transpose into standard defences if White chooses to play an early P–Q4 or P–K4. Likewise,. many potential switches into "closed" lines of the Semi-open Games, or into the King's Indian Attack must constantly be kept in mind.

THE DUTCH-RÉTI (cols. 27–9) covers lines whereby Black strives for a Dutch formation without quite achieving a Dutch Defence as White refrains from P–Q4. Features of the English may arise in instances of P–QB4. The system has been frequently used lately as is manifest from the respective columns and notes.

THE KING'S INDIAN ATTACK (cols. 30–5) represents the latest type of dilatory manoeuvring, whereby both sides almost by mutual consent refrain from any premature occupation of the centre squares.

THE DOUBLE FIANCHETTO (cols. 37–8) is, however, a very frequent outgrowth of the Nimzowitsch Attack, or may independently evolve by means of a delayed Queen's fianchetto on both White's and Black's part (cols. 37–8).

THE NIMZOWITSCH ATTACK (cols. 39–40) is another child of the Réti and the forerunner of the King's Indian Attack. In certain respects similar to Bird's Opening, it is more flexible. Black can actually establish a classical pawn-centre and often stand firm against White's wing strategy. It represents a kind of delayed "Larsen Attack" but with Nimzowitsch owning the right of precedence.

As may be logically deduced from these overlappings, the Réti Opening, just like the English, has in recent years been serving as an important launching pad for transposition into many other Indian or Queen's Gambit, or Pirć and Robatsch lines, often allowing for sudden favourable switches and surprises when the opponent has in routine fashion followed an orthodox opening pattern, unaware of possible diversions.

The good old times of "orthodoxy" have now passed away.

1 N–KB3, P–Q4; 2 P–B4

	1	2	3	4	5
	P–QB3 . . ⎫	. . . .	P × P	P–Q5 The Benoni "Reversed"	
3	P–QN3 ⎬	The London	N–R3 (*h*)	P–K3 (*l*)	
	N–B3 (*a*) ⎭	System	P–QB4	N–QB3.	P–QB4
4	P–N3		N × P	P × P (*m*)	P × P!
	B–B4	B–N5 (*d*)	N–QB3	N × P	P × P
5	B–KN2	B–KN2 (*e*)	P–KN3 (*i*)	N × N	P–KN3
	P–K3	P–K3	P–K4	Q × N	N–QB3
6	B–N2	B–N2	B–N2 (*j*)	N–B3	B–N2
	QN–Q2	QN–Q2	P–B3	P–K4	P–KN3
7	O–O	O–O	P–N3	P–Q3	P–Q3
	B–Q3!	B–K2 (*f*)	KN–K2	B–QB4	B–N2
8	P–Q3	P–Q3	B–N2	B–K3	O–O
	O–O	O–O	N–Q4	Q–Q3	P–K4
9	N–B3! (*b*)	QN–Q2	O–O	N–N5	R–K1
	Q–K2	P–QR4	B–K2	Q–K2	P–B3!
10	R–K1	P–QR3	N–R4!	B × B	P–QN4
	P–K4 (*c*)	Q–N3 (*g*)	O–O (*k*)	Q × B (*n*)	N × P (*o*)

(*a*) 3 . . . B–N5?! 4 B–N2, P–K3; 5 P–K3, N–B3; 6 B–K2, B–Q3; 7 N–B3, QN–Q2; 8 P × P (Larsen-Ivkov, Büsum 1969), KP × P = . This is the same early Black's bishop thrust as in col. 2, but it prevents White's immediate double fianchetto—whatever meaning it may have other than a psychological or stylistic one.

(*b*) 9 QN–Q2, P–K4! 10 P × P, P × P; 11 P–K4, also evens out.

(*c*) 11 P × P, P × P; 12 P–K4, P × P; 13 P × P, B–N3 (or 13 . . . B–N5!) = . Müller-Lilienthal, Budapest 1933.

(*d*) (A) 4 . . . P × P; 5 N–R3, P–K3; 6 N × P, B–K2 = . (B) 4 . . . P–K3; see Neo-Catalan. (C) 4 . . . P–KN3; 5 B–KN2, B–N2; 6 B–N2, O–O; 7 O–O, B–N5; 8 P–Q3, B × N; 9 B × B, QN–Q2; 10 B–N2, R–B1; 11N–Q2, P–QR4 = . Larsen-Uhlmann, match 1971.

(*e*) 5 N–K5?! B–R4; 6 B–KN2, QN–Q2; 7 N × N, Q × N; 8 B–N2, P–K3; 9 O–O, B–Q3; 10 P–Q3, Q–K2; 11 Q–B2, O–O; 12 P–K4, P × KP = . Réti-Torre, Moscow 1925. Compare also cols. 17, 19 and 25.

(*f*) Or 7 . . . B–Q3; 8 P–Q3, O–O; 9 QN–Q2, Q–K2; 10 P–QR3, P–K4 = .

(*g*) 11 Q–B2, P–KR3; 12 B–B3, KR–B1; 13 KR–K1, Q–Q1; 14 P–K4, Q–B1 = . Bilek-Geller, Sousse 1967.

(*h*) The "bizarre" but authentic answer to Black's acceptance of this gambit. (A) A "natural" try is 3 P–K3, P–QB4 (3 . . . N–QB3; 4 B × P, P–K4; 5 P–Q4! P × P; 6 P × P, B–N5†; 7 N–B3 ±); 4 B × P, P–K3; 5 O–O, N–KB3; 6 P–QN3 (6 P–Q4, see Queen's Gambit Accepted), N–B3; 7 B–N2, P–QR3; 8 P–QR4, B–K2; 9 N–K5, N–QR4; 10 P–Q4, N × B = . Keres-Fine, Zandvoort 1936. (B) 3 Q–R4†, N–Q2; 4 P–KN3, N–B3; see col. 10, note (*k*).

(*i*) (A) 5 QN–K5, N × N; 6 N × N, N–B3; 7 P–K3, P–K3; 8 P–QN3, N–Q2; 9 B–N5, B–Q3; 10 B–N2, O–O; 11 N × N, B × N; 12 Q–N4, P–B3 = . Keres-Fine, Semmering 1937. (B) 5 P–QN3, P–B3; 6 B–N2, P–K4; 7 P–N3, reverts to the column.

(*j*) White could accept Black's sacrifice, e.g. 7 QN × P, N × N; 7 N × N, Q–Q4; 8 N–B3, B–N5; 9 Q–R4†, B–Q2; 10 Q–B2 ∞.

(*k*) 11 Q–N1! R–B2; 12 N–B5, B–K3; 13 P–B4, P × P; 14 P × P, N–N3! 15 B–K4, B × N/5 = . Botvinnik-Fine, Nottingham 1936.

(*l*) (A) There is no target here for the wing attack 3 P–QN4, P–KB3 (or 3 . . . P–KN3; 4 B–N2, B–N2; 5 P–K3, P–K4 =); 4 P–K3, P–K4; 5 Q–N3, P–QB4; 6 P × BP, B × P; 7 P × P, P × P; 8 B–R3, Q–K2†; 9 B–K2 ± . (B) 3 P–Q3, N–QB3; 4 P–KN3, N–B3; 5 B–N2, P–K4; 6

O–O, P–QR4! = . (c) 3 P–KN3, N–QB3; 4 B–N2, P–K4; (1) 5 P–Q3, N–B3; 6 O–O, N–Q2; 7 N–R3, B–K2; 8 N–B2, O–O; 9 P–K3, B–B3; 10 P × P, N × P; 11 QN × N, P × N + . Ivkov-Sosonko, Amsterdam 1974. (2) 5 O–O, N–B3; 6 P–QN4, P–K5; 7 N–N5, B–N5; 8 N × KP, N × N; 9 B × N, B–R6 = .

(*m*) 4 P–QN4!? N × P; 5 P × P, P–K4! 6 P–QR3, P–K5; 7 P × N, P × N; 8 Q × P, Q × P; 9 R–R4 ∞ with scurrilous gambiteering throughout. *Comments.*

(*n*) 11 P–Q4, P × P; 12 Q × P, Q × Q; 13 N × Q, B–N5 = . Katětov-Alekhin, Prague 1943.

(*o*) 11 Q–R4†, N–B3; 12 N × QP, Q × N; 13 B × N†, B–Q2 = . *Comments.*

1 N–KB3, P–Q4; 2 P–B4, P–K3; 3 P–KN3 (*a*)

	6	7	8	9	10
	N–KB3...................................				P × P (*i*)
4	B–N2				Q–R4† (*j*)
	B–K2..................		QN–Q2	..... P × P	B–Q2 (*k*)
5	O–O........	N–B3 (*e*)	P–N3	Q–R4†	Q × BP
	O–O	O–O	P–B3	B–Q2	P–QB4
6	P–N3 (*b*)	P–N3	O–O	Q × BP	N–K5 (*l*)
	P–B4 (*c*)	P–B4	B–Q3	B–B3	N–QB3
7	P × P	B–N2	B–N2	O–O	N × B
	N × P	N–B3	O–O	B–Q4	Q × N
8	B–N2	P × P	N–B3 (*f*)	Q–R4†	B–N2
	N–QB3	P × P	P–QN3	Q–Q2	N–B3
9	P–Q4 (*d*)	R–QB1	P–Q3	Q–B2	P–Q3
	KN–N5	B–K3	B–N2	N–B3	B–K2
10	P–QR3	O–O	P–K4	N–B3	O–O
	N–R3	R–B1	P × KP	B × N	N–Q5
11	P × P	P–Q4	P × P	B × B	N–B3
	Q × Q =	R–K1 =	Q–B2 (*g*)	N–Q5 (*h*)	R–Q1 (*m*)

(*a*) For P–Q4 on White's 3rd, 4th, 5th or even 6th move see Queen's Catalan.

(*b*) 6 Q–B2, QN–Q2; 7 P–N3, P–B3; 8 B–N2, N–K5! *Comments.* If 8 . . . P–QR4; 9 N–B3, P–QN3; 10 P–Q3 ± . Smyslov-Kurajica, Skopje 1969.

(*c*) (A) 6 . . . P–QN3; 7 B–N2, B–N2; 8 P–Q3, P–B4 = . (B) 6 . . . P–Q5; 7 P–K3, N–B3; 8 P × P, N × P; 9 B–N2, N × N†; 10 Q × N, R–N1 = . Botvinnik-Ståhlberg, Amsterdam 1954.

(*d*) 9 N–B3, B–B3; 10 Q–B1, P–QN3; 11 N × N, P × N; 12 P–Q4, B–R3; 13 R–K1, N × P = . Flohr-Stoltz 1931. The column is Sliwa-Pachman, Katovice 1948. In the column, more flexible than 7 P × P is 7 B–N2, (1) 7 . . . N–B3; 8 P–K3, P–QN3; 9 N–B3, B–N2; 10 P × P, N × P; 11 N × N, Q × N; 12 P–Q4, QR–Q1; 13 N–K5 ± . (2) 7 . . . P–QN3; 8 P–K3, B–N2; 9 P–Q3, QN–Q2; 10 N–B3, R–B1; 11 Q–K2, Q–B2; 12 P × P ± , Ribli-Saren, Helsinki 1972.

(*e*) If 5 P–N3, P–B4; 6 B–N2, N–B3; 7 O–O, P–QN3; 8 N–R3, B–N2; 9 N–B2, Q–B2; 10 P × P, N × P = . The column is Larsen-Penrose, Mallorca 1969.

(*f*) 8 P–Q4, N–K5; 9 QN–Q2, P–KB4; 10 N × N, BP × N = . Réti-Vajda, Semmering 1926.

(*g*) 12 Q–K2, KR–Q1; 13 KR–Q1, Kashdan-Horowitz, New York 1931, P–K4 = .

(*h*) 12 Q–Q3, P–B3 = . Abroshin-Krykov corr. 1960.

(*i*) With the counterthrust of P–QN4 eliminated (see col. 4 notes (*i*) and (*j*)). Black may try 3 . . . P–Q5; 4 B–N2, N–KB3; 5 P–Q3, P–B4; 6 O–O, N–B3; 7 P–K4, P–K4; 8 N–K1, P–KN3; 9 P–B4, B–N5 = . *Comments.*

(*j*) 4 B–N2, N–KB3; (A) 5 N–R3, B × N; 6 P × B, P–QR3; 7 B–N2, P–QN4; 8 N–K5, N–Q4; 9 P–QR4, B–N2 ∞. *Comments.* (B) 5 Q–R4†, N–Q2; see note (*k*).

(*k*) The other main line is 4 . . . N–Q2; 5 B–N2, N–B3; 6 Q × BP, P–QR3; 7 Q–B2, P–B4; 8 P–QR4, P–QN3; 9 O–O, B–N2; 10 N–B3, B–K2; 11 P–N3, O–O; 12 B–N2, R–B1; 13 KR–Q1, R–B2; 14 P–Q3, Q–R1; 15 P–K4, N–N1; 16 N–K5, N–B3 = . Panno-Keres, Moscow 1956.

(*l*) 6 P–Q4, P × P; 7 N × P, N–QB3; 8 B–N2, R–B1; 9 O–O, N–B3 = . Olafsson-Cirić, Wijk aan Zee 1969.

(*m*) 12 P–QR4, N–Q4 = . Réti-Tartakover, Semmering 1926. Also 8 . . . R–QB1 equalizes.

1 N-KB3, P-Q4; 2 P-KN3, N-KB3; 3 B-N2

	11	12	13	14	15
	B-B4		P-B4	P-KN3 (g)	
4	O-O (a)		O-O	O-O	P-Q4 (j)
	P-B3 (b)		P-K3	B-N2	B-N2
5	P-B4	P-Q3	P-Q3 (e)	P-Q3	O-O
	P×P (c)	QN-Q2	N-B3	O-O	P-B3
6	N-R3	QN-Q2	QN-Q2	QN-Q2	P-N3
	P-K4	P-KR3	B-K2	N-B3 (h)	QN-Q2
7	N×BP	Q-K1	P-K4	P-K4	B-N2
	P-K5	P-K3	O-O	P-K4	P-K4!
8	N-K1	P-K4	R-K1	P-B3	P×P
	B-B4	B-R2	Q-B2	P-QR4	N-N5
9	P-Q3	Q-K2	P-K5	R-K1	QN-Q2
	O-O	B-K2	N-Q2	P×P	KN×KP
10	B-K3	P-K5	Q-K2	P×P	N×N
	QN-Q2 =	N-KN1 (d)	P-QN4 (f)	N-Q2 (i)	N×N =

(a) 4 P-B4, (A) 4 . . . P-K3! 5 Q-N3, N-B3 (5 Q-B1; 6 N-B3, P-B3; is very confining); 6 P×P, P×P; 7 O-O, R-QN1; 8 P-Q3, B-K2; 9 P-K4, P×P; 10 N-N5, O-O; 11 P×P, B-KN5; 12 P-B3, N-Q5; 13 Q-Q1, B-QB4 = . Shiyanovski-Sokolski, USSR Chp. 1960. (B) 4 . . . P-B3; 5 P×P, P×P; 6 Q-N3, Q-B1; (6 . . . Q-N3? 7 Q×Q, P×Q; 8 N-B3, P-K3; 9 P-Q3, N-B3; 10 O-O, B-K2; 11 B-B4, P-KR3; 12 N-QN5, O-O; 13 KR-B1 ± . Barcza-Opočenský, Karlovy Vary 1948); 7 N-B3, P-K3; 8 P-Q3, N-B3; 9 B-B4, B-K2; (1) 10 R-QB1, O-O; 11 N-QN5, N-KR4; 12 B-K6! ± . (2) 10 N-KR4, B-N3; 11 N-N5, O-O; 12 N×B, RP×N; 13 B-Q6!, Q-Q2; 14 B×B, Q×B; 15 R-QB1, P-N4; 16 P-K3!, (3) 10 O-O, O-O; 11 QR-B1, B-N3?! (11 . . . P-QR3!?); 12 N-K5!, N-Q2! 13 N×B, RP×N; 14 P-KR4!, N-B4; 15 Q-Q1, Q-Q1; 16 P-Q4, N-Q2; 17 P-K4, N-N3; 18 P-K5, R-B1; 19 B-R3!, P-R3; 20 K-N2, N-B5; 21 P-N3, N-R6; 22 N-R4, N-N5; 23 Q-Q2, P-QN4 (23 . . . N/5-B7 would allow White to prevail finally); 24 N-B5, B×N; 25 P×B?? (25 R×B! +) N-B3; 26 KR-K1? (26 B-N4!, P-Q5; 27 B-B3 ±), P-Q5!, 27 B-N4 (27 K-N1!), Q-R4; 28 Q×Q (28 Q-Q3!, KR-Q1; 29 P-R5 ±), N×Q; 29 B-Q2, N-B3; 30 B-KB3, P-Q6; 31 R-K3, N-B7; with a draw at the 47th move. Korchnoi-Karpov, 15th match game 1974. The game revealed the practical and psychological backdrop of championship battles (*Comments* by Korn in *Atlantic Chess News* 1975/5).

(b) 4 . . . P-K3; 5 P-Q3, P-B3; 6 QN-Q2, N-R3; 7 P-QR3, B-K2; 8 Q-K1, N-B4 = . Tsvetkov-Smyslov, Amsterdam 1954.

(c) A King's fianchetto against a Slav Defence developed after 5 . . . P-K3; 6 P-Q4, QN-Q2; 7 QN-Q2, P-KR3; 8 P-QR3, B-Q3; 9 Q-N3, Q-B2; 10 P-B5, B-K2; 11 Q-B3, P-QN4 = . Reshevsky-Simonson, New York 1950. The column is Tartakover-Rossolimo, match 1948. Compare with the Queen's Gambit, Tarrasch Defence, and with the Catalan.

(d) 11 N-N3, B-B1; 12 P-B4, N-K2; 13 QN-Q4, N-KB4; 14 N×N, B×N; 15 P×P, BP×P; 16 P-Q4, P-QR4; 17 B-K3, B-K2; 18 KR-B1, O-O = . Benko-Petrosian, Curaçao 1962.

(e) 5 P-Q4, (A) 5 . . . B-K2; 6 P×P, B×P; 7 P-B4, see Queen's Catalan. (B) 5 . . . P×P; 6 N×P, P-K4; 7 N-KB3, N-B3; 8 P-B4, P-Q5; 9 P-K3, B-K2; 10 P×P, P×P; 11 P-N3, O-O = . Kottnauer-Gligorić, Moscow 1947. (c) 5 . . . Q-N3; 6 P-K3, N-B3; 7 P-N3, B-K2. Santasiere-Fine, New York 1938.

(f) 11 P-KR4, P-QR4; 12 N-B1, B-R3; 13 N/1-R2, N-N5; 14 P-R5? (Bronstein-O'Kelly, Beverwijk 1963)?, P-R5; 15 P-R6, P-N3; 16 N-N4, P-B5 = . The position at 8 R-K1 is also reached via the French Defence, col. 111, with 8 . . . P-QN4! to follow.

(g) (A) 3 . . . QN–Q2; 4 P–B4, P–K3; 5 O–O, B–K2; 6 Q–B2 (6 P–Q4, ? see Queen's Catalan), O–O (or 6 . . . P–B4); see col. 6. (B) 3 . . . P–QN3; 4 P–B4. See col. 24. (C) 3 P–K3 see col. 32, note (b)-(B)-(1)). (D) 3 . . . P–B3; 4 P–Q3, B–B4; 5 P–N3, P–K3 = .

(h) 6 . . . P–B4; ? 7 P–K4, P × P; 8 P × P, N–B3 = .

(i) 11 Q–K2, P–N3; 12 N–B4, B–QR3; 13 B–B1, Q–B3 = . Evans-Olafsson, Dallas 1957.

(j) 4 P–QN4, B–N2; 5 B–N2, O–O; 6 O–O, B–N5; 7 P–B4, P–B3; 8 N–R3, QN–Q2 = . Smyslov-Spasski, USSR Chp. 1961. The column is Eliskases-Najdorf, Mar del Plata 1948.

1 N–KB3, P–Q4; 2 P–KN3

	16	17	18	19	20
	P–QB4	B–N5			
3	B–N2	B–N2			
	N–QB3	N–Q2	N–KB3 (*i*)		
4	O–O	P–B4 (*e*)	P–B4		O–O (*l*)
	P–K3 (*a*)	P–QB3	P–B3		P–B3
5	P–Q3	P × P	P × P	Q–B2	P–B4
	P–KN3	P × P	B × N	P–K3	P–K3
6	N–QB3 (*b*)	N–B3 (*f*)	B × B	O–O	P × P
	B–N2	P–K3	P × P	B–K2	B × N
7	P–QR3 (*c*)	Q–N3 (*g*)	Q–N3	P–QN3	B × B
	KN–K2	Q–N3	Q–Q2	QN–Q2	BP × P
8	R–N1	Q × Q	N–B3	B–N2	N–B3
	O–O	N × Q	P–K3	O–O	N–B3
9	B–Q2	P–Q3	O–O	P–Q3	P–Q3
	R–N1 (*d*)	R–B1 (*h*)	N–B3 (*j*)	P–QR4 (*k*)	B–K2 = (*m*)

(*a*) This position may also arise from the Sicilian or French Defence. More aggressive is 4 . . . P–K4, leading to King's Indian Reversed, e.g. 5 P–Q3, P–B3; 6 P–K4, KN–K2; 7 P × P, N × P; 8 P–B3, B–K2; 9 P–Q4 = .

(*b*) 6 P–K4, B–N2; 7 Q–K2, KN–K2; 8 P–K5, Q–B2; 9 R–K1, P–KR3; 10 P–B3, B–Q2. = . Bronstein-Botvinnik, match 1951.

(*c*) 7 B–N5, N–B3; 8 N–Q2, O–O; 9 N–N3, Q–K2; 10 P–K4, P–Q5; 11 N–K2, P–KR3 ∞. Feuerstein-Martinovsky, Atlantic Open, New York 1971.

(*d*) 10 P–QN4, P × P; 11 P × P, P–QN4; 12 P–K4, P–QR4 ∞. Larsen-Mecking, Mallorca 1969. The position arose from a King's fianchetto. In the column, for 5 N–KB3 refer to col. 13. If White, instead of 5 P–Q3, pushes the pawn to 5 P–Q4, he creates a "Grünfeld Defence Reversed" with a move in hand, e.g. 5 . . . P × P; 6 N × P, B–B4; 7 N–N3, B–N3; 8 P–B4, N–B3 = . Korchnoi-Mecking, 7th match game 1974.

(*e*) (ᴀ) 4 O–O, P–QB3; 5 P–Q3, P–K4; 6 P–KR3, B–R4; 7 P–B4, P × P; 8 P × P, KN–B3; 9 B–K3, Q–B2; 10 N–B3, B–QN5 = . Benko-Keres, Curaçao 1962. (ʙ) 4 P–Q3, P–QB3; 5 P–KR3, B × N; 6 B × B, KN–B3; 7 O–O, P–K3; 8 N–Q2, B–B4; 9 P–B3, O–O = . Benko-Darga, Amsterdam 1964. Observe the different stratagems in (ᴀ) and (ʙ). For (ᴄ) 4 P–N3, P–QB3; 5 B–N2, KN–B3; 6 P–B4, refer to col 2.

(*f*) 6 O–O, KN–B3; 7 N–B3, P–K3; 8 P–KR3, B–R4; 9 P–Q3, B–B4; 10 P–K4, O–O = . Olafsson-Keres, Los Angeles 1963.

(*g*) 7 Q–R4, KN–B3; 8 P–Q3, B–QB4; 9 O–O, O–O (Barcza-Keres, Tallin 1969); 10 P–K4 = .

(*h*) 10 B–K3, B–Q3; 11 N–QN5, B–N1; 12 O–O, N–K2; 13 KR–B1, R × R†; 14 R × R, N–B3; 15 KN–Q4, K–Q2 = . Benko-Bisguier, US Chp. 1963.

(*i*) For 3 . . . P–QB3 see col. 23, note (*d*-ʙ).

(*j*) 10 B–N2, B–K2; 11 P–Q3, O–O = . Keene-Basman, Hastings 1966–7.

(*k*) 10 QN–Q2, P–R5; 11 B–B3, P × NP; 12 P × NP, Q–N3 = . Benko. An English-Réti Double Fianchetto, again similar to col. 2.

(*l*) (ᴀ) 4 P–Q3, P–B3; 5 P–KR3, B × N; 6 P × B, P–KN3; 7 O–O, B–N2; 8 P–KB4, O–O; 9 N–Q2, P–K3; 10 N–B3, P–B4 = . Kotov-Ivkov, Sarajevo 1966. (ʙ) 4 P–N3 (or 4 . . . P–B3; 5 P–N3), again see col. 2.

(*m*) 10 B–N2, with a Bishop's pair (Larsen).

1 N–KB3, P–Q4

	21	22	23	24	25
2	(P–KN3)......................................				P–QN3 (h)
	N–QB3......	P–K3	N–Q2 (e)	.... N–KB3	B–N5 (i)
3	P–Q4 (a)	B–N2	P–B4 (f)	B–N2	B–N2
	B–B4	P–QB4	P–K3	P–QN3!?	N–Q2
4	B–N2	O–O	B–N2	P–B4!	P–B4
	N–N5!?	N–QB3	KN–B3	P–K3!	P–K3
5	N–R3	P–Q3	N–B3	P × P	P–K3
	P–K3	B–Q3	B–K2	P × P	KN–B3
6	O–O	P–K4 (c)	O–O	O–O	B–K2
	N–KB3	KN–K2	O–O	B–Q3?	P–B3
7	N–R4	QN–Q2	P–Q3	P–Q4	N–Q4
	B–N5	O–O	P–B4	O–O	B × B
8	P–QB4	N–R4!	P × P	N–B3	Q × B
	P–B3	P–QN3	P × P	P–B3	B–Q3
9	N–B2	P–KB4	B–N5	N–K5!	P–B4
	N × N (b)	P × P (d)	P–QN3 ∓	B–N2 (g)	O–O = (j)

(a) A Man vs. Computer game went 3 P–Q3! P–K4; 4 QN–Q2, N–B3; 5 B–N2, B–K2; 6 O–O, O–O; 7 P–K4—White has arrived at a Piré Defence Reversed (see Piré Defence, col. 26) with a tempo ahead. Black continued 7 . . . K–R1?! 8 P–QB3, B–KN5 (8 . . . KN–K1 and 9 . . . P–B4); 9 P–KR3, B–K3; 10 P–QN4? P × P; 11 P × P, Q–Q6; 12 B–N2, N × KP; 13 N × N, Q × N/5; 14 N–Q4, Q–N3; 15 N × N, P × N; 16 R–K1, P–QR4; 17 B × P, QR–Q1; 18 Q–R4, Q–B3 (18 . . . B–Q3!) 19 R–K2? B–B5; 20 R–B2, B–Q6; 21 R–Q2, B–N4!! + . P. Benjamin (2050) vs. Chess 4.9, Stanford Univ. 1980.

(b) 10 Q × N, B–K2; 11 P–KR3, B–R4; 12 P–KN4, B–N3; 13 N × B, RP × N = . Savon-Aronin, USSR 1963.

(c) A modern "Closed Sicilian Defence Reversed" has now been reached with White a move in hand.

(d) 10 P × P, B–R3; 11 R–K1, P–B5; 12 P–B3! (Fischer-Ivkov, Santa Monica 1966) R–B1∞ . Compare col. 32, note (b) and French Defence, Closed Systems.

(e) (A) 2 . . . P–KN3; 3 B–N2, B–N2; 4 P–Q4, N–KR3; 5 O–O, O–O; 6 P–B3! N–B4; 7 QN–Q2, P–N3; 8 P–K4, P × P; 9 N × P, B–N2; 10 N–R4! ± . Barcza. (B) 2 . . . P–QB3; 3 B–N2, B–N5; (1) 4 P–QN3, N–B3; 5 O–O, QN–Q2; 6 B–N2, P–K3; 7 P–Q3, B–K2 (or 7 . . . B–QB4 =); 8 QN–Q2, O–O; 9 P–KR3, B × N! = . Keene. This is a "Double Fianchetto" without White's P–B4, as distinct from col. 2. But compare cols. 18–20. (2) 4 P–Q3, N–Q2; 5 P–KR3, B–R4! = or 5 QN–Q2, P–K3; 6 O–O, KN–B3; 7 P–K4, B–K2; 8 Q–K1, O–O; 9 P–KR3, B × N! = . Ivkov.

(f) (A) 3 B–N2, P–K4! (B) 3 P–Q4, P–K3; 4 B–N2, P–QB4; 5 P–B4, P × BP; 6 N–R3, KN–B3; 7 N × P, P–QN4; 8 QN–K5, B–N2 = . The column is Kraus-Korn, corr. 1965.

(g) 10 B–N5, P–KR3; 11 B × N, Q × B; 12 P–B4, R–Q1; 13 P–K4! ± . Benko-Bisguier, US Chp. 1966–7. The position after Black's eighth move is a Caro-Kann Exchange Variation with reversed colours but a weak move . . . P–QN3. Safer was 6 . . . B–K2; with . . . P–B4 to follow. An instructive example of transposition.

(h) 2 P–QN4, N–B3 see Unorthodox Flank Openings, col. 16. If 2 . . . Q–Q3; 3 P–N5 or P–QR3. If 2 . . . P–KB3; 3 P–K3 (3 P–Q4, P–K4!), P–K4; 4 P–B4, P–Q5 . *Comments*.

(i) 2 . . . P–QB4; 3 B–N2, P–B3; 4 P–B4, P–Q5; 5 P–Q3, P–K4; 6 P–K3, N–K2; 7 B–K2, KN–B3; 8 QN–Q2, B–K2; 9 O–O, O–O; 10 P–K4, P–QR3; 11 N–K1, P–QN4. Petrosian-Fischer, 6th match game, 1971.

(j) Rabinovich-Rauzer, Moscow 1934. The column is akin to the Nimzowitsch Attack.

1 N–KB3

	26	27	28	29	30
	P–QB4	P–KB4	(The "Dutch" Réti)		P–KN3 (q)
2	P–KN3 (a)	P–KN3 (f)			P–KN3 (r)
	N–QB3 (b)	N–KB3			B–N2
3	B–N2	B–N2			B–N2 (s)
	P–KN3	P–KN3	P–K3 (i)		P–K4!
4	O–O	P–Q3 (g)	P–B4		P–Q3
	B–N2	B–N2	B–K2 (j)		N–QB3
5	P–K4	QN–Q2	O–O		P–K4 (t)
	P–Q3	P–Q3	O–O (k)		P–Q3
6	P–B3	P–K4	P–Q3	P–N3! (n)	N–QB3
	P–K4 (c)	P–K4	P–Q3	P–B4 (o)	KN–K2
7	P–Q3	N–B4	N–B3	B–N2	B–K3
	N–R3 (d)	O–O	N–B3 (l)	N–B3	O–O
8	N–K1	P×P	R–N1	N–B3	Q–Q2
	O–O	P×P	P–QR4	P–K4	N–Q5 (u)
9	P–KB4	B–K3	P–QR3	P–K3!	
	P×P (e)	N–B3 (h)	Q–K1 (m)	P–Q3 (p)	

(a) (A) 2 P–K4 makes it an elementary Sicilian. (B) 2 P–B4 turns it into an English Opening with the potential for a Sicilian Defence, Maróczy Bind, and (c) 2 P–QN3 see Nimzowitsch Attack, cols. 39–40; or arrives out of a Queen's Fianchetto (Unorthodox Flank Openings, col. 9).

(b) For 2 . . . N–KB3 see also King's Indian Attack, cols. 31–4 and for other answers see Fianchetto Openings.

(c) 6 . . . N–B3; 7 P–Q3, O–O; 8 QN–Q2, B–Q2; 9 R–K1, P–QN4; 10 P–QR4, P–N5; 11 N–B4, P×P; 12 P×P, N–K1; 13 P–K5, R–B1; 14 B–B4, P–Q4 = . Larsen-Deutsch, Boston 1970.

(d) (A) 7 . . . N–B3; see Sicilian Defence, cols. 51–5. (B) 7 . . . KN–K2 is also good.

(e) 10 B×P, N–KN5; 11 N–R3, KN–K4; 12 K–R1, Q–N3; 13 Q–Q2, B–K3 = . Evans-Najdorf, Dallas 1957.

(f) (A) 2 P–Q4, P–QB4 again see English Opening, cols. 26–34. (B) 2 P–QN3, N–KB3; 3 P–B4, P–QN3; (1) 4 P–N3, B–N2; 5 B–KN2, P–K3; 6 N–B3, B–N5; 7 B–N2, O–O; 8 O–O, B×N; 9 B×B, P–Q3; 10 P–Q3, Q–K1; 11 P–K3, QN–Q2; 12 P–QN4, Q–K2 = . Korchnoi-Spasski, 9th match game 1977–8 (with transposition from 1 P–QB4). (2) 4 P–K3, B–N2; 5 B–N2, P–K3; 6 B–K2 (i) 6 . . . B–Q3; 7 O–O, O–O = . Andersen-Larsen, match 1974. (ii) 6 . . . P–QR4; 7 O–O, P–R5; 8 P–Q3, P×P; 9 P×P, R×R; 10 B×R, B–N5; 11 N–B3, O–O; 12 N–R2, B–Q3; 13 B–B3, N–B3; 14 P–QN4, N–K2! 15 N–B1, N–N3; 16 N–N3, Q–K2; 17 Q–Q2, N–N5; 18 P–N3, P–R4; 19 P–B5, P×P; 20 P×P, B×BP; 21 P–R3, N–B3; 22 N×B, Q×N; 23 B–N4, Q–Q4; 24 B×R, N–K4; 25 P–K4, N×KP; 26 Q–K3, N–Q7; 27 resigns. Fraguela-Larsen, Las Palmas 1976. (c) 2 P–K4! (The Wagner Gambit) P×P; 3 N–N5, N–KB3; 4 P–Q3! P–K6! 5 B×P! N–B3; 6 P–Q4, P–K4; 7 P–Q5, N–K2! 8 B–Q3! (8 P–QB4, N–N3), P–Q3 ∞ . Pachman-Clemens, Hamburg 1980.

(g) 4 P–B4, B–N2; 5 O–O, O–O; 6 N–QB3, P–B3 (Ftačník-Sweig, Amsterdam 1977) with transposition from the 1 P–QB4. Now 7 P–Q4 would transpose into the Dutch Defence.

(h) 10 P–Q4, P–K5 = . Van den Pol-Barden, Holland v. England 1960.

(i) . . . P–Q3; 4 P–Q4, P–B3; 5 O–O, Q–B2; 6 P–B4, (A) 6 . . . QN–Q2; 7 Q–B2, P–KN2 = . Comments. See Dutch Defence, Antoshin Variation. Weaker is (B) 6 . . . P–K4; 7 N–B3, B–K2; 8 P–B5! Udovčić-Lombardy, Zagreb 1969.

(j) 4 . . . P–QN3; 5 P–N3, B–N2; 6 O–O (6 P–Q4 again brings about a true Dutch Defence, Dutch Indian variation, similar to col. 8 there), B–Q3, 7 N–B3, O–O; 8 B–N2,

P-B4; 9 P-Q4, P×P; 10 Q×P, B-B4; 11 Q-B4, N-B3; 12 P-QR3, Q-K2; 13 P-QN4, B-Q3;
14 Q-Q2, QR-B1; 15 KR-Q1, B-N1; 16 QR-B1, QR-Q1; 17 P-K3, Q-B2; 18 Q-K2, Q-N3;
19 R-B2, Q-R3; 20 N-QN5, N-K5; 21 N-Q2, P-Q4; 22 P×P, P×P; 23 N-KB3, B-R3; 24
N/3-Q4, N-K2; 25 Q-K1, R-Q2; 26 P-QR4, B-N2; 27 N×BP, N×N; 28 B×N, N-R5; 29
B-KR1!! P-Q5; 30 P-K4, P-Q6; 31 R/2-Q2, N-B6†; 32 B×N, R×B; 33 N-Q4, R-B1; 34
R×P, Q-N3; 35 N-B5, R/2-KB2; 36 R-Q7, R-K1; 37 R-Q8, Q-K3; 38 P-B3, P-QN4; 39
R×R†, Q×R; 40 P×P, B-B2; 41 Q-B3, resigns. Rogoff-Rodriguez, Orense 1976.

(k) If at once 5 . . . P-B4; 6 N-B3, N-B3; 7 P-Q4! P×P; 8 N×P, O-O; 9 P-K4 ± .

(l) An earlier *MCO* suggestion, not shown in practice but still valid, was 7 . . . Q-K1; 8
P-K4, P-K4 = .

(m) 10 P-QN4, P×P; 11 P×P, P-K4 = . Gufeld-Bokuchava, USSR Chp. prelims 1968.

(n) (A) 6 P-Q4, P-Q3; 7 P-N3, QN-Q2; see Dutch Defence. (B) 6 N-B3, N-B3! = .

(o) 6 . . . P-Q4; 7 B-N2 (7 P-Q4 see Dutch Defence), (A) 7 . . . P-B3; 8 P-Q3! QN-Q2; 9
QN-Q2, Q-K1; 10 Q-B2 ± . Necessary again seems (B) 7 . . . N-B3; or (C) 7 . . . P-Q3; with
. . . QN-Q2 and . . . P-K4 to follow. But thus 3 . . . P-K3 might prove to be a loss of time.

(p) 10 P-Q4! ± . Lundin-Tartakover, Groningen 1946.

(q) For 2 P-QN3 see Unorthodox Flank Openings, cols. 8-10, without . . . P-KB4.

(r) 2 P-K4, P-QB4; see Sicilian Defence, col. 174.

(s) A weaker variant of the King's Indian Attack, which is handled in cols. 31-35. Good
seems first 3 P-B4 with an "English" character, or 3 P-Q4 (to prevent . . . P-K4).

(t) 5 P-B4, KN-K2; 6 N-B3, P-Q3; 7 O-O, P-KR3; 8 R-N1, B-K3; 9 P-QN4, Q-Q2; 10
P-N5, N-Q1; 11 N-Q2 (Quinteros-Ljubojević, Yugoslavia 1970), P-R3 = .

(u) 9 N-K2?! (9 O-O!?) B-R6; 10 N/3×N, B×B; 11 R-KN1, P×N; 12 N×P, P-QB4; 13
N-N5, B-B6; 14 P-KN4, P-Q4; 15 B×P, R-B1; 16 B-R3, P×P; 17 P×P, Q-N3; 18 B×N,
Q×N; 19 B×R, Q×P; 20 B×B, K×B; 21 R-QB1, R-Q1; 22 Q-K3, Q×BP; 23 K-B1,
R-Q8†; 24 resigns. Barcza-Tal, Tallinn 1971.

1 N-KB3, N-KB3

	31	32	33	34	35
2	P-KN3..P-QB4 (*i*)				
	P-QN4...... P-KN3 (*b*)				P-KN3
3	P-QR4	P-QN4...... P-N3 .... P-QB4			P-QN4
	P-N5	B-N2	B-N2	P-Q3 (*f*)	B-N2
4	P-Q3	B-QN2	B-QN2	B-N2	B-N2
	B-N2	O-O (*c*)	O-O	B-N2	O-O
5	P-K4	B-N2	B-N2	O-O	P-K3 (*j*)
	P-Q3	P-Q4	P-Q3	O-O	P-Q3
6	B-N2	O-O	P-Q4	N-B3	B-K2
	QN-Q2	B-N5	KN-Q2	QN-Q2	P-K4
7	O-O	P-B4	N-B3	P-Q3 (*g*)	O-O
	P-K3	P-B3	P-K4	P-K4	R-K1
8	P-R5	N-R3	Q-Q2!	B-Q2!	N-B3
	R-QN1	QN-Q2	R-K1	N-B4	QN-Q2
9	QN-Q2	R-B1	P×P	P-QN4	P-Q3
	B-K2 (*a*)	P-QR4 (*d*)	N×P (*e*)	N-K3 (*h*)	P-B3 =

(*a*) 10 N-B4, O-O = . Petrosian-Spasski, 14th World Chp. match game 1966.

(*b*) Most other replies transpose into one of the systems dealt with elsewhere, or into "closed treatments" of Semi-open K'sP games. E.g. (A) 2 . . . P-QB4; 3 B-N2, P-Q4, see col. 13; or (B) 2 . . . P-Q4; 3 B-N2 (as in col. 14), and now (1) 3 . . . P-K3; 4 O-O, B-K2; 5 P-Q3, O-O; 6 QN-Q2, P-B4; 7 P-K4, N-B3; 8 R-K1 just as in (A), or (2) 3 . . . P-QN3!? see col. 24. (c) 2 . . . P-K3; 3 B-N2, B-K2; 4 P-Q4, P-Q4; see Queen's Catalan and for 4 P-B4 see cols. 6-10. For 3 P-Q3, P-Q4; 4 QN-Q2, B-K2; 5 P-K4 see French Defence, Closed System. (D) 2 . . . P-Q3; 3 P-Q4, QN-Q2! (aiming for a Pirć or an Old Indian Defence without White's P-QB4); 4 B-N2, P-K4; 5 O-O, (1) 5 . . . B-K2; 6 QN-Q2, O-O; 7 P×P, P×P; 8 N-B4! P-K5 . Andersson-Larsen, 6th match game, Stockholm 1975. (2) 5 . . . P-KN3; 6 P-N3!? B-N2; 7 P-B4, O-O; 8 Q-B2, R-K1; 9 N-B3, P-B3; 10 P×P, P-QR3; 11 P×P, P×P; 12 B-N2, N-B4; 13 KR-Q1, Q-B2; 14 N-Q2, B-N5 ∞. Andersson-Kavalek, match, Washington 1978. (E) 2 . . . P-QN3!? 3 B-N2, B-N2; 4 O-O, (1) 4 . . . P-B4; 5 P-Q3, P-N3 (5 . . . P-Q4); 6 P-K4, P-Q3; 7 N-R4, N-B3; 8 P-KB4, B-N2; 9 N-QB3, O-O; 10 P-B5 (10 P-KN4!), N-K4; 11 B-N4, P-K3; 12 Q-Q2, Q-Q2 = . Hübner-Adorjan, Candidates match 1980. (2) 4 . . . P-K3; 5 P-B4, etc. see Queen's Indian Defence, col. 4.

(*c*) (A) 4 . . . P-B3; 5 B-N2, P-QR4; 6 P-QR3, P×P, 7 P×P, R×R; 8 B×R, Q-N3; 9 P-B3, O-O; 10 O-O, P-Q4 = . Smyslov-Bronstein, Amsterdam 1964. (B) 4 . . . P-QR4; 5 P-N5, P-B3; 6 N-R3, O-O; 7 R-QN1, P-Q4; 8 P-B4, QN-Q2; 9 B-KN2, Q-B2; 10 O-O, N-K5 = . Smyslov-Alvarez, Havana 1962.

(*d*) 10 P-N5, P-R5; 11 P-Q3, P-K4 = . Smyslov.

(*e*) 10 N×N, B×N ∞. Olafsson-Kavalek, Wijik aan Zee 1969. The column has features of (deferred) Nimzowitsch Attack and a Double Fianchetto. Compare cols. 37-8.

(*f*) For 3 . . . P-QB4 see English Opening, Symmetrical Variation. For 3 . . . P-Q4; see Réti Opening, col. 14.

(*g*) For 7 P-Q4, P-K4; see King's Indian Defence, col. 57.

(*h*) 10 R-N1, N-K1; 11 P-QR4, P-B3; 12 P-R5, KN-B2 = . *Comments.*

(*i*) For 2 P-QN4 see Unorthodox Flank Openings, 1 P-QN4.

(*j*) 5 P-Q3, P-B3; 6 P-K3, P-QR4; 7 P-N5, P×P; 8 P×P, P-R5; N-R3, P-Q4 = . Benko-D. Byrne, Mallorca 1968. For 3 P-QN3 see Nimzowitsch Attack. The column is R. Byrne's analysis.

1 N–KB3, N–KB3

	36	37	38	39	40
2	(P–QB4)............................			P–QN3 (Nimzowitsch Attack)	
	(P–KN3).....	P–QN3 (e)	(Double Fianchetto)	P–KN3......	P–Q4 (k)
3	N–B3 (a)	P–KN3		P–B4	B–N2
	P–Q4 (b)	B–N2		B–N2	P–K3 (l)
4	P×P	B–N2		B–N2	P–K3
	N×P	P–B4	P–K3 (g)	O–O	B–K2 (m)
5	Q–R4† (c)	O–O	O–O	P–N3	P–B4
	B–Q2!	P–N3	B–K2	P–B4 (i)	O–O
6	Q–N3	P–N3	P–N3	B–N2	P–Q4
	N–N3	B–N2	O–O	P–N3 (j)	P–QN3
7	P–Q4	B–N2	B–N2	O–O	B–Q3 (n)
	B–N2	O–O	P–Q4	B–N2	B–N2
8	B–B4	N–B3	P–K3	N–B3	O–O
	B–K3	P–Q4	QN–Q2	P–K3	QN–Q2
9	Q–B2	N×P	N–B3	R–N1	QN–Q2
	N–B3 (d)	N×N (f)	N–K5 (h)	Q–K2 =	P–B4 (o)

(a) (A) 3 P–QN3, B–N2; 4 B–N2, O–O; 5 P–K3 (5 P–KN3, P–B3 =), P–Q3, and if 6 P–Q4, see King's Indian Defence. (B) 3 N–QB3, P–Q4; see Grünfeld Defence.

(b) 3 . . . B–N2; 4 P–K4, P–Q3; 5 P–Q4, see King's Indian Defence. But this order of moves prevents Black's transposing into the Grünfeld Defence.

(c) 5 P–K4, N×N; 6 QP×N, Q×Q†; 7 K×Q, N–Q2 = .

(d) 10 R–Q1 with a minimal advantage, according to Pachman.

(e) (A) 2 . . . P–QB4; (1) 3 P–KN3, P–K3; 4 B–N2, B–K2; 5 P–N3, P–QN3; 6 B–N2, B–N2; 7 O–O, O–O; 8 N–B3, P–Q4 = ; see English Opening col. 27. (B) 2 . . . P–K3? 3 N–B3, P–QN3? 4 P–K4, B–N2; 5 B–Q3! P–Q3; 6 B–B2, P–B4; 7 P–Q4, P×P; 8 N×P, B–K2; 9 O–O, O–O; 10 P–QN3 ± . Polugayevski-Gheorghiu, Manila 1976. See English Opening, col. 21 note (a–B). The move 5 B–Q3 is a kind of Kopec variation (see Index).

(f) 10 B×B, K×B; 11 P×N, Q×P; 12 P–Q4, N–R3 = . A "double" Double Fianchetto, also in cols. 33–4. Compare English Opening, col. 25. In the column, 6 N–B3 or 6 P–Q3 are alternatives.

(g) (A) 4 . . . P–N3; 5 P–Q4, see Queen's Indian Defence. (B) 4 . . . P–K4!? 5 N–B3, B–N5! 6 Q–B2, O–O; 7 O–O, B×QN! 8 NP×B, P–K5; 9 N–Q4, R–K1; 10 P–QR4, P–B4 = . Pachman-Smyslov, Moscow 1967.

(h) 10 P×P, N×N; 11 B×N, P×P! = . Geller-Kholmov, Moscow 1969. A "double" Double Fianchetto. Also compare Indian Catalan. In the column, 8 . . . N–R3; 9 P–K3, P–Q4 is also equal.

(i) (A) 5 . . . P–B3; 6 B–N2, P–Q4; 7 O–O, QN–Q2; 8 Q–B2, R–K1; 9 N–B3, N–B1; 10 P–Q4, B–B4; 11 Q–B1, N–K5 = . Botvinnik-Ståhlberg, Moscow 1956. (B) 5 . . . P–Q3; 6 B–N2, P–K4; 7 P–Q3, P–B3! 8 N–B3, Q–K2! 9 O–O, QN–Q2; 10 P–K3, P–QR3 = .

(j) 6 . . . N–B3; 7 O–O, P–Q3; 8 N–B3, B–Q2; 9 P–Q4 ± . The column is a Nimzowitsch Attack (2 P–QN3). The position may also arise from the English Opening, or as a transposition from the Fianchetto Openings (col. 5 of the Unorthodox Flank Openings).

(k) 2 . . . B–N5; 3 P–K3, N–KB3; 4 B–N2, P–K3; 5 P–KR3, B–R4; 6 P–Q3, P–B4; 7 P–KN4, B–N3; 8 N–K5; QN–Q2; 9 N×B, RP×N; Korchnoi-Mecking, 6th match game 1974.

(l) (A) 3 . . . B–N5; 4 P–B4, P–B3; see col. 2 (B) 3 . . . B–B4; 4 P–K3, P–K3; 5 B–K2, P–KR3; 6 O–O, QN–Q2; 7 P–Q3, B–K2; 8 QN–Q2, O–O; 9 N–K5, P–B4 = . Comments.

(m) 4 . . . P–B4; 5 P–B4, B–K2; 6 N–B3, O–O; 7 P×P, N×P; 8 N×N, P×N; 9 P–Q4, P–QN3 = . Comments.

(n) 7 B–K2, B–N2; 8 O–O, P–B4; 9 P × QP, KP × P; 10 QN–Q2, N–B3; 11 R–B1, N–K5; 12 P × P, B × P; 13 B–N5?! R–B1∞. Andersson-Langeweg, Wijk aan Zee 1976. The opening moves actually were 1 N–KB3, N–KB3; 2 P–QB4, P–K3, 3 P–QN3, P–Q4; 4 B–N2, B–K2; 5 P–K3, O–O; 6 B–K2, P–B4; 7 O–O, N–B3; 8 P × P, P × P; 9 P–Q4, P–QN3; 10 QN–Q2, B–N2, etc. These transpositions demonstrate the stable flexibility that applies to coordinated Flank Systems, and their ability to switch into centralization at expedient moments, or deviate into another tactical experiment—veering from ultra-modern initiative to a conservative set-up; here, a Tarrasch-type of hanging but potent centre pawns of Black's.

(o) 10 Q–K2, N–K5; 11 QR–B1, R–B1 = . Lombardy-Burger, US Chp. 1969–70.

Unorthodox Flank Openings

As compared to the previous edition, the first section has been greatly expanded into seven columns for the King's Fianchetto, and the second section newly created, with three columns of the Queen's Fianchetto.

THE KING'S FIANCHETTO OPENING
1 P–KN3 (cols. 1–7).

As distinct from the Réti-King's Indian Attack, this chapter deals with lines where White omits the thematic move N–KB3, and plays N–K2 or N–KR3 instead, or maintains these options but plays N–KB3 at a later date and in a position different from other Flank Opening lines.

One of these different stratagems is the "Paris Attack" which crops up in a variety of circuitous transpositions; so do other "reversed" formations, as pointed out in the various footnotes. (col. 7).

THE QUEEN'S FIANCHETTO OPENING
1 P–QN3 (cols. 8–10)

This dates back to Nimzowitsch and has in our times been practised at periodic intervals by Benko and Larsen. It may also result in a "double or "triple" Fianchetto" (cols. 9–10).

BIRD'S OPENING
1 P–KB4 (cols. 11–15)

This was popularized by the English master H.E. Bird towards the end of the nineteenth century. His attack is rarely tried by modern masters because it is nondeveloping, does not secure a lasting hold on the centre, and slightly weakens the king's field.

It is often played by outright devotees who want to follow a set strategy, well known to them, in order to avoid surprises. Nevertheless, its affinity with contemporary closed Flank Openings and the transpositions to and from Fianchetto Attacks have rejuvenated this début.

In conjunction with 1 . . . P–Q4 (cols. 11–13), the Bird is a kind of "Dutch Attack," as it then is a Dutch Defence in reverse, White having a move in hand. Col. 11 is Capablanca's suggestion and col. 12 originates with Schlechter. Column 13 tries a line-up with the Fianchetto Attack and col. 14 is a sort of Queen's Indian Reversed in answer to White's classical formation.

While 1 P–KB4 is an attempt to control K5, Black may impudently challenge this assertion at once and try to wrest the initiative. *From's Gambit* 1 P–K4 serves this purpose (col. 15). While considered unsound, with White generally holding the gambit pawn, it still discourages a lot of players from playing the Bird and risking the From! Moreover, recent experience supports Black's initiative.

THE SOKOLSKI OPENING
1 P–QN4 (cols. 16–18)

This is the only choice of relevance in this sector, if only by sheer weight of analysis and practice put into it by the Russian master in the third quarter of this century. Sporadically played by the neo-romantics Alekhin, Réti, Tartakover (who called it the "Orang Utan Opening"), *et al.*, it was employed in the United States by S. Bernstein and by Santasiere, and otherwise analysed also by Pachman. It is also known as the "Polish" Attack or Opening.

THE DUNST OPENING, 1 N–QB3 (col. 19) evokes memories of the Kevitz-Trajkovic Defence and requires talent for patient trench warfare after 1 . . . P–Q4?!

THE VAN'T KRUYS OPENING, 1 P–K3 or 2 P–K3 (col. 20) invites a French Defence reversed, but 1 . . . N–KB3 is the most neutral waiting move.

THE SARAGOSSA OPENING, 1 P–QB3, (col. 19 note (g)), propagated by the Spaniard Juncosa is a Caro-Kann in reverse if Black consents. It has no independent functional characteristics but may gain in interest for players with a flair for the recent trend of manoeuvring behind the lines, with a waiting move in hand.

1 P-KN3 (King's Fianchetto Opening)

	1	2	3	4	5
	P-KN3		P-K4	N-KB3	P-Q4
2	B-KN2 (a)		B-N2	B-N2	B-N2 (l)
	B-N2		P-KN3 (g)	P-KN3	N-KB3
3	N-QB3	P-K4 (e)	N-KB3 (h)	P-K4 (j)	P-QB3?!
	P-QB4 (b)	P-QB4	B-N2	P-Q3	P-K4
4	P-Q3	P-Q3	O-O	P-Q4	P-Q3
	N-QB3	N-QB3	P-Q3	B-N2	N-B3
5	P-QR3 (c)	N-KB3	P-Q4	N-K2	N-Q2
	N-B3	P-Q3	N-QB3	O-O	B-QB4
6	R-N1	O-O	P×P	O-O	P-K3?!
	P-QR4	P-K4	P×P	P-K4	O-O
7	P-QR4	P-B3	Q×Q†	QN-B3	P-QN4
	O-O (d)	KN-K2 (f)	N×Q (i)	P×P (k)	B-K2 (m)

(a) 2 P-KB4, P-Q4! leads into Bird's Opening, col. 13. If 2 . . . B-N2; 3 B-N2, P-QB4; 4 P-K4! N-QB3; 5 P-Q3, P-K3 (5 . . . P-Q3! and 6 . . . N-R3); 6 N-Q2, KN-K2; 7 N-KR3! P-Q4; 8 O-O, O-O; 9 P-K5 ± . Petrosian-Pachman, Moscow 1967. The line resembles the "Paris Attack."

(b) 3 . . . P-K4; 4 P-Q3, N-QB3; 5 P-B4, P-Q3; 6 N-B3, KN-K2; 7 O-O, O-O; 8 P-K4, P-KR3; 9 B-K3; 9 B-K3, N-Q5; 10 Q-Q2, K-R2 = . Larsen-Panno, Mallorca 1969.

(c) 5 N-B3, P-K3; 6 O-O, P-Q4; 7 P-QR3, KN-K2; 8 R-N1, O-O; 9 B-Q2, R-N1; 10 P-QN4, P×P; 11 P×P, P-QN4; 12 P-K4, P-QR4 = . Larsen-Mecking, Mallorca 1969.

(d) 8 N-B3, P-Q3; 9 O-O, N-K1 = . Larsen-Lehmann, Mallorca 1968.

(e) (A) 3 P-Q4, P-QB4; 4 P-Q5, see Benoni Defence. (B) 3 P-QB4! P-K4; 4 N-QB3, P-KB4 (otherwise see English Opening); 5 P-K3, P-Q3; 6 KN-K2, N-KB3; 7 P-Q4, O-O; 8 P-QN3, QN-Q2; 9 P-QR4, R-K1; 10 R-R2, P-K5 = . D. Byrne-R. Byrne, USA 1971. (C) 3 N-KB3 see Réti Opening, col. 30.

(f) 8 QN-Q2, O-O; 9 P-QR4, P-KR3; 10 R-QN1, B-K3; 11 P-QN4, P-N3; 12 P-N5, N-R4 = . Reshevsky-R. Byrne, US Chp. 1969-70. Compare also Réti Opening, col. 26, and Sicilian Defence, cols. 51-5. Playable is 6 . . . N-B3; 7 R-K1, O-O; 8 QN-Q2, R-N1; 9 P-QR4, P-N3; 10 N-B4, B-N2 = . A type of Sicilian, hardly arrived at in the P-KB4 line, is achieved here after 5 P-KB4, P-Q3; 6 N-KB3, P-K3?! 7 O-O, KN-K2; 8 P-B3, P-K4; 9 QN-Q2 ± . DeFotis-Reshevsky, US Chp. 1972.

(g) (A) 2 . . . P-Q4! 3 P-QB4! P-QB3; 4 P-N3, P×P; 5 P×P, Q-Q5; 6 N-QB3, Q×P; 7 N-B3, B-Q3; 8 O-O, N-B3 ∞. Gufeld-Zilberstein, USSR 1969. (B) 2 . . . P-Q3; 3 P-QB4, P-KB4; or 3 . . . P-KN3; 4 N-KR3; or 4 N-QB3, N-KB3; see English Opening, cols. 8 and 9.

(h) 3 P-QB4, B-N2; 4 N-QB3, P-KB4; 5 P-Q4, P×P; 6 N-N5, N-QB3; 7 N-KB3, N-B3; 8 O-O, N-K5 = . Benko-Petrosian, Curaçao 1962.

(i) 8 N-B3, P-KR3; 9 N-Q5 (Smyslov-Boleslavski, USSR 1968), N-K3 = .

(j) 3 P-KB4, B-N2; 4 N-KR3, P-B4; 5 N-B2, N-B3; 6 P-B4, R-QN1. Lombardy-Daniels, New York 1968. A Bird's Opening (Paris Attack), which bypasses From's Gambit. Also see col. 7, note (e).

(k) 8 N×P, R-K1; 9 P-KR3, QN-Q2; 10 K-R2, P-B3; 11 N-N3, Q-B2 = . Gonzales-Ciocaltea, Havana 1962. The line is a King's Indian Defence but White has omitted the weakening P-QB4

(l) (A) 2 N-KB3, N-KB3; 3 B-N2, P-QN3, see Réti Opening, cols. 24 and 37. (B) 2 P-KB4, P-KN3; 3 N-KB3, B-N2; 4 P-QB4 is a Bird's Opening but may also be here called a "Dutch Defence in Reverse."

(m) 8 P-N5, N-N1; 9 B-N2, B-KB4! ∞. Simagin-Lilienthal, Moscow 1967.

	6	7	8	9	10
1	(P-KN3). (King's Fianchetto) P-QN3 (Queen's [and Double] Fianchetto)				
	(P-Q4) P-QB4		P-K4 . . . . . . N-KB3 . . . . . . P-QN3 (j)		
2	(B-N2)	B-N2	B-N2	B-N2	B-N2
	P-QB3	N-QB3	P-Q3 (f)	P-KN3	B-N2
3	P-QB4	P-Q3	P-N3	P-K4	N-KB3 (k)
	P-KN3 (a)	P-KN3	P-KN3	P-Q3	P-K3
4	Q-R4!? (b)	N-KR3?!	P-QB4 (g)	P-N3	P-N3 (l)
	P-Q5	B-N2	N-KB3	B-N2	N-KB3
5	N-KB3	P-K4 (d)	B-N2	B-N2	B-N2
	B-N2	P-K3	B-N2	O-O	B-K2
6	O-O	P-KB4?!	N-KB3	KN-K2	O-O
	P-K4	KN-K2	O-O	P-K4	O-O
7	P-Q3	N-B2	N-B3	O-O	P-B4
	N-K2 (c)	P-B4 (e)	P-B3 (h)	N-B3 (i)	Q-B1 (m)

(a) 3 . . . P-K4!? 4 P×P, P×P; 5 Q-N3, N-KB3; 6 N-QB3, N-B3!? 7 P-Q3 (7 N×P, N-Q5; 8 N×N†, Q×N; 9 Q-Q1, B-KB4; 10 P-Q3, R-B1; 11 K-B1, Q-QR3! 12 B-Q2, B-B4; 13 B-QB3, O-O; 14 N-B3, N×P!∓), P-Q5; 8 N-N1, B-N5†; 9 B-Q2, P-QR4!∓. Bukal-Benko, Sarajevo 1970.

(b) 4 P×P, P×P; 5 P-Q4, see Queen's Catalan.

(c) 8 QN-Q2, O-O; 9 P-QN4, N-Q2 = . Larsen-Korchnoi, Mallorca 1969.

(d) 5 P-KB4, N-KB3; 6 N-B2, R-QN1; 7 P-B4, P-QR3; 8 N-B3, P-QN4; 9 O-O, O-O; 10 R-N1, P×P = . 6 P-K4! is old and solid.

(e) An alternative is 7 . . . P-K4; 8 N-B3, O-O; 9 P-KN4, P×BP! 10 B×P, P-Q3; 11 P-N5, N-K4! = . The column continues 8 N-Q2, R-QN1!? 9 P-KN4, P-Q4; 10 O-O, O-O = . Lombardy-Mednis, New York 1968. The whole line, including note (D), is the "Paris Attack" so called and advocated by Lombardy and exemplified by the configuration P-KB4, P-KN3 and N-KR3 (followed by 6 N-KB2). It may also be entered by 1 N-KR3, P-Q4, but the whole strategy is altogether too rigid. For transpositions refer to the Index.

(f) The other alternative is to play for . . . P-Q4 by 2 . . . N-QB3! 3 P-QB4 with the choices (A) 3 . . . P-Q3; 4 P-K3, P-KN3; 5 P-N3, B-N2; 6 B-N2, KN-K2; 7 N-QB3, B-K3; 8 KN-K2, P-Q4! 9 P-Q3, O-O = ; Archives; or (B) 3 . . . N-B3; (1) 4 N-QB3! P-Q4; 5 P×P, N×P; 6 P-QR3, N×N; 7 B×N, B-Q3; 8 P-K3, O-O; 9 P-Q3, Q-K2; 10 B-K2, P-QR4 with initiative. Simagin-Pachman, Sarajevo 1963. (2) 4 P-K3, B-K2; 5 P-QR3, O-O; 6 P-Q3, P-Q4; 7 P×P, Q×P; 8 N-QB3, Q-Q3; 9 N-B3, B-B4 = . Fischer-Tukmakov, Buenos Aires 1970. (3) 4 P-N3, P-Q4; 5 P×P, N×P; 6 B-N2, B-K3; 7 N-KB3, B-Q3; 8 O-O, P-B3; 9 P-K4, N/4-K2; 10 P-Q4, P×P; 11 N×P, N×N; 12 B×N, N-B3 = . R. Byrne-Shipman, Boston 1970. Also compare with Réti Opening (Nimzowitsch Attack), col. 34. (4) N-KB3? P-K5; 5 N-Q4, B-B4; 6 N×N, QP×N; 7 P-K3, B-B4; 8 Q-B2, Q-K2; 9 B-K2, O-O-O; 10 P-B4, N-N5; 11 P-N3, P-KR4; 12 P-KR3, P-R5; 13 P×N, P×P; 14 R-N1, R-R8; 15 R×R, P-N7; 16 R-B1, Q-R5†; 17 K-Q1, P×R(Q)†; 18 resigns. Larsen-Spasski, Belgrade 1970 (5) 4 P-Q3! seems the safest move.

(g) 4 P-Q4, B-N2; 5 P×P, B×P; 6 N-QB3, N-QB3; 7 N-B3, B-N2; 8 B-N2, N-B3; 9 N-Q4, B-Q2 = . Larsen-Hort, Monte Carlo 1968.

(h) 8 O-O, R-K1; 9 P-K3, B-B4; 10 P-Q3, Q-Q2 = . Larsen-Benko Monte Carlo 1969.

(i) 8 P-QB4, B-N5; 9 P-B3, B-Q2; 10 QN-B3, Q-B1 = . Larsen-del Corral, Mallorca 1968.

(j) Other choices are (A) 1 . . . P-QB4; 2 B-N2, (1) 2 . . . N-QB3; 3 P-QB4, P-K4; 3 . . . P-K3; 4 N-KB3, N-KB3; 5 P-N3, B-K2; 6 B-N2, O-O; 7 N-B3, P-Q4 = ; see Réti Opening, col. 7; 4 P-N3, N-B3; 5 B-N2, P-Q4; 6 P×P, N×P; 7 N-QB3, B-K3 = . (2) 2 . . . P-K3; 3 P-KB4, P-Q4; 4 P-K3, N-QB3; 5 N-KB3, N-B3 = , similar to Bird's Opening. (3) 2 . . .

P–Q4; 3 N–KB3. See Réti Opening. (4) 2 . . . N–KB3; 3 P–QB4, P–KN3; 4 B × N!? Karpov-Browne, San Antonio 1972. (B) 1 . . . P–Q4; 2 B–N2, N–KB3; 3 N–KB3, P–K3; 4 P–N3, B–K2; 5 B–N2, O–O; 6 O–O, P–B4 (6 . . . P–QN3; 7 P–B4, B–N2 = . Benko-Portisch, Monte Carlo 1968); 7 P–B4, N–B3; 8 P–K3, P–QN3; 9 N–B3, B–N2 = . Compare Catalan or English Opening.

(k) Harmless is 3 P–KB4, P–KB4; 4 P–K3, P–K3! = .

(l) 4 P–K3, P–KB4; 5 B–K2, N–KB3; 6 P–B4 etc., see Réti Opening, col. 27, note (f). Another "Dutch-Réti."

(m) 8 P–Q4 with a Queen's Indian Defence and equal chances.

1 P–KB4

	11	12	13	14	15
	P–Q4			N–KB3	P–K4 (*j*)
2	P–K3 (*a*)		P–KN3	P–K3	P × P
	P–KN3	N–KB3	N–KB3	P–KN3	P–Q3
3	N–KB3 (*b*)	N–KB3	B–N2	P–QN3 (*g*)	P × P
	N–KB3	B–N5 (*d*)	P–B4 (*f*)	B–N2	B × P
4	P–QN4?! (*c*)	B–K2	N–KB3	B–N2	N–KB3
	B–N2	B × N	N–B3	O–O	P–KN4 (*k*)
5	B–N2	B × B	P–B3	N–KB3	P–Q4
	O–O	QN–Q2	P–KN3	P–B4	P–N5
6	B–K2	P–B4	O–O	B–K2	N–N5!? (*l*)
	B–N5	P–K3	B–N2	P–Q4 (*h*)	P–KB4! (*m*)
7	O–O	P × P	P–Q3	O–O	P–K4
	P–B3	P × P	O–O	P–N3!	P–KR3
8	P–QR4	N–B3	QN–Q2	N–K5	P–K5
	QN–Q2	P–B3 (*e*)	Q–B2 =	B–N2 (*i*)	B × P! (*n*)

(*a*) (A) 2 P–B4, P × P; 3 N–QR3, P–K4; 4 P × P, B × N; 5 Q–R4†, N–B3 = . (B) 2 P–QN3, B–N5; 3 P–N3, N–KB3; 4 B–KN2, P–B3; 5 N–KB3, B × N; 6 B × B, P–KN3 = .

(*b*) 3 P–B4, N–KB3; 4 N–QB3, B–N2; 5 N–B3, O–O; 6 Q–N3, P × P; 7 B × P, N–B3; 8 N–K5, P–K3; 9 N × N, P × N; 10 P–Q4, Q–Q3; 11 B–Q2, P–B4 = . *Comments*.

(*c*) 4 P–Q4, B–N2; 5 B–Q3, O–O; 6 O–O, P–B4; 7 P–B3, P–N3; 8 Q–K2, B–N2; 9 QN–Q2, Q–B2 = .

(*d*) 3 . . . P–B4; 4 B–K2 (4 B–N5†, B–Q2!), N–B3; 5 O–O, P–KN3; 6 P–Q4, B–N2; 7 P–B3, O–O; 8 Q–K1, Q–B2 is a reverse Dutch Stonewall.

(*e*) 9 O–O, B–K2; 10 P–Q3, N–N3; 11 P–K4, P × P; 12 P × P, B–B4† = . Tartakover-Grünfeld, Vienna 1917. A typical classic of the Bird.

(*f*) A solid bulwark is created by 3 . . . P–B3! 4 P–N3!? P–QR4! 5 B–N2, P–KN3; 6 N–KB3 (6 N–KR3 and 7 N–B2 is a possibility), B–N2; 7 O–O, O–O; 8 K–R1, P–R5 = . Hartoch-Keene, Hastings 1968–9. The column is *Comments*.

(*g*) 3 N–KB3, B–N2; 4 P–Q4, P–Q3; 5 B–B4, QN–Q2; 6 O–O, O–O; 7 N–B3, P–B4 = .

(*h*) 6 . . . P–N3; 7 O–O, B–N2; 8 P–B4, P–Q4 = . A reversed Queen's Indian Defence.

(*i*) 9 P–Q3, N–B3; 10 B–KB3, Q–B2; 11 N–Q2, QR–Q1; 12 Q–K2, N–K1; 13 P–Q4 = . Pirć-R. Byrne, Helsinki 1952.

(*j*) From's Gambit. If (A) 1 . . . P–KB4; 2 P–K4! (tame is 2 P–QN3, P–Q3; 3 B–N2, N–KB3; 4 P–B4, P–KN3; 5 N–KB3, B–N2 = . Larsen-Bilek, Büsum 1969), P × P; 3 P–Q3, P–K6; 4 B × P, N–KB3; 5 P–Q4, P–K3; 6 B–Q3, N–B3; 7 P–QR3, N–K2; 8 N–R3, P–QN3; 9 O–O, B–N2; 10 N–Q2, P–N3; 11 B–B2 ± . Pelikan-Alekhin, Poděbrady 1936. (B) 1 . . . P–KN3; see King's Fianchetto Opening. (C) 1 . . . P–QB4; 2 N–KB3, P–KN3; 3 P–K4, B–N2; 4 B–K2, N–QB3; 5 O–O, P–Q3; 6 P–Q3, P–K3; 7 N–R3, KN–K2; 8 P–B3, O–O; 9 B–K3, P–QR3; 10 P–Q4, P × P; 11 N × P, P–QN4; 12 N × N, N × N; 13 Q–Q2, Q–B2 = . Larsen-Fischer, match 1971. 1 P–KN3, P–Q4; 2 P–KB4 avoids the From, but invites 1 . . . P–K4.

(*k*) The customary reply, besides (A) 4 . . . N–KR3; 5 P–Q4, N–N5; 6 Q–Q3, P–QB4; 7 N–B3, P × P; 8 Q × QP, O–O = . *Informator 8*. (B) 4 . . . N–KB3; 5 P–Q4, N–N5; 6 Q–Q3, P–QB4; 7 P–B3, P × P; 8 P × P, N–QB3; 9 N–B3, O–O; 10 P–K4, R–K1 = . Or 7 Q–K4†!, B–K3; 8 N–N5! ± .

(*l*) Less colourful but safe is 6 N–K5, B × N; 7 P × B, Q × Q†; 8 K × Q, N–QB3; 9 B–N5, N × P; 10 N–B3, B–K3; 11 P–K3, P–KB3; 12 B–R4, O–O–O† = .

(*m*) 6 . . . Q–K2; 7 Q–Q3, P–KB4; 8 P–KR3! N–QB3; 9 P × P, N–B3; 10 P–B3, N–K5; 11 N × N, P × N; 12 Q–K3, B × P; 13 N–Q2, B–KB4 = .

(*n*) 9 P × B, Q × Q†; 10 K × Q, P × N; 11 B × P, B–K3. Popp.

	16	17	18	19	20
1	P-QN4 (Sokolski Opening)			N-QB3 (g)	
	P-Q4 ......P-K4 ....N-KB3			P-Q4 ......P-K4 (i)	
2	B-N2	B-N2	N-KB3 (d)	P-K4	P-K3
	N-KB3	P-KB3?! (b)	P-K3 (e)	P-Q5	P-Q4
3	P-K3	P-N5	P-QR3	QN-K2	P-Q4
	B-B4	P-Q4	P-QR4	P-K4	P×P
4	N-KB3	P-K3	P-N5	N-N3	Q×P
	P-K3	B-K3	P-Q4	B-K3	N-KB3
5	P-B4	P-Q4	P-K3	P-Q3	P-K4
	N-B3	P-K5	P-B4	N-QB3	P×P (j)
6	P-QR3	QN-Q2	B-N2	P-QR3	Q×Q†
	P×P	P-B3	QN-Q2	P-KN3	K×Q
7	B×P	P-QR4	P-B4	P-KB4	B-KN5
	B-Q6 (a)	B-Q3 (c)	B-Q3 (f)	P×P (h)	B-KB4 =

(a) 8 B × B, Q × B; 9 Q-K2, Q × Q†; with near equality. In the column, if 2 . . . Q-Q3; 3 P-N5! The opening move 1 P-QN4 is also known as the "Polish Attack" and was originally called by Tartakover the "Orang-Utan" opening.

(b) Safest is 2 . . . P-Q3, e.g., 3 P-QB4, P-KB4; 4 P-K3, N-KB3; 5 N-KB3, B-K2 = ; or 3 . . . N-KB3; 4 N-KB3, P-KN3 = .

(c) 8 P-QB4 with a complicated untried position—Sokolski.

(d) This variation, also arrived at after 1 N-KB3, N-KB3; 2 P-QN4, is also known as "Santasiere's Folly." The other main line is 2 B-N2, P-KN3; 3 P-QB4, B-N2; 4 P-K3, P-Q3; 5 N-KB3, O-O; 6 P-Q4, QN-Q2; 7 B-K2, P-K4; with a King's Indian formation.

(e) (A) 2 . . . P-Q4; (1) 3 P-K3, P-KN3; 4 P-Q4, B-N2; 5 P-B4, O-O; 6 QN-Q2, P-QR4; 7 P-N5, P-B4; 8 B-K2. Santasiere. (2) 3 B-N2, P-K3; 4 P-QR3, P-B4; 5 P × P, B × P; 6 P-K3, O-O; 7 P-B4, N-B3 is Alekhin-Drewitt, Portsmouth 1923. (B) 2 . . . P-KN3; 3 P-QB4, B-N2; 4 P-Q4, P-Q3; 5 P-K3, O-O; 6 B-N2, QN-Q2 = .

(f) 8 P-Q4, O-O; 9 QN-Q2, P-QN3; 10 B-K2, B-N2; 11 O-O, R-B1; 12 R-B1, Q-K2; 13 Q-N3, B-N1; 14 N-K5, N × N; 15 P × N, N-Q2; 16 P-B4, P-B3 = . Santasiere-Gonzales, Cocoa Open Chp. Florida 1969.

(g) The Dunst Opening. Other rare eccentricities are (A) 1 P-QB3—The Saragossa Opening researched by Juncosa—1 . . . P-K4; 2 P-Q4, P × P; 3 P × P, P-Q4; 4 N-QB3, P-QB3; 5 N-B3, B-Q3; 6 Q-N3, Q-N3; 7 Q-B2, N-K2 = . Or 1 . . . P-KB4; 2 P-Q4, P-K3; 3 N-B3, P-QN3; 4 P-KN3, B-N2; 5 B-N2, B-K2 = . Other answers may transpose into Orthodox Openings. (B) 1 P-K3 here or also in col. 20, constitutes the Van't Kruys Opening, aiming at a French Defence in reverse. (c) 1 P-KN4? is "The Spike" or Grob's Attack, which craves originality but is ineffective, e.g. 1 . . . P-Q4; 2 B-N2, P-QB3! 3 P-KR3, P-K3; 4 P-Q3, B-Q3; 5 N-KB3, N-K2; 6 P-K4, N-R3 = . It has been lately analysed by C. F. Bloodgood. (D) 1 N-KR3 is Tartakover's "Paris" Gambit in its original form, e.g. 1. . . P-Q4; 2 P-KN3, P-KN3!, (E) 1 P-QR4 is Ware's 19th century "Meadow Hay Opening." Its best version is 1 N-KB3, P-Q4; 2 P-QR4 and another form is 1 P-QR4, P-K4; 2 P-QB3, P-Q4; 3 P-Q4, P-K5; 4 B-B4, B-Q3; 5 B × B, Q × B; 6 P-K3. (F) 1 P-Q3 (Mieses) is seen occasionally. (G) 1 P-QR3 is the Adolph Anderssen Attack as used by him once against Morphy. It allows White, with a move in hand, to "defend" against a few selected King's Pawn Openings in reverse. Also see Mengarini's Opening. (H) 1 N-QR3 is the Durkin Attack. 1 P-Q3 is the Pirć Defence Reversed.

(h) 8 B × P, B-Q3; 9 Q-Q2, Q-K2 = . Petrov-Ragozin, Semmering 1937.

(i) (A) A noncommittal answer altogether is 1 . . . N-KB3, waiting for White to tip his hand. (B) 1 . . . P-QN3; 2 P-K4, B-N2; 3 P-Q3, N-KB3 is a Queen's Fianchetto Defence which may also arise after 1 P-K4, P-QN3; 2 P-Q3, B-N2; 3 N-QB3, N-KB3, e.g. (1) 4

P–K5, N–Q4; 5 B–Q2 (5 KN–K2!), P–N3; 6 N–B3, B–N2; 7 P–KN3, N × N; 8 B × N, P–QB4 ∞. Richter-Korn, corr. 1968. (2) 4 P–KN3, P–Q4; 5 B–N2, P–K3; 6 B–N5, B–K2; 7 KN–K2, O–O; 8 O–O, P × P! ∞. Another type of Queen's Fianchetto may come about by transposition from or into the French Defence after 1 P–K4, P–K3; 2 P–Q4, P–QN3!?. See French Defence, cols. 106–110.

(j) 5 . . . N–QB3 leads into a Nimzowitsch Defence Reversed. The column is Nimzowitsch's analysis of the Van't Kruys Opening.

Index

Index

INDEX